PEACE
AND
WAR

Other Books by Anthony H. Cordesman

Transnational Threats from the Middle East, US Army War College, Carlyle, 1999

Iraq and the War of the Sanctions: Conventional Threats and Weapons of Mass Destruction, Praeger, Westport, CT, 1999

Iran in Transition: Conventional Threats and Weapons of Mass Destruction, Praeger, Westport, CT, 1999

Bahrain, Oman, Qatar and the UAE: Challenges of Security, Westview, Boulder, 1997

Kuwait: Recovery and Security after the Gulf War, Westview, Boulder, 1997

Saudi Arabia: Guarding the Desert Kingdom, Westview, Boulder, 1997

US Forces in the Middle East: Resources and Capabilities, Westview, Boulder, 1997

Iran: Dilemmas of Dual Containment, with Ahmed Hashim, Westview, Boulder, 1997

Iraq: Sanctions and Beyond, with Ahmed Hashim, Westview, Boulder, 1997

Perilous Prospects: The Peace Process and Arab-Israeli Balance, Westview, Boulder, 1996

The Lessons of Modern War: Volume Four—The Gulf War, with Abraham R. Wagner, Westview, Boulder, 1995, paperback 1999

Iran and Iraq: The Threat from the Northern Gulf, Westview, Boulder, 1994

US Defense Policy: Resources and Capabilities, London, RUSI Whitehall Series, 1993

After the Storm: The Changing Military Balance in the Middle East, Boulder, Westview, 1993

Weapons of Mass Destruction in the Middle East, Brassey's, London, 1991

The Lessons of Modern War: Volume One—The Arab-Israeli Conflicts, with Abraham R. Wagner, Westview, Boulder, 1990

The Lessons of Modern War: Volume Two—The Iran-Iraq Conflict, with Abraham R. Wagner, Westview, Boulder, 1990

The Lessons of Modern War: Volume Three—The Afghan and Falklands Conflicts, with Abraham R. Wagner, Westview, Boulder, 1990

The Gulf and the West, Boulder, Westview, 1988

NATO Central Region Forces, RUSI/Jane's, London, 1987

The Iran-Iraq War and Western Security, 1984–1987, RUSI/Jane's, London, 1987

The Arab-Israeli Military Balance and the Art of Operations, American Enterprise Institute (AEI)/ University Press of America, Washington, D.C., 1986

Western Strategic Interests and Saudi Arabia, Croom Helm, London, 1986

The Gulf and the Search for Strategic Stability, Westview, Boulder, 1984

Jordanian Arms and the Middle East Balance, Middle East Institute, Washington, D.C., 1983

Deterrence in the 1980s, Extended Adelphi Paper, International Institute for Strategic Studies, London, 1982

Imbalance of Power, Shifting U.S.-Soviet Military Strengths, with John M. Collins, Presidio, Monterey, 1978

PEACE
AND
WAR

The Arab-Israeli Military Balance
Enters the 21st Century

ANTHONY H. CORDESMAN

Westport, Connecticut
London

Library of Congress Cataloging-in-Publication Data

Cordesman, Anthony H.
    Peace and war : the Arab-Israeli military balance enters the 21st century / Anthony H. Cordesman.
      p. cm.
    Includes bibliographical references.
    ISBN 0–275–96939–8 (alk. paper)
    1. Arab countries—Armed Forces. 2. Israel—Armed Forces. 3. Middle East—Armed
Forces. 4. Arab-Israeli conflict—1993– I. Title.
UA854.C67 2002
956.05'4—dc21   2001021180

British Library Cataloguing in Publication Data is available.

Library of Congress Catalog Card Number: 2001021180
ISBN: 0–275–96939–8

First published in 2002

Praeger Publishers, 88 Post Road West, Westport, CT 06881
An imprint of Greenwood Publishing Group, Inc.
www.praeger.com

Printed in the United States of America

The paper used in this book complies with the
Permanent Paper Standard issued by the National
Information Standards Organization (Z39.48–1984).

10 9 8 7 6 5 4 3 2 1

To Richard Fairbanks

The author would like to thank Carolyn Mann, Rebecca Litt, and Jeff Leary for their work in research, analysis, editing, and contribution to this book.

Contents

1

Assessing the Conventional Balance

The uncertain Arab-Israeli peace process has scarcely put an end to the threat of war or the Arab-Israeli arms race. Israel's peace agreements with Egypt and Jordan have not led to major reductions in force numbers and have had no effect in ending the race to improve force quality. In fact, the peace between Israel and Jordan is the only part of the peace process that has so far produced anything approaching "warm" relations, and even this peace has not led to either stable political relations or major economic relations and trade. The peace between Egypt and Israel is a "cold peace," and while both sides seem committed to preserving it, both also treat the opposing state as a potential threat in their military planning.

In the case of the partial peace between the Palestinians and Israel, it is difficult to tell the difference between the "Cold War" that preceded the Camp David and Oslo Agreements and the "Cold Peace" that has followed. Something approaching a Second Intifada began on September 29, 2000, and there are many "final settlement" issues that have not been fully addressed, much less resolved. Palestinian support for the peace process is still heavily dependent on the leadership of one man—Yasser Arafat—and there is a continuing risk of a shift in power to an anti-peace leadership. Israel faces its own political uncertainties, and there are deep divisions within Israel over what kind of peace Israel should accept, or whether a true peace is even possible.

At this writing, Israel and Syria have failed to make a major breakthrough in negotiating a peace. Israel is also involved in a low-level war with the Hizbollah, in which the Hizbollah has become a proxy for Syria and Iran. If Israel and Syria do reach such a peace, they will still retain massive war fighting capabilities and weapons of mass destruction, and any disengagement and force limitation agreements will be limited to reducing the risk of surprise attacks, rather than the ability to go to war. As a result, it will be years before it is clear whether a peace that results in Syria's reoccupation of the Golan brings lasting stability and peace.

There is political instability in Egypt, Jordan, and Syria, and incidents of terrorism or repression can undermine public support and pro-peace leaders. The nations of the region also face growing threats from outside the confrontation states. Proliferation is a regional and not simply an Arab-Israeli problem. The "linkage" between Iranian, Iraqi, Israeli, Libyan, and Syrian proliferation is creating a new set of region-wide threats. Iran is acquiring long-range missiles that can strike Israel, and Iraq may reemerge as a threat with both conventional forces and long-range missiles and weapons of mass destruction.

In short, peace is neither inevitable nor will it bring an end to history. While history may teach that "all wars must end," history is equally consistent in warning that "all peaces fail." It is likely to be a decade or more before Israel and its Arab neighbors make a major reduction in their current war fighting potential.

In the interim, the peace process may freeze into an uneasy status quo, fail in part, or fail altogether. If any aspect of the peace process does fail, the political and military risks of war are almost certain to increase. The present conventional arms race and the search for weapons of mass destruction are almost certain to accelerate. Almost regardless of the progress in the peace process, proliferation, advances in conventional military technology, asymmetric warfare, and the need to adjust force postures to any peace settlement will lead to continuing changes in the military balance and the risks it poses for future wars. A failing peace is likely to discredit and undermine moderate secular Arab regimes, encourage both Israel and Arab extremists, lead to violent exchanges of terrorism and counterterrorism, and possibly drag outside Arab and Islamic states into any future conflict.

Even if all the elements of the peace process do move forward, the end result will still be "peace with violence." Peace cannot eliminate all terrorism and extremist violence. There will be many future incidents of violence between Israel, the Palestinians and Hizbollah before the final stages of a peace settlement are agreed upon and fully implemented. "Peace" may sometimes escalate to low-intensity warfare.

True peace will require fundamental shifts in the present security policies of the nations in the region, major reductions in future military spending, and a process of confidence building measures and arms control to reduce the potential destructiveness of any future conflict. This will not be an easy task. "Peace" will inevitably increase some aspects of the regional arms race as nations attempt to adapt their force postures to the new demands of peace. Israel, for example, may have to make significant military investments to compensate for the loss of the Golan and territory in the West Bank. It may also have to shift its nuclear posture to new basing modes like submarines to ensure its survivability.

Even if arms reductions are agreed to, it will be many years before even the most successful peacemaking effort can reduce the capability to fight major wars. During this process, any asymmetries that unilateral force cuts or arms control create in the military balance may also lead to more extreme forms of escalation. Lower levels of arms may also lead to less technology-oriented conflicts that last longer and involve more close combat—fighting which inevitably produces higher casualties and more risk of involving civilian targets than brief intense wars directed at destroying key weapons and military facilities.

The wrong forms of confidence building measures, or moves towards "parity," could encourage risk-taking or reduce deterrence in a political crisis. Reductions in conventional military power may encourage irregular warfare or the use of weapons of mass destruction. A rise in the military power of the Gulf states at a time when Israel and its neighbors are disarming may encourage interventions by radical states like Iran or Iraq.

Finally, the trends in the military balance will have a continuing major domestic political and economic impact on Egypt, Israel, Jordan, Lebanon, the Palestinians, and Syria—regardless of the outcome of the peace negotiations. At least in the near-term, Israel and its neighbors will continue to spend some 10% to 25% of their central government expenditures, as much as 10% of their GNP, and as much as 10% of their annual hard currency imports on military forces. Such expenditures will remain a critical drain on their capability for development at a time when their total population will increase by over 50% during the coming decade.[1]

THE CONVENTIONAL BALANCE

The Arab-Israeli balance is still shaped largely by the conventional balance between Israel and its immediate neighbors—Egypt, Jordan, Lebanon, and Syria—the so-called "ring" or "confrontation" states. At the same time, a wide range of different factors are reshaping the way in which the Arab-Israeli balance must be measured and the contingencies that must be examined in determining that balance.

Some of the factors are positive. Israel's continuing peace with Egypt and Jordan, Israel's withdrawal from Lebanon and Lebanon's growing internal stability, the impact of the end of the Cold War on the regional arms race, the impact of the Gulf War, and the decline in Syria's arms imports and conventional war fighting capability. They include the relative weakness of the conventional threats to Israel from states like Iran, Iraq, and Libya. They also include the election of Prime Minister Ehud Barak in a pro-peace platform in the spring of 1999 and limits to Israeli defense spending, and the new security agreements that helped to lead to the Israeli and Palestinian agreement to move forward in implementing the Wye Accords in September 1999. It is striking that peace talks continued even after the outbreak of Israeli-Palestinian violence that began on September 29, 2000.

Other factors, however, act to increase the probability and/or possible intensity of a conflict. The most notable is the same outbreak of new violence between Israelis and Palestinians that has led to the risk of a prolonged Intifada, and which has again created broad anti-Israeli feeling in the Arab world. Other factors include the impact of the rise of Islamic extremism, the political and economic instability in the Arab states surrounding Israel, and the deep divisions within the Palestinian movement. They include religious divisions with Israel, Israeli extremists and political divisions between "doves" and "hawks." They include the weakening of the peace process after the assassination of Yitzhak Rabin and terror bombings in 1996, and the "peace fatigue" and loss of confidence that followed.

Israel and its neighbors remain ready for war. They maintain large standing military forces, they invest in massive levels of force modernization, and they maintain their military capabilities in combat ready postures. There is still a threat of the kind of major conventional war that occurred in 1948, 1956, 1967, and 1973. At the same time, the peace process brings new threats of low-level conflict, and proliferation and the acquisition of long-range missiles inside and outside the Arab-Israeli "ring states" creates the risk of new types of war. So does a growing Arab capability for asymmetric warfare.

This mix of trends makes it increasingly difficult to characterize and predict the Arab-Israeli balance, and there are many other problems that affect an analysis. Ever since 1948, the Arab-Israeli balance has been determined primarily by uncertainty and "intangibles," not force numbers.

Disarray and disunity prevented Arab forces from being effective in 1948. A sudden British and French intervention over the Suez Crisis shaped the outcome in 1956. Israeli surprise and tactical innovation, coupled with Egyptian unprepared-ness, led to a massive Israeli victory in 1967. The Canal War of 1970 was an unexpected battle of attrition shaped largely by major Soviet deliveries of new air defense weapons. Arab surprise shaped the initial outcome of the 1973 war, only to see the course of the fighting reversed by a daring Israeli thrust across the Suez Canal supported by major US resupply efforts. The outcome was then affected, in turn, by Russian threats to move missiles to the region and pressures on the US to push Israel towards partial withdrawals as part of the cease-fires. In 1982, a fundamental Israeli misreading of the situation in Lebanon, and a rogue effort to transform a limited action against the PLO into an attack on Syria, turned an initial Israeli victory into a war of occupation and a strategic defeat. Russia then altered the balance with a massive flow of aid to Syria. In each case, the course of the fighting and its final outcome was shaped as much by the specific scenario as by force quality or force quantity.

At the same time, "intangibles" like leadership, training, manpower quality, tactics, innovation, flexibility, effective use of combined arms and jointness, command and control capability, and battle management skills shaped the out-come of each conflict. No Arab-Israel conflict has ever had an outcome determined by easily quantifiable force ratios or pre-conflict orders of battle.

Uncertainty and "intangibles" are likely to be equally important in the future. The peace process, proliferation, and end of the Cold War make future scenarios even more unpredictable, and make sweeping comparisons of the total size of Arab and Israeli forces even less relevant. At the same time, the changes now taking place in tactics, training, and technology emphasize the value of force quality relative to force quantity. As the Gulf War has demonstrated, the "revolution in military affairs" is changing the nature of warfare and large inventories of older or mediocre equipment are more likely to be targets than assets.

COUNTING TOTAL FORCES

"Intangibles" do not mean that comparisons of force strength are not important. Numbers still tell. Force ratios, manpower, and equipment numbers have an important impact on both political perceptions of the balance, and they have value in estimating war-fighting capabilities. Force numbers can be particularly valuable when they show the full range of major combat weapons, and show the different force mixes involved in different countries. Simple counts of total manpower, or a few weapons categories like tanks and combat aircraft, often disguise as much as they reveal.

Deciding What to Count

Much, however, does depend on which forces are counted. For example, Table 1.1 reflects a "classic" Israeli estimate of the military balance that was made before Israel's peace with Jordan and the Palestinians, and that is based on the total conventional forces the Arab states can deploy against Israel. This is now a dated, "worst case" method of comparison that exaggerates the probability of such coalitions and the total forces they can deploy. Few Israeli analysts and planners now base their assessments on comparisons of Israel's total forces with the total forces that all Arab states could conceivably deploy against Israel.[2]

Table 1.1 illustrates the problems inherent in force counts that include too many countries and forces. The total Arab forces include the total forces of Egypt, Jordan, Lebanon, the PLO, Syria, the entire Libyan Navy, and selected forces from the Saudi Army, Iraq, Kuwait, the Algerian Army, Morocco, Libya, and minor elements of land forces from Iran. Any such comparisons include large numbers of undeployable and unsustainable Arab forces, and imply a degree of Arab unity that never existed during the period before Egypt, Jordan, and the PLO signed peace agreements with Israel. Further, many of the Arab states involved have long been as concerned with other enemies and internal enemies as with Israel.

There are several reasons why such "region-wide" counts of Arab forces should not be used as a key measure of war-fighting capabilities, and should be reserved for low probability worst cases:

- Egypt and Jordan seem firmly committed to the peace process. They retain significant war fighting capability against Israel, but no longer train, deploy, and create support structures tailored to such operations.
- Syria is the key component in an "Arab-Israeli balance" but only a limited fraction of the strength of Arab states like Iraq could come to Syria's assistance.
- Lebanon is not a real military force in the sense of meaningful capability for joint, armored, or combined arms warfare.

Table 1.1

The Arab-Israeli Balance: A Past Israeli View of the Arab Threat as One Including All of the Arab Forces in the Region

Category/ Weapon	1984 Arab	1984 Israel	1984 Ratio	1994 Arab	1994 Israel	1994 Ratio
A. Land Forces						
Divisions						
Armor	10	11	0.9	16	12	1.3
Mechanized	10	-	-	14	-	-
Infantry	3	-	-	3	4	0.8
Total	23	11	2.1	33	16	2.1
Independent Brigades	51	20	2.5	44	13	3.4
Tanks	8065	3650	2.2	10400	3850	2.7
Other Armored Vehicles	8470	8000	1.1	13250	8100	1.6
Artillery & Mortars	6050	1000	6.0	6100	1300	4.7
B. Air Forces and Air Defense						
Interceptors						
High Quality	130	40	3.3	215	75	2.9
Others	620	-	-	478	-	-
Total	750	40	18.8	693	75	9.5
Strike/FGA						
High Quality	496	445	1.1	72	204	0.4
Others	354	185	1.9	467	463	1.1
Total	850	530	1.6	539	667	1.2
Total Combat Aircraft	1635	670	2.4	1236	742	1.8
Helicopters						
Attack	161	55	2.9	280	115	2.4
Other	324	133	2.4	362	138	2.6
Total	485	188	2.6	642	253	2.5
Military Airfields	48	11	4.4	65	11	5.9
C. Naval Forces						
Major Missile Surface	8	0	-	14	0	-
Major Non-Missile Surface	8	0	-	2	0	-
Submarines	18	3	6.0	17	3	5.7
Missile Patrol Boats	67	24	2.8	67	19	3.5
Landing Craft						

Source: Adapted by the author from Shlomo Gazit, Zeev Eytan, *The Middle East Military Balance,* 1984-1994, JCSS/Westview, Tel Aviv/Boulder, 1995, pp. 494–499.

- Algeria, Morocco, Kuwait, Saudi Arabia, and Tunisia are very unlikely to contribute significant military forces to an Arab-Israeli conflict, and face major potential threats from Iran and Iraq.

- Libya's forces have never been adequately manned, have little power projection capability and sustainability, and are steadily deteriorating in equipment quality and overall modernization.

- No Arab state can deploy all of its forces against Israel without removing the security forces that are critical to the regime. This is particularly important in the case of Iraq and Syria, where the presence of troops supporting the regime plays a critical factor in ensuring the regime's day-to-day survival.

At the same time, the risk of "region-wide" coalitions cannot be totally ignored. Iraq did play a significant role in the October War. There is no "right" count of Arab-Israeli forces. As this book explores in depth, there are many different comparisons, which represent valid pictures of possible scenarios. These can range from counts of the forces that might be involved in a relatively low-intensity conflict between Israel and the Palestinians to counts estimating the forces in a theater-wide conflict with many elements of the Israeli "worst case" scenario. Even contingency-oriented counts do, however, have their limitations. Counts of total national forces do not reflect the portion of the total force that a given country can actually deploy and sustain in combat, and ignore many aspects of force quality.

The Strengths and Weaknesses of Manpower Numbers

Even if one does make the right decisions as to which forces should be counted, there are other limitations to the value of the resulting figures. Total manpower numbers do provide a rough picture of the level of effort given nations devote to their military forces and of the war fighting capabilities of armies. At the same time, manpower training and experience are as important as manpower numbers. The quality of a given force's NCO, technician, and junior officers shape the ability to use modern combat equipment effectively. The value of conscript forces depends heavily on their funding and training. For example, Egypt and Syria grossly underfund conscript training, and most of their conscripts have too little experience and training, and never realistically train in complex war fighting scenarios and exercises.

Active manpower is hard to compare to reserve manpower. Much of the reserve manpower in Arab forces has limited value due to a lack of training, modern equipment, sustainability, and adequate C^4I/BM capability. The Israeli reserve system is far more effective than that of any of its Arab neighbors, in part because Israel has such a small population that it has no alternative. Even Israel, however, has found it increasingly difficult to give reserve forces the training they need to maintain a capability for advanced maneuver warfare, and most Arab land force reserve manpower has little training, second or third rate equipment, and little capability in maneuver and demanding combined arms warfare.

Money is a steadily increasing problem. Modern military forces are so expensive that Middle Eastern states cannot afford to use much of their total manpower pool because they cannot fund suitable equipment, training, and sustainability. At the same time, states cannot use much of the manpower in their military forces in missions tailored to large-scale wars with their neighbors. Internal security and low-intensity operations degrade training for war fighting, and this presents a serious manpower quality problem for Israel, Egypt, and Syria. It is a problem both countries face difficulties addressing because of the need to avoid additional unemployment and the feeling that mass conscription aids in political indoctrination and "nation-building."

The Strengths and Weaknesses of Equipment Numbers

Comparisons of equipment numbers have similar strengths and weaknesses. Past Arab-Israeli conflicts, the Iran-Iraq War, and the Gulf War have all shown that equipment quality is often more important than force numbers. For example, the comparisons of Arab and Israeli forces shown in Table 1.1 are the result of a major build-up in Middle Eastern land force numbers that continued from the late 1940s to the early 1990s. Holdings of armored forces and artillery increased significantly in size. However, much of the increase in the total inventory of Arab land weapons is the result of the fact that some Arab states continue to retain older and low quality systems that have only limited capability. The value of much of this equipment is uncertain, and so is the ability of Arab forces to man it effectively.

Force quality can also improve strikingly even as force numbers drop or remain constant. Israel has cut aircraft numbers to fund major improvements in the quality of its combat aircraft. Reductions have taken place in the size of Arab forces in response because of factors like attrition and the rising cost of aircraft. At the same time, the Arab combat aircraft have also improved strikingly in relative quality.

Changes in force mix affect the meaning of equipment numbers as well as any counts of major combat unit strength. For example, the counts of fixed-wing aircraft in Table 1.1 do not reflect the fact that both sides now have significantly larger numbers of attack helicopters. Further, such totals overstate the strength of both Israel and Arab air forces by counting some aircraft in storage or training units.

Dealing with Force Quantity and Force Quality

The analysis that follows is based on the thesis that a meaningful assessment of the military balance must look far beyond simple quantitative comparisons of the total size of Arab and Israeli forces. It examines the Arab-Israeli balance many different ways. These include a detailed look at the level of resources available to each country and the flow of arms into the region over a period of decades. These comparisons show that various countries have grossly different total military expenditures and access to modern arms, and that the forces of Israel and Egypt have benefited far more from recent arms transfers than those of Jordan, Lebanon, and Syria.

The analysis examines different ways to count conventional forces, and possible ways of relating force numbers to force quality. It examines the quality of manpower and weapons by country and service, and the impact of changes in military technology. It then integrates such analysis with an examination of the kinds of contingencies and scenarios most likely to affect the future, and how changes in both force quantity and force quality are likely to affect future wars.

2

Arab–Israeli Military Efforts and Arms Transfers

Comparisons of military effort, defense expenditures, and arms sales provide important insights into the broad trends in military effort—and set the stage for the analysis of both force numbers and force quality. Countries differ sharply in the size of their economy, and in the relative military effort they make at any given time. Figure 2.1, for example, shows a declassified US intelligence estimate of the trends in Arab-Israeli military spending in current dollars from 1967 to 1995—the most recent year for which directly comparable declassified data are available. These comparisons provide a broad picture of the trends in military spending, but they do not correct for inflation and the figures are not directly comparable from year to year. Figure 2.2, in contrast, shows a similar declassified intelligence estimate of the trends in military spending measured in constant dollars. The use of constant dollars compensates for the impact of inflation and provides figures that are directly comparable over time.

The patterns in these figures show that Israel's military spending has dropped since the mid-1980s, but still approaches the military spending of all its immediate neighbors combined. When these military expenditures are compared to the size of the forces they fund, it becomes equally clear that most Arab states spend relatively little in comparison to the total size of their armed forces, and that key countries like Syria have made sharper cuts since 1985 than Israel. These spending trends affect Arab-Israeli force modernization, readiness, sustainability, and every other aspect of force quality. They also provide an important picture of each nation's ability to "recapitalize" its holdings of weapons, military equipment, munitions, and infrastructure.

Figure 2.1
Trend in Total Arab-Israeli Military Spending by Country: 1967–1997
(in $US Current Millions)

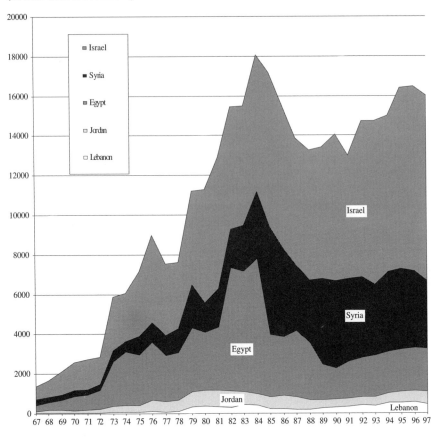

Source: Adapted by Anthony H. Cordesman from US State Department, Bureau of Arms Control, *World Military Expenditures and Arms Transfers*, Washington, GPO, various editions, Table I. Note that the author has made extensive estimates for Syria and Lebanon, and that the ACDA data differ in definition over time. The author has made extensive adjustments using editions in an attempt to make the data more comparable over the entire period, but this is not fully possible for the period from 1967 to 1973.

DIFFERENCES IN THE SIZE OF NATIONAL ECONOMIES AND IN THE LEVEL OF MILITARY EFFORT

Military spending is a function of both economic capability and perceived risk. The economies of Israel, Egypt, Jordan, Lebanon, and Syria differ sharply in size, structure, and relative wealth. Israel is the only highly industrialized state in the

Figure 2.2
National Trends in Arab-Israeli Military Spending in Constant Dollars: The Decline in Arab Forces as a Share of Total Spending: 1985–1997
(In $US 1997 Constant Millions)

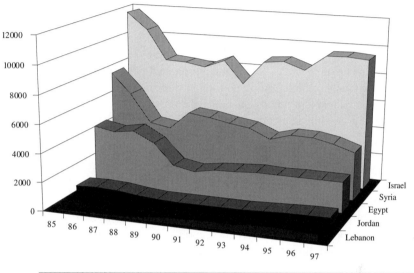

	85	86	87	88	89	90	91	92	93	94	90	96	97
■ Lebanon	120	85	75	120	150	370	400	471	428	541	556	561	465
■ Jordan	870	910	813	626	523	471	478	470	477	535	581	609	626
▣ Egypt	4430	4150	4380	3600	2160	1840	2070	2150	2230	2190	2180	2170	2180
▣ Syria	7750	6320	4280	4000	5240	5045	4720	4500	3870	4260	4210	3920	3400
□ Israel	11750	10555	8400	8280	8060	8620	7040	8730	8880	8330	9440	9490	9340

Source: Adapted by Anthony H. Cordesman from US State Department, Bureau of Arms Control, *World Military Expenditures and Arms Transfers*, Washington, GPO, Table I, various editions.

region, with industrial production worth 22% of the GDP and growing at an annual real growth rate of 8%. Although Israel had a population of only 5,842,000 in 2000, the CIA estimates that Israel had a GDP worth $105.4 billion in 1999 in purchasing power parity terms, and a per capita GDP of $18,300. Its exports were worth $23.5 billion, and consisted largely of industrial goods and light manufactures. Israel's imports were worth $30.6 billion.[3]

In contrast, Egypt had a population of 68,360,000 in 2000, a GDP worth $200 billion in 1999, in purchasing power parity terms, and a per capita income of only $3,000. More than 30% of its workforce was employed by the state sector, and industrial production was a relatively low percentage of the economy. Egypt's exports were only worth $4.6 billion, while its imports cost $15.8 billion. Egypt had more than 10 times Israel's population, but substantially less than twice its GDP and less than 20% of Israel's per capita income. As a result, Egypt faces much more severe limits in allocating money to military expenditures and manufactures than Israel.[4]

Jordan and Lebanon have much smaller economies than both Israel and Egypt. Jordan had a population of 4,999,000 in 2000, and a GDP worth $16.0 billion in 1999. Its per capita GDP was $3,500. Jordan's exports were worth $1.8 billion, while its imports cost $3.3 billion. Jordan is one of the few countries in the region to make significant economic reforms and has improved its economic performance since a recession following the Gulf War. It has improved its debt serve and debt to export ratios to some of the best in the region, and has passed new investment, financial market corporate taxes, and foreign exchange laws. This still, however, has not overcome the problems caused by the stalemate in the peace process and high population growth. Jordan's per capita GNP showed little real growth between 1994 and 1998, its annual budget deficit increased steadily, and its trade balance remained sharply negative—with imports averaging about twice exports.[5]

Lebanon had a population of 3,578,000 in 2000 and a GDP worth $16.2 billion in 1999, when measured in terms of purchasing power parity. Its per capita GDP was $4,500. Lebanon's exports were worth only $0.866 billion, while its imports cost $5.7 billion. Syria's economy was less than half the size of that of Israel, although its population was nearly three times larger. Syria had a population of 16,306,000 in 2000, and a GDP worth $42.2 billion in 1999. Its per capita GDP was $2,500. Syria's exports were worth $3.3 billion, while its imports cost $3.2 billion.[6]

In total, Egypt, Jordan, Lebanon, and Syria had a combined GDP worth over $270 billion, or about 2.6 times larger than that of Israel. They had a population of nearly 95 million, or 16 times larger. These comparisons, however, have never had much impact on the military balance because the Arab states have never approached Israel's efficiency in mobilizing its economy to fund military forces. Although Egypt and Jordan are moving towards reform, the rigid state sectors of Israel's major Arab neighbors have crippled both their economic development and their ability to fund military forces.

The regional data on military spending as a percentage of GNP and national budgets are a morass of classified or partial reporting, and definitional and comparability problems. Nevertheless, enough data are available to make it clear that there is little correlation between the size of total national military spending and the burden it places on the economy and state budget. While Israel leads all states in cumulative spending on military forces, Syria's percentage of central government expenditures devoted to military spending is the highest in the region. Jordan's economic problems have forced it to cut the amount of its budget it devotes to defense, and its peace with Israel has made it possible to reduce spending still further. More is involved, however, than economic efficiency. Israel and Egypt are only able to limit military spending as a percentage of central government expenditures as much as they do because they receive large amounts of US military aid.

A mix of economic pressures and the "peace dividend" made possible by Israel's peaces with Egypt, Jordan and the Palestinians have led Israel and its Arab neighbors to make significant reductions in the amount of their total economies they devote to military spending. Figure 2.3 shows the latest declassified US intelligence trends in military spending as a percentage of GNP. While these data only go up to 1977, a comparison of these data with national and other sources reveals several trends:

- A significant decline took place in total real military spending after 1982. A massive drop took place in the percent of GDP that Israel and Syria spend on military forces. Shortly after the 1982 war, the level of total GDP allocated to military spending in both countries is less than half of what it was in the early 1980s.

- Israel continues to outspend any individual Arab ring state by a large margin, and is the only regional state to sustain the military spending levels necessary to both pay for significant military modernization and to fund a relatively high level of force quality by the standards of the developed world. At the same time, Israel's costs for manpower, operations, and maintenance are substantially higher than those of Arab states.

- Egypt is the only Arab state to sustain the military spending levels necessary to both pay for significant military modernization and to fund a relatively high level of force quality by the standards of the developing world.

- Jordan, Lebanon, and Syria have spent so little on military forces since the early 1990s that they have failed to compete with Israel in force modernization and readiness.

- While the percentages have dropped considerably since 1983, each country in the region continues to spend significant percentages of their GNP on their military forces.

The data in Figure 2.3 show that there has been a major drop in Arab-Israeli military efforts since the crisis years following Israel's 1982 invasion of Lebanon, although the spending levels shown in these figures still reflect major military efforts by all of the nations concerned. Figure 2.3 also shows that there has been a similar drop in military spending as a percent of the gross national product. Military spending makes up less than 50% of the portion of state spending than it did a decade ago.

Taken together, Figures 2.1 to 2.3 show the priority each government gives military spending relative to its total budget. Israel, in particular, has cut the burden on its economy and budget by over 50%. This level of military effort is very different from the period between 1948 and 1984, when the Arab-Israel ring states generally pushed their military expenditures to the highest levels their economies could tolerate. At the same time, it is clear that Egypt, Israel, Jordan, Lebanon, and Syria all have demonstrated in the past that they can rapidly raise their military spending to much higher percentages of their GNPs and national budgets if they choose to do so at the expense of economic development and civil spending.

Figure 2.3
Trend in Percent of GNP Spent on Military Forces: 1983–1997: Half the Burden of
the Early 1980s

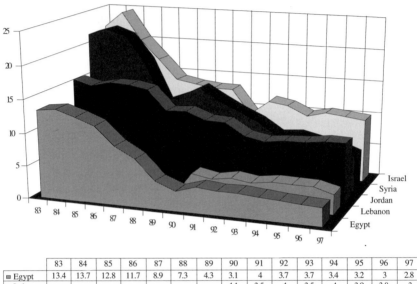

	83	84	85	86	87	88	89	90	91	92	93	94	95	96	97
Egypt	13.4	13.7	12.8	11.7	8.9	7.3	4.3	3.1	4	3.7	3.7	3.4	3.2	3	2.8
Lebanon	-	-	-	-	-	-	-	4.1	3.5	4	3.5	4	3.9	3.8	3
Jordan	15.6	14.9	15.5	15.4	14.8	12	12	10.8	10.7	8.8	8.3	8.6	8.7	9	9
Syria	21.8	22.7	21.8	18	11.7	12.9	14.4	12.6	11.1	9.7	7.8	8	7.4	6.7	5.6
Israel	22.2	24.5	20.3	17.3	14.2	13.6	13.2	13.2	9.4	11.7	11.2	9.8	10.5	10.1	9.7

Source: Adapted by Anthony H. Cordesman from US State Department, Bureau of Arms Control,
World Military Expenditures and Arms Transfers, Washington, GPO, Table I, various editions.

PROBLEMS IN DOLLAR COMPARISONS OF MILITARY
EXPENDITURES AND ARMS SALES

There are important uncertainties in the data in Figures 2.1 through 2.3, and in
all of the data available on military efforts and military expenditures. There are
three major sources for directly comparable data on the military expenditures and
arms sales of Egypt, Israel, Jordan, Lebanon, and Syria: the Bureau of Arms
Control in US State Department (formerly the Arms Control and Disarmament
Agency or ACDA), the Stockholm International Peace Research Institute (SIPRI),
and the International Institute of Strategic Studies (IISS). Out of all these sources,
only the Bureau of Arms Control has access to US intelligence data, and can draw
on the major analytic effort that goes on within the US intelligence community.
The SIPRI data have to be based largely on the estimates of a small group of private
analysts. The IISS data rely on a mix of official sources, but only report on military
expenditures, and sometimes vary in definition from year to year and country to

country in ways that limit the value of both trend and inter-country comparisons.[7]

While the State Department data are taken from material provided by the US intelligence community, they too have problems. These problems include:

- They often do not track with national reporting on military expenditures in budget documents, and the data on military expenditures for Egypt, Jordan, Lebanon, and Syria are exceptionally rough estimates.[8]

- The data on military expenditures are not fully comparable in definition from country to country. They generally exclude expenditures on weapons of mass destruction, and exclude many imports of long-range missiles.

- The data are not fully comparable in terms of the amount of military imports included or in terms of the extent to which they include new foreign debt and/or past interest payments on military foreign debt—data excluded from the budget reporting of all of the Arab states listed.

- The data are not fully comparable in terms of the amount of non-military goods and services used by the military, and include very different levels of military infrastructure expenditures.

- There is no way to adjust for the very different costs each country pays for manpower. Israel, for example, pays for high quality regular manpower, but is primarily a reserve force. Arab states pay almost nothing for conscripts and very low salaries for other ranks and many junior officers.

Table 2.1 shows the most recent IISS estimates of Arab-Israel military spending and a comparison of the data in this table with Figures 2.1 to 2.3 illustrates the range of uncertainty in the two best sources of comparable data on military spending. While some of the estimates are sometimes similar, the estimates can be different because of changes in the definition used by given countries, and because the IISS tended to report the figures given countries make public while the ACDA figures are based on intelligence estimates of total actual spending in directly comparable terms. Nevertheless, several key trends emerge in both sets of data:

- Israeli spending is high relative to that of individual countries.
- Egypt is the only Arab state spending enough to fund large effective forces.
- Jordan, Lebanon, and Syria face major funding problems.
- Iraqi military spending has decreased significantly as a result of the Gulf War although it continues to spend a high level of its GDP for military purposes.
- Lebanon has increased military spending, but its expenditures remain too low to buy significant military capability.
- Libyan expenditures remain relatively high for a nation with so little military capability, but reflect a severe drop relative to the period in the 1980s when Libya was a major arms importer.

Table 2.1

IISS Estimate of Military Spending and Manpower Trends: 1985–2000

Trend: 1985 versus 1995 * ($US are in Constant 1995 prices)

Country	Military Expenditures is $US Millions			Military Spending Per Capita ($US)			Military Spending as a % of GDP			Military Manpower (1,000s) Active		Reserve	Para
	85	94	95	85	94	95	85	94	95	85	95	85	95
Israel	6,899	6,842	7,197	1,630	1,286	1,279	21.2	9.1	9.2	142.0	172.0	430.0	6.1
Egypt	3,527	2,234	2,417	73	40	42	7.2	4.3	4.3	445.0	436.0	254.0	174.0
Jordan	822	441	440	235	100	100	16.9	7.2	6.7	70.3	98.6	35.0	10.0
Lebanon	273	370	407	102	92	102	9.0	5.1	5.3	17.4	44.3	-	18.5
Syria	4,756	2,165	2,026	453	155	142	16.4	7.6	6.8	402.5	423.0	650.0	8.0
Iraq	17,573	2,748	2,700	1,105	138	128	25.9	14.6	14.8	520.0	382.5	650.0	24.8
Libya	1,844	1,413	1,401	490	280	259	6.2	5.5	5.5	73.0	80.0	40.0	0.5

Annual Expenditures in Dollars ** ($US are in Current Billions)

	1990	1991	1992	1993	1994	1995	1996	1997	1998	1999	2000
Israel	6.16	5.0	7.4	6.2	6.7	9.3	11.0	11.3	9.2	8.9	-
Egypt	1.57	1.65	2.1	2.48	2.2	2.5	2.7	2.7	2.8	3.0	-
Jordan	0.571	0.415	0.525	0.430	0.537	0.448	0.451	0.496	0.548	0.569	-
Lebanon	0.140	0.176	0.233	0.275	0.363	0.490	0.484	0.676	0.594	0.560	-
Palestinian Authority	-	-	-	-	0.084	0.170	0.248	0.250	0.300	0.500	-
Syria	1.62	4.5	2.2	2.38	2.1	1.7	2.0	2.2	1.7	1.9	-
Iraq	8.61		2.5	2.6	2.7	1.3	1.3	1.3	1.3	1.4	-
Libya	1.82	2.7	2.3	1.091	1.4	1.4	1.3	1.3	1.5	1.3	1.2

*Source: Adapted by Anthony H. Cordesman from International Institute for Strategic Studies, *Military Balance*, 1996–1997, London, IISS/Oxford, 1996.

**Source: Adapted by Anthony H. Cordesman from International Institute for Strategic Studies, *Military Balance*, various editions. Data for the Palestinian Authority is the security budget and includes police and law enforcement. Figures in parenthesis are the military budget and normally use a different definition from the estimate of actual spending shown in earlier years.

WHAT CAN BE LEARNED FROM COMPARISONS OF MILITARY EXPENDITURES

The data available are so uncertain or different in definition that it is difficult to go beyond these broad trends. Nevertheless, there are some additional sources of data on individual countries that are of value. When these sources are used to supplement the ACDA and IISS data on national trends they offer additional insights into Arab-Israeli military efforts that have a high degree of credibility:[9]

- Israel is the only country that publicly debates its military spending in any detail, and where it is possible to supplement outside estimates with a summary of domestic figures. Israeli military spending dropped from $12 billion annually in 1985, in constant 1997 dollars, to around $9.5 billion in the mid-1990s, and further cuts took place during much of the late 1990s. Israeli reporting which uses somewhat different definitions and conversion factors, indicates that the Israeli military budget was $8.25 billion in current dollars in 1995 and $8.28 billion in 1996. This cut for 1996 came after a major debate within the Israeli cabinet, a debate that illustrated some of the problems Israel faces in making peace. The Israeli military had requested an additional $492.6 million to cover current and planned withdrawals from Gaza and the West Bank. However, the IDF's military budget was cut by $56.5 million for the Fiscal Year 1997. In July 1997, the Israeli Ministry of Defense was forced to cut $58 million from its annual spending budget and $14 million from its internal security budget. This was to accommodate an across-the-board one percent cut in the Israeli budget.[10] Similar debates and cuts took place in FY 1998. In FY1999, the Ministry of Defense aggressively sought to increase its defense budget by 5%. It sought to raise the defense budget by an additional $500 million and provide Israel with financing for long-term projects. The IDF claimed that the difference in deficit between real defense spending and defense requirements would grow to around $15 billion by 2010.[11] The IDF did not get the money it sought, and faced new cuts in its budget requests for FY2000. Its spending request was cut by 950 million New Israel Shekels (NIS), or $224 million.[12]

- Syrian military spending dropped from around $7.4 billion annually in the mid-1980s—in constant 1997 US dollars—to around $4 billion in 1995. It was below $3.5 billion in 1997.

- Jordanian military spending, which was always low by the standards of its neighbors, declined steadily after 1987 and remained below $500 million until 1993. It then gradually crept back to over $600 million after 1996. Even so, financial pressures forced Jordan to downsize its forces after it ceased to receive significant amounts of aid after 1990, in reaction to its political support for Iraq during the Gulf War. The renewal of US aid in 1996 gave Jordan some relief, but much of the money went to buy F-16 aircraft and the resulting support costs for the F-16 put additional strains on the Jordanian defense budget. Funding problems still seriously limit the readiness and modernization of the Jordanian forces—particularly the army.[13]

- Egyptian domestic military spending dropped from around $4.4 billion annually during the mid-1980s to $2.2 billion in 1995, and remained below $3 billion through FY2000.

This cut was made possible only by high levels of US aid, and the Egyptian military was increasingly forced to depend on this aid for new acquisitions because so much of Egypt's lower domestic military budget had to be used to pay for personnel and maintenance costs.

- Lebanese military spending showed a slight recovery after Syrian intervention put an end to Lebanon's civil war, but continues to be so low that Lebanon has little hope of developing serious military capabilities unless it can find a source of large amounts of foreign military aid. Lebanese spending ranged from around $500 million to $700 million in the mid to late 1990s, and was below $600 million in 1998 and 1999.

Syrian Military Expenditures

It is useful to look at some of the other factors shaping military spending on a country-by-country basis. Syria—Israel's major remaining rival—has consistently had some of the worst economic leadership, highest levels of corruption in allocating its military and arms expenditures, and most excessive state interference in the economy of any developing state. It has never implemented effective economy reform, and state interference has crippled its economic growth and development for roughly a quarter of a century. The agricultural sector accounts for 40% of the labor force and 26% of the GNP, and remains underdeveloped. The CIA estimates that roughly 80% of agricultural land is still dependent on rain-fed sources. While Syria currently has sufficient water supplies at normal levels of precipitation, the great distance between major water supplies and population centers poses serious distribution problems and serious annual fluctuations in rainfall.

Syria's water problems are compounded by rapid population growth, industrial expansion, and increased water pollution. Private investment is badly needed to expand and modernize the agricultural, energy, and export sectors, but many barriers still exist to both domestic and foreign investment, and the state interferes in many aspects of business operations—sometimes in the form of serious corruption and forced nepotism. Oil production is leveling and will probably decline, and development of non-oil exports has been poor. The CIA reports that Syria has an inadequate infrastructure, outmoded technological base, and weak educational system. At the same time, a high population growth rate well in excess of 3.0% a year has limited any increase in its real per capita income and its ability to raise discretionary spending on defense.

Syrian reporting on its military budget has little meaning. For example, Syria reported spending only $878 million for 1998, although this was still over 25% of the national budget. This figure does not seem to have included procurement, however, and it is not clear how Syria financed its presence in Lebanon.[14]

Syria was able to seek numerical parity with Israel in conventional forces until the mid-1980s because of a combination of aid from the Gulf and arms from the

Soviet Union and the Warsaw Pact. These arms, however, were provided through grant aid and favorable long-term loans. Syria ceased to accept such aid from the Soviet Union and the Warsaw Pact in the mid- to late 1980s, and had to buy on credit. Syria also found that it could not meet its arms debt to Russia that had reached a total that many experts estimated as approaching $11 billion. This effectively halted Russian credit to Syria, and Syria had only limited ability to buy arms from Russia because of its debt problem.

Although Syria did receive an allotment of aid close to $1 billion at the time of the Gulf War, it received little military aid from the Gulf states after 1991. The money it did receive for supporting the Coalition against Iraq was only sufficient to allow it to continue to modernize some of its armor and self-propelled artillery. It was not sufficient to allow it to fund the other major force improvements it needed, and Syria has now been unable to find any major source of outside aid for nearly a decade.

Jordanian Military Expenditures

Jordan received significant Arab aid during the oil boom of the late 1970s and early 1980s, and its annual real GNP growth then averaged more than 10%. Jordan never received anything approaching the level of Gulf and Soviet bloc aid provided to Syria, however, and reductions in Arab aid and worker remittances slowed its real economic growth to an average of roughly 2% per year during the rest of the 1980s. Jordan's imports—mainly oil, capital goods, consumer durables, and food—sharply outstripped its exports and Jordan had to finance the difference with aid, remittances, and borrowing.[15]

As a result, Jordan's economy entered a crisis from which it has not yet recovered. The Jordanian Government began debt-rescheduling negotiations in mid-1989, and agreed to implement an IMF-supported program designed to gradually reduce the budget deficit and implement badly needed structural reforms.[16]

Jordan supported Iraq during the early phase of its invasion of Kuwait, and this put an end to aid from the Gulf while worker remittances, and trade contracted; in addition refugees flooded the country. This forced Jordan to put an end to the IMF program, created serious balance-of-payments problems, reduced GDP growth, and created a major new burden on government resources. Jordan had to halt its debt payments and suspend rescheduling negotiations. The Jordanian economy did grow in 1992, but only because of a one-time influx of capital repatriated by workers returning from the Gulf, but this spending did not sustain development.

Jordan's external debt—which had been $348 million in 1975 and $4.0 billion in 1985—rose to $6.9 billion in 1993 and $7.4 billion in 1994. It was still at $7.5 billion in 1999, in spite of austerity measures.[17] Jordan reached a new agreement with the IMF in early 1999, which should provide new loans over the next three years. It is not clear, however, that either these loans or the current scale of economic reform will lead to significant growth, and overcome the problems posed by debt, poverty, and unemployment.

Jordan's economic problems led to a British-Jordanian study in 1994 of how to cut Jordanian forces to a more affordable level, which involved a $10 billion restructuring plan designed to trade manpower cuts for the funds necessary to buy more equipment. Although Jordan did make some cuts in its forces, it still cannot afford to fund munitions, spares, and modernization—much less major amounts of new equipment. Further, Jordan had to cut its domestic civil and military spending sharply in 1990 as a result of the cuts in aid coming from the Gulf states and western states as well.

Jordan continued to operate under sharp spending constraints in the late 1990s.[18] For example, Jordan raised its military spending from 318 million Dinars in 1997 to 347 million Dinars in 1998; the loss of value of the Dinar reduced spending in dollars from $488 million to $447 million.[19] As a result, net Jordanian military expenditures—including foreign aid to buy military equipment—have dropped far more than the data in Figure 2.1 indicate.[20]

Jordan will benefit, however, from its peace with Israel, gradual rapprochement with the Gulf states, and post-Gulf War opposition to Saddam Hussein. This led to the renewal of US military assistance to Jordan. As a result, Jordan embarked on a military restructuring program aimed at redefining the image and purpose of the military. Jordan hoped to fund this program with increased US aid and a possible renewal of aid from the Gulf States.[21] FMF assistance from the US in 1999 totaled $45 million and increased to $75 million in the 2000 budget. Jordan received an additional $100 million in 1999 and another $100 million over the next two years.[22] In 1999, the US offered Jordan a new 5-year, $575 million military aid package. US aid is planned to reach $170 million annually during FY1998–FY2000, with $200 million more now that the Wye Memorandum of 1998 is to be implemented.[23]

Egyptian Military Expenditures

Egypt still suffers badly from the legacy of Arab socialism under Nasser and a conversion to a state-controlled economy that effectively crippled its economic development for nearly a quarter of a century. Even in the late 1980s, Egypt had critical problems with poor productivity and economic management. The CIA reports that these problems were compounded by excessive population growth, high inflation, and massive urban overcrowding. In 1991, however, Egypt began to undertake wide-ranging macroeconomic stabilization and structural reform measures. Its reform efforts have since been supported by three agreements with the IMF, the last of which expired in September 1998. Egypt's reform efforts—and its support of the UN Coalition in the Gulf—gave it massive debt relief under the Paris Club arrangements.[24]

Since that time, Egypt has made growing progress. It has controlled inflation, reduced its budget deficits, and built up substantial foreign reserves. Its structural reforms—including privatization, easing investment constraints, and reducing the barriers to forming new businesses have lagged behind the schedule under the IMF program, but Egypt's shift to a market-oriented economy has led to increased foreign investment. Egypt's improving internal stability also seems to be overcoming the impact of incidents like the November 1997 killings of foreign tourists in Luxor, as has the rise in world oil prices that began in the spring of 1999.

Any effort to analyze the Egyptian military illustrates the problems inherent in trying to determine the trends in nations that do not make the details of their military spending public. As is the case with the other Arab states that affect the Arab-Israeli balance, the details of the Egyptian defense budget are secret, and Egypt's reporting tends to change without any clear public explanation.

For example, work by the US State Department indicates that Egypt did not report any expenditures for defense and security in its 1998/1999 budget.[25] If all other listed expenditures in the budget are subtracted, this leaves LE 22 billion (USD $6.47 billion). This figure, however, contains more than just the defense/interior/justice accounts. The Government of Egypt (GOE) has combined expenditures on the military, internal security, and justice over the past several years and provided only one figure. The unspecified military portion of this figure has traditionally included military wages, local purchases and maintenance but does not include the value of US aid. This US aid includes USD $1.3 billion in annual direct benefits through USG Foreign Military Financing (FMF) or security assistance, and the indirect benefits of an additional $800 million in annual Economic Support Funding.

In past years, defense, interior and justice had been reported together. Since the amount for 1998/1999 was almost double the amount reported for the same three agencies in 1997/1998, it must be assumed that additional expenditures were included. At the same time, there may have been some dual-use expenditures that were part of other line items. In any event, it is clear that the LE 22 billion figure is not a true reflection of what the GOE spends on defense, which is probably considerably lower.

It is equally hard to be precise about the economic burden imposed by Egyptian military spending. Egypt's economy has shown real growth in recent years, but its population growth has been so rapid that it has experienced little growth in per capita income. Egypt, however, has received in excess of $1 billion annually in Foreign Military Funds (FMF) and over $800 million in Economic Support Funding (ESF) from the US. If the 1998/1999 defense spending figure is used, Egypt spent 7.4% of its GDP on defense, but this is almost double the figure for last year, and contains other funding. Egypt reported that it spent 24.2% of its budget on defense during this year.

Egypt has never made data on other (non-FMF) military procurement, debt servicing, and support for the military available to the public and it is not known what other expenditures were left out as well. About half of recent Egyptian military spending seems to be provided by USG FMF assistance (USD 1.3 billion annually since FY 1987). Egypt received a total of $1.3 billion in FMF and $815 million in ESF in FY 1999, for an annual total of $2.1 billion. The 2000 FMF budget request includes $1.3 billion for FY 2000.[26] The Senate foreign aid bill that was being debated in July 1999 slightly reduces aid to Egypt for the first time (by $40 million), but Egypt is still slated to receive $1.3 billion in military aid and $775 million in economic aid.[27] Only a small portion of this aid seems to be counted in Figure 2.1, and most of Egypt's spending on arms is now funded through US aid in ways which add significantly to the figures shown.[28] While the level of US aid is high, it has already lost at least 50% of its peak value due to inflation.

Lebanese Military Expenditures

Lebanon's military budget increased after the end of its civil war, following Syrian intervention in 1990. Lebanon has had French, US, and other military aid. Lebanon's military development, however, is controlled by Syria, and Table 2.1 shows that military expenditures had to be reduced at the end of the 1990s because of Lebanon's growing economic problems.

It is difficult to talk about the Lebanese military budget in any normal way because of the unique conditions inside the country. The Lebanese Armed Forces (LAF) have benefited from the seizure of vast quantities of weapons used by the warring militias during the war, and the CIA estimates that it has extended central government control over about one-half of the country. However, the Hizbollah, the radical Shi'a party, retains its weapons and conducted a successful proxy war against Israel and the Israeli-backed South Lebanon Army (SLA) in the southern border area. Syria maintains about 25,000 troops in Lebanon based mainly in Beirut, North Lebanon, and the Beka'a Valley.

Lebanon's future military spending will be shaped by whether it can recover from the broader economic effects of its 1975–1991 civil war, and by whether Israeli withdrawal from Lebanon and the collapse of the SLA leads to greater stability or a new and more demanding form of proxy war along the Israeli-Lebanese border. The CIA estimates that the civil war seriously damaged Lebanon's economic infrastructure, cut national output by half, and all but ended Lebanon's position as a Middle Eastern entrepôt and banking hub. Since that time, the central government has restored control over Beirut, has collected taxes, and has restored its control over the key ports and government facilities. The banking system and some small and medium-scale manufacturers are recovering, and family remittances, banking services, exports, and international aid have provided substantial foreign exchange.

There are serious questions about the success of Lebanese recovery programs such as "Horizon 2000"—the government's $20 billion reconstruction program. This program began in 1993, and the CIA estimates that Lebanon's GDP grew 8% in 1994 and 7% in 1995. Annual inflation fell from more than 100% to 5% during 1992–98, and foreign exchange reserves jumped to more than $6 billion from $1.4 billion.[29] In April 1996, Israel's Operation Grapes of Wrath sharply reduced economic activity and Lebanese growth slowed.

Much of "Horizon 2000" also involved vast infrastructure projects and efforts to support development in areas chosen by the government. Extensive corruption and nepotism affected the way in which projects were chosen and contracts were allocated. The government funded reconstruction by drawing down on the country's foreign exchange reserves and increasing its borrowing in spite of massive foreign aid—$3.5 billion in 1998. The gap between rich and poor also widened during the reconstruction effort, forcing the government to shift its focus from rebuilding infrastructure to improving living conditions. A massive gap has developed between imports and exports ($711 million versus $7.5 billion in 1998, although this gap has since been reduced).[30]

Israeli Military Expenditures

Israel is the only country shaping the Arab-Israeli balance that publishes relatively open data on military spending, and the Israeli defense budget is in the public domain as part of the regular budget. The US State Department reports that these public figures seem to be accurate and include broad functional breakdowns of military spending (e.g., salaries, procurement, pensions, etc.) and specific policy changes for the new budget year and their estimated budgetary effects. The overall military budget and its major components are approved by the Knesset. Its relative transparency also is enhanced by press reporting. In addition, the Office of the State Comptroller serves as an internal control mechanism by overseeing all government ministries and presenting an annual report to the Knesset.

If one examines recent US State Department reporting on the Israeli military budget, it reports that Israel spent 30.0 billion in current New Israeli Shekels (NIS) on military forces during 1996, 32.2 billion in 1997, 34.8 billion in 1998, and 36.4 billion in 1999. This is equivalent to $9.4 billion in 1996, $9.3 billion in 1997, $9.1 billion in 1998, and $8.9 billion in 1999. The State Department estimates that there was no meaningful real increase in Israeli defense spending between 1990 and 1999.[31]

Defense spending continues to place a serious burden on Israel's economy in spite of economic growth and US aid. The US State Department estimates that

Israel spent 9.9% of its GDP on military forces during 1996, 9.6% in 1997, and 9.0% in 1998. It spent 20.6% of its total budget on military forces during 1996, 19.5% in 1997, and 19.8% in 1998. Israel's overall economic performance was good during much of the 1990s. According to the Israeli Embassy, Israel's gross domestic product grew nearly 82% from the beginning of 1980 to the end of 1997. The Israeli Finance Ministry estimated that Israel's economy grew by 7% in 1995 and 9.5% in 1996. However, other reports have estimated that it dropped from 4.6% growth in 1996 to an estimated 1.5% growth in 1998.[32]

Israel's per capita income, which ranged under $10,000 during the 1980s, has grown to nearly $18,000 in current dollars—putting it in the top twenty most prosperous states. Foreign investment has expanded very rapidly, almost doubling in two years from 1995 to 1997 and reaching a total of $3.04 billion by the end that year. Foreign investors have invested more than $1 billion in the stock market alone in 1997 and Israeli companies were able to double earnings from stock markets both domestically and abroad. Exports rose to $32.5 billion in 1997.[33]

Nevertheless, Israel has had serious structural economic problems.[34] Israel's economy has a strong private sector and has a level of productivity and technology approaching that of the US and Western Europe, but it is still burdened with a large, inefficient state sector. Israel still normally has large current account deficits, which it must deal with by aid, transfer payments from abroad, and by foreign loans. The CIA estimates that roughly half of the government's external debt is owed to the US.[35]

Israel's economy was stimulated during much of the 1990s by the influx of some 750,000 Jewish immigrants from the former USSR. As a result, the FSU portion of the total population of Israel now exceeds one million, one-sixth of the total population. The resulting stimulation of the economy, however, led to unprecedented real growth in the value of the shekel, which grew at a compound rate of 11% after 1993. This severely damaged the profitability of exports and production, presented a problem in capital markets, encouraged the growth of consumption, hurt long-term savings, and caused a $5.5 billion balance of payments deficit.[36]

Growth began slowing in 1996, when the government imposed tighter fiscal and monetary policies and the immigration slowed, and then remained weak during 1996–1999 because problems in the peace process limited foreign investment and tourism. Israel had to cut spending in 1997 and 1998 as tax revenues fell far behind forecasts and the government struggled to keep the budget deficit within 2.4% of the GNP.[37] The slowdown in growth increased unemployment, which returned to 1988 levels of 8–9%.[38]

In 1997, these problems led to cuts in the defense budget request that caused the State Controller (General Auditor), the Minister of Defense, and the Chief of Staff to claim that they were producing serious problems in the IDF's readiness. These Israeli officials claimed that Israel needed some $667 million a year more to fund both the necessary conventional war fighting capability and the ongoing problem of border security. The Ministry of Defense also requested a one-time funding allocation of $910 million. Other studies in 1997 and 1998 indicated that a deficit of $1.5 billion had built up in equipment modernization funding over the previous 4–5 years, and that there was a $425 million deficit in aircraft and related systems modernization.[39]

Similar problems occurred in 1998, and in 1999, and the debate over the 1999 cuts illustrates their importance in affecting Israeli military capabilities. In September 1999, Israeli defense officials claimed that the Barak government's decision to cut 1.2 billion shekels from the proposed 34 billion shekel defense budget would seriously jeopardize Israel's ability to fund the multi-year defense program that the previous Netanyahu government had approved in 1998. Prime Minister Barak held the portfolio of Minister of Defense and the Cabinet approved the cuts, but Deputy Defense Minister Ephraim Sneh described the cuts as "dangerous." He stated that Lt. General Shaul Mofaz, the Chief of Staff of the IDF, had already trimmed defense spending as much as possible as a result of its defense reorganization plans, and was already cutting some 3,000 personnel and eliminating older armored units.[40]

Mofaz, in turn, claimed that he had saved 850 million shekels and that the IDF needed 5–6 billion more shekels to preserve readiness and execute its modernization plans. He stated that the IDF needed some $2–4 billion more for air force modernization even though it had just spent $2.5 billion on additional F-16 fighters. Other Ministry of Defense officials raised questions about the IDF's ability to fund new missile defenses. Brigadier General Moti Betzer, the economic advisor to Mofaz, claimed that it would be impossible to meet the Epoch 2003 force and modernization goals if the 1.2 billion shekel cut was made in the new defense budget. This helped reduce the cuts to the 950 million shekels mentioned earlier.[41]

There is no question that the IDF has faced considerable fiscal pressure in meeting all its goals. At the same time, every ministry has a natural desire to demand a larger share of the budget, and the complaints about the 1999 cuts in military spending were made about a relatively limited cut in the Israeli defense budget. They were also made at a time when the US had offered $1.2 billion in additional aid when Israel fully implemented the 1998 Wye Accords.

Nevertheless, Israel went through a similar scenario in 2000. The command of the IDF requested in August 2000 that the defense budget be raised by NIS 5 billion ($1.25 billion) over the next five years, and Major General Moshe Ivri-Sukenik, the general officer commanding the Ground Forces Command, warned that the IDF would not be ready for war without a stronger modernization program. He claimed that the armored and logistics corps were deteriorating, emergency supplies were being depleted, and new systems were not being developed. He stated that thousands of M-2/M-3 half-tracks had been retired during the previous year without replacement. Major General Yitzhak Ben-Yisrael, the head of the Defense Ministry's intelligence directorate, gave similar warnings about the IDF's intelligence equipment.[42] Other sources claimed that the IDF could not fund its goal of 600,000 many days of reservist training, and that 50% of the 10,000–15,000 troops in the West Bank and Gaza did not have adequate personal protection gear.[43]

The IDF Chief of Staff, Shaul Mofaz, warned the Knesset in early September 2000 that the IDF needed a real increase in defense, but that the total defense budget would only be around NIS 37.2 billion ($9.25 billion), and that at least one billion shekels more was needed. While the budget appeared to reflect an increase of NIS 780 million ($171.6 million), it produced a real increase of only NIS 90 million ($22.4 million) because of prior cuts and adjustments. As a result, the increase in the real defense budget was less than the projected 4.5% increase in the GDP.[44] This lack of Israeli effort led President Clinton to issue an unusual call to Israel for more defense spending as a prerequisite for a US response to a request for $800 million in additional US military aid.[45]

The compensating factor is that Israel does not have to depend on its own economy and continues to receive massive amounts of US aid. This aid includes both Foreign Military Financing (FMF) and Economic Support Fund (ESF). Israel has long received $1.8 billion in annual Foreign Military Sales (FMS) grant aid and $1.2 billion in ESF grants. As a result, it has received $3 billion a year, only part of which is counted in the totals shown for Israeli military spending. Israel's actual defense effort is considerably larger than its current reporting indicates, although there is no way to determine its exact size.

This US aid is shifting away from economic aid and towards added military assistance. A plan to restructure aid to Israel was announced in July 1999. This plan will phase out the $1.2 billion a year Israel receives in economic assistance over the next 10 years. During the same time, the amount of military aid will increase from the current $1.8 billion to $2.4 billion.[46]

The US FMF budget for 2000 included a $1.92 billion grant for Israel, as well as an additional $600 million in 1999 and another $100 million over the next 2 years.[47] In exchange for Israel's compliance with the Wye Accords, the US has also pledged a further $1.2 billion dollars to Israel, which will be spent on advanced equipment, construction, and engineering work. However, a new foreign aid bill being debated in the Senate in July 1999 did not include the $500 million requested by Clinton to support the Wye Accords. It also, for the first time, reduced aid to Israel by $60 million, but Israel will still receive $1.08 billion in economic aid and $1.86 billion in military aid.[48]

It is also clear that Israel could spend much more on military forces in an emergency. Israeli defense spending has dropped from over 20% of the GNP in the mid-1980s to well under 10% in the late 1990s. Its strong private sector, improved economic relations with other countries, Russian immigration, and some $10 billion in US loan guarantees have since helped make Israel a fully developed country. As a result, many of its present military spending problems are more the result of the way it chooses to allocate its resources than of any basic constraints forced upon it by its economic capabilities.

"Haves" versus "Have Nots"

All of these data reinforce the message of the broad comparative trends shown in Figures 2.1 to 2.3, and Table 2.1 The current trends in military expenditures sharply favor Israel and Egypt—proven partners in the peace process. This difference in military resources affects every aspect of military capability, but it has a particularly important impact on the modernization and recapitalization of Egyptian, Israeli, Jordanian, Lebanese, and Syrian forces.[49]

The end result is that the region is dividing into military "haves" and "have nots":

- Israel is the only state to sustain high enough overall expenditures to maintain most force levels and improve quality.
- Egypt is well off in terms of arms and technology imports but has not funded manpower quality or the other aspects of force quality.
- Syria has lost the Soviet bloc as a patron and has massive capitalization and force modernization problems and has not funded manpower quality or the other aspects of force quality.
- Jordan's military reflects the loss of aid after the Gulf War. It too has massive capitalization and force modernization problems and has not funded manpower quality or the other aspects of force quality.
- Lebanon's military reflects the impact of years of civil war. Like Syria and Jordan, it too has massive capitalization and force modernization problems and has not funded manpower quality or the other aspects of force quality.

It is also important to understand that such differences in military spending have had a powerful cumulative effect. The gap between Israel and Egypt and the other Arab states has grown with time. Israel and Egypt have continued to modernize and maintain their readiness. In contrast, Jordan, Lebanon, and Syria have lacked the funds to compete in modernization and maintain their existing force structure for nearly a decade.

Relative Efficiency in Using Military Expenditures

These issues relating to the size of military spending are only part of the equation. Each nation also differs in the relative efficiency with which it uses its military budget, and the differences in efficiency reinforce the division of the region into "haves" and "have nots." The problems that the Arab states face in military spending are compounded by:

- Efforts to preserve force size even though the money is lacking to maintain force quality.
- Internal political problems.
- Keeping too many types of equipment in service, often with low-grade modifications—compounding cost, sustainability, interoperability, and operations and maintenance problems.

Egypt, for example, has the advantage of being able to manage its defense acquisition efforts with the knowledge that it can count on a substantial flow of US aid and something approaching Israel's level of access to advanced US military technology. Egypt also has the advantage of a substantial industrial base and low-cost manpower. Egypt, however, has highly bureaucratic military forces with many fiefdoms and rivalries. It is only beginning to acquire modern management systems. Manpower and training management is poor; the potential advantages of low-cost manpower are more than offset by a failure to fully modernize training programs, make proper use of trained manpower, develop strong and respected NCO and technical cadres, and properly encourage the career development of junior and mid-level officers.

Egypt still attempts to support far too large an active force structure for its financial resources, and maintains a large number of units with low-grade Soviet and European-supplied equipment—which places a further burden on its inadequate logistic and maintenance system. Although Egypt has been phasing out its dependence on Soviet bloc arms and equipment for nearly twenty years, it cannot hope to complete this conversion before 2005 at the earliest.[50] If Israel's military industries are often of only moderate efficiency, Egypt's are generally of low efficiency and lack effective management and capital. Egypt's military facilities and infrastructure have often been allowed to decay—because funds are allocated to new acquisitions instead—and Egypt lacks a "maintenance ethic" that ensures its equipment has proper readiness.

Jordan uses its resources more efficiently than Egypt, but it has few resources. It has had to adopt successively smaller modernization plans ever since the late 1970s and has still been unable to fund any of these plans. These shifts from year-to-year have disrupted Jordan's efforts to create an efficient acquisition effort and the development of its military maintenance and modernization facilities. It has also meant that Jordan has had only limited access to advanced technology. This, however, has the potential to change in the future, but stability in that country will only become a realistic possibility if the US and other countries in the region decide that Jordan is firmly on the path to peace.

Although Jordan has relatively high quality manpower, the divisions between Trans-Jordanians and Palestinians limit its ability to exploit its manpower skills on the basis of merit, or to create a large pool of reserves. Jordan is also faced with a steadily growing problem in dealing with diseconomies of scale and aging and obsolete equipment. Its force structure is too small in many areas to allow the efficient use of resources, and it is forced to either retire equipment from service or to spend more and more to service and modify aging equipment to get less and less in terms of relative effectiveness. The most recent Jordanian acquisition and restructuring plan may change this. Its campaign to acquire new or more modern weapons from the US has been met with increasingly favorable results from the US Congress and has subsequently resulted in relatively substantial aid increases. For example, Jordan received $30 million in military aid in 1997, a figure which has risen to $45 million in 1998 and 1999.[51]

Lebanon has made some progress in improving the inadequate management of its heavily politicized, and often corrupt, military forces. However, it has never had anything approaching an effective acquisition and maintenance capability. Its officer corps is still heavily recruited from the "failed sons" of Lebanese families, and it has recently turned its training system into a military disaster by reducing conscription to a single year of service. It must now also contend with the fact that it was the Hizbollah and Amal that drove Israel out of Lebanon and not the central government or regular armed forces.

The problems in using military spending effectively have been most serious in the case of Syria, which has chosen to maintain very large forces even at the cost of letting underfunding make them progressively more "hollow." Syria has many effective small combat formations, particularly in its land forces, but it has a highly inefficient central structure, and does not use its military expenditures efficiently. It has been less successful than Egypt in modernizing its overall manpower management and training system, in developing strong and respected NCO and technical cadres, and in developing effective training and career systems for its junior and mid-level officers. It does a poor job of funding the training of senior officers.

Inter-service and inter-branch rivalries present major problems for Syria and corruption and the political use of funds is common throughout the Syrian armed forces. Syria's acquisition policy strongly favors the purchase of large numbers of modern weapons at the expense of effective sustainability, maintenance, infrastructure, and support. Large amounts of low-grade equipment which cannot be deployed effectively in virtually all foreseeable scenarios, and which consume financial and manpower resources, are retained in the force structure.

If Egypt sometimes lacks a "maintenance ethic," Syria sometimes lacks a basic consciousness of basic maintenance requirements—particularly for equipment in storage or units with older equipment. Syria has only limited domestic major military repair, overhaul, and modernization capability and its military management system is organized around dependence on imports, rather than the manufacture of spares, support equipment, etc. Much of the manufacturing resources Syria does have either produce aging Soviet light weapons and ammunition for older Soviet systems, or are devoted to Syria's effort to acquire weapons of mass destruction and the means to deliver them.

In contrast, Israel compensates for high manpower costs by heavy reliance on conscription and reserves, and through efficient manpower management. It has a large and efficient manufacturing base, a modern infrastructure, and the ability to import the latest military technology from the US with minimal constraints on technology transfer. Unlike its Arab neighbors, Israel has the domestic resources to develop or modify the technology and complex systems needed to create the advanced command, control, communications, computer, intelligence, and battle management (C^4I/BM) systems. It is able to take advantage of those aspects of the "revolution in military affairs" it feels are necessary to meet its strategic and tactical objectives.

COMPARISONS OF ARMS SALES AND IMPORTS

Comparing the data available on arms imports presents many of the same problems as comparing military expenditures. In addition to the problems mentioned earlier, the data on arms purchases exclude many expenditures on weapons of mass destruction, and exclude many imports of long-range missiles. They are not comparable in terms of the kind of contractor services and advisory efforts, military construction, and civil/dual use equipment included.

Comparing data on the dollar value of arms imports presents further problems because there often is only a limited correlation between the dollar figure and the number of weapons transferred or the importance of technology transferred. Dollar-oriented comparisons can be particularly misleading in examining the Arab-Israeli balance because Israel has a major military industry and often imports components which are not included in the figures for arms imports. Egypt is the only Arab "ring state" with significant military industrial output, but the sophistication of its output does not approach that of Israel.

Much of the data on arms sales has to be based on educated guesses about the very different prices given nations pay for given weapons. It may or may not properly adjust for the fact that some countries get weapons that are provided as surplus equipment or pay far less for given types of weapons than other countries. These factors need to be kept in mind in comparing the data in Figures 2.3 through 2.13. The trends in the figures are probably broadly accurate but they do not portray directly comparable data.

Throughout the Cold War the Arab states buying from the Soviet bloc paid far less per weapon than states buying from the West. Since the end of the Cold War,

Figure 2.4
Arab-Israeli Arms Imports as a Percent of Total Imports: 1984–1997
(In Percent)

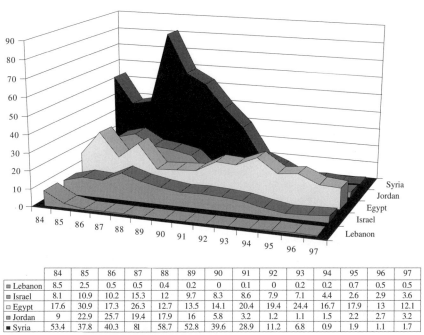

	84	85	86	87	88	89	90	91	92	93	94	95	96	97
▥ Lebanon	8.5	2.5	0.5	0.5	0.4	0.2	0	0.1	0	0.2	0.2	0.7	0.5	0.5
▥ Israel	8.1	10.9	10.2	15.3	12	9.7	8.3	8.6	7.9	7.1	4.4	2.6	2.9	3.6
▢ Egypt	17.6	30.9	17.3	26.3	12.7	13.5	14.1	20.4	19.4	24.4	16.7	17.9	13	12.1
▥ Jordan	9	22.9	25.7	19.4	17.9	16	5.8	3.2	1.2	1.1	1.5	2.2	2.7	3.2
■ Syria	53.4	37.8	40.3	8l	58.7	52.8	39.6	28.9	11.2	6.8	0.9	1.9	1.1	1.7

Source: Adapted by Anthony H. Cordesman from US State Department, Bureau of Arms Control,
World Military Expenditures and Arms Transfers, Washington, GPO, Table I, various editions.

states buying from Russia, the PRC, and Central Europe had to pay more than in
the past, but have still paid far less per weapon than nations buying similar types of
weapons from Western countries. These price differences were so striking in the
case of some arms transfers to the Middle East that there was sometimes an inverse
correlation between the trends reflected in cost estimates of the size of the arms
transfers to given states and the trends in the number of weapons transferred.[52]

Egypt and Israel present special problems. The data available on their total arms
imports rarely track with the data available on the size of the US military assistance
provided to Egypt and Israel, and there is no way of relating dollar values to the
value of the weapons technologies being purchased. There is an uncertain
correlation to actual expenditures in foreign currencies, and to data on military
foreign assistance and borrowing. There is little correlation between the ACDA
(now State Department) arms import estimates and the flow of FMS aid. ACDA's
estimates of Egypt's *total* annual arms imports from some countries are sometimes
lower than the value of the arms delivered through US FMS aid alone.

Figure 2.5
National Trends in Arab-Israeli Arms Deliveries in Current Dollars
($US Current Millions)
($97 Constant Millions)

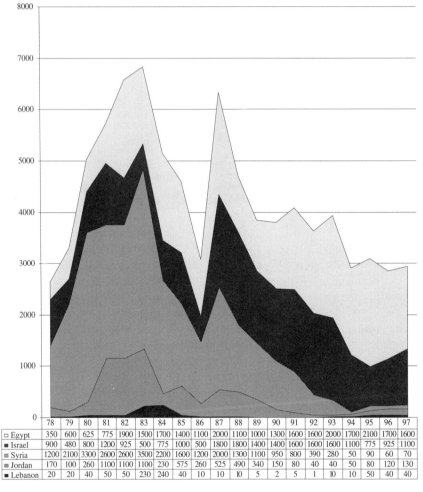

	78	79	80	81	82	83	84	85	86	87	88	89	90	91	92	93	94	95	96	97
□ Egypt	350	600	625	775	1900	1500	1700	1400	1100	2000	1100	1000	1300	1600	1600	2000	1700	2100	1700	1600
■ Israel	900	480	800	1200	925	500	775	1000	500	1800	1800	1400	1400	1600	1600	1600	1100	775	925	1100
▨ Syria	1200	2100	3300	2600	2600	3500	2200	1600	1200	2000	1300	1100	950	800	390	280	50	90	60	70
▨ Jordan	170	100	260	1100	1100	1100	230	575	260	525	490	340	150	80	40	40	50	80	120	130
■ Lebanon	20	20	40	50	50	230	240	40	10	10	10	5	2	5	1	10	10	50	40	40

Source: Adapted by Anthony H. Cordesman from US State Department, Bureau of Arms Control, *World Military Expenditures and Arms Transfers*, GPO, Washington, various editions.

Once again, however, the broad patterns in new arms orders and arms transfers reflect strategically important trends that are valid in spite of these problems in the data. Figures 2.4 through 2.7 show the patterns in Arab-Israeli arms transfers using the ACDA (now State Department) data. These patterns are complex, and it is easy to misinterpret the importance of a given comparison, or to exaggerate its

Figure 2.6
National Trends in Arab-Israeli Arms Deliveries in Constant Dollars
($97 Constant Millions)

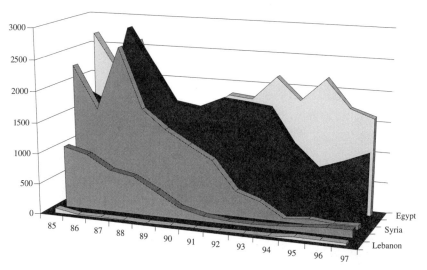

	85	86	87	88	89	90	91	92	93	94	95	96	97
▢ Lebanon	79	16	13	13	6	2	6	3	11	11	52	41	40
▪ Jordan	1013	912	686	619	414	176	91	44	43	53	83	122	130
▪ Syria	2278	1585	2613	1643	1339	1113	906	432	302	53	93	61	70
▪ Israel	1785	1585	2874	2275	1704	1640	1812	1774	1728	1163	802	940	1100
▢ Egypt	2690	2105	2613	1390	1217	1522	1812	1774	2159	1798	2174	1728	1600

Source: Adapted by Anthony H. Cordesman from US State Department, Bureau of Arms Control,
World Military Expenditures and Arms Transfers, GPO, Washington, various editions.

importance. Accordingly, the data are shown in both current and constant dollars,
as individual national and as cumulative totals, and as patterns over a period of
time, rather than simply as annual figures.

While the data are complex, the figures cumulatively reveal the following patterns:

- Although the data on Israeli arms exports exclude most US aid because it does not come
  in the form of finished major weapons, Israeli new agreements and deliveries remained
  high while Syria's declined. Syria experienced a steady and massive drop in arms imports
  over the period from 1983 to 1999. Its deliveries in the early 1990s were so low that they
  only equaled a small fraction of the deliveries necessary to sustain or modernize Syria's
  massive force structure. Although any such judgments are speculative, deliveries seem to
  be less than 15% of the volume required to maintain and "recapitalize" Syria's forces. If
  trends continue, Syria, lacking a sufficient military industry, could face a severe lack of
  usable military hardware in the future.

Figure 2.7
Shifts in Arab-Israeli Arms Deliveries from War to War by Country: 1973–1996
(In $US Current Millions)

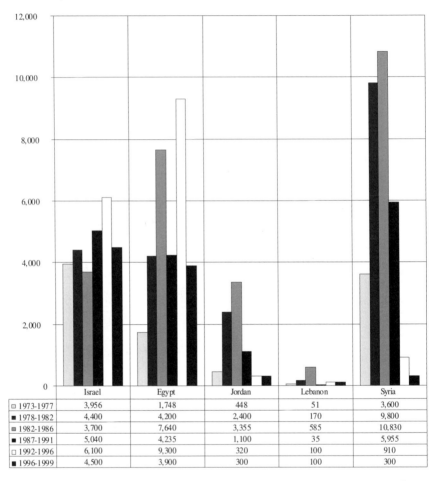

	Israel	Egypt	Jordan	Lebanon	Syria
□ 1973-1977	3,956	1,748	448	51	3,600
■ 1978-1982	4,400	4,200	2,400	170	9,800
▨ 1982-1986	3,700	7,640	3,355	585	10,830
■ 1987-1991	5,040	4,235	1,100	35	5,955
□ 1992-1996	6,100	9,300	320	100	910
■ 1996-1999	4,500	3,900	300	100	300

Source: Adapted by Anthony H. Cordesman from ACDA, *World Military Expenditures and Arms Transfers*, various editions.

- Like Israel, Egypt benefited from massive US aid, and its new agreements and deliveries remained high. The figures for Egypt reflect this aid more accurately because Egypt generally imports finished weapons and military equipment, while Israel often used aid to buy components for its defense industry.

- Jordan received a significant amount of deliveries in the period 1988–1990. As a result of the Gulf War, however, deliveries decreased to minimal levels and Jordan experienced a crippling loss in the volume of its arms imports. Jordan, however, is receiving US aid as a

Figure 2.8
Total New Agreements By Arab-Israeli Buyer: Before and After Gulf War
(In $US Current Millions)

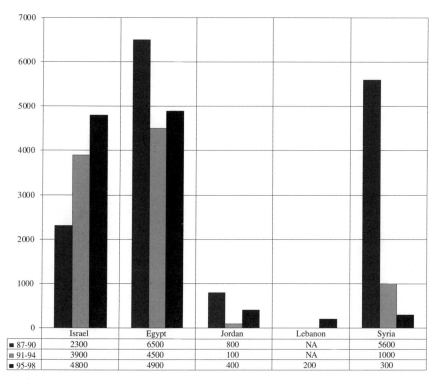

	Israel	Egypt	Jordan	Lebanon	Syria
■ 87-90	2300	6500	800	NA	5600
▣ 91-94	3900	4500	100	NA	1000
■ 95-98	4800	4900	400	200	300

Note: 0 = less than $50 million or nil, and all data rounded to the nearest $100 million.

Source: Richard F. Grimmett, *Conventional Arms Transfers to the Developing Nations*, Congressional Research Service, various editions.

result of its peace agreement with Israel. Outside aid is the only way that Jordan will be able to either maintain its present force levels or improve their rate of modernization.

• After the US withdrawal from Lebanon in the mid-1980s, Lebanon's arms imports were so low that Lebanon's already largely ineffective military forces became even more hollow. Imports fell to zero in the years 1990 and 1992 and have only risen to minimally adequate levels since 1995.

• Egypt appears to have had substantially higher levels of arms deliveries than Israel. These figures reflect the fact that Egypt is the only Arab state to have had anything approaching the level of arms imports necessary to maintain and modernize its forces.

Figures 2.4 through 2.7, however, tell only part of the story. The discussion of the data in these tables needs to be supplemented by data on the source of Egyptian,

Israeli, Jordanian, Lebanese, and Syrian arms imports, and data on US military assistance. Table 2.2 provides some of these data. It is based upon more current data, which are drawn from the work of Richard F. Grimmett of the Congressional Research Service. Like the ACDA data, they are taken from unclassified estimates made by the US intelligence community.[53]

Additional data are shown in graphic form in Figures 2.9 to 2.11. The data in these figures cover a range of different four-year periods before and after the Gulf War. These periods roughly correspond to periods before and after the break-up of the Soviet Union and the Warsaw Pact. They also illustrate the very different relationships between new arms sales agreements and new arms deliveries.

These figures reveal the following patterns:

- Only Israel and Egypt approach the levels necessary to recapitalize and modernize their forces.

- Israel is still unable to fund full modernization of armored mobility and naval modernization.

- Egypt overfunds weapons at the expense of other aspects of military technology; it also preserves far too much obsolete Soviet-bloc and low-grade European weaponry.

- Syria is crippling itself by maintaining large force size and funding 5–10% of the level of arms imports needed for modernization and recapitalization.

- Jordan has made some compromises by withdrawing equipment from active service, but its air force and much of its land-based air defense system is obsolescent, and it cannot fund army modernization.

- Lebanon is still funding more of an internal security force than a real army. It has no meaningful air and naval equipment and no plans to fund them.

- No state has succeeded in creating a viable military industry, although Egypt can produce small arms and some heavy weapons, and Israel's problem is over-capacity, not quality and efficiency in meeting internal needs.

- Arms transfer data exaggerates the size of Egyptian imports relative to Israel because Israel's imports of the components for its arms industry are not counted as arms. Israel actually has larger military imports than Egypt.

The implications of these data are particularly striking in the case of Syria. For example, Table 2.2 and Figure 2.10 show that Syria signed orders for $5.6 billion worth of arms between 1987–1990. In contrast, Syria only signed orders for $1,000 million during 1991–1994 and only $300 million during 1995–1999—30% of the level it had signed during the earlier period.[54] Similarly, Syria received far fewer deliveries after the Gulf War than it did during 1987–1990. Syrian new arms agreements fell far behind those of Egypt and Israel. They totaled $1,600 million during 1991–1994 because of the momentum from earlier orders, but they dropped to only $500 million during 1995–1999.[55] Further, Table 2.2 shows that Syria only

Table 2.2
Arms Sales Affecting the Arab-Israeli Balance (Millions of Current US Dollars)

Recipient Country	US	Russia	PRC	Major West European	All Other European	All Others	Total
New Arms Transfer Agreements							
1987–1990							
Israel	2,300	0	0	0	0	0	2,300
Egypt	5,900	500	0	0	100	0	6,500
Jordan	100	200	100	100	200	100	800
Lebanon	0	0	0	0	0	0	0
Syria	0	5,300	0	0	100	200	5,600
1991–1994							
Israel	3,000	0	100	1,200	0	0	4,300
Egypt	4,000	300	0	200	100	200	4,800
Jordan	100	0	0	0	0	0	100
Lebanon	0	0	0	0	0	0	0
Syria	0	500	0	0	200	200	900
1995–1998							
Israel	2,600	0	0	100	0	200	2,900
Egypt	4,500	400	0	100	0	0	5,000
Jordan	300	300	0	0	0	100	700
Lebanon	100	0	0	100	0	0	200
Syria	0	200	0	0	100	0	300
Arms Transfer Deliveries							
1987–1990							
Israel	2,400	0	0	0	0	0	2,400
Egypt	2,300	500	100	400	200	200	3,700
Jordan	200	400	100	400	100	100	1,300
Lebanon	0	0	0	0	0	0	0
Syria	0	5,000	0	0	200	0	5,200
1991–1994							
Israel	2,800	0	100	400	0	0	3,300
Egypt	4,400	100	0	0	100	200	4,800
Jordan	100	0	0	0	0	0	100
Lebanon	0	0	0	0	0	0	0
Syria	0	1,000	0	0	100	300	1,400
1995–1998							
Israel	2,400	0	0	100	0	300	2,800
Egypt	4,000	500	0	200	200	100	5,000
Jordan	200	0	0	0	0	100	300
Lebanon	100	0	0	0	0	0	100
Syria	0	100	0	0	100	100	300

Source: Adapted by Anthony H. Cordesman, CSIS, from Richard F. Grimmett, *Conventional Arms Transfers to Developing Nations*, Washington, Congressional Research Service, various editions. All data are rounded to nearest $100 million. Major West European states include Britain, France, Germany and Italy.

Figure 2.9
New Arab-Israeli Arms Orders by Supplier Country: 1992–1999
($US Current Millions)

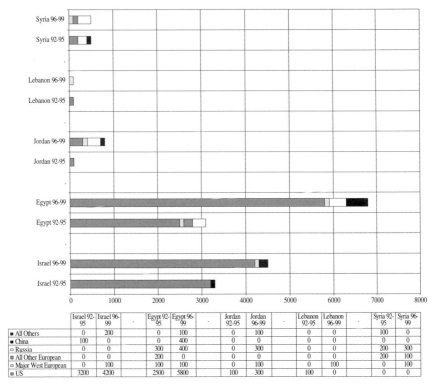

	Israel 92-95	Israel 96-99		Egypt 92-95	Egypt 96-99		Jordan 92-95	Jordan 96-99		Lebanon 92-95	Lebanon 96-99		Syria 92-95	Syria 96-99
■ All Others	0	200		0	100		0	100		0	0		100	0
■ China	100	0		0	400		0	0		0	0		0	0
☐ Russia	0	0		300	400		0	300		0	0		200	300
▣ All Other European	0	0		200	0		0	0		0	0		200	100
☐ Major West European	0	100		100	100		0	100		0	100		0	100
▥ US	3200	4200		2500	5800		100	300		100	0		0	0

Note: 0 = less than $50 million or nil, and all data rounded to the nearest $100 million.

Source: Adapted by Anthony H. Cordesman, CSIS, from Richard F. Grimmett, *Conventional Arms Transfers to the Developing Nations*, Congressional Research Service, various editions.

received limited deliveries of arms from Russia, and no major deliveries from the West.

The drop in Syrian imports is described in more detail in Figures 2.11 through 2.12, which show the trend in new arms orders and delivery by supplier country, and which highlight the radical changes in Russia's role as an arms supplier. The deliveries to Syria clearly reflect the combined impact of the end of the Cold War, Syria's continuing problems in meeting its past arms debt to Russia, Russia's insistence on cash payments for arms, reductions in outside aid to Syria, and Syria's inability to control its balance of payments deficit.

Syria was still able to modernize many of its tanks and some of its aircraft during the early 1990s, largely because of aid Syria received during the Gulf War.

Figure 2.10
Arab-Israeli Arms Deliveries by Supplier Country: 1992–1999
($US Current Millions)

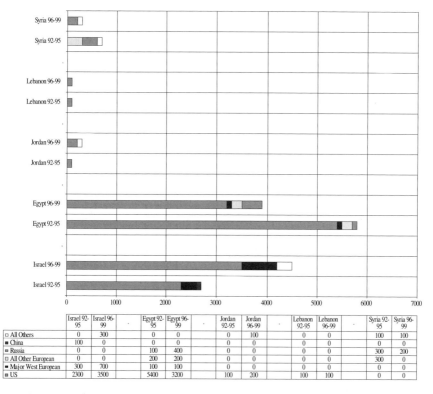

	Israel 92-95	Israel 96-99		Egypt 92-95	Egypt 96-99		Jordan 92-95	Jordan 96-99		Lebanon 92-95	Lebanon 96-99		Syria 92-95	Syria 96-99
□ All Others	0	300		0	0		0	100		0	0		100	100
■ China	100	0		0	0		0	0		0	0		0	0
▦ Russia	0	0		100	400		0	0		0	0		300	200
□ All Other European	0	0		200	200		0	0		0	0		300	0
■ Major West European	300	700		100	100		0	0		0	0		0	0
▦ US	2300	3500		5400	3200		100	200		100	100		0	0

Note: 0 = less than $50 million or nil, and all data rounded to the nearest $100 million.

Source: Adapted by Anthony H. Cordesman, CSIS, from Richard F. Grimmett, *Conventional Arms Transfers to the Developing Nations*, Congressional Research Service, various editions.

Nevertheless, it accumulated a debt to Russia for past arms deliveries totaling between $13 billion and $16 billion. When Syria sought another $2 billion deal with Russia in 1992, the deal collapsed because of Russia's insistence on cash payments. The deal would have included 24 more MiG-24 fighters, 12 Su-27 fighter-bombers, 300 T-72 and T-74 tanks, and an unspecified number of SA-16 and SA-10 missiles.[56] Despite Syria's debt to Russia, the two countries held serious talks in 1999 to discuss expanding military cooperation and the sale of advanced weapons systems to Syria.[57] A five year, $2 billion contract to replace Syria's aging Soviet equipment was under discussion.[58] Syria asked for Su-27 fighters and S-300 air defense systems, but was offered MiG-29 fighters and the Tor-M1 air defense systems.[59]

Figure 2.11
The Gap Between Aid and Arms Deliveries: ACDA Reporting on Arms Import
Deliveries to Israel vs. US Aid and Commercial Arms Sales: 1986–1997
(In $US Current Millions)

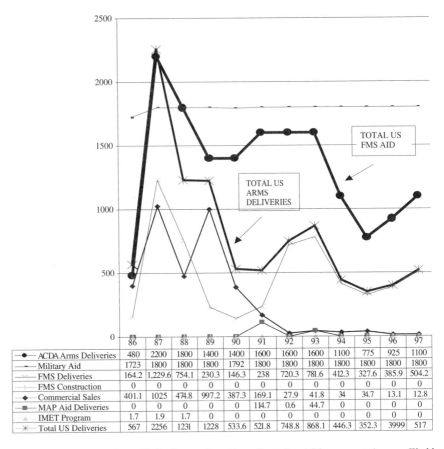

	86	87	88	89	90	91	92	93	94	95	96	97
ACDA Arms Deliveries	480	2200	1800	1400	1400	1600	1600	1600	1100	775	925	1100
Military Aid	1723	1800	1800	1800	1792	1800	1800	1800	1800	1800	1800	1800
FMS Deliveries	164.2	1,229.6	754.1	230.3	146.3	238	720.3	781.6	412.3	327.6	385.9	504.2
FMS Construction	0	0	0	0	0	0	0	0	0	0	0	0
Commercial Sales	401.1	1025	474.8	997.2	387.3	169.1	27.9	41.8	34	34.7	13.1	12.8
MAP Aid Deliveries	0	0	0	0	0	114.7	0.6	44.7	0	0	0	0
IMET Program	1.7	1.9	1.7	0	0	0	0	0	0	0	0	0
Total US Deliveries	567	2256	1231	1228	533.6	521.8	748.8	868.1	446.3	352.3	3999	517

Source: Adapted by Anthony H. Cordesman from Arms Control and Disarmament Agency, *World Military Expenditures and Arms Transfers*, Washington, GPO, 1996, various editions; and DSAA database.

Syria has been able to continue to buy some arms since the mid-1990s, but outside aid has dropped from an average of $800 million per year during 1973–1993, to an average of $55 million a year since 1993. Syria has not been able to obtain major new sources of aid since the Gulf War. In fact, promises made during the Gulf War that Syria would get aid for a major new steel mill and phosphate fertilizer plant were never kept and the projects have remained in the tender stage ever since.

As Table 2.2 and Figures 2.10 and 2.11 show, these developments have led to a lack of funding which has crippled the development of Syria's conventional forces. Syria is gradually reforming its fiscal institutions to improve its borrowing capability, but it has had to reschedule its past civil debts to limit its arrears on payments due on past loans to $400 million. Its current account balance dropped from a surplus of $1.7 billion in 1990, and $700 million in 1991, to a surplus of $55 million in 1992, and a deficit of $607 million in 1993, $930 million in 1994, and $875 million in 1995.[60] Syria has no prospect of paying off all of its past arms debts to the Former Soviet Union (FSU)—which total $7 to 11 billion—although it does seem to have reached some accommodation with Russia over the issue in 1997.

Although Russia has not made major new arms deliveries, Russia and Syria have had high-level talks. For example, in September 1999, Syria's Defense Minister Lieutenant General Mustafa Tlas met with a Russian delegation headed by General Alexander Grabelnikov, director of the general surveillance department in Russia. The talks covered ways of developing military cooperation, and how to bolster ties between the Syrian and Russian armies. The Russian general and the accompanying delegation later held similar talks with the Chief of Staff of the Syrian Army Lieutenant General Ali Asslan. No details are available on these talks, but Syria does seem to have raised its desire to buy advanced weapons systems like the Russian S-300 surface-to-air missile.[61]

In spite of the moderate growth in Syria's GDP resulting from some liberalization and privatization following the Gulf War, Syria has been in a poor position to generate anything like the resources it needs to maintain and modernize its force structure. Furthermore, Syria is in the midst of its worst drought in 25 years. The drought, combined with low oil prices, will most likely cause severe damage to the Syrian economy.[62] Both the decline in new arms agreements and deliveries, and the lack of access to high technology systems, will steadily weaken Syrian forces in the future.

Jordan faced a similar level of austerity, but for very different reasons. Table 2.2 and Figures 2.9 through 2.12 show a massive cut in Jordanian new arms agreements after 1990. Much of this cut resulted from the near total cut-off of foreign aid to Jordan from both gulf and western states following Jordan's tilt toward Iraq during the Gulf War. This aid had totaled up to $1.2 billion a year, although it declined in the period before the Gulf War.[63]

Jordan had to devote most of its economic resources to dealing with the loss of aid and the massive influx of Jordanian and Palestinian workers forced to leave the Gulf as a result of Jordan's support of Iraq. This burden helped drive Jordan's civil debt up to $8 billion in 1992. While a rescheduling of this debt and an improving economy brought the debt down to $6 billion in 1995, the rescheduling came at the cost of an IMF-imposed austerity program that sharply limited Jordan's flexibility in using its domestic resources to buy arms.[64] Since that time, Jordan's external debt has risen to $6.5 billion.

As a result of these factors, Jordan was unable to sign any arms agreements between 1989–1992. The situation improved in the mid-1990s. Jordan signed only

$100 million worth of new arms agreements during 1991–1994, but $800 million worth during 1995–1999.[65] Jordan signed $400 million in two major new arms agreements between 1993–1996 alone, largely with the US and Russia.

Deliveries, on the other hand, declined from $400 million in 1989–1992 to $100 million in 1991–1994. Because of the long delays that often occur between signing an agreement and actual deliveries, they only rose to $300 million during 1995–1999.[66] Jordan has acquired better access to Western arms and technologies as a result of its peace agreement with Israel, but lacks the funds it needs to recapitalize and modernize its forces.

Since the mid-1990s, Jordan has received continuing aid from the US, but not enough to offset the high cost of new weapons like the F-16. The Wye Accords of 1998 did call for additional aid to Jordan, and President Clinton asked the Congress to expedite approval of $100 million in economic aid and $200 million in military aid after King Hussein's death in February 1999. He took this action to support King Abdullah and help ensure Jordan's stability. The program, however, is spread out over three years, giving Jordan's military forces $50 million in FY1999, $50 million in FY2000, and $100 million in FY2001. This is hardly enough to meet Jordan's goals for buying more F-16s, much less its desire for Patriot missiles, and modern chemical and biological protection equipment.[67]

Jordan has also encountered some growing economic problems in spite of its peace with Israel. As a result, arms imports barely keep peace with urgent needs and there is little funding to provide the imports necessary to modernize the Jordanian Army, buy new land-based air defenses, or complete the modernization of the Jordanian Air Force. Jordan has halted much of its military decline, but there are few prospects that it will have the arms imports to do more than replace its most obsolescent equipment.

Table 2.3 shows that these patterns affect Arab states that do not border on Israel as well. They also show that the states that have not made peace with Israel have suffered from far more serious procurement and modernization problems than the states that have. The figures are particularly striking in the case of Iraq, which is perhaps the only major Arab power outside the Arab-Israel ring states capable of reinforcing Syria and posing a significant threat under worst case conditions.

THE IMPACT OF US MILITARY ASSISTANCE

All of the previous comparisons are problematic to the extent they understate the true nature of Israeli military imports. It is sometimes difficult to determine why the estimates of Israeli arms deliveries are so sharply understated, but the reason seems to be that the arms import data generated by the US intelligence community reflects only the value of fully assembled weapons at the price the US charged, and does not reflect the total value of FMS grants.

As has been discussed earlier, Israel has received major amounts of aid from the US. Some estimates put the total aid since 1949 at $81–92 billion. Israel has received $1.8 billion in annual FMS grant aid for most of the 1990s and this is

Table 2.3
Arms Transfer Deliveries Affecting the Overall Arab-Israeli Balance: 1992–1997
(Millions of Current US Dollars)

Supplier	Israel	Egypt	Jordan	Lebanon	Syria	Iran	Iraq	Libya
1992-1994								
United States	2,600	3,800	90	50	0	0	0	0
Canada	0	0	0	0	20	0	0	0
France	0	0	0	0	0	0	0	0
Germany	310	5	0	0	0	40	0	10
United Kingdom	0	10	0	0	0	0	0	0
Other Western Europe	0	0	0	0	0	0	0	0
Russia	0	30	0	0	300	1,000	0	0
Eastern Europe	0	210	0	0	170	30	0	20
China	0	0	0	0	30	525	0	50
Other East Asia	0	0	5	0	80	110	0	0
Middle East	0	0	0	0	0	20	0	0
Others	0	5	5	0	0	40	0	0
Total	2,970	4,060	100	50	600	1,765	0	80
1994-1996								
United States	2,600	5,000	170	90	0	0	0	0
France	0	130	0	0	0	0	0	0
Germany	150	0	0	0	0	0	0	0
United Kingdom	0	0	0	0	0	0	0	0
Other NATO	5	0	0	0	0	10	0	0
Other Western Europe	0	0	0	0	0	10	0	0
Russia	0	210	0	0	110	320	0	0
Other Eastern Europe	10	150	0	0	0	80	0	0
China	0	0	0	0	0	500	0	0
Other East Asia	0	10	0	0	10	50	0	10
Middle East	0	0	70	0	80	10	0	10
Others	80	5	0	0	10	5	0	0
Total	2,865	5,675	245	90	230	1,025	0	25
1995-1997								
United States	2,600	4,600	220	120	0	0	0	0
France	0	130	0	0	0	0	0	0
Germany	0	0	0	0	0	0	0	0
United Kingdom	0	0	0	0	0	0	0	0
Other NATO	5	150	0	0	0	10	0	0
Other Western Europe	0	0	0	0	0	10	0	0
Russia	0	360	0	0	0	320	0	0
Other Eastern Europe	10	40	0	0	110	80	0	0
Other East Asia	0	30	0	0	10	50	0	10
Middle East	0	0	110	0	60	10	0	10
Others	170	0	0	0	10	5	0	0
Total	2,875	5,330	330	120	220	1,025	0	25

Source: Adapted by Anthony H. Cordesman from US State Department, Bureau of Arms Control, *World Military Expenditures and Arms Transfers*, Washington, GPO, Table III, various editions.

reflected in the data shown in Table 2.4 and Figure 2.11. Israel received a total of $19.8 billion in FMS grant aid during 1987–1997. If one examines recent trends, it is clear that Israel got $7.2 billion worth of FMS aid during 1994–1997, although the previous tables indicate that Israel signed only $4.4 billion worth of new agreements during this period and received only $1.6 billion worth of deliveries.

This aid has been accompanied by steadily improving Israeli ties with the US, and a growing US commitment to helping Israel preserve its military "edge." For example, the first meeting of the US-Israeli Defense Policy Advisory Group (DPAG) was held in Tel Aviv, Israel, on September 30, 1999.[68] The meeting was co-chaired on the US side by Under Secretary of Defense for Policy Walter Slocombe and on the Israeli side by Director General of the Ministry of Defense Ilan Biran. President Clinton and Prime Minister Barak had agreed to create the group when they met in Washington in July. The purpose of the DPAG is to coordinate and plan the cooperation between the US Department of Defense and the Israeli Ministry of Defense by consolidating the channels of defense cooperation and dialogue between the two defense and military establishments under the group. One key aim was to jointly meet the challenges posed by new and emerging threats from missiles and weapons of mass destruction. The US delegation is comprised of senior civilian and policy officials from the Office of the Secretary of Defense, the Joint Chiefs of Staff, and the US European Command. The Israeli side is comprised of senior Ministry of Defense and Israel Defense Forces civilian and military officials.

Furthermore, Israel received $1.2 billion annually in ESF grants, which allowed it to shift its own funds away from domestic spending to areas like its arms industries. The US has also provided Israel with $10 billion in loan guarantees since FY1993, at a rate of $2 billion per year. While these loan guarantees have been subject to penalties for Israel's funding of new settlements on the Occupied Territories, these penalties have been reduced to help Israel pay for the cost of the peace process and have been changed to exclude the value of any "private" construction. As a result, their net impact has dropped from $437 million in penalties in FY1993 to $60 million in FY1995. Further, the government of Israel has been allowed to use the entire $4 billion due during FY1996 and FY1997 to finance its national budget deficit.

The US has invested several hundred million dollars more in development of the Arrow, which allowed Israel to procure more arms, and the appropriations bill of November 5, 1990, provided Israel with grant military equipment valued at $700 million.[69] In addition, Israel has allocated the $1.2 billion it will receive from the US for its participation in the Wye Accords for the purchase of AH-64D Apache Longbow attack helicopters, detection and surveillance equipment, and engineering and construction work for a new Reserve Armored Division and infantry training facilities.[70] This package was frozen when former Prime Minister Netanyahu failed to honor commitments made in the Wye Accords. However, the US has reopened these projects since Prime Minister Barak, upon taking office, pledged to uphold the Wye Accords.[71]

Table 2.4

The Comparative Size of US Military Assistance and Commercial Arms Sales to the Arab-Israeli Ring States: 1986–1997

	87	88	89	90	91	92	93	94	95	96	97
Israel											
Foreign Military Financing Program	1,800.0	1,800.0	1,800.0	1,800.0	1,800.0	1,800.0	1,800.0	1,800.0	1,800.0	1,800.0	1,800.0
Payment Waived	1,800.0	1,800.0	1,800.0	1,800.0	1,800.0	1,800.0	1,800.0	1,800.0	1,800.0	1,800.0	1,800.0
FMS Agreements	100.5	130.9	327.7	376.7	361.4	98.4	163.3	221.4	664.8	883.3	524.9
Commercial Sales	1.024.8	474.8	997.2	387.3	169.1	27.9	41.8	33.96	14.2	7.7	32.2
FMS Construction Agreements	-	-	-	-	-	-	-	-	-	-	-
FMS Deliveries	1,229.6	754.1	230.3	146.3	239.0	720.6	782.0	446.6	329.1	388.2	504.2
MAP Program	-	-	-	74.0	43.0	47.0	491.1	166.0	80.0	22.0	-
MAP Deliveries	-	-	-	-	114.7	0.6	44.7	-	-	-	2.0
IMET Program/ Deliveries	1.9(0)	1.7(0)	1.9(0)	2.1(0)	1.1(0.2)	0.6(0)	0.5(0)	0.8(0)	0.8(0)	-	-
Egypt											
Foreign Military Financing Program	1,300.0	1,300.0	1,300.0	1,300.0	1,300.0	1,300.0	1,300.0	1,300.0	1,300.0	1,300.0	1,300.0.
Payment Waived	1,300.0	1,300.0	1,300.0	1,300.0	1,300.0	1,300.0	1,300.0	1,300.0	1,300.0	1,300.0	1,300.0
FMS Agreements	330.9	1306.1	2646.3	969.5	1,631.7	631.5	447.3	443.0	1,051.7	1,397.7	1,065.5
Commercial Sales	55.4	73.1	252.5	206.0	75.6	31.0	18.7	9.6	3.7	1.7	3.2

Table 2.4 (continued)

	87	88	89	90	91	92	93	94	95	96	97
Egypt											
FMS Construction Agreements	112.4	118.8	65.1	48.2	269.7	107.5	14.0	1.4	15.4	61.6	21.4
FMS Deliveries	955.1	473.0	296.8	368.1	482.3	1,026.7	1,238.6	890.0	1,536.4	1,112.4	1,180.7
MAP Program	-	-	-	-	-	-	-	13.5	-	-	.
MAP Deliveries	-	-	-	-	-	-	-	1.4	-	-	.
IMET Program/ Deliveries	1.7	1.5	1.5	1.5	1.8	1.5	1.7	0.8	1.0	1.0	1.0
Jordan											
Foreign Military Financing Program	-	-	10.0	67.8	20.0	20.0	9.0	9.0	7.3	100.3	30.0
Payment Waived	-	-	10.0	67.8	20.0	20.0	9.0	9.0	7.3	100.3	30.0
DoD Guaranty	81.3	-	-	-	-	-	-	-	-	-	-
FMS Agreements	33.9	28.7	9.4	26.7	0.4	6.9	15.6	39.1	15.0	216.6	18.3
Commercial Sales	73.4	18.3	23.5	12.1	0.9	2.0	1.3	1.0	1.4	3.2	3.3
FMS Deliveries	49.7	55.4	59.5	42.1	22.9	19.5	25.0	31.5	47.0	15.7	52.3
MAP Deliveries	1.1	0.8	-	-	0.4	-	0.1	-	-	16.0	20.8
IMET Program/ Deliveries	1.9	1.7	1.9	2.1	1.1	0.6	0.5	0.8	1.0	1.2	1.7

Lebanon

FMS Agreements	4.9	0.5	-	-	-	-	3.4	29.7	65.0	16.1	22.0
Commercial Sales	0.1	0	0.2	0.1	0.5	0.4	0.9	0.8	0.4	0.1	0.1
FMS Deliveries	12.1	11.9	3.9	2.0	0.3	1.3	4.9	3.6	40.9	31.7	33.0
MAP Deliveries											
IMET Program/ Deliveries	-	0.3	0.3	0.1	-	-	0.5	0.3	0.4	0.4	0.5

Syria

FMS Agreements	-	-	-	-	-	-	-	-	-	-	-
Commercial Sales	-	-	-	-	-	-	-	-	-	-	-
FMS Deliveries	-	-	-	-	-	-	-	-	-	-	-

Source: Adapted from US Defense Security Assistance Agency (DSAA), *Foreign Military Sales, Foreign Military Construction Sales and Military Assistance Facts*, Department of Defense, Washington, various editions.

Table 2.4 shows the recent annual levels of new FMS agreements and deliveries, and commercial military imports. Any comparison of these data on annual US aid with the annual data on Israeli arms imports in Figure 2.3 reinforces the point that current estimates of Israeli arms imports do not provide a valid picture of the size of Israel's military effort. Further, Israel has been able to tailor many of its imports to support its military industries and has often received large amounts of US technology at little or no cost. Figure 2.11 reflects the diversity and number of aid packages showing the current Israeli arms deliveries compared to US aid and commercial sales.

Israel had made effective use of most of this aid, although US aid has sometimes been wasted or abused. In 1991 and again in 1997, top level military officials were investigated for embezzling millions of dollars of US assistance. There is also some speculation that funds have been diverted to allow Israel to purchase foreign-made weapons with US funding.[72] During the 1980s, Israel used US aid to subsidize inefficient military industries and projects like the Lavi fighter, which were more grandiose than practical. In other cases, however, Israel was able to increase the efficiency of its arms imports by combining US technology and domestic production into systems tailored specifically to Israel's strategic and tactical needs.

Most "IDF-driven" decisions to produce equipment in Israel also produced equipment that did a more cost-effective job of meeting Israel's special military needs than simply importing equipment tailored to the global needs of US forces. Figure 2.11 breaks down the different aid packages that the Israelis receive in terms of both FMS aid, military aid and other forms of aid packages resulting in deliveries.

Changes are taking place in the flow of aid. The US and Israel tentatively agreed to a plan that began in 1999, and that will phase out economic aid to Israel by the year 2008 while increasing military aid to an estimated $2.4 billion per year. This plan stipulates that the annual $1.2 billion in economic aid would be cut by $120 million each year until the end of the program. During this time period, military aid to Israel would be increased $60 million per year until the completion of the program. While details about this plan still need to be agreed upon, Israel seems to be the ultimate beneficiary of this deal in the long run.[73]

For example, Israel gave up $120 million in economic aid for FY2000, but the Congress increased military aid by $60 million. As a result, Israel got $960 million in economic aid (ESF), $1.92 billion in military (FMS) aid, and $60 million for refugee resettlement—a total of $2.94 billion. Israel also benefits from getting all of its aid in the first month of each fiscal year, which allows it to invest in US Treasury notes and earn another $50 million a year, and has considerable flexibility in using the aid for purchases outside the US. It also has been promised an additional $1.2 billion in economic aid for fully implementing the Wye Accords.

Table 2.4 shows that Egypt has also received massive amounts of US military assistance, as part of a total aid package that was worth $2.035 billion in FY2000. The resulting arms deliveries have done much to modernize Egypt's forces and they are continuing. In March 1999, the US and Egypt agreed to an arms sale involving $3.2 billion worth of new American weapons, including 24 F-16C/D Block 40 fighter jets, 200 M-1A1 tanks and 32 Patriot missiles.[74] The deal was negotiated by US Secretary of Defense William Cohen during his talks in Cairo with President Hosni Mubarak and Defense Minister Mohamed Hussein Tantawi.

The 100 M-1A1 tanks were estimated to cost around $654 million and the coproduction program was to include 100 M-256 120-mm smooth bore guns, 100 M2 12.7-mm machine guns, 200 M240 7.62-mm machine guns, spare parts, test equipment, and training equipment. Egypt had already coproduced 555 M-1A1s at its Egyptian Tank Plant. The order for 100 more tanks represented a major cutback relative to an original plan to produce 200 more weapons. There are practical limits on how many more tanks Egypt can produce without changing the configuration of the M-1A1s. The production lines for the Textron Lycoming AGT 1500 1500-horsepower engine have been closed, and the engines for the additional 100 tanks will have to come from US Army stocks.[75]

The 24 F-16 fighters, made by Lockheed Martin, cost $1.2 billion, and were additions to an existing force of 196 F-16s already in the Egyptian Air Force. The battery of Patriot-3 missiles, made by Raytheon, would cost $1.3 billion. It consisted of eight firing units, each containing four missiles. The 200 M-1A1 tanks cost nearly $700 million, and were to be assembled in Egypt. They were additions to Egypt's 555 existing M-1A1 tanks. Secretary Cohen said of the sale that, "Egypt has been a role model for some 20 years now since the Camp David accords and you can look to the Egyptian-Israeli relationship as a model for others to follow. We believe this relationship is very important and that is the reason we continue support and (have) friendship with Egypt."[76]

It is important to note that deliveries of this scale never make quick changes in a nation's forces or the regional military balance. Deliveries take some years and absorption or "conversion" of new weapons and technologies can take several years longer. The Patriot 3, for example, was still being developed in the form that Egypt ordered, and the F-16 planes still had to be built. Deliveries were also tied to Egypt's ability to pay for the arms from the $1.2 billion a year it got in US military aid, and the memorandum of understanding still had to receive Congressional approval and be translated into specific contracts. The Pentagon had approved the sale in principle but no deal had been signed.

It is equally important to note that the data in the previous tables and figures do not understate the value of Egyptian arms imports by anything approaching the extent to which they understate Israel's arms imports. This is because almost all of the US aid was provided in the form of fully manufactured military goods and FMS services that are counted in the estimates in Figure 2.2. As a result, Figures 2.2 and 2.12 are almost certainly correct in showing that Egypt's arms imports have been significant relative to those of Israel, and that Egypt received far more arms than Jordan, Lebanon, and Syria.

Table 2.2, for example, indicates that Egypt signed about sixteen times more new arms agreements during 1994–1997 than Syria, and 11 times more than

Jordan. Such figures are hardly surprising, given the fact that Table 2.4 shows Egypt received $1.3 billion a year in FMF Grant Aid, or $5.2 billion in aid over the four-year period, plus substantial value from the delivery of excess defense articles and commercial sales.[77]

Table 2.4 does not reflect significant US aid to Jordan or Lebanon, or any meaningful aid to Syria, but US and Jordanian relations have improved in recent years—particularly since Jordan's peace agreement with Israel. This has resulted in both the forgiveness of all but $63 million of Jordan's $702.3 million debt to the US and an increase in US aid.[78] The Clinton Administration requested $15.5 million worth of US aid be given to Jordan in FY1995 ($7.2 million in ESF, $7.3 million in FMF, and $1.0 million in IMET), and $38.4 million worth of US aid be given to Jordan in FY1996 ($7.2 million in ESF, $30.0 million in FMF, and $1.2 million in IMET), all of which it later received.[79] Aid has been set at $225 million which the US State Department had approved for 1998 and which it plans to continue for FY1999. Seventy-five million dollars of the total will include military aid consisting of $25 million in credits for US military draw down equipment with the remaining $50 million to be used for direct military aid.[80]

On September 27, 1995, King Hussein met with US Secretary of Defense William Perry to discuss a larger aid program. This program involved the transfer of up to 72 used USAF F-16 fighters, upgrades to Jordan's tanks including 200 Abrams M1A2 tanks, conversion of its IHawk surface-to-air missiles to the Pip-3 version, and upgrades to its air defense C^{4}I/BM system. It also involved conversion of Jordan's M-113A1 armored personnel carriers to the M-113A3 version, upgrades of its anti-tank guided missiles, the provision of rocket assisted artillery rounds, supply of 18 UH-1H scout helicopters, and the supply of spare parts.[81]

Since that meeting in 1995, Congress has approved the sale of 12 F-16As and four F-16Bs that cost $220 million. These fighters were delivered to Jordan in March 1998 with final funding being provided out of FY1999 military aid. Additional aid has come through excess equipment released by the US. This includes 50 M60A3 tanks, 250 trucks, 18 UH-1H helicopters, one C-130 transport, 1,180 night vision sights and 107 radios. Other aid currently under review could provide Jordan with AIM-9 Sidewinder air-to-air missiles and AIM-7 Sparrow anti-radar missiles under the $25 million draw down authority in the FY1998 budget.[82] Another aid package could provide $300 million worth of upgrades to Jordan's fixed IHawks and obsolete aid defense system. Furthermore, the US has discussed a mission to upgrade Jordan's military training effort and further military exercises in the region to include Turkey and Israel. However, not all of the Jordanian "wish-list" was met with US aid. Jordan also asked for "A-10 tank-killing aircraft, M60A3 tanks, antitank missiles, armored personnel carriers, and some monitoring equipment for the borders."[83]

Since that time, additional US funding provided to the Jordanians (taking $50 million apiece from Israeli and Egyptian aid packages) has alleviated Jordan's problems, but scarcely solved them. Jordan had to use virtually all of the funds to buy F-16 fighters and then had trouble finding the money to support them. Jordan has received continuing aid from the US, but not enough to offset the high cost of new weapons like the F-16. The Wye Accords of 1998 did call for additional aid to Jordan, and President Clinton asked the Congress to expedite approval of $100 million in economic aid and $200 million in military aid after King Hussein's death in February 1999. The $200 million in military aid, however, is out over three years, giving Jordan's military forces $50 million in FY1999, $50 million in FY2000, and $100 million in FY2001. This is hardly enough to meet Jordan's goals.[84] Jordan has not had major deliveries of land weapons since 1980, except for captured Iranian equipment transferred by Iraq. Its only purchase of a new combat aircraft before the US F-16s consisted of the moderate performance Mirage F-1s it bought from France in 1979.[85]

Since 1993, the US has provided Lebanon with 32 UH-1 helicopters, more than 800 M-113 APCs, spare parts for Lebanon's M-48 tanks, 3,000 jeeps and trucks, and other non-lethal military equipment worth more than $80 million. This aid, however, is only sufficient to make the Lebanese forces more effective for internal security purposes. The US will not help Lebanon build up serious modern military forces as long as it remains under Syrian occupation, and permits Iran and Syria to supply and fund the Hizbollah in attacks on Israel.[86]

Since the initial success in receiving US aid, former Prime Minister Rafiq Hariri expressed an interest in buying 500 M113 armored personnel carriers, attack helicopters (in particular the UH-1N twin-engine utility chopper), communication systems, P-3 Orion naval reconnaissance aircraft and more training for Lebanese military officers by US military personnel.[87] US officials are planning to gradually increase military sales to Lebanon in order to prepare Lebanese troops for expansion into southern Lebanon following a possible Israeli withdrawal from its security zone. The Pentagon will focus on training and mobility, but the Lebanese military must still wait for a peace agreement before moving into the area.[88]

Aid is certain to play an important role in the future of the peace process. There is a broad consensus among those who are actively involved in the peace process that the future size and nature of US economic and military aid to Israel, Egypt, Jordan, and the Palestinians will play a critical role in ensuring the stability of the Camp David accords, the Oslo accords, and the Israeli-Jordanian peace agreement. Something close to current US levels of aid to Egypt and Israel will probably be needed for half a decade or more simply to underpin the current peace agreements. Military aid to Jordan will be needed to provide both security and internal stability, and economic aid to the Palestinians will be needed to reduce the risk of internal upheavals and create a stable Palestinian Authority.

Israeli officers and officials are divided over whether Israel will need a major increase in US aid to adjust to its withdrawal from the West Bank and any future withdrawal from Lebanon and the Golan. Politicized Israelis, and those who base their assessments on worst case threats, feel that withdrawal from the Golan will result in an increase in the risk to Israel that requires significant additional aid. Some indicate that they intend to use withdrawal as an excuse for asking for a massive new aid package worth up to $5 billion.

Those Israeli officers and officials who have analyzed the military situation in detail generally seem to have more modest demands. They feel the current mix of grant aid and loan guarantees will be largely sufficient as long as Israel is not suddenly forced to withdraw before it can restructure its forces. Most do, however, feel added aid will be needed and that either a direct US role in ensuring the peace accords or some increase in US military aid will be needed to compensate Israel for full withdrawal.

Much, however, would depend on any force limitation agreements, confidence building and warning measures, verification regimes, and international peacekeeping forces that become part of any Israeli-Syrian peace agreement. There also is little prospect that the US will provide significant aid to Syria, even if Syria agrees to a comprehensive peace agreement with Israel. This could, however, present problems. Syrian implementation of a strong force limitation agreement could be expensive, and require some additional equipment like improved air defenses as compensation. This may mean Syria will need aid from a third party to implement the military aspects of a peace agreement.

3

Comparing Arab–Israeli Forces by Service and Country

While economics can provide important insights into the trends in the balance, it is military forces, not economics, that determine current war fighting capabilities. Table 3.1 provides a more realistic picture of the military forces that must be considered in assessing the trends in the balance than does Table 1.1. The figures in this table are based on a combination of information provided by US experts and information taken from the International Institute of Strategic Studies (IISS).

Table 3.1 also compares Israel's forces with those of potential Arab threats by country and not in terms of unrealistic totals for Arab forces. Such a country-by-country breakdown avoids the assumption that the balance should be measured in terms of the total forces of a combination of Arab states relative to Israel. The figures that follow provide similar data as well as the details of each nation's holdings of some of the key weapons that shape the balance.

There are several broad conclusions that can be drawn from such data:

- *Syria remains a major regional military power in spite of its recent problems in financing arms imports*. Syria's military build-up after the October War—which was given further impetus by its defeat in 1982—has still left it with near quantitative parity in many areas of land force strength, and numerical superiority over Israel in a few areas like armored infantry fighting vehicles, anti-tank weapons launchers, and artillery. Syria also has rough parity in total combat aircraft and attack helicopters.

  The sheer mass of Syrian forces cannot be ignored, and could be particularly important in a surprise attack or a defensive land battle. At the same time, there are many qualitative differences between Israeli and Syrian forces which almost universally favor Israel.

Table 3.1

The Arab-Israeli Balance: Forces in the Arab-Israeli "Ring" States in 2001

Category/Weapon	Israel	Syria	Jordan	Egypt	Lebanon
Defense Budget					
(In 2000, $Current Billions)	$7.0	$1.8	$0.488	$2.5	$0.846
Arms Imports: 1996–1999 ($M)					
New Orders	4,500	500	800	6,800	100
Deliveries	4,500	300	300	3,800	100
Mobilization Base					
Men Ages 13-17	281,000	1,042,000	274,000	3,634,000	213,000
Men Ages 18-22	270,000	853,000	245,000	3,437,000	195,000
Manpower					
Total Active	172,500	316,000	103,880	448,500	63,750
(Conscript)	107,500	-	-	322,000+	22,600
Total Reserve	425,000	396,000	35,000	254,000	-
Total	597,500	7120,000	139,000	702,000	60,670
Paramilitary	8,050	108,000	10,000	230,000	13,000
Land Forces					
Active Manpower	130,000	215,000	90,000	320,000	60,670
(Conscripts)	85,000	-		250,000+	22,600
Reserve Manpower	400,000	300,000	30,000	150,000	-
Total Active & Reserve Manpower	530,000	515,000	120,000	470,000	60,670
Main Battle Tanks	3,900	3,650 (1200)	1,246 (300)	3,960	327
AIFVs/Armored Cars/Lt. Tanks	408	3,305	241	740 (220)	125
APCs/Recce/Scouts	5,900	1,500	1,450	2,990 (1,075)	1,338
WWII Half-Tracks	500 (3,500)	0	0	0	0
ATGM Launchers	1,300	3,390+	610	2,660	250
SP Artillery	855	450	412	251	0
Towed Artillery	520	1,600	132	971	151
MRLs	198	480	0	156	23
Mortars	6,440	4,500+	800	2,400	377
SSM Launchers	48	72	0	18-24	0
AA Guns	850	2,060	416	834	220
Lt. Sam Launchers	1,298	4,055	1,184	1,146	-

Table 3.1 (continued)

Category/Weapon	Israel	Syria	Jordan	Egypt	Lebanon
Air & Air Defense Forces					
Active Air Force Manpower	36,000	40,000	13,400	30,000	1,700
Active Air Defense Command	0	60,000	0	80,000	0
Air Force Reserve Manpower	20,000	92,000	-	90,000	-
Air Defense Command Reserve		-	0	70,000	0
Manpower	0				
Aircraft					
Total Fighter/FGA/Recce	446	589	106	583	(16)
	(250)				
Fighter	0	310	41	363	0
FGA/Fighter	405	0	0	0	0
FGA	25	154	65	133	0
Recce	10	14	0	20	0
Airborne Early Warning (AEW)	6	0	0	5	0
Electronic Warfare (EW)	37	10	0	10	0
Fixed Wing	37	0	0	6	
Helicopter	0	10	0	4	
Maritime Reconnaissance (MR)	3	0	0	2	0
Combat Capable Trainer	26	111	2	64	3
Tanker	6	0	0	0	0
Transport	37	27	12	32	2
Helicopters					
Attack/Armed	133	87	16	129	0
SAR/ASW	6	-	-	-	-
Transport & Other	160	110	52	158	30
Total	299	197	68	287	30
SAM Forces					
Batteries	28	150	14	38+	0
Heavy Launchers	79	848	80	628	0
Medium Launchers	0	60	0	36-54	0
AA Guns	0	4,000	-	72+	-
Naval Forces					
Active Manpower	6,500	6,000	480	18,500	1,200
Reserve Manpower	5,000	4,000	-	14,000	0
Total Manpower	11,500	10,000	480	34,000	1,200
Naval Commandos/Marines	300	0	0	0	0
Submarines	2	0	0	4	0
Destroyers/Frigates/Corvettes	3	2	0	11	0
Missile	3	2	0	10	0
Other	0	0	0	1	0
Missile Patrol	12	10	0	25	0
Coastal/Inshore Patrol	32	8	6	15	7

Table 3.1 (continued)

Category/Weapon	Israel	Syria	Jordan	Egypt	Lebanon
Naval Forces					
Mine	0	5	0	13	0
Amphibious Ships	1	3	0	3	0
Landing Craft/Light Support	4	5	(3)	9	2
Fixed-wing Combat Aircraft	0	0	0	0	0
MR/MPA	0	0	0	0	0
ASW/Combat Helicopter	0	24	0	24	0
Other Helicopters	-	-	-	-	-

Note: Figures in parentheses show additional equipment known to be in long-term storage. Some
   Syrian tanks shown in parentheses are used as fire points in fixed positions.

Source: Adapted by Anthony H. Cordesman from data provided by US experts, and the IISS,
   Military Balance.

Syria is also unquestionably wasting resources in preserving low capability forces that
would be better spent on new equipment, or making its better units more effective.

- *Egypt remains a major Middle Eastern power, and has made considerable advances in
  modernization and war fighting capability.* Egypt has near numerical parity with Israel in
  terms of total force strength. It has fewer tanks than Israel or Syria, but it is well equipped
  with other armored fighting vehicles, and anti-tank guided weapons. Egypt also has large
  numbers of modern US weapons, although it does not match Syrian artillery in mass or
  Israel artillery in mobility.

- *Jordan is now a small military power relative to Egypt, Israel, and Syria.* It adopted a
  five-year plan, which went into effect on January 1, 1995. This plan called for Jordan to
  make major cuts in its headquarters, training, and support functions, and to consolidate its
  land forces from four divisions to three. It consolidated logistics centers and depots under
  a single directorate, it combined the air and army staff colleges, and placed weapons
  acquisition under a single directorate. The 1995 five-year plan also restructured the
  Jordanian military staff system from one based on British models to one using the G-1 to
  G-5 organization of the US Joint Chiefs of Staff—a measure designed to make Jordanian-
  US cooperation more effective in operations like peacekeeping. Since that time, Jordan
  has made further force changes, emphasizing special forces.

  Jordan still has considerable armored and artillery strength, but it only has a small air
  force and negligible naval capability. It has been able to improve the mobile and
  manportable SHORAD coverage of its ground forces, but it lacks modern fighters and
  mobile medium-range surface-to-air missiles and can only provide its land forces with
  very limited air defense coverage.

- *Lebanon's regular military forces are too small to be a meaningful player in the Arab-
  Israeli balance.* Lebanon has only negligible military strength by the standards of Egypt,
  Israel, Jordan and Syria. It does have some 300 tanks and 620 other armored fighting

vehicles, but its armored and mechanized forces have very limited training, sustainment, and actual war fighting capability. Similarly, Lebanon has little ability to mass, manage, and sustain its artillery assets. It has no operational combat aircraft, and armed helicopters in its air force. The 3,000-odd men in the Iranian and Syrian-backed Hizbollah, and the 2,500-odd men in the Israeli-backed South Lebanon Army are far more active in the Arab-Israeli conflict than Lebanon's regular forces, and are likely to remain so.

UNDERSTANDING THE DETAILS BEHIND QUANTITATIVE COMPARISONS OF TOTAL FORCES

At the same time, the kind of force totals shown in Table 3.1 require consider-able additional explanation and analysis if their implications are to be fully understood and kept in the proper perspective. First, there are many ways to count the balance, and each tends to provide a different picture of relative capability. Second, there are many possible sources of such data, and the estimates of the force strengths and equipment holdings used throughout this paper differ significantly according to the source. The primary source of these estimates is a series of interviews and comments by Western, Israeli, and Arab experts, as well as *Military Balance* by the IISS.[89] Third, quantitative comparisons tend to be most meaningful when they are organized to portray important aspects of force capability that can be related to possible scenarios, and put in a broader analytic context.

Total Force Strength and Differences in National Force Structure

There are many important measures of force numbers that cannot be compared in direct quantitative terms. Table 3.1—and the rest of the tables and figures in this analysis—do not attempt to compare numbers of major combat units because each nation involved defines its combat units so differently. Numerical comparisons of formations that have such different individual manpower and equipment strengths are virtually meaningless. Some divisions may be twice the size as others. Furthermore, some countries have "brigades" and "regiments" that are as large as other countries' divisions or as small as other countries' large battalions.

The only thing that Israel, Syria, Jordan, and Egypt have in common in organizing their major combat units is that they all structure the organization of their land forces with a common emphasis on armored and mechanized land units, supported by some element of elite airborne and special forces units.

Israeli Command Structure and Land Forces Major Combat Unit Strength

The Israeli command structure is in a considerable state of flux as the result of a major review of Israeli strategy and the Israeli Defense Forces (IDF) discussed in

Chapter 6. At present, the chain of command passes down from the Minister of Defense to the Chief of the General Staff to the Deputy Chief of Staff and then to the Military Regional Commands, Army Command, Air Force Command, and Naval Command. The Intelligence, Plans, Operations, Logistics, and Personnel branches report directly to the Deputy Chief of Staff.[90]

The Israeli Army Commander is based in Tel Aviv. He commands a General Reserve, consisting of the 96th Division (Airborne) and 60th Division (Air Mobile). Most of the army's combat units, however, are assigned to three regional commands: The Northern Command headquartered at Zefat, the Central Command headquartered at Neva Yaccout, and the Southern Command headquartered at Bersheba. Each command effectively acts as Corps, supported by territorial border defenses.

The Northern Command headquarters at Zefat is about eight miles south of the border. This command is responsible both for Israel's proxy war with the Hizbollah and its defense of the Golan. It has some of Israel's best combat units, including the heavy Golani brigade, which is the combat ready unit in place in the Golan Heights. This front has the highest priority of any front in wartime, and the Northern Command would be assigned a contingency-oriented mix of major combat units to meet its needs, including as many as six to eight armored divisions. In addition to regular combat units, it acted as the de facto command of the South Lebanon Army (SLA) and had a Territorial Division responsible for border security and supporting the SLA in the Israeli security zone in southern Lebanon. This area extended about 10–15 kilometers beyond the Israeli border with Lebanon. There were numerous check points, surveillance systems and sensors, and barriers like ditches, tank obstacles, and barbed wire. Israeli withdrawal from Lebanon, and the collapse of the SLA, have deprived the Northern Command of this defensive buffer, although the deployment of UN peacekeeping forces may act as a substitute.

The Central Command has been continuously restructured to reflect Israeli withdrawals from the West Bank. It used to have District Headquarters in Hebron, Nablus, and Benjamin, but the status of these headquarters is unclear. The Central Command would be assigned three to four division equivalents in an all-out mobilization, but the precise force-mix would be contingency-oriented. It too has a Territorial Division, which is responsible for border security and for protecting the settlements in the West Bank.

The Southern Command has been restructured to reflect the Israeli withdrawal from Gaza, and the Gaza Security Force that occupied the Gaza Strip has been restructured to provide border security, protect the settlements, and help organize for possible seizure and reoccupation of the Gaza. The Southern Command would be assigned a contingency-oriented force mix, and it is this command that must also deal with the contingency of a war with Egypt. It has a Territorial Division, which is responsible for border security and for protecting the settlements.

The IDF has a force structure with a total of 12 armored divisions (3 active, 8–9 reserve), and three regional mechanized infantry divisions with 10 reserve regional brigades and elements of a fourth opposite Lebanon. It has two additional division headquarters for internal security operations against the Palestinians, and four active independent mechanized infantry brigades (1 training for airborne operations). Israel has a nominal reserve air mobile/mechanized infantry division (the 96th). This division has three brigades manned by paratroop-trained reservists. The IDF has seven artillery battalions (3 active—with MLRS—and 4 reserve) with the reserve battalions armed with 203-mm self-propelled M-110s.

The IDF has a fluid force structure that rapidly adapts its force mix to a given task or threat. A typical active Israeli armored division, however, has three armored brigades (one usually reserve), one mechanized brigade (usually reserve), a recce battalion, and logistic, maintenance, engineering, medical and aviation battalions or elements. A division would have a wartime strength of about 12,000 men, 330 main battle tanks, and 64 self-propelled guns. The reserve armored divisions have 2–3 armored brigades, one affiliated mechanized brigade, and an artillery brigade. Each of the 10 reserve regional brigades has a special unit to deal with border security.

Syrian Command Structure and Land Forces Major Combat Unit Strength

Syria has a highly centralized command structure designed to give maximum authority to President Hafez al Assad, who was both President and Supreme Commander of the Armed Forces, and which his son, Bashar, inherited after Assad's death in June 2000. The Deputy Prime Minister acts as Minister of Defense and Deputy Commander in Chief of the Armed Forces. The Syrian Defense Minister, Mustafa Tlas, is a Sunni. However, he studied with Assad at Syria's Military College, and rose to power with Assad. He often seems subordinate to less visible Alawite generals and served in the same position for nearly 30 years as Hafez Assad's proxy and close supporter. All major decisions and command activities now pass through Bashar Assad, and there are numerous internal intelligence and security elements to guard against a coup, and ensure the loyalty of major combat units and senior commanders.[91]

Syria organizes its ground forces into two corps that report to the Land Forces General Staff and Commander of the Land Force. The chain of command then passes up to the Chief of the General Staff and Deputy Defense Minister, Minister of Defense (Deputy Commander in Chief of the Armed Forces), and Supreme Commander of the Armed Forces. The Syrian 1st Corps is headquartered near Damascus, and commands forces in southeastern Syria, opposing Israel. The 2nd Corps is headquartered near Zabadani, near the Lebanese border, and covers units in Lebanon. The command relationships involving Jordan, Turkey, and Iraq are unclear. The 1st Corps has two armored and three mechanized divisions. The 2nd Corps has three armored and two mechanized divisions.

The Syrian army has a total of five to seven armored divisions, including the 1st, 3rd, 9th, 11th, and 569th. Syrian armored divisions vary in size. They have 2–3 armored brigades, 1–2 mechanized brigades, and one artillery regiment. A typical division has around 8,000 men. A typical armored brigade has 93 main battle tanks, and 30 other armored fighting vehicles like the BMP. The Syrian army has 3 mechanized divisions. They normally have about 11,000 men, but vary in structure. They have 1–2 armored brigades, 2–3 mechanized brigades, and 1 artillery regiment. A typical mechanized brigade has 40 main battle tanks, and 90 other armored fighting vehicles like the BMP.

Syria also has 1 Republican Guard division, with 3 armored brigades, 1 mechanized brigade, and 1 artillery regiment that reports directly to the Commander of the Land Forces, plus a special forces division with 3 special forces regiments and eight independent special forces regiments.

Syria's other independent formations include three independent infantry battalions, two independent artillery brigades, and two independent anti-tank brigades. Its active smaller formations include 1 border guard brigade, 3 infantry brigades, 1 anti-tank brigade, 1 independent tank regiment, 8 special forces regiments, three surface-to-surface missile brigades with an additional coastal defense brigade, and 2 artillery brigades. According to some reports, it has one reserve armored division, and 30 reserve regiments, including infantry and artillery formations.[92]

There are major army bases in Aleppo, Damascus, Dar'a, Dumayer, Hamah, Al Harrah, Al Hasakah, Homs, Idlib, Quabon, Quatanah, As Suwayda, and Zabadani. The exact Syrian order of battle is unclear, but the army has heavy divisions at Al Hasakah in the far northeast; at Aleppo, Idlib, Hamah, and Homs, in the north and west; and near Damascus, Dar'a, Dumayer, Al Harrah, Al Hasakah, Quabon, Quatanah, As Suwayda, and Zabadani opposing the Golan and Lebanon.[93]

Jordanian Command Structure and Land Forces Major Combat Unit Strength

Jordanian military forces report directly to the King, but the formal chain of command passes through the Prime Minister and Minister of Defense, and the Commander-in-Chief of the Armed Forces. The Chief of the General Staff, Armed Forces Inspectorate, commanders of the Army, Air Force, Coast Guard, and People's Army report to the Commander-in-Chief. There are Military District headquarters in Irbid, Al Balqa, Al Asimah, Al Karak, and Maan.

The Jordanian Army has restructured from a force with a large number of conscripts to a leaner, 100,000-man and largely professional force. It still has two armored (3rd Armored and 5th Armored) and two mechanized divisions (4th Mechanized "Aman" and the 5th Mechanized), but these have been "leaned out" to use only Jordan's more modern equipment. Their lower-quality combat elements and weapons have been dropped out of the force structure.

The armored divisions have about 9,500 men and 222 tanks, and have two armored brigades, one mechanized brigade, an artillery group, and recce, engineering, transport, medical, and maintenance battalions. The mechanized divisions have about 11,000 men, one armored and two mechanized brigades, and similar support elements. The mechanized divisions are deployed forward in the Jordan River Valley area. The armored divisions are kept in reserve and under the cover of Jordan's air defenses.

Jordan is, however, converting to a lighter force structure emphasizing smaller combat formations and fewer tank battalions. This force will be more professional, cheaper, more mobile, and better able to deal with internal security problems and the defense of Jordan's borders against threats like the constant pressure of smuggling and infiltration across the Jordanian border. As part of this conversion, Jordan is putting more emphasis on special forces, and on equipment like the AB3 Black Iris light utility vehicle, and remotely piloted helicopters for border surveillance.[94]

Jordan also has a Special Operations Command that includes its special forces brigade. This unit was under the command of King Abdullah II before he became king. It has been extensively reorganized since 1992, has two special forces battalions with counter-terrorist training (71 and 101) and two parachute battalions (81 and 91), plus a 105-mm artillery battalion and a psychological operations unit. The unit conducts joint training with the British 5th Airborne Brigade and Parachute Regiment. The Special Operations Command also includes the royal guard brigade, elements of the police, and an air wing with AH-1F attack helicopters and UH-1H utility helicopters. The Special Operations Command plays a critical role in securing the Iraqi border, where almost nightly clashes take place with Iraqi smugglers, and in blocking infiltration across the Syrian border.

Its other major elements include one independent royal guard brigade and one forward artillery brigade. It has three additional infantry battalions in its Southern Military Area. It also has 10,000 men in its Public Security Directorate, which is under the command of the Ministry of the Interior and includes the police and Desert Patrol. The Desert Patrol has about 2,500 men, 25 EE-11, and 30 aging Saracen armored infantry and scout vehicles. The People's Army is a broad pool of reserves with some military training which would assume part of the internal security mission in time of war. It has some 90,000–200,000 men, most of whom have little equipment and training.

Jordan's regular army forces have high quality manpower and relatively high readiness by regional standards. Jordan does, however, face severe financial pressures. Jordan has reorganized its land force deployments to improve coverage of the Iraqi and Syrian borders, and provide a lighter border force to cover its border with Israel which will emphasize border security over defense against Israel. This new border force will be highly mobile, will have improved surveillance technology, and may be supported by an electrified border fence and systems of thermal TV cameras. These efforts are mainly to provide protection from infiltration and smuggling from Iraq and Syria as well as to counter terrorist threats. Talks are under way between Israel and Jordan on cooperative border surveillance.[95]

According to some reports, Jordan is considering reducing the army's combat unit strength to one armored, one mechanized, and one lighter strategic reserve division to be used as a frontier force. These three divisions combined will have the same number of combat elements as the previous divisions, but will convert three tank battalions to units better suited for border surveillance and will have sharply reduced support and headquarters strength. They will be relatively heavily mechanized if Jordan can obtain suitable aid. Jordan may not make such cuts, however, because of the troubled peace process, problems on its border with Iraq, and pressure from Syria.

Lebanese Command Structure and Land Forces Major Combat Unit Strength

The Lebanese military forces are slowly beginning to recover from years of civil war and sectarian divisions. Lt. General Emile Lahoud, who served as Commander-in-Chief of the Armed Forces after 1990 and is now President, is credited with making major progress in creating a true national army. At the same time, Lebanon remains under partial Syrian occupation in most of the country and was occupied in the south by Israel and the South Lebanese Army (SLA) until May 2000. It was Islamic Shi'ite groups, such as the Hizbollah and Amal, and not the Lebanese forces that did the fighting against Israel and the SLA, and they received extensive arms and training from Iran and Syria.[96]

Israeli withdrawal from Lebanon in late May 2000, and the collapse of the SLA, may lead to added stability or may heighten tensions on the border. UNIFIL is being strengthened to play a peacekeeping role in the border area, but much depends on whether the Hizbollah choose to carry on its fight with Israel and how the Lebanese political system deals with the fact that Lebanon's only military victory in its national history was won primarily by a Shi'ite faction, the Hizbollah. Much also depends on the extent to which Bashar Assad can consolidate power in Syria, his interest in continuing to use Lebanon in a proxy war against Israel, and whether Iran seeks to go on supporting the Hizbollah.

The command structure is highly political. The President is the nominal commander, but cannot act without Syrian approval. The commander of the army is Maronite Christian, the Deputy Commander is a Muslim (Shi'ite), and the Army Council has Druze and Sunni members.

Lebanon has a "paper strength" of 11 infantry brigades, 1 Presidential Guard Brigade, 1 commando/ranger regiment, three special forces regiments, 2 artillery regiments, and 1 air assault regiment. Each brigade is supposed to have three infantry battalions, one armored battalion, a logistics battalion, and an engineer company. In fact, the formations of the Lebanese Army differ widely in actual manning, equipment, and readiness, and some of its brigades are close to being nothing more than reinforced battalions.[97]

President Lahoud did, however, eliminate much of the past tendency to man given brigades by religion and leave combat elements in fixed sectarian areas where they became tied to a given religious group or party and not to the nation when he served as the general commanding Lebanon's military forces. He gradually expanded the coverage of the army to secure most of the country aside from the Syrian-controlled Beka'a Valley and the Israeli-SLA–controlled security zone in South Lebanon. The Lebanese Army has also disarmed virtually all militias except the Amal and Hizbollah and has some troops present with the UN peacekeeping force (UNIFIL) in south Lebanon. US training and aid is also improving the proficiency and equipment of the better brigades.

Egyptian Command Structure and Land Forces Major Combat Unit Strength

The Egyptian command structure is headed by the president, who has a military advisor, and is supported by the National Defense Council and High Armament Council. The formal military chain of command reports through the Ministry of Defense, although the President acts directly in many cases. The Ministry of Defense includes the Minister for Defense and Military Production, Field Marshall Hussein Tantawi. Command then passes down through the Chief of Staff of the Armed Forces, the Armament Authority, and the Secretary General for Defense. The army staff, and commanders of the navy, air force, and air defense force report to the Chief of Staff of the Armed Forces. Each service has its own chief of staff and separate staff departments, but the Chief of Staff of the Armed Forces is generally the chief of staff of the army. There is also a separate Ministry of Military Production which reports directly to the president and which includes the Arab Organization for Industrialization and the National Organization for Military Production.[98]

The Egyptian army has been steadily restructured since the end of the October War in 1973 and the Camp David Accords in 1979. Many of its mid-level and junior officers are US trained, and its National Training Center near Cairo is in some ways similar to the US National Training Center at Fort Irwin, California. Egypt has also tested its command structure and training levels in depth through a series of annual joint exercises with the US called the "Bright Star" series. Much of the senior command of the Egyptian forces did, however, have Soviet training and preserves the hierarchical rigidity of the Soviet system.[99]

A major reorganization of Egypt's command structure did take place in the mid-1980s, however, and created a structure with five military zones: The Central Zone (Cairo), the Eastern Zone (Ismailiya), the Western Zone (Meksa Matrun), the Southern Zone (Alexandria), and the Northern Zone (Aswan). In spite of the fact that Egypt has strictly adhered to the terms of its peace with Israel, the Eastern Zone and defense of Suez and the Sinai is still its major military priority. Its two field armies (the 2nd Field Army and 3rd Field Army) are placed under the Eastern Zone Command.

Egypt's combat strength emphasizes heavy forces. It has four armored and eight mechanized infantry divisions, one Republican Guard armored brigade, four independent armored brigades, one air-mobile brigade, four independent mechanized brigades, two independent infantry brigades, fifteen independent artillery brigades, two surface-to-surface missile brigades, one paratroop brigade, and six commando groups. Like Syria, a substantial part of this order of battle is composed of relatively low-grade and poorly equipped units, many of which would require substantial fill-in with reservists—almost all of which would require several months of training to be effective.[100]

Each military zone has one armored division with two armored and one mechanized brigades, except for the Central Zone. The mechanized divisions are concentrated in the Eastern Zone, but some are in the other zones. Each mechanized division has two mechanized and one armored brigade. The Republican Guard is under the command of the Central Zone, but takes its orders directly from the President. The air mobile and paratroop units also seem to be under presidential command. The army's main bases are in Cairo, Alexandria, El Arish, Ismailiya, Luxor, Matruh, Port Said, Sharm el-Sheik, Taba, and Suez.

There are a wide range of paramilitary forces, including the National Guards, Central Security Force, Border Guards, Internal Security Forces, General Intelligence Service, and Department for Combating Religious Activity. The National Guard, Central Security Force, and Border Guards are all under the command of the Ministry of Interior. Egyptian military intelligence has a separate, and large, internal security force to preserve the loyalty of the armed forces.

The National Guard has some 60,000 personnel. Its training and effectiveness have improved steadily in recent years, and it has become a key element of Egypt's efforts to suppress violent Islamic extremists. It is dispersed throughout the country and has automatic weapons, armored cars, and some 250 Walid armored personnel carriers. The Central Security Force is also under the Ministry of Interior and plays a major role in fighting Islamic extremists. It has some 325,000 men, and it was this force that mutinied near the pyramids in 1986. It remains relatively poorly trained, paid, and equipped and is given lower-grade conscripts while the army gets the better-educated intake. The Border Guards include some 12,000 men in 18 regiments.

Internal Security Forces and General Intelligence Service play a major role in dealing with Islamic extremists, other militant opposition groups, and foreign agents. Both services report to both ministers and the president. The Department for Combating Religious Activity is under the command of an army general, and has focused on the most extreme religious groups. These include the Islamic Jihad,

Gamaat Islamiya (Islamic Group), and Vanguards of Conquest. The Moslem Brotherhood is the subject of considerable government activity, but is more a political party than an extremist movement.

The Importance of Reserve Forces and Strategic Warning

The manpower data in Table 3.2 and Figures 3.1 and 3.2 reflect another important aspect of the regional balance. The data in Table 3.2 provide a rough measure of the comparative size of each nation's current military establishment. Figure 3.1 provides a rough picture of the trends in total active military manning since the 1973 war. As noted previously, there is more to consider between forces in the Middle East than just their military strength. Table 3.2 provides data on population and demographics regarding men reaching military age.

Israel, however, organizes its forces and military manpower in different ways from those of its Arab neighbors, and comparisons of either total active manpower or total active and reserve manpower have only limited meaning in measuring military effectiveness. Israel has only about 175,000 active men and women in its peacetime force structure, and this total includes some 138,500 conscripts. Israeli male conscripts serve a total of 36 months (21 months women, 48 months officers), and a significant number are still in training or gathering combat experience at any given time. Israel's military effectiveness depends heavily on the ability to call up the key elements of a reserve manpower pool of about 430,000 men. In fact, nine of Israel's 12 armored "divisions" are reserve forces, as are one air mobile mechanized division, four artillery brigades, and the 10 regional infantry brigades it uses to guard its borders. Figure 3.2 shows the comparison between the total Israeli active units and the other Arab countries. This comparison illustrates the dependency that Israel has on its reserve units as an offset to the superior numbers of the surrounding Arab countries.

Syria, Jordan, and Egypt also have reserve forces. Syria has some 500,000 reservists, including 400,000 in the army, 92,000 in the air force, and 8,000 in the navy. Jordan has 35,000 men (30,000 in the army), and Egypt has 254,000. These reserves provide a pool of hundreds of thousands of men, but the war fighting capability of most Arab reserves is limited. They receive little call-up training and most are not integrated into an effective unit structure or mix of active and reserve force elements. Syria has never made effective use of most of its reserves, and Egypt and Jordan have steadily cut back on reserve activity—in part for financial reasons.

On paper, Syria has one low-grade reserve armored unit with about half the effective strength of its active divisions, plus 30 infantry and one artillery reserve regiment. Most of these Syrian reserve units are poorly equipped and trained. Those Syrian reserves that do train usually do not receive meaningful training above the company to battalion level, and many train using obsolete equipment

Table 3.2
Arab-Israeli Military Demographics and Forces in 2001

Country	Total Population	Males Reaching Military Age Each Year	Males Between the Ages of 13 and 17	18 and 22	23 and 32	Males Between 15 and 49 Total	Medically Fit
Egypt	68,360,000	704,000	3,634,000	3,218,000	5,067,000	18,164,000	11,767,000
Gaza	1,132,000*	-				-	-
Israel	5,842,000	50,348	281,000	270,000	526,000	1,499,000	1,227,000
Jordan	4,999,000	55,742	274,000	245,000	4447,000	1,399,000	994,000
Lebanon	3,578,000	-	213,000	195,000	391,000	958,000	592,000
Palestinian	2,900,000*	-	163,000	140,000	233,000	-	-
Syria	16,306,000	197,000	1,042,000	853,000	1,210,000	4,221,000	2,359,000
West Bank	2,020,000*	-				-	-
Iran	65,620,000	801,000	4,587,000	3,827,000	5,771,000	17,762,000	10,546000
Iraq	22,676,000	260,000	1,498,000	1,281,000	1,894,000	5,675,000	3,177,000

Note: Totals include non-nationals, Total population, males reaching military age, and males between 15 and 49 are generally CIA data, the rest are IISS data. * Totals for Palestinians are IISS, totals for Gaza and West Bank are CIA.

Source: Adapted by Anthony H. Cordesman, CIA *World Factbook, 2000*, IISS, *Military Balance, 2000–2001,*

Country	Total Active Manpower	Total Active Army Manning	Tanks	OAFVs	Artillery	Combat Aircraft	Armed Helicopters
Egypt	448,500	320,000	3,960	3,730	1,378	583	129
Israel	172,500	130,000	3,900	6,300	1,537	446	133
Jordan	103,880	90,000	1,246	1,691	544	106	(16)
Lebanon	63,750	65,000	327	1,463	174	(3)	0
Palestinian	(35,000)	(35,000)	-	45	-	-	-
Syria	316,000	215,000	3,650	4,805	2,530	589	87
Iran	513,000	475,000	1,410	1,105	3,224	304	100
Iraq	387,500	350,000	2,700	3,400	2,200	353	120
Libya	65,000	35,000	985	2,620	1,870	420	65

Note: Totals count all "active" equipment, much of which is not operational. They do not include stored equipment, but are only approximate estimates of combat-ready equipment holdings. Light tanks, APCs, AIFVs, armored recce vehicles, and misc. AFVs are counted as OAFVs (Other Armored Fighting Vehicles). Artillery counts towed and self-propelled tube weapons of 100-mm+ and multiple rocket launchers, but not mortars. Only fixed wing combat aircraft in combat, COIN, or OCU units are counted, not other trainers or aircraft.

Source: Adapted by Anthony H. Cordesman, CIA *World Factbook*, various editions and IISS, *Military Balance*, various editions.

Figure 3.1
Total Arab-Israeli Active Military Manpower: 1973–2001

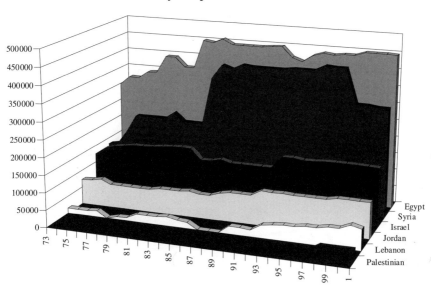

Source: Adapted by Anthony H. Cordesman from the IISS, *Military Balance*, various years. Some data adjusted or estimated by the author.

that is different from the equipment in the active units to which they are assigned. The Syrian call-up system is relatively effective, but the Syrian army is not organized to make use of it. Virtually all of the Syrian reserves called up in the 1982 war had to be sent home because the Syrian army lacked the capability to absorb and support them.

Egypt has a 254,000-man reserve (150,000 in the army, 20,000 in the air force, 70,000 in the air defenses, 14,000 in the navy). The Egyptian reserve system has been allowed to collapse into near decay since the 1973 war. Reserves still have nominal assignments to fill in badly undermanned regular units, but they have little training for their mission. Like Syria, those Egyptian reserves that do train usually do not receive meaningful training above the company to battalion level, and many train using obsolete equipment that is different from the equipment in the active units to which they are assigned. These problems are made worse by the fact that Egypt provides adequate training funds for its active officers, but not for reserve officers and NCOs, and Egypt faces major command burdens in dealing with its active force because of its lack of force-wide exercise training.

Jordan cannot significantly increase its combat unit numbers with reserves. It has had to cut back on reserve training to the point where its reserves now have little effectiveness, and has recently frozen its intake of conscripts for its active

Figure 3.2
Arab Active versus Israeli Mobilized Army Manpower: 1973–2001

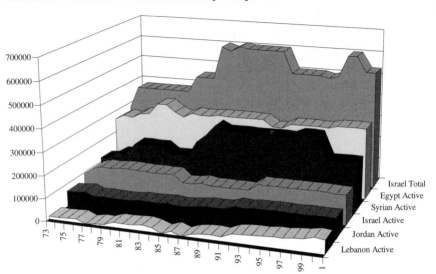

Source: Adapted by Anthony H. Cordesman from the IISS, *Military Balance*, various years. Some
data adjusted or estimated by the author.

forces to reduce the cost of its forces. This freeze effectively ensures that Jordan's
active and reserve forces will not grow with its population, and Jordan may have to
make additional cuts in both its active and reserve strength. Lebanon has no
meaningful reserve system.

Where Israel's high quality reserves are an important key to its military
effectiveness, the cost of maintaining Syrian and Egyptian reserve forces may
actually reduce the total military effectiveness of each country by wasting
resources on low-grade forces that would be better spent on more effective units.

Figure 3.2 illustrates the resulting impact of Israel's reserves on the balance by
showing how both the active and mobilized strength of Israel's land forces
compares with the active manpower in Arab armies. The Israel total that includes
reserves shows just how much Israel can increase its pool of highly trained
manpower in an emergency, and it is that total that should really be compared to the
Arab armies. As a result, Israel has more real world manpower strength than its
total active military manpower would indicate.

At the same time, Israel's use of reserves makes it dependent on timely
mobilization for its war fighting capability, and Israel requires 36–48 hours of
strategic warning and reaction time to fully prepare its defenses in the Golan—its
most vulnerable front. Only about one-third of Israel's total manpower consists of

Figure 3.3
Arab-Israeli Operational Armored Forces in 2001

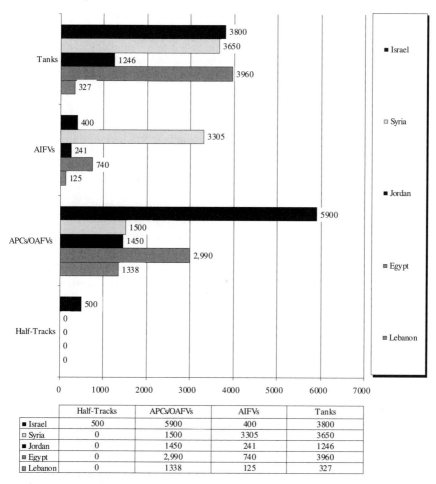

	Half-Tracks	APCs/OAFVs	AIFVs	Tanks
■ Israel	500	5900	400	3800
□ Syria	0	1500	3305	3650
■ Jordan	0	1450	241	1246
▣ Egypt	0	2,990	740	3960
▨ Lebanon	0	1338	125	327

Source: Prepared by Anthony H. Cordesman, based upon discussions with US experts.

full-time actives, and much of this manpower consists of conscripts. Some of Israel's best troops consist of its younger reserves.[101]

High-Quality Weapons versus Total Weapons

There are many different ways to count weapons, and many sources of different estimates of weapons numbers. Unfortunately, efforts to score or "weight" the war fighting value of different weapons systems using either static or dynamic analysis fail to provide a convincing picture of present force-wide effectiveness or future combat capability. The author has been involved in many efforts to "score" weapons by type since the development of the revised firepower scores in the 1960s, and the development of the weapons effectiveness indicators (WEI). None of these have been able to accurately compare direct and indirect fire weapons, deal with weapons upgrades and modifications, trade off one aspect of weapons effectiveness against another, assess the value of modern fire control systems, or aggregate very different mixes of combined arms in units with very different tables of equipment. Such systems may simplify the problem of developing databases for war games, or aggregating weapons data into simple scores for entire combat units, but they do so at the cost of both transparency and credibility. A "black box" effectiveness score is ultimately less useful than a straightforward count of weapons strength.

Table 3.1 has provided a "snap shot" of the current balance, based on the estimate of US experts. Several of the following figures provide a graphic portrayal of the same data, highlighting key aspects of weapons numbers. Several of these figures show the trend in equipment numbers from 1973 to the present, based largely on data provided by the International Institute of Strategic Studies (IISS). Other figures provide a more selective picture of force strengths, based on counts of the highest performance weapons. Total numbers are still important measures of war fighting potential. The Gulf War and past Arab-Israeli conflicts have shown, however, that high quality weapons tend to dominate modern conflicts. Accordingly, these figures provide a very different picture of the force strength on each side, and provide a rough measure of how force quantity is affected by force quality.

At the same time, any counts of high performance or modern weapons are inherently controversial. One man's definition of "high performance" is almost inevitably different from another's. For example, Figure 3.6 provides an estimate of high quality tanks. The data excludes all older generation Soviet tanks, but includes all M-60s and Chieftains. Many experts would argue that the M-1 and Merkava II and III are the only truly advanced tanks that should be counted in the balance, while others would argue that the Chieftain and M-60A1 are not equal to the M-60A3 and T-72.

The count of true armored fighting vehicles portrayed later is even more controversial. Many experts would argue that Figure 3.7 should include more types of armored reconnaissance vehicles, particularly those armored vehicles that have heavy weaponry. This count is highly selective, and only includes the vehicles US experts classify as high performance, based on recent combat experience.

Similarly, the counts of high performance aircraft and advanced attack helicopters in Figure 3.20 and Figure 3.23 differ sharply from many estimates, which define all supersonic aircraft as "high performance." Such distinctions are obsolete and never reflected the realities of air combat. Supersonic speed is largely a measure of intercept or escape speed for most combat aircraft, which are forced to fly at subsonic speeds the moment they engage in air-to-air combat and lose energy of maneuver. Only a few modern aircraft are effective if they fly attack missions at supersonic speeds. In contrast, modern avionics play a critical role in determining situational awareness, night and poor weather mission capability, the ability to fly look-down, shoot-down missions, carry out beyond-visual-range intercepts, and use precision-guided weapons effectively. As a result, Figure 3.20 is based on modern mission capability and not aircraft speed.

Main Battle Tanks

Figure 3.4 shows the trends in each nation's total holdings of main battle tanks, and Figure 3.5 shows current holdings by type. Figure 3.6 provides a count of the portion of this total that can be categorized as high quality armor, and is perhaps the most important measure of land force strength. These figures provide a broad index of the most important single measure of maneuver and direct-fire warfare capability. It should be noted that the totals for high quality tanks in all Arab forces are about 75% higher than the total for Israel, but that no Arab state individually equals the total for Israel.

A comparison of Figure 3.6 with the data in Figures 3.4 and 3.5 shows how different the tank strength of each nation is when one looks only at high quality tank forces. Israel's total tank strength includes about 2,100 Merkavas and M-60s. This total includes at least 1,200 Merkava I/II/IIIs, 300 M-60A1s, and 600 M-60A3s. This is a total of 2,100 high quality tanks out of a total strength of 3,900, or 54%.

Israel's percentage of high quality tanks would drop significantly if one only included its Merkavas and M-60A3s, but Israel continues to build Merkavas and is getting deliveries of additional M-60A3s.[102] Israel has also fitted many of its M-60s with "Blazer" modular armor that has greatly improved their protection. The upgrade M-60s and Merkava II have proven to be unexpectedly vulnerable to the Soviet AT-4 (Spigot, Faggot or 9K111) anti-tank guided missile, and the IDF suffered three losses to such missiles during its fighting with the Hizbollah in Lebanon in 1997. Israel may have eliminated this vulnerability by adding more armor to a 60° frontal arc of the M-60 and Merkava I/II.[103] Israel has also shown prototypes of a Sabra Mark II conversion of the M-60 to use a 120-mm MG251 smoothbore gun, day/night thermal sight, laser rangefinder, and the Elbit/El-Op Knight III computerized fire control and electric gun control and stabilization for advanced fire-on-the-move capability. It carries 40 120-mm rounds.[104]

Israel's Merkava IIIs have an extra protective coating of passive armor, and additional passive armor fitted to the forward part of the turret roof to protect against top attack missiles. They also have a CL-3030 self-screening system and a laser detector that fires smoke shells to make it impossible to track the tank with guided missiles. The Merkava III has survived repeated hits by anti-guided missiles and RPGs in Lebanon, and both the Merkava II and III are evidently being upgraded to use fourth-generation sloped-sided armor packs that fit to the sides of

Figure 3.4
Arab-Israeli Main Battle Tanks: 1973–2001

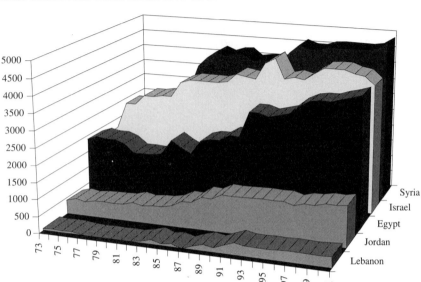

Note: The totals include large numbers of vehicles that are in storage or are fixed in place. In 2000,
   these included 300 M-47/M-48A5s for Jordan, 1,200 tanks for Syria and an unknown number for
   Egypt, Israel, and Lebanon.

Source: Adapted from the IISS, *Military Balance*, various years. Some data adjusted or estimated by
   the author. Data differ significantly from estimates by US experts.

the turret in place of the current slab-sided packs. The Merkava III has also been
upgraded to use a new stabilized sight and gun with daylight, infrared and thermal
sensors. It also has a commander's day/night stabilized panoramic sight with a
second-generation FLIR to give it a hunter-killer engagement capability, a new
image processing automatic target tracker to aim the gun, an improved 120-mm
smoothbore gun, and two 7.62-mm machine guns.[105]

A fourth generation of Merkava armor is also being deployed, which is being
retrofitted on the Merkava II. The use of modular composite armor modules is
making it much cheaper to upgrade Israeli tanks and a number of other weapons
systems. The protection of fuel tanks and internal ammunition is also being
improved. The IDF has also deployed a new armor-piercing, fin stabilized,
discarding sabot (APFSDS) round and an advanced high explosive, anti-tank,
multipurpose (HEAT-MP) round with pop-out fins that allows HEAT ammunition
to be as accurate as an APFSDS round. The fire control system is also being
upgraded to give the gunner's sight day and thermal channels, a laser rangefinder,
and a line of sight capability which is independently stabilized about two axes.

Figure 3.5
Israel versus Egypt, Syria, Jordan, and Lebanon: Tanks in Total Inventory by Type: 2001 (Includes large numbers of tanks in storage or fixed positions)

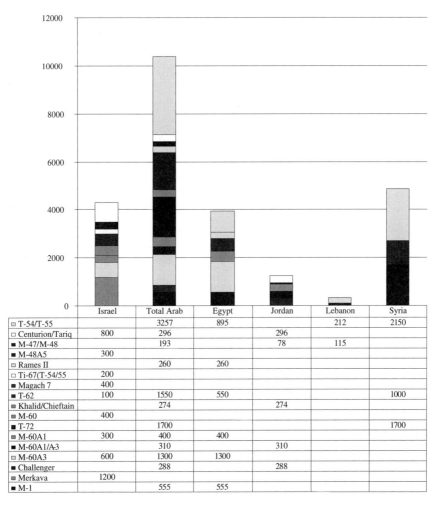

	Israel	Total Arab	Egypt	Jordan	Lebanon	Syria
▫ T-54/T-55		3257	895		212	2150
▫ Centurion/Tariq	800	296		296		
▪ M-47/M-48		193		78	115	
▪ M-48A5	300					
▫ Rames II		260	260			
▫ Ti-67(T-54/55	200					
▪ Magach 7	400					
▪ T-62	100	1550	550			1000
▨ Khalid/Chieftain		274		274		
▨ M-60	400					
▪ T-72		1700				1700
▨ M-60A1	300	400	400			
▪ M-60A1/A-3		310		310		
▫ M-60A3	600	1300	1300			
▪ Challenger		288		288		
▨ Merkava	1200					
▪ M-1		555	555			

Note: The totals include large numbers of vehicles that are in storage or are fixed in place. In 2000, these included 300 M-47/M-48A5s for Jordan, 1,200 tanks for Syria and an unknown number for Egypt, Israel, and Lebanon.

Source: Adapted from the IISS, *Military Balance*, various years. Some data adjusted or estimated by the author. Data differ significantly from estimates by US experts.

Figure 3.6
Israel versus Egypt, Syria, Jordan, and Lebanon: High Quality Tanks by Type
(High-Quality Tanks include T-62s, T-72s, M-60s, M-1s, Merkavas, Challengers)

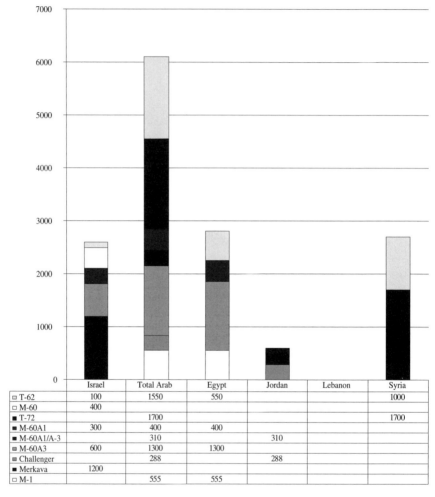

	Israel	Total Arab	Egypt	Jordan	Lebanon	Syria
▫ T-62	100	1550	550			1000
▫ M-60	400					
▪ T-72		1700				1700
▪ M-60A1	300	400	400			
▪ M-60A1/A-3		310		310		
▪ M-60A3	600	1300	1300			
▪ Challenger		288		288		
▪ Merkava	1200					
▫ M-1		555	555			

Source: Adapted from the IISS, *Military Balance*, various years. Some data adjusted or estimated by the author. Data differ significantly from estimates by US experts.

This allows the Merkava to engage at ranges well over 2,000 meters. There is also an autotracking capability, protection against laser attack, and an independently stabilized panoramic sight for the tank commander, giving the tank commander a hunter-killer capability. The use of steel-tired road wheels has also improved the suspension system, and the engine is being upgraded from 1,200 horsepower to 1,500. While the weight has increased to 64 tons, the power-to-weight ratio will still be 23 horsepower per ton. In short, the duel between armor and anti-armor continues—although it is far from clear how many new or retrofitted Merkavas Israel can afford.[106]

Israel has another advantage over its potential opponents which goes beyond the specifications of its tanks. Modern tanks are capable of engagements during both day and night at ranges well over 2,000 meters, and maneuver far faster than previous tanks. This, however, requires highly advanced training for both tank crews and armored formations. In 1997, the IDF's Field Unit Training Center in Negev Desert created its own version of the advanced computerized simulation center the US has at its National Training Center at Fort Irwin. The Israeli center at Matbat occupies an area of about 2,500 square kilometers. It is not as advanced as the US center, but it is the first truly modern, instrumented armored training center in the Middle East.

Syria has given its tank forces high priority and it has a total of about 4,850 main battle tanks, and this total includes some 1,700 relatively capable T-72 and T-72M tanks. It has also upgraded about 200 T-55s to the T-55MV, most of which are deployed in units near the Golan. The T-55MV is a Ukrainian upgrade with a Bastion 9M-117 laser-guided projectile that can be fired through its 100-mm gun. It carries a high explosive anti-tank warhead. The Ukraine claims this warhead can penetrate up to 550-mm of armor at a maximum range of 4,000 meters and a version with a tandem warhead is believed to exist. The T-55MV also has upgraded running gear, a Volna computerized fire control system, and napalm protection. It is unclear whether the tanks have Kontact 5 explosive reactive armor. Some analysts believe that the Bastion can defeat the frontal armor of the Merkava, and the T-55MV has protection that can now defeat the US M829 APFSDS 120-mm depleted uranium round used in the M-1A2 and Merkava.[107]

The remaining tanks include 2,150 relatively low quality T-54s and T-55s, and 1,000 obsolescent T-62M/Ks. About 1,200 of these T-54, T-55, and T-62 tanks are also placed in revetments or in storage, and are not part of Syria's operational or maneuver forces. Syria has, therefore, emphasized numbers over quality and war fighting capability. Further, many of the tanks Syria has in storage, or assigned to its reserve units, have never been properly prepared for storage, and are stored in the open. A number of experts believe they would now require extensive rebuilding to become operational.

In August 1997 Moscow offered to upgrade the rest of Syria's arsenal of T-55s, claiming they could achieve the capability of the T-72 for several hundred thousand dollars each. A modern Russian MBT, in contrast, would cost $2 million. Additionally, Syria has been eager to upgrade its 1500 T-72/-72Ms, which lack a night-fighting capability, an improvement that could cost as much as $630 million. As yet, however, Syria has made very slow progress in upgrading the rest of its armor, and serious questions have emerged about the ergonomics and operational effectiveness of such upgrades. The technical ability to fit a capability to a tank does not mean that it is easy to operate or results in the effectiveness of a tank designed to use advanced fire control, sensor, and night vision devices as original equipment.

Jordan's tank strength includes 1,246 tanks, but most of its 300 M-47 and M-48 tanks are now in storage. This total also includes 280 obsolete Tariq (Centurion) tanks that have been upgraded, but are strikingly inferior to Israel's tanks, and would have severe difficulties in successfully engaging Syria's T-62s and T-72s. They also include 274 aging Khalid/Chieftains. As a result, only about half of Jordan's tanks are really modern. Like Syria, many of the tanks Jordan has placed in storage are stored in the open.

Jordan's upgraded M-60A1s and M-60A3s may still be effective against tanks like the T-72, but its Khalids (Chieftains) are worn and have a number of power and training problems. Consideration has been given to upgrading Jordan's M-60 A1s to the same level as the A3. This would provide the tanks with thermal capability as well as the option for increased armor. In March 1999 Jordan and Switzerland completed a prototype of the M-60A1 fitted with a new 120-mm smoothbore compact tank gun.[108] Trials continued into 2000, and Jordan indicated that the "M-60–120" would use a 120 CTG L50 120-mm gun and a Raytheon AB9B1 integrated fire control system with a dual-axis stabilized gunner's sight, thermal viewer, and laser rangefinder. It would also have a Cadillac-Gauge turret stabilization system to give it an advanced fire-on-the-move capability, CDC ballistic computer, advanced databus, and laser warning receiver.[109]

Jordan has experimented with conversions of its other Centurions to use a smoothbore high-pressure CTG 120-mm gun with a 10-round autoloader, Helio SWARM stabilized self-defense weapon, and stabilized day/night sight, and stowage is provided for another 14 rounds. It has also looked at possible conversion of its Khalids and Al-Husseins to use the CTG high-pressure gun and one-piece ammunition instead of the present medium-pressure L11 gun and two-piece ammunition.[110] On the other hand, Jordan has not been able to finance the upgrading of most of its Khalids, although it still hopes to upgrade their armor. The King Hussein Military Works outside Amman has capacity to rebuild 80 main battle tanks, plus 120 M113s, a year. This military complex can also provide heavy and light maintenance of both the Khalid and Tariq. While this is an option for Jordan, funding for these projects is scarce.[111]

One division uses about two-thirds of Jordan's upgraded Chieftains, or Khalids. The Khalids were originally built for the Shah of Iran as the Shir 1 tank, but were sold to Jordan instead after the Shah's fall in 1979. The Khalid is a modified British Chieftain armed with a 120-mm L11 rifled gun, an uprated suspension and power pack, and computerized fire control; they did have advanced Chobham armor or pneumatic suspension. Another division will use Jordan's upgraded M-60A1/A3s. Many of its remaining M-47M-48s and upgraded Centurions (Tariqs) will be dropped from service and sold, or undergo extensive conversion into heavy infantry fighting vehicles.[112]

These problems help explain Jordan's reorganization to lighter armored divisions. Jordan has, however, improved its armor during the last few years. Britain agreed in March 1999 to give Jordan at least 150 Challenger I tanks that it is replacing with Challenger IIs—which Jordan will rename the Al Hussein. It later raised the offer to at least 288.[113]

The Challenger Is have 120-mm L11 rifled guns and computerized fire control systems. They are overhauled to field standard by the British Army Base Repair Organization, and will evidently be transferred with the Chobham armor package on the British version of the tank. Jordan is further upgrading them at the King Hussein Main Workshop in Jordan with improved auxillary power units and reconditioned thermal sights, and possible improvements to the fire control system. This will give Jordan tanks with guns and armor that are superior to any tank in Iraqi and Syrian service and some of the capabilities of the Israeli Merkava.

The first Jordanian armored battalion was equipped with Al Husseins early in 2000, and 288 are now in service in Jordanian forces. Britain has not announced how many tanks it will transfer, but it produced a total of 420 Challenger Is. This number is not high enough to threaten any neighboring state, but they will greatly improve Jordanian defense capabilities.[114]

Lebanon has 115 aging M-48A2 and 212 T-54/T-55 main battle tanks. None are capable of engaging first-line modern tanks with high rates of kill or survivability.

Egypt has a large number of modern tanks. These include 400 M-60A1, 1,300 M-60A3, and 555 M-1A1 tanks, or more than 50% of Egypt's total of 4,960 tanks. Egypt had coproduced a total of 555 M-1A1s at its Factory 200 near Cairo by the end of 1998. It will get further deliveries of Egyptian-assembled M-1A1s and a number of surplus US M-60s. In March 1999, the US and Egypt agreed to a sale of 200 more M-1A1s at a cost of $700 million, to be assembled in Egypt.[115] These deliveries were later cut back to only 100 more tanks for cost reasons, although Egypt evidently still plans to assemble at least 50 M-88A2 armored recovery vehicles and possibly up to 100.[116] The US also agreed to build 10,500 rounds of 120-mm smoothbore KEW-A1 ammunition to be used by Egypt's M-1A1s.[117] Egypt is also considering whether to use its tank production plant to upgrade its M-60s and M-113s with new turrets.[118] It is coproducing 50 M-88A2 tank recovery vehicles.[119]

Egypt does, however, still have 895 worn and obsolete T-54 and T-55 tanks in its active force structure, 550 worn and obsolescent T-62s, and 260 Ramses conversions of the T-54 and T-55—a conversion of uncertain value in combat against first-line tanks. These lower-quality tanks might be of value against a low-grade enemy like Libya or the Sudan, but they have doubtful value against an opponent like Israel. They may well represent a waste of Egyptian resources in which Egypt invests in useless mass at the cost of force equality. Like Syria and Jordan, many of the tanks Egypt has in storage, or assigned to its reserve units, have never been properly prepared for storage, and are stored in the open. Moreover, there is no indication that Egypt has plans for such storage facilities or the military budget to accomplish such a task.

More generally, it should be noted that many of the tanks shown in Figures 3.4 to 3.6 reflect equipment that can be up to 40 years old, that has had extensive combat

and exercise wear, and that has now had a decade or more of uncertain maintenance and upgrading. Some have reached the point where they are in permanent
storage, placed in fixed defenses, or useful only as equipment for low-grade
reserves. Israel generally sets much higher maintenance and upgrade standards
than its Arab neighbors. Jordan has a good refit program, but it has faced serious
financial problems and the overall readiness of its armor and other major weapons
has decayed significantly since 1991. Egypt has very erratic maintenance standards, and concentrates its resources on its latest and most modern equipment. Its
upgrade programs are much more effective in terms of technical rhetoric than war
fighting performance. Syrian standards are low, and Lebanese efforts are negligible.

These problems affect virtually all of the rest of the major weapons in each
country and they are compounded by several other problems. Figures 3.5 and 3.6
show that several countries retain too many types of tanks, and the fact that older
Soviet-made tanks have a common model name does not mean that they are
standardized in every detail. Israel and Jordan are the only states that place a proper
emphasis on battlefield recovery and repair. For the other armies, this means that
maintenance failures and limited combat damage can result in the total loss of
tanks and other major weapons under conditions where it should be possible to
bring a weapon back into rapid service. Most Arab countries are badly under-
equipped with armored recovery vehicles, and no country has an adequate number
of tank transporters to reduce road wear and maintenance problems in moving
tanks long distances. This is not critical in the case of forces deployed near the
areas where they are likely to fight, but it does sharply limit the rapid deployment
capability of a nation like Egypt.

Figures 3.5 and 3.6 also illustrate the importance of the points made throughout
the rest of this analysis regarding the importance of advanced combined arms and
joint warfare training and realistic maneuver warfare training, as well as the need
for tactical air and attack helicopter support. Nations can compensate for older
equipment and poor standardization by providing given units with dedicated or
tailored missions, and through realistic training in complex maneuver warfare and
realistic sustainment exercises. Even Israel, however, cannot afford such training
for all of its forces, particularly its less well-equipped units. Arab states face much
more severe resource problems, and the standards in Arab forces are often poor.
Jordan has attempted to compensate by reducing its operational strength to
conserve resources, but once again, standards have dropped since the Gulf War.

Night warfare, communications, and battlefield management problems are also
compounded by the reliance on older and less well-equipped tanks, and by the fact
that other armor and artillery are often less well-equipped than tanks. This
compounds the problems in fighting combined arms warfare at night and in poor
weather, as well as in areas like mountains, rough terrain, and cities where modern
tanks often have to rely on support from artillery and other vehicles, or need careful
coordination to maintain battlefield situational awareness. Poor training and
exercise standards compound these problems, particularly in Arab forces, as do
weak battlefield management and coordination links to attack helicopters.

While a number of Arab forces now have some elements equipped to make effective use of remotely piloted vehicles, GPS, computerized battlefield management systems, and "netted" approaches to maneuver warfare, only Israel has made major progress in using its armor in such operations. Arab progress is largely limited to a comparatively few elements in the Egyptian army.

Other Armored Fighting Vehicles

The data on armored fighting vehicles (AFVs) shown in Figures 3.7 and 3.8 reflect even greater differences in the mix and quality of each nation's forces than the data on tanks. Egypt, Israel, Jordan, and Syria have all emphasized the main battle tank, and Lebanon has sought to increase its holdings of each weapon. The story is very different in the case of AFVs. Each country has taken a different path towards mechanizing its infantry, support, and artillery, and acquiring specialized reconnaissance and infantry fighting vehicles.

Taken together, Figures 3.7 to 3.9 reflect very different levels of mobility and different national emphasis on armored fighting vehicles either to support tanks or serve as a substitute. There is also a striking lack of standardization and the data on weapons types often reflects major problems in interoperability. While a detailed discussion must be reserved for the expert level, many armies retain equipment that is so old that it lacks the speed, endurance, and rough terrain capability to maneuver with a given nation's tanks, other armored vehicles, and self-propelled artillery. Many countries also have far too many types, and this creates problems in training, maintenance and sustainment.

This is one area where Israel does not have a qualitative "edge," at least in terms of its overall inventory. Israel has an inventory of nearly 9,900 APCs and half-tracks, but this high total is misleading. Only about 6,300 of these weapons are really capable of acting as OAFVs in combat and 5,900 are armored personnel carriers (APCs) with limited weaponry and armor. These include low-grade systems like the BRDM-2 and BTR-50 as well as better performing systems like the M-113A1/A2, Nagmashots Nagmachons, and Nakpadons, Achzarits, Fuchs, and Ramta conversion of the M-113. Israel also still has 4,000 obsolete M-2 and M-3 half-tracks, many of which are in storage and have little, if any, operational value. Only about 500 of these half-tracks can be counted as fully operational. This is why Figure 3.9 shows a lower total for Israel's operational force strength.

Some of Israel's more modern AFVs and APCs have been up-armored, are relatively well-armed, and can support tanks from positions only slightly to the rear in direct tank engagements. Some were developed to provide exceptional survivability even under difficult ambush conditions like those during the fighting in Lebanon. The IDF has converted many of its captured T-55s to 44-ton Achzarit AFVs, which are now in service with a number of Israel's infantry battalions. They have a clamshell rear access hatch, and are used to transport infantry across fire zones.[120]

Figure 3.7
Arab-Israeli Other Armored Fighting Vehicles (Lt. Tanks, AFVs, APCs, Scouts, Recce, OAFVs): 1973–2001

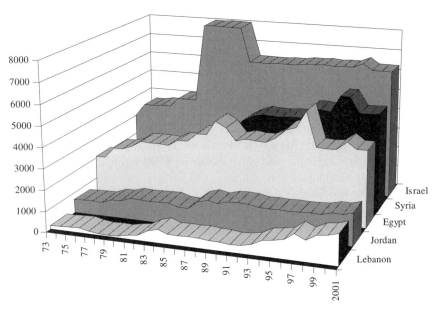

Note: Includes APCs, scouts cars, half-tracks, mechanized infantry fighting vehicles, reconnaissance
vehicles and other armored vehicles other than tanks. The totals include large numbers of vehicles
that are in storage or not operational. After 1986, the totals do not count some 4,000 obsolete half-
tracks Israel still held in inventory, and many of which were operational in the reserves or
undemanding support roles. In 2001, the totals included 3,000-3,500 half tracks for Israel, 220
BMP-1s and 1,075 BTR-60/OT-62s for Egypt, and an unknown number for Lebanon and Syria.

Source: Adapted by Anthony H. Cordesman from the IISS, *Military Balance*, various years. Some
data adjusted or estimated by the author.

The Nagmashot is a conversion of the Centurion tank chassis that can carry up to
eight infantrymen, and has four fixed 7.62 or 12.7-mm machine guns in a "pillbox"
with explosive reactive armor cassettes instead of the Centurion's turret. There is
also another conversion of the Centurion called the Nagpadon, which is extremely
heavily protected, and which was developed to deal with the Hizbollah threat in
Lebanon. It can carry up to 10 infantrymen, has four machine guns, and is so
heavily protected that it weighs 55 tons. The engines in these vehicles have been
upgraded to the 900-horsepower engine used in the Merkava I.[121] This makes it
difficult to distinguish their war-fighting capability from systems that were
originally designed as armored fighting vehicles like the BMP and Scorpion, and
some almost certainly can outperform the BMP in armored maneuver warfare.
Another version called the Puma is used by combat engineers. The Nakpadon has

Figure 3.8
Israel versus Egypt, Syria, Jordan, and Lebanon: "True AFVs" in 2001
(AFVs include Light Tanks, MICVs, AIFVs, and Reconnaissance)

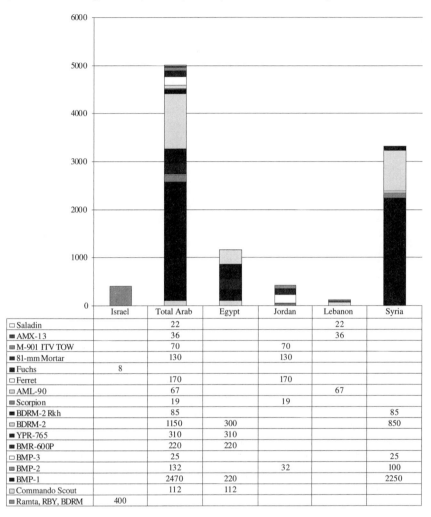

	Israel	Total Arab	Egypt	Jordan	Lebanon	Syria
□ Saladin		22			22	
■ AMX-13		36			36	
▨ M-901 ITV TOW		70		70		
■ 81-mm Mortar		130		130		
■ Fuchs	8					
□ Ferret		170		170		
▨ AML-90		67			67	
▨ Scorpion		19		19		
■ BDRM-2 Rkh		85				85
□ BDRM-2		1150	300			850
■ YPR-765		310	310			
■ BMR-600P		220	220			
□ BMP-3		25				25
▨ BMP-2		132		32		100
■ BMP-1		2470	220			2250
□ Commando Scout		112	112			
▨ Ramta, RBY, BDRM	400					

Source: Adapted by Anthony H. Cordesman from the IISS, *Military Balance.* Some data adjusted or
   estimated by the author.

passive armor on its fighting compartment, rather than the reactive armor used in
the Nagmachon. Both use reactive armor on their sideskirts. Both carry up to four
7.62-mm machine guns and a 60-mm mortar.[122]
   Nevertheless, most US experts feel that Israel should not be counted as having
large holdings of the kind of other armored fighting vehicles which have the armor,

Figure 3.9
Operational Arab-Israeli Armored Personnel Carriers in 2001

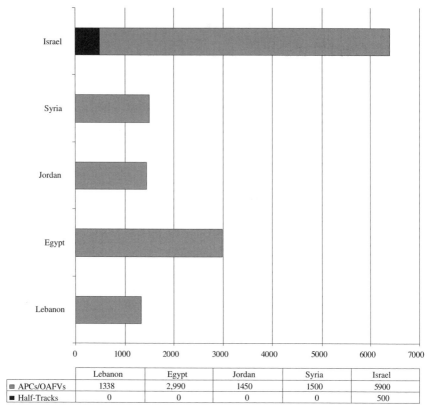

	Lebanon	Egypt	Jordan	Syria	Israel
▦ APCs/OAFVs	1338	2,990	1450	1500	5900
■ Half-Tracks	0	0	0	0	500

Includes APCs, scouts cars, half-tracks, mechanized infantry fighting vehicles, reconnaissance vehicles and other armored vehicles other than tanks. The totals do not include large numbers of vehicles that are in storage or not operational. In 2000, they included 3,000-3,500 half tracks for Israel, 1,075 BTR-60/OT-62s for Egypt, and an unknown number for Lebanon and Syria

Source: Adapted by Anthony H. Cordesman from the IISS, *Military Balance.* Some data adjusted or estimated by the author on the basis of comments by US experts.

firepower, and mobility to directly support its best tanks in maneuver combat or engage well-armed and well-placed infantry with modern anti-tank weapons. They only classify around 400–800 of Israel's other armored fighting vehicles as designed for this role, although Israel is now deploying more armored vehicles modified to provide direct support of tanks and is giving the procurement of an advanced APC/AFV a higher priority.[123]

Syria has purchased large numbers of other armored vehicles, although these are of very mixed quality. Syria has 850 obsolescent BDRM-2s that it uses as armored reconnaissance vehicles. These vehicles performed relatively poorly in Afghanistan. They have limited visibility and poor angles of fire for rough and mountainous terrain of the kind on the Golan and in the Galilee, are highly vulnerable even to light anti-tank weapons, and are difficult to exit rapidly once the vehicle is hit. Syria also has 1,500 obsolescent and relatively low quality BTR-40s BTR-50s, BTR-60s, and BTR-152 armored personnel carriers which are Korean War vintage designs.

Syria's most capable armored fighting vehicles consist of 2,250 BMP-1s and 1000 BMP-2s, and some BMP-3s that it uses as armored infantry fighting vehicles (AIFVs). The BMP is a Soviet-designed weapon intended to support tanks in combat. It is an effective system in some respects, but has light armor and the BMP-1 proved to have severe ergonomic problems in the design of its fire ports, and in the operation of its main gun and anti-tank guided weapons system.

The BMP-1 and BMP-2 performed relatively poorly in the Iran-Iraq War, the Gulf War, and the fighting in Afghanistan. Russian armored vehicles have been extensively modified as a result of these conflicts, and the BMP-3 seems to have corrected many of the crippling ergonomic problems that limited the effectiveness of the BMP-1 and BMP-2. The BMP-3 has a much more effective 100-mm gun and its use of a gun-launched variant of the AT-10 "Bastion" (9M117) missile may give it the first effective anti-tank guided missile capability ever deployed on a BMP. Syria, however, has no immediate ability to buy the BMP-3 or upgrade its existing BMPs, and even the BMP-3 is relatively heavy for its power train and has demonstrated serious reliability problems.[124]

Like Israel, Jordan has comparatively large numbers of APCs, many of which carry heavy weapons. However, it has relatively few other armored vehicles suitable for the direct forward support of tanks, and is much better equipped for armored personnel movement and dismounted support of tanks than the direct support of tanks. Its holdings include 19 Scorpion light tanks, and 32 relatively modern BMP-2 armored infantry fighting vehicles. It seems to have withdrawn 170 obsolete Ferret armored reconnaissance vehicles from service. The rest of Jordan's holding consists of 1,400 variants of the M-113 APC and 50 BTR-80s/ BTR-94s. Some of these M-113s have improvements in armor, some have been equipped with cannon/machine guns and mortars, and 70 have TOW anti-tank weapons. The BTR-94s are Ukrainian 8x8 armored vehicles with twin 23-mm guns and a 7.62-mm machine gun. They have firing ports and are closer to AFVs than most APCs.[125]

Jordan is actively seeking US aid to convert its M-113A1s to M-113A3s, to improve their survivability and firepower in combined maneuver operations, and to upgrade the armor of its M-113s. It also, however, plans to cut its total operational strength of M-113s by about 15% to free resources to maintain its remaining forces. In addition, Jordan has been testing an upgraded Scorpion Combat Vehicle Reconnaissance. The upgraded version has a turbocharged diesel engine, a 7-speed transmission, a new electrical system, and a thermal fire-control system.[126] Jordan is also acquiring a family of vehicles suited for special forces operations and low-intensity combat. These include up to 100 AB3 Black Iris 4x2 light utility vehicles, which can carry TOW launchers, 106-mm recoilless rifles, and 12.7-mm machine guns.[127]

Lebanon has a mix of different armored vehicles, some of which are severely worn or which have been confiscated from various militias. They include 36 worn and obsolete AMX-13s, 81 worn VAB-VCIs, 81 AMX-VCIs, and 37 Panhard M3/VTTs. The bulk of Lebanon's holdings consist of 1,164 M-113/A1/A2 armored personnel carriers. Many have been modified to carry mortars, anti-tank weapons, and machine guns.

Egypt has comparatively large numbers of armored fighting vehicles, but much of its strength is worn and/or obsolete. Egypt has some 2,990 operational APCs, including 2,320 M-113s. The M-113s come in a wide range of variants, including the M-113A2 armored ambulance, M-548A1 ammunition carrier, and M-577A2 armored command post. Egypt also has over 650 Walids, 70 YPR-765 and over 165 Fahds. It has 1,075 BTR-50/OT-62s, but most are in storage.

Egypt's armored reconnaissance vehicles include 300 obsolescent BRDM-2s and 112 light armored Commando Scouts that are not suited for missions in areas with modern anti-tank weapons and tanks. Its holdings of armored infantry fighting vehicles include 220 BMR-600Ps, 310 YPR-765s with 25-mm guns, plus 220 worn BMP-1s which are largely in storage.

These totals reflect the fact that Egypt is absorbing 611 YPR-765 armored infantry fighting vehicles, which it ordered from the Netherlands in 1994. This order is being delivered in three batches which will include 304 YPR 765 PRIs, with a turret equipped with 25-mm guns and a coaxial 7.62-mm machine gun, 6 YPR 765 PRCO-Bs armored command vehicles, 210 YPR 765 PRAT-TOW with dual-TOW launchers, and 79 YPR 765 PRCO-Cs with 0.50 caliber machine guns. Egypt is also absorbing 12 M-577 command vehicles. The Netherlands is also providing technical and training assistance.[128]

Egypt is developing its own Infantry Fighting Vehicle that is designed to operate across the country in coordination with the M1A1 tank, and trials of this IFV are currently under way. So far Egypt has only built the relatively simple Fahd wheeled armored vehicle—which is a 4x4 Mercedes-Benz truck chassis equipped with an armored shell. There are something like 1,000 Fahds in service, although most are in service in low-grade units, support functions, and the security services. The IISS estimates that only 165 are in active service with the army. They are to replace older, low-grade systems like the Wahlid and BTRs. Most are armed with 7.62-mm and 12.7-mm machine guns, although there is a mine-laying variant that can lay up to 250 anti-tank mines by dropping them through a chute at the rear of the vehicle.[129]

If Egypt does succeed in producing the IFV it is now developing, it will be the only IFV in the Egyptian military truly capable of coordinating and supporting main battle tanks in combat.[130] The IFV chassis is based on an updated and stretched version of the M-113A with six road wheel stations and a greatly improved suspension. It uses a 400-horsepower engine and automatic transmission and has a combat weight of 17,690 kilograms, and a power to weight ratio of 22.62 horsepower per ton—better than the US Bradley. It uses much the same armor as the M-113 but has an applique layer of titanium armor, which gives the vehicle full protection against a 14.5-mm weapon. The turret is similar to that fitted to the Bradley with 25-mm chain gun, twin TOW launcher, and twin 7.62-mm machine gun.[131]

There are differences of opinion over just how important the weaknesses in Israeli and Jordanian armored fighting vehicles are. Some Israeli and Jordanian officers do not feel that their respective lack of an advanced armored fighting vehicle is likely to be significant in combat on the West Bank, on the Golan, or in Lebanon. They feel that advanced armored fighting vehicles may be useful in supporting tanks and direct fire in the relatively open terrain of the Sinai, but that moving through rough terrain requires infantry to dismount from armored vehicles, or allows AFVs with softer armor and less speed to be positioned where their anti-tank weapons and mortars can be used "hull down" or in less vulnerable positions.

They feel that both tanks and AFVs fighting in the Golan, much of the West Bank, and Lebanon will have to advance along the same relatively predictable routes for terrain reasons and will have to compete for maneuver room in major engagements. Also, armed helicopters, close air support, and rapidly responding precision fire artillery will provide more effective support for tanks in hunting down and suppressing enemy tanks and anti-tank weapons than AIFVs. US experts also question the value of Syria's emphasis on massing direct fire armored weapons in the vicinity of the Golan Heights and the Galilee because of the geographic factors that limit cross-country movement and "channel" armored vehicles.

Israeli officers with extensive experience with unattended airborne vehicles (UAVs) also stress the new degree of situational awareness that modern sensors can give combined arms forces in locating and suppressing both tanks and AFVs. In contrast, Egyptian officers who served in the Gulf War are more impressed with the advantages of weapons like the M-2 Bradley and the impact of a mix of M-1A1 tanks and the M-2 in armored maneuver combat. In short, Egypt, Israel, Jordan, and Syria not only have different views of their desired relative mix of tanks and AFVs, but differ over the role of AFVs in combined arms.

Anti-Tank Weapons

There is no way to develop exact counts of Israel's, Egypt's, Jordan's, Lebanon's, and Syria's holdings of anti-tank guided weapons, but all of the countries involved have acquired relatively large numbers of modern crew-served, vehicle-mounted, and manportable anti-tank guided weapons. These systems play a major role in shaping the balance of armored warfare capabilities.

Israel had at least 300 modern crew-served TOW anti-tank guided missile launchers in 2000 (some mounted on Ramta M-113s), 900 aging man-portable

Dragon anti-tank guided missile launchers, 25 Mapats, and some captured AT-3 Saggers. It also has large numbers of B-300 82-mm rocket launchers, Carl Gustav 84-mm rocket launchers, and 250 M-40A1 106-mm rocket launchers.

Israel is developing systems that can rapidly modernize these holdings. Israel's Rafael Armament Development Authority has developed a new family of anti-tank guided missiles that are designed to "kill any target on the battlefield" and which may eventually replace the US TOW missiles. The three new weapons in this family are called the Gill (Small Spike), the Spike, the Dandy, and the Excalibur. This new family of anti-tank weapons uses fiber optics as a means of concealing the launch position, using non-line-of-sight firing, and developing an arc trajectory to penetrate targets from their upper surface.[132] The Gill has a maximum range of 2,500 meters in its fire-and-forget mode and the Spike has a range of 4,000 meters in its fiberoptic mode.[133] The Gill is already in IDF service. Targets may include all tanks or helicopters located at ranges of 2–3 kilometers away from the position of firing.

The Dandy is a helicopter and vehicle-mounted system that is just entering service. It has two methods of engagement.[134] The helicopter version comes in pods of four missiles, the basic launcher weighs 55 kilograms, and the missile weighs 33 kilograms. It can be used as a fire-and-forget system, or in-fire and engagement. In the fire-and-forget mode, the target is detected using a charge-coupled device and the gunner locks the missile on track, allowing the missile to follow the sensor image to its target. In the in-fire and engagement mode, the combination of a nose-mounted charge coupled device and infrared sensor, and an optical fiber data link allows the gunner to update the guidance all the way to the target. The missile is said to have a range of 400–6,000 meters, and to use a tandem high explosive anti-tank warhead that can defeat reactive armor. Four Dandy missiles were fired in southern Lebanon in early 1998, and reports from these firings suggest that the range of these missiles may be much greater than the six kilometers originally projected.[135] The Dandy was successfully tested in three "fire and forget" firings from an AH-1 helicopter in September 2000. The Excalibur is an artillery-fired, top-attack tank-killer with 105-mm and 120-mm versions. It is a fire-and-forget weapon with a homing sensor that can be fired at long ranges and which does not require a line of sight to destroy a tank from the top.[136]

Israeli Aircraft Industries (IAI) is also developing the Laser Homing Anti-Tank (LAHAT) missile, which completed a series of firing tests and was ready to enter the pre-production phase in August 1999. The LAHAT can be fired from 105-mm and 120-mm guns on the M60A3 and Merkava Mk III main battle tanks.[137]

While anti-tank weapons are not as glamorous as tanks, Israel's holdings of advanced weapons and procurement of fire-and-forget weapons gives it a greatly improved capability to defend against a Syrian armored attack and to allow its infantry, light vehicles, and helicopters to engage at long ranges with minimum risk.

Syria too has made striking advances in its anti-tank weapons capability in recent years—one of the few areas where its forces have had major modernization.

It still has 3,000 low-quality Soviet-bloc AT-3 Sagger anti-tank guided weapons with second-generation guidance systems. Roughly 2,500 of these systems are mounted on its armored fighting vehicles. It does, however, have 200 modern manportable Milans, 150 modern AT-4 Spigots, and 200 AT-5 Spandrel anti-tank guided weapons with third generation guidance systems. Syria also has an estimated 2,000 AT-10s and an unknown number of AT-14 Kornets.

Jordan has emphasized anti-tank weapons as a way of offsetting its weakness in armor. It has 330 TOW launchers (70 mounted in APCs) and 310 Dragons. It also has some 2,500 LAW-80 94-mm rocket launchers, 2,300 112-mm APILAS rocket launchers, and 330 M-40A1 106-mm rocket launchers. Jordan is seeking to upgrade its TOW missiles to the TOW-2A, and find a replacement or upgrade package for its Dragons. Jordan plans on using some of its estimated $575 million in US military aid to upgrade its TOW missiles and to purchase Maverick and Hellfire anti-armor weapons.[138]

Egypt has a mix of low- and high-quality anti-tank guided weapons. Its low-quality weapons include Soviet-bloc and British anti-tank guided weapons with second-generation guidance systems. These include 1,400 AT-3 Sagger launchers (some on BRDM-2s) and 200 Swingfire launchers. The AT-3s and Swingfires are obsolescent and are another case where Egypt has tended to maintain force numbers at the expense of force quality.

Its high quality weapons include 220 Milan launchers and 530 TOW launchers, including improved TOWs and TOW-2As. Most are vehicle mounted, including 52 mounted on M-901 armored vehicles, and 210 on YPR-765 PRAT-TOWs. Egypt bought 2,372 TOW-2A missiles in 1997. Egypt is seeking major future deliveries of the improved TOW-2B as one of its highest procurement priorities.[139] These missiles attack armored units from the top surface, and present a potential political problem. They could enable Egypt to improve its capability to strike Israel's Merkava tanks, which are particularly vulnerable because of the lack of protection in that area.

Lebanon has 20 TOW launchers, and ENTAC and Milan anti-tank guided weapons. It has large inventories of RPG-7 and M-65 anti-tank rocket launchers, and recoilless weapons like the M-40A1 106-mm recoilless rifle.

Egypt, Israel, Jordan, and Syria all recognize the advantages of modern anti-tank guided weapons that combine high lethality, long range, and ease of operation. They also mix the use of AFVs that can fire anti-tank guided weapons at long ranges with an emphasis on defensive tactics that use anti-tank weapons in fortifications and pre-surveyed locations.

Israel and Syria have made anti-tank guided weapons a key part of their fortifications on the Golan, and Jordan relies heavily on such weapons for the defense of the slopes on the Eastern Bank of the Jordan. Israel, however, does a far better job than Syria of supporting its anti-tank guided weapons crews with C⁴I/ BM systems, and of training its crews for integrated combined arms operations.

According to some American experts, Syria now sees equipping its commandos and special forces with modern anti-tank guided weapons, and other advanced crew and manportable weapons, as one way of countering Israel's edge with asymmetric warfare. Small lightly equipped units are much harder to attack with modern targeting sensors and precision-guided weapons, and can have considerable lethality in both defense and covert operations.

Artillery Forces

Figures 3.10 through 3.12 provide a broad picture of the relative artillery strength of Israel, Egypt, Jordan, Lebanon and Syria, and a rough measure of their indirect fire capability. Figures 3.13 through 3.16 break these data down into more detail. They compare total holdings of self-propelled artillery and multiple rocket launchers, and then show holdings of self propelled, towed, and multiple rocket launcher artillery by type. The data show striking differences in each country's mix of advanced artillery weapons, artillery maneuver capability, and ability to mass fire. They also often reflect a striking lack of interoperability in terms of standardization on ammunition by caliber and by weapons type.

These figures illustrate the fact that Israel has emphasized artillery maneuver warfare since the 1973 War, while its Arab neighbors have tended to place more emphasis on massing artillery and sheer weight of fire. One important aspect of this table that may have considerable impact in future wars is that maximum artillery ranges now extend from 27 to over 45 kilometers.[140] This is a significant increase in range since 1973, and a near doubling of range since 1967. It means both sides can fire at military and civilian targets much deeper in their opponent's territory.

Egypt and Syria have massive total artillery forces. At the same time, the data in Figure 3.11 reflect the fact that Israel has built up a considerable force of modern self-propelled artillery weapons, including some 855 self-propelled weapons out of a total of 1,537 self-propelled, towed, and multiple rocket launcher weapons— or roughly 55%. Israel's best artillery weapons include 530 M-109A1/A 155-mm, and 35 M-110 203-mm weapons. Israel also has 520 towed weapons, including 70 M-101 105-mm, 100 D-30 122-mm, 100 M-46 130-mm, and 50 Soltam M-68 to 71, 50 M-839–845P, and 50 M-114A1 155-mm weapons. Soltam has developed some very advanced 155-mm designs and rounds, although the IDF has lacked the funds to buy its products in large numbers. It claims that its extended-range full-bore base-bleed (ERFB-BB) projectiles have a maximum range of 41 kilometers, and its L-15 high-explosive round has a maximum range of 31 kilometers.[141]

Israel has an additional advantage in artillery battle management technology because it has much better counter-battery, long-range targeting and battle management and fire control systems and capabilities than Egypt, Jordan, and Syria, and conducts much more realistic combined arms exercises than its Arab neighbors. It has particularly advanced real-time targeting systems, including a steadily more sophisticated range of unmanned aerial vehicles (UAVs), and battle management computers.

Figure 3.10
Arab-Israeli Artillery Forces by Category of Weapon in 2001

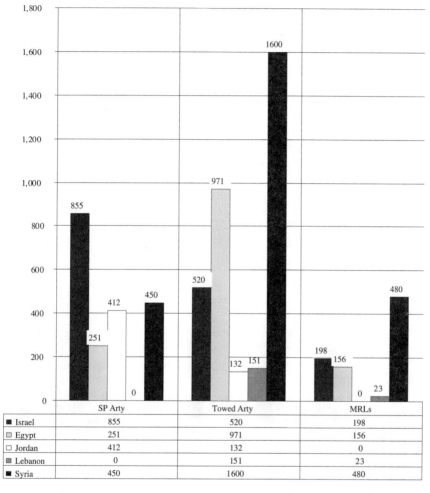

	SP Arty	Towed Arty	MRLs
■ Israel	855	520	198
▢ Egypt	251	971	156
▢ Jordan	412	132	0
▦ Lebanon	0	151	23
■ Syria	450	1600	480

Source: Prepared by Anthony H. Cordesman, based upon the IISS *Military Balance* and discussions with US experts.

Syria has improved its artillery to add more maneuver capability, and now has 400 122-mm S21 self-propelled artillery weapons, and 50 152-mm S23 self-propelled artillery weapons. It does, however, remain reliant on some 1,630 older Soviet-bloc supplied towed artillery weapons. These towed weapons include 100 M-1931 and M-1937, 150 M-1938, and 450 D-30 122-mm weapons. They also include 700 M-46 130-mm weapons, 20 D-20 and 50 M-1937 152-mm weapons, and 10 S23 180-mm siege guns. A substantial number of Syria's towed weapons

Figure 3.11
Arab-Israeli Artillery Forces By Country in 2001

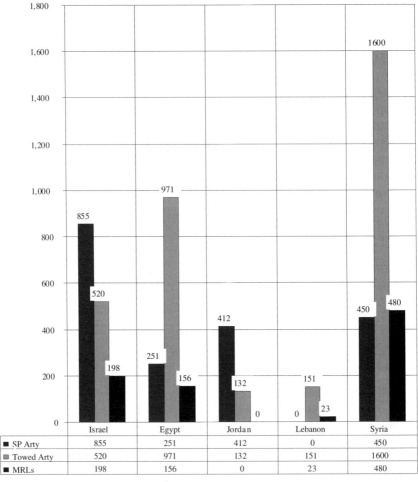

	Israel	Egypt	Jordan	Lebanon	Syria
■ SP Arty	855	251	412	0	450
▨ Towed Arty	520	971	132	151	1600
■ MRLs	198	156	0	23	480

Source: Prepared by Anthony H. Cordesman, based upon the IISS *Military Balance* and discussions
with US and regional experts.

are in storage or low-grade reserve units. According to some Israeli exports, Syria
also has significant inventories of chemical rounds for its artillery. US experts do
not confirm Syrian stockpiling of such chemical rounds.

Syria does have counterbattery radars and some long-range target acquisition
capabilities, but it is much less sophisticated in organizing and training its artillery
forces for maneuver warfare than Israel, and is significantly less sophisticated than
Egypt and Jordan. Syria still divides much of its artillery command structure and

Figure 3.12
Arab-Israeli Total Artillery Strength 1986–2001
(Towed and Self-Propelled Tube Artillery of 100-mm+ and Multiple Rocket Launchers)

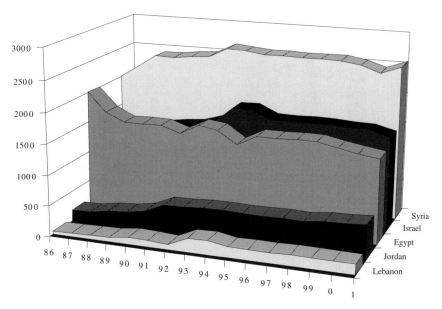

Source: Prepared by Anthony H. Cordesman, based upon the IISS *Military Balance* and discussions with US and regional experts.

training in ways that do not involve combined arms capability, and fails to conduct realistic training above the battalion and regiment level. Syria places more emphasis on bringing sustained, high rates of fire against pre-surveyed or relative static targets than it does on rapidly locating targets, rapidly bringing precision fire to bear, and then rapidly shifting fires to meet combined arms needs.

Jordan has low total artillery holdings by the standards of its Arab neighbors, but it has joined Israel in emphasizing self-propelled artillery and the role of artillery in combined arms. Jordan has 544 major artillery weapons, 412 of which are self propelled. Its holdings include 35 obsolescent M-52 105-mm weapons, 23 M-44 155-mm weapons, 234 relatively modern M-109A1/A2 155-mm weapons, and 120 M-110 203-mm weapons. A number of Jordan's towed artillery weapons seem to be in storage, but it still has 54 M-102 105-mm, 38 M-114 155-mm, 18 M-59/M-1 155-mm, plus 22 M-115 203-mm weapons in storage. Jordan has AN TPQ-36 and AN TPQ-37 counter-battery radars, and has shown good capability to use them. (Jordan has deployed a company with TPQ-37s in its peacekeeping forces in Bosnia.) Jordan also has a French artillery fire control and battle management system. It is seeking rocket-assisted projectile rounds for its 155-mm weapons to

Figure 3.13
Israel versus Egypt, Syria, Jordan, and Lebanon: High Performance Artillery in
2001

Modern Self Propelled Artillery

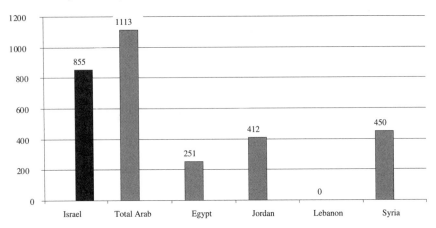

Multiple Rocket Launchers

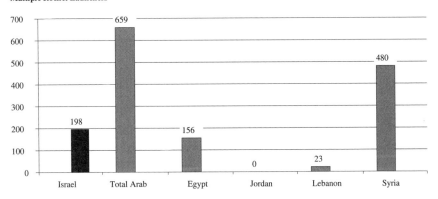

Source: Prepared by Anthony H. Cordesman, based upon the IISS *Military Balance* and discussions
with US and regional experts.

compensate for the range advantage of Iraqi and Syrian artillery, and is at least
experimenting with UAVs for artillery targeting.

Lebanon has no self-propelled tube artillery weapons. It has 174 towed artillery
weapons, including 13 M-101A1 105-mm; 26 D-30 and 36 M-1938 122-mm; 11
M-46 130-mm; and 12 Model 50, 18 M-114A1, and 35 M-1938 155-mm weapons.

Egypt has an operational strength of 251 self-propelled and 971 towed tube
artillery weapons, although it has a total inventory of around 2,200 towed
weapons—some of which are in reserve units. It has 175 to 196 modern self-

Figure 3.14
Arab-Israeli Self-Propelled Artillery By Caliber in 2001

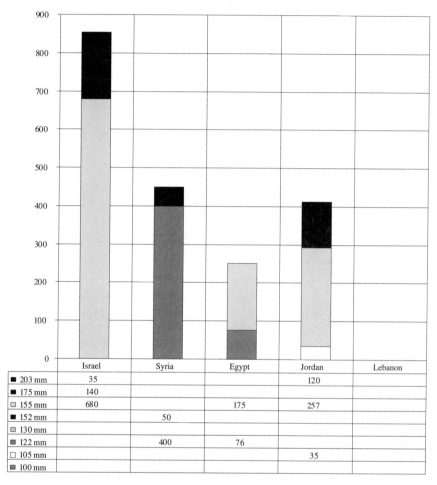

	Israel	Syria	Egypt	Jordan	Lebanon
■ 203 mm	35			120	
■ 175 mm	140				
▫ 155 mm	680		175	257	
■ 152 mm		50			
▫ 130 mm					
■ 122 mm		400	76		
▫ 105 mm				35	
▤ 100 mm					

Source: Prepared by Anthony H. Cordesman, based upon the IISS *Military Balance* and discussions with US and regional experts.

propelled M-109A2 artillery weapons (sources differ and only 164 seem to be operational), and its best artillery units—which are equipped with these weapons—reflect a new emphasis on improved training, combined arms doctrine, more sophisticated target acquisition, and more rapid shifts of fire. Egypt announced in June 2000 that the US had agreed to sell it 179 more surplus M-109A2/A3s for $48 million. This would more than double its present M-109 force and allow Egypt to get rid of a substantial number of aging Russian towed artillery weapons. Egypt is also buying 76–100 SP-122 122-mm weapons. These mount Egyptian-made 122-

Figure 3.15
Arab-Israeli Towed Artillery By Caliber in 2001

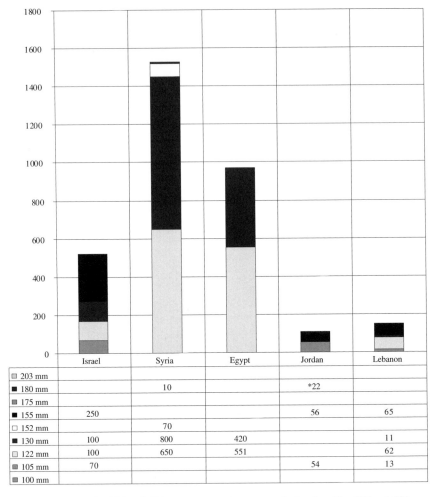

	Israel	Syria	Egypt	Jordan	Lebanon
☐ 203 mm					
■ 180 mm		10		*22	
☐ 175 mm					
■ 155 mm	250			56	65
☐ 152 mm		70			
■ 130 mm	100	800	420		11
☐ 122 mm	100	650	551		62
■ 105 mm	70			54	13
■ 100 mm					

Note: Syria has 100 additional 122-mm weapons in storage. Jordan has 25 additional 203-mm weapons in storage.

Source: Prepared by Anthony H. Cordesman, based upon the IISS *Military Balance* and discussions with US and regional experts.

mm weapons on the chassis of the United Defense M-109A2 self-propelled howitzer. The first 23 were due to be delivered in 2000.[142]

Egypt does not have Israel's proficiency in using its self-propelled weapons to acquire targets at long ranges, or to use its artillery to rapidly shift and mass fires, and maneuver its artillery. It does, however, have modern counterbattery radars

Figure 3.16
Arab-Israeli Multiple Rocket Launchers By Caliber in 2001

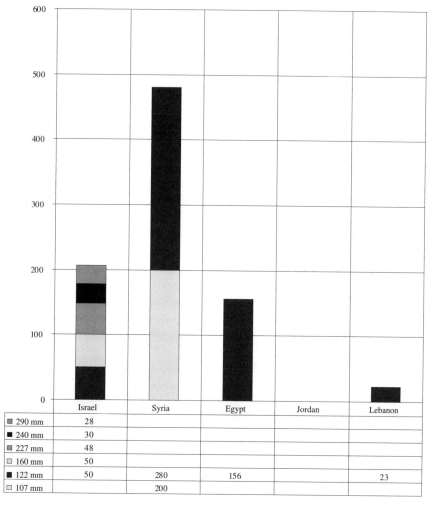

	Israel	Syria	Egypt	Jordan	Lebanon
■ 290 mm	28				
■ 240 mm	30				
▩ 227 mm	48				
☐ 160 mm	50				
■ 122 mm	50	280	156		23
☐ 107 mm		200			

Source: Prepared by Anthony H. Cordesman, based upon the IISS *Military Balance* and discussions with US and regional experts.

like the AN/TPQ-37, and uses modern artillery fire management vehicles like the Rasit.

Egypt is continuing to seek more self-propelled artillery. According to some reports, it has signed a $21 million agreement with Finland to buy and/or coproduce the 155 GH 52 APU towed 155-mm field gun. The weapon has a 42 kilometer range, a semiautomatic breech block and an advanced pneumatic flick rammer loading system which allows it to fire three rounds every 12 seconds.[143] Other reports indicate that it is buying 24 more chassis for its 122-mm weapon from United Defense.[144]

Egypt, however, is still largely dependent on towed Soviet-bloc weapons. Its operational towed artillery assets in active combat units include 36 M-31 and M-37 122-mm weapons, 359 M-1938 122-mm weapons, 156 D-30M 122-mm weapons, 420 M-46 130-mm weapons, and an unknown number of larger weapons of mixed size. Some are 152-mm M1937s. Many of these weapons are obsolete Soviet-supplied weapons with awkward ergonomics and limited rates of fire. They are not supported by artillery radars and advanced fire control systems, although Egypt does have the ability to manufacture artillery barrels and refurbish such weapons.[145] The artillery units using these towed weapons continue to use relatively obsolete tactics, lack more fire control support, and lack mobility and effective combined arms training. They have substantially less effectiveness than Egypt's units with self-propelled weapons. Egypt has the capacity to manufacture chemical rounds, but there is no evidence it has large numbers in inventory, or that its forces train to use such rounds.

Multiple Rocket Launchers

The data in Figure 3.10 show that Israel, Egypt, Jordan, Lebanon, and Syria have large inventories of multiple rocket launchers (MRLs). The numbers of the weapons in these figures are somewhat misleading, however, because they disguise a fundamental asymmetry between Israel's artillery forces and those of Egypt and Syria. Israel emphasizes maneuver and precision; Syria—and to a lesser degree Egypt—emphasize volume of fire and surge capability over precision and mobility.

Israel has around 156 multiple rocket launchers. They include 50 122-mm BM-21s, 160-mm LAR-160s, 48 227-mm Multiple Launch Rocket Systems (MLRS), and more than 20 190-mm MAR 190s. Israel's LAR family of multiple rocket launchers now uses a new 160-mm round that has a trajectory control system to improve its accuracy, and an improved warhead with 104 anti-personnel or anti-materiel bomblets. This improvement is typical of Israel's growing emphasis on relatively precise, long-range area fire using rockets with advanced warheads which can be targeted with great precision in near real-time using UAVs and GPS.[146] Israel seems to have some longer-range systems with ranges of up to 90 kilometers or more.

Israel has acquired the Multiple Launch Rocket System (MLRS) from the US—a system with far greater accuracy and warhead lethality than any deployed in the forces of the Arab "ring states." It has ordered over 40 MLRS launchers and 1,500 tactical rockets, at a cost of $103.5 million in US FMF aid.[147] More batteries are to be sold to Israel as part of a contract worth $50 million that, with upgraded guidance systems, greatly enhances the accuracy of its artillery.[148]

Israel is also developing its own MLRS system that will allow last minute course correction of rockets still in flight. The Minatezt MLRS launcher has two pods with six rockets each, and has a crew of three. It is designed to increase the range of Israeli artillery rockets from 32 kilometers to 45 kilometers, and increase accuracy from a 350-meter CEP to one of 40 meters using a Trajectory Corrected System developed by Lockheed-Martin. This increase in accuracy allows smart submunitions to be more effective, and the IDF is discussing plans to retrofit all MLRS equipped units with such capabilities by 2002.[149] Israel has also developed trajectory correction systems which it claims can give its rockets the same accuracy as conventional artillery weapons.[150]

Syria has at least 480 multiple rocket launchers. These include 200 Type 63 107-mm Chinese weapons and 280 BM-21 Soviet bloc weapons. The Type 63s are towed weapons, and the BM-21s are mounted on trucks. Multiple rocket launchers have historically been most effective in terms of their shock effect on relatively static troops, and have only had high lethality against exposed infantry forces or large, static area targets. Syria's holdings can provide a considerable amount of surge fire to harass and suppress enemy activity or attack area targets, but it has not modernized its C^{4}I/BM capabilities to improve the accuracy and rapid reaction capabilities of its MRL forces or to support them effectively with real-time beyond-visual-range targeting. According to some Israeli experts, Syria has significant inventories of chemical rounds for its multiple rocket launchers. US experts do not confirm Syrian stockpiling of such chemical rounds.

Jordan has no multiple rocket launchers, and Lebanon has 23 BM-21 122-mm weapons.

Egypt has at least 156 multiple rocket launchers. These include 96 BM-11 122-mm weapons and 60 BM-21, as Saqr 10, 18, and 36 barrel 122-mm weapons. Egypt has substantially cut its number of operational multiple rocket launchers in recent years—partly because of their lack of precision, high logistic demands, and relatively slow movement rates. It does, however, manufacture modern 122-mm rockets with enhanced stability and possibly enhanced lethality warheads. Egypt has the capability to manufacture chemical warheads for its MRLs, but there is no evidence that such rounds are currently deployed.

Mortars

Both Israel and the Arab "ring states" use extensive numbers of mortars, which add a significant firepower capability. Israel has some 7,740 mortars, including 1,600 81-mm mortars, 900 120-mm mortars, and 240 160-mm mortars. A number of these weapons are mounted in APCs. Israel also relies heavily on about 5,000 smaller caliber 60-mm mortars that are useful for maximum maneuverability.

Syria has over 4,500 mortars, but it is not clear how many are actively deployed. Syria's holdings include 82-mm mortars, 350 M-1943 120-mm mortars, 100 M-160 160-mm mortars, and 8 M-240 240-mm mortars.

Jordan has a total of 800 mortars, including 450 81-mm mortars, about 130 of which are mounted on APCs. Jordan also has 50 M-30 107-mm mortars, and 300 Brandt 120-mm mortars.

Lebanon has around 380 mortars, including 158 81-mm, 111 82-mm, and 108 120-mm weapons.

Egypt has well over 2,400 mortars. These include some 1,800 M-43 120-mm mortars, around 540 82-mm mortars (at least 50 mounted on armored vehicles); a number of 107-mm mortars (at least 50 mounted on armored vehicles); and a number of 160-mm mortars (at least 60 mounted on M-160 armored vehicles).

Mortars are important in urban warfare, static infantry combat, and in rough terrain. They allow rapid reaction direct fire at targets in visual range, and the use of suppressive fire without complex command and control problems. This eliminates many of the organizational and tactical problems that countries like Syria face in coordinating the use of longer-range systems, and mortars have produced as many casualties as long-range artillery in a number of clashes between Israel and Arab forces.

Advanced Artillery Warfare Capability

As is the case with armor, Arab and Israeli holdings of artillery weapons are often more impressive than actual warfighting capability. This is not simply a matter of the differences in mobility and counter-battery capabilities discussed earlier; it is also a function of training, sustainment, and doctrine.

Israel is the only regional state to broadly train and equip its forces to rapidly acquire targets, allocate artillery fire efficiently in support of armored and maneuver forces, organize and train for night warfare, emphasize high levels of prolonged sustainment, and concentrate on firing against known, precisely located targets in ways that allow indirect fire to have some of the precision and lethality of direct fire weapons. Israel is also the only country which has demonstrated a consistent capability to use sensors like UAVs and effective battle management systems to acquire targets in near real-time at long ranges. Even Israel, however, often lacks advanced equipment and training for such operations and must concentrate on improving the combined arms and joint warfare capability of its best forces.

In many cases, Israel must use less sophisticated systems that are patched together for warfare in carefully defined parts of given fronts, and which do not have the broad capabilities common in US forces. Israelis argue, probably with considerable justification, that Israel has no need for the kind of global flexibility of US equipment, and can achieve better results with much less sophisticated equipment tailored to the specific areas where Israel must fight. At the same time, the resulting solutions often seem to be an awkward mix of different levels of equipment, and the IDF cannot afford to provide the same level of capability to all of its forces.

Jordanian doctrine recognizes the value of such sophisticated sensors, fire control, and battle management systems, but Jordan simply cannot afford the level of training, equipment, and sustainment it needs. Its forces using its 155-mm M-109A1/A2s and 203-mm M-110s are better equipped and trained than its other units, but Jordan's artillery is better organized for defensive warfare than offensive combat.

Although Egypt is modernizing its artillery branch, it still tends to be slow to maneuver, weak in target acquisition and battlefield management capability, and limited in night warfare and sustainment capability. Egyptian exercises have steadily improved combined arms operations, particularly for the forces equipped with US weapons and those which participate in joint exercises with the US. Its M-109-equipped forces are notably more proficient than its other forces, and many Egyptian artillery units are still best suited to static or slow-moving massed area fire—a notably inefficient approach to modern artillery warfare.

Syrian artillery forces suffer sharply from a Soviet-era heritage emphasizing massed fires and towed artillery. Joint and combined arms warfare training is poor, overall maneuver warfare capability is weak, and sustainment is best suited to defensive operations or combat in the Golan area—where Syrian forces can rely on existing stockpiles. Overall night warfare training is poor, battle management is poor, and Syria is just beginning to try to exploit GPS and UAVs effectively to take advantage of long-range fire capabilities. The Syrian forces equipped with Russian-made, self-propelled 122-mm 2S1s and 152-mm 2S3s are, however, more proficient than the rest of Syrian artillery and some Syrian heavy divisions seem to have effective mobile artillery support in combat exercises.

The Lebanese Army is beginning to make slow improvements, but its limited in resources and must concentrate on fundamentals.

Combat Aircraft

Table 3.3 shows the manning of Arab and Israeli air and air defense forces. Gross manpower numbers, however, tell little about the war fighting capabilities of these forces. The war fighting capability of air forces is shaped largely by the quantity and quality of its pilots and technicians, combat aircraft and air munitions of each force, by the quality of its command and control system, and by support systems such as basing and sustainability.

Figures 3.17 through 3.19 provide data on the trends in aircraft strength and total current holdings, although it should be noted that estimates of the total inventory of fixed-wing combat aircraft differ sharply according to source. Estimates of the number of aircraft that are actually operational in combat units are even more controversial. The difference between these two sets of figures is critical because many of the combat aircraft in each country are in storage or are assigned to training units. Many of the older aircraft in Egypt and Syria are assigned to very low-grade units with token or no combat capability against an air force with surviving air defense capabilities.

Table 3.3
Arab-Israeli Land-Based Air Defense Systems in 2001

Country	Major SAM	Light SAM	AA Guns
Egypt	664 launchers 40/282 SA-2 53/212 SA-3 14/56 SA-6 12/78 I Hawk (4 Div./100 Btn.)	2,100 SA-7 Ayn as Saqr 20 SA-9 26 M-54 Chaparral SP 14/36 Crotale 18 Amoun Skyguard/ RIM-7F 36 quad SAM Ayn as Saqr 57mm, 85mm, 100mm	200 ZPU-2/4 14.5mm 280 ZU-23-2 23mm 118 ZSU-23-4 SP 23mm 36 Sinai SP 23mm 200 M-1939 37mm 200 S-60 57mm 40 ZSU-57-2 SP 57mm 14/- Chaparral 2000 20mm, 23mm, 37mm, 36 twin radar guided 35mm guns Sinai radar-guided 23mm guns
Israel	3/18 Patriot Bty. 17/102 I Hawk Bty. 1 Arrow ATBM Bty	250 Stinger 1,000 Redeye 8/48 Chaparral 8 Stinger Bty. (IAF)	850 20 mm: including 20mm, Vulcan, TCM-20, M-167 35 M-163 Vulcan/ Chaparral 150 ZU-23 23mm 60 ZSU-23-4 SP M-39 37mm 150 L-70 40mm 8 Chaparral Bty. (IAF
Jordan	2/14/80 I Hawk	SA-7B2 52 SA-8 92 SA-13 300 SA-14 240 SA-16 260 Redeye	416 guns 100 M-163 SP 20mm 52 ZSU-23-4 SP 264 M-42 SP 40mm
Lebanon	None	SA-7 SA-14	20mm ZU-23 23mm 10 M-42A1 40mm
Syria	25 Ad Brigades 130 SAM Bty. 11/60/600 SA-2/3 11/27/200 SA-6 1/2/48 SA-5	35 SA-13 20 SA-9 4,000 SA-7 60 SA-8	2,060 guns 650 ZU-23-2 400 ZSU-23-4 SP 300 M-1938 37mm 675 S-60 57mm 10 ZSU-5-2 SP 25 KS-19 100mm 4.000 guns (?)

Source: Adapted by Anthony H. Cordesman from the *IISS, Military Balance*. Light SAMs and AA guns, weapons below line for Egypt, Syria, and Israel, are weapons operated by air force.

Figure 3.17
Arab-Israeli Air Force and Air Defense Manpower in 2001

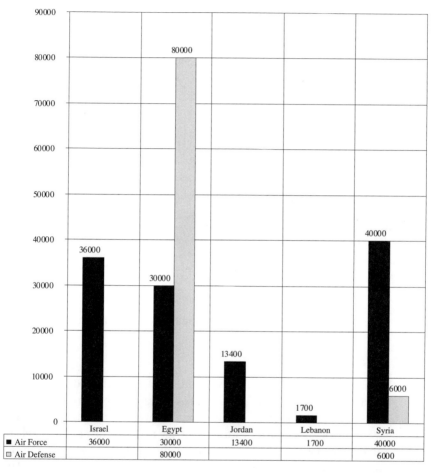

	Israel	Egypt	Jordan	Lebanon	Syria
■ Air Force	36000	30000	13400	1700	40000
□ Air Defense		80000			6000

Source: Prepared by Anthony H. Cordesman, based upon the IISS *Military Balance* and discussions with US and regional experts.

It should be noted that US experts believe that counts which lump fighters, fighter ground attack (FGA), dual role, reconnaissance, and special purpose aircraft into one total for combat aircraft are virtually meaningless as a measure of war fighting capability, and that only mission-related counts of operational aircraft have value in assessing the balance. They also question the value of the kind of breakdown of combat aircraft strength into fighters, fighter ground attack (FGA), and dual role aircraft shown in Table 3.1. Many believe that unclassified estimates of such missions ignore real-world training and mission allocations.

Figure 3.18
Trends in Total Arab-Israeli Combat Aircraft: 1973–2001

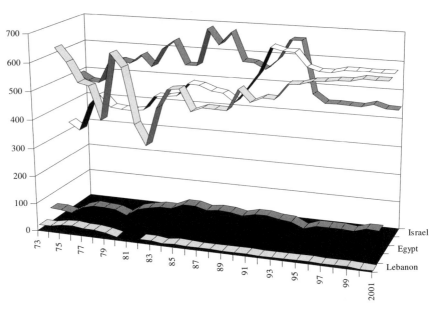

Source: Prepared by Anthony H. Cordesman, based upon the IISS *Military Balance* and discussions with US and regional experts.

At the same time, Figure 3.18 does show that Egypt, Israel, Jordan, and Syria have made no major increases in gross combat aircraft numbers in recent years. This reflects a growing emphasis on aircraft quality over aircraft quantity, and the combined impact of losses through attrition and the need to limit aircraft numbers in order to pay for aircraft that have grown far more costly in constant dollars, as well as more capable and sophisticated. Lebanon, in contrast, has withdrawn all of its aging Hunters and attack helicopters from service and is attempting to slowly build up its air force using trainer-light attack aircraft as a first step.

Figures 3.20 to 3.22 show current strength by aircraft type. Figure 3.20 is particularly important because it shows relative strength in terms of high quality combat aircraft. While experts will always argue over what aircraft should be included, and each type provides a unique mix of mission capabilities, this figure provides a rough measure of modern air warfare capability. As has been discussed earlier, it emphasizes total mission capabilities, and the sophistication of avionics over speed.

The aircraft included in Figure 3.20 have significant mission capabilities that were not widely available in 1973 or 1982. Many of the fixed-wing aircraft shown

Figure 3.19

Total Operational Arab-Israeli Combat Fighter, Attack, Bomber, FGA, and Reconnaissance Aircraft by Type in 2001 (Does not include stored, unarmed electronic warfare and AC&W, and transport aircraft)

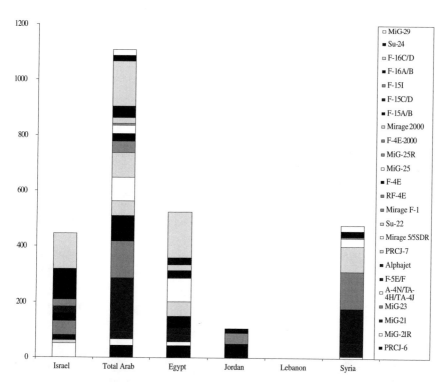

Source: Prepared by Anthony H. Cordesman, based upon the IISS *Military Balance* and discussions with US and regional experts.

now have significant beyond-visual-range air combat capability. Many also have the ability to use advanced precision air-to-surface weapons at ranges outside the coverage of many short-range air defenses, and aircraft like the F-15 and Su-24 are capable of very long-range strikes—with or without refueling.

Force quality is more important in shaping war fighting capability than either manpower or aircraft numbers. The Arab-Israeli air balance is shaped by the following key qualitative factors:

- Israel is the only Middle Eastern state to fund the mix of training, technology, readiness, C⁴I/BM/AEW/EW capability, and sustainability necessary to exploit the revolution in military affairs.

Figure 3.20
High-Quality Operational Arab-Israeli Combat Aircraft in 2001 (Does not include stored, unarmed electronic warfare and AC&W, and transport aircraft)

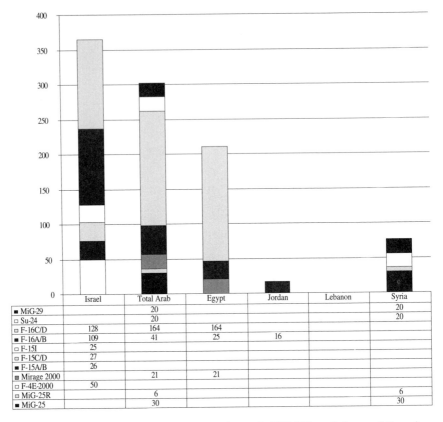

	Israel	Total Arab	Egypt	Jordan	Lebanon	Syria
■ MiG-29		20				20
□ Su-24		20				20
□ F-16C/D	128	164	164			
■ F-16A/B	109	41	25	16		
□ F-15I	25					
□ F-15C/D	27					
■ F-15A/B	26					
▩ Mirage 2000		21	21			
□ F-4E-2000	50					
□ MiG-25R		6				6
■ MiG-25		30				30

Source: Prepared by Anthony H. Cordesman, based upon the IISS *Military Balance* and discussions with US and regional experts.

- Israel now has the most advanced mix of land-based air and ATBM defenses in the region.

- Egypt has many of the elements of a modern air force but as yet lacks overall force quality and cohesion and emphasizes aircraft numbers over balanced force quality.

- Egypt's land-based air defenses have weak C4I/BM capability and mix 78 modern I Hawk launchers with 282 SA-2, 212 SA-3, and 56 SA-6 launchers supplied before 1975.

- Jordan's air force will remain obsolete until its F-16s are fully in service.

- Jordan's "fixed" I Hawk units actually have some mobility, and its C4I/BM system has some modernization, but the overall system is weak.

- Syria's air force is obsolete in concept, organization, training, and equipment. It has only a token strength of first-generation export versions of the MiG-29 and Su-24 and

Figure 3.21
Low/Moderate Quality Arab-Israeli Combat Fighter, Attack, Bomber, FGA, and Reconnaissance Aircraft in 2001 (Does not include stored, unarmed electronic warfare and AC&W, and transport aircraft)

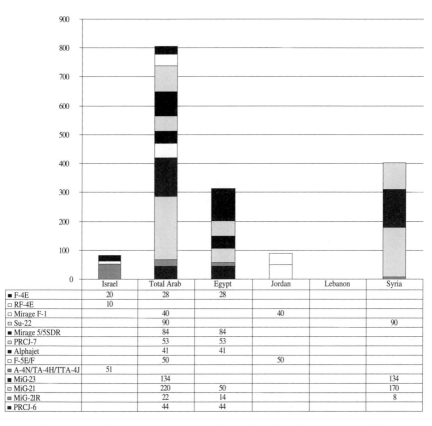

	Israel	Total Arab	Egypt	Jordan	Lebanon	Syria
■ F-4E	20	28	28			
□ RF-4E	10					
□ Mirage F-1		40		40		
□ Su-22		90				90
■ Mirage 5/5SDR		84	84			
□ PRCJ-7		53	53			
■ Alphajet		41	41			
□ F-5E/F		50		50		
■ A-4N/TA-4H/TTA-4J	51					
■ MiG-23		134				134
□ MiG-21		220	50			170
■ MiG-21R		22	14			8
■ PRCJ-6		44	44			

Source: Prepared by Anthony H. Cordesman, based upon the IISS *Military Balance* and discussions with US and regional experts.

proficiency training is poor. It has not modernized attack helicopter training even though Israel uses modern tailored tactics.

- Syria's land-based air defense systems are obsolete in terms of deployment C^4I/BM, and most fire units.

Qualitative Factors Shaping the Effectiveness of the IAF

Israel has the only air force that heavily emphasizes dual-capability squadrons with both air combat and attack capabilities—although Egypt and Jordan have such units and Egypt has steadily improved the dual-capability of its F-16 units.

Figure 3.22

Unarmed Fixed and Rotary Wing Recce, Electronic Warfare, and Intelligence Aircraft in 2001

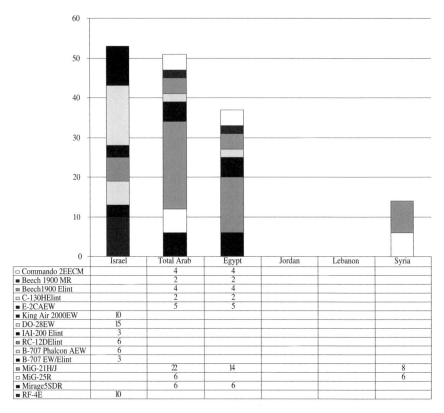

	Israel	Total Arab	Egypt	Jordan	Lebanon	Syria
□ Commando 2EECM		4	4			
■ Beech 1900 MR		2	2			
▣ Beech1900 Elint		4	4			
□ C-130HElint		2	2			
■ E-2CAEW		5	5			
■ King Air 2000EW	10					
□ DO-28EW	15					
■ IAI-200 Elint	3					
▣ RC-12DElint	6					
□ B-707 Phalcon AEW	6					
■ B-707 EW/Elint	3					
▣ MiG-21H/J		22	14			8
□ MiG-25R		6				6
■ Mirage5SDR		6	6			
■ RF-4E	10					

Source: Prepared by Anthony H. Cordesman, based upon the IISS *Military Balance* and discussions with US and regional experts.

The IAF now has some 36,000 men and women, 12 major active combat air bases, and 13 dispersed operating bases and emergency airfields. It has main bases at Tol Nov/Bacha, Sid Dov, Hatzor, Lod, Nevatim, Hatzerim, Ramat David, Palmachim, Ramon, Ovda, Kefar Zekharya, and training detachments at Meggido, Ein Shemer, Tel Nov, and Sde Kedem.

The IAF is headquartered in Tel Aviv, and normally deploys its aircraft in standard squadrons that are based to group aircraft of a given type on bases designed to support them. The IAF also has squadrons for UAVs (146, 155, and 200 squadrons) and three squadrons that operate Israel's nuclear-armed Jericho missiles. These include 150, 199, and 248 squadrons, all of which are nominally based at Kefar Zekharya, and 151 squadron, which supports missile trials at

Palmachim.[151] Much of the ground unit structure includes emergency mobilization forces. The IAF operates most of Israel's land-based air defense units.

The IISS counts 446 active combat aircraft and 250 stored. Jane's counts 619 active and stored aircraft and 470 active aircraft. Israel's combat aircraft are more modern and more capable than those of its Arab neighbors, with the exception of Syria's MiG-29s and Su-24s, and Egypt and Jordan's F-16Cs. Israel also took delivery on 25 F15-I long-range strike aircraft in early 1998.[152] These aircraft are now part of Squadron 69, the Hammer (Patishim) squadron, and began operation with night strikes against targets in Lebanon on January 11, 1999.[153]

The F-15I is specially configured for the IAF, and has a maximum strike range of 1,620 kilometers—although this range is significantly lower when the F-15I is loaded with precision-guided munitions. Israel will receive the AIM-120 Advanced Medium Range Air-to-Air Missile (AMRAAM) from the US for use on the F-15I and its other advanced fighters. It will also receive advanced air-to-ground attack munitions like 700 GPS-guided Joint Direct Attack Munition (JDAM) guided strap-on kits for its Mark-84 2,000-pound bombs.[154] The F-15-I gives Israel an all-weather long-range, pre-emptive strike capability for the first time.[155]

The IAF's first line combat aircraft strength consists of 25 F-15Is, 73 F-15C/Ds, 109 F-16A/Bs, and 128 F-16C/Ds. The F-15-I gives Israel an all-weather, long-range, pre-emptive strike capability for the first time.[156] Israel also has 50 relatively modern Phantom F-4E 2000s plus 20 F-4Es. Its reconnaissance, airborne command and control, and electronic warfare assets include 10 RF-4Es, 2 F-15DRs, 6 Phalcon AEW aircraft which are somewhat similar to the AWACS in function, and up to 37 electronic warfare and signals intelligence aircraft (3 B-707 ELINT/ECM, 6 RC-12D, 3 IAI-200, 15 DO-28, and 10 King Air 2000). This gives Israel roughly 440 highly sophisticated active combat aircraft.[157] In addition, Israel seems to have well over 120 Kfir C2/C7s in storage, plus 25 active A-4Ns in the ground-attack role and up to 130 more A-4Ns in storage.

While Israel does not have modern trainers, it compensates by extending its training in dual-seat versions of its combat aircraft. It makes extensive use of simulated air-to-air combat at the large formation, squadron, small unit, and individual pilot level, and has its own equivalent of "aggressor squadrons" which it uses in training over the Negev and other areas. It has at least one MiG-29, and IAF fighters have flown simulated dogfights against the MiG-29 since late 1996.[158] Air space is, however, a problem and one that grows as the range of air-to-air and air-to-ground weapons grow as aircraft become involved in complex task-oriented groups that must practice over a considerable range. Losing the air space over the West Bank and Gaza in a peace agreement with the Palestinians could create some significant training problems.

During the late 1990s, the Israeli Air Force (IAF) considered possible purchase of up to 100 new US-made F-22 air superiority aircraft to replace these aircraft. It then debated whether to spend $2 to $2.5 billion on 25–40 more F-15Is or 50–110 F-16 Block 60s, or some mix of F-15Is and F-16s in a series of new arms buys.[159] One possible deal included a package of 60 F-16C/D Block 50/52s with PW-229 or

F100-GE-129 engines, 60 AN/APG-68(V)7 radars, 30 LANTIRN navigation and targeting pods, and AIM-9 and AIM-120 missiles. Another included 30 F-15Is, 30 AN/APG-70 PR AN/APG-63(V)I radars and 30 LANTIRN navigation and targeting pods.[160]

Much of the debate over whether to purchase F-15Is or F-16s centered around the fact that Israel can get nearly twice as many F-16s for the same money, but that the F-15I has the ability to strike at long-range targets like Iran without refueling. Other debates included possible offset programs, whether Israel could mount its own radars in the F-16, the possibility of funding an extended range F-16 with a 1,500-kilometer range similar to the F-15I, and the nature of Israel's access to advanced classified versions of the AIM-120 AMRAAM beyond-visual-range air-to-air missile.[161]

Although the Israeli press reported the IAF was leaning towards the F-16s in late 1998, the final decision was put off until after the May 1999 elections. When Ehud Barak won, he asked Defense Minister Moshe Arens to delay the decision until after he formed a government.[162] In the end, Barak and the IAF decided to buy 50 F-16I Block 50/52 fighters in an estimated $2.5 billion deal. The deal called for deliveries to begin in 2003, and included an option to order up to 60 more F-16s within two years for an additional $2 billion.[163] The F-16Is will be equipped with AMRAAM, the Rafael Python 4, and Popeye II missiles.[164]

The IAF may have favored the F-16 because it is considering upgrading its existing F-16s as part of an Avionics Capabilities Enhancement (ACE) program developed by Israeli Aircraft Industries (IAI) and Elbit Systems. This program could enter the fleet as early as 2001. Israel is developing the program for both the IAF and export to foreign air forces. It includes an upgrade cockpit configuration with multifunction liquid crystal displays, a sight helmet, a synthetic aperture radar optimized for air-to-ground operations, advanced data links, new electronic defense systems, and beyond-visual-range (BVR) instrumentation systems. It also includes a 600-gallon external fuel tank offering a 50% increase in range, and new armaments options like the VER-2 vertical ejection bomb rack, improved weapons pylons, the Python 4 air-to-air missile, and the Popeye-Lite air-to-surface missile. The IAF also solved other range problems by developing a capability to use its F-15Is to refuel the F-16 in midair for long-range strike missions.[165]

Israel will develop advanced reconnaissance pods for the F-16 and upgrade its F-16s as part of the USAF Common Configuration Implementation Program and the Lockheed-Martin Tactical Aircraft System upgrades to the Block 40 and 50 models of the F-16. These upgrade options illustrate Israel's unique ability to take an advanced fighter and upgrade it in ways that greatly improve its performance over the "stock" model and extend its useful life as a first-line fighter.[166] Israel has also examined the possible upgrading of its new F-16 buys to the Block 60 model, although this would raise the cost of its new buy by at least $200 million.[167]

Israel is now looking well beyond its current acquisition of the F-16. It has joined the US-British Joint Strike Fighter (JSF) program, and will act as a "major participant" in the development of this new strike-attack fighter. The JSF has significant "stealth" characteristics, and will have very advanced sensors, avionics, secure data links, ECM, and long-range attack munitions delivery capabilities.[168] Israel will also be the first foreign country to acquire the US Joint Direct Attack munition (JDAM), which is a long-range air-to-surface weapon which provides global positioning system (GPS) guidance to 1,000- and 2,000-pound bombs. Israel is planning to buy 700 of the missiles, which performed well even in extremely poor weather conditions in Kosovo. It has a range of 12–50 miles, depending on launch aircraft speed and altitude and an accuracy of around 40 meters.[169]

More is involved than the quantity and quality of fighter and attack aircraft. Figure 3.22 shows that Israel also has significant airborne early warning (AEW), airborne command and control, airborne intelligence and electronic warfare (EW), and advanced reconnaissance capabilities. As was the case for Coalition aircraft during the Gulf War, these special purpose aircraft help Israel to manage its combat aircraft as an integrated force rather than as a series of individual squadrons. This allows it to manage sophisticated beyond-visual-range combat, to maintain force cohesion in large scale air-to-air combat, to conduct near-real-time targeting and rapid reaction missions, and to allocate interdiction and act missions effectively in complex joint operations. The only Arab air force to support its combat aircraft with modern command, control, communications, intelligence and battle management (C[4]I/BM) and reconnaissance capabilities is Egypt.

Israel has also integrated its combat aircraft into the kind of "system of systems" that is essential to take advantage of modern air power. It has developed and modified a large number of guided offensive weapons. These include a large rocket boosted glide bomb called "Popeye" which the US used as the AGM-142 or "Have Nap" on the B-52s flown in Desert Storm.[170] It is a TV-guided missile that uses a Mark 84 bomb as a warhead, and has a large 895-kilogram warhead, a digital data link, and a maximum range of about 80 kilometers. It can be launched by the Kfir, F-15, and F-16. The F-16 uses a lighter version called the AGM-142B "Have Lite," which entered service in 1995.[171] There are different warheads for the missiles with TV or imaging infrared seekers, conventional blast fragmentation or penetrating warheads, and possibly a nuclear warhead. The Rafael Armaments Authority, an Israeli military production company, produces Popeye missiles for its own air force and exports it to other countries including Turkey. There are unconfirmed reports of the development of a turbojet version with ranges up to 300 kilometers which would use a small INS platform with GPS updates.

Like the US Air Force, the IAF has also developed advanced kits to convert regular bombs into guided glide weapons. These include systems like the SPICE (smart, precision-impact, cost-effective) bomb guidance system. It is claimed to have a CEP of 50 centimeters at a range of more than 42 kilometers from a launch altitude of 12,200 meters (40,000 feet). It adds the same AGM-142 TV seeker to the guidance for a strap-on kit to the Mark 84 2,000-pound bomb that is used in the Popeye, and is said to have a cost roughly 20% that of the Popeye.[172]

There are several air-to-air missiles that could help give Israel a strategic edge. One is the AIM-120 Advanced Medium-Range Air-to-Air Missile (AMRAAM) mentioned earlier.[173] This missile incorporates new technology that Israel will undoubtedly be using in its own missile program. Israel has purchased 64 of these missiles for $28 million. This purchase has been approved by the US Congress, and may raise the stakes in the air balance and could possibly start a new weapons race in terms of air power. Israel is seeking to buy an additional 42 AIM-120 Bs from the US for an estimated $18 million.[174]

The Python 4 is another important missile. It has been operational with the IAF since 1994. The IAF claims this missile can maintain controlled flight at about twice the angle of attack and sustain twice the turn rate of third-generation infrared guided air-to-air missiles like the Python 3, MICA, and current Russian-made designs. It is said to have a range of up to 40 kilometers and to complement beyond-visual-range missiles like the AIM-120. Some reports indicate that its guidance can be slaved to the aircraft's radar to track at ranges of up to 120 kilometers, pull up to 9 "Gs," provide full frontal and rear hemisphere coverage, and launch at ranges as short as 400 meters.[175] The Python 4 has been integrated with several key types of aircraft, including the F-5, F-15, F/A-18, F-16, and Kfir.[176] A more advanced air-to-air missile called the ISRAAM is under development.[177]

It is sometimes difficult to separate reality from Israeli technical propaganda. There have also been reports about a new air-to-air missile that Israel is developing on its own which is highly classified. This system has code names like Derby, Firefly, and Glory, and is reported to be linked to an Israeli F-16 upgrade program called Netz. While it is known that this weapon will eventually be available for Israel to export, military experts have only described this new weapon as smaller, lighter, and more maneuverable than the US AIM-120. It is reported that Israel plans to incorporate this weapon with the F-15 and F-16.[178]

Israel has an air-launched version of the Gabriel anti-ship missile with a range of 35 kilometers, sea skimming capabilities, and a 150-kilogram semi-armor piercing warhead. A medium-range laser-guided air-to-surface missile called the Nimrod is in development. It has a range of 25 kilometers and a 15-kilogram warhead suited for anti-armor or small point target killing.[179]

Israel has continued to make improvements in its ability to use aircraft to support ground forces. It is steadily improving the lethality and range of its air-to-ground munitions and is emphasizing high volumes of accurate delivery of dumb, but more lethal, munitions in low vulnerability attack profiles. It has taken full advantage of its access to US air-to-air and air-to-ground avionics and weapons. It has steadily improved the tactics and avionics it uses to deliver precision guided weapons and is buying advanced all-weather navigation and targeting systems like LANTIRN. Israel is also producing the LITENING airborne laser target designator and navigation pod. This pod, mounted on an F-16, is designed to use laser capabilities for acquiring a target and guidance for airborne launched missiles.

Israel has already placed an order for 13 of these units with a total potential for 60 units in the future.[180]

Israel has also demonstrated an Elta synthetic-aperture radar pod to the US Air Force called the EL/M-2060P that has a range of 120 kilometers and the capability to scan up to 50,000 square kilometers an hour and identify targets even in the worst weather conditions. The pod currently transmits data to a ground station, but plans exist to allow direct transmission of targeting data to aircraft in flight for real-time attack mission targeting.[181]

Israel is one of the few Middle Eastern air forces capable of providing a full range of defensive countermeasures for its aircraft, and has heavily modified these countermeasures to suit local combat conditions or introduced designs of its own. It regularly deploys on-board chaff and flare dispensers, and radar homing and warning receivers. It has both its own and US active countermeasure systems and ECM pods.[182] Pilots receive excellent training in using these systems and they normally have high standards of maintenance and operational readiness.

The IAF has steadily improved its reconnaissance, electronic warfare, and C4I/ battle management capabilities as a result of the lessons of the 1982 and the Gulf War. The IAF now has 10 RF-4Es dedicated to the reconnaissance role, although some reports indicate that it also has two specialty F-15s.[183] Compared with the other ring states, Israel is by far the leader, as shown in Figure 3.15, which gives it a distinctive advantage over other countries in these respective fields.

The IAF's electronic intelligence and ECM squadrons include a number of specially modified aircraft and UAVs, including 6 E-707s, 6 RC-12Ds, 3 IAI-200s, 15 Do-28s, and 6 King Air 2000s. The E-707s seem to use Elta electronic support measure (ESM) and communications support (CSM) equipment for electronic intelligence, communications intelligence, and command analysis. According to some reports, they can cover a band-width of 70 megahertz to 40 gigahertz over a 360° area, and sense transmitters up to 450 kilometers away from the aircraft. They provide a continuously updated electronic display at communications intelligence and ELINT consoles and have a secure air-ground data link. Some may have special naval electronic support measure or ELINT systems.[184] According to some reports, IAF is seeking US aid in developing a more advanced version using a different aircraft body from the B-707.[185]

The IAI 200 and RC-12D are configured for tactical signals intelligence missions. The IAI-200s carry ELINT and signals intelligence equipment. The RU-21As are fitted for airborne direction finding against hostile communications nets. The RC-12Ds are fitted with the US Guardrail V target location and identifica-tion system.[186]

In the past, the IAF operated four updated and Israeli modified E-2C airborne early-warning aircraft. The E-2Cs were fitted with AN/APS-125/138 surveillance radars and AN/ALR-73 passive detection systems.[187] Israel's E-2Cs played a critical role in large-scale air combat. They provided a much better capability to allocate for Israeli fighters and vector them towards possible targets than could be done by regional control centers on the ground. They performed electronic intelligence missions, helped reduce the IFF problem, and managed overall IAF fighter deployments according to the need of the battle. Israel also used the radars in the E-2Cs along with its long-range radars on its F-15s so that an F-15 in the rear could help direct forward deployed Israeli fighters into combat without having to risk direct engagement.

The E-2Cs did not have the same range or capability to detect aircraft flying over land as the E-3A AWACS, however, and Israel's version used the AN/APS-124 radar, rather than the AN/APS-138 used by the US Navy. They still, however, provided Israel with good low altitude radar coverage, filling in the gaps left by land-based radars and greatly extending the range of detection and IAF battle management capability. They allowed Israeli fighters to take advantage of their excellent low altitude combat training.

The IAF has now introduced a new variant of the AWACS called the Phalcon that combines Israeli-designed early warning and command and control equipment with improved radars, IFF equipment, ELINT equipment, electronic warfare systems, and a variety of display systems. Six are now deployed, and the Phalcon is the first AWACS-type aircraft to eliminate the radar dome above the aircraft.

The Phalcon is advanced enough so that the US put intense pressure on Israel to halt its sale to China.[188] It uses an Elta EL/M-2075 phased array radar of about 800 transmit/receive modules in six antenna arrays molded to conform with the fuselage of a modified B-707. This allows 360° operation without interference from the wings, engines, or tail. It is claimed to be able to detect a 5-square-meter target at ranges of up to 350 kilometers, ships at up to 500 kilometers, and cruise missiles at up to 230 kilometers. It also allows all of the arrays to be concentrated in one area, provides tracking within 4 seconds versus 20–40 seconds for a rotating dome radar, and is supposed to be more sensitive to slow moving and hovering helicopters.[189] The sale of a version of this system to the PRC has provoked serious tensions with the US. Israel has denied that any such sale would involve a transfer of US technology.[190]

Israeli forces are now equipped with modern high speed anti-radiation missiles, and advanced on-board jamming and chaff systems. The IAF may also retain some "Wild Weasel" F-4Es which are specially equipped to carry the US AGM-78B Standard anti-radiation missile. These aircraft were used extensively in the Beka'a Valley operations in 1982, and reflect the fact that one of the key lessons that Israel drew from the 1973 fighting was the need for effective anti-radar missiles as a key air defense suppression weapon. The Wild Weasel F-4Es can carry four AGM-78Bs each. They have special J79–17B engines, AN/APQ-120(V)4 radars, and TISEO long-range optical visual identification systems. There are special displays and provision for the launch of AGM-65 missiles. The aircraft do not have emitter location equipment separate from the missile, and Israel put its own improved Purple Heart seeker on the AGM-78Bs as a result of the lessons it learned in 1982. Some experts suggest that Israel has a number of other aircraft that can deliver anti-radiation missile (ARM) systems and is phasing out the F-4Es.[191]

Israel continues to expand its use of unmanned airborne vehicles (UAVs) or remotely piloted vehicles (UAVs). It currently operates hundreds of the Mastiff, Scout, Teledyne Ryan 124R, MQM-74C Chukar I, Chukar II, Samson, Pioneer, Searcher, and Delilah (decoy) UAVs. These systems perform a wide range of targeting and intelligence functions, and use photo, IR, ELINT, and possibly small radar sensors. Israel is the world's first major user of UAVs, and its Mastiffs and Scouts had logged some 10,000 flight hours and over 1,000 sorties by the mid 1980s, including the several hundred sorties they flew in 1982. It is believed that Israel has some UAVs modified for attack purposes, including some designed to home in on radar emitters.[192]

Israel has deployed third and fourth generation UAVs. These include the Searcher, which has been used extensively in Lebanon, and the Pioneer. The Pioneer has a payload of 45 kilograms versus 38 for the Scout, and an endurance of eight to nine hours versus four to six hours for Israel's older UAVs. Its speed is increased from 60 to 70 nautical miles per hour, and its airframe is made from composite materials rather than metal to reduce its radar signature. Like previous Israeli UAVs, the Pioneer is very silent and normally is hard to see. It has a ceiling of 15,000 feet and a video transmission range of up to 200 kilometers.

The equipment on the Pioneer includes a TV camera, a thermal imager, electronic warfare equipment, and a laser range finder or designator. It will be deployed in field units with four Pioneers each, and can be launched with a pneumatic catapult and rocket booster or on any 250-meter-long stretch of road. It can land on a 70-meter road using a catch net. The Pioneer has a greatly improved down link and display system and can be turned over to remote forward-deployed control stations. The normal range of the down link is 30 to 40 kilometers.[193] It gives Israel an even greater advantage in tactical reconnaissance and surveillance capability than it had in 1982, and allows the IDF to carry out such missions without exposing personnel.[194]

Israel has more advanced systems in deployment and development. In 1992, it began to deploy the Searcher, a 318-kilogram system that builds on the lessons learned from the Scout and Pioneer. Systems in development include a twin engine system with about twice the range-payload of the Pioneer. This system is called the Impact, and can operate at ranges from 150 to 300 kilometers beyond Israel's front lines. It is designed to have a much lower radar cross section than previous UAVs, has a 150-pound payload, an endurance of 12 hours, a maximum speed of 120 knots, a loiter speed of 60 knots, and a multi-mission stabilized TV/FIR sensor payload. It can be deployed as a containerized unit of the back of a pickup truck. It has a long loiter system called the Heron with a demonstrated world endurance record of 51 hours and 21 minutes, and has claimed to have UAVs with the ability to fly at altitudes as high as 30,000 feet.[195]

The Israeli UAV fleet may include a system like the Hermes 1500. This is a medium-altitude endurance UAV with a maximum take-off weight of 1,500 kg and the possibility of flying a mission up to 40 hours. Fuel is stored in the wings, which enables the fuselage to be used for storage during flight. Israeli planners envision this plane to assume a variety of roles currently performed by other UAV designs. Signals intelligence, imagery intelligence, synthetic-aperture radar and electronic countermeasures are some of these possible missions.[196]

Several Israeli UAVs have been developed for air defense suppression. The Delilah is a modular system that can either be used with an active payload to simulate the presence of an attack aircraft—and draw enemy fighters, surface-to-air missiles, and anti-aircraft fire away from real attack aircraft—or with a passive payload to saturate an area with chaff to blind enemy air defense radars. It uses both active elements in the A, C, and L radar bands to simulate aircraft and a passive Luneberg lens reflector to expand its apparent size to enemy radars. It weighs only 180 kilograms, and can be carried by an attack fighter like the F-4. It can fly at speeds of Mach 0.4 to 0.8, has a range of up to 400 kilometers, and can simulate fighter maneuvers in the target area with a positioning accuracy of better than 91 meters.

Israel has also developed a remotely piloted vehicle or drone called the Harpee or STAR-1. This would be able to loiter for extended periods over the battlefield and then home in immediately on any radar that started to operate in the area, even if it only emitted for very short periods of time.[197] The Harpee is similar in concept to the US Seek Spinner and Tactic Rainbow missiles. While the details are classified, the system evidently can loiter for several hours waiting for a threat radar to emit and then home in on it and kill it. This would allow it to replace the much more costly, aging, and vulnerable F-4E Wild Weasels. It seems to have been tested in simulated missions where it did home in and hit military radars. Such a system would give Israel a greatly improved capability to destroy Arab air defense systems without exposing high cost aircraft, and would confront an Arab force with the fact that it could never predict when its air defense systems would be attacked.[198]

Israel has already made extensive use of UAVs for asymmetric and low-intensity warfare in both Lebanon and in the fighting against the Palestinians that began in September 2000. It has coupled the use of UAVs for surveillance and targeting with the use of computers that integrate data from ground-based radars and unattended ground sensors. According to some reports, Israel has used long-loitering UAVs with day and night vision devices to monitor the headquarters of Hizbollah and hostile Palestinian leaders and to conduct special forces operations to seize or kill them.

All of these various airborne or flying assets are linked to battle management and fusion centers and to field mobile C^4I/BM systems that can directly support the land forces. It is important to note that the IDF's integration of land and air intelligence, sensor, and battle management systems gives it a further advantage in the air-land battle. They are backed by a range of active and passive electronic warfare systems. Israel has succeeded in improving its edge over Syria in every aspect of electronic warfare. Israel has also greatly increased the sophistication of its ground-based forward electronic warfare and targeting efforts, although the details remain classified.

Israel has eight tanker aircraft, which provide a significant refueling and long-range strike capability—although some are only equipped for probe and drogue recovery and cannot refuel the F-15 and F-16.[199] It has five B-707, 12 C-47, 24 C-130E/H, and seven IAI-201 fixed wing transport aircraft—making it and Egypt the only air forces with real airlift capability. Israel is seeking 12 new C-130Js and 10 C-27Js from Lockheed over the next decade at a cost of around $1 billion, but funding is uncertain. Its existing 17 C-130Es and five KC-130H tanker/transports date back to 1971, and at least five C-130Es are in long-term storage.[200]

Qualitative Factors Shaping the Effectiveness of the Syrian Air Force

The Syrian Air Force is divided into an air force and air defense command. It has a complex and highly bureaucratic structure that is more function than mission-oriented. Its main operational combat bases are at Doumier, Hamah, Khal Khalah, Sayqal, Sheyrat, and Tiyas. Its transport forces and electronic brigade are based near Damascus. Its helicopter units are based near Damascus, Hama, and Quaar al Sitt. There is an air academy or central training base at Neirab air base, which is near Aleppo. There are other bases at Abu a-Dhur, An Nasiryah, Dier ez Zor, Jirah, Kamishly, Lattakia, Marj Ruhayyil, Qasayr, Rasin el About, As West, Tabqa, and Tudmur. Most bases have good quality shelters and good dispersal facilities, plus some hardened command sites and munitions storage areas.[201]

Syria has long emphasized numbers over quality, tactics, and training. It currently has about 40,000 men and 589 operational combat fixed-wing aircraft, with well over 100 more that are not operational, derelict, or in storage. While such estimates are highly uncertain, the IISS estimates that Syria has nine fighter-ground attack squadrons, equipped with 44 obsolete MiG-23BNs, and 70 moderate capability Su-22s. Syria also has 17 fighter-air defense squadrons equipped with 170 MiG-21 and 90 MiG-23 fighters that have low-grade avionics and radars and limited air-to-air combat capability.

Syria has been unable to afford major modernization of its forces for nearly a decade, and has failed to obtain the MiG-31s and Su-27s it has sought from Russia.[202] Syria's front-line strength does, however, include 20 modern Su-24 long-range strike-attack aircraft, 30 MiG-25s, which are effective at medium-high altitudes, and 20 modern MiG-29 fighters that are capable of beyond-visual-range combat and effective look-down, shoot-down capability. Syria's only reconnaissance aircraft are six MiG-25Rs with low quality sensor packages, and 8 obsolete MiG-21H/Js. Syria's only electronic warfare aircraft include 10 Mi-8J/K helicopters.

Syria's MiG-29s and Su-24s illustrate the path it must take to modernize its air force and make it competitive with Israel. Its MiG-29 aircraft are designed for forward area air superiority and escort missions, including deep penetration air-to-air combat. Their flight performance and flying qualities are excellent, and are roughly equivalent to that of the best Western fighters.[203] They have modern avionics and weapons (although they are now more than a decade old), and an advanced coherent pulse-Doppler radar with look-down, shoot-down capabilities that can detect a fighter-sized, two-square-meter target at a range of 130 kilometers (70 nautical miles), and track it at 70 kilometers (38 nautical miles).

The MiG-29 also has a track-while-scan range of 80 kilometers (44 nautical miles) against a 5-square-meter target and is designed to operate with the radar off or in the passive mode, using ground-controlled intercept.[204] It has an infrared search and track system collimated with a laser range finder, a helmet-mounted sight, internal electronic countermeasure systems, SPO-15 radar warning receiver, modern inertial navigation, and the modern Odds Rod IFF. The range of the infrared search and track system is 15 kilometers (8.2 nautical miles) against an F-16-sized target. The maximum slant range of the laser is 14 kilometers (7.7 nautical miles) and its normal operating range is 8 kilometers (4.4 nautical miles).

The MiG-29 can carry up to six air-to-air missiles, a 30-mm gun, a wide mix of bombs, and 57-mm, 84-mm, and 240-mm air-to-ground rockets. A typical air combat load would include 250 rounds of 30-mm gun ammunition, 335 gallons of external fuel, 4 AA-8 Aphid infrared guided missiles, and 2 AA-10 Alamo radar-guided medium-range air-to-air missiles. Iran may have acquired AA-8, AA-10, and AA-11 Archer air-to-air missiles from Russia.

The MiG-29s in Syrian service have a number of ergonomic problems. The cockpit frames and high cockpit sills limit visibility. The cockpit display is fussy and uses outdated dials and indicators similar to those of the F-4. There is only a medium angle heads-up display and only partial hands-on system control. The CRT display is dated and the cockpit is cramped. The helmet-mounted sight allows the pilot to slave the radar, IRST, and heads-up display (HUD) together for intercepts and covert attacks using off-boresight cueing, but the weapons computer and software supporting all combat operations are several generations behind those in fighters like the F-15C.[205] Therefore, it is doubtful that even a well-trained MiG-29 pilot has the air-to-air combat capability of a well-trained pilot flying an F-16C/D, F-15C, F/A-18D, or Mirage 2000 in long-range missile or beyond-visual-range combat, or in any form of combat when only the other side has the support of an AWACS type aircraft.

The Su-24 is a twin seat, swing wing strike-attack aircraft that is roughly equivalent in terms of weight to the F-111, although it has nearly twice the thrust loading, and about one-third more wing loading. The Su-24 can carry payloads of up to 25,000 pounds and operate on missions with a 1,300-kilometer radius when carrying 6,600 pounds of fuel. With a more typical 8,818-pound (4,000-kilogram) combat load, it has a mission radius of about 790 kilometers in the LO-LO-LO profile, and 1,600 kilometers in the LO-HI-LO profile. With extended range fuel tanks and airborne refueling by an aircraft like the F-14, the Su-24 can reach virtually any target in Iraq and the southern Gulf.[206]

Although it is not clear what variant of the Su-24 has gone to Syria, it seems likely to be an export version of the Su-24D, which includes a sophisticated radar warning receiver, an improved electronic warfare suite, an improved terrain avoidance radar, satellite communications, an aerial refueling probe, and the ability to deliver electro-optical, laser, and radar-guided bombs and missiles.[207]

The Su-24D provides excellent range-payload capabilities for delivering air-to-surface missiles and biological, chemical, and nuclear weapons, but its avionics, sensors, and displays now represent technology well over a decade old. It can carry a wide range of air-to-ground missiles including up to three AS-7 Kerry radio command guided missiles (5 kilometers range), one AS-9 Kyle anti-radiation missile with passive radar guidance and an active radar fuse (90 kilometers range), three AS-10 Karen passive laser-guided missiles with an active laser fuse (10 kilometers range), three AS-11 Kilter anti-radiation missiles with passive radar guidance and an active radar fuse (50 kilometers range), three AS-12 Kegler anti-radiation missiles with passive radar guidance and an active radar fuse (35 kilometers range), three AS-13 Kingposts, and three AS-14 Kedge semi-active laser-guided missiles with an active laser fuse (12 kilometers range). It can also carry demolition bombs, retarded bombs, cluster bombs, fuel air bombs, and chemical bombs. Some experts believe that Russia has supplied Iran with AS-10, AS-11, AS-12, and possibly AS-14/AS-16 air-to-surface missiles.

At this point in time, even the Su-24 and MiG-29 that Syria has received are dated in comparison to Israel's latest F-15s and F-16s, or Egypt's F-16s. Syria needs the most advanced technology available to overcome Israel's edge in C⁴I/SR, training, munitions, and sustainability, and this would mean either a very advanced new version of the Su-24 or MiG-29, or a next generation aircraft.

Even then, it will scarcely be enough for Syria to buy advanced fighters, attack aircraft, and reconnaissance aircraft. Even if one ignores "intangibles" like leadership and training, Syria lags far behind the West and its most advanced neighbors in the ability to command an air force in large-scale battle. If Syria is to compete effectively with Saudi and US forces in air combat it will also need an airborne warning aircraft, advanced beyond-visual-range missiles, advanced stand-off air attack ordnance, a new C⁴I/BM system, and much more advanced electronic warfare capabilities.

The practical problems are whether Syria can obtain such aircraft from Russia, afford them in sufficient numbers, manage the complex conversion from US to Russian aircraft efficiently, and fully understand and accomplish the need to convert from an air force organized to fight at the squadron, or small flight level, to one that can conduct coherent force-wide operations and fight modern joint warfare.

Equally important, the problems Syria faces go far beyond modernizing its air order of battle, and require fundamental changes in its ability to conduct force-on-force warfare. Where Israel has integrated its air force into a "system of systems," the Syrian air force still consists of "pieces of pieces." Where Israel stresses joint operations, Syria cannot even conduct effective battle management of its air forces in large scale individual air operations.

It is far from clear that Syria can accomplish all these tasks in the near to mid-term. Syria is also unlikely to obtain any assistance from the US and Europe as a substitute for Russia. Further, Chinese capabilities are unlikely to evolve to the point where China can be an adequate supplier of advanced aircraft, munitions, and technology before 2010.

Qualitative Factors Shaping the Effectiveness of the Jordanian Air Force

The Jordanian air force is headquartered in Amman, and has separate operation and training commands and a royal flight. All combat aircraft are under the Operations Command. The main operating bases include Al Mater, Mowafaq Al Salti, King Feisal Bin Abdul Aziz, and Prince Hassan Air Bases. Key locations include Amman/Marka, Al Jafr, H-5, and El Azraq. The Training Command is based at Al Mafraq. There is also a small public security air wing based in Amman.

Jordan now has only a limited strength of combat aircraft, including 106 operational fixed-wing fighters and 16 attack helicopters. The core of its force consists of 3 fighter ground-attack squadrons with 50 F-5Es and F-5Fs, and two air defense squadrons with 35 operational Mirage F-1CJs and F-1EJs. Jordan has no dedicated reconnaissance and electronic warfare aircraft. In 1999, Jordan announced it was leasing two CASA CN-235 tactical transport aircraft from Turkey.[208]

Jordan has, however, begun to deploy modern ground-attack fighters that include 12 F-16As and 4 F-15Bs from the US as surplus equipment. Delivery of these planes started in 1997 and Jordan now deploys 16 in a new fighter squadron. These are its only defense fighters with advanced radars and beyond-visual-range air combat capability, and were part of a $575 million US aid package that started deliveries in 1999. The Air Force is expected to receive about 40 percent of this total, which it will use on obtaining more F-16s, 3-D radars and improved communications equipment.[209] Jordan has done a good job of absorbing its F-16 aircraft, although they have proved to be very costly in terms of training, maintenance, and facility expenses.

Jordan has long had problems in financing its aircraft modernization plans. In 1989, it had to cancel an $860 million order for 8 Tornado attack aircraft it had placed in September 1988. In September 1991, Jordan had to cancel a $1 billion order it placed with France in April 1988 because it lost Saudi funding as a result of the Gulf War. This deal would have given it 12 Mirage 2000s, with an option to buy eight more and would have upgraded 15 of its Mirage F-1Js. Jordan denies reports that it has signed a $21 million contract with Singapore Aerospace to upgrade up to 40 of its F-5s with look-down, shoot-down Doppler radars and advanced avionics. It has financed this order by selling Singapore Aerospace seven other F-5E/Fs.[210]

Jordan is still negotiating with the US over whether it can obtain additional new combat aircraft from the US. It has sought a total 60 to 72 ex-USAF Block 10 F-16A/Bs as US aid.[211] This might allow Jordan to remove all of its 25 remaining Mirage F-1s and 50 F-5Es from its combat units, and to standardize on the F-16— although it would keep one squadron of F-5Es for training purposes. Jordan feels that it could support such an F-16 force more cheaply than its present combination of F-1s and F-5Es and has even held informal talks with Israel about cooperative efforts at major overhaul and maintenance.[212]

Jordan has requested the A-10 fighter from the US in the past, but the prospects for any deliveries are uncertain at best. The A-10 is a heavily armored tank-killer that was used by the US during the Gulf War on low-flying missions primarily to destroy Iraqi tanks. While the A-10 is no longer being built and use is being phased out in the USAF, Jordan hopes to acquire these used aircraft. It is unclear, however, whether Jordan will get this level of aid from the US.[213]

Qualitative Factors Shaping the Effectiveness of the Egyptian Air Force

Egypt has one of the largest air forces in the Middle East, with 30,000 men in the air force and another 80,000 in the air defense force. This compares with 32,000 for Israel, 13,500 for Jordan, 800 for Lebanon, and 40,000 men in the Syrian air force and another 60,000 in the Syrian air defense force. The air force is headquartered in Cairo, and is generally organized into regiments of two squadrons each, both of which normally have the same aircraft and mission. The F-16A/B and F-16C/D squadrons form the elite core of the EAF.

Egypt has a wide range of main operating and dispersal bases. Many are sheltered, but a large number of the shelters have obsolete designs and are vulnerable even to relatively small (500–1,000 pound) precision-guided munitions. The main combat bases include Abu Suwayr, Al Mansurah, Beni Suef, Berigat, Bibays, Birma, Cairo West, Faid, Gebel-el Basur, Inshas, Jiyanklis, and Mersa Matruh. There are training, transport, and support bases at Amaza, Bibays 2, Cairo East, El Minya, and Kom Awshim. Most bases are in the northwest—a heritage of World War II and past Arab-Israeli conflicts. The EAF's attack helicopters and some of its Alphajets are specially organized and trained for the counterinsurgency as well as the close support mission.

Egypt has an operational strength of 580 fixed-wing combat aircraft, and 129 armed helicopters. It is one of the few Arab air forces organized and equipped with modern air control, reconnaissance, and electronic warfare assets. It also has a large force of 179 operational, modern F-16 fighters, which now make up the core of the Egyptian Air Force (EAF). These aircraft are equipped with modern munitions, including the AGM-84 Harpoon anti-ship missile.[214]

The Egyptian Air Force has seven squadrons of fighter ground-attack aircraft with 41 Alphajets, 28 F-4Es, 44 Chinese J-6s, and 20 Mirage 5E2s. These forces have significant problems because the J-6s have limited payload, endurance, and avionics, and are very low performance aircraft. The Alphajets are light daytime attack aircraft, which are only effective in line-of-sight visual close-support missions. The Mirage 5E2s have limited-range payload and mediocre avionics, and Egypt would like to replace its entire original inventory of 50 aircraft. Egypt's F-4Es are worn and aging aircraft that have not been modernized to improve their attack and electronic warfare capabilities.

Egypt also has 21 air defense squadrons. Nine of these squadrons are equipped with modern aircraft including 135 F-16Cs, 29 F-16Ds, 25 F-16As, 10 F-16Bs, and 18 Mirage 2000Cs. The remaining fighters are low quality forces largely limited to visual intercepts. They include 53 obsolete low-performance Chinese J-7s, 60 obsolete low-performance MiG-21s, and 53 aging and marginal-performance Mirage 5D/Es. The J-7s, MiG-21s, and Mirage 5D/Es are supersonic, but lack the radar, avionics, and missiles to be highly effective. Egypt has extensive stocks of modern US Aim-9 IR-guided air-to-air missiles and some 271 Aim-7M radar-guided air-to-air missiles. It is seeking to buy HARM anti-radiation missiles and is discussing the future purchase of the AMRAAM with the US.[215]

Egypt's reconnaissance aircraft are largely obsolete photo-reconnaissance aircraft, including six Mirage 5SDRs, and 14 MiG-21Rs. Egypt does, however, have 5 modern E-2C airborne early warning and control aircraft, and a number of electronic warfare aircraft—including 2 CH-130s, 4 Beech 1900s, and 4 Commando 2 ECM helicopters. It is considering a major upgrade for its E-2Cs that would involve considerable improvements in situational awareness, missile tracking, IFF, passive detection, precision navigation, and interoperable/joint communications.[216]

Egypt gives high priority to the modernization of its air force. It hopes to acquire a total of 190 F-16 fighters, as part of the Peace Vector program, and almost 80% of the US military aid it has received under the second and current US-Egyptian military modernization programs has gone to the Egyptian Air Force. In March 1999, the US and Egypt agreed to the sale of 24 more F-16C/D Block 40 fighter jets (12 F-16C and 12 F-16D). The 24 F-16 fighters, made by Lockheed Martin, will cost $1.2 billion and will be delivered after 2000.[217] They will include advanced IFF, Harpoon anti-ship missile capabilities, AN/APG-68 radars, heads-up displays, multiple boresight indicators, F110-GE-100B engines, ALR-56M radar-warning receivers, and an ALE-47 countermeasure dispenser.[218]

These deliveries will take place under a new Peace Vector VI program, and will have a value of nearly $1 billion. They will expand the Egyptian F-16 force to nearly 220 aircraft, but Egypt will badly need to retire its remaining MiG-21s and Mirage 5s by the time the F-16 deliveries are completed.[219] Egypt is also seeking to phase out its F-4Es, which present severe maintenance and spare parts problems.

Egypt has said in the past that it would like to acquire a total of 40 Mirage 2000 fighters and 48 L-29 advanced trainers that have dual capability in the close support role, but there is little chance it can fund such a purchase.[220] It has discussed buying F-15s with the US, but the US is resisting the sale of a limited number of new types of aircraft, while at the same time it is tempting Egypt to buy added support capabilities for its F-16s and a depot-level maintenance program to ensure the F-16s are kept properly combat ready and sustainable.[221]

It hopes to extend its long-range strike capability and combat air patrol capability by requesting KC-135 aerial tankers from the US. This would not give Egyptian fighters more ability to attack Israel, but Egypt's real motive is probably to improve its capability to attack targets in the Southern Sudan and Libya. It is doubtful that Egypt can afford this level of modernization, but it is clear that Egypt recognizes the seriousness of its modernization problems.[222]

More generally, Egyptian officers recognize that the equipment of the Egyptian air forces can be organized into three different forces: an obsolete and ineffective force using its older Soviet-bloc aircraft; a somewhat more capable force using its newest Soviet-bloc aircraft, Mirage 5s, and Alphajets; and a relatively modern force using its F-16s and Mirage 2000s. Some officers recognize that the retention of the older Soviet-bloc aircraft does little more than waste financial and skilled manpower resources on militarily ineffective units, but others see force size as a matter of Egyptian prestige.

Egypt has made progressively better use of its E-2Cs for large-scale air defense operations. Egyptian pilot training and maintenance have also improved as a result of cooperation with the US, and Egypt has many pilots equal to those of the USAF in individual training. Nevertheless, Egypt does not approach Israeli standards of maintenance, squadron, and force-on-force training nor the ability to support its best combat aircraft with the special purpose aircraft, electronic warfare, and C^4I/ BM technology necessary to integrate them into a "system of systems" and provide effective large-scale joint warfare capabilities.

Syria, Jordan, and Egypt also lack the facilities, equipment, trained ground crews, and doctrine to generate anything approaching Israel's surge and sustained sortie rates—although Egypt's F-16 forces are significantly more capable than any Syrian air units. This is a critical technical and organization defect. Both past Arab-Israeli conflicts and the Gulf War have shown that combat air strength is as much a function of the ability to generate and effectively allocate sorties as are aircraft numbers. Historically, Israel has been able to sustain up to three times as many combat sorties per operational aircraft as Egypt, and four to five times as many as Syria.

Attack and Armed Helicopters

Attack and armed helicopters are playing an important role in changing the nature of any future Arab-Israeli conflict. They provide a considerable increase in maneuver and long-range strike capability that had been lacking in past Arab-

Israeli conflicts. They also allow operations deep into the battlefield which are not limited by terrain or defensive barriers, and they can be combined with troop-carrying helicopters to seize key points or bypass ground troops. Figure 3.23 shows the number of attack and armed helicopters in each force.

It should be noted, however, that attack and armed helicopters differ as much in combat capability as fixed-wing aircraft. Only a relatively small number of the armed helicopters on each side have the avionics, armor, maneuverability, anti-armor missiles, night and poor weather sights, and ergonomics to allow rapid acquisition of targets, high lethality strikes, and rapid evasion of air defenses. With the exception of the AH-64 and AH-1s, the combat helicopters in Egyptian, Israeli, Jordanian, Lebanese, and Syrian forces have only limited anti-armor capability and are highly vulnerable to short-range air defenses. Many use semi-obsolete missile guidance systems that require exceptional training to be effective and which force the exposure of the aircraft for relatively long periods during the attack phase. Some are large slow-flying helicopters, while others have ergonomic problems in attacking from map-of-the-earth and pop-up profiles unless the pilot has exceptional proficiency and training.

Israeli Combat Helicopter Forces

The IAF has an extensive helicopter fleet, including 41 AH-64A, 21 AU-1G, 36 AH-1F, and 30 Hughes 500MD armed/attack helicopters. It has 4 AS-565A and two SA-366 maritime helicopters with limited ASW capability. Its transport helicopters include 38 CH-53Ds, 10 UH-60s, 15 S-70A Blackhawks, 54 Bell-212s, and 43 Bell 206s. The IDF is acquiring a total of 15 UH-60s.[223] It has requested the approval of the purchase of 35 more UH-60Ls.[224]

These forces give Israel a total of 133 attack and armed helicopters. The AH-64s give Israel a major new long-range strike and maneuver weapon, and Israel has sought to buy 24 more and convert its entire force to use the Longbow "fire-and-forget" anti-armor missile.[225] The IAF is seeking to buy at least one additional squadron of AH-64 Apache Longbow attack helicopters, with all-weather and night avionics and sensors and Longbow fire-and-forget anti-armor missiles. This would give it a total force of 51–66 AH-64s, and it hopes to eventually convert all its AH-64s to use the Longbow. It has already submitted a formal request to the US to convert 24 of its existing AH-64As to the AH-64D Longbow standard. This would include installation of AN/APG-78 fire control radars, APR-48A radar-interferometers, T-700-GE-701C engines, target acquisition designation sight/pilot night vision sensor (TADS/PNVS) systems, and the purchase of 480 AGM-114L3 Hellfire II missiles.[226]

According to press reports, Israel agreed to purchase 12 more AH-64 Longbows in January 2000, at a cost of $400 million. The US approved an Israeli buy of eight AH-64Ds, 10 AN/APG-78 Longbow radars, and conversion kits to upgrade 70 M-272 Hellfire missiles to the M-299 standard in October 2000.[227]

Figure 3.23
Operational Arab-Israeli Attack and Armed Land Warfare Helicopters in 2001

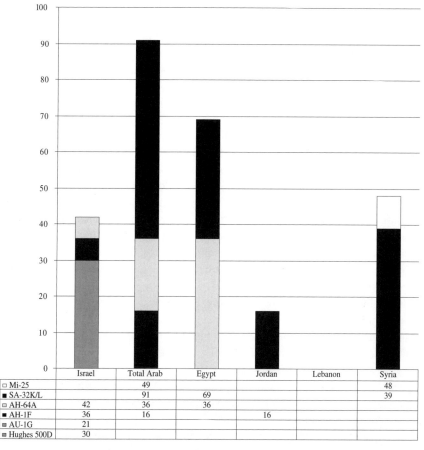

	Israel	Total Arab	Egypt	Jordan	Lebanon	Syria
□ Mi-25		49				48
■ SA-32K/L		91	69			39
□ AH-64A	42	36	36			
■ AH-1F	36	16		16		
▣ AU-1G	21					
▥ Hughes 500D	30					

Source: Prepared by Anthony H. Cordesman, based upon the IISS *Military Balance* and discussions with US and regional experts.

There are, however, differences over price and the transfer of the AH-64D software codes between Israel and the US. It is considering the purchase of AH-1W Super Cobras as a possible fall-back position.[228] Israel is considering buying 24 more AH-1W Super Cobras if it cannot afford more Longbows.[229] Its 40 AH-1F(1G-1S)s remain relatively effective attack aircraft, and may be equipped with the Hellfire anti-tank guided missile.[230]

Israel is closely studying the creation of a separate attack helicopter command under its new Field Forces Command to attack armor as a separate force, although the IAF feels this would present major logistic, training, and command and control problems.[231] It is seeking to buy advanced trainers to replace its A-4s and Mystere Tzukits.[232] With luck, the IAF should eliminate its remaining low-to-moderate performance Kfir C2/C7s, A-4Ns, and F-4Es by the year 2000.

Unlike its Arab neighbors, Israel has done an effective job of integrating its attack helicopters into joint operations and its C^4I/BM system. This ensures that they have the training and suppression systems to deal with the steady improvement in threat short-range air defenses, and ensuring that its ground forces have suitable training to recognize and kill threat attack helicopters. While Israel has taken full advantage of its sometimes painful lessons from the 1982 War, Syrian doctrine, training, and C^4I/BM capabilities have remained static in many ways.

Israel has excellent heliborne mobility by regional standards, with 38 heavy lift CH-53Ds; 15 medium lift S-70A Blackhawks, 10 UH-60s, and 54 Bell 212s; and 39 light Bell 206s. Israeli helicopter readiness standards are very high and its CH-53s are being upgraded to the CH-53–2000 following a collision between two CHH-53s that killed 73 soldiers in 1997. The modified CH-53s will have structural modifications to improve their survivability, crash-proof fuel tanks, titanium rotor blades, improved night vision and collision avoidance systems, improved communications, and improved tactical planning systems. New video systems and ground-based battle management systems will be used to improve situational awareness and survivability.[233]

Israel has made procurement of more Blackhawk UH-60s a high priority. It received 14 UH-60s in 1997 and continues to bolster the numbers and quality of its force. In 1997, Israel notified Congress of its intent to buy 15 to 34 UH-60 engines for a total estimated deal at $200 million.[234] Israel is also buying an upgrade package for its AH-64A Apache helicopters. This improvement would allow the helicopters to have the same features as the AH-64D model. Israel also has recently looked to France for supplying helicopter support. It received five AS-565SAs in 1997 and continues to request even more.

The IAF has relatively good proficiency in helicopter missions, particularly in using its attack helicopters—where its tactics are more advanced and flexible than those of its Arab neighbors. It has, however, had problems in training and crewing its transport and utility helicopters.

Arab Combat Helicopter Forces

The Arab states cumulatively have larger total numbers of attack and armed helicopters, but only Egypt is getting helicopters that equal Israel's first-line attack helicopters in effectiveness and Syria has no modern attack helicopters. Syria has 48 Mi-25s and 39 SA-342Ls. These forces do not have advanced sensors, targeting, and night combat systems, but Syria has trained these forces relatively well. IDF officers developed considerable respect for Syrian armed helicopter forces during the fighting in Lebanon in 1982, although they note that Syria has been very slow to modernize its equipment, tactics, and training, and joint warfare training and exercises have made little progress since the mid-1980s.

Jordan has 16 relatively high performance AH-1S attack helicopters armed with TOW. This force has had high readiness, but has lacked effective scout helicopters. This explains why Jordan has obtained agreement from the US to provide 18 UH-1H helicopters to use as scouts. It also plans on upgrading its Cobra helicopters with night vision capability.[235] Jordan has moderate heliborne mobility for its ground forces—it has 9 AS-332M Super Pumas 3 Bo-105s, 8 Hughes 500Ds, 18 UH-1Hs and eight UH-60 Blackhawks. Jordanian helicopter pilot and ground crew training standards have been high, but inadequate funding has created some problems in sustaining operations and advanced training.

Egypt has a number of armed Mi-8s and Mi-25s, but these are not true attack helicopters. Its largest assets of true attack helicopters now include four squadrons of 69 SA-342Ks. About 44 of these SA-342Ks are armed with HOT anti-tank guided weapons, but the avionics and guidance systems for these missiles present moderate ergonomic problems. The rest of Egypt's 342Ks are armed with 20-mm guns. The forces equipped with SA-342Ks have moderate training and readiness standards. Egypt also has 9 SA-342Ls, 5 Sea Kings, and 10 SH-2G maritime surveillance weapons.

Egypt does have 36 AH-64s armed with Hellfire. While conversion to such an advanced attack helicopter has proved difficult, largely because of the complex maintenance and training profile for the AH-64, US advisors have found the Egyptian officers and crews to be highly motivated. This AH-64 force will give Egypt significant modern attack helicopter capabilities once it becomes fully trained and capable of operating in demanding missions.

Major Surface-to-Air Missile Defenses

There is no easy way to count surface-to-air missile and other air defenses. There are significant differences in the data, and the systems involved have little comparability. Table 3.3 does, however, provide an overview of each nation's air defense forces, showing its strength by weapons type. This table illustrates the fact that surface-to-air missile defenses are a vital part of Egyptian, Israeli, Jordanian, and Syrian air defenses. While quantitative measurements do not give a complete picture, the fact that Egypt has twice the amount of manpower in its air defense force alone as Israel does in its entire air force is an indicator of the degree to which Egypt and Syria see land-based forces as compensation for Israel's superiority in aircraft.

At the same time, effective surface-to-air missile defenses require integration into a system of overlapping defenses supported by a highly sophisticated and fully integrated C[4]I/BM system. They require modern sensors and electronic warfare support, sophisticated central and regional command and control centers, and the capability to simultaneously manage air-to-air combat, surface-to-air missile combat by different types of missiles, and different types of anti-aircraft guns. In practice, fighting an effective air war also requires a nation to have the capability to rapidly suppress at least part of its opponent's air defense system and achieve enough air superiority to allow effective attack operations.

Israeli Land-Based Air Defenses

Once again, Israel is the only state that has the resources, technology, organizational skills, war planning capability, and leadership to provide such a comprehensive approach to air defense and air warfare. Jordan has the technical understanding, but lacks the equipment and resources. Egypt again combines some modern capabilities with large obsolete forces, and a lack of overall systems integration and military coherence. Syria relies on aging Soviet systems, the most modern of which date back to the early 1980s. Its air defense deployments and battle management systems are poorly executed in detail, and lack effective systems integration, electronic warfare capability, and modern C^4I/BM capabilities.

Israel has long emphasized air power over land-based surface-to-air missile forces. It now, however, has 17 batteries of MIM-23 Improved Hawk surface-to-air missiles, and 3 batteries of upgraded Patriot missiles with improved anti-tactical ballistic missile capabilities, and is deploying three Arrow battalions. The Patriot batteries have three multiple launcher fire units each. Israel also has eight short-range Chaparral missile fire units and units with large numbers of Stinger, Grail, and Redeye manportable missiles and Vulcan anti-aircraft guns.

The IAF operates Israel's land-based air defense units. These are organized into six brigades covering five geographic regions (central, northwestern, southeastern, southwestern, and northeastern), plus a training unit. Weapons are deployed into battalions organized by weapons type. This includes Israel's Patriot/I Hawk battalions (136, 138, and 139 battalions) which have one Patriot battery and three IHawk batteries each,

Israel integrates these systems and its air defense aircraft into an effective air defense battle management, and command, control, communications, computers, and intelligence system. This system may lack the full sophistication of US systems, but it is believed to make use of the Hughes technology developed for the USAF, including many elements of the USAF 407L tactical command and control system and Hughes 4118 digital computers. The system has main control centers in the Negev and near Tel Aviv. It has a mix of different radars, including at least two AN/TPS-43 three dimensional radars with three AN/MPQ-53 radar sets and three AN/MSQ-104 engagement control stations bought in 1998. This system is tailored to Israel's local threats and has sufficient technology to meet these threats in combat. Israel also has the ability to coordinate its air defenses from the air, has superior electronic warfare and systems integration capability, and has a clear strategy for suppressing enemy land-based air defenses and the ability to execute it. Israel also has plans to integrate its attack helicopters with UAVs carrying weapons, and stand-off weapons like the IMI Modular Stand-Off Vehicle, so they can provide prolonged forward defense until armored forces can arrive.[236]

Syrian Land-Based Air Defenses

Syria has a large separate Air Defense Command with nearly 60,000 personnel. Its forces are organized into 25 regional brigades and a country-wide total of 130 air defense batteries. There are two major air defense commands, a North Zone and a South Zone. The defenses are concentrated to protect the south, but Syria has recently redeployed some forces to strengthen the North Zone and defenses against Turkey and Iraq. Some forces are deployed to cover Lebanon.

These forces include large numbers of worn, obsolete Soviet-bloc systems which have only had limited upgrading. These assets include 11 SA-2 and SA-3 brigades with 60 batteries and some 480 launchers. They include 11 brigades with 27 batteries that are armed with 200 SA-6 launchers and some air defense guns. In addition, there are two regiments that have two battalions with two batteries each, and which are armed with 48 SA-5 and 60 SA-8 surface-to-air missile launchers. The SA-5s seem to be deployed near Dumayr, about 40 kilometers east of Damascus, and at Shansur near Homs.

The SA-2 and SA-3 are effectively obsolete. They are hard to move, large enough to be easy to target, and are vulnerable to Israeli, Jordanian, and Egyptian countermeasures. The SA-5 is an obsolescent long-range system whose primary value is to force large, fixed-wing aircraft like Israel's E-2Cs to stand off outside their range. The SA-6 is Syria's only moderately effective long-range system. The SA-8 is a mobile medium-range system that is effective, but limited in capability.

Syria badly needs a new type of missile system to develop the range of air defense capabilities it requires. Its SA-2s, SA-3s, SA-6s, SA-5s, and SA-8s are vulnerable to active and passive countermeasures. If Syria is to create the land-based elements of an air defense system capable of dealing with the retaliatory capabilities of the Israeli air force, it needs a modern, heavy surface-to-air missile system that is part of an integrated air defense system. Such a system will not be easy for Syria to obtain. No European or Asian power can currently sell Syria either an advanced ground-based air defense system, or an advanced heavy surface-to-air missile system. The US and Russia are the only current suppliers of such systems, and the only surface-to-air missiles that can meet Syria's needs are the Patriot, S-300 series, and S-400.

Syria has no hope of getting the Patriot system from the US, making Russia the only potential source of the required land-based air defense technology. This explains why Syria has sought to buy the S-300 or S-400 heavy surface-to-air missile/anti-tactical ballistic missile systems and a next generation warning, command, and control system from Russia.[237] The SA-10 (also named the Fakel 5300PMU or Grumble) has a range of 90 kilometers, or 50 nautical miles. It has a highly sophisticated warning radar, tracking radar, terminal guidance system and warhead, and has good electronic warfare capabilities. The SA-10 is a far more advanced and capable system than the SA-2, SA-3, SA-5, or SA-6.[238]

Much depends on Russian willingness to make such sales in the face of Syria's debt and credit problems. Russia has the capability to provide Syria with the SA-300 or S-400 quickly and in large numbers, as well as to support it with a greatly improved early warning sensor system, and an advanced command and control system for both its fighters and land-based air defenses.

Syria and Russia have repeatedly discussed a deal involving the S-300 system, but as of July 1999 no agreement had been finalized.[239] Such an advanced land-based Russian air defense system would, however, give Syria far more capability to defend against retaliatory or preemptive raids. It would allow Syria to allocate more fighter/attack aircraft to attack missions and use its interceptors to provide air cover for such attack missions. It would also greatly complicate Israel's problem in using offensive air power against Syria, require substantially more Israeli forces to conduct a successful air campaign, and increase Israel's air losses.

Such a Russian-supplied system would, however, still have important limits. Russia has not fully completed integration of the S-300 or S-400 into its own air defenses. It also has significant limitations on its air defense computer technology, and relies heavily on redundant sensors and different, overlapping surface-to-air missiles to compensate for a lack of overall system efficiency. A combination of advanced Russian missiles and an advanced sensor and battle management system would still be vulnerable to active and passive attack by the US.

It would take Syria at least three to five years to deploy and integrate such a system fully, once Russia agreed to the sale. Its effectiveness would also depend on Russia's ability to both provide suitable technical training, and to adapt a Russian system to the specific topographical and operating conditions of Syria. A Russian system cannot simply be transferred to Syria as an equipment package. It would take a major effort in terms of software, radar deployment and technology—and considerable adaptation of Russian tactics and siting concepts—to make such a system fully combat effective. As a result, full-scale modernization of the Syrian land-based air defense system is unlikely to occur before 2005 under the most optimistic conditions, and will probably lag well beyond 2010.[240]

Jordanian Land-Based Air Defenses

Jordan has modernized some aspects of its ground-based air defense C⁴I/BM system with US aid, but has lacked the funds to compete with Israel in systems integration, sensor and sensor integration capability, digital data links, and electronic warfare capabilities. It now has two incompatible air defense systems:

its air force and Improved Hawk forces use a US system supplied by Westinghouse, and its land forces use a Russian system. Jordan has 4 batteries of Improved Hawk launchers, organized into two brigades with a total of 24 launchers.

Jordan's Improved Hawk forces, however, have important limitations. They are not mobile, they have blind spots in their low altitude coverage, and Israel can easily target them. The Improved Hawks have not been upgraded in recent years, and are vulnerable to Israeli and Syrian electronic countermeasures. Jordan is seeking to upgrade its US-supplied Improved Hawks to the Pip (product improvement program) 3 version, to upgrade its Westinghouse-supplied system, and to replace its Russian-supplied system with a US-supplied system for its land forces. Jordan will probably use money from a new US military aid package to upgrade the Hawk System to Phase 3.[241]

Egyptian Land-Based Air Defenses

As a result of the Canal War of 1970, Egypt has developed one of the largest dedicated air defense forces in the Middle East. It has a separate Air Defense Command with nearly 80,000 personnel. Its forces are organized into four divisions with regional brigades and a country-wide total of 100 air defense battalions. These forces include large numbers of worn, obsolete Soviet-bloc systems that have had only limited upgrading. These assets include 40 SA-2 battalions with 282 launchers, 53 SA-3 battalions with 212 launchers, and 14 SA-6 battalions with 56 launchers. These Egyptian forces have low readiness and operational sustainability, and only limited capability to resist modern jamming and other air defense suppression techniques. They are vulnerable to modern anti-radiation missiles.

Egypt does have substantial holdings of more modern and more effective Western-supplied systems. They include 12 batteries of Improved Hawks with 78 launchers. Egypt is also developing an integrated command and control system, with US assistance, as part of Program 776.[242] This system is not highly advanced by US standards, but it will allow Egypt to (a) integrate airborne and land-based air defenses into a common air defense system, (b) create a single C^4I/BM network, and (c) manage a defense against air attacks that bring a moderate number of sorties together at the same time and near the same area.

Egypt has long been trying to upgrade its older air defense systems and will improve its surface-to-air missile capabilities in the near future. Egypt first considered trying to update some of its systems with modern Russian-made S-300 or S-400 surface-to-air missiles.[243] In 1997, Egypt is reported to have submitted a proposal to Russia whereby it would purchase the S-300 in a package containing 224 missiles and nearly 100 mobile launchers and radar systems at a cost of at least $700 million.[244] The S-300 is not only an effective surface-to-air missile, but also a competent anti-tactical ballistic missile system and defense against cruise missiles. Egypt lacked the funds to complete this contract, however, and could not use US

aid funds for such a purpose It limited its buys from Russia to a $125 million
contract to upgrade 50 Egypt's SA-3A missile launchers and their associated
units by 2003.[245]

As a result, Egypt turned to the US. In March 1999, the US agreed to sell Egypt
$3.2 billion worth of new American weapons, including 24 F-16C/D Block 40
fighter jets, 200 M-1A1 tanks and 32 Patriot missiles.[246] The sale gave Egypt its
first battery of Patriot-3 missiles at a cost of $1.3 billion. The battery consisted of
eight firing units, each containing four missiles. At the same time, the US
announced that it would provide Egypt with the same warning data on the launch of
any hostile ballistic missile that it provided to Israel. Egypt will almost certainly
acquire several more batteries over time, acquiring far better air, cruise, and
tactical ballistic missile defenses than it has today.

Egypt is also upgrading its AN/TPS50(V)2 air defense radars to the (V)3
standard. This will provide new software and hardware, including new signal
processing centers. It will also give Egypt considerably more ballistic missile
attack warning and tracking capability, and advanced long-range, three dimensional air-surveillance capabilities. The radars are linked to 12 operations centers
in Egypt which will be able to pass intercept data to both airborne and ground-
based air defenses and anti-ballistic missile warning data to Egypt's IHawks and
Patriots.[247]

Short-Range Air Defenses

Egypt, Israel, and Syria have large numbers of anti-aircraft guns and light
surface-to-air missiles. These systems are not highly sophisticated, but can provide
considerable defense against attack helicopters, and low altitude coverage against
attacking fighters of a kind that is not reliant on radar. They also can force most
attack aircraft to use very high-speed attack profiles that lack accuracy, or to use
long-range precision guided missiles to attack at stand-off ranges. Many of the
attack aircraft in Arab forces lack the range to conduct such attacks. Even Israel,
however, faces problems in trying to suppress such defenses, and faces low altitude
survivability problems in attacking targets with sophisticated short-range air
defenses (SHORADS).

Israeli Short-Range Air Defenses

The Israeli Army has large numbers of Stingers, 1,000 obsolescent Redeye
manportable surface-to air missiles, and 45 Chaparral crew-served missile launchers. It also has some 850 20-mm anti-aircraft (AA) guns—including TCM-20s and
M-167 Vulcans. It has 35 M-163 Vulcan/M-48 Chaparral gun-missile systems,
100 ZU-23 23 and 60 ZSU-23–4 23-mm AA guns and some M-39 37-mm and L-

70 40-mm AA guns. The IAF has eight Stinger batteries and eight Chaparral batteries. These assets give Israel only limited total forces and air defense mobility relative to its neighbors, but Israel relies primarily upon its air force for such defense.

Syrian Short-Range Air Defenses

Syria extensively reorganized its short-range air defenses after Israel proved able to suppress them during the fighting in 1982. Like all Arab states, however, Syria is keenly aware that Iraqi short-range air defenses proved relatively ineffective in the Gulf War, and that Israel is now equipped with stand-off air-to-ground missiles, high speed anti-radiation missiles (HARMs), UAVs that can target mobile and concealed systems, and extensive countermeasures.

The Syrian army has roughly 4,000 manportable light surface-to-air missiles, including SA-7s. It has a number of vehicle-mounted, infrared systems that include 20 SA-9s and 35 SA-13s. Syria's 60 radar guided SA-8 fire units are assigned to its Air Force as part of its Air Defense Command. Like all similar weapons in Arab forces, these systems have low individual lethality, but help keep attacking aircraft at stand-off distances, can degrade the attack profile of aircraft they are fired at, and have some cumulative kill probability.

The Syrian Army has over 2,000 anti-aircraft guns, including some 400 radar-guided 23-mm ZSU-4–23s, and 10 57-mm unguided ZSU-57–2 self-propelled guns. It also has 650 23-mm ZU-23, 300 M-1939 37-mm, 675 57-mm S-60, and 25 100-mm KS-19 unguided towed guns. These anti-aircraft guns have limited lethality even at low altitudes, except for the ZSU-23–4. They can, however, be used effectively in "curtain fire" to force attacking aircraft and helicopters to attack at high altitudes or at stand-off ranges.

Jordanian Short-Range Air Defenses

Jordan has attempted to use purchases of large numbers of short-range air defense systems to compensate for its lack of modern air defense aircraft and survivable surface-to-air missile defenses. Its lower quality manportable surface-to-air missile launchers include large numbers of SA-7Bs and 250 Redeyes. Its more effective manportable weapons include 300 SA-14s and 240 SA-16s. Its vehicle-mounted surface-to-air missile forces include 50 SA-8s and 50 SA-13s. Its 360 AA guns include 100 20-mm M-163 Vulcans, 44 23-mm ZSU-23–4s, and 216 40-mm M-42 self-propelled weapons. These assets give the Jordanian army considerable air defense mobility, which partially compensates for its static Improved Hawk defenses.

Egyptian Short-Range Air Defenses

The Egyptian ground forces have large numbers of AA weapons. The army's surface-to-air missile assets include some 2,000 obsolete SA-7s and slightly better performing Egyptian-made variants of the SA-7 called the Ayn-as-Saqr. The Army also has 12 batteries of short-range Chaparrals with 26 M-54 self-propelled Chaparral fire units, 14 batteries of short-range Crotales with 36 launchers, and at least 20 SA-9 fire units. Egypt is acquiring a system called the Avenger, which consists of Stinger missiles mounted on a HMMWV with IFF systems, an IR range finder, and machine guns.[248]

The Egyptian Army's holdings of air defense guns include 200 14.5-mm ZPU-2/4, 280 23-mm ZU-23-2/4, 200 37-mm M-1939, and 200 57-mm S-60 towed-unguided guns. They also include 118 ZSU-23–4 and 36 Sinai radar-guided self-propelled guns. The SA-9s, Chaparrals, ZSU-23–4s, and Sinais provide the Egyptian Army with maneuverable air defenses that can accompany Egyptian armored forces.

In addition, Egypt's Air Defense Command has some 2,000 Soviet-bloc supplied unguided towed AA guns ranging from 20-mm to 100-mm, and a number of light air defense systems. These include 18 Amoun (Skyguard/RIM-7F Sparrow) systems with 36 twin guns and 36 quad launchers, a number of ZSU-23–4s, and Sinai-23 systems which are composed of Dassault 6SD-20S radars, 23-mm guns, and short-range Ayn-as-Saqr missiles. These weapons provide low-altitude defense of military installations and critical facilities, and can often be surprisingly effective in degrading attack sorties or destroying attack aircraft that attempt to fly through a "curtain" of massed anti-aircraft fire.

The Size and Role of Naval Forces

The manning of Egypt, Israel, Jordan, Lebanon, and Syria's navies is summarized in Figure 3.24, and total combat ship strength is shown in Figure 3.25. Figure 3.26 shows strength by major category, and it is clear that all of these navies lack strong "blue water" navies of the kind that can play a decisive role in controlling the flow of supplies to an enemy power or dominating lines of communication. Egypt and Israel do, however, have considerable anti-ship capability in local waters, Egypt has considerable strength relative to other Red Sea powers, and Israel and Egypt have some "blue water" capability in the Eastern Mediterranean.

While no nation can ignore sea power, it is doubtful that the navies of this region will ever play a large role in most serious conflicts. The following key factors affect the Arab-Israeli naval balance:

- Any attack on Israel or Egypt could lead to decisive intervention by the US navy.
- It is unclear that the balance at sea will play a major or decisive role in most contingencies. Most key combat will be decided by air-land combat.
- Naval forces are most important in limited power projection and sea control operations.
- Egypt is the only regional power seeking to create a major naval surface force.

Figure 3.24
Arab-Israeli Naval Manpower in 2001

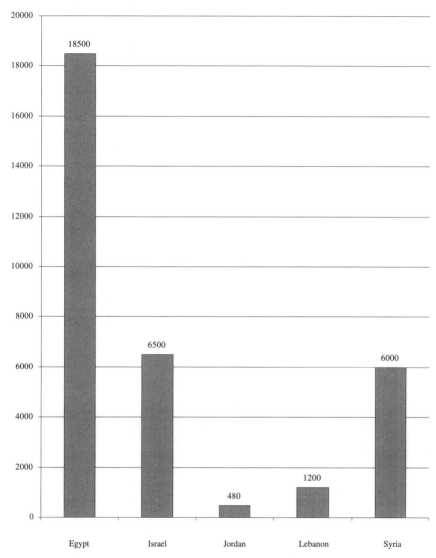

Source: Prepared by Anthony H. Cordesman, based upon the IISS *Military Balance* and discussions with US and regional experts.

- Israel is probably still strong enough to dominate its waters and those of Lebanon and Syria.
- Key issues like relative skill in surface-to-surface missile warfare may be dominated by airborne systems; air power may be the real key to naval power.

Figure 3.25
Arab-Israeli Total Naval Combat Ships by Category in 2001

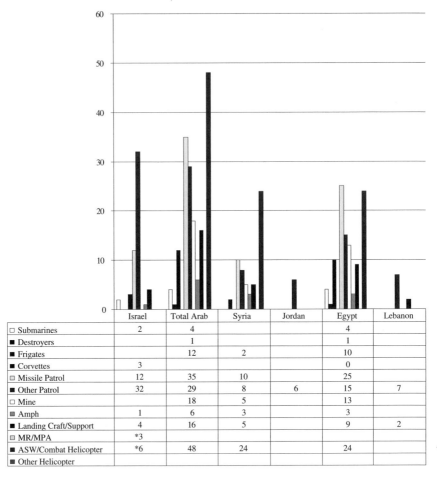

	Israel	Total Arab	Syria	Jordan	Egypt	Lebanon
□ Submarines	2	4			4	
■ Destroyers		1			1	
■ Frigates		12	2		10	
■ Corvettes	3				0	
□ Missile Patrol	12	35	10		25	
■ Other Patrol	32	29	8	6	15	7
□ Mine		18	5		13	
▨ Amph	1	6	3		3	
■ Landing Craft/Support	4	16	5		9	2
□ MR/MPA	*3					
■ ASW/Combat Helicopter	*6	48	24		24	
■ Other Helicopter						

Source: Prepared by Anthony H. Cordesman, based upon the IISS *Military Balance* and discussions
   with US and regional experts.

- Submarines seem to be sought more for prestige than their war fighting capabilities.
- Mine warfare presents a major threat in some scenarios; real-world mine detection and
  sweeping capabilities may be low.

Israeli Naval Forces

Israel's naval forces have 6,500 actives, and up to 11,500 men upon full
mobilization. Conscripts serve three years. Its forces are based at Haifa, Ashdod,
and Eilat. At this point in time, Israel has little or no capability in the Red Sea—

Figure 3.26
Arab-Israeli Major Combat Ships by Category in 2000

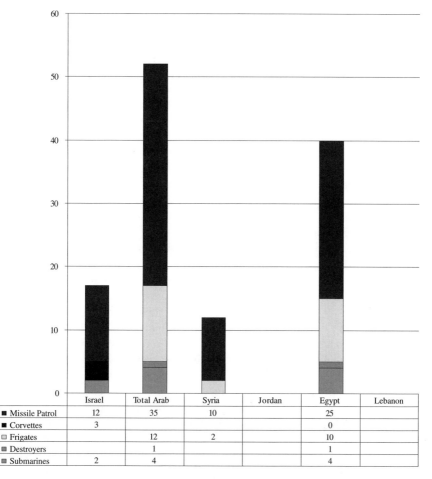

	Israel	Total Arab	Syria	Jordan	Egypt	Lebanon
■ Missile Patrol	12	35	10		25	
■ Corvettes	3				0	
▢ Frigates		12	2		10	
▨ Destroyers		1			1	
▨ Submarines	2	4			4	

Source: Adapted by Anthony H. Cordesman from the IISS, *Military Balance* and Jane's *Fighting Ships*, various editions.

reflecting its peace with Egypt and Jordan. Israel does, however, have two operational Gal-class submarines and one under maintenance in the Mediterranean, all of which are armed with Mark 37 torpedoes and Harpoon anti-ship missiles.[249]

Israel is replacing its three Gal-class submarines with three modern Dolphin-class submarines. These are currently undergoing testing, and should have all been delivered and in service by the end of 2000. The German government funded the construction of two of the submarines, and Israel paid for the third. The original delivery schedule slipped, but the first Dolphin finally set out for Israel from Germany in late June 1999, and arrived off Haifa on July 27.[250] The second, the *Leviathan (Livaytan)*, sailed from Germany and arrived in October 1999.[251] The third, the *Tekuma* began trials in the Baltic in the fall of 1999, and arrived in October 2000.[252] Israeli Navy plans originally called for Israel to maintain all five submarines to do this, but it is unclear that such a force is affordable. Its Gal submarines will probably be retired by the end of 2001.[253] Vice Admiral Yedidya Ya'ari, the commander-in-chief of the Israeli Navy made it clear in an interview in November 2000 that the navy wanted to either buy two more Dolphins or buy two subs from the US if the US resumed the production of conventional submarines as part of a deal with Egypt.[254]

The Dolphins will give Israel considerably greater strategic depth in operating in Mediterranean waters. They can be operated at ranges of up to 8,000 miles and have an endurance of up to 30 days. They have modern sonars, wire-guided torpedoes, and facilities for the launch of Harpoon anti-ship missiles. Some experts like General Israel Tal have also advocated that Israel use these submarines to provide a secure and relatively invulnerable launch platform for nuclear armed missiles—presumably new long-range cruise missiles. Israel has denied that the Dolphins will be nuclear armed.[255]

The Dolphins will be the most advanced submarines in the Middle East. They weigh 1,700 tons and are twice the size of the currently used Gal-class subs.[256] In addition, Israel is to receive German Seahake heavyweight torpedoes to be embarked on the Dolphins as part of a $65 million Foreign Military Funding (FMF) deal.[257] There are indications that several modifications will be made in Israel, possibly including fitting a sea-launched cruise missile with a nuclear warhead.[258]

Israel has three new Sa'ar 5 (Eliat or Sa'ar V)-class missile corvettes. These are 1,227-ton ships, each of which has two quad launchers for Harpoon missiles with a range of up to 130 kilometers, eight IAI MBT Gabriel anti-ship missiles with radar and optical homing and ranges of up to 36 kilometers, two 32 cell launchers for Barak air defense missiles, 1 76-mm gun, a Dauphin SA-366G helicopter, a Phalanx close-in defense system, and six torpedo launchers.[259] The Sa'ar 5s also have modern electronic support and countermeasure systems, and advanced software for target tracking and identification.[260] These facilities include a sophisticated command information center (CIC) sheltered deep within the ship that can act as task group command centers, as well as fight the individual ship. The sea and air tracking and battle management system is also advanced for a ship of this class.[261] The ships give Israel additional "blue water capability," and are superior to any similar missile ships in service with Israel's Arab neighbors.[262]

Israel has 12 additional operational missile craft—including four Sa'ar 4.5 (Hetz)-class ships with eight Harpoons and six Gabriels each. It has two Sa'ar 4.5 (Aliya)-class ships with 4 Harpoons and 4 Gabriels, and 4 Sa'ar 4 (Reshef)-class ships with 2–4 Harpoons and 4–6 Gabriels. The Sa'ar 4.5s and 4s have been extensively modernized under the Nirit (4.5)-class upgrade program which incorporates a "modernization by cannibalization" approach, scrapping much of the material from the Sa'ar 4s while outfitting the vessels with new hulls, low-radar-signature masts, new fire-control detectors, updated sensors, and four eight-cell launchers for Barak point-defense missiles (JDW 2 Sept. 1998). All Sa'ar 2s and 3s have been retired.[263] Israel also has 11–14 operational Dvora-class fast attack craft with 20-mm guns and short-range Hellfire missiles, and 1–315 Dabur-class coastal patrol boats. There are three small Bobcat (coastguard)-class patrol boats. The Israeli Navy has one Ashdod-class LCT (400-tons, 730-tons fully loaded). It may lease a Newport-class LST from the US.

The IAF's six Phalcons can provide maritime surveillance, as well as airborne early warning, and it has 19 Bell 212 helicopters for coastal surveillance tasks. It has 2 Sea Panther helicopters for its Sa'ar 5s, and Sea Scan UAVs for maritime surveillance and targeting.[264]

Israel is the only navy in the Middle East supported by an industrial base that has advanced electronic warfare design and modification capabilities, and with the ability to manufacture and design its own sensors and anti-ship missiles. These developments should allow Israel to maintain a decisive edge over Syria in the Mediterranean and more limited advantage in tactics, training, and technology over the Egyptian Navy—although the Egyptian Navy is now receiving significant modernization.

Syrian Naval Forces

Syria has a small 4,000–6,000-man navy, manned largely by conscripts with 18 months of service. It is based in Latakia, Tartus, Baniya, and Minet el-Baida. Junior naval officers receive training at the Jableh Naval Academy. Senior officers receive training as part of the normal program of the general staff's center at Quabon. Petty officer and enlisted training is conducted at Minet el-Baida, Lattakia, and on ship. Training standards are low. Syria has some 2,500–4,000 naval reserves, but they have little training and war fighting capability. The navy has 18 surface ships and three non-operational Romeo-class submarines moored at Tartus.[265]

Syria's only significant surface ships include two obsolete Petya III class frigates. These ships can still go to sea, and are equipped with torpedo tubes and rocket launchers, but have no modern air defense capability or anti-ship missiles. It has two obsolescent Osa I and eight Osa II missile patrol boats dating back to the 1970s. Each is equipped with four SS-N-2 Styx anti-ship missiles. Since these ships date back to the 1970s, many have only limited operational capability while others are on the edge of being laid up. At least two may already lack operational capability. Syria did, however, modernize some of its Osas in the mid-1980s.[266]

Syria also has eight light Soviet Zhuk-class patrol boats. These light coastal patrol boats have little firepower and combat capability. It has ten obsolescent FSU-supplied mine warfare craft, including one Natya-class, one T-43, one Sonya, and three Yevenya-class ships. Only five to seven of these mine craft are operational; at least one has had its minesweeping gear removed. They can lay mines, but have little minesweeping capability except for the one Sonya-class vessel. Syria has three relatively modern medium Polnocny-class landing ships (LSMs) with a lift capacity of 100 troops and 10 tanks.

There is a small naval aviation branch with 24 armed helicopters. These include 11–20 operational Mi-14P Hazes and four Kamov Ka-28 Helixes, and are manned with air force operators. The Mi-14 does have dipping sonar, radar, MAD, and can use sonobuoys, and can launch torpedoes, depth bombs, or mines. The Ka-28s are relatively modern and also have dipping sonar, radar, MAD, and can use sonobuoys, and can launch torpedoes, depth bombs, or mines.

The coastal defense force was placed under naval command in 1984. It has two infantry brigades for coastal surveillance and defense, two artillery brigades with 18 130-mm M-46 coastal guns and around six KS-19 anti-aircraft guns. Its main armament consists of 8–12 batteries of aging SSC-1B Sepal and SS-N-2 Styx anti-ship missiles.[267]

The Syrian Navy's primary mission is the defense of Syria's ports at Lattakia and Tartous, coastal surveillance and defense, and peacetime patrol missions. Its major bases are at Banias, Mina el-Beida, Lattakia, and Tartous, with small marine detachments at Banias, Lattakia, and Tartous. There are Scuba and UDT units at Mina el-Beida. Most surface forces are based at Lattakia and Tartous, and the submarines at Tartous.[268] Overall readiness, training, and funding levels are low. It rarely practices meaningful exercises, has almost no joint warfare training, and it has little war fighting capability against either Israel or Turkey.[269] It is largely a coastal surveillance and patrol force.

Jordanian Naval Forces

Jordan's small naval forces report to the Director of Operations at the headquarters of the general staff and consist of a 480-man force with ten coastal patrol boats. Most patrol boats are based at Aqaba, but they also deploy to the Dead Sea.[270] Its vessels include three 30-meter, Al Hussein-class boats built by Vosper. These are 124-ton boats with twin 30-mm guns, radars, and chaff launchers. They also include up to four small 8-ton, Faysal-class boats with machine guns. Jordan also has three Rotork-class, 9-ton craft capable of carrying 30 troops each.[271]

Jordan currently sees its navy as a coastal patrol force designed to provide inspection for incoming cargo ships and guard its coasts and ports against infiltration. It is not designed to have a war fighting capability against Israel or any neighboring state.

Lebanese Naval Forces

Lebanon has about 1,000–1,200 men assigned to its navy, including 100 marines. Its forces are based in Beirut and Jounieh. It has seven coastal patrol craft, including five British-made, 38-ton, Attacker-class inshore patrol craft with radars and twin 20-mm guns. It also has two British-made, 31-ton Tracker-class inshore patrol craft with radars and twin 23-mm guns. It has two aging 670-ton Sour-class (French Edic-class) landing craft, which can carry about 33 troops each. The navy has some 27 other small armed boats in inventory, including 13 6-ton inshore patrol craft and two more Tracker-class boats in the Customs service. It is not clear how many are operational.[272]

The Lebanese Navy has a coastal patrol capability, and some troop lift capability, but no war fighting capability against Israel or any neighboring state. It can perform a surveillance role, inspect cargo ships, and intercept small infiltrating forces along a limited part of Lebanon's coastline.[273]

Egyptian Naval Forces

Egypt has a 19,000–20,000-man navy, including a 2,000-man coast guard. About half of this force consists of conscripts with limited experience and training. Its headquarters is in Alexandria, and its forces are based primarily at Port Said, Mersa Matruh, Safaqa, Port Tewfiq, and Hurghada. In the past, the navy has tended to emphasize force quantity over force quality, and to try to retain its past strength levels even at the cost of obsolescence and limited readiness.

This focus on force numbers is reflected in Figure 3.25, which shows Egypt's forces are much larger than those of Israel—four submarines and nine principle surface combatants versus three submarines and five principle surface combatants for Israel.[274] While the Egyptian navy has impressive combat strength for the region, this force strength comes at the cost of holding onto aging and low-capability ships and limited overall effectiveness—although the navy is improving as it continues to modernize.

Egypt's major combat ships include four ex-Chinese, Romeo-class submarines. These are badly aging designs, although they have been modernized to use Western periscopes, trailing GPS, passive sonars and fire control systems; fire modern wire-guided torpedoes and Harpoon missiles (130-kilometer maximum range); and use modern torpedoes. Egypt examined replacing them with two former Royal Dutch-Navy Zwaardvis-class submarines, which could be specially refitted for Egypt. Egypt also examined ways to use its US FMF grants to buy two new RDM-designed Moray 1400 submarines or German Type-209s. Egypt signed a letter of intent to buy two Morays in October 2000, and they will be built at the Ignalls shipyards in Pascagoula, Mississippi, with delivery in 5–7 years. The subs will be Dutch designs, but will have the Lockheed-Martin SBICS-900 combat system.[275]

Egypt's other combat ships include one obsolete British Z-class destroyer that dates back to 1955, and which lacks modern air defenses and anti-ship missiles. They also include one British Black Swan-class frigate dating back to the late 1940s. Both of these vessels are now restricted to use as training ships.

Egypt has two low-quality 1,425-ton Jianghu 1-class Chinese frigates dating back to the early 1980s, and which have never been upgraded and refitted as the Egyptian Navy once planned. Each is equipped with 4 HY-2 anti-ship missiles (with a maximum range of 80 kilometers) and four 57-mm guns. These ships are both active in the Red Sea, where no other regional navy except Saudi Arabia deploys more modern major combat vessels.

Egypt does, however, have two El Suez (Spanish Descubierta-class) frigates. The ships date back to the early 1970s, but each was modernized in the early 1980s. These are 1,479-ton ships equipped with 8 Harpoon anti-ship missiles (maximum range 70 nautical miles, 130 kilometers) in two quadruple launchers, an octuple Albatros anti-air missile launcher, a 76-mm gun, two triple torpedo tubes, and anti-submarine mortars. Their combat data systems, air search, and fire control radars were updated in 1995–1996. They can be modified to carry up to eight Otomats.

Egypt has two 3,011-ton Damyat (ex-US FF-1051 Knox)-class guided missile frigates. While they date back to the 1970s, they were recommissioned in 1995–1995. Each has eight Harpoon missiles, ASROC anti-submarine rocket launchers, Phalanx close-in air/missile defenses, and a 127-mm gun. They have two twin torpedo tubes, and relatively modern combat data systems, electronic countermeasures, search and surface radars, and fire control systems. Each can carry one Kaman Seasprite SH-2G helicopter. They have had boiler problems that seem to have been fixed, the ASROC system is now dated, and they lack long-range air defenses.

In 1996 the Egyptian Navy began to acquire four Oliver Hazard Perry-class frigates in a $600 million deal with the US. These frigates are 2,750-ton vessels. They are now in service as the Mubarak-class, and are armed with four Harpoon anti-ship missiles, 76-mm guns, Standard SM-1 surface-to-air missiles, Vulcan, and six torpedo tubes with Mk 46 anti-submarine torpedoes. All of these ships date back to the early 1980s, but they have been upgraded and have relatively modern radars, sonars, fire control, combat data management, and electronic warfare capability. Each can carry two Kaman Seasprite SH-2G helicopters. Egypt has sought the transfer or lease of surplus FFG-7s, but there have been Congressional objections to providing the ships as grant aid because they cost $60 million each to procure.[276]

Egypt has 24–25 operational missile patrol craft, 12 of which are relatively modern ships armed with the Harpoon and Otomat anti-ship missile. These include six 307-ton Ramadan-class ships, each with four Otomat I anti-ship missiles and 76-mm guns. They also include six 82-ton October-class craft with two Otomat I missiles and 30-mm guns.

Egypt has six aging 68-ton Hegu-class (the Chinese version of the FSU Komar-class) vessels with SY-1 missiles. They were refitted with improved electronic support measures in 1995–1996, but one seems to be laid up on what may be a permanent basis. Egypt may still have four obsolete Osa I-class with four SS-N-2A Styx missiles and 2 Komar-class vessels with SS-N-2A missiles in reserve. Several of these Osa and Komar-class ships have had serious combat damage or been taken out of service at some point, but two Osa-class seem to have been refitted to the point where they are operational. Egypt is buying four 400-ton missile patrol boats from the US, which will have TRS-3D/16 lightweight three-dimensional radars, and integrated combat systems.[277]

Egypt has 18 other patrol ships (4 Shanghai-class, 6 Shershen-class, and 8 Hainan-class). Some are armed with 122-mm multiple rocket launchers, torpedoes, or 57-mm guns. They can also be used to lay mines. These have some value in the patrol mission and fire support mission in secure waters. Only about 15 of these ships, however, are regularly operational.

Egypt has 13 operational mine vessels, including three relatively modern Swiftsure coastal mine hunters. The rest of its mine vessels can lay mines, but its 4 ex-Soviet Yurka and 6 T-43-class mine vessels have little modern mine detection and mine sweeping capability. Plans to modernize their capabilities have never been implemented.

The Egyptian navy has three major Polnocny-class amphibious vessels (100 troops and 10 tanks capacity each) and nine Vydra-class landing ships (200 troops capacity each). It has some 20 support ships, including diving and support ships. There are six specialized Seafox ships for deliveries of underwater demolition teams.

The army operates three land-based, truck-mounted batteries of Otomat anti-ship missiles with Plessey targeting radars, and two brigades of 100-mm, 130-mm, and 152-mm SM-4-1 coastal defense guns. These defenses are located near major ports and the approaches to the Suez Canal and are under Egyptian Navy command.

In addition, the Egyptian Air Force is equipping a limited number of F-16s to carry Harpoon anti-ship missiles, and Egypt wants to acquire 10 anti-submarine warfare helicopters. It currently has nine operational SA-342L anti-ship missile-equipped helicopters (out of a total of 12) armed with AS-12 guided missiles, and 10 SH-2(G)E Seasprite helicopters equipped for anti-submarine warfare, which carry sonars and two torpedoes or depth charges. It also has five Mark 47 Sea Kings equipped for both the anti-ship and anti-submarine warfare roles. The EAF has five E-2C Hawkeyes with search and warning radars and both electronic support and countermeasures, and two Beech 1900C surveillance aircraft with surveillance radars and electronic support measures that it can use in the maritime patrol role.[278]

The Egyptian navy is improving, but it has not yet received the funding necessary to fully modernize its ships, or to carry out the levels of advanced joint warfare training it needs. It has difficulties in maintaining ships from so many different countries, and many of its ships and boats are worn and obsolete and have little operational effectiveness.

The Egyptian navy has the capability to pose a limited to moderate threat to Israel, although it would face major problems. It does not have the training, electronic warfare, or navy–air force joint operations capabilities to challenge Israel's best Sa'ar-class vessels in joint operations, except in Egyptian waters, where Egyptian ships might have air cover and protection from its submarines.

The Egyptian navy is, however, the dominant regional naval power in the Red Sea. It has moderate capability to defend the approaches to the Suez Canal. Egypt can play an important role in dealing with the less sophisticated naval and air forces of potentially hostile Red Sea countries and in securing the Egyptian coastline and approaches to the Suez Canal. The better-crewed and funded Egyptian ships have drawn considerable praise from their US counterparts during joint exercises.

THE INEVITABLE LIMITS OF QUANTITATIVE COMPARISONS

The previous qualifications regarding the composition and employment of the weapons held by each country show that even the most detailed quantitative force comparisons retain some of the defects of the data in Table 1.1. As the previous discussion has shown, even the most detailed break out of weapons strengths inevitably includes equipment with a wide range of different capabilities.

The previous tables and figures also count total inventories, and not total operational forces. Much of the equipment counted in these totals is deployed in low-grade active and reserve units with only limited readiness and limited combat capability. A substantial amount of the total equipment in Israeli and Arab inventories is in storage or has only limited operational readiness. Unfortunately, there is no way to make accurate estimates of deployable forces, to relate these estimates to mobilization times and readiness rates, or estimate which portion of a given national force can be deployed in a given contingency or on a given front. While it is possible to make intelligent guesses, estimates of the balance always have this defect.

These tables and figures focus on weapons numbers at a time when the integration of weapons with other technologies into war fighting systems is increasingly more critical in shaping actual war fighting capability. Force numbers alone have never determined the Arab-Israeli balance. Since the Suez War of 1956, the outcome of conflicts between Israel and various Arab states has been determined primarily by Israel's "edge" in integrating superior tactics, training, and technology. The first phase of Egypt and Syria's surprise attack on Israel in October 1973 is the only notable exception.

The key missing dimension in all quantitative comparisons is the synergy between numbers, technology, tactics, sustainability, and training—an area where Israel often has a significant advantage. There is no way to quantify or reflect very different capabilities in modern command, control, communications, computers, intelligence and battle management (C^4I/BM), electronic warfare (EW), and reconnaissance (recce) capabilities. These differences are equally critical to joint operations, combined arms, and the other synergies of modern warfare, and in all of these areas Israel again enjoys a significant advantage.

At the same time, Israel's fighting against the Hizbollah and Amal in Lebanon, and the Palestinians in the West Bank and Gaza, has shown that forces designed for conventional war are not always dominant in low intensity combat and asymmetric warfare. As is the case with the US, the IDF's qualitative edge in conventional forces pushes opponents to adopt other approaches to warfare. The following chapters on Lebanon and Palestinian forces show that such Arab forces have often had considerable success.

4

"Intangibles": Arab–Israeli Force Quality

Table 4.1 provides a very different picture of the relative capabilities of Arab-Israeli forces from the previous tables. It provides a qualitative ranking of their war fighting capabilities in the critical areas shaping the balance judged by Western standards. It should be clear that the judgments made in Table 4.1 are highly subjective, and are anything but easy to make and validate. Further, such comparisons inevitably raise the question of whether peak US military capabilities are the proper standard of reference for judging Arab-Israeli forces. Many Arab forces that have severe limitations by Western standards have moderate to good capability if they are judged by their ability to fight other Arab states, and some might argue that this is the proper standard of comparison.

THE ISRAELI "EDGE"

One of the key factors shaping the judgments in Table 4.1 is Israel's qualitative superiority or "edge" over most Arab conventional military forces. Israeli forces have many limitations of their own, but the fact remains that Israel has dominated Arab forces in every war it has fought. The Suez War of 1956, the June War of 1967, the Canal War of 1970, the October War of 1973, and the Lebanon conflict of 1982 all show that the Arab-Israeli balance cannot be judged by force numbers or by the standards of military effectiveness set by military powers in the developing world. Egypt achieved high technical proficiency in areas like land-based air defense during the Canal War. Egypt and Syria demonstrated consider-able innovation and military competence during their initial surprise attacks in 1973, and Syrian attack helicopter units and special forces fought well in 1982. It is

Table 4.1
The War Fighting Capabilities of the Individual "Ring" States Judged By Western Standards

Capability & Quality	US	Israel	Syria	Jordan	Egypt	Lebanon
Active Manpower						
Officer quality	VG-E	G-E	P-VG	M-E	P-E	N
NCO Quality	VG-E	G	P-M	M-E	P-E	N
Enlisted quality	G-VG	G-VG	VP-M	M-G	P-M	N
Reserve Manpower						
Officer quality	G	G-VG	P	M	P	N
NCO Quality	G	G	P	P	P	N
Enlisted quality	G	G	VP	P	VP	N
Combined operations	VG	VG	VP	P	P	N
Land Forces						
Combined arms	G-VG	G-VG	P-M	M	P-M	N
Advanced Maneuver	VG-E	G-VG	P-M	M	P-M	N
Armored Warfare	VG	VG	P-M	M	P-M	N
Infantry Warfare	G	G	P-VG	G	P-G	N-M
Advanced Artillery	E	G	P	P	P-G	N
Heliborne	VG	VG	P-M	P	P-M	N
Advanced Night	VG	VG	P	P	P	N
Unconventional	VG	E	M-E	M	M-E	N
C4I/BM	E	VG	P	P	P-M	N
Sustainability	VG	VG	P	M	P-M	N
Standardization	E	VG	M	P	VP-M	N
Interoperability	E	VG	P	M	P-M	N
Naval Forces						
Combined Operations	VG-E	M	VP	N	VP	N
Anti-Ship Missile	G-E	G	P-M	N	P-M	N
ASW	G-E	P	VP	N	VP	N
Offensive Mine	P-M	P	M	N	P	N
Defensive Mine	P	P	P	N	P	N
Amphibious	VG	M	P	N	P	N
C4I/BM	E	M	P	N	P	N
Sustainability	VG	P-M	P	N	P	N
Standardization	E	G	G	N	P	G
Interoperability	VG	P	P	N	P	G
Air Forces						
Combined Operations	E	VG	P	P	P-M	N
Day air defense	E	E	P-G	P-G	P-VG	N
AWX/BVR air defense	E	E	VP	N	VP-M	N
Day attack	E	E	P	P	P-M	N
Close support	E	VG	P	M	P-M	N
Advanced anti-armor	VG	VG	VP	VP	VP-P	N
Night/AWX attack	E	VG	VP	P	P-M	N
Reconnaissance	E	E	P	P	P-M	N

Table 4.1 (continued)

Capability & Quality	US	Israel	Syria	Jordan	Egypt	Lebanon
Air Forces						
Electronic warfare	E	G	P	N	P	N
Attack helicopter	G-E	G	P	P	P	VP
C4I/BM	VG-E	E	VP	P-M	P-M	N
Sustainability	VG	E	VP	P	P-M	N
Standardization	E	E	M	P	VP-M	N
Interoperability	VG	VG	P	P	VP-M	N
Strategic Mobility						
Air	VG	M	VP	VP	P-M	N
Sea	G	P	N	N	N	N
Prepositioning	M	-	-	-	-	-
Counterproliferation						
Missile Defense	P-M	P-M	N	N	N	N
Bio. Offensive	N	N	P	N	P	N
Bio. Defensive	VP-N	P	P	N	P	N
Chem. Offensive	VP	P	M	N	P	N
Chem. Defense	M-G	P-M	P-M	N	P	N
Nuclear Offensive	E	E	N	N	N	N
Nuclear Defensive	M-VP	N	N	N	N	N
Conventional Retaliation	VG	E	P	VP	P	N

Note: E = Excellent, VG = Very Good, G = Good, M = Moderate, P = Poor, VP = Very Poor , N = Negligible.

Interoperability refers to the Israeli ability to interoperate broadly with other Gulf and Western forces, and an Arab country's ability to operate flexibly with other Arab forces. *Standardization* refers to whether equipment pool in a given service in given country is standardized enough to permit effective cross-service and resupply. *C4I/BM* refers to overall command, control, communications, intelligence, and battle management capabilities.

Israel's overall ability to match Western military quality, however, which has proven decisive in every Arab-Israeli conflict.

Israeli military forces are closer to Western forces in tactics, training, and technology than they are to the forces of Middle Eastern countries. The standard of comparison used in judging the trends in the Arab-Israeli military balance must be based on the force with the highest qualitative standards since it is most likely to dominate the outcome of combat.

Arab countries have put more emphasis on manpower quality in recent years. Egypt has established a National Training Center, Jordan has sacrificed manpower numbers to keep training levels high, and Syria has emphasized training and manpower quality in specific units, particularly the commando and special forces units it believes would be effective in asymmetric warfare. Nevertheless, Arab forces have not kept pace with Israel, particularly in using high technology training systems. For example, Israel's Advanced Training and Simulations, Ltd. has a partnership with Siemens Nederlands called Simagine Simulation Systems for the export of gunnery, training simulators for tanks, the Dragon and TOW anti-tank guided weapons, field artillery observers, and light air defense systems like the Stinger and Vulcan.[279] The outcome of the Gulf War reinforces this conclusion. While capabilities for guerrilla, asymmetric, low intensity, and some aspects of urban warfare are less subject to changes in training, tactics, and technology, the Gulf War has demonstrated that the military balance is changing strikingly for those nations that can begin to exploit the relevant aspects of the "revolution in military affairs."

Since 1990, Israel has done a much better job of taking advantage of the advances in tactics, training, and technology than its Arab neighbors. As a result, Israel has many of the same strengths that Western forces enjoyed at the time of the Gulf War. These are strengths which, as the Gulf War showed, are fundamentally changing the importance of the following: joint and combined operations, the tempo and precision of air power, beyond-visual-range combat, rates of armored maneuver and ranges of armored engagement, the use of precision-directed long-range artillery, sustainability in armored maneuver and air operations, and the ability to conduct "24 hour" warfare.

Israel has also been able to exploit a wide range of political, economic, and strategic problems in the Arab world. These problems include:

- The end of the Cold War and the lack of any replacement for FSU support and aid.
- Continuing political divisions within the Arab world.
- Egypt's commitment to the peace process.
- Egyptian reliance on US aid. (While US aid greatly improves Egyptian force quality, it also makes Egypt somewhat dependent on continued US support and maintaining its peace with Israel.)
- Jordan's severe economic problems, and therefore lack of military modernization and investment.
- Syria's lack of recent investment in new arms and critical new military technologies.
- Lebanon's long-standing military weakness.
- Iraq's defeat in the Gulf War and the impact of seven years of no military resupply coupled with the efforts of UNSCOM and IAEA.
- The lack of any meaningful military assistance and commitment by other Arab powers.
- Politicized military forces that undercut much of the military effort to modernize and create professional military forces.

ARAB ORGANIZATIONAL, RESOURCE, POLITICAL, AND "CULTURAL" PROBLEMS

The judgments in Table 4.1 reflect the fact that the Arab states have strength in numbers, but that they have not as yet translated this advantage into real world war fighting capability. While the Arab states—particularly Egypt—have steadily improved their forces over time, they still suffer from a lack of effective organization, realistic large scale combat training, overemphasis on mass relative to quality, emphasis on attrition over maneuver, emphasis on weapons numbers over C^{4}I/BM systems and capabilities, and a lack of proper emphasis on standardization and sustainability.

Part of this Arab failure to develop force quality that can compete with Israel is the result of a lack of resources and/or access to first-line Western technology. Jordan, for example, has lacked the resources to modernize and equip its forces with high technology weapons and systems. Syria has been denied Western weapons and technology for political reasons, not the least of which are its opposition to the peace process and its ties to the former Soviet Union. There is no question that Jordan and Syria would have far more effective forces if they had the same level of aid and access to advanced technology the US provided to Egypt and Israel.

Many of the problems in the Arab forces, however, are the result of national and/or cultural failures to come to grips with the demanding realities of making modern military forces effective. In general, the Arab states have not yet acquired the mix of resources, educational base, and emphasis on management and technical skills that is necessary to transform their large holdings of equipment into effective forces. They have tended to emphasize equipment purchases over tactics, training, manpower management, and sustainability. Procurement and promotion have been politicized and subject to corruption and nepotism.

Each Arab "ring state" has individual military problems. Syria has made progress in reshaping its forces, and has shifted away from a futile search to obtain direct military parity with Israel. It has put a growing stress on asymmetric warfare in the form of ballistic missiles and weapons of mass destruction. It is also creating small elite units in including commando and special forces units that are well trained, equipped with advanced crew and manportable weapons, and which can be dispersed in defensive or covert operations in ways that Israel finds more difficult to attack than forces with large, easily targetable weapons. Nevertheless, Syria still emphasizes sheer force size, and the acquisition of lead technology weapons systems with a high "glitter factor," over a balanced and effective approach to force modernization.

Jordan has excellent special forces and pays close attention to manpower quality. However, its forces lack the technology and resources to fully modernize and develop effective combined operations and joint warfare capabilities. At almost every level, Jordan faces resource problems that keep it from pursuing the level of military modernization and effectiveness it desires.

Egypt is improving some aspects of its manpower quality and management, and has created a National Training Center. Officers are steadily better trained and given more initiative. Egypt has not, however, made the necessary improvements in conscript training. Egypt is steadily improving its systems integration, C^{4}I/BM, and sustainability, but it still pays too much attention to the "glitter factor" of the latest technology and sheer mass. For example, Egyptian forces would be significantly more effective if Egypt did not try to support a large bloc of low-grade forces equipped with obsolete Soviet bloc equipment supplied before 1974, and concentrated its resources on making its Western supplied forces as effective as possible.

Such generalizations are dangerous because they can disguise the fact that there is a wide range of quality within Arab forces, and individual Arab units can be as effective as Israeli or US forces. These problems do not mean that Arab forces are incapable of strategic innovation or military effectiveness. The Egyptian-Syrian surprise attack on Israel in October 1973 was one of the major feats of arms of the 20th century and involved considerable strategic and tactical innovation. Today, Syria has several effective armored divisions and some elite special forces units. Jordanian forces have a high degree of military professionalism within their technical limits. Egypt has developed several high quality land and air units that are equipped with modern American arms, and has gained experience in US concepts of warfare through its experience during the Gulf War and its participation in joint exercises.

It is also impossible to ignore the fact that most Arab governments, ministries of defense, and military leaders fail to place a realistic emphasis on "intangibles." While Arab forces have steadily improved in quality over time, they still fail to properly emphasize aggressive leadership and the need for innovation and change. Ministries of Defense are still too bureaucratic and rigid, and there is extensive inter-service and intra-service rivalry and over-compartmentalization of procurement, manpower, and other functions. The layering of new functions and responsibilities over older bureaucratic structures is confused with effective reorganization.

Bureaucracy, favoritism, and politicization add to the problem over time. Far too often, Arab officers become progressively less competitive with their Israeli counterparts, and other officers in the world's most effective military forces, as they rise in rank. Senior commanders and officials usually serve too long, lack effective professional training to update their experience and technical capability, and are often chosen for political skills or loyalty, rather than professional competence.

With the exception of Jordan and the elite elements of Egyptian and Syrian forces, Arab forces have not yet succeeded in creating a strong and respected corps of NCOs and technicians for their overall manpower pool. The gap in social status and command authority between officer and NCO is still too great—particularly in units where the experience and technical competence of other ranks is critical to the effective use of new technologies. Many junior and mid-ranking officers do not receive sufficient training, and they are rarely subjected to realistic exercises that force them to innovate and become aggressive and competent leaders and administrators. They are still promoted as much for time in service and political ties to senior commanders as for professionalism.

Arab officers are increasingly encouraged to assume personal responsibility for technical tasks and to work with their troops in areas involving manual labor and administrative detail. However, initiative and "hands on" attention to detail is still a problem. One serious by-product of these problems is that Arab forces have far too great a tendency to blame foreign support and equipment, and accept conspiracy theories as a substitute for technical competence. They often exhibit an obsessive focus on efforts to procure the latest and most advanced weapons system but then underinvest in the required training and simulation systems, spare parts and sustainability, and overall systems integration.

Improvements are taking place in training at the squad to battalion level but the outcome of most exercises is still predetermined, and units are not tested in realistic field exercises. Progress at lower levels is not usually matched by equally demanding training at the regimental or wing level and above. Both large-scale field exercises and command post exercises are generally undemanding, limited in effort, and without penalty for anything other than the most mediocre performance.

The end result is that there is too little realistic adversary training that forces officers to accept the reality of defeat for their mistakes, and to learn to innovate in the face of superior forces. Within most Arab military services there is little acceptance of the need for "make or break" exercises that ruthlessly identify those field grade officers that can or cannot command, and to force inferior field grade officers out of the military. The need to make a major investment in realistic, large unit training and to force effective joint and combined arms performance on the training process is not understood, or limited to elite units like commandos and special forces that cannot, by themselves, successfully fight an armor-heavy combined arms action.

Once again, it is important to stress that Arab forces are improving with time, and their quality differs sharply according to country and service. As the following chapters show, Israeli forces have many problems of their own—as do those of the US and any other armored forces. Nevertheless, many Arab states still fail to recognize that training and sustainability are often more important aspects of war fighting capability than numbers. They confuse the technical advantages of buying the latest new weapon with the war fighting advantages to be gained from integrating weapons into a "system of systems" that ensures overall force-on-force effectiveness. There is insufficient attention to the need to support weapons systems and combat units with service support, sustainability and maintenance, associated technologies for targeting and intelligence, and effective C^4I/BM systems. There is insufficient understanding of the need to integrate firepower, maneuver capability, and sustainability as three pillars of high intensity, "24 hours a day" combat operations.

THE QUALITATIVE WEAKNESSES IN MOST MIDDLE EASTERN MILITARY FORCES

The Gulf War and the Arab-Israeli conflicts of 1967, 1973, and 1982 all revealed a fundamental disparity between the limited number of nations who can use new methods of warfare, and the vast majority of nations who cannot. This disparity is an important strategic reality that no nation can ignore. It raises serious questions about the value of many of the force structures and weapons systems in the Arab states surrounding Israel, and about the ability of such states to engage "First World" states like Israel in mid to high intensity, high technology conflict.

The following weaknesses in Arab forces are steadily declining with time—and Egypt and Jordan have some excellent units—but they seem likely to play an important role in shaping the outcome of any future war:

- *Authoritarianism and over-centralization of the effective command structure*: The high command of many countries is dependent on compartmentalized, over-centralized C^4I/ BM systems that do not support high tempo warfare, combined arms, or combined operations and lack tactical and technical sophistication. Many forces or force elements report through a separate chain of command. C^4I/BM systems often are structured to separate the activity of regular forces from elite, regime security, and ideological forces. Systems often ensure major sectors and corps commanders report to the political leadership, and separations occur within the branches of a given service. Intelligence is compartmentalized and poorly disseminated. Air force command systems are small, unit-oriented and unsuited for large scale force management. Coordination of land-based air defense and strike systems is poorly integrated, vulnerable, and/or limited in volume handling capability. Combined operations and combined arms coordination are poor, and command interference at the political level is common.

- *Lack of strategic assessment capability*: Many Middle Eastern nations lack sufficient understanding of Western war fighting capabilities to understand the impact of the revolution in military affairs, the role of high technology systems, and the impact of the new tempo of war. Other countries have important gaps in their assessment capabilities reflecting national traditions or prejudices.

- *Major weaknesses in battle management, command, control, communications, intelligence, targeting, and battle damage assessment*: No Middle Eastern country has meaningful access to space-based systems, or advanced theater reconnaissance and intelligence systems. Most lack sophisticated reconnaissance, intelligence, and targeting assets. Beyond-visual-range imagery and targeting is restricted to largely vulnerable and easily detectable reconnaissance aircraft or low performance UAVs. Many rely on photo data for imagery, and have cumbersome download and analysis cycles in interpreting intelligence. Many have exploitable vulnerabilities to information warfare. Most are limited in the sophistication of their electronic warfare, SIGINT, and COMINT systems. Their communications security is little better than commercial communications security. They have severe communications interconnectivity, volume handling, and dissemination problems. Additionally, they cannot provide the software and connectivity necessary to fully exploit even commercial or ordinary military systems. They lack the C^4I/BM capability to manage complex deep strikes, complex large-scale armor and artillery operations, effective electronic intelligence, and rapid cycles of reaction in decision-making.

- *Lack of cohesive force quality*: Most countries' forces have major land combat units and squadrons with very different levels of proficiency. Political, historical, and equipment supply factors often mean that most units have much lower levels of real-world combat effectiveness than the best units. Further, imbalances in combat support, service support, and logistic support create significant additional imbalances in sustainability and operational effectiveness. Many states add to these problems, as well as lack of force cohesion, by creating politicized or ideological divisions within their forces.

- *Shallow offensive battlefields*: Most states face severe limits in extending the depth of the battlefield because they lack the survivable platforms and sensors, communications, and data processing to do so. These problems are particularly severe in wars of maneuver, in wars involving the extensive use of strike aircraft, and in battles where a growing strain is placed on force cohesion.

- *Manpower quality*: Many states rely on the mass use of poorly trained conscripts. They fail to provide adequate status, pay, training, and career management for NCOs and technicians. Many forces fail to provide professional career development for officers and joint and combined arms training. Promotion often occurs for political reasons or out of nepotism and favoritism.

- *Slow tempo of operations*: Most Middle Eastern military forces have not fought a high-intensity air or armored battle. They are at best capable of medium tempo operations, and their pace of operations is often dependent on the survival of some critical mix of facilities or capabilities.

- *Lack of sustainability, recovery, and repair*: These initial problems in the tempo of operations are often exacerbated by a failure to provide for sustained air operations and high sortie rates, long-range sustained maneuver, and battlefield/combat unit recovery and repair. Most Middle Eastern forces are heavily dependent on re-supply to deal with combat attrition whereas Western forces and Israeli forces can use field recovery, maintenance, and repair.

- *Inability to prevent air superiority*: Many regional states have far greater air defense capability on paper than they do in practice. Most have not fought in any kind of meaningful air action in the last decade, and many have never fought any significant air action in their history. C^{4}I/BM problems are critical in this near real-time environment. Most countries lack sophisticated air combat and land-based air defense simulation and training systems, and do not conduct effective aggressor and large-scale operations training. Efforts to transfer technology, organization, and training methods from other nations on a patchwork basis often leaves critical gaps in national capability, even where other capabilities are effective.

- *Problems in air-to-air combat*: Air combat training levels are low and unrealistic. Pilot and other crew training standards are insufficient, or initial training is not followed up with sustained training. There is little effective aggressor training. AWACS and ABCCC capabilities are lacking. EW capabilities are modified commercial grade capabilities. Most aircraft lack effective air battle management systems, and have limited beyond-visual-range and look down shoot down capability. Most Soviet/Communist supplied air forces depend heavily on obsolete ground-controlled vectoring for intercepts. Key radar and control centers are static and vulnerable to corridor blasting.

- *Problems in land-based air defense*: Most Middle Eastern states must borrow or adapt air defense battle management capabilities from supplier states, and have limited independent capability for systems integration—particularly at the software level. They lack the mix of heavy surface-to-air missile systems to cover broad areas, or must rely on obsolete systems that can be killed, countered by EW, and/or bypassed. Most Middle Eastern short-range air defense systems do not protect against attacks with stand-off precision weapons or using stealth.

- *Lack of effective survivable long-range strike systems*: Many Middle Eastern nations have the capability to launch long-range air and missile strikes, but also have severe operational problems. Refueling capabilities do not exist or are in such small numbers as to be highly vulnerable. Long-range targeting and battle damage assessment capabilities are lacking. Training is limited and unrealistic in terms of penetrating effective air defenses. Platforms are export systems without the full range of supplier avionics or missile warheads. Assets are not survivable, or lose much of their effective strike capability once dispersed.

- *Combined (joint) operations, combined arms, and the air-land battle*: Many states fail to emphasize the key advances in the integration of war fighting capabilities from the last decade. When they do emphasize combined arms and joint operations, they usually leave serious gaps in some aspects of national war fighting capability.

- *Rough/special terrain warfare*: Although many Middle Eastern forces have armed helicopters, large numbers of tracked vehicles, and can create effective rough terrain defenses if given time, they have problems in conducting high tempo operations. Many tend to be road-bound for critical support and combined arms functions, and lack training for long range, high-intensity engagements in rough terrain. Many are not properly trained to exploit the potential advantages of their own region. They are either garrison forces, or forces that rely on relatively static operations in pre-determined field positions. These problems are often compounded by a lack of combat engineering and barrier crossing equipment.

- *Night and all-weather warfare*: Most Middle Eastern forces lack adequate equipment for night and poor weather warfare, and particularly for long-range direct and indirect fire engagement, and cohesive, sustainable, large scale maneuver.

- *Armored operations*: Most countries have sharply different levels of armored warfare proficiency within their armored and mechanized forces. Few units have advanced training and simulation facilities. Most land forces have interoperability and standardization problems within their force structure—particularly in the case of other armored fighting vehicles where they often deploy a very wide range of types. Many are very tank heavy, without the mix of other capabilities necessary to deploy infantry, supporting artillery, and anti-tank capabilities at the same speed and maneuver proficiency as tank units. Most forces have poor training in conducting rapid, large-scale armored and combined operations at night and in poor weather. Effective battle management declines sharply at the force-wide level—as distinguished from the major combat unit level—and sometimes even in coordinating brigade or division-sized operations.

- *Artillery operations*: Many Middle Eastern states have large numbers of artillery weapons, but serious problems in training and tactics. They lack long-range targeting capability and the ability to rapidly shift and effectively allocate fire. Many rely on towed weapons with limited mobility, or lack off-road support vehicles. Combined arms capabilities are limited. Many units are only effective in using mass fire against enemies that maneuver more slowly than they do.

- *Combat training*: Regional training generally has serious problems and gaps, which vary by country. Units or force elements differ sharply in training quality. Training problems are complicated by conversion and expansion, conscript turnover, and a lack of advanced technical support for realistic armored, artillery, air-to-air, surface-to-air, and offensive air training. Mass sometimes compensates, but major weaknesses remain.

- *Inability to use weapons of mass destruction effectively*: Any state can use weapons of mass destruction to threaten or intimidate another, or to attack population centers and fixed area targets. At the same time, this is not the same as having an effective capability and doctrine to obtain maximum use of such weapons, or to manage attacks in ways that result in effective tactical outcomes and conflict termination. Many states are acquiring long-range missiles and weapons of mass destruction with very limited exercise and test and evaluation capabilities. This does not deny them the ability to target large populated areas, economic centers, and fixed military targets, potentially inflicting massive damage. At the same time, it does present problems in more sophisticated military operations. Many will have to improvise deployments, doctrine, and war fighting capabilities. In many cases, weaknesses and vulnerabilities will persist and they will only be able to exploit a limited amount of the potential lethality of such systems.

THE QUALITATIVE ADVANTAGES OF ISRAELI FORCES

It is difficult to create such a generic list of weaknesses without making highly subjective judgments about the capabilities of Israeli, Syrian, Egyptian, and Jordanian forces that are unfair to important elements of each Arab nation's order of battle. Nevertheless, a great deal is known about the doctrine, training, and/or exercise performance of Israeli and individual Arab forces and US, French, British, and Russian advisors and experts have reviewed and agreed with many of these points—as have a number of Arab officers.

Furthermore, some of the weaknesses in Syrian, Egyptian, and Jordanian forces are products of limits in deployed weapons and technology and not "intangibles." Past Arab-Israeli conflicts have also shown that some of these factors are likely to be equally relevant in future Arab-Israeli conflicts—*if* Israeli forces have the time to deploy and fully organize and prepare, and *if* they do not face major challenges in terms of threats from weapons of mass destruction or guerrilla, urban, and revolutionary warfare—areas where many of the qualitative advantages of Israeli forces do not apply.

The potential cost of the weaknesses in Arab forces have also been illustrated by the lessons of the Gulf War (and Kosovo). They include:

- *Decoupling of political and military responsibility*: No war is ever free of command controversy or friction between political and military leadership. However, the Coalition forces fought the Gulf War with effective delegation of responsibility for military decisions to military commanders. Israel is likely to enjoy the same advantage in mid- to high-intensity wars. Syrian military forces are highly politicized, and organized more to suit the regime's internal security needs than to conduct modern joint operations. Jordan's small forces are under tight political control, but are selected for their professionalism. Egypt's military forces are involved in politics, but operational units are under professional, rather than political command. Egypt still, however, has a severe problem in reporting objectively through its chain of command—particularly when it has to report bad news. Egyptian intelligence is often politicized.

- *Unity of command*: The level of unity of command, and "fusion," achieved during the Gulf War was scarcely perfect, but it was far more effective than that possible in most Arab states. Israel has steadily improved its unity of command and ability to conduct joint operations since 1973. Syrian command is still over-compartmentalized by command, service, and branch. Jordan has a limited combined operations capability, but lacks the technology and resources to develop a high degree of effectiveness. Egyptian command is also heavily over-compartmentalized by command, service, and branch.

- *Combined operations, combined arms, and the "air-land battle"*: While US doctrine had always placed a pro forma emphasis on combined operations, many US operations in Vietnam did not properly integrate combined arms. Common inter-service training in combined operations was limited, and air operations were not properly integrated into land operations. In the years that followed, the US reorganized to place far more emphasis on combined arms and combined operations. It greatly strengthened combined operations training and career rotations into joint commands. At the same time, it developed tactics that closely integrated air and land operations into what the US came to call the "air-land battle." These tactics were critical to the success of the ground battle. Israel cannot afford the level of technology and sophisticated training systems used by the US, but it has adopted lower cost and equally effective methods to its theater of operations. Israel's major problems now lie in improving the coordination between its manpower forces and support by a mix of long-range artillery and fixed and rotary-wing aircraft. Syria has not made similar advances. Jordan's military doctrine recognizes the need for such advances, but Jordan lacks the resources and technology to move beyond defensive operations. Some Egyptian units equipped with US weapons and technology have performed adequately during preplanned exercises, but overall Egyptian capabilities are poor.

- *Emphasis on maneuver*: The US had firepower and attrition warfare until the end of the Vietnam War. In the years that followed, it converted its force structure to place an equal emphasis on maneuver and deception. This emphasis was supported by Britain and France, and was adopted by Saudi Arabia. Israel has long emphasized wars of maneuver, although it faces obvious limits in using such techniques in offensive land warfare against entrenched Syrian forces on the Golan. Syria still emphasizes preplanned tactics and maneuvers. These might prove adequate on the Golan if the Syrians achieve strategic surprise, but Syrian forces lack true maneuver capability and flexibility. Jordanian land forces recognize the importance of maneuver doctrine, but Jordan lacks the resources to adequately equip and train for modern maneuver warfare. Egypt's best units have moderate maneuver capability but even these units still need to improve their combined operations and sustainability. The bulk of Egyptian forces are relatively static and defensive in capability.

- *Emphasis on deception and strategic/tactical innovation*: No country has a monopoly on the use of deception and strategic/tactical innovation. The Coalition, however, demonstrated capabilities that were far superior to those of Iraq. Egypt and Syria made brilliant use of deception and innovation against Israel in the opening battles of the October War, but this operation took long preplanning and lacked operational flexibility once the initial battle plan was executed. Israel now has the technology and tactical sophistication to conduct "soft strike" air and land-based weapons attacks that are likely to achieve a high degree of "surprise," and has a distinct advantage in crisis-driven innovation. Syria retains the ability to use deception in preplanned operations, and has some elite units that showed considerable tactical flexibility in 1982, but lacks overall flexibility and speed of reaction. Jordan has considerable skill, but faces severe technical limits on its range of action. Egypt also retains the ability to use deception and innovation in preplanned operations, but only a relatively few elite units seem to exhibit tactical innovation and flexibility under pressure. In some ways, Egypt seems to have become more rigid since 1973—perhaps because of the problems inherent in trying to operate forces with such diverse equipment and training levels and such limited interoperability.

- *"24-hour war"—Superior night, all-weather, and beyond-visual-range warfare*: "Visibility" is always relative in combat. There is no such thing as a perfect night vision or all-weather combat system, or way of acquiring perfect information at long ranges. US and British air and land forces, however, have far better training and technology for such combat than they ever had in the past, and were the first forces designed to wage warfare continuously at night and in poor weather. Equally important, they were far more capable of taking advantage of the margin of extra range and tactical information provided by superior technology. Israel cannot afford all of the systems and high technology training aids available to the US, but does have a distinct advantage in technology and training over its neighbors. Syria is still largely a daytime, visual-range, military force. Jordan has many similar limitations, although Jordanian land forces have night warfare training superior to Syria's. Egyptian capabilities are mixed. Some elite land units have night warfare capability, and some US supplied air units have good all-weather and beyond-visual-range aircraft and training. Overall Egyptian proficiency is limited to moderate.

- *Near real-time integration of $C^4I/BM/T/BDA$*: The Coalition took advantage of major US $C^4I/BM/T/BDA$ organization, technology, and software to integrate various aspects of command, control, communications, computers, and intelligence (C^4I); battle management (BM); targeting (T); and battle damage assessment (BDA) to achieve a near real-time integration and decision-making–execution cycle. Israel is far less sophisticated than the US in some aspects of such systems, but it has enough technology to achieve many of these same capabilities at the tactical level while its neighbors lack a similar combination of organization, technology, and training. Syrian ground forces use techniques at least a decade old, Syrian air units still rely primarily on obsolete ground controlled intercept techniques and slow, grinding cycles of air attack planning. Syrian surface-to-air missile $C^4I/BM/T/BDA$ systems are a decade out of date. Jordan has lacked the resources to adequately modernize its $C^4I/BM/T/BDA$ systems, although it has sometimes adapted low cost solutions to obtain partial capability. Egypt has modernized some aspects of its $C^4I/BM/T/BDA$ systems, but its integration of these capabilities is uncertain and its improvements in $C^4I/BM/T/BDA$ systems only affect the US-equipped portion of its forces. Egypt has poor force-wide $C^4I/BM/T/BDA$ capabilities.

- *A new tempo of operations*: The Coalition exploited a superiority in every aspect of targeting, intelligence gathering and dissemination, integration of combined arms, multiservice forces, and night and all-weather warfare to achieve both a new tempo of operations and one far superior to that of Iraq. Israel has long emphasized tempo of operations while Syria remains a relatively low tempo force, Jordan lacks the air and artillery capabilities to support high tempo armored operations, and Egyptian forces have mixed quality. Syria can only briefly sustain high tempo land operations under conditions where it has previously planned and trained for the specific operation involved and its battle plans are not disrupted by preemption or massive enemy air superiority. Jordan has had the training and doctrine for high-intensity land operations, but now lacks the resources to keep most of its land forces at this level of proficiency. It can only briefly surge air operations. Egyptian capabilities to sustain high tempo operations are limited to moderate and many Egyptian force elements still lack detailed doctrine, training, support capabilities, and supply capabilities for such operations.

- *A new tempo of sustainability*: Coalition forces had maintainability, reliability, reparability, and the speed and overall mobility of logistic, service support, and combat support force activity that broadly matched their maneuver and firepower capabilities. The benefits of these new capabilities were reflected in such critical areas as the extraordinarily high operational availability and sortie rates of US aircraft, and the ability to support the movement of heliborne and armored forces during the long thrust into Iraq from the West. Israel has long demonstrated it has the ability to sustain high-intensity air and land operations. Syria lacks the doctrine, training, specialized equipment and support vehicles, and stocks and supply system to give sustainability the emphasis needed in modern warfare. Jordan lacks the resources to fund adequate levels of sustainability for its land and air units. Egypt has placed a proper conceptual emphasis on sustainability, but lacks the detailed doctrine, training, specialized equipment and support vehicles, and stocks and supply system to give most of its forces the sustainability needed in modern warfare.

- *Beyond-visual-range air combat, air defense suppression, air base attacks, and airborne C^4I/BM*: The Coalition had a decisive advantage in air combat training, beyond-visual-range air combat capability, anti-radiation missiles, electronic warfare, air base and shelter and kill capability, stealth and unmanned long-range strike systems, IFF and air control capability, and airborne C^4I/BM systems like the E-3 and ABCCC. These advantages allowed the Coalition to win early and decisive air supremacy. Israel has a mix of aircraft, E-2Cs, UAVs, electronic warfare systems, and command and control assets that give it many of the same advantages in its particular theater of operations against the forces of its Arab neighbors. Virtually every aspect of Syrian operations in these forms of combat is a decade behind the state of the art. Jordan lacks the equipment to implement such combat effectively, Egypt can use its E-2Cs effectively in air defense missions, but only with its US-supplied air and surface-to-air missile units. Its F-16s are capable of good beyond-visual-range (BVR) combat capability, but are limited by their rules of engagement and a concern for fratricide, and cannot compete with Israel in overall battle management capability and air defense suppression and air field suppression/attack capabilities.

- *Focused and effective interdiction bombing*: While the Coalition strategic bombing effort during the Gulf War had limitations, the tactical and interdiction aspects of the Coalition's use of offensive air power was highly successful. The interdiction effort was successful in many respects. The Coalition organized effectively to use its deep strike capabilities to carry out a rapid and effective pattern of focus strategic bombing where planning was sufficiently well coupled to intelligence and meaningful strategic objectives so that such strikes achieved the major military objectives that the planner set. At the same time, targeting, force allocation, and precision kill capabilities had advanced to the point where interdiction bombing and strikes were far more lethal and strategically useful than in previous conflicts. Israel has given tactical offensive and interdiction capabilities high priority since the 1973 war. It does not have all of the targeting, intelligence, and advanced stand-off munitions of capabilities of US forces, but it has advanced conventional bombing or "soft strike" capabilities, and has the technology, tactics, and training to conduct similar operations in its theater of operations. Syria has yet to demonstrate anything approaching modern doctrine, tactics, and training for using its strike and attack aircraft, although it has some effective attack helicopter units. Jordan has developed a more sophisticated doctrine, but lacks virtually every technical capability needed for advanced attack and interdiction missions. Egypt has improved the capability of its Western equipped fighter-ground attack and F-16 units, but has poor overall doctrine and training for force-wide air attack and interdiction missions. It also seems to lack advanced targeting and striking planning techniques, and has a force mix filled with many low capability Soviet bloc and European aircraft and weapons.

- *Expansion of the battlefield: "Deep Strike"*: As part of its effort to offset the Warsaw Pact's numerical superiority, US tactics and technology emphasized using air-land battle capabilities to extend the battlefield far beyond the immediate forward "edge" of the battle area (FEBA). The Coalition exploited the resulting mix of targeting capability, improved air strike capabilities, and land force capabilities in ways that played an important role in attriting Iraqi ground forces during the air phase of the war, and which helped the Coalition break through Iraqi defenses and exploit the breakthrough. This achievement is particularly striking in view of the fact that the US was not yet ready to employ some "deep strike" targeting technologies and precision strike systems designed to fight the Warsaw Pact that were still in development. Israel has long emphasized long-range conventional air strikes, or "soft-strike" capabilities and should be able to penetrate and/or suppress Syrian and Jordanian air defenses early in the air war. Syria has done little to refine its capabilities beyond developing the ability to fire missiles at area targets. It has not exploited its acquisition of Su-24 strike aircraft by providing effective training and doctrine. Jordan lacks modern strike aircraft and weapons. Egypt has some capability to use rockets against targets of moderate depth, and modern dual-capable aircraft, but has concentrated its modern aircraft in air defense units and does not seem to have developed an effective doctrine—and suitable targeting and battle management capabilities—for "deep strike" missions.

- *Technological superiority in many critical areas of weaponry*: The US scarcely had a monopoly on effective weapons during the Gulf War, but it had a critical "edge" in key weapons like tanks, other armored fighting vehicles, artillery systems, long-range strike systems, attack aircraft, air defense aircraft, surface-to-air missiles, space, attack helicopters, naval systems, sensors, battle management, and a host of other areas. As has been discussed in Chapter 1, this superiority went far beyond the technical "edge" revealed by "weapon on weapon" comparisons. Coalition forces exploited technology in "systems" that integrated mixes of different weapons into other aspects of force capability and into the overall force structures of the US, Britain, France, and the Saudi Air Force to a far greater degree than Iraq and most military forces in Middle Eastern states. Israel has a similar overall mix of technological superiority, while Syria and Jordan lack anything approaching a broad base of high technology systems, and Egyptian forces are split between forces with modern US equipment and forces with obsolete and/or worn Soviet bloc and European supplied equipment.

- *Integration of precision-guided weapons into tactics and force structures*: The Coalition exploited a decisive US technical "edge" in the ability to use precision-guided weapons against Iraq. US forces had far more realistic training in using such weapons, and the US had the ability to link their employment to far superior reconnaissance and targeting capability. Israel does not have the same level of sophistication as US forces, but it has created substitutes tailored to its own tactical needs to provide the equivalent of capabilities similar to those of the US. With the exception of a few units that use anti-tank guided missiles, Syrian capabilities to use precision guided weapons, and related targeting and battle management systems, are poor. Jordanian capabilities are severely limited by a lack of equipment and sophisticated training aids. Egypt has a few well trained units, but most elements of all four Egyptian services are not trained effectively to use such weapons—particularly in complex, combined and joint operations.

- *Realistic combat training and use of technology and simulation*: During the Gulf War, the US and Britain used training methods based on realistic combined arms and air-land training, large-scale training, and adversary training. These efforts were far superior to previous methods and were coupled to a far more realistic and demanding system for ensuring the readiness of the forces involved. Equally important, they emphasized the need for the kinds of additional training that allowed US forces to adapt to the special desert warfare conditions of Desert Storm. Israel has long emphasized realistic training, and has adapted US techniques and systems for simulation using lower cost technology where it feels these meet its needs plus innovations of its own. Syrian units differ sharply in training quality, and even the most highly trained Syrian units use obsolete training methods with inadequate technical support. Jordan trains relatively well, but lacks the resources and organization for realistic aggressor training and simulation. Egypt has some units with high training levels, and some Egyptian units perform well in joint exercises with the US. Most Egyptian forces in all four Egyptian military services, however, have low levels of training with poor technical aid and support, and a lack of realistic aggressor training.

- *Emphasis on forward leadership and delegation*: During the Gulf War, virtually all of the successful Coalition forces were aggressively led from the front. In contrast, Iraqi forces were often led from the rear and the officers in forward units were sharply constrained in terms of delegation of authority, overall information on the battlefield situation, and the ability to take independent action. The performance of the forces in the Arab "ring states" is constrained by the same problems even though Jordanian commanders, as well as the best Egyptian and Syrian commanders, do lead from the front. Israel, however, has made this a force-wide doctrine and long demonstrated its excellence in this area of operations. Furthermore, delegation of command authority is a problem in the Jordanian Army and in all of the Egyptian and Syrian services. The lack of emphasis on command initiative is compounded by a lack of realistic force-wide exercise training.

- *Heavy reliance on NCOs and enlisted personnel*: There was nothing new about the heavy reliance that Western forces placed on the technical skills, leadership quality, and initiative of non-commissioned officers (NCOs) and experienced enlisted personnel. This is a reliance which is common to virtually every Western military force, and which has given them a major advantage over Soviet and those Middle Eastern forces which do not give the same authority and expertise to NCOs and career enlisted personnel. Educated, trained, and experienced NCOs and enlisted personnel are critical to the ability to exploit technology, and sustain high tempo operations. Israel recognizes the need for a strong, well-trained force of other ranks, although it faces increasing problems in getting the level of training it needs because of its heavy reliance on conscription. Syria has done a poor job of developing well trained and professional NCOs and technicians, and has generally done a poor job of training junior officers and forcing them to work closely with enlisted men in training and technical tasks. Egyptian manpower management and training policies have been erratic. There are some good Egyptian units, but in broad terms, Egyptian NCO, technician, and junior officer cadres are poorly paid and their training and technical level is significantly lower relative to Israel than it was during 1971–1974. Jordan is the only Arab state which has consistently emphasized the development of a cadre of high quality NCOs and technical personnel, and Jordan has lacked the funds and equipment to approach Israel's recent levels of training and proficiency.

- *High degree of overall readiness*: Military readiness is a difficult term to define since it involves so many aspects of force capability. Western forces entered the Gulf War, however, with two great advantages. The first was far more realistic standards for measuring readiness and ensuring proper reporting. The second was adequate funding over a sustained period of time. Israel emphasizes overall readiness while its neighbors tend to emphasize force size or major weapons procurement. Syria has not been able to fund full-scale modernization and high overall standards of readiness since the mid-1980s. Jordan used to emphasize readiness over force size, but can no longer afford high overall force readiness. Egypt maintains higher readiness standards for its best US-equipped units, but has low force-wide readiness.

THE LIMITS OF ISRAEL'S QUALITATIVE "EDGE"

At the same time, Israel is going through a major debate over its own weaknesses and vulnerabilities, and the importance of Israel's qualitative advantages should not be exaggerated. There are serious debates over the quality of Israel military leadership, training, and readiness. There are inherent limits in the IDF's present structure, imposed by limited financial conscript forces, and a low ratio of actives to reserves.

Israel's experience against the Hizbollah has shown that the IDF cannot win a decisive victory in dealing with unconventional warfare, politically dominated low-intensity and guerrilla conflicts, urban warfare, and other specialized types of conflict. Israel has little strategic depth and room for maneuver, and faces a significant risk of urban and mountain warfare. The Arab states are more aware of many of their own weaknesses and are unlikely to attack under the conditions where they are most vulnerable.

The Israeli list of vulnerabilities and weaknesses is different from that for Arab forces, but it still can have an important impact in virtually any contingency.

- *Sudden or surprise attack*: Israel is dependent on strategic warning, timely decision making, and effective mobilization and redeployment for much of its military effectiveness. Egypt and Syria achieved a level of strategic and military surprise during their initial attacks in October 1973 that confronted Israel with its most serious threat of defeat to date, and remains one of the most significant achievements in modern warfare. Some key lessons that Arab states are likely to draw from both the October War and Desert Storm are the potential advantage of sudden and decisive action, and the potential value of exploiting the problems Israel faces in mobilizing and deploying its forces. Any attack that succeeds in its initial objectives before Israel can mobilize gives an Arab attacker significant advantages. New developments in surface-to-surface missiles and weapons of mass destruction are constantly making Arab countries capable of such decisive actions. Furthermore, attack can come from Iran, Iraq, or states further from Israel's borders.[280]

- *Saturation*: There is no precise way to determine the point at which mass, or force quantity, overcomes superior effectiveness, or force quality—historically, efforts to emphasize mass have been far less successful than military experts predicted at the time. Even the best force, however, reaches the point where it cannot maintain its "edge" in C4I/battle management, air combat, or maneuver warfare in the face of superior numbers or multiple threats. Further, saturation may produce a sudden catalytic collapse of effectiveness, rather than a gradual degeneration from which the Israeli Defense Force could recover. This affects forward deployment, reliance on mobilization and reliance on defensive land tactics versus preemption and "offensive defense."

- *Dependence on reserves and warning*: Israel cannot afford to maintain an active force structure large enough to defend against an all-out Syrian attack, much less a contingency that includes Egypt. Israel is dependent on both warning and acting on that warning in time to mobilize and deploy its reserve. As the events of October 1973 demonstrate, warning is not a certainty. Israel's reliance on reserves also creates growing problems at a time when forces require more and more advanced training to take advantage of advanced military technology. Israel faces a major challenge in reshaping its reserves so they can maintain Israel's qualitative edge.

- *Taking casualties*: War fighting is not measured simply in terms of whether a given side can win a battle or conflict, but how well it can absorb the damage inflicted upon it. Israel is highly sensitive to casualties and losses. This sensitivity may limit its operational flexibility in taking risks, and in sustaining some kinds of combat if casualties become serious relative to the apparent value of the immediate objective.

- *Inflicting casualties*: Israel's dependence on world opinion and outside support means it must increasingly plan to fight at least low and mid-intensity conflicts in ways that limit enemy casualties and collateral damage to its opponents, and show that Israel is actively attempting to fight a "humanitarian" style of combat.

- *Low-intensity combat*: Israel has had more recent practical experience in low-intensity conflict than the US, but it cannot exploit most of its technical advantage in such combat—because low-intensity wars are largely fought against people, not things. Low-intensity wars are also highly political. The battle for domestic Israeli, Palestinian civilian, and Western public opinion is as much a condition of victory as killing the enemy. The outcome of such a battle will be highly dependent on the specific political conditions under which it is fought, rather than Israeli capabilities.

- *Hostage taking and terrorism*: Like low-intensity warfare, hostage-taking and terrorism present the problem that the IDF cannot exploit their conventional strengths, and must fight a low-level battle primarily on the basis of infantry combat. HUMINT is more important than conventional military intelligence, and much of the fight against terrorism may take place in urban or heavily populated areas.

- *Urban and built-up area warfare:* Israeli military forces have never come fully to grips with the problem of urban warfare. They did not perform particularly well in urban warfare in Egypt and Lebanon, and have far fewer technical advantages in fighting in populated areas. Western forces are not trained or equipped to deal with sustained urban warfare in populated areas during regional combat—particularly when the fighting may affect large civilian populations on friendly soil.

- *Extended conflict and occupation warfare*: Not all wars can be quickly terminated, and many forms of warfare—particularly those involving peacekeeping and peace enforcement—require prolonged military occupations. Israel faces severe economic problems in fighting any war or major confrontation that compels mobilization for more than a few weeks, and has nothing to gain from prolonged military occupation of enemy territory. It also faces major risks in any conflict where it would have to attempt to attack into Egypt or Syria. Both nations have defensive capabilities that are much better than their offensive capabilities. Syria demonstrated the risks Israel faces in an extended campaign during the 1982 fighting in Lebanon. Hizbollah and Amal forces drove Israel out of Lebanon in June 2000.

- *Weapons of mass destruction*: The UN Coalition emerged from Desert Storm claiming a victory over Iraq in destroying its weapons of mass destruction that, in fact, it never achieved. It had firmly identified only two of 21 major Iraqi nuclear facilities before the war, struck only eight by the time the war ended, did not properly characterize the functions of more than half the facilities it struck, and never completed effective BDA. Coalition strikes on Iraqi chemical facilities left 150,000 chemical munitions intact—most of which suffered far more from design defects than Coalition attacks. Iraq's biological warfare capabilities seemed to have been evacuated, and remain largely intact. The Coalition "Scud Hunt" failed and never produced a confirmed kill. It is far from clear that Israel has any better ability to target and destroy Syrian and Egyptian chemical and biological warfare facilities and capabilities, and it has only limited ability to defend effectively against Syrian missiles or less conventional delivery means.

- *Dependence on foreign assistance and technology transfer*: Israeli dependence on US military and economic assistance, and technology transfer, constitutes a strength in many ways. US military assistance and technology transfers have played a key role in giving Israel its present "edge," and in allowing Israel to simultaneously develop its economy and maintain strong military forces. Israel's ties to the US also provide an intangible security guarantee that no Arab state can ignore. While the US has no formal commitment to Israel's security, the 1973 war showed that the US will re-supply Israel in an emergency, and the process of American diplomacy has focused on Israel's security virtually since the existence of Israel as a state. It is doubtful that the US would ever allow Israel's naval and air lines of communication to be threatened or allow any combination of Arab navies to dominate Israeli waters. It is also doubtful that the US would stand by if Israel faced an existential threat as the result of either conventional defeat or attacks with weapons of mass destruction. At the same time, dependence is dependence. Aid levels can vary and the need to pay close attention to US views and public opinion does impose significant constraints on Israel's possible tactics and levels of escalation.

- *The inability to win an ultimate grand strategic victory*: Israel faces the problem that no military victory can—in itself—bring it security. Israel can—and has—used military force to defeat Arab forces, and occupy Arab territory. It has the nuclear capability to threaten and destroy the existence of given regimes. As all of the Arab-Israeli wars have shown, however, each military victory breeds new threats and new problems. As Israel's 1982 invasion of Lebanon has shown, victory and occupation cannot force lasting new political structures on even a weak and divided Arab state. The Intifada has shown that Israel cannot ignore the political costs of even decisive military victory in the territory it already occupies. No amount of military superiority can compensate for one central strategic reality that affects all the trends in the Arab-Israeli balance. Only a mix of peace supported by a stable balance of deterrence—Sun Tsu's "perfect victory" of winning without fighting and not Clausewitz's strategy of destroying enemy forces—can bring Israel lasting security.

5

Comparing Arab–Israeli War Fighting Capability

The preceding analysis of quantitative and qualitative factors that shape the military balance can provide considerable insight into the factors that must be considered in moving from peace to arms control, or the possible war fighting consequences if peace fails. At the same time, no assessment of total national military strength—regardless of the mix of quantitative strength and qualitative factors used in the assessment—can accurately measure the military balance, describe its impact on the peace process, or predict the nature and outcome of future wars.

Aggression, deterrence, and defense are not products of how leaders and nations calculate total national force strengths. They are products of different calculations about the outcome of war fighting in given contingencies. An analysis of contingency capabilities, however, presents serious analytic problems of its own. Crisis and war fighting behavior has rarely been predictable.

While foreign policy analysts sometimes talk about the end of the Cold War as having created new sources of conflict, the reality is very different. Roughly 20 to 30 low-intensity civil wars and international conflicts have gone on every day since the end of World War II. The end of the Cold War did not create a "new world disorder." All it did was remove the West's central focus on the East-West conflict, and expose an underlying reality that was already there.

Such conflicts also are not just endemic to the Middle East. Some 900 conflicts took place between 1945 and 1988, ranging from low-level civil wars to major combat.[281] During this period, a total of 105 states intervened in other states and territories a total of 131 times. At least 639 military interventions were serious enough to involve clashes between armed forces. A total of 269 conflicts escalated to the point where they had some international and military significance.

While the Middle East is often thought of as a key center of such conflicts, these clashes and conflicts were spread throughout the world. There were eight in the Caribbean, 15 in Central America, 14 in South America, 12 in Europe, 13 in West Africa, 18 in Central Africa, 11 in the Horn of Africa, 20 in East Africa, 14 in Southern Africa, 15 in North Africa, 14 in the Persian Gulf, 27 in the Arab-Israeli confrontation states and the Levant, 13 in Southern Arabia, four in Southwest Asia, 17 in East Asia, 20 in South Asia, 26 in Southeast Asia, and three in Oceania.[282] It is impossible to accurately estimate the total deaths that these wars caused—from direct casualties, famine, and disease, but the total almost certainly exceeds five million lives.

It is equally important to note that most of these wars and crises occurred with only limited warning, and took on a form that at least one of the nations involved never intended or predicted. They involved very different kinds of forces and levels of intensity, and the opponents often had very different types of forces and technology. The pattern of the conflicts within given nations and sub-regions has also varied sharply over time, and low-level conflicts have sometimes suddenly escalated into major struggles.

Ironically, state-of-the-art technology is not necessarily the key to victory. Two of the most publicized wars, Vietnam and Afghanistan, were decisively lost by technologically advanced modern forces fighting against relatively primitive forces organized more for guerrilla combat than regular war. In addition, the losing side in both Vietnam and Afghanistan spent most of each war reporting that they had won every battle. We need to remember this when we consider the role of new technologies in combat, and the "revolution in military affairs."

Further, the outcome of such wars has had little to do with pre-war force ratios and there has so far been little correlation between the use of modern technology and the number of casualties in a conflict—although this may be a result of the fact that most recent wars involving high technology have been wars in which one side had a major lead over the other. The outcome of war has been determined more by skill than size. While there have been some exceptions, conflicts involving prolonged infantry combat and guerrilla warfare have tended to be far more bloody than direct conflicts between states which both employ high technology forces. Similarly, "static" wars of attrition between ground forces that have been fought under tactical conditions that prevented decisive battles have tended to be far more bloody than quick and decisive wars of maneuver.

Sun Tsu warned nearly 2,500 years ago, "there never has been a protracted war from which a country has benefited," and this fact is reflected in part by Arab-Israeli conflicts. The 1948 War was a prolonged infantry conflict, and was the most costly of all the Arab-Israeli conflicts. The 1982 War involved high levels of military technology, but most Israeli and Syrian losses took place after Israel had achieved its initial objectives in a war of maneuver and the conflict had bogged down in a prolonged slow-moving effort to occupy parts of Lebanon. In contrast,

Table 5.1
Losses in the Arab–Israeli Wars: 1948–1982

A. 1948-1973 Wars

	1948		1956		1967	
	Arab[a]	Israel	Arab	Israel	Arab	Israel
Killed	4,800	4,500	1,000	189-210	4,296	750-983
Wounded	25,000	15,000	4,000	899	6,121	4,517
Total[b]	40,000	21,000	5,000	1,088-1,109	10,417	5,267-5,500

Equipment Losses

Main Battle Tanks[c]	–	–	30	40	965-1,000	200-394
Aircraft	–	–	215-390	15-20	444-500	40
Combat Vessel	–	–	2	0	?	0

B. Land, Air, and Naval Losses: 1973 War

	Israel	Total Arab	Egypt	Syria	Jordan	Iraq	Other Arab
Casualties							
Killed	2,838	8,528	5,000	3,100-3,500	28	218-260	100
Wounded	8,800	19,549	12,000	6,000	49	600	300
Prisoners/Missing	508	8,551	8,031	370-500 500	–	20	?
Equipment Losses							
Main Battle Tanks[d]	400-840	2,554	1,100	1,200	54	100-200	?
Other Armor	400	850+	450	400	–	?	?
Artillery Weapons	?	550+	300	250	–	?	?
SAM Batteries	–	47	44	3	–	–	?
Aircraft	102-103	392	223	118	–	21	30
Helicopters	6	55	42	13	–	?	?
Naval Vessels	1	15	10	5	–	–	–

Table 5.1 (continued)

C. Land, Air, and Naval Losses: 1982 War

	Israel	Total Arab	Syria	PLO
Killed	368	3,000	1,000	2,000
Wounded	2,383	6,000	3,000	3,000
Total	2,751	11,000	4,000	7,000
Prisoners of War	7	-	250	-
Tanks, OAFVs, and				
Trucks	-	-	-	2,600[e]
Tanks	150	-	350-400	-
OAFVs	175	-	350-400	-
Artillery Weapons	-	-	-	1,700[e]
Aircraft	2	92	92	0
Helicopters	3	-	?	0
Munitions (Tons)	-	-	-	6,000[e]

Notes: a. Includes only Egyptian casualties in fighting with Israel. Equipment losses include total Egyptian losses, including those to France and the United Kingdom.

b. Prisoner of war and missing data are too unreliable to be included.

c. Lower end of range often reflects losses that could not be returned to combat by the end of war. Higher end shows "kills" that put tank temporarily out of combat.

d. Lower end of range often reflects losses that could not be returned to combat by the end of war. Higher end shows "kills" that put tank temporarily out of combat.

e. Totals are equipment and munitions captured by Israel. No total is available for combat losses.

Sources: Estimates for 1948-1973 losses differ widely from source to source, which is the reason for not comparing all data in the same section of the table. The figures shown are adapted from Trevor Dupuy, *Elusive Victory*, New York, Harper and Row, 1978; Chaim Herzog, *The Arab-Israel Wars*, New York, Random House, 1982; and from various editions of the *Born in Battle Series*, Tel Aviv, Eshel Drammit.

The estimates for 1982 are drawn from Anthony H. Cordesman, *The Lessons of Modern War, Volume I*, Boulder, Westview, 1990, pp. 152-153, data provided by the IDF Spokesman and Embassy of Lebanon, and Yezid Sayigh, "Israel's Military Performance in Lebanon, June, 1982," *Journal of Palestine Studies*, Vol. 13, No. 1 (Fall 1983).

high technology conflicts like the Gulf War and October War have tended to be quick and decisive and to produce far fewer casualties. Table 5.1 shows the size of these casualties, and illustrates the lack of any predictable outcome from given wars and pre-war force ratios.

This pattern could easily change in future Arab-Israeli conflicts. There have been two major restraints on the use of high technology in most conflicts since the end of World War II that may not apply in the future. The first is that states have made only very limited use of weapons of mass destruction. The second is that most high technology conflicts have not involved major attacks on non-military targets in population centers or national populations. As Iraq's use of gas warfare has demonstrated, however, nations are capable of using this technology with far less discrimination.

In short, such discussions can illustrate potential war fighting capability, but cannot predict the point at which current tensions will explode into a future conflict. No amount of static analysis, modeling, or war gaming can reliably estimate the outcome of conflicts between forces that have not fought a major conflict since 1973 or 1982. Their composition, training, C^{4}I/BM systems, weapons and technology, and objectives have changed so much in character since that time, that many aspects of Arab and Israeli war fighting capabilities are uncertain.

No one can predict whether the dominant weapon will be the tank or the rifle, the chemical weapon or the car bomb. No one can predict timing, duration, or intensity of existing wars or new ones. War simply is not predictable in terms of its timing, duration, intensity, and cost. This is a truth that far too many political leaders and military planners ignore. History provides a myriad of examples of unpredictability.

These analytic problems are compounded by the fact that it is not possible to translate many of the negative trends in the balance into a particular contingency based on clear military incentives to fight a given type of conflict. The fact that the overall trends in the Arab-Israeli balance, and the success of the peace process, currently favor deterrence has an ironic side effect. If war does occur, it may be the result of miscalculation or a serious failure in crisis management. This can lead to highly unpredictable patterns of conflict and escalation.

At the same time, neither the current state of the military balance nor the peace process provide any assurance that more predictable forms of war will not occur. It is possible to make rough subjective estimates of the potential outcome of a range of conflicts that illustrate the current and near-term risks in the balance, as well as possible considerations for force planning. While such estimates are scarcely a means of predicting the future, they do highlight the importance of key trends in the balance and illustrate how the character of a future war could differ from a past conflict. They also help illustrate the fact that wars involving Israeli and Palestinian forces, or Israel and different combinations of the Arab ring states have very different probabilities and are likely to have very different outcomes.

6

The Israeli "Edge": Strengths and Weaknesses

Israel's current and future war fighting capabilities set the baseline for any analysis of possible scenarios simply because Israel is the one common denominator in a very wide range of potential conflicts. These capabilities have already been discussed in broad terms, but the details of Israel's strengths and weaknesses are critical to understanding what might happen in future conflicts, and the trends in Israel's forces are shown in Table 6.1.

Many of Israel's strengths have now shaped the regional military balance for several decades. Israel's weaknesses, however, are compounded by the fact that Israel faces a wide range of new challenges. It must deal with the growing threat of long-range missiles and weapons of mass destruction, not only from Syria but from powers like Iran, Iraq, Libya, and indirectly, Pakistan. It faces asymmetric threats of low-intensity combat like the possibility of a new Intifada with the Palestinians and the war it has fought with the Hizbollah in Lebanon. It must deal with the continuing threat of terrorism from the opponents of the peace process.

Like its Arab neighbors, Israel must decide how to restructure its forces to deal with the peace process and how to revise its strategy doctrine and force structure. In Israel's case this translates to a restructuring of its forces to deal with withdrawals from the West Bank and Gaza. It also means planning for possible withdrawals from the Golan, and for possible arms control and confidence building measures. This means adjustments to deployments and basing, changes in C^{4}I/BM systems, and changes in readiness. Additionally, Israeli security forces must adjust to a new and dynamic role, one that demands far more concern over dealing with the Palestinian security services. Inevitably, it means finding ways to optimize Israel's deterrent and war fighting capabilities within the structure of any

Table 6.1
Force Trends in Israel

Category/Weapon	1975	1980	1985	1990	1995	2000	2001
Manpower							
Total Active	156,000	169,600	142,000	141,000	172,000	175,000	172,500
(Conscript)	(125,000)	(125,300)	-	(110,000)	(138,500)	(138,500)	(107,500)
Total Reserve	275,000	-	370,000	504,000	430,000	430,000	4250,000
Total Actives &							
Reserves	400,000	400,000	512,000	645,000	602,000	605,000	597,500
Paramilitary	9,000	9,500	4,500	6,000	6,050	6,050	8,050
Land Forces							
Active Manpower	135,000	135,000	104,000	104,000	134,000	134,000	130,000
(Conscripts)	(120,000)	(120,000)	(88,000)	(88,000)	(114,700)	(114,700)	(85,000)
Reserve Manpower	240,000	-	310,000	494,000	365,000	365,000	400,000
Total Reserve &							
Active Manpower	375,000	375,000	414,000	598,000	499,000	499,000	530,000
Main Battle Tanks	2,700	3,050	3,600	4,288	4,095	4,300	3,900
(Static & In Storage)	-	-	-	-	-	-	
AIFVs/Armored							
Cars/Lt. Tanks	365	80+	300	400	408	408	408
APCs/Recce/Scouts	3,000*	4,000*	4,000	5,980	5,980	5,980	5,900
WWII Half-Tracks	*	*	4,000	4,400	3,500	500(4,000)	500
ATGM Launchers	-	-	-	-	1,005	1,005	1,300
SP Artillery	660**	228	488	816	1,150	1,150	855
Towed Artillery	**	950	570	579	400	400	520
MRLs	**	-	180	175	160	160	198
Mortars		900+	900+	-	2,740	2,740	6,440
SSM Launchers	-	-	-	112	100+	48-96	48-96
AA Guns		900+	900+	850+	850	850+	850+
Lt. SAM Launchers	-	-	-	945+	945+	1,298	

Table 6.1 (continued)

Category/Weapon	1975	1980	1985	1990	1995	2000	2001
Air & Air Defense Forces							
Active Air Force Manpower	16,000	38,000	28,000	28,000	32,000	37,000	36,000
	-	-	-	-	-	-	
Active Air Defense Reserve Manpower	4,000	9,000	9,000	9,000	20,000	20,000	20,000
Air Defense Command Reserve	-	-	-	-	-	-	-
Aircraft							
Total Fighter/FGA/Recce	481	535	684 (90)	553	449	459(250)	446(250)
Fighter	0	0	0	0	0	0	0
FGA/Fighter	275	265	402	393(+83)	373(+120)	405	405
FGA	200	200	130	121(+14)	50(+150)	25	25
Recce	6	14	15	14	22	10	10
Airborne Early Warning (AEW)		4	4	4	4	6	6
Electronic Warfare (EW)		-	10	26	36	37	37
Fixed Wing						37	37
Helicopter						0	0
Maritime Reconnaissance (MR)		0	0	5	3	3	3
Combat Capable Trainer	25	74	123	48	14-24	19	26
Tanker	2	2	2	7	8	8	6
Transport	54-98	58-70	45	58	47	36	37
Helicopters							
Attack/Armed/	-	6	58	74	116	133	133
ASW/SAR	-	-	37	2	2	6	6
Transport & Other	97	145	92	143	145	160	160
Total	97	151	187	219	263	299	299
SAM Forces							
Batteries	15	15	15	17	17	28	28
Heavy Launchers	90	60	60	68	68	79	79
Medium Launchers	-	-	-	-	-	-	-
Naval Forces							
Active Manpower	5,000	6,600	10,000	9,000	6,000-7,000	6,500	6,500
Reserve Manpower	1,000	3,400	10,000	1,000	10,000	5,000	5,000
Total Manpower	6,000	10,000	20,000	10,000	16,000-17,000	11,500	11,500

Table 6.1 (continued)

Category/Weapon	1975	1980	1985	1990	1995	2000	2001
Submarines	2	3	3	3	2	4	2
Destroyers/Frigates/							
Corvettes	0	0	6	0	3	3	3
Missile	0	0	6	0	3	3	3
Other	0	0	0	0	0	0	0
Missile Patrol	18	22	24	26	23	14	12
Coastal/Inshore Patrol	36	38	45	37	40	36	32
Mine	0	0	0	0	0	0	0
Amphibious Ships	0	3	3	0	1	1	1
Landing Craft/Light							
Support	10	6	9	9	4	4	4
Naval Forces							
Fixed-wing Combat							
Aircraft	0	0	0	0	0	0	0
MR/MPA	0	3	0	0	0	0	0
ASW/Combat Helicopter	0	0	0	0	0	0	0
Other Helicopters	-	-	-	-	-	-	-

Notes: * Includes all types of other armed vehicles except tanks and self-propelled artillery.

**Includes all medium and heavy self-propelled and towed weapons.

Source: Adapted by Anthony H. Cordesman from data provided by US experts, and the IISS, *Military Balance.*

new arms control and confidence building measures. It also means considering how to deal with the possibility that Israel may formally declare that it is a nuclear power and that it has significant chemical and biological weapons capabilities.

Israel's peace with Egypt, Jordan, and the Palestinians requires careful attention to reinventing its strategy and doctrine. Israel must structure its war fighting concepts around the fact that preemptive attacks or the occupation of Arab territory may threaten its peace settlements. At the same time, any new occupation of Lebanon, Palestinian territory, and/or Syria can create as many problems as it solves—forcing Israel into the role of an occupation army in nations where its primary goal must be to establish peace and secure borders.

Changes in military technology affect critical aspects of Israel's force planning. Advanced military systems often require more training and proficiency than is possible with conscript forces, and impose training costs that make retention a critical issue. Joint warfare and demanding combined arms combat also require more experience and training than is possible with conscript forces and usually means that officers, senior NCOs, and key technicians require several years' more experience in demanding training and exercises than in the past. This not only presents problems in terms of conscripts, it raises growing questions about the value of reserve forces in many critical military roles and tasks.

The speed and intensity of modern combat requires new levels of proficiency in night and poor weather warfare, and new types of sustainability and logistic support. These too require added training and professionalism. They also require faster speeds of reaction and new mobilization systems when they depend heavily on reserves.

Israel may not achieve a stable and secure peace on all its borders, but it no longer is a garrison state that is threatened by every neighbor. Social and political attitudes are changing. A constant focus on security has given way to a concentration on economic development and conditions of life. This inevitably affects the prestige of the armed forces and the willingness of Israelis to serve as conscripts, to volunteer for military service, and to stay in the armed services. It also increases Israel's traditional concern over casualties. At least one Israeli official believes that Israel's biggest threat is now the deep social divisions between Arabs and Jews, secular and religious Jews, and left and right, rather than a lack of weaponry or resources.[283]

KEEPING THE "EDGE"?

Israel continues to emphasize many of its classic strengths: Leadership, demanding exercise training, promoting on the basis of competence, maintaining a relatively young and aggressive officer corps, and insisting on forward leadership. It uses training that develops battlefield initiative, and it allows flexibility in executing orders. In contrast, Arab forces often require highly detailed written orders and systems of accountability in order to ensure that orders are obeyed, and commanders are taught not to deviate from orders when presented with new battlefield opportunities or unanticipated problems. Most exercises have predetermined outcomes that sharply limit the initiative of the officers involved, and make it impossible to determine the relative effectiveness of the forces involved.

Israeli Military Technology, Equipment Buys, and Arms Transfers

Israel makes good use of advanced military technology, and of its access to arms transfers from the US. Israel's current equipment holdings are summarized in Figure 6.1. Once again, however, it is quality that counts..

Figure 6.2 shows the historical trend in arms deliveries to Israel, and the decline in the value of such sales since the peak buildup in the mid-1980s, following Israel's invasion of Lebanon. The decline after 1990 reflects the broadening of Israel's peace with its Arab neighbors, and the reduced need to compete against nations like Syria and Iraq following the breakup of the Soviet Union and the destruction of much of Iraq's military capability during the Gulf War.

Figures 6.3 and 6.4 show the sources of Israel's arms imports, and Figure 6.5 provides the necessary context in terms of comparative military expenditures. Israel's arms imports reflect the impact of massive US military aid, and that the US has long been Israel's dominant arms supplier. Much of this equipment is more advanced than the equipment the US deployed during the Gulf War, and Israel has the industrial base to modify much of this equipment to meet its specialized tactical needs, as well as supplement it with a wide range of Israeli-designed equipment and munitions. In addition, Israel is able to take advantage of virtually all of the upgrades the US military services develop as part of their multi-stage improvement programs (MSIPs).

Israel has done more than procure high technology equipment. While some Arab states focus on the "glitter factor" inherent in buying the most advanced weapons systems, Israel has given the proper weight to battle management, sustainability, and systems integration. Israel integrates technology into its force structure in ways that emphasize tactics, training, and all aspects of technology rather than relying on force strengths and weapons performance.

There are, however, some Israeli experts that feel Israel is not spending enough of its own funds on research and development. A Defense Ministry committee headed by Major General Moshe Peled examined Israel's spending on its defense industries and reported in December 1999. It concluded that Israel was spending some three times as much on defense R&D a decade earlier, and only 8% of its defense budget—versus about 13% in the US. The committee was particularly concerned with underspending on programs like intelligence and reconnaissance satellites.[284] Israel's dependence on US technology has also led to a long series of arguments over whether Israel is selling US-based technology to nations like China.[285] At one point, the US State Department notified Congress that Israel had sold China US Patriot and advanced avionics technology. It did not, however,

Figure 6.1
Israeli Major Operational Military Equipment in 2001

Land Forces

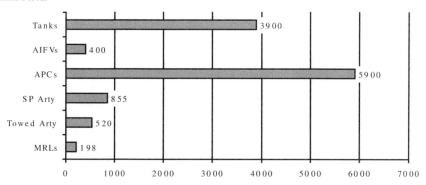

Air Forces

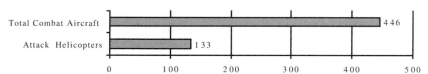

Naval Forces

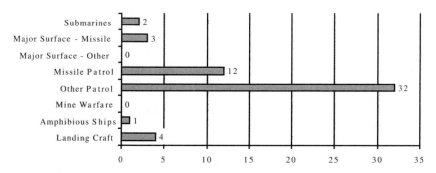

Source: Prepared by Anthony H. Cordesman, based upon the IISS *Military Balance* and discussions with US and regional experts.

provide supporting evidence and there has been no public confirmation of other charges.

ISRAELI FORCE TRENDS

Israeli force trends have long reflected an emphasis on force quality as well as force quantity, and Israel has often been willing to trade numbers for quality when

Figure 6.2
Israeli Arms Deliveries: 1985–1996
($97 Constant Millions)

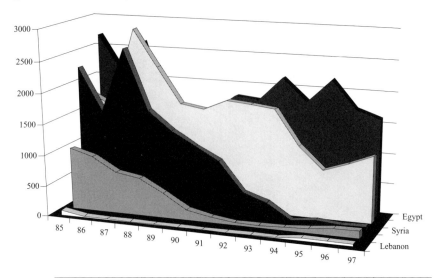

	85	86	87	88	89	90	91	92	93	94	95	96	97
▫ Lebanon	79	16	13	13	6	2	6	3	11	11	52	41	40
▨ Jordan	1013	912	686	619	414	176	91	44	43	53	83	122	130
▪ Syria	2278	1585	2613	1643	1339	1113	906	432	302	53	93	61	70
▫ Israel	1785	1585	2874	2275	1704	1640	1812	1774	1728	1163	802	940	1100
▪ Egypt	2690	2105	2613	1390	1217	1522	1812	1774	2159	1798	2174	1728	1600

Source: Adapted by Anthony H. Cordesman from US State Department, Bureau of Arms Control,
   World Military Expenditures and Arms Transfers, GPO, Washington, various editions.

it felt this could provide it with a more effective force. This involves a constant
series of trade-offs between force numbers and force quality, however, and Figure
6.5 shows that neither are cheap. Furthermore, Israel faces growing problems in
making trade-offs between manpower numbers and high quality, combat-effective
active manpower in a climate where funds are sharply restricted. Israel may have
outspent the individual Arab states by a significant margin, but there have been no
major increases to offset the steadily higher real cost of advanced military
technology. While total spending has not dropped significantly, Israeli military
spending has dropped from 19.1% of the GDP in 1982, to 11.2% in 1991 and to
9.7% in 1997.

   Money will remain a major issue, in spite of US military assistance. The cost of
modern military technology and weapons is rising far more quickly than the
average rate of inflation. As the Israeli force trends in Table 6.1 show, this means
force quality often has to be traded for force quantity, and that additional trade-offs
have to be made in deciding just what military technology is both critical and

Figure 6.3
Israeli Arms Agreements and Deliveries By Major Supplier
($Current Millions)

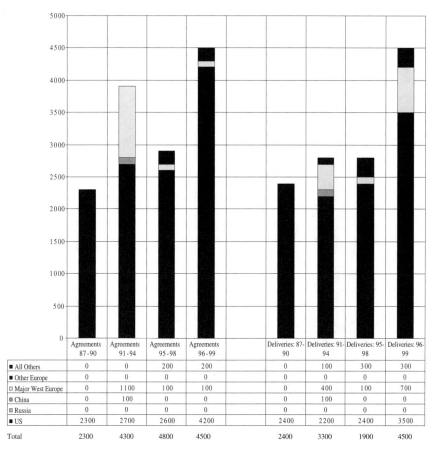

	Agreements 87-90	Agreements 91-94	Agreements 95-98	Agreements 96-99		Deliveries: 87-90	Deliveries: 91-94	Deliveries: 95-98	Deliveries: 96-99
■ All Others	0	0	200	200		0	100	300	300
■ Other Europe	0	0	0	0		0	0	0	0
▢ Major West Europe	0	1100	100	100		0	400	100	700
▨ China	0	100	0	0		0	100	0	0
▨ Russia	0	0	0	0		0	0	0	0
■ US	2300	2700	2600	4200		2400	2200	2400	3500
Total	2300	4300	4800	4500		2400	3300	1900	4500

Notes: Includes Gulf states, Arab-Israeli states, North Africa, and Yemen.
0 = less than $50 million or nil, and all data rounded to the nearest $100 million.

Source: Richard F. Grimmett, *Conventional Arms Transfers to the Developing Nations,*
Congressional Research Service, various editions.

affordable. This problem is compounded by rising training costs, more expensive
facilities and logistics, and by a growing need to replace conscripts and military
professionals with career professionals. The end result is that Israeli forces are
being reshaped by debate over the need to change Israel's strategy, to create a
"smaller but smarter" conventional force structure, and to deal with the growing
threat of proliferation and long-range missiles.[286]

Figure 6.4
Trend in Supplier's Share of Israel's Arms Market Before and After Gulf War
(New Arms Sales Agreements in $US Current Millions)

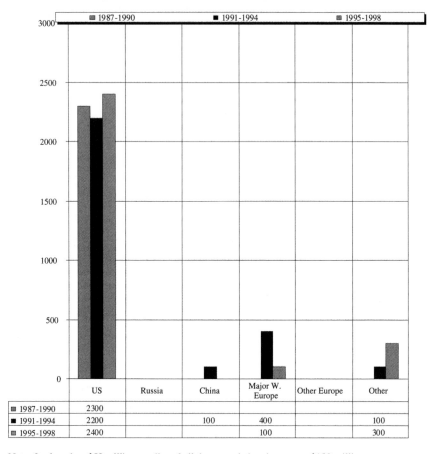

	US	Russia	China	Major W. Europe	Other Europe	Other
1987-1990	2300					
1991-1994	2200		100	400		100
1995-1998	2400			100		300

Note: 0 = less than $50 million or nil, and all data rounded to the nearest $100 million.

Source: Adapted by Anthony H. Cordesman from Richard F. Grimmett, *Conventional Arms Transfers to the Developing Nations*, Congressional Research Service, various editions.

Israeli Military Manpower

Israel modeled its post-independence manpower system partly on Swiss practices and partly on its own experience in the pre-state period of operating a large underground militia. The IDF created an army in which, in the words of a former chief of staff, Israelis are, in effect, "soldiers on eleven months' annual leave." Traditionally, men as well as women have performed two or three years' active duty in the army. This has constituted a rite of passage to adulthood and full

Figure 6.5
Cumulative Trends in Arab-Israeli Military Spending in Constant Dollars: The Decline in Arab Forces as a Share of Total Spending: 1985–1995 (In $US 1997 Constant Millions)

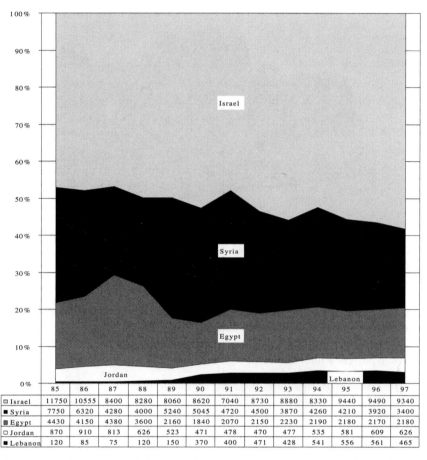

	85	86	87	88	89	90	91	92	93	94	95	96	97
□ Israel	11750	10555	8400	8280	8060	8620	7040	8730	8880	8330	9440	9490	9340
■ Syria	7750	6320	4280	4000	5240	5045	4720	4500	3870	4260	4210	3920	3400
■ Egypt	4430	4150	4380	3600	2160	1840	2070	2150	2230	2190	2180	2170	2180
□ Jordan	870	910	813	626	523	471	478	470	477	535	581	609	626
■ Lebanon	120	85	75	120	150	370	400	471	428	541	556	561	465

Source: Adapted by Anthony H. Cordesman from US State Department, Bureau of Arms Control, *World Military Expenditures and Arms Transfers*, Washington, GPO, Table I, various editions.

membership in society. Reserve service has, for decades, been a constant feature in the life of Israeli men through their forties and fifties.[287]

Israel's recent manpower trends are shown in Figure 6.6. These trends reflect Israel's long-standing emphasis on conscripts and reserves to make up for a lack of active manpower. Even so, the active manpower Israel does maintain is very expensive and has come to account for nearly half of the defense budget. Israel has already converted some of its force structure into a smaller "peacetime" force that

Figure 6.6
Israeli Active and Total (Active & Reserve) Army Manpower: 1973–2001
(Men and Women in Uniform)

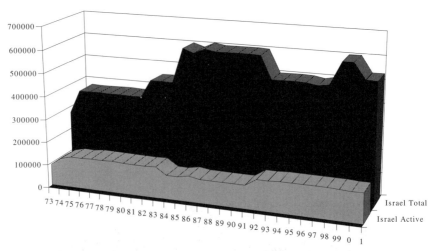

Source: Adapted by Anthony H. Cordesman from the IISS, *Military Balance*, various years. Some
   data adjusted or estimated by the author.

reflects its peace with Egypt and Jordan, but it still faces many challenges in
finding the right balance between conscripts, reservists, and career actives. The
end result has been a continuing debate over both the quantity and quality of IDF
"person power" within Israel.

The Problem of Peace and Bureaucratization

Some of this debate focuses on the fact that today's IDF lacks the combat
experience that Israeli forces had in the past, and charges that the IDF is becoming
bureaucratized and has eased its standards. At least some retired Israeli commanders are increasingly critical of what they see as a shift away from a "war fighting" to
a "garrison" mentality, and to an over-reliance on technology. Other critics feel
that the morale of the IDF still suffers from the impact of the Intifada and the
quagmire in Lebanon. They charge that the peace process is leading to a relaxation
of standards, that there is a tendency to shift to more defensive tactics, that
conscript and reserve training are no longer as demanding as in the past, and that
the government is taking peace dividends at the expense of overall readiness and
capability.

Since 1982, the IDF has faced the challenge of remaining a lean combat-capable
force in peacetime. It has not always done well. Israeli studies in the early 1990s
found that a once lean IDF had acquired 600 colonels performing headquarters and
staff functions by the early 1990s.[288] While repeated efforts have been made to

pare down headquarters and support manning since that time, many Israeli experts still feel the IDF is too "bureaucratic" a force and new efforts were made to cut the size and rank structure of the IDF's center headquarters facilities in 1999.[289]

The Problem of Conscription

Restructuring and resizing conscription is an even more important challenge. In theory, Israel conscripts all physically able young men who are not eligible for a religious exemption for three years and drafts many women for 20 months. In practice, Israel's manpower pool has increased by 20% since 1990 alone, and it now has too many men to draft them all and retain them for three years.

Although a future drop in immigration might change this situation, Israel currently no longer needs to be a 'garrison state' and rely on universal conscription. As a result, the number of secular young Israeli males expecting to be drafted dropped from 93% in the mid-1980s to 75% in the mid-1990s. The percentage of males actually conscripted dropped 88% even in the early 1980s, and dropped to 83% by the mid-1990s—with another 15% receiving early discharges for various reasons.[290]

These figures show that IDF still calls up most eligible young men, but it has reduced the number of men and women called up for conscript service. Nevertheless, many IDF planners argue that the IDF is still forced to take too many conscripts even though conscription is waived for a larger and larger percent of eligible people.[291] The end result is that the IDF is examining plans for either a selective draft or increased reliance on career soldiers.[292]

These proposals are not necessarily popular with the Israeli public. Many Israelis feel that reducing the draft will shatter national unity. They are already angry that ultra-orthodox Jews are exempt from the draft, contributing to the growing tensions between secular and religious Jews. In response, the army created a new, all-religious platoon, which it hopes will help to ease tensions and to solve this particular draft problem.[293]

The IDF also faces a growing problem in terms of conscript morale and motivation. In broad terms, a substantially smaller number of young Israelis now want to serve as conscripts or go on to career service. Consequently, the IDF faces growing retention problems, and there are fewer volunteers for ordinary combat units, as distinguished from elite units or rear area and headquarters functions where military service is relatively easy.[294]

This decline in motivation seems to be most pronounced among the native-born youth from a secular and middle-class background that supply the majority of the IDF's annual intake.[295] The IDF has been compelled to take a number of steps to try to reduce this decline in motivation, including improving the monetary compensation conscripts receive. Since 1995, conscripts attached to combat units have received almost double the remuneration paid to rear echelons.[296]

At the same time, Israel has less and less need for total numbers as its technology improves and it focuses on force quality. This has proven to be true even though the

IDF's conscripts serve for a relatively long time and are well-educated, particularly in comparison with the manpower intake of its Arab neighbors. By the early 1980s, some 65% of Israelis aged 18–24 had some secondary education and an additional 20% had some post-secondary schooling.

The IDF still pays its conscripts relatively little by US standards—it only costs about $16,500 to feed and clothe a male conscript for three years. Nevertheless, the total training, pay, and support costs are now high by Israeli standards. They limit what the IDF can pay for equipment and career actives. The IDF still calls up most eligible young men, but it has reduced the number of men and women called up for conscript service and is examining plans for either a selective draft or increased reliance on career soldiers.[297]

The IDF has not resolved any of these issues regarding conscription. They also are not simply military issues. They interact with a host of political issues in Israeli society, ranging from military service as a nation-builder to ethnic and religious divisions within Israeli society. They also involve questions about economic opportunity. In the past, those who served in the IDF were eligible for low cost loans and had an advantage in getting many jobs. It is not clear that the same advantages can be offered if many young Israelis do not serve because they are not needed.

The Uncertain Role of Women

The need for skilled, experienced, and well-trained manpower raises additional questions about the role of women. The IDF does have three general officers that are women, and a significant number of women serve in support roles.[298] Female conscripts now serve for only 20 months, however, and Israel can only afford to put them through expensive training programs if they then provide at least a year more of service. The IDF already only takes about 50% of eligible women for military service, and many feel that they do make work projects that waste their time.[299]

This situation may change because Israel's Supreme Court upheld a female conscript's claim to be granted entry into the IAF's pilot training course in 1995, although no women now serve as pilots on active duty.[300] Israel also announced in August 1999 that it was seeking approval from the Knesset to open 100 new job classifications to women starting in July 2000. While women were still precluded from serving outside Israel, the additional classifications included NBC disposal, bomb disposal, active duty in the Corps of Artillery, and service as tank crew members in the Armored Corps. The IAF would also accept women as electronic warfare operators. The Navy would allow women to serve on coastal combat vessels, but not on submarines.[301]

At the same time, military forces are not the proper forum for social experiments, and women must be properly assigned to use their skills in real jobs and on a competitive basis. The challenge the IDF faces in finding the proper role for women is not one of dealing with "sexism," but rather finding the best way to use an even larger pool of potential conscripts in a wider range of roles.

The Changing Role of Reserves

Similarly, reserve manpower now requires much more frequent and sophisti-cated training, and career forces need to be kept out of headquarters and support functions and be given full "warrior" training. This has led the IDF to cut the maximum age for reserves in combat units from 54 to 42 and to reduce the number of times a year that most reserve units are activated. The IDF has cut its reserve training hours by some 50% since 1990.

Even so, Israeli reserves have absenteeism of up to 20% in some combat units and 40% in some support elements. Many reservists now evade service for reasons that various IDF surveys have found to be false, and one Israeli newspaper claimed in 1996 that half of those in the reserves would not serve unless they were forced to do so. Further, some estimates claim that a small cadre of about 10% of the reservists perform about 90% of all active duty for reserve forces.[302]

There are reports that the IDF is examining plans to cut the size of its reserves from around 430,000 in the mid-1990s to future levels below 230,000. These force cuts could achieve considerable savings, but they will inevitably increase Israel's vulnerability to saturation through sheer mass, and raise questions about Israel's ability to fully mobilize against an all-out Syrian or broader attack.[303] Ultimately, Israel may need fewer and better reserves, but cannot eliminate its strategic dependence on reserve manpower.

Israel's real challenge is to choose the right kind of reservists and use them over shorter periods. Many reservists who have left recent service can still be of great value if they received adequate training in service, undergo continuing call-ups and training, and remain fit. In many cases, such reservists will have a higher average level of training and proficiency than most actives for several years, simply because they have more experience. They tend to rapidly decline in relative effectiveness after that time, however, and mobilizing vast numbers of aging men (and potentially women) who lack at least several weeks of truly demanding refresher and exercise training can waste assets just as easily as inflating the number of conscripts.[304]

Furthermore, some IDF officers feel that reliance on full mobilization to defend against an all-out attack now has steadily less contingency value. They feel reliance on reserves puts too high a premium on strategic early warning to permit the mobilization of forces before the outbreak of war. At the best of times, this has confronted Israel's leaders with an unenviable choice: mobilize the reserves and be safe, but strain the economy and the army's citizen-soldiers, or continue normal deployments and run the risk of surprise attack. Today, Israel may get little strategic warning of a major clash with the Palestinians or a sudden clash on the Golan. Peace with Egypt, Jordan, and the Palestinians gives it far less ability to preempt, and future wars may be determined as much by missiles as by manpower. Once again, the changing nature of warfare has a major impact on manpower needs and policies.

Morale, Motivation, and Money

Other problems affect those who do serve. Morale, conscript conversions to career status, retention of career personnel, and willingness to serve in the reserves have all been affected by the Intifada, the peace process, the protracted struggle in southern Lebanon, and competition from the private sector. They have also been affected by growing religious and ethnic tensions. For example, during the 1960s, some nine out of ten young Israelis who were offered promotions to platoon commander of paratroops in the regular army would accept. This figure has slowly dropped to one in ten in 1995. Reserve call-ups are shorter and less demanding, and some of the IDF's best regular officers now leave early for civilian careers.[305] Even pilot retention has become a growing problem.

The end result is that the IDF has also had to steadily increase the pay and privileges of actives and reservists. They now receive payment commensurate with the priority of the national service they perform and this trend is a departure from the past view of military duty as a civic obligation, for which the monetary rewards were limited.[306] These new costs explain the seeming paradox in which manpower costs have risen as manpower numbers have dropped. The total cost of all types of personnel rose from 19% of the IDF budget in 1984 to 29% in 1991, and 48% in the mid-1990s.[307]

Willingness to Serve and Willingness to Take Casualties

There are equally important questions about the peace process, the kind of service the IDF should perform, and willingness to accept casualties. The IDF now has a steadily increasing percentage of relatively conservative officers and other ranks who take a somewhat hard line on the peace process. It does not face any crisis in enforcing the terms of the peace accords, dealing with terrorism, or taking military action against the Palestinians.

Even so, service involving military or security action against the Palestinians in the West Bank and Gaza is not popular and few members of the IDF have any desire to see a repetition of the Intifada in any form. These problems interacted with the general unpopularity of service in Lebanon, in dealing with the South Lebanese Army, and fighting the Hizbollah. The IDF had to be careful to screen the troops it used in Lebanon, and severely limit the use of conscripts and reservists. This is as much to ensure a high level of professionalism as for morale reasons, but it reflects a general need to minimize "police" and "security" functions. Any operations that depend on the character of low-intensity combat now present a growing manpower problem.

The issue of casualties is a complex one, which again involves issues that go far beyond manpower. Israel has always been willing to take casualties when it is essential to Israel's survival. Somewhat ironically, Israel proved it was willing to take very high casualties during the fighting in 1948, when it had the least manpower relative to enemy forces. It also demonstrated in 1956, 1967, 1973, and 1982 that a reluctance to take casualties did not mean a reluctance to take substantial military risks, and that its commanders fully realized that over-caution can increase net casualties over time just as much as recklessness.

At the same time, a more secure Israel is increasingly unwilling to take casualties for non-existential fighting and risk manpower in training and low-intensity combat. Furthermore, high technology forces with soldiers that costs hundreds of thousands of dollars to train, and years to give proper proficiency, require tactics and strategies that preserve military manpower for purely military reasons. This requires complex new trade-offs between exposing men and using technology, protection and firepower, and tactical aggressiveness and risk that the IDF is now debating at many levels.

This situation has been complicated by progressively less social and media acceptance of casualties at any level. Every accident and combat loss in Israel tends to provoke a short fire storm of media second-guessing and some officer is virtually always found to be to blame—even if the IDF does not draw such a conclusion. Parental complaints and interference have become chronic and there is much of the same tendency to demand "perfect war" as in the US.

Some very experienced IDF officers do feel this inhibits realistic training and tactical innovation and risk taking, with the end result that more losses are sometimes taken in bureaucratic and media safety by going by the book than would otherwise be the case. They note that adequate training will inevitably impose demands that force accidents and fatalities, and that demanding joint and combined operations lead to friction that in turn leads to accidents and losses from friendly fire. Also, some forms of combat—like urban warfare, the campaign in Lebanon, and sudden clashes against Palestinians—must be conducted under conditions where Israel lacks a decisive edge and cannot avoid casualties without remaining on the defensive.

Numbers versus Quality versus Money

It seems likely that it will take at least half a decade for the IDF to establish lasting policies and plans regarding future numbers of Israel's active career soldiers, the conscript intake, the size of Israel's reserves, and the future role of women in Israel's combat forces. Career soldiers are expensive, but almost all combat troops must now have very high levels of technical and operational training to make use of Israel's technological edge and exploit it to the fullest possible degree. Israel must pay for the career personnel it needs almost regardless of the cost, but this means low-quality active, conscript, and reserve manpower consumes assets that the IDF cannot afford to waste.

A shift to a much larger career force would also raise questions regarding recruitment and retention. Career forces are expensive at the best of times, but if Israel becomes a society where young men and women are not obligated to serve as conscripts, it will be hard to obtain an initial intake. Similarly, high levels of retention require progressively higher incentives for those with skill and experience, which is essential to maintaining force quality and making expensive training cost-effective. A major shift in the percentage of career personnel in the IDF entails a significant shift from a focus on "patriotism" to a focus on the military as a "profession"—particularly since military service has lost some of the popular status it had at a time when Israel was perceived as being constantly under siege.

Israeli Land Forces

Israel is actively debating missions, organization, and structure of its land forces as part of a general review of its strategy. While it has not taken firm decisions on many issues, it does seem to be examining ways to integrate its maneuver units, sensors, and battle management systems into an integrated system for its managing forces. It is examining low cost options for creating a "digital battlefield" and the application of Internet-like concepts to the management of land forces.[308]

The IDF increasingly emphasizes joint operations in its training and doctrine, and seems likely to develop fully mobile and air mobile infantry units that match or exceed the maneuver capability of its armored forces. It is still a 12-division force, of which some nine divisions are manned by reserves. However, it seems to be moving towards a more flexible task force concept in which the independently controlled infantry brigades could be placed under the overall control of the armored divisions in order to enhance armored combat under fire-saturated battlefield scenarios. The resulting units could operate independently in a number of scenarios.

Israel also is one of the few armies in the Middle East with anything approaching the advanced training facilities that the US Army has at Fort Irwin or that the US Marine Corps has at Twenty-Nine Palms. The Israeli army has a computer corps called Mamram.[309] It has a training center at Mabat in the Negev desert, which uses a modern computerized training range, an advanced command and control simulator, an area-weapons effect system, and over 1,000 MILES II instrumented player outfits for infantry, anti-tank weapons, and armored vehicles. There are other MILES systems for infantry and special forces training, and some form of equipment is used to simulate helicopter and fixed wing aircraft in joint training. The facility is scarcely as advanced as its US counterparts, but has well over $50 million worth of equipment.[310]

The IDF seems to want to restructure its support and logistic elements to allow more rapid support of maneuver operations at the brigade or task force level. Such forces would be re-equipped with a mix of specialized armored and tracked support vehicles like the Achsarit, Puma, and Nakpadon to provide both better mobility and some degree of NBC protection.

The IDF is examining different ways to man "high alert" forces. Some include larger numbers of career actives and fewer reserves. Others seem to involve more use of attack helicopters, air support, and long-range firepower systems like rockets with advanced conventional warheads. A high degree of emphasis seems to be placed on improving joint operations at every tactical level.

Money, however, is a major issue. Israel does not face recapitalization problems that approach those of Jordan or Syria, but it does have problems. It cannot afford to convert its armor to a coherent force of first-line systems. Israel's 1100 Merkavas and 600 M-60A3s are the only tanks which are likely to have a decisive "edge" over the T-72—although some analysts argue that its Magach 7s are equal to the M-60A3 in many areas. Roughly 1,100 of Israel's 3,800 tanks are relatively low-grade Centurions, T-54s, T-55s, or T-62s.[311] Israel is expanding its Merkava force, but some sources indicate rates as low as 60 per year.

Israel has had to choose between funding improved tanks and funding improvements of other armored fighting vehicles. As a result, it has few modern AIFVs to supplement its tanks. It only has a small number of Nagmashots and Achzarits—although large numbers of its 5,900 M-113s have been converted from APCs to AIFVs. While Israel has built up a massive modern artillery force of some 1,150 self-propelled weapons and more than 100 modern multiple rocket launchers—and is acquiring the US MLRS—it is still dependent on large numbers of obsolete half-tracks for support vehicles and reserves.

The IDF also has not been able to modernize its artillery forces at the rate it desires. It is steadily upgrading its battle management and targeting systems, self-propelled artillery force, and is enhancing its long-range strike capabilities with advanced multiple rocket launchers, but it would still like to acquire much larger stocks of advanced and specialized ammunition, upgrade to weapons like an upgunned version of the M-109 and Soltam Slammer self-propelled 155-mm howitzers, and increase its number of MLRS and other advanced multiple rocket launchers. At this point, however, it may have to concentrate on upgrading its targeting sensors like radars and UAVs and battlefield management systems.

The IDF has also faced a continuing strain because of the need to train and equip for both major conventional wars and asymmetric conflicts. As is described in later chapters, its long involvement in Lebanon forced it into an exceptionally expensive military effort that required specially tailored forces and large amounts of specialized equipment. While it withdrew from Lebanon in 2000, it still faces a major potential challenge from the Hizbollah, Amal, and Palestinians along its northern border. The outbreak of a second Intifada on September 29, 2000, created a new asymmetric threat in Gaza and the West Bank, and even within Israel. Long before this fighting actually began, the IDF was forced to create a mock Palestinian hill town and train continuously for low intensity combat against the Palestinians in urban areas. It also had to train large numbers of troops and reservists to protect Israeli settlements.[312]

Israeli Air Forces

Israel has long stressed joint warfare, and combines its skills in land maneuver warfare with one of the most effective and modern air forces in the world. It has systematically improved its conventional attack—or "soft strike"—capability. It now has many of the advantages US airpower enjoyed during the Gulf War, plus a wide range of subsystems and weapons tailored to deal with threats like Syria and the special conditions in its theater of operations. The IAF has recently absorbed 20–24 F-15Is, 50 surplus USAF F-16s, additional AH-64s, 10 Black Hawk helicopters, advanced new UAVs, and ongoing Israeli upgrades to existing aircraft like the F-15, F-16, and Phantom 2000.[313] The IAF announced on July 18, 1999, that it had decided to buy 50 F-16s from the US for approximately \$2 billion.[314]

Israel may be the only Middle Eastern air force that combines all of the elements of modern air power into an efficient and integrated whole. Israel has advanced combat, electronic warfare, intelligence and targeting, and battle management aircraft. These are supported by a host of advanced and special purpose weapons systems, combat electronics, unmanned airborne vehicles, night and all weather combat systems, and command and control facilities.

The Israeli Air Force (IAF) has an unequalled record in air-to-air combat. It destroyed many of its opponent's aircraft on the ground in the 1967 war and then scored 72 air-to-air kills over the rest. It destroyed 113 Egyptian and Syrian aircraft in air-to-air combat during the war of attrition, and killed 452 Egyptian, Syrian, Iraqi, and Jordanian aircraft during the October War in 1973. It killed at least 23 Syrian aircraft between 1973 and 1982, and killed 71 fixed-wing aircraft during the fighting in 1982. It shot down three Syrian fighters between 1982 and 1992. While it has lost 247 aircraft in combat since the beginning of the 1948 war, only 18 have been lost in air-to-air combat. In contrast, Arab forces have lost at least 1,428 fixed-wing and rotary-wing aircraft in combat, and 817 have been lost in air-to-air combat.[315]

The IAF is aided in such missions by access to advanced US air-to-air ordnance and air-to-ground weapons. Israel is also one of the few countries capable of creating advanced chaff, electronic warfare, and electronic supporting measures and its own guided air weapons. The Python has long competed with the US AIM-9 as one of the most advanced infrared guided air-to-air missiles available. The IAF feels that its Python 4 offers unique advantages in terms of range and the ability to target enemy aircraft over a wide range from both the front and the rear.[316]

Israel has modern versions of the IHawk, surface-to-air missiles, advanced Patriot surface-to-air missiles with limited anti-tactical ballistic missiles, and its first deployments of Arab anti-theater ballistic missiles. Israel is the only country in the Middle East with the technical resources to steadily modernize and improve the capability of its electronic warfare and reconnaissance aircraft. At the same time, Israel has the C^4I/BM, training, night warfare, electronic warfare, support, sustainability, and other specialized qualitative capabilities necessary to exploit the revolution in military affairs. Its superior technology is fully supported by superior tactics and training, and this gives it all of the qualitative advantages over Syria that were discussed earlier.

Israeli pilot and aircrew selection and training standards are the highest in the Middle East and some of the highest in the world. Nearly 90% of those who are selected as possible pilots do not make the grade as fighter pilots. Israel has a ruthless selection process to keep its pilots at a high standard. It promotes on the basis of performance, rather than seniority. High quality pilots and aircrews now serve in a reserve capacity after leaving active service, giving Israel a significant ability to expand its combat air strength in wartime—particularly with attack aircraft. El Al, the national airline, can be mobilized immediately for transport and resupply missions and to provide added technical personnel, as can skilled workers in Israel's defense industries.

The Israeli Air Force has over two pilots per combat aircraft versus less than one in most Arab air forces. It is equipped with first line aircraft like the F-15 and F-16. It continues to emphasize training and has one of the most advanced combat training systems in the world, as well as the advantage of US training centers. The IAF's excellence in pilots is supported by excellence in the human dimension at all levels. Some Arab air forces have good training standards for a limited to moderate number of their pilots, but the IAF has the most demanding pilot training and performance standards of any air force in the Middle East. In fact, initial selection for pilot training is so demanding that the IAF has attrition levels approaching 90%. The IAF has equally demanding standards for maintenance, logistics, command and control, intelligence and targeting, and all of the other functions necessary to maintain effective air operations.

In addition, Israel has developed a reserve system that requires exceptional performance from its air force reservists. There are no reserve squadrons in the IAF, and all squadrons can operate without mobilization. However, about one-third of the air crew in each squadron are reservists. Reserve aircrews train 55–60 days a year, and fly operational missions with the squadron to which they are assigned. In the event of a call-up, the reserve air crews and operations support personnel report first, and then support personnel for sustained operations. About 60% of the IAF reserves are in air and ground defense units.

In contrast, other Middle Eastern forces are weakened by their failure to enforce rigorous selection procedures for assignments other than combat pilot, and by their failure to create a highly professional class of non-commissioned officers that are paid, trained, and given the status necessary to maintain fully effective combat operations. In most cases, these problems are compounded by poor overall manpower policies and promotion for political and personal loyalty. Other Middle Eastern air forces also tend to be weakened by a failure to see command and control, intelligence and targeting, high-intensity combat operations, and sustainability as being equal in importance to weapons numbers and quality. While Egypt, Iraq, and Saudi Arabia have moved towards the idea of force-wide excellence in supporting an overall concept of operations, they still have a long way to go before approaching Israel's level of capability.

While the Israeli air defense system is scarcely leak proof—a fact it demonstrated some years ago when a defecting Syrian pilot flew undetected deep into Israeli air space—a fully alert Israeli air defense is capable of coordinating its sensors, fighters, and land-based defenses with a level of effectiveness that no other Middle Eastern air force can approach.[317] Israel has a better overall mix of systems, better trained personnel, and a far better ability to integrate all its assets with its own technology and software than any other Middle Eastern air force.

Israel's advantages in strategic and long-range offensive operations are even greater. The IAF is the only air force in the Middle East that is seriously organized for strategic attacks on its neighbors. Other Middle Eastern air forces may have long-range strike aircraft, effective munitions, and even a limited refueling capacity. They are, however, essentially amateurs in using their assets to inflict strategic damage on an enemy nation or in conducting effective long-range strategic strikes.

Israel has the ability to strike deep into the Arab world, and has greatly improved its long-range strike capability since its attacks on Osirak in 1981 and on Tunisia in 1985.[318] It has the F-15I and greatly improved refueling capability, targeting capability, stand-off precision munitions, and electronic warfare capability. Israel could probably surgically strike a limited number of key targets in virtually any Arab country within 1,500 nautical miles of Israel, and could sustain operations against western Iraq. It would, however, probably be forced to use nuclear weapons to achieve significant strategic impact on more than a few Iraqi facilities, or if it has to simultaneously engage Syrian and Iraqi forces.

Nevertheless, several Arab forces now have combat elements with moderate to high capabilities. Two Arab air forces—Egypt and Saudi Arabia—have relatively good training standards, modern combat aircraft, and advanced battle management systems like the E-3A and E-2C. The IAF faces growing problems over the cost of advanced new aircraft, munitions, sensors and battle management systems.

Modernization will continue to present financial challenges. The IAF must eventually upgrade its remaining older fighters with up to 100 new fighters like F-15Is, F-16 Block 60s, or JTF. It would like to buy up to 42 more AH-64 Apache or AH-64D Longbow attack helicopters, including at least one more squadron equipped with Longbow long-range, all-weather, fire-and-forget, anti-armor missiles.[319]

The IAF is considering creating a separate attack and assault helicopter force under the new Field Forces Command that would include its attack helicopters.[320] The IAF is also seeking new transport helicopters and additional helicopters tailored to special forces missions. It is upgrading its 42 existing CH-53 helicopters to reduce their vulnerability. These upgrades include titanium rotor blades, improved night vision, improved communications, Popeye air-to-ground missiles, and more advanced mission planning systems.[321] This will extend their life, but at some point the IAF will also have to modernize its helicopter lift capabilities.

More generally, the IAF faces two evolving challenges that could erode its present almost decisive superiority. One is the risk that a nation like Syria will acquire large numbers of truly modern surface-to-air missiles like the S-300 or S-400, and the necessary command and control system and sensors. The other is proliferation. Long-range missiles and weapons of mass destruction pose a risk to all of Israel's conventional forces, but they pose a particular challenge to Israel's air forces because they (a) provide the ability to strike directly at Israel's densely packed main operating bases, and (b) bypass its air combat capabilities. Israel's very strengths drive its opponents towards asymmetric warfare, and to use proliferation as a way to exploit its remaining areas of vulnerability.

Israeli Naval Forces

The overall capabilities of the Israeli Navy have already been discussed in detail. Sea power is not likely to be a significant issue in any near-term Arab-Israeli conflict—particularly one between Israel and Syria. Israel has massive naval superiority over Syria and Lebanon. It also can probably use joint naval-air operations to win superiority over Egypt except in Egyptian waters.[322]

It should be noted, however, that Israel has effectively ended its naval presence in the Red Sea, and has had to make trade-offs that have reduced its naval capabilities. It has had to cut its procurement of new Sa'ar corvettes from eight to three and may have problems in funding all three Dolphin-class submarines. It also had to cut back substantially on its Barak ship defense missiles—although these are armed with Harpoon and Gabriel ship-to-ship missiles.[323] The practical issue is whether this matters given the strategic partnership between the US and Israel and US dominance of the sea. It simply is not clear that any of Israel's naval trade-offs erode its edge in any probable contingency.[324]

The most interesting conceptual challenge is whether Israel will decide to try to equip its Dolphins with nuclear-armed missiles as has been suggested by General Israel Tal. Quite frankly, this seems to be extremely difficult given the small size of the Dolphin and the fact the Harpoon missiles now on the Dolphins are small missiles with 130-kilometer ranges. It might be possible to create some kind of deck-mounted pod for one long-range missile, but even an advanced cruise missile with an advanced boosted warhead would probably still have to be small enough to be restricted in range if Israel attempted to fit it to the Dolphin. A surface-launch from a Sa'ar 5-class missile might be substantially easier.[325]

Israeli Long-Range Missiles and Weapons of Mass Destruction

Since the 1960s, Israel has been an undeclared nuclear power that relies primarily on a conventional war fighting "edge." The nature of Israel's nuclear capabilities are discussed later in this analysis, but Israel cannot ignore the fact that even the best conventional "edge" is not an effective defense or deterrent against proliferation in Syria and Egypt, or in nations like Iran, Iraq, and Libya. This is particularly true because the threats can be asymmetric in many ways.

Israel is already beginning to deploy the Arrow missile as a point defense against theater ballistic missiles. The Arrow is not, however, capable of theater-wide defense against advanced long-range ballistic missiles, and Israel would require some form of layered defense to be effective. Israel's small territory also makes it highly vulnerable, and it is essentially a "one-bomb country" in the sense that it is uncertain whether Israel could reconstitute itself as a viable nation after a major nuclear strike on Tel Aviv.

This not only creates a potentially impossible requirement for "leak-proof" missile defenses, it also creates the problem that unconventional delivery means such as smuggling a weapon into Israel, a short-range cruise missile launch from a ship near the coastline, or the remote detonation of a weapon in a shipping container entering Haifa harbor, could bypass extremely expensive defense systems.

Asymmetric attacks with advanced biological weapons will also offer a steadily more attractive approach to attacking Israel's population and existence as a state. As Chapter 15 describes in some detail, small amounts of agent, which are extremely difficult to detect, can kill a high percentage of the population of the greater Tel Aviv area simply by being disseminated from high-rise buildings with the right wind patterns. Tests of this type of delivery using particulates the same size as dry Anthrax agent proved successful long before the signing of the Biological Weapons Convention in 1975. It is possible that such an attack could not only go on without being detected, but that Israel might not be able to firmly and conclusively identify its attacker for some time—creating serious questions about retaliation.

Israeli strategic and arms control literature is filled with various proposals to deal with these problems, but many ultimately depend on the kind of trust and political climate that is more a function of the success of the peace process than the military balance. One of the difficulties with most proposed solutions is that they may simply end up in "squeezing the balloon." They will contain or limit part of the problem, but drive opponents to use other tactics, weapons of mass destruction, and delivery systems in the areas where deterrence and defense are weakest. Much then depends on the willingness of potential opponents to take major risks in areas where there are few precedents and the end result of given actions remains unknown, but military history is essentially the history of the willingness to take such risks.

These issues affect Israel's "edge" in two fundamental ways. First, it must deal with the new threat posed by weapons of mass destruction and the widely different ways in which they can be delivered and employed. Second, however, there is the constant risk that conventional combat can transition to the use of such weapons, and that the very size of Israel's edge in conventional weapons encourages its potential enemies to proliferate and employ asymmetric warfare. Furthermore, there is no way to predict the point at which a conflict may begin to involve some use of weapons of mass destruction or the way and intensity with which they will be employed.

At present, Israel's nuclear superiority and superior long-range strike assets, and Arab and Iranian unwillingness to risk employing such weapons, limit the risk that Israeli deterrence will fail, and war fighting and the military balance are still likely to be determined by conventional forces. There is no guarantee, however, that this will be the case in the future, or even that the rate of proliferation in the region will be determined by the main players in the Arab-Israeli arms race, as distinguished from players in the arms race and tensions in the Gulf.

ISRAELI CRITICISMS OF THE IDF AND FEARS THAT ISRAEL IS LOSING ITS "EDGE"

For all of its strengths, Israel is scarcely "10 feet tall." In addition to the broad qualitative problems that have just been discussed, there have been major struggles for resources within the IDF between services and branches of a given service, debates over strategy and tactics, and arguments over organization and command. Indeed there have been severe problems that the Israeli military has had to face regarding budgetary issues and the allocation of the budget to the IDF.[326]

Table 6.2 illustrates some of the major concerns expressed by officers in the IDF regarding these budget issues. These debates have been interwoven with the broader debates in Israeli society. They have taken place over trading territory for peace or preserving control of the Occupied Territory, the Intifada and relations with the Palestinians, civil versus military spending, economic reform, and Israel's relations with the US and its dependence on US aid.

For more than a decade, the IDF has had to debate a number of basic military issues:

- The trade-offs between force size and force quality, particularly in an era where financial problems and manpower quality problems tend to force an emphasis on "small and smart" forces.
- The trade-offs between full-time active professionals, conscripts, and reservists, given the steadily increasing demands modern military equipment places on training exercises and experience.
- The extent to which Israel's land forces should be capable of decisive sudden offensive action against Syria—or any combination of Syria, Lebanon, and Jordan—as distinguished from being capable of defending Israeli territory by halting any invasion.
- The specific contingencies Israel should plan for, and the level of capability of Syria, or Syria in combination with other Arab states, to carry out a surprise attack on Israel across the Golan or through Lebanon and/or Jordan.
- The level of readiness Israel needs within its land and air forces to deal with a surprise or limited warning attack.
- The ability of the Israeli Air Force and advanced conventional technology to inflict a decisive series of strikes on the Syrian military and Syrian economy within a few days using conventional weapons and without a major land offensive, or to inflict similar damage on any other neighbor.
- The level and type of force that should be used to control Palestinian activity within Gaza and the West Bank, what level of compromise or relations with the Palestinian Authority will preserve Israeli security, and what war fighting options to plan for if peace should fail.

- The amount of territory that might be traded for peace, and the conditions under which such a trade might take place, and the resulting options for force planning.

- The level of forces and other resources, if any, that Israel should commit to south Lebanon.

- How the IDF should plan to deal with contingency of hostile regimes in Egypt and Syria, and a catastrophic breakdown in the peace process.

- How to deal with other regional threats like Iran, Iraq, and Libya.

- The extent to which Israel needs a "blue water" navy that is capable of securing its lines of communication and long-range strike capability, as distinguished from securing its coasts and immediate waters.

- The level of anti-tactical ballistic missile defense that can be provided, and the broader question of how to create the defensive aspects of a counterproliferation strategy.

- The level of defense Israel can provide its soldiers and population against biological, chemical, and nuclear weapons.

- The extent to which Israel should reveal or publicize its nuclear and missile capabilities. The changing structure of deterrence as nations like Iran, Iraq, and Syria continue to proliferate.

- The extent to which the Israeli defense industry should be encouraged both to reduce dependence on the US and to create a technology base for advanced exports overseas.

- The level of resources that should go to defense versus absorbing the Russian Jews and economic development.

The Wald Report

These debates have taken place at every professional level within the IDF, and have been going on through the early 1980s. Perhaps the most serious public critique of Israeli capabilities, however, is still the one written by Colonel Emanuel Wald. In a report originally written for Israel's then chief of staff Moshe Levi, Wald argued that the IDF had evolved into a slow-moving and feuding bureaucracy that lost the 1982 war. Wald claimed the IDF was unable to effectively manage combined arms and combined operations, and make effective decisions at the command level.[327]

The more severe critics of the IDF claimed that it has lost its professionalism at the command and combat unit level, has fragmented along branch and service lines and promoted according to bureaucratic performance. They claimed the IDF no longer realistically trained its officers for combat, and could not effectively coordinate or manage operations at the corps level. Other charges include questions about the readiness of conscripts and reserves and their ability to operate modern military technology. They stated that the IDF could not sustain a high tempo of continuous operations, wastes resources on a large and unproductive staff and support structure, and inflates its number of high-ranking officers. They charged the IDF could not effectively maneuver to engage all of its forces with the enemy, had limited night combat capability, had uncertain ability to use its

Table 6.2
Israeli Concerns About Readiness and Force Quality

- Israel doubled its presence in Southern Lebanon to 2,000 men. In 1997 the reinforcement came as a response to an increasingly effective campaign by the Hizbollah. Nevertheless, the Hizbollah forced the Israelis to restrict their movements for fear of ambush, and then to withdraw from Lebanon. The "proxy war" in Lebanon imposed a major drain on Israeli resources.

- Reports like the 1997 report of the State Controller's office in the spring of 1997 stated there were serious deficiencies in the combat readiness of the IDF. The report said that training has deteriorated; many AFVs are not battle-ready; many air force helicopters have malfunctions; and that emergency stockpiles of weapons and ammunition have been depleted.

- Senior officers like Major General Matan Vilnai have expressed concern that most IDF combat troops spend less time preparing for war and more time occupied with anti-terrorist and other duties. Officers who have risen to field commands have only been involved in Lebanon and the Intifada. While this experience has exercised their basic skills, it has no relevance to their efficiency in modern war.

- The growing concern that older elements of the air force fighter fleet faces major fatigue problems. Geography and IDF operational philosophy involves more high-G loading than USAF fighters. Israeli-made 600-gallon jettisonable fuel tanks have increased stress of wing root sections. Israeli-designed weapon pylons and engine modifications also contribute to fighter fatigue. Due to fatigue there is a constant need within the IDF air force for new fighters and service life extension programs.

- Some officers complain that the IDF involvement in the peace negotiations has put it in an awkward and controversial position. This has embroiled the IDF in controversial issues such as withdrawal from the West Bank and the Golan Heights.

- Lt. General Amnon Shahak, the former Chief of Staff, warned in July 1997, that training days had been cut by two-thirds in recent years, and that civil defense against a chemical and biological attack by Syria was inadequate. Similar warning surfaced during the 1998 budget debates.

Source: Various media reports.

intelligence collection in effective battle management, and lacked the ability to set meaningful politico-military objectives for battle and pursue them to a meaningful conclusion.

The Barak Reforms

The IDF responded to many of these concerns and criticisms by steadily improving its use of technology, and by acting aggressively to take advantage of the lessons of the 1982 war and the Gulf War. It eliminated many career officer and civilian positions from the IDF—particularly in headquarters, support, and "bureaucratic" functions. It has reduced or phased out IDF functions, including the Training Branch, Women's Corps, Education Corps, and Gadna Youth Corps.

Several reforms took place after Lt. General Ehud Barak was appointed as Chief of Staff of the IDF on April 1, 1992. Barak immediately summoned 3,000 officers from Lt. Colonel to Major General to a meeting. He issued a message that the IDF had become too fat and over-manned, lacked sufficient rigor and training, needed to tighten discipline, had to focus on arming and training for the high technology battlefield of the 1990s, and had to plan to live within tighter resources. Barak then proceeded to slash headquarters and rear area support functions by 10–20%, cut paperwork, abolished some 30 out of 32 IDF publications, remove officers who failed in command exercises or who failed to react quickly to terrorism. He also cut reserve service and training to provide added funds for high technology modernization. Barak's changes came very close to many of those recommended by Wald.[328] His successors have supported similar reforms since that time.[329]

Reform Since Barak

Under Minister of Defense Yitzhak Mordechai, Major General Shaul Mofaz succeeded Wald as Chief of Staff of the IDF in July 1998.[330] In spite of a major budget crisis and political turmoil, Mofaz continued to streamline IDF headquarters and improve efficiency in 1999, most notably through his Zahal 2000 plan.

As a result, both efficiency and morale have improved since the early 1990s. Although there has been a decline in interest in the military, 86% of eligible young Israelis still served in the military in 1995, and service was still three years for men and 22 months for women. Elite combat units still get adequate numbers of volunteers in spite of arduous service conditions, and the number of Israelis who do not report for service has increased by only 1.5% over the last four years— including Israeli Arabs and those Orthodox Jews who refuse all military service.[331]

Many Israeli officers and experts feel that some of the more recent criticism of the IDF's conventional war fighting capabilities and readiness ignores both the reforms that have taken place since 1982, and the fact that the IDF is now a high technology force with different needs. They feel that modern combined arms and joint warfare training must emphasize different skills and technical competence over physical effort. They feel that Israel's technical edge necessarily requires a far more sophisticated support and administrative structure that past IDF forces, and that the kind of emphasis on aggressive armored warfare that was decisive during 1967–1973, must be modified to deal with different Arab forces, equipment, and tactics. They also feel that some reductions in military spending are justified given the high level of US aid, the limitations of the Syrian threat, and the success of the peace process.

Nevertheless, Table 6.2 summarizes a wide range of Israeli concerns that the IDF might be encountering new challenges and new situations for which it is not fully prepared. Many were raised in a report by the Israel State Controller's Office in May 1997—long after the Wald report and Barak reforms. The report indicated that the IDF could not simultaneously perform its present border security mission and prepare for war. It severely criticized the reserve training program, particularly the quality and experience of instructors, and the readiness of key active elements like the Golani brigade, which it said was no longer ready to fight a conventional war with Syria because of the burden of border defense. It said the IDF lacked sufficient transport helicopters, and had to upgrade some of its combat aircraft and the expense of the readiness of others. It criticized the lack of training, doctrine, and exercise experience in aircraft-helicopter operations, and reported that a spot-check of 103 main battle tanks in a reserve unit showed that they were not properly protected and combat ready. It also said that many AFVs might break down in the first two days of combat, and that the IDF lacked the trained personnel to maintain and store heavy weapons and other equipment.[332]

Some of this criticism was almost certainly exaggerated. It seems to have overstated the IDF's training and readiness problems for political purposes and to help increase its budget. Nevertheless, these criticisms and the ongoing budget debate led the Minister of Defense Itzchak Mordechai to state that the IDF was being crippled by underfunding, and needed $667 million dollars to bring it to acceptable readiness levels. Lt. General Amnon Lipkin-Shahak, then the Chief of Staff, called for more funds to deal with "intolerable gaps" in the IDF's ability to fight a conventional war.[333] The end result was that senior Israeli officers like General Itzchak Mordechai, Lt. General Amnon Lipkin-Shahak (the former Chief of Staff), Major General Matan Vilani (Deputy Chief of Staff of the IDF), and Rear Admiral Micha Ram (the former Commander of the Navy) have raised the issues and concerns listed in Table 6.3.

Israel's Continuing Strategic Debate

There is a broad consensus among Israeli planners that Israel must steadily evolve and improve its conventional war fighting strategy and force posture. Israel is less capable of using offensive maneuver and preemption to rapidly win a decisive land battle while many of its Arab adversaries are improving their destructive and lethal capabilities. Surface-to-surface missiles are becoming priority procurements in many Arab nations and with these acquisitions, weapons of mass destruction programs become more focused and developed.[334] The Intifada, the proxy war in Lebanon, and continued terrorist attacks all show that Israel faces a continuing problem with asymmetric warfare.

Many Israeli military planners indicate that Israel should now focus more on creating an effective land defense supported by advanced long-range strike capabilities. There are real questions about the value of conscripts and reserve forces with limited training and technical proficiency and the need to trade mobilization capability for increased high-technology regular forces. Counterproliferation has become a major issue. Early-warning systems and antiballistic missile programs are also the trends of the future.

Table 6.3
Israeli Concerns Over Israel's Military Edge: Views Expressed in Interviews with General Itzchak Mordechai (MOD), Lt. General Amnon Lipkin-Shahak (COS), Major General Matan Vilani (DCOS), and Rear Admiral Micha Ram (Former Commander of the Navy)

Egypt

- "Peace with contingency plans": Can never ignore Egyptian "front," but can never discuss it or publicly plan for it.
- Risk of breakdown of peace process; radicalization of Egypt.
- Parity in many aspects of equipment, particularly tanks, AFVs, and aircraft.
- Growing understanding of C^4I/BM, erosion of Israeli edge.
- Potential problem of Patriot/SA-10 upgrade of air defenses.
- E-2C, electronic warfare, F-16, BVR missile air defenses.
- Knowledge of US methods and tactics, experience gained in training with US forces.
- Lessons of Gulf War.

Hizbollah/Proxy War in Lebanon

- Improved ordnance and technology. ATGMs, SHORADs, long-range rockets, mines, night vision, radio control. Added Iranian shipments and Syrian support.
- Loss of edge in LIC. Near parity in casualties, with far more sensitivity to losses on Israeli side.
- Corruption and uncertain loyalty of much of SLA.
- Uncertain future of Syria: "Fourth front" under Syrian control?

Iran

- No Dongs, refueling, attacks on Israel.
- Nuclear "time window."
- Support of Hizbollah/PIJ.
- Ability to use commercial satellite technology.
- Targeting and strike challenge posed to IDF for preemption and retaliation.

Iraq

- Can strike Israel with missiles.
- Retention of WMD capabilities, future breakout.
- Retention of missiles and long-range strike aircraft.

Table 6.3 (continued)

Iraq

- Breakdown in peace process, rapprochement with Syria and/or Jordan.
- Ability to use commercial satellite technology.
- Targeting and strike challenge posed to IDF for preemption and retaliation.

Israel

- Breakdown of peace process; Palestinian despair.
- Problems in obtaining adequate manpower intake and retention: 1/3 no longer serve as conscripts. 15% get early out.
- Growing manpower costs.
- Caserne mentality, lack of aggressive edge. Conscripts compete to serve in rear areas, near home, not in prestige combat units.
- Bureaucratic problems: Colonels up by 17%, Brigadier Generals by 60%, Generals as a whole by 41%. High salaries and retirement bonuses for officers (Colonel earns $5,900 a month. Retirement bonus of $282,200 for Colonel as early as age 42).
- Loss of readiness due to funding issues. Dead-lined aircraft and armor, stockpiles down. Mordechai has publicly said it would cost $667 million in FY1998 to restore the IDF to proper readiness.
- Time problems grow in relying on mobilization and this creates windows of vulnerability.
- Shahak has warned of sharp decline in reserve training activity; loss of combat experienced cadres; poor reserve exercise performance and adaptation to new technology/C^4I/BM systems.
- Sensitivity to casualties.
- "Who's a Jew" divisions within Israel affecting military; Rabbis who interfere in operations dealing with settlements.
- Last war was 1973 (1982). Loss of generations with combat experience.
- Inadequate military spending.
- Inability to fund "necessary" upgrades of OAFVs/APCs and helicopter force.
- Loss of edge in stand-off attack capability, targeting, and electronic warfare?
- What comes after E-2C, current ECM/recce aircraft/UAVs?
- Underfunding of navy.

Table 6.3 (continued)

Israel

- Shift of resources to security missions; Morale problems in dealing with Palestinians.

- Vulnerability to attacks with WMD, particularly terrorism.

- Hobson's TABM: The financial cost of funding the Arrow versus the military risks of not having the Arrow.

- Lag in Satellite program.

- Uncertain future of defense industry; political interference in IDF force plans to serve needs of industry.

Jordan

- Breakdown in peace process, rapprochement with Egypt, Syria and/or Iraq.

- Uncertain political future: After King Hussein?

- Role in "new Intifada."

- Spoiler or added front role, particularly as gets new US equipment.

Libya

- Minor "Spoiler" role.

New Intifada

- Jibril.

- Rapid recruiting and training of suicide bombers.

- Hamas/PIJ.

- Palestinian Authority security forces turn on Israel.

- Trying to enforce isolation of Palestinian enclaves. Mid- to long-term LIC war similar to Northern Ireland.

North Korea

- No Dong missile.

Syria

- Fear Syria might make a lasting strategic shift away from the peace process.

- Proxy war in Lebanon.

- Shift of land forces to aid in sudden attack on Golan/Mt. Hermon "four hours from the border." Shift 14th Special Forces Division from Lebanon to Golan similar to steps taken in 1973.

Table 6.3 (continued)

Syria

- Build-up of armored forces (1,500 T-72s), risk of surprise attack, "Golan grab."

- Air force minor threat, but major improvement to SAM defenses could affect balance.

- Purchase of new missile craft and 27 naval attack helicopters.

- Scud Cs, No Dongs?

- VX gas.

- Chemically armed missiles: Volley fire against key Israeli targets?

- IDF estimate of at least 80 SSM launchers, many mobile and/or sheltered, and more than 1,000 missiles by 2000.

- Biological weapons?

- Ability to use commercial satellite technology.

- Targeting and strike challenge posed to IDF for preemption and retaliation in dealing with SSM/WMD threat.

Russia/Ukraine

- Potential sale of advanced aircraft, refueling capabilities, AWACS.

- Potential SA-10 system sale.

- Security of nuclear materials.

Saudi Arabia

- Purchase of submarines.

- Qualitative parity in air with Tornadoes, F-151, US support and training. Long-range strike and AWAACS/BVR capability.

- Patriot air defense system.

UAE

- Potential transfer of AMRAAM to Arab country.

US

- Uncertain future of 6th Fleet.

- Decline in US defense investment, rate of modernization and innovation contributing to Israel's edge.

- Constant rises in real price of US weapons and military equipment.

Some of the specific problems that the IDF has felt it needs to address with the development of a new doctrine are as follows:[335]

- The IDF needs to reshape its grand strategy, strategy, tactics, and peacetime posture into a coherent concept for the future. It must develop a new five-to-10-year force and budget plan that makes hard trade-offs between technology and force size, mass intakes of conscripts for "nation building" and real war fighting needs, and high quality, long-call-up reserves and large reserve forces.

- Peace provides added security but it limits flexibility and training and preparation for offensive and counteroffensive operations. The IDF must take account of peace with Egypt, Jordan, and the Palestinians in terms of perceptions, peacetime action, and war fighting. It must minimize collateral damage and Arab criticism where possible, and plan for the reestablishment of peace even if peace should temporarily fail. This limits preemption, occupation, and any change in Israel's de facto borders.

- Israel must choose between defense at its borders and invasion or counterattack into Arab territory, and decide how to use its new deep-strike air and missile capabilities, and air mobile/air assault forces to defeat Arab enemies or force them to peace. This may lead to more emphasis on airpower, missiles, and long-range artillery to attrit attacking land forces before IDF armor begins a counterattack or to complex joint operations. It also may force the IDF to adapt its tactics and joint force mix under enemy attack, rather than impose it by preempting.

- Israel has unique potential regional advantages in sensors ranging from satellites to UAVs, in cyberwarfare, and in information warfare. These assets can be used to extend the range and/or intensity of the battlefield, to minimize the exposure of manned vehicles and combat forces, or to use forms of information warfare that may not inflict human casualties on either side. At the same time, they are often extremely costly, unproven, and involve the risks inherent in any experimental form of warfare. Revolution may involve unacceptable costs and risks but evolution is absolutely essential.

- Israel must plan for warfare with the Palestinians even as it seeks to cement a true peace and plans for withdrawal from Gaza and the West Bank. A sovereign Palestinian state or entity changes the strategic geography of Israel at virtually every level and a failed peace could mean massive problems in terms of terrorism and urban, asymmetric, and occupation warfare. The Palestinian Authority is already a far more serious threat than an unarmed population was during the *Intifada*.

- Israel must simultaneously plan to deter Syria, to fight Syria, and to make peace with Syria, with or without peace with Lebanon. It must also prepare for low-level war, large-scale conventional combat, and warfare involving chemical and biological weapons. Under worst cases, this could involve outside Arab intervention.

- The IDF must plan for an extended low-intensity war on its border with Lebanon. The army's commanders failed to use their high-tech superiority to develop flexible enough new tactics to minimize continuing losses to guerrilla attacks in southern Lebanon from the Hizbollah militia. While the IDF often achieved tactical superiority for a period, the Hizbollah adapted and was able to exploit the repetitiveness of IDF tactics and delays in the IDF decision-making cycle.

- Israel cannot count on coalition warfare, but it must decide how to strengthen alliances and secure its peace with Egypt, Jordan, and the Palestinians. So far, this means closer strategic cooperation with the US and Turkey, but the IDF must also be prepared to rethink the way in which it would assist Jordan in the event of Iraqi or Syrian pressure or attack, and the possibility of extending missile defense over Jordan and Palestinian territory.

- The IDF must look beyond defense against its neighbors, most of whom now have peace treaties with Israel, to a broader range of threats like Iran and Iraq which will acquire very long-range strike capabilities and which can support proxies in asymmetric warfare.

- Nuclear and retaliatory survivability is becoming a growing problem, as is reliance on an undeclared nuclear deterrent. Israel continued to use its limited resources to build more nuclear warheads, but its shelters are not hardened silos and do not protect its existing warheads and Jericho medium-range missiles from a pre-emptive surprise nuclear attack.

- Counterproliferation involves both offense and defense. In 1981, the IAF was able to destroy an Iraqi nuclear reactor before it could start to produce material or waste that could be used for atomic weapons. Now Iran has been successful in using Chinese and Russian support to develop a nuclear program that is spread out and not susceptible to long-range attack. This requires a shift to missile defense, but it also requires a broader counterproliferation strategy and possibly a new approach to deterrence and retaliation—making nuclear deterrence more overt and mixing it with credible long-range precision conventional strikes.

The Creation of a National Security Council, "Zahal 2000," "Idan 2003," and "Idan 2010"

Since 1997, Israel has conducted an intense series of planning efforts to determine the best way to deal with these issues. Israel's former Defense Minister Yitzhak Mordechai stated in early 1997 that high-level discussions were in progress to talk about the changing military situation that Israel faces and what a newly revised military doctrine might cover. At the same time, senior Israeli officials gave interviews that made it clear that the IDF felt it must take an evolutionary approach towards change issues, and that it felt it could afford the kind of change that might involve strategic, tactical, technical, or financial risks. The IDF's decision-making process was also caught up in the turbulence and uncertainty surrounding the Arab-Israeli peace process and Israeli domestic politics. As a result, a number of studies and plans were delayed, and several decisions were deferred until after the 1999 election.[336]

One potentially important choice about defense organization was made in February 1999. Former Prime Minister Netanyahu formed a new National Security Council, chaired by Major General David Ivry, to advise the prime minister on all matters of defense and strategic security.[337] The cabinet approved the National Security Council in March 1999.[338] The timing of this decision was heavily influenced by Mordechai's resignation in political opposition to Netanyahu. His resignation gave Netanyahu the opportunity to create the National Security

Council—a decision he had advocated since coming to office, but which Mordechai had opposed. It is still too soon to tell, however, what changes, if any, the creation of a National Security Council has really made in Israel's strategy, and some Israelis feel the Council could be abolished if Netanyahu does not win the election. An unrelated organizational study is also reported to have recommended cutting 2,000 administrative and management jobs from the General Headquarters and to removing eight general officer-level and 20 colonel-level positions from General Headquarters to strengthen combat manning and leadership.

According to press reports, the Chief-of Staff of the IDF, Lt. General Shaul Mofaz, also presented a draft of a new Israeli strategic defense plan to the government in early 1999. Press reports have variously referred to the plan as "Zahal (IDF) 2000," "Idan (Epoch) 2003," and "Idan 2010."[339] In practice, there seems to have been a phased plan with different time goals: Early measures for the year 2000, a "five-year plan" for the year 2003, and a longer-term set of goals for 2010.

The details were kept secret and only a small group of officials and experts were given access. Press reports indicated, however, that the studies focused on Israel's need to deal with the growing threat posed by proliferation, and particularly by nations like Iran, Iraq, and Syria—which have long-range strike systems and weapons of mass destruction. They examined the consequences of peace with Egypt, Jordan, and Israel and the advantages and risks involved, and the impact of a post–Cold War Middle East and the lack of Russian arms transfers and military intervention in the region. They also examined the broad force planning, manpower, and military spending issues that have just been discussed.

Several reports indicate that the IDF plans and studies examined the concept of three concentric circles of threats to Israel. The first circle included the potential danger from Islamic militants, such as Hamas, Islamic Jihad, and Hizbollah. The second circle included Syria as a potential aggressor in full-scale war, with or without reinforcements from other Arab countries. The third circle included the risk of air or long-range ballistic missile strikes from anywhere in the region, possibly with NBC warheads hitting strategic population centers. It focused on the need to give continuing priority to missile defense and to a broad counterproliferation policy for dealing with weapons of mass destruction.

This concern with proliferation seems to have led to a detailed examination of ways in which Israel could reduce the vulnerability of its nuclear forces and ensure their retaliatory survivability, and a wide range of options for reinforcing their deterrent effect in a crisis and for actually employing forces at different levels of escalation. It also seems to have involved a compartmented effort to examine Israel's response over time to further demonstrative attacks like the Iraqi missile attacks on Israel in 1990, as well as specific options for striking at nations like Iran, Iraq, and Syria using both conventional precision strikes at high value strategic targets and nuclear weapons. These studies seem to have examined both possible disarming strikes, preemptive options, and options for dealing with successful enemy strikes against Israeli population centers.

Key Israeli officials like David Ivry were still discussing Israel's planning efforts as "ongoing" in May 1999. One detailed report did indicate, however, that the IDF plans and studies had proposed a major structural reorganization of the Israeli Armed Forces to meet the three circles of threats.[340] It seems to have triggered a personnel reform program signed in June 1999. The goal of this program was to streamline manpower, enhance combat units, and reduce the size of rear and headquarter units. It was expected to save the IDF about $197 million in the next five years, and result in the loss of 3,000 jobs by 2003.[341] It was also to introduce short-service commissions for officers, restructure the reserve system, and improve the conditions of service to ensure the retention of officers and skilled personnel.[342]

As part of other related changes, the IDF's Ground Forces Command was converted into a senior Ground Forces Service, which was inaugurated on June 29, 1999.[343] The Ground Forces Service, known as Mazi, was given responsibility for training, doctrine, weapons development, manpower, and acquisitions for all ground-fighting elements under a senior major general. Day-to-day operational responsibility remained under the regional territorial commands: Northern, Central, and Southern. The Northern Command was to deal with the Lebanese and Syrian borders; the Central Command for the West Bank and Jordan. The Southern Command was given responsibility for policing the Gaza Strip and Egyptian border, although an option was presented under which it might be disbanded and given to the Central Command. The Rear Area Command was given enhanced responsibility for protecting Israel's population centers.

Various IDF plans and studies seem to have called for other changes that may still be under consideration—although much of the IDF's attention since early 1999 has been focused on the very different problems of trying to plan for possible peace settlements with Syria and the Palestinians, low intensity combat in Lebanon, and asymmetric warfare with the Palestinians:

- Giving the Deputy Chief of Staff day-to-day responsibility for running the army, to allow the Chief of Staff to focus on long-range planning, strategy and prepare for war. Some experts believe that no Chief of Staff would choose to focus on planning and leave operational control up to his deputy.

- Reorganizing the General Headquarters to include new branches for Logistics, which directs several ordnance and supply corps, and for a new branch for Operations, which would take over all operational directives and co-ordinate all branches and services for combined activities. These changes and consolidations were intended to result in enhanced efficacy for all combat service support elements and help prevent redundancies in and multiplication of materiel. Administration was to be streamlined by the elimination of many senior posts and the reassignment of staff responsibilities.

- Creating a separate Strategic Command to encompass all aspects of strategic threats and take responsibility for strategic strikes using conventional weapons and weapons of mass destruction (WMD) and for deterring WMD attacks. The Strategic Command would have authority over Israel's missile forces, long-range strike fighters, submarines (with the option of upgrading them to launch nuclear-armed cruise missiles, and missile defenses). It was intended to develop a more coherent strategy for deterrence, using Israel's first- and second-strike capabilities, for the military approach to arms control, and for conflict termination.[344]

- Press reports indicated that Ytzhak Mordechai, who resigned from his post as Minister of Defense in January 1999, over political differences with former Prime Minister Netanyahu, wanted this separate Strategic Command. The command was to deal with the threats posed by missiles and weapons of mass destruction, active missile defenses, passive civil defenses, and deterrent and retaliatory use of Israel's conventional and nuclear strike forces. According to this report, the Strategic Command was to absorb the Rear Area Command dealing with civil defense that Israel had established to deal with Iraq's Scud strikes in 1991, but which had never been given the status of a major national effort. Related reports indicated that the IDF was also examining the possible use of naval basing of part of Israel's nuclear-armed missile force as part of related studies.[345] The creation of a strategic command was advocated by a number of top serving officers in the IAF in interviews in August 2000.[346]

There were also reports that the IDF examined ways to help Israel confront the difficulty of dealing with the strategic reliability of US assistance in an emergency. US interests may sometimes clash with those of Israel, as was demonstrated in the case of the Gulf War when the US was reluctant to provide Israel with vital intelligence information to prevent Israeli retaliation. Israel evidently studied new ways to expand US and Israeli strategic ties, but also studied what might happen in a crisis where Israel could not rely on the US for strategic defense and the possible need for purely autonomous missile defenses.[347]

Another aspect of the IDF plans and studies is reported to have involved the examination of new tactics and strategies for the Armored Corps, Navy, and Air Force. Under this proposal, every aspect of the Israeli command structure would be further streamlined to reduce manning and costs and ensure efficient independence of action. This would involve eliminating many overlapping and duplicative senior posts, and creating separate deputy commands to deal with Lebanon and Palestinian security issues.[348]

As part of this examination, a high degree of emphasis seems to be placed on improving joint operations at every tactical level. The army was to use its Field Force Command to examine new approaches to training and doctrine that integrate the use of new technologies in a form somewhat similar to the US Army TRADOC command. The IDF would develop fully mobile and air mobile infantry units to match the maneuver capability of its armored forces, and its support and logistic elements would be reorganized and equipped to allow rapidly maneuvering operations at the brigade or task force level. The support and logistic elements would be given a mix of specialized armored and tracked support vehicles to provide both better mobility and some degree of NBC protection. At the same time, independently controlled infantry brigades could be placed under the overall control of the armored divisions in order to enhance armored combat under fire-saturated battlefield scenarios. The resulting "task force" could then operate independently in a number of scenarios.

Other Israelis argued that Israel's armored divisions are inherently too big and unwieldy, and they should be broken up into smaller combined arms units, while Israel puts more emphasis on joint warfare, helicopters, and modern artillery and crew weapons.[349]

The IDF seems to have examined different ways to man "high alert" forces. Some include larger numbers of career actives and fewer reserves. Others seem to involve more use of attack helicopters and high speed, long-range firepower systems like rockets with advanced conventional warheads. These include ideas like "1,000 little missiles" that would create the equivalent of a smart, relatively long-range barrage capability to defeat enemy armored forces.

The IDF does not seem to have considered anything as ambitious as the US Army "digital battlefield." It does seem to have examined ways to "net" its maneuver units, sensors, and battle management systems into an integrated system for managing forces, dealing with force allocation and friendly fire, acquiring long-range targets, and allocating artillery fire and air support. This seems to have involved a new approach to situational awareness with some of the aspects of the integrated "C^{4}I/SR" concepts the US is examining as part of the "revolution in military affairs."

The future mission of the Air Force was to be multi-faceted, covering strategic deterrence to offensive attack, ground support and special forces operations. Several new purchases are planned under the IDF plans and studies, including at least one more squadron of AH-64 Apache attack helicopters, which would be AH-64Ds with Longbow "fire and forget" missiles, and the purchase of either F-15I or F-16 Block-60 fighters to replace more than 100 front-line aircraft, including the A-4 Skyhawk and the Kfir.

Many of these recommendations were put on hold, however, as it became clear that the May 1999 election might bring a new government to power. According to some sources, the IDF officials working on the study also delayed forwarding some of the recommendations to the Netanyahu government, and the new Minister of Defense Moshe Aarons. They indicate they feared they would be leaked and become an election issue and that this might polarize any new government politically in ways that would mean rejecting the recommendations of the studies.

The Barak Government and Idan 2010

It is one of the ironies of history, that the May 1999 election brought a new government to power that was far more interested in reaching a broad peace with both the Palestinians and Syria, but which then became involved in kinds of warfare that the IDF had given only secondary consideration in much of its previous planning. The first shift in emphasis was one to giving higher priority to planning for withdrawal from the Golan and peace with the Palestinians. This, however, was followed by a de facto Israeli defeat in low intensity combat with the

Hizbollah and Amal in Lebanon and then the outbreak of a highly asymmetric war with the Palestinians.

The new Prime Minister, Ehud Barak campaigned on a strong peace platform and on withdrawal from Lebanon. His security agenda was expected to focus on high-technology deterrence, re-establishing ties with the White House, and reinvigorating the peace process.[350] Barak rapidly made good on some of his campaign promises. Soon after his election, he formed a "peace administration" to handle Israel's major security issues and to manage peace negotiations.[351]

The administration was to consist of three working groups. The first, led by Amnon Lipkin-Shahak, was to conduct negotiations with the Palestinian Authority; the second, led by Uri Saguy, was to conduct negotiations with Syria; and the third, led by Yossi Peled, was to negotiate with Lebanon once the talks with Syria made this possible.[352] While Barak was not able to make quick progress with Syria, he did reach an agreement in September 1999 that put the Wye Accords back on track and which seem to create a climate where Israel and the Palestinians might move forward in serious discussions of the "final settlement" issues. As for Lebanon, the IDF was forced first to plan for unilateral withdrawal, and then rush out of Lebanon following the collapse of the SLA.

According to press reports, Barak also moved forward in reforming Israel's planning for conventional and nuclear war. He approved a new long-term strategic plan in August 1999, called Idan (Epoch) 2010.[353] Press reports indicated that the five separate working groups were formed to implement the plan. One dealt with advanced war fighting technologies and was headed by Major General Yitzhak Ben-Israel, Chief of Research and Development and Technological Research and Development and War Fighting Equipment within the MOD. A second dealt with rear area defense and was headed by Retired Chief of Staff Moshe Levi.

The full details of the Israeli plan and its implementation were not made public, but it seemed to be a phased plan that would build on the steps called for in ZAHAL 2000 and Idan 2003. Press reports indicate that Idan 2010 had the following features:[354]

- The IDF would not attempt anything as sophisticated as the US "Revolution in Military Affairs," and would stress inserting new technologies into existing platforms in its existing force structure, rather than fielding new technologies in new platforms in a new force structure. Its emphasis on new technologies included smart munitions, unmanned aerial vehicles (UAVs) and unmanned aerial combat vehicles (UACVs), plus sophisticated information warfare technologies. It would introduce space-based intelligence systems that would provide reliable, real-time warning and intelligence.

- The Army would retain its emphasis on armor, build up its inventory of Merkava 3 tanks, and probably introduce a new Merkava 4 with enhanced firepower and protection. At the same time, it was not clear that Israel could afford to upgrade its older 2,000 main battle tanks, and the IDF seems to have felt that its present heavy armored divisions were too large and unwieldy. Some thought is evidently being given to a more flexible brigade group structure comprising modern main battle tanks, attack helicopters, stand-off support weapons, infantry units equipped with heavy armored fighting vehicles and personnel carriers, and armored engineers. Some IDF officers seem to believe that such a force mix would be more flexible and allow Israel to react more quickly to threats from Syria and the West Bank.

- The Israeli Air Force would have 110 new F-16Is and advanced combat aircraft like the F-22 or Joint Strike Fighter. It would introduce the AH-64D and upgrade the F-15I and AH-64A. The UN-60 Blackhawk would become the standard multi-purpose helicopter. The IAF would modernize its transport fleet, buy new in-flight refueling tankers and AEW aircraft, and buy at least one or two new airborne surveillance aircraft.

- At least three full Arrow batteries will be in service, supported by the Patriot PAC-3 and other systems. Israel could be reinforced by US Navy Aegis theater missile defense ships off shore. Consideration would be given to procurement and deployment of boost phase intercept and anti-mobile surface-to-surface missile programs being developed in cooperation with the US.

- A new strategic command would be set up with long-range strike aircraft, in-flight refueling, new sensor and battle management systems, and dedicated unmanned aerial vehicles (UAVs) and unmanned aerial combat vehicles (UACVs). This might involve special long-range ground elements designed to attack and destroy threats like weapons of mass destruction and mobile missiles.

- A special force formation would be created for counterinsurgency operations including air, ground, and possibly naval forces designed for deep insertion operations and to deal with threats like possible Hizbollah attacks from Lebanon. Another specially trained formation would be created to deal with the problems created by an agreement with the Palestinian Authority equipped with high technology equipment for urban warfare.

Press reports often prove inaccurate, however, and it is still far from clear how Israel will actually implement its military reforms, and what kind of new forces Israel can afford. One of the key ongoing lessons of the IDF's studies is just how costly new forces and technology really are, and how difficult it is to find the money and manpower resources to keep Israel's "edge." Another is that a nation involved in complex peace negotiations that could radically change its deployments, and its military capabilities on the Golan, in Lebanon, and in the West Bank, can scarcely plan for the future with any certainty. Reports in early 2000, from officers like Lt. General Shaul Mofaz (then Chief of Staff of the IDF) indicated that Israel had adopted a much more flexible ten-year plan that would be revised annually to meet the evolving needs of the IDF.[355]

Israel's State Comptroller, Eliezer Goldberg, added another dimension to this debate in late 1999: Intelligence. In October 1999, the State Comptroller issued a report calling upon the government to form a panel of intelligence chiefs, headed by the prime minister, to conduct a comprehensive reform of all of Israel's intelligence agencies and their data bases. The report charged that their organization was outdated, that they failed to cooperate effectively, and tended to produce identical threat assessments for political reasons. This criticism applied to the research divisions of the Mossad, General Security Services, military intelligence, and Foreign Ministry's research division, and noted that they often duplicate their efforts without coordination. It also charged the Foreign Ministry lacked the intelligence to conduct the peace negotiations, and attacked the quality of the national assessment that Israeli military intelligence prepared for the prime minister.[356]

Perhaps the key uncertainty Israel now faces is whether it will or will not be on the Golan, since it seems committed to withdrawing from much of the West Bank. This is leading the Israeli government to rethink its current strategic relationship with the US, and there were reports in November 1999 that Israel and the US had agreed on a new strategic relationship. This would involve joint study by a number of working groups to develop a joint memorandum of understanding (MOU) to look at the prepositioning of US forces and supplies in Israel, missile defenses, cooperation on non-conventional weapons, and how to best preserve Israel's strategic edge. It was not clear whether this meant any major changes in the existing Israeli-US Defense Policy Advisory Group and Strategic Policy Planning Group, or older bodies like the Joint Political-Military Planning Group, Joint-Security Assistance Planning Group, and Joint Economic Development Group.[357] Later discussions in February 2000 explored the idea of a US-Israeli defense pact as part of a comprehensive peace settlement.[358]

In early 2000, Israel announced that it would need substantial additional US aid to cover the cost of withdrawing from the Golan and making suitable force improvements. At one point, figures as high as $30 billion were quoted. A figure of $17.4 billion then appeared in the Israeli press. This figure was to cover an aid package of new weapons like the Tomahawk cruise missile, more AH-64s, UH-60 transport helicopters, and a wide range of advanced long-range air-to-ground and land-based US munitions and strike systems. It also included US aid in building new military bases. According to some reports, Israel indicated that the cost of the package could be reduced to $16.9 billion if Israel could keep some kind of monitoring presence on the Golan, even if this was a presence in an international monitoring team on Mount Hermon. Others indicated that the cash cost to the US could be closer to $10 billion if Israel was given what it needed out of surplus US equipment.[359]

All of these debates have gone on in spite of the IDF's involvement in withdrawal from Lebanon and a Second Intifada.[360] At present, however, it is anyone's guess as to what Israel actually needs or how it should reform its strategy and force posture. Peace is still possible, but no one can foresee the actual security conditions that will evolve. Israel faces a new kind of asymmetric warfare with the same Palestinians who may be a peace partner. Moderate Arab states may become far less reliable peace partners if a "Second Intifada" persists, and the proliferation of chemical, biological, radiological, and nuclear weapons, and long-range missiles, throws yet another wild card into the game. It is a military cliché that the battle plan never survives engagement with the enemy. It seems to be an equal reality that plans to reform strategy and forces never survive the realities of actual events.

7

Israeli–Palestinian Conflicts

One of the many tragedies of the crisis between Israel and the Palestinians that began in late September 2000 is that a "Second Intifada" has now become a reality. The events of September and October 2000 have reversed trends that once seemed far more positive. The election of Prime Minister Barak in the spring of 1999 gave Israel a government committed to creating a full peace with the Palestinians, peace with Syria, and peace with Lebanon. Prime Minister Barak repeated this pledge in his Yom Kippur speech on September 19, 1999.[361] Chairman Arafat and the Palestinian Authority made similar efforts to reach a peace agreement, both sides continued to improve the quality of their security efforts, and movement took place towards resolving many of the "final settlement" issues.

Israel and the Palestinian Authority made considerable progress in restarting the peace process by signing the Sharm el Shiekh Memorandum on September 4, 1999. The Sharm el Shiekh Memorandum had a significant impact on Israeli-Palestinian security arrangements. It called for the full implementation of the previous Wye and Hebron agreements, and called for completing the final status talks by September 13, 2000. It moved the transfer of land to the Palestinians forward, although it allowed Israel to do this in three stages rather than two. It included an oral agreement on releasing Palestinian prisoners, and expedited the effort to sign a protocol providing the Palestinians with two safe passage routes between the West Bank and Gaza, with the southern route to open on October 1, 1999. It expanded the Hebron agreement, called for the rapid construction of a port in Gaza, strengthened Israeli-Palestinian security agreements, and effectively delayed the issue of Palestinian statehood until at least September 2000.

Further progress was made at a summit meeting between Prime Minister Barak, Chairman Arafat, and President Clinton at Camp David in July 2000. Both sides addressed the "final settlement" issues in some depth for the first time since the signing of the Oslo Accords. They addressed the future of Jerusalem, the status of the West Bank, borders, Israeli settlements, Palestinian refugees and their right of return, water issues, Palestinian sovereignty, and future security arrangements. While the talks failed to reach an agreement and exposed deep differences between the two sides, they seemed to make sufficient progress to indicate a peace agreement might be possible.

There is still hope for an eventual peace, but any chronology of what happened after the Camp David meeting in July and November 2000 shows just how unstable the peace process is and how quickly it can turn to war:

- July 11—President Clinton launches peace summit with Palestinian President Yasser Arafat and Israeli Prime Minister Ehud Barak at Camp David. Both sides make progress in compromising on the final settlement issues, seeking to meet a September 13 deadline for a peace agreement.

- July 25—The Camp David summit ends after 15 days without an agreement. The fate of Jerusalem and Palestinian refugees are the main obstacles. Palestinians want Arab East Jerusalem as the capital of their planned state. Israel, which seized East Jerusalem in the 1967 war, regards it as an indivisible capital.

- July 29—Arafat begins visits to foreign states in an effort to gain support for the Palestinian position. Many Arab states support his refusal to make concessions over Jerusalem, but many Arab and Western leaders urge him not to declare a Palestinian state before reaching a peace deal with Israel.

- September 6—Clinton fails to resolve the differences between Barak and Arafat during his separate meetings with the leaders during the UN Millennium Summit in New York.

- September 10—The 129-member Palestinian parliament decides to delay the planned declaration of a Palestinian state, saying this will allow more time to reach a peace deal. It says it will meet to consider the matter again by November 15.

- September 13—Israelis and Palestinians fail to meet a deadline they had agreed on for reaching a peace deal.

- September 27—An Israeli soldier is killed by a roadside bomb in Palestinian-ruled Gaza.

- September 28—A visit by right-wing Israeli leader Ariel Sharon to the al-Aqsa mosque and temple mount, a holy site in Jerusalem sacred to both Jews and Muslims, leads to major clashes between Palestinian protesters and Israeli security forces. Dozens of police and several Palestinians injured.

- September 29—Palestinians clash with Israeli security forces. The Israelis open fire with rubber-coated metal bullets in the al-Aqsa mosque compound in Jerusalem's walled Old City. Six Palestinians killed and close to 200 wounded.

- September 30—Major clashes erupt in the Gaza Strip and West Bank. Fatah Hawks, Hamas, and Palestinian Islamic Jihad supporters, as well as some Palestinian Authority security personnel, join in mass violence and stone throwing against the IDF. Fourteen Palestinians killed by Israeli fire, including 12-year-old Mohammed Aldura, whose death is broadcast around the world (the IDF would first contend that his death was accidental, and later would revise its position claiming that Palestinians may have shot Mohammed Aldura for sympathy purposes). Scattered sniping by Palestinians.

- October 1—Clashes erupt between Israeli Arabs and Jews in Umm al-Faheh and Arab-populated towns in northern Israel. Cease-fire agreed on but collapses. Twelve killed, including an Israeli border policeman who bleeds to death inside Joseph's Tomb in West Bank city of Nablus as Palestinian gunmen keep medics away.

- October 2—Nineteen are killed. Israeli Arabs protest in solidarity with Palestinians. Israelis barred from travel in Palestinian territories.

- October 3—Reports of another cease-fire agreement. Clashes resume, and six killed.

- October 4—Israeli Prime Minister Ehud Barak and Palestinian leader Yasser Arafat meet US Secretary of State Madeleine Albright and French President Jacques Chirac in Paris. Arafat declines to sign an agreement because of a failure to agree on terms for an international inquiry or fact-finding mission into the violence. Both sides order military forces away from flashpoints. Seven killed.

- October 5—Arafat attends talks with Egyptian President Hosni Mubarak and US Secretary of State Madeleine Albright, but Barak sees no point in going to the talks because of Arafat's refusal to sign the agreement in Paris. Israeli tanks move back from positions in West Bank. Three killed.

- October 5—Malaysia presents draft UN resolution condemning the violence committed by Israeli security forces. The UN Security Council adopts a modified resolution condemning Israel's "excessive use of force" against the Palestinians. The United States abstains. Barak says the Palestinians must end their wave of protests within two days or Israel will consider the peace process dead.

- October 6—Israel seals West Bank and Gaza Strip. Israeli troops seize a Jerusalem shrine after the Palestinians raise their flag. One killed in clash with police outside the shrine, nine die in West Bank and Gaza.

- October 7—Barak extends the ultimatum when it expires. Palestinian demonstrators storm Joseph's Tomb after Israeli withdrawal, set fires and tear up holy Jewish books. Hizbollah abducts three Israeli soldiers. Barak issues 48-hour ultimatum to Arafat—stop the violence or peace talks will end and Israeli troops will act with full force. Four Palestinians killed. Confrontations take place on the Israeli-Lebanese border and Lebanese guerrilla group Hizbollah seizes three Israeli soldiers in cross-border raid. The guerrillas used a vehicle and uniforms with fake UN markings and flags. These were most likely obtained at one of the many souvenir shops in Lebanon.

- October 8—Israeli forces blow up two apartment buildings and a factory building in Gaza used by Palestinian gunmen. Jewish settler Hillel Lieberman is found dead in a cave near a West Bank highway. Two Palestinians and one Israeli Arab killed.

- October 9—Secretary-General Kofi Annan and Russian Foreign Minister Igor Ivanov travel to the region for meetings with Israeli and Palestinian officials and crisis talks with Barak and Arafat. Clashes in Jerusalem, Nazareth and Hebron continue through Yom Kippur. Annan Barak's 48-hour deadline is extended to avoid a prolonged armed conflict. Violence between Israeli Arabs and Jews erupts across the country. Three Palestinians killed.

- October 10—Barak says it is too early to tell whether a slight fall in level of violence is enough to resume negotiations. A 12-year-old Palestinian boy is shot in the head in Gaza; rioting continues in the West Bank.

- October 11—Violence continues, as does diplomatic activity. An effigy of Barak is burned at a Palestinian march in Hebron. Israelis and Palestinians exchange gunfire in cities, villages and along West Bank highways. Three Palestinians killed.

- October 12—A Palestinian mob kills two Israeli soldiers inside a Palestinian police station in Ramallah, and throw one of their bodies out the window in front of television cameras. Israeli helicopters rocket Palestinian targets including Yasser Arafat's residential compound, police stations, and broadcasting centers. The 12-year-old boy shot on October 10 dies.

- October 13—Israeli security forces and Palestinians fight in sporadic clashes. Annan intensifies peace efforts, says he expects a summit in 48 hours. Palestinians staged marches across the West Bank and Israel prevents Muslims under the age of 45 from participating in Friday prayers at Jerusalem's al-Aqsa mosque. Efforts continue to bring Barak and Arafat together for a summit. Two Palestinians killed in clashes in Hebron, West Bank. Palestinian State Television broadcasts an inflammatory sermon instructing Palestinians: "Wherever you are, wherever you find them (Jews), kill them."

- October 14—Barak and Arafat agree to attend a summit meeting in Sharm el-Sheikh. Clinton says he will also attend, with Egyptian President Hosni Mubarak, Annan and European Union foreign policy representative Javier Solana. Clashes in West Bank and Gaza Strip are isolated.

- October 14—Hizbollah says it has lured an Israeli intelligence officer and reserve colonel into Lebanon and has taken him captive. Low-level violence continues in the West Bank and Gaza Strip.

- October 16—Arafat joins Barak, Clinton, President Mubarak, and King Abdullah in Jordan for a summit meeting in Sharm el-Sheikh in a bid to end the violence. Low-level violence continues in the West Bank and Gaza Strip.

- October 17—Clinton announces at the end of the summit that both sides have agreed to halt violence, set up an inquiry into its causes and explore a return to peace negotiations, "take immediate, concrete measures" to end the 19-day conflict, which has killed more than 100 people, mostly Palestinians, and endangered once promising peace negotiations. The measures include immediate statements from Arafat and Barak urging an end to violence, elimination of points of friction, redeployment of Israeli forces, an end to incitement, restoration of security cooperation between the two sides and a lifting of an Israeli closure of Palestinian towns that has kept residents confined there during the violence. But the "statement of understandings" read out by Clinton is a report on oral undertakings that officials said were not put on paper. It includes no specifics about what is supposed to happen—or in what order—leaving it uncertain whether the two struggling leaders left the summit at this Egyptian resort with the same set of expectations about what they had committed to do.

- October 18—Neither Barak nor Arafat announces the details of his position on the agreement. Arafat has the Palestinian Authority issue statements but personally remains silent. The IDF does ease constraints on Palestinian movement, but tensions only ease moderately. Sporadic violence continues.

- October 19—Marwan Barghouti, the head of the Fatah movement on the West Bank, says that the Fatah armed militia or Tanzeem, will continue the struggle against Israel in spite of the Sharm el-Sheikh agreement.

- October 20—Arab leaders arrive in Cairo for summit meeting. Fighting leaves as many as 10 Palestinians dead. Barak threatens to suspend the peace process. The UN General Assembly resolution condemns Israel for the "excessive use of force." The non-binding resolution is adopted with only 92 votes in favor—an unusually low number for resolutions on the Middle East. Six countries vote "no" votes, and 46 countries abstain. Some 30 countries don't vote at all. The resolution was the third adopted by the United Nations since the violence began on September 28, following a similar one in the Security Council. The Israeli Foreign Ministry calls the resolution "completely one-sided," saying it ignores the mob killing of two Israeli soldiers and the desecration of Jewish holy sites in Nablus and Jericho.

- October 21—Arab leaders at the summit in Cairo condemn Israeli violence, but call for pressure on Israel to support the peace process on Palestinian terms. Libya walks out. Iraq condemns moderation. Crown Prince Abdullah of Saudi Arabia calls for $1 billion in aid to Palestinians, and offers $250 million. Voice of Palestine radio and television switches to simultaneous FM transmission on several frequencies, after having its primary transmitter destroyed by Israeli retaliatory strikes following the mob killings of two Israeli soldiers, reaching an even larger audience. These transmissions frequently show clashes between Israeli forces and Palestinian young people, as well as eulogies for Palestinians who have died fighting for the cause.

- October 22—The final statement of the Arab League condemns Israel: "The Arab leaders confirm that the Aqsa Intifada erupted as a result of continuing occupation and the Israeli violation of Haram al Sharif, and the rest of the Islamic and Christian holy sites in the Palestinian land. . . . They also affirm the Palestinian people's right to just compensation from Israel for moral, human and material losses. . . . Arab leaders demand forming a neutral international committee in the framework of the United Nations that will report to the Security Council, and the Human Rights Committee, on the reasons and the responsibility for the dangerous deterioration in the occupied Palestinian Land, and the massacres committed by the Israeli occupying forces. . . . They also ask that the Security Council and General Assembly take charge of providing protection for the Palestinian people under Israeli occupation, through discussing forming a force or any international presence for this purpose. . . . Arab Leaders affirm that Arab nations shall pursue, in accordance with international law, those responsible for these brutal practices and demand that the Security Council form an international tribunal dedicated to trying Israeli criminals of war who committed massacres against the Palestinians and the Arabs in the occupied land like the former tribunal formed for criminals of war in Rwanda and the former Yugoslavia. . . . Arab leaders express their deep resentment and deprecation of the Israeli escalation in aggression and its provocation in a time when the region was getting ready for comprehensive and just peace, especially after the Arabs decided since the Madrid conference that a comprehensive and just peace is their option and opens the way for a final settlement. . . . Arab leaders affirm that a comprehensive and just peace shall not be achieved without the return of Jerusalem to Palestinian sovereignty and without granting the Palestinians legitimate rights including the founding of an independent state with Jerusalem as its capital. . . . And without restoring all Arab land occupied, including a full Israeli withdrawal from the West Bank and Gaza and from Golan to the borders of June 4, 1967, and the completion of the Israeli withdrawal from southern Lebanon to the international borders including Shabaa plantation. And without the release of Arab prisoners held in the Israeli prisons. . . . Arab leaders affirm that achieving durable peace and security in the region requires Israeli accession to the nuclear non-proliferation treaty. And to submit all Israeli nuclear installations to international inspection system. They stress the importance of making the Middle East free of nuclear weapons and weapons of mass destruction."

Barak is quoted as saying at the weekly cabinet session: "We will have to take a time-out the purpose of which is to reassess the peace process in response to the events of recent weeks." Barak says Israel needs a time-out from peacemaking with the Palestinians because the emergency Arab summit used what he called threatening language against Israel. "Israel totally rejects the language of threats that came out of the summit and condemns the call, folded into the decisions, for continued violence." Israeli government spokesman Nachman Shai acknowledges reports that taking a time-out from peacemaking could allow Barak to negotiate with right-wing opposition leader Ariel Sharon to form a national emergency government.

Arafat responds by saying that Barak's decision is no surprise and anyone blocking the Palestinian path to an independent state with Jerusalem as its capital can "go to hell." President Clinton calls Barak to urge him "to get past the violence and ultimately get back to the peace process." Four Palestinians, including a 14-year-old, are killed in clashes with Israeli forces in the West Bank and Gaza Strip bringing the number of dead in three weeks of bloodshed to 125, of which only eight are Israelis. Shooting takes place on the outskirts of Jerusalem, where police said at least 12 Israeli apartment buildings on West Bank territory were strafed by gunfire from Beit Jalla village near Bethlehem. No one was hurt. Israeli attack helicopters fired machine guns at targets in the village in response. Israeli Army Radio says several Palestinians are wounded. Arab leaders end the summit in Cairo by calling for a war crimes tribunal to investigate Israel's handling of the crisis: "Arab states will prosecute according to international law those who caused these barbaric practices and demand that the Security Council form a special international criminal court to try Israeli war criminals." Tunisia severs its low-level diplomatic relations with Israel.

- October 23—Israeli army imposes a blockade on Beit Jalla, a Palestinian town from which machine guns were fired Sunday night into the nearby Jerusalem neighborhood of Gilo. The army responds with machine-gun fire from tanks and infantry and missiles fired from attack helicopters. A factory in Beit Jalla is destroyed and Beit Jalla and Bethlehem are plunged into darkness. Hundreds of civilians flee from Beit Jalla and the nearby Aida refugee camp. Gilo has repeatedly come under fire from Beit Jalla. On Sunday night, Palestinian gunmen fire at streets that had not been hit before. Nobody is hurt but 16 apartments were damaged. Lt. Gen. Shaul Mofaz, the army chief of staff, says "If they make it impossible to conduct a normal life on the Israeli side I do not think we can tolerate such a situation." Mofaz said the blockade was imposed to block the entry of armed Palestinian militants into Beit Jalla. The army said neighboring Bethlehem would not be sealed. Palestinians attack Israeli army positions and bases in both regions. These attacks are also intended as a deterrent to future violence from the city, the Palestinians contend that there were no hostile armed forces in Beit Jalla. The Israeli army spokesman says a Palestinian shooting attack on an Israeli army position in the southern Gaza Strip was "massive." The Israelis respond with small arms and anti-tank rockets.

Syrian spokesmen attack Barak's decision to take time out to reassess the peace process. One Syrian official says, "The peace process is in fact frozen. Barak is not a man of peace. . . . He does not want peace and his call for a time-out is only a meaningless threat. Sharon's provocative visit to the holy Aqsa Mosque in Jerusalem which came in full coordination with Barak, and with his blessing, proves that the Israeli premier does not care about peace and that he does not care about the feelings of Arabs and Muslims."

- October 24—Palestinian killed in Hebron, Israel claims that the man was part of the Tanzim militia; the Palestinian authority claims that he was simply a bystander. Additionally, 3 Palestinian teenagers are killed in fighting in the West Bank and Gaza. Arafat gives Palestinian Islamic Jihad and Hamas leadership decision-making authority in the Palestinian National Authority and al-Fatah by placing them on the High Committee of the Follow-Up Intifada of Nationalist Islamic Organizations.

- October 25—Sporadic violence continues. President Clinton states that Arafat could dramatically lower the level of violence if he so chooses. Gun sales in Israel are reported to have increased threefold and weapons training courses have increased by five times in the last month. Polls in Israel reveal that most Israeli citizens believe that the army has thus far showed restraint in its dealings with the Palestinian protesters. US House of Representatives passes a resolution (365–30) of support of Israel, while condemning both the use of force by both sides and blaming the Palestinian leadership for the recent outbreak of violence. Israel releases its rules of engagement: Tear gas and stun grenades are used first. Should these fail to disperse the protest, rubber-coated metal bullets are used, which are supposed to be shot at the lower body from a distance of 25 meters or more. Live ammunition is used in response to firebombs, shooting at the lower body and when encountering shooting and/or grenades Israeli soldiers will shoot to kill.

- October 26—Palestinian Islamic Jihad claims credit for a suicide bombing of an Israeli Army post in Gaza killing the bomber and wounding an Israeli soldier. It was carried out on the fifth anniversary of the assassination of the group's leader, Fathi Shiqaqi, although the PIJ claimed this was only a coincidence. The PIJ also renews its pledge to liberate all of Palestine, not just the West Bank and Gaza, therefore their attacks would not be confined to the occupied territories in the future.

A low-intensity cyber-conflict develops when Israel teenagers brag that they sabotaged the Hizbollah Web site by placing Israeli flags, posting Zionist articles and having the site play the Israeli national anthem when a user logs on. Soon after, the Israeli Defense Forces and the Prime Minister's Web site crashes after being bombarded by a huge number of e-mails. The Knesset Web site has files tampered with by hackers, possibly from Saudi Arabia.

Praising Morocco's decision to sever ties with Israel, the Secretary General of the Arab League Ismat Abdul Miguid calls on all Arab states which have relations with Israel to cut these relations. He, however, stresses that each nation has the right to make its own decisions about its foreign relations.

- October 27—Sporadic fighting continues. Hizbollah calls for more bombings like that of the PIJ bombing the previous day.

- October 28—One month anniversary of Ariel Sharon's visit to Temple Mount/Haram al-Sharif, to date 149 dead, the vast majority being Palestinian. Sporadic fighting continues with heavier fighting near Beit Jalla after Israeli forces began to take small arms fire. Israeli helicopter and armor support are called upon to suppress the fire. Talks between Ariel Sharon and Ehud Barak to form a national unity government fall apart. Recent polls in Israel demonstrate a declining popularity of both leaders, while having increased support for Benjamin Netanyahu.

- October 29—Five Palestinians are killed in ongoing fighting. Israel deploys armor to the Gaza Strip. Al-Fatah urges the Palestinian people to "continue and escalate the Intifada."

- October 30—Two Israelis are killed; both were armed civilians in the greater Jerusalem area. Several Palestinians are wounded in continuing clashes. Israeli Defense Forces admit that lethal force may have been inappropriately used in the deaths of 2 brothers in the West Bank. The brothers may have been simply throwing rocks and Israeli rules of engagement require that there be immediate danger to military or civilian lives.

Barak's government does not collapse, despite efforts of Ariel Sharon after the Shahs party announces that it would not use its block of votes for a no-confidence vote against Barak. This leaves Barak with a minority government of 30 MPs in a 120-seat Knesset.

Israeli helicopters launch a series of strikes against al-Fatah headquarters installations. Rather than being retaliatory in nature, these are initiated to send a message to al-Fatah. These represent a change in Israeli tactics according to Deputy Defense Minister Ephraim Sneh to "more sophisticated measures" and that strikes will no longer necessarily be retaliatory in nature. The air strike against the al-Fatah office in El-Bireh in the West Bank missed and hit a Palestinian home.

New more aggressive attacks are authorized for the IDF land forces. These allow specialized anti-guerilla units to operate and capture suspects in shooting incidents in Palestinian-controlled areas.

- October 31—Six Palestinians die in fresh fighting in Gaza. Palestinian forces from al-Fatah and Tanzim make use of anti-tank weapons for the first time. Israel forces respond with heavy machine-gun fire and by bulldozing the al-Fatah outpost with military bulldozers. Israel begins to fortify Jewish towns within Israel against possible Arab attack.

- November 1—Three Israeli soldiers are killed in fighting in the West Bank near Bethlehem and Jericho. Israel begins retaliatory strikes. These damage a casino and the Palestinian training facilities in Jericho. The settlement of Gilo near Beit Jalla comes under the heaviest fire since the violence began. Negotiations between Shimon Peres and Yasser Arafat yields a truce despite heavy fighting. Israeli forces are to withdraw from their positions at dawn on November 2.

- November 2—A car bomb explodes in the Jerusalem marketplace killing two; the PIJ claims responsibility. This blast kills the daughter of the National Religious Party leader Rabbi Yitzhak Levy. Israeli tanks begin to withdraw from positions in the occupied territories.

- November 3—Two Palestinians die amid new clashes, however, the overall number of clashes declines. The Web site of the American-Israeli Public Affairs Committee (AIPAC) is hacked; 3,500 credit card numbers are stolen, and this spreads the low-intensity cyber-conflict to America.

- November 4—Sporadic clashes continue. Two Palestinians die, one is a 14-year-old girl who dies due to previously sustained gunshot wounds; the other is a baby who dies of tear gas inhalation. Palestinian and Israeli leaders both announce that they are ready to meet with Clinton to end the violence.

- November 5—Al-Fatah leadership declares that the Intifada should continue and there cannot be any negotiations. Two Palestinians are killed in renewed clashes. Two Israeli settlers are killed near Ramallah. IDF sources report an increased targeting of settlements and IDF soldiers by Palestinian gunmen, however Arafat orders that gunmen take a reduced role in the rock-throwing segments of the uprising.

- November 6—Two Palestinians die in continuing clashes. Barak rejects Arafat's call for an international peacekeeping force.

- November 7—One Palestinian dies when a fishing boat explodes near an Israeli patrol boat off of the Gaza Strip near the Egyptian-Israeli border in what IDF sources call a fumbled suicide bombing. There are no Israeli casualties. The Israeli government reports that there has been a 40 percent reduction in the number of clashes since the most recent truce was signed.

- November 9—Israeli forces successfully kill Hussein Abayat, a local military commander in Fatah. He was believed to be responsible for 6 separate shooting incidents involving Israeli soldiers including one which killed three IDF soldiers. Abayat was traveling in a van in Beit Sahur when an Israeli attack helicopter destroyed the van with two Hellfire missiles. The IDF hoped that this would have a deterrent effect on other upper and mid-level Fatah officers involved in the recent violence. Two Palestinian women are killed by shrapnel from the explosion. Bill Clinton and Yasser Arafat meet in Washington, D.C. hours after the missile strike; very little progress is made.

- November 10—Palestinian leader Yasser Arafat appeals to the United Nations Security Council to send a UN force. Four more Palestinians, an Israeli Arab and an Israeli soldier are killed in clashes.

- November 12—In Gilo a rare daylight attack against the settlement; this represents a more aggressive use of military force by the Palestinians. Crown Prince Abdullah of Saudi Arabia demands that all Arab States cut off their ties with Israel and with any nation that moves its embassy to Jerusalem. However, no unified Muslim voice seems to come from the Organization of the Islamic Conference summit in terms of policy, but they are able to generate a strong statement of condemnation.

- November 13—Four Palestinians, including the nephew of Mohammed Dahlan, the head of Preventative Security, and four Israelis die, including two female civilians. Palestinian gunmen are increasingly targeting settlers and soldiers in ambushes, moving towards a possible Lebanonization of the conflict. Israel once again shuts down non-emergency access to and from the West Bank and Gaza.

- November 15—Palestinian Independence Day, eight Palestinians are killed, the Israeli government announces that it will abandon its "policy of restraint" that it previously had towards the conflict. Yasser Arafat calls on Fatah activists to stop shooting at Israeli soldiers. Israeli helicopters attack four Fatah positions in the territories. A German citizen is killed in these attacks.

- November 17—For the first time, Arafat makes a call for cessation of shooting the Palestinian-controlled areas via radio. This, however, is not satisfactory to the Israeli government because it calls for a ban only on weapons firing in Area A, but Areas B and C were noticeably excluded from Arafat's ban.

- November 19—An Israeli embassy official is shot and wounded in Amman Jordan.

- November 20—A roadside bomb in Gaza is detonated next to a school bus killing two adults and wounding 5 children. Omar Al-Mukhtar, the military wing of the Syrian-based Fatah Uprising, claimed responsibility. Israel retaliates by launching numerous missile strikes against Fatah buildings in the West Bank and Gaza marking the heaviest bombardment to date.

- November 21—Gunfire escalates in the wake of the missile strikes and Egypt recalls its ambassador in protest to recent Israeli aggression.

- November 22—Four Palestinians which Israel claimed were Tanzim militia gunmen are ambushed by IDF infantry with mechanized support while driving in civilian vehicles. The Palestinian Authority claimed these men are not Tanzim and are in fact civilians. Jamal Abdel Razek, a Fatah officer, is among the dead. There are conflicting statements on whether or not the party was armed or attempting to run a checkpoint. A car bomb explodes in Hadera killing two and wounding 55. Ezzedin al-Qassam Brigades of Hamas claim responsibility for the bombing.

- November 23—An Israeli-Palestinian liaison office is killed by a mortar shell. This almost immediately results in Israel ordering all Palestinian police and security officers to leave all liaison offices throughout the West Bank and Gaza. This temporarily ends security cooperation between the Palestinians and Israelis. In a gun battle between an Israeli patrol and Palestinian forces one Israeli and one Palestinian are killed.

- November 24—Israeli-Palestinian liaison offices are re-opened after a telephone conversation between Barak and Arafat. While "cooperation" is officially resumed the situation remains tense and little to no actual cooperation is taking place. Six Palestinians, an Israeli major (the highest-ranking officer killed to date) and a Jewish settler are slain in continuing violence.

- November 26—Israeli soldiers attack a carload of Fatah members carrying small arms, killing all five individuals in the car; another unrelated Palestinian dies of previously sustained wounds.

- November 27—UN human rights commissioner Mary Robinson delivers a highly critical address to the UN General Assembly condemning Israel's excessive use of force and calls for an international monitoring force. For the first time in almost 3 weeks no one on either side dies.

- November 28—Barak agrees to early elections after his bid to pull together a national unity government fails.

- November 29—Four Palestinians are killed attempting to enter Israel; Sharon begins to make plans to run against Barak.

- November 30—Barak proposes that a Palestinian state be formed in the West Bank and Gaza, but leaving the status of Jerusalem, refugees and final border to be resolved by future negotiations over the next three years. The Palestinian Authority is quick to reject this plan, saying only a comprehensive peace plan can be successful.

- December 1—As it is the first day of Ramadan Israel lifts its ban on those younger than 40 praying at the Al-Aqsa Mosque Complex. Both sides show restraint in this sector; however violence continues elsewhere. Mohammed Dief, a Hamas bomb maker, escapes from a Palestinian jail with the help of his guards. This is not disclosed to the public until a week later.

- December 2—Head of Fatah in the West Bank, Marwan Barghouti, declares that the Palestinians will not stop the uprising as a condition of resumed negotiations.

- December 3—Under strong pressure from the Clinton administration, Israel lifts its opposition to an inquiry panel investigating the causes of the recent violence.

- December 4—Yasser Arafat is seen in public for the first time since 1994 holding his sub-machine gun. Jewish settlers block his route by throwing stones at his convoy and he continues to hold the weapon after the incident while reviewing troops. The settlers are detained by the IDF. US Ambassador to Israel Martin Indyk publicly states that the continued violence in the occupied territories and Hizbollah attacks in violation of UN Security Council 425 increase the risk of a new regional war.

- December 5—An Israeli embassy employee is shot and wounded while leaving a supermarket parking lot in Jordan. He was driving an unmarked car. This is the second such incident in 3 weeks.

- December 6—Fatah leader Marwan Barghouti states that negotiations should not be restarted and that the current uprising should be escalated. Also, he says that Arafat has rescinded the order not to fire from Palestinian-controlled areas.

- December 7—A Palestinian man is sentenced to death by a Palestinian court in Nablus for spying for Israel and assisting opposing security forces with the November 23 assassination of local Hamas leader Ibrahim Bani Oudeh. The World Bank authorizes a 12 million dollar grant to the Palestinian Authority to offset the growing economic problems stemming from Israeli travel restrictions.

- December 8—Ten people die in the worst violence since the original outbreak of violence on September 28, 2000. Three are Israeli settlers and seven are Palestinians.

- December 9—Iraq promises 1 billion Euros (approximately $900 million US) in food and medical aid to the Palestinians.

- December 10—Barak resigns as Prime Minister in an effort to outflank Netanyahu, as one must be a sitting member of the Knesset in order to run for Prime Minister in an early election. Polls show Netanyahu would crush Barak by an almost 2 to 1 margin in the election, if the two ran against each other.

  In the West Bank Israeli soldiers kill a Palestinian man who is planting a roadside bomb. Palestinian gunmen ambush Chief Rabbi Meir Lau. The IDF convinces the rabbi to travel in an armored bus instead of his usual car; therefore the rabbi arrives at his destination unharmed.

- December 11—Bill Mitchell's probe into the causes and solutions to the recent violence begins, but is overshadowed by the drama of Israeli election policy. Israeli soldiers kill Anwar Hamran, a suspected bombing suspect for the PIJ, while waiting for a taxi-cab in Narblus.

- December 12—IDF infantry kill Yousef Abu Swayeh, a local Fatah leader, in front of his house.
- December 13—Claiming that they were pursuing a shooting suspect IDF forces cross into a Palestinian-held sector of the Gaza Strip. They cross only about 100 meters into Area A. Chief of General Staff Lt.-Gen. Shaul Mofaz said on Wednesday that the IDF is carrying out intensive clandestine actions to foil attempts by Palestinian gunmen to attack Israeli civilians and soldiers in the territories. Abbas al-Awewi, Hamas member, is shot by the IDF on streets of Hebron. He has previously been arrested several times by both Israeli and Palestinian authorities.
- December 14—Israeli soldiers stop and shoot at a checkpoint, Hani Abu Bakr, a Hamas member, after he attempted to draw a pistol.
- December 19—Israeli and Palestinian officials meet in Washington, DC to discuss the prospects for peace. The UN Security Council votes against deploying UN observers to the disputed regions after only receiving 8 of the 9 votes necessary in the 15-member body. France, Namibia, Malaysia, Bangladesh, Jamaica, Tunisia, Mali, Ukraine, and China all support the resolution. Argentina, Canada, the Netherlands, Britain, Russia, and the US abstains. Benjamin Netanyahu declares that he will not seek the office of Prime Minister saying he would only run if Parliament disbanded and parliamentary elections were held. This leaves Ariel Sharon and Shimon Peres as potential rivals to Barak in February.

It is now all too clear that the peace process *is* reversible and that the peace negotiations can fail entirely, or become locked in an explosive stalemate that could last months or years. Even before the September 2000 fighting between Israelis and Palestinians, Prime Minister Barak stressed that he was seeking "peace with security," and would only negotiate a peace that he felt left Israel militarily secure. The Palestinians made many political demands of their own and made it clear that a new struggle was one of their options in reaction to any failure in the peace process.

Even the best outcome seems likely to be a tragedy for both sides in which they return to positions very similar to those raised at Camp David, and reach compromises that remain unsatisfactory to both sides. Such a peace is nearly certain to be "cold," and involve the constant threat of violence from extremists and terrorists on both sides. It will leave a legacy of hatred and hundreds, if not thousands, of casualties that will take years to overcome. It is all too possible, however, that the "Second Intifada" may last for months or years, and leave both sides sadder, but not wiser, or that there will be an awkward and unstable end to open violence without a real peace and with continued terrorism and extremism.

PEACE WITH VIOLENCE VERSUS A SECOND INTIFADA: THE NATURE OF ASYMMETRIC WARFARE

Both the fighting that began in September 2000 and the earlier failure of the Camp David summit exposed the fact that Israelis and Palestinians still have deeply asymmetric goals and expectations, not only over Jerusalem but over all of the final settlement issues. The steps that Israel proposed at Camp David went further than Israel had ever gone before, but they were not a return to the 1967 boundary that the Palestinians sought. They did not meet Palestinian expectations regarding East Jerusalem, the Mosques on the Temple Mount, Palestinian sovereignty, borders, an Israeli military presence in the West Bank and Gaza, or treatment of the Israeli settlements in the Occupied Territories. Israel, on the other hand, felt that it had proposed dramatic concessions that represented the absolute limits to its negotiation position. In fact, Prime Minister Barak may have gone further at Camp David than the Israeli people were willing to go without truly bridging the gap, and both sides may then have come closer than they will be able to come for months or years.

Even if a peace settlement can now be reached in spite of the Israeli-Palestinian fighting that began in September 2000, it will still leave major problems and the near certain threat of at least low-level continuing violence. Any compromise acceptable to both sides must leave Jerusalem and the West Bank deeply divided. Much of the West Bank would remain under Israeli control and at least the greater Jerusalem area would remain open for Israeli settlement.

No peace can meet the economic and political expectations of the younger Palestinians for years to come. It was young Palestinians, however, that created the first Intifada, and that turned the events that began in September 2000 into something approaching a popular uprising. The Israelis, in turn, will have to live with the uncertainty that a peace would give the Palestinian Authority steadily growing power without necessarily bringing lasting security and peace, and with the specter of some kind of uprising by Israeli Arabs.

Such a peace will be "peace with violence," and signing an agreement will only be the first step. Any peace based on such divisions will be the prelude to years of further agonizing tension over the situation in the West Bank and Gaza, and Palestinian rights to full sovereignty. Israelis and Palestinians could be faced with a new political and military struggle for power even after such a "peace."[362] Alternatively, peace could proceed in a way in which Israel continued to deal with a Palestinian entity that supported the peace process, but where extremist elements within the Palestinian community continued to attack and murder pro-peace Palestinians and Israelis, while Israeli Jewish extremists opposed movement towards compromise, the creation of a Palestinian state, a halt to and/or roll-back of settlements, economic integration to aid the Palestinians and Jordan, with equal violence.

Regardless of whether a Second Intifada continues, or a cold peace occurs, leadership problems and internal disputes will affect both the Palestinian Authority and Israel. It is possible that Arafat's death and the struggle for the succession could create a low-level civil war among Palestinians that could spill over into attacks on Israel or bring an anti-peace Palestinian leader to power. It is equally possible that Israeli opposition to the peace process, and anti-government extremism, would grow in response to the transfer of territory in the West Bank and negotiations over the Golan, Jerusalem, and the future of the settlements. The bitter internal tensions in both the Palestinian movement and Israeli society will be equally troublesome.

Israeli politics could bring a government that opposes peace to power, or one that would not take the risks necessary to make a peace work. It could couple the deep divisions in Israeli society and politics to the debate over peace and turn every effort to implement and improve a peace into a bitter partisan political debate in Israel that increased the risk of Israeli extremism and terrorism and/or delayed or blocked the implementation of given aspects of a peace agreement. It is one of the tragedies of current events that "peace," or any interim security agreement that brings an end to violence, may be a two-edged sword.

The most dangerous scenario, however, is not the problems created by peace, or an interim security agreement, but rather a scenario where a lasting breakdown of the peace process takes place. It is a scenario leading to the creation of a sustained "Second Intifada." This would be a low intensity war fought partly as a popular Palestinian uprising, and partly as low intensity conflict by armed Palestinians, against the Israel Defense Forces (IDF) and Israeli society. The events of September through November 2000 have shown how quickly such violence can escalate and how sudden the transition can be from peace negotiations to something approaching war. It also showed that asymmetric expectations and asymmetric war can be a terrible combination.

Events have already shown the fundamentally asymmetric character of the fighting. Israel has an overwhelming advantage in terms of conventional arms. It has the military strength to defeat the Palestinians by the direct application of military force, although such fighting could take weeks or months of intensive combat, and the IDF could take heavy casualties and lose the political war in doing so. While Israel continues to examine plans for a reoccupation of the Palestinian population centers in the West Bank, it has determined that even with the use of advanced helicopters, tanks and troops, such a reoccupation would be extremely costly to both the Palestinians and Israelis and that the legacy of such a "victory" would have major strategic and political costs. It might well polarize the entire Arab and Islamic world against Israel, and cost it many of its allies in the West.

The IDF has conducted a number of simulations of a possible retaking of part of the Palestinian land if such a situation was to develop. It seems clear from these exercises that Israel would be the eventual *military* victor in any given battle for the control of a Palestinian town or city. However, the political image of Israel would suffer serious damage, there would be serious potential casualties the moment the IDF had to fight in built-up areas against armed Palestinians, and the end result would be maintaining strong points for an occupation army in a sea of hostile Palestinians.

As a result, the IDF has focused more on a strategy of containment and isolation than on reoccupation. It has focused on plans to isolate key Palestinian population centers, securing access roads and lines of communication, and improving the security of the settlements and military installations in the West Bank. It has examined ways to combine military isolation with economic measures like freezing financial operations and transit between Palestinian areas, cutting off communications, and limiting the shipment of goods. It has emphasized the use of helicopters and standoff precision weapons, while seizing and destroying key Palestinian strong points or facilities that could be used to attack Israel.

Israel has already begun to apply many of these tactics. During October 2000, for example, Israel made its first extensive use of attack helicopters to strike targets in Gaza and the West Bank. AH-64A Apaches were used to hit targets in Nablus and in Gaza, including Chairman Arafat's compound. The AH-64 was used instead of the AH-1G/S Cobra because of its superior range, sensors, and weapons, and ability to better distinguish between civilians and "combatants."[363] "Precision," however, is always relative and any attack on built up and urban areas risks killing innocent civilians. Unfortunately in some cases the AH-64s have failed to hit the desired targets and inflicted collateral damage. For example, an AH-64 attack against the al-Fatah in El-Bireh in the West Bank in October 2000 hit the house next door.[364]

IDF tactics on the ground would also have to become more aggressive in comparison to the previous Intifada. For example, Israel deployed special anti-guerrilla units in October 2000 that could be used for more aggressive penetration and counter-guerrilla missions. The problem with such units, however, is that they require superb human intelligence (HUMINT) if they are to be directed against the right targets, avoid striking at civilians or young men caught up in the Intifada, and avoid taking casualties. It is far easier to call for raids and commando missions than execute them, the political costs of collateral damage and casualties can be high, and even success can simply increase Palestinian political hatred and commitment to violence and an uprising.

Despite the inherent difficulties of commando raids, Israel is employing them on a limited basis with a good success rate. Anwar Hamran, a PIJ bombing suspect, was killed while waiting for a taxicab on December 11, 2000. The IDF has denied pursuing a policy of killing members of Hamas and Fatah; however IDF spokesperson Yarden Vatikay reminded reporters that the IDF would "target anyone who plans terrorist actions against Israelis" and Lt. General Mofaz admitted that the IDF was involved in "major clandestine action" to hunt down Palestinian forces which attack IDF positions. Deputy Defence Minister Ephraim Sneh told Israeli radio in regards to the recent deaths "You can't beat terror with symposiums at the university. The most effective and just way to deal with terror is the elimination or incarceration of the people who lead these organizations." Hamas members Abbas al-Awewi and Hani Abu Bakr and Yousef Abu Swayeh, a local Fatah leader, were all recently killed by Israeli forces. Whether or not these individuals were armed is disputed. These raids resulted in no Israeli casualties or collateral damage. These commando raids have been more successful in public relations terms than the previous killings using AH-64 due to their lower profile compared to helicopter strikes. Furthermore, a misfire of an M-16 is far less dangerous than a misfire of a laser-guided anti-tank missile making these raids more favorable in terms of collateral damage. However, these raids present a greater intelligence challenge due to the need for HUMINT on the habits and locations of the targets.[365]

Gaza is less of a military problem for the IDF than the West Bank, but presents political difficulties because of the IDF's need to defend isolated Israeli settlements. The IDF has no desire to reoccupy the Gaza, and senior Israeli officers privately make it clear that they would like to see an end to all of the remaining Israeli settlements in the Gaza Strip. They regard these settlements as a useless drain on Israel's security assets, just as they do many of the small hardline Israeli settlements deep in Palestinian territory in the West Bank. Nevertheless, the political reality is that the IDF cannot pursue such a strategy. Domestic politics in Israel mean that it cannot evacuate and isolate, and must adopt a strategy of isolating the Palestinian areas of Gaza as much as possible, and provide expensive and dangerous protection to Israeli settlements. It has already begun to implement this strategy by the division of the Gaza Strip into four separate security zones, thereby preventing Palestinian travel between these four areas.[366]

Both Israelis and Palestinians regard the other side's goals as unfair and use of violence as excessive, and both exploit the other side's excesses and apparent excess to try to gain the support of world opinion. Here, Israel has political disadvantages that partially offset its military advantages.

Far more of the world opposes Israeli settlements and the Israeli presence in the West Bank and Gaza than supports it. UN Security Council resolutions largely endorse the Palestinian demand for Israeli withdrawal to the 1967 boundary. What is even more important from a military point of view is that the struggle between Israeli and Palestinian is as much a battle of perceptions as a military and security struggle. The fighting between well-equipped Israeli soldiers and Palestinian civilians using sniping, rock throwing, and physical attacks, is a political battle in which the IDF can only use decisive force at the cost of media images of Palestinian suffering that severely damage Israel's political position. As a result, any form of Intifada becomes asymmetric warfare where Palestinian "martyrs" become political weapons that can be as effective in their own way as Israeli heavy weapons. Furthermore, this asymmetry in terms of force and the need to make use of the media as a weapon makes de-escalation difficult, even when both sides sincerely seek to limit violence.

There are severe limits to what an IDF force seeking to minimize its casualties can do to avoid inflicting casualties on the Palestinians. Non-lethal force is highly limited in scope, and the phrase "non-lethal" can be misleading. Weapons like CS gas and rubber bullets have limited range. They often are not effective in stopping large groups, but gas can be lethal in a small number of cases and rubber bullets produce serious trauma in 5–20% of actual hits even within their limited range. They are much more lethal at close ranges. As a number of experts have privately pointed out, the resulting problems are compounded by Israel's failure to develop large, well-trained, and well-equipped units dedicated to riot control and the non-lethal use of force, and the lack of joint training for such missions by both the IDF and Palestinian Security forces. Ironically, the climate of peace negotiations before September 2000, coupled to a heavy emphasis on counterterrorism, left both sides poorly prepared to both minimize violence during an uprising and enforce efforts to halt the violence.

Israel's acute sensitivity to casualties compounds the problem, and observers that have never been in a violent riot or watched clashes between violent civilian groups and troops often ignore the grim realities that sometimes develop on the ground. Troops cannot let mobs armed with stones or Molotov cocktails close on their positions, or rely on their riot control gear used in dealing with civil disobedience. They must use lethal fire if they risk being overrun by a group that may kill. The problems grow steadily more serious if there is any risk of sniping or small arms fire, where lethal and non-lethal force can easily become mixed and it is almost impossible to separate innocent civilians, Palestinians throwing rocks, and Palestinians using lethal force.

These problems are poorly understood in the media, while exploiting the media and world opinion is critical in the Palestinian ability to turn tactical military defeats into a political and strategic victory. The Palestinian side can only "win" in terms of major gains in a peace process or settlement if it can capture world opinion, and uses Palestinian suffering and "martyrs" to gain political support. At the same time, violence provokes violence and the current fighting has already evolved beyond the ability of Chairman Arafat and the Palestinian Authority leadership to exercise tight control, if such a capability ever existed. Palestinian young men do not fight because they are part of some guiding strategy; they fight because of years of resentment and growing feelings of hatred. Almost inevitably, the fighting has also strengthened the hand of true opponents of peace like Hamas and the Palestinian Islamic Jihad, given outside movements like the Hizbollah more influence, and pushed elements of Arafat's own supporters like the Fatah Hawks towards a commitment to continued armed struggle.

In broad terms, however, the Second Intifada is developing into a strategic tragedy where neither side can be given the primary blame for the consequences. One side—Israel—has a goal of minimizing its casualties and establishing control. The other side—the Palestinians—has the political goal of using their own suffering, if not actually encouraging their own casualties, to create political instability and tension. The end result is that Israel seems to use excessive force while the Palestinians seem to provoke it.

This is a remarkably poor combination of strategy and tactics for ending violence, and one where both sides are confronted with the fact that the media images they want to create mean higher casualties, if for totally different reasons. Given these circumstances Israel has officially adopted the following rules of engagement: Tear gas and stun grenades are used first. Should these fail to disperse the protest, rubber-coated metal bullets are used, which are supposed to be shot at the lower body from a distance of 25 meters or more. Live ammunition is used in response to firebombs and when encountering shooting and/or grenades Israeli soldiers will shoot to kill.

Palestinian sources claim that Israeli forces are not abiding by these rules and are more frequently making use of lethal shots aimed at the upper body or head.[367] Other observers claim that IDF troops deliberately aim at the legs of young men, seek to cripple them, and even prevent effective emergency medical services. For example, Palestinian sources are quoted as reporting that as of November 12, 21.4% of the 4,448 Palestinians admitted to a hospital were shot in the legs, and the Physicians for Human Rights are quoted as saying that the existence of a similar pattern of injuries over time reflects an ongoing policy.[368]

Many of these reports are extremely controversial, and reflect a total lack of military experience. Leg wounds often occur when troops are trying to avoid hits on the head or body, and require the target to be exposed—making the target more difficult to acquire. Talking about the finer details of wound patterns implies a degree of accuracy in combat that no army has ever achieved, as well as a degree of control over individual soldiers in a firefight or close combat that at best is possible only with small cadres of elite forces. War is not a computer game; it is fought in a climate of emotion, fear, and misperception. No army in history has ever been able to create a force composed entirely of sharpshooters, or keep a significant percentage of its troops from panicking and over-reacting.

That said, the Report of the UN High Commissioner on Human Rights on her visit to the occupied Palestinian territories during November 8–16, 2000, illustrates the real-world human cost of asymmetric warfare.[369] It notes a high number of rubber bullet hits on the eyes of Palestinians, and the risks inherent in using rubber bullets and tear gas. It quotes figures provided by the Minister of Health of the Palestinian Authority stating that some 6,958 people (3,366 in the West Bank and 3,592 in Gaza) had been wounded between September 29 and November 9, and that 1,016 Palestinians had been wounded in Israel. It also notes that 13 Arab-Israelis were killed following street demonstrations in late September and early October, and over 1,000 were imprisoned.[370]

According to these Palestinian figures, 40% of those wounded were under 18 years of age, and 41% of the wounds were caused by rubber bullets, 27% by regular ammunition, 27% by tear gas, and 11% by heavier weapons like rockets. At the same time, the report notes that the IDF had found that rubber (plastic coated) bullets, tear gas, and water cannons were not effective at ranges over 50–100 meters, and that, "The IDF have over the last few months tested dozens of weapons but have concluded that less than lethal weapons effective to range of 200 meters do not currently exist."[371]

The asymmetric nature of the casualties and effects of the fighting are illustrated by the fact that the UN report notes that the Palestinian Red Crescent Society reported that 236 Palestinians had been killed, and 9,353 had been wounded, between September 27 and November 23. In contrast, Israel reported 30 Israelis killed and 375 wounded, although the IDF claimed there had been a total of 5,085 attacks on Israelis and 1,400 had involved live fire, including machine guns and the use of fire bombs.[372] The UN also reports that the Palestinians have suffered far more in terms of economic restrictions, curfews, and other civil and economic costs.

While both side's dispute such statistics, it is clear that far more is involved in such efforts than a battle for the media and world opinion. Every Israeli use of lethal force builds Palestinian hatred and resentment. This fuels Palestinian extremism in societies that are extremely young. The Palestinian Authority did far less to educate its population and try to reduce such extremism between the Oslo accords and September 2000 than the Israelis and this can easily lead to lethal violence against IDF soldiers and Israeli civilians that is not under the control of the Palestinian Authority. At the same time, various Israeli settler groups and many private Israelis are arming themselves, taking gun lessons, and creating a climate where untrained civilians may shoot at innocent Palestinians, carry out vigilante justice or take "revenge," regardless of any real justification.[373] The rise in popular violence on both sides can create and add to cycles of reaction and counter-reaction that is beyond either side's control.

This, in turn, creates a climate which extremists on both sides can exploit, and where incidents of terrorism or violence against the other side's civilians can be used to block efforts to bring ceasefires or any return to the peace process. Words are weapons in such asymmetric conflicts and so are political gestures. Both sides have a natural tendency to add a religious and ethnic dimension of the conflict. The risk of a secular Palestinian struggle becoming Islamic is particularly great, but the "Jew versus Jew" struggle inside Israel brings Judaism into such a struggle as well.

Physical containment and economic warfare create further problems. Containment means isolating Palestinians and crippling the economy of any area facing containment. Given the already weak economies in Gaza and the West Bank, this has an immediate and brutal human impact and affects all involved, not simply those who are violent. So does the destruction of buildings and facilities to clear lines of sight or fire for the IDF, punish attackers, or prevent sniping—all of which inevitably becomes part of the political battle for media attention.

When Israel closes off the West Bank and Gaza, some 125,000 Palestinian workers have been unable to reach their jobs, and unemployment has risen from 11% to over 30%. The Palestinian economy has been losing $10 million a day and the lucrative tourist trade has all but dried up. Furthermore, foreign investment has slowed dramatically; a disaster, as this foreign capital accounts for 70% of the new economic ventures.

At the same time, Israelis suffer economically as well as Palestinians and the economic dimension of the conflict builds tension on both sides. So far the economic cost has been great to both sides. Some estimates indicate the Israeli economy will lose $2 billion in exports and its forecasted growth rate has dropped from 7 to 5%. Especially hard hit is the agricultural industry that depends on Palestinians for 20% of its labor. In the end, however, the continuation of the closings of the territories costs the Palestinians more economically than their Israeli counterparts. Israel is only dependent on the PNA territories for one percent of its GDP, while the Palestinian economy is dependent on the Israeli economy for over 25% of its GDP.[374]

Enforcing containment of hostile populations makes the problem of both actual violence and images of the asymmetric character of that violence worse. It means the forward deployment of overwhelming force in the form of armor and artillery, the use of helicopters to reduce vulnerability and provide a platform for precision fire. It means IDF bunkers and deployments become natural targets, and that there is a further incentive for Palestinian bombings and "terrorism," Palestinian efforts to kidnap or attack IDF soldiers and civilians anywhere along the perimeter of containment areas, and clashes between Israeli and Palestinian civilians. This can lead to low-level night battles and overreaction at all times by both sides, as well as involving innocent civilians. Securing Israeli settlers presents another dilemma for Israel. They must be equipped for defense and armed accordingly, but they are not subject to military discipline and can easily overreact. Many of the more isolated settlers tend to be ideological extremists, which scarcely helps.

In short, every step that continues or escalates violence and Israeli-Palestinian clashes compounds the tragedy of conflict, makes peace or a ceasefire more difficult to reach, and makes any kind of peace or ceasefire more difficult to enforce.

THE "MILITARY BALANCE": THE ACTORS THAT WOULD CHALLENGE THE IDF IN A SECOND INTIFADA

The political and strategic outcome of an enduring "Second Intifada" is almost impossible to predict. So much depends on the role of outside actors and political events that there is no way to predict who would "win," and how much both sides would actually lose. There are, however, some aspects of the military balance that would have a powerful impact if a "Second Intifada" ever did escalate to prolonged conflict.

Normal measures of the conventional military balance have only limited meaning under such conditions. Conflicts in Afghanistan, Cambodia, Kashmir, Lebanon, Northern Ireland, the Sudan, Sri Lanka, Vietnam, and the Western

Sahara have shown that long, bloody, guerrilla wars and low-level conflicts can be fought by small, poorly equipped extremist elements even when they face massively superior conventional armies. Even highly trained and well-equipped Israeli forces never entirely succeeded in enforcing security during the Intifada, just as similarly trained and equipped British forces were never able to halt the violence in Northern Ireland.

Many low-intensity wars have occurred where the "guerrillas" initially seem to be defeated. In many cases, however, the military or paramilitary capabilities of guerrilla forces evolved during the conflict, adapting and re-adapting to the military and internal security techniques used to suppress them. Thus, the balance at the beginning of such a conflict proved to be little indication of the balance that will exist at its end. "Winning" the first round of battles only led to years of political and military struggle with constant changes in tactics, weapons, and levels of engagement. The paramilitary and guerrilla organizations that exist at the start of such conflicts also can change radically in leadership, tactics, and equipment under the pressure of events. At the same time, the IDF has examined how to fight a "Second Intifada" ever since the ending of the first uprising. It created special facilities like a mock Palestinian hill town and trained units continuously for low intensity combat against the Palestinians in urban areas. It also trained large numbers of troops and reservists to protect Israeli settlements.[375]

Palestinian Paramilitary Groups

At present, there is a wide range of Palestinian military and paramilitary forces that could shape a Second Intifada. These forces include different factions with shifting alignments, almost all of which make grandiose claims about their active manpower, their combat equipment, and the size of their combat formations.[376]

Many are forces that supported peace and counterterrorism operations before September 29, are deployed in Gaza and the West Bank, and are controlled by the Palestinian Authority. These forces are summarized in Figure 7.1 and described in detail in Table 7.1, which lists the total pro-peace forces as of mid-1999. The totals are up from 1995, when there were some 16,500 to 18,000 police officers and security personnel, including 7,000 men in the Public Security Force, 4,000 men in the Civil Police, and 2,500 men in the Preventive Security Force.

As Figure 7.2 shows, there are additional pro–Palestinian Authority/PLO forces including the security, military and paramilitary elements of Fatah, Palestine Liberation Front (PLF), Arab Liberation Front (ALF), Popular Front for the Liberation of Palestine (PFLP), Democratic Front for the Liberation of Palestine (DFLP), and Palestine Popular Struggle Front (PPSF). Some forces like the Palestine National Liberation Army (PNLA) still exist as cadres, but much of their manpower has been incorporated in the forces of the Palestinian Authority.

Most of the pro–Palestinian Authority/pro-peace forces outside Gaza and Jericho lost much of their strength and income since the Gulf War. Syria and the

Figure 7.1
Palestinian Authority Paramilitary Forces in 2000

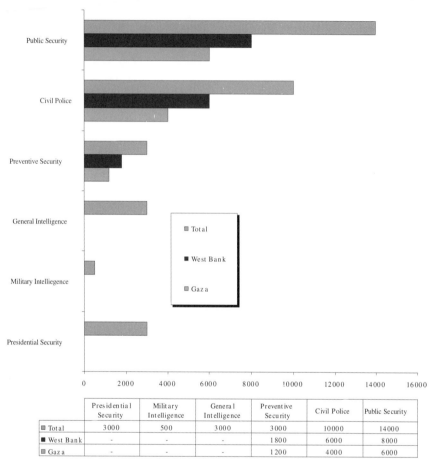

	Presidential Security	Military Intelligence	General Intelligence	Preventive Security	Civil Police	Public Security
Total	3000	500	3000	3000	10000	14000
West Bank	-	-	-	1800	6000	8000
Gaza	-	-	-	1200	4000	6000

Source: Prepared by Anthony H. Cordesman, based upon the IISS *Military Balance* and discussions
with US and regional experts.

Lebanese Army partially disarmed many of the pro-PLO Palestinian factions in
Lebanon in 1991, and took away their heavier arms like tanks, APCs, and
artillery—although Syria and the Lebanese Army left pro-Syrian factions like the
PFLP-GC (General Command) alone. The Lebanese Army has continued these
efforts since 1991, and conducted new operations against the Fatah Revolutionary
Council in 1994. Syria and Iraq maintain tight control over the operations and
weapons of all Palestinian forces based on their territory.

Some Palestinian factions within the PLO, and most factions outside the PLO,
opposed the peace process before September 29. These factions are also shown in

Table 7.1
Military and Paramilitary Strength of Key Palestinian Factions and the Hizbollah

Palestinian Authority

35,000 Security and paramilitary pro-PLO forces enforcing security in Gaza and Jericho, including:
  Public Security (14,000)—6,000 in Gaza and 8,000 in West Bank
  Civil police (10,000)—4,000 in Gaza and 6,000 in West Bank
  Preventive Security (3,000)—1,200 in Gaza and 1,800 in West Bank
  General Intelligence (3,000)
  Presidential Security (3,000)
  Military Intelligence (500)
  Additional forces in Coastal Police, Air Force, Customs and Excise Police Force,
    University Security Service, and Civil Defense.
Equipment includes 45 APCs, 1 Lockheed Jetstar, 2 Mi-8s, 2 Mi-17s, and roughly 40,000 small arms. These include automatic weapons and light machine guns. Israeli claims they include heavy automatic weapons, rocket launchers, anti-tank rocket launchers and guided weapons, and manportable anti-air missiles.

Pro-PLO

Palestinian National Liberation Army (PNLA)/Al Fatah—5,000-8,000 active and semi-active reserves that make up the main pro-Arafat force, based in Algeria, Egypt, Iraq, Lebanon, Libya, Jordan, Sudan, Syria, and Yemen under the tight control of the host government.
Palestine Liberation Front (PLF)–Abu Abbas Faction—300-400 men led by Al-Abbas, based in Syria.
Arab Liberation Front (ALF)–300-400 men based in Lebanon and Iraq.
Democratic Front for the Liberation of Palestine (DFLP)—400-600 men led by Naif Hawatmeh, which claims eight battalions, and is based in Syria, Lebanon, and elsewhere.
Popular Front for the Liberation of Palestine (PFLP)—800 men led by George Habash, based in Syria, Lebanon, West Bank, and Gaza.
Palestine Popular Struggle Front (PSF)—600-700 men led by Samir Ghawsha and Bahjat Abu Gharbiyah, based in Syria.

Anti-PLO

Palestinian Islamic Jihad (PIJ)—350 men in various factions, led by Assad Bayud al-Tamimi, Fathi Shakaki, Ibrahim Odeh, Ahmad Muhana, and others, based in the West Bank and Gaza.
Hamas—military wing of about 300 men, based in the West Bank and Gaza.
As-Saiqa—600-1,000 men in pro-Syrian force under Issam al-Qadi, based in Syria.
Fatah Revolutionary Council (FRC)/Abu Nidal Organization (ANO)—300 men led by Abu Nidal (Sabri al-Bana), based in Lebanon, Syria, and Iraq.
Popular Front for the Liberation of Palestine–General Command (PFLP-GC)—600 men led by Ahmad Jibril, based in Syria, Lebanon, and elsewhere.

Table 7.1 (continued)

Anti-PLO

Popular Front for the Liberation of Palestine–Special Command (PFLP-SC)—50-100
  men led by Abu Muhammad (Salim Abu Salem).
Palestine Liberation Army (PLA)—4,500 men, based in Syria.
Fatah Intifada—400-1,000 men led by Said Musa Muragha (Abu Musa). Based in Syria
  and Lebanon.

Hizbollah (Party of God)

About 300-5000 actives with 3,000 men in support, Shi'ite fundamentalist, APCs,
  artillery, MRLs, ATGMs, rocket launchers, AA guns, SA-7s, AT-3 Saggers.

Source: Adapted from US Department of State, "Patterns of Global Terrorism, 1998," Washington,
  GPO, April 1999; IISS, *Military Balance,* 1998–1999 and 1999–2000.

Figure 7.3. At least ten organizations with some kind of military, paramilitary, or
terrorist element have rejected the peace process, and declared themselves part of
the "opposition front" at a meeting in Damascus in September 1992. At the time,
this list included the Hamas-Islamic Resistance, elements of the Palestine Popular
Struggle Front (PPSF), the Palestinian Islamic Jihad (PIJ), the Revolutionary
Communist Party, DFLP, elements of the People's Liberation Front (PLF), al-
Saiqa and Fatah-Intifada in 1999. However, this list may not be currently accurate
since the organizations that oppose the peace process tend to change over time.

   Palestinian forces that are not aligned with the PLO include forces belonging to
the Fatah dissidents, Fatah Revolutionary Council/Abu Nidal Organization (FRC/
ANO), Fatah Intifada (Abu Musa), Palestine Liberation Army (PLA), PFLP-GC
(General Command), and PFLP-SC (Special Command). Some of these forces are
based in, and under the direct control of, Syria.

   The current military strength of these various factions is difficult to estimate.
Table 7.1 and Figure 7.3 provide a rough estimate of their manpower strength.
Even where such units have significant manpower strength, however, they have
little conventional military strength and cannot use most of the medium and heavy
weapons (if any) they possess. Their capabilities are limited to terrorism, unconventional warfare, and low-intensity combat in built-up areas and mountainous
terrain. In the past most such radical Palestinian forces had low levels of activity in
terms of casualties, although no meaningful incident account seems to be available. In fact, many such forces are now little more than political tools or ideological
sinecures.[377]

   Further, even if current estimates of the size and capabilities such factions were
reliable, they only would be valuable as rough indicators of the kind of forces that
might become involved in a future conflict. The key issue shaping this aspect of the
Arab-Israeli military balance is not the current size and activity of Palestinian

Figure 7.2
Other Pro-PLO/Palestinian Authority Palestinian Paramilitary Forces in 2000

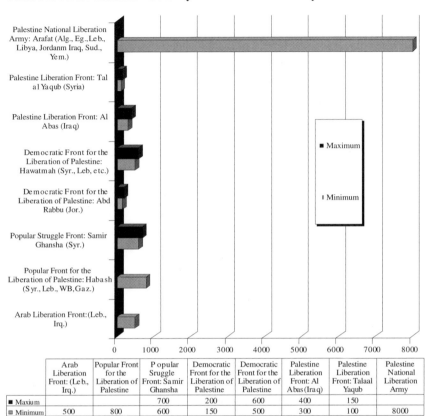

	Arab Liberation Front: (Leb., Irq.)	Popular Front for the Liberation of Palestine	Popular Sruggle Front: Samir Ghansha	Democratic Front for the Liberation of Palestine	Democratic Front for the Liberation of Palestine	Palestine Liberation Front: Al Abas (Iraq)	Palestine Liberation Front: Talaal Yaqub	Palestine National Liberation Army
■ Maxium			700	200	600	400	150	
▣ Minimum	500	800	600	150	500	300	100	8000

Source: Prepared by Anthony H. Cordesman, based upon the IISS *Military Balance* and discussions with US and regional experts.

military and paramilitary forces. It is rather the future actions of various extremist groups that use terrorism and random violence, and the new forces that might emerge as a result of a breakdown of the peace process.

The Role of Hamas and the Islamic Jihad

Hamas and the Islamic Jihad are the two Palestinian organizations that have been most active in attacks on Israelis and pro-peace Palestinians in recent years. The fact that many elements of these organizations have been "freed" since September 29, or given more military freedom of action, constitutes a continuing threat to efforts to rebuild the peace process and means they could become a far

Figure 7.3
Anti-PLO/Palestinian Authority Palestinian Paramilitary Forces in 2000

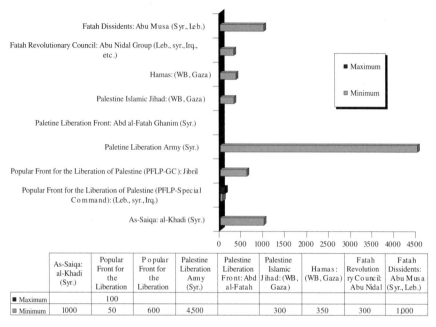

	As-Saiqa: al-Khadi (Syr.)	Popular Front for the Liberation	Popular Front for the Liberation	Palestine Liberation Army (Syr.)	Palestine Liberation Front: Abd al-Fatah	Palestine Islamic Jihad: (WB, Gaza)	Hamas: (WB, Gaza)	Fatah Revolution ry Council: Abu Nidal	Fatah Dissidents: Abu Musa (Syr., Leb.)
■ Maximum		100							
▣ Minimum	1000	50	600	4,500		300	350	300	1,000

Source: Prepared by Anthony H. Cordesman, based upon the IISS *Military Balance* and discussions with US and regional experts.

more serious threat in a "Second Intifada." Their acts of terrorism before September 29 showed that lightly armed insurgents inside the West Bank, Gaza, and Israel can conduct acts of terrorism and extremism, and can strike successfully against their fellow Palestinians and the West, as well as Israel. While they have not yet been able to block the peace process, they have repeatedly shown that they can sometimes slow its pace and weaken both Israeli and Palestinian support for the process.

There has been a long history of Israeli-Palestinian violence. The causes of this violence, and the rights and wrongs on each side, are not the subject of this analysis, but some of the recent history has direct relevance to a military assessment. Since Oslo, a total of 140 Israeli civilians and soldiers were killed between the signing of the Declaration of Principles between Israel and the PLO on September 13, 1993, and September 13, 1995. These deaths included 27 civilians and soldiers in Judea, Samaria and the Gaza Strip, and 62 civilians and 26 soldiers within the Green Line. Palestinian extremist groups killed a total of 73 Israeli soldiers during 1994, and wounded more than 100 additional Israelis—a slightly higher total than in 1993. At least 20 additional Palestinians were killed, and well over 100 were wounded. Hamas and Islamic Jihad were the source of virtually all of this violence.

After 1994, most terrorist attacks were sporadic and occurred largely as reaction to political events. A record high of 87 Israelis were killed around the time of the inauguration of former Prime Minister Binyamin Netanyahu. In 1997, there were only 31 reported Israeli fatalities as a result of terror attacks. Nevertheless, the Israeli Foreign Ministry claimed in September 1998 that[378]

Although peace talks between Israel and the Palestinians have been taking place over the last five years, terrorism still remains a major threat. Since the exchange of *letters of mutual recognition* between Israel and the PLO on September 9, 1993, the threat of terrorism against Israelis has dramatically increased. In fact, more Israelis have been killed by Palestinian terrorists in the 5 years since the *Oslo Accord*, than in the 15 years preceding it.

... While five years have passed since the first agreement was reached with the Palestinians, and the framework of PA responsibilities was adopted, terrorism remains, and the number of its victims has grown. The Israel Government Press Office has recently released figures showing that during this 5-year period, 279 men, women and children have been killed in 92 lethal attacks carried out against Israelis by Palestinian terrorists. This is 50 percent more than the number of Israelis killed in the six years of the Intifada ('87-'93), and surpasses the number of those killed in the entire 15 years preceding the signing of the agreements.

In 1998, President Yasser Arafat made overtures to include Hamas and Islamic Jihad in the new Palestinian Authority administration. Both parties refused to join the new cabinet on the grounds that they would not participate in any government that approved of agreements limiting Palestinian sovereignty, including the Oslo accords.[379] Hamas leaders did express approval of Arafat's desire to consult with opposition groups, but this approval in no way signifies warm relations between Hamas and the Palestinian Authority. It now seems doubtful that Hamas and the Islamic Jihad will truly renounce violence unless the peace process offers the Palestinians far more rewards than it has to date, such as a complete Israeli withdrawal from the occupied territories and dismantlement of all Israeli settlements.[380]

A study by the Washington Institute that was published in October 1999 helps put the history of such violence in perspective. The study compared a period of 69 months before the signing of the Oslo Declaration of Principles in September 1993 (December 9, 1987-September 13, 1993) with the 70-month period that followed (September 14, 1993-July 6, 1999). It found that there were 152 lethal incidents in the earlier period, or 2.2 a month. There were a total of 973 lethal incidents involving Palestinians killed, or 14.1 per month. The totals dropped strikingly after the Declaration. In the 70 months that followed, there were 116 lethal incidents involving Israelis, or 1.6 a month. There were a total of 254 lethal incidents involving Palestinians killed, or 3.6 per month.[381]

These positive trends towards peace and mutual security have been reversed by the outbreak of violence on September 29, and the result has been far more brutal than the outbreak of the previous Intifada. The number of people killed in the first two weeks following Sharon's visit to the Temple Mount/Sharam Al-Sharif was the same as the number killed in the first four months of the 1987–1993 Intifada.

Drops in the number of incidents did not lead to similar cuts in fatalities, largely because of the use of larger bombs in attacks against Israelis and a reduction in intra-Palestinian feuds and killings. There were 212 Israelis killed in the earlier period, or 3.1 a month. There were 1,236 Palestinians killed, or 17.9 per month. The totals dropped strikingly after the Declaration. In the 70 months that followed, there were 287 Israelis killed, or 4.1 a month. In contrast, there were 391 Palestinians killed, or 5.6 per month. The percentage of Israelis killed by bombs rose from 2.1% under the Shamir government to 47.2 under Rabin/Peres and 33.8% under Netanyahu. In contrast, well over 90% of the Palestinians who died were killed by gunfire under all three governments.[382]

The other patterns revealed in the Washington Institute study show the impact of the crisis in terrorism following the Declaration, and the rise in anti-peace Palestinian terrorism. This was followed by a sharp drop in incidents as the Israeli government pushed for stronger security measures and the security efforts of the Palestinian Authority improved.[383] These cycles of violence are another indication of the risk of the sudden outbreak of new tensions and conflict:

- The number of Israeli fatalities per month rose from 2.7 per month under the Shamir government to 6.0 under the Rabin/Peres governments, and then dropped to only 1.9 under the Netanyahu government.

- The number of Palestinian fatalities per month dropped from 18.7 per month under the Shamir government to 10.1 under the Rabin/Peres governments, and then dropped to only 3.3 under the Netanyahu government.

- Terrorist bombings killed only 2.4% of the Israelis killed before the Oslo Declaration and 54% after the Declaration, reflecting the impact of anti-peace terrorist groups.

- The number of Israeli civilians killed dropped from 70.5% of the total under the Shamir government (103) to 66.7% under the Rabin/Peres governments (188), and then to 63.4% (45) under the Netanyahu government.

- The number of Israeli military killed rose from 22.6% of the total under the Shamir government (33) to 32.6% under the Rabin/Peres governments (92), and then to 36.6% (26) under the Netanyahu government.

These patterns show that the progress toward peace alters the pattern of violence, but does not always reduce it. At the same time, they reflect the fact that the Palestinian Authority did steadily improve its security efforts and that the main cause of violence was anti-peace Palestinian movements trying to block further progress in the peace process. It is also clear that stronger Palestinian and Israeli security measures sharply limit the capabilities of extremists, and that it proved possible to have both peace and a high degree of security. However, none of these rules apply if the Palestinian Authority security forces overtly or covertly support extremists or insurgents, or are willing to fight the IDF. The clashes in both 1996 and 2000 have shown that this is a very real possibility. Moreover, the clashes in 2000 have shown that there can be alliances between the Palestinian Authority forces of groups like Fatah and far more hostile groups like Hamas and the Islamic Jihad.

Hamas

The Hamas organization is the most politically powerful of the two organizations. Hamas is both an acronym for "Harakat Al-Muqawwama Al-Islamia"—Islamic Resistance Movement—and a word meaning "zeal" or "courage and bravery." Hamas has several other names, including the Islamic Stream ("Al-Tiar Al-Islami"), or the Islamic Trend ("Al-Athja Al-Islami"). Hamas is a radical Islamic fundamentalist organization that has stated that its highest priority is a Jihad (holy war) for the liberation of Palestine and the establishment of an Islamic Palestine "from the Mediterranean Sea to the Jordan River." Hamas has stated that the transition to the stage of Jihad "for the liberation of all of Palestine" is a personal religious duty incumbent upon every Muslim, and rejects any political arrangement that would relinquish any part of Palestine. Its central goal is the establishment of an Islamic state in all of Palestine.[384]

Hamas first became active during the early stages of the Intifada. It was formed in early 1987, out of the religious-social "Al-Majama Al-Islami" (Moslem Brotherhood) association in the Gaza District. Many senior members of "Al-Majama" helped form Hamas, and used the existing infrastructure of Al-Majama as a basis for semi-covert activity once the Intifada began. Hamas then expanded its activity into the West Bank and at least some cells in Israel proper, becoming the dominant Islamic fundamentalist organization in the occupied territories. Its elements have used both political and violent means, including terrorism, to pursue the goal of establishing an Islamic Palestinian state in place of Israel.

The US State Department reports that Hamas is a loosely structured organization, with some elements working clandestinely while others working openly through mosques and social service institutions to recruit members, raise money, organize activities, and distribute propaganda. Its strength is concentrated in the Gaza Strip and a few areas of the West Bank. It has, however, engaged in peaceful political activity, such as running candidates in West Bank Chamber of Commerce elections.

Hamas's operations in Gaza and the West Bank currently consist of a combination of regional and functional organizations. It has several identical, parallel frameworks that operate in each region. Hamas has a well-organized fund-raising apparatus in Gaza, the West Bank, and Jordan, as well as outside the region. It has a framework called "Dawa," literally "call" or "outreach," which engages in recruitment, distribution of funds, and appointments. It has another framework called security ("Amn"), which gathers information on suspected collaborators during the Intifada. This information was passed on to "shock committees," which interrogated and sometimes killed suspects. Amn is now a key element in Hamas's rivalry with the Palestinian Authority and in intelligence-gathering operations.

The paramilitary elements of Hamas have played a major role in violent fundamentalist subversion and radical terrorist operations against both Israelis and Arabs. Its "shock troops" ("Al-Suad Al-Ramaya"—the "throwing arm") were responsible for popular violence during the Intifada, and still play a role in violent opposition to the peace process. Hamas also has two paramilitary organizations for more organized forms of violence. The first is the Palestinian Holy Fighters ("Al-Majahidoun Al-Falestinioun")—a military apparatus that includes the "Iz al-Din al Qassam Brigades." The second is the Security Section ("Jehaz Amn").

According to Israeli government sources, the "Al-Majihadoun Al-Falestinioun" was established by Sheik Ahmed Yassin in 1982. It procured arms, and began to plan an armed struggle against both Palestinian rivals and Israel. This activity was uncovered in 1984, and Yassin was sentenced to 13 years in prison but was released shortly afterwards as part of the Jibril prisoner exchange (May 1985). Yassin then resumed his effort to set up a military apparatus. He began by focusing on the struggle against "heretics" and collaborators, in accordance with the view of the Muslim Brotherhood that Jihad should come only after the purging of rivals from within. At the same time, he prepared a military infrastructure, and stockpiled weapons for war against Israel. Shortly before the outbreak of the Intifada, operatives were recruited to carry out the military Jihad and regular terrorist attacks. The new military apparatus carried out a large number of attacks of various kinds, including bombs and gunfire, mostly in the northern part of the Gaza District.

The Security Section ("Jihaz Amn") of Hamas was established in early 1983. Its function was to conduct surveillance of suspected collaborators and other Palestinians who acted in a manner which ran counter to the principles of Islam (drug dealers, sellers of pornography, etc.). In early 1987, it began to set up hit squads, known as "MAJD"—an Arabic acronym for "Majmu'at Jihad wa-Dawa"—Holy War and Sermonizing Group—which became the operational arm of the Security Section. Its purpose was to kill "heretics" and collaborators. Yassin instructed the leaders of these sections that they must kill anyone who admitted under interrogation to being a collaborator, and reinforced this instruction with a religious ruling.

After the outbreak of the Intifada, Hamas began to organize military action against Israeli targets as well. The "MAJD" units then became part of the "Al-Majahadoun" network. At the same time, the military apparatus of Hamas underwent several changes as a result of preventive measures and exposure by the Israeli forces following major terrorist attacks. The military apparatus formed the "Iz al-Din al Qassam" Squads or "Brigades," which have been responsible for most of the serious attacks carried out by Hamas since January 1, 1992. These squads were formed out of dozens of proven personnel from Gaza who later began to operate in the West Bank as well. Palestinians from the West Bank were recruited to carry out attacks inside the Green Line. Since the peace accords, these groups have been formed into cells that sometimes recruit young Palestinians, and form smaller cells to carry out attacks and suicide bombings.

During the Intifada, Hamas used its overt political operations to recruit members into the units that engaged in riots and popular violence. Those who distinguished themselves were then recruited into the military apparatus, which carried out attacks against Israelis and Palestinians.

While the source of some terrorist incidents is unclear, the military wing of Hamas (the Izz al-Din al-Qassam) claimed responsibility for the April 6, 1994, bus bombings in Afula and Hadera, which killed 14 Israelis and wounded nearly 75. It also claimed responsibility for the kidnapping of Israeli Corporal Nachshon Wachsman, the shooting of people on the streets of Jerusalem on October 9, a suicide bombing of a commuter bus in Tel Aviv on October 19 that killed 22 Israelis, an April 9, 1995, suicide bombing that killed seven Israelis and an American tourist, a July 24 suicide bombing on a commuter bus in Ramat Gan that killed six people, and an August 21 bomb explosion on a bus in Jerusalem that killed five and injured more than 100.[385]

There is no way to know exactly how many Arabs Hamas has killed since the signing of the Olso Declaration of Principles in September 1993, but the Israeli government estimates that Hamas killed 20 Israelis and one Jewish tourist from the beginning of the Intifada (December 9, 1987) and December 1992, and assassinated close to 100 Palestinians. It also lists the following incidents of violence as having been caused by the Hamas:[386]

- April 6, 1994—Car bombing in Afula—8 killed and 44 injured.
- April 13, 1994—Suicide bomber on bus in Hadera—5 killed.
- October 19, 1994—Suicide bomber on No. 5 bus in Tel Aviv—21 killed.
- April 9, 1995—Car bomb in Kfar Darom—8 killed.
- July 24, 1995—Suicide bomber on bus in Ramat Gan—6 killed and 32 injured.
- August 21, 1995—Suicide bomber on No. 26 bus in Jerusalem—4 killed.
- February 25, 1996—Suicide bomber on No. 18 bus in Jerusalem—26 killed.
- March 3, 1996—Suicide bomber on Jerusalem bus—19 killed.
- July 30, 1997—Two terrorists carried out suicide bombing in Mahane Yehuda Market, Jerusalem—16 killed and 170 injured.
- September 4, 1997—Three terrorists carried out suicide bombing in Ben Yehuda pedestrian mall, Jerusalem—5 killed and 164 injured.

A separate analysis by the Washington Institute indicates that Hamas was responsible for 27.7% of the deaths that have occurred since the signing of the Olso Declaration of Principles versus 9.8% for the Palestinian Islamic Jihad (PIJ), 6.3% for the Palestine Front for the Liberation of Palestine (PFLP), 0.9% for the Democratic Front for the Liberation of Palestine (DFLP), and 0.0% for Fatah. These figures indicate that 49.1% of the killings cannot be attributed and 6.3% have to be assigned to smaller splinter groups and individuals.[387]

This violence caused a considerable backlash within the Palestinian community, and gave Hamas a reason to limit its violent actions. A combination of the Palestinian desire for peace, and the loss of jobs and income as a result of Israeli economic retaliation, led to a steady drop in Hamas's public support. Public opinion polls show that support has dropped from nearly 40% in 1993, to 18% in June 1995, and 11% in some polls in October 1995. As a result, Hamas began to hold talks with the Palestinian Authority in the summer of 1995.[388]

There were reports in late 1995 that a meeting in Khartoum might have produced an accord between Hamas and the Palestinian Authority, and that Hamas might either convert to a peaceful political party or form such a party under a separate name.[389] In October 1995, the Palestinian Authority released Dr. Mahmoud al-Zahar—the main Hamas spokesman in Gaza—from three months in prison after Hamas indicated that it might become a peaceful political party.[390] Hamas was also allowed to resume the publication of its newspaper, although it declared in October 1995 that its willingness to resume a dialogue with the Palestinian Authority did not mean it had rejected its armed struggle against the Jewish state.[391]

Hamas, however, continued its terrorist and paramilitary operations. Like the Hizbollah in Lebanon, it always maintained a distinction between the overt and covert aspects of activity of its various sections. It always had strong civil elements that perform charitable roles and have little or no direct connection to violence. At the same time, it used its charity committees—and the ideological instruction, propaganda, and incitement it delivered in the mosques and other institutions and through leaflets—as a recruiting base for violence and terrorism. The first step seems to be to involve young men in organized elements that engage in riots and popular violence. Those who prove loyal and active are then recruited into the paramilitary cells. The civil side of Hamas also supports their families and relatives if they are killed or arrested. In short, even if Hamas makes a formal public commitment to peaceful political action, it may simply make its violent elements more covert without changing its real nature and behavior.[392]

It is interesting to note in this regard that Hamas issued a leaflet after Rabin's assassination "congratulating the Palestinian people for the assassination. . . . " and stating that, "The assassination proves that the Zionists are not ready for real peace and the next period of time will prove the Zionists want the Palestinians to give up more and more. . . . Our people have to be happy for the assassination of Rabin." Another leaflet issued shortly afterwards called for a "serious national dialogue" with the Palestinian Authority, but also announced that Hamas would not give up the "struggle against occupation."[393] In December 1999, Hamas was caught preparing major new terrorist attacks against Israelis and Americans in Jordan, and it is scarcely surprising that it has played an active role in the new violence that began in September 2000.

Hamas has received extensive monetary support from Islamists outside Israel, and has received significant funding from various Islamists in Saudi Arabia,

Europe, and the US. Israeli sources estimate that the government of Iran contributes approximately three million dollars per year for all Hamas activities.[394]

There are also four central Hamas charity funds in the West: The Palestine Relief and Development Fund—"Interpol" in Britain; the "Holy Land Foundation" in the US; the "Al Aqsa Foundation" in Germany, with branches in Belgium and Holland; and the "Comité de Bienfaisance et Solidarité avec la Palestine" in France. Hamas also receives funding from other Islamic organizations. These include non-governmental charitable organizations in the Gulf states that collect charity for Muslims throughout the world, and support Hamas's social and welfare institutions. They also include aid groups in the West like the Muslim Aid, and the Islamic Relief Agency—ISRA. The Muslim Brotherhood established the "Muslim Aid Committee to the Palestinian Nation" in the 1980s in order to aid Hamas. Only a relatively small portion of Hamas funds come from a limited number of profitable economic projects: sewing and weaving centers, cattle farms, and symbolic payment for services, but it does conduct fund-raising activities throughout the occupied territories.

Hamas has had considerable support from Syria, which extends to allowing it to train and operate in Lebanon and Iran. A report on Syria's role in terrorism by Dr. Reuven Ehrlich (Avi-Ran) of the International Policy Institute for Counter-Terrorism in Israel notes that:[395]

The "Islamic Jihad" and Hamas maintain a propaganda and political presence in Lebanon alongside of which they also carry out military activities. The founding of these organizations in Lebanon, while cooperating with the Iranians and the Hizbollah, was made possible by the approval of Syria, which controls what takes place in Lebanon. It is our opinion that the Syrians view the activity of these organizations in Lebanon to be advantageous as it blurs the Syrian connection with these organizations somewhat [and] "diverts evidence" from Syria. We believe that this will be an even greater consideration as political pressures on Syria increase to terminate the presence and activity of these terror organizations on its soil. One may assume that the Palestinian Muslim organizations reciprocate on the operational level by assisting the Hizbollah in its operations in Israel through the infrastructure which exist in the Palestinian population in Judea, Samaria and Gaza.

Lebanon is an important arena for these organizations. They perceive Lebanon as an additional important arena from which operational activities in Israel and the "territories" can be conducted, with the assistance of friendly organizations, mainly the Hizbollah. The presence of a large population of Palestinian refugees, the position of Lebanon as an important communication and financial center in the Arab world and the freedom prevailing there (in comparison to Syria) make it also a more convenient political, organizational and propaganda center for these organizations. The senior official of Hamas in Lebanon is Mustafa Lidawi. The senior official of the "Islamic Jihad" is Ziad Nahaleh, Dr. Shalah's deputy. Alongside, lower-ranking activists work in the region of Beirut and South Lebanon in the political-propaganda sphere and in the military-operational field.

In the framework of operational cooperation between the "Islamic Jihad" and the Hizbollah, the latter enables the "Islamic Jihad" to operate in south Lebanon; and in some cases, there were even joint operations by both organizations. Since 1990, the "Islamic Jihad" has carried out 9 terrorist attacks in the Security Zone, the last one on October 24, 1997 (attempted assault on South Lebanese Army post in the central sector, with the assistance of the Hizbollah).

Likewise, Hizbollah has publicly announced that it is training Hamas and "Islamic Jihad" members in Hizbollah bases in the Lebanese Beka'a region. Furthermore, a prisoner of the "Islamic Jihad" Shkaki faction who was captured by the IDF following a clash with a terrorist squad north of Netua (October 30, 1991), admitted during the investigation that the members of the squad were trained at a Hizbollah base near Janata' in the Beka'a region.

Hamas has gradually developed ties to Iran. Initially, it ignored or rejected the Iranian revolution as Shi'ite—although a few leaders of Al-Majama quoted leading Iranian revolutionaries—and focused almost exclusively on Sunni groups and issues. It also took a relatively ambiguous position on the Gulf War because of its dependence on rich Gulf donors and its rivalry with the PLO. Iran actively began to court Hamas after the Gulf War, and meetings took place between a Hamas delegation and Iran's foreign minister in October 1992. While it is unclear just how much Iranian support Hamas actually obtained, Hamas did set up a small office in Iran and its leaders began to visit there regularly. The leaders of Hamas also began to meet regularly with the leaders of the Hizbollah in Lebanon. Iran seems to have begun to provide Hamas with up to several million dollars a year from 1993 onwards, and some Israeli estimates go as high as $20 to $30 million. Palestinian police reported that Hamas might have already received $35 million to carry out sabotage operations against Israelis in the Gaza Strip.[396] However, it is doubtful that Iran has provided large amounts of arms and military training. It is also doubtful that there is extensive cooperation between Hamas and Hizbollah in training or operations, although there certainly is some coordination.[397]

These contacts between Hamas and Iran did not stop after President Khatami's election in Iran and new Iranian claims that it was not supporting terrorism. The US State Department reported in April 1999 that, "Iran continued to provide support to a variety of terrorist groups, including the Lebanese Hizbollah, Hamas, and the Palestinian Islamic Jihad, which oppose the Middle East peace process through violence. Iran supports these groups with varying amounts of training, money, and/or weapons. In March 1998, a US district court ruled that Iran should pay $247 million to the family of Alisa Flatow, a US citizen killed in a PIJ bomb attack in Gaza in April 1995. The court ruled that Iran was responsible for her death because it provided funding to the PIJ, which claimed responsibility for the act. Palestinian sources said Iran supported the PIJ's claimed attack in Jerusalem in early November 1998, in which two suicide bombers injured some 21 persons."[398] Hamas also made an attempt to launch a new series of bombings in early September 1999, just after Israel and the Palestinian Authority met and signed the Sharm el Sheik memorandum.[399]

A report by the International Policy Institute for Counter-Terrorism on Iran's role in terrorism notes that:[400]

The Palestinian organization most loyal to the Iranian revolutionary ideology is the Palestinian Islamic Jihad. In spite of it being a Sunni organization, the Iranian revolution sees in it an example to be followed. After the deportation of its leader, Fathi Shqaqi, from the Gaza Strip, the ties between Iran and the organization have been strengthened, particularly in the field of Iranian military assistance. Instructors of the Guardians of the Revolution give regular military instruction courses to the organization's activists from the Territories and abroad, as well as in the Hizbollah camps in Lebanon and Iran. Iran also provides the organization's activists with logistic support, including Iranian identification papers.

. . . . Iran also aided The PIJ in laying the groundwork for terrorist attacks abroad. At the beginning of 1996, the organization's representative in Iran visited Turkey to prepare for the training in Iran of several of the organization's activists. These activists were due to infiltrate back into Israel in order to carry out terrorist attacks. The Turkish security authorities arrested some of the PIJ militants and one of them, Khalil 'Atta, was arrested in Israel. 'Atta was one of nine PIJ militants who underwent training in Iran in the period of July—September 1995.

Since 1992, Iran has drawn closer to Hamas, which it perceives as the leading Islamic movement in the Territories. At the foundation of their relationship lies their common interest in the disruption of the political process, and their efforts to undermine the PLO. These common goals transcend the ideological variance between them due to religious differences between the Sunni Hamas and the Shi'ite Iran. These ties are manifest themselves in frequent high-level meetings between the two sides, and the relative importance of the Hamas representative in Tehran. For example, a Hamas delegation headed by two top activists, "Imad 'Alami (Chairman of the Internal Committee) and Mustafa Qanu" (the representative in Syria) visited Iran in October 1995 and met with high ranking Iranian officials.

In addition to political ties, Iran also provides Hamas with military assistance. The movement's activists train on a regular basis at the camps of Hizbollah and the Guardians of the Revolution in Lebanon, as well as in Iran. This includes training for suicide attacks. Several Iranian-trained militants succeeded in infiltrating back into the Territories under Palestinian Authority control. Israel has arrested Hamas activists who admitted that they were trained by Iranian instructors in the Beka'a Valley, in Lebanon, and in Iran. The training included the use of light weapons, photography and sabotage. Iran also gives Hamas financial assistance . . . including money originating from the Iranian "Fund for the Martyrs," which grants assistance to victims of the "Palestinian Uprising."

While Israeli commentary on a Palestinian terrorist group must always be considered with some reservations, Hamas also had growing problems with Jordan before the outbreak of violence on September 29. King Hussein had extended Hamas the same tolerance he showed to the Jordanian Muslim Brotherhood. Ever since 1993, Hamas had been allowed to keep an office in Jordan as long as there was no tie between the Hamas presence in Jordan and any acts of violence. In November 1998, however, Jordan began to warn Hamas that its efforts to build up a support base and network in Jordan would not be tolerated. In August 1999, the Jordanian government shut down many of its offices, arrested a number of its leaders, and issued arrest warrants for three leaders who were visiting Iran—

Khaled Meshal, Ibrahim Ghosheb, and Abu Marzook. Khaled Meshal and Ibrahim Ghosheb were arrested when they returned from Iran on September 22, and Abu Marzook was deported.

The Jordanian security services acted partly because of evidence that Hamas was planning acts of terrorism in Israel from its bases in Jordan, partly because it was smuggling arms through Jordan from Iraq to Gaza and the West Bank, and partly because it supported hard-line Islamists opposed to King Abdullah. According to Jordan, Jordanian security officials also found that Hamas had stockpiled arms in warehouses in Jordan, had developed massive computer files on Jordanian officials and political contacts—including many Jordanian Palestinians, and had managed to raise some $70 million during the last five years.[401]

Hamas had also expanded its operations in Jordan to use it as a base to develop contacts and cells among Israeli Arabs in Israel proper—leading to strong new Israeli objections to the Hamas presence in Jordan.[402] This was one reason that Israeli Prime Minister Barak praised the arrests and said, "The very attitude of King Abdullah to Hamas is an example of security awareness, an anti-terror approach, and of courageous standing that puts a limit on the operational latitude of an extremely dangerous organization."[403] It is far too soon to determine whether Hamas will work out some compromise with Jordan, but it seems likely that King Abdullah will continue to show little tolerance of any efforts to prepare and stage acts of terrorism against Israel, or create the kind of political network that might affect Jordan's internal security.

It is difficult to determine how popular Hamas will be in the future, and much depends on the course of the present fighting and success of ceasefire efforts and any future peace process. Many Palestinians made it clear that they were sick of violence and constant economic disruption even during the period when former Prime Minister Netanyahu seemed to have halted the peace process. Hamas leader Sheik Ahmed Yassin does, however, seem to retain considerable personal popularity among Palestinians.[404] His ability to raise millions of dollars in funds for Hamas and his virulent anti-Israel stance have led many to fear that he will eventually rival Arafat for power over the Palestinian Authority, although Yassin denies such rumors.[405]

The Palestinian Authority was careful to keep Yassin under close observation and scrutiny. Following the signing of the Wye Accords, hundreds of Hamas activists were detained and Yassin was placed under house arrest in November 1998. This spurred an angry response from Hamas members and Palestinians, vowing violent retaliation against Arafat and the Palestinian Authority.[406] Although Yassin was released in late December 1998, relations between Hamas and the Palestinian Authority remained strained. After that time, both sides remained political rivals. The fighting since September 2000, however, has shown that any major incident can suddenly make Hamas and pro-Arafat forces allies in fighting the IDF.

Islamic Jihad

The Islamic Jihad movement has a different history and character from Hamas. Like Hamas, it began as an ideological element within Sunni Islam, primarily within the Moslem Brotherhood, and was formed in reaction to the Brotherhood's loss of militancy. It is committed to violence in the struggle to establish an "Islamic alternative." Like Hamas, its struggle is directed against both non-Muslims and Arab regimes which have "deviated" from Islam and which have attacked or suppressed the Moslem Brotherhood.[407]

Islamic Jihad is not, however, simply a Palestinian group. Elements of the Islamic Jihad have appeared in almost all the Arab states and in some parts of the non-Arab Islamic world under various names. These groups have been influenced by the success of the revolution in Iran, and by the growth of Islamic militancy in Lebanon and in Egypt. According to Israeli sources, the Palestinian factions of the Islamic Jihad are part of the Islamic Jihad movements that appeared in the Sunni part of the Arab world in the 1970s. These movements are characterized by a rejection of the Brotherhood's "truce" with most of the existing regimes in the Arab world. They see violence as a legitimate tool in changing the face of Arab societies and regimes.

Unlike the Islamic Jihad movements in Arab countries, the Palestinian factions of the Islamic Jihad see the "Zionist Jewish entity" embodied in the State of Israel as the foremost enemy and their primary target. They see "Palestine" as an integral and fundamental part of the Arab and Moslem world, where Muslims are "subjected" to foreign rule. The fact that Israel is seen as foreign and non-Moslem allows the Islamic Jihad to use different methods of resistance than those adopted by similar groups operating against Moslem and Arab regimes. The Palestinian Jihad calls for armed struggle against Israel through guerrilla groups composed of the revolutionary vanguard. These groups carry out terrorist attacks aimed at weakening Israel and "its desire to continue its occupation." These attacks lay the groundwork for the moment when an Islamic army will be able to destroy Israel in a military confrontation.

The Islamic Jihad movement is divided into factions, and the dominant faction that has emerged since the signing of the Declaration of Principles between Israel and the PLO, is the one that was headed by Dr. Fathi Shekaki until his assassination in Malta on October 26, 1995. Shekaki had succeeded in pushing aside Abd al-Aziz Ouda, the co-founder of the organization and its spiritual leader.

Shekaki and Abed el-Aziz Ouda were both from Gaza, and founded their faction because of the influence of similar political groups in Egyptian universities. They began to coordinate similar groups in Gaza when they returned from their studies, and may have had some responsibility for the grenade attack on an Israeli army induction ceremony at the Wailing Wall in October 1986, which killed one person and wounded 69. They were deported from Gaza to Lebanon in 1988. They then reorganized their faction to establish a military unit to carry out attacks against Israeli targets, alongside the existing political unit. These forces seem to have played a role in the assault on an Israeli tourist bus in Egypt in February 1990 that killed nine Israelis and two Egyptians, and wounded 19. They also seem to have been responsible for killing two people and wounding eight in a knifing attack in Tel Aviv in March 1993.

Islamic Jihad has made no secret of its commitment to violence since the peace accords, or of its close ties to Iran.[408] It has distributed propaganda material and tapes, and used the mosques as centers of its activity. It has also created a newspaper called "Al-Istiqlal," which appears in the area under the jurisdiction of the Palestinian Authority, which is edited by Ala Siftawi. Until his assassination, Dr. Shekaki resided in Damascus, and his organization remains one of the ten Palestinian opposition factions based in Syria.

Shekaki often boasted of his ties with Iran—which, according to him, were strengthened following his first visit to Teheran in December 1988. (He visited Iran again in October 1993—following the signing of the Israeli–PLO peace accords.) Unlike Hamas, his faction also had close ties to the Hizbollah.[409] Shekaki praised the Islamic Republic, and its political and spiritual support of the Palestinian people's efforts to continue the jihad and to achieve independence. In 1994, he stated that Islamic Jihad did not receive Iranian military aid and did not have a base in Iran, but claimed that Iranian support for his organization and Hamas amounted to $20 million a year.[410]

Islamic Jihad intensified the tone of its anti-Israeli statements after the murder of Islamic Jihad activist Hani Abed in Gaza on February 11, 1994. Shekaki said, "The continuation of the jihad against the Zionist occupation is our primary concern and the center of our lives," and "we shall raise arms against the criminal Israelis wherever they may be in the autonomous territory and outside it. We have a new reason which justifies the continuation of our struggle." In another statement, he announced the establishment of a group of 70 people prepared to commit suicide "in order to carry out attacks against the occupation forces in the self-governing areas. Such attacks in the Gaza Strip will cease only when the Israeli settlements in the area will be disbanded. . . . If this will occur, the suicide attacks will be transferred to other areas, because our fight against the occupation will continue."[411]

The Palestinian Islamic Jihad (PIJ)–Shekaki faction has killed dozens of Israelis since the 1993 peace accords. It claimed responsibility for killing two Israelis at a bus stop in Ashdod in April 1994 and for 17 other attacks on Israelis. These included killing an Israeli soldier on foot patrol in Gaza on September 4, 1994, killing three Israeli officers in a suicide bombing at the Netzarim junction in the Gaza on November 11, 1994, and a bombing that killed 20 Israeli soldiers and a civilian at a bus stop in Beit Lid near Netanya in central Israel on January 22, 1995. Both the Palestinian Islamic Jihad and Hamas claimed responsibility for a suicide bombing on April 9, 1995, where two Palestinians on buses blew themselves up near Kfar Darom, a Jewish settlement in the Gaza Strip. Seven Israeli soldiers and an American student were killed, and 40 other Israelis were wounded. Eleven other Israelis were hurt in two suicide bombings on November 1, 1995, that were conducted as revenge for Shekaki's assassination.

Since that time, the Palestinian Islamic Jihad has been less successful, but it has scarcely abandoned violence. Like Hamas, it also changed the character of its operations, focusing heavily on suicide bombers. This emphasis on the use of suicide bombings has since been seen in the recent violence in September through November 2000. On October 26, 2000, the PIJ claimed responsibility for a suicide bombing in Gaza that injured one Israeli soldier. Additionally, on November 2, 2000, a car bomb exploded in the Jerusalem marketplace killing many, including the daughter of the National Religious Party leader Rabbi Yitzhak Levy. The PIJ claimed responsibility.

Ironically, a quarter of a century of paramilitary training and "terrorist" training camps has had only a limited impact on Israel for more than a decade. Untrained youths, however, had a major impact during the Intifada. Since that time, Hamas and the Palestinian Islamic Jihad have found that using Islamic organizations to locate idealistic "true believers," giving them a short indoctrination to prepare them, and then sending them out on suicide missions gives the Palestinian Authority and Israel far less warning than using trained personnel.

The Islamic Jihad does, however, have important foreign support. While Iran is often seen as its key foreign sponsor, Syria is also a major sponsor. When Islamic Jihad joined in the protests of the Jordanian crackdown against Hamas in September 1999, it did so out of its office in Damascus and in cooperation with the Popular Front for the Liberation of Palestine (PFLP), the Popular Front for the Liberation of Palestine-General Command (PFLP-GC) and Fatah Uprising.[412]

The US State Department summarizes this aspect of Syria's role in terrorism as follows:[413]

There is no evidence that Syrian officials have engaged directly in planning or executing international terrorist attacks since 1986. Syria, nonetheless, continues to provide safe haven and support to several terrorist groups, allowing some to maintain training camps or other facilities on Syrian territory. Ahmad Jibril's Popular Front for the Liberation of Palestine-General Command and the Palestine Islamic Jihad, for example, have their headquarters in Damascus. In addition, Syria grants a wide variety of terrorist groups— including Hamas, the PFLP-GC, and the PIJ—basing privileges or refuge in areas of Lebanon's Beka'a Valley under Syrian control.

. . . Although Damascus claims to be committed to the Middle East peace process, it has not acted to stop anti-Israeli attacks by Hizbollah and Palestinian rejectionist groups in southern Lebanon. Syria allowed—but did not participate in—a meeting of Palestinian rejectionist groups in Damascus in December 1998 to reaffirm their public opposition to the peace process. Syria also assists the resupply of rejectionist groups operating in Lebanon via Damascus. Nonetheless, the Syrian Government continues to restrain the international activities of some groups and to participate in a multinational monitoring group to prevent attacks against civilian targets in southern Lebanon and northern Israel.

A report on Syria's role in terrorism by Dr. Reuven Ehrlich (Avi-Ran) of the International Policy Institute for Counter-Terrorism in Israel notes, however, that:[414]

. . . "Islamic Jihad" began operating in Syria upon the arrival of Fathi Shkaki in 1989 and the establishment of his headquarters in Damascus. Permitting Shkaki to operate from Syrian territory, marked Damascus' transformation into the center of Palestinian-Islamic activity in the 90's, as it was the center for Palestinian left-wing organizations in the 70's and 80's. Unlike Hamas, which has military and political infrastructure in various countries, the "Islamic Jihad's" infrastructure outside Judea, Samaria and Gaza is concentrated mostly in the area of Damascus, from where operational activity is being directed.

In this framework, Dr. Ramadan Shalah, Secretary-General of the organization, currently resides in Damascus. Also in Syria is the operational leadership of the organization. Outstanding among the organization's leadership are Ziad Nehaleh, Shalah's deputy, responsible for the "Lebanon arena" and Ibrahim Shehadeh, a senior figure responsible for operations in the organization. These operational activists initiate, plan and carry out terror attacks in Israel and Judea, Samaria and Gaza, an activity that found its expression in five lethal suicide bombings of the last three years. In addition to directing the operational activity, the organization's leadership in Syria maintains contact with other terrorist organizations (mainly the Hizbollah and the PFLP-GC).

The interrogation of "Islamic Jihad" recruits arrested in Judea, Samaria and Gaza in recent years revealed that most of them maintain some direct or indirect link to Islamic Jihad operational headquarters in Damascus. Some of them confessed to having been recruited in Syria, from where they were sent for training in Iran or Lebanon. Further, specific guidelines govern communications between these recruits and headquarters in Syria. Upon returning to the territories, these men regularly received operational orders from Damascus.

Outside Actors: Palestinians in Lebanon, the Hizbollah, and Iran

Israel faces potential threats from Palestinian movements in Lebanon, as well as from the Hizbollah. A report by Dr. Reuven Ehrlich (Avi-Ran) on hard-line Palestinian activity in Lebanon tracks closely with the estimates of many US intelligence experts:[415]

. . . the destruction of the Palestinian military infrastructure during the Lebanon war and the imposition of the "Syrian order" in the framework of which the Syrians encourage the Lebanese government to establish its control and sovereignty over considerable parts of Lebanon and confine the military organizations of the Palestinians within the refugee camps. This has weakened the Palestinian left-wing organizations, which are subject to close supervision by the Lebanese army and intelligence agencies. The exception is the PFLP-GC that, under Syrian supervision, enjoys relative freedom of action in organizing and carrying out terrorist attacks.

- P.F.L.P.-GC—Of all the left-wing organizations in Lebanon, this has the most highly developed infrastructure. It has several hundred active members in Lebanon, among them more than one hundred fighters. The organization has bases, camps, and offices in Lebanon from which it carries out terror activities against the IDF in Southern Lebanon (in close cooperation with the Hizbollah and with other Palestinian terror organizations). It has training camps and arsenals containing both light and heavy weaponry. In addition, the organization has a marine unit in Lebanon.
- D.F.L.P./Na'if Hawatmeh—The Democratic Front has been operating in Lebanon since the 1970s. In the 1990s there has been a gradual decline in the organization's scope of activities in Lebanon as a

result of the general weakening of the left-wing organizations among the Palestinian public, restrictions placed on it by the Lebanese Army, the organization's financial difficulties, and repeated failed attempts at acts of terror. Today, the organization has several hundred active members in Lebanon, several dozen of which are "fighters" and the rest involved in the political-propaganda and logistic-organizational fields. A number of bases and offices serve as arsenals and launching points for the organization's operational activities. Because of reduced operational capability, members are often assisted by their counterparts, particularly the Hizbollah and Habash's "PFLP."

- P.F.L.P./George Habash—This organization has a few dozen military activists and other members involved in the areas of politics, propaganda, and logistics. The organization has offices and bases in Lebanon, including arsenals, training camps, and operations bases.

- "Fatah—Revolutionary Council"/Abu Nidal—Since the beginning of the 1980s, Abu Nidal's organization has had an operational infrastructure in Lebanon (originally secretively and later openly). In the '80s the organization's ranks numbered several hundred operatives, with camps and bases at its disposal in Beirut, Beka'a, and Northern and Southern Lebanon. In the 1990's the organizations infrastructure in Lebanon was damaged and weakened because of loss of prestige with the Syrians and various additional reasons: internal disputes, violent conflict with "Fatah"/Arafat, and vigorous efforts against it by the Lebanese army and the Lebanese intelligence agencies (particularly after the 1994 murder of the First Secretary of the Jordanian Embassy in Lebanon, which was ascribed to the organization). The organization continues to maintain an operational infrastructure in Beirut and in refugee camps throughout Lebanon, however, in the past few years it has kept a low profile and conducted its activities in utmost secrecy. According to the annual US State Department report (as of April 1998), the organization has refrained from attacking Western targets since the end of the 1970s.

- "Fatah"/Abu Mussa faction—The organization numbers a few dozen military activists in Lebanon, and has several offices and bases in Lebanon including weapons arsenals and training camps.

The Hizbollah in Lebanon is becoming an actor that could play a major role in a Second Intifada. It has concentrated on the "liberation" of Southern Lebanon in the past, and has not been a major player in the Israeli-Palestinian struggle, but it easily could become one in the future. The Hizbollah's defeat of the IDF and South Lebanon Army in Southern Lebanon in May 2000 made it a regional force, and the visit of Ariel Sharon to the Muslim holy sites in Jerusalem that triggered the fighting in September 2000 seems to have also helped unite the Hizbollah and the Palestinians. Sharon organized the Israeli invasion of Lebanon in 1982, and is widely held responsible for creating the climate that led to the massacres of Palestinians in the Sabra and Shatilla refugee camps by Christian militias.

The Hizbollah reacted strongly to the fighting that began in September 2000. Its television and radio station in Lebanon broadcast speeches by its leader, Sheik Hassan Nasrallah, deliberately designed to inflame Palestinian hatreds and which included a call to stab Israelis to death: "If you don't have bullets, who among you doesn't have knives? Hide the knife, and when he comes close to the enemy let him stab him. Let the stab be fatal." Sheik Nasrallah appeared on the independent satellite television station al-Jazeera, in Qatar, and addressed the Palestinians as "holy war comrades-in-arms" and proposed a strategy of gradually escalating the Intifada from stones to daggers to firearms and other means of military combat.[416]

Press reports indicate that the Hizbollah flag has been used in many Palestinian demonstrations in the Gaza since Israel's withdrawal from Lebanon and is sold at the Palestine Liberation Organization flag shop. They also indicate that Palestinian protesters in Ramallah shouted slogans like, "Hizbollah our beloved/Destroy, destroy Tel Aviv." The Hizbollah's victory is seen as a model by some among Palestinians, even though virtually all are Sunni Muslims or Christians. There are reports that Sheik Nasrallah and other Hizbollah leaders went to Iran after the Israeli withdrawal and Iran's religious leader, Ali Khamenei, told them they should now struggle for the Muslim liberation of Jerusalem.[417]

The Hizbollah seized three IDF soldiers in a disputed part of the Israeli-Lebanese border after the fighting began in September 2000, and kidnapped an Israeli reservist. The three soldiers were seized by Hizbollah forces allegedly disguised as UN soldiers with a mock UN vehicle. The necessary uniforms, badges, decals, and license plates for the operation can be bought at a number of souvenir shops throughout the region. The kidnapping was performed in the disputed region of Chebaa Farms in the foothills of Mount Hermon. The United Nations and Israel used a border demarcation based on the French and British Mandate division of territory which places the Chebaa Farms in Syria; therefore a withdrawal from Lebanese territory does not include a withdrawal from Chebaa. However, Hizbollah, the Lebanese, and Syrian governments claim Chebaa belongs to Lebanon and not Syria. This makes the Chebaa Farms a potential point of conflict in the future.[418]

There were unconfirmed reports in October 2000 that the Hizbollah was seeking to find ways of sending arms to Fatah, and to the police force as well as to Hamas and Islamic Jihad. Other reports indicated that the younger street fighters in Al Fatah—Fatah Hawks and the Tanzeem—distributed a leaflet declaring a "popular war" against Israel, and were cooperating with Hamas and the Hizbollah. This was particularly important because Marwan Barghouti, the head of the Tanzeem, was a key hardliner who called for prolonged violent struggle against Israel.

Iran has also played a hand. The Iranian foreign minister, Kamal Kharazi, consulted in early October 2000 with Sheik Nasrallah. Kharazi told reporters that, "The issue of Jerusalem is not only important for the Palestinians, but all the Muslims of the world. This indicates how deep the Israeli provocation was in its attack on Al Aqsa Mosque." The Iranian foreign minister also met with Secretary General Kofi Annan in October. Mr. Kharazi is reported to have asked Annan to deliver a warning about an Israeli retaliatory attack against Lebanon or Syria, "Please convey this warning to Israel The counter reaction will be extremely violent, and no one will be able to stop Lebanon's Islamic resistance movement from retaliating."[419]

It is important to note, however, that the Hizbollah scarcely has a free hand. Syria and the Lebanese government have been very cautious about provoking

Israel in the past. The Lebanese Army, and Palestinian refugee camp officials in Lebanon, made an effort to limit demonstrations in October 2000. The army strengthened its control points on the roads going into the south, along the coast road between Sidon and Tyre, and near Palestinian refugee camps.

This could have an impact on Palestinian activity as well. The Lebanese army also controls most of the arms once held by the Palestinians and maintains particularly tight control over the Rashidiye camp near Tyre.[420] In fact, the Fatah commander in Lebanon—Sultan Abu Alaynen—is forced to remain in the camp because he is under sentence of death by the Lebanese Army. As a result, both Hizbollah and Lebanese Palestinian support for a Second Intifada may be more political than military.

Palestinian Hard-Line Movements in Syria and Jordan

Syria has not permitted any Palestinian activity in the Golan, but it has allowed a variety of hard-line and extreme groups to operate from Syrian territory. These have included four major categories of groups:

- Hizbollah;
- Palestinian Islamic organizations: Hamas, Palestine Islamic Jihad/Shkaki;
- Radical left-wing Palestinian organizations: the PFLP-GC/Jibril, the PFLP/Habash, the DFLP/Hawatmeh, The Palestine Liberation Front, the Fatah Revolutionary Council/Abu Nidal, Fatah/Abu Musa and an extremist faction of the Popular Struggle Front;
- Other Middle Eastern and International terrorist groups: Kurdistan Workers Party (PKK), Japanese Red Army and other terrorist organizations.

The Palestinian groups in Syria that could have the most impact on the Palestinian aspects of the Arab-Israeli balance in a Second Intifada include hard-line organizations like the Palestine Liberation Front (PLF—Abd al-Fatah Ghanim faction), Popular Front for the Liberation of Palestine-General Command (PFLP-GC), Popular Front for the Liberation of Palestine-Special Command (PFLP-SC), Hamas, and Palestinian Islamic Jihad. Iraq supports Palestinian extremist groups like the ANO, the Palestinian Liberation Front (PLF). It also permits Abu Abbas and Abu Ibrahim to live in Iraq. The Sudan and Libya also give these groups at least some support.[421]

A report on Syria's role in terrorism by Dr. Reuven Ehrlich (Avi-Ran) notes that:[422]

Syria currently serves as a center for eight Palestinian terror organizations which reject the peace process and the peace accords and oppose Arafat. Five of these Palestinian terror organizations are among the most radically leftwing: the "Popular Front for the Liberation of Palestine-General Command (PFLP-GC)"/Ahmed Jibril, the "Democratic Front for the Liberation of Palestine (DFLP)"/Na'if Hawatmeh, the "Popular Front for the Liberation of Palestine (PFLP)"/George Habash, "Fatah"/Abu Mussa, and the radical segment of the "National Struggle Front"/Khaled Abd al-Majid faction. Three of the eight organizations belong to the pro-Iranian Islamic stream: "Islamic Jihad in Palestine"/Shkaki faction, "Hamas" and "Hizbollah in Palestine"/Ahmed Mah'anah faction. Damascus and its vicinity provide a haven for most of the leadership and the political and military infrastructure of these eight terror organizations, as well as for other Palestinian terrorist groups. Further-more, these organizations have established—with Syrian approval of course—representa-tions and operational infrastructures in the Syrian controlled area of Lebanon.

. . . Damascus is the primary center of left-wing Palestinian organizations opposed to the Palestinian Authority and the Oslo Accords. Syria serves as an important area of activity for Hamas outside of Judea, Samaria and Gaza, and senior Hamas officials carry out operational, political and propaganda activities from Damascus. The infrastructure of the "Palestine Islamic Jihad" outside of Judea, Samaria and Gaza is primarily located in the vicinity of Damascus, from where its operations and activities in the "territories" are directed.

The leaders of most of these terrorist organizations reside in Syria, from where they oversee and direct the military, political and propaganda activities of their organizations against Israel and other Arab states. Among the senior leaders and activists of the terror groups residing in Damascus are: Dr. Ramadan Shalah, Secretary-General of Islamic Jihad and his deputy Ziad Nehaleh; Imad al-Alami, chairman of Hamas' "Interior Committee", who is a dominant figure in activating the organizations' military apparatus for carrying out attacks; Ahmed Jibril, George Habash and Nayef Hawatmeh, leaders of the three main left-wing Palestinian terrorist organizations. Also active in Syria are middle- and low-ranking military activists of all the above mentioned groups.

The Syrians permit these groups to maintain their military and political infrastructure in areas under their control in Lebanon. The most widespread infrastructure belongs to Hizbollah, which is also the leading group that concentrates attacks in southern Lebanon. The Syrians also permit some limited activity by the left-wing Palestinian terrorist groups. With Syrian approval, the Beka'a Valley continues to serve as an organizational and training center for Middle East and international terrorist groups.

. . . Popular Front for the Liberation of Palestine—GC/ Ahmed Jibril—perceived in the 1990's by the Syrians as the primary Palestinian left-wing organization. The organization's headquarters, its main offices and training camps are located in Syria. In these bases, activists from other terror groups undergo training. For example, Sami Kamel al-Habib, an "Islamic Jihad" member arrested by Israel and interrogated in March 1995, said that he had gone to Syria in 1992 with other "Islamic Jihad" members to undergo military training at a camp run by PFLP-GC leader Ahmed Jibril. Jibril lives in Syria and bases his activity from there. A PFLP-GC aerial unit of gliders is also active in Syria. A radio station is at the organization's disposal ("Radio Al-Quds"), operated in southern Syria, aimed at the residents of Judea, Samaria and Gaza, whose broadcasts often sharply attack Arafat and the Palestinian Authority.

In the 1970's and 1980's the Syrians often used Jibril's organization as a "terrorist subcontractor" for terror missions abroad. But following the exposure of the organization's operational activities in Germany (the "Dalkamuni affair," October 1988) when Syria's "fingerprints" were exposed and after the explosion of the Pan Am aircraft, imputed to the organization (December 1988), Syria imposed a series of restrictions on its members and ceased activating it as a "terrorist subcontractor" abroad. Since then, the PFLP-GC focuses its activities in Lebanon, Israel and the "territories" and avoids carrying out terrorist operations abroad—constituting clear evidence of Syria's ability to influence the terror policies of the groups under its aegis, when it is in the Syrian interest to do so.

In addition to the PFLP-GC, the following left-wing Palestinian organizations are active in Damascus:

- Popular Front for the Liberation of Palestine/George Habash—the leadership's institutions are located in Syria as are its leaders: George Habash, the organization's Secretary General; Abu Ali Mustafa, another senior official who was involved in the past in directing operational activities; and Abu Ahmad Fuad, in charge of terrorist attacks, all of whom maintain permanent residence in Syria. The organization has a number of offices in the Damascus area; arsenals and military camps in which activists from the "territories", among others, are trained, are located in Syria as well.

- Democratic Front for the Liberation of Palestine/Na'if Hawatmeh—The political and military infrastructure of the organization is located in Syria. Na'if Hawatmeh, Secretary-General of the organization, and Khaled Abd al-Majid, in charge of terrorist operations, maintain permanent residence in Syria. The organization has a number of offices in the Damascus region, as well as arsenals and training camps in which activists from the territories, among others, are trained.

- Other Palestinian organizations—The operational and political infrastructure of other Palestinian terrorist organizations are located in Syria, including that of the "Palestine Liberation Front," Fatah/ Abu Mussah and the Popular Struggle Front/the rebel faction (faction headed by Khaled Abd al-Majid, who opposes the peace process). The Syrians have not allowed Abu-Nidal's organization to operate in Syria since its expulsion in 1987 (but have allowed it to operate in Lebanon while maintaining a low profile).

Jordan has allowed a number of Palestinian rejectionist groups to operate offices within Jordan. At various times, these groups have included the PFLP, PFLP-GC, DFLP, PIJ, and Hamas. Jordan has, however, restricted the actions of such groups. Jordan arrested 30 Palestinians, including 15 members of the Abu Nidal Organization (ANO), on February 25, 1994, and an Islamic extremist for stabbing tourists on February 27. Jordan declared Hamas to be an illegal organization in April, and arrested another 25 Islamists, or Arab "Afghans," during 1994 for planning the assassination of Jordanian officials. More than 20 other Palestinian Islamic extremists suspected of planning terrorist acts against Israel were arrested after Jordan signed a full peace treaty with Israel on October 26, 1994. Jordan launched a similar crackdown on Hamas in January 2000.

Iraq and Libya serve as a base for hard-line Palestinian elements. Iran has some links to the Popular Front for the Liberation of Palestine (PFLP), as well as to the Hizbollah, PIJ, and Hamas.[423] It continues to provide regular shipments of funds and arms to the Hizbollah.[424] A report by the International Policy Institute for Counter-Terrorism on Iran's role in terrorism notes that:[425]

The Palestinian organization most loyal to the Iranian revolutionary ideology is the Palestinian Islamic Jihad. In spite of it being a Sunni organization, the Iranian revolution sees in it an example to be followed. After the deportation of its leader, Fathi Shqaqi, from the Gaza Strip, the ties between Iran and the organization have been strengthened, particularly in the field of Iranian military assistance. Instructors of the Guardians of the Revolution give regular military instruction courses to the organization's activists from the Territories and abroad, as well as in the Hizbollah camps in Lebanon and Iran. Iran also provides the organization's activists with logistic support, including Iranian identification papers.

. . . Iran also aided The PIJ in laying the groundwork for terrorist attacks abroad. At the beginning of 1996, the organization's representative in Iran visited Turkey to prepare for the training in Iran of several of the organization's activists. These activists were due to infiltrate back into Israel in order to carry out terrorist attacks. The Turkish security authorities arrested some of the PIJ militants and one of them, Khalil 'Atta, was arrested in Israel. 'Atta was one of nine PIJ militants who underwent training in Iran in the period of July-September 1995.

ISRAELI HARD-LINE MOVEMENTS AND EXTREMISTS

Israel has violent extremists of its own. Baruch Goldstein, a Kach member, killed 29 Palestinian worshipers and wounded more than 200 in a Hebron mosque on February 25, 1994. Israel declared Kach and Kahane Chai to be terrorist organizations, and arrested 11 Jewish extremists for planning attacks on Palestinians in September 1994.[426] This, however, did little to halt the activities of Israeli extremists whose rhetoric grew progressively more violent as the peace accords were implemented.

Their verbal and physical attacks came to include Israel's leaders, and created a major problem for the peace process. Yigal Amir, an Israeli with ties to an extreme right-wing group, assassinated Israel's Prime Minister, Yitzak Rabin, on November 4, 1995.

There have been many serious incidents of Israeli violence against Palestinians, and these included attacks on Israeli Arabs during the fighting in September-October 2000. Each new case of violence by one side tends to trigger even more violence and extremism by the other. Tomorrow's factions may prove to be more of a threat than any of the current factions listed in Table 7.1.

THE HISTORY AND EFFECTIVENESS OF THE
PALESTINIAN AUTHORITY SECURITY FORCES

The Palestinian Security forces will be another key factor determining the outcome of either peace or a Second Intifada. They are now caught between the possible need to challenge the IDF and the need to reestablish control over movements like Hamas and the Palestinian Islamic Jihad. On the one hand, they may have to fight an asymmetric war in which they must seek to use media coverage of the martyrdom and suffering of all factions of Palestinians, Israeli casualties to combat and terrorism, and the economic and political strain on Israel to defeat a military force that is otherwise militarily superior in every way. On the other hand, they must seek to retain control over the Palestinian movement and preserve the option of reaching some kind of ceasefire peace settlement. Trying to find the proper balance will be an extremely difficult challenge in dealing with the Palestinian people, other Palestinian groups, and Israel; and the fact that many aspects of the Second Intifada reflect a true popular uprising, limits the ability of the Palestinian Security forces to act.

The Palestinian Authority versus Hamas and the PIJ

This exercise in "riding the tiger" was scarcely easy even before the crisis of September 2000. The combined activity of Hamas and Islamic Jihad had a massive impact on Israeli public opinion, threatening to bring an end to the peace process, long before the Israeli-Palestinian clashes in September 2000. Terrorist attacks during 1993 and the first part of 1994 steadily shifted Israeli opinion against further withdrawals. On January 22, 1994, two bombs exploded at a bus stop at Beit Lid, killing 21 and wounding 60. The Palestinian Islamic Jihad claimed responsibility for the attack. On January 27, an unidentified assailant wounded three Israelis near Netzarim, in Gaza. On February 6, an unidentified gunman killed an Israeli in Gaza. On March 20, unidentified assailants fired on a bus near Kiryat Arba, killing two Israelis.

This violence escalated sharply in April 1994. In early April, several Hamas members were killed in Gaza when a bomb they were making exploded prematurely. Then, on April 9, a suicide bomber linked to the Palestinian Islamic Jihad drove an explosives-laden car into a bus near Kfar Darom in Gaza, killing seven Israelis and one American and wounding 34. Another attack on the same day near Netzarim left 11 Israelis wounded. Hamas claimed responsibility for this second attack.[427]

A US State Department investigation of these events concluded that, "We have no information that incidents of terrorism were perpetrated or organized by PLO elements under Arafat's control during the period covered by this report." Further, former Prime Minister Rabin stated during a speech on May 15, 1994, that, "Fatah groups under the Palestinian Authority headed by Arafat have not taken part in any murderous terrorist attacks against Israelis."

The State Department investigation also concluded that Palestinian and PLO officials had denounced these acts of terrorism as they occurred. For example, Chairman Arafat telephoned former Prime Minister Rabin to express his condolences in response to the Beit Lid attack on January 22, 1994, and called the attack a "criminal act that threatens the peace process." The Planning Minister of the

Palestinian Authority, Nabil Sha'ath, called the act a "criminal deed which we resolutely condemn." The Health Minister of the Palestinian Authority reacted to the March 20, 1994, attack in Hebron by stating that the Palestinian Authority "shares the grief of the families" of the victims, and stressed that no terror attack would stop the peace process. The Housing Minister called the attack on civilians "deplorable." Arafat responded to the April 9 bombings in Kfar Darom and Netzarim, by stating he would "make war on the perpetrators of terrorist attacks who seek to thwart the peace process."

Words, however, were not enough. Each attack by Hamas and Islamic Jihad undermined the peace process, and it took time for the Palestinian Authority to realize that it had to match its words with action. The particularly bloody terrorist incident on Israel civilians on April 9, 1995, was a key catalyst in this process.[428] The Israeli response made it clear that the peace process could only continue as long as the Palestinian Authority improved the quality of its security options and was seen to publicly and constantly crack down on violent movements like Hamas and Islamic Jihad. Israel threatened to enforce prolonged travel bans in Gaza and West Bank that affected tens of thousands of Palestinian jobs and businesses—and even partial bans cost Gaza at least $1.5 million a day.[429]

This Israeli response cost Hamas and the Palestinian Islamic Jihad a considerable amount of popular Palestinian support because of the loss of jobs and trade. It also led the Palestinian Authority to take a much firmer line in reacting to attacks. Its security forces improved their cooperation with Israeli security forces, conducted ruthless interrogations and quick trials, and expanded their prisons. These actions reduced the number of terrorist incidents, and weakened Islamic Jihad, which also lost some of its leaders to assassinations overseas. They also showed that the Palestinian Authority and PLO could crack down effectively on the Hamas and Islamic Jihad without losing significant public support or major reprisals.[430]

The Effectiveness of the Palestinian Authority Security Forces

State Department officials and US intelligence experts indicate that the Palestinian Authority has continued to improve its performance since mid-1995, although none describe any element as well-trained, properly organized, or truly professional. At the same time, Israeli officials remain far more critical, and events have shown that the Palestinian Authority was still years away from developing fully effective internal security forces when the violence began in September 2000.[431] In spite of assistance from the CIA, Palestinian Authority security forces continue to have problems with internal discipline, corruption, and human rights issues, and there was some infiltration by anti-peace elements. In addition, there was a significant risk that the loyalty of the security forces could be threatened or undermined by a collapse or delay of the peace process, by being asked to take action against fellow Palestinians that was too extreme, or by extreme Israel security actions which sharply infringed on Palestinian rights.

Creating effective security forces is anything but easy even without the challenge posed by the Second Intifada. The Palestinian Authority had to convert paramilitary elements that were anti-Israeli before the peace accords to an effective security force that can provide security and law enforcement for a secular Palestinian Authority. It had to expand its capability to conduct joint patrols with Israeli security forces, prevent attacks on Israelis, disarm and suppress violent extremist movements like the Islamic Jihad, and prevent conflict between Palestinians. At the same time, it had to preserve the support of the Palestinian people, and learn how to act in an environment where the Palestinian Authority was moving towards true sovereignty, and where the need to reflect more democratic methods, preserve human rights, and resist corruption and power brokering was becoming steadily more important.

It is important to note that cooperation between Palestinian and Israeli security forces did lead to a significant decline in terrorism before the clashes of September 2000. Even Israeli sources that have often been critical of the Palestinian Authority have generally recognized that this cooperation was a main reason why terror, especially Hamas activity, has declined since 1997. In 1996, there were 60 Israeli victims of terrorist acts. By 1997, the number was down to 29 and there were only 12 in 1998. Furthermore, the Palestinian Authority is credited with thwarting a large-scale terrorist attack in Tel Aviv in February. Israeli officials say that previous ineffectiveness was due to inexperience, and they now recognize the improvement in the Palestinian security forces.[432]

The CIA played a major role in the peace process after the mid-1990s by encouraging greater security cooperation and by assisting in the development of concrete means to implement joint security endeavors and other cooperative agreements. The agency's critical role was further highlighted during the negotiations at the Wye Plantation in the fall of 1998 which culminated in a memorandum that set the stage for further Israeli redeployments from the West Bank and a strengthened commitment to joint Israeli-Palestinian security arrangements. This training and liaison not only improved the effectiveness and credibility of Palestinian operations, it also helped the Palestinian security forces reduce the use of arbitrary arrests and forces and to adopt more effective and modern methods of counterterrorism.

Prime Minister Barak initially sought to reduce the role of the CIA after his election in the spring of 1999 because he felt that Israel and the Palestinian Authority must learn to work together and the fear that this was creating independent ties between the US and the Palestinians that undercut US-Israeli ties and limited Israeli freedom of action.[433] However, the CIA still played a role after Barak's efforts, and played a significant role in trying to contain Palestinian-Israeli violence when the clashes began in September 2000. The CIA was charged with continuing this role as part of the October 17 summit agreement, and it is clear that the Palestinian Authority security forces will need continuing aid and liaison from the CIA or some similar outside group to effectively enforce any ceasefire or peace agreement.

There are unconfirmed reports that Jordanian, Egyptian, Israeli, Palestinian, and US cooperation in counterterrorism was greatly strengthened by the formation of a "joint framework" to deal with terrorism in the fall of 1999. According to one report, this framework was established at the urging of King Abdullah of Jordan, with the support of President Clinton, President Mubarak, Prime Minister Barak, and Chairman Arafat. This effort has not been confirmed, however, and few details are available.[434]

In any case, past and future progress cannot be expected to produce perfection. A fundamentally unpopular peace or ceasefire will be unenforceable. Virtually any achievable agreement will now create an ongoing risk that new terrorist attacks and low-intensity fighting between Palestinians and Israelis, or between Palestinians, will escalate to major proportions.

Far too much of the Palestinian Authority political structure is still built around the influence of one man, Yasser Arafat, who may or may not survive and who may or may not be able to make the difficult transformation from leader of an opposition in exile to someone who can both govern and be a statesman. Further, the Palestinian Authority's ability to enforce security measures is highly dependent on Palestinian public support, progress in the peace process, progress in reducing Israeli control over the Palestinians, and belief that the peace will bring jobs and economic development.

The Organization of the Palestinian Security Forces in Gaza and the West Bank

The Palestinian Authority has absorbed much of the Palestinian personnel and administrative structures that worked in Gaza under the Israeli civil administration, and has steadily improved its administrative efforts in Gaza since 1993. There are now a total of thirteen different Palestinian Authority security forces, twelve of which are official. Ten of these are controlled by the Palestinian Police Force Directorate or General Security Service under the leadership of Nasr Yusuf. These are the Civil Police (Shurta), National Security Forces, Preventive Security, General Intelligence, Military Intelligence, Military Police, Local Governorate Security and Emergency Services, as well as small elements like the Air Guard and the Maritime Police in Gaza. The Presidential Security Detail (Amn al-ri-asa) and the Special Security (Al-An al-Khass) are both independent units that answer directly to Yasser Arafat. In addition to the officially recognized security forces, the Tanzim, or "Organization" under the leadership of Marwan al-Barguti forms an unofficial militia for Fatah, the primary base of political support for the Palestinian Authority and Yasser Arafat's original group.

Under the Oslo accords, the Palestinian Authority could deploy 12,000 men on the West Bank, out of a total Palestinian Authority security force of 30,000 men—including the 18,000 men in Gaza. This force could have a total of 5,000 men recruited from Palestinians abroad. A total of 6,000 could be deployed initially to Area A and limited parts of Area B, with the other 6,000 to be deployed later. The force could have a total of 4,000 rifles, 4,000 pistols, 120 machine guns of .30 to .50 caliber and 15 light unarmed riot vehicles.

Under the initial deployment schedule, the Palestinian Authority was allowed to deploy up to 6,000 men, and increase this total as it took control over the seven largest Arab cities. The Palestinian Authority could deploy 1,000 men in the Jenin District, 400 men in the Tulkarm District, 1,200 men in the Nablus District, 400 men in the Qalqilyah District, 1,200 men in the Ramallah District, 850 men in the Bethlehem District, and 950 men in the Hebron District (including 400 men in the zone under Palestinian Authority control within the city limits). It could deploy up to 600 men in the Jericho District, which are counted as part of the 18,000 men who can be deployed in Gaza.[435]

In practice, the Palestinian Authority built up substantially larger numbers of men and weapons than the accords formally permitted. There was also substantial smuggling of weapons like AK-47s from Iraq through Jordan into the West Bank, many of which went into private hands or were given to Fatah, the Palestinian Authority militias like the Tanzim, as well as other militant groups such as Hamas and the PIJ. The Palestinian Authority probably also seems to have obtained some unauthorized artillery rockets, anti-tank rocket launchers, anti-tank guided missiles, and possibly manportable surface-to-air missiles like the SA-7. It is impossible to separate Israeli charges and Palestinian denials and establish the truth. What is known is that Fatah and Tanzim activists used anti-tank weapons against IDF tanks and armored personnel carriers in Gaza on October 31, 2000, although their fire was largely ineffective.

The agreements did, however, lead to some progress. They established national, regional, and district security liaison offices that are manned on a 24-hour basis and have special communications links. These agreements also established a Joint Security Committee (Joint Coordination and Cooperation Committee for Mutual Security or JSC) with 5 to 7 members from each side, which were to operate on the basis of agreement by both sides, and to develop the comprehensive plans for the transfer of regional authority. Joint Regional Security Committees (JRSCs) were created for the West Bank and for Gaza, and joint District Coordination Offices (DCOs) for each district.

The DCOs were set up with six officers from each side, a commander, and five duty officers. They coordinated affairs in the individual districts, and reported to the JRSCs and the JSC. They directed the Joint Patrols and Joint Mobile Units that were to ensure "free, unimpeded, and secure movement" along key roads and provide a rapid reaction to any incidents. Each Joint Patrol had an Israeli and a Palestinian vehicle with an officer and three guards. The JRSCs, DCOs and joint patrols were supposed to share intelligence, and support joint liaison bureaus at the key crossing points along the border with Jordan. The Palestinian Police Forces and Israeli Security Forces were to cooperate fully in the areas of security and forensics. The PFF was also to submit a complete list of its policemen to Israeli forces.[436]

This policy of joint patrols was terminated on November 23, 2000, after a grenade or mortar shell killed an Israeli officer at a DCO in the Gaza Strip. Suspecting that Palestinians within the DCO had cooperated with the attack, Palestinian forces were instructed to leave the security office. Within hours the IDF had submitted a formal request for the Palestinian Authority to remove all of its security forces from all of the DCOs in the territories. The next day, via telephone, Barak and Arafat agreed to re-implement the security patrols; however the patrols have yet to resume in practice due to the continuing violence.

The accords sometimes gave Israel more advantages than were readily apparent. They specified that the IDF and Israelis should continue to move freely on roads in the West Bank and Gaza. In Area A, Israeli vehicles were accompanied by joint patrols. Israelis could not, under any circumstances, be arrested or placed in custody by the Palestinian police, and may only be required to present identity and vehicle documentation. On roads that were jointly patrolled, only the Israeli side of a joint patrol shall make any request for identification. Both sides shall cooperate, lend assistance to one another in the search for missing persons, and share pertinent information. Such arrangements effectively gave Israel—the side with armor, heavy weapons, and helicopters—a major advantage in a Second Intifada. The Palestinians could still operate from urban cover and survive, but the accords never equipped the Palestinian Authority to challenge the IDF's ability to seize and secure lines of communication outside of urban areas.

As for the structure of the Palestinian security forces, they were something of an organizational nightmare and sometimes committed significant abuses. The services in Gaza and the West Bank were placed under the direction of the General Security Service (GSS), an umbrella organization that coordinates and maintains ten Palestinian security services, as well as nine administrative departments, from two separate headquarters. The GSS, together with the Special Security Force (SSF) and the Presidential Security Force, constituted the Palestinian Security Services (PSS).

The National Security Force (NSF) became the largest security service and is responsible for missions along the borders of Area A and inside cities, including Israeli-Palestinian Joint Patrols and checkpoints at city limits. Key elements of the force were formed largely out of the elements from the Palestinian Liberation Army (PLA) and Fatah forces, based throughout the world.

The Civil Police Force became the main law enforcement tool in the Palestinian Authority (PA) and is responsible for ordinary police functions such as directing traffic, arresting common criminals, and keeping public order. It employed more than 10,000 officers in both the West Bank and Gaza and can deploy its forces in 25 selected villages in the areas of the West Bank known as Area B+. The Civil Police also headed a 700-man special police unit to handle complex crises, such as severe riots and counterterrorism operations.

The constituent elements of these forces presented problems from the start. Remnants of the PLA and Fatah that formed the NSF had little cohesion and little training for their new mission, either in dealing with extremists like those in Hamas or the PIJ or dealing with crowd and riot control. The forces included a large number of men who were aging bureaucrats living on a PLO income rather than official paramilitary personnel. Both forces initially had little money, equipment, or training. Many members of the forces had little or no training, but some received training in Jordan or Egypt. These training efforts only involved limited numbers of personnel and were slow to develop. They did not create the kind of force that could find the best balance between necessary operations and human rights, and corruption was sometimes a problem.

The regular police force combined volunteers from Gaza and the West Bank, including some former violent opponents of Israel like the Fatah Hawks and Black Panthers. It is scarcely surprising therefore that members of al-Fatah militia have exchanged gunfire with IDF forces during the recent clashes and its leaders declared that they strongly support the need for continued uprising of the Palestinian people. Some elements in the security forces have divided loyalties and this makes the prospects for enforcing a ceasefire or peace more fragile.[437] It is also important to note that the Palestinian Authority continued to run some 90 two- and three-week "summer camps" for Palestinian youth in which personnel associated with its security forces provided training for mock attacks on Israeli sentry posts and mock kidnappings of Israelis, as well as some basic weapons training. The camps trained some 1,000 teenagers a year.[438]

These problems are compounded by internal difficulties and problems in the structure of the command of the forces involved. Within the PSS, responsibilities of several units often overlapped, leading to street clashes, confusion, inefficiency, and sometimes battles over blurred jurisdictions. Rivalries within the various security and paramilitary forces were sometimes tied to longstanding rivalries within the PLO and Arafat's immediate entourage. Coordinating the services to prevent such problems was complicated by Arafat's insistence on personally directing and arbitrating between the groups, and use of their divisions to ensure that no rival could emerge.

In addition, three groups of generals are represented in the security establishment. The first group consists of "outsiders"—generals who arrived in the territories in 1994 as part of the Oslo accords and did not actively participate in the Intifada. A second group is made up of prominent figures in the Palestinian struggle for independence during the Intifada. This group enjoys great popular support and one of its members may be chosen as Arafat's successor. A third group consists of officers brought to the territories by Arafat from abroad to command the most sensitive security bodies, primarily intelligence services.

By placing the security forces under the command of a heterogeneous group of generals who are often at odds with each other, Arafat managed to prevent the formation of a cohesive general staff with authoritative power. In this way, he reduced the possibility that his power will ever be challenged by a united military coup, as has occurred in several Arab regimes in the Middle East. However, the efficacy and utility of the PSS is compromised by such a structure.[439]

While the Palestinian security structure was supposed to be professional, Arafat also created overlapping groups that were highly political in character and spied on each other. In many cases, there has been considerable corruption, internal violence, and feuding within the security services. The security services are supposed to enforce the rule of law, but they are as subject to family and clan interests as every other aspect of the Palestinian Authority. While the security forces have been accused of preparing for war, for expanding beyond the Oslo limits, they also had to co-opt young Palestinians to keep them from joining the opposition. This hiring of low-grade personnel to create jobs and offer positions for patronage purposes may have helped ensure their loyalty, but it has also made corruption, feuding, and human rights abuses worse.

Israel too faced problems. It was able to rapidly adapt its forces to the problem of controlling Palestinian movement in and out of Gaza, as well as securing its access to Gaza, key lines of communication, Israeli settlements, and mixed areas. At the same time, it had to develop and enforce extremely complex arrangements with the Palestinian Authority to define the right of hot pursuit, and secure key roads inside Gaza, as well as the perimeter of several key settlements. Israel's concentration on security and counterterrorism also led it to underestimate the political, economic, and social pressures inside Gaza and the West Bank that led to the outbreak of mass violence on September 29, 2000.

Israel was slow to address the potential causes of violence, and it did not prepare to deal with a mass popular uprising, as distinguished from terrorism. It failed to train and prepare effectively for riot control and the outbreak of a Second Intifada, and act in ways that minimized the use of lethal force. It pressured the Palestinian security forces to take hard-line action without sufficiently considering the fact that the Palestinian Authority had to keep its popular support and it often delayed implementing the Oslo and follow-on accords on security grounds without fully considering the linkage between such delays and the lack of Palestinian support for the peace process.

Progress also took place in a climate of acute mutual suspicion. Members of the IDF and Israeli security forces that dealt with the new Palestinian security forces initially had serious reservations about whether the Palestinians could become effective in and conduct counterterrorism operations. Over time, however, they felt that the various Palestinian security and police forces gained experience, improved their training and equipment, set up intelligence and informer networks, and improved their cooperation with Israel.

Some of this improvement was forced on the Palestinian Authority by the growing risk that tolerance of Palestinian terrorism would lead to a breakdown of the peace process. The Palestinian security forces only began to take decisive action after the April 9, 1995, suicide attack on Israelis. Nevertheless, the Palestinian security operation in Gaza and Jericho built up total forces of 9,000 regular police and 12,000 security police by late 1994, and demonstrated that a number of its cadres had at least moderate effectiveness.[440]

The new "Oslo II" peace accords signed by Israel and the Palestinian Authority on September 13, 1995, further strengthened the role of the Palestinian security forces in Gaza. They allowed the Palestinian Authority to deploy 18,000 men in Gaza out of a total security force of 30,000, and to recruit up to 7,000 men from Palestinians abroad. The agreement allowed them to be armed with rifles and pistols, possess a total of 7,000 light personal weapons, 120 machine guns of .30 to .50 caliber, and 45 wheeled armored vehicles.[441] In practice, the Palestinian Authority built up significantly larger forces than the accords permitted by 1997, and continues to maintain them.

The new agreements between Israel and the Palestinian Authority made as part of the Wye Accords in 1998 built on the experience both sides had gained since 1993. They expanded regional and district security liaison offices that are manned on a 24-hour basis and have special communications links. The agreements called for the sharing of intelligence, joint patrols on key roads, joint mobile units for rapid response to disturbances and terrorist attacks, and joint liaison bureaus at the key crossing points.

The Wye Accords strengthened the role of the CIA in training the Palestinian Authority, and led to more stringent Palestinian Authority action in dealing with extremists and terrorists. They also created a more formal role for the CIA as an arbiter and buffer between the two sides. The CIA was not, however, supposed to be involved in an operational role and claims that it has not departed from advisory and liaison functions.

The Sharm el Shiekh Memorandum of September 4, 1999, did not involve much public detail about new security arrangements. It did, however, remove a number of causes of friction between the Palestinians and Israel, and did call for full implementation of the Wye Accords. It also called for the two sides to act to ensure the immediate, efficient, and effective handling of any incident involving a threat or act of terrorism, violence or incitement by either Israelis or Palestinians. It also called for the Palestinians to fully implement their responsibilities for security, security cooperation, ongoing obligations and other issues—particularly those called for in the Wye River Memorandum. Specifically, it called for a continuation of the Palestinian program to collect all illegal weapons, provide reports on the apprehension of suspects, and for forwarding a full list of Palestinian policemen to Israel no later than September 12, 1999. A revitalized Israeli-Palestinian Monitoring and Steering Committee was to review this compliance.

The end result, however, was to demonstrate that security forces are no substitute for a peace that both sides regarded as acceptable and just. The clashes between IDF forces and Palestinian security forces since September 2000 were scarcely the first sudden outburst of violence. In September of 1996, Netanyahu refused to close the tunnel of Al-Aqsa, one of the Islamic holy sites in Jerusalem. Fighting between the Palestinians and Israelis broke out for three days, leaving 72 people dead. This event was particularly notable, because it was the first time Palestinian forces turned against Israeli forces and began to fire on them.[442] It is also important to note that the Palestinian security forces did relatively little to train and organize for riot control before September 2000 and the risk of a Second Intifada. They concentrated on counterterrorism. As a result they lacked the riot equipment, security posts, communications equipment, and experience to deal with a major Palestinian uprising.

CONFLICT IN GAZA

The division of Gaza and the West Bank creates two different kinds of security problems for Israel and the Palestinians in either peace or war. The Gaza is an area slightly more than twice the size of Washington, DC. The current political status of the Gaza is defined by a number of agreements between Israel and the Palestinian Authority. The Israel-PLO Declaration of Principles on Interim Self-Government Arrangements (the DOP), which was signed in Washington on September 13, 1993, provides for a transitional period of Palestinian interim self-government in the Gaza Strip and the West Bank that does not exceed five years. Under the DOP, Israel agreed to transfer certain powers and responsibilities to the Palestinian Authority, which includes a Palestinian Legislative Council elected in January 1996, as part of interim self-governing arrangements in the West Bank and Gaza Strip.

The security arrangements to date have given the Palestinian authority extensive control with the Gaza, but have also left Israel with extensive security capabilities. A transfer of powers and responsibilities for the Gaza Strip and Jericho took place pursuant to the Israel-PLO Cairo Agreement on the Gaza Strip and the Jericho

Area of May 4, 1994. It took place in additional areas of the West Bank pursuant to the Israel-PLO Interim Agreement of September 28, 1995, the Israel-PLO Protocol Concerning Redeployment in Hebron of January 15, 1997, the Israel-PLO Wye River Memorandum of October 23, 1998, and the Sharm el-Sheikh Agreement of September 4, 1999. The DOP provided that Israel would retain responsibility during the transitional period for external security and for internal security and public order of settlements and Israeli citizens. Permanent status was to be determined through direct negotiations. These resumed in September 1999 after a three-year hiatus but did not resolve any issues before the Israeli-Palestinian clashes that began in September 2000.

Fighting in an Economic and Demographic Time Bomb

The geography and demography of the Gaza virtually ensure that a future Israeli-Palestinian conflict will take different forms in the Gaza and West Bank. Gaza is an area of about 360 square kilometers, sharing a 51-kilometer border with Israel, an 11-kilometer border with Egypt, and 40 kilometers of coastline.[443] These borders are relatively compact and easy for the IDF to secure, provided that Egypt enforces the control of its borders with the same strictness as Israel. Even without Egyptian cooperation, the Gaza's southern border can be secured with considerable effectiveness.

Unlike the West Bank, the Gaza is an almost totally Palestinian entity. There were 1,132,063 Palestinians in the Gaza at the end of 1999, but only 6,500 Israeli settlers. These were, however, scattered in 24 Israeli settlements and civilian land use sites. The Palestinian population is overwhelmingly Muslim, and the religious composition of the Gaza is 98.7% Muslim, 0.7% Christian, and 0.6% Jewish.[444]

At the same time, the Gaza has become an economic and demographic time bomb. According to CIA estimates, the economy has deteriorated steadily since the early 1990s. Real per capita GDP for the West Bank and Gaza Strip (WBGS) declined 36% between 1992 and 1996 owing to the combined effect of falling aggregate incomes and robust population growth. The CIA estimates that this downturn in economic activity led to a nearly two year decrease in life expectancy and a significant increase in child mortality between 1997 and 2000.[445] The population growth rate was an extremely high 3.97%, in spite of economic conditions and gross overcrowding in the available housing. The population is extremely young: 50% is 14 years of age or younger. The CIA describes the Gaza's economic situation as follows:[446]

. . . largely the result of Israeli closure policies—the imposition of generalized border closures in response to security incidents in Israel—which disrupted previously established labor and commodity market relationships between Israel and the WBGS. The most serious negative social effect of this downturn has been the emergence of chronic unemployment; average unemployment rates in the WBGS during the 1980s were generally under 5%; by the mid-1990s this level had risen to over 20%. Since 1997 Israel's use of comprehensive closures has decreased and, in 1998, Israel implemented new policies to reduce the impact of closures and other security procedures on the movement of Palestinian goods and labor. In October 1999, Israel permitted the opening of a safe passage between the Gaza Strip and the West Bank in accordance with the 1995 Interim Agreement. These changes to the conduct of economic activity have fueled a moderate economic recovery in 1998–99.

The GDP of the Gaza was only $1.17 billion in 1999, even when measured in purchasing power parity terms. The per capita income was $1,060. In spite of major water, desertification, and sewage problems, roughly one-third of the economy was still tied to agriculture. Another 25% worked in light industry; the rest work in "services," largely consisting of temporary work.[447] Most water and electricity are imported from Israel and are under Israeli control. Israel has the power to shut off most power and water, as well as cut most communications. The Israeli company BEZEK and the Palestinian company PALTEL are responsible for communication services in the West Bank. The is a total of a little over 100,000 telephone landlines in the entire WBGS area, although there are many cellular phones.[448]

Table 7.2 provides a profile of the geographic, economic, and population profile for the Gaza, West Bank, Jordan, and Israel. As a result of the September 13, 1993, accords between Israel and the Palestinian Authority, and the Cairo Agreement of May 4, 1994, it is divided into a mix of common roads, Israeli-controlled entry points and roads, Israeli settlements, Palestinian Authority–controlled areas, and other areas.[449]

The Gaza presents a continuing risk of internal instability. Peace and sovereignty alone cannot feed its people. Gaza has no natural resources, and no significant internal industrial activity or exports except souvenir production, a few showpiece factories, and citrus fruits—many of which are grown by Israelis.[450] Gaza's economy has been highly dependent on Israel in the past. Gaza provided most of the roughly 50,000 Palestinian workers who worked in Israel during 1994, and over 43% of all Gazan employment came from Israel during the peak employment year of 1992.[451] Remittances accounted for roughly 40% of the Gaza's GNP.[452] Israel has accounted for about 90% of Gaza's external trade.

Total Palestinian unemployment rose by as much as 10% per year during the mid-1990s and unemployment and disguised unemployment in Gaza varied from 35% to 40% during 1995–1999.[453] The official figures ranged from 20% to 30%, but only because nearly 80% of the Palestinian Authority's expenditures went to wages for civil servants and the security forces.[454] Unemployment was particularly high among young Gazans, who accounted for over half of the total of the unemployed Palestinians on the West Bank and Gaza.[455] The Gaza's unemploy-

Table 7.2
CIA Profile of Gaza and West Bank

Category	Gaza	West Bank	Israel	Jordan
Total Area (sq. km)	360	5,860	20,770	89,213
Land Area (sq. km)	360	5,640	20,330	88,884
Land Boundaries (km)	62	404	1,006	1,619
Egypt	11	-	255	-
Gaza	-	-	51	-
Iraq	-	-	-	181
Israel	51	307	-	238
Jordan	-	97	238	-
Lebanon	-	-	79	-
Saudi Arabia	-	-	-	728
Syria	-	-	76	375
West Bank	-	-	307	97
Coastline (km)	40	0	273	26
Land Use (Percent)				
Arable	24	27	17	4
Permanent Crops	39	0	4	1
Meadows & Pastures	0	32	7	9
Forest & Woodland	11	1	6	1
Other	26	40	66	85
Irrigated (sq. km)	120	-	1,800	630
Population	1,132,063	2,020,298	5,842,454	4,998,564
(% 0-14 years)	50	45	28	38
(% 15-64 years)	47	52	63	59
(% 65+ years)	3	3	9	3
Growth Rate (%)	3.97	3.38	1.67	3.1
Birth Rate (per 1,000)	43.14	36.73	19.32	26.24
Fertility Rate (Per Woman)	6.55	5.02	2.60	3.44
Net Migration Rate (per 1,000)	0.83	1.51	3.63	7.4
Death Rate (per 1,000)	4.31	4.49	6.22	2.63
Infant Mortality (per 1,000)	25.97	22.33	7.90	21.11
Life Expectancy (yrs.)	70.82	72.08	78.57	77.36
Ethnic Divisions	99.4	83	19.9	98
Arab	-	-	-	1
Armenian	-	-	-	1
Circassian	0.6	17	80.1	-
Jew				
Religion	0.7	8	2.1	4
Christian	0.6	17	80.1	-
Jew				

Table 7.2 (continued)

Category	Gaza	West Bank	Israel	Jordan
Muslim	98.7	75	14.6	96
Other	-	-	3.2	-
Literacy	-	-	95	86.6
Labor Force	-	-	2,300,000	1,150,000
Construction (%)	-	8.0	-	10.0
Agriculture (%)	13.0	13.0	2.6	7.4
Industry (%)	21.0	13.0	20.2	11.4
Commerce (%)	-	12.0	25.9	10.5
Other Services (%)	66.0	54.0	13.1	52.0
Public Services (%)	-	-	31.2	-
GDP (PPE in $billion)	1.17	3.3	105.4	16.0
Real Growth Rate	4.62	4.6	2.1	2.0
GDP Per Capita ($US)	1,060	2,050	18,300	3,500
Inflation Rate (%)	5	7.6	1.3	3
Unemployment Rate (%)	26.8	17.3	9.1	20-30
Budget ($B)				
Revenues	(1.6 ——— 1.6)		40.0	2.8
Expenditures	(1.73 ——— 1.73)		42.4	3.1
Trade ($M)				
Exports	(62 ——— 6821)		23,500	1,800
Imports	(2,500 ——— 2,500)		30,600	3,3900
External Debt ($M)	(108 ——— 108)		18,700	8,400
Economic Aid ($M)	(800 ——— 800)		1,100+	850
Transportation				
Railroads (km)	0	0	610	677
Roads (km)	-	4,500	15,464	8,000
Paved (km)	-	2,700	15,464	8,000
Airports	2	2	31	16
Runways 1,500M+	-	1	7	4
Runways 3,000M+	1	0	2	9
Telephones	(95,229 ——— 95,279)		2,800,000	402,600
Cellular	-	-	2,500,000	75,000
Televisions	-	-	1,690,000	500,000
Stations	-	-	24	8
Radios	-	-	3,070,000	1,660,000
AM Stations	-	-	23	6
FM Stations	-	-	15	5
Short-wave	-	-	2	1

Note: *In addition, there are 171,000 Jewish settlers in the West Bank and 172,000 in East Jerusalem, and 6,500 in Gaza.

Source: Adapted from CIA Internet database as of October, 2000 by Anthony H. Cordesman.

ment problems are certain to remain critical unless there is heavy outside investment and/or Gaza can develop close economic ties to Israel.

Gazan employment in Israel dropped sharply after 1992, because of Israeli actions to halt terrorism. Palestinian employment in Israel was only about one quarter of its peak level in mid-1995, and remittances accounted for only about 20% of Palestinian GNP. Changes in Israeli policy in 1998 did allow Palestinians to find new jobs in Israel and contributed to a drop in unemployment; nevertheless, the GNP per capita remained at only $1,100—even using the purchasing power parity method.[456]

Israeli control of access to the Gaza is a powerful economic weapon, and it was not always used wisely or with proper regard for the human costs of Israeli action before the fighting in September 2000 created new problems. The Gaza is an enclave that requires a high volume of peacetime traffic across its borders for the Gazan economy to function. Some 30,000 Palestinian workers with work permits, and 500 trucks crossed the border daily before violence began in September 2000.[457] This regular traffic takes place at known checkpoints, but it is still possible to smuggle in some small arms, explosives, and manportable weapons through other areas.

Plans to create a port and transit route between Gaza and the West Bank will complicate the IDF's capability to isolate the Gaza in this situation if the peace process is restored. So will a past history of sometimes deliberately delaying the clearance procedure, using searches to put political pressure on the Palestinian Authority, and deploying troops with inadequate training and regard for Palestinian dignity.

At the same time, Israel had begun to use more sophisticated security procedures to minimize some of the problems and delays before the fighting began in September. More advanced technology is also available which can handle greatly increased volumes of traffic with equal or greater speed and equal or greater security. These tools include UAVs, unattended ground sensors, ground-based radars, and night vision and surveillance equipment. No set of procedures can perfectly secure the Gaza in the sense of preventing all arms smuggling and infiltration, but there are a wide range of technical measures that can improve security without extensive physical searches and delays.

The Forms the Fighting Might Take in the Gaza

Given these conditions, much depends on whether fighting in the Gaza takes place as part of a Palestinian effort under the direction of the Palestinian Authority or is part of a broader popular uprising. The Palestinian Authority security forces were able to maintain a high degree of control in Gaza as long as they remained under the direction of leaders who supported the peace process, and as long as most

Gazans either supported the peace process or at least opposed violence. The events of September 2000 have shown, however, that this situation can change with little warning unless a peace is popular and/or efforts to reduce Palestinian violence address Gaza's human and economic problems.

Hamas and the PIJ can scarcely be counted out simply because there is another ceasefire or some kind of peace agreement, and young Palestinians may take events into their own hands. Even if this does not happen, the eventual death of Arafat (and the inevitable struggle over who would succeed him) could lead to either a new leadership in Gaza, or to a violent, broad-based popular uprising in which the Palestinian Authority might divide.

Containment is not an issue. Almost regardless of what happens *within* the Gaza, however, the IDF has the military strength to quickly seal it off from the rest of Israel, and control its coasts and border with Egypt. The IDF can probably also protect the Israeli settlers within Gaza and the necessary lines of communication. The IDF has shown it can fortify strong points, clear fields of fire, and secure key roads under crisis conditions.

The primary problem that Israel faces is the political reaction of the world to any prolonged isolation and containment of the Palestinians in Gaza and their suffering. The IDF could also face growing problems in protecting Israeli settlers in the Gaza, and much would depend on the scale of Palestinian popular support for violence, and Palestinian willingness to take casualties.

A number of Israeli military experts feel that securing the remaining Israeli presence in Gaza is extremely costly even in peacetime, and a needless source of provocation. The defense of the settlements requires one soldier to be stationed for every two settlers. Furthermore, they feel it will present growing problems for the IDF if the Palestinians sustain any kind of Second Intifada, and particularly if the Palestinians gradually acquire significant numbers of long-range rocket launchers, mortars, and anti-tank guided weapons. Some IDF experts privately believe that Israel should fully withdraw from the Gaza, and others believe that at least a temporary evacuation might be necessary.

There are several possible evacuation routes that the IDF could use for Israeli settlers in Gaza. The most desirable would be to evacuate the settlers directly into Israel on land. However, due to the close quarters created by the urban environment other routes remain a possibility. One route moves directly along the Israeli-Egyptian border, rather than through the heart of Gaza like more traditional evacuation routes. Another route uses a combination of air and naval forces to rapidly extract the population in the event of a very sudden and dangerous escalation.[458] The settlement of Netzarim, south of Gaza City, was unable to be reached by land for 2 weeks and visitors caught in the 400-person settlement were evacuated by helicopter. However, the settlers themselves do not seem to have any intention of leaving. They have erected electrical warning fences, paved patrol

Map 7.1
The Gaza

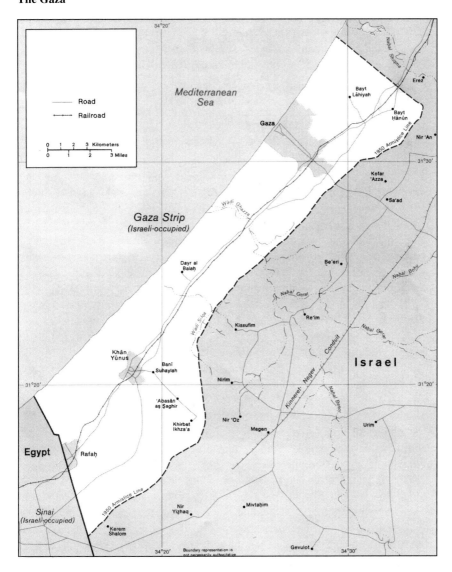

roads around the settlement, improved the observation system and fortified its outposts with new roofs to prevent damage from incendiary weapons.[459]

There are also scenarios in which the Palestinians might be more effective in opposing the IDF by concerted operations in Gaza and the West Bank. Yuval Stienitz has raised a scenario in which armed Palestinians, particularly those security forces with military training, infiltrate into Israel to disrupt mobilization against another Arab enemy and force Israel to disperse its forces. Such infiltration would be easier from the West Bank than Gaza, and the IDF has an excellent record in blocking infiltration by sea, but Palestinian forces in Gaza might be able to penetrate deeply enough to disrupt at least some mobilization activity and/or threatening movement along Israel's main north-south routes (Highways 1 & 4) during a critical point in Israeli troop movements. The Palestinians in Gaza might also attack the settlements simultaneously to force the IDF to deploy. If such attacks should precede major attacks from within the West Bank or from other Arab states, they might lead the IDF to overcommit forces to Gaza.

It is more likely, however, that such Palestinian attacks would have a limited effect of short duration even if they were initially successful. The IDF could probably resecure the settlements relatively quickly with limited amounts of force. It could also probably resecure many of the Palestinian areas in Gaza in a matter of days if it chose to do so—although isolating these areas seems to be a far more likely IDF tactic. The main problem for the IDF is that it would have to be willing to take casualties and would face political problems in dealing with world public opinion. These casualties could be serious if the IDF had to fight prolonged urban warfare in Gaza in the middle of a hostile population, and/or if the IDF had to confront most of the Palestinian Authority security forces. Any initial IDF victory could prove illusory, however, and lead to Gazans regrouping, reorganizing, and shifting to the kind of low-level war that took place in Lebanon and Ulster.

Street-by-street fighting is the worst case for the IDF, and one it would almost certainly seek to avoid by containing Gaza, rather than occupying it. The Palestinian Authority forces in Gaza and the West Bank are now relatively well armed for urban warfare, and an effort to suppress a sustained, armed popular uprising would be far more difficult than defeating the known elements of the Palestinian Authority security forces. IDF studies and exercises show that any prolonged form of low-level urban warfare in the Gaza could be bloody, difficult, and lead to high casualties, although the Palestinian Authority forces are not well trained to fight this kind of conflict.

The IDF might also face growing problems in maintaining control over the border areas of Gaza if the Palestinians adapt to hit-and-run tactics, ambushes, booby traps, and the use of rocket launchers. Fighting the urbanized equivalent of the Hizbollah in a war of attrition confronts the IDF with major problems since its technical advantages would often provide little tactical superiority and the Palestinians could choose the time and place of their attacks. The IDF has also lost much of its former intelligence network and access to informants in Gaza.

On December 13, 2000, a battle involving hundreds of armed combatants from both sides with the Israelis supported armor and mechanized infantry. The IDF believed the previous night an earth embankment on the edge of the Khan Yunis refugee camp had been used to shoot at the community center in the Neve Dekalim settlement. The IDF, therefore, resolved to bulldoze the embankment with armored support. The Palestinians perceived this as an invasion of their sovereign territory and soon hundreds of armed Palestinians were resisting the Israeli advance. After seven hours and the use of tank shell and heavy machine gun fire, the IDF forced a Palestinian withdrawal and demolished the embankment. Four Palestinian police were killed and two dozen were wounded in the engagement; there were no Israeli casualties.[460]

Despite its seeming success of operations, the cost and manpower requirements would also be a problem for Israel. If Israel had to defend the settlements in Gaza for weeks or months under such low-intensity warfare conditions, the IDF would have to expand its presence to create a series of complex security zones. At the same time it would have to enforce a wide range of security measures to defeat violent elements within the Palestinian population in Gaza while pacifying the rest. It would probably also have to make further improvements to the security of key lines of communication, and almost completely substitute other workers for the Palestinians. The other side of this issue is Israel's control over electricity and water and ability to seal off the Gaza economy.

Intelligence will be a problem for Israel. The IDF and the Israeli General Security Services (GSS), or Shin Bet, have lost a considerable amount of their intelligence on Palestinian activities in Gaza, and the Palestinian towns and cities in Gaza could become places of refuge.[461] Once again, UAV sensors, radars and other devices can help. They are not, however, a substitute for human intelligence. They also cannot eliminate the risk of civilian casualties and collateral damage. Targets do not remain fixed in war. Threats change location, and so do innocent civilians. As a result, strikes and raids can fail and/or have high costs in terms of media coverage and world opinion, while even successes can breed more resentment and counterviolence than they are worth. Precision weapons do not mean precision tactics or precision consequences.

The security along the Gazan border with Egypt has deteriorated since the peace accords, and there are reports of tunnels and arms smuggling. In spite of a major Jordanian effort to halt it, there is still a flow of smuggled arms from Iraq through Jordan to both Gaza and the West Bank. The opening of both an airport and seaport in Gaza has created further opportunities for smuggling, and the creation of safe passage routes between Gaza and the West Bank could make this situation worse in the future.

Much will also depend on just how sophisticated the flow of arms into Gaza has already been and becomes in the future. Israeli reports may be exaggerated, but there do seem to be substantial numbers of unauthorized arms in Gaza, and a considerable amount of military explosives.[462] Most sources agree that the Palestinian Authority forces are amassing stocks of light anti-armor weapons, rocket-propelled grenades, anti-tank missiles, and SAM-7 anti-aircraft missiles— all of which are forbidden under the Oslo Accords. The Palestinian Authority now seems to have an ability to use anti-tank weapons. Moreover, the Fatah and Tanzeem militia forces in Gaza, and Hamas and PIJ cadres, can be given large numbers of small arms, automatic weapons, and explosives and the Tanzeem are reported to already have thousands of small arms.[463] Furthermore, the Tazeem and

Fatah forces have demonstrated a willingness to engage IDF forces with small arms fire and have made use of anti-tank weapons.

Further, Israel cannot plan in the mid- to long-term to deal with Palestinian Authority forces and other Palestinian elements in Gaza as if they will remain under the control of a popular secular leader like Arafat. The IDF must now plan for a future where Arafat and/or pro-peace secular leaders in the Palestinian Authority may lose control of Gaza or the Palestinian Authority's security forces. The armed clashes between the IDF and Palestinian Authority security forces that took place in 1996 and 2000 show that Israelis must also plan for a future where large elements of currently pro-PLO/pro-Palestinian Authority Gazans could turn firmly against the peace process and/or Israel.

It is not clear that either side could achieve a strategic victory through asymmetric warfare in the Gaza, or even that either would be notably wiser and more able to achieve a secure peace after prolonged fighting. At best, there would be a high price tag in memories, suffering, distrust, and blood. At worst, both sides could become locked into endemic violence or some kind of ceasefire arrangement that would do nothing to address Gaza's need for development and acceptable living standards.

As is the case with fighting on the West Bank, the ultimate irony surrounding fighting between the IDF and Palestinians in Gaza is that both sides may end up almost exactly where they began in September 2000, but with even more problems in reaching a peace. One thing is certain. They will eventually have to deal with virtually the same issues affecting Gaza that they were negotiating at Camp David. This means the following issues will still be of major concern to both parties with or without a Second Intifada:

- Future security arrangements within the Gaza and between the Palestinian Authority in Gaza and Israel.
- Israel's ability to secure its access to Gaza and to control Palestinian movement in and out of it.
- Arms smuggling and infiltration into Gaza.
- The future of around 6,000 Israeli settlers in 24 different settlements.
- Coping with Palestinian population growth.
- Palestinian support of religious extremist groups.
- Poor economic conditions and high unemployment for Palestinians.
- Gaza's economic dependence on Israel.

CONFLICT ON THE WEST BANK

The West Bank presents many of the same problems as Gaza, but the West Bank has far more strategic importance to Israel, consists of scattered urban areas rather than one large entity, has borders that make it more open to infiltration, mixes Arab and Jew far more closely and in many areas, is far harder to contain, and has settlements that are far more valuable and important to Israel.

The West Bank is normally defined to include the West Bank, Latrun Salient, and the northwest quarter of the Dead Sea, but to exclude Mt. Scopus, East Jerusalem and Jerusalem. It is slightly smaller than Delaware. It has 5,860 square kilometers, and 5,640 square kilometers of land area. It has 307 kilometers of boundaries with Israel and a 97-kilometer border with Jordan.[464] This compares with an area of 20,700 square kilometers for all of Israel within its 1967 borders. Its highlands are the main recharge area for Israel's coastal aquifers.

The West Bank is also a significant military barrier to any attack on Israel from the East. Its north-south ridge may only reach heights of about 3,000 feet, but the Jordan River and Dead Sea descend 1,200 feet below sea level—resulting in an incline of 4,700 feet over a space of 15 miles. There are only five major east-west routes connecting the Mediterranean to Jordan, which makes any route of armored advance across the West Bank predictable and easier to target.[465]

Unlike Gaza, a struggle for the West Bank cannot be a relatively simple struggle based on a war of containment. The problem of maintaining security and reaching a secure peace for both sides is complicated by a greater intermingling of the two populations, the existence of a significant population of Israeli-Arabs, settlements in the West (some by Israeli extremists), the problem of Jerusalem, population growth issues, and problems in dividing key resources like water, and problems in dealing with Israeli and Palestinian immigration. There are far greater difficulties in implementing the final settlement issues, and in deciding how much territory will be traded for peace (an issue that includes Jerusalem).

There are different ways to count the number of Palestinians and Israelis involved. The CIA estimates that the total Palestinian population in the West Bank was around 2,020,298 in mid-2000. There were 171,000 Jewish settlers in 231 settlements and land use sites in the West Bank, and another 172,000 Jewish settlers in 29 areas in East Jerusalem.[466] Table 7.3 shows the growth in Israeli settlement, in Gaza and the West Bank during the period from 1990–2000. As is the case in Gaza, the Palestinian population has an extremely high birth rate. It was 3.38% in 2000, and 45% of the total Palestinian population was 14 years of age or younger.

The religious and ethnic composition of the West Bank is significantly more complex than that of Gaza. The population is 83% Palestinian Arab and 17% Jewish, and the religious distribution is 75% Muslim (predominantly Sunni), 17% Jewish, and 8% Christian and other. There is a significant shift within the Palestinian population towards the Muslim faith because of lower Christian birth rate and high rates of emigration.[467] There are another 1,051,641 Palestinians and other Arabs within Israel's 1967 boundaries—about 18–20% of the total population. This population growth, however, has blurred the geographic separation of Israeli and Palestinian in many areas of the West Bank, the greater Jerusalem area, and in Israel proper.

Table 7.3

Changes in Israeli Settlers in Gaza and the West Bank: 1992–1998 (not including Israelis in annexed Jerusalem)

Growth of Settlements

	West Bank	Gaza	Total
January 1, 1992	97,800	3,410	101,210
June 1, 1996	145,000	5,500	150,500
June 1, 1998	163,173	6,166	169,339
July , 1999 (CIA)	166,000	6,000	172,000
Population Increase	65,373	2,756	68,129
Percentage Increase	67%	81%	67%
Number of settlements gaining population since 1992	-	-	109
Number of settlements losing population since 1992	-	-	13

The CIA estimated that in July 1999 there were 216 Israeli settlements and land use sites in the West Bank, 42 in the Golan Heights, 24 in the Gaza Strip, and 29 in East Jerusalem. In addition to the settlers shown, there were 19,000 in the Golan and 176,000 in East Jerusalem.

Status of Occupancy

	Residential Units	Empty Units	Vacancy Rate in Percent
West Bank			
CIA Estimate	41,000	9,939	26
Israeli Central Bureau of Statistics	31,763	3,312	10.4
Gaza Strip			
CIA Estimate	2,300	1,300	56
Israeli Central Bureau of Statistics	1,847	754	41
Katfi Bloc Settler Council	1,500	340	22
Peace Now, Nov, 96	-	-	25
Golan Heights			
CIA Estimate	-	-	28
Golan Settler Council	-	-	6

Note: There are roughly 15,000 Israeli settlers in the Golan. Ariel Sharon called for an expansion of this total to 25,000 on September 26, 1996, and for building roughly 600 new dwelling units a year. The Likud government has indicated that Israel plans to increase the population of the settlements in the West Bank and Gaza by 50,000 over the next four years, and build 10,000 new dwelling units at a rate of 2,500 per year.

Source: Adapted from data developed by the Foundation for Middle East Peace and Ha'aretz, May 20, 1997 and May/June 1999. Some data adjusted or estimated by the author.

The West Bank Version of the Economic and Demographic Time Bomb

Once again, economic and demographic conditions combine to create a time bomb in the Palestinian population. The GDP of the West Bank is only $3.3 billion, even in purchasing power parity terms, and this compares with $14.5 billion for Israel. The per capita income is about twice that of Gaza, at $2,050. However, this compares with $18,300 for Israel. The total unemployment rate in the West Bank and Gaza was at least 15% before the fighting in September-November 2000, but this figure is almost totally misleading. Much of the employment is very sporadic and large numbers of Palestinian youths are not counted in these figures even though they seek jobs. The true figure for direct and disguised unemployment is at least 25% and probably exceeds 30%.[468] At the same time, this situation does make Palestinian labor vulnerable to Israeli reprisals. Some 120,000 Palestinians worked in Israel or Israeli-occupied areas before the fighting began in September 2000—roughly 60,000 had work permits and 60,000 worked there illegally.[469]

Like the Gaza, most water and electricity services are under Israeli control. Most electricity is imported from Israel. The East Jerusalem Electric Company buys and distributes electricity to Palestinians in East Jerusalem and its concession in the West Bank. The Israel Electric Company directly supplies electricity to most Jewish residents and military facilities. Some Palestinian municipalities, such as Nablus and Jenine, do generate their own electricity from small power plants, and most cities—like Ramallah—have some generators. Israel has the power to shut off most power and water, as well as cut most communications. The Israeli company BEZEK and the Palestinian company PALTEL are responsible for communication services in the West Bank. There are a total of a little over 100,000 telephone landlines in the area, although there are many cellular phones.[470]

Israeli settlements are a major source of tension, and the steady growth of both the Palestinian and Israeli population has pushed both peoples closer together. Tables 7.3 and 7.4 show the increase in settlements and settlers after the signing of the Declaration of Principles. Israeli settlements have always been a contentious issue. Even though the Oslo accords bar Israel and the Palestinians from taking unilateral action that would alter the status quo, Israel has continued to expand its settlements on the West Bank and to settle new areas. Settlement growth has accelerated since 1991, when the peace process began.[471]

More than a dozen new settlements have been established since the 1998 Wye Accords, although former Prime Minister Netanyahu supposedly promised Clinton that he would halt expansion.[472] Prime Minister Barak pledged to curtail settlement building, but he did not promise to completely halt activity.[473] In July 1999, Barak suspended financing for the construction of new factories in the West Bank and Gaza.[474] On the other hand, he insisted that most, but not all, existing settlements would remain under Israeli sovereignty after final status negotiations.[475] The end result is steady Israeli demographic pressure that matches Palestinian pressure. It has both contributed to the risk of a Second Intifada, and

Table 7.4
Status of Settlements in the Occupied Territories in 1994–2000

Growth of Settlements

	1994	1995	1996	1997–1998	2000
Settlement population beyond Green Line	290,00	301,000	313,000	-	-
Settlements beyond Green Line	250	250	300	-	-
Settlers in West Bank	121,000	127,600	136,000	161,000	171,000
Yearly increase in settlers in West Bank	9,400	3,500	6,000	-	-
Residential sites in West Bank	181	180	190	207	-
Israeli population in 20 neighborhoods of East Jerusalem	149,000	153,700	166,800	180,000	(172,000)
Yearly increase in Israelis in East Jerusalem	9,000	4,700	2,600	-	-
Israeli population in 20 neighborhoods of Gaza Strip	4,800	5,000	5,000	6,000	6,500
Yearly increase in Israelis in Gaza Strip	300	200	0	-	-
Settlers in Golan Heights	14,700	14,800	15,000	17,000	20,000
Yearly increase in settlers in Golan	700	100	200	-	-
Settlements in Golan	36	34	36	42	-
Israeli settlers as percent of total population in the Occupied Territories	12	11	13	-	-
Unoccupied housing units in existing Israeli settlements	15,000	15,600	17,000	-	-
Housing starts in settlements beyond the Green Line	3,700	4,100	3,100	-	-
Housing completions in settlements beyond the Green Line	2,600	3,800	3,500	-	-

Source: Adapted from statistical Yearbook, Jerusalem, 1996; US reports to Congress on the status of the disbursement of loan guarantees to Israel, Foundation for Middle East Peace, and CIA *World Factbook.*

has made any military, political, and economic separation of the two peoples more difficult. At the same time, it has created a growing security incentive for Israel to use forced separation in the event of a conflict.

Major Security Issues on the West Bank

Unlike Gaza, any future fighting cannot be based simply on sealing off the West Bank. Israel is unprepared to accept anything like a total withdrawal from the area. There are far larger and more important Jewish settlements and Israel will seek to maintain control of all of greater Jerusalem. Israel would lose much of its present strategic depth if it returned all of the Occupied Territories. (It would then be only 14 kilometers wide from west to east in its narrowest area near Tel Aviv.)

This is why continued fighting raises at least some threat that Israel could attempt some form of forced separation over much of the West Bank. Israel was reported to be studying such a separation plan in late October 2000 if the fighting continued to escalate. According to a report in the *New York Times*, Prime Minister Barak directed Ephraim Sneh, the Israeli deputy defense minister, to develop contingency plans to deal with a total breakdown of the peace effort. These plans could be executed in the event of either the transformation of a Second Intifada into a low intensity war or in reaction to a unilateral Palestinian declaration of statehood under war or near-war conditions.[476]

While such a separation plan would also affect the Gaza, what the Israelis call "unilateral separation," would primarily affect the West Bank. It would mean halting all Palestinian labor movement, while relocating some exposed settlements and making others Israeli territory. A combination of security and economic measures would be coupled to Israeli efforts to create its own "borders." This would initially mean an extended close of the "border" areas to seal off Palestinian areas, and the IDF would create or strengthen checkpoints on the border area and severely limit any movement of goods and labor across the borders.[477]

It is hard to judge how serious Israel really is about a Palestinian declaration of statehood, but some sources indicate that this could lead Israel to formally annex the large blocks of settlements and protect them with troops, check points, border fences, sensors, mines, and surveillance systems like UAVs and ground-based sensors. Such a move might also lead to Israel severely curtailing delivery of electric power and water, and using separation as a form of economic warfare to counter the Intifada.

According to the *New York Times* report, Barak also directed Avi Ben-Bassat, staff director for the Finance Ministry, to assemble an "interministerial task force and assess the feasibility and cost of a 'separation' strategy." This task force is said to have concluded that Israel could sharply reduce the need for Palestinian laborers in agriculture and construction, and that this would produce higher base wages and lower unemployment for unskilled Israeli workers.[478]

Israel sometimes announces or leaks such contingency planning efforts in an attempt to intimidate the Palestinians and push them towards halting violence and

Map 7.2
Jerusalem

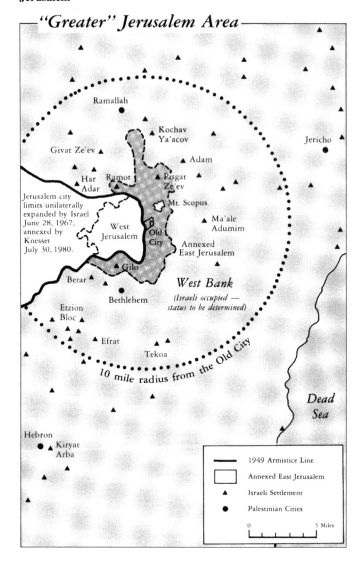

"Greater" Jerusalem Area

Ramallah

Kochav
Ya'acov

Givat Ze'ev

Jericho

Adam

Har   Ramot   Pisgat
Adar   Ze'ev

Jerusalem city
limits unilaterally
expanded by Israel
June 28, 1967;
annexed by
Knesset
July 30, 1980.

Mt. Scopus

West
Jerusalem

Old
City

Ma'ale
Adumim

Annexed
East Jerusalem

Gilo

West Bank

Betar

*(Israeli occupied —
status to be determined)*

Bethlehem

Etzion
Bloc

Efrat

Tekoa

10 mile radius from the Old City

*Dead
Sea*

Hebron
Kiryat
Arba

1949 Armistice Line

Annexed East Jerusalem

Israeli Settlement

Palestinian Cities

0   5 Miles

towards peace negotiations. Such a plan also would present major problems
because there are such large Israeli settlements and land holdings in areas outside
Israel's 1967 boundaries, and Israelis and Palestinians intermingle or live in close
proximity in many areas. It is important to note, however, that Israel has given at
least some contingency study to even more Draconian plans involving forced
Palestinian deportations out of the East Jerusalem, greater Jerusalem, Bethlehem,

and Nablus areas, and away from the 1967 border areas and Jewish settlements, and pushing the Palestinian population towards the West Bank.

The practical problem for both Israel and the Palestinians, however, is that any Israeli separation effort almost certainly means that the Second Intifada would continue indefinitely, and that Israel would face massive hostility from much of the world. At the same time, any alternative means both sides must ultimately deal with the same basic West Bank security issues they faced before violence broke out in September 2000. Any future agreement must ultimately deal with Palestinian sovereignty or non-sovereignty, demographics, water rights, future boundaries, security measures, the Israeli settlement and Palestinian refugee problem, creating new security arrangements, and the political, physical, and religious aspects of Jerusalem and the other holy areas.

The Problem of Palestinian Sovereignty and the Final Settlement Issues

One key issue is the uncertain evolution of a Palestinian government on the West Bank. The "final settlement" negotiations over Jerusalem and the rest of the West Bank were supposed to begin in 1996, and lay the groundwork for resolving the issue of Palestinian sovereignty. However, Israel and the Palestinian Authority made little progress after September 1995 and only token progress in the Wye River Memorandum concluded in November 1998. While progress was made in 1999 and 2000, the failure of the Camp David talks in the summer of 2000 and Israeli-Palestinian clashes of September through November 2000 have left the West Bank's future unresolved.

This does not mean that there has not been major progress towards creating a Palestinian state. The Palestinian Authority has a functional chief executive and an elected 82-member Palestinian Council.[479] The Palestinian Authority has the power to tax, to zone land, to control some aspects of communications, to control local radio and TV broadcasts, to regulate many aspects of commerce, to issue passports, to have foreign currency reserves, to enter into some types of international agreements, and to set up courts and enforce their judgments over Palestinians.[480]

Nevertheless, Israel and the Palestinian Authority still have to resolve the issue as to whether the Palestinians are to become a fully independent and sovereign state, and there is a growing risk that the Palestinian Authority will declare statehood without Israeli approval. At an April 1999 meeting, the Palestinian Authority discussed unilaterally declaring statehood by the year 2000. It put off this decision in both the hope that a final peace settlement would lead to Israeli agreement to such a declaration and because Israel threatened reprisals, including the unilateral declaration of its own new borders.

Prime Minister Barak was considerably more receptive to negotiations over statehood than Netanyahu had been.[481] Barak said in an NBC interview on July 18, 1999, that he did not rule out the possibility of a Palestinian state, but asked Arafat to delay a declaration until after a final settlement.[482] His receptiveness was also conditional on the success of peace negotiations. Since September 2000 the Israelis have created the dilemma in which they have made a unilateral Palestinian declaration more likely, and under conditions where it will be part of a Second Intifada. As has been discussed earlier, this could push Israel towards trying to execute a separation plan at the same moment the Palestinians seek to create a state.

Regardless of what happens in terms of a unilateral Palestinian declaration of sovereignty, moving towards peace will not be easy and any form of security must still address the underlying issues affecting the West Bank that existed before the Second Intifada. Israel and the Palestinian Authority will have to work with other Arab governments to resolve the rights and treatment of Palestinians outside the West Bank and Gaza. A decision will have to be made regarding what rights the Palestinian entity will have to develop military forces or paramilitary forces. These issues interact with other equally serious problems in the West Bank which all have security implications and where Israelis also have asymmetric values:

- Demographics and population growth.
- Poor economic conditions and high unemployment for Palestinians.
- The threat of major immigration to areas controlled by the Palestinian Authority or government by Palestinian refugees, and the strain such immigration would put on the water supply.
- Control over Jerusalem and adjustments to Israel's boundaries.
- The strategic value of the Jordan River area, which makes Israel reluctant to give up control over its security.
- Competition for water, which is compounded by the fact Israelis now use three times more water per capita than Palestinians.
- Resolving the issue of whether there should be any form of confederation with Jordan. Such a confederation now seems extremely unlikely, but the issue remains and would have a major potential impact on the future role of Jordanian military and Jordan's role in the peace process.

The Problem of Demographics and the Right of Return

As has been touched upon earlier, Palestinian demographics present security problems in terms of both military manpower and economic pressure. Projections by the US Census Bureau indicate that the total Palestinian population in the West Bank and East Jerusalem will increase to 1.5 million in 2005, and 1.7 million in 2010. Similarly, the total Palestinian population in Gaza is projected to increase from 0.73 million in 1995, to 0.95 million in 2005, and 1.1 million in 2010. The total Palestinian population in Lebanon is projected to increase from 0.39 million in 1995, to 0.46 million in 2000, 0.53 million in 2005, and 0.6 million in 2010.[483] More recent estimates by the World Bank indicate that the total population of the West Bank and Gaza doubled between 1980 and 1996, and will double again by 2010.[484]

This population growth poses daunting problems for the political and economic success of any peace settlement. It also compounds the problem of giving Palestinians outside the West Bank and Gaza any right of return. Estimates indicate that there are up to 1.5 million people outside the West Bank and Gaza that are registered as Palestinian refugees and who might claim the right of return, and the UN has registered a total of over three million refugees.

In 1999, the CIA estimated that this included 367,610 Palestinians in Lebanon (200,707 in refugee camps). This total amounted to 10.5% of the country's population and had an annual growth rate of 2.9%. There were 370,035 people in Syria (2.6% of the country's population with an annual growth rate of 3.0%, and 107,931 in camps), and 1,487,449 people in Jordan (33.9% of the country's population with an annual growth rate of 3.6%, and 272,257 in camps). There are over 562,000 registered refugees in the West Bank and East Jerusalem (30.1% of the population with an annual growth rate of nearly 5.0%, and 150,904 in camps). There were over 785,000 registered refugees in Gaza (77% of the population with an annual growth rate of over 3.5%, and 427,840 in camps).[485]

The total Palestinian population in Jordan is projected to increase from 1.9 million in 1995 to 2.3 million in 2000, 2.7 million in 2005, and 3.1 million in 2010. The total Palestinian population in Lebanon is projected to increase from 0.39 million in 1995 to 0.46 million in 2000, 0.53 million in 2005, and 0.6 million in 2010. The total Palestinian population in Syria is projected to increase from 0.36 million in 1995 to 0.41 million in 2000, 0.46 million in 2005, and 0.51 million in 2010.[486]

These demographic realities make the problems of agreeing on any form of Palestinian "right of return" as a part of any peace agreement extremely serious. Meaningful compensation for nearly 3.8 million refugees would also involve massive costs. Both sides also are still bitterly divided over the extent to which the refugees fled because of Israeli military action and persecution, on their own, or because Arab leaders encouraged them to do so. There is also the fact that most of these Palestinians have never seen any part of "Palestine." More than 70% of the refugees have been born since their parents left Israel, and this raises questions as to whether refugee status can be inherited.

These pressures help explain why Israel is not prepared to absorb more Palestinians into Israel proper. At the same time, there are massive development and absorption problems in Gaza and the West Bank. Both are already under extreme demographic pressure and have few prospects of getting the water, development funds, and infrastructure they need to deal with their current population. At the same time, it is far from clear that Jordan, Lebanon, and Syria are prepared to deal with the political, social, and economic problems of moving the refugees out of the camps into their territories and fully assimilating them as citizens with local or dual nationality. Some experts have proposed compensation, but there are serious questions as to who should be compensated and how it would be paid out in a region where corruption is not totally unknown and refugees are little able to appeal to governments and the courts.

At the same time, any Palestinian struggle with Israel will involve Palestinians outside Israel and the Gaza and the West Bank, and such action could escalate or lead to new acts of terrorism if the issue is not resolved. Many groups representing Palestinian refugees have long demanded the right of return and/or compensation from Israel, as have the registered refugees in the West Bank and Gaza. Palestinian refugees help fund and support the Palestinian Authority, secular Palestinian movements, Hamas, and the PIJ. They sometimes infiltrate into Gaza and the West Bank as "freedom fighters," and sometimes secular extremist/terrorist movements. Others, particularly Palestinians in Lebanon, might be organized into a paramilitary force that could attack across the border into Israel proper or infiltrate into the West Bank, possibly with support from Hizbollah, Syria and/or Iran.

The Problem of Economics

Economics are both an incentive for a Second Intifada and popular uprising, and a major problem for any peace settlement. Palestinian population on the West Bank currently has relatively low living standards and has seen little benefit from the seven years of peace negotiations following the Oslo Accords. Per capita income is about $2,000—much higher than Gaza, but much lower than Israel's $18,300. While some figures put Palestinian unemployment as low as 12%, true unemployment and disguised unemployment on the West Bank can vary from around 35% to 40%, depending upon political conditions.

After the first Oslo agreement, World Bank studies recommended a minimum of $1.35 billion in short-term investment, and $1.6 billion in long-term investment to improve living standards in the West Bank and Gaza over the next five years. Such investment would not, however, make more than a limited reduction in the gap between Palestinian and Israeli living standards and estimates in 2000 come closer to $10 billion. Finding jobs and career opportunities for both older Palestinians and the large and volatile younger Palestinian population will still be a major problem.[487]

Even the most favorable projections of economic development in the region indicate that there is only a moderate chance that the living standards of Palestinians already in East Jerusalem, the West Bank, and Gaza can be improved at a rate that will reduce the security problems inherent in the gap between their present per capita income and that of Israelis.[488] Any major immigration by Palestinians from outside the West Bank and Gaza would sharply increase the economic problem, while major immigration to Israel will also mean more competition for water.[489]

The Problem of Jerusalem

The final settlement negotiations have shown that Israel and the Palestinian Authority differ fundamentally over control of Jerusalem and the extent to which Israel will seek substantial adjustments in its pre-1967 boundaries. As recently as the spring of 1999, former Israeli Prime Minister Netanyahu continued plans to make a Jewish settler enclave in Hebron, 80% of which has been turned over to Palestinian rule in 1997, permanently.[490] While Prime Minister Barak advanced a far more generous proposal at Camp David, neither side has as yet shown that it can compromise over control of the Temple Mount, East Jerusalem, or the greater Jerusalem area. The Hebron issue is as contentious with Israelis as Palestinians and led to new incidents of violence on both sides in September through November 2000.

Religion is always a problem between Israeli and Palestinian. Tolerance is always tentative, and passions run deep. This reality became all too clear during the fighting in September through November 2000, which rapidly made religion a major issue. There are many areas and shrines to fight over, including Hebron, Bethlehem/Rachel's tomb, and Joseph's tomb, but Jerusalem is as much a matter of religion as one of territory.

Both violence and a peace process must deal with a deeply divided city. There are approximately 200,000 Palestinians with ID cards registered in Jerusalem, while approximately only 86,000 Palestinians actually live in the city (about 2,400 Jews and 27,000 Palestinians live in the old city).[491] The Israeli population of the greater Jerusalem area is approximately 433,000, with two-thirds of the population actually in Jerusalem.[492] Israelis have long been moving into settlements that surround Arab East Jerusalem in order to separate the Arabs of Jerusalem and those of the West Bank, while the Palestinians had built around 5,000 houses in the area without Israeli permission by late 1999—around 2,500 of which had pending demolition orders.

The present area of East Jerusalem is about 10 times the size it was under Jordanian administration in 1967. It extends to Kafr Aqab, about 10 kilometers to the north of the old boundary, and then about two kilometers west of the old boundary—almost as far west as Abu Dis. It extends to Umm Tuba and Har Homa in the south, roughly four kilometers to the south of the old boundary. As a result, modern East Jerusalem is larger in territory than the entire Jewish-occupied area around Jerusalem was in 1967. East Jerusalem, however, also now includes about 100,000 Palestinian residents, and isolated Palestinian villages like Um Tuba and Sur Baher.[493]

Demographics again are a problem. The Jewish population only grew by one percent in 1998, while the Palestinian population had a natural increase of around 3.5%. Israel attempted to reduce the number of Palestinians with Jerusalem ID cards between 1995 and 1999—although it claims to have confiscated only around 2,800 ID cards while Palestinian sources talk about over 11,000.[494] As a result, it is almost impossible for the IDF to secure the Arab areas in East Jerusalem or the greater Jerusalem area without either urban warfare or the forced evacuation of a large number of Palestinians.

Until the Camp David summit in July 2000, Israel insisted on undivided control over Jerusalem and its Israeli-occupied suburbs, although this can mean very different things. The Israeli government has not yet defined precisely how much of "greater Jerusalem" it will seek to retain. Former Prime Minister Rabin made it clear that he regarded control of Jerusalem as non-negotiable in a speech he gave on October 25, 1995, at Israel's celebration of the 3,000th anniversary of King David's establishment of Jerusalem as the capital of Israel. He told an audience of Israeli lawmakers and leading Jewish figures that, "There is only one Jerusalem. For us, Jerusalem is not a subject of compromise, and there is no peace without Jerusalem. Jerusalem . . . was ours, is ours, and will be ours forever. . . ."[495]

This position was also endorsed by former Prime Minister Peres and former Prime Minister Netanyahu. It is also an issue where Israel has strong US political support. On October 24, 1995, the US Senate voted 93 to 5 to move the US Embassy to Jerusalem by 1999.[496] However, President Clinton exercised his waiver authority under this act on June 18, 1999, saying that the issue of Jerusalem should be resolved through direct negotiation between Israel and the Palestinians, and the US should not take steps that would prejudice the negotiations or make them harder. However, he implied the US would support moving the capital after the failure of the Camp David talks in the summer of 2000.[497]

Prime Minister Barak did offer significant compromises at Camp David, but the violence that broke out in September 2000 has shown there are few indications that the Palestinians are willing to accept the Israeli position. Regardless of the justice of the arguments on both sides, and the legality of the issue, this is perhaps the most difficult single case of asymmetric values and one where it is far easier to pose innovative solutions and compromises, or legal and historical arguments, than create a realistic basis for a mutually agreed settlement. Going beyond Camp David requires one or both sides to accept a result that has so far been fundamentally unacceptable.

The problems in reconciling the Israeli and Palestinian positions are compounded by the fact that Jerusalem is not easy to define in either religious or geographic terms. The old city involves complex religious issues regarding the control of Jewish and Muslim holy places. The Jewish and Palestinian population of greater Jerusalem now extends far beyond the former administrative boundaries of Jerusalem and involves suburbs and settlements beyond the boundaries of several Palestinian cities.

This fundamental asymmetry in goals and values presents problems regardless of whether a state of violence exists, or both sides can negotiate a peace. "Jerusalem" will remain a large area with very complex demographics and economics. Metropolitan Jerusalem has a population of nearly half a million, and spreads over more than 100 square kilometers (42 square miles) of hills and valleys.[498] East Jerusalem, in the West Bank, occupies about 67 square kilometers. In addition, the Israeli-occupied suburbs in the West Bank now extend beyond Ramallah and Bethlehem. There are four major Jewish settlement complexes in the greater Jerusalem metropolitan areas, including Betar-Gush Etzion-Tekoa in the south (16,713 Israelis), Ma'aleh Adumim-Mishor Adumim in the East (21,348 Israelis), Beit El-Kochav Ha Shahar in the north (7,573 Israelis) and Givon-Beit Horon in the west (17,644 Israelis). Israeli settlements as far away from the old city as Beit Shemesh in the west, Almog junction in the east, Ofra in the north, and Tekoa in the south are still within a 30-minute commute of modern Jerusalem.[499]

Given the background, it seems likely that any prolonged Second Intifada will mean a complex mix of battles of containment and low-level urban warfare over a broad area around and within Jerusalem. Any such battle would also mean dealing with the fact that the Israeli definition of "Jerusalem" is likely to remain at least 60% larger than the Jerusalem of 1967, and the Israeli-controlled area around Jerusalem could grow to include much more territory during the course of a long struggle. Many Israeli analysts believe it is likely to include a zone that begins at Gush Etzion in the south and extends north to Givat Ze'ev, and some Israelis have argued that it should extend to Beit El. This, however, would mean dealing with municipal areas that mix at least 160,000 Jews and 150,000 Palestinians, and leave at least 64,000 Israelis in settlements in the greater Jerusalem area.[500]

Given the violence that broke out in September 2000, any Israeli Prime Minister is likely to insist on firm 'red lines' in making any final peace deal with the Palestinians: Israel will not withdraw all the way to its pre-1967 borders, Jerusalem will remain entirely under Israeli rule, most Jewish settlers will remain in West Bank blocs, and no foreign army will be allowed west of the Jordan River.[501]

The Problem of West Bank Security

The West Bank security presents roughly the same security issues for Israel and the Palestinians in both a Second Intifada and in creating and enforcing a peace. The Jordan River Valley forms a natural security barrier between Israel and Jordan, and effectively acts as a giant anti-tank ditch. Giving up this defensive line affects the amount of time Israel has to mobilize and therefore its ability to ensure control over the West Bank in the event of a war. This is why former Prime Minister Rabin stated that Israel would never give up control of this area in an October 5, 1995, speech to the Knesset shortly before his assassination. It is also why the IDF will maintain a major presence in the area in any Second Intifada and seek to remain a part of any peace settlement.

The ability to occupy key areas in the West Bank also gives the IDF major military advantages. Israel now occupies "Green Areas" that run through the Jordan Valley and that are approximately 60 kilometers long from north to south and 10 kilometers deep. Israel also has created two security corridors from west to east that separate the Palestinian-controlled areas into four parts. One runs from the Ariel settlement to the Shilo settlement to the Jordan Valley and separates the Ramallah and Nablus-Jenine areas. The other runs from East Jerusalem through the Ma'ale Adumim settlement to the Jordan and separates Ramallah, Bethlehem-Hebron, and Jericho. As a result, the IDF can control virtually every key communication route and junction and will do so in a Second Intifada.

From a Palestinian viewpoint, the ideal answer is simple: a return to the 1967 boundaries, or something very close to it, and full Palestinian sovereignty. The Palestinians have every incentive to seek to create a contiguous state on the West Bank, and obtain the return of as much territory as possible. This is not merely a matter of percentages or UN resolutions; it is a matter of status and security for the Palestinians, and their ability to limit the growth of Israeli settlements.

It is sometimes said that the Palestinians want peace with dignity and sovereignty while Israel wants peace with security and separation. The problem is that both sets of demands are just in theory, but may not be achievable in practice. From an Israeli viewpoint, each sacrifice of control over the routes up to the heights above the West Bank and down to Israel's pre-1967 territories, reduces both this control over the West Bank, and the ease with which the IDF can deploy, increasing the potential risk of a Jordanian, Palestinian, or Syrian force being able to deploy into the heights. Control of access of the heights above the Jordan River Valley provides a major military advantage in terms of sensor coverage, warning, artillery operations, and armored warfare.

This explains why Israel has long resisted giving up control of the Jordan River area north of Jericho, positions on the heights on the West Bank that provide sensor and intelligence coverage of Jordan and the West Bank, and a substantial strip of the West Bank to the east of its 1967 boundary south of Tulkarm and north of Ramallah. Former Prime Minister Rabin indicated in his October 5, 1995 speech that Israel would retain a security border in the Jordan Valley and annex the west bank of the Jordan and the settlement blocs of Ma'ale Adumim, Givat Zeev, and Gush Etzion around Jerusalem. This would put the homes of about 48,000 Jews, or one-third of the current settlers, under full Israeli sovereignty.[502]

At the same time, securing the West Bank does have its costs to the IDF, and costs that will steadily increase if a Second Intifada continues or any peace settlement or ceasefire is broken by sporadic violence. It means dealing with complex and sometimes overlapping enclaves of both Palestinian and Israeli settlers. Securing any strong point or settlement can leave the IDF and settlers isolated in any given battle, and a major West Bank–wide Second Intifada would force the IDF to disperse into a wide range of areas. The Palestinians are relatively easy to isolate in much of the West Bank, but the Israelis are extremely sensitive to casualties. This, in turn, reinforces each side's incentives to adopt asymmetric tactics and methods of warfare.

The events of September and October 2000 have revealed just how real these problems are. It is now clear that any combination of a Second Intifada and Israeli separation program would force both sides to struggle or fight along each of these "fracture lines" in the West Bank for their own different objectives.

At the same time, adequate security issues will be equally important in terminating a conflict, and it is unclear that any past offers will remain on the bargaining table in the same form. If peace negotiations do resume, it seems likely that Israel will seek to occupy part of the West Bank along the upper part of the Jordan River, and keep the Jordan River Valley as its security border. Even though the Camp David talks have shown Israel is willing to make some concessions in this regard, Israel is virtually certain to demand an agreement that limits the growth of Palestinian paramilitary capabilities to levels only slightly higher than those allowed in the 1995 accords. Israel is likely to demand that no regular Palestinian or Jordanian military forces be permitted in the West Bank area, or deployed closer to Israel than Jordanian forces are today. Israel will almost certainly demand that there be fixed force limitations, force deployment and disengagement agreements, limits on the nature and size of military exercises, and warning and pre-notification agreements.

At the same time, the Palestinian entity is likely to resist every such concession and compromise that does not go back to the 1967 border, and seek the maximum amount of flexibility and sovereignty. This means that even a successful compromise could be highly unstable for years, and that extremists on both sides are likely to try to undermine a peace with terrorism and violence.[503]

The Problem of Water

Control of the West Bank involves serious water issues that can easily affect any future fighting or move towards peace. Water is both an economic weapon for war and a key economic problem in peace. Israel clearly controls most of the flow of water to the Gaza, but the division and control of water between Israelis and Palestinians is particularly visible and contentious in the West Bank area. While various reports differ significantly over the amounts of water involved, a large system of mountain aquifers supplies both the West Bank and Israel's pre-1967 territory. This system of aquifers can supply about 970 million cubic meters of renewable water per year. It currently provides about 40% of the water Israel uses for agriculture and 50% of its drinking water—much of it for Tel Aviv and its suburbs.

While the West Bank has over 600 million cubic meters (21 billion cubic feet) of this water, much of it drains into Israel's pre-1967 boundaries and is easier to collect there. The Palestinian Authority has made claims for a total of roughly half of the entire 970 million cubic meters. However, virtually all of the water collected within Israel's pre-1967 boundaries goes to Israelis, and about 470–480 cubic million meters of the 600 million cubic meters' worth of water available from the mountain aquifers on the West Bank was used by Israel in 1994—about 80–83%. About 50 million cubic meters of the 600 million cubic meters was given solely to Jewish settlers on the West Bank. The average per capita water use in Israel is 12,040 cubic feet, compared to 3,290 cubic feet in the West Bank and Gaza.[504] Thus, Israelis use at least three times more water per capita than Palestinians do.

In contrast, the entire Palestinian population was only given about 120–130 million cubic meters (4.2 billion cubic feet)—16% to 20%. This allocation forced many Palestinian villages on the West Bank to severely ration water, and 37% of the Palestinian villages were entirely without running water. Only a few Israeli and Palestinian towns had wells in addition to piped water.[505]

The allocation of West Bank water to the Palestinians increased as part of the accords signed by Israel and the Palestinian Authority in September 1995, but the new allocation scarcely met Palestinian demands and the control of water remained a major security issue. It is both a potential political and economic weapon in a Second Intifada and a source of asymmetric values in a peace process. Population growth is steadily reducing the amount of water per capita. Even if no outside immigration takes place, World Bank studies indicate that current population growth levels in Israel, Gaza, and the West Bank will restrict renewable water use for human consumption and light industrial needs by 2010. However, as mentioned earlier, there are up to 1.5 million people who claim Palestinian refugee status who could, upon returning to Israel, sharply increase the water problem.

Some experts have indicated that shifting water use away from agriculture, making better use of recycled water, and creating major new desalination plants could solve this problem. Other experts have claimed such shifts are costly and impractical for Israel. They could take up to a decade to accomplish, and could involve an investment in excess of $10 billion. The one thing that is certain is that the combination of water and security problems is likely to present major strategic complications well beyond the year 2000.

The Impact of the Security Arrangements on the West Bank

The risk of a conflict and Second Intifada on the West Bank is also shaped by the security arrangements that have evolved under the Oslo Accords, and the history of tensions between the Palestinian Authority and Israel.

The Israeli-Palestinian Accords

The Security Annex of the September 1995 accords specified the commitment of Israel and the Palestinian Council to cooperate in the fight against terrorism and the prevention of terrorist attacks. It specifies that the Palestinian police is the only Palestinian Security Authority that will act systematically against all expressions of violence and terror, and will arrest and prosecute individuals suspected of perpetuating acts of violence and terror. It specifies that the Palestinian Council will issue permits in order to legalize the possession and carrying of arms by civilians and that the Palestinian police will confiscate any illegal arms.

The September 1995 accords also began major trades of territory for peace on the West Bank that went far beyond the token control of Jericho the Palestinian Authority obtained in 1993. They divided the West Bank into three areas. The Palestinian Authority was to gradually acquire control over seven largely Palestinian cities and some 450 Palestinian towns. According to the accords,

- Area A included Jenin, Nablus, Tulkarm, Kalkiyla, Ramallah, and Bethlehem. Special security arrangements were set up for Hebron, with one district largely under the authority of the Palestinian civil police and another—where the Israeli settlers live—under Israeli control. The Palestinian Council was given full responsibility for internal security and public order, as well as full civil responsibilities.
- Area B comprised roughly 450 Palestinian towns and villages of the West Bank. In these areas, which contained some 68% of the Palestinian population, the Palestinian Council was granted full civil authority as in Area A. As a result, the Palestinian Authority was to

have authority over nearly 98% of the Palestinian population. The Council was charged with maintaining the public order, while Israel had overall security authority to safeguard its citizens and to combat terrorism. This responsibility was to take precedence over the Palestinian responsibility for public order. Twenty-five Palestinian police stations, each with 25–40 civil police, could be established in specified towns and villages to enable the Palestinian Authority to exercise its responsibility for public order. These included stations in Yamun, Meithalun, Kafr Ray, Jalqamus, and Burqin in the Jenin Districts; Asirat al-Shamaliyya, Talouza, Tell, Talfit, Tamun, and Aqraba in the Nablus District; Shuweika, Kafr Zibad, Anabta, and Illar in the Tulkarm and Qalqilya Districts; Tuqo'a in the Bethlehem District; and Yata, Dhahiriyya, Nuba, Dura, and Bani Na'im in the Hebron District. The agreement contained provisions fixing the number of police at each station and requiring that the movement of the Palestinian police in Area B be coordinated and confirmed with Israel.

- Area C comprised about 68% to 70% of the West Bank, and included unpopulated areas, Jewish settlements, future Jewish settlement areas, strategic roads, strategic high points along the West Bank hill ridge, and areas used by the IDF such as military depots, deployment areas, early warning and intelligence facilities, and training areas. Israel was to retain full responsibility for security and public order. The Palestinian Council, however, was to assume all civil responsibilities not related to territory, such as economics, health, education, etc. in the parts of Area C that are eventually turned over to the Palestinian Authority.

The Wye agreement called for Israel to transfer 13% of Area C (full Israeli control) to the Palestinians, with 1% going to Area A (full Palestinian control) and 12% going to Area B (joint control). Further, it called on Israel to transfer 14.2% of Area B to Area A. These transfers were to take place in three stages.

Early progress was rapid. According to the original schedule agreed to in September 1995, the Palestinian Authority was to take over in Jenin on February 11, 1996, in Tulkarm on February 18, in Nablus on February 25, in Qalqilyah on March 3, in Ramallah on March 10, in Bethlehem on March 17, and in Hebron on March 24. The entire Israeli withdrawal was to be completed by March 24, 1996. In the course of these redeployments, additional parts of Area C were to be transferred to the jurisdiction of the Palestinian Council, so that by the completion of the redeployment phases Palestinian territorial jurisdiction would cover West Bank territory, except for areas where the jurisdiction is to be determined by the final status negotiations (settlements, military locations, etc.).[506]

Some aspects of this schedule were accelerated in the early days of the peace process. Partly as a result of the assassination of Prime Minister Rabin, Israel has speeded up its withdrawals from Jenin, Bethlehem, Tulkarm, Nablus, and Qalqilya. Virtually all of the transfers in Areas A and B were completed by early January 1996.[507] After that time, however, former Prime Minister Netanyahu slowed and then halted the withdrawals. He completed the first stage of the Wye Accords, withdrawing from approximately one percent of the West Bank. However, when this triggered a revolt in his hard-line coalition, he froze the agreements, claiming the Palestinians had not upheld their end of the agreement. As a result, Israel completed only the first stage of the transfers, moving 2% from Area C to Area A, and 7.1% from Area B to Area A, before it froze further withdrawals.

Although this was not specified in the various accords, the IDF seems to have planned to retain the right to set up checkpoints and roadblocks around Palestinian cities and villages. The September 1995 accords also call for the PLO to revoke those articles of the Palestinian Covenant calling for the destruction of Israel within two months of the inauguration of the Palestinian Council. The Palestinians seem to have taken major steps in this direction in 1998, but their actions still do not satisfy Israel.

The near breakdown in the peace process during Netanyahu's time in office then led to a major new US negotiating effort that resulted in the Wye agreement of 1998. The Wye agreement called for Israel to resume withdrawals in return for Palestinian concessions relating to timing and security.[508] It called for greater cooperation among the Palestinian security forces in the crackdown against terrorism, an Israeli troop redeployment from an additional thirteen percent of the West Bank (to take place within a ninety-day period), and a transfer of more than fourteen percent of jointly controlled land to full Palestinian control. Also included in the memorandum are such elements as the opening of a Palestinian airport in Gaza, the guarantee of two corridors of safe passage between Gaza and the West Bank, and a third Israeli troop redeployment from the West Bank.

The agreement also called for Israel to remove a number of military camps, including Fahme, Bezek, Sanur, Majnounei, and Nahal Ginat. The agreement called for new Israeli bases to be constructed, but each was to be smaller in size than the ones they replaced. Newspaper reports stated that several small bases would be established throughout the West Bank, particularly near isolated settlements in the heart of Palestinian areas without an army base nearby. These camps were to separate the territory under Palestinian control from the settlements.[509] The Wye agreement also called for the withdrawal of Israeli troops from roughly thirteen percent of the West Bank in exchange for specific security actions by the Palestinian Authority, in particular cracking down on terrorist groups.[510]

The failure to fully implement the Wye agreement was one of the factors that eventually led to the collapse of Netanyahu's government.[511] Netanyahu was defeated in May 1999, and the new Prime Minister, Ehud Barak, was elected in a landslide victory. His commitment to the peace process was a major factor leading to the Sharm el-Shiekh Memorandum of September 4, 1999, in which Israel and the Palestinian Authority agreed that Israel would resume its withdrawals according to a new schedule.

- Israel to transfer 7% from Area C under full Israeli control to Area B under joint control between September 11 and 13, 1999. (Israel completed the transfer on September 10, 1999.)

- The Palestinian Authority to report on the collection of illegal weapons and arrested terrorist suspects on October 15, 1999.

- Israel to transfer 2% from Area B under joint control to Area A under full Palestinian control, and 3% from Area C under full Israeli control to Area B on November 15, 1999.

- Israel to transfer 1% from Area C under full Israeli control to Area A under full Palestinian control, and 5.1% from Area B under joint control to Area A on January 20, 1999.

- Target date for completion of final agreement is September 13, 2000. (The original deadline set in the Oslo Agreement of September 13, 1993 was May 4, 1999.)

In return, the Palestinians agreed to implement an effective legal framework to criminalize the importation, manufacturing, or unlicensed sale, acquisition or possession of firearms, ammunition, or weapons in Palestinian-controlled areas.

If one examines the actual history of territorial transfer in terms of percentages, Oslo II put 2% of the West Bank in Area A (Palestinian military and civil control), 26% in Area B (Palestinian civil control and Israeli military control), and 72% in Area C (Israeli military and civil control). The first Sharm el-Sheikh agreement raised the percentage to 9.1%, 27.9%, and 70%, respectively. The second Sharm el-Sheikh agreement raised the percentages to 11.1%, 28.9%, and 60%, and a third Sharm el-Sheikh agreement on March 21, 2000 raised the percentages so that 17.2% of the West Bank was under Palestinian military and civil control, 23.8% was under Palestinian civil control and Israeli military control, and 59% was under Israeli military and civil control. While these percentage increases were important, and left only about 40,000 Palestinians in Area C, they still left the West Bank deeply divided.

Israel and the Palestinians signed another agreement affecting Palestinian-Israeli security on October 5, 1999. This agreement established a "safe passage" corridor along a 44-kilometer (27-mile) route using Israeli roads between Gaza and the southern part of the West Bank near Hebron. A second route, between Gaza and the northern part of the West Bank was to open in late January 2000. The agreement was signed by Shlomo Ben-Ami, the Israeli Public Security Minister, and Jamil Tarifi, the Palestinian Civil Affairs Minister, and came after weeks of hard negotiating over what Israel saw as a major security risk. The agreement also involved a compromise in which Palestinians would apply to the Palestinian Authority for transit cards, rather than Israel, but Israel would have the final authority over the list of approved applicants forwarded by the Palestinian Authority.[512]

The Israeli cabinet approved the handover of a further 6.1% of the West Bank on March 19, 2000, with 5.1% of the West Bank handed over to total Palestinian control. In the remaining 1%, the Palestinians will have administrative control while Israel will retain responsibility for security. This put 39.8% under full or partial Palestinian control. The 39.8% was divided roughly equally between full and partial self-rule. Some 60% of West Bank Palestinians will be living in areas under full Palestinian control after this step, and this will include all major Palestinian cities and towns. The towns to come under full self-rule included Salfit, Beitounia, Halhoul, Yatta, Dura and Dahariyah. A bridge between Hebron and Halhoul was put under full Palestinian control, but the highway over which the bridge crosses will remain under full Israeli control. No areas adjacent to Jerusalem were handed over in the withdrawal.[513] Prime Minister Barak talked later about building an elevated superhighway between Gaza and the West Bank to provide secure, high speed, high volume access between the two sectors.

Possible Wars on the West Bank

It was clear long before the fall of 2000 that the security of the West Bank hinged on a delicate and unstable relationship between the Palestinian Authority and the Israeli government. Any number of changes in the political and economic structure could potentially upset the balance and provoke conflict. The Palestinian urban areas on the West Bank could quickly become a sanctuary for extremist military groups operating within Palestinian areas.

The IDF planned for this possibility from the start of the Oslo Accords. It knew it would retain the military strength to quickly seal off urban areas on the West Bank in a conflict and to secure key routes and junctions in all of the greater Jerusalem area. It also planned to secure the Israeli settlements outside the greater Jerusalem area. As was the case with Gaza, a number of IDF experts privately felt that securing small, exposed settlements would not be worth the effort because it would be too costly and dangerous. They felt that it would be a needless source of provocation, and would present growing problems if the Palestinian Authority acquires significant numbers of long-range rocket launchers and anti-tank guided weapons. Many privately believed that Israel should fully withdraw from such settlements and a number of Israeli experts believed that the Israeli presence in Hebron is a particularly serious problem.

Nevertheless, Israeli politics forced the IDF to plan to secure the entire West Bank, and the IDF had very real military options. The IDF spokesman provided some of the possible details of such Israeli contingency plans to reoccupy large parts of the West Bank in a statement made in June 1997.[514] Many of these details tracked closely with the plans tested in "Operation Field of Thorns," a plan the IDF spokesman had made public in September 1996.

Israeli Tactics in a West Bank Conflict

Israel tested some of these plans in clashes with the Palestinians during that period, and began to apply many of the measures in them in September 2000. The measures that fall short of a major "separation program," but that could also be combined with it, include:

- Mobilization and deployment of armored and other land forces in the face of a massive Palestinian rising.
- Massive reinforcement of IDF troops at points of friction.
- Use of armor and artillery to isolate major Palestinian population areas, and to seal off Palestinian areas, including many areas of Zone A.
- Use of other forces to secure settlements, key roads, and terrain points.
- Use of helicopter gunships and snipers to provide mobility and suppressive fire.
- Use of extensive small arms, artillery, and tank fire to suppress sniping, rock throwing and demonstrations.
- Bombing, artillery strikes, and helicopter strikes on high value Palestinian targets and to punish Palestinian elements for attacks.
- Search and seizure interventions and raids into Palestinian areas in the Gaza and West Bank to break up organized resistance and capture or kill key leaders.
- Use of military forces trained in urban warfare to penetrate into cities if necessary—most probably in cases where there were Jewish enclaves like Hebron.
- Arrest PA officials and imposition of a new military administration.
- Introduction of a simultaneous economic blockade with selective cutoffs of financial transactions, labor movements, and food/fuel shipments.
- Selective destruction of high value Palestinian facilities and the clearing of strong points and fields of fire near Palestinian urban areas.
- Use of Israeli control of water, power, communications, and road access to limit the size and endurance of Palestinian action.
- Regulation and control of media access and conduct a major information campaign to influence local and world opinion.
- Carrying out "temporary" withdrawal of Israeli settlers from exposed and low value isolated settlements like Hebron.
- Forced evacuations of Palestinians from "sensitive areas."

Israeli exercises and studies after the Oslo accords did conclude that Israel might suffer hundreds of casualties in using such tactics to deal with any major Palestinian and Israeli Arab uprising, but that the Palestinians would suffer thousands. They also concluded that new security measures needed to be taken to protect lines of communication and Israeli settlements. The IDF requested $90 million in additional funds for the 1997 budget to improve defenses around West Bank settlements. The Israeli treasury granted only $19 million but roughly $53 million had been granted earlier in 1994–1995 and many of these measures were implemented.

Yet, these costs should not be exaggerated. Israel began to develop many of the capabilities it concluded it needed long before the Oslo Accords. After the Six Day War in 1967, Israel also built an extensive road network connecting the coastal plains to the strategic Jordan Valley, including many high-speed roads that bypass Palestinian towns and cities. However, roads are still vulnerable to attack. Many of these network roads link the Palestinian townships of Jenin, Nablus, Ramallah, Bethlehem and Hebron, which now contain most of the Palestinian Arab population. Hebron became a particularly difficult problem since roughly 500 hard-line Israelis insisted they had a religious right to live in a city of some 120,000 Palestinians. However, the IDF still controls the interconnecting territories and could cut the vital lifelines to these cities in the event of conflict.[515]

As has been touched upon earlier, Israel has almost finished establishing an extensive net of new security roads that bypass Arab cities, to help secure the settlements, and allow the IDF to redeploy into the West Bank and reinforce its positions at the Jordan River. At least 12 new bypass roads are being constructed under the Wye Accords, at a cost of $70 million.[516] This road net raises questions about how many settlements will actually be withdrawn from the West Bank area. Hebron is the exception, not the rule. Hebron is a city where 415–450 Israelis—including a number of radical Jewish militants—live in an overwhelmingly Palestinian city of 120,000, with a large number of Islamic fundamentalists.[517]

As a result, the IDF can probably now establish a dominating military presence in all the Palestinian areas in the West Bank within 48–96 hours if it is willing to pay the cost in casualties and hostile media coverage and public opinion. However, it would have to be willing to take more serious casualties if it also had to establish strong points inside hostile Palestinian towns and cities and if the IDF had to confront the Palestinian Authority security forces in urban firefights. Furthermore, the IDF would then have to face the consequences of even more hostile world and public opinion.

The Palestinian Response

Israel's main problem, however, is not dealing with short-term threats. Once the Israelis "win" an initial "victory" in containing the West Bank, the real danger for the IDF lies in becoming involved in a prolonged, ongoing low-level war. This type of more prolonged war allows the Palestinians to organize and to use ambushes, terrorism, and urban clashes to exploit the vulnerabilities of the IDF, whose technical advantages would be much less of a tactical advantage in an urbanized guerilla war.

The Palestinians cannot really plan for armed struggle or warfare in the West Bank in the conventional sense of military planning. They must improvise and evolve, and the essence of asymmetric warfare is to find Israeli political, military, and economic vulnerabilities in the face of superior military force and exploit them as effectively as possible.

The quality and nature of political leadership and control over the fighting on the Palestinian side will be a major variable in determining how well the Palestinians can do this. Much will depend on whether the Palestinians remain under the control of a popular secular leader like Arafat or devolve into disparate elements that may be more innovative and harder to control. The Palestinian militias in the West Bank and Gaza have exhibited a considerable degree of independence early in the fighting since September 2000. Much of the actual struggle was managed by two emergency committees—one in each area—that did include senior members of Fatah, but also included some radical elements and younger and more aggressive Palestinian leaders like Marwan Barghouti, who commands the Tanzeem forces on the West Bank.[518]

Israel would have least difficulty in fighting a low-level terrorist or guerrilla war against a mass Palestinian uprising backed only by relatively small extremist groups like Hamas and/or Islamic Jihad. The situation becomes much worse for Israel if the Palestinian Authority security forces become violently hostile to Israel, divide so that some elements are hostile, or tolerate large-scale armed violence by other Palestinians. The same will be true if the Palestinian people violently reject the peace accords on a lasting basis. The resulting level of conflict will then be a function of (a) the level of arms and military supplies available to Palestinian forces, (b) the unity within the Palestinian side, (c) which key elements of the PLO and security forces of the Palestinian Authority joined the conflict, (d) the amount of territory already ceded to Palestinian control in the peace process, and (e) the level of violence Israel was willing to use in suppressing Palestinian attacks.

A Second Intifada on the West Bank or future outbreaks of Palestinian "armed struggle" could thus range in intensity from a repeat of the Intifada to a serious low-intensity war in which Israel would be forced to make extensive use of the IDF and employ methods such as reoccupation, expulsion, and/or creating security zones that isolated Israelis from the Arabs. Further, if the IDF was not content to isolate Palestinian cities and towns, such fighting could lead to bloody urban warfare. Much would then depend on just how much light weaponry the Palestinians were able to obtain before the fighting began, and the amount of anti-tank weapons, light artillery, and light anti-aircraft weapons they had available. Even a relatively limited number of such weapons could allow a Palestinian force to make the IDF fight some initial battles on a "house-by-house" basis.

Palestinian tactics centered on the use of rock throwing by teenage boys encouraged to risk their lives by their peers, the Palestinian media, and a deep desire to assist in the liberation of Palestine. These groups seem to primarily target military outposts and settlers as they travel. This creates tense situations in which the probability for errors in judgment and misassessment of threats is very high for both sides. These rock throwers are accompanied, some of the time, by armed Fatah activists who, whether they engage the IDF forces or not, increase the underlying tension and risk in already volatile and potentially tragic situations as they make the IDF more likely to use lethal ammunition. This creates an environment to sway international public opinion through the martyrdom of Palestinian young men that serves the interests of Palestinian Authority.

In addition to the traditional rock throwing clashes, the recent violence has shown the beginnings of low intensity conflict. Palestinian forces have made a strong effort to deny the use of roads to the settler community and have had some successes. The Gaza settlement of Natzarim was denied vehicular access for two weeks in October of 2000. Furthermore, the use of roadside bombs and ambushes has increased fears among the settlers that the army cannot fully ensure their safety when they travel. For example, on November 13, 2000, in two separate incidents, unarmed Israeli female civilians were shot while driving. On November 20, 2000, a roadside bomb killed two adults and wounded seven children, dismembering some, on their way to school. On December 10, 2000, Palestinian gunmen ambushed an important rabbi; he, however, escaped unharmed. These incidents demonstrate that the IDF cannot control all of the access routes, all of the time and serve to highlight the potential vulnerability of the Israeli settlers, especially those in more isolated settlements.

Another tactic being used by the Palestinians is the use of low-level attacks on settlements themselves, primarily at night; according to IDF officials, as of December 5, 2000, there have been 600 such incidents. These so far have yet to prove to be a significant threat to the actual overrunning of the Israeli settlements and are not as effective in terms of casualties inflicted on the settlers or the IDF as attacks on the access routes, although Palestinian attacks have become better coordinated. The IDF specifically expressed this concern over a "very well coordinated and orchestrated attack" on December 4, 2000 against Rachel Tomb that was the "most dangerous" event so far in the conflict.[519] The attack involved a coordinated attack from three directions on the settlement from 1 A.M. to 4 A.M., and was on such a scale that the Israeli forces called in air support. Palestinians dispute the claim that any such attack was made, and instead claim that the gunfire was from an Israeli offensive against Palestinians in Bethlehem.[520]

A key "wild card" shaping the outcome of Palestinian action in such conflict will be the level of the problems the IDF actually encounters in securing greater Jerusalem and the other heavily populated areas where Israelis and Palestinians either intermingle or live in such close proximity that it would be difficult to separate them or isolate the Palestinians. Israel's use of helicopters, precision-guided missiles and bombs, and precisely directed radars—coupled with its use of UAVs—gives it the ability to acquire and strike targets in any purely Palestinian area with negligible Israeli casualties and to do so both day and night.

Greater Jerusalem, however, has an intermingled population and any use of major weapons has special religious and political sensitivities. Securing the area of

East Jerusalem could force Israel to (a) rely on a combination of police and paramilitary operations on a community-by-community—and sometimes house-by-house—basis, (b) rely on curfews and strict limitations on local movement, (c) return to demolitions and limited expulsions, (d) suppress all signs of violence or protest with force, often deadly force, (e) hunt down and seize or kill suspected enemies, and/or (f) expel large blocs of Palestinians from such areas. Such tactics would benefit the Palestinian side in terms of world political reactions, although not necessarily in terms of any practical advantages on the ground. Furthermore, any prolonged low-intensity conflict involving Jerusalem will raise serious questions about the future of the Palestinians living in the old city and suburbs. If a conservative, hard-line party controls the Israeli government, there is also a danger that the Israeli government will simply continue to escalate, and that a Second Intifada will take place under conditions where both sides turn firmly from a peace process to a war process without moving towards any resolution beyond sporadic cease-fires.

Similar problems could include fighting outside the greater Jerusalem area. Bethlehem, Ramallah, Hebron, Nablus, Jericho, and Jenin are already examples of how the Palestinians can create a multifront approach to an uprising on the West Bank, and they are all possible Palestinian centers for urban warfare. The Tul Karm and Kaikilia areas could present serious problems in terms of possible firebases for rocket attacks on Israel. Depending on the final settlement, even Tel Aviv could come within range of artillery rockets. (It is only about 22 kilometers from the 1967 boundary at its narrowest part.) Fighting an urban war of attrition in such areas tends to favor the Palestinians, for the same reasons discussed earlier in analyzing a similar war in the Gaza Strip.

Systematic armed Palestinian infiltration of Israel proper from the West Bank might also present a problem, particularly if it took place covertly and with support from Israeli Arabs, and in cooperation with some other Arab state like Syria. As is the case with Gaza, it seems unlikely that this infiltration could do more than disrupt limited aspects of the IDF's activities or conduct occasional attacks on civilians, but more serious fighting in Israel proper is possible. Any coordinated series of Palestinian attacks could also make it more difficult for the IDF to concentrate its forces, and one logical Palestinian tactic might be to try to pin down as much of the IDF as possible by launching sporadic, low level attacks on a wide range of Israeli settlements.

The exact extent of the flow of unauthorized arms to the West Bank will be a factor. It is unclear how large and sophisticated this flow has already been, but arms have been smuggled into the West Bank across Jordan from Iraq, and there are certainly far more arms in both the West Bank and Gaza than are publicly re-ported. The Tanzeem seems to have thousands of unauthorized small arms in reserve.

A Palestinian human rights group (LAW) charged that a flood of unlicensed weapons had led to the death of 12 people in the areas of the West Bank under

Palestinian control in 1999. The same group also charged that the use of unlicensed weapons by Palestinian security forces without the authority to use them or be trained to use them was "alarmingly frequent." It complained that rivalries between the nine Palestinian security agencies led to shootings in densely populated areas, militia-style violence, armed family feuds, and using guns to settle scores. One such incident included Osama al-Keilani, the Attorney General in Jenin who the group was protesting. This was intra-Palestinian violence, but its protest reflected the fact that arms had become far more common and they might be used against Israel.[521]

The Costs of Fighting and Possible Aftermaths

The economic costs of such fighting are already serious for both sides. Israel faces major economic problems. At the same time, as is discussed in more detail later, the Palestinians have suffered more quickly and more deeply in economic terms, in terms of dependence on Israeli control utilities, and in terms of possible relocation. Other aspects of the regional peace process and military balance are also involved. Any major conflict on the West Bank poses a political threat to Israel's peace with Jordan. Furthermore, any enduring low-level conflict in the greater Jerusalem area could pose a political threat to Israel's relations with the entire Arab world, and encourage action by the Hizbollah. The basic asymmetry in the war fighting methods of both sides also means that any unnecessary harshness or incidents involving innocent Palestinians will have an explosive effect in the world's media.

Given all these interactive variables, conflict termination could become an oxymoron on both the West Bank and Gaza if the situation escalates sharply. Even a relatively short period of serious conflict could lead to a broad breakdown of the peace process by making each side's values and negotiating position far more asymmetric than when the fighting began. A forced or compromise peace could easily be no peace at all and simply create a pause before new fighting. Even the best halt to the fighting would raise questions about how many peaces can be made and shattered before the best peace can be little more than an enduring cold war.

Peace is likely to become almost impossible if the fighting on the West Bank triggers the forced separation of Palestinians and Israelis discussed earlier. This would mean much larger deportations of Palestinians, the relocation of some Israeli settlements, the creation and strengthening of IDF strong points to enforce separation, and the creation of electronic "fences," physical fences, mined areas, and deployment of sensor systems and UAV day and night surveillance of "border" areas in both the countryside and built-up areas. It would mean forced clearing of boundary areas to create free fire zones and improve line of sight and create a buffer between Palestine and Israel. It could also involve changes in economic laws and regulation to block the use of Palestinian labor and make Palestinian economic growth and development difficult or impossible.

In short, neither side seems to have any military alternative that would allow it to truly "win" a Second Intifada. It is far from clear that the short-term military advantages to the IDF of improving the separation of Israelis and Palestinians in a crisis could offset the political cost in terms of lasting Palestine hatred and resentment. One way or another, any probable outcome of future fighting will leave Israel and Palestine extremely close neighbors and often intermingled, and any mass deportations might trigger a broader regional war. The Palestinian economy on the West Bank, in Jerusalem, and Gaza cannot be separated from the Israeli economy, and Jordan's economy can only develop and ensure internal stability in Jordan if there is growing integration of the Jordanian, Palestinian, and Israeli economy.

CYBER-CONFLICT ON THE WEB

While it is scarcely a critical aspect of the military balance, the use of cyber-attacks against Web sites on both sides of the conflict is a new aspect in the Israeli-Palestinian conflict since the outbreak of violence in September of 2000. This so-called "cyber war" is now really a minor cyber-low-intensity conflict, but it still illustrates the changing nature of war. This struggle began when pro-Israeli hackers crashed the Hizbollah Web site on October 6, 2000, by causing the site to reload itself several times every minute, making the site inoperable. This was followed by the defacing of the site with Israeli flags, Zionist information and a recording of "Hatikva," the Israeli national anthem. Since then pro-Palestinian hackers have attacked and crashed the sites of the Israeli Defense Forces, the Knesset, and the Israeli Foreign Ministry. Other sites have been hit in retaliation such as the Palestinian National Authority and Hamas.[522]

The trend, especially with the Pro-Palestinian hackers, has been to broaden the scope of their attacks and hit targets that are more "civilian" in nature. These include the sites of the National Bank of Israel and the Tel Aviv Stock Exchange. Unity, the largest pro-Palestinian group, has threatened to escalate the conflict further by attacking Israeli e-commerce sites. This conflict has also spread to the US. The primary pro-Israeli lobby group, the American-Israeli Public Affairs Committee, was attacked and 3,500 credit card numbers and many confidential emails were stolen, as well as the site itself being defaced.[523]

This conflict was different than previous cyber-conflicts such as what was seen during the Kosovo bombings. This is because far more Internet users, some of which have limited or no hacking experience, have been participating. In such a situation Israel has 1.1 million Internet hookups, more than all of the 22 Arab states combined. This gives Israel a manpower and technological advantage in the conflict. With this technological advantage, however, comes increased liability in terms of Internet infrastructure and actual Web sites. Ultimately, although it is impossible to determine if this conflict will continue to escalate, recent attacks have only had the effect of denying possible outlets of information to the Internet community. Thus far, neither side has attacked critical infrastructure; if such a development did take place it would represent a new development in asymmetric warfare.

IF PEACE SHOULD FAIL FOR YEARS: "VIOLENCE WITHOUT PEACE"

It is painfully clear that the balance of political power could also shift firmly in favor of a prolonged war. Such violence could stretch out over years. Such a Second Intifada and prolonged Israeli-Palestinian conflict could create a hostile or divided Palestinian Authority. It would create one that tolerated the creation of significant extremist forces and cadres, encouraged constant low-level violence, and which resorted to large-scale violence when it thought this would influence world opinion.

A Possible Drift Towards Military and Political Extremism

If this happens, any action by Israel that gave control of the Arab cities or loosened control over the border could also give Palestinian extremists—like the military wing of Hamas and Islamic Jihad—the equivalent of sanctuaries and better access to weapons and explosives. It could increase the risk that Palestinian extremist groups outside the West Bank and Gaza—like those listed in Table 7.1— would supply and train new cadres of Palestinians.

At the same time, Israel is also likely to move towards extremism. Any such prolonged low-intensity war could trigger some serious form of the Israeli separation plan. At the same time, it would force Israel to expand its presence in the West Bank and to enforce a wide range of security measures in order to defend all of the settlements. The IDF would be forced to find a difficult balance between a long-term effort to defeat the violent elements of the Palestinian population and trying to pacify the rest. Striking selectively against an increasingly better organized and sheltered force in urban and built-up areas is likely to be especially difficult because the IDF has lost much of its intelligence capability to cover Palestinian activities in the areas under control of the Palestinian Authority.[524]

Israeli settlers have already demonstrated the depth of these risks. On October 7, 2000, Israeli settlers ransacked 8 villages in the Qalquilya area of the West Bank, killing two Palestinians and kidnapping two others. On December 6, 2000, an Israeli settler and schoolteacher were killed in a drive-by shooting by Palestinian gunmen, this to demands from the settlers that Palestinian cars should not be allowed to drive on the highways. Furthermore, protests were sparked when the son and daughter-in-law of deceased Israeli extremist leader Meir Kahane were killed in a Palestinian ambush on December 31, 2000. Not only did his supporters call for more Arab blood to be spilled, but denounced Barak as a traitor. This rhetoric is similar in tone from what was seen just before the assassination of Prime Minister Rabin. Baruch Goldstein, the Jewish extremist who killed 26 Muslims in a Hebron mosque was also part of this movement.[525]

Israeli officers and officials indicate that Israel lost much of its former intelligence-gathering network when it gave up the Palestinian-occupied areas on the West Bank, and that UAVs, communications intelligence, and other technical aids are not a full substitute for HUMINT. Lt. General Amnon Shahak, former Chief of Staff of the IDF, stated that the Oslo II accords would make an effective counterterrorist strategy, ". . . far harder than it is now, particularly in the field of intelligence." Brigadier General Ya'akov Amidror, then head of the analysis section of Israeli military intelligence, has said that, "Israel's intelligence capability in the Gaza Strip has dropped to zero, and a similar situation could develop in Judea and Samaria, when we transfer control to the Palestinian Authority."[526]

The longer the fighting goes on, the more areas are likely to become extremist sanctuaries. Long before September 2000, there were also examples of Palestinian extremists using the Palestinian Authority–controlled areas as a lasting sanctuary. When two Israelis—Ohad Bachrach and Ori Shavord—were killed in the Wadi Kelt on July 18, 1995, the suspects—Yussef and Shaher Ra'ii—took refuge in Jericho. The Palestinian Authority claimed the two were imprisoned after a rapid trial, and were not subject to a "transfer of suspects." At least one of the suspects may, however, have then been released from prison.[527]

At the same time, Israel no longer has to maintain control from within the Arab towns and cities that presented the greatest problems during the Intifada. Under many long-term conflict scenarios, the IDF could largely avoid involvement in such areas, and concentrate on less politically and militarily dangerous operations, like securing routes of communication, perimeter operations, and protecting the settlements. It could steadily improve its ability to isolate Palestinian towns and cities, and cripple the Palestinian economy, until violence halted. This might well reduce the morale problems that arose in dealing with the kind of civil disorder that took place during the Intifada, as well as the problems of media exposure and public opinion.

The Palestinian political and media advantage will be at least partially countered by the fact that Israel will retain overwhelming military strength, and be able to continue to control much of the actual land on the West Bank.[528] It will retain military control over the Jordan River and a strong presence in the Jordan River area, in heavily Jewish areas near the Jordan River, near the Jerusalem Metropolitan District, and in areas near Israel's 1967 boundaries.

Possible Israeli Tactics in a Prolonged Conflict

There is no consensus among Israelis as to the exact tactics that Israel should employ in any prolonged Second Intifada or "no peace" scenario. However, various Israeli experts have suggested the following possible approaches in dealing with such problems:

- *Isolating the Gaza Strip*—Israel would seal the borders with Gaza, and use the crisis as a rationale to remove any remaining Israeli settlements in the Gaza Strip. These settlements currently cost more to protect in military and economic terms than they contribute to the Israeli economy.

- *Walling or sealing off the Palestinian areas*—Israel would seal off Palestinian areas to ensure they could not cross into Jewish areas and Israel proper, effectively creating a series of walls or security fences to prevent or restrict Israeli-Palestinian contact. The concept of an elevated secure superhighway between Gaza and the West Bank is a variation on this theme.

- *Ending remaining dependence on Palestinian labor*—Israel would use labor permits largely as a political weapon, having imported Asian and East European labor as a substitute for Palestinian labor.

- *Removing or marginalizing small Israeli settlements in the middle of Palestinian populations that do not serve security purposes*—Like the Israeli settlements in Gaza, IDF experts feel many of these settlements are an expensive ideological liability.

- *Securing lines of communication*—Israel would fully secure its strategic lines of communication and major routes into the area, and use travel permits as a lever to push the Palestinian Authority to crack down on violence and extremism.

- *Using economic infrastructure as a lever*—Similarly, Israel would use international phone links, power generation, international postal services, external water flow, and similar levers to pressure the Palestinians into ending attacks on Israel.

- *Secure the perimeter of Palestinian cities and towns*—The IDF would stay out of populated areas wherever possible, but would seal off the perimeter of towns where violence took place and punish towns felt to be centers of violence or extremism.

- *Mobilize "border" defenses of Israel proper, the greater Jerusalem area, and Israeli settlements on the West Bank*—Israel would create strong security defenses that tightly controlled entry and movement into Israeli areas. It would seal off Palestinian areas felt to be centers of violence and effectively halt all economic activity until such violence ceased. Such efforts would be highly selective and would seek to rely largely on non-violent means.

- *Use trained security forces*—The IDF and security forces would avoid mass call-ups or the use of troops without special training. It would emphasize the identification and tracking of actual threats, and the use of the GSS and Border Police, and officers and forces with counter-insurgency training. It would utilize the improved equipment it obtained during the Intifada.

- *Use non-intrusive surveillance methods*—Israel would use its UAVs and SIGINT capabilities to provide surveillance of Palestinian activity without sending IDF forces into Palestinian areas except to deal with known targets or in hot pursuit. Although Israel's network of informers and covert operatives in Palestinian areas has been sharply reduced, use would still be made of such techniques where possible.

- *Emphasize a willingness to continue the peace process and good relations with Arab states*—Israel would seek to politically and diplomatically isolate the violent and extremist elements within the Palestinians.

- *Reward Palestinians who support the peace process and/or are non-violent*—Restrictions would be minimized in any area or case where the Palestinian Authority or some town or company did not present security problems. Labor permits and investment would be encouraged in such areas.

Israel could also apply steadily more powerful economic weapons. It will retain long-term control over movement, utilities, transport, and water. It will be able to set the terms by which Palestinians can work in Israel, if at all. Israel has already demonstrated that it will try to use low-cost Asian and East European labor as a substitute for Palestinian labor. Israel issued labor permits to over 55,000 non-Palestinian foreign workers in 1994, and nearly 70,000 in 1995, versus less than 5,000 a year during 1992 and 1993.[529] In 1998, the Israeli government issued 80,000 permits to non-Jewish foreign workers, a cutback of 23% in the past two years. Only 38,000 Palestinian workers are legally allowed to work in Israel.[530]

The economic outcome of the fighting that began in September 2000 has also shown that any Palestinian political advantage in terms of media and the world is offset by economic costs as well as the cost in blood. UN estimates indicate that only two months of violence following the outbreak of fighting on September 29 cut the Palestinian gross domestic product by 10 percent, and project rate of growth in the GDP for 2000 from +4% to 10%. They also indicate that the violence, and the measures Israel imposed as security measures and diplomatic pressure, cost the Palestinians more than $500 million in lost wages and sales.[531] This is equal to roughly $9 million a day, and the estimates do not include the impact of the bulldozing of hundreds of acres of Palestinian orchards by the Israeli army to clear the line of sight in security areas, or the destruction of Palestinian buildings, homes, infrastructure and property. Furthermore, the average Palestinian worker supports four other persons and the loss of income forces all of these individuals to cut back consumption dramatically, thus affecting the income of other segments of the economy.[532]

The same report indicates that Israel is also paying an economic cost and has dropped a full percentage point in its growth estimates for the year, which is a billion-dollar correction. It shows a major cut in tourism, problems for farmers and contractors who depend on Palestinian workers, and cutbacks in the technology sector. However, the same estimates indicate that the $100 billion Israeli economy would still grow by more than four percent, and raise Israel's average per capita income above $18,000. And, these figures did not reflect the fact that the Clinton administration sought to add an additional $450 million to Israel's annual $2.9 billion aid package.[533]

As has been discussed earlier, the Palestinian economy is only about 5 percent the size of Israel's, and estimates indicate that normal economic activity was cut by as much as 50%. The UN report estimated a $388 million drop in local economic output, plus another $117 million in the lost wages of some 110,000 workers who had jobs in Israel. Direct unemployment in Gaza and the West Bank rose from 70,000 (11%) to 260,000 (30%). These costs are two and a half times greater than the total foreign aid received by Palestinians from all sources. This totaled $183 million during the first six months of 2000.[534]

New aid will help. Reporting in the *New York Times* indicates that the World Bank will provide a $15 million grant, the European Union will provide emergency aid to help pay Palestinian Authority employees, and Gulf businessmen have donated more than $20 million for a special Palestinian unemployment fund. Arab governments have pledged $693 million in new economic aid to the Palestinians since the fighting began, with most of it coming from Saudi Arabia ($250 million), Kuwait ($150 million), and the United Arab Emirates ($150 million). The United States continues to provide more than $75 million annually to the Palestinians under a long-term aid commitment, though most of the programs it underwrites have been paralyzed for the last two months.[535]

Nevertheless, the UN estimated that Palestinian poverty would increase sharply and that nearly half of the population would live on $2.10 a day or less.[536] Reports estimate that unemployment nearly quadrupled in only two months, soaring from about 70,000 jobless workers before the outbreak of violence to about 260,000. This means that two in five Palestinian workers are unemployed, including 100,000 barred from their day jobs in Israel. The estimates indicate that the poverty rate among Palestinians has jumped by 50% between late September and December. Nearly 33% of the three million Palestinians in Gaza and the West Bank lived below the poverty line in early December, up from around 20% before the violence erupted. Before the outbreak of violence the poverty rate declined from 25% in 1997.

A prolonged struggle would be far more costly and impact on a Palestinian economy with few reserves. If current conditions persist, according to the previously discussed UN report, the poverty rate will climb by an additional 33% to 43.8% by the end of 2001. Aid is often promised that is not delivered or spends years in a pipeline. For example, the World Food Program asked wealthy donor countries in November 2000 to provide $3.9 million in additional funding for food for impoverished Palestinians and the request was not met. Israel can take far more serious steps in the form of economic warfare. It can cut off the flow of aid deliveries, and take steps like imposing a near total economic embargo, limiting water and electricity, freezing finances, and limiting access to communications.

There is no way to predict which mix of military, political, and economic tactics Israel would use in a prolonged conflict, or the long-term effectiveness of any given mix of such tactics, any more than it is possible to predict how the Palestinian response will evolve under pressure. It is important to remember, however, that past low-level conflicts have shown that hatred can be remarkably creative. In fact, the worst outcome of a prolonged Second Intifada would probably be that it institutionalized the levels of hatred exhibited in Bosnia.

Prolonged Conflict, "Separation," and Evacuation

The worst-case outcome for both sides would be for Israel to combine such tactics with more extreme versions of a "separation" program. Some Israeli analysts believe that Israel could go beyond separation and permanently re-secure the West Bank through a combination of further separation between Israelis and Palestinians, limited reoccupation of key areas, improved security measures, selective deportations and economic and political pressures on the Palestinians. They believe that this would entail some Israeli casualties, and some continuing low-level problems with terrorism, but this might well be enough to restore something approaching a cold peace at a political, military, and economic cost that is actually lower than that of the Intifada.

Some Israeli analysts also have privately proposed deportations and/or the idea of building a series of walls or a continuing security "wall" within the Old City and the greater Jerusalem area to separate Jew and Palestinian—a concept that might aid security in the physical sense but which would do much to prevent the development of stable social and economic relations and which might undermine security in other ways. A few hardliners have raised the issue of forced large-scale deportations of Palestinians from the greater Jerusalem, East Jerusalem, Bethlehem, and Nablus areas, but it is unclear that the IDF has ever translated conceptual studies of such options into even preliminary contingency plans.[537]

At the same time, some IDF analysts have privately said that Israel might also have to evacuate some of its more exposed settlements. On October 7, 2000, the IDF "temporally evacuated" Joseph's Tomb in Nablus after five days of fighting, after brokering a deal with PA security forces to protect the site. The PA forces were either unwilling or unable to defend the site and were overrun by Palestinian protesters who set it on fire. The images of Palestinians burning prayer books appeared on Israeli televisions prompting increased public pressure not to evacuate more settlements under similar conditions.[538] Securing and defending roads could be a problem, particularly if the Palestinians develop sophisticated hit-and-run tactics. Maintaining the force to secure the small Israeli enclaves near the Jordan would take men and resources. These are areas where the only alternatives are for the IDF to maintain a major continuous presence and draconian security checks or forcibly relocate large numbers of Palestinians.

The end result of warfare might be a situation where the Palestinian response would explode to a point so serious that the only solution available to the IDF would be a state of massive armed occupation in which the IDF had to occupy most Palestinian cities, react with extreme force, and deal with constant low-level violence. Such a "reoccupation" would be far more costly than containment, and could lead to the equivalent of "ethnic cleansing" and Israeli security measures that would drive large numbers of Palestinians out of Israeli security zones or the Gaza and West Bank. Much would depend on the character of the Israeli government involved. A total break down of the peace process, combined with a hard-line Israeli government would also certainly involve the execution of most of the "separation" option and could conceivably result in a more humane but very real form of "ethnic cleansing."

One thing is certain. Each new level of prolonged conflict will make it progressively harder for both sides to reach either a "cold" or "warm" peace. Each level of conflict will also be a test of the political costs Israel is willing to pay for giving up parts of the West Bank, and how long it is willing to fight a prolonged low-level or antiterrorist conflict that is much more violent than the Intifada.

The Role of Egypt, Syria, Jordan, Iran, and Hizbollah in a Longer Conflict in Gaza or the West Bank

There is another dimension to a prolonged conflict. Arab states are fully aware of Israel's conventional military superiority and that it possesses nuclear weapons. Even so, both the short and long versions of a Second Intifada create the risk that Israeli action against large numbers of Palestinians in either Gaza or the West Bank would threaten Israel's peace with Egypt and Jordan, and create a lasting block on further progress in the peace negotiations with Syria.

Egypt withdrew its ambassador, Muhammad Bassiouny, "indefinitely" in protest over Israeli actions. This damaged a key communication line between the Israeli government and the Palestinian Authority and disrupted the US ability to place pressure on Arafat through his ties with Egypt. However, President Mubarak remained active in attempting to broker a peace between the two sides.[539]

Furthermore, Jordan, the only other Arab state with full diplomatic relations with Israel, delayed appointing a new ambassador to Israel since September, despite the obvious prominence of the post to Jordanian foreign policy. Further-more, late on November 21, 2000, an Israeli missile attack damaged the official residence of the Jordanian representative to the Palestinian Authority.[540] Internal pressure against the peace process is built up in the Hashimite Kingdom as well.

Repeated protests took place in Amman that threatened the US and Israeli embassies and forced the Jordanian army to deploy troops for their protection.[541]

Things could escalate further. A bloody conflict over and within Gaza would present problems for Egypt, and might eventually be serious enough to affect the Camp David Accords. A major struggle between Israel and Palestinians on the West Bank might end the peace between Jordan and Israel as well as impact on Jordan's internal stability. Either war would probably trigger new action by Iran and Shi'ite extremists in Lebanon like the Hizbollah or Sunni extremists such as Islamic Jihad. It also could make Israel's Arabs shift to a much more active political and military role in opposing Israel.

As a result, what might start as a low-level war between Israeli and Palestinian extremists could produce longer-term and more serious shifts in the regional military balance. An escalation to involve Arab states would, in fact, almost certainly become the goal of Palestinian extremists if they were given the opportunity.

This does not mean that outside Arab support would succeed in helping the Palestinians win a conflict or sustain a long-term low-level war against Israel, or be able to give them enough additional military strength to force a better peace settlement. Israel can defeat its neighbors, and there are severe limits to how many arms or other forms of military support outside states could give to the Palestinian forces as long as Israel controlled the security of its borders and could seal off Gaza and access to the West Bank.

Palestinian forces might, however, gain significant additional political leverage if they could broaden their struggle to include Israel's Arab neighbors, dominate the Palestinian community and defeat the Palestinian supporters of the peace process, and/or obtain major supplies of arms, money, and training from extremist nations and movements outside the West Bank and Gaza.

IF PEACE DOES EVER COME: THE COST OF LIVING WITH "PEACE WITH VIOLENCE"

A Second Intifada is not the only risk that the Palestinian Authority and Israel must deal with. Even if a peace can be reached in the future, both sides will be forced to conduct aggressive security operations for years to come. These operations not only will be the price for peace; they are essential to prevent any new crises and confrontations from escalating to large-scale violence or war. At the same time, such operations can have a high price tag in terms of human rights and will present risks of their own. There have been potentially explosive incidents and clashes between the IDF and the Palestinian Authority in every year since 1993, and a significant armed clash in 1996 preceded the far more serious violence that began in September 2000.

Palestinian Authority Security Operations and "Mission Impossible"

In the past, Israel has demanded that the Palestinian security forces must maintain almost perfect order among a population with significant elements that strongly oppose the peace process and deny the legitimacy of the Palestinian Authority and the PLO. This will be "mission impossible" in the near to mid-term. Establishing an effective security structure takes time and experience, and the Palestinian Authority initially lacked both. In contrast, the Palestinian security forces had to deal with elements like Hamas and the Palestinian Islamic Jihad, which have a lot of experience in the use of violence, and cells of well-trained paramilitary extremists. This meant their opposition was often better trained and difficult to locate.

Any peace settlement will mean Palestinian security forces will now be confronted with the same series of contradictory goals they faced before the fighting began in September 2000. They will have to demonstrate to Israel that they will act immediately and decisively to prevent violence and will arrest and punish terrorists to reassure Israel. At the same time, they will have to try to maintain popular support and meet the demands of human rights activists. The contradictions involved are illustrated by the fact that Colonel Jibril Rajoub, the commander of the security service who reports to Arafat, was often attacked for laxness by Israelis before the fighting in 2000, but Palestinian extremists have accused him of being "a big agent of the Israeli police."[542]

Both the Palestinian and Israeli security forces have already encountered severe criticism over human rights issues when they acted decisively, and they will receive equally severe political and partisan criticism if they free suspected terrorists or pardon convicted ones. Both the Israeli and Palestinian security services have also sometimes confused excessive and extreme action with decisive and effective action. For example, the Palestinian Preventive Security forces have often been accused of the arbitrary arrest and torture of Palestinians—in many cases Palestinians whose business interests conflicted with those of Palestinian Authority officials, or who publicly criticized Arafat and the Palestinian Authority.

It is easy to minimize the costs and risks involved in choosing between effective counterterrorism and peace enforcement, and civil liberties, to ignore the violent nature of political movements and focus solely on state abuses, or to claim that international norms can be applied in spite of the level of violence and hatred involved and the potential cost to peace and human security.

Important as civil liberties are, they are only one of the human rights that nations and the world must try to protect. Certainly, every effort should be made to preserve human rights and make the best possible trade-offs between peace, physical security, and civil liberties. However, it is dangerous to assume that no dilemma exists and that civil liberties must always have first priority. Peace and security from terrorism are also human rights.

Any valid assessment of human rights cannot consist solely of an indictment of the violations of governments, no matter how important or valid. It must explicitly consider the level of overall violence involved, the role of various non-governmental groups in using violence and terrorism, and the level of risk to civilians, peace, and civil order. It must examine the military, paramilitary, and overall security conditions involved, and specifically assess the options open to governments and how well they deal with the trade-offs between civil liberties and other human rights. They must also address the extent to which both governments and their opponents attempt to use claims about law, democracy, terrorism and human rights as political weapons in a world where such efforts have become a routine aspect of asymmetric warfare.

It is also important to note that there is a significant gap in such efforts in dealing with Israel and the Palestinians. Israel's supporters often view the problem solely in terms of counterterrorism and the right to security. Palestinian supporters often see the issue almost solely in terms of the rule of law and human rights, while the opponents of both Israel and the Palestinian Authority tend to issue blanket condemnations of both while ignoring both the overall security conditions and the violent nature of many of the political movements and groups involved. A similar gap emerges in outside reporting on violence and terrorism and human rights. For example, the annual State Department report on terrorism tends to ignore civil liberties and state abuses of human rights while the annual report on human rights tends to minimize or ignore the problem of civil violence and terrorism. The reporting of the UN Commissioner on Human Rights has striven for more balance, but focuses far more on civil liberties than security.

Reasonable people can disagree sharply in assessing the situation and the kind of trade-offs each side will have to make between civil liberties and security. At the same time, any valid assessment must come fully to grips with the issue and not simply consist of a focus on one aspect of the issue. Any cease-fire or "peace" between Israelis and Palestinians is likely to involve years in which a cold peace cannot be distinguished from a cold war, and in which new violence and terrorism is a constant threat.

Both sides may find that there are no solutions that are both pleasant and workable. No security force in history has been able to do a perfect job facing similar threats. The British forces in Ulster are perhaps the most successful example of a security force working with similar problems. By and large, the British security services did an excellent job of balancing the conflicting problems of effective security and a concern for human rights. At the same time, there were still many incidents of violence and terrorism, and many cases where the British used excessive force, abused human rights, and used extreme interrogation methods and torture in ways that simply exacerbated the situation. It is scarcely surprising, therefore, that the Palestinian Authority often failed.

Israeli Criticisms and the Art of the Possible

This means Israel may have to revise its standards for security and for judging the Palestinian Authority. Israeli diplomats, military officials, and intelligence analysts have repeatedly criticized the Palestinians in the past for their lack of effort, neglect in pursuing terrorists and extremists, and release of such persons after detention or serving a limited portion of their sentence. A senior serving Israeli security official once stated, "Arafat has long had a policy of containing Hamas and the PIJ and making them part of his camp. . .Whenever he knows of any specific case of an attack that is planned by Hamas or the PIJ, he is going to do his best in order to foil it. But he knows, and we know also, that you cannot know about every single attack."

Typical Israeli charges against the Palestinian Authority security forces include:[543]

- The actual size of the security forces totals 45,000 and is 27,000 more than permitted in the Oslo Accords.
- Palestinian police cooperated in operations to kill Israeli settlers in the West Bank during 1997. Intercepts and the confession of one of the policemen involved confirm this.
- Brigadier General Ghazi Jabali, the Commander of the Police in Gaza, provided a car and weapons for this operation. State Department spokesman says on August 2, 1997, that the US has no intelligence to confirm this charge.
- The Palestinian Authority has far more weapons than authorized, including anti-tank missiles.
- The Palestinian Authority may have Katyusha rockets and SAM-7 anti-aircraft missiles.
- Arms' smuggling is continuing.
- Arafat has used the diplomatic immunity of his car and helicopter to smuggle in arms.
- Palestinian security forces have systematically attacked the network of informers that Israeli intelligence had developed before the transfer of the territories.
- The Palestinian Authority tacitly tolerates recruiting and training operations by Hamas and the Palestinian Islamic Jihad.
- Arafat has often freed known terrorists, including some 120 in the spring of 1997.

Israeli security officials have differed over the seriousness of these charges in ways that reflect the divisions in Israeli politics. For example, Carmi Gillon, a former chief of Shin Bet, put some of the blame on Netanyahu and his lack of support for the peace process. In contrast, Gidon Ezra, a former Deputy Shin Bet chief and Likud legislator, blames Arafat for putting good relations with Hamas and PIJ before security cooperation. Any post–September 2000 efforts to deal with these problems, however, will have to deal with far more serious doubts on both sides. Any major firefights between the IDF and Palestinian security forces will also create a legacy of lasting hatred and distrust. While both sides may well be equally to blame, if blame can be assigned in asymmetric war, it is also very unlikely that either side will show much empathy for the other.

"Peace With Abuses" versus "Peace With Violence"

Both sides will almost certainly face painful problems in choosing between peace and security and civil liberties. There is no magic or right trade-off between the improved security and counterterrorism needed to create and enforce a peace, and provide both Israelis and Palestinians with physical security and civil liberties. Effective counterterrorism and peace enforcement is extremely difficult in the best of times, and both Israel and the Palestinians will have to approach the enforcement of either a cease-fire or peace in a climate of extremism and hatred, and with an uncertain history in dealing with security issues.

As has been discussed earlier, Israeli pressure and Palestinian politics led the Palestinian Authority security forces to emphasize security over human rights long before the crisis that began in September 2000, although they often did so to maintain the present ruling elite rather than to preserve the peace process. The three main Palestinian security forces had six prisons by 1998. The civil police, under Nasir Yusef and Brigadier General Ghazi Jabali, has two prisons. The chief of the preventive security force in Gaza, Mohammed Dahlan, has two prisons. In addition, the director of military intelligence, Mousa Arafat, has two prisons. Suspects in these prisons have been subject to long detentions without trial, and there are reports of torture and violent interrogations. For example, Mahmoud Zohhar, the chief spokesman of Hamas, was arrested in June 1995 and held at the military intelligence prison at Saraya for 105 days. His head and beard were shaved, and there were reports he was beaten and had several broken bones.[544]

The Palestinian Authority Response

Critics of Palestinian Authority security forces must understand that such problems may remain the rule, not the exception. If the Palestinian security forces do not react quickly and decisively in dealing with terrorism and violence, there probably will be no future peace, or stable peace process. This will be essential if they are to preserve the momentum of future Israeli withdrawals, the expansion of Palestinian control and sovereignty, and the stability of the peace process.

In this context, the Palestinian Authority security forces will probably use excessive force by the standards of Western police forces. Efforts to halt terrorist and paramilitary action by Hamas and Islamic Jihad may involve interrogations, detentions, and trials that are too rapid and lack due process by Western standards. Conversely, the failure to act effectively could have a high net cost to both peace and the human rights of most Palestinians. Israeli leaders have clearly focused on

Table 7.5
Key Incidents of Terrorism Since the Oslo Accords in September 1993

September 12, 1993: A Palestinian Islamic Jihad (PIJ) suicide bomber crashes an explosives-laden car into a bus carrying soldiers at Sheik Ajlun in Gaza. The car failed to explode, and the only casualty was the driver of the car.

October 4, 1993: A Palestinian Islamic Jihad (PIJ) car bomb is detonated in proximity to a bus on the No. 173 line. Thirty people are slightly injured.

October 24, 1993: Two small explosive charges detonate near the French embassy in Tel Aviv. There was no damage or casualties. A member of the Jewish extremist Kahana Hay movement claimed responsibility for the explosions, saying the attack was carried out to protest PLO leader Yasser Arafat's visit to France and agreements he signed there.

January 29, 1994: A Jordanian diplomat was shot and killed outside his home in Beirut. The government of Lebanon arrested and prosecuted Abu Nidal Attacker terrorists for the attack.

April 6, 1994: Car rigged with explosives detonates next to a bus in Afula in Northern Israel. 9 Israelis killed and 45 wounded. Hamas claims responsibility.

April 13, 1994: A Palestinian suicide bomber triggers bomb in bus in Hadera in central Israel. 6 Israelis killed and 45 wounded. Hamas claims responsibility.

April 16, 1994: A Hamas (Islamic Resistance Movement) car bomb is detonated at the roadside kiosk at Mehola, Israel in the Jordan valley. One person is killed and nine injured.

July 18, 1994: A car bomb explodes at the Israeli-Argentine Mutual Association (AMIA), killing 100 persons and wounding more than 200 others. The explosion causes the seven-story building to collapse and damages adjacent buildings.

July 19, 1994: A commuter plane explodes in flight over the Santa Rita Mountains in Panama, among the 21 victims are Israeli nationals, dual Israeli-Panamanian citizens, three US citizens and 12 Jewish persons.

July 23, 1994: Two unknown Palestinians stab and seriously injure an American woman in the Arab quarter of the Old City of Jerusalem. The assailants escape unharmed.

July 26, 1994: A car bomb explodes at the Israeli Embassy in London, injuring 14 persons. The bomb is planted by a woman who was driving an Audi car.

July 27, 1994: A car bomb detonates outside a building that houses Jewish attackers in London. Five persons are injured in the attack.

October 9, 1994: Hamas (Islamic Resistance Movement) terrorists opened fire with automatic weapons in Jerusalem's Nahalat Shiva'a business district. An off-duty soldier and an Israeli Arab were killed in the attack. One of the attackers was shot by bystanders and the other captured. Fourteen are injured

October 19, 1994: Palestinian suicide bomber triggers bomb in bus in Tel Aviv. 22 Israelis killed and 48 wounded. Hamas claims responsibility.

Table 7.5 (continued)

November 11, 1994: Palestinian suicide bomber on a bicycle in the Gaza Strip kills 3 Israeli soldiers. Palestinian Islamic Jihad claims responsibility.

December 25, 1994: Palestinian suicide bomber triggers bomb in bus in Jerusalem. 12 Israelis wounded. Hamas claims responsibility.

January 22, 1995: Two Palestinian suicide bombers trigger bomb in Beit Lid junction in central Israel. 21 Israelis killed. Palestinian Islamic Jihad claims responsibility.

April 9, 1995: Two Palestinian suicide bombers trigger bombs outside two Israeli settlements in Gaza Strip. 7 Israeli soldiers and one American killed. Hamas and Palestinian Islamic Jihad claim responsibility.

June 25, 1995: A Palestinian Islamic Jihad (PIJ) activist detonates an explosives-laden cart near an I.D.F. vehicle, injuring 3 soldiers.

July 24, 1995: Palestinian suicide bomber triggers bomb in bus in Tel Aviv. 6 Israelis killed and 28 wounded. Hamas claims responsibility.

August 21, 1995: Palestinian suicide bomber triggers bomb in bus in Jerusalem. 4 Israeli soldiers and 1 American killed. More than 100 wounded. Hamas claims responsibility.

February 25, 1996: Palestinian suicide bombers trigger bombs in bus in Jerusalem and at a soldier's hitchhiking post near Ahkelon along the coast, killing 23 Israelis, 2 Americans, and 1 Palestinian. Wound more than 80. Hamas claims responsibility.

February 26, 1996: American Arab drives rental car into Jerusalem bus stop. 1 Israeli killed and 23 wounded. Driver is shot and killed. Seems to have acted on own but Hamas claims responsibility.

March 3, 1996: Palestinian suicide bomber triggers bomb in bus in Jerusalem. 18 Israelis killed and 10 wounded. The Students of Yehiye Ayyash, a splinter group of Hamas, claim responsibility for the attack.

March 4, 1996: Palestinian suicide bomber triggers bomb outside shopping center in Tel Aviv. 12 Israelis killed and more than 100 wounded. Both Hamas and the Palestine Islamic Jihad (PIJ) claim responsibility for the bombing.

May 13, 1996: Hamas (Islamic Resistance Movement) gunmen open fire on a bus and a group of Yeshiva students near the Beth El settlement, killing a dual US/Israeli citizen and wounding three Israelis. No one claims responsibility for the attack, but Hamas is suspected.

June 9, 1996: Unidentified gunmen opens fire on a car near Zekharya, killing a dual US/Israeli citizen and an Israeli. The Popular Front for the Liberation of Palestine (PFLP) is suspected.

February 23, 1997: A Palestinian gunman opens fire on tourists at an observation deck atop the Empire State Building in New York City, killing a Danish national and wounding visitors from the United States, Argentina, Switzerland and France before turning the gun on himself. A handwritten note carried by the gunman claimed this was a punishment attack against the "enemies of Palestine."

Table 7.5 (continued)

March 21, 1997: Palestinian suicide bomber killed 3 Israeli women in Tel Aviv.

July 30, 1997: Two Palestinian suicide bombers trigger bombs inside the Mahane Yehuda bazaar, the central produce market in Jerusalem. 13 Israelis killed, and 170 wounded. Hamas appears to claim responsibility.

September 4, 1997: Three Palestinian suicide bombers trigger bombs on the Ben Yehuda pedestrian mall in Jerusalem. Four Israelis are killed and nearly 200 wounded. Hamas claims responsibility.

November 20, 1997: Unknown gunmen shoot and kill a Hungarian Yeshiva student and wound an Israeli student in the Old City of Jerusalem. No one claims responsibility.

January 14, 1998: A booby-trapped videocassette explodes at Israel-Lebanon border near Metulla. Intended target was a senior Israeli intelligence officer. 3 Israelis and 3 Lebanese wounded. Amal claims responsibility.

April 2, 1998: An Israeli vehicle was fired upon near Telem, Israel. There are no casualties.

April 30, 1998: A firebomb is thrown at the parking lot of the Jerusalem hotel in Amman, Jordan. The Jordanian authorities arrest eight members of a foreign-backed Islamic group, accusing them of being behind a wave of recent arson attacks.

May 3, 1998: A pipe bomb explodes in front of the apartment of three Arab students in the Mussrara neighborhood of Jerusalem. A fire in the stairwell is the only damage caused. Israeli police suspect right-wing extremists.

June 1, 1998: Two terrorists ambush and fire six shots at an Israeli vehicle. No casualties are reported.

August 20, 1998: Rabbi Shlomo Raanan is stabbed to death by a Hamas terrorist in his home in Tel Rumeiyda, Israel. The attacker enters the house through a window and escapes after throwing a Molotov cocktail which sets fire to the house.

September 24, 1998: An IDF soldier was injured when a Hamas (Islamic Resistance Movement) bomb explodes in a bus station near the Hebrew University in Jerusalem. The explosion destroys the bus shelter.

September 30, 1998: Fourteen IDF soldiers and 11 Palestinians are wounded when a Hamas (Islamic Resistance Movement) terrorist hurls two grenades at a border police jeep in Hebron. The patrol shoots the attacker in the leg and pursues him into the Palestinian-controlled part of Hebron, but he manages to escape.

October 1, 1998: Thirteen soldiers and five Palestinians are injured in a Hamas (Islamic Resistance Movement) grenade attack in Hebron. A Palestinian from the Palestinian-controlled H-1 area lobs two grenades at the soldiers. One explodes close to where the men were standing, injuring several Palestinian passers-by, soldiers, and border policemen. The second hits two cars parked on a sidewalk and injures nearby Palestinians. Two border policemen and one soldier suffer moderate injuries, while ten others were only slightly hurt. Five Palestinians were taken to Hebron hospitals. The

Table 7.5 (continued)

soldiers give chase to the assailant and one of them opens fire and apparently hits him in the leg. However, he manages to escape back into the H-1 area.

October 19, 1998: Two grenades are hurled into crowd at Central bus station at Be'er Sheva, Israel during rush hour. At least 59 people are wounded. Most of the injured are lightly or moderately wounded, though two were seriously hurt. The attacker is overwhelmed by several bystanders, who turn him over to civil guard policemen. Hamas claims responsibility.

October 27, 1998: Mohmoud Majzoub, a senior member of the Islamic Jihad Attacker in Lebanon, is seriously injured in a car bomb assassination attempt. The car bomb also injures his wife, their nine-month-old son and a Syrian passerby.

October 29, 1998: A Hamas suicide bomber targets a school bus carrying children from the community of Kfar Darom to a regional school near the Gush Katif Junction. The bus is escorted before and aft by army jeeps, and is transporting children. A suicide bomber driving an explosives-laden vehicle attempts to collide head-on with the bus. The driver of the leading jeep moves to block the suspicious car from reaching the bus, and the bomber detonates the explosives near the jeep. At least one person in the jeep is killed, along with the suicide bomber. Two passengers of the jeep are seriously injured. Six people sustain light-to-moderate injuries, including three young people and three children.

October 31, 1998: Khaled Kurdiyeh, a Fatah activist, survives an assassination attempt in Lebanon. The car bomb explodes at a Palestinian refugee camp. No one is injured.

November 6, 1998: Two suicide bombers drive car bomb into Mahane Yehuda market in Jerusalem. 20 people injured. Palestinian Islamic Jihad claims responsibility.

September 5, 1999: Two car-bomb explosions occur within minutes of each other in Tiberias and Haifa at around 5:30 P.M., killing three terrorist bombers and seriously wounding a 73-year-old woman. The car-bomb attacks occurred less than 24 hours after the signing of the Sharm e-Sheik Memorandum.

Source: US Department of State, "Patterns of Global Terrorism," various editions, Washington, GPO; Institute for Counter-Terrorism, "Middle Eastern Terror Attacks," http://www.ict.org.il/. ARAB_ISR/attackresults.cfm; International Policy Institute for Counter Terrorism in Israel (www.ict.org.il).

the very issue of terrorism as a means of evaluating the Palestinian Authority's commitment to the peace process.

Table 7.5 shows that decisive measures also tend to work. It shows the record of such incidents of terrorism since the Oslo Accords and up to the fighting that began in September 2000. This table shows the problems that the Palestinians encountered in dealing with terrorism during the critical period before the election that brought former Prime Minister Netanyahu to office. However, there was a significant drop in terrorism since 1997, and Israeli sources cite security cooperation between the Palestinian and Israeli forces as the major reason for this decline.

Israeli officials say that the Palestinian Security forces were ineffective at first because they were inexperienced, but improved significantly with time. Even former Prime Minister Netanyahu gave Chairman Arafat and the Palestinian Authority credit for foiling a terrorist attack in Tel Aviv, for the decline in Hamas activity, and for the decline in terror in general.[545]

The Israeli Security Response

The Israeli security forces face many of the same dilemmas. Although these forces are under much tighter control and are less prone to arbitrary human rights abuses, they often have had to choose between a strict interpretation of the law and effectiveness. They have done so with the knowledge that effectiveness has been the price of both maintaining Israel's security and political support for a peace process. More broadly, Israeli security forces have operated, and will continue to operate, against extremist and terrorist forces that have learned to cloak their activities under "respectable" political cover, in order to manipulate the rhetoric of human rights and democracy, as well as human rights groups and the media, and to exploit every weakness in the law and legal procedures.

This is why former Prime Minister Rabin once described such Israeli security operations as "war without quarter" shortly before his assassination, why former Prime Minister Netanyahu gave the issue so high a priority, and why Israeli counterterrorist activity was often swift and violent even before the fighting in the fall of 2000.

At the same time, Israel shares the same need as the Palestinian security forces to avoid excessive measures and ones that simply end in creating added opposition and willingness to use terrorism. Israeli officials like Attorney General Michael Ben-Yair have stated publicly that security organizations like the Shin Bet have used violence during interrogations and have sometimes killed those being interrogated.[546] Such measures not only tend to be ineffective in any given case, they breed more violence than they eliminate.

It is also common knowledge that Israeli intelligence has fought its side of asymmetric warfare by killing or assassinating terrorist leaders. A probable list of such assassinations includes:[547]

- *April 1973*: Israeli commandos land on Beirut beach and drive into city to kill PLO officials Kamal Nasser, Mohammed Najjar, and Kamal Adwan.
- *January 1979*: PLO special forces head Abu Hassan, a.k.a. Ali Salameh, who was involved in the 1972 Munich Olympics massacre of 11 Israelis, killed in car bombing in Beirut.
- *July 1979*: Zuhayr Mohsen, PLO operations wing chief, killed in Cannes, France.
- *December 1979*: Samir Tukan, second secretary in PLO office in Nicosia, Cyprus, and Abu Safawat, another top PLO official, are murdered.

- *October 1981*: Majed Abu Sharar, head of the PLO information office, killed by bomb at Rome Hotel.

- *June 1982*: PLO deputy Kamel Hussein killed by bomb in Rome.

- *July 1982*: Fadel el-Daani, deputy of the PLO representative in France, killed by car bomb.

- *August 1983*: Mamoun Muraish, aide to Abu Jihad, No. 2 in Yasser Arafat's Fatah movement, shot to death in car.

- *June 1986*: Khaled Ahmed Nazal, of the Marxist Democratic Front for the Liberation of Palestine, gunned down at Cyprus hotel.

- *October 1986*: Munzer Abu Ghazala, PLO navy commander, killed in Athens.

- *February 1988*: Three senior PLO officers killed by car bomb in Limassol, Cyprus.

- *April 1988*: Khalil al-Wazir, a.k.a. Abu Jihad, killed in his home in Tunis, Tunisia by Israeli commandos.

- *December 1988*: Israel kidnaps Hizbollah leader Jawad Kaspi from south Lebanon.

- *August 1989*: Israeli commandos kidnap Hizbollah spiritual leader Sheik Abdul Karim Obeid from south Lebanon.

- *February 1992*: Israeli helicopters kill Hizbollah chief Abbas Musawi, firing rockets at his car in south Lebanon.

- *May 1994*: Mustafa Dirani, head of the Believers Resistance Group, kidnapped from home in Lebanon.

- *October 1995*: Dr. Fathi Shakaki, head of Islamic Jihad, shot and killed in Malta by gunman on motorbike.

- *January 1996*: Yehya Ayyash, Hamas's bomb-maker, known as the "engineer," killed when a cellular phone packed with 50 grams of explosives detonates near his head.

Two other Palestinians have sometimes been added to this list, although they seem to have been killed by Abu Nidal. These include Said Hamami, a top PLO official who was murdered in London in January 1978; and Nayim Kader, a PLO representative in Belgium who was killed on a Brussels street in June 1981.

Recent US State Department reporting on human rights provides further insight into this aspect of Israeli security operations, and gives what seems to be an accurate picture of the trade-offs Israel has made between security operations and human rights:[548]

Internal security is the responsibility of the General Security Service (Shin Bet), which is under the authority of the Prime Minister's office. The police are under the authority of a different minister. The Israel Defense Forces (IDF) is under the authority of a civilian Minister of Defense. It includes a significant portion of the adult population on active duty or reserve status and plays a role in maintaining internal security. The Foreign Affairs and Defense Committee in the Knesset reviews the activities of the IDF and Shin Bet.

The Government generally respects the human rights of its citizens, who enjoy a wide range of civil and other rights. Israel's main human rights problems have arisen from its policies and practices in the occupied territories and from its fight against terrorism. The redeployment of the IDF from most major Palestinian population areas in the West Bank in December 1995 and its previous withdrawal from Gaza and Jericho have significantly reduced the scope of these problems.

Nonetheless, there continued to be problems in some areas. Security forces abused Palestinians suspected of security offenses. During the year, the High Court of Justice heard 46 abuse-related cases (almost all asking for an injunction to halt the torture of a specific individual). In no case did the High Court issue an injunction prohibiting the use of "moderate physical pressure." The Government continues to detain without charge numerous Palestinians. Detention and prison conditions, particularly for Palestinian security detainees held in Israel, in some cases do not meet minimum international standards. However, new legislation took effect in May that set tighter limits on the length and grounds for pretrial detention. During the year, discussion continued on proposed legislation to define the basis for and limits of GSS activities after a 1996 version was widely criticized by human rights groups and legal experts because it authorized the Government to use force during interrogation and to issue secret guidelines defining the methods of interrogation. The revised legislation, which had not been formally submitted to the Knesset by year's end, omits this clause. Although there continues to be no explicit legal basis for the use of "special measures," i.e., force during interrogation, the Government justifies such practices as necessary in "special circumstances" when thought necessary to save lives in the fight against terrorism.

The Government responded to terrorist and security incidents by periodically tightening existing restrictions on movement across borders with the West Bank and Gaza and between Palestinian Authority–controlled areas inside the West Bank, detaining hundreds of Palestinians without charge and demolishing the homes of some suspected terrorists and their families in the occupied territories.

Israeli security forces abused, and in some cases tortured, Palestinians suspected of security offenses. Human rights groups and lawyers say that abuse and torture is widespread and that Israeli security officials use a variety of methods designed to coerce confessions that threaten prisoners' health and inflict extreme pain, including the use of violent shaking. Prison conditions are poor, and Israeli authorities arbitrarily arrest and detain persons. Prolonged detention, limits on due process, and infringements on privacy rights remained problems. In some cases, Palestinians were able to challenge successfully the length of their administrative detentions and in July the Israeli High Court of Justice ruled that judges, rather than senior Israeli military officers, are authorized to extend a detainee's administrative detention order. Israeli authorities placed some limits on freedom of assembly. The Israeli Government places limits on freedom of movement.

Although laws and administrative regulations prohibit the physical abuse of detainees, they are frequently not enforced in security cases. Interrogation sessions are long and severe, and solitary confinement is used frequently for long periods. The GSS systematically uses interrogation methods that do not result in detectable traces of mistreatment of the victims, or which leave marks that disappear after a short period of time. Common interrogation practices include hooding; forced standing or squatting for long periods of time; prolonged exposure to extreme temperatures; tying or chaining the detainee in contorted and painful positions; blows and beatings with fists, sticks, and other instruments;

confinement in small and often filthy spaces; sleep and food deprivation; and threats against the detainee's life or family. Israeli interrogators continued to subject prisoners to violent "shaking," which in at least one past case resulted in death. In 1997 B'tzelem, a respected Israeli human rights group, found that a large percentage of Palestinian detainees whom it surveyed had been tortured while in Israeli detention.

The GSS was responsible for the widespread abuse of Palestinians suspected of security offenses. The head of the GSS is empowered by government regulation to authorize security officers to use "moderate physical and psychological pressure" (which includes violent shaking) while interrogating detainees. These practices often led to excesses.

The State Department cites a very real list of civil rights problems, and many actions that are almost certainly ultimately counterproductive in terms of the Palestinian reaction. The other side of this reporting, however, is that no one should ignore the level of violence on the other side, and often by groups that have long attempted to claim they are purely political organizations or which have tried to exploit civil rights as a political weapon.

Israel had to deal with very real problems and threats even when there was little sign of a Second Intifada. On March 21, 1997, a suicide bomber killed 3 Israelis and wounded 48 in an attack on a Tel Aviv cafe. On July 30, two suicide bombers killed 16 persons and wounded 178 in an attack on a Jerusalem market. On September 4, 3 suicide bombers killed 5 persons and wounded 181 in an attack on a Jerusalem pedestrian shopping mall. During 1998, 8 Israelis were killed and over 100 were wounded in terrorist attacks carried out by Palestinian groups or individuals seeking to halt the Middle East peace process. In September 1999, there were two bombings by Hamas on the same day that Israel and the Palestinian Authority reached a new agreement to move forward with the Wye Accords.

At the same time, Israel has made progress. The Israeli Supreme Court voted 9–0 to place important new constraints on Israeli use of force against suspected terrorists in a decision on September 6, 1999.[549] The Court concluded that the Shin Bet or General Security Service had misused a variety of torture-like techniques like violently shaking interrogees, sleep deprivation, beatings, and violent disorientation techniques.

As a result, Israeli security forces will face the same and very real dilemma as the Palestinian security forces, and that is inherent in virtually every intensive internal security effort that must take place in a climate of extremism, terrorism, and social violence. Israel cannot hope to create future stability in Gaza, the West Bank, or Jerusalem if it ignores the need to preserve Palestinian dignity and create a security climate that promotes economic cooperation and an improvement in Palestinian living conditions. Yet, history has shown that Israel security forces can only have mid- and long-term effectiveness if they do not constantly consider the broader political implications of their actions and remember that any excesses undermine outside support for Israel, breed Palestinian hostility and violence, and undercut Palestinian and Arab support for the peace process and Palestinian security operations.[550] In short, both Israel and Palestinian security forces must try to walk the same narrow line in a climate of crisis and uncertainty in which neither can hope to be fully successful.

Both Israelis, and Israel's supporters, also need to remember that Israeli terrorism is a problem as well as Palestinian terrorism. Israeli extremist violence against Palestinians and Israeli Arabs broke out in the fighting in the fall of 2000. Even when Israeli extremists do not use violence however, Israeli and pro-Israeli extremists operate in a climate where their verbal violence can be as deadly as the use of bombs and weapons. Israeli extremists use rhetoric that is as violent and extreme as that of the Palestinian extremists. They have charged leaders like Yitzak Rabin and Shimon Peres with "treason," and one of their members murdered Yitzak Rabin on November 4, 1995. Similar charges were made about former Prime Minister Benjamin Netanyahu after the Wye Accords and about Israeli moderates during the 1999 election campaign. Israeli extremists have threatened to kill Palestinians who interfere with their actions and drive them out of their homes or the entire West Bank. A few have beaten or murdered innocent Palestinians.

Groups like the Action Committee for the Abolition of the Autonomy Plan, Kach, Kahane Chai, Eyal, radicals in the more extreme settlements such as Hebron and Kiryat Arba, and the more extreme members of settler groups not only commit occasional direct acts of terrorism, but they constantly and directly provoke extreme Palestinian actions. In the process, they have done just as much to kill their own countrymen as the Palestinians who have actually used a bomb or pulled the trigger. Unfortunately, there is little prospect that any Israeli government can bring a complete halt to such Israeli extremist activity, and there is equally little prospect that Israeli extremists will see that they have often played a direct role in terrorism.[551]

The Cost-Effectiveness of Security Measures

Even a successful cease-fire or peace will enforce its own tragedies on both Palestinian and Israeli security efforts. Both sides will have to learn to live with the bitterness of a cold peace and continuing violence. At least for several years, they will have to choose between acting decisively and sometimes violently and having terrorists or extremists succeed. There will be the constant specter of having to choose between threats to peace and security, and the kind of counterterrorism that relies on interrogation methods that border on psychological and/or physical torture, arrests and detentions that are "arbitrary" by the standards of civil law. If "peace" means that extremists and terrorists go on with levels of violence that approach low intensity combat, then it will be difficult to establish the norms of civil society.

Map 7.3
The West Bank

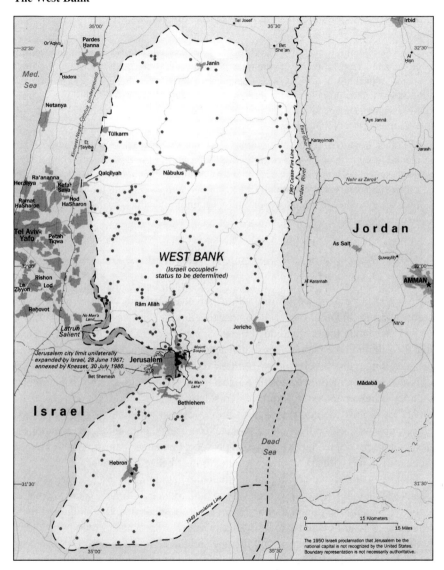

   In the case of such a "peace," both sides—and world opinion—will have to
decide whether extreme security measures will sometimes be used, and whether
they are sometimes necessary. In such an event, the key issue will be how many
such acts occur, how targeted they are on those who directly commit terrorism,
and, therefore, how justified they appear to be in terms of their near-term

effectiveness and long-term impact on all forms of human rights, including peace
and physical security as well as civil liberties.

There are two possible ways to reduce these dilemmas:

- One is a much more massive effort to improve the quality of the Palestinian security
  effort and create effective communication between Israeli and Palestinian security
  forces, of the kind the CIA, as well as elements of the EU and other advisory groups, have
  already carried out. In general, every improvement in the quality of each side's security
  forces and the cooperation between them, should reduce the need for tradeoffs between
  effectiveness and civil liberties.

- The other is to recognize that no security effort is likely to succeed that is not based on the
  mutual perception of the vast majority of Israelis and Palestinians that any compromise
  resulting in a cease-fire or peace is better than continued fighting. New words or lines on
  a map will not be enough. Similarly, even the best compromise will probably fail if both
  sides do not address the demographic and economic problems of the Palestinians in Gaza
  and the West Bank.

A Cold Peace and the Possible Role of Neutral Observers

No one can predict when or if Israeli-Palestinian peace negotiations can now
have a real hope of succeeding, or limit Israeli-Palestinian violence to sporadic
confrontations and civil unrest. It is clear that any final peace will take months or
years longer than the original deadline of September 13, 2000. It is equally clear
that the full implementation of any such accords will then likely take years or even
decades longer and involve many further incidents of violence.

Issues such as the right of return, repatriations, water, definitions of sovereignty,
security arrangements, the future of Jerusalem, and the fate of the Israeli settlements are simply too controversial to firmly resolve with one set of accords and
any compromise is too likely to provoke extremists on both sides. Even under the
best conditions, there is little near-term prospect that either Palestinians or Israelis
can avoid living with "peace with violence" and "peace with abuses."

There have been two developments since the beginning of violence in September 2000 that may, however, offer a way to both reduce the time it takes to create a
stable peace and the dilemma inherent in creating security and ending terrorism.
First, the Mitchell Commission offers a possible precedent in creating a neutral
body that can assess the causes of violence and the nature of the military response
on both sides without being seen as biased in favor of one side or the other, and
turning the assessment of the actions of each side and its use of force into a political
extension of asymmetric warfare by other means.

It is important to recognize both the validity of Israeli and Palestinian fears that
such efforts will become such a "weapon" for the other side in a war of perceptions,
and the grim reality that each side has also long used "terrorism" and "human
rights" issues as political weapons against the other. There is a risk that any effort
to monitor violence and the actions of both sides to counter it can become more of a

problem than a solution. This is particularly true if such an effort continues both sides' efforts to use history and law to make purely partisan arguments, rather than focus on creating a just and secure peace and future for Palestinian and Israeli. The issue is the future and not the past, and one should remember the famous historical indictment of the Bourbon rulers of France: "They forgot nothing and they learned nothing."

Yet, both sides can benefit from having some neutral body to turn to, if one can be created and sustained that is acceptable to both sides during periods of violence and during efforts to create a lasting cease-fire or peace. Both sides can benefit from transparency in executing the terms of a cease-fire or peace agreement, and in conducting their security efforts and improving their effectiveness while reducing the cost to civil liberties. Objective, mutual criticism may still be painful, but it can also be constructive. Ideally, Israelis and Palestinians should be able to communicate without any such neutral third party. In practice, they have not done well to date, and a truly neutral observer body or commission might be useful *if* one can be created that both sides trust.

The use of any kind of military cadres to enforce a peace or cease-fire is even more controversial. At this point, Israel feels—and not without reason—that many calls for such forces are simply a call for security efforts that will aid the Palestinians. Certainly, this is an area where the UN's political record may make it difficult for the UN to play such a role. At the same time, Palestinians have equal reason to question whether any such group that is acceptable to Israel will be truly neutral and evenhanded in dealing with the Palestinians. Peacekeeping too can become an extension of war by other means.

There may still, however, be a case for international military observers who can not only assess the military actions of each side in any future outbreaks of violence, but each side's compliance with those terms of a cease-fire or peace agreement that involve military risks and issues. Once again, the problems in creating a truly neutral and trusted group of military observers are legion, and even the best-intentioned group will face constant pressures to back one side against the other. Yet, the question increasingly arises as to how each side can really trust the other and deal with the legacy of the current violence without outside help. It seems as dangerous to reject any possible solution out of hand as it is to assume such solutions will be easy or even possible.

The end result is the greatest challenge to finding new approaches to peacekeeping since Bosnia and Kosovo. Nothing useful can come out of efforts that attempt to refight the past, and debate either the Holocaust or every event since the 1967 war. Nothing good can come out of efforts that take sides or efforts that divide along pro-Israeli or pro-Palestinian lines. The Balkans and Somalia have already demonstrated the cost of demonizing one side while sanctifying another, and the attacks on French and US barracks in Lebanon have shown how quickly perceptions of a humanitarian intervention can change, and make it the target of terrorism. At the same time, abandoning the use of international commissions and some form of military observer force because the mission is extremely difficult, means abandoning tools that might well help create a more stable cease-fire and peace and speed the transition from a cold peace that is virtually undistinguishable from cold war to one that offers Israelis and Palestinians a secure future.

One further issue must also be addressed. As the previous analysis has shown, the Oslo accords tacitly assumed that peace would somehow address the economic and demographic crisis in Gaza and the West Bank. Peace is a desirable end in itself, but it does not bring economic growth and development. Neither will any foreseeable solution to the final settlement issues, and any peace or cease-fire based on "separation" risks permanently crippling Palestinian economic development and severely hurting the economic development of Jordan. Israel, the Palestinians, and the world will have to address the extent to which any peaceful outcome of the Israeli-Palestinian struggle can be made stable without a massive exercise in economic aid, development, and nation building, and some deliberate effort to develop Israeli, Palestinian, and Jordanian economic cooperation, if not partial integration. Like peace, security, and civil liberties, the "right" to economic well-being can never be perfectly implemented. Economics, however, are ultimately as critical to security as any treaty.

8

Israeli–Syrian Conflicts

The risk of another Israeli-Syrian conflict currently seems limited. Prime Minister Barak has repeatedly called for peace with Syria, and praised Syria's President Assad as "a man of his word . . . of honor, of dignity." Syria has made several offers to resume peace talks since Barak's election, and President Hafez Assad's death in June 2000 has created a new level of political instability in Syria which makes it seem Syria will prefer peace to adventures—at least until Syria's new president, Bashar Assad, or some other leader can consolidate power.[552] Syria also has made no major progress in finding a new source of military aid or arms, and its economy remains too weak to fund the modernization of its existing force structure, much less compete with Israel in creating new war fighting capabilities.

Nevertheless, such a conflict still poses one of the most serious threats to peace, along the risk of a "Second Intifada" and the escalation of the proxy war in Lebanon. Camp David, Jordan's peace with Israel, and Iraq's defeat in the Gulf War have made the "Arab-Israeli Balance" largely a "Syrian-Israeli Balance." Barring some massive shift in the current political situation, neither Egypt nor Jordan are likely to initiate a conflict with Israel, and neither would offer Syria significant military support if a conflict did begin.

The current Syrian-Israeli balance is summarized in Table 8.1 and Figure 8.1. While it is clear that Syria has built up massive military forces, a balance limited to an Israeli-Syrian conflict is far less threatening to Israel than any comparison based on the strength of all the Arab "ring states." This balance is even less threatening when recent trends in military expenditures and arms transfers are considered. Syria's military efforts and modernization have fallen steadily behind Israel since

Table 8.1
The Syrian-Israeli Balance in 2001

Category/Weapon	Israel	Syria
Defense Budget		
(In 2000, $Current Billions)	$7.0	$1.8
Arms Imports: 1996-1999 ($M)		
New Orders	4,500	500
Deliveries	4,500	300
Mobilization Base		
Men Ages 13-17	281,000	1,042,000
Men Ages 18-22	270,000	853,000
Manpower		
Total Active	172,500	316,000
(Conscript)	107,500	-
Total Reserve	425,000	396,000
Total	597,500	7120,000
Paramilitary	8,050	108,000
Land Forces		
Active Manpower	130,000	215,000
(Conscripts)	85,000	-
Reserve Manpower	400,000	300,000
Total Active & Reserve Manpower	530,000	515,000
Main Battle Tanks	3,900	3,650 (1200)
AIFVs/Armored Cars/Lt. Tanks	408	3,305
APCs/Recce/Scouts	5,900	1,500
WWII Half-Tracks	500(3,500)	0
ATGM Launchers	1,300	3,390+
SP Artillery	855	450
Towed Artillery	520	1,600
MRLs	198	480
Mortars	6,440	4,500+
SSM Launchers	48	72
AA Guns	850	2,060
Lt. SAM Launchers	1,298	4,055
Air & Air Defense Forces		
Active Air Force Manpower	36,000	40,000
Active Air Defense Command	0	60,000
Air Force Reserve Manpower	20,000	92,000
Air Defense Command Reserve Manpower	0	-
Aircraft		
Total Fighter/FGA/Recce	446(250)	589
Fighter	0	310
FGA/Fighter	405	0

Table 8.1 (continued)

Category/Weapon	Israel	Syria
Air & Air Defense Forces		
FGA	25	154
Recce	10	14
Airborne Early Warning (AEW)	6	0
Electronic Warfare (EW)	37	10
Fixed Wing	37	0
Helicopter	0	10
Maritime Reconnaissance (MR)	3	0
Combat Capable Trainer	26	111
Tanker	6	0
Transport	37	27
Helicopters		
Attack/Armed	133	87
SAR/ASW	6	-
Transport & Other	160	110
Total	299	197
SAM Forces		
Batteries	28	150
Heavy Launchers	79	848
Medium Launchers	0	60
AA Guns	0	4,000
Naval Forces		
Active Manpower	6,500	6,000
Reserve Manpower	5,000	4,000
Total Manpower	11,500	10,000
Naval Commandos/Marines	300	0
Submarines	2	0
Destroyers/Frigates/Corvettes	3	2
Missile	3	2
Other	0	0
Missile Patrol	12	10
Coastal/Inshore Patrol	32	8
Mine	0	5
Amphibious Ships	1	3
Landing Craft/Light Support	4	5
Fixed-wing Combat Aircraft	0	0
MR/MPA	0	0
ASW/Combat Helicopter	0	24
Other Helicopters	-	-

Note: Figures in parentheses show additional equipment known to be in long-term storage. Some Syrian tanks shown in parentheses are used as fire points in fixed positions.

Source: Adapted by Anthony H. Cordesman from data provided by US experts, and the IISS, *Military Balance.*

Figure 8.1
Israeli Versus Syrian Operational Force Strength in 2001

Land Weapons

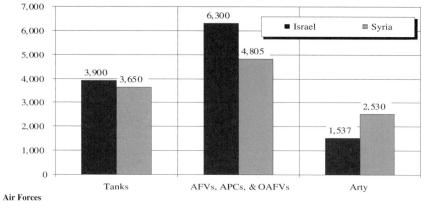

Air Forces

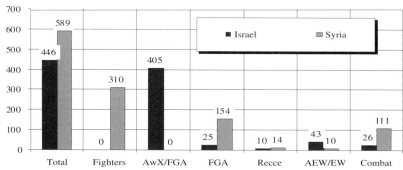

Note: Total Artillery includes towed and self-propelled tube artillery and multiple rocket launchers. Total air forces include only operational fixed wing fighter, fighter-attack, and reconnaissance aircraft in combat units, less aircraft in combat training units.

Source: Adapted by Anthony H. Cordesman from data provided by US experts, and the IISS, *Military Balance.*

the mid-1980s, and Syria has had only limited military modernization during the 1990s.

Figure 8.2 shows that Syrian military expenditures have shrunk from about two-thirds of Israel's in the mid-1980s to only about half the Israeli level. Similarly, Figure 8.3 shows that Syrian arms imports have shrunk from levels much higher than Israel's in the late 1980s to levels that are only a fraction of Israel's. One of the major reasons for this drop has been the end of the Cold War, and Russia's growing financial problems. Russia has cut back on scheduled deliveries and has refused new orders that are not paid in cash since the Syrians defaulted on their

Figure 8.2
Trends in Syrian-Israeli Military Spending: 1985–1997
(In $US 1997 Constant Millions)

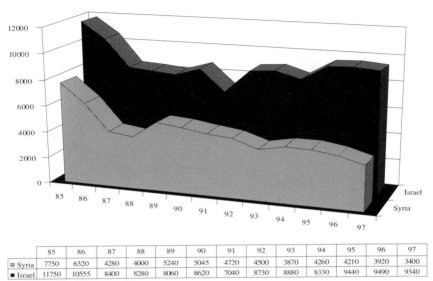

	85	86	87	88	89	90	91	92	93	94	95	96	97
Syria	7750	6320	4280	4000	5240	5045	4720	4500	3870	4260	4210	3920	3400
Israel	11750	10555	8400	8280	8060	8620	7040	8730	8880	8330	9440	9490	9340

Source: Adapted by Anthony H. Cordesman from US State Department, Bureau of Arms Control, *World Military Expenditures and Arms Transfers*, Washington, GPO, Table I, various editions.

loans to Russia.

Another major reason is corruption. Much of the outside military aid Syria received at the time of the Gulf War went directly into the hands of its senior political and military officials. In fact, until Bashar Assad began his anti-corruption drive in 1998, the steady growth in the misappropriation of military budgets, and corruption and nepotism within the Syrian leadership and high command, was leading to a steady decline in Syria's ability to maintain and improve its war fighting capabilities.

It is still unclear whether Hafez Assad's death will affect this situation. Both the continuity in much of the Syrian command, and the limited number of purges, seem designed more to secure Bashar Assad's succession to the Presidency than to improve Syrian military capabilities. While some changes have been associated with an anti-corruption drive that began in 1998, such changes may have begun in early 1995, when Ali Haydar, the Special Forces Commander, was fired for "insubordination."[553] Hafez Assad's brother Rifat was finally stripped of the title of Vice President in February 1998, when Hafez Assad seems to have become more serious about preparing for a shift in power. Hikmat al-Shihabi was replaced as Chief of Staff in 1998 by Ali Aslan, who had been Deputy Chief of Staff and who was not only an Alawite but also a member of the same Kalbiyya tribe as Assad.

Figure 8.3
Annual Trends in Syrian Israeli Arms Deliveries: 1985–1997
($US 1997 Constant Millions)

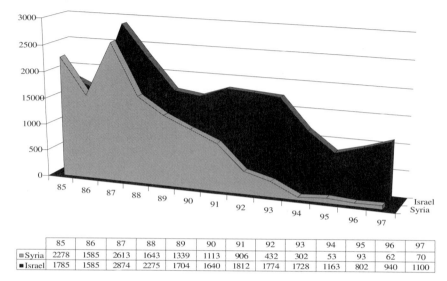

	85	86	87	88	89	90	91	92	93	94	95	96	97
▣ Syria	2278	1585	2613	1643	1339	1113	906	432	302	53	93	62	70
▪ Israel	1785	1585	2874	2275	1704	1640	1812	1774	1728	1163	802	940	1100

Source: Adapted by Anthony H. Cordesman from US State Department, Bureau of Arms Control, *World Military Expenditures and Arms Transfers*, Washington, GPO, various editions.

General Bashir Najjar, the head of the General Intelligence Department, was fired, and eventually sentenced to 11 years for corruption. General Ali Huri replaced him, and General Muhammed Nasif was made Huri's deputy. Nasif had been head of Internal Security and had long been an Assad loyalist. In January 1999, Assad had raised the retirement age for the Chief of Staff from 69 to 70 to keep both Aslan and Minister of Defense Mustafa Tlas in office. Tlas had long been viewed as little more than an Assad stooge.[554]

In 1999, Assad seems to have kept other loyalist officers in their positions past their retirement age, while forcing others out. The eventual "exile" of ex-Military Chief of Staff General Hikmat Sehahabi, full retirement of officials like Chief of the Military Security Service Ali Dubah, and removal of Air Force Commander Muhammad Khuli, all seem to have been carried out largely to ensure full support for Bashar's succession, although it scarcely represented a loss of military competence by any standard.[555]

Ironically, Bashar came to full power shortly after an anti-corruption purge led to the "suicide" of ex-Prime Minister Muhammad Zubi—one of the less corrupt officials in the Syrian leadership. Bashar was made commander of the armed forces after his father's death by Abdul Halim Khaddam, the acting president and ex-vice president, and one of the more corrupt officials in Syria. Defense Minister

Mustafa Tlas helped bring Bashar to power, and remained in office. Tlas's son may also be promoted to a new security position. Intelligence officials like General Bahjat Suleiman also emerged as supporters of Bashar and have remained in power.

Some analysts close to the Syrian regime indicate that it may take more than five years for Bashar to fully consolidate his position and such a consolidation may come at the cost of military effectiveness. Bashar scarcely has the military credibility of his father. He was 29 when he suddenly became Hafez's heir as the result of the death of his elder brother in a car accident in 1994, and he had been trained as an ophthalmologist. While he was being rushed to the top of Syria's power structure even before his father's death, his 10-year apprenticeship still left him only 38 at the time of his father's death and he was so young that the Syrian constitution had to be amended to allow him to become President. He had nothing approaching King Abdullah of Jordan's military experience and credentials.

Bashar faces other problems. Syria has been so much of a strongman state that the meeting of the Syrian Baath Party on June 17, 2000, that gave Bashar official power was the first meeting in 15 years. Bashar is an Alawite, which is part of an 11% minority in a country that is overwhelmingly Sunni, and a sect which Sunni factions like the Moslem Brotherhood have regarded as unfit to rule. Bashar may face some challenge from his uncle Rifat Assad, although Rifat is in exile and it is not clear what power base Rifat Assad still retains in Syria, if any. He also will have to deal with his sister, Bushra, and her husband Assif Shawkat, the Chief of Military Intelligence for Ground Forces.[556]

While many experts feel that Bashar is far more interested in serious economic reform than his father, money is almost certain to be a continuing problem. Figure 8.4 shows that Syria's new orders have been cut even more than its deliveries, in part because of the delivery of past orders after 1990. As a result, the impact on Syrian war fighting capabilities will increase steadily over time. In contrast, Israel has maintained a relatively constant flow of aid from the US, its major supplier, and the fluctuations in Israeli orders are largely a function of the fact that major orders or deliveries in any given year usually mean a cut in the next.

SYRIAN CAPABILITIES IN WAR FIGHTING

The trends in Syrian military forces are shown in more detail in the tables and figures which follow, which also help explain the previous comparisons of Syrian force numbers and force quality with those of other regional states. Table 8.2 shows the changes in the size of Syria's forces from a period shortly after the October War to the present. Figure 8.5 provides a graphic summary of Syria's current force strength.

The trends in Figures 8.6 and 8.7 are particularly striking since it is brutally clear that Syria has not gotten anything like the arms deliveries necessary to maintain and modernize its current force structure.[557] The impact of such cuts in arms imports are even more severe because Syria's force structure and procurement planning still suffer from many of the problems chronic to Soviet bloc–supplied

Figure 8.4
Syrian-Israeli Arms Agreements and Deliveries: 1986–1999
($Current Millions)

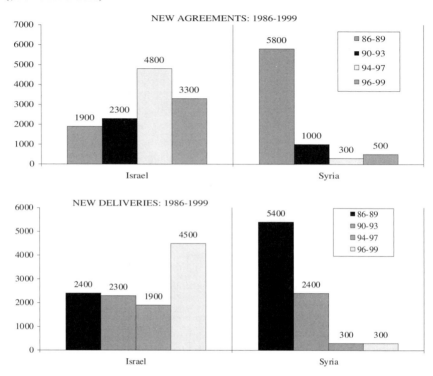

Source: Adapted by Anthony H. Cordesman, CSIS, from Richard F. Grimmett, *Conventional Arms Transfers to Developing Nations,* Washington, Congressional Research Service, various editions.

forces during the Cold War, and which led to many of Iraq's problems during the Gulf War. While some Syrian forces fought well in 1973 and 1982, and Syria has managed to improve some aspects of its air and land force equipment in recent years, it simply has not been able to compete with Israel's military modernization efforts.

Syrian Modernization, Military Spending, and Arms Imports

Syrian economic liberalization may someday give it added resources to spend on its military forces and arms, but its economic reform under Hafez Assad was corrupt, ineffective and faltering. Syria has yet to make any of the major increases it must make in its expenditures to improve the quality of its existing forces. Although Syrian reporting on military and security expenditures sharply understates the true scale of its expenditures, it does provide a rough indication of the

Table 8.2
Force Trends in Syria

Category/Weapon	1975	1980	1985	1990	1995	2000
Manpower						
Total Active	177,500	247,500	402,500	404,000	423,000	320,000
(Conscript)	-	-	-	-	-	-
Total Reserve	102,500	-	273,500	400,000	650,000	500,000
Total	280,000	-	676,000	804,000	1,073,000	820,000
Paramilitary	9,500	9,500	6,300	10,800	8,000+	8,000+
Land Forces						
Active Regular						
Manpower	150,000	200,000	270,000	300,000	315,000	215,000
(Conscripts)	-	(140,000)	(135,000)	(130,000)	(250,000)	-
Republican Guards	-	-	-	10,000	-	
Reserve Manpower	100,000	-	270,000	392,000	550,000	400,000
Total Reserve &						
Active Manpower	250,000	-	540,000	702,000	865,000	615,000
Main Battle Tanks	1,400	2,920	4,200	2,900	3,200	3,450
(Static & in Storage)		-	-	(1,100)	(1,200)	(1,200)
AIFVs/Armored						
Cars/Lt. Tanks	70	700	1,400	2,800	3,310	3,010
APCs/Recce/Scouts	1,100	1,600	1,600	1,500	1,500	1,500
WWII Half-Tracks	0	0	0	0	0	0
ATGM Launchers	-	-	-	1,100	3,390	3,390
SP Artillery	75	800*	-	186	450	450
Towed Artillery	700	*	-	2,000	1,630	1,630
MRLs	57	-	-	250	480	480
Mortars	-	-	-	-	658+	4,500+
SSM Launchers	-	54	54	61	62	
AA Guns	-	-	1,000	1,700	2,060	2,060
Lt. SAM Launchers	-	-	-	-	4,055	4,055
Air & Air Defense Forces						
Active Air Force						
Manpower	25,000	45,000	70,000	40,000	40,000	40,000
Air Force Reserve						
Manpower	-	-	-	-	92,000	92,000
Active Air Defense						
Command	-	(15,000)	60,000	60,000	60,000	60,000
Air Defense						
Command Reserve	-	-	-	-	-	-

Table 8.2 (continued)

Category/Weapon	1975	1980	1985	1990	1995	2000
Air & Air Defense Forces						
Aircraft						
Total						
Fighter/FGA/Recce	400	395	500	558	579	589
Bombers	4	0	0	0	0	0
Fighter	250	225	280	312	300	310
FGA/Fighter	0	60	0	0	9	0
FGA	140	110	193	170	154	154
Recce	0	0	10	6	14	14
Airborne Early						
Warning (AEW)	0	0	0	0	0	0
Electronic Warfare						
(EW)	0	0	-	8	10	10
(Fixed Wing)						
(Helicopter)						
Maritime						
Reconnaissance						
(MR)	0	0	0	0	0	0
Combat Capable						
Trainer	-	20	10-60	76-96	111	111
Tanker	0	0	0	0	0	0
Transport	9	17	23	28	34	49
Helicopters						
Attack/Armed	0	0	100	100	100	72
ASW/SAR	0	35	23	25	0	0
Transport & Other	60	82	160	155	118	110
Total	60	117	283	280	218	182
SAM Forces						
Batteries	-	75	126	126	130	130
Heavy Launchers	-	-	658	640	728	728
Medium Launchers	-	-	-	60	60	60
AA Guns	-	-	-	-	-	-
Naval Forces						
Active Manpower	2,500	2,500	2,500	6,000	8,000	6,000
Reserve Manpower	2,500	-	2,500	8,000	8,000	4,000
Total Manpower	5,000	-	5,000	14,000	16,000	10,000
Submarines	0	0	0	3	3(2)	0(3)

Table 8.2 (continued)

Category/Weapon	1975	1980	1985	1990	1995	2000
Naval Forces						
Destroyers/Frigates/						
Corvettes	0	0	0	2	2	2
Missile	0	2	2	2	2	2
Other	0	0	0	0	0	0
Missile Patrol	6	18	22	12	18	10
Coastal/Inshore Patrol	12	9	7	8	11	8
Mine	1	3	4	9	7	5
Amphibious Ships	-	-	2	3	3	3
Landing Craft/Light						
Support	-	-	-	-	-	5
Fixed Wing Combat						
Aircraft	0	0	0	0	0	0
MR/MPA	0	0	0	0	0	0
ASW/Combat						
Helicopter	-	-	-	17	29	24
Other Helicopters	-	-	-	-	-	-

Note: *Includes all types of towed and self-propelled artillery, but not multiple rocket launchers.

Source: Adapted by Anthony H. Cordesman from data provided by US experts, and the IISS, *Military Balance*.

trend in spending. According to the US Arms Control and Disarmament Agency, Syrian military spending totaled about 14% of its GNP in the early 1990s, but dropped to 7% by 1995. The most recent Syrian reports indicate that military and security expenditures were lower than $3.6 billion out of a total GNP of $49.5 billion in 1995. Once inflation is considered, these expenditures were lower than in 1995 and significantly lower than in the early 1990s—when Syria had the benefit of concessional sales and aid from the former Soviet Union.[558]

Figure 8.9 shows the decline in arms deliveries to Syria since 1985, through the end of the Cold War, and the most recent slight rise due to steadily increasing arms agreements with Russia.

- Syrian arms deliveries reached their peak in 1987 with a total of almost $2.6 billion.

- The lowest point in Syrian arms deliveries occurred in 1994 with a total of only $41 million.

- Some experts then put Syria's arms debt to Russia at $11 billion, although Syrian sources claim it was much lower—although they refuse to cite a more accurate figure.[559]

- Since 1994, Syrian deliveries have been estimated to be growing slightly. In 1995 deliveries equaled $70 million.

Figure 8.5
Syrian Major Military Equipment in 2001

Land Forces

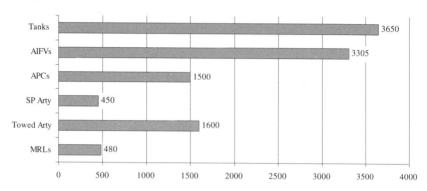

Air Forces

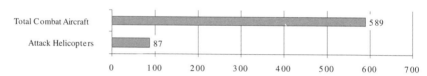

Naval Forces

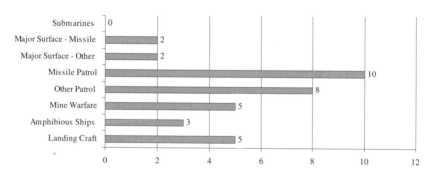

Source: Adapted by Anthony H. Cordesman from data provided by US experts, and the IISS, *Military Balance*.

- Deliveries averaged $400 million a year during 1991–1994, but only $75 million a year during 1995–1999.

While deliveries have increased slightly since that time, Syrian military spending has plateaued. Figure 8.2 shows the trend in military spending over the period from 1985 to 1995. This figure clearly shows the current gap in spending between Israel and Syria. It is unclear whether Syria can hope for significant Russian aid at

Figure 8.6
Syrian Arms Agreements and Deliveries By Major Supplier: 1987–1999
($Current Millions)

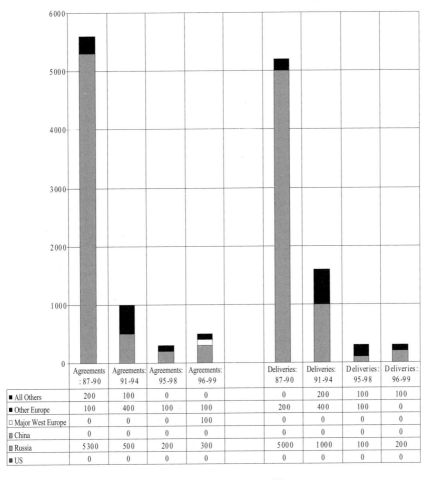

	Agreements :87-90	Agreements: 91-94	Agreements: 95-98	Agreements: 96-99	Deliveries: 87-90	Deliveries: 91-94	Deliveries: 95-98	Deliveries: 96-99
■ All Others	200	100	0	0	0	200	100	100
■ Other Europe	100	400	100	100	200	400	100	0
□ Major West Europe	0	0	0	100	0	0	0	0
▨ China	0	0	0	0	0	0	0	0
▨ Russia	5300	500	200	300	5000	1000	100	200
■ US	0	0	0	0	0	0	0	0

Notes: Includes Gulf states, Arab-Israeli states, North Africa, and Yemen.
0 = less than $50 million or nil, and all data rounded to the nearest $100 million.

Source: Richard F. Grimmett, *Conventional Arms Transfers to the Developing Nations,*
Congressional Research Service, various editions.

any point in the foreseeable future, and without such aid, Syria is likely to
experience continued spending and arms import problems.

- In 1984, both Syrian and Israeli military spending was estimated to be around $12 billion.
- Between 1984 and 1989, Israeli and Syrian military spending both declined but remained

Figure 8.7
The Syrian Recapitalization Crisis: Arms Deliveries During 1985–1996
($US 1997 Constant Millions)

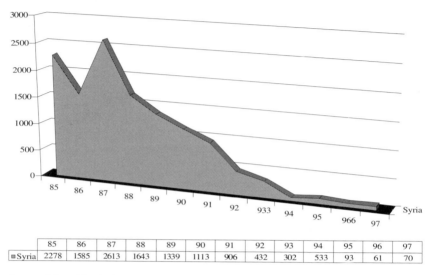

	85	86	87	88	89	90	91	92	93	94	95	96	97
▣Syria	2278	1585	2613	1643	1339	1113	906	432	302	533	93	61	70

Source: Adapted by Anthony H. Cordesman from US State Department, Bureau of Arms Control, *World Military Expenditures and Arms Transfers*, GPO, Washington, various editions.

relatively equal.

- After the Cold War ended in 1989, Syrian military spending declined at a greater pace while Israeli spending increased.

- By 1995, Israeli military spending was estimated at $8.7 billion while Syrian spending was estimated to be around $3.5 billion.

- By 2000, Israeli military spending was estimated at well over $8.0 billion while Syrian spending was estimated to be around $3.0 billion.

These financial pressures have forced Syria to abandon its search for conventional parity and make four shifts in its strategy and procurement effort that reflect a new focus on "asymmetric warfare":

- Emphasize the procurement of long-range ballistic missiles and weapons of mass destruction as a relatively low cost offset to Israel's conventional superiority while giving Syria a limited counterweight to Israel's nuclear strike capability.

- Give priority to elite commando and special forces units that can be used to defend key approaches to Syria and spearhead infiltrations and attacks. Many of these forces are equipped with modern anti-tank guided weapons and other modern crew and manportable weapons that allow them to disperse without relying on armored weapons and other systems Israel can target more easily. They are supported by attack helicopters.

- Maintain a large tank force both as a deterrent to any Israeli attempt to penetrate Syria and to maintain a constant threat to the Golan, even if Syria has no hope of achieving overall parity.
- Use the Hizbollah and Amal as proxies to attack Israel and the SLA in Southern Lebanon.

Syria has attempted to remedy some of its growing modernization problems by procuring upgrades and technology from Russia and the West, but Syria has not done well in obtaining such help. Its only major conventional force improvements during the mid and late-1990s were some Ukrainian modifications for part of the T-55 tank fleet and AT-14 Kornet anti-tank guided missiles. Syria has not yet succeeded in negotiating major new arms agreements with Russia and other suppliers. Western firms want firm cash guarantees and are reluctant to sell to Syria. China and North Korea cannot supply the quality of conventional arms Syria needs, and any purchase of equipment that does not come from Russia will create interoperability problems that will compound Syrian weaknesses in sustainability and combined arms.

Russia is Syria's most logical source of new conventional arms, and there were reports during the early 1990s that indicated that Syria would be able to spend some $1.4 billion on military modernization between 1992 and 1994. Russia failed to fill a major arms deal in 1992 for some 24 MiG-29s. 12 Su-27s, 3 T-72s, and T-74s, and an unknown number of S-300 and SA-16 missiles because of Syria's lack of finances.[560] There were new reports that Syria negotiated with Russia in 1994 to buy 30 Su-24s, 50 MiG-29s, 14 Su-17s, 300 T-72s and T-74s, S-300 multiple rocket launchers (a Russian system similar to the MLRS) and S-300 missiles.[561]

Syria found, however, that post-Communist Russia did not make concessionary arms sales that approached the level of gifts, or show the past tolerance for unpaid loans. This was a major stumbling block throughout the 1990s. Syria had piled up a massive debt over the years. It owed Russia roughly $7–11 billion for past arms purchases, and a total of $20 billion for both its military and civil debt. Russia was well aware that there was little prospect that it would ever be paid and this had a chilling impact on Syria's ability to obtain arms.[562]

Russia and Syria have claimed on several occasions to have resolved the issue. Syria signed a new cooperation agreement with Russia in April 1994, for "defensive weapons and spare parts." Syria held extensive new arms purchasing talks with Russia in 1997 and 1998. In February 1999, Syria announced plans to spend as much as $2 billion on a range of Russian armaments, including more anti-tank systems—which seem to have included deliveries of more AT-5 Spandrels, thousands of AT-10s, and AT-14 Kornets.[563]

Syria and Russia held talks in May 1999 to discuss expanding military cooperation, and in particular to arrange the sale of Russian advanced weapons systems to Syria.[564] According to some reports, Russia now seemed willing to put repayments of its debt on hold.[565] A five-year, $2 billion contract was under discussion.[566] According to one report, Syria apparently requested Su-27 fighters and the S-300 air defense system, but was offered the cheaper MiG-29 fighters and Tor-M1 air defense systems.[567] Syrian President Hafez Assad visited Moscow in July 1999, and Syria and Russia held new high level talks on military cooperation in September 1999. These talks seem to have again involved a $2–2.5 billion deal over five years, and the possible purchase of the S-300 surface-to-air missile defense system, the Sukhoi Su-27 multirole fighter, MiG-29SMT fighters, T-80 tanks, and more anti-tank weapons. Once again, however, the contractual status of such agreements, the weapons involved, and delivery schedules remained unclear.[568]

It is not clear how Hafez Assad's death, and Bashar's succession, will affect this situation. Even if the reports of major new Russian arms sales prove true, any foreseeable new agreements will still leave Syria with far fewer funds than it needs to recapitalize its current force structure and compete with Israel in modernization. It is hard to see how Syria can finance even half the funds and projected deliveries necessary to replace its older land force equipment and aircraft in the near to mid-term. Furthermore, if Syria could order all of the arms it wants, it would still take some three to five years to fully absorb all of the new technology it needs, integrate it into effective combat systems, and retrain its forces—assuming it recognizes the need to do so. Barring massive outside aid, Syrian forces are almost certain to continue to go "hollow" for the foreseeable future, although moderate deliveries of advanced modern aircraft, tanks, and surface-to-air missile systems like the S-300 could still help correct key Syrian weaknesses.

Syria's limitations will be further compounded by its problems in absorbing new equipment. These include the endemic corruption discussed earlier. They also include its politicized and compartmented command structure, inadequate military pay, poor manpower management, poor technical training, and poor overall training—particularly in realistic combat exercises and aggressor training. Syrian forces have inadequate combat and service support, equipment for night and poor weather warfare, long-range sensors and targeting systems, and mobile rapidly maneuverable logistics, recording, and combat repair capability. While individual Syrian officers have shown a keen understanding of many of these problems, Syria has never taken effective action to deal with them.

These trends have not gone unnoticed by Israeli analysts, including the experts of the Jaffee Center for Strategic Studies. Its latest assessment of the balance, the *Middle East Military Balance, 1999–2000*, notes that Syria has failed to modernize its conventional land forces, has not purchased any new planes since the mid-1980s, and its submarines are unusable and its surface ships are aging.[569]

It should be noted, however, that the IDF does not see this situation as fixed, and that senior officers, like Israeli Air Force Commander, Major General Eitan Ben-Eliahu, have warned that the military stability affecting a settlement on the Golan could be upset by the transfer of a modern air defense system like the Russian Almaz S-300 surface-to-air missile system. Major General Amos Malka, the chief of Israeli military intelligence has warned that the Syrian army continues to improve its readiness (US military intelligence analysts seem to sharply disagree), that Syria has improved its anti-armor capability and electronic countermeasures

(US military intelligence analysts agree), and that the Syrian army could improve sharply in readiness over one to two years (US military intelligence analysts agree).[570]

Syrian Land Forces

Syria has put increasing emphasis on asymmetric warfare, on creating high quality commando and special forces, and on training and equipping small infantry formations with modern anti-tank and other crew-served weapons to make its units harder for Israel to attack with precision weapons and artillery. Nevertheless, Syria's greatest strength remains its armored forces.

The previous analysis has shown why Syria has had to emphasize quantity over quality. Although Syria now has a total of some 4,850 tanks, at least 1,200 of these tanks are in static positions or in storage. Roughly half are relatively low-grade T-54s and T-55s, and only 1,700 are relatively modern T-72s. Even the T-72s lack the advanced thermal sights, fire control systems, and armor to engage the Israeli Merkavas and M-60s on anything like a 1:1 basis. The T-72 also performed surprisingly poorly in Iraqi hands during the Gulf War. Its armor did not prove to be as effective against modern Western anti-tank rounds as was previously expected, and its sensors and fire control systems proved inadequate for night and poor visibility combat and could not keep up with Western thermal sights in range and target acquisition capability.[571]

Syria has some 2,350 BMPs. These armored fighting vehicles can supplement and support Syria's tanks in combined arms combat, and increase its potential ability to overwhelm unmobilized Israeli forces with sheer mass. Only about 100 of these BMPs are the more modern BMP-2s, plus a limited number of BMP-3s. Nearly half of Syria's other armor consists of low-grade BRDM-2 and BTR-40, 50, 60, and 152 reconnaissance vehicles and APCs. Even the BMP-2 has relatively light armor, and retains many of the ergonomic problems in fighting from the vehicle and using its guns and anti-tank guided missile launchers as with the BMP-1. The BMP has only moderate ability to escort tanks in a combat environment where the opponent has modern sensors and anti-tank guided weapons.

US experts believe Syria has made relatively limited progress in improving its combined arms and armored war fighting capabilities since 1982, although it does have more advanced anti-tank guided weapons like the Milan, AT-10, and AT-14. They believe that Syrian exercise and command post training is weak above the battalion or regimental level, that Syrian tactics are rigid, and that Syrian reaction times are slow.

Syria can mass large numbers of towed artillery weapons and multiple rocket launchers. This could have a major impact in an area like the Golan where ranges are relatively short and where Syria normally deploys much of its artillery. At the same time, massed artillery fire has only limited lethality against well dug in defenses and armor, and Syria lacks the sensors and battle management systems to concentrate its artillery fire with great precision and to rapidly switch fires. Syria will also have problems in maneuvering its artillery. Only about 28% of Syria's artillery consist of modern self-propelled weapons.

Syria does have good physical defenses of its own positions on the Golan. Syria has spent decades in improving its terrain barriers and creating anti-tank barriers and ditches, and many of its units in the area between Damascus and the Golan have considerable readiness and effectiveness. However, Syria has not come close to Israel in developing the kind of capabilities for combined operations that the IDF takes virtually for granted. For example, Syria's only modern third-generation anti-tank guided missile launchers consist of 200 Milans, 40 AT-5s, and an unknown number of AT-10s and AT-14s out of total holdings of some 3,390 anti-tank guided missile launchers.[572] Most of its systems are still relatively low-grade anti-tank guided missiles systems that can hardly be ignored, but they greatly reduce the effectiveness of Syrian anti-tank forces both in the defensive mode and in providing mechanized infantry support for armored operations.

Syrian Air and Air Defense Forces

The Syrian Air Force and Air Defense Command have more severe problems than Syrian land forces. Syria's 20 Su-24s are its only truly modern attack fighters and they lack the avionics and precision all-weather strike capabilities of first-line Israeli attack aircraft. Similarly, Syria's 20 MiG-29s are its only modern fighters with advanced beyond-visual-range and look-down shoot-down capabilities, and Syria so far has shown little ability to use such aircraft effectively in training and simulated combat or to generate high sortie rates. The bulk of Syria's air defense fighters have poor look-down, shoot-down capabilities and beyond-visual-range combat capability, and still operate largely using obsolete and electronically vulnerable ground-controlled intercept (GCI) techniques.

Syria has also been slow to modernize its attack helicopter tactics. While Syria's attack helicopter tactics were successful in the 1982 war, they were successful largely because the IDF did not expect them and was often trying to rush its advances without adequate coordination. The IDF has now greatly improved its counterattack helicopter training and tactics, has armed its helicopters to attack other helicopters, and improved its anti-aircraft systems and light air defense weaponry.

Syria has no airborne early warning and electronic intelligence and warfare aircraft that approach Israel's capabilities. Syria has vast holdings of land-based air defenses, but these consist largely of obsolescent SA-2, SA-3, SA-5, and SA-6 surface-to-air missile systems and shorter-range systems. Israel was able to defeat all of these systems in 1982, except for the SA-5, which was only deployed late in 1982, after the fighting.

Syria has not modernized its C^{4}I/BM system to anything approaching a high capability automated system, and virtually all of its systems require active radar to operate—which makes them very vulnerable to Israeli anti-radiation missiles, target location and identification systems, and electronic warfare capabilities.

While such land-based air defenses can scarcely be disregarded, and are certain to both force Israel to conduct a massive air defense suppression campaign and fly attack missions that avoid or minimize exposure to surviving defenses, Syrian air defenses do not have the quality necessary to match their quantity.

THE STRATEGIC AND TACTICAL IMPACT OF
THE GOLAN

The Golan has significant strategic importance to both Syria and Israel. It was Syrian territory until Israel conquered it during the Arab-Israel war of June 1967, and it provides strategic depth in defending the approaches to Damascus. The Golan once had some 147,000 Syrian residents, although this number dropped to around 17,000 in the portion Syria retained after the 1967 and 1973 wars. Israel has now occupied most of the Golan since 1967, and the Israel Knesset annexed it on December 14, 1981.

There are now some 18,000 Jews settled on the Golan in 33 Jewish communities (27 kibbutzim and moshavim, 5 communal towns, and 1 city), and some 15,000 Druze and four Druze villages.[573] The largest Israeli town is Katzrin, with some 7,500 residents. According to Israeli sources, this town alone claims some $2.5 billion in civilian assets. The Golan gives Israel de facto control over the headwaters of the Jordan and Sea of Galilee and access to the critical water resources in the region. Control of the Golan also affects control of the waters of the Hatzbani River and any diversion of the Banias River. As a result, any peace settlement must deal with both settlement and water issues in the area.

Israeli control of the Golan confronts Syria with the fact that Israel has a springboard to launch an attack into Syria, a platform for artillery and rocket attacks, and the ability to target movement and military positions from the Golan to Damascus. The Golan also provides Israel with an excellent platform for artillery and missile fire, and for launching UAVs and other sensor systems that can help direct attacks on Syria's land-based air defenses and air force.

There are still good prospects for a peace between Israel and Syria that might transfer virtually all of the Golan to Syria.[574] Even if such a peace does not occur, or is deferred while Syria deals with problems like the succession to President Hafez Assad, war does not seem highly likely. Syria is ill-prepared for any kind of large-scale conventional war with Israel, and its problems are compounded by geography. Syria can at least consider striking at Israel through Lebanon and Jordan, but any strike through Lebanon would require a massive redeployment and restructuring of Syria's support structure and force it to fight through rough terrain and highly defendable territory. Jordan has never shown any interest in permitting Syrian forces to move through its territory, and most potential lines of advance would require Syrian forces to move down narrow valleys and routes that are almost perfect killing grounds for the IAF.[575]

In practice, any major Syrian advance would now have to come through the Golan Heights, one of the most critical strategic areas in the Middle East. It is a high plateau that rises between the Galilee and Damascus of about 1,150 square kilometers.[576] It is situated to the extreme southwest of Syria and northeast of Israel. It overlooks the lower branch of the Yarmuk River on the south, and Mount Hermon that draws the Syrian Lebanese boundaries, on the north, and reaching Lake Tabaraya to the south—forming a border with Israel. To the east lies Al Raquad Valley, in Syria. It is roughly 67 kilometers long from north to south, and a maximum of 25 kilometers wide from the buffer zone between Syrian and Israeli-occupied territory on the Golan to Israel and the Galilee. Prior to the 1967 war, the Syrian-Israeli border along the Golan was 72–76 kilometers long—depending on various views of the border.[577]

The topography of the Golan is a natural extension of the convex slope of Mount Hermon, and an area of volcanic eruptions.

- The Golan area is formed by a number of hills that are originally volcanic cones. Some of these hills form a mountain chain (Al-Qunaitra-Al-Rafeed), the highest of which is Bir-Ajam (1,158 meters).

- The highest point, which offers an excellent surveillance area for sensor coverage of Syria, is Mount Hermon that reaches a height of 2,814 meters. Damascus is only 60 kilometers to the east, and Israel established surveillance facilities in 1967 that have been steadily upgraded in sensor coverage and which now provide signals intelligence, radar coverage, and electronic intelligence.[578]

- There are other hill ranges, such as: Al-Sheika (1,211 meters), Sidral-Arous (1,198 meters), A'ram (1,171 meters), Aboul-Nada (1,204 meters), Al-Khanzeer (1,977 meters), and Al-Azas (927 meters).

- From an Israeli perspective, key tactical points include Hermonit (1,200 meters) in the north and Tel Fares in the south (1,250 meters). Israel has electronic observation points in these areas.

- From a Syrian viewpoint, the Golan offers Israel the shortest attack route into the Damascus Basin, although Damascus can be defended along the Awaj River to the west, and can also be attacked through Jordan. This helps explain why some estimates indicate that Syria deploys 70% of its forces to defend the Golan and Damascus Basin, which make up only 3% of its territory.[579]

- There are several valleys, such as: Halawa, Ainel-Teeneh, Daboora, Hawa, Al-Samak, and Jalbina.

- There are several plains such as: Al-Mansoura, Ain Ziwan, Al-Aul, Kafar Alma, Faik, and Kafer Harib.

The Golan is situated between a subtropical arid zone in the south and east and the tropical wet zone prevailing from the Mediterranean nearby coast in the north. There are sharp climatic contrasts which can affect combat depending on the time of year. The average annual temperature in Al-Qunietra is 20° centigrade, but it snows in the winter and clouds, rain, and fog are common from fall to spring. The annual rain and snow fall in the Golan is estimated at around 105 billion cubic meters. Rain falls between October and May and snow between January and March. Most rain water evaporates due to the nature of land, the volcanic rocks and the little permeability of its clay composition. This affects both terrain trafficability and visibility for air and land combat.

Terrain is a far more serious issue than the impact of weather on trafficability. Movement through the Golan area is limited by Mount Hermon in the north, and by the Ruqqad and Yarmuk River wadis in the far south. In the south, it rises from below sea level at the Jordan River to 929 meters at Mount (Tel) Fares and 780 meters at the plateau at Aniam, although the southern end sometimes slopes down to heights of 350–450 meters. The central Golan has a relatively gentle slope down toward Damascus, but it rises sharply above the Sea of Galilee, Jordan River, and the surrounding land below Mount Hermon. In the space of less than 20 kilometers, it rises to 780 meters at Shaal and 1,204 meters at Mount Avital. In the north, it rises from 100 meters in Israel to peaks as high as 2,814 meters at Mount Hermon ("Mitzpe Shlagim" to Israel and "Jabal Ash-shayk" to Syria), and 890 to 950 meters on the Golan plateau at Khan Arnabah. The Golan descends sharply to the Jordan River and the Huleh Valley, and is difficult to approach through Jordan.

Movement through the Golan can occur through two main high-speed highways and a total of five main east-west routes, but each route presents problems. The terrain on the Golan is relatively smooth at the top, and armor can move through many areas in the north, but the center and south are broken up with small volcanic cones that make natural sites for defensive positions and strong points.

Syria has created a formidable series of fortified positions, fire points, mine fields, and anti-tank ditches and barriers on its side of the Golan. This would place serious limits on Israel's ability to advance down the slope of the Golan towards Damascus, but it is a Syrian attack to recover the Golan that represents a far more likely contingency.

In this contingency, Israel can also exploit terrain. It occupies the key line of volcanic peaks to the west of Quneitra, and in wartime Israeli ground forces could be deployed on the high ground on the Golan to the east of the line of volcanic mounds that defines the Golan watershed. This is the most favorable line of defense on the Golan, and Israel has created an extensive network of fire points, anti-tank obstacles, and mine fields.

Israel can exploit both defenses and terrain. In the south, the Yarmuk and Ruqqad riverbeds constitute a natural obstacle for armored combat vehicles, and even for the movement of infantry forces. Observation posts and light forces are sufficient for the defense of this sector. In the eastern Golan, a chain of hills extending from Tel Saki near Ramat Magshimim to Mt. Hermon in the north forms a reasonable defense line. The IDF positions on these hills—Tel Faris, Bashanit ridge, Mt. Shipon, Mts. Avital, Bental, and Hermonit, Mt. Odem and Mt. Hermon—make it easy to detect any Syrian military effort and to respond to it rapidly. The topography permits a Syrian breakthrough at only two points: the Tel Faris area and the Quneitra area, and the Golan gives Israel strategic depth to defend the Huleh and Jordan Valleys.

The Golan provides the IDF with excellent high ground positions for radars and observation points to observe both Israel and Syria. Israel has observation points on Mount Hermon (1,121 meters) in the northwest, on the volcanic mound at Tel Avital (1,024 meters) in the central Golan, and on Tel Faris (929 meters) in the southern Golan. These posts not only provide a relatively clear picture of Syrian military activity near Israel, the post on Mount Hermon provides surveillance of part of Lebanon.[580] The Golan is only 50 kilometers from Damascus, and Israeli sensors have a direct line of sight to downtown Damascus, as well as direct line of sight and line of sensor observation of threatening movements from Lebanon and Syria.[581] The Israeli signals and electronic intelligence sensors on the Golan are an integral part of Israel's early warning system, and provide good intelligence coverage of much of Syria and some of western Iraq.

THE GOLAN AND ISRAEL'S OVERALL SUPPLY OF WATER

The Golan is also strategically important because of its influence on Israel's water supply. Syrian sources estimate that 1.5 billion cubic meters of relatively heavy rain falls annually through the Golan. Evaporated water constitutes about 81% of the annual fall, whereas about 10% is absorbed into the land and about 9% flows on the surface and forms rivers or lakes. The water is absorbed into the Golan land, feeds the underground aquatic reservoir existing among the land strata, and thereby forms important reserves of water. The surface water, estimated at about 135 million cubic meters, eventually flows into the lakes and river beds. Most of the Golan springs are adjacent to Mt. Hermon which is known to be a huge aquatic reservoir.[582]

In spite of the fact that most rain and snow fall evaporates, the Golan has significant springs and water sources, the head waters of the Jordan River and tributaries such as Al-Wazan River and Banias River are in the Golan. The largest lake in the area is the Masada Lake that holds about 3 million cubic meters of water, and has a depth of 8–9 meters. There are 80 springs in the Golan area, with a total flow of hundreds of liters per second, but most rivers don't pass through the Golan area; they pass along the borders because of the Golan's rocky terrain and impermeable basalt stone. As a result, the water runs on the surface to the surrounding valleys. The better agricultural land lies in the south. The stony foothills of Mt. Hermon (north) with patches of woodland shrub, are a stock-raising area. About 280 square kilometers of the Golan are wood-covered land, making up almost 15% of the Golan district. The trees in Golan are short, slow growing, and highly resistant to the great climatic contrasts of the area.

Control of the Golan potentially affects a critical aspect of Israel's water supplies. Israel depends on three sources of water: The Sea of Galilee (Lake Kinneret) catchment basin, which is fed by sources in the Golan area and which is the only surface source of water, and two underground reservoirs—The Mountain Aquifer and the Coastal Aquifer.[583]

The basin of the Sea of Galilee is around 2,700 square kilometers, about 25% of which is located in Lebanon. The basin's average annual output is 610 million cubic meters, with 500 million cubic meters coming from the Jordan River and its sources, 300 cubic meters coming from the Hatsbani, Dan and Banias Rivers, and 100 cubic meters coming from streams and wadis, mostly from the Golan Heights), which drain into the Jordan and the Kinneret. Rain also falls directly on the Kinneret, and there are additional minor sources. This provides a total of 900 cubic meters. Even though over 250 million cubic meters a year evaporate in Lake Galilee, its basin supplies Israel's with about one-third of its total annual supply. It is also high quality water, usable for both drinking and agriculture.

The sources of the Jordan and the water in Lake Tiberius (Galilee) are in or near the Golan. The Banias and the Dan Rivers now flow through Israeli territory. Syria formerly controlled the sources of the Banias, however, and the sources of the Dan were right on the Israeli-Syrian border. Most of the tributary streams flowing into the Jordan and Lake Galilee (Tiberius) originate on the Golan slopes, including the Zachi, Yehudiya, Daliot and Meshushim. The Hatsbani River rises in Lebanon, which is now under Syrian control.

All of these issues also affect any Syrian-Israeli agreement on a new boundary, and the past history of border disputes leaves both sides with a case to argue. The original 1923 boundary was designed to ensure that Palestine had control over the Jordan River, although it made no effort to consider defensive issues. It gave all of Lake Tiberius and a 10-meter strip along its Eastern Shore to Palestine, and the border was 50–400 meters east of the Jordan from Lake Tiberius north to Lake Hula.[584]

The July 20, 1949 armistice line was a compromise based on the location of forces rather than the international boundary. It called for Syrian forces to withdraw east of the international boundary, and for Israeli forces not to enter the areas Syria withdrew from, which were to become a demilitarized zone. It created three separate enclaves. The first was in the far northeast between Banias and Dan, the second on the west bank of the Jordan near Lake Hula, and the third along the eastern-southeastern shores of Lake Tiberius (Galilee) extending to Al Hamma. The 1923 border only applied in the two places between these three sectors, which took up a total of 66.5 square kilometers.

This created a climate in which Israeli-Syrian clashes were almost inevitable. There were major clashes in 1951, and efforts to reach a new secret agreement in 1952–1953 failed. Israel began an active effort to win back the territory to the 1923 boundary in 1953 that continued until it recaptured the Golan on June 4, 1967. By

1966, the two countries had made a total of some 66,000 official complaints about each other to the UN. Syria still held roughly 18 of the 65.5 kilometers that differed from the international boundary when the June 1967 war began. As a result, Syria's insistence on Israeli withdrawal to the line of June 4, 1967 would mean Syria would occupy the northeastern shore of Lake Tiberius (Galilee) and along the eastern bank of the Jordan River from Lake Tiberius to the now drained area of Lake Hula.[585]

The situation affecting the shore of Lake Galilee (Tiberius) is equally complex. The agreements that France and Britain reached between 1920 and 1923 put the Galilee in Palestinian territory, but the populations of Syria and Palestine were never consulted and an independent Syria never agreed to the 1923 boundary. The fighting in 1948 left Syria in control of the eastern shore down to the water, but the Israeli-Syrian General Armistice Agreement of June 20, 1949 gave Israel nominal control of the entire Galilee and its shore. Even so, Syria never gave up control of the shore and Syrians continued to swim, boat, and fish along the shore, often leading to confrontations with Israeli patrol boats. Syria claimed in 1954 that its jurisdiction extended 250 meters into the lake, and UN efforts to broker an agreement failed. Syria still controlled a 10-meter strip along the entire northeastern shore and in part of the demilitarized zone in the south at the beginning of the 1967 war.

It is also scarcely surprising that both Israel and Syria have long sought to control these sources of water. While Israel has dominated the area since 1967, Syria made an effort in the 1960s to divert the three riverbeds to a new water carrier, and to divert the Banias to the Golan Heights and from there to the Yarmuk basin. Israel now uses virtually all of the water it has available, and does not have enough in drought years. It reduced the flow to Jordan in 1999, in spite of the peace treaty. Israel also faces problems with its other supplies of water.

The mountain aquifer is an underground reservoir, composed mainly of limestone, at the central mountain backbone of Judea and Samaria. The water produced by it is of very high quality, and is utilized for domestic consumption. However, full utilization of the mountain aquifer water has not been expanded for household use, in order not to create a dependency on it as the exclusive future water source for the population of the coastal region. Israel may have to allocate more of this water to Jordan or to the Palestinians.

The coastal aquifer is an underground reservoir extending from Mount Carmel in the north to the Gaza Strip in the south, from the shoreline in the west to the foothills in the east. There are 1,700 wells scattered throughout the coastal strip, pumping water from depths ranging from 50 to 150 meters, and providing about 450 million cubic meters per year. The quality of this groundwater is deteriorating because there are many sources of pollution. There are nearly two million residents in this region, mostly in urban centers, and many industrial zones and agricultural land cultivated intensively by modern methods. Most Israeli sewage is produced in the coastal plain, and most of the farmland irrigated with treated wastewater is located there as well. Over-pumping during the past 25 years has caused a drop in groundwater levels and penetration of seawater from the west. Thus the aquifer's western edge has become salinated to a distance of up to four kilometers from the shoreline, and many wells have had to be shut down.

THE IMPACT OF GIVING UP THE GOLAN

Israel will have to give up its settlements, military advantages, and some aspects of the security of its water supplies if it withdraws from the Golan. It will also have to accept an increase in the vulnerability of northern Israel. The Golan is within 20 kilometers of Israeli cites like Tiberias, and 60 kilometers of less difficult terrain from Haifa and Acre. The Golan would be a good observation platform for Syria, which could locate visual and signals intelligence observation posts at Mount Hermon, Tel al-Hara, Tel al-Sha'ar, and Tel al-Jalbiya. Syria could also use the Golan for artillery and missile attacks on northern Israel. Syria never repopulated its former provincial capital of Quneitra after the 1974 disengagement, but would not have to worry about Israeli fire on Syrian towns in the Golan.

This is why many Israeli military experts have opposed returning the entire Golan, and have suggested compromises such as a border that leaves Israel in possession of the cliffs over the Jordan rift valley and overlooking the Sea of Galilee, and in control of the sources of the Jordan River at Banias. Syria, in contrast, has insisted on returning to the international border of 1967, including the control of the eastern shore of the Sea of Galilee.[586]

Even if a peace agreement restricted Syrian deployments and created a demilitarized zone, the terrain might give Syrian ground forces an advantage in a "race for the Golan." Syrian armor could exploit the fact that the Syrian side of the Golan consists of relatively flat or smooth undulating terrain while the western "edge" of the Golan plateau rises in steep increments of hundreds of feet in something approaching a vertical "wall." This allows Syrian armor to descend the western edge relatively quickly, but makes it difficult for the IDF to use armor and infantry to fight its way up the "wall" to the heights.

Further, if Syria were able to achieve a breakthrough, advance into the Galilee, and then dig in, Syrian forces could prove costly to dislodge despite the fact that there are only a limited number of routes Syria could take, and any advance along these routes and into the Huleh Valley would make Syrian forces vulnerable to Israeli air attacks. Already, during the period from 1996 to 1997 Syria has threatened Israel at least 7 times by using aggressive tactics throughout the area as shown in Table 8.3. Control of the Golan could also give Syrian radar improved sensor coverage of Israel, while complicating the IAF's problems in air operations, in suppressing Syrian surface-to-air missiles, and in deploying radars to improve its air warning and control of Syrian fighter intercepts.

These complex issues affecting strategic vulnerability and relative advantage help explain why it is so difficult to reach a peace settlement, and why Israel has

Table 8.3
Syrian Moves Affecting War with Israel over the Golan: 1996–1997

- In September 1996, the 51st Brigade of the 10th division deployed from base on the outskirts of Beirut to a staging area south of Zahle in the Beka'a Valley.

- This move tightened control of the Beirut-Damascus road and places the unit under the cover of Syrian land-based air defense missiles.

- Some 10,000 men in 14th Special Forces Division moved from the Beirut area into the Golan area.

- Unit is now near the foothills of Mt. Hermon.

- Three-four Syrian divisions in forward positions near Golan improved in readiness in late 1996 and 1997.

- In May 1997, Syria moved tanks and BMPs out of the Beka'a back into Syria through the Masna border crossing.

- Forces are believed to have gone to strengthen positions along Syria's border with Turkey.

- Maneuvers in June 1997 in the area enhanced Syrian capability for a sudden or surprise attack capability.

- On June 2, 1997, Syria opens border with Iraq for the first time since 1982.

- Lt. General Amnon Shahak warns that Syria is "talking about a surprise attack" in July 1997.

previously insisted on maintaining Israeli-manned observation posts on the Golan. It also explains why any contingency analysis of a conflict on the Golan is highly dependent on whether a Syrian attack takes place before a peace settlement, or after Syrian recovery of the Golan.

WAR FIGHTING ON THE GOLAN

Israel and Syria fought major wars over the Golan in 1967 and 1973. The October War, in particular, showed that the balance of forces that each side could bring to bear in the critical 24-hour period before the attack began and after it commenced is a critical factor in assessing the Israeli-Syrian balance. Israel miscalculated the compromises it could make in reducing the size and readiness of its reserve forces between 1970 and 1973. As a result, Syria successfully launched a surprise attack with 1,400 tanks and 28,000 other weapons and vehicles against unprepared Israeli forces on the Golan, and thrust 15 kilometers into Israeli territory.

It has been over 20 years since the IDF faced the kind of challenge that forced it to fully mobilize under true wartime conditions and test its system *in extremis*—a "learning experience" that military history shows is inevitably more demanding than even the best peacetime exercises and training. Much has changed since 1973, however, and any new war would have a very different character.

Mobilization, Surprise, and Mass

Israel's main challenge in defending the Golan is providing sufficient mobility and killing capability over the entire battlefield. Israel must be able to commit the IDF and Israeli Air Force in ways which react to initial warning indicators on a near "hair trigger" basis to prevent significant initial Syrian gains. Much of the Syrian Army is forward deployed and could rapidly mobilize and attack across the Golan with roughly 6 armored division equivalents. This attack could potentially be supported by a thrust through Jordan and/or Lebanon, although such a thrust is now politically unlikely.

Israel has greatly improved its defenses and fortifications on the Golan, and Syria cannot prevent Israel from retaliating with powerful air strike capabilities. Even so, the IDF can only halt an all-out Syrian surprise attack with minimal casualties if it has time to redeploy its active forces and mobilize its reserves. The IDF needs at least 24 hours of strategic warning of a Syrian attack to mobilize and man its forward defenses. It needs 36 to 48 hours of reaction time to complete its plans.

This makes the success of any Syrian attack highly dependent upon whether Syria can attack with enough surprise or speed to prevent Israel from mobilizing before Syria creates new facts on the ground, such as seizing back the Golan or even penetrating into the Galilee and then using diplomatic pressure to reach a cease-fire. If Syria could attack before Israel fully mobilized and deployed, such an attack might make serious initial gains, and Syria might then be able to hold the territory it seized, dig in, and try to obtain a political settlement.

As Table 8.3 shows, Syria has large forces near the Golan area, with an active strength of nearly 40,000 men. Although Syria would need sustained training and exercise activity to properly prepare its forces for a massive all-out attack, and some 48 to 72 hours of intensive mobilization and redeployment activity to properly support and sustain such an attack, it might still take the risk of attacking with the forces on hand and supporting them with follow-on echelons. Under these conditions, Syria could use its existing forces to attack with minimal warning and amass large amounts of artillery to support its armored advance.

The Syrian I Corps, which is headquartered in Damascus, has the 5th and 7th Mechanized Divisions in the Golan area, the 9th Armored Division in support, the 1st Armored Division northeast of Qatana, and the 569th Armored Division and a Republican Guards Division near Damascus. Three more armored divisions—the 11th, 17th, and 18th—are located in the general area between Homs and Hama.[587]

Syria could put simultaneous pressure on Israel by attacking across the Lebanese border with the 30,000 men it stations in the Beka'a, or using the men in the Hizbollah.[588] Syria does have at least two high-quality heavy divisions and three Special Forces regiments that performed well in 1982, and could bring two

other heavy divisions to bear in support. It could reinforce such units relatively
rapidly, although the readiness and training of many of these Syrian reinforcements would be limited. Virtually all heavy units in the Syrian army now suffer
from a sustained lack of spare parts and outside support, a result of Syria's lack of
funds and the break-up of the Soviet Union.

Syria would face other mobilization, deployment, and sustainability problems.
The Israeli-Syrian disengagement agreement signed on May 31, 1974 limits the
forces Israel and Syria can deploy in the Golan area. There is a 3–6 kilometer-wide
disengagement zone where no forces are permitted, except for a UN disengagement observer force (UNDOF) of about 1,000 men assisted by some 80 military
observers of the United Nations Truce Supervision Organization (UNTSO)
Observer Group Golan. This force has been in place since May 31, 1974, and has
manning from Austria, Canada, Japan, Poland, and the Slovak Republic, and has a
budget of roughly $33.7 million a year.[589]

Israeli and Syrian forces are then separated by a 10-kilometer-wide force
limitation zone where each side can deploy a maximum of 6,000 soldiers, 75 tanks,
and 36 short-range howitzers (122-mm equivalent). There is a third 10-kilometer-
wide force limitation zone where both sides are limited to 450 tanks and 162
artillery weapons with a range not exceeding 20 kilometers. Finally, each side is
forbidden to deploy surface-to-air missiles closer than 25 kilometers from the
disengagement zone.

Expanding the Depth of the Golan Battlefield

A "race for the Golan" would still be a high-risk strategy for Syria even if it
could achieve a substantial degree of surprise. The IDF completely reorganized its
defenses on the Golan after 1973, and it has progressively improved these defenses
ever since. Although the May 31, 1974 separation of forces agreement between
Israel and Syria cost Israel about 600 square kilometers of territory on the Golan,
particularly control over the dominant Bahta ridge line in the south and Rafid
junction, Israel is also aided by the fact it no longer is forced to split its forces to
defend against both Egypt and Syria.

It is also unclear how much surprise Syria could achieve, even if it practiced
substantial deception and attacked during a supposed training exercise. The IDF
has deployed a wide range of all-weather sensors, and can detect virtually any
major Syrian movement in time to mobilize and react—although such indicators
can never assure that the IDF makes the right assessment of Syrian moves, or
whether its political leaders choose to react. Israeli coverage of Syria includes
advanced airborne radar reconnaissance that extends north of Damascus from
positions in Israeli air space, coverage from advanced UAVs which include
electronic intelligence (ELINT) as well as imagery systems, airborne ELINT
coverage capable of characterizing and precisely locating any Syrian electronic
emitter including radars, and land-based sensors in the Golan and on Mt. Hermon.

The IDF has built up major strong points in the Golan, specially tailored heavy armored brigades designed to blunt any initial attack, and improved its mining and artillery capabilities in the Golan. It has significantly improved its ability to rapidly reinforce its forward-deployed forces, and to provide artillery and rocket support. It has developed much stronger attack helicopter forces, and fixed-wing air attack capabilities that can attack Syrian armor with considerable precision and lethality even at night or in relatively poor weather. Israel has also improved its real and near real time long-range surveillance and battle management capabilities.

The IDF now shows much less interest in meeting engagements between massed armored forces, and preserving the option to drive forward into Syrian territory. Armored wars of maneuver and the counteroffense are still an option, but defense in depth offers higher attrition of Syrian forces with fewer Israeli casualties. Defense in depth also allows Israel to decide whether to counterattack, rather than rely on such attacks and to vary its mix of armor, artillery, close air support, and air interdiction to strike deep into Syria while defending forward.

The IAF has learned from its mistakes and successes in the 1973 and 1982 wars, and from the Gulf War. It has steadily improved its coordination with the land forces in combined operations. It can do a much better job of coordinating the air-land battle in both tactical operations and at the strategic level. Its C^{4}I and battle management systems may lack all the sophisticated technology and techniques used by US forces, but they are tailored to a unique area and set of missions and allow given assets to be used with great effectiveness. At least some Israeli planners have argued since 1973—reinforced by Israel's experience in 1982—that Israel must either fight very limited military actions or strategically decisive ones.

The approaches to the Golan force Syria to channel its armor in any major offensive and it has little ability to provide effective air defense or even prevent the IAF from making intensive air-to-ground strikes deep into the battlefield without waiting to win an air battle for air supremacy. Israel not only has advanced anti-tank weapons and attack helicopters, it can now use rockets and submunitions to kill advancing armor in large numbers at ranges well over 60–80 kilometers. Night and poor weather would no longer be Syria's friend. Israel has superior night warfare capability, and warning and intelligence assets that can function in virtually any weather. The confusion factor Syria would face in operating under such conditions would, on the other hand, slow Syrian movement and allow Israel to inflict more attrition during an advance.

The IAF does, however, face certain basic operational constraints in using such a defense. The IAF alone cannot destroy all of the land forces of a major enemy like Syria within a short period, although it might be decisive in cooperation with the IDF in an air-land offensive. It can contribute to the land battle, but Syria's forces near the Golan are too close to the border and too large for any combination of interdiction bombing and close air support to act as a substitute for effective defensive action by the IDF's land forces.

There also are limits to Israel's ability to exploit some of its technical capabilities at lower thresholds of conflict. If the IAF is to minimize its losses and inflict maximum damage on Syria, it must achieve a high degree of technological surprise in air defense suppression—either through preemption or deception. As Israel learned in 1982, it does not make sense to reveal its air defense suppression capabilities in limited attacks with limited objectives, and give an enemy time to improve its own defense and develop countermeasures.

Israeli "Soft Strike" Capabilities in Strategic Bombing

Israel also could escalate to targets outside the Golan. Any major Syrian success in an attack on the Golan would involve the risk of Israeli strategic retaliation using conventional forces. Israel currently has so large a qualitative "edge" in air, precision attack, and electronic warfare capabilities that it could probably win air superiority in a matter of hours and break through part of Syria's land-based air defenses in a day. Israel could then strike high value targets in Syria with relative impunity in a conventional war—and Syria would only be able to launch limited numbers of air and missile attacks in retaliation.

Since 1973, the IDF has organized its targeting, battle management, and strike plans for both conventional and nuclear strategic strikes on key potential enemies. Israel gives high priority to destroying and suppressing the enemy's air and land-based air defense capability during the initial stages of the battle. The potential scale of Israel's success in suppressing Syrian air defenses in a future battle over the Golan is indicated by the fact that during the 1982 war, Israel essentially broke the back of the Syrian surface-to-air missile network in the Beka'a Valley in one day, on June 9. Israel shot down over 80 Syrian fighters, and only lost one A-4 in flying a total of over 1,000 combat sorties—including the sorties delivered against Syrian ground-based air defenses in the Beka'a. Israel also was able to devote an extraordinary percentage of its total sorties to the attack mission, although it should be noted that even in the 1973 war, some 75% of all IAF sorties were attack sorties.[590]

Israel has sufficient long-range precision munitions, land-based missile and rocket systems, and UAVs to then use conventional weapons to cripple the power, water, refining, key communications and command centers, and critical industrial facilities of either or both confrontation states before the US or outside powers could intervene. If Israel was to launch such attacks on a surprise or preemptive basis, or do so before Syrian and/or Jordanian air forces were fully alert and dispersed, it would achieve nearly certain success. It would have a very high probability of success even against fully alert Syrian and Jordanian forces.

Such strategic attacks would, however, risk Syrian escalation to biological and chemical weapons. They might require a level of Israeli strategic commitment to achieving rapid strategic success that could force Israel to escalate to weapons of mass destruction if conventional IAF attacks failed. Further, they would involve sudden unilateral Israel military action under conditions where Israel must expect US and outside pressure to limit such military action. On the one hand, the IAF would have to operate under political conditions that deter large-scale action. On the other hand, the IAF would have to operate under military conditions that could lead it towards sudden and massive escalation.

The existence of Israeli nuclear weapons might also succeed in deterring Syrian use of biological and chemical weapons in response to conventional strategic air attacks. Furthermore, Israel might have no other way to achieve a decisive victory over Syria. It is unclear that any land victory over Syria would be sufficient to force Syria to accept a peace or so weaken it that it could not recover as a threat in a few years.

A New Type of War?

The IDF can be counted on to make further improvements to warning and the sensors and battle management capabilities necessary to fight intense "24-hour-a-day" battles in all-weather conditions.[591] Many of the sensors and other assets that improve Israel's warning and ability to characterize Syrian movements provide all-weather targeting capabilities that make it much more difficult for Syria to take advantage of weather and terrain masking. Israel also plans to steadily improve its air, missile, and rocket assets in ways that allow Israel to strike far deeper into the Golan battlefield, and even near Damascus. In contrast, Syria lacks matching intelligence, warning, battle management and strike capabilities. It is half-blind compared to Israel.

The use of UAVs, other sensors, smart precision munitions, and more lethal area munitions, will increasingly allow the IDF to simultaneously engage a Syrian advance at virtually every point from the forward edge of the battle to the limits of its rear areas. Long before such attacks defeated Syria through attrition, they would seriously degrade or break up the coherence of its military advance. In a number of simulations, they would create movement problems that froze substantial Syrian forces of armor and vehicles in place in the open, allowing Israeli forces to destroy them in detail without directly engaging Syrian forces in a war of maneuver.

Syrian Risk Taking

Given this background, a Syrian attack on the Golan is not a particularly attractive option for either side, particularly if there is hope for serious peace negotiations. Nevertheless, Syria might still risk war—if it felt it could achieve strategic surprise and hold a significant amount of the Golan long enough for world opinion to bring a halt to fighting and use such "shock therapy" to achieve its goals in the peace process. Syria might be reluctant to take such a risk without a superpower patron to support it diplomatically, but it might try to use the threat of escalation to chemical warfare as a substitute for outside diplomatic and military support.

Even though Syria cannot hope to penetrate much beyond the Golan, it might still launch such an attack in an effort to create new facts on the ground and at least shallow defenses and emergency fortifications. Syria might also attempt to use

such an attack to alter the outcome of peace negotiations, to respond to a failure of
the peace negotiations, or to try to exploit a peace agreement that disrupted or
weakened the IDF presence on the Golan without placing compensating limitations on Syria.

These two options are scarcely particularly desirable, and do not seem to present
a high near-term risk of war. At the same time, few wars have begun because of
careful rational calculations about risk and possible outcomes.

AN ATTACK THROUGH THE GOLAN AFTER A SYRIAN-ISRAELI PEACE SETTLEMENT

Any change in the military deployments on the Golan resulting from the peace
process could shift the balance between Israel and Syria. It is one thing to fight
from prepared positions on the Golan, and another thing to fight up the Golan
Heights against well-positioned Syrian forces which would have time in which to
create limited defensive barriers. The entire Golan is only 20–24 kilometers
wide—and the terrain limits the potential combat area to about 240 square
kilometers.[592]

These risks take on considerable importance because Israeli military intelligence warned the Israeli cabinet in January 2000 that Israel cannot count on a
warm or stable peace with Syria, and Israeli military planners claim that any
withdrawal would require a substantial investment in added Israeli military
readiness and capability to make up for the loss of the Golan.[593]

The Value of the Golan to Syria in an Attack on Israel

Syria would not have to take large amounts of territory to increase the ability of
its artillery to cover northern Israel. Syria has large numbers of FROGs, and much
of Syria's artillery and multiple rocket launchers have effective ranges of 35
kilometers or more.[594] Syria can also target accurately against fixed targets at such
ranges using UAVs. As a result, the Golan has potential military significance in
allowing Syria to use artillery to attack Israel and increasing the risk of a surprise
Syrian attack against the Galilee—although any such use of the Golan would be
targetable by Israeli sensors and vulnerable to massive retaliation by Israeli air and
artillery forces.

If Syria could succeed in advancing to the base areas it occupied on the edge of
the Heights in 1967, it would have an altitude advantage of about 120 meters over
the surface of the Sea of Galilee and about 100 meters over the heights of lower
Galilee. Such a terrain advantage has lost some of its meaning in an era of high
performance tanks, attack helicopters, attack aircraft, and artillery with beyond-
visual-range precision fire capability, but dug in forces would still present
problems for Israel and could not be dislodged without casualties.

Israeli and Syrian military planning and peace negotiations must also take
account of the fact that a Syrian attack through the Golan might also become more

feasible as a result of future weapons transfers to Syria. Syrian armor would be considerably more effective in armored battles if all of the advancing forces were equipped with modern thermal sights, fire control systems, anti-armor rounds, and armor. However, it is far from clear that any of the T-72s in Syria's inventory can currently be adapted to match the capabilities of the Merkava in these areas. A major improvement in target acquisition and fire management systems could also greatly improve the suppressive and direct fire capabilities of Syrian artillery.

Equally important, Syria might blunt some of the IAF's "edge" in the air if it could actually obtain its reported orders of 30–50 additional MiG-29s, 24–37 SU-24s, and the S-300 or S-400 surface-to-air missiles and if Israel did not react by strengthening its own forces. Deployment of an advanced heavy surface-to-air missile like the Russian S-300 or S-400 might reduce the IAF's ability to rapidly suppress Syrian air defense capabilities, and the ability of the Israeli Air Force to use attack aircraft and helicopters to halt Syrian armor—although Israel's anti-radiation missiles and stand-off precision-guided weapons would still have considerable capability in destroying and suppressing land-based air defense weapons.

Giving up the Golan also reduces the strategic threat Israeli land forces can pose to Syria, and increases the strategic risk to Israel. From a Syrian perspective, such a shift in the balance may be essential for a peace agreement or any concessions on arms control. Israel's positions on the Golan not only occupy Syria's territory, they also give Israel a major advantage in using artillery or missiles to attack Syria, in any land or helicopter assault on Syria, in providing intelligence coverage of civil and military developments from the Golan to Damascus, and in targeting Syrian forces and positions.

At the same time, it is important to note that if Israel continues to improve its long-range surveillance, targeting, and strike capabilities, many of the advantages of possessing the Golan will be sharply reduced. Even well dug-in Syrian forces are now vulnerable, in fact they are fixed targets that make it easier to plan some kinds of attacks. Syrian forces moving down the Golan would be channeled into even more concentrated killing grounds than forces moving up the Golan in the previous scenario. It would also be possible to combine direct fire weapons with indirect weapons with smart submunitions and real-time targeting and battle management. The end result could be notably unpleasant for Syria.

Some Israeli officers advocate an approach to the problems raised by withdrawing from the Golan that would turn such a withdrawal into a potential military advantage to Israel. They feel that the "revolution in military affairs" can be exploited to give the IDF relatively long-range artillery rockets filled with "smart" anti-armor submunitions and antipersonnel submunitions. These can be supplemented with hunter-killer UAVs, and a combination of satellites, UAVs, and other sensors that would both provide a reliable picture of Syrian military activities without access to points on the Golan and precision targeting and strike capabilities. In most scenarios, this killing capability could be reinforced by mobilized IDF forces with systems like the MLRS and long-range smart anti-tank killers, attack aircraft, and AH-64s.

The end result would be to turn the Golan into a "killing ground" where Syrian forces would be targeted from above, where Syrian artillery could not survive, and where any descent into the valley below the Golan would expose Syrian armor and forces to massive Israeli stand-off attacks. While such a decisive reversal of the military importance of the Golan depends on sensors and weapons the IDF does not yet have, it is at least technically possible. It also would greatly increase the value of demilitarizing the Golan, since this would force Syria to carry out massive exposed movements to prepare for any kind of attack and potentially attack down the Golan using exposed chokepoints that Israel would be able to exploit as targets.

The IAF would also face far fewer political protests and constraints in conducting an all-out strategic attack on Syria's political structure, economy, and infrastructure if Syria advanced into Israel in violation of a peace agreement than if Syria attempted to reoccupy the Golan. An IAF strategic soft strike option would be far easier to implement. Any major Syrian success would also confront the risk of Israeli escalation to the use of nuclear weapons in the tactical role, and/or risk major US intervention. If Israel no longer has anything to gain from pressing forwards toward Damascus, Syria has much to lose by pressing forward into the Galilee.

Can the Golan Stay Partially Divided?

Hafez Assad made it clear that Syria would not accept any peace settlement with Israel that did not involve the return of virtually all of the Golan as long as he was in power. Syria rigidly held to this position in its preliminary peace talks and formal negotiations with Israel in late 1999 and early 2000. It attempted to make a return to the line of June 4, 1967 the *sine qua non* for any negotiation with Israel. It did so although this line only corresponded with the international boundary that France and Great Britain agreed to in 1923 along one 15-kilometer stretch, and did not correspond to the demarcation line that Israel and Syria had agreed to in 1949. Syria also claimed that Prime Minister Rabin had offered the return of virtually all of the Golan—a position that Prime Minister Barak formally confirmed for the first time in January 2000.[595]

The Israeli public remains deeply divided on the issue, as do Israeli politicians. An Israeli poll found in March 1999 that 75% of Israelis would agree to a partial withdrawal from the Golan in order to make a deal with Syria over Lebanon and 59% would support conceding territory to Syria, but it also found that more than 60% opposed handing back all of the Golan. In contrast, Syria demanded full withdrawal to the legal 1967 boundary.[596] Public opinion polls on the issue are often in conflict, but seem to show a slow, but steady shift against giving up the Golan since late 1999. The Israeli Knesset also passed legislation over Prime Minister Barak's objection in February 2000 that required an absolute majority of Israeli voters to approve a referendum to give up the Golan (which could require approval by up to 63% of the popular vote including Israeli Arabs). The legislation also required that the Knesset approve giving up the Golan by a similar "super majority."

The tensions in Israel over the risks imposed by withdrawal from the Golan is scarcely surprising, although such a peace has many advocates, and even some of the settlers in the Golan seem resigned to the idea that the Golan will probably be ceded in a peace agreement with Syria. These settlers appear willing to leave the Golan in exchange for full peace, and demonstrated this by voting for Barak in the May 1999 elections.[597]

Those Israelis who oppose giving up the Golan argue that this would impose unacceptable security risks, and that there is no parallel between a peace settlement with Egypt and one with Syria. They argue that the Sinai demilitarization agreement had substantial security significance, with a depth of some 200–300 kilometers. This means that even if Egypt should violate the peace treaty, the IDF could immediately enter into a war of maneuver with air and surface forces and halt the Egyptians while they were still deep inside Sinai.

These Israelis argue that even if the Golan Heights were fully demilitarized when they were handed over to Syria, and Syria agreed to demilitarize an additional 40-kilometer belt within its own territory, such force limitation measures would have little security value. They argue that the Syrian army would be capable of advancing rapidly on level ground and could move at least 2–3 divisions to the front overnight, from their staging points in the Damascus area. Furthermore, they argue that Syria has developed commando units intended to occupy key junctions on the Golan Heights with the objective of delaying Israel's reserve forces, and is capable of using Scud C missiles against Israel's reserve assembly and equipment storage areas and to significantly delay access to the front by reserve forces. This might allow Syria to penetrate into the Galilee and/or fully militarize the Golan, while the IDF would then have to respond by fighting back up the Golan Heights from its bases in the Huleh and Jordan valleys, and do so in spite of decisive topographic inferiority.

They also argue that any agreement which attempts to treat Israel and Syria equally in defining the disengagement and force limitation zones could push the IDF into deploying outside of the Galilee and Samaria, creating major problems for Israel in responding to any Syrian build-up on the Golan. This leads many to argue that Israel must retain significant forces in the northern Galilee and its military camps and equipment and supply storage areas in the Jordan Valley.

Given such arguments, it is not surprising that Israeli experts argue over how much of the Golan can safely be traded for peace. Some Israelis have argued for a compromise that would only give the four key Druze villages in the Golan, and control of the volcanic peaks of Tel al-aram and Tel Abu al-Nada (which overlook Quneitra) back to Syria. This compromise would allow Israel to keep its settlements and some strategic depth. Others have argued for a staged withdrawal from the Golan that would keep positions on the Heights for a matter of years.

Some Israeli and US military experts who have analyzed and modeled such conflicts believe that a rapid withdrawal would be acceptable. They feel that Syria would need at least 12 to 24 hours of very visible movements to move up the necessary engineering equipment into the Golan, redeploy artillery batteries, move ammunition stores, redeploy forward air defense elements, and make armored units ready for combat. More probably, this process could take a matter of days. They believe there is little chance of Syria achieving surprise if there are reasonable limits on the Syrian military presence in the Golan area, and Israel takes prudent warning and surveillance measures.

They also feel that Syria would take so long to mass and move its armored forces in the forward area that it would be very vulnerable to Israeli air attack in the process, as well as attack using long-range artillery weapons with "smart" anti-armor submunitions. They believe that Syrian armor could not descend the Golan quickly in strength, and that the terrain would channel such a Syrian advance into natural killing grounds for the IDF. Further, they feel the Huleh and Jordan River valleys, and the area above them, would make excellent defensive barriers.

These analysts feel that Israel can give up most or all of the Golan and still preserve most of its sensor and advanced attack capabilities. They also feel that the IAF has the capability to do decisive strategic damage to Syria's economy using conventional weapons, and that such strategic strikes would have a far greater deterrent effect than any attempt to fight back up the Golan. It is the latter view that seems most likely to be correct, given the acute weaknesses and problems in Syria's military capabilities.

The experts who have shaped the present Israeli approach to the peace negotiations with Syria have taken this general line. They feel that Israel might be able to withdraw completely in one step if such a withdrawal was coupled with clear limits on Israeli and Syrian deployments in the area, "transparency" in terms of guaranteed warning of major movements and surveillance of preparations for a build-up in the rear, and confidence-building measures like limitations on military exercises and pre-notification of military movements.

At the same time, most of the experts involved in planning the negotiations with Syria, believe that the Golan needs to be demilitarized, and that the area immediately east of the Golan along the Quneitra-Rafid axis needs to be nearly demilitarized. Force-limitation zones need to be established in the areas east and west of the Golan. One idea is to limit Syria to two armored divisions in the area from the 1974 armistice line to the Damascus-Zanamin-Dera'a line, while Israel would be able to deploy one division in the panhandle of the Galilee. The bulk of the remaining IDF forces in the area would have to be deployed west of the Jordan River to the Safed area. These experts also argue for a US or US-led UN observer force in the Golan, an Israeli-Syrian observer Commission to monitor each side's actions, and for force limitations on the Syrian presence in the Beka'a Valley.[598]

Those who feel Israel can remain secure after giving up the Golan also warn that such a conclusion must be based on the condition that Israel attacks on strategic warning and reacts with massive and decisive force the moment Syria carries out any major deployment for attack or violation of any peace accords. The military need for an early and massive Israeli response to any major Syrian violation of a peace agreement is a critical point, and one that needs to be understood by all concerned. Israel's defense after the return of the Golan will have to be based on preemption, and the need for immediate and decisive action grows with each improvement in Syrian readiness and pre-movement preparation. Further, the time-urgent need for decisive action increases in direct proportion to how much of the Golan Israel gives up, and how many concessions it makes on warning, demilitarization and/or on force limitations.

CREATING A SECURE PEACE ON THE GOLAN

There is no way to predict whether a peace will make these security concerns an ongoing issue. The election of Ehud Barak may have created a political climate in which Syria or Israel can move forward toward peace in the near future. After the Israeli elections, Syrian President Hafez Assad indicated that he was willing to reopen talks with Israel.[599] Israeli Prime Minister Barak was even more emphatic about the need for peace, and agreed on July 22, 1999 to resume talks from the point where they broke off three years ago. Syria had demanded this condition for renewed negotiations. In mid-July, reports surfaced that Syrian Vice President Abdel-Halim Kaddam asked several Palestinian guerrilla groups to stop their armed struggle against Israel. Although the Palestinian groups denied this report and the Syrian government has not confirmed it, it still seems that Syria made a gesture to prove its willingness to reopen talks.[600] Talks then began between Israel and Syria at both the informal and formal level, and US-mediated talks took place in the US in January 2000 that produced something approaching a strawman agreement.[601]

Syria felt that Israel was not forthcoming enough, however, and new questions arose about the depth of President Hafez Assad's commitment to reaching a peace agreement. Bashar Assad's succession to power creates new uncertainties, Prime Minister Barak's coalition is divided, and the status of the proxy war in Lebanon involves a whole new set of problems now that Israel has withdrawn from Lebanese territory. Furthermore, there are serious military problems that affect the negotiations, including the nature of any disengagement and force limitation zone and whether Israel can maintain some kind of de facto observer presence on Mt. Hermon.

While much of the debate over the Golan is political and economic, the military risks to Israel increase sharply if Syria is not bound by detailed arms control agreements that:[602]

- Severely limit the number and type of military forces that Syria could deploy in the Golan.
- Allow Israel comparative freedom in building up its defenses and military forces below the Golan.

- Provide for sensor and warning systems that ensure Israel could detect any significant change in Syrian readiness and movement towards the Golan in near real time.

- Place limits on Syrian exercise activity, mobilization, and large-scale offensive training.

There are perceived threats on both sides. Syrian officers and arms control negotiators have not expressed detailed public opinions on Syria's perceptions of its military vulnerabilities and there has been little meaningful dialogue since 1996. It seems likely, however, that Syria feels threatened by the current status quo on the Golan just as the IDF feels threatened by the prospects of withdrawal.

It also seems likely that Syria has drawn its own lessons from the Gulf War, including its vulnerability to precision artillery fire, Israel's precision air attack capabilities, and Syria's lack of night and poor-weather warfare capability. In fact, the Syrian army conducted tactical maneuvers in May 1999 and was told to "remain vigilant" by an army leader.[603] If Israel feels threatened by surprise and mass, Syria may feel equally threatened by surprise and quality, and may well argue that some of the warning data and "transparency" Israel may want from a peace agreement translates into targeting data for an Israeli offensive against Syria.

The Military Aspects of the Israeli and Syrian Positions

The full details of previous Israeli and Syrian negotiations over these issues have not been made public. However, several major issues have surfaced where their relative positions seem clear, at least in terms of the positions they took during their peace talks in Shepherdstown, West Virginia in January 2000:[604]

- Israel is primarily concerned with military security, the normalization of relations with Syria, and water. Syria is primarily concerned with sovereignty and the potential impact of an agreement on Syrian political stability and a stable succession to Assad. Syria has also demanded that any agreement be at least as favorable in terms of territory, timing, and other arrangements as the Israeli accords with Egypt over the Sinai.

- Syria's most important single demand is full Israeli withdrawal and de facto or de jure annulment of the international border demarcated in 1923, and its replacement with the boundary of June 4, 1967.[605] As recently as March 1999, Syria stated that Israel would not enjoy security unless it withdrew its troops from the Golan Heights and south Lebanon.[606] Former Prime Minister Rabin unofficially indicated before his assassination that Israel was willing to fully withdraw, although he preferred withdrawal to the international boundary, and not the June 4, 1967 boundary—which would give Syria control of part of the Eastern shore of Lake Tiberius.[607] Peres and Barak were also prepared to withdraw to the international border, although they too did not reject Syria's demand to return to the 1967 border. Although Syria has generally been inflexible in demanding withdrawal to the June 4, 1967 boundary, at least one report indicated that it seemed ready to consider the international border for the first time in exchange for concessions elsewhere.[608]

- Both sides agree in broad terms to a demilitarized zone and force limitation zone that would modify the Agreement on Disengagement Between Israeli and Syrian Forces of May 31, 1973, and a no overflight of the DMZ without notification agreement. Syria argues that all security arrangements on the Golan must be "reciprocal, balanced, and equal." In practice, this meant that any disengagement and forced limitation zones must be the same on both sides. Israel argued that the relative size of the zones should be 9:1 in Israel's favor. In June 1995, Israel announced that Syria seemed to accept the idea that a settlement would have to recognize Israel's need to limit Syria's capability for sudden or surprise attack, and would accept an asymmetry that was 5:3 in Israel's favor. However, Israel and Syria remain divided over the details of any such arrangements and such issues as the presence of Israeli inspection and warning posts on the Golan, other early warning systems, demilitarized areas, troop pullbacks, weapons deployment limits and other security arrangements.

- Both sides agree that there should be no alliances with a third party of a hostile military character, or use of their territory by a hostile third party, but Syria is concerned with Israel's ties to the US and Turkey, while Israel is concerned about Syria's ties to the Arab world.

- Both parties claim to oppose terrorism, but cannot agree in substance on which this means in terms of Lebanon, Palestinian anti-peace groups, or Syria's role in the area. They also agree a peace agreement should preclude organizing, instigating, inciting, assisting, or participating in any acts of violence against the other party, and that both parties should take active measures to prevent any such action by third parties on their soil, but there is no practical agreement on how this should be implemented.

- Syria originally pressed for full Israeli withdrawal in six months while Israel pressed for a period of eight years. Syria has since asked for a complete one stage withdrawal in 18 months, while Israel pressed for a two stage withdrawal over three years and eight months—the same period Israel took to withdraw from the Sinai.[609]

- Israel pressed for Israeli warning posts on Syrian soil. Syria rejected such proposals and said that only aerial surveillance would be acceptable.

- Israel pressed for full normalization of relations after the first stage of its withdrawal—as was the case with Israel's peace treaty with Egypt—while Syria only agreed to full normalization after completed withdrawal. However, Syria seems to have accepted a compromise calling for low-level relations after the first stage of withdrawal.

- Israel is concerned with control of the ten-meter strip along the eastern shore of Lake Tiberius that is part of the international boundary, and gives it control over the entire lake. It is also concerned with the control of the eastern bank of the Jordan River and the flow of waters from the Banias River, which have an important impact on Israel's water supplies.

Force Limitation Measures and Confidence-Building Measures

While it is possible to discuss a long list of possible force limitation measures and confidence building measures that Israel and Syria might agree on to secure a peace agreement, such a discussion is moot. Israel has already developed a detailed list of options and negotiating measures, and Syria almost certainly has a list of its own.

What is clear is that such measures are necessary and that they reflect the geographic and strategic differences between the two parties. Further, it is clear that the strength of such measures will play a critical role in determining the extent to which Israel and Syria can cut military spending in the future, in reducing the incentive for preemption or a race for the Golan in a crisis, and in reducing the risk that peace on the Golan may become a political pawn in some unrelated Arab-Israeli crisis or confrontation.

Given Israeli planning to date, the key issues that are likely to emerge from the military disengagement aspects of Israeli-Syrian negotiations over the Golan are the:

- Nature of the observation points, sensors, and transparency measures.
- Character and role of an international peacekeeping or observation force.
- Role of the US in securing or monitoring a Golan agreement.
- Choice of force limitations and their ability to secure against first strikes, preemption, and races to deploy into the area.
- Future disengagement and force separation agreements, and future of the Israeli-Syrian disengagement agreement signed on May 31, 1974, which establishes the present force limitation and disengagement zones.
- Limitations on exercises, redeployments, and other potentially threatening activities and related "transparency" measures.
- Joint military bodies and liaison groups, direct communications, and other measures designed to increase transparency and mutual confidence.
- Changes in military doctrine and technology designed to reduce the risk of attacks across the Golan.
- Security of the eastern shore of Lake Tiberius and the entire lake. Control of the eastern bank of the Jordan River and the flow of waters from the Banias River, which have an important impact on Israel's water supplies.

Observation Points, Sensors, and Transparency

The transparency of any security regime will be critical, particularly to Israel. This has led many Israelis to argue that full withdrawal from the Golan would only be acceptable if Syria accepted Israeli observation posts on the Golan, and/or if the IDF was given major advances in weapons technology and new targeting and surveillance systems like the J-8 JSTARS. They feel that airborne platforms are not an adequate substitute for the permanent, line-of-sight and SIGINT collection centers necessary to analyze Syrian VHF communications, or to ensure reliable all-weather, day and night coverage. They believe that any international monitoring group might be infiltrated, deceived, or pressured to withdraw or limit its activities and that Syria might then wait some time to attack to restore an element of surprise.

There is some justification in these views. Virtually without exception, the proponents of airborne surveillance have made claims about cost, capability, reliability, and endurance that have proved to be untrue. This has been particularly true of claims made for aerostats and long-endurance UAVs. While modern technology can deal with virtually any weather conditions, the Golan does present complex weather problems. Further, full "transparency" in intelligence collection and warning cannot depend on a narrow range of sensors. It requires a range of different collection assets and considerable human analysis and intervention.[610]

More broadly, it is in both Israel's and Syria's interest that this transparency be as great as possible. The risk of misunderstanding is simply too great—given the cost of reacting or not reacting on a time urgent basis, and of not reacting with large amounts of force. Prestige and sovereignty make good ideological slogans but avoiding an accidental war or de-stabilizing misunderstandings is far more important.

"Military science" is almost as uncertain an art as political science, and the fact that Israelis with years of military experience differ over such issues is a reflection of valid uncertainty and the immense importance of the technical details of the security agreements that must underpin a Syrian-Israeli peace accord. There is no wrong or right view on such issues, and no perfect agreement will ever be possible.

Some Israeli experts feel that a suitable verification regime should include satellite based systems and a US monitoring unit with tailored sensors similar to the unit in the Sinai, unattended ground sensors, and tight restrictions on exercises. Others have indicated that a small international peacekeeping force would be adequate. Some Israeli experts argue for US aid in providing satellite intelligence systems, UAVs, attack helicopters, long endurance UAVs, aerostats, and other military and sensor assets as compensation for Israeli withdrawal from the Golan. Others have raised the possibility of acquiring an aircraft-mounted long-range ground surveillance radar capability like the US Air Force J-8 (JSTARS).

Syrian views on these issues are less clear, partly because Syria has stressed sovereignty over the Golan, and has not articulated its security views in detail. It does seem likely, however, that Syria is deeply concerned with the risk that some crisis might lead Israel to move its forces to the edge of the Golan, preemptively attack Syria, or overreact to Syrian actions and warning indicators. Transparency is ultimately as important to Syria as it is to Israel.

The Role of a Peacekeeping or Observer Force and the Role of the US

The character and role of a peacekeeping or observer force on the Golan will be another important factor affecting contingency capabilities on the Golan. The United Nations Disengagement Observation Force (UNDOF) has been in the Golan for 25 years.[611] Neither Israel nor Syria has publicly indicated what kind of peacekeeping or observer force it would like to replace UNDOF, if any. However, on June 24, 1999, Syria asked Canada to keep troops along the border with Israel even if Syria and Israel sign a peace deal.[612] The major options seem to be:

- Replace the UNDOF with a US-French observer force, possibly with the same name, and with a major observation post on Mount Hermon, supported by US intelligence.
- Create a similar observer force with de facto Israeli and possibly Syrian participation.
- Retain the UNDOF.
- Strengthen the UNDOF or some new multinational force to provide a much more capable observer force.
- Strengthen the UNDOF or some new multinational force to provide both a much more capable observer force and a force strong enough to act as a "tripwire" that would make any incursions across the Golan a clear act of international aggression.
- Strengthen the UNDOF or some new multinational force to verification functions that would ensure full inspection of Israeli and Syrian activity within the disengagement and force limitation zones and verification of confidence building measures.
- Strengthen the UNDOF or some new multinational force to add a combat force strong enough to delay or resist any incursions across the Golan.
- Formalize the US-Israeli strategic alliance to provide formal security guarantees and/or deploy US forces to guarantee the border.
- Any of these options could include de jure or de facto Israeli and Syrian elements or liaison teams to strengthen Israeli and Syrian confidence in their effectiveness.
- These options could also be supported by dedicated intelligence assets, the use of high resolution commercial satellites, and/or guaranteed intelligence reporting by the US and Russia, or some other mix of countries.
- They could also be supported by a more formal set of bilateral security guarantees or by an alliance between the US and Israel, designed to give Israel guarantees of US support after it withdraws from the Golan.

US Presence in a Peacekeeping Force

There is no easy way to evaluate the merit or risk of having the US deploy a peacekeeping and warning force on the Golan as part of UNDOF or as the core of some French-US replacement force. A US presence has a symbolic value, and access to national technical intelligence systems no other nation can match. To Israel, it offers reassurance the US would intervene in the event of a Syrian violation, something no other power can do with equal authority. To Syria, it offers a reassurance that Israel's strongest ally would pressure it to fully comply.

Syria probably did play a major role in the attack on the US Marine Corps barracks in Beirut. That was 15 years ago, however, and the fact that such a US force might be at risk is scarcely a reason not to deploy it. In fact, the obsessive concern of some analysts with the risk of American casualties is almost an insult to the Americans who have volunteered to serve in the armed forces or other hazardous duties overseas. The merit of the cause and the capability to perform the mission are more serious issues than the risk of casualties.

The UNDOF force has taken similar risks for more than 20 years, and such missions are typical of the peacekeeping missions other countries have manned for many years. Canada and Japan have already volunteered to send such forces to the

Golan. Reaching an Israeli-Syrian peace accord, and ensuring that Israel will have adequate warning is a legitimate strategic interest of the US, and one where many members of the US military would volunteer to accept the risk. This is the position endorsed by former Secretary of Defense William Perry and it seems to be correct.

At the same time, much will depend on exactly what type of US force is asked to perform a given function under a given peace agreement. For example, the US could perform missions as diverse as manning observer and sensor posts on the Golan as a substitute for Israeli and Syrian forces, reinforcing UNDOF, providing a US-only observer force, or heading a non-UN multinational force. All of these options might provide Israel with added confidence that such an observer force would remain in a crisis and provide full warning, and might provide Syria with confidence that it would not face the risk of Israel over-reacting or preempting.

One thing is clear: the US should strongly resist making any choices about whether to commit US personnel or forces in reaction to the arguments of hard-line Jewish Americans who attempt to use "scare tactics" in describing the risk to US forces. These arguments do not reflect legitimate concerns with military and political risks; they are simply a means of disguising the fact that they oppose the peace process and any Israeli withdrawal from the Golan. As experts like former US national security advisor, General Brent Scowcroft, have argued, the US must judge the cost-benefits of a US role in the Golan on the basis of US strategic interests.[613] Similarly, the choice of whether Israel should agree to a given peace is a choice that Israelis should make and not Jewish-Americans.

A US-Israeli Strategic Alliance

Somewhat similar issues apply to an Israeli request for a more formal alliance or set of security guarantees from the US. Such an alliance could do a number of things to underpin the peace process and formally guarantee Israel:

- US presence in a peace monitoring force.
- US aid over a period of time long enough to ensure the IDF could adjust to withdrawal from the Golan.
- Rapid US resupply of Israel in the event of a conflict.
- US support in developing effective defensive counterproliferation capabilities—such as anti-tactical ballistic missile defenses and nuclear-chemical-biological defense equipment.
- US intelligence support in key areas related to strategic and tactical warning, and real time tactical intelligence support in the event of an attack on Israel.
- US guarantees to preserve Israel's air and naval lines of communication.

As has been noted earlier, there were reports in November 1999 that Israel and the US had agreed on a new strategic relationship. This would involve joint study by a number of working groups to develop a joint memorandum of understanding (MOU) to look at the prepositioning of US forces and supplies in Israel, missile defenses, cooperation on non-conventional weapons, and how to best preserve Israel's strategic edge. It was not clear whether this meant any major changes in the existing Israeli-US Defense Policy Advisory Group and Strategic Policy Planning Group, or older bodies like the Joint Political-Military Planning Group, Joint-Security Assistance Planning Group, and Joint Economic Development Group.[614] Later discussions in February 2000 explored the idea of a US-Israeli defense pact as part of a comprehensive peace settlement.[615]

There is an equally good case for a US aid package to help Israel pay for the costs of peace, although such a package should scarcely be open-ended or offered as a blank check. In early 2000, Israel announced that it would need substantial additional US aid to cover the cost of withdrawing from the Golan and making suitable force improvements. A shopping list formulated by Israeli Chief of Staff, Lt. General Shaul Mofaz for Prime Minister Barak was then leaked to the Israeli press. The items on the list had a potential price tag of $17.4 billion over a period of five years.[616]

According to Israeli sources, this aid request was based on the thesis that Israel would have to continue to be ready to fight a two-front war with Egypt and Syria even after a comprehensive peace. The head of the Israeli Air Force, Major General Eitan Ben-Eliahu, also noted that, "The goal is not to be the best air force in the world. The goal is to ensure that our air force is good enough to stop a massive ground and missile offensive even if we are taken by surprise. . . . Being able to work around the clock, with no limitations of darkness or weather, might be an adequate solution, or compensation for withdrawing from the Golan Heights."[617]

As a result, the Israelis included a package of new weapons like the Tomahawk cruise missile, aid in developing Israeli intelligence and reconnaissance satellites, more AH-64s, and a wide range of advanced long-range air-to-ground and land-based US munitions and strike systems. It also included US aid in building new military bases. According to some reports, Israel indicated that the cost of the package could be reduced to $16.9 billion if Israel could keep some kind of monitoring presence on the Golan, even if this was a presence in an international monitoring team on Mount Hermon.[618] Some items on the Israeli list, like the cruise missile, would be a violation of the Missile Technology Control Regime and would send the message that the US was helping Israel add a whole new dimension to the regional race to acquire weapons of mass destruction. Other items represent an almost random collection of items cut out of past IDF budget requests. In broad terms, however, it does seem that Israel will need in excess of $10 billion in incremental aid to make up for withdrawal from the Golan.

On the other hand, neither Israel nor the US should have any illusions about US ability to provide Israel with a substitute for strategic self-reliance. There are severe limits on what US power projection capabilities can do during the first hours and days of an attack on Israel. The US could provide Israel with powerful

Map 8.1
The Golan

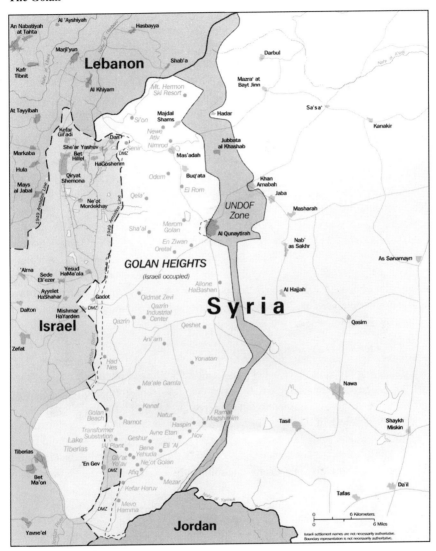

political-military support during a crisis and could play a major role in limiting any outside reinforcement of Syria. However, it would take major US heavy combat units in place in Israel for the US to play a significant role in opposing a massive Syrian advance.

There are several problems with a large US military presence in Israel. First of all, it would be expensive for the US and would potentially involve the US directly in every new crisis in the region. Second, it would probably alienate many friendly Arab states. Finally, it would almost inevitably be less efficient than an integrated mix of IDF forces, would create inevitable C⁴I/BM problems in coordinating with Israeli forces, and would raise major potential problems in terms of when such a US force should engage in battle.

Token US forces would have great value as a symbol and in providing political leverage, but they could not immediately halt a full-scale war. Even a full US heavy brigade could only delay a Syrian advance, rather than halt one. The bulk of the defensive task would still fall on the IDF, and the IDF might well end up devoting resources to trying to protect the US force. The US could not deploy additional heavy land forces into Israel in less than several weeks. A limited US air presence would compete directly with the IAF for basing space, and present serious C⁴I/BM problems. While the US could reinforce Israel relatively rapidly with air units, naval forces, and cruise missiles—this reinforcement would still not be a substitute for a strong IAF with a decisive technical edge.

There may be a case for a symbolic US combat presence if Israel should feel such symbolism was vital to the peace process, but the war fighting limits of such a US force must be kept carefully in mind. The tyranny of time and space preclude the US from providing security guarantees to Israel based on US reinforcement within the period of hours or days that would be necessary for such a force to have major contingency value. A strong IDF, supported by continued US aid, is a much more realistic alternative.

US "Extended Deterrence"

Similarly, proposals that the US provide Israel with an explicit or tacit guarantee of "extended deterrence" seem to have uncertain credibility and pose major problems in terms of implementation. It is virtually certain that Israel would massively retaliate in the event of any attack using weapons of mass destruction that threatened Israel's existence. Any such "guarantee" by the US would be far less credible and would present the problem that there is little chance the US would ever act preemptively or before it could fully characterize the nature of an attack on Israel.

Such a US guarantee would also present the problems that (a) Israel would probably have to receive massive damage before the US would act, (b) US retaliation would be uncertain in the case of ambiguous attacks on Israel or ones where the use of covert attacks made it difficult to immediately and conclusively identify the attacker, and (c) the US would be confronted with the political problems inherent in retaliating in punishment or revenge without a clear strategic objective which would undermine the credibility of US retaliation.

Including Arab States

There are political and grand strategic dangers in allying the US directly with Israel to the exclusion of Arab participants in the peace process like Egypt and

Jordan. The US has spent nearly two decades convincing friendly Arab states that US ties to Israel can be compatible with US ties to friendly Arab states. These efforts have been vital both in allowing the peace process to move forward and in serving US strategic interests outside Israel.

Any US participation in the peace process that formalizes the US-Israeli strategic relationship in ways that favor Israel at the expense of Syrian security, or favor Israel to the exclusion of proven friends like Egypt, will have a significant political and strategic price tag for both the US and Israel. As a result, any US participation in a peacekeeping force must be "neutral" to the extent that it offers Syria guarantees of strategic warning, and that the US will act as a stabilizing presence to help ensure there is no repetition of the Israeli adventurism that took place in 1982.

Similarly, any more formal US-Israeli strategic relationship must be explicitly linked to US military support only in the event of an attack on Israel or an imminent threat of attack. Serious consideration should also be given to providing similar guarantees to Egypt, Jordan, and any other participant in the peace process who demonstrates a full commitment to peace, to providing confidence building measures and regional arms control efforts, and to eliminating terrorism and violent extremism. It is in every nation's interest that a peace agreement be based on a mix of self-reliance and regional security negotiations, and not on over-exclusive strategic relationships or over-dependence on the US.

9

Wars Involving Lebanon

While the Golan is the usual focus of discussions of the Arab-Israeli military balance and future Arab-Israeli conflicts, Lebanon has long been the scene of actual fighting. Israel's sudden withdrawal from Lebanon in May 2000 may do little to change this situation, and Israel is only one of Lebanon's problems. Lebanon's destiny will also be affected by the future of any factional struggles and the role the Hizbollah plays in Lebanon's internal politics, any broader confrontations between Syria and Israel, Syria's continuing military role as an occupying power, and the ultimate success or non-success of the peace talks between Israel and Syria. At the time, fighting between Israel and Palestine that began in September 2000 shows that Lebanon could also become involved in any Second Intifada.

One key issue is whether a successful Israeli-Syrian peace agreement will lead to full Syrian withdrawal from Lebanon, or will be based on the de facto acceptance of continued Syrian occupation after Israel withdraws. Another issue is whether today's anti-Israeli forces like the Hizbollah and Amal will halt their military action against Israel—even if a broader peace is reached in the future. There is now a serious risk that Israel's clashes with the Palestinians will shift the mission of the Hizbollah from seeking to "liberate" Southern Lebanon to attacks on Israel proper.

A HISTORY OF CIVIL WAR

Whatever happens, the tragedy of war will not be new to Lebanon. Even a capsule history of recent events illustrates the depth of the problems involved.

There have been serious tensions between and within Lebanon's diverse ethnic groups since France first carved the country out of Syria in an effort to create a Christian-dominated state that would be easier to govern. It is unclear that Lebanon ever had a Maronite Christian majority, but it was clear by the late 1950s that it had more Moslems than Christians. It was also clear that there was little unity among the feuding Maronite warlords, and that the largest Muslim faction—the Shi'ites— had been denied political power and wealth.

Serious civil violence began in the late 1960s, and Beirut first divided into Christian and Moslem zones in April 1975. The first major Syrian intervention took place in June 1976, and Israel established its first occupation zone under Major Saad Haddad in March 1978. Israel invaded Lebanon in June 1982, and took Beirut in September 1982, only to have its position disintegrate after the assassination of Bashir Gemayel and Christian massacres of Palestinians in Sabra and Shatila.

These same massacres led to the deployment of an international peacekeeping force, only to see the peacemakers become part of the problem. More than sixty Americans died in the bombing of the US embassy in Beirut in April 1983. Israel signed a meaningless peace agreement with the Maronite Christian government of Lebanon on May 17, 1983, but was forced to withdraw from its positions near Beirut. Shi'ite suicide bombers killed 241 US Marines and 58 French paratroopers on October 23, 1983—leading to the evacuation of the peacekeeping mission.

In February 1984, new conflicts between the Christian and Muslim militias split the country and the Lebanese army. Syria forced the new head of the Lebanese government, Amin Gemayel to cancel the peace agreement with Israel and accept a growing Syrian influence. This same month, an anti-Israeli Shi'ite militia, the Hizbollah, made its first major public appearance. The resulting period of civil war and near chaos led Israel to withdraw to its present security zone some 15 kilometers from the border in 1985, while another Shi'ite militia, the Amal, started a 2-year campaign against the Palestinians in the refugee camps. Civil fighting and assassinations continued through February 1987, when Syrian forces were again sent to West Beirut to try to end the fighting by the militias.

A new set of problems began in early 1988, when the Lebanese parliament could not agree on a new president to replace Amin Gemayel. Gemayel appointed General Michael Aoun, the commander of the Christian part of the army, to head a military cabinet. The remaining Moslem officers largely quit the army. In March 1988, Aoun took control over many of the Christian militias, declared a naval blockade on Moslem ports, and declared a "war of liberation" to force Syrian forces to leave the country. The end result was a long series of clashes and artillery duels between the Maronite forces and those of the Moslems and Syria that resulted in over 1,000 killed and thousands more wounded.

A truce in September 1989 came after a de facto Syrian victory over Aoun. A meeting under the sponsorship of the Arab League at Taif in Saudi Arabia brought Lebanese Christians and Moslems together and led to an accord in October that sharply reduced the power of the Maronite minority. Aoun refused to accept the agreement because it left Syrian forces in Lebanon, but an agreement was reached to make Rene Muawad the new president. Muawad lasted less than a month and was assassinated in November. The Parliament then elected Elias Hrawi, only to have Aoun refuse to accept his authority.

During February-May 1990, open civil war again took place in Lebanon as militias fought to control the Christian enclave. The Vatican arranged a cease-fire in May, after Aoun was largely defeated, and the Parliament accepted the terms of the Taif Accord in August 1990. The Syrian struggle against Aoun reached its culmination in October, when Syrian planes bombed his headquarters, and he fled to the French Embassy. In November 1990, Syrian forces forced the Christian and Moslem militias to withdraw from Beirut, and Syria took de facto control of all of the country except the Israeli occupied zone in the south. Syria began to disarm the militias, and gave the now Syrian-backed Lebanese army control of Beirut in December 1990.

Most of Lebanon is now under Syrian control due to Syrian intervention in the Lebanese civil war in 1990 and the Lebanese-Syrian treaty of friendship and cooperation of 1991. This deployment was approved by the Arab League during the civil war and by the Taif Accord. Syria claims that the continued weakness of the LAF, requests by the Lebanese Government, the terms of the Lebanese-Syrian treaty of friendship and cooperation, and the failure of the Lebanese Government to implement all of the constitutional reforms in the Taif Accord force it to maintain its presence in Lebanon. The CIA estimated that Syria maintained about 25,000 troops in Lebanon based mainly in Beirut, North Lebanon, and the Beka'a Valley in 1999.[619]

Unfortunately for Lebanon, civil war was followed by a "proxy war" on Lebanon's border with Israel. After the Syrian intervention in 1990, the focus of the fighting became the small Israeli-controlled security zone in southern Lebanon, along the Israeli border. Such a security zone was first created in 1978, when Israel invaded southern Lebanon to halt Palestinian attacks on Israel in what Israel called Operation Litani. The occupation zone was expanded as part of Israel's invasion of Lebanon in 1982, and took on its present form in 1985, after Israel withdrew from most of Lebanon.

After that time, Israel maintained a limited forward troop presence in southern Lebanon but relied heavily on an Israeli-supported proxy militia called the South Lebanon Army or SLA (also known as the Army of South Lebanon or ASL). Israeli and SLA forces were deployed along a narrow stretch of territory contiguous to the Israeli-Lebanese border. This enclave was a self-declared security zone extending about 20 kilometers north to the strategic town of Jazzin.[620]

From the mid-1980s onwards, Israel and the SLA faced attacks by two Lebanese Shi'ite movements, the Hizbollah and Amal. These two forces—particularly the Hizbollah—had the support of both Iran and Syria. The result was a low-level war between Israel and its ally the South Lebanon army, and the Lebanese Shi'ites in the Hizbollah and some elements of the Amal.

This struggle was a "proxy war" in the sense that Syria used it to put diplomatic and military pressure on Israel, while Iran used it to demonstrate its support for the Lebanese Shi'ites, Muslim "legitimacy," and its opposition to Israel's very existence.

Israel's withdrawal from Lebanon in May 2000 made the future of this "proxy war" problematic, but it came at a painful political and military cost to Israel and the IDF, and the Israeli decision also did not come easily. From 1996 to 1999, Israel examined and seemingly rejected the option of ending its support of the South Lebanon Army and withdrawing from southern Lebanon. While most Israeli military leaders still supported the occupation of Lebanon during this period, rising casualties led Israeli public opinion to increasingly shift against continued involvement.

The key catalyst leading to actual withdrawal was the fact that neither the IDF nor SLA could find a way to halt the growing success of the Hizbollah in the late 1990s. As a result, Prime Minister Ehud Barak won the May 1999 Israeli elections in part because he promised to withdraw from Lebanon within a year. This helped trigger a catalytic process of collapse. In early June 1999, the Israeli-backed SLA retreated from the northern outpost of the security zone. Israeli defeats in January and February 2000 shifted public opinion further in favor of withdrawal, with or without a peace settlement. The Israeli cabinet unanimously endorsed such a withdrawal on March 5, 2000. Israel began the first steps in its withdrawal in the next month, and the knowledge that this withdrawal had become inevitable led to the collapse of the SLA in late May 2000, and forced Israel to immediately withdraw.

It is still unclear, however, how the Lebanese government, Hizbollah, and Amal, will ultimately react to this Israeli withdrawal and whether it will bring a lasting end to the fighting. Syria's long-range intentions in Lebanon also remain unclear. Some discussions of an Israeli-Syrian peace agreement assume that Syria will withdraw from Lebanon. Others assume such an agreement will restrict the Syrian military presence to the Beka'a and to positions far enough north of the Israeli border so that they would only pose a limited threat to Israel. Such an agreement would not require any adjustment in the deployment and strength of Israeli forces. Other discussions assume that a peace agreement will not place explicit limits on either Israeli or Syrian deployments to the west of the Golan. Under such conditions, the IDF would always have to deal with the risk that Syria might exploit its control of Lebanon to create a new axis of attack on Israel if a peace should fail.

Peace is anything but a certainty. It is more than possible that Syria will remain in tacit control of Lebanon with or without a peace settlement, although an Israeli-Syrian peace agreement would probably have to include some formal or informal agreement regarding the size, structure, and deployment of Syrian forces. There are now roughly 300,000 Syrian workers and soldiers, and 500,000 Palestinian "refugees" in a country with a total population of a little over 4.3 million, leaving a total native population of 3.4–3.7 million. Syria is slowly but steadily integrating Lebanon into its economy and would make major economic sacrifices if it fully withdrew.[621]

Some Israelis also feel that a continued Syrian military presence, and Syrian guarantee to support the Lebanese military in checking any action by Amal or the Hizbollah, would be preferable to an independent Lebanon. As a result Lebanon may prove to be a "sacrifice pawn" in Israel-Syrian negotiations.

Finally, the situation is complicated by the legacy of Palestinian involvement in Lebanon. There is a large population of Palestinian refugees living in camps ruled by their own lightly armed militias. The UN reports that there are approximately 367,000–370,000 Palestinian refugees located in 12 different camps in Lebanon, although the vast majority of these "Palestinians" were born in Lebanon.[622] These Palestinians lost most of their arms and military strength during Israel's invasion of Lebanon in 1982. The so-called commander of the Palestinians in Lebanon— Brigadier General Sultan Abu Alaynen is also under a sentence of death by the Lebanese government, and normally cannot leave the Rashidiyah refugee camp for fear of arrest.[623]

Nevertheless, the camps are still places where the Lebanese police and army find it difficult to operate.[624] Some experts also feel that Syria might try to use the Palestinians as a new proxy in attacks across the Lebanese-Israeli border if Israel does not return the Golan.[625] They point out that most Palestinians cannot find legal jobs in Lebanon, are disliked or hated by the Lebanese Shi'ites, and are forced to live on $50–66 dollars a month in UN aid per family. Lebanese President Emile Lahood warned of the possibility of such attacks in early 2000 if Israel did not reach an agreement with Syria to return the Golan Heights.[626] Syria and Lebanon might use them as a proxy, possibly along with the Hizbollah. They may act on their own in any Second Intifada.

Other experts feel, however, that the Lebanese government will do everything possible to resist any rearming of the Palestinians. They also feel that the Palestinians would not be willing to attack Israel unless (a) the Israeli-Palestinian peace process totally collapsed, and/or (b) a peace failed to both give them a right of return or some legal status as citizens of Lebanon, Palestine, or some other Arab state. As a result, they feel that Palestinian military action against Israel would only come in the form of small groups directly supported and controlled by Syria, and then only if Syria could no longer use the Hizbollah or some other Shi'ite group as a proxy.

THE LEBANESE MILITARY FORCES

Given this background, an assessment of Lebanon's military forces has only secondary importance. The Lebanese army and air force are perhaps the least destabilizing force in the country. It is impossible to disregard the possibility that Lebanon's regular forces might eventually become an active threat to Israel, but this seems so doubtful at the present time that it only merits limited contingency analysis. Lebanon's regular military forces are so weak, and so internal security-oriented, that they cannot currently be taken seriously as part of the Arab-Israeli balance.

Lebanese military forces total some 68,000 active men, including some 27,400 conscripts. It is unclear, however, that all of this strength is actually present in its assigned units, and Lebanese forces are lightly armed, poorly trained and organized for maneuver warfare, and lack both a meaningful air force and modern land-based air defense assets.[627] The current status of Lebanon's regular military forces is summarized in Table 9.1 and Figure 9.1. These tables show that Lebanon is making some progress towards rebuilding its national military forces. Additionally, since the Israeli pullout from Southern Lebanon, the Lebanese government has authorized deployment of a joint force of 500 army commandos and military police to join its 500 internal security personnel already in the south.[628]

Lebanon, however, must still consider its long history of civil war, and the risk of dividing its military forces if they are used for any mission that all major factions do not perceive as being in Lebanon's national interest. The past cost of this history is reflected in the irregular patterns in force development shown in Table 9.2, which covers the period from 1975 to the present. It is also reflected in the fact that no reliable data are available on Lebanese military spending during much of the 1970s and 1980s because of civil war, and the low rate of more recent military spending and arms transfers shown in Figures 9.2 through 9.4.

The Lebanese Army

The Lebanese Army is the only element of Lebanon's military forces that has any serious potential war fighting capability against a well-organized military force. It has played a steadily more important internal security role since the final battles of the civil war in October 1990. It has deployed south from Beirut and occupies Lebanese territory as far south as Sidon and Tyre, north to Tripoli, and in the Shuf Mountains. Most militias have been contained to their local territory, and most are largely disarmed. Some militias have been integrated into the Army, and most have turned over or sold their heavy weapons. Furthermore, the command structure is tightly linked to Syria (to the dismay of many Lebanese) and might deploy in support of Syria if it came under intense pressure to do so.

The army has an authorized strength of about 65,000 men. Its order of battle has 11 regular infantry brigades, a Presidential Guard Brigade, a Ranger Regiment, three Special Forces regiments, an air assault regiment, and two artillery regiments. It also has 304 tanks—with estimated 92 M-48A1 and M-48A5 tanks and 212 T-54 and T-55 tanks.

It has phased out its AMX-13 light tanks and Saladin, Ferret, and Staghound light armored reconnaissance vehicles. It does, however, have 67 AML-90 and 1,281 APCs, including the operational portion of an inventory of 1,164 M-113s, 20 Saracens, 80 VAB-VCIOs, and 37 Panhards. It has 203 towed artillery weapons—of which a little over 151 are operational, 23–25 multiple BM-11 and BM-21 rocket launchers, and over 280 mortars. It has 20 BGM-71A TOWs and an unknown number of Milan and ENTAC anti-tank guided missiles, plus large numbers of light anti-tank weapons and light air defense weapons.[629]

Table 9.1
Current Status of Lebanese Military Forces

- Lebanese army is fragmented along sectarian lines and has been largely confined to an internal security role with the support of 25,000-35,000 Syrian troops.

- Heavily influenced by Syria. Syrian military intelligence is believed to have many active agents in Lebanese forces and Lebanese military intelligence.

- Total strength of roughly 63,570.

- Army has 60,670 actives authorized, 11 infantry brigades, 1 Presidential Guard Brigade, 1 commando/ranger regiment, 5 special forces regiments, 2 artillery regiments, 1 commando regiment, and 1 air assault regiment.

- Equipment readiness and sustainability is improving, but is still poor. Standardization and spare parts situation very poor.

- Main Battle Tanks: 115 M-48A1/A5s, 212 T-54/T-55s.

- Other Armored Fighting Vehicles: 36 AMX-13s, 67 AML-90s, 22 Saladins.

- Armored Personnel Carriers: 1,164 M-113s, 81 VAB-VCIs, 81 AMX-VCIs, 12 Panhard M3/VTTs.

- Towed Artillery: 13 M-101As 105-mm, 36 M-1938s, 26 D-30 122-mm; 11 M-46s, 130-mm, 18 M-114A1s, 35 M-198s, 12 M-50s 155-mm.

- Multiple Rocket Launchers: 23 BM-21s 122-mm.

- Mortars: 158 81-mm, 111 82-mm, 108 120-mm.

- Anti-tank Weapons: ENTACs, Milans, and 20 BGM-71 TOW ATGMs, RPG-7s, M-65 89-mm rocket launchers; M-40A1 106-mm recoilless rifles.

- Air Force has some 1,700 actives. Has no real fixed wing combat capability. Limited fair-weather helicopter capability with limited survivability, firepower, and tactical skill.

- Grounded aircraft in storage include: 6 Hunters, 10 Mirage EL-3s (possibly sold to Pakistan).

- Attack Helicopters: Once included 4 SA-342s with AS-11 and AS-12 air-to-surface anti-armor missiles in inventory, evidently no longer active.

- Other Helicopters: 16 UH-1H. Operational status of 5 Bell-212, 3 SA-330, 1 SA-318, and 2 SA-342s unclear.

- Training Aircraft: Include 5 CM-170s, 3 Bulldogs.

- Transports: Once included 1 Dove, 1 Turbo-Commander 690A.

- Navy has some 1,200 personnel. Is largely ineffective except in light patrol role against smugglers and guerrillas.

- Bases at Juniye, Beirut, and Tripoli.

Table 9.1 (continued)

- Combat Ships: 5 UK-made *Attacker* in-shore patrol craft; 2 UK-made *Tracker* in-shore patrol craft; 27 armed boats.

- Amphibious: 2 Sour-class LCTs, capable of carrying 33 troops each.

- Ministry of Interior security force has 13,000 men. Includes Beirut and regional Gendarmerie and Judicial Police. Equipped with small arms, automatic weapons, and 30 Chamite APCs.

- Customs: Equipped with 2 *Tracker* and 5 *Aztec* in-shore patrol craft.

Its equipment is improving. Since the end of Lebanon's civil war in 1990, Beirut has been able to capitalize on an increasingly positive relationship with the US military. The US has either donated, or sold at minimal prices, 16 Huey helicopters, and earmarked another 16 for future delivery, comprising the entirety of Lebanon's air force. The US has furnished 80 percent of Lebanon's ground transportation, including 850 armored personnel carriers, 3,000 trucks and jeeps and 60 ambulances. The Pentagon has provided much equipment, labeled as "excess defense articles," which has included small weapons, spare parts, grenade launchers, night-vision goggles, and communications equipment to Lebanon for sums totaling nearly $30 million a year.[630] Recent reports say that US officials are planning gradual increases in military sales in Lebanon, and focusing on training and mobility so that the Lebanese Army will be able to expand into border areas now that Israel has withdrawn from its security zone.[631]

In 1997, the Lebanese army underwent a massive reorganization, integrating Muslim and Christian brigades in an attempt to end factional rivalries and bias. It did so under the direction of General Lahoud, now Lebanon's president. Units became subject to rotation to prevent any regional bias from forming and commanders within units are rotated regularly to ensure that religious prejudice does not create informal hierarchies.[632] Although these changes will not compensate for Lebanon's weaknesses in materiel or client relationship with Syria, many hope they will insulate the military from the religious tensions that plague the country.

In spite of these improvements, the army is still slowly emerging from the chaos of civil war. Lebanon may have some excellent individual officers and some good combat elements, but there are still ethnic and sectarian divisions within its forces. Its "brigades" and "regiments" are often badly undermanned. Conscripts train for only one year. Career soldiers still tend to be politicized, are generally low in quality, and receive limited training for anything other than defensive infantry combat. The Lebanese Army's seemingly impressive equipment pool is worn, often obsolescent, and much of it is inoperative.

The army is seeking to re-create itself as an independent national force and many Lebanese officers are struggling hard to maintain the army's independence. The

Figure 9.1
Lebanese Major Military Equipment in 2000

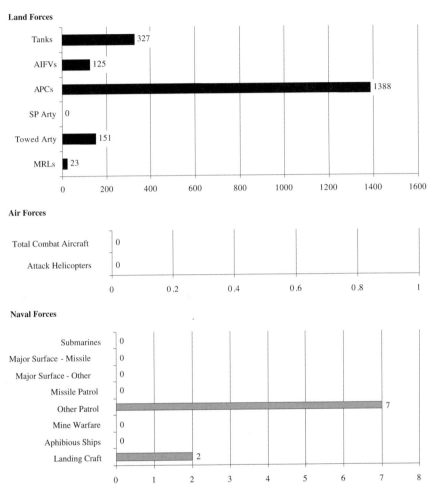

Source: Adapted by Anthony H. Cordesman from data provided by US and regional experts, and the IISS, *Military Balance*.

fact remains, however, that it still is heavily under Syrian influence, and even the best leaders cannot quickly overcome its heritage of incompetence, corruption, and ethnic divisions. It will be years before the Lebanese Army can emerge as an independent fighting force that could engage Israeli or Syrian forces in anything other than well positioned defensive combat.

Table 9.2
Force Trends in Lebanon

Category/Weapon	1975	1980	1985	1990	1995	2000	2001
Manpower							
Total Active	15,300	23,000	17,400	21,000	44,300	67,900	63,750
(Conscript)	-	-	-	-	-	(27,400)	(22,600)
Total Reserve	-	-	-	-	-	-	-
Total	-	-	17,400	21,000	44,300	67,500	63,750
Paramilitary	5,000	-	13,000	8,000	13,000	13,000	13,000
Land Forces							
Active Manpower	14,000	22,250	16,000	21,000	43,000	65,000	60,670
(Conscripts)	-	-	-	-	-	-	22,600
Reserve Manpower	-	-	-	-	-	-	-
Total Reserve &							
Active Manpower	14,000	22,250	16,000	21,000	43,000	65,000	60,670
Main Battle Tanks	60	0	50	200	300	304	327
(Fixed & in Storage)	-	-	-	-	-	-	-
AIFVs/Armored							
Cars/Lt. Tanks	43	17	150	102	175	67	125
APCs/Recce/Scouts	180	80	420	340	740	1,285	1,388
WWII Half-Tracks	0	0	0	0	0	0	0
ATGM Launchers	-	-	-	-	200	250	250
SP Artillery	0	0	0	0	0	0	0
Towed Artillery	50	28	125	111	200	151	151
MRLs	0	0	0	-	30	23	23
Mortars	-	-	200	120	280	280	377
			+	+	+	+	
SSM Launchers	0	0	0	0	0	0	0
AA Guns	-	-	-	-	-	220	220
Lt. SAM Launchers	-	-	-	-	-	-	-
Air & Air Defense Forces							
Active Manpower	1,000	500	1,100	800	800	1,700	1,700
Reserve Manpower	-	-	-	-	-	-	-
Aircraft	19						
Total							
Fighter/FGA/Recce		7	7	3	3	(16)	(16)
Fighter	6(5)	(9)	0	0	0	0	0
FGA/Fighter	0	0	0	0	0	0	0

Table 9.2 (continued)

Category/Weapon	1975	1980	1985	1990	1995	2000	2001
Air & Air Defense Forces							
FGA	13	7	7	3	3	0	0
Recce	0	0	0	0	0	0	0
Airborne Early Warning (AEW)	0	0	0	0	0	0	0
Electronic Warfare (EW)	0	0	0	0	0	0	0
Maritime Reconnaissance (MR)	0	0	0	0	0	0	0
Combat Capable Trainer	0	0	0	0	0	3	3
Tanker	0	0	0	0	0	0	0
Transport	3	2	2	2	2	2	2
Helicopters							
Attack/Armed	0	4	4	1	4	0	0
ASW/SAR	0	0	0	0	0	0	0
Transport & Other	16	17	28	15	46	16	30
Total		21	32	16	50	16	30
SAM Forces							
Batteries	0	0	0	0	0	0	0
Heavy Launchers	0	0	0	0	0	0	0
Medium Launchers	0	0	0	0	0	0	0
Naval Forces							
Active Manpower	300	250	300	-	500	1,200	1,200
Reserve Manpower	0	0	0	-	0	0	0
Total Manpower	300	250	300	-	500	1,200	1,200
Submarines	0	0	0	-	0	0	0
Destroyers/Frigates/Corvettes	0	0	0	-	0	0	0
Missile	0	0	0	-	0	0	0
Other	0	0	0	-	0	0	0
Missile Patrol	0	0	0	-	0	0	0
Coastal/Inshore Patrol	5	6	4	-	9	7	7
Mine	0	0	0	-	0	0	0
Amphibious Ships	0	0	0	-	0	0	0
Landing Craft/Light Support	1	1	1	-	2	2	2
Fixed Wing Combat Aircraft	0	0	0	-	0	0	0
MR/MPA	0	0	0	-	0	0	0
ASW/Combat Helicopter	0	0	0	-	0	0	0
Other Helicopters	0	0	0	-	0	0	0

Note: Lebanese combat aircraft shown in parentheses are in storage or are for sale.

Source: Adapted by Anthony H. Cordesman from data provided by US experts, and the IISS, *Military Balance*.

Figure 9.2
Trends in Lebanese Military Spending: 1986–1997
(In Constant $US 1997 Millions)

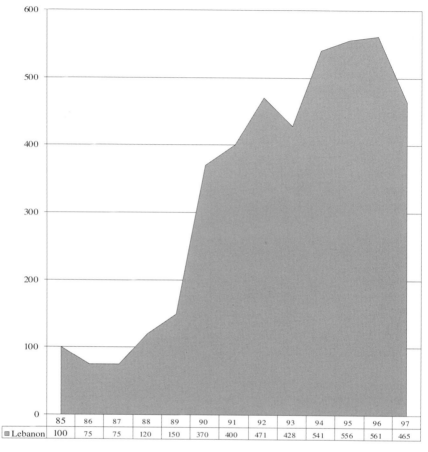

	85	86	87	88	89	90	91	92	93	94	95	96	97
Lebanon	100	75	75	120	150	370	400	471	428	541	556	561	465

Source: Adapted by Anthony H. Cordesman from US State Department, Bureau of Arms Control,
World Military Expenditures and Arms Transfers, various editions, Table I.

The Lebanese Air Force and Navy

Lebanon has no real air force or navy. Its air force has 800 men on paper, but its
real strength is much lower. It only has three worn, obsolete, low-capability Hunter
light attack aircraft and four SA-342 attack helicopters armed with obsolete short-
range AS-11 and AS-12 missiles. It has no significant surface-to-air missile
defenses. The only significant assets of the Lebanese air force are its transport
helicopters, which consist of about 16 UH-1Hs, 5 AB-212s, 3 SA-330s, and 4 SA-

Figure 9.3
Trends in Lebanese Arms Import Deliveries: 1985–1997
(In Constant $US 1997 Millions)

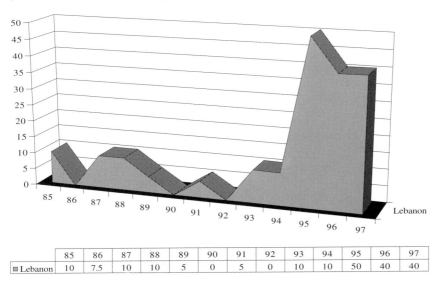

	85	86	87	88	89	90	91	92	93	94	95	96	97
▣ Lebanon	10	7.5	10	10	5	0	5	0	10	10	50	40	40

Source: Adapted by Anthony H. Cordesman from US State Department, Bureau of Arms Control, *World Military Expenditures and Arms Transfers*, 1995, Washington, GPO, 1996, Table II.

319s. A substantial number of these helicopters need major overhauls or are only semi-operational.

The Navy has 1,000 men based at Juniye, Beirut, and Tripoli. It has five worn, lightly armed Attacker-class inshore patrol craft, two Tracker-class inshore patrol craft, and around 27 other armed small craft.

It is doubtful that Syria has any near-term prospect of using regular Lebanese forces in creating a new front. Some elements might, however, support a Syrian attack through the Golan by attacking along Lebanon's 79-kilometer border with Israel, but Syria would have to be desperate to push the Lebanese forces into such an attack. Such pressure might also trigger a mutiny by the Lebanese forces and lead to the breakup of Syrian influence and the Lebanese-Syrian treaty of friendship and cooperation of 1991, the arrangements that give Syria de facto control over all but southern Lebanon.

THE SYRIAN MILITARY PRESENCE IN LEBANON

Syria is now the real military power in Lebanon. Syria's military involvement with Lebanon began in June 1976, but de facto Syrian military occupation of

Figure 9.4
Lebanese Arms Agreements and Deliveries By Major Supplier: 1996–1999
(In $US Current Millions)

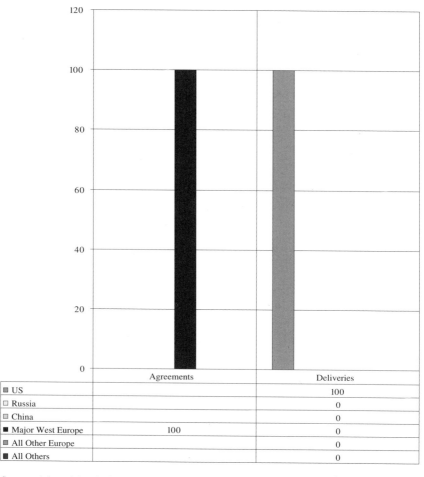

	Agreements	Deliveries
▣ US		100
☐ Russia		0
☐ China		0
■ Major West Europe	100	0
▨ All Other Europe		0
■ All Others		0

Source: Adapted by Anthony H. Cordesman from Richard F. Grimmett, "Conventional Arms Transfers to Developing Nations, 1992–1999," Washington, Congressional Research Service, RL30640, August 18, 2000.

Lebanon north of the Litani River was formalized with the Saudi-brokered Taif accord in 1989, which acknowledged legitimate Syrian interests in the country and provided a role for Syrian troops. In May 1991, Syria and Lebanon signed a Treaty of Brotherhood, Co-operation, and Co-ordination.[633]

Syria decisively defeated the Maronite forces under General Aoun in October 1990, and was able to disarm Lebanon's militias or bring them under tight Syrian control. Most of Lebanon's former warlords are now partially financed by Syria or are partially under Syrian control. Syria demonstrated its power in Lebanon in October 1995 by unilaterally forcing Rafiq Hariri, then Prime Minister of Lebanon, and Nabih Berri, the speaker of the Lebanese parliament, to amend the constitution to allow the term of office of Lebanon's pro-Syrian president—Elias Hrawi—to be extended by three years.[634]

Syria and Lebanon cooperate closely in public, but neither side shows much affection for the other in private. Syria keeps a tight, if low profile, rein on the Lebanese military and the actions of Lebanese militias and paramilitary groups. Senior Lebanese officials make it clear that they want Syria to leave. Syrians make it clear that they see Lebanon's very existence as a colonial artifact of French imperialism. Some Syrian officials make it clear that they feel that Lebanon is incapable of independence without civil violence, and Syrian contempt for Lebanon is not always kept under tight control. Syria's vice president, Abdel-Karim Khaddam, once summarized Syrian attitudes towards Lebanon with unusual frankness.[635]

. . . the Lebanese don't want to work, they want a luxurious standard of living, they send their children to private schools, import maids and labor, evade taxes and duties, and then stand up and say the government is responsible for the budget deficit and the rise in the cost of living.

Syrian Forces in Lebanon and Possible Creation of a Second Front against Israel

If the fighting should resume along the Israeli border, or the Hizbollah and Lebanese Palestinians become involved in a Second Inifada, Syria is much more likely to continue its proxy war than to launch an attack on Israel, unless Israel escalates the border war to the point of major attacks on Syrian forces or targets. Syrian intelligence and security forces operate throughout most of Lebanon. Syria has strong military forces in Beirut, just south of Beirut, in Northern Lebanon, and in the Beka'a Valley. Some estimates put the total as high as 35,000 men, but the real world manning of combat-capable Syrian forces seems to be substantially lower than 30,000 men.[636] The most likely figure is 20,000 to 25,000, and much of the Syrian military presence in Lebanon is now involved in control of Lebanon, black market operations, and/or quasi-commercial activity.

The unclassified data available on Syria's force structure in Lebanon are now dated. The IISS estimates a total of 22,000 men. It reports that elements of one mechanized infantry brigade and five special forces regiments are deployed in the Beirut area; elements of one mechanized infantry brigade are deployed in the Metn area; and a mechanized infantry division headquarters and elements of one armored and two mechanized brigades are deployed in the Beka'a Valley. One special forces regiment is deployed near Tripoli, another near Batrum, and two near Kpar Fallus.[637]

At one time, Syrian forces included the headquarters of the II Corps at Shtawrah, a mechanized division headquarters, and the 62nd and 85th Mechanized Brigades. It had elements of the 51st Armored Brigade, and special forces division with four special forces regiments in the area around Beirut (including the 55th, 54th, 46th, and 35th regiments). Syria had the 44th Special Forces regiment near Shikka, the 53rd Special Forces regiment south of Halba and east of Tripoli, and the 804th and 41st Special Forces Regiments east of Juniyah. It had the 18th Mechanized Brigade in the Beka'a, and the 556th Special Forces Brigade north of Rashayya. All of these forces were kept north of the 1976 "red line" that Israel and Syria agreed to in 1976, and which runs from Sidon to Jazzin through Rashayya. Syria also has the 13th Rocket Artillery brigade, and two artillery regiments. All of the Syrian forces near the coast are north of Ad Damur.[638]

Some elements of these forces seem to have been withdrawn to Syria. Some may have been moved closer to the Turkish border with Syria before Syria agreed to cease supporting Turkish Kurdish insurgents in 1999, and forced their leader to leave Syria. Most of the Syrian forces remaining in Lebanon seem to be concentrated in the Beka'a. Syria has established and retained a large military infrastructure in Lebanon, although this structure is largely defensive and is not designed to supply and sustain heavy forces in a major attack on Israel.

Syrian forces in Lebanon could still, however, drive towards Tyre and Sidon with little warning and create a new source of military pressure on Israel's northern border. Syria also could deploy three more divisions into the Beka'a on relatively short notice, although it would take about 48 hours simply to move such units and about 96 hours to deploy them for any kind of attack. Even then, it would take substantially longer to assemble all combat elements in a properly organized attack-ready and sustainable position, and Syria would have to divert assets from forces it might use in attacking the Golan.[639]

Such a Syrian movement towards the Lebanese border with Israel might help divert Israeli forces from concentrating on a Syrian attack across the Golan, but a sudden Syrian deployment would risk massive, early losses to Israeli air power. Syria would not be able to deploy fully integrated heavy surface-to-air missile defenses in less than two to six weeks, and Israeli targeting capabilities and long-range strike assets have improved strikingly since 1982.

An Israeli army counterstrike would probably be very effective if Syrian forces should make a serious attempt to cross the Israeli border. The result of such a Syrian attack might delay or limit the scale of an Israeli victory on the Golan, but would be unlikely to have any success unless Syria could achieve a massive degree of strategic surprise and Israel failed to mobilize and deploy in response to the attack. The Syrian Army is also generally slow-moving and has rarely shown much initiative in major force movements. It would take weeks of concerted buildup and training effort for Syria to create a sustainable, integrated attack capability. Even then, Syrian forces would have to attack through relatively narrow corridors and across rough and easily defensible terrain without adequate air support and air defense capability.

The risk of some Syrian thrust at Israel through Lebanon cannot be totally disregarded, but it would take fundamental changes in the nature of the Syrian presence in Lebanon for Syria to be able to put serious pressure on the IDF. This situation could change over time, however, if Lebanon came under even more direct Syrian control, if Syria could build up a modern land-based air defense system in the region, and if Syria gradually built up a mix of Syrian and Lebanese forces and infrastructure designed to support such an attack. Syria might also be able to use Lebanese forces to create the infrastructure and support capabilities needed to sustain a Syrian attack. Even the effort to make these changes would complicate Israel's defensive tasks and there is at least some possibility that Syria might try to pursue this option as an alternative to demilitarization of the Golan.

THE HIZBOLLAH AND THE PROXY WAR IN LEBANON

The future of the Hizbollah and the proxy war in Lebanon raise equally important issues. The low-level proxy war between Syria and Israel lasted more than 15 years, and the main proxies have included the Syrian-Iranian–backed Hizbollah and Islamic Jihad, and the Israeli-backed South Lebanese Army (SLA).[640] While Iran is sometimes given sole blame for foreign support of the Hizbollah, the flow of Iranian money and arms was only part of the story. Any movement of Iranian and Revolutionary Guard personnel into and out of Lebanon only occurred with Syrian permission. In early 2000, the Iranian training and support effort probably involved less than 100–150 people, and Syrians and pro-Syrian Lebanese played a much more active role in supporting the Hizbollah and Islamic Jihad. Furthermore, much of the financial support of the Hizbollah has come through Syrian front groups and from independent donors in Europe, the US, and the rest of the Arab world. At least some arms and training are provided directly by Syria.[641]

It is also important to note that this proxy war involved many human tragedies. While the fighting in the proxy war in Lebanon generally remained at low levels during 1985–2000, it often flared into serious clashes and it had serious cumulative consequences. Lebanese sources claim as many as 20,000 Lebanese have been killed by Israelis since 1978, including Hizbollah and other Shi'ite forces. However, these figures include the claim that over 17,000 Lebanese and Palestinians died in the 1982 invasion. There is no way to determine the accuracy of such figures or to determine how many Lebanese have died in southern Lebanon as a result of the IDF/SLA campaign against the Hizbollah.[642]

What is clear is that the civilians on both sides suffered, and more was involved than body counts. Only about 100,000 of the roughly 250,000 former residents of southern Lebanon remained in the area at the time of the Israeli withdrawal, and economic development south of the Litani has been crippled. More broadly, the recurrent Israeli raids deep into Lebanon had a continuing impact on foreign investment and tourism and weakened Lebanon's recovery from its civil war.[643] At the same time, 9 Israeli civilians died in related violence between 1985 and 1999, and 248 were wounded. The need to take to shelters during rocket and mortar attacks had a major impact in terms of workdays lost in Israeli villages near the border.

Estimates of total military losses are uncertain, but they too have been significant. There have been well over 1,200 Israeli soldiers killed and wounded.[644] The ratio of Hizbollah killed to IDF killed also shifted from 5:1 during the 1980s and early 1990s to less than 2:1 in the late 1990s. An average of 20–30 IDF soldiers a year have died in recent years, and 12 were killed and 57 were wounded in 1999.[645] A total of 410 South Lebanon Army soldiers were killed, and 1,318 wounded, between 1985 and 1999. It seems likely that the Hizbollah and other guerrillas lost 700–1,200 killed and had many more wounded during this same period but no reliable figures are available.[646] It is also virtually impossible to separate Hizbollah militia casualties from those of civilian "sympathizers."

The Evolution of the Hizbollah

Much also depends on the future willingness of the Hizbollah and Amal to engage in a future conflict with Israel. The history of these movements and of their past fighting with Israelis is critical to understanding this aspect of the Arab-Israeli balance. The Hizbollah was established following Israel's invasion of Lebanon in 1982, as an organizational body for Shi'ite fundamentalists. It was formed by religious clerics, who saw the adoption of Iranian doctrine as the solution to Lebanon's political problems and who saw the use of armed force and terrorism as a legitimate means of attaining political objectives. Iran soon sent Revolutionary Guards to assist these clerics in the establishment of a revolutionary Islamic movement in Lebanon, with the understanding that this movement would participate in the 'Jihad' against Israel. These Revolutionary Guards forces were centered in the area of Ba'albek in the northern Beka'a Valley, and still aid the Hizbollah in maintaining a training apparatus throughout the Shi'ite villages in Lebanon and their surroundings, as well as in some training outside of Lebanon.

Once the IDF withdrew from most of Lebanon in 1985, the Hizbollah established storage depots for weapons, recruited more activists and fighters, and broadened its base of support through the donation of money, equipment, medical supplies, etc. Its militias spread into the Shi'ite neighborhoods in southern and western Beirut as well as into southern Lebanon.

The growth of the Hizbollah made it the natural rival of another Shi'ite militia, the Amal. This led to fighting and near defeat of the Hizbollah in the Beka'a in 1988. The Hizbollah responded by demonstrating that it could defeat the Amal in the outskirts of Beirut, and only Syrian intervention saved Amal from a much broader defeat. The Syrian intervention demonstrated that Syria could constrain the Hizbollah's freedom of action, and Syria established de facto control over the supply of Hizbollah's forces after the "Taif Agreement" in 1989. Iran and Syria negotiated an arrangement in January 1989, however, that allowed the Hizbollah to resume operations in southern Lebanon, and gave it Syrian permission to make use of active bases in the Beka'a near Ba'albek, Nabi Shit, and Jantra.

It is important to note that Amal remained popular with many Lebanese Shi'ites in the south because it was more secular and because many Shi'ites had no desire to be the victims of Israeli reprisals. A survey after Operation Grapes of Wrath, a major IDF intervention in southern Lebanon in April 1996, found that half the town of Qana—a main target of Israeli shelling—supported Amal. Much broader public opinion surveys of Lebanese Shi'ites in February 1999, found Hizbollah had far more support away from the fighting in Beirut than it did in areas near the Israeli border and SLA security zone—although this may have changed as a result of the collapse of the security zone and Israeli withdrawal.[647]

In any case, the Hizbollah dominated the attacks on the SLA and IDF from the early 1990s to the Israeli withdrawal. The Hizbollah actively attacked IDF and SLA forces, and tried to extend the conflict into Israeli territory. In contrast, the Amal (afwaj al-muqawama al-lubnaniyya or Lebanese Resistance Battalions) was more political, with a more secular and moderate political program, and seems to have competed with the Hizbollah in military operations to win political support as often as it acted with any real desire to liberate the south or to engage it in combat.

Throughout this period, the Hizbollah acted as a political organization as well as a military and paramilitary force. It described itself as a political party serving Lebanon's 1.2 million Shi'ites, with seven members in Lebanon's 128-member parliament. It also describes itself as a social and welfare organization, and it operates nine schools, three hospitals, and 13 dental clinics, helps finance the rebuilding of homes and businesses destroyed in the fighting in the south, and sometimes rebuilds roads.[648]

The fact that it is an umbrella organization of various radical Shi'ite groups and organizations has made it easier to operate at a number of levels. Hizbollah acted as a major Lebanese political party, and a large Shi'ite social and educational organization, as well as an armed force. It has its own radio and television stations and thousands of activists and members are located in the Beka'a valley, Beirut, and southern Lebanon. Its civil and religious activities are a major part of Shi'ite life in Lebanon, although they also provide a base for the recruitment of additional activists and fighters among the local Shi'ite populations.

The question the Hizbollah must decide, now that Israel has withdrawn from Lebanon, is what it will be in the future. While the Hizbollah sometimes tries to present a public image as a welfare organization and as a body seeking the liberation of Lebanon, it has made the establishment of a pan-Islamic republic headed by religious clerics a key ideological goal. Its political platform, which was published in February 1985, saw the establishment of an Islamic republic as the only type of regime that could secure justice and equality for all of Lebanon's citizens. Its literature has also supported the fight against Western imperialism and its eradication from Lebanon, and sees conflict with Israel as a central concern. Its writings and actions focused on ending the IDF presence in Lebanon, but some of its leaders and literature have called for the complete destruction of the State of Israel and the establishment of Islamic rule over Jerusalem and actively supported the ideology of a Second Intifada in September and October 2000. The Hizbollah has also supported the use of terrorism against its enemies as a legitimate weapon of the weak and oppressed against strong aggressors.[649] Ideologies change with victory, however, and much also depends on Syria and Iran.

Foreign Support for the Hizbollah

The Hizbollah receives significant support from Syria, which sees the Hizbollah as a tool it can use to indirectly challenge Israel without provoking a major Israeli military response. Syria has used the Hizbollah both as a method of punishing Israel and pushing it towards a settlement on the Golan on Syrian terms. Some argue that Syria's support of the Hizbollah was also used to help force Israel to continue to maintain a presence in southern Lebanon that justified Syria's presence in Lebanon and helped gain external Arab support.

While Iran has gotten much of the blame for the Hizbollah's operations and "terrorism," a report on Syria's role in terrorism by Dr. Reuven Ehrlich (Avi-Ran) of the International Policy Institute for Counter-Terrorism notes that:[650]

An analysis of Syria's assistance to Hizbollah indicates that the most important service that the Syrians have made and are making is their readiness to allow it to exist as an organization with a military infrastructure within the framework of the "Syrian order" in Lebanon—in complete contrast with the dismantling of the other Lebanese militias. In order to facilitate Hizbollah's ongoing military activity in Lebanon, the Syrians have refrained from disarming it in the wake of the "Taif Agreement" (1989) and have left it as the only organization that maintains an established military infrastructure.

Furthermore, at the end of the 1980s, when there was a sharp military and political conflict between Hizbollah and the Amal movement (the more pragmatic of the Shi'ite groups), the Syrians helped Hizbollah to emerge from the confrontation as the victors. After a short period in which Amal succeeded in removing Hizbollah military infrastructure from southern Lebanon (1988) and bringing about a sharp drop in Hizbollah's military activity against Israel, the Syrians and Iran mediated the "Second Damascus Agreement." This agreement enabled Hizbollah to re-establish its military infrastructure in southern Lebanon (1991) and marked its becoming the leading organization in operational military activity against Israel from Lebanon in the 1990s. Lebanese Prime Minister Rafik Hariri's attempt—following "Operation Accountability" (1993)—to send Lebanese army forces to the area south of the Litani River in order to restore control of the area to the Lebanese administration, was torpedoed by the Syrians. The Syrian regime saw, and continues to see, Hizbollah as an important tool in advancing its policy, and therefore opposes any weakening or dismantling of its operational capability.

In contrast to the Palestinian leftist organizations whose exclusive loyalty was usually given to Syria, and which were ideologically close to Syria, Hizbollah was, and remains, a problematic organization from the Syrian point of view. This is because its basic loyalty is to Iran and its ideology is in strong contrast to the Ba'athist ideology of the Syrian regime. Additionally, Hizbollah's objectives in Lebanon are not identical with the "Syrian order" currently in place there. Syria needed to bind Hizbollah to the agreed "rules of the game" vis-à-vis what is permissible and what is prohibited regarding the patterns of action against Israel, and to maintain ongoing control over its activities in order that they fit in with its policy and not harm Syrian interests. During the 1990s, these "rules of the game" were formulated, in some cases after disagreements among the parties and after Syria applied pressure to Hizbollah. Following are the characteristics of the "rules of the game" which Syria and Hizbollah formulated and remain in force until today:

- Syria has encouraged Hizbollah to maintain ongoing and continuous warfare against the IDF and SLA in the Security Zone and the Jezzine enclave. The main expressions of this warfare are: mortar, anti-tank and small arms fire at IDF and SLA positions or at IDF and SLA forces in the Security Zone or the laying of explosive charges. "Quality" operations to take over SLA outposts or infiltrate car bombs into the Security Zone are carried out less frequently.

- Syria is not directly involved in Hizbollah's daily, ongoing activity, but suffices with determining its general line. In our analysis, Syria lays down general guidelines in accordance with its interests regarding the "heating up"—or relaxation—of the situation in southern Lebanon, and takes care that there are no prominent exceptions in Hizbollah activities which could harm its interests. In contrast to the Syrians' deep involvement in the terrorist actions carried out in the 1970s and 1980s by the Palestinian groups, their involvement in Hizbollah's ongoing activity has been indirect and vague, and therefore also more difficult to prove. It seems that the Syrians are not actively involved in choosing the organization's tactical targets, and in defining the nature and timing of most Hizbollah attacks as long as these jibe with Syrian policy and do not cause the Syrians political damage or are liable to lead to a military deterioration under circumstances not to Syria's liking.

- Syria encourages Hizbollah to refrain from actions which may harm Syrian interests vis-à-vis the conflict with Israel or its relations with the US, or which may cause an uncontrollable deterioration. Thus, for example, the Syrians encourage Hizbollah to refrain from firing Katyusha rockets at Israel as part of its ongoing confrontation with the IDF in southern Lebanon within the framework of the "Grapes of Wrath" understandings as well as their basic interest in preventing a deterioration of the situation. At the same time, the Syrians do not prevent Hizbollah from placing their military infrastructure within Lebanese villages and launching attacks from within the villages, something that violates the "Grapes of Wrath" understandings.

- Syria has ensured that Hizbollah moderates, or even halts, its terror activities in southern Lebanon for short periods of time when Syrian interests so demand: This has been the case with respect to the peace process, its relations with the United States (such as when senior American officials visit Syria or the region, or during the course of important political contacts with Israel), and internal Lebanese events impacting on the "Syrian order" in Lebanon (such as the elections for the Lebanese parliament on 18 August 1996, preceded by a noticeable drop in the number and "quality" of Hizbollah attacks), or during periods such as the Gulf War, when Syria had an interest in keeping things quiet in southern Lebanon.

. . . Beyond the political sanction for Hizbollah's maintenance of a military infrastructure, and for its actions against the IDF and the SLA in southern Lebanon, there are a series of practical spheres in which Syria offers assistance to Hizbollah. Following are the primary characteristics of Syria's assistance:

- Permission for Hizbollah to locate its military-political infrastructure in the Syrian-controlled areas of Beirut and the Lebanese Beka'a Valley. Hizbollah's headquarters, training bases, arsenals, broadcast stations and other infrastructure facilities are located in areas under uncontested Syrian control—in the central Beka'a Valley (Ba'albek, Nabi Sheet, Janta, Brital) and in the Shi'ite quarters of southern Beirut. In these areas, where the authority of the Lebanese government is weak, the Syrians allow Hizbollah to maintain partially autonomous areas under its control and to fulfill various governmental functions thanks to large cash infusions that Hizbollah receives from Iran. The proximity of this infrastructure to Syrian army bases, mainly in the Beka'a, offers Hizbollah a Syrian "aerial umbrella" and provides the organization with Syrian security assistance.

- Permission for the Iranian Revolutionary Guards and other Iranian terrorist elements to operate in areas under Syrian control, and to guide and assist Hizbollah terrorism. The Syrians also allow the Iranian Revolutionary Guards—which play an important role in rendering military assistance to Hizbollah—to operate in the Ba'albek region (while this contingent once consisted of several hundred men, it currently numbers just a few dozen.)

- Syria allows Iran to supply aid to Hizbollah (including significant quantities of weapons and ammunition) through Damascus' international airport, via the Iranian-Syrian military transport channel created when the Revolutionary Guards arrived in Lebanon in 1982. Since Operation Grapes of Wrath in April 1996, dozens of Iranian flights have landed in Damascus bearing military and civilian aid for Hizbollah, allowing the organization to rehabilitate itself and strengthen its hold over southern Lebanon in the wake of Grapes of Wrath. This link has been Hizbollah's "life-line"—which, if severed, could present Hizbollah with harsh operational and logistical problems. (In fact, Hizbollah has tried to reduce this dependence on Syria; in January 1996, Turkey intercepted six truckloads of weapons, including rocket launchers, destined for Hizbollah in Lebanon. Iran also appears interested in a direct Tehran-Beirut air-link, in order to convey the weapons to Hizbollah directly and without having to go through Damascus.)

- Weapons arriving from Iran are unloaded at the airport in Damascus and shipped to Hizbollah bases in the Beka'a Valley and Beirut. The London-based Al-Hayat newspaper (02.02.97) reported that Iranian air transports do not undergo any form of inspection in Damascus and are delivered to the Revolutionary Guards in Ba'albek. Moreover, in some instances, Iranian aircraft returned with coffins—which the Syrians suspect were used to smuggle illegal equipment or Lebanese and foreign hostages from Lebanon to Iran; Syria, however, did not intervene, for fear of impairing its relations with Tehran. These transfers from Tehran to Damascus also enable Syria to supervise the flow of weapons to Hizbollah, giving the Syrians effective leverage over both Hizbollah and Iran. Syria thus serves as a lifeline for Hizbollah.

- Syria allows the unfettered passage of Hizbollah fighters and arms reinforcements from the Beka'a Valley and Beirut to the frontline in southern Lebanon. Members of Hizbollah who travel from their bases to the front in southern Lebanon are furnished with travel permits signed by senior Syrian officials. Syrian and Lebanese military checkpoints allow Hizbollah members with these permits to move freely between their rear-guard bases and the front lines.

- Existing cooperation between Hizbollah and the intelligence branches of Syria and Lebanon. This cooperation benefits all parties concerned, while directly impacting on Hizbollah military actions against the IDF and the SLA in southern Lebanon. Some of the information gathered by Syrian and Lebanese intelligence on the IDF and the SLA in the Security Zone and Jezzine area is transferred to Hizbollah and then exploited for operational needs. Over time, established forums—such as the Quadripartite Committee (to which Amal is also a partner), which periodically convenes in Ramaile, south of Beirut—have been created for consultation and intelligence exchanges.

- Syria encourages operational cooperation between Hizbollah and left-wing, pro-Syrian Palestinian organizations. Hizbollah allows these left-wing groups to deploy in territory under its control, from which they carry out attacks, sometimes in conjunction with Hizbollah. This holds particularly true for Ahmed Jibril's PFLP-GC, a group with a rich history as "terror subcontractors" in the service of Syria.

- Syria acts in the informational and political spheres to legitimize Hizbollah activity in the Lebanese, inter-Arab and international arenas. This effort aims to present Hizbollah (and the other organizations acting against Israel from Lebanon) as a legitimate "national liberation movement" and as "resisting the occupation." The Syrian-sponsored Lebanese administration also offers political and informational backing for Hizbollah—for example, cooperating with Hizbollah in the discussions of the committee monitoring the "Grapes of Wrath" understandings, sometimes even representing its positions and interests. This legitimacy is particularly vital for Hizbollah, being defined by the

United States as a "terrorist organization" in the service of Iran, and having been implicated in past kidnappings of Westerners and terrorist attacks against American and Western targets in Lebanon.

... Until recently, it appeared that the Syrians did not encourage Hizbollah to operate outside of Lebanon. However, attempted infiltrations from Syria to Lebanon by Hizbollah terrorists in the first few months of 1998 may indicate changes in Syrian policy. Our assessment is that in those exceptional cases in the past where Hizbollah did operate outside of Lebanon, its actions were coordinated with Iran and not with Syria. This, with regard to terror attacks carried out by Hizbollah in 1992–94 against the Israeli embassy and the Jewish community center in Buenos Aires, and two other attempted attacks which were thwarted in Israel: the first, in April 1996, by Hussein Makdad, a Shi'ite Hizbollah member, and the second in November 1997 by Stephen Josef Smirek, a German citizen who had converted to Islam.

US experts that have reviewed these views feel they are broadly correct. They note that the US government has tended to downplay some aspects of Syria's role in support of the Hizbollah, Amal, and terrorist operations because the US has sought the cooperation of Syria in the peace process.

At the same time, it is clear that Iran has played a major role in providing the Hizbollah with arms and training. While Syria and Iran cooperate in supporting the Hizbollah, and high level Iranian and Syrian officials meet regularly together with Hizbollah leaders, Iran's motives for supporting the Hizbollah differ somewhat from Syria's. Iranian support is more ideological. It is based on a common Shi'ite faith, ideological opposition to Israel's existence, and a historical solidarity based on the fact that a former Shah imported Lebanese Shi'ite clergy to help convert much of Persia to the Shi'ite sect in order to create a religious barrier to military pressure from Turkey.

Iran flew regular supply flights to Syria in recent years, and its support for the Hizbollah does not seem to have diminished since the election of President Khatami. Iranian, Syrian, and Hizbollah leaders continued to meet regularly through late 1999, and early 2000. The Iranian Foreign Minister, Kamal Kharrazi, stated in February 2000 that the Hizbollah had a right to attack the Israelis as they stayed in Lebanon, and there is considerable evidence that Iran shipped new weapons systems like the TOW-1A anti-tank guided missile to the Hizbollah in early 2000.[651] Iran also actively supported Hizbollah efforts to support the Palestinians in September and October 2000.

Iran seems to have provided several millions of dollars in aid to the Hizbollah each year, and the General Secretary of the Hizbollah, Hassan Nasrallah, has publicly stated that the organization receives financial and political assistance for "the legitimate struggle against Israel."[652] Claims that Iranian support equaled well over $30 million a year, however, seem to be exaggerated and the figure is based upon little more than speculation. There is little evidence that the Hizbollah has received anything approaching this level of arms or that the civil branch of the Hizbollah gets this level of Iranian support, and it is clear that the Hizbollah also gets money from a wide range of sources in Lebanon, Europe, and the US.

Iran is the main supplier of weapons and explosives to Hizbollah and has provided mortars, Sagger anti-tank rockets, mines, explosives, small arms, and munitions. It sent a large arms consignment to the Hizbollah forces in Lebanon in February/March 1992, after clashes between Israel and the Hizbollah. Since then, it does not seem to have sent large amounts of arms consignments by air, possibly because of Syrian objections to the highly visible political profile of such flights. It did, however, continue ground shipments. For example, six trucks carrying arms from Iran to Lebanon, were apprehended in Turkey in mid-January 1996.[653]

Iran continued to support the Hizbollah's training program, but the organization's militants now carry out the most basic instruction. The Guardians of the Revolution (more explicitly the training arm of the al-Quds Forces) provided higher level training in Iran. According to Israeli sources this was done mainly at the al-Quds Force training base "Imam Ali" in northern Tehran. This training included courses for officers, company commanders, commandos, and courses in communications and powered-gliders.[654]

The Size and Armament of Hizbollah

Hizbollah forces have clashed with the IDF and the South Lebanon Army ever since 1984, but the Hizbollah did not become an effective force for low intensity combat until the 1990s. The Hizbollah steadily improved its weaponry after the Syrian-Iranian-Hizbollah agreement of 1989.[655] As a result, Hizbollah attacks became steadily more intensive in the late 1980s and early 1990s. The Hizbollah fired rockets and artillery across the border with Israel, and carried out low-level attacks on Israeli civilians and attacks both inside and outside the region.

Unlike the various Palestinian paramilitary forces, the Hizbollah forces gained significant military experience and developed an effective training, intelligence, and command and control base. As a result, Hizbollah forces slowly learned how to conduct successful ambushes, and demonstrated that they could use anti-tank guided weapons to kill Israeli Merkava tanks. Israeli sources say that the Hizbollah took some of its training lessons from Israel's planning manuals and from the Pentagon's writing on the Revolution in Military Affairs, making it even harder for Israeli forces to counter its attacks.[656] In any case, Hizbollah forces were well trained by the late 1990s, and generally had years of combat experience.

In fact, many active elements had considerably more experience in guerrilla warfare than the IDF forces deployed against them. Israel estimates that the Hizbollah was responsible for 19 attacks in 1990, 52 attacks in 1991, 63 attacks in 1992, and 158 attacks in 1993. From 1992 onwards, the Hizbollah began to conduct ambushes with increasingly more successful remotely detonated bombs and explosives, some of which involved highly sophisticated devices like artificial rocks filled with explosives. In August 1993, the Hizbollah carried out its first successful large-scale ambush of IDF forces near Shifin. Many others followed. During the course of "Operation Accountability" in 1993, Hizbollah forces fired hundreds of Katyusha rockets into the Security Zone and Israeli territory. It kept up this pressure during 1994 and 1995. Hizbollah attacks killed 21 Israeli soldiers in 1994 and 22 in the first ten months of 1995.[657]

In early 2000, Hizbollah and Islamic Jihad were a mix of small full-time forces, cadres that could be called up for particular operations in given areas, and militia. While any estimates are speculative, the Hizbollah seemed to have full-time forces that total about 300–400 men, plus some 2,500–3,000 part-time soldiers or militia. The Hizbollah also had the ability to mobilize much larger numbers of less-experienced and well-trained personnel. The size and armament of these Hizbollah forces is summarized in Table 9.3.

Before the collapse of the SLA in May 2000, the Hizbollah forces were equipped with a limited number of armored fighting vehicles and artillery weapons, and with large numbers of light weapons, including AT-3, AT-4, and TOW anti-tank guided missiles, 106-mm recoilless rifles, and 81-mm and 120-mm mortars. They had SA-7 and some Stinger manportable surface-to-air missiles, and anti-aircraft guns—including some Zu-23s mounted on trucks. It is not clear how many weapons and munitions the Hizbollah captured after the collapse of the SLA, but it is clear that the SLA abandoned much of its equipment.

The Hizbollah also had 107-mm and 122-mm rockets and many experts felt they had 240-mm rockets with ranges of up to 40 kilometers. The 107-mm and 122-mm rockets gave the Hizbollah the capability to strike at Israeli towns like Metulla, Kiryat Shmona, Ma'alot, and Nahariya, before the collapse of the Israeli security zone and Israeli withdrawal. Rockets placed near the border can reach Acco, Safed, and Carmiel. If the Hizbollah do have 240-mm rockets, they can reach as far south as Haifa, Tiberius, and Katzin.

Until the SLA's collapse and Israel's withdrawal, Hizbollah forces were normally deployed in the Beka'a and in southern Lebanon in the Shi'ite areas near the zone occupied by Israel and the South Lebanon Army.[658] It is not yet clear how Hizbollah forces will redeploy as a result of the SLA's collapse and Israeli withdrawal, but it seized three IDF soldiers in the border area in October 2000, and has kept its forces active in the border area while the Lebanese Army has stayed only loosely engaged.

The Role of the Hizbollah in Military and Terrorist Actions

The Hizbollah has not always acknowledged its military and terrorist actions. It has used cover names such as "Islamic Jihad," "The Revolutionary Justice Organization," and "The Islamic Resistance."[659] It is clear, however, that Hizbollah has supported terrorism and many experts believe that the "Islamic Jihad," "The Revolutionary Justice Organization" and "The Islamic Resistance" are simply separate elements of the Hizbollah's military structure. Some experts feel that these elements have had direct support from Syria and Iran, and a few feel that Syrian and/or Iranian Revolutionary Guards intelligence officers have played at least a liaison role in their operations.

Table 9.3
Developments in Hizbollah Military Forces in Lebanon in 1998–2000

- Roughly 2,500-3,500 men, heavily dependent on part-time and irregular forces. Many are now highly experienced, often well-educated forces.

- Composed of a core of around 300 guerrillas. Has deliberately cut its force over the past years to prevent infiltration and leaks.

- Hizbollah fighters are old by comparison to Israeli fighters. Any age up to 35, usually married, often university students or professional men.

- Roughly 150 Iranian Revolutionary Guards as advisors. Heavily supplied and financed by Iran, but Syrian personnel seem to be involved in training and in coordinating with Iran. Iranian and Syrian coordination of support for military supply and possibly operations of Hizbollah seems to occur at the general officer, deputy minister level.

- Iran has flown up to three 747 cargo jets monthly to Hizbollah via Syria in an effort to upgrade their arms capabilities. Weapons include the Russian-made Sagger and Strella antitank missiles. Iran's military camps in Lebanon appear to be offering training on the more advanced systems.

- Conflicting intelligence reports estimate Iranian aid to Hizbollah to be an exaggerated $65 to $100 million a year.

- Forces carry out an average of two operations a day against the SLA and Israeli forces. Some missions involve long-range shelling while others have included sophisticated roadside bombings and commando missions involving 40 well-trained guerrillas operating as a team.

- Equipped with APCs, artillery, multiple rocket launchers, mortars, anti-tank guided missiles (including AT-3s), recoilless rifles, SA-7s, anti-aircraft guns. Captured some equipment from IDF and SLA when SLA collapsed and IDF withdrew in summer 2000.

- Guerrilla mortar strikes have improved in both accuracy and range, indicating better range-finding systems, low signature weapons, and the use of mortar boosters that enable consistent hits for 2 to 3 miles.

- New anti-tank weapons capable of burning through the armor plate of Israel's M-60 tanks.

- Acquisition of anti-tank weapons with a longer range.

- Supply of Katyusha rockets is estimated to have risen to 1,000. These include 30 Iranian-produced 240-mm rockets with a range of 40 km, according to Israeli intelligence reports. Most of the rockets are 120-mm and 127-mm variants with a maximum range of 22 km.

- Improved radio detonated roadside bombs proved effective against the Israelis. Some are disguised as large rocks. The rocks are reportedly produced in Iran.

- Hizbollah has attacked across the Israel-Lebanese border in the Shebaa Farms area since Israel withdrew from Lebanon. The Lebanese Army's presence in southern Lebanon has not disarmed or weakened the Hizbollah.

It is virtually certain that elements of the Hizbollah attacked American and Multinational Forces targets in Lebanon. These operations included the truck bombing of the American Embassy in April 1983, the attack on the US Marine Corps and French barracks in October 1983, and the bombing of the US Embassy annex in September 1984. They were probably responsible for the hijacking of TWA Flight 847 in 1985, and were certainly responsible for many kidnappings, hostage takings, and killings. They have also supported some Palestinian extremist groups such as Hamas and the Palestinian Islamic Jihad. The Hizbollah publicly admitted to training Hamas members in Lebanon in October 1997.[660]

The Hizbollah may also have operated far outside of Lebanon. It may have played a role in the bombing of the Israeli Embassy in Buenos Aires, in terrorist activity in Thailand, and in the attack on the Argentine-Israeli Mutual Association (AMIA) in Buenos Aires on July 18, 1994. The attack on the Argentine-Israeli Mutual Association was one of the bloodiest guerrilla attacks in 1994, and is a potential warning that such warfare does not have to be conducted inside the region. Hizbollah may also have carried out these attacks with Iranian assistance—although the evidence is uncertain and recent disclosures relating to the attack on the Argentine-Israeli Mutual Association have done more to implicate the Argentine military than outside groups. These uncertainties are a significant problem in assessing both the Hizbollah's commitment to terrorism, and the role Iran has played in encouraging it.[661]

Amal in Military and Terrorist Actions

Amal is not as well organized and armed as the Hizbollah, but it does have as many as 2,000 fighters, and it has often used mortars and bomb ambushes to attack Israeli and SLA forces. While it has generally been more moderate politically than the Hizbollah, its rivalry with the Hizbollah has forced it to compete in carrying out military operations. Amal came under fire for its lack of operations against Israel in the mid-1990s, and according to one source, it nearly quadrupled its operations against Israel in 1998 and 1999.[662]

The South Lebanon Army

The South Lebanese Army was a significant player in the military equation in Lebanon until its collapse during May 21–24, 2000. It was always little more than a mercenary force. It was formed in 1985 as part of the Israeli effort to broker an agreement that would allow it to end the last vestiges of its occupation of southern Lebanon. As IDF forces withdrew, Israel created a security zone placed under the command of Major General Antoine Lahad, a former senior officer in the Lebanese forces. Lahad was attempting to protect a Christian enclave in the south, centered on Marjayoun and which ranged from En Naqoura in the West to Bent Jbail in the center, and Kafr Shuba in the northeast.

Over time much of the Christian population left and much of the remaining population saw less and less future in the SLA. The South Lebanese Army was roughly 80–90% Christian when it was formed. By the time it collapsed, it was still under the direction of Israeli-paid Christian warlords, but its forces were 50–70% Shi'ite Muslim.[663] These forces no longer worked for a Christian Lebanon, or even to protect a Christian enclave. They worked for Israeli pay and privileges— including medical services, housing, education and the ability to buy goods in Israel. The SLA never represented a significant political force in Lebanese politics.

The creation of the SLA allowed the IDF to turn over much of the burden of forward defense to the SLA. The IDF had to actively man only 8 of the 43–47 strong points in South Lebanon, and it trained the SLA to operate tanks, towed artillery, and heavy mortars. This allowed the IDF to concentrate on providing air support, artillery support, and using mobile patrols to cover the most vulnerable areas.

At the time of its collapse, and for most of its existence, the South Lebanon Army had a nominal strength of 2,500 men, although some estimates put its full time active strength at a maximum of 1,400–1,800 men—many of which were Shi'ite or Druze. Its armor includes some 30 T-54 and T-55 tanks, some M-113s and BTR-50s and BTR-60s. It also had D-30 122-mm, M-46 130-mm, and M-1950 155-mm artillery weapons, and heavy mortars. It was not, however, capable of acting as an independent force, and could not function or survive without cadres of Israeli advisors and intelligence officers, military support from the IDF, and IDF funds.[664]

The collapse of the SLA began long before Israel announced it was withdrawing from Lebanon. The SLA lost any meaningful support from Christian politicians in Lebanon well before the late 1980s, and did not have support from any other ethnic faction. Its motivation became increasingly mercenary, and was heavily dependent on Israel's aura of invincibility and taking low casualties. Between 1985 and 1999, however, the cumulative number of casualties built up to 420 killed and 1,200 wounded. This is a very high casualty rate for such a small force—even when spread out over 15 years.[665]

The Hizbollah and Amal also steadily improved their performance after 1995, while the Hizbollah and Lebanese political leaders raised increasing questions about whether the members of the SLA should be punished as traitors. This led some members of the SLA to desert and others to obtain foreign passports, but many—particularly those who were Shi'ites—took steps to protect themselves by contacting Hizbollah. The end result bore a striking resemblance to the latter days of Vietnam.

By the late 1990s, the SLA became a divided organization with very high levels of pro-Hizbollah sympathizers and extremely poor internal security. While IDF officers publicly denied that the SLA provided the Hizbollah with extensive data on IDF operations, senior IDF officers made it clear that they regarded much of the

SLA as a threat to Israel rather than an ally. In spite of continuing efforts to purge the SLA by Israeli intelligence, it became steadily more difficult for Israel to conduct operations involving the SLA that were not fully reported in advance to the Hizbollah—a major factor in the Hizbollah's ability to ambush IDF and SLA forces or avoid their attacks.[666]

Things were not helped after Prime Minister Barak's election by Israel's ambiguity over how the SLA would be treated once Israel withdrew from Lebanon, and the situation became worse once it became clear that Israel would withdraw from Lebanon no later than the summer of 2000. Prime Minister Ehud Barak announced on February 27, 2000, that Israel might withdraw troops from southern Lebanon without a security arrangement or peace agreement with Syria. On April 17, 2000, Israel officially informed the United Nations it planned to withdraw from Lebanon by July. For most members of the SLA, this series of events left them no choice other than trying to flee to Israel or leave the region, to fortify ties to the Hizbollah or Amal, or to risk trial for treason. It created a situation where the IDF's goal of a neat phased withdrawal became hopeless. Few in the SLA had any incentive to be left behind or be seen as the last willing defender of Israel.[667]

The end result was that the SLA collapsed like a house of cards when the IDF began to conduct its phased withdrawal. It first collapsed in the middle of the security zone, and then collapsed throughout the entire area during May 21–24. By the 24th, Shi'ite Muslim guerrillas had reclaimed the entire Israeli-occupied zone in southern Lebanon today, and had seized many of the SLA's abandoned tanks.

While the IDF had originally planned to take six more weeks to shut down the military buffer zone, it suddenly faced total collapse. By May 23, its only remaining position was Beaufort Castle, on a bluff in Lebanon overlooking northern Israel. By May 24, it had to withdraw from Beaufort, its other small outposts in Lebanon, and bring home its remaining troops. Shortly after sunrise on May 24, the last IDF tank armored vehicles crossed the border, and the border fence was locked. Lebanese television reported that, "There is only one headline in Lebanon tonight, 'The liberation of the land.' The slinking, servile withdrawal by Israel."[668] At the same time, Hizbollah forces and a large column of civilians followed the IDF's withdrawal. There were miles-long parades of supporters, including villagers returning to the south for the first time in two decades. Villagers sacked the villa of General Lahad, and raised the Hizbollah flag over it.[669]

As for the SLA, Lebanese officials claimed that at least 620 defected, and announced that the Lebanese Army was now detaining them, and that many members of the SLA faced charges of treason. More than 3,000 members of the SLA, and their relatives, fled to Israel.[670] One soldier who fled to Israel stated, "For 25 years we worked together and we shed our blood together, and this is the respect we get in the end. . . . The Israelis did what was right for them, and we got the raw end of the deal." Another stated, "They promised us 100 percent support, they said they wouldn't leave us until United Nations troops took over our positions, but the opposite happened and they just put us on buses and brought us here. . . . We're not traitors, we were defending our land."[671]

While the IDF had planned to blow up its strong points before completing its withdrawal, as it had done when it pulled out of the village of Jezzine, in 1999, the SLA effectively vanished. In at least one case, the SLA soldiers disappeared so quickly that they left tanks with their motors running. As a result, the Hizbollah was able to forage through the IDF and SLA's deserted posts, seizing rocket launchers, ammunition, and military equipment. In some cases, Hizbollah soldiers jostled with those of Amal over who got to keep the IDF and SLA equipment. The Hizbollah was able to send a convoy of newly captured Israeli tanks and armored vehicles back to Bint Jbail, in the zone's center, and the IDF was forced to deploy attack helicopters, which then bombarded some of the abandoned IDF and SLA posts.[672]

Villages in the security zone also stormed Khiam prison, which the SLA had used to hold and interrogate Hizbollah and other Shi'ite prisoners and suspects. The SLA guards had fled, turning their prisoners over to the Red Cross. Hassan Nasrallah, the Secretary-General of the Hizbollah, told the ex-prisoners, "You can raise your heads high now. We have regained the land, starting an era of Arab triumphs. . . . This is the first glorious victory in 50 years of Arab-Israeli conflict. By morning you will see the photographs of the last Israeli soldiers leaving Lebanon, humiliated."[673]

While Israeli sources estimated that at least 5,000 members of the SLA and their dependents fled to Israel during the entire period of the collapse, many did not. In Christian towns like Marjayoun, many were forced to surrender to the Lebanese police, the Hizbollah or other militias. Well over 160 SLA soldiers surrendered in Marjayoun alone.[674] The only reassurance was that Hizbollah officials like Sheik Nabil Kawouk stated, "We in Hizbollah feel that we are responsible for the safety of all our sons, Moslems and Christian. Israel is the enemy and now all the Lebanese must unite as one. This is an historic day, a day that we have been waiting for years. We welcome our brothers in the resistance."[675]

ISRAEL'S DEFEAT IN LEBANON: AN ISRAELI VIETNAM?

To many, the situation in southern Lebanon resembles an Israeli version of Vietnam. In fact, one senior advisor to Prime Minister Barak not only drew this parallel long before the collapse, he stated that, "We may be the only country in the world whose judgment regarding Lebanon is even worse than that of the Lebanese. We suffered a major strategic and political defeat in 1982 that we are still paying for, and we are headed for another in 2000." Some Palestinians also see this struggle as a model for victory in a Second Intifada. This makes it important to understand why the IDF was "defeated," why any parallels to "Vietnam" may be limited, and what the collapse says about the future.

The Basic Military Situation

Israel's problems in the security zone were legion and were sharply influenced by its lack of any real political support in Lebanon. The SLA became progressively less trustworthy and effective. The IDF was better armed and better trained than its opponents, but could only use a small part of its sophisticated weapons arsenal and lacked its traditional superior professional skill in dealing with its opponents. While it restructured its personnel in Lebanon so that all were regulars or volunteers with special anti-guerrilla training, most served for only a comparatively limited period of time. The Hizbollah often had years more service and experience than their IDF counterparts. The Hizbollah forces had a nearby sanctuary in the north and foreign sponsors in Iran and Syria. They could use nearby friendly villages as bases, could fight on familiar territory, and could use a wide range of ruses and decoys to outwit IDF forces whose retaliatory capacity was constrained by an agreement to refrain from attacking civilian targets.[676]

In contrast, Israel had to defend a porous 300-kilometer border along the northern edge of the security zone. The Israeli-controlled "Security Zone" had a total area of 850 square kilometers. It was roughly 10 kilometers deep just north of its border with Lebanon. It ran for 70 kilometers from Al Bayyadah on the Mediterranean coast eastwards to the slopes of Mount Hermon. This peak was of strategic value to the IDF not only because it provides a commanding position overlooking the Golan plateau and much of northern Israel and southern Syria, but because it covered south Lebanon. The northern border of the security zone was covered by the UNIFIL peacekeeping effort, but UNIFIL had no war fighting capability and limited effectiveness.[677]

The SLA became progressively more exposed and vulnerable with time as the Hizbollah gained confidence and capability and the population in the South lost its fear of major Israeli reprisals. There were many positions where the SLA's strong points were badly located and deployed, and the Hizbollah had the advantage in terrain or the high ground. This increasingly forced the IDF to defend the SLA, which tended to withdraw to security points and rarely patrolled aggressively. As a result, the IDF effectively became the protector of Israel's protector.[678] Military activity within the security zone was also difficult. Roads tend to follow routes that make ambushes easy. The hilly countryside is filled with wadis, or dry stream beds, covered with thick brush. There are many built-up areas and small villages. Once the Hizbollah penetrated into the zone, there were many positions along the border with Israel where the Hizbollah had the high ground, and could use it for rocket launches or to observe activities in Israel.

Political conditions in Lebanon and in the Arab world, and international agreements, increasingly forced the IDF to be extremely sensitive to collateral damage. At the same time, Israeli public support for operations in Lebanon was also increasingly marginal and public opinion was extremely sensitive to casualties. The smallest mistake could lead a hypercritical Israeli media to destroy an officer's career. This forced many IDF operations to be conducted in direct-fire engagements against forces that had proven themselves to be hostile, rather than allowing the IDF to stand off and attack suspected targets, and many engagements occurred in unfavorable areas with a possible sanctuary for the Hizbollah in settled areas.

The Fighting Through 1995

The Hizbollah was never passive or ineffective. Israel estimates that the Hizbollah was responsible for 19 attacks in 1990, 52 attacks in 1991, 63 attacks in 1992, and 158 attacks in 1993. From 1992 onwards, the Hizbollah began to conduct ambushes with increasingly more successful remotely detonated bombs and explosives, some of which involved highly sophisticated devices like artificial rocks filled with explosives. In August 1993, the Hizbollah carried out its first successful large-scale ambush of IDF forces near Shifin. Many others followed.

The IDF responded with major assaults into southern Lebanon. This began with a 7-day operation in July 1993 called "Operation Accountability." It involved a major air and artillery campaign that often struck deep into Lebanon, but which led to little more than a temporary drop in Hizbollah activity and an agreement between the two sides that they would not target civilians. Even during "Operation Accountability," Hizbollah forces fired hundreds of Katyusha rockets into the security zone and Israeli territory. The Hizbollah kept up this pressure during 1994 and 1995. Hizbollah attacks killed 21 Israeli soldiers in 1994 and 22 in the first 10 months of 1995.[679]

During the mid-1990s, Israeli mistakes also aided the Hizbollah in several ways. The IDF provided economic and medical benefits, but many Israelis treated the South Lebanese Army as a mercenary force, rather than a true ally. Israel did little to give the SLA even the image of representing a patriotic force. Many IDF personnel in the area were poorly briefed and trained to deal with the Lebanese and were often arrogant and aggressive in dealing with Lebanese citizens in the SLA area or in nearby settlements with family connections.

During this period, IDF raids, artillery fire, and air strikes were often carried out with minimal attention to their possible effect in creating a political backlash. The Hizbollah learned to react faster than IDF forces and to rapidly disperse in the face of Israeli air or ground attacks. In contrast, Israel continued to reply with air or artillery attacks against Shi'ite villages. One such IDF operation in 1993 killed 130

Lebanese civilians and created thousands of refugees.[680] Israel also did little to win the hearts and minds of the ordinary Lebanese. It did not provide aid to create meaningful business ties to the Lebanese, or provide benefits in terms of roads and services. It instead labeled many signs in south Lebanon in Hebrew.

The IDF did improve its intelligence and targeting to focus more on striking Hizbollah facilities. At the same time the IDF was slow to change many of its tactics, and provide advanced anti-guerrilla warfare training. It often exposed its forces without proper planning and support, and found the South Lebanese Army progressively less reliable and effective. During the mid-1990s, the Hizbollah located and executed much of the IDF's intelligence network in Southern Lebanon as well as security officials in the South Lebanese Army. At the same time, Hizbollah intelligence began to heavily penetrate the South Lebanese Army and obtain intelligence on SLA and IDF operations.

The Disaster of Operation Grapes of Wrath

Operation Grapes of Wrath, which began on April 11, 1996, proved to be something of a turning point. The IDF took strong reprisals against Hizbollah operations in Southern Lebanon, and rocket attacks on Northern Israel. By April 17, IAF fighters and attack helicopters had flown more than 1,000 sorties against targets in southern and eastern Lebanon, and Israeli artillery had fired some 10,000 shells. A combination of UAVs and TPQ-37 counterbattery radars gave the IDF strike considerable effectiveness in some instances. The Hizbollah, however, was using single Grad artillery rockets which took moments to set up, could be remotely detonated, and had ranges of 20 kilometers. This gave the Hizbollah far too great a launch area for the IDF to cover and it still fired more than 200 rockets at Israel, hit hard at Kiryat Shmone, and forced the evacuation of some towns in Northern Israel.[681]

Unfortunately, the main casualties of Operation Grapes of Wrath were Lebanese civilians, most of whom had no clear ties to the Hizbollah. Nearly 60 were killed and 200 were injured in the first 7 days of the fighting, and nearly 400,000 fled the area. Things were made worse by IAF strikes on two Beirut power stations, which forced the city's 1.2 million inhabitants to ration power. The operation then turned into a public relations disaster for Israel when 5 Israeli shells from IDF 155-mm counterbattery fire against the Hizbollah killed 91 Lebanese civilians sheltering in a UNIFIL compound.[682]

This was not a result of Israeli negligence or carelessness. Even the most modern counterbattery techniques, and use of radars like the AN/TPQ-37 Firefinder, still presented a major risk of collateral damage if the Hizbollah fired from within or near populated areas. On April 18, 1996, an IDF targeting error of only 200–250 meters caused the Israeli 155-mm artillery fire to hit civilians sheltering near the UNIFIL base at Qana in South Lebanon and killed 102 people.

The IDF also found that the use of UAVs and IDF commandos on the ground near a Hizbollah operation often could not provide the targeting data needed in time and/or in reliable enough form to guarantee there would not be collateral damage. Unless helicopters or tanks were already in the area, the Hizbollah could generally strike and disperse before the IDF could react. Even then, Israel originally used artillery to strike at the suspected Hizbollah position at Qana and had to call them back because of the weather. The Hizbollah became highly adept at using decoys or ruses to lure IDF forces into ambushes or mined areas, and made use of remotely detonated Claymore mines, explosive devices and rocks, and sudden short mortar barrages to strike from a distance.

The end result was the IDF did some military damage to the Hizbollah and Amal, but a great deal more damage to Lebanese civilians and the IDF's reputation. The operation never came close to inflicting severe damage on the Hizbollah, and the resulting collateral damage did at least as much to alienate various Lebanese factions as intimidate them. A separate cease-fire agreement ended the 17-day bout of fighting between the IDF and Hizbollah, but did little to end the war of ambush, counter-ambush, and assassination discussed earlier.

Trying to Fight Guerrillas on Their Own Terms

The IDF began to pursue new tactics in 1997, but these did not achieve notable successes. It introduced greatly improved surveillance and targeting to detect Hizbollah operations and strike at them while they were under way. It set up a new commando training school just across the border from Lebanon under Major General Aviram Levine, shifted to anti-guerrilla force tactics, and strengthened a special anti-guerilla unit tailored to fight in Lebanon called Egoz. Nevertheless, Hizbollah carried out 104 operations in July 1997—the highest number for a one-month period in years. Roughly 96 of these attacks were long-range missile or mortar attacks and only four were close quarters attacks.

These changes were controversial within the IDF. Various Israeli experts had spent years arguing over whether it is possible to overcome and counter these disadvantages. Some IDF officers felt fixed positions should have been reduced to the absolute minimum necessary to maintain area control. Operational activities would then revert to small mobile unit actions, mounted with a high level of local initiative, responding to situations and real-time intelligence which would attack Hizbollah with their own tactics.[683]

Others argued for more specialized anti-guerrilla forces and deep penetration raids against the leadership of the Hizbollah and Amal, and for new anti-guerrilla warfare tactics. For example, a study by Colonel Shmuel Gordon suggested ways to radically alter anti-guerrilla warfare concepts to solve many of the problems encountered by the IDF. He has suggested placing overall anti-guerrilla warfare under the command of a combined three-pronged task force. One wing of the task force would consist of a small staff in charge of planning, intelligence, real-time command, and control. The second prong would consist of airborne platforms such as attack aircraft, attack helicopters, assault helicopters, UAVs, reconnaissance and target-acquisition systems, precision munitions, and a commando unit. The third component would consist of intelligence gathering assets connected to available information systems. Such a task force would not be bound by the chain of command controlling ground forces, and thus could react more quickly to real-time intelligence opportunities. The new organization was supposed to enable the IDF to minimize the rate of casualties, while inflicting high losses on the Hizbollah.[684]

Still others argued for relocation along a new line of contact chosen for its defensive value with minimal regard at most for the location of the villages supporting the SLA, and maximum surveillance of hostile villages. Some argued for greatly improved real-time surveillance and intelligence gathering, and small mobile strike forces supported by attack helicopters and precision artillery fire. Some called for joint air-ground strike forces with the ability to react immediately under liberal rules of engagement. The IDF even argued over how to introduce a new tactical training program to prepare troops for anti-guerrilla combat before they went to the security zone. This new training was meant to prevent friendly fire incidents, possibly a result of inadequate training.[685]

In any case, none of the approaches the IDF tried actually worked. While Israel's involvement became increasingly costly, the only impact of Israel's efforts to change the situation was to further alienate the SLA and Lebanese population. Even when the IDF won battles, it continued to lose the politics and the "war." The end result was that Israel faced the same ultimate choice as the US did in Vietnam: To declare victory and run.

The IDF also found that taking high risks to penetrate deep into Lebanon to try to attack the leadership of hostile factions resulted in the death of 12 IDF commandos at Insariyeh in October 1997. Although the attack was on a high-level Amal militia chief, it was part of a broader strategy that had already helped result in the death of 35 IDF troops in combat (plus 73 in a helicopter accident) during 1997.[686] By the end of 1997, 39 IDF members were killed in combat and 99 were wounded. In 1998, it lost 24 Israelis, and 33–45 members of the South Lebanese Army, for an estimated loss of 30–38 members of the Hizbollah.[687] A total of three Israeli and 22 Lebanese civilians were killed. The casualty figures for 1999 were 12 IDF soldiers, 20 SLA soldiers, 30 members of the Hizbollah, 1 Israeli civilian, and 24 Lebanese civilians.[688]

These figures, however, understate the true cost of the fighting, and the pressure on an IDF force that was extremely sensitive to casualties. In addition to those killed, the IDF had 103 wounded in 1998 and 56 in 1999. The SLA had 46 wounded in 1998 and 81 in 1999. No such figures are available for the Hizbollah. A total of 33 Israeli and 88 Lebanese civilians were wounded in 1998, and 16 Israelis and 175 Lebanese in 1999. Israel won the body count according to such figures, but the problem for Israel was that there were any bodies at all.

Sheik Nabil Qauok, the senior Hizbollah commander in southern Lebanon, described the impact of this situation in forcing an Israeli withdrawal in an interview in July 2000. He stated that, "The use of media as a weapon had an effect parallel to a battle. By the use of these films, we were able to control from a long distance the morale of a lot of Israelis." Qauok felt that demoralization as much as defeat helped to drive the Israelis from southern Lebanon.[689]

Qauok claimed that the most critical reason for the Hizbollah victory was that its fighters "were always ready for martyrdom," but that the Israeli soldier "probably wasn't ready to die for this. . . . More important than everything is that the Israeli soldier didn't believe in the war."[690] He mentioned the use of suicide bombers to crash cars into Israeli installations beginning in the mid-1980's and that the improving use of ambushes, assassinations and roadside bombs had a major impact on the IDF. He noted that the ambush of a raid by elite Israeli naval commandos in which a dozen were killed led the IDF to stop such raids for more than a year. Qauok stated that the Hizbollah had also put out word that it had penetrated Israeli intelligence, and this further reduced Israeli counterinsurgency operations and helped keep the Israelis in their strong points and give up control of the countryside and initiative to the Hizbollah.

Qauok stressed the importance of a good intelligence network. The effectiveness of that network was demonstrated with the assassination on February 28, 1999, of Brig. Gen. Eretz Gerstein, the top Israeli Army liaison officer to the South Lebanon Army, by a roadside bomb as his car passed in a military convoy. Gerstein was the highest-ranking Israeli officer killed during the occupation. He also noted that the Hizbollah had killed the SLA's second-ranking commander, Col. Akl Hashem, with a bomb at his house in Merj 'Uyun, in January 2000.

Sheik Qauok stated that the guerrillas had been able to steadily improve their effectiveness by studying each operation, learning from their mistakes, and developing new uses for weaponry. He also outlined the Hizbollah's reliance on low technology methods, "The two kinds of wars: guerrilla war and conventional war. By alternating tactics, Hizbollah was able to maintain the initiative and, after a clash, melt away into a largely sympathetic populace. By limiting the firing, we were able to keep the cards in our hands. . . . Even the rockets the resistance used had to be used intelligently. . . . We would do an action only in the time and place where it had an impact."

Qauok cited a number of Hizbollah innovations, which included roadside bombs made of fake plastic rocks, which could be bought in Beirut garden stores for $15, moving farm animals across areas monitored by Israeli motion sensors, and using low-cost jammers against Israeli radar and closed-circuit television monitors. He claimed an old Soviet T-55 tank was hidden in a cave and fired sporadically, and took the Israelis months to find because it was never driven and did not show up on Israeli heat sensors. He also indicated that Hizbollah fighters discovered that wire-guided antitank rockets could be steered in flight into small openings in Israeli concrete bunkers. "Even the man who invented these rockets did not know this." He refused to say, however, whether the Hizbollah had American-made TOW missiles, in addition to Russian Saggers.

UN military sources in Lebanon agreed with many of Qauok's points and stated that the impact of the Hizbollah strikes was amplified by the fact that they were videotaped by hidden cameramen and that the tapes were then given to Israeli television, sometimes even the videotapes were rushed to Beirut, where copies were delivered to Lebanese television and Western news agencies like the Associated Press and Reuters, which made them widely available. They were, however, sometimes shown first on Hizbollah's own television station for internal propaganda purposes. Showing the videos on the nightly television news in Israel helped show the cost of the occupation, and made a sharp contrast to the censored coverage allowed to Israeli military reporters. The UN source also claimed that the tapes would never have been taken at all without the improved intelligence gathering and combat skills Hizbollah developed over the years. "When they first started, they thought they could do it with a bunch of people on a hill yelling 'Allah-u akbar,' They would lose 40 in an operation. Now they are very sophisticated, very disciplined."[691]

Blundering Towards Withdrawal

In March 1998, Israel made its first major public announcement that it was considering plans to leave southern Lebanon, but stated that it could not withdraw without security guarantees from the Lebanese government and a comprehensive agreement with Syria.[692] However, Lebanon rejected Israel's offers, stating that Israel was already obliged to withdraw from the area under United Nations Security Council Resolution 425.[693] Many experts feel that the reason why Lebanon did not attempt to guarantee the security of Israel's border was that Syria wanted to force a peace settlement including Syria. It wanted to use Southern Lebanon as a bargaining chip because it is the only place where Israel faced military pressure to make peace on Syrian terms, which would mean surrendering the Golan. If Lebanon had been able to secure the borders and crack down on the Hizbollah, Israel may have been able to retreat unilaterally, and Syria would lose its leverage.[694]

For Israel, a unilateral withdrawal without Syrian and Lebanese forces to secure the border area presented new implications because it might give the Hizbollah free range in the border area. While some Israelis argued that the Hizbollah would stop military action once southern Lebanon was "liberated," others concluded that it would be under strong Iranian and Syrian pressure to continue its proxy war against Israel, and would need the conflict to provide domestic political support.[695]

These security issues help explain why Israeli public opinion fluctuated so sharply over the issue of withdrawal. For example, one poll taken over a two-week period in February 1997, before and after an air accident in the area that killed 73 Israelis, found that 65–79% of Israelis opposed unilateral withdrawal from Lebanon, and 16–25% supported it. At roughly the same time period, however, a poll found that 78% of Israelis questioned whether the IDF could defeat the Hizbollah in South Lebanon. Roughly 76% favored using stronger methods, but 74% supported withdrawal if these methods failed. Polls since that time have shown the same sudden shifts and ongoing uncertainties.[696]

The IDF was increasingly concerned that the deployment of long-range artillery rockets could provide the Hizbollah with a way to strike at Israel proper with considerable effectiveness, and that the high ground and rough terrain in the border area might simply mean moving the existing low-intensity conflict south and into Israel. In late December 1998, IDF commanders unanimously accepted Chief-of-Staff Mofaz's view that withdrawal from the security zone would place Israel's northern border settlements under constant threat from Hizbollah and other hostile groups.[697] In early January 1999, the Israeli cabinet adopted an official policy of retaliatory air and artillery strikes on Lebanon in response to any cross-border Hizbollah attack.[698]

A new review of Israel's position in February 1999 again led the IDF to the conclusion that any withdrawal without a formal agreement with Syria, Lebanon, and the Hizbollah would be worse than staying. In a statement made after a Hizbollah attack in February 1999, former Prime Minister Netanyahu stated that Israel would be glad to leave the zone if the Lebanese army would take up the positions it vacated. However, he also stated that Israel was aware that Lebanon was not able to take such action.[699]

As might be expected, the killing did not stop. The Hizbollah successfully ambushed and killed three elite IDF paratroopers in February 1999. It then killed Brigadier General Erez Gerstein, two IDF soldiers, and an Israeli journalist a few days later. Erez Gerstein was the senior officer in the south Lebanon border zone. The most the IDF could do in reprisal was to bypass its agreement with the Hizbollah not to strike targets in the rear, and use the pretext of Hizbollah rocket attacks to launch a series of air raids on Hizbollah targets in the Beka'a—a strategy that had little deterrent effect.[700]

New international talks produced the April 1999 understanding which included a formal version of the 1993 agreement not to attack civilians. It established a monitoring group with representatives from France, Israel, Lebanon, Syria, and the

US to meet at regular intervals to review any violation of the agreement. The practical effect was to limit Hizbollah rocket attacks on Israel, but it did little to halt day-to-day Hizbollah activity in Southern Lebanon. It did equally little to halt Israeli air raids on Lebanon and IDF/SLA attacks on the Hizbollah. Reports by the multinational monitoring group in charge of implementing the agreement indicate that both sides violated the agreement.[701]

Sheik Hassan Nasarallah, the head of Hizbollah, said after Nasiryah that,[702]

> During the Nasiryah attack the citizens came down the streets brandishing their weapons and ready to fight the enemy. . . . Do you remember the time when people used to bury their weapons and escape to Beirut when Israeli forces attacked? We are getting stronger!

In contrast, Major General Matan Vilnai, then Deputy Chief of Staff of the IDF, said,[703]

> We have no illusions. You won't defeat Hizbollah. You won't exterminate them. They won't start loving you. They'll continue to be there, living their miserable lives. Our mission is to stave off their attacks, which we do.

The Hizbollah refused to accept a temporary truce during the run-up to the Israeli elections on May 17, 1999. It defended its right to use roadside bombs and Katyusha rockets.[704] In fact, on April 27, Hizbollah guerillas launched a wide-scale offensive and hit 22 outposts in Lebanon.[705]

These events led to new calls for withdrawal from those in favor of Israel's withdrawal, including calls from politicians as diverse as the head of the Labor Party, former Chief of Staff Ehud Barak, and even from the Likud's Ariel Sharon.[706] Nevertheless, public opinion polls found that 61% of Israelis still opposed unilateral withdrawal, although 75% favored a negotiated withdrawal. The Israeli government also stated repeatedly that it planned to remain in Lebanon until some formal agreement could be reached with Lebanon (and Syria).[707]

As has already been discussed, Barak's victory in the May elections had a major impact on Israeli policy. During the campaign, Barak had pledged that Israel would withdraw by July 2000. While he recognized the same risks as IDF planners, he felt there were good military reasons to question the military costs of continuing Israel's presence. The key factor was casualties. In spite of the IDF's efforts to change its tactics, it continued to take losses, and the death of Brigadier General Erez Gerstein was soon followed by the deaths of other IDF soldiers.[708]

Israel attempted to create a forward line that was easier to defend.[709] The IDF announced in April 1999 that it planned to reduce security forces in Lebanon, and that 80 percent of outposts had already been handed over to the SLA.[710] In late May 1999, the SLA "decided to withdraw" from the northern tip of the security zone, the area around Jezzine, because the area had become too dangerous to hold.[711] By June 3, 1999, the SLA pulled back to just south of Kfar Houne.[712]

Nevertheless, the worst fighting since operation Grapes of Wrath broke out between the Hizbollah and the IDF on June 24 and 25.[713] The Israeli army carried out air strikes in the Beirut area in response to Hizbollah rocket attacks on Northern Israel. The bombs caused a blackout in Beirut and destroyed several key bridges.[714] The Hizbollah responded by targeting the Northern Galilee. The fighting reportedly killed 8 and wounded 64 Lebanese and killed 2 and wounded 12 Israelis.[715] The attacks—which occurred after the Israeli elections but before Barak took office—apparently were ordered by Netanyahu without Barak's consultation.[716]

Once the immediate backlash from these events died down, Barak repeated his pledge to get Israel out of Lebanon. He made this pledge in a speech in September 1999, although both Barak and his Deputy Defense Minister, Ephraim Sneh, added important qualifications. Sneh stated on September 29, 1999, that Israel would only withdraw from Syria as part of a comprehensive security arrangement with Syria.

When Sneh's speech led the press to question Barak's commitment to withdrawal, he gave a press conference the next day in which he stated, "The answer is yes. By July 2000, we will withdraw the Israeli Defense Forces from Lebanon, with an agreement, and put them on the international border and defend the northern settlements. . . . I don't recommend that anyone test us or our reaction after we are on the international border." Barak did not, however, make clear what would happen if there was not agreement. Somewhat ironically, the IAF was striking targets in Lebanon while Barak was speaking. This marked the fourth straight day of such attacks.[717]

Sensors and Electronic Fences

Meanwhile, Israel made a further change in its tactics.[718] Israel had the SLA stay largely in its strongholds, giving the IDF added freedom of action. It then greatly expanded the "electronic fence" of ground and air-based sensors (including UAVs and aerostats) it used to cover the region. This system became pervasive enough so that the IDF became convinced it could spot unusual movements of any kind.

The IDF ceased to routinely use IDF forces as counterguerrillas to patrol the ground and fight the guerillas in their own way. The IDF had found that far too often such patrols were too large and cumbersome, and became a target. The IDF often took one IDF casualty for every two Hizbollah, and this accompanied growing internal political problems in Israel. Similarly, fixed forces in 120-mm-proof IDF and SLA pillboxes became vulnerable to attacks by Hizbollah forces using weapons like 160-mm mortars.

Instead, the IDF attempted to use its new sensor system to ensure there was no place the Hizbollah forces could hide. This meant even small, fragmented units with demolition charges, sniper rifles, and thermal sights could be tracked in rough terrain—in fact, Israeli sensors began to pick up the Hizbollah use of thermal sights as targets. The IDF then deployed aircraft, helicopters, or mobile ground troops to the precise area of Hizbollah operations, rather than attempt combat patrols.

These changes took four to six months to implement, and the new sensor system was extremely costly. Initially, it seemed to work. The sensors could operate day and night and through foliage. The UAVs were modified to fly high enough so that they were virtually silent, and long-endurance UAVs were combined with moored aerostats and ground-based seismic and IR sensors. New SIGINT systems were also employed to take advantage of Hizbollah's increasing reliance on electronic communication as the range of their weapons increased, and forward observers had to communicate to the rear.

New C^3 centers tied the data together in computer consoles, and could provide targeting data accurate within a few meters, providing an improved way to use airpower and artillery with less risk of collateral damage. It was sometimes possible to use the remote platforms to laser-illuminate Hizbollah, and TV images from other sensors to provide targeting data to fixed wing aircraft and the Apache attack helicopter for precision strikes. Vulnerable patrols could be reduced or eliminated and focused strike forces could attack known targets.

As was the case with similar US systems in Vietnam, however, the advantages of such a system were greatest during the first few months. Hizbollah agents within the SLA began to get a precise picture of what was happening, and Iran provided longer-range precision strike systems like the TOW-1A anti-armor guided missile.[719] As a result, the Hizbollah began to focus on long-range ambushes where it could strike at high value human targets with a minimal presence and great precision, and used its growing number of spies in the SLA as its human equivalent of Israel's electronic fence. One of the most successful of these attacks occurred on January 30, 2000, when they killed Colonel Akl Hashem, the second in command of the SLA forces with a remotely triggered roadside bomb. When IDF troops attempted to retaliate, the Hizbollah successfully ambushed and killed five IDF soldiers.

Air Raids, "Massive Retaliation, " and Collapse

Somewhat ironically, Israel then reacted by reverting back to its tactics of several years earlier and launched a series of major air raids on February 7–8, 2000. These strikes went deep into Lebanon and hit three power plants near Beirut. Just as the Israeli electronic fence bore a resemblance to the McNamara line the US had used in Vietnam, its failure led to a resumption of strategic bombing and to major new domestic demands in Israel to bring the troops home. It also led to largely futile peace talks on February 11, which ended when the Hizbollah killed the seventh IDF soldier in three weeks.

The end result was to create a massive increase in the public demand in Israel for withdrawal from Lebanon—although few in Israel seemed to know what would happen once the withdrawal took place. Prime Minister Barak again promised to withdraw by the end of July 2000, and on March 5, the Israeli cabinet unanimously voted to withdraw all Israeli troops by that date—*if* an agreement could be reached with Lebanon and Syria. At the same time, Iran, Syria, and the Hizbollah left their positions unclear as to whether the Hizbollah and Amal would continue to fight against Israel proper once the IDF withdrew. The Israeli Foreign Minister threatened that Lebanon would "burn" if more Israelis died, and the IDF talked about further massive retaliation on rear area targets in Lebanon and striking at Syrian forces in Lebanon.[720]

About the only hopeful signs in March 2000 were reports that Israel and Lebanon would hold direct talks if Israel and Syria agreed on a peace, and attempts to define how the two states should deal with each other. Neither state, however, had defined a clear vision of its policy on key issues like borders, water, the nature of a "peace," the future of some 367,000 Palestinian refugees in Lebanon, the future role of the Lebanese Army and Syria in securing the border, the future of the SLA, and the future of the Hizbollah and Amal. Lebanon either could or would not look beyond the narrow terms of UN Security Council Resolution 425, which called for unconditional Israeli withdrawal from Lebanon and peace and security along the border.[721] About the only hopeful sign was President Lahood's statement that Lebanon was prepared to guarantee a peace along its southern border *if* Israel reached a comprehensive peace settlement with Syria, and if Israel granted a right of return to all of the Palestinian refugees in Lebanon.[722]

The resulting failure of Israeli-Syrian peace talks led Israel to shift to a policy of unilateral withdrawal, and triggered the process of collapse of the SLA discussed earlier. Israel was first forced to change its deadline for withdrawal from July 7 to June 1, and then the SLA defense of Taibah and Houla collapsed on May 22, 2000—bringing Hizbollah forces within less than four kilometers of the Israeli border town of Misgav Am, cutting the security zone in half, and leading to the total collapse of the Israeli and SLA security zone two days later.[723]

In contrast to some of the reports in the media, the IDF did have contingency plans. It had three basic plans: First, "Operation New Horizon" foresaw an orderly withdrawal with Syrian consent, and the deployment of Lebanese forces into the positions the IDF had left. Second, Operation "Morning Twilight" anticipated an accelerated withdrawal under fire, and third, "Operation Stamina" planned for the worst case scenario in which the SLA would totally disintegrate and result in an immediate IDF withdrawal.

Following the collapse of the SLA, the IDF moved its convoys using armored bridge-layers over the Litani River to avoid Hizbollah ambushes as special guides and low-light markers helped drivers using night-vision equipment to see in the total darkness.[724] This brought an end to 22 years of Israeli occupation, but it left all of the states and parties involved without a peace agreement and as many reasons to continue a low-level conflict as to accept the new situation. It also placed the struggle directly on the Israeli border, and increased the risk of escalation.

SYRIA, ISRAEL, AND LEBANON WITH OR WITHOUT THE PEACE PROCESS

There is no way to predict whether a new form of border war will emerge from these events. The proxy war may resume unless Israel can reach a peace with Syria, and make some formal accommodation with Syria and Lebanon that places tight constraints on any future fighting. The war between Israel and the Hizbollah may continue for ideological reasons within Hizbollah, because of encouragement from Iran, or in sympathy with a Palestinian Second Intifada. Syria has also made it clear since the collapse that only the return of the Golan on its terms will bring peace to the region, and Lebanon must follow where Syria leads.

Israeli Defense Options

The current thinking of the IDF seems to center around mixing forward defense at the border with massive retaliation by air or missile. This could take the form of attacks on Hizbollah targets in Southern Lebanon, but it might well take the form of attacks on high value targets around Beirut designed to force the Lebanese government to intervene against the Hizbollah or to put pressure on Syria by hitting targets in Lebanon of value to Syria. The IDF has also refined targeting plans to strike against Syrian targets in Lebanon as part of a similar effort to force Syria to intervene against the Hizbollah.

The newest Israeli version of border defenses, and the use of an "electronic fence," have already exposed their limitations, and the strategic problems presented by the close proximity of Israeli civilians to the border, and the uneven borderline and terrain, make any "leak-proof" defense of the zone difficult. There are many areas along the nearly 300-kilometer borderline where the Lebanese skyline dominates Israeli territory, ideal for short-range attack not only of the villages close to the border, but also of the roads connecting settlements and military installations in the border area. South Lebanon's hilly countryside, with deep dry riverbeds covered with thick brush, offers excellent hideouts for the small fighting teams of the Hizbollah. If the Hizbollah and Amal operate in the border area in small, well-armed groups, they may be able to continue to fire long-range rockets and ambush Israeli citizens or troops and then retreat into safe havens in the underbrush or nearby villages.[725]

Given the past history of the Hizbollah and Amal, they may well rely more on rocket attacks than on attempts to actively infiltrate. Israel is seeking to develop the THEL laser as a defense against such attacks and to deploy it in the near future. Active counterbattery fire and surveillance, however, are very difficult challenges in dealing with small scattered individual rockets, and Israel has a number of vulnerable towns and civilian targets within rocket range:[726]

- There are eight Israeli cities and towns near the border with more than 5,000 residents. Most targets are collectives and Arab villages with populations of less than 1,000. Cities in the forward area near the border include Kiryat Shmona (24,000 residents); Nahariya (35,000); and Ma'alot (35,000). These targets will be vulnerable to 107- and 122-mm rockets in Hizbollah and Amal forces even if they are fired from areas 5–10 kilometers away from the border.

- Rockets near the border can reach 64 additional populated targets with a population of around 150,000. There are 10 residential areas with more than 5,000 people. The largest is Safed, with a population of 23,000.

- If the Hizbollah and Amala have longer-range 240-mm rockets, they can reach any target in the Golan and upper Galilee and cities like Acco, Haifa, and Tiberias.

- Conventional artillery rockets are so inaccurate and have such a limited payload that they produce only limited, random casualties, and are more terror weapons than a critical threat. This would not be true, however, if the Hizbollah should acquire chemical or biological warheads.

Much depends on the course of the peace process, Syrian policy, and the actions of the Hizbollah and other militias. The IDF did, however, react to these problems by making plans for a new defense line, and a withdrawal, with a potential total cost of $234–500 million, depending on the option chosen. This compares with a cost of about $250 million a year to fund the IDF and SLA presence in Lebanon.[727]

Brigadier General Giora Iland, the former IDF chief of operations, completed a study of Israel's military options for withdrawal in the fall of 1999. The study called for a major new shelter program, a new sensor system and electronic fence on the border, other electronic detection systems, improved roads, and other protective measures. It called for the increased use of air power and attack helicopters in retaliatory strikes that did not expose the IDF and increase casualties—a tactic that Israel implemented in April 1999. It also called for the development of advanced armor that required less IDF infantry protection and manpower to protect armored patrol units against anti-tank weapons. The plan also examined resettling some 2,000 members of the SLA—with paid compensation for some, resettlement in Israel for some, and help in immigrating for others.[728] It should also be noted that Lt. General Shaul Mofaz, the Israeli Chief of Staff, and Major General Amos Malka, the chief of military intelligence, both expressed reservations about this plan. They warned it would only be safe after a broad agreement was reached with Syria and Lebanon, and Hizbollah and Palestinian guerillas would continue to attack unless Syria and Lebanon forced them to stop.[729]

Since the debate over the land plan, some Israeli and US experts believe that enough progress has been made with the THEL anti-rocket defense laser to significantly improve these defensive capabilities. The Tactical High Energy Laser or THEL program was originally a $100 million program, with the US paying $70 million and Israel paying $30 million. At present it is primarily a defense against unguided rockets, rather than guided missiles. It is still unclear that it will work, since current versions need to hold a rocket in flight for nearly 15 seconds, and the average flight time of an 80–240-mm rocket is generally less than 30 seconds. It is also dependent on a clear line of sight, so haze and smoke present major problems.[730]

Tests at White Sands in February 1996 proved that a laser could track a missile for the required time, and that a deuterium fluoride laser beam could destroy a missile in flight. The THEL program did run into trouble in 1999 when a series of technical difficulties encountered during initial tests and chemical leaks caused by faulty valves delayed the project by up to a year.[731] The delays resulted in cost overruns totaling $30–50 million over the $130.8 million ceiling. The cost overruns jeopardized the future of the project as the contractor and the US government argued over who was responsible for the extra cost.[732] THEL was saved when the Israeli Ministry of Defense and the US Army agreed to each pay a quarter of the overruns while the contractor is still responsible for the other half.[733]

The THEL deuterium fluoride laser has since been successful in tests against incoming Katyusha rockets, and the demonstrator is being dismantled and shipped to Israel for operational testing.[734] Major Gen. Isaac Ben-Israel of the Israeli Ministry of Defense said of these tests that THEL had taken "the crucial first step necessary to help protect the communities along our northern border against the kind of devastating rocket attacks we've suffered recently."[735] The system is still a developmental fixed-site system, however, and it may be several more years before its cost effectiveness is fully established.

Israel may well have no choice other than active defense and "massive retaliation," but such options could just as easily lead to escalation into a war on the Northern front as force Lebanon and Syria to put pressure on the Hizbollah. The IDF has talked very publicly about such a retaliatory bombing effort, and the IAF has already demonstrated that it can hit targets in Lebanon with near immunity. Israel also chose to make public on April 30, 2000 that it was training its pilots to attack two scale models of Syrian air bases in the Negev. It also announced that its F-15s had conducted mock attacks on one base in February 2000, while Israeli-Syrian peace talks were still going on.[736] The tacit message was that the IAF would strike at Syria if the situation in Lebanon grew serious enough.

The real question is whether such IAF strikes can really pressure Lebanon and Syria enough to force an end to the proxy war, or will end in provoking new levels of escalation and embarrassing Israel in terms of world opinion. President Assad of Syria was as willing as Saddam Hussein to take substantial damage if it supported his political goals, and if he felt that riding out such attacks would eventually push Israel towards returning the Golan. Bashar Assad's succession makes Syria's response more uncertain, but it seems unlikely that he would do anything in conflict with his father's goals (at least until after he gains leverage domestically).

Israeli strikes would also affect other nations. Previous air strikes have led President Mubarak to visit Beirut to show solidarity against such strikes. In March 2000, the Arab foreign ministers met in Beirut for the first time in years to attack Israel's air raids against Lebanese power plants and its "dangerous words"—a reference to Israeli Foreign Minister David Levy's remark that Lebanon would "burn" unless the Hizbollah was controlled.[737] As a result, Lebanon may represent a much broader threat to peace than simply a continuation or escalation of the Israeli-Syrian proxy war.

Peace as a Defense

The best defense would be a stable peace, but any peace between Israel and Syria still has uncertain prospects, and any such peace that ignored Lebanon might end in leading to new kinds of fighting. The Lebanese problem can scarcely be ignored. The future presence of Syrian forces in Lebanon confronts Israel and Syria with the need to negotiate a peace that at least tacitly considers Syria's future role in Lebanon, and the risk that some elements in Lebanon might turn against both Israel and Syria is at least a possibility.[738]

Much depends on the answer to the broader question of whether Syria will give up de facto control of Lebanon after peace is established with Israel, or whether such a peace will formally or tacitly recognize Syria's "special role" in that country. Syrian withdrawal from Lebanon is essential if Lebanon is to emerge as a truly independent state, but it also presents risks. Lebanon still has strong warlords and ethnic-religious factions. It is possible that Syrian withdrawal from Lebanon could trigger a new round of fighting between these factions, and lead to attacks by some factions on Israel.

Any peace agreement between Israel and Syria must also take account of the risk Syria's remaining military presence in Lebanon poses to Israel. This risk includes Syria's ability to attack through Lebanon and/or explicitly limit both Syrian deployments in Lebanon and Israel's support of the South Lebanon Army. At a minimum, a peace would have to formalize the present agreements that limit the presence of Syrian forces in southern Lebanon and add limits on the total size of Syrian forces in Lebanon. They might not have to be as formally or carefully defined as a peace on the Golan, but they would almost inevitably involve some of the same verification and disengagement issues.

Assad's death, and his son Bashar's succession, may also affect Syria's policy. Bashar may wish to accompany his succession with a peace deal, but he may find it difficult to agree to any terms that give Syria less than those set by his father.[739] Whatever happens, the devil will lie in the details, and a truly stable peace will prove anything but easy to negotiate. Finally, one cannot ignore the Hizbollah's deep antagonism to Israel, the influence of Iran, and the risk the Hizbollah will become engaged in a Second Intifada.

The UNIFIL Option

The current United Nations force in Lebanon will also play a role in determining whether new conflict will break out between Israel and Lebanon. The UN has long deployed a force in the area called the UN Interim Force in Lebanon (UNIFIL). Until June 2000, it was more of a monitoring, mediating, and humanitarian buffer force than a true peacekeeper. It was established in March 1978 to monitor the Israeli withdrawal from Lebanon after an attack on Palestinian forces. United Nations Security Council Resolution 425 gave UNIFIL the mission of "confirming the withdrawal of Israeli forces, restoring peace and international security, and assisting the Government of Lebanon in the return of its effective authority in the area." After Israel invaded Lebanon in 1982, UNIFIL remained behind Israeli lines, with its role limited to providing protection and humanitarian assistance to the local population.[740]

The mandate of the force has been regularly renewed by the UN Security Council ever since. It has generally had an authorized strength of about 6,000 men, but only about 4,500 men in actual service. UNIFIL has had six small infantry battalions—with one battalion each from different countries, plus support elements from other nations. There has also been a small contingent of 70 men from the UN Truce Supervision Organization (UNTSO) which acts as the Observer Group in Lebanon. This force was originally established in 1948 to observe the application of the 1949 Arab-Israel armistice agreements.[741] After Israel invaded Lebanon in 1982, it was deployed in a buffer strip north of the Israeli-SLA occupation zone, but some battalions did have operating areas inside the zone.

During the fighting between Israel, the SLA, and Hizbollah, UNIFIL's forces helped to reduce the level of conflict and protect civilians. Some 239 UN personnel were killed during these efforts, including 235 military personnel, one military observer, two international civilian staff, and one local staff. At the same time, UNIFIL suffered from the classic limitations to any small peacekeeping force. It had no enforcement capability or peacemaking mission. UNIFIL could never use force and lacked the intelligence data to effectively enforce the separation of the various sides. Further, it had to operate in a relatively narrow area, without a clearly defined force limitation and disengagement zone and without the full support of Israel and Syria.[742]

The role of the UNIFIL has changed significantly, however, since the Israeli withdrawal. UN Secretary-General Kofi Annan proposed at the time of the collapse that some elements of such a force be deployed into the south. He stated that the United Nations could verify the Israeli withdrawal. He also recommended that the 4,515-strong peace force then in Lebanon be immediately reinforced to 5,600 men and then increased to 7,900, in order to help the Lebanese government regain control of the area.

Key European states expressed reservations about the creation of a more effective force. France had about 240 soldiers in the existing UN Interim Force in Lebanon (UNIFIL), and French Foreign Minister Hubert Vedrine said shortly after the collapse that it was now up to the Lebanese state to demonstrate it could control its own territory. He added that French participation in a strengthened UNIFIL was dependent on the attitudes of Israel, Syria and Lebanon and on the commitments made in the Security Council. He stated that, "All the countries are looking to France to play a major role in UNIFIL. . .both to confirm our presence and possibly boost it. We have never rejected this demand, but all three protagonists must have a responsible behavior to manage this new situation which is a positive move. . . . We are entering a phase where it is now up to the Lebanese state to exert its authority over the territory."[743]

In practice, it soon became clear that Lebanon could not control its own border, and the UN was the only alternative. This led to a complex deal where Israel agreed to allow the UN to demarcate the border, and to withdraw to the border even when this meant its forces would be exposed. The Lebanese government agreed to send in at least a token military presence, and the Hizbollah agreed to accept the UN's border demarcation and security presence. While this did not bring total peace to the border area, it did reduce violence to minimal levels through September 2000.

Some of these UN activities had begun before Israeli withdrawal. The Secretary-General had received formal notification on April 17, 2000, that Israel would withdraw its forces from Lebanon by July, "in full accordance with Security Council resolutions 425 (1978) and 426 (1978)." The Secretary-General informed the Security Council of this notification on the same day, stating that he had initiated preparations to enable the United Nations to carry out its responsibilities under those resolutions. The Council had endorsed the Secretary-General's decision to initiate those preparations on April 20, 2000.[744]

During April 26-May 9, the Secretary-General had also sent a Special Envoy, the Force Commander of UNIFIL, and a team of experts to meet with the governments of Israel and Lebanon and concerned Member States in the region, including Egypt, Jordan, and the Syrian Arab Republic. The delegation also met with the PLO and the League of Arab States. During this mission, United Nations cartographic, legal, and military experts examined the technical issues that would need to be addressed in the context of the implementation of resolution 425 (1978). Parallel to that mission, which took place between April 26 and May 9, 2000, the Secretary-General consulted with interested Member States, including those contributing troops to UNIFIL.

This effort took on a whole new meaning on May 16, when the IDF began to withdraw. By May 21, large crowds of Lebanese, with some armed elements, had entered villages in the Israeli-controlled area. At the same time, a large number of the SLA forces and their families were crossing into Israel, while others surrendered to the Lebanese authorities. As a result, Israel notified the Secretary-General on May 25 that Israel had already redeployed its forces in compliance with Security Council resolutions 425 (1978) and 426 (1978) instead of July.

Events forced the UN into a sudden border demarcation effort. From May 24 to June 7, a United Nations cartographer and his team, assisted by UNIFIL, worked on the ground to identify a line to be adopted for the practical purposes of confirming the Israeli withdrawal. While this was not a formal border demarcation, the aim was to identify a line on the ground conforming to the internationally recognized boundaries of Lebanon, based on the best available cartographic and other documentary evidence. This UN effort was particularly important. The Hizbollah initially threatened to continue post-withdrawal, cross-border anti-Israeli violence, on the grounds that Lebanon was still "occupied" by the IDF.

Fortunately, much of the border was not disputed. The line from Ra's an Naqura (Rosh HaNikra) on the Mediterranean to Jisr al-Ghajar on the Hasbani was set in 1920, surveyed and demarcated in 1921, described officially in 1922, ratified in 1923, and brought fully into effect in 1924 incorporating several Shi'ite villages forming the Galilee "panhandle." The British and French redemarcated this line in the early 1940s because France failed to maintain the border markers. At Lebanon's request, the 1949 Israel-Lebanon General Armistice Agreement established the 1923 Palestine-Lebanon border as the "Armistice Demarcation Line" (ADL) between the two states, and ILMAC (Israel Lebanon Mixed Armistice Commission) in 1949–1951. According to UN reporting, the entire ADL was marked except for the five kilometers just south of Metulla (boundary pillar 38) and Jisr al-Ghajar. Additionally, both Israel and Lebanon said in June 2000 that they would adhere to the 1923/1949 international boundary, or ADL.

The main remaining controversy over the border line occurred because the 1921 border gave no consideration to security or defense. It went across the fields and ridges of the Upper Galilee and was drawn with little thought given to controlling cross border traffic or to erecting security barriers. After Lebanon lost control of its boundary in the 1970s, Israel sought to "improve" on the line, and it attempted to do so again in July 2000. The IDF initially asked the UN to accept a plan called

Operation "Morning Twilight" that allowed for withdrawal to a "purple" line instead of the "red" or international line. Although this plan would have left more Israeli land on the Lebanese side than Lebanese land on the Israeli side, Lebanon would have severely criticized it.[745]

Lebanon also expressed reservations "on the UN view related to positions between Rmaish and Metulla [in the central sector], in addition to verifying the Israeli withdrawal from the eastern sector of the border." Another important issue was control over the Shebaa Farms area. This is a plateau situated on the Lebanese and Syrian border but which had been occupied by Israel since 1967. Israel took the position that Shebaa Farms was Syrian when it took control in 1967, and that its fate should be the subject of bilateral negotiations with Damascus.[746]

Nevertheless, a map showing the withdrawal line was formally transmitted by the Force Commander of UNIFIL to his Lebanese and Israeli counterparts on May 7. With some reservations about the line, Israel and Lebanon then confirmed that identifying this line was solely the responsibility of the UN and they would respect the line as identified.

UNIFIL teams commenced the work of verifying the Israeli withdrawal behind the line on June 8, 2000. The Secretary-General reported to the Security Council on June 16 that Israel had withdrawn its forces from Lebanon in accordance with resolution 425 (1978). He also stated that it had met the requirements defined in his report of May 22, 2000—and had completed the withdrawal in conformity with the line identified by the UN, that the SLA had been dismantled, and that all detainees held at the Al-Khiam prison had been freed. The Secretary-General also said that the government of Lebanon had moved quickly to re-establish its effective authority in the area through the deployment of its security forces, and had informed the United Nations that it would send a composite force composed of army and internal security personnel to be based in Marjayoun. It also stated that it would consider deploying its armed forces throughout southern Lebanon following confirmation by the Secretary-General of Israel's withdrawal.

On June 18, the Security Council endorsed the work done by the UN and called on all parties concerned to cooperate with the United Nations and to exercise restraint. It also noted that the United Nations could not assume law and order functions that were properly the responsibility of the Lebanese government. The Council welcomed the government's first steps in that regard, and called on it to proceed with the deployment of its armed forces into the Lebanese territory vacated by Israel as soon as possible, with the assistance of UNIFIL.

This uneasy compromise gave Lebanon far more responsibility than it was able to actually assume. UNIFIL also found a number of violations after the verification of the Israeli withdrawal, where the Israeli technical fence crossed the withdrawal line and the Israel Defence Forces used patrol tracks that also crossed the line. This halted the deployment of UNIFIL and the Lebanese troops to the vacated areas. As a result, the Secretary-General visited the region again in late June, and his Special Envoy followed up on those discussions in July. The net result was that Israel committed itself to the removal of all Israeli violations of the withdrawal line by the end of July 2000.

It is impossible to predict the future, but some developments have been positive. The situation in the area of UNIFIL operation remained generally calm from the end of May 2000 to September 2000. The Lebanese army, gendarmerie, and police established checkpoints in the vacated area, and took formal responsibility for controlling movement and maintaining order. The Lebanese army did retrieve some heavy weapons abandoned by the IDF and SLA, and UNIFIL carried out joint patrols with the Lebanese authorities. UNIFIL monitored the line of withdrawal on a daily basis, by means of ground and air patrols. It examined possible violations from both sides of the line, as many of the areas could only be accessed from the Israeli side, owing to the presence of mines and unexploded ordnance on the Lebanese side. It had liaisons that provided a constant link with the Chief of Operations of the IDF and the Director of Lebanese General Security, as well as with the normal chain of command on each side. Any violations of the withdrawal line were immediately brought to the attention of the side concerned.

On July 24, the Secretary-General informed the Security Council that the Israeli authorities had removed all violations of the line of withdrawal. On the same day, in a meeting with the Secretary-General's Special Envoy, Lebanese President Emile Lahoud and Prime Minister Selim el-Hoss gave their consent to the full deployment of UNIFIL on July 26, which was followed by the deployment to the formerly Israeli-controlled area of the composite Lebanese unit, comprising army and internal security personnel.

The Secretary-General had mixed success in his efforts to strengthen UNIFIL. He asked in May 2000 that total UNIFIL troop strength increase from 4,513 to approximately 5,600. He also asked that UNIFIL be reinforced bringing its strength to a total of eight battalions plus appropriate support units, or approximately 7,935 peacekeepers, once the Israeli withdrawal was confirmed. On July 20, the Secretary-General said that the first phase of this reinforcement of UNIFIL was under way, and that the mine-clearance capacity of UNIFIL had been reinforced with two units from Sweden and Ukraine. In addition, an engineer battalion of 600 from Ukraine came at the end of July. The units from Finland, Ghana, Ireland, and Nepal were reinforced, and Fiji and India undertook to reinforce their units.

No nation, however, volunteered to provide the additional two infantry battalions needed to provide a high degree of self-sufficiency and the capability to deploy to the mission area using national assets. The Commander of UNIFIL had to devise a deployment plan using existing resources and reinforcements to cover the area vacated by the Israel Defence Forces with a combination of mobile patrols, patrol bases, and temporary observation posts. As of July 14, 2000, UNIFIL comprised 5,075 troops, from Fiji (592), Finland (632), France (251), Ghana (783), India (619), Ireland (656), Italy (46), Nepal (712), Poland (630), Sweden (44), and Ukraine (110). UNIFIL was assisted in its tasks by some 50 military observers of UNTSO. UNIFIL also employed 464 civilian staff.

The basic problem remained that Lebanon was not strong enough to play its proper security role in the south, and UNIFIL was too weak to enforce a peace. As a result, the IDF forward deployed at the border in near readiness for war. Repeated low level clashes took place, and the Hizbollah retained a major presence. The risk involved became all too clear in September 2000 when the Hizbollah reacted to the outbreak of Israeli-Lebanese fighting by kidnapping three IDF soldiers in the Shebaa Farms area, although it claimed that it had acted in an area of Lebanon that Israel was still occupying.

THE FUTURE THREAT TO ISRAEL PROPER—WITH AND WITHOUT A PEACE

The risk of low level war is real, but major conflict seems less probable than a Second Intifada. Hizbollah and other Lebanese guerilla forces have not proved effective in infiltrating into Israel in the past, and have been restricted largely to sporadic artillery and rocket attacks on Israeli territory. The Hizbollah and Amal may, however, become much more dangerous if it can operate directly from territory on Israel's borders, and they may have artillery rockets with ranges of well over 60 kilometers.

One critical issue will be whether the Hizbollah feels committed to its ideological opposition to Israel's existence or whether it will accept a peace agreement that results in Israel's withdrawal from southern Lebanon. Hizbollah has declined to say whether it would keep fighting Israel now that the IDF has withdrawn from southern Lebanon.[747] Its speeches and public statements immediately after the collapse were equally ambiguous.[748] Sheik Hassan Nasrallah made it clear that the Hizbollah would seek to attack Shebaa farms.[749]

The Hizbollah could play a major role in a Second Intifada, although it has concentrated on the "liberation" of southern Lebanon. The Hizbollah's "defeat" of the IDF has made it a regional actor and the Hizbollah did play a role in the Israeli-Palestinian fighting that began in September 2000. It seized three IDF soldiers in a disputed part of the Israeli-Lebanese border and lured an Israeli intelligence officer and reserve colonel into Lebanon where it kidnapped him.

Sheik Hassan Nasrallah delivered a series of speeches calling for a Second Intifada: "If you don't have bullets, who among you doesn't have knives? Hide the knife, and when he comes close to the enemy let him stab him. Let the stab be fatal." Sheik Nasrallah addressed the Palestinians as "holy war comrades-in-arms" and proposed a strategy of gradually escalating the Intifada from stones to daggers to firearms and other means of military combat.[750]

Iran—including some of Iran's "moderates"—has played a role in encouraging the Hizbollah. Nasrallah very publicly announced in July 2000 that he had met with Iran's President Khatami, and that the Iranian government opposed any efforts to disarm Hizbollah after Israel's withdrawal from Lebanon.[751] The Iranian foreign minister, Kamal Kharazi, consulted in early October 2000 with Sheik Nasrallah and Kharazi told reporters that, "The issue of Jerusalem is not only important for the Palestinians, but all the Muslims of the world. This indicates how deep the Israeli provocation was in its attack on Al Aksa Mosque."[752] There were unconfirmed reports in October 2000 that the Hizbollah was seeking to find ways of sending arms to Fatah and to the police force as well as to Hamas and Islamic Jihad.

The Hizbollah has shown, however, that it can negotiate with Israel under some circumstances. In 1993, it accepted an agreement negotiated by US Secretary of State Warren Christopher in which the Hizbollah and Israel agreed not to attack each other's population centers in areas around the Israeli security zone. This agreement sharply cut the number of attacks on Shi'ite villages and the Israeli towns in the northern Galilee, although there have been some violations.[753] The Hizbollah repeatedly participated in further such negotiations through 1999. In June 2000, Nasrallah also stated that the Hizbollah would give negotiators time to try to work out a full Israeli withdrawal and clarification of the situation on the border, and Hizbollah was relatively careful to only attack IDF targets in disputed areas even during the Palestinian-Israeli violence in September and October 2000.[754]

Another key issue is whether Syria and the Lebanese Army will seek to keep the Hizbollah and other Lebanese guerillas from attacking Israel and/or whether Israel can find some form of military pressure—such as strategic bombing—that will force them to try to exercise such control. The Lebanese Army did not fully deploy into the Lebanese-Israel border area after June 2000, but it did establish some points in the border zone on July 9, its first actual deployment in the area in 22 years.[755]

As of September 2000, the Lebanese Army had one battalion of around 5,000 troops in the area, although these forces only went in as a political gesture, and as part of the bargain that allow UNIFIL to deploy to the border, and remained largely in their casernes. The Lebanese Army left security up to the UN, Amal, and Hizbollah. It also had a police presence, although only one government policeman was present even in an important town like Jezzine. The military tribunal tried some 2,000 supporters and members of the SLA after Israeli withdrawal was held in Beirut.[756] The various disputes over the policing of the border area have also been left largely to the UN.[757]

Syria is a more important player. Most experts currently believe that Syria can exercise such control over the Hizbollah *if* it chooses to do so. They believe that

Map 9.1
The Lebanon Frontier

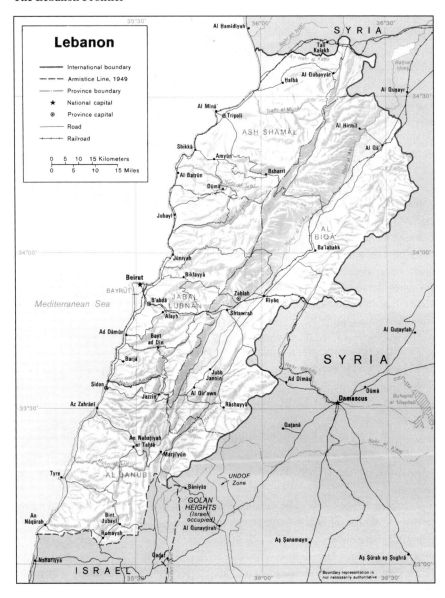

Syria can exercise similar control over the other militias in Lebanon, including other Shi'ite militias like Amal. It is not clear, however, that Syria could continue to extend such control if it ever proved willing to remove its military forces from Lebanon. Furthermore, Syria's authority in Lebanon may be eroding. The landslide victory of Rafik Hariri over the Syrian-backed candidate for Prime Minister in September 2000, indicates that Bashar al-Assad does not have the authority of his father.[758]

Syria may, however, prefer to support increased Hizbollah activity against Israel in order to try to push Israel into giving up the Golan and/or divert Israeli forces from the Golan and pin more IDF units down in Southern Lebanon. It could continue to use the Hizbollah in such a role while maintaining the status quo on the Golan or even participating in a peace agreement. As long as Syria can maintain some degree of plausible deniability, it can make some use of the threat from the Hizbollah almost regardless of the situation. Further, if a catastrophic breakdown should occur in the peace talks, Syria might be able to both expand the Hizbollah and Amal militias. These forces could not invade Israel or even hope to maintain a successful pattern of infiltration, but they could conduct more low-level attacks across the border and outside the region and present an additional security problem.

The Palestinian refugees in Lebanon and Syria are another wild card. The Lebanese Army has shown far more concern with limiting the operations of the Palestinians in the refugee camps in Lebanon than with securing the border, but it might tolerate Syrian and/or Iranian backing of the Palestinians in operations against Israel if this did not mean massive Israeli air strikes or reprisals. If the Second Intifada grows bad enough, Lebanon may also have no choice other than to let the Palestinians vent their anger against Israel. Certainly, Syria and Lebanon's firm opposition to any peace settlement that does not involve the return of the Palestinian refugees to "Palestine" presents a problem. They cannot oppose a peace and then easily oppose some form of Palestinian action.

Finally, it is possible that Iran and Syria might split over a peace settlement with Israel, and that Iran might try to use the Hizbollah to break up or resist the peace process. It is not clear whether Iran has the leverage to do so, particularly since Syria has considerable influence over the Hizbollah and controls the Amal—which might counterbalance any extremist Shi'ite forces. Nevertheless, this is one more risk in an already long list.

10

Jordanian–Israeli Conflicts

A conflict between Jordan and Israel is substantially less likely than a conflict between Israel and Syria. Jordan has shown little interest in risking strategic attacks or further losses of territory since 1967. It held secret talks with Israel long before it reached a formal peace agreement. The threat of Israeli intervention helped keep Syria from intervening in Jordan's battle with the Palestinians in 1970, and although Jordan sent a brigade to help Syria in 1973, it took no action across its border.

Jordan signed a peace accord with Israel on July 25, 1994, called the Washington Declaration. This agreement has led to a rapid normalization of Jordanian-Israeli relations, is leading to important further changes in Jordan's forces, and is leading both nations to adopt new confidence-building measures. Article 3 of the Washington Declaration has led Jordan and Israel to resolve their remaining differences over the border between Jordan and Israel's defense lines in Israel and on the West Bank. Furthermore, it has led to agreement on the use of air space, water, and the delimitation of their boundary in the Gulf of Aqaba.

Article 4 not only calls for the adoption of bilateral confidence-building measures, but also for regional efforts. It formalizes the long-standing tacit agreement between the two countries to avoid the use of force, suppress terrorist and extremist activity, and avoid the support of hostile third parties or groups. It precludes Jordan and Israel from allowing third party military forces or groups on their soil that, "adversely prejudice the security of the other Party." It has led Jordan and Israel to establish strong liaison groups to deal with security issues, and cooperate in the Multilateral Working Group on Arms Control and Regional Security (ACRS).

Jordan has little to gain from war and much to lose. Jordan has no near-term prospect of being able to integrate the Palestinians in the West Bank and Jerusalem into Jordan, and Jordan is vulnerable to Israeli air and artillery attacks. Jordan also faces more of an Arab threat from Iraq and Syria than from Israel. Since 1992, Jordan has been fighting an almost nightly low-level battle with Iraqi smugglers, many of whom are trying to move arms into or through Jordan. Jordan is concerned about missile defense in any future clash between Israel and Iraq and Iran. It is discussing the possible creation of some form of missile defense umbrella with Israel and the US. It also seems likely that Jordan, Israel, and the US would cooperate in dealing with any more serious Iraqi threat to Jordan, any post-Hafez Assad rebirth of a Syrian threat to Israel, or Islamist extremist-led conflict on the West Bank.

The current balance of Israeli and Jordanian forces is shown in Table 10.1, and is summarized in Figure 10.1. The disparity in force strength is striking, and scarcely gives Jordan any incentive to plan for war with Israel. So is the disparity in military spending shown in Figure 10.2, the disparity in arms imports shown in Figure 10.3, and the massive problems in the recapitalization of Jordan's forces shown in Figure 10.4.

Figure 10.5 shows that Jordanian arms imports have recovered slightly since the Gulf War, largely due to US aid. At the same time, it is obvious that Jordan cannot hope to compete with Israel in force quantity and force quality or in any conflict where Jordan does not have massive support from other Arab states. Furthermore, Jordan is currently planning to create small and lighter land forces which will be better equipped to deal with threats like the smuggling and infiltration problems it faces along its border with Iraq, but which will mean smaller tank forces and lighter major combat units. This is just the opposite of the force mix it would need to fight Israeli heavy armor.

JORDAN'S MILITARY FORCES

The trends in Jordan's force strength are shown in Table 10.2. It is clear that Jordan has made some important improvements in its capabilities since 1996, including the acquisition of F-16s. It is equally clear that it has not been able to begin to compete with Israel in either military expenditures or military modernization. Since 1990, Jordan has faced an economic crisis that has severely limited its ability to maintain its military forces, much less increase them.[759] However, Jordan has seen an increase in foreign aid since its peace with Israel.

Jordan has one of the best-planned force structures in the Middle East, and it has been able to retain significant defensive and war fighting capabilities in spite of its economic problems. At the same time, its first line tanks now consist of 354 M-60A1/A3 conversions and 288 Challenger Is, supported by 270 much less capable Khalid (Chieftain) tanks.[760] Jordan's other armored fighting vehicles consist of 19

Table 10.1
The Jordanian-Israeli Balance in 2001

Category/Weapon	Israel	Jordan
Defense Budget		
(In 2000, $US Current Billions)	$7.0	$0.488
Arms Imports: 1996-1999 ($M)		
New Orders	4,500	800
Deliveries	4,500	300
Mobilization Base		
Men Ages 13-17	281,000	274,000
Men Ages 18-22	270,000	245,000
Manpower		
Total Active	172,500	103,880
(Conscript)	107,500	-
Total Reserve	425,000	35,000
Total	597,500	139,000
Paramilitary	8,050	10,000
Land Forces		
Active Manpower	130,000	90,000
(Conscripts)	85,000	-
Reserve Manpower	400,000	30,000
Total Active & Reserve Manpower	530,000	120,000
Main Battle Tanks	3,900	1,246(300)
AIFVs/Armored Cars/Lt. Tanks	408	241
APCs/Recce/Scouts	5,900	1,450
WWII Half-Tracks	500(3,500)	0
ATGM Launchers	1,300	610
SP Artillery	855	412
Towed Artillery	520	132
MRLs	198	0
Mortars	6,440	800
SSM Launchers	48	0
AA Guns	850	416
Lt. SAM Launchers	1,298	1,184
Air & Air Defense Forces		
Active Air Force Manpower	36,000	13,400
Active Air Defense Command	0	0
Air Force Reserve Manpower	20,000	-
Air Defense Command Reserve Manpower	0	0
Aircraft		
Total Fighter/FGA/Recce	446(250)	106
Fighter	0	41
FGA/Fighter	405	0

Table 10.1 (continued)

Category/Weapon	Israel	Jordan
Air & Air Defense Forces		
FGA	25	65
Recce	10	0
Airborne Early Warning (AEW)	6	0
Electronic Warfare (EW)	37	0
Fixed Wing	37	0
Helicopter	0	0
Maritime Reconnaissance (MR)	3	0
Combat Capable Trainer	26	2
Tanker	6	0
Transport	37	12
Helicopters		
Attack/Armed	133	16
SAR/ASW	6	-
Transport & Other	160	52
Total	299	68
SAM Forces		
Batteries	28	14
Heavy Launchers	79	80
Medium Launchers	0	0
AA Guns	0	-
Naval Forces		
Active Manpower	6,500	480
Reserve Manpower	5,000	-
Total Manpower	11,500	480
Naval Commandos/Marines	300	0
Submarines	2	0
Destroyers/Frigates/Corvettes	3	0
Missile	3	0
Other	0	0
Missile Patrol	12	0
Coastal/Inshore Patrol	32	6
Mine	0	0
Amphibious Ships	1	0
Landing Craft/Light Support	4	(3)
Fixed-wing Combat Aircraft	0	0
MR/MPA	0	0
ASW/Combat Helicopter	0	0
Other Helicopters	-	-

Note: Figures in parentheses show additional equipment known to be in long-term storage. Some Syrian tanks shown in parentheses are used as fire points in fixed positions.

Source: Adapted by Anthony H. Cordesman from data provided by US experts, and the IISS, *Military Balance.*

Figure 10.1
Israel versus Jordan in 2001

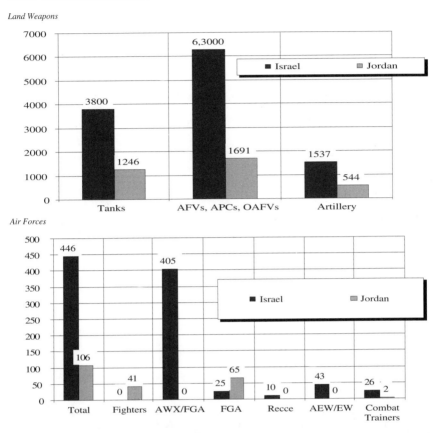

Land Weapons

Air Forces

Note: Total Artillery includes towed and self-propelled tube artillery and multiple rocket launchers. Total air forces include only operational fixed wing fighter, fighter-attack, and reconnaissance aircraft in combat units, less aircraft in combat training units.

Source: Adapted by Anthony H. Cordesman from data provided by US experts, and the IISS, *Military Balance.*

aging Scorpions and 32 BMP-2s. It has converted some of its roughly 1,400 M-113s from APCs to AIFVs, but a substantial number of the rest of its M-113s are not fully operable.[761]

Jordan does have 412 relatively modern US-made self-propelled artillery weapons and 132 towed artillery weapons, but it cannot support most of its artillery with advanced target acquisition, fire and battle management, and counter-battery capabilities. It is well armed with modern TOW and Dragon anti-tank weapons, but these are more valuable in the defense than in the attack.

Figure 10.2
Trends in Jordanian-Israeli Military Spending: 1985–1997
(In $US 1997 Constant Millions)

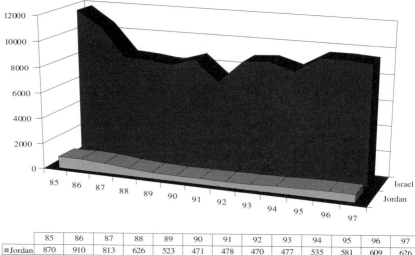

	85	86	87	88	89	90	91	92	93	94	95	96	97
▣ Jordan	870	910	813	626	523	471	478	470	477	535	581	609	626
▪ Israel	11750	10555	8400	8280	8060	8620	7040	8730	8880	8330	9440	9490	9340

Source: Adapted by Anthony H. Cordesman from US State Department, Bureau of Arms Control,
World Military Expenditures and Arms Transfers, Washington, GPO, Table I, various editions.

Jordan has significant numbers of AA guns—including 52 ZSU-23–4 radar-guided guns, 100 self-propelled SA-8s and SA-13s, and 240 SA-16 manportable surface-to-air missile launchers, but these are only capable of protecting ground troops at short ranges and low altitudes. Jordan's IHawk missile launchers are obsolescent Mark II versions which would take $100 million to fully modernize, and which are fixed and vulnerable to Israeli low altitude attacks, using anti-radiation missiles (ARMs), and electronic countermeasures.[762]

Jordan's air force is now limited to roughly 106 fully operational combat aircraft. Only its 25 Mirage F-1s and the 12 recently acquired F-16s from the US have significant air-to-air combat capability—although its 50 F-5E-IIs may be upgraded as a result of a recent agreement with Singapore. The Mirage F-1 aircraft cannot hope to engage IAF F-16s and F-15s with any success, and Jordan lacks any form of AEW aircraft and its ground-based air battle management capabilities have severe technical limitations. Jordan does have 16 AH-1S attack helicopters, but these could not fly evasive attack profiles over most of the border with Israel because they would be highly vulnerable.[763]

Jordan had to cut its armed forces from 130,000 troops in 1991 to 90,000 troops in 1997, although it has since built back up to nearly 104,000 men. It has severe parts and/or munitions shortages for some of its tanks, TOW ATGMs, US-supplied

Figure 10.3
Trends in Jordanian-Israeli Arms Import Deliveries: 1985–1997
($US 1997 Constant Millions)

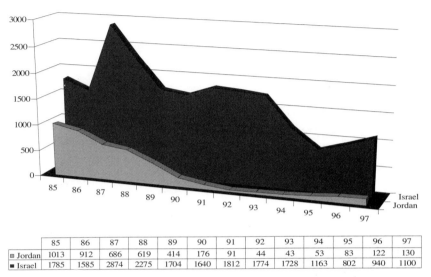

	85	86	87	88	89	90	91	92	93	94	95	96	97
Jordan	1013	912	686	619	414	176	91	44	43	53	83	122	130
Israel	1785	1585	2874	2275	1704	1640	1812	1774	1728	1163	802	940	1100

Source: Adapted by Anthony H. Cordesman from US State Department, Bureau of Arms Control, *World Military Expenditures and Arms Transfers*, GPO, Washington, various editions.

trucks, and 50 F-5E/F fighters, and is trying to sell its 200 oldest M-48 tanks.[764] Jordan is expected to finance the improvement and modernization of its armed forces using increased US military aid to purchase advanced equipment such as more combat aircraft, M-60A3 tanks and border monitoring equipment.[765] Jordan is trying to improve its military relations with moderate Arab states.

King Abdullah is pursuing closer ties with the Persian Gulf states in hopes of mending relationships damaged during the Gulf War in order to increase joint military training.[766] In addition, he is exploring maintenance and upgrading cooperation with Egypt. This cooperation would help Jordan since Egypt's military industry is considerably more advanced than Jordan's.[767]

Figure 10.6 summarizes Jordan's current equipment strength and it is surprising that Jordan has been able to maintain numbers this large. Jordan has been starved of arms imports from many of its key suppliers in past years for nearly a decade, and it would take years to rebuild Jordan's military forces even if major new orders were placed over the next few years.

Such orders are unlikely. Jordan has begun to restore its military relations with the West and moderate Arab states, and is receiving some important aid and arms transfers from the US. Nevertheless, it still lacks the funds to buy major amounts of new armor and high technology artillery and air defense equipment. Jordan is

Figure 10.4
The Jordanian Recapitalization Crisis: Arms Deliveries: 1985–1997
($US 1997 Constant Millions)

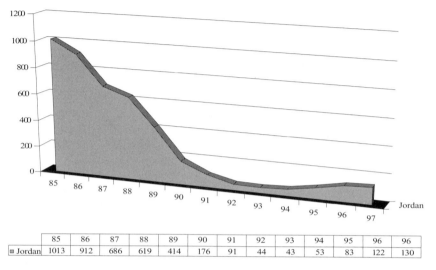

	85	86	87	88	89	90	91	92	93	94	95	96	96
▣ Jordan	1013	912	686	619	414	176	91	44	43	53	83	122	130

Source: Adapted by Anthony H. Cordesman from US State Department, Bureau of Arms Control, *World Military Expenditures and Arms Transfers*, GPO, Washington, various editions.

seeking totals of surplus equipment as high as 36–72 F-16s and 200 M-1A2s, but it will at best take several years before Jordan gets such aid and it is unlikely that Jordan will get all the aid it desires.[768] As a result, much of the new equipment Jordan does obtain is likely to do more to offset the impact of Jordan's steady aging of its existing inventory of major combat weapons than increase Jordan's offensive power against Israel.[769]

JORDANIAN SUPPORT OF PALESTINIAN FORCES IN THE WEST BANK, JERUSALEM, AND ISRAEL

Nevertheless, it is still possible to conceive of conditions under which Jordan might go to war with Israel. King Abdullah II is a proven army officer with considerable experience and leadership capability and began to reorganize the Jordanian Army to ensure its loyalty and efficiency shortly after coming to the throne.[770] Even so, King Hussein's death and Jordan's continuing economic problems create uncertainties about the future character of the regime, and Jordan cannot ignore events in the West Bank or Gaza. Any war would be a worst case contingency, but there are three forms that such a conflict could take: Support of Palestinian forces, a unilateral attack on the West Bank, and joint action with Syria in an "Eastern Front."

Figure 10.5
Jordanian Arms Agreements and Deliveries By Major Suppliers: 1987–1999
($Current Millions)

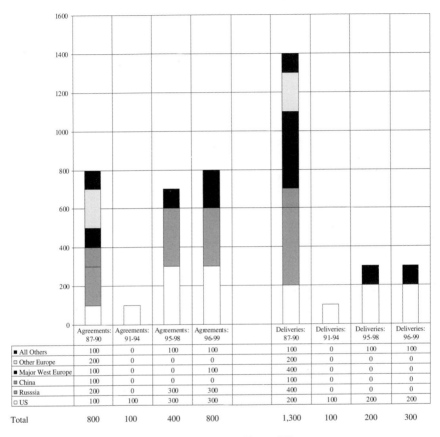

	Agreements: 87-90	Agreements: 91-94	Agreements: 95-98	Agreements: 96-99	Deliveries: 87-90	Deliveries: 91-94	Deliveries: 95-98	Deliveries: 96-99
■ All Others	100	0	100	100	100	0	100	100
□ Other Europe	200	0	0	0	200	0	0	0
■ Major West Europe	100	0	0	100	400	0	0	0
▨ China	100	0	0	0	100	0	0	0
▨ Russsia	200	0	300	300	400	0	0	0
□ US	100	100	300	300	200	100	200	200
Total	800	100	400	800	1,300	100	200	300

Notes: Includes Gulf states, Arab-Israeli states, North Africa, and Yemen.
0 = less than $50 million or nil, and all data rounded to the nearest $100 million.

Source: Richard F. Grimmett, *Conventional Arms Transfers to the Developing Nations*, Congressional Research Service, various editions.

The first type of conflict—which would involve the least risk for Jordan—would be a low-level conflict in which Jordan actively and covertly supported Palestinian attacks on Israel, but did not overtly use its military forces. Jordan has not acted as a sanctuary for hostile Palestinian elements since 1970, and put serious new limits on the Hamas operations in Jordan in 1998 and 1999. Nevertheless, some radical collapse of the peace process, or series of violent clashes between the IDF and Palestinians, might create political conditions which undermine the peace

Table 10.2
Force Trends in Jordan

Category/Weapon	1975	1980	1985	1990	1995	2000	2001
Manpower							
Total Active	80,200	67,200	70,300	82,250	98,800	104,500	103,880
(Conscript)	-	-	-	-	-	-	-
Total Reserve	-	-	35,000	35,000	35,000	30,000	35,000
Total Active & Reserve	-	-	105,300	117,250	133,800	134,500	139,000
Paramilitary	10,000	10,000	11,000	17,000	10,000	10,000	10,000
Land Forces							
Active Manpower	75,000	60,000	62,750	74,000	90,000	90,000	90,000
(Conscripts)	-	-	-	-	-	-	-
Reserve Manpower	-	-	30,000	30,000	30,000	30,000	30,000
Total Reserve & Active Manpower	-	-	92,750	104,000	120,000	120,000	120,000
Main Battle Tanks	440	609	795	1,131	1,141	1,217	1,246
(Fixed & in Storage)			-	(260)	(270)	(300)	(300)
AIFVs/Armored Cars/Lt. Tanks	240	140	32	188	204	224	241
APCs/Recce/Scouts	440	962	850	1,244	1,100	1,100	1,100
WWII Half-Tracks	0	0	0	0	0	0	0
ATGM Launchers	-	162	610	640	640	640	610
SP Artillery	55	173	144	237	370	406	412
Towed Artillery	160	90	91	89	115	115	132
MRLs	0	0	0	0	0	0	0
Mortars	-	400	500	600	450+	800	800
SSM Launchers	0	0	0	0	0	0	0
AA Guns	200	200	366	408	360	360	416
Lt. SAM Launchers	-	-	-	-	890	965+	1,184
Air & Air Defense Forces							
Active Air Force Manpower	5,000	7,000	7,200	10,000	8,000	13,600	13,400
Active Air Defense	-	-	-	-	(2,000)	(3,400)	(3,400)
Air Force Reserve Manpower	-	-	-	5,000	5,000	-	-
Air Defense Reserve Manpower	0	0	0	0	0	0	0

Table 10.2 (continued)

Category/Weapon	1975	1980	1985	1990	1995	2000	2001
Air & Air Defense Forces							
Aircraft							
Total							
Fighter/FGA/Recce	42	58	121	104	82	93	106
Fighter	18	24	35	32	30	41	41
FGA/Fighter	0	0	0	0	0	0	0
FGA	24	24	68	72	50	50	65
Recce	0	0	0	0	0	0	0
Airborne Early							
Warning (AEW)	0	0	0	0	0	0	0
Electronic Warfare (EW)	0	0	0	0	0	0	0
(Fixed Wing)	-	-	-	-	-	-	-
(Helicopter)	-	-	-	-	-	-	-
Maritime							
Reconnaissance (MR)	0	0	0	0	0	0	0
Combat Capable							
Trainer/OCU	7	10	18	0	2	2	2
Tanker	0	0	0	0	0	0	0
Transport	11	9	10	13	20	14	12
Helicopters							
Attack/Armed	0	0	0	24	24	16	16
ASW/SAR	0	0	0	0	0	0	0
Transport & Other	13	17	38	32	20	46	52
Total	13	17	38	56	44	62	68
SAM Forces (operated							
by Army)							
Batteries	0	14	14	14	14	14	14
Heavy Launchers	0	-	-	126	80	80	80
Medium Launchers	0	-	20	40	-	-	-
AA Guns	-	-	-	-	-	-	-
Naval Forces							
Active Manpower	250	200	350	250	600	480	480
Reserve Manpower	-	-	-	-	-	-	-
Total Manpower	250	200	350	250	600	480	480
Submarines	0	0	0	0	0	0	0
Destroyers/Frigates/							
Corvettes							
Missile	0	0	0	0	0	0	0
Other	0	0	0	0	0	˙0	0
Missile Patrol	0	0	0	0	0	0	0
Coastal/Inshore							
Patrol	12	9	9	1	5	3	6
Mine	0	0	0	0	0	0	0

Table 10.2 (continued)

Category/Weapon	1975	1980	1985	1990	1995	2000	2001
Naval Forces							
Amphibious Ships	0	0	0	0	0	0	0
Landing Craft/Light							
Support	0	0	0	0	3	7	(3)
Fixed Wing Combat							
Aircraft	0	0	0	0	0	0	0
MR/MPA	0	0	0	0	0	0	0
ASW/Combat							
Helicopter	0	0	0	0	0	0	0
Other Helicopters	0	0	0	0	0	0	0

Source: Adapted by Anthony H. Cordesman from data provided by US and regional experts, and the IISS, *Military Balance.*

process. Jordan might then be willing to provide bases, training facilities, and arms to Palestinian extremists on the West Bank. Such Jordanian support for a low-intensity war in the West Bank might significantly complicate Israel's internal security problems.

Jordan could also escalate its involvement in such a conflict by sending in cadres of lightly armed special forces from the Jordanian Army under civilian cover. Such Jordanian covert forces would be easier for Israel to identify than native Palestinians, but would have far more training than the Palestinians. They could make a significant contribution to any Palestinian military effort that involved urban warfare, or terrorism that required high levels of discipline and technical expertise. Cadres of trained advisors and troops have played a significant role in previous guerrilla and low-level wars—often under conditions where they preserved "plausible deniability." Such a use of Jordanian forces would allow Jordan to exploit its strengths—a highly trained and well-disciplined army—with less risk than other uses of Jordanian forces.

At the same time, Israel has established a secure perimeter along the border with Jordan in the past, and the terrain favors such a security perimeter as long as a Palestinian entity does not exist on the West Bank that cannot be cut off from Jordan. Israel can also retaliate with the kind of air and artillery strikes it has used against the Hizbollah in Lebanon, and retaliate economically by sealing off the border between Jordan and Israel. Anything but very low-level covert Jordanian support of a Palestinian conflict would be detected by Israel in a matter of hours or days, and would also present major problems in terms of US reactions and those of other states. Jordan would risk serious problems in terms of access to foreign investment, trade, loans, and aid.

As a result, low-level Jordanian support of Palestinian military efforts does not seem likely to have any significant effect on the military balance unless the

Figure 10.6
Jordanian Major Military Equipment in 2001

Land Forces

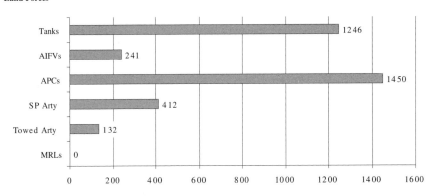

Air Forces

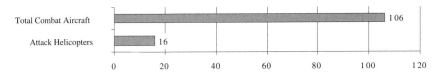

Naval Forces

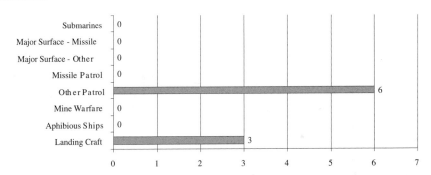

Source: Adapted by Anthony H. Cordesman from data provided by US and regional experts, and the IISS, *Military Balance*.

Palestinian entity on the West Bank becomes so strong that Israel can no longer secure the present border with Jordan, the final settlement talks between Israel and the Palestinians fail after the Palestinian Authority has established full control over most Palestinian population centers, or a hard-line Israeli government comes to power and halts the peace process. Under these conditions, the IDF might take time to reestablish a firm control over movements from Jordan into the West Bank, and

Map 10.1
Israel and Jordan

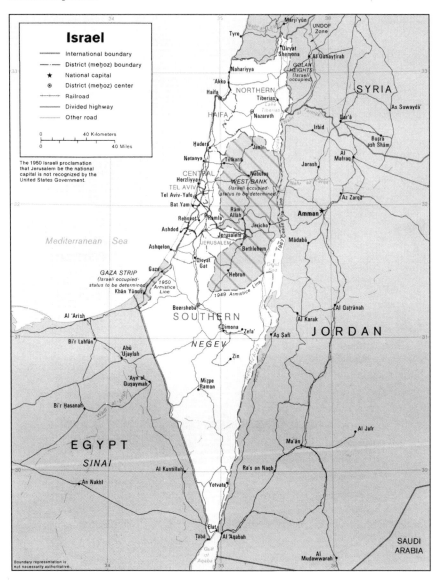

might be unable to deal with any covert Jordanian presence on the West Bank. Even so, such a contingency is something of a contradiction in terms. Israel is only likely to give up its ability to secure the border after it secures and tests a "warm peace" with both Jordan and its Palestinians. Further, Jordan's current regime is unlikely to cooperate with any Palestinian entity that falls under Islamist extremist or other radical control because such an entity would be as much of a threat to Jordan as it would to Israel.

JORDANIAN "RESCUE" OF PALESTINIANS IN THE WEST BANK: JORDANIAN RE-OCCUPATION OF THE WEST BANK

The second contingency would be a crisis-driven Jordanian intervention in the West Bank. Such a contingency is extremely unlikely under current conditions. It would either require Israel to abandon the peace process so catastrophically that Jordan would feel compelled to go to the aid of the Palestinians or a massive change in the character of Jordan's government. Even then, Jordan would only be willing to take risks of this kind if Islamic extremists dominated it, or extreme Israeli provocation threatened Jordan's existence. This would effectively require a contingency like a forced Israeli expulsion of the Palestinians living in the West Bank. Such events are conceivable, but they presently strain the limits of political credibility.

If such a battle did occur, Jordan would almost certainly lose decisively during the first day or days of combat. Jordan's forces are well trained and disciplined, with some of the best officers, NCOs, and career troops in the developing world. They have significant defensive capability against limited to mid-intensity Israeli attacks that attempt to move across the Jordan and up the East Bank. Jordanian forces have performed well in exercises with US troops, such as the desert warfare exercises the US and Jordan have conducted since August 1995. In fact, Israel might find it as painful and futile to attack deep into Jordan, and particularly into the area above the East Bank of the Jordan River, as Jordan would find it to attack Israel.[771]

Air power, technology, and force ratios do, however, decisively favor Israel. Jordan could only attack across the Jordan by moving virtually its entire land forces down to the East Bank. This would provide clear strategic warning and allow Israel to use its air force extensively with only limited resistance by the Jordanian air force and ground-based air defenses. Jordanian land forces would then have to fight their way across the Jordan, and up the West Bank, in the face of overwhelming Israeli superiority in the air, a high level of Israeli superiority on the ground, and Israeli ability to exploit a wide range of defensive barriers.

Jordan does not come close to having the kind of forces that could survive a move down to the Jordan River through narrow and predictable routes, cross a relatively open river plain averaging about 30 kilometers wide with a water barrier in the middle, and fight through Israeli forward defenses and then up in the heights on the West Bank. Only a few roads go down the 900 meters from the heights above the East Bank and the 400–600 meters up from the Jordan River. Israel can also couple its advantage in modern UAVs, reconnaissance and strike aircraft, and AEW to extraordinarily short flight times from Israel to land targets moving through the West Bank. Flight times vary from 2 to 5 minutes once an aircraft is airborne, and Israel has demonstrated excellent capabilities to surge high sortie rates and manage large numbers of sorties.

The only area where the Jordanian army could hope to take advantage of rough terrain is in the far northwestern part of Jordan at the junction of the Yarmuk and Jordan Rivers, just south of Lake Tiberius. The Jordanian heights of Umm Qays also overlook Lake Tiberius and the Galilee and would allow Jordan to use its artillery against targets in Israel. This, however, is an area where there are no easy routes up and down the heights, and where Israel has excellent surveillance capabilities. The Yarmuk River is also a significant terrain barrier with only a few crossing points, and any attack through Irbid that involved armored or mechanized forces would be highly vulnerable to air power, systems like the MLRS, and attack helicopters.

The Jordan River Valley becomes progressively harder to fight across at any point about 10 kilometers south of the junction between the Yarmuk and Jordan Rivers. It opens up into a plain 5 to 40 kilometers wide. Israel is geographically vulnerable through the Beit Shean or Jezreel Valley, but forces attacking in this direction also become vulnerable to Israeli air and armor. Furthermore, it would take Jordan days to mass a sustainable force to launch such an attack, and at least six hours to cross the terrain and river barrier.

The distances involved are short by the standards of most wars, but they are still long enough for Israel to employ air power with great effect. It is roughly 40 kilometers from Irbid to Beisan/Beit Shean, 85 kilometers from Jerash to Irbid, 55 kilometers from Salt to Amman, 55 kilometers from Amman to Jericho via the King Hussein Bridge, and 45 kilometers by the King Abdullah Bridge. The southern route along the Dead Sea is 100 kilometers from Amman and the route to Eilat through Aqaba and Maan is 130 kilometers.

ARMS CONTROL AND SECURITY IMPLICATIONS

Israel can scarcely ignore Jordan's capabilities in structuring its peace and security agreements with the Palestinians, or its arms control negotiations. At the same time, Israel can scarcely ignore Jordan's participation in the peace process, and cooperation with Israel in bilateral and regional arms control efforts.

Jordan cannot by itself pose anything approaching an existential threat to Israel. Jordan's present and projected forces do not force Israel to seek the same kind of complex security arrangements it insisted upon in reaching a peace settlement with Egypt, and is certain to insist upon in reaching a peace settlement with Syria. In spite of their peace agreement, both nations are faced with the need to maintain strong deterrent and defensive capabilities relative to the other. However, Jordan is far more of a problem for arms control in terms of its potential impact in combination with other Arab states than as an independent military power.

If anything, Jordan became so weak in the mid-1990s that this threatened its ability to maintain armed forces which can firmly deter any pressure from Iraq and

Syria. Jordanian self-sufficiency and self-reliance are also critical to obtaining Jordanian public support for the peace process and convincing the Palestinian Authority that Jordan can be a strong partner in any regional security arrangements.

There is a good case for providing Jordan with enough military equipment and both military and economic aid to ensure that it can play its proper role in preserving regional stability and securing its peace settlement with Israel. There is an equally good case for ensuring that Jordan has enough military prestige to allow Jordanian military forces to act as a substitute for Palestinian forces. Such prestige is essential to underpin Jordan's monarchy, and create a climate for some form of federation or confederation between Jordan and a Palestinian entity.

11

A Jordanian–Syrian Alliance, Turkey, and Wars on the Eastern Front

The final contingency that might involve Jordan in any near-term conflict is a Jordanian alliance with Syria, and the creation of a broader Arab "Eastern Front." The possible total forces that could be drawn upon in such contingencies are shown in Table 11.1 and summarized in Figure 11.1, but such comparisons again list total potential forces, and not the forces that would actually be deployed in war.

In practice, there seems to be little real world political prospect that Jordan and Syria would join forces in such a war. Israel might just as easily join Jordan to defend it from Syria. Syria has long posed a potential threat to Jordan and Jordanian planning spends as much time on this contingency as a war with Israel.

IF JORDAN SHOULD JOIN SYRIA

Even if Jordan and Syria did fight as allies, they would have problems in fighting effectively and developing an effective joint command. Their forces are not standardized, do not have interoperable land or air forces, and have no joint training. Rather than achieve any military synergy, an alliance might actually add to the qualitative problems of each separate force by leaving gaps in capability, or creating coordination problems.

The IAF is now organized and equipped to use a combination of electronic intelligence aircraft, jammers, stand-off munitions, land-based strike systems, UAVs, ground-based radars, unattended sensors and other measures to suppress both Syrian and Jordanian air defenses. It has steadily improved its technology bases to reflect the lessons of the Gulf War, while Syria and Jordan have made

Table 11.1
Israel Versus Jordan and Syria in 2001: The "Eastern Front" Balance

Category/Weapon	Israel	Syria + Jordan	Syria	Jordan
Defense Budget				
(In 2000, $Current Billions)	$7.0	2.288	$1.8	$0.488
Arms Imports: 1996-1999 ($M)				
New Orders	4,500	1,300	500	800
Deliveries	4,500	600	300	300
Mobilization Base				
Men Ages 13-17	281,000	1,316,000	1,042,000	274,000
Men Ages 18-22	270,000	1,098,000	853,000	245,000
Manpower				
Total Active	172,500	419,800	316,000	103,880
(Conscript)	107,500	-	-	-
Total Reserve	425,000	431,000	396,000	35,000
Total	597,500	851,000	712,000	139,000
Paramilitary	8,050	118,000	108,000	10,000
Land Forces				
Active Manpower	130,000	305,000	215,000	90,000
(Conscripts)	85,000	-	-	-
Reserve Manpower	400,000	330,000	300,000	30,000
Total Active & Reserve				
Manpower	530,000	636,000	515,000	120,000
Main Battle Tanks	3,900	4,896	3,650 (1200)	1,246 (300)
AIFVs/Armored Cars/Lt. Tanks	400	3,545	3,305	241
APCs/Recce/Scouts	5,900	2,950	1,500	1,450
WWII Half-Tracks	500(3,500)	0	0	0
ATGM Launchers	1,300	4,000	3,390+	610
SP Artillery	855	862	450	412
Towed Artillery	520		1,600	132
MRLs	198	1,732	480	0
Mortars	6,440	5,300	4,500+	800
SSM Launchers	48	72	72	0
AA Guns	850	2,476	2,060	416
Lt. SAM Launchers	1,298	5,239	4,055	1,184

Table 11.1 (continued)

Category/Weapon	Israel	Syria + Jordan	Syria	Jordan
Air & Air Defense Forces				
Active Air Force Manpower	36,000	53,400	40,000	13,400
Active Air Defense Command	0	60,000	60,000	0
Air Force Reserve Manpower	20,000	113,400	92,000	-
Air Defense Command Reserve Manpower	0		-	·0
Aircraft				
Total Fighter/FGA/Recce	446(250)	695	589	106
Fighter	0	351	310	41
FGA/Fighter	405	0	0	0
FGA	25	219	154	65
Recce	10	14	14	0
Airborne Early Warning (AEW)	6	0	0	0
Electronic Warfare (EW)	37	10	10	0
Fixed Wing	37	0	0	0
Helicopter	0	10	10	0
Maritime Reconnaissance (MR)	3	0	0	0
Combat Capable Trainer	26	113	111	2
Tanker	6	0	0	0
Transport	37	39	27	12
Helicopters				
Attack/Armed	133	87	87	16
SAR/ASW	6	-	-	-
Transport & Other	160	110	110	52
Total	299	197	197	68
SAM Forces				
Batteries	28	150	150	14
Heavy Launchers	79	848	848	80
Medium Launchers	0	60	60	0
AA Guns	0	4,000	4,000	-
Naval Forces				
Active Manpower	6,500	6,480	6,000	480
Reserve Manpower	5,000	4,000	4,000	-
Total Manpower	11,500	10,480	10,000	480
Naval Commandos/Marines	300	0	0	0
Submarines	2	0	3	0
Destroyers/Frigates/Corvettes	3	2	2	0
Missile	3	2	2	0
Other	0	0	0	0
Missile Patrol	12	10	10	0
Coastal/Inshore Patrol	32	14	8	6
Mine	0	5	5	0

Table 11.1 (continued)

Category/Weapon	Israel	Syria + Jordan	Syria	Jordan
Naval Forces				
Amphibious Ships	1	3	3	0
Landing Craft/Light Support	4	5	5	(3)
Fixed-wing Combat Aircraft	0	0	0	0
MR/MPA	0	0	0	0
ASW/Combat Helicopter	0	24	24	0
Other Helicopters	-	-	-	-

Note: Figures in parentheses show additional equipment known to be in long-term storage. Some Syrian tanks shown in parentheses are used as fire points in fixed positions.

Source: Adapted by Anthony H. Cordesman from data provided by US experts, and the IISS, *Military Balance.*

virtually no significant improvement in their air defenses since the 1980s. As a result, the IAF could probably win almost immediate freedom of action over the Golan and West Bank, win air superiority over critical areas of Syria and Jordan in 24–48 hours, and then maintain air supremacy over much of Syria and all of Jordan.

At the same time, Jordan does have a 238-kilometer border with Israel. Even if Jordan did nothing more than deploy in ways that forced the IDF to deploy and the IAF to keep assets in reserve, this might assist Syria in a grab for the Golan. Syria could also reduce the IDF's concentration of force if Jordan gave Syrian troops free passage, and Syria could deploy armor reinforced with heavy mobile air defenses to attack through northern Jordan. Also, Syria could expand the area of attack by striking across the Lebanese border from positions in the Beka'a.

The main problem Israel would face in this contingency is that it would increase the strain on the IDF in deploying across a broader front. At the same time, the Syrian-Jordanian forces would not have a significant probability of defeating Israel, and Syrian-Jordanian movements would be even more exposed to Israeli air attack than a concentrated Syrian movement through the Golan, and have significantly less heavy surface-to-air missile protection. Any Syrian-Jordanian attack would require significant political changes in Jordanian-Syrian relations and long preparation to be effective. As a result, any military advantages to the Arab side might well be offset by the added strategic warning and preparation time provided to the IDF.

Such a large scale Syrian-Jordanian attack might also remove many of the constraints Israel might have in terms of launching strategic attacks on Jordan and Syria. It would be closer to all-out war, and Israel might well preempt or strike at critical economic targets in a systematic effort to force early conflict termination. It is also unlikely that the US would attempt to exercise any major restraint on Israel in making such attacks as long as Israel was directly threatened.

Figure 11.1
Israel Versus Jordan and Syria in 2001

Land Weapons

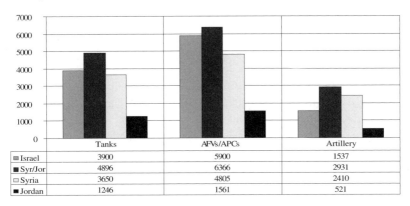

	Tanks	AFVs/APCs	Artillery
Israel	3900	5900	1537
Syr/Jor	4896	6366	2931
Syria	3650	4805	2410
Jordan	1246	1561	521

Air Forces

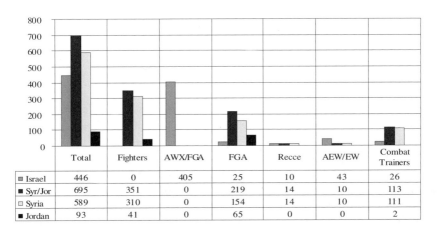

	Total	Fighters	AWX/FGA	FGA	Recce	AEW/EW	Combat Trainers
Israel	446	0	405	25	10	43	26
Syr/Jor	695	351	0	219	14	10	113
Syria	589	310	0	154	14	10	111
Jordan	93	41	0	65	0	0	2

Note: Total Artillery includes towed and self-propelled tube artillery and multiple rocket launchers. Total air forces include only operational fixed wing fighter, fighter-attack, and reconnaissance aircraft in combat units, less aircraft in combat training units.

Source: Adapted by Anthony H. Cordesman from data provided by US experts, and the IISS, *Military Balance*.

A JORDANIAN ROLE IN A BROADER ALLIANCE AGAINST ISRAEL

As for some kind of broader "Eastern Front" contingency involving Jordan, of the kind discussed in more detail in Chapter 13, it is difficult to see this contingency as anything other than game-theoretic. The Jordanian-Israeli peace treaty forbids the kind of Iraqi-Jordanian joint exercises and Iraqi movements to Jordan that took place before the Gulf War. Iraq might deploy significant land and air forces at some indefinite point in the future, but any such attack in the near term would be likely to trigger US intervention with air strikes and cruise missile strikes. Iran is highly unlikely to cooperate with Iraq, or deploy significant forces.

Saudi Arabia, the other Gulf states, Libya, and the other Maghreb states have only made token deployments in the past Arab-Israeli conflicts and seem even less likely to make significant military contributions today. The force ratios in the "Eastern Front" columns of Table 11.1 cannot be ignored—quantity does influence combat—but the current trends in the balance make it less, not more, relevant to possible war fighting contingencies.

There is one final caution, however, that must be applied to all of the Jordan versus Israel scenarios that have just been examined. It is dangerous to examine military balances in terms of "probable" wars. Little about the history of the 20th century indicates that war is the product of calmly planned grand strategies or processes of escalation based on rational ladders. At the same time, any of these conflicts would be a tragedy for both Jordan and Israel. A Jordanian war with Israel would probably be devastating for Jordan, in spite of the considerable professionalism of Jordan's military forces. Such a war would, however, complicate Israel's military problems, and Jordanian support of Palestinian forces in the West Bank might put considerable strain on the IDF and Israel's economy.

This, in turn, affects the problem of arms control in the region. No agreement related to the Golan can totally ignore Jordan's potential, any more than it can ignore the risk of attacks through Lebanon and the Beka'a Valley. This does not mean that such agreements must explicitly take account of this risk. It might well be possible to create arms control agreements that dealt with these issues through tacit understanding about the risks involved, and such agreements might also aid in developing arms control options that reflected Israel's different perception of the risks from Jordan and Syria. At the same time, it is equally possible that Israeli and Syrian perceptions could differ fundamentally on this issue: That Israel would insist on considering the Jordanian threat and Syria would see the balance purely in terms of the threat posed by Israel.

THE ISRAELI (JORDANIAN) ALLIANCE WITH TURKEY

The other wild card in this particular scenario is Turkey. Turkey has no more love for Syria than Israel or Jordan, and Israel and Turkey have developed close ties. Turkey has long had friction with Syria over water issues, Syria's support of hostile Turkish Kurdish movements like the Kurdish Democratic Party, and traditional rivalries for power dating back to the breakup of the Turkish Empire after World War I. Turkey has seen Israel as a way of containing Syria and pressuring it and as a source of military technology and intelligence—interests which virtually mirror those of Israel.

These pressures helped lead to steadily improving relations between Turkey and Israel as Turkey became more deeply involved in a civil war with its Kurds. Turkish-Syrian tensions grew to the point where Turkey deployed troops to the Syrian border in June 1998. Lt. General Hussein Kivrikoglu, the Chief of the Turkish General Staff, stated on October 2, 1998, that, "There is a state of undeclared war between us and Syria." Turkey only withdrew after Syria ended support for the Kurdish Democratic Party forces fighting Turkey and expelled its leader from the country.[772]

Turkey and Israel signed a Security and Secrecy Agreement on May 31, 1994. They signed a new memorandum of understanding so that each could train its pilots in the other's airspace on September 18, 1995. They signed an Enhanced Military Training Agreement on February 22, 1996, and a Defense Industry Cooperation Agreement on August 28, 1998. The new Barak government held further talks to strengthen Israeli and Turkish cooperation in July 1999.[773]

It is an open secret that the two nations closely share intelligence and counter-terrorism data. The heads of military intelligence on both sides seem to exchange semi-annual visits.[774] Israel was one of the top contenders for Turkey's $7 billion main battle tank program until Israel gave in to US pressure and agreed not to sell its tanks to Turkey. The US was concerned about what Syria's reaction would be if Israeli tanks were deployed on both its northern and southern borders.[775]

Syria is deeply concerned about this "encirclement." It seems highly doubtful that either country will cooperate directly in a major attack, or allow the other's forces to attack from bases in its country. Syria found in 1998, however, that it could not make major deployments to respond to the Turkish movement to its borders because it could not leave a gap opposing Israel on the Golan. It is also clear that Syria has no operational sanctuary in its north where it can deploy, reorganize, and train without Israel receiving Turkish intelligence. There is also no question that the joint training of F-16s by each air force in the other's country improves the *potential* capability to cooperate against Syria. On the other hand, Turkey has some concern that Israel might reduce cooperation as part of its quest for peace with Syria. Turkey has threatened to curb potential military projects if this happens, but Israeli officials insisted that strategic cooperation with Turkey will continue even if a peace does eventually become possible.[776]

Furthermore, Jordan has relations with Turkey that long predate its peace with Israel. Jordan and Turkey signed a military cooperation agreement in 1984. This agreement became much more active after the Gulf War, at which time Jordan and Turkey began to exchange intelligence data on Syria, the Kurdish Democratic Party, and Iraq. They began biannual military cooperation talks. Jordan was an observer in the US-Israeli-Turkish naval exercises in January 1998. The Jordanian Air Force began to train its F-16s in Turkey in 1998 and Turkish F-16s will train in Jordan in 1999. Turkey leased F-16 simulators to Jordan and may lease two CN-235 tactical transport aircraft. Although King Abdullah II has downplayed this cooperation with Turkey since coming to the throne, Turkey and Jordan exchanged training battalions, and Turkey provides Jordan with technical assistance and help in some aspects of military construction.

It is dangerous, therefore, to see a future war between Syria and Israel in terms of a Syrian-Jordanian alliance. Syria has no real friends on any of its borders and is unlikely to gain them unless it reaches a full peace with Israel and establishes much better relations with Jordan, Iraq, and Turkey. So far, such improvements are almost solely cosmetic. The current Syrian rapprochement with Iraq is more of an effort by both nations to break out of political encirclement than anything approaching friendship. Turkey is unlikely to reach a stable settlement on water issues, and King Abdullah II is unlikely to quickly forget that Syria sponsored potential terrorist attacks on the Jordanian royal family in 1997.

There are some senior Israeli defense planners, like David Ivry, who have at least speculated about broader Israeli strategic alliances. They look towards Pakistan at the eastern edge of the Middle East, and even at Iran—a potential threat, but also a nation which faces a continuing threat from Iraq, which in turn threatens Israel and Jordan. As one Israel planner pointed out, the clashes within Middle Eastern nations have usually been more serious than the clashes "between civilizations." Israel has natural allies in the region in terms of the interests of the ruling regime, economic interests, and strategic interests. Alliances based on intelligent self-interest, rather than the difference between Israeli and Arab, or Jew and Muslim, may ultimately offer Israel the security it needs to reach a lasting peace—or at least a lasting level of stable deterrence.[777]

12

Egyptian–Israeli Conflicts

Worst cases are worst cases, and there is no doubt that the Arab-Israeli balance changes strikingly if Egypt is added to the Arab side. These changes are a matter of both force ratios and geography. Even the Jordanian-Syrian contingency allows Israel to fight on something approaching a single front. Any war that involves both Syria and Egypt, however, forces Israel to fight on two fronts of very different character over long distances, and the resulting problems would be compounded in the case of any Palestinian rising and Hizbollah attacks across the border. These risks are obvious from any map of the region, but Figures 12.1 and 12.2 provide a rough idea of the different geography involved in terms of both borders and geographic depth.

Egypt is a major military power. Table 12.1 and Figure 12.3 compare the present strength of Egyptian and Israeli forces, and it is clear that Egypt has near parity with Israel in land numbers. Unlike most other Arab states, Egypt also has a large pool of advanced, high quality military equipment. This is partly the result of its relatively high levels of military spending and arms imports. Figure 12.4 shows a comparison of Egyptian and Israeli military expenditures, and Figure 12.5 shows a similar comparison of their recent arms imports.

Egypt is also the Arab state that has been most successful in military modernization. Egypt had no tanks equivalent to the Merkava in 1990. It is now acquiring a total of 755 M-1A1s. It had 67 F-16s compared to Israel's 53 F-15s and 145 F-16s in 1990; it now is acquiring a total of 220 F-16s.[778] While Egypt does not approach Israel's overall force quality, it has both impressive overall force numbers and large elements of its force structure with first-rate arms. This has led at least some Israeli analysts to say that Egypt is using its aid for peace to support an arms race.

Figure 12.1
Arab-Israeli Borders
(Total Length Kilometers)

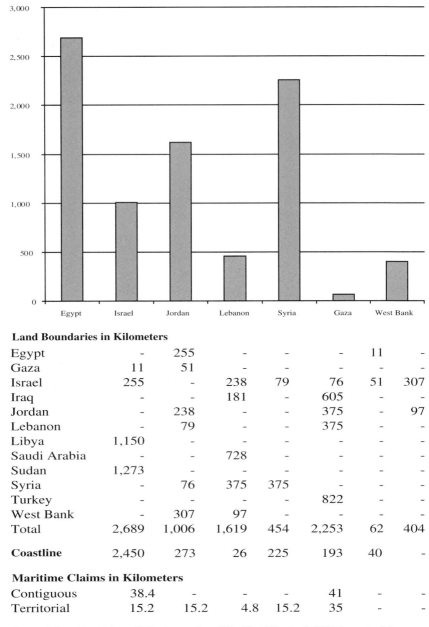

Land Boundaries in Kilometers

	Egypt	Israel	Jordan	Lebanon	Syria	Gaza	West Bank
Egypt	-	255	-	-	-	11	-
Gaza	11	51	-	-	-	-	-
Israel	255	-	238	79	76	51	307
Iraq	-	-	181	-	605	-	-
Jordan	-	238	-	-	375	-	97
Lebanon	-	79	-	-	375	-	-
Libya	1,150	-	-	-	-	-	-
Saudi Arabia	-	-	728	-	-	-	-
Sudan	1,273	-	-	-	-	-	-
Syria	-	76	375	375	-	-	-
Turkey	-	-	-	-	822	-	-
West Bank	-	307	97	-	-	-	-
Total	2,689	1,006	1,619	454	2,253	62	404
Coastline	2,450	273	26	225	193	40	-

Maritime Claims in Kilometers

	Egypt	Israel	Jordan	Lebanon	Syria	Gaza	West Bank
Contiguous	38.4	-	-	-	41	-	-
Territorial	15.2	15.2	4.8	15.2	35	-	-

Source: Adapted by Anthony H. Cordesman from CIA, *World Factbook, 2000*, Internet edition.

Figure 12.2
Arab-Israeli Geography
(Total Territory in Square Kilometers)

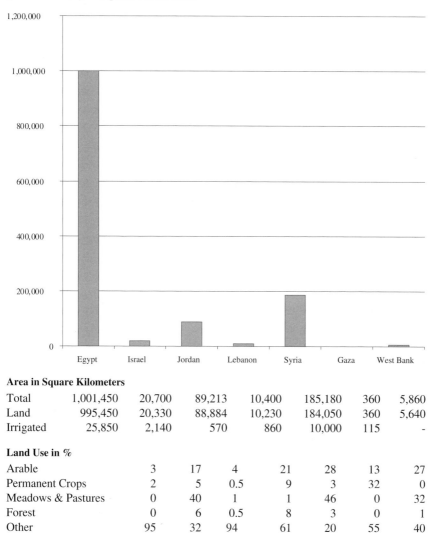

Area in Square Kilometers							
Total	1,001,450	20,700	89,213	10,400	185,180	360	5,860
Land	995,450	20,330	88,884	10,230	184,050	360	5,640
Irrigated	25,850	2,140	570	860	10,000	115	-
Land Use in %							
Arable		3	17	4	21	28	13	27
Permanent Crops		2	5	0.5	9	3	32	0
Meadows & Pastures		0	40	1	1	46	0	32
Forest		0	6	0.5	8	3	0	1
Other		95	32	94	61	20	55	40

Source: Adapted by Anthony H. Cordesman from CIA, *World Factbook, 2000*, April 2000.

That said, it is at least as hard to create a convincing war fighting contingency between Egypt and Israel as it is to create one involving Israel and Jordan. Like Jordan, Egypt has a moderate secular government. It has fully adhered to its peace with Israel in spite of crises like Israel's 1982 invasion of Lebanon. It has

Table 12.1
The Egyptian-Israeli Balance in 2001

Category/Weapon	Israel	Egypt
Defense Budget		
(In 2000, $Current Billions)	$7.0	$2.5
Arms Imports: 1996-1999 ($M)		
New Orders	4,500	6,800
Deliveries	4,500	3,800
Mobilization Base		
Men Ages 13-17	281,000	3,634,000
Men Ages 18-22	270,000	3,437,000
Manpower		
Total Active	172,500	448,500
(Conscript)	107,500	322,000+
Total Reserve	425,000	254,000
Total	597,500	702,000
Paramilitary	8,050	230,000
Land Forces		
Active Manpower	130,000	320,000
(Conscripts)	85,000	250,000+
Reserve Manpower	400,000	150,000
Total Active & Reserve Manpower	530,000	470,000
Main Battle Tanks	3,900	3,960
AIFVs/Armored Cars/Lt. Tanks	408	740(220)
APCs/Recce/Scouts	5,900	2,990(1,075)
WWII Half-Tracks	500(3,500)	0
ATGM Launchers	1,300	2,660
SP Artillery	855	251
Towed Artillery	520	971
MRLs	198	156
Mortars	6,440	2,4000
SSM Launchers	48	18-24
AA Guns	850	834
Lt. SAM Launchers	1,298	1,146
Air & Air Defense Forces		
Active Air Force Manpower	36,000	30,000
Active Air Defense Command	0	80,000
Air Force Reserve Manpower	20,000	90,000
Air Defense Command Reserve Manpower	0	70,000
Aircraft		
Total Fighter/FGA/Recce	446(250)	583
Fighter	0	337
FGA/Fighter	405	0

Table 12.1 (continued)

Category/Weapon	Israel	Egypt
Air & Air Defense Forces		
FGA	25	133
Recce	10	20
Airborne Early Warning (AEW)	6	5
Electronic Warfare (EW)	37	10
Fixed Wing	37	6
Helicopter	0	4
Maritime Reconnaissance (MR)	3	2
Combat Capable Trainer	26	64
Tanker	6	0
Transport	37	32
Helicopters		
Attack/Armed	133	129
SAR/ASW	6	-
Transport & Other	160	158
Total	299	287
SAM Forces		
Batteries	28	38+
Heavy Launchers	79	628
Medium Launchers	0	36-54
AA Guns	0	72+
Naval Forces		
Active Manpower	6,500	18,500
Reserve Manpower	5,000	14,000
Total Manpower	11,500	34,000
Naval Commandos/Marines	300	0
Submarines	2	4
Destroyers/Frigates/Corvettes	3	11
Missile	3	10
Other	0	1
Missile Patrol	12	25
Coastal/Inshore Patrol	32	15
Mine	0	13
Amphibious Ships	1	3
Landing Craft/Light Support	4	9
Fixed-wing Combat Aircraft	0	0
MR/MPA	0	0
ASW/Combat Helicopter	0	24
Other Helicopters	-	-

Note: Figures in parentheses show additional equipment known to be in long-term storage. Some Israeli and Egyptian vehicles shown in parentheses are used as fire points in fixed positions.

Source: Adapted by Anthony H. Cordesman from data provided by US experts, and the IISS, *Military Balance*.

Figure 12.3
Israel Versus Egypt in 2001

Land Weapons

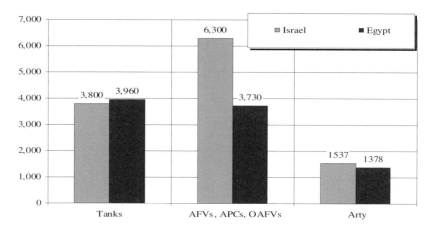

Air Forces

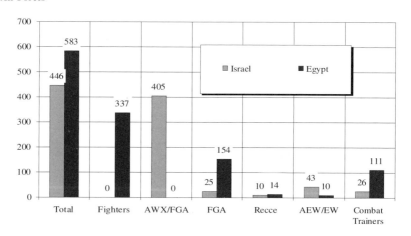

Note: Total artillery includes towed and self-propelled tube artillery and multiple rocket launchers. Total air forces include only operational fixed wing fighter, fighter-attack, and reconnaissance aircraft in combat units, less aircraft in combat training units.

demonstrated its commitment to peace during several crises between Israel and its other Arab neighbors, and has helped lead other Arab states into the peace process.

There is also the issue of intelligent self-interest. Egypt has gained every strategic advantage from peace that it was denied as the result of war. It gained great prestige, as well as massive aid and debt forgiveness, from supporting the US and the UN Coalition during the Gulf War. President Mubarak has shown that

Figure 12.4
Trends in Egyptian-Israeli Military Spending: 1985–1997
(In $US 1997 Constant Millions)

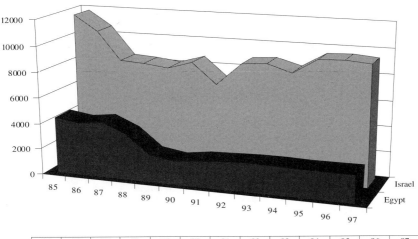

	85	86	87	88	89	90	91	92	93	94	95	96	97
■ Egypt	4430	4150	4380	3600	2160	1840	2070	2150	2230	2190	2180	2170	2180
▨ Israel	11750	10555	8400	8280	8060	8620	7040	8730	8880	8330	9440	9490	9340

Source: Adapted by Anthony H. Cordesman from US State Department, Bureau of Arms Control, *World Military Expenditures and Arms Transfers*, Washington, GPO, Table I, various editions.

Egypt can also maintain its Arab identity and reassert its role as a leader of the Arab world, and still do everything possible to encourage a broadened peace between Israel and its other Arab neighbors.

Egypt has one of the best proven records in peacekeeping in the modern world, and it seems likely to stick to its commitment to peace as long as it retains a moderate secular government. For now this is likely because there seems to be a decreasing prospect that Islamic extremists will come to power. Egypt has done a far better job of reestablishing its internal security than Algeria, and has sharply reduced the capability of its extremists to threaten its armed forces.

Such a contingency also presents the problem that many of Egypt's best educated military officers would strongly resist any such Islamic takeover, which could only take place after a massive disruption of Egypt's officer corps of the kind that crippled Iran's forces after the fall of the Shah. Egypt's secular government is one of the most institutionalized in the Middle East, and its military forces not only lead its government but have shown a consistent commitment to peace.

Even so, there is still *some* risk that Egyptian economic and political problems could eventually lead to the kind of political upheaval that could bring an extremist Islamic government to power. This might conceivably be triggered by a combination of a cut-off or major reductions in US aid, the collapse of Egypt's international

Figure 12.5
Trends in Egyptian-Israeli Arms Import Deliveries: 1983–1997
($US 1997 Constant Millions)

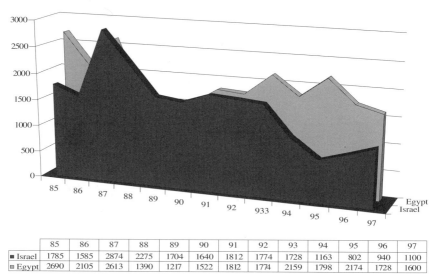

	85	86	87	88	89	90	91	92	93	94	95	96	97
■ Israel	1785	1585	2874	2275	1704	1640	1812	1774	1728	1163	802	940	1100
▣ Egypt	2690	2105	2613	1390	1217	1522	1812	1774	2159	1798	2174	1728	1600

Source: Adapted by Anthony H. Cordesman from US State Department, Bureau of Arms Control,
   World Military Expenditures and Arms Transfers, GPO, Washington, various editions.

credit position, the rise of other Islamist extremist governments, or some catastrophic breakdown of the peace process followed by extreme Israeli use of force
against the Palestinians. Egypt has also made enough progress in its military
modernization so that Israeli officers are beginning to publicly warn of an Egyptian
buildup. For example, Brigadier General Amos Gilead, the director of Israel's
military division has warned of both Egypt's conventional buildup and efforts to
buy extended-range Scud missiles from North Korea.[779]

Even without political upheaval resulting in an extreme Islamist government,
there is a chance for conflict between Egypt and Israel. A halt or sharp reduction in
US aid might be enough to cause a conflict between a secular Egyptian government
and Israel. Similarly, some other crisis in the Arab world could force Mubarak or
his successor to take a much more strident line over problems in the peace process
or issues like Israel's possession of nuclear weapons. Egypt might also alter the
balance without attacking, if it responded to some crisis in the peace process by
remilitarizing part or all of the Sinai, perhaps over an issue like Jerusalem. Such
cases seem unlikely, but not impossible.

EGYPTIAN WAR FIGHTING CAPABILITIES

Egypt has formidable military forces. Table 12.2 shows that Egypt retains much
of the force levels it had during the October War in 1973, and it has benefited from

Table 12.2
Force Trends in Egypt

Category/Weapon	1975	1980	1985	1990	1995	2000	2001
Manpower							
Total Active	322,500	367,000	445,000	450,000	450,000	450,000	448,500
(Conscript)	-	-	(250,000)	(252,000)	(320,000)	(320,000)	(322,000)
Total Reserve	-	-	380,000	623,000	254,000	254,000	254,000
Total	-	-	825,000	1,073,000	704,000	704,000	703,500
Paramilitary	120,000	49,000	139,000	374,000	230,000	230,000	230,000
Land Forces							
Active Manpower	275,000	245,000	320,000	320,000	320,000	320,000	320,000
(Conscripts)	-	-	(250,000)	(180,000)	(250,000+)	(250,000+)	(250,000+)
Reserve Manpower	500,000	350,000	323,000	500,000	150,000	150,000	150,000
Total Reserve & Active Manpower	775,000	595,000	643,000	820,000	470,000	470,000	470,000
Main Battle Tanks (Fixed & in Storage)	1,945	1,600	2,159	3,190	3,500	3,855	3,960
AIFVs/Armored Cars/Lt. Tanks	130	580	747	770	1,080	982 (220)	740 (220)
APCs/Recce/Scouts	2,500	2,550	2,550	2,745	3,834	3,205(1,075)	3,990(1,075)
WWII Half-Tracks	0	0	0	0	0	0	0
ATGM Launchers	-	1,000	-	3,340	2,785	2,350	2,660
SP Artillery	200	200	200	185	200	251	251
Towed Artillery	1,300	1,500	1,500	1,120	971	971	971
MRLs	420	300	300	300	296	156	156

Table 12.2 (continued)

Category/Weapon	1975	1980	1985	1990	1995	2000	2001
Land Forces							
Mortars	-	-	-	-	-	2,400	2,400
SSM Launchers	18+	54	-	13	21	24	18-24
AA Guns (Army + ADC)	2,500	2,500+	2,500+	1,070+	1,677+	1,074	834
Lt. SAM Launchers	-	-	-	1,226+	2,046	2,146	1,146
Air & Air Defense Forces							
Active Air Force Manpower	30,000	27,000	25,000	80,000	30,000	30,000	30,000
Air Defense Command	(75,000)*	75,000	80,000	30,000	80,000	80,000	80,000
Total Reserve Manpower	20,000	-	42,000	109,000	90,000	90,000	90,000
Aircraft							
Total Fighter/FGA/Recce	608**	363(305)	427	475	564	583	583
Bomber	30	23	13	0	0	0	0
Fighter	-	45	164	272	339	363	363
FGA/Fighter	200	92	103	0	0	0	0
FGA	205-253	201	73	139	135	133	133
Recce	-	-	34	20	20	20	20
Airborne Early Warning (AEW)	0	0	0	5	5	5	5
Electronic Warfare (EW)	0	2	2	10	10	10	10
Maritime Reconnaissance (MR)	0	0	0	2	2	2	2
Combat Capable Trainer/OCU	153	50	38	48	70	64	64
Tanker	0	0	0	0	0	0	0
Transport	70	65	37	25	32	32	32

Table 12.2 (continued)

Category/Weapon	1975	1980	1985	1990	1995	2000	2001
Air & Air Defense Forces							
Helicopters							
Attack/Armed	0	0	48	74	103	129	129
ASW/SAR	0	0	5	0	14	0	0
Transport & Other	138	168	108	118	115	158	158
Total	138	168	161	192	232	287	287
SAM Forces							
Batteries	-	-	-	-	-	38+	38+
Heavy Launchers	635	635	727	808	702	628	628
Medium Launchers	-	20	16	50	36	36-54	36-54
Naval Forces							
Active Manpower	17,500	20,000	20,000	20,000	16,000	20,000	18,500
Reserve Manpower	15,000	-	15,000	14,000	14,000	14,000	14,000
Total Manpower	32,500	-	35,000	34,000	30,000	34,000	34,000
Submarines	12	10(1)	14	10	4	4	4
Destroyers/Frigates/Corvettes	8	8	10	5	7	11	11
Missile	-	5	7	4	6	9	10
Other	-	3	3	1	1	2	1
Missile Patrol	13	22	30	21	25	24	25
Coastal/Inshore Patrol	42	38	32	18	18	15	15
Mine	12	14	15	9	7	14	13
Amphibious Ships	-	3	3	3	3	3	3

Table 12.2 (continued)

Category/Weapon	1975	1980	1985	1990	1995	2000	2001
Naval Forces							
Landing Craft/Light Support	14	17	13	-	11	9	9
Fixed Wing Combat Aircraft	0	0	0	0	0	0	0
MR/MPA	0	0	0	0	0	0	0
ASW/Combat Helicopter		6	(5)	(17)	(14)	24	24
Other Helicopters	-	-	-	-	-	-	-

Notes: *Included in the army total.
** Includes 108 fighters in the Air Defense Command.

Source: Adapted by Anthony H. Cordesman from data provided by US experts, and the IISS,
   Military Balance.

well over a decade of large amounts of US grant aid. Further major force developments are under way that will make further improvements in Egyptian forces. At the same time, Egypt's military forces suffer from outdated equipment, and a wide range of qualitative problems.[780]

Egyptian Military Expenditures and Arms Transfers

Egypt's greatest strength lies in its pool of advanced modern equipment. The previous figures have shown that Egypt maintains a relatively high level of military spending, although its spending levels have dropped relative to Israel. Figure 12.6 summarizes Egypt's current holdings of major weapons. Figure 12.7 shows that Egypt has been able to compete with Israel in arms imports during the 1990s. These tables also show that Egypt has had massive supplies of US and other Western arms, and that it has a substantial backlog of new orders.

At the same time, these figures reflect Egypt's dependence on US aid. This dependence will present problems if US aid declines in the future, or if Egypt should ever back away from the peace process. Egypt would face an immediate cut-off of US aid if it should come under extremist Islamic rule, and this would present major near-term problems in Egypt's effort to support US-supplied systems as well as probably lead to an immediate internal economic crisis.

Egyptian Land Forces

The Egyptian army has large holdings of modern equipment and continues to modernize. In early 2001, Egypt had 555 M-1A1 tanks, plus 400 M-60A1s and 1,300 M-60A3s. This is a total of 2,225 relatively modern tanks out of a total of 3,960, or nearly 60%. It compares with 1,200 Merkavas, 300 M-60A1s and 600 M-60A3s for Israel, which had a total of 2,100 modern tanks out of overall holdings of 3,900 tanks, or roughly 55%. A decade earlier, Egypt only had 785 M-60A3s out of a total of 2,425 tanks.

Neither Egypt nor Israel had large numbers of other modern fighting vehicles. Egypt's operational armored fighting vehicles outnumbered Israel's—300 BDRMs, 112 Commandos, 220 BMR-600Ps, and 310 YPR-765s armed with 22-mm guns—but its holdings of operational APCs were far smaller: 2,320 M-113s, 600 Walids, 165 Fahds, and 70 YPR-765s. Israel had 400 Ramta, Fuchs, and other fighting vehicles. Its holding of APCs consisted of some 5,500 M-113A1/A2s, 200 Nagmashots, and 200 Achzaits, Pumas, and BTR-50Ps.

Egypt has, however, weakened its ability to use its modern weapons effectively by over-extending its force structure. It tries to support far too large a land force structure at the cost of relying on low quality conscripts, poor training for most of its forces, and increasingly underpaid officers and other ranks.[781] In spite of a decade of ongoing modernization, about 35–40% of Egypt's total inventory of

Figure 12.6
Egyptian Major Military Equipment in 2001

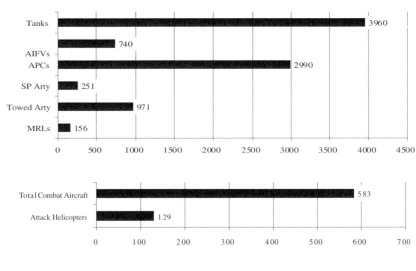

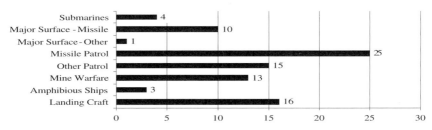

Source: Adapted by Anthony H. Cordesman from data provided by US experts, and the IISS, *Military Balance*.

major land combat weapons still consist of obsolete and badly worn Soviet bloc systems supplied in the late 1960s, and none of its Soviet bloc inventory was supplied after 1974.

For example, the rest of its tanks consisted of obsolete to obsolescent Soviet bloc models. These included 1,100 T-54/T-55s, only 260 of which had had any real upgrading, and 550 T-62s. The most Egypt could do to modernize the rest of these tanks was to obtain British aid in upgrading their ammunition.

Similarly, the 310 YPR-765s were the only part of Egypt's holdings of nearly 1,200 AIFVs that had significant war fighting capability—although a total of 600 YPR-765s may eventually be delivered. Roughly 200 more AIFVs were in storage, and Egypt was forced to try to upgrade its low quality Fahd-30 AIFVs with BMP-2 turrets. Only about half of its total holdings of some 4,065 APCs were relatively modern types, and at least 1,000 of the total were in storage.

Figure 12.7
Egyptian Arms Agreements and Deliveries By Major Supplier: 1987–1999
($US 1999 Current Millions)

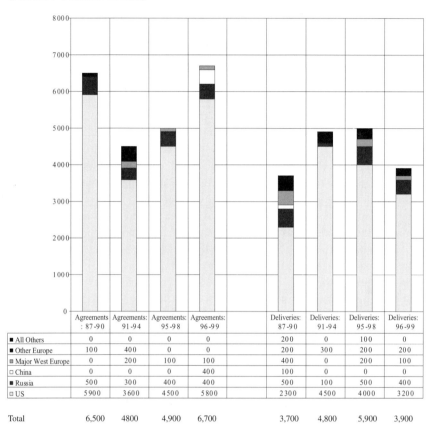

	Agreements : 87-90	Agreements: 91-94	Agreements: 95-98	Agreements: 96-99		Deliveries: 87-90	Deliveries: 91-94	Deliveries: 95-98	Deliveries: 96-99
■ All Others	0	0	0	0		200	0	100	0
■ Other Europe	100	400	0	0		200	300	200	200
▨ Major West Europe	0	200	100	100		400	0	200	100
☐ China	0	0	0	400		100	0	0	0
■ Russia	500	300	400	400		500	100	500	400
☐ US	5900	3600	4500	5800		2300	4500	4000	3200
Total	6,500	4800	4,900	6,700		3,700	4,800	5,900	3,900

Notes: Includes Gulf states, Arab-Israeli states, North Africa, and Yemen.
0 = less than $50 million or nil, and all data rounded to the nearest $100 million.

Source: Richard F. Grimmett, *Conventional Arms Transfers to the Developing Nations*, Congressional Research Service, various editions.

Egypt had 175 modern self-propelled M-109A2 155-mm howitzers. It also had AN/TPQ-37 counterbattery radars, UAVs, and RASIT artillery support vehicles to support this artillery in maneuver warfare. However, the rest of its artillery consisted of 76 aging FSU-supplied 122-mm self-propelled weapons, 971 towed weapons, and 156 operational multiple rocket launchers, only a limited number of which had been modernized.

Egypt had large numbers of advanced US TOW anti-tank guided weapons (including the TOW-2A that has a significant capability against reactive armor), many mounted on M-901 armored vehicles, and was seeking TOW-2B missiles. It also, however, had 1,300 aging, second-generation AT-3 Saggers and 200 Swingfires. This was a total of 1,500 obsolete to obsolescent anti-tank guided weapons out of a total of roughly 2,350.

It had truly massive numbers of short-range air defense weapons, which include over 1,000 anti-aircraft guns and thousands of manportable surface-to-air missiles. The most combat-effective portion of this total, however, consisted of only 117 radar guided ZSU-23–4s and 46 modern surface-to-air missile fire units.[782]

In spite of its successes in force modernization, the Egyptian Army is still heavily dependent on aging and obsolescent Soviet-supplied systems, many of which are inoperable or incapable of sustained combat. Ironically, the Egyptian army could probably be much more effective against Israel if it concentrated its manpower and training resources on a much smaller and better-equipped force. It could also use the resulting savings in military spending to either improve its readiness and sustainment or for economic development.

Egypt also has never effectively trained and organized the forces using these weapons into a modern war fighting force and it lacks modern support vehicles, C⁴I, battle management and fire control, and target acquisition and counter-battery radars and sensors. Many of its forces are not trained or equipped for effective BVR targeting, counter-battery fire, and rapid shifts of mass fire.

The Egyptian army has not organized for war with Israel. In spite of ongoing improvements, it has never modernized its infrastructure, support, and sustainment capabilities near the Suez Canal in ways that would allow it to efficiently mobilize and assemble a massive armored force that could rapidly thrust across the Sinai and then sustain itself in intense combat. It has emphasized acquisition and modernization over overall readiness and sustainment, and it is much better postured to defend in depth than to attack in a massive war of offensive maneuver.

Egyptian Air Forces

Egypt has the only air force in the Arab "ring states" with large numbers of modern fighters capable of advanced strike/attack missions and BVR/look-down shoot-down air-to-air combat. In early 2001, Egypt had 35 F-16A/Bs, 164 F-16C/Ds, and 21 Mirage 2000B/Cs. This was 220 advanced aircraft out of a total of 580 combat aircraft or nearly 40%. Egypt had only had 83 modern F-16 and Mirage-2000 fighters out of 517 combat aircraft a decade earlier (16%). Egypt's holdings compared with 73 F-15A-Ds, 25 F-15Is, 237 F-16A-Ds, and 50 F-4E 2000s for Israel. Israel had a total of 385 advanced combat aircraft out of a total of 446, or over 85%.[783]

Egypt is the only Arab air force with AEW aircraft and some modern electronic warfare, intelligence, and reconnaissance aircraft—including 5 E-2Cs, 2 C-130Hs01, and 4 Beech 1900s. It also has modern self-propelled versions of the

IHawk surface-to-air missiles. Egypt has significant force improvements under way. It is currently scheduled to receive a total of 220 F-16s. Egypt has a wide range of modern air munitions and has the technology to make Fuel-Air-Explosive (FAE) weapons, although it is not clear it has done so.[784]

The Egyptian air force could do a better job of supporting a land attack on Israel than the Syrian or Jordanian air force, and some Egyptian squadrons have excellent pilots. However, the 580 combat aircraft in the Egyptian air force included 44 low quality PRC-made J-6s and 53 J-7s, and over 74 worn-out Soviet bloc MiG-21s.[785] The EAF had not done well in keeping its Mirage 5s at a high degree of combat readiness. Egypt also still had 41 aging Alpha Jets, and 20 well-worn F-4Es. Egypt also had 36 AH-64 and 44 SA-342K anti-tank/attack helicopters, but the AH-64s were still completing advanced training, the operational readiness of many of its SA-342K armed helicopters was limited, and the HOT weapons suite on the SA-342K had significant operational limitations.

More generally, the Egyptian air force cannot compete with the Israeli air force in overall battle management, the exploitation of modern sensors and targeting systems, electronic warfare, beyond-visual-range warfare, and in using precision strike and attack munitions. The Egyptian air force is a good air force but it is up against the best. It is also an air force that is still transitioning to joint warfare, particularly at levels above the squadron.

Egyptian land-based air defense capabilities were far more effective as a static defense in depth than in protecting Egyptian offensive operations. While Egypt has some 638 heavy surface-to-air missile launchers, most are obsolete SA-2s and SA-3s, and only 78 are IHawks. This will change because Egypt has ordered a battery of Patriot-3 missiles, with eight firing units, each containing four missiles and has a deal with Russia to upgrade its SA-3As.[786] It will take years before the Patriot-3 is integrated into Egyptian forces, however, and Egypt will require far more than one battery, needing new radars and C^{4}I/BM/SR systems to take full advantage of the capabilities of the Patriot-3.[787]

Egypt cannot project large mobile land-based surface-to-air missile forces into the Sinai without having to operate individual fire units outside the full sensor and C^{4}I/BM capabilities of its central air defense command and control system. It would have to support its advancing land forces with individual surface-to-air missile units which would become progressively more vulnerable to the IAF as they moved across the Sinai. Unless Egypt had months in which to build up its forces near Israel's border, they would become progressively more vulnerable to air attack in terms of both Israel's ability to rapidly suppress Egyptian air defenses and target and attack Egyptian land units.[788]

Egyptian Naval Forces

Egypt cannot defeat Israel at sea. The Egyptian navy has many capable vessels, and a steadily increasing capability to defend Egypt's coast, the approaches to the

Suez Canal, and Egypt's interests in the Red Sea. However, its naval moderniza-tion is still limited and its training and sustainability have had comparatively limited funding. Most importantly, Egypt's navy would not have the air cover and air defense capability necessary to protect itself from the Israeli Air Force.

AN EGYPTIAN-ISRAELI CONFLICT IN THE SINAI

The outcome of any Egyptian-Israeli war would be heavily shaped by the geography of the Sinai. Unlike Israel's boundaries with Gaza, Jordan, Lebanon, Syria, and the West Bank, the force limitations in the Sinai affect a relatively large territory which could easily become a killing ground for Egyptian land forces, and where Israel would require near air supremacy and very fast deployment to avoid an engagement during any advance towards the Suez Canal.

The Suez Canal, the Mediterranean Sea, the Gulfs of Suez and Aqaba, and the border with Israel define the Sinai. The distances are about 190 km from the Suez Canal to the Israeli border, about 145 km along the Suez Canal and the Great Bitter Lakes, and about 370 km from the coast of the Mediterranean down to the southern-most tip of the Sinai. The terrain is very barren and rugged.

Movement through the Sinai is limited in ways which increase the difficulty in moving forces and sustaining them, and increase their vulnerability to air attack. There are only a limited number of roads through the Sinai. The main roads go along the northern coast, and through two passes, the Giddi in the north and Mitla in the south. The two passes are about 20 kilometers apart. The Mitla pass is about 32 kilometers long and the Giddi pass is about 29 kilometers long. The Mitla pass is more open and has a relatively wide slope. The Giddi pass has rough terrain and narrows down to as little as 100 meters. South of these passes, the terrain becomes very rugged and large-scale armored movement becomes very difficult. The north coast road is vulnerable to air and land attacks. The ocean blocks northern movement and extensive southern movement is highly restricted by "seas of sand." Further, Egypt's border with Israel is far from most Israeli population centers, and the Negev Desert gives Israel strategic depth.

The paved and graded roads in the north central Sinai are channeled through the Giddi and Mitla passes, and bypassing them is difficult. This makes them the preferable route for large mechanized forces, and such movements involve hundreds of armored vehicles and nearly 600 support vehicles for each heavy division. Combat and service support units must also accompany combat units to sustain them in combat and provide artillery support, and most Egyptian support vehicles are wheeled rather than tracked. This further limits the areas in which they can move and makes the passes more important. Further, unless Egypt moves its heavy land-based air defenses forward to create the kind of defensive belt it had near the Suez in 1970–1973, its forces would be exposed to the IAF—which would be far more effective against armor than in any previous Arab-Israeli conflict.

Egyptian Defensive Capabilities

Egypt has been most successful in developing the combat capability it needs to defend or deter against an Israeli attack through the Sinai. As long as the Sinai remains largely demilitarized, Israel might be able to move rapidly into the area, just as Egypt could move north. At some point, however, it would have to engage Egyptian armor in large numbers as well as fight a massive battle for air superiority. Egypt might lose the Sinai—as it did in 1973—but the cost would probably be far higher to Israel than in the October War. Israel might be able to retake the Suez Canal, but it would involve significant military risks. It would also confront Israel with then having to either hold the area at immense political, economic, and military cost or repeat its past withdrawal.

While such an Israeli attack on Egypt seems even more improbable than an Egyptian attack on Israel, Egypt's deterrent and defensive strength is important both in terms of Egyptian perceptions and those of moderate and friendly Arab states. It demonstrates that Egypt's support of the peace process does not mean that it had to accept strategic inferiority or the kind of "edge" that gives Israel offensive freedom of action as distinguished from defensive security, and that Arab strategic alliances with the US can involve parity in technology transfer. Egypt's military modernization also gives it a decisive edge over regional rivals like Libya and Sudan, and makes it a major potential player in any coalition involving Arab forces in the Gulf.

Egyptian Offensive Capabilities

At the same time, Egypt would have little to gain from attacking Israel. Any near-term Egyptian land attack on Israel would have to be preceded by massive redeployments of armored and mechanized forces across the Suez and through the Sinai. Egypt would have to carry out these redeployments without anything approaching the required major support and staging facilities in the Sinai.

Even if a new, radical Islamic government should come to power in Egypt, or Egypt should be driven to attack by some breakdown in the peace process or new Arab-Israeli crisis, any buildup in its capabilities for such an attack would give Israel ample strategic warning. Furthermore, Egypt could only prepare for such an attack and execute it, by violating an international treaty, thereby risking the almost certain loss of US aid.

Once Egypt moved into the Sinai, it would also be exposed to an Israeli attack in far more depth than a Syrian force advancing into the Golan. The Sinai is an exposed killing ground where land forces are exposed and/or must move through narrow predictable routes. The IAF is now organized and equipped to use a combination of electronic intelligence aircraft, jammers, stand-off munitions, land-based strike systems, UAVs, and other countermeasures to suppress Egyptian air defenses. If the Golan has become a high technology killing ground, it is even truer of the Sinai and the Negev.

Egypt *might* be more successful in advancing under the defensive envelope of its surface-to-air missiles than in 1973. More probably, it would find that the Israeli Air Force could use a combination of electronic warfare, anti-radiation missiles, UAVs, and precision strike systems to strip away such land-based air defenses before Egyptian troops could come close to the Israeli border. Similarly, the Egyptian air force is not strong and effective enough to provide survivable air cover. The end result would probably be to turn the Sinai into a killing ground for the Israeli air force, which would be supported by Israel's long-range artillery and multiple rocket launchers. These attacks would seriously degrade the cohesion of any Egyptian advance and delay or potentially halt it. This part of the fighting would be expensive to both sides, but Israel would almost certainly win.

If the armored forces of both nations did close in the Sinai, the resulting massive armored engagement between Israel and Egypt would be a tragic, bloody mess. Egyptian armored and artillery forces are now good enough so that the resulting attrition would be high for both sides. Egypt, however, would almost certainly take far greater losses than Israel. Egypt still needs to make major improvements in its manpower quality, emphasize joint warfare and combined arms, change many of its training methods above the brigade and squadron level, and allocate funds to buy the high technology equipment necessary to support more advanced training methods.

Egypt's land forces remain vulnerable to a combination of Israeli air and artillery attacks and armored maneuver. They would be relatively exposed and have to operate in an environment where Israel's superior sensors, UAVs, and battle management capabilities would give it the equivalent of information dominance. Israel's superior targeting and battlement systems would probably allow it to out-range and out-kill Egyptian artillery, and its Merkavas would certainly out-range all Egyptian armor except the M-1A1. Even then, superior Israeli training, battle management, and situational awareness might give the IDF a decisive edge in range and kill capability. It would be an exceedingly unpleasant war for both sides, but it is not a war that Egypt can now win.

Unless Israel passively allows Egypt to redeploy in the Sinai without reacting with its own deployments, Israel would be likely to win any conflict relatively quickly and decisively, and Egypt's resulting losses would be far higher than in a defensive battle. Egypt might well again be confronted with the loss of both the Sinai and Suez.

Egypt would also be strategically vulnerable. It has far better air defenses than Syria, but Israel could probably win enough air superiority in several days to launch the same kind of strategic strikes using conventional weapons that have been described in the case of Syria. In this case, geography is both one of Egypt's strengths and weaknesses. Egypt has a larger total area than any other country of territory in the ring states. This means that Egypt is forced to defend a large amount of air space. At the same time, Egypt's economy, infrastructure, and population centers are heavily concentrated in the Cairo area and lower Egypt, and in areas well within the range of Israel strikes.

Map 12.1
Egypt and the Sinai

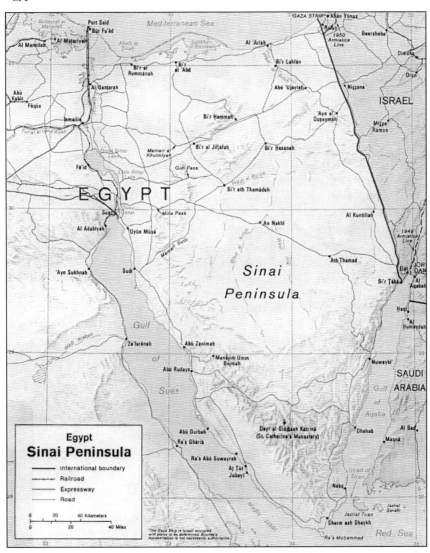

At the same time, Israel would probably require the luxury of a one-front war and considerable freedom of action to be able to concentrate enough armor to advance through the Sinai without taking major losses. Unless Israel was free to react quickly and decisively, any battle could become a two-way race for the passes or have to be fought further north and close to Israel. The situation would also become progressively more difficult for Israel as the IDF advanced towards the Suez. An Israel fighting on more than one front—or with a large portion of its forces tied down on other fronts—would then face an Egyptian army organized to fight a defense in depth, and which could be a formidable opponent.

Israel and Egypt would also confront a common strategic problem. A conflict would lead to almost immediate US political and possibly military intervention. Any tactical or theater victory would confront Egypt with the reality that no defeat of the IDF in the Sinai is going to lead to total victory or the occupation of a nuclear-armed Israel, and confront Israel with the reality that a return to the edge of Suez does not amount to a total victory over Egypt. Although many previous conflicts were not prevented by knowledge that war would be pointless, it is especially hard in this case to see any form of such a war as anything other than a mutually self-defeating strategic disaster for both Egypt and Israel.

In the longer run, Egypt's dependence on US aid would create major problems for any regime that contemplated an attack on Israel. Egypt's current modernization plans and resources will not allow Egypt to modernize on a scale that can offset its severe problems in maintaining its current force structure even with US aid. Such a regime would need a massive new source of arms and years to convert. It would also face the problem that Israel would react with its own force improvements, and would be even more likely to resist any Egyptian remilitarization of the Sinai.

ARMS CONTROL IN THE SINAI

These factors make it almost impossible for either Egypt or Israel to win any major strategic advantage from another war. It is also important to remember that the Sinai is the site of one of the world's most successful arms limitation agreements and peacekeeping operations. Long before the Egyptian-Israeli peace treaty, Egypt and Israel reached two different disengagement agreements and agreed to the deployment of a small multinational monitoring force in the key passes in the Sinai.

When Egypt and Israel reached a full peace treaty on March 26, 1979, the treaty called for the withdrawal of all Israeli forces from the Sinai and demarcated the Sinai into military zones. Annex I, Article VI of the treaty proposed that UN forces and observers supervise these security arrangements, and the US made a commitment during the Camp David negotiations to ensure the establishment of an acceptable alternative force if the UN failed to agree on such a force. In the months that followed, the UN Security Council did fail to agree on the proposal to establish UN forces and observers, and reported this lack of agreement on May 18, 1981. As a result, Egypt and Israel agreed to a protocol to their peace treaty on August 3, 1981, which established a Multinational Force and Observers (MFO).

Since that time, the MFO has enforced the following provisions of the peace treaty:[789]

- There are four force limitation and disengagement zones in the Sinai that progressively limit the size of Egyptian forces in the Sinai relative to the distance from the Israeli border.
- Egyptian forces in Zone A, which extends 50–60 kilometers from the Suez Canal, are limited to one mechanized division (consisting of three mechanized brigades and one armored brigade with up to 230 tanks), 126 artillery weapons, 126 anti-aircraft guns, a very limited number of surface-to-air missiles, and limits on other materiel.
- Egyptian forces in Zone B, which extends to the east of Zone A for 100–130 kilometers, are limited to four border battalions with light weapons.
- Zone C extends from Zone B to the international border with Israel and is 16 to 30 kilometers wide. Only UN forces and Egyptian police units may be in this zone. The Egyptian police are limited to light weapons.
- Zone D is a narrow strip several kilometers wide on the Israeli side of the border. The Israeli forces in this zone are limited to four infantry battalions, and may not include tanks, artillery, or surface-to-air missiles other than portable weapons.
- No Egyptian overflights or reconnaissance flights may take place east of Zone A and no Israeli flights may take place west of Zone D.
- Egypt may only operate early-warning systems in Zone A, and Israel may only operate them in Zone D.

These arrangements divide each side's forces by roughly 150 kilometers, and place significant limits on Egypt's logistic and support capabilities in the Sinai, land-based air defenses, and air power. These limitations mean that the bulk of Egypt's ground forces are located on the other side of the Suez Canal and are a minimum of 210 kilometers from the Israeli border. They place powerful restrictions on Egypt's ability to conduct a surprise attack, or to even prepare for such an attack without major preparations and taking actions that would give Israel extensive strategic warning. They also effectively remove any major incentive for Israel to preempt in a crisis, and prevent any surprise Israeli land attack on Egypt.

Since 1982, the MFO has enforced these provisions of the treaty by manning observation posts in the Sinai, conducting ground and air surveillance, and conducting naval patrols in the Straits of Tiran. The MFO has also used sensors, and has been supported by US intelligence data. In 1995, there were eleven countries in the MFO, each with its own participation agreement. The MFO consisted of roughly 2,000 men, of which nearly half were US soldiers.[790]

While there have been minor technical violations of the zone agreements, Egypt and Israel have complied with the limitations in the Egyptian-Israeli peace treaty ever since Israel withdrew from the Sinai on April 25, 1982.[791] As a result, the MFO and the force limitation agreements of the Egyptian-Israeli peace treaty create significant further obstacles to both an Egyptian attack on Israel and an Israeli attack on Egypt. They also serve as a useful precedent for an Israeli-Syrian agreement—although the Golan and Lebanese border area have far less strategic depth and the terrain and distance from Israel's major mobilization areas make it far more difficult for air and land forces to disrupt an offensive.

EGYPT'S IMPACT ON PEACE NEGOTIATIONS AND
ARMS CONTROL

Egypt's conventional capabilities are so large that no Israeli planner can afford to ignore them in any arms control agreement and/or view the Arab-Israeli balance solely in terms of Syria and Jordan. They are strong enough to give Egypt powerful defensive and deterrent capabilities. They do not, however, represent the kind of threat that requires Israel to take any additional military measures or consider them in reaching the kind of peace agreement with Syria discussed earlier.

Israel must consider Egyptian capabilities in structuring Israeli-Syrian and Israeli-Jordanian disengagement, deployment, warning, and force limitation agreements but has no need to make this consideration an explicit part of such agreements. It can create arms control agreements with Jordan and Syria that deal with the contingency threat posed by Egypt through tacit understandings about the risks involved. In fact, such bilateral agreements may be easier to negotiate in ways that reflect Israel's perception of the different levels of risk from Egypt, Jordan, and Syria than broader multi-lateral agreements.

Once again, Egypt and Israel are likely to have very different perceptions of risks that could present serious problems in structuring and agreeing upon an arms control agreement. Major arms reductions would force Israel to consider the full range of threats from the Arab "ring states" while Egypt might have different perceptions of the risk posed by Israel and insist on some form of near parity.

It is interesting in this light to consider the statements of two senior Israeli defense officials after the US announced the sale of $3.2 billion worth of modern arms to Egypt in March 1992. Israeli Defense Minister Moshe Arons, a hawkish member of the Likud Party said, "Egypt is a country with whom we are at peace. We understand the reasons why the Egyptian government would like to modernize its defense forces in order to take care of its security interests."[792]

At the same time, a senior official in the Ministry of Defense and new National Security Council stated that, "Egypt is not in our 'threat' calculus; however, it is in our 'risk' column. The Middle East remains a largely over-armed region. These are huge militaries. In the case of states such as Egypt, Saudi Arabia, Qatar and Kuwait, they get their arms largely from Western sources, the bulk of it the United States. They have become huge arsenals."[793]

It is hardly necessary to point out that Egypt is equally ambivalent about Israel. A senior Egyptian official in the Foreign Ministry commented on these quotations as follows, "They talk of 'cold peace' and ignore 1982 and their own failure to move forward with peace with the Palestinians. They talk of our arms and build up their nuclear weapons behind a shield of missile defenses. They talk of deterrence and they help stimulate a race to proliferate throughout the region. They talk of Arab attacks and they occupy Lebanon and try to assassinate people in a friendly Jordan. We believe in peace, we like it, and we will keep it. They give us little reason to like them."

13

"Worst Case" Conventional Wars: Israel Fights Egypt, Jordan, and Syria with Support from Other Arab States

Table 13.1 illustrates a "worst case" conflict involving a massive broadening of an Arab-Israeli war to include Israel and all of the Arab "ring states," but it does not include the forces of Iraq, Algeria, and the other Arab states that are included in some Israeli worst case estimates of the balance. Any conflict involving this array of Arab forces would require a massive change in the political and strategic situation. It would probably require the systematic breakdown of the entire peace process, the conversion of all the Arab "ring states" into aggressive powers interested in war fighting capability, and a level of unity the Arab world never approached in any of the previous Arab-Israeli wars. The end result would either be years of strategic warning and the development of a new regional military balance, or to force the Arab side to improvise a multi-front war in a crisis in ways that would make many of their military actions a disorganized and poorly coordinated mess.

It is important to note that while Israel can deploy most of the forces shown in Table 13.1 in actual combat, the Arab states cannot. Only about half of the forces shown for Egypt and Syria could be committed in any strength without a massive military buildup over a period of at least nine months to a year. It is credible that such forces might be supplemented by other Arab forces, and by a Palestinian force that simultaneously engaged the IDF in low-intensity combat, but any major reinforcements are unlikely. Nevertheless, the ratio between the Israeli and Arab forces shown in Table 13.1 cannot be dismissed in any assessment of the current trends in the balance. A conventional Arab-Israeli conflict is inherently asymmetric in two critical grand strategic dimensions. First, Israel's existence can be

Table 13.1
The Broader Arab-Israeli Balance

Category/Weapon	Israel	Syria	Jordan	Egypt	Lebanon
Defense Budget					
(In 2000, $Current Billions)	$7.0	$1.8	$0.488	$2.5	$0.846
Arms Imports: 1996-1999 ($M)					
New Orders	4,500	500	800	6,800	100
Deliveries	4,500	300	300	3,800	100
Mobilization Base					
Men Ages 13-17	281,000	1,042,000	274,000	3,634,000	213,000
Men Ages 18-22	270,000	853,000	245,000	3,437,000	195,000
Manpower					
Total Active	172,500	316,000	103,880	448,500	63,750
(Conscript)	107,500	-	-	322,000 +	22,600
Total Reserve	425,000	396,000	35,000	254,000	-
Total	597,500	7120,000	139,000	702,000	60,670
Paramilitary	8,050	108,000	10,000	230,000	13,000
Land Forces					
Active Manpower	130,000	215,000	90,000	320,000	60,670
(Conscripts)	85,000	-	-	250,000 +	22,600
Reserve Manpower	400,000	300,000	30,000	150,000	-
Total Active & Reserve					
Manpower	530,000	515,000	120,000	470,000	60,670
Main Battle Tanks	3,900	3,650 (1200)	1,246 (300)	3,960	327
AIFVs/Armored Cars/Lt.					
Tanks	408	3,305	241	740 (220)	125
APCs/Recce/Scouts	5,900	1,500	1,450	2,990 (1,075)	1,338
WWII Half-Tracks	500 (3,500)	0	0	0	0
ATGM Launchers	1,300	3,390 +	610	2,660	250
SP Artillery	855	450	412	251	0
Towed Artillery	520	1,600	132	971	151
MRLs	198	480	0	156	23
Mortars	6,440	4,500 +	800	2,400	377
SSM Launchers	48	72	0	18 -24	0
AA Guns	850	2,060	416	834	220
Lt. SAM Launchers	1,298	4,055	1,184	1,146	-

Table 13.1 (continued)

Category/Weapon	Israel	Syria	Jordan	Egypt	Lebanon
Air & Air Defense Forces					
Active Air Force Manpower	36,000	40,000	13,400	30,000	1,700
Active Air Defense Command	0	60,000	0	80,000	0
Air Force Reserve Manpower	20,000	92,000	-	90,000	-
Air Defense Command Reserve					
Manpower	0	-	0	70,000	0
Aircraft					
Total Fighter/FGA/Recce	446 (250)	589	106	583	(16)
Fighter	0	310	41	363	0
FGA/Fighter	405	0	0	0	0
FGA	25	154	65	133	0
Recce	10	14	0	20	0
Airborne Early Warning (AEW)	6	0	0	5	0
Electronic Warfare (EW)	37	10	0	10	0
Fixed Wing	37	0	0	6	-
Helicopter	0	10	0	4	-
Maritime Reconnaissance (MR)	3	0	0	2	0
Combat Capable Trainer	26	111	2	64	3
Tanker	6	0	0	0	0
Transport	37	27	12	32	2
Helicopters					
Attack/Armed	133	87	16	129	0
SAR/ASW	6	-	-	-	-
Transport & Other	160	110	52	158	30
Total	299	197	68	287	30
SAM Forces					
Batteries	28	150	14	38 +	0
Heavy Launchers	79	848	80	628	0
Medium Launchers	0	60	0	36 -54	0
AA Guns	0	4,000	-	72 +	-
Naval Forces					
Active Manpower	6,500	6,000	480	18,500	1,200
Reserve Manpower	5,000	4,000	-	14,000	0
Total Manpower	11,500	10,000	480	34,000	1,200
Naval Commandos/Marines	300	0	0	0	0
Submarines	2	0 (3)	0	4	0
Destroyers/Frigates/Corvettes	3	2	0	11	0
Missile	3	2	0	10	0
Other	0	0	0	1	0
Missile Patrol	12	10	0	25	0
Coastal/Inshore Patrol	32	8	6	15	7
Mine	0	5	0	13	0

Table 13.1 (continued)

Category/Weapon	Israel	Syria	Jordan	Egypt	Lebanon
Air & Air Defense Forces					
Amphibious Ships	1	3	0	3	0
Landing Craft/Light Support	4	5	(3)	9	2
Fixed-wing Combat Aircraft	0	0	0	0	0
MR/MPA	0	0	0	0	0
ASW/Combat Helicopter	0	24	0	24	0
Other Helicopters	-	-	-	-	-

Note: Figures in parentheses show additional equipment known to be in long-term storage. Some Syrian tanks shown in parentheses are used as fire points in fixed positions.

Source: Adapted by Anthony H. Cordesman from data provided by US experts, and the IISS, *Military Balance*.

threatened; that of its Arab neighbors cannot. Second, this existential threat raises the constant specter that Israel will never accept a decisive conventional defeat. At some point, it will escalate to nuclear war.

The situation is also scarcely static, and much depends on the success of the Arab-Israeli peace process. The Arab side might make more serious efforts to develop an effective and well coordinated attack using all the forces shown in Table 13.1 if it felt there was no chance of a successful peace. The numbers develop far more serious war fighting capabilities over a period of three to five years if significant transfers of new weapons and technology to Egypt, Jordan, and/or Syria overcome the technical limitations in these forces.

A multi-front war of this kind would put severe strains on Israel. This is true even if one allows for the fact that the level of political change necessary to make such a worst case alignment of an Arab force possible would probably give Israel several years of strategic warning to make crash improvements in its own war fighting capabilities. Israel cannot fight with the same intensity on all its borders at once. Israel does not have the numbers to concentrate decisive force simultaneously against Egypt, Jordan, and Syria, and would have to adopt a defensive posture in some areas to concentrate its forces on others. At the same time, Israel can use its short lines of communication to redeploy forces quickly and effectively, and can exploit any major gap in the timing of attacks on its northern and southern borders. Israel also can shift air power very quickly from one front to another, and the IAF is far more capable of attacking armor and ground forces than it was in 1973 or in 1982.

The strength of the IAF would be limited relative to the sheer number of its opponents in such a war and its ability to win rapid air supremacy and conduct strategic attacks would be radically different if it confronted both a hostile Syria and a hostile Egypt. The IAF cannot be used as flexibly in attacks on populated areas, and any effort to conduct precision bombing in urban warfare raises a serious risk of collateral damage. It cannot normally locate and destroy guerrilla forces or play a decisive role in low-intensity conflict.

The practical question would be the extent to which Arab forces could act in unison and put maximum strain on Israel's defense capabilities. The degree of Arab success would be determined by the level of coordination and interoperability that Arab forces developed in building up for such an attack, and the level of technology and weapons transfers they received. Today, that coordination would be severely limited and inept. However, several factors will be critical in determining whether Arab forces can collectively erode Israel's qualitative "edge" in the future:

- The level of improvement in advanced interceptors, AEW aircraft, electronic warfare, and air-to-air missiles.
- The level of improvement in self-propelled advanced surface-to-air missiles such as the S-300 or S-400 and Patriot.
- The improvement of tank capabilities to match the IDF in range, all-weather night combat, and rate of engagement capability.
- The number of advanced anti-tank weapons with third or fourth generation guidance systems and the ability to defeat advanced armor.
- Shifts in artillery equipment to provide advanced BVR and counterbattery targeting capability, more lethal rounds, and an MLRS-like capability, coupled with advanced C^{4}I/BM capabilities to use advanced targeting systems and to mass and switch fires.
- Shifts in armored infantry fighting vehicle capabilities to provide better support for armor.
- Improvements in attack helicopter capability to provide better sensors and targeting capability, all-weather-night operations capability, and effective long-range anti-armor capability.
- Improved air attack forces capable of stand-off precision attacks on IDF armor and aircraft shelters.
- Cruise missile or similar precision conventional-strike capability against strategic targets in Israel.
- The risk of escalation to the use of weapons of mass destruction.
- The role of Palestinians and internal Arab resistance.

All of these developments are possible over a period of time. It is important to note, however, that they will only be effective to the degree that the Arab forces in each country go beyond the "glitter factor" of acquiring new systems and technology, and actually transform them into an integrated set of sub-systems that can support combined operations, and match new technology with new tactics and new training methods. So far, Egypt is the only nation making significant progress in this regard. Jordan has the force quality, but not the funds and force modernization.

A Palestinian Authority armed with a few light armored vehicles and small arms cannot threaten Israel militarily or play a major role in reducing Israel's ability to defend at the West Bank or prevent a Syrian drive around the Golan. This would require Palestinian forces to be large enough and well armed enough to seriously limit the mobility of Israeli armor and pose a threat to the Israeli air force. At a minimum, this would require the Palestinian forces to have large numbers of guided anti-tank weapons, mines, and modern light surface-to-air missiles like the Stinger or SA-14/SA-16. Even then, such a force would be largely defensive and could only harass and delay Israeli forces, not challenge them in any form of prolonged combat. While such Palestinian forces might be able to fight effectively in urban warfare, Israel would have little reason for house-to-house fighting in most contingencies or even to enter most Arab cities, and could rapidly overrun such Palestinian forces in the field, on near roads, or in small towns.

Palestinian forces could only be highly effective in disrupting Israel's overall military capabilities if they acquired substantial amounts of artillery, armor, and anti-aircraft weapons to delay the IDF long enough for Syria and Jordan to massively reinforce the Palestinian forces, or pose enough of a threat on the West Bank to pin down a large amount of Israel's ground forces and limit its capabilities against other Arab armies. Palestinian forces are unlikely to have these capabilities until well after the final peace negotiations are completed, and even then it seems unlikely that Israel would accept such a level of armament, or ignore any change in the combined capabilities of Palestinian and other Arab forces.

The peace process could also weaken Israeli capabilities to fight in such a contingency if such a peace collapsed after Israel had withdrawn from most of the West Bank and the Golan. As discussed earlier, trading territory for war is different from trading territory for peace. Any peace that restored the Golan to Syria, created a sovereign or near-sovereign Palestinian entity, created free right of passage between Jordan and the Palestinian entity, *and which did not involve substantial arms control measures*, would create risks for Israel. This will be particularly true if Israel did not react preemptively to any significant Arab buildup on its new borders. Such a peace would improve Syria's military position in the Golan, potentially ease Jordanian deployments on the West Bank, create a potential terrorist or unconventional warfare threat to Israel's mobilization centers, air bases, and other critical facilities, and to Israel's roads and lines of communication. A simultaneous uprising in the West Bank, Gaza, and Jerusalem during a major Arab attack might then complicate IDF mobilization and movements and seriously weaken Israel's defensive capabilities.

Such a peace seems unlikely, however, and the key to the security of a peace agreement will be how Israel deals with the most serious threat in a multi-front war. Israel will not give up the Golan casually, and will ignore the need for warning, disengagement arrangements, new rapid reaction contingency capabilities, and acting upon strategic warning. A war that involved a "race for the Golan" in which Israel and Syria raced to redeploy forces would not expose most IDF forces to major interference from any Palestinian uprising in the Gaza and West Bank. Syria's advantage in distance and terrain would be offset by Israel's superior air and precision weapons delivery capabilities, and Syria would find it difficult to

Figure 13.1
Israel Versus Egypt, Syria, Jordan, and Lebanon in 2001

Operational Land Weapons

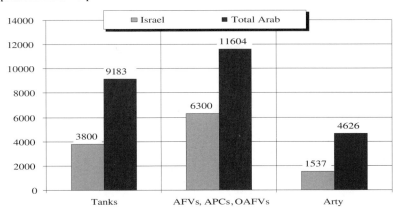

Operational Combat Aircraft

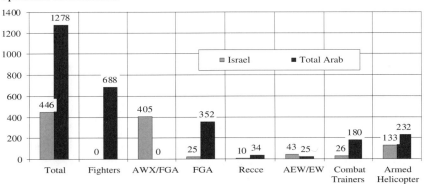

Notes: Total artillery includes towed and self-propelled tube artillery and multiple rocket launchers.
  Total air forces include only operational fixed wing fighter, fighter-attack, and reconnaissance
  aircraft in combat units, less aircraft in combat training units.

Source: Adapted by Anthony H. Cordesman from data provided by US experts, and the IISS,
  Military Balance.

either sweep around the Golan through Jordan or penetrate down through the
Golan and achieve any significant gains in the Galilee.

The risks posed by a Syrian attack from the Golan in either a Syria-only attack or
a multi-front Arab attack are more an argument for coupling arms control and
security measures to a peace settlement, than arguments against a peace settlement.
While some increase in military risk may be inevitable during some stages of the
peace process, there is no inherent reason that arms control cannot make a peace as

Map 13.1
Israel and the Arab "Ring States"

RINGS AROUND JERUSALEM, January 1992			
Settlement	Population	Housing under Construction	Current Number of Housing Units
Betar	1,800	500	300
Gush Etzion*	7,530	1,123	1,750
Ma'ale Adumim	15,500	2,000	3,300
Mikmash	450	250	120
Adam	400	630	100
Abir-Yaacov	300	189	75
Givat Ze'ev	5,675	250	1,050
Har Adar	1,100	0	290
TOTAL	32,755	4,942	6,985

* Gush Etzion—the Etzion Bloc— includes 16 separate settlements.

secure or substantially more secure than the present status quo and prevent another "arms race" of the kind that led Egypt and Israel to buy many new arms after the Camp David agreement. In fact, measures that reduced the costs of military forces and arms imports offer a potential way of providing the kind of "peace dividend" that may be necessary to secure the peace process. Such arms control options are an important part of the current peace negotiations.

There is no way to anticipate the success of the linkage between arms control and the peace process at this time, or the extent to which confidence building measures and constraints on exercises and deployments can be coupled to actual reductions in military forces and changes in military technology. This linkage will, however, be a critical factor in determining the shifts in the military balance. The preceding analysis indicates that Israel's "edge" is not sufficiently large to secure the peace process militarily without arms control, or to preserve the current level of deterrence of war.

Finally, it is important to note that Israel is not bound to defend against such a "worst case" Arab attack on Arab terms. Israel can launch strategic conventional strikes against critical economic and leadership targets, attacking the nation rather than the nation's forces. Israel's nuclear forces would also act as a significant deterrent to any full exploitation of the conventional forces shown in ratios illustrated in Figure 13.1, even if Arab forces could win an initial conventional victory on at least one front.

Israel's existential vulnerability gives credibility to Israeli nuclear escalation if Arab forces begin to win a decisive conventional victory. Similarly, such an Arab victory becomes steadily more likely to trigger massive US intervention of some kind and diplomatic initiatives by other states. There are important limiting factors on Arab military success, even if Israel should be defeated. It is far from clear that even a worst case Arab attack—under worst case conditions—could ultimately be exploited to the point of a successful end game.

14

Wars Involving Libyan, Iranian, Iraqi, and Other Arab Conventional Forces

There is often a sharp difference between perceptual threats and war fighting threats. As discussed earlier, some Israelis tend to see the military balance in terms of large parts of the entire Arab world, and have often exaggerated the kind of forces Arab states outside the region can bring to bear against Israel. This tendency has declined since the peace treaties with Egypt, Jordan, and the PLO, and after a growing informal dialogue with the states of North Africa.

There are, however, three nations whose forces do merit serious discussion: Libya, Iran, and Iraq. Libya, Iran, and Iraq are unquestionably hostile to Israel and all three have large inventories of conventional weapons. In each case, however, there are good reasons to assume that Libya, Iran, and Iraq could only make a limited contribution to a conventional Arab-Israeli conflict. This situation is also only likely to change significantly in the case of Iraq, and then only if it can break out of UN sanctions and rebuild and modernize some of its forces.

Tables 14.1, 14.2, and 14.3 provide further insight as to the total pool of Arab forces that might be involved. Table 14.1 shows the total forces of Algeria, Iran, Iraq, and Libya. Tables 14.2 and 14.3 show the total pool of forces in the Arab world. These tables do not make any attempt to portray the balance of forces that might actually engage in combat. Instead, they show the size of Israel relative to the total military demographics of the greater Middle East and the total military forces of all the countries involved.

It should be clear that the comparisons of military demographics in Table 14.2 have only a limited impact on the military balance, largely because the states in the region are limited by the number of troops they can pay for, train, equip, and

Table 14.1
Algerian, Iranian, Iraqi, and Libyan Forces in 2001

Category/Weapon	Algeria	Libya	Iran	Iraq
Manpower				
Total Active	124,000	76,000	513,000	429,000
(Conscript)	75,000	40,000	220,000	-
Total Regular	-	70,000	378,000	429,000
Revolutionary Guard and				
Other	0	?	135,000	0
Total Reserve	150,000	40,000	350,000	650,000
Total Active and Reserve	274,000	116,000	763,000	1,079,000
Paramilitary	181,200	?	40,000	45,000-50,000
Land Forces				
Active Manpower	107,000	45,000	400,000	375,000
(Revolutionary Guards)	-	-	(100,000)	-
(Conscripts)	75,000	25,000	-	450,000
Reserve Manpower	-	-	350,000	825,000
Total Manpower	-	-	750,000	
Main Battle Tanks	1,006	985 (1,040)	1,135	2,200
AIFVs/Armored Cars/Lt.				
Tanks	1,032	1,630 *	555	2,000
APCs/Recce/Scouts/Half-				
Tracks	680+	990 *	590	2,400
ATGM Launchers	-	3,000 *	420+	480+
SP Artillery	185	450 *	290	150
Towed Artillery	416	720 *	1,950	1,900
MRLs	126	700 *	664+	500
Mortars	330+	-	6,500	2,000+
SSM Launchers	-	120	46	6-24
AA Guns	895	600+*	1,700	5,500
Lt. SAM Launchers	1,000+	2,500+*	700	1,100
Air & Air Defense Forces				
Active Manpower	10,000	22,000	40,000	52,000
(Air Defense Only)	NA	?	(15,000)	(17,000)
Reserve Manpower	-	-	−	-
(Air Defense Only)	NA	?	-	-
Aircraft				
Total Fighter/FGA/Recce	181	420	291	353
Bomber	0	6	0	6?
Fighter	110	212	157	180
FGA/Fighter	50	194	690	130
Recce	10	11	15	8

Table 14.1 (continued)

Category/Weapon	Algeria	Libya	Iran	Iraq
Air & Air Defense Forces				
Airborne Early Warning (AEW/EW)	0	0	(1)	0
Maritime Reconnaissance (MR)	15	0	5	0
Combat Capable Trainer	8	21	35	155
Tanker	0	0	4	2
Transport	27	78	65	34
Helicopters				
Attack/Armed/ASW	65	52	(100)	(120)
Other	63	98	512?	380
Total	138	150	612?	500
SAM Forces				
Batteries	9	39		
Heavy Launchers	43	236	155	340
Medium Launchers	-	?	52	200
AA guns	-	?	-	6,000
Naval Forces				
Active Manpower	7,000	8,000	40,600	2,000
Regular Navy	-	8,000	20,600	2,000
Naval Guards	-	-	20,000	0
Marines	-	-	2,600	-
Reserve Manpower	-	-	-	-
Total Manpower	-	-	-	2,000
Submarines	2	2(2)	5	0
Destroyers/Frigates/Corvettes	8	5	5	0
Missile	5	5	3	0
Other	3	0	2	0
Missile Patrol	9(2)	13(8)	20	1
Coastal/Inshore Patrol	3	-	42	5
Mine	0	6	7	4
Amphibious Ships	3	4(1)	9	0
Landing Craft/Light Support	3	12	9	-
MPA/ASW/Combat Helicopter	0	-/32	-/29	(6)

Notes: *Extensive, but unknown amounts inoperable or in storage.

Figures in parentheses are additional equipment in storage. Total equipment holdings for the Iranian land forces include 470 tanks, 620 other armored vehicles, 360 artillery weapons, 40 rocket launchers, and 140 anti-aircraft weapons with the land units of the Revolutionary Guards. Iranian & Iraqi attack helicopters are in the army. Only about 60% of the US supplied fixed wing combat aircraft in Iran and 80% of the Chinese supplied aircraft are operational.

Source: Adapted by Anthony H. Cordesman from data provided by US experts, and the IISS, *Military Balance*.

Table 14.2

The "Perceptual Balance"–Military Demographics of the Greater Middle East in 2000

Country	Total Population	Males Reaching Military Age Each Year	Males Between the Ages of 13 and 17	18 and 22	23 and 32	Males Between 15 and 49 Total	Medically Fit
Egypt	68,360,000	704,000	3,634,000	3,218,000	5,067,000	18,164,000	11,767,000
Gaza	1,132,000*	-	-	-	-	-	-
Israel	5,842,000	50,348	281,000	270,000	526,000	1,499,000	1,227,000
Jordan	4,999,000	55,742	274,000	245,000	4447,000	1,399,000	994,000
Lebanon	3,578,000	-	213,000	195,000	391,000	958,000	592,000
Palestinian	2,900,000*	-	163,000	140,000	233,000	-	-
Syria	16,306,000	197,000	1,042,000	853,000	1,210,000	4,221,000	2,359,000
West Bank	2,020,000*	-	-	-	-	-	-
Iran	65,620,000	801,000	4,587,000	3,827,000	5,771,000	17,762,000	10,546000
Iraq	22,676,000	260,000	1,498,000	1,281,000	1,894,000	5,675,000	3,177,000
Bahrain	634,000	5,699	33,000	26,000	40,000	221,000	121,000
Kuwait	1,974,000	17,919	120,000	103,000	147,000	7498,000	447,000
Oman	2,553,000	25,527	131,000	106,000	154,000	763,000	425,000
Qatar	744,000	6,471	25,000	21,000	35,000	307,000	161,000
Saudi Arabia	22,024,000	221,000	1,348,000	1,133,000	1,670,000	5,786,000	3,226,000
UAE	2,369,000	24,506	86,000	84,000	143,000	785,000	4223,000
Yemen	17,479,000	234,000	974,000	788,000	1,293,000	3,936,000	2,209,000
Algeria	31,194,000	374,000	1,955,000	1,787,000	2,871,000	8,523,000	5,220,000
Libya	5,115,000	62,200	375,000	310,000	475,000	1,415,000	841,000
Morocco	30,122,000	335,000	1,750,000	1,583,000	2,698,000	7,962,000	5,026,000
Tunisia	9,593,000	102,000	524,000	496,000	856,000	2,670,000	1,524,000
Chad	8,425,000	79,595	396,000	324,000	508,000	1,749,000	916,000
Mauritania	2,668,000	-	145,000	119,000	189,000	605,000	293,000
Western Sahara	245,000	-	-	-	-	-	-
Afghanistan	25,839,000	244,958	1,451,000	1,178,000	2,014,000	6,402,000	3,432,000
Djibouti	451,000	-	41,000	34,000	55,000	106,000	62,000
Eritrea	4,136,000	-	246,000	205,000	311,000	-	-
Ethiopia	64,117,000	687,000	3,8426,000	3,083,000	4,617,000	14,184,000	7,393,000
Somalia	7,253,000	-	607,000	494,000	707,000	1,773,000	984,000
Sudan	35,080,000	386,000	1,9408,000	1,644,000	2,471,000	8,144,000	5,014,000
Turkey	65,667,000	664,000	3,266,000	3,254,000	6,098,000	18,524,000	11,228,000

Note: Totals include non-nationals, total population, males reaching military age, and Males between 15 and 49 are generally CIA data, the rest are IISS data. * Totals for Palestinians are IISS, totals for Gaza and West Bank are CIA.

Source: Adapted by Anthony H. Cordesman, CIA *World Factbook, 2000*, IISS, *Military Balance*, 2000–2001.

Table 14.3
The "Perceptual Balance": Military Forces of the Greater Middle East

Country	Total Active Manning	Total Active Army Manning	Tanks	OAFVs	Artillery	Combat Aircraft	Armed Helicopters
Egypt	448,500	320,000	3,960	3,730	1,378	583	129
Israel	172,500	130,000	3,900	6,300	1,537	446	133
Jordan	103,880	90,000	1,246	1,691	544	106	(16)
Lebanon	63,750	65,000	327	1,463	174	(3)	0
Palestinian	(35,000)	(35,000)	-	45	-	-	-
Syria	316,000	215,000	3,650	4,805	2,530	589	87
Iran	513,000	475,000	1,410	1,105	3,224	304	100
Iraq	387,500	350,000	2,700	3,400	2,200	353	120
Bahrain	11,000	8,500	106	411	107	24	26
Kuwait	15,300	11,000	385	455	68	76	20
Oman	43,500	31,500	141	219	109	40	0
Qatar	11,100	8,500	44	284	44	18	12
Saudi Arabia	162,500	127,000	1,055	4,285	568	432	33
UAE	64,500	59,000	237	1,138	289	99	49
Yemen	66,300	61,000	1,030	1,290	702	89	8
Algeria	124,000	107,000	1,006	1,712	727	181	65
Libya	76,000	45,000	985	2,620	1,870	420	52
Morocco	198,500	175,000	644	1,344	484	89	24
Tunisia	35,000	27,000	84	417	123	44	7
Chad	30,350	25,000	60	63+	5	4	0
Mauritania	15,650	15,000	35	105	75	7	0
Afghanistan	-	-	-	-	-	-	-
Djibouti	9,600	8,000	0	31	6	0	0
Eritrea	200,000 -250,000	200,000 -250,000	89	175	160	179	0
Ethiopia	352,500	350,000	160	200	300	53	16-18
Somalia	35,900?	35,900?	-	-	-	-	-
Sudan	104,500	100,000	1700	608	300?	30	5
Turkey	609,700	495,000	4,205	2,616	2,883	505	37

Note: Totals count all "active" equipment, much of which is not operational. They do not include stored equipment, but are only approximate estimates of combat-ready equipment holdings. Light tanks, APCs, AIFVs, armored recce vehicles, and misc. AFVs are counted as OAFVs (Other Armored Fighting Vehicles). Artillery counts towed and self-propelled tube weapons of 100-mm+ and multiple rocket launchers, but not mortars. Only fixed wing combat aircraft in combat, COIN, or OCU units are counted, not other trainers or aircraft.

Source: Adapted by Anthony H. Cordesman, CIA *World Factbook*, various editions and IISS, *Military Balance*, various editions.

support more than they are limited by their total manpower pool. Most of the forces shown in Tables 14.1 and 14.3 cannot be deployed to fight against Israel in any combat effective form. They represent the impact of arms races and conflicts between Arab, North African, and Gulf states that have nothing to do with Israel. And, they include the forces of many nations that recognize Israel's right to exist and/or have never played a role in past Arab-Israeli conflicts.

LIBYAN CAPABILITIES

Libya has military forces with an active strength of 76,000 men and some 40,000 reserves. Libya also has a larger inventory of combat equipment than it can actually man, including 2,225 tanks (1,040 in storage), 1,630 other armored fighting vehicles, 990 armored personnel carriers, 720 towed artillery weapons, 450 self-propelled artillery weapons, and over 650 multiple rocket launchers. Libya has 420 combat aircraft and 52 armed helicopters. These forces include 6 Su-24s, 29 Mirage F-1s, 45 Su-20s and Su-22s, 60 MiG-25s, 40 Mi-25s and 12 Mi-35s.[794]

Libya's teeth, however, are far worse than its bite. Its land forces only have 45,000 men and only about 985 of its main battle tanks have even limited operational status. The Libyan air force has little combat proficiency and even less power projection capability. It is not trained or organized to be indirectly interoperable with any of the Arab air forces surrounding Israel, and its long-range strike capabilities consist of its Su-24s, which have a limited refueling capability.

Libya is little more than a military farce. It has the worst led, worst managed, worst trained, and least effective forces in the Arab world. It has never created effective land and air forces and cannot use its aircraft and major land weapons effectively. Most of its already limited military capabilities have degenerated steadily since the breakup of the Soviet Union and Warsaw Pact, and the imposition of the UN sanctions.

A combination of wretched organization and training, a cutoff of most arms imports because of UN sanctions, and cutbacks in military spending has meant its forces have gone from terrible to worse. At least 55% of Libya's tanks and combat aircraft are in storage or have negligible operational capability. Libya has virtually ceased modernizing many of its conventional weapons, and has lacked organized flows of spare parts and force-wide maintenance efforts.

Most of Libya's operational armor and combat aircraft have little or no sustainable combat capability. Its active forces have only token levels of combined arms training, and Libya is little more than a massive military parking lot. It might be able to transfer some arms to other Arab forces and deploy a few ships and combat aircraft, but it could not deploy or sustain combat effective formations. In fact, the political cost to any host Arab nation of supporting Libyan reinforcements would probably be far greater than its military value.

IRANIAN CAPABILITIES

Iran's attitudes towards Israel are politically ambiguous. There seems to be a consensus in the Iranian government that Iran must be hostile towards Israel as long as it occupied Southern Lebanon and Syria is not at peace with Israel. There have been no signs that the more moderate faction in Iranian politics, led by President Hojjat ol-Eslam Ardakani (Ali) Mohammad Khatami, opposes Iranian cooperation with Syria in supporting the Hizbollah. In fact, officials close to President Khatami have repeatedly taken this position. A similar consensus seems to have emerged in Iranian talks with Turkey over the perception that Israel might use its long-range strike capabilities against Iran.

The uncertainties lie in what seems to be a split between the moderates under Khatami, and the "hard-liners" under the Supreme Leader, the Ayatollah Ali Hoseini Khamenei, over whether Iran should remain hostile to Israel now that it has withdrawn from Lebanon if Israel reaches a peace with Syria. The "moderate" faction seems to support ending active hostility under such circumstances. Some senior "moderates" say they believe that better Iranian-Israeli relations would serve as a counterweight to Iraq and defuse both nations' current focus on the other's possession of weapons of mass destruction and missile and long-range strike capability. The "hard-line" faction at least claims to firmly oppose Israel's right to exist, and to see it as a religious and ideological enemy regardless of whether it makes peace with Syria, and makes a full peace with the Palestinians. Such hard-liners mention the Israeli missile and nuclear threat to Iran almost as often as they deny that Iran is seeking nuclear capabilities of its own.

Iran has mixed military capabilities. It has large conventional military forces with an active strength of over half a million men. It is slowly rebuilding the quality of its forces after massive losses in the final battles of the Iran-Iraq war, and is acquiring modern T-72 tanks and combat aircraft like the MiG-29 and Su-25. Since the end of the Iran-Iraq War, Iran has obtained hundreds of modern T-72 tanks and it is seeking hundreds more. It is acquiring self-propelled artillery, and more modern armored fighting vehicles.[795]

It can now deploy Su-24 strike aircraft, with better avionics and range-payload capabilities than the Russian medium bombers of the 1960s, and MiG-29s with advanced beyond-visual-range combat capability. It has acquired SA-5 and SA-6 missiles to supplement its US supplied IHawks. It is acquiring advanced air-to-surface and air-to-air missiles, and more advanced radars and command, control, communications, computer, and intelligence (C^4I/BM) systems.

Iran has acquired three relatively advanced conventional submarines with wire-guided torpedoes and "smart" mines. It has acquired more advanced anti-ship missiles that can attack ships virtually anywhere in southern Gulf waters from relatively small ships, from land positions near the Strait of Hormuz, and from the islands it seized in the lower Gulf. It now has large numbers of smart non-magnetic mines that include types that can be moored in shallower waters, and "bounding mines" that can rise from the bottom to attack ships in deep channels. Iran is also steadily receiving additional advanced versions of the Scud that can attack targets across the Gulf, and has ordered the No Dong missile, which has nearly twice the range of the Scud C and can reach targets deep into the Southern Gulf.

In 2001, Iran had about 513,000 full-time actives in its forces, plus 350,000 men in its reserves. It had 325,000 actives in the regular army, 125,000 men in its Islamic Revolutionary Guards Corps (Pasdaran Inquilab), 18,000 in the navy, and 45,000 in the air force. It also had 200,000 in its Basiij (Popular Mobilization Army), 150,000 in its internal security forces, and around 8,000 men in an Iranian trained and funded Kurdish Democratic Party militia.[796]

Iran had an inventory of around 1,135 tanks—reflecting a rise of nearly 350 tanks over its strength in 1993 and 410–530 tanks over 1992.[797] Iran seems to have had about 550 operational armored personnel carriers, 555 armored infantry fighting vehicles, and 290 self-propelled medium and heavy artillery weapons, 2,170 towed artillery weapons and over 764 multiple rocket launchers.

The Iranian air force and air defense force had around 50,000 men, a total inventory of around 2,904 combat aircraft, plus 100 armed helicopters in its army. These forces included 24 Su-24s, 7 Su-25Ks, 30 MiG-29s, 66 F-4D/Es, 25 F-14s, and 100 AH-1Js. It had 30 Improved Hawk fire units (150+ launchers), 50–55 SA-2 and HQ-23 (CSA-1) launchers (Chinese-made equivalents of the SA-2), and 25 SA-6 launchers. The air force also had three Soviet-made long-range SA-5 units with a total of 10–15 launchers, enough for six sites.

Iranian conventional capability has, however, often been exaggerated. Iran has spent far less on arms imports in recent years than it did during the Iran-Iraq War. Iran has not come close to being able to replace its losses of land force equipment during the final battles of the war in 1988—losses which US experts estimate reached 40–60% of its entire inventory of armor and artillery. Much of its remaining inventory of land and air weapons is now 15–25 years old, has been severely worn in combat, and has lacked any orderly maintenance and modernization since the fall of the Shah.

Iran has little strategic mobility and meaningful power projection capability, and its equipment and command and control assets are not interoperable with the equipment and systems of any Arab "ring state." The limited reinforcements Iran could actually provide would probably cost an Arab host nation far more in support effort than their military effectiveness would be worth.

As a result, it is Iran's proliferation of long-range missiles, acquisition of weapons of mass destruction, and ties to Islamic extremist movements like Hamas, the Islamic Jihad, and the Hizbollah which pose the greatest threat to Israel and the peace process.[798] Iran does have the ability to support an unconventional war against Israel, even though it presents little near-term threat of being able to deploy significant effective conventional military forces.

IRAQI CAPABILITIES

Iraq has been a major threat to Israel in the past. It deployed a total of four brigades against Israel by the end of the 1948 War, which was fought in Samaria. It deployed a reinforced division, composed of an armored brigade, a mechanized brigade, and two infantry brigades in 1967—as well as a Palestinian contingent. This force only failed to engage Israeli land forces because the lead Iraqi mechanized brigade was badly hurt by the IAF while it was still on the East Bank.[799]

Iraq deployed several divisions and significant air power in 1973. This Iraqi force played a significant role in limiting the IDF advance towards Damascus, and might have been far more effective if Iraq had been better able to move and sustain its forces and Syria had provided more effective overall C^4I and battle management assistance. Iraq acquired enough tank transporters and logistics equipment, and improved its infrastructure in Western Iraq, to the point where it could have rapidly moved and sustained four divisions in a conflict with Israel by the mid-1980s. Iraq also began to exercise air units and small land headquarters units in Jordan before the Gulf War, although Jordan is now forbidden to allow the deployment of Iraqi forces on Jordanian soil as part of its peace agreement with Israel.

Iraq is still a major power by regional standards. In 2001, it had 429,000 active troops and a 375,000-man army. It had some 2,200 tanks, 700–1,000 BMP-1/BMP-2 armored infantry fighting vehicles, 1,000 armored reconnaissance vehicles, 2,400 APCs, 150 self-propelled and 1,900 major towed artillery weapons, 150 multiple rocket launchers and FROG rockets, thousands of light surface-to-air missiles and anti-aircraft guns. It still retained roughly 350 combat aircraft, including 1 Su-24 and some MiG-29s, large numbers of armed helicopters, and extensive surface-to-air missile defenses.

Nevertheless, Iraq's capabilities to intervene in an Arab-Israeli conflict are currently limited. Iraq suffered massive losses during the Gulf War, losing 40–60% of its inventory of armor, artillery and aircraft and many of its most advanced systems. While Iraq has rebuilt and reorganized its forces since 1991, these efforts have not come close to offsetting the damage inflicted by the Gulf War and nine years of sanctions. Iraq also now deploys much of its army where it can deal with the threat from Iran, and internal security missions against its Kurds and Shi'ites. It has had steadily growing problems with morale and desertions, and at least some senior officers have been involved in coup attempts.

While Iraq has extensively reorganized its Republican Guard and conventional forces since the Gulf War, it has had no major new arms imports since August 1990 and suffered significant damage after the Gulf War as the result of Desert Fox. This has had a steadily more serious impact on Iraq's readiness. Iraq never developed an effective large-scale maintainable support system before the Gulf War. It relied on vast imports of new weapons and parts to substitute for effective support, logistics, and maintenance capabilities.

Its reconstruction of its military industries since the Gulf War has not been able to correct these problems, and it lacks the capability to provide large numbers of heavy weapons or technically sophisticated equipment and parts. Iraq has been unable to import the new technology it needs to react to any of the major lessons of its defeat in the Gulf War. Its air force and air defense forces have had very limited training, and much of its land forces have been tied up in operations in the marshes or in securing the perimeter of the Kurdish security zone.[800]

These problems do not mean that Iraq could not deploy a force as large as several heavy divisions or several squadrons of combat aircraft to Syria and/or Jordan. Iraq has the infrastructure in Western Iraq, and the tank transporters, to move at least two divisions relatively quickly. However, in order to be effective, any such deployments would force Iraq to deploy several of its best divisions, which might affect Saddam Hussein's security. Such a deployment would also require a sudden political rapprochement between Saddam Hussein and Bashar Assad and/or King Abdullah II—a now unlikely contingency. Even then, such Iraqi deployments would have limited sustainability and real-world combat power, would present many of the same battle management and coordination problems that arose in 1973, and could not obtain effective air cover and support from the Iraqi Air Force.

Iraq may well reemerge as a threat to Israel once current sanctions are lifted and it has the opportunity to fully rebuild its forces. This, however, will require several years at a minimum, and much will depend on Iraq's political leadership and policies at that point, including whether it chooses to thrust itself back into the Arab-Israeli confrontation as well as deal with its problems in the Gulf.

THE IMPACT OF LIBYAN, IRANIAN, IRAQI, AND OTHER ARAB CONVENTIONAL CAPABILITIES

Libyan and Iranian conventional capabilities cannot be totally disregarded, and Iraq may emerge as a significant mid-term threat. Israel must consider these threats in its military and arms control planning—at least on a contingency basis. At the same time, the current threat of any major deployment of conventional forces by radical states outside the region seems very limited, and it does not seem meaningful to attempt detailed contingency analysis. If such nations pose a near-term threat, it is more likely to come in the form of unconventional warfare or aid to a ring state in acquiring or using weapons of mass destruction.

The practical problem for both Israel and its immediate Arab neighbors is not so much the near-term war fighting threat from Libya, Iran, and Iraq, but rather their potential impact on arms control. Arms control agreements between Israel and its neighbors cannot be based simply on current capabilities. It takes years to build up military forces and war fighting capabilities, and Israel must consider this in reviewing any agreement that ignores threats from states outside the region, particularly Iraq. Further, the more Israel cuts its forces, the easier it will be for limited Iraqi reinforcements to influence war fighting or crisis outcomes since they will be large relative to Israel's remaining capabilities.

This problem will not be an easy issue for Israel and its Arab neighbors to deal with. Syria sees Iraq as a potential threat—as well as a possible ally—and would have to consider this in developing its arms control positions. Jordan cannot ignore the Iraqi threat, and Egypt has regional concerns about Iran's intentions and capabilities. At least in the near term, the "greater Middle East" may present more risks and problems for the Arab-Israeli military balance than it does economic or political opportunities.

15

Wars Using Weapons of Mass Destruction

Conventional wars are certainly capable of destroying whole nations, particularly small ones like Israel, Jordan, and the emerging Palestinian entity. In the real world, however, the probable outcome of conventional warfare in any of the previous contingencies is likely to be limited—at least in the sense that such wars are unlikely to escalate to levels of conflict which threaten the existence of one or more states, or produce massive civilian casualties. The slow proliferation of weapons of mass destruction, however, poses a growing risk of wars that could threaten the major population centers of Israel and its Arab neighbors. Proliferation could destroy the very existence of Israel and change beyond all recognition the leadership and character of any Arab state that became involved in a large-scale exchange using biological or nuclear weapons.

This process of proliferation extends far beyond Israel and its immediate Arab neighbors. Iran, Iraq, and Libya are all proliferators. It also involves weapons of mass destruction that have fundamentally different lethalities from those of conventional weapons, and there are important differences between chemical biological, and nuclear weapons. Tables 15.1 to 15.6 describe the war fighting effects, possible targets and missions, and limitations of each type of weapon of mass destruction.

ISRAELI WEAPONS OF MASS DESTRUCTION

Israel is the only state in the region that currently has nuclear weapons and which can deliver them with effective long-range missiles. While other proliferators are

Table 15.1
Strengths and Weaknesses of Weapons of Mass Destruction

Chemical Weapons

Destructive Effects: Poisoning skin, lungs, nervous system, or blood. Contaminating areas, equipment, and protective gear for periods of hours to days. Forcing military units to don highly restrictive protection gear or use incapacitating antidotes. False alarms and panic. Misidentification of the agent, or confusion of chemical with biological agents (which may be mixed) leading to failure of defense measures. Military and popular panic and terror effects. Major medical burdens which may lead to mistreatment. Pressure to deploy high-cost air and missile defenses. Paralysis or disruption of civil life and economic activity in threatened or attacked areas.

Typical Military Targets: Infantry concentrations, air bases, ships, ports, staging areas, command centers, munitions depots, cities, key oil and electrical facilities, desalinization plants.

Typical Military Missions: Killing military and civilian populations. Intimidation. Attack of civilian population or targets. Disruption of military operations by requiring protective measures or decontamination. Area or facility denial. Psychological warfare, production of panic, and terror.

Military Limitations: Large amounts of agents are required to achieve high lethality, and military and economic effects are not sufficiently greater than carefully targeted conventional strikes to offer major war fighting advantages. Most agents degrade quickly, and their effect is highly dependent on temperature and weather conditions, height of dissemination, terrain, and the character of built-up areas. Warning devices are far more accurate and sensitive than for biological agents. Protective gear and equipment can greatly reduce effects, and sufficiently high numbers of rounds, sorties, and missiles are needed to ease the task of defense. Leave buildings and equipment reusable by the enemy, although persistent agents may require decontamination. Persistent agents may contaminate the ground the attacker wants to cross or occupy and force use of protective measures or decontamination.

Biological Weapons

Destructive Effects: Infectious disease or biochemical poisoning. Contaminating areas, equipment, and protective gear for periods of hours to weeks. Delayed effects and tailoring to produce incapacitation or killing, treatable or non-treatable agents, and be infectious on contact only or transmittable. Forcing military units to don highly restrictive protection gear or use incapacitating vaccines as antidotes. False alarms and panic. High risk of at least initial misidentification of the agent, or confusion of biological with chemical agents (which may be mixed) leading to failure of defense measures. Military and popular panic and terror effects. Major medical burdens, which may lead to mistreatment. Pressure to deploy high-cost air and missile defenses. Paralysis or disruption of civil life and economic activity in threatened or attacked areas.

Typical Military Targets: Infantry concentrations, air bases, ships, ports, staging areas, command centers, munitions depots, cities, key oil and electrical facilities,

Table 15.1 (continued)

Biological Weapons

desalinization plants. Potentially fare more effectively against military and civil area targets than chemical weapons.

Typical Military Missions: Killing and incapacitation of military and civilian populations. Intimidation. Attack of civilian population or targets. Disruption of military operations by requiring protective measures or decontamination. Area or facility denial. Psychological warfare, production of panic, and terror.

Military Limitations: Most wet agents degrade quickly, although spores, dry encapsulated agents, and some toxins are persistent. Effects usually take some time to develop (although not in the case of some toxins). Effects are unpredictable, and are even more dependent than chemical weapons on temperature and weather conditions, height of dissemination, terrain, and the character of built-up areas. Major risk of contaminating the wrong area. Warning devices uncertain and may misidentify the agent. Protective gear and equipment can reduce effects. Leave buildings and equipment reusable by the enemy, although persistent agents may require decontamination. Persistent agents may contaminate the ground the attacker wants to cross or occupy and force use of protective measures or decontamination. More likely than chemical agents to cross the threshold where nuclear retaliation seems justified.

Nuclear Weapons

Destructive Effects: Blast, fire, and radiation. Destruction of large areas and production of fallout and contamination—depending on character of weapon and height of burst. Contaminating areas, equipment, and protective gear for periods of hours to days. Forcing military units to don highly restrictive protection gear and use massive amounts of decontamination gear. Military and popular panic and terror effects. Massive medical burdens. Pressure to deploy high-cost air and missile defenses. Paralysis or disruption of civil life and economic activity in threatened or attacked areas. High long-term death rates from radiation. Forced dispersal of military forces and evacuation of civilians. Destruction of military and economic centers, and national political leadership and command authority, potentially altering character of attacked nation and creating major recovery problems.

Typical Military Targets: Hardened targets, enemy facilities and weapons of mass destruction, enemy economy, political leadership, and national command authority. Infantry and armored concentrations, air bases, ships, ports, staging areas, command centers, munitions depots, cities, key oil and electrical facilities, desalinization plants.

Typical Military Missions: Forced dispersal of military forces and evacuation of civilians. Destruction of military and economic centers, and national political leadership and command authority, potentially altering character of attacked nation and creating major recovery problems.

Table 15.1 (continued)

Nuclear Weapons

Military Limitations: High cost. Difficulty of acquiring more than a few weapons. Risk of
    accidents or failures that hit friendly territory. Crosses threshold to level where nuclear
    retaliation is likely. Destruction or contamination of territory and facilities attacker
    wants to cross or occupy. High risk of massive collateral damage to civilians if this is
    important to attacker.

Source: Adapted by Anthony H. Cordesman from Office of Technology Assessment, *Proliferation of
    Weapons of Mass Destruction: Assessing the Risks,* U.S. Congress OTA-ISC-559, Washington,
    August, 1993, pp. 56–57.

more threatening to regional stability and the peace of the region, Israel is the
region's most successful case and the only current regional nuclear power.

Israeli Nuclear Weapons

US intelligence concluded that Israel had, or was on the edge of deploying,
nuclear weapons in 1966. US experts are virtually certain that Israel had combat-
ready nuclear weapons deployed at the time of the June War in 1967. Furthermore,
a number of reports and studies conclude that Israel prepared its nuclear strike
forces for a possible launch during the greatest period of Egyptian and Syrian
success in the October 1973 War. According to some US experts, preparation of
missile forces was detected on October 8, 1973. Israelis say that the weapons were
prepared after US intelligence detected the Soviet shipment of more Scuds and
possibly nuclear warheads towards Egypt and Syria later in the fighting.[801]

Many US experts believe that Israel has at least 50 to 90 plutonium weapons,
and could have well over 135, provided that it was forced to use the normal amount
of plutonium in such weapons.[802] A few experts estimate Israel may have as many
as 200 to 400 weapons, but these high estimates seem to be based more on
theoretical estimates of production and storage capability than detailed estimates
of Israeli activities.[803]

Israel obtained significant amounts of fissile material from a US company called
Numec in the early 1960s. It has long produced fissile material at its secure reactor
facility in Dimona. Israel has deliberately concealed the history of Dimona's
output and expansion since 1958, and at one point systematically provided US
officials with false data on the reactor. But disclosures by Mordechai Vanunu in
1986 strongly indicate that Dimona was producing at least 40 kilograms of fissile
grade plutonium a year by the early 1980s. If the Vanunu disclosures are correct,
Israel may also have the capability to boost the yield of its fission weapons to yields
in excess of 100 kilotons, reduce the amount of material it required per bomb, or
even build a fusion weapon.[804]

Table 15.2
Major Chemical Agents[805]

NERVE AGENTS: Agents that quickly disrupt the nervous system by binding to enzymes critical to nerve functions, causing convulsions and/or paralysis. May be ingested, inhaled, and absorbed through the skin. Very low doses cause a running nose, contraction of the pupil of the eye, and difficulty in visual coordination. Moderate doses constrict the bronchi and cause a feeling of pressure in the chest, and weaken the skeletal muscles and cause fibrillation. Large doses cause death by respiratory or heart failure. Reaction normally occurs in 1-2 minutes. Death from lethal doses occurs within minutes, but artificial respiration can help and atropine and the oximes act as antidotes. The most toxic nerve agents kill with a dosage of only 10 milligrams per minute per cubic meter, versus 400 for less lethal gases. Recovery is normally quick, if it occurs at all, but permanent brain damage can occur:

> Tabun (GA)
> Sarin (GB) - nearly as volatile as water and delivered by air. A dose of 5 $mg/min/m^3$ produces casualties, a respiratory dose of 100 $mg/min/m^3$ is lethal. Lethality lasts 1-2 days.
> Soman (GD)
> GF
> VR-55 (Improved Soman) A thick oily substance which persists for some time.
> VK/VX - a persistent agent roughly as heavy as fuel oil. A dose of 0.5 $mg/min/m^3$ produces casualties, a respiratory dose of 10 $mg/min/m^3$ is lethal. Lethality lasts 1-16 weeks.

BLISTER AGENTS: Cell poisons that destroy skin and tissue cause blindness upon contact with the eyes, and which can result in fatal respiratory damage. Can be colorless or black oily droplets. Can be absorbed through inhalation or skin contact. Serious internal damage if inhaled. Penetrates ordinary clothing. Some have delayed and some have immediate action. Actual blistering normally takes hours to days, but effects on the eyes are much more rapid. Mustard gas is a typical blister agent and exposure of concentrations of a few milligrams per meter over several hours generally at least causes blisters and swollen eyes. When the liquid falls onto the skin or eyes it has the effect of second or third degree burns. It can blind and cause damage to the lungs leading to pneumonia. Severe exposure causes general intoxication similar to radiation sickness. HD and HN persist up to 12 hours. L, HL, and CX persist for 1-2 hours. Short of prevention of exposure, the only treatment is to wash the eyes, decontaminate the skin, and treat the resulting damage like burns:

> Sulfur Mustard (H or HD) A dose of 100 $mg/min/m^3$ produces casualties, a dose of 1,500 $mg/min/m^3$ is lethal. Residual lethality lasts up to 2-8 weeks.
> Distilled Mustard (DM)
> Nitrogen Mustard (HN)
> Lewisite (L)
> Phosgene Oxime (CX)
> Mustard Lewisite (HL)

Table 15.2 (continued)

CHOKING AGENTS: Agents that cause the blood vessels in the lungs to hemorrhage, and fluid to build up, until the victim chokes or drowns in his or her own fluids (pulmonary edema). Provide quick warning though smell or lung irritation. Can be absorbed through inhalation. Immediate to delayed action. The only treatment is inhalation of oxygen and rest. Symptoms emerge in periods after exposure of seconds up to three hours:

> Phosgene (CG)
> Diphosgene (DP)
> PS Chloropicrin
> Chlorine Gas

BLOOD AGENTS: Kill through inhalation. Provide little warning except for headache, nausea, and vertigo. Interferes with use of oxygen at the cellular level. CK also irritates the lungs and eyes. Rapid action and exposure either kills by inhibiting cell respiration or it does not – casualties will either die within seconds to minutes of exposure or recover in fresh air. Most gas masks have severe problems in providing effective protection against blood agents:

> Hydrogen Cyanide (AC) A dose of 2,000 mg/min/m^3 produces casualties, a respiratory dose of 5,000 mg/min/m^3 is lethal. Lethality lasts 1-4 hours. Cyanogen Chloride (CK) A dose of 7,000 mg/min/m^3 produces casualties, a respiratory dose of 11,000 mg/min/m^3 is lethal. Lethality lasts 15 minutes to one hour.

TOXINS: Biological poisons causing neuromuscular paralysis after exposure of hours or days. Formed in food or cultures by the bacterium clostridium Botulinum. Produces highly fatal poisoning characterized by general weakness, headache, dizziness, double vision and dilation of the pupils, paralysis of muscles, and problems in speech. Death is usually by respiratory failure. Antitoxin therapy has limited value, but treatment is mainly supportive:

> Botulin toxin (A) Six distinct types, of which four are known to be fatal to man. An oral dose of 0.001 mg is lethal. A respiratory dose of 0.02 mg/min/m^3 is also lethal.

DEVELOPMENTAL WEAPONS: A new generation of chemical weapons is under development. The only publicized agent is perfluoroisobutene (PFIB), which is an extremely toxic odorless and invisible substance produced when PFIB (Teflon) is subjected to extreme heat under special conditions. It causes pulmonary edema or dry-land drowning when the lungs fill with fluid. Short exposure disables and small concentrations cause delayed death. Activated charcoal and most existing protection equipment offers no defense. Some sources refer to "third" and "fourth" generation nerve gases, but no technical literature seems to be available.

Table 15.2 (continued)

CONTROL AGENTS: Agents which produce temporary irritating or disabling effects
    when in contact with the eyes or inhaled. They cause a flow of tears and irritation of
    upper respiratory tract and skin. They can cause nausea and vomiting and can cause
    serious illness or death when used in confined spaces. CN is the least toxic gas,
    followed by CS and DM. Symptoms can be treated by washing of the eyes and/or
    removal from the area. Exposure to CS, CN, and DM produces immediate symptoms.
    Staphylococcus produces symptoms in 30 minutes to four hours, and recovery takes
    24-48 hours. Treatment of Staphylococcus is largely supportive:

> Tear
> Chlororacetophenone (CN)
> O-Chlorobenzyl-malononitrile (CS)
> Vomiting: Cause irritation, coughing, severe headache, tightness in chest, nausea.
> Adamsite (DM)
> Staphylococcus

INCAPACITATING AGENTS: Agents, which normally cause short-term illness,
    psychoactive effects, (delirium and hallucinations). Can be absorbed through inhalation
    or skin contact. The psychoactive gases and drugs produce unpredictable effects,
    particularly in the sick, small children, elderly, and individuals who already are
    mentally ill. In rare cases they kill or produce a permanent psychotic condition. Many
    produce dry skin, irregular heart beat, urinary retention, constipation, drowsiness, and a
    rise in body temperature, plus occasional maniacal behavior. A single dose of 0.1 to 0.2
    milligrams of LSD-25 will produce profound mental disturbance within a half-hour
    that lasts 10 hours. The lethal dose is 100 to 200 milligrams:

> BZ
> LSD
> LSD Based BZ
> Mescaline
> Psilocybin
> Benzilates

At least some Israeli nuclear weapons work took place in cooperation with
South Africa, and there may have been at least one test that was detected by the US
Vela satellite in 1979. Israel obtained extensive reactor and weapons design
support from France beginning in 1957, and seems to have obtained considerable
French and US weapons design data as well as extensive data drawn from the
French nuclear weapons tests at Ekker and Reggan in Algeria up until 1964.[806] As
a result, Israeli stockpiles may have included some highly efficient weapons by the
early 1980s, as well as other enhanced yield weapons with variable yields of up to
100 kilotons or more.[807] Many US experts believe that Israel's cooperation with
South Africa also extended to the design of small tactical nuclear weapons with
yields of only several kilotons or less.

Table 15.3
Typical War Fighting Uses of Chemical Weapons

Mission	Quantity
Attack an infantry position: Cover 1.3 square kilometers of territory with a "surprise dosage" attack of Sarin to kill 50% of exposed troops.	216 240-mm rockets (e.g. delivered by 18, 12-tube Soviet BM-24 rocket launchers, each carrying 8 kilograms of agent and totaling 1,728 kilograms of agent.
Prevent launch of enemy mobile missiles: Contaminate a 25-square-kilometer missile unit operating area with 0.3 tons of a persistent nerve gas like VX per square kilometer.	8 MiG-23 or 4 Su-24 fighters, each delivering 0.9 ton of VX (totaling 7.2 tons).
Immobilize an air base: Contaminate a 2-square-kilometer air base with 0.3 tons of VX twice a day for 3 days.	1 MiG-23 with six sorties or any similar attack aircraft.
Defend a broad front against large scale attack: Maintain a 300-meter-deep strip of VX contamination in front of a position defending a 60-kilometer-wide area for 3 days.	65 metric tons of agent delivered by approximately 13,000 155-mm artillery rounds.
Canalize 1st and 2nd Echelon attacking forces: Force attacking or retreating forces into fixed lines of movement. Guard flanks. Disrupt rear area operations.	8 MiG-23 or 4 Su-24 fighters, each delivering 0.9 ton of VX (totaling 7.2 tons).
Terrorize population: Kill approximately 125,000 unprotected civilians in a densely populated (10,000-square-kilometer) city.	8 MiG-23 or 4 Su-24 fighters, each delivering 0.9 ton of VX (totaling 7.2 tons) under optimum conditions.

Source: Adapted by Anthony H. Cordesman from Victor A. Utgoff, *The Challenge of Chemical Weapons*, New York, St. Martin's, 1991, pp. 238-242, and Office of Technology Assessment, *Proliferation of Weapons of Mass Destruction: Assessing the Risks*, U.S. Congress OTA-ISC-559, Washington, August, 1993, pp. 56–57.

Israel has extensive nuclear facilities. It has major nuclear research and weapons design facilities at Nahal Soreq (south of Tel Aviv) and the Negev. Uranium phosphate is mined in the Negev, near Beersheba, and yellowcake is produced at two plants in the Haifa area as well as at a phosphate plant in Southern Israel. Dimona has an experimental pilot-scale centrifuge and laser enrichment facility. It

Table 15.4
Key Biological Weapons that May Be in the Middle East

Disease	Infectivity	Trans-missibility	Incubation Period	Mortality	Therapy
Viral					
Chikungunya fever	high?	none	2-6 days	very low (-1%)	none
Dengue fever	high	none	5-2 days	very low (-1%)	none
Eastern equine encephalitis	high	none	5-10 days	high (+60%)	developmental
Tick borne encephalitis	high	none	1-2 weeks	up to 30%	developmental
Venezuelan equine encephalitis	high	none	2-5 days	low (-1%)	developmental
Hepatitis A	-	15-40 days	-	-	-
Hepatitis B	-	40-150 days	-	-	-
Influenza	high	none	1-3 days	usually low	available
Yellow fever	high	none	3-6 days	up to 40%	available
Smallpox (Variola)	high	high	7-16 days	up to 30%	available
Rickettsial					
Coxiella Burneti (Q-fever)	high	negligible	10-21 day	low (-1%)	antibiotic
Mooseri	-	-	6-14 days	-	-
Prowazeki	-	-	6-15 days	-	-
Psittacosis	high	moderate-high	4-15 days	mod-high	antibiotic
Rickettsi (Rocky mountain spotted fever)	high	none	3-10 days	up to 80%	antibiotic
Tsutsugamushi	-	-	-	-	-
Epidemic typhus	high	none	6-15 days	up to 70%	antibiotic/vaccine
Bacterial					
Anthrax (pulmonary)	mod-high	negligible	1-5 days	usually fatal	antibiotic/vaccine
Brucellosis	high	none	1-3 days	-25%	antibiotic
Cholera	low	high	1-5 days	up to 80%	antibiotic/vaccine
Glanders	high	none	2-1 days	usually fatal	poor antibiotic
Meloidosis	high	none	1-5 days	usually fatal	moderate antibiotic
Plague (pneumonic)	high	high	2-5 days	usually fatal	antibiotic/vaccine
Tularemia	high	negligible	1-10 days	low to 60%	antibiotic/vaccine
Typhoid fever	mod-high	mod-high	7-21 days	up to 10%	antibiotic/vaccine
Dysentery	high	high	1-4 days	low to high	antibiotic/vaccine

Table 15.4 (continued)

Disease	Infectivity	Trans-missibility	Incubation Period	Mortality	Therapy
Fungal					
Coccidioido- mycosis	high	none	1-3 days	low	none
Coccidiodes Immitis	high	none	10-21 days	low	none
Histoplasma Capsulatum	-	-	15-18 days	-	-
Norcardia Asteroides	-	-	-	-	-
Toxins[a]					
Botulinum toxin	high	none	12-72 hours	high neromus-cular paralysis	vaccine
Mycotoxin	high	none	hours or days	low to high	-
Staphylococcus	moderate	none	24-48 hours	incapacitating	-

Note: *a.* Many sources classify as chemical weapons because toxins are chemical poisons.

Source: Adapted by Anthony H. Cordesman from *Report of the Secretary General*, Department of Political and Security Affairs; *Chemical and Bacteriological (Biological) Weapons and the Effects of Their Possible Use*, New York, United Nations, 1969, pp. 26, 29, 37–52, 116–117; *Jane's NBC Protection Equipment*, 1991–1992; James Smith, "Biological Warfare Developments," *Jane's Intelligence Review*, November, 1991, pp. 483–487.

also purifies Uranium (UO$_2$), converts UF$_6$, and fabricates fuel for weapons purposes. The two significant reactor projects are the five megawatt research reactors fueled with highly enriched uranium called the IRR-1 at Nahal Soreq, and the 40–150 megawatt heavy water, IRR-2 natural uranium reactor used for the production of fissile material at Dimona. However, only the IRR-1 is under IAEA safeguards.

In addition, there is a major plutonium reprocessing facility at Dimona, as well as hot cell facilities and a pilot-scale plutonium extraction facility at Nahal Soreq and in the Negev. Rehovot has pilot-scale heavy water production and the Negev Center has a pilot plant for extracting uranium from phosphates. There are facilities for the storage of nuclear weapons at Kefar Zekharya, Eilabun, and Tel Nof, and a nuclear weapons assembly facility at Yodefat.

US experts believe Israel has highly advanced implosion weapons. Israel is known to have produced Lithium-6, allowing production of both tritium and lithium deuteride at Dimona. However, this particular facility may no longer be

Table 15.5
The Thermal and Blast Effects of Nuclear Weapons
Radius of Effect in Kilometers

Yield in Kilotons	Metals Vaporize	Metals Melt	Wood Burns	3rd Degree Burns	5 psi/160 mph Winds	3 psi 116 mph Winds
10	0.337	0.675	1.3	1.9	1.3	1.6
20	0.477	0.954	1.9	2.7	2.0	2.5
50	0.754	1.6	3.0	4.3	2.7	3.3
100	1.0	2.0	4.3	5.7	3.5	4.3
200	1.5	2.8	5.7	8.0	4.5	5.4

Source: Adapted by Anthony H. Cordesman from the Royal United Services Institute, *Nuclear Attack: Civil Defense*, London, RUSI/Brassey's, 1982, pp. 30–36.

operating. This would give Israel the capability to make "boosted" fission weapons with yields well in excess of 100 kilotons and possibly thermonuclear weapons.

Israeli Nuclear Delivery Systems

Many of the details of Israel's potential nuclear weapons delivery systems are as uncertain as the details of its nuclear weapons. Israel is not a signatory to the Nuclear Non-Proliferation Treaty and the only facility where it permits IAEA inspection is the IRR-1.[808] However, it is certain that Israel has had long-range strike fighters since it first acquired nuclear weapons, and some reports indicate that it had nuclear capable F-4 units deployed at the Tel Nof air base by the late 1960s.

Israel can deliver nuclear weapons with its F-4Es, F-16s, and F-15s, and has the technology to adapt air-to-surface missiles like the Popeye to carry nuclear warheads with ranges in excess of 30 miles—although there is no evidence that it has done so.[809] It can refuel its strike aircraft with KC-130 and B(KC)-707 tankers, and give its strike aircraft the range to launch missions of over 1,500 kilometers. Israel's strikes on Iraq and Tunisia have shown that it can execute long-range missions with great military skill. Israel also has excellent electronic warfare capabilities, and can provide excellent fighter cover using its F-15s and special purpose aircraft. A small number of Israeli attackers could probably penetrate the air defenses of virtually any nation in the region.[810]

There are convincing indications that Israel has deployed nuclear armed missiles on mobile launchers. Most outside sources call the first of these missiles the "Jericho I," but Israel has never publicly named its long-range missile systems.[811] These missiles were near-copies of the two-stage, solid-fueled, French MD-620 missile. Some reports claim the first 14 were built in France.[812] A number of sources indicate that Israel deployed up to 50 "Jericho I" (YA-1) missiles on

Table 15.6

The Comparative Effects of Biological, Chemical, and Nuclear Weapons Delivered Against a Typical Urban Target in the Middle East

Using missile warheads: Assumes one Scud-sized warhead with a maximum payload of 1,000 kilograms. The study assumes that the biological agent would not make maximum use of this payload capability because this is inefficient. It is unclear if this is realistic.

	Area Covered in Square Kilometers	Deaths Assuming 3,000-10,000 people Per Square Kilometer
Chemical: 300 kilograms of Sarin nerve gas with a density of 70 milligrams per cubic meter	0.22	60-200
Biological: 30 kilograms of Anthrax spores with a density of 0.1 milligram per cubic meter	10	30,000-100,000
Nuclear: One 12.5 kiloton nuclear device achieving 5 pounds per cubic inch of over-pressure	7.8	23,000-80,000
One 1 megaton hydrogen bomb	190	570,000-1,900,000

Using one aircraft delivering 1,000 kilograms of Sarin nerve gas or 100 kilograms of anthrax spores: Assumes the aircraft flies in a straight line over the target at optimal altitude and dispensing the agent as an aerosol. The study assumes that the biological agent would not make maximum use of this payload capability because this is inefficient. It is unclear if this is realistic.

	Area Covered in Square Kilometers	Deaths Assuming 3,000-10,000 people Per Square Kilometer
Clear sunny day, light breeze		
Sarin Nerve Gas	0.74	300-700
Anthrax Spores	46	130,000-460,000
Overcast day or night, moderate wind		
Sarin Nerve Gas	0.8	400-800
Anthrax Spores	140	420,000-1,400,000
Clear calm night		
Sarin Nerve Gas	7.8	3,000-8,000
Anthrax Spores	300	1,000,000-3,000,000

Source: Adapted by Anthony H. Cordesman from Office of Technology Assessment, *Proliferation of Weapons of Mass Destruction: Assessing the Risks*, US Congress OTA-ISC-559, Washington, August, 1993, pp. 53-54.

mobile launchers in shelters in the hills southwest of Jerusalem, with up to 400 miles range with a 2,200 pound payload, and with possible nuclear warhead storage nearby. The current deployment of the "Jericho I" force is unclear. Some sources say it has been phased out for the Jericho II missile.[813]

Israel has since gone far beyond the Jericho I in developing long-range missile systems.[814] It has developed and deployed the "Jericho II" (YA-2). The "Jericho II" began development in the mid-1970s, and had its first tests in 1986.[815] Israel carried out a launch in mid-1986 over the Mediterranean that reached a range of 288 miles (460 kilometers). It also seems to have been tested in May 1987. A flight across the Mediterranean reached a range of some 510 miles (820 kilometers), landing south of Crete.[816] Another test occurred on September 14, 1989. Israel launched a missile across the Mediterranean that landed about 250 miles north of Benghazi, Libya. The missile flew over 800 miles, and US experts felt it had a maximum range of up to 900–940 miles (1,450 kilometers)—which would allow the Jericho II to cover virtually all of the Arab world and even the southern USSR.[817] The most recent version of the missile seems to be a two-stage, solid-fueled missile with a range of up to 900 miles (1,500 kilometers) with a 2,200 pound payload. Some Jericho IIs may have been brought to readiness for firing during the Gulf War.

Commercial satellite imaging indicates the Jericho II missile may be 14 meters long and 1.5 meters wide. Its deployment configuration hints that it may have radar area guidance similar to the terminal guidance in the Pershing II.[818] According to other reports, the new single stage missile uses strap-down inertial guidance. *Jane's Intelligence Review* speculates that the Jericho II may use radar terminal guidance similar to the radar area guidance (RADAG) used in the Pershing II, but provides no evidence for this beyond the fact that Jonathan Pollard sold some of the required satellite imagery to Israel. This guidance would allow numerous targets to be stored in the missile guidance system and allow very rapid retargeting of the missile.

Israel began work on an updated version of the Jericho II no later than 1995 in an effort to stretch its range to 2,000 km. At least part of this work may have begun earlier in cooperation with South Africa. Israel is also seeking technology to improve its accuracy, particularly with gyroscopes for the inertial guidance system and associated systems software. Israel is actively examining ways to lower the vulnerability of its ballistic missiles and nuclear weapons. These include improved hardening, dispersal, use of air-launched weapons, and possible sea-basing. There are reports of the development of a long-range, nuclear armed version of Popeye with GPS guidance and of studies of possible cruise missile designs that could be both surface-ship and submarine based.[819]

There are also reports that Israel is developing a Jericho III missile, based on a booster it developed with South Africa in the 1980s. The tests of a longer-range missile seem to have begun in the mid-1980s.[820] A major test of such a booster seems to have taken place on September 14, 1989, and resulted in extensive reporting on such cooperation in the press during October 25 and 26, 1989. It is possible that both the booster and any Israeli-South African cooperation may have focused on satellite launches.[821] Since 1994, however, there have been numerous reports among experts that Israel is seeking a missile with a range of at least 4,800 kilometers, which could fully cover Iran and any other probable threat. *Jane's* estimates that the missile has a range of up to 5,000 kilometers and a 1,000 kilogram warhead. This estimate is based largely on a declassifed DIA estimate of the launch capability of the Shavit booster that Israel tested on September 19, 1988.[822]

Reports of how Israel deploys its missiles differ. Initial reports indicated that 30–50 Jericho I missiles were deployed on mobile launchers in shelters in the caves southwest of Tel Aviv. A source claimed in 1985 that Israel had 50 missiles deployed on mobile erector launchers in the Golan, and/or launchers on flat cars that could be wheeled out of sheltered caves in the Negev. (This latter report may confuse the rail transporter used to move missiles from a production facility near Be'er Yaakov to a base at Kefar Zeharya, about 15 kilometers south of Be'er Yaakov.)

More recent reports indicate that Jericho II missiles are located in 50 underground bunkers carved into the limestone hills near a base near Kefar Zekharya. The number that are on alert, command and control, and targeting arrangements, and the method of giving them nuclear warheads has never been convincingly reported.[823]

Jane's Intelligence Review published satellite photos of what it said was a Jericho II missile base at Kefar Zekharya several miles southeast of Tel Aviv in September 1997.[824] According to this report, the transport-erector-launcher (TEL) for the Jericho II measures about 16 meters long by 4 meters wide and 3 meters high. The TEL is supported by three support vehicles, including a guidance and power vehicle. The other two vehicles include a communications vehicle and a firing control vehicle. This configuration is somewhat similar to that used in the US Pershing II IRBM system, although there are few physical similarities.

The photos in the article show numerous bunkers near the TEL and launch pad, and the article estimates a force of 50 missiles on the site. It also concludes that the lightly armored TEL would be vulnerable to a first strike, but that the missiles are held in limestone caves behind heavy blast-resistant doors. It estimates that a nuclear-armed M-9 or Scud C could destroy the launch capability of the site.[825] This is theoretically possible, but it is unlikely that the targeting capabilities of regional attackers, the yield of the nuclear weapons they can develop, and the inherent systems accuracy of their missiles will give them such a first strike capability in the near to mid-term.

The same article refers to nuclear weapons bunkers at the Tel Nof airbase, a few kilometers to the northwest. The author concludes that the large number of bunkers indicates that Israel may have substantially more nuclear bombs than is normally estimated—perhaps up to 400 weapons with a total yield of 50 megatons.[826] This estimate, however, seems to be based on filling every bunker with nuclear weapons, rather than the dispersal of a much more limited number of weapons that both are stored in other locations and only fill a much smaller portion of the bunkers involved.

While Israel's small size and dense population concentrations make it highly vulnerable to weapons of mass destruction, the same is true of Arab countries and Iran. Their political structures, cultural and educational systems, and economies are extremely vulnerable to nuclear strikes on key cities. Tables 15.6 and 15.7 show a 20-kiloton to 50-kiloton weapon could destroy any city in the region, as well as any major air base.[827] The same tables provide data on the other thermal and blast effects of nuclear weapons. A single high-yield weapon of 100 kilotons or more could effectively destroy a Syrian city like Damascus, Aleppo, or Homs; a Jordanian city like Amman, Irbid, or Zarqa; an Iraqi city like Baghdad, Basrah, or Mosul; a Libyan city like Tripoli or Benghazi; or most of the larger Egyptian cities of Cairo, Alexandria, or Gaza.

Iran, Iraq, and Libya are also vulnerable to ethnic targeting. Estimates put Iran's Persian population at anywhere from 51–65%, depending upon definitions. Targeting ethnic Persian areas would shift the ethnic balance in favor of large minorities like the Azeri. Iraq is currently ruled by a Sunni elite, many of whom come from the area around Tikrit. The nation already has a Shi'ite Arab majority and an additional 20–25% of its population are Kurds. Nuclear strikes on primarily Sunni cities could decisively shift the ethnic balance and striking the area around Tikrit would have a political impact out of all proportion to the region's total population. Strikes targeting Qadahfi's tribal supporters in Libya would have a similar impact.

Contrary to some opinions, Israel can also use its nuclear weapons in tactical and theater situations, even near its borders. It is now remarkably easy to use simple remote sensors and other data to create extremely precise weather and wind models in very small areas. If Israel took advantage of this technology, and varied the yield and height of the burst, it could make extensive use of nuclear weapons even in a neighboring area like the approaches to the Golan. It could use low heights of burst and fallout to safely produce catastrophic wide area casualties in a nearby target area like the greater Damascus area.

Most nuclear weapons effects manuals tend to stress direct or short-term nuclear kills because these have maximum impact on the immediate tactical military situation. However, it is important to note that the use of nuclear fallout to make massive increases in the long-term death rate in predictable areas is a well-known nuclear weapons effect. It is possible to create synergistic effects by mixing nuclear and biological weapons. It is also possible to create major increases in the near and mid-term death rate by mixing different types of biological weapons or by targeting nuclear and or biological weapons against areas where medical services are already strained or where there are water and malnutrition problems.

Table 15.7
Unconventional Attacks Using Weapons of Mass Destruction

- A radiological powder is introduced into the air conditioning systems of Cairo's high-rise tourist hotels. Symptoms are only detected over days or weeks and public warning is given several weeks later. The authorities detect the presence of such a powder, but cannot estimate its long-term lethality and have no precedents for decontamination. Tourism collapses, and the hotels eventually have to be torn down and rebuilt.

- Parts for a crude gun-type nuclear device are smuggled into Israel or bought in the marketplace. The device is built in a medium sized commercial truck. A physics student reading the US Department of Defense weapons effect manual maps Tel Aviv to maximize fallout effects in an area filled with buildings with heavy metals and waits for a wind maximizing the fallout impact. The bomb explodes with a yield of only 8 kilotons, but with an extremely high level of radiation. Immediate casualties are limited but the long-term death rate mounts steadily with time. Peace becomes impossible and security measures become draconian. Immigration halts and emigration reaches crisis proportions. Israel as such ceases to exist.

- Several workers move drums labeled as cleaning agents into a large shopping mall, large public facility, subway, train station, or airport. They dress as cleaners and are wearing what appear to be commercial dust filters or have taken the antidote for the agent they will use. They mix the feedstocks for a persistent chemical agent at the site during a peak traffic period. Large-scale casualties result, and draconian security measures become necessary on a national level. A series of small attacks using similar "binary" agents virtually paralyze the economy, and detection is impossible except to identify all canisters of liquid.

- Immunized terrorists visit a US carrier or major Marine assault ship during the first hours of visitor's day during a port call in the Middle East. They are carrying anthrax powder in bags designed to make them appear slightly overweight. They slowly scatter the powder as they walk through the ship visit. The immediate result is 50% casualties among the ship's crew, its Marine complement, and the visitors that follow. The US finds it has no experience with decontaminating a large ship where anthrax has entered the air system and is scattered throughout closed areas. After long debates over methods and safety levels, the ship is abandoned.

- A terrorist seeking to "cleanse" a nation of its secular regime and corruption introduces a modified type culture of Ebola or a similar virus into an urban area – trusting God to "sort out" the resulting casualties. He scatters infectious cultures for which there is no effective treatment in urban areas. By the time the attack is detected, it has reached epidemic proportions. Medical authorities rush into the infected area without proper protection, causing the collapse of medical facilities and emergency response capabilities. Other nations and regions have no alternative other than to isolate the nation or center under attack, letting the disease take its course.

- A terrorist group modifies the valves on a Japanese remote-controlled crop spraying helicopter which has been imported legally for agricultural purposes. It uses this system at night or near dawn to spray a chemical or biological agent at altitudes below radar coverage in a line-source configuration. Alternatively, it uses a large home-built UAV with simple GPS guidance. The device eventually crashes undetected into the sea

Table 15.7
Unconventional Attacks Using Weapons of Mass Destruction

or in the desert. Delivery of a chemical agent achieves far higher casualties than any conventional military warhead. A biological agent is equally effective and the first symptoms appear days after the actual attack—by which time treatment is difficult or impossible.

- A truck filled with what appears to be light gravel is driven through the streets of Tel Aviv or Cairo during rush hour or another maximum traffic period. A visible powder does come out through the tarpaulin covering the truck, but the spread of the powder is so light that no attention is paid to it. The driver and his assistant are immunized against the modified form of anthrax carried in the truck that is being released from behind the gravel or sand in the truck. The truck slowly quarters key areas of the city. Unsuspecting passersby and commuters not only are infected, but carry dry spores home and into other areas. By the time the first major symptoms of the attack occur some 3-5 days later, anthrax pneumonia is epidemic and some septicemic anthrax has appeared. Some 40-65% of the exposed population dies and medical facilities collapse causing serious, lingering secondary effects.

- A terrorist group scatters high concentrations of a radiological, chemical, or biological agent in various areas in a city, and trace elements into the processing intakes to the local water supply. When the symptoms appear, the terrorist group makes its attack known, but claims that it has contaminated the local water supply. The authorities are forced to confirm that water is contaminated and mass panic ensues.

- Immunized terrorists carry small amounts of anthrax or a similar biological agent onto a passenger aircraft like a B-747, quietly scatter the powder, and deplane at the regular scheduled stop. No airport detection system or search detects the agent. Some 70-80% of those on the aircraft die as a result of symptoms that only appear days later.

- Several identical nuclear devices are smuggled out of the FSU through Afghanistan or Central Asia. They do not pass directly through governments. One of the devices is disassembled to determine the precise technology and coding system used in the weapon's PAL. This allows users to activate the remaining weapons. The weapon is then disassembled to minimize detection with the fissile core shipped covered in lead. The weapon is successfully smuggled into the periphery of an urban area outside any formal security perimeter. A 100-kiloton ground burst destroys a critical area and blankets the region in fallout.

- The same device is shipped to Israel or a Gulf area in a modified standard shipping container equipped with detection and triggering devices that set it off as a result of local security checks or with a GPS system that sets it off automatically when it reaches the proper coordinates in the port of destination. The direct explosive effect is significant, but "rain out" contaminates a massive local area.

- Iraq equips a freighter or dhow to spread anthrax along a coastal area in the Gulf. It uses a proxy terrorist group, and launches an attack on Kuwait City and Saudi oil facilities and ports. It is several days before the attack is detected, and the attacking group is never fully identified. The form of anthrax involved is dry and time encapsulated to lead to both massive prompt casualties and force time consuming

Table 15.7 (continued)

decontamination. Iraq not only is revenged, but benefits from the resulting massive surge in oil prices.

- A terrorist group scatters small amounts of a biological or radiological agent in a Jewish area during critical stages of the final settlement talks. Near panic ensues, and a massive anti-Palestinian reaction follows. Israeli security then learns that the terrorist group has scattered small amounts of the same agent in cells in every sensitive Palestinian town and area, and the terrorist group announces that it has also stored some in politically sensitive mosques and shrines. Israeli security is forced to shut down all Palestinian movement and carry out intrusive searches in every politically sensitive area. Palestinians riot and then exchanges of gunfire follow. The peace talks break down permanently.

- The Iranian Revolutionary Guard equips dhows to spread anthrax. The dhows enter the ports of Dubai and Abu Dhabi as commercial vessels – possibly with local or other Southern Gulf registrations and flags. It is several days before the attack is detected, and the resulting casualties include much of the population of Abu Dhabi and government of the UAE. The UAE breaks up as a result, no effective retaliation is possible, and Iran achieves near hegemony over Gulf oil policy.

Israeli Chemical and Biological Weapons

Israel has the capability to manufacture and deploy other weapons of mass destruction and may have done so. Israel denies that it has chemical and biological warfare capabilities, but American experts feel there have been repeated intelligence indicators that Israel has at least brought such weapons to the full development/production-ready stage.

According to some reports, Israel revitalized its chemical warfare facilities south of Dimona in the mid-1980s, after Syria deployed chemical weapons and Iraq began to use them in the Iran-Iraq War. Israel has at least one major research facility with sufficient security and capacity to produce both chemical and biological weapons.[828] There are extensive reports that Israel has a biological weapons research facility at the Israel Institute for Biological Research at Nes Ziona, about 12 miles south of Tel Aviv, and that this same facility also has worked on the development and testing of nerve gas. This facility has created enough public concern in Israel so that the mayor of Nes Ziona has asked that it be moved away from populated areas. The facility is reported to have stockpiled anthrax, and to have provided toxins to Israeli intelligence for use in covert operations and assassinations like the attempt on a Hamas leader in Jordan in 1997.[829]

An El Al 747–200 cargo plane crashed in southern Amsterdam on October 4, 1992, killing 43 people in the apartment complex it hit. This led to extensive examination of the crash and the plane was found to be carrying 50 gallons of dimethyl methylphosphonate (DMMP), a chemical used to make Sarin nerve gas.

The chemical had been purchased from Solkatronic Chemicals in the US and was being shipped to the Israeli Institute for Biological Research. It was part of an order of 480 pounds of the chemical. Two of the three other chemicals used in making Sarin were shipped on the same flight. Israel at first denied this and then claimed it was only being imported to test gas masks. The fact was, however, that the aircraft manifest did not list the suspect cargo, and Israel refused to provide detailed manifests after the crash. The voice recorder seems to have been stolen from the crash site and El Al rushed jets to Schipol to airlift out part of the wreckage.[830]

Israel may have the contingency capability to produce at least two types of chemical weapons and has certainly studied biological weapons as well as chemical ones. According to one interview with an Israeli source of unknown reliability, Israel has mustard gas, persistent and non-persistent nerve gas, and may have at least one additional agent. Some US experts privately state that Israel is one of the nations included in US lists of nations with biological and chemical weapons. They believe that Israel has at least some stocks of weaponized nerve gas, although they may be stored in forms that require binary agents to be loaded into binary weapons.

They believe that Israel has fully developed bombs and warheads capable of effectively disseminating dry, storable biological agents in micropowder form and has agents considerably more advanced than anthrax. Opinion differs over whether such weapons are actively loaded and deployed. Few US experts believe that this is the case. There have been unconfirmed reports in the British *Sunday Times*, however, that IAF F-16s are equipped for strikes using both these weapons and chemical weapons. In practice, however, any fighter with bomb racks can be equipped with such weapons.[831]

Israeli Deterrent and Strategic Doctrine and Planning

Israel has long relied on a doctrine of undeclared nuclear deterrence, which has left its nuclear capabilities deliberately ambiguous. At the same time, the term "ambiguous" has been relative. Prime Minister Levi Eshkol was asked to make a pledge that Israel would not deploy nuclear weapons in the Middle East during a visit to the White House in 1964, and agreed only "not to be the first to introduce nuclear weapons to the Middle East." This was broadly taken to be a veiled threat and to refer to first use, not deployment and it is a doctrine that has been followed by every Israeli prime minister since that time, including former Prime Minister Netanyahu.[832]

The closest a senior Israeli official has come to openly saying that Israel would use nuclear force have been the statements of Shimon Peres—whom many regard as the original driving force behind Israel's nuclear effort. Peres stated in 1995 that Israel might give up nuclear weapons for a true peace. He stated in an interview in July 1996 that, "Our deterrent is the Arab suspicion. They are not quite sure what our true capabilities are. They have an idea of what is the nature of our strength they do not know . . . and it is this uncertainty that has its own strength." He also referred back to a meeting with President Kennedy in 1961: "President Kennedy quizzed us on our nuclear capabilities and intentions, and we assured him that Israel would not be the first country to introduce nuclear weapons in the region . . . and (this) is a formula that works."[833]

Peres said many of the same things in an interview on Danish television in April, 1998. He was asked whether it was necessary for Israel to have nuclear weapons and replied that,[834]

Yes, otherwise we would not have arrived to peace. And if we wouldn't start then, 40 years ago in Dimona, the nuclear option, we wouldn't have arrived to Oslo with the peace option for the region . . . Israel by the way, never said that we have nuclear weapons. Look, we never declared it. We said that we would not introduce nuclear weapons to the Middle East.

Peres also said that Amr Moussa, the Egyptian foreign minister, had asked to visit Dimona while Peres was prime minister and that Peres told him that if he went he would find nothing, "Then he will stop fearing and we shall lose our deterrent . . . I mean that your suspicion is my deterrent." When Peres was asked if Israel had ever planned to use its nuclear capability, he replied that, "No, not for war. For peace. Our nuclear potential is to deter war so we can arrive to peace."[835]

This kind of ambiguity served Israel's interests well for many years. Arab nations without nuclear and biological weapons understood that Israel possessed such weapons, but did not make it a major issue. Israel's nuclear monopoly helped deter any kind of attack that might lead to a nuclear response. The uncertainties regarding the size and nature of Israeli military forces tended to exaggerate estimates of what Israel might do in given scenarios without provoking a major Arab response.

Official ambiguity about the possession of nuclear weapons has not prevented Israel from making threats that are less ambiguous. Many believe that the Israeli government deliberately leaked the fact it was preparing its nuclear forces to the world press in 1973. At the time of the Gulf War, then Israeli Chief of Staff Dan Shomron warned that the IDF could "strike hard" at anyone who struck Israel.[836] The same day, Defense Minister Moshe Arens warned that Israel's response would not be "low profile" if it were attacked, and Prime Minister Yitzhak Shamir warned Iraq that an attack on Israel, "will be likely to bring upon himself a heavy disaster."[837] President Eizer Weizman, former Prime Minister Benjamin Netanyahu, and former Minister of Defense Yitzhak Mordecai issued very similar warnings in February 1998, when it seemed possible that US and British strikes on Iraq might lead Iraq to lash out with new missile strikes or terrorism.[838]

Several factors do seem, however, to have led Israel to reexamine this policy. Iraq's use of missiles and chemical weapons during the Iran-Iraq War made many nations take proliferation more seriously and stimulated a low–level arms race, "creeping proliferation," among a number of nations in the region. The debate over the renewal of the Nuclear Non-Proliferation Treaty (NNPT) in 1995 highlighted the disparity between Israel and its Arab neighbors and led Egypt to demand that Israel sign the NNPT. Israel refused to do so, and there have been continuing Israeli-Egyptian debates over Israel's nuclear role and relevant arms control measures ever since. The rising threat of proliferation from Iran and Syria, and the UN's inability to disarm Iraq, have also led to growing Israeli concern that an ambiguous deterrent might be too weak and too vague to have credibility in some scenarios.

The end result is that several reports indicate that Israel's strategic review during 1997–1998 involved a review of Israeli nuclear strategy that included Prime Minister Netanyahu's Office, the Ministry of Defense, and Foreign Ministry. This effort seems to have decided that Israel should keep the nature of its weapons of mass destruction and missiles secret, strengthen its missile defenses, and reduce the vulnerability of its nuclear strike forces.[839] At the same time, Israel eased its censorship. The Israeli paper *Yedioth Ahronoth*, was allowed to print excerpts from the classified portions of the trial of Mordecai Vanunu, a former technician at Dimona, in November 1999. Israel held its first parliamentary debate on nuclear weapons on February 2, 2000, at the request of Issam Mahoul, a member of the Knesset from the largely Arab Hadash party.[840] Mahoul provided the first statistics and description of Israel's nuclear program ever mentioned in the Knesset, although the government rejected the numbers and the debate rapidly turned into an Arab-Israeli shouting match.[841]

Israel also seems to be considering ways to reduce the vulnerability of its nuclear strike force, and to reduce the incentive for any strike on its delivery system. These seem to include new forms of dispersal, hardening some facilities, and the possible use of Israel's new Dolphin submarines to deliver cruise missiles.

Israel still refuses to openly discuss its deterrent or the nuclear issue in various regional arms control talks, although it has increasingly supported arms control measures that do not force it to declare its nuclear capability. It has agreed to abide by the terms of the Missile Technology Control Regime (MTCR), it signed the Chemical Weapons Convention (CWC) in January 1993, and the Comprehensive Test Ban Treaty in September 1996.[842] In May 1997, Israel also carefully leaked an interview given by Gideon Frank, the former head of the Atomic Energy Commission in the Prime Minister's office. Frank said Israel could only give up its nuclear weapons when it reached a peace with Egypt, Syria, and other states similar to the one reached between Argentina and Brazil. Frank said that it would require a proven framework for mutual cooperation, particularly in the economic area, a "process of democratization" in the Arab world, and "a long, phased confidence-building process."[843]

ISRAELI MISSILE DEFENSES

The possibility of an Arab or Iranian attack using weapons of mass destruction puts Israel at risk because of Israel's small size, its concentrated urban population, and the fact that 85% of its population is condensed into a triangle in Northern

Israel. This triangle is a maximum of 68 miles wide in the south and 130 miles long. In addition, the Arab countries and Iran have the ability to target Israel's two main coastal urban areas because they are largely non-Arab. These population concentrations make Israel acutely vulnerable to the direct effects of nuclear and biological weapons and fallout. It also makes it acutely vulnerable to both direct missile attacks on its coastal cities, and asymmetric ship based attacks from coastal waters.

It is hardly surprising, therefore, that Israel has given careful study to active and passive defense, and particularly to missile defense. Israel is one of the few nations in the world to have developed its own national missile defenses. Israel has also begun to examine the missile defense implications of its peace with Jordan, and the fact that Jordan could be the deliberate or inadvertent target of Iranian and Iraqi missile launches.

Israeli National Programs

Israel has developed a comprehensive missile defense plan, including a 10-year funding plan. The Arrow missile defense program forms the core of this plan, but it involves layered defense, a possible boost-phase interceptor, new battle management systems and sensors, and close cooperation with the US. It also involves consideration of extending the defense umbrella to cover Jordan, reducing the vulnerability of Israeli missile and nuclear forces, and possible cooperation with Turkey.[844]

The resulting Homa (barrier) project now calls for both tactical and theater defenses to be overlayed in ways that combine Israeli systems with US reinforcements. Israel recognizes, however, that any program must be technology and threat driven and respond to new developments and events. It also recognizes that effective defense against long-range missiles involves terminal velocities that severely limit the effectiveness of the anti-tactical ballistic missiles it can afford to develop. As a result, Israel is faced with the challenge of finding either some form of boost phase defense or an "upper tier" wide-area threat defense with a high intercept capability even against missiles closing from ranges in excess of 1,000 kilometers. (Missile launch ranges from Iraq, Libya and Syria are under 1,000 kilometers and have closing velocities suited to lower tier theater missile defenses and which still give tactical ballistic missile defenses some effectiveness in point defense over a reasonably wide range of deployment locations. Iran must generally launch from ranges in excess of 1,000 kilometers, and the closing speeds of more modern and longer-range missiles like the Shahab are faster and present much more serious intercept problems.)

The Tactical High Energy Laser (THEL) or Nautilus

The Tactical High Energy Laser or THEL program was originally a $100 million program, with the US paying $70 million and Israel paying $30 million. At present it is primarily a defense against unguided rockets, rather than guided missiles. It is far from clear that it will work, since current versions need to hold a rocket in flight for nearly 15 seconds, and the average flight time of an 80–240-mm rocket is generally less than 30 seconds. They are also dependent on a clear line of sight, so haze and smoke present major problems.[845]

Nevertheless, tests at White Sands proved in February 1996 that a laser could track a missile for the required time, and that a deuterium fluoride laser beam could destroy a missile in flight. This led the US to push the concept forward, largely in an effort to provide defenses against Hizbollah rocket attacks on northern Israel. Rockets can also be used to launch large numbers of biological and chemical weapons, however, and THEL provides a tactical layer of defense.[846]

The THEL program ran into trouble in 1999 when a series of technical difficulties encountered during initial tests and chemical leaks caused by faulty valves delayed the project by up to a year.[847] The delays resulted in cost overruns totaling $30–50 million over the $130.8 million ceiling. The cost overruns jeopardized the future of the project as the contractor and the US government argued over who was responsible for the extra cost.[848] THEL was saved when the Israeli Ministry of Defense and the US Army agreed to each pay a quarter of the overruns while the contractor is still responsible for the other half.[849]

While costs reached $185 million by May 2000, with $64 million coming from Israel, the THEL deuterium fluoride laser proved to be successful in tests against incoming Katyusha rockets in June 2000. As a result, the demonstrator was dismantled and shipped to Israel for operational testing in October 2000. It then became a static fire unit as part of the Homa or "barrier" multilayered defense system that Israel is deploying along its border with Lebanon. The creation and deployment of a mobile operational THEL test bed is unlikely to be complete before early 2001, however, and the cost-effectiveness of the program remains uncertain.[850]

The Patriot and PAC-3

Israel currently deploys three Patriot batteries using systems and missiles whose anti-tactical ballistic missile (ATBM) defenses have been upgraded since the Gulf War. They now have software that allows them to distinguish between the missile booster and warhead far more accurately, and they have a much greater kill probability against an oncoming warhead. Each battery has three missile launch vehicles. It is receiving new equipment with a value estimated at $73 million, which was approved by the US Department of Defense in June 1998. This equipment includes three AN/MPQ-53 radar sets, three AN/MSQ-104 engagement control stations, three M-983 tractors, nine M931A2 trucks and other equipment. It is also developing its own ATBM defenses.

The Patriot is an air defense system with moderate capabilities in a largely point defense mode as a tactical ballistic missile defense system. It also provides considerable defense against cruise missiles, adding a key layer to Israeli defenses, and is being steadily improved to widen its coverage against Scud-type threats. Its speed and range are limited, however, and cannot be particularly effective against IRBM-type threats like the Shahab-3 which have closing velocities that limited the Patriot's defense area coverage to a much narrower radius near the missile launcher.

The Patriot's capability will be further enhanced by the PAC-3 upgrade. The PAC-3 upgrade expands the area from which Patriot can intercept a missile, reduces the risk of "leakage" against ballistic missiles, introduces a superior direct hit to kill system, and improves defense against cruise missiles. The system has had major development problems and cost overruns, but did have a successful hit-to-kill intercept in March 1999.[851] The US Department of Defense licensed the new Patriot technology for export in November 1999.[852]

The Arrow

The Arrow missile is an anti-tactical ballistic missile defense with limited area coverage that is tailored to Israel's needs and limited geographic area. The Arrow-2 is supposed to intercept incoming missile warheads at ranges, which have been variously reported as being from 10–40 kilometers or 33,000–131,000 feet. The missile is a two-stage, hypersonic, solid-fuel missile with a fragmentation warhead. Each Arrow-2 battery has four missile launchers with six missile tubes each, and will normally be equipped with at least 50 missiles. The system uses a Green Pine search and track radar, a Citron Tree fire control center, a Hazelnut Tree launch control center, and the Arrow-2 launcher. Its manning requires about 100 personnel.

Plans call for three batteries, although only two are fully funded. Israel calculates that two batteries can defend "most populated areas in Israel." The official program cost is often said to be around $1.6 billion, although some Israelis feel the true total system-related cost will be in excess of $3 billion.[853]

The program is constantly evolving to respond to changes in technology, the development and test program, and changes in the threat. As of March 1999, it was a three-phase program with the following features:

- Phase I: Validate defense concept and demonstrate pre-prototype missile

  - Fixed price contract: $158 million.
  - The US pays 80%; Israel pays 20%.
  - Completed in December 1982.

- Phase II: Demonstrate lethality, develop and demonstrate tactical interceptor and launcher.

  - Fixed price contract: $330 million.
  - The US pays 72%; Israel pays 28%.
  - Began in July 1991.
  - Successfully completed.

- Phase III: Develop and integrate tactical system, conduct weapon system tests, and develop and implement interoperability.

  - Program cost estimated at: $616 million.
  - The US pays 48%; Israel pays 52%.
  - Began in March 1996.
  - System integration in progress.

Israel originally planned to deploy the Arrow in two sites near Tel Aviv and Haifa which could cover up to 85% of Israel's population. It expanded this plan to include a third site in June 1998, with an additional $57 million allocated to this battery. Partly because of the increasing pace of the threat from Iran and Syria, Israel accelerated work on the Arrow. It then planned to deploy the system in mid-1998. However, a fire at a plant near Tel Aviv caused an estimated $30 million in damage and delayed the program. As a result, the first Arrow 2 missile battery was activated on November 29, 1998, and began training in December 1998.[854] In 1999, Israel urged the US to consider expanding the Arrow system into a regional defense by including additional batteries in Jordan and Turkey. With additional batteries, the Arrow would protect all of Turkey, Jordan, and Israel against attacks from a country such as Iran. However, it is unlikely that the US will agree to this and it is unclear that Jordan even wants the Arrow.[855]

It is difficult to put the Arrow-2 into technical perspective. Like all systems this complex, it has had a troubled life in terms of its original technical design, management and system integration problems. It has had some successful tests, notably in an integrated weapon system test and fly out against a simulated target on September 14, 1998. It also destroyed an Israeli seal-launch TM-91 missile, which was simulating an Iraqi Al Hussein missile, during its first comprehensive system test in November 1999. However, the Arrow has also had test failures and severe management and development problems. It has had only seven firing tests as of the end of 1999, and its current test program calls for less than one-fifth of the tests necessary to fully validate its reliability and effectiveness.[856]

The development schedule that Israel has adopted is a high-risk program with limited testing that raises serious questions about the extent to which even successful follow-up tests will provide highly reliable data on its operational probability of intercept, particularly under real-world conditions against different types of missiles and different types of "volleys." It seems possible that it may prove highly effective against Scud type missiles. However, it clearly has only limited capability against newer systems like the Iranian Shahab series, which is already forcing Israel to develop a follow-on version of the Arrow-2. Occasional Israeli claims that the Arrow can provide a reliable defense capability against the regional missile threat seem to be designed to deter possible enemies from launching, rather than claims that the Israeli advocates of the Arrow feel are technically credible.[857]

There has been some limited progress. On September 15, 2000, Arrow-2 (ATBM) achieved its first frontal interceptions of a target missile aimed at Israel.[858] According to executives of Israel Aircraft Industries (IAI), "the system is operational and, when we need it, the system will function."[859] The president of IAI further commented the system will be fully operational by 2001.

The Arrow-2's growth capability to deal with missiles like the No Dong, Shahab-3, Taepo Dong-1, CSS-4, and Shahab-4 is questionable. Under these conditions, the launch footprint or defensive area the Arrow can cover with a high probability of intercept might well be so restricted in area that Israel would have to rely primarily on other layers of its missile defense system.[860]

The Integrated Boost-Phase Intercept System and Moab

Israel is examining a number of options for an integrated boost-phase intercept system and gave such programs a high priority in its security talks with the US in 1999. Israel is closely studying the US airborne laser program, but its leading candidate for an Israeli system is the Moab. The Moab is a missile that can be carried on an F-15 or UAV, and that is designed to engage theater ballistic missiles at ranges of around 100 kilometers soon after launch. The Moabs would be a modified form of the Python 4 with a new booster to accelerate the missile to speeds of 1.5–2 kilometers per second. Maximum firing range is stated to be 80 kilometers from a firing altitude of 30,000 feet and up to 100 kilometers from 50,000 feet.[861]

The Moab would initially be deployed on the IAF's F-15Is, but would eventually use a high altitude UAV that would loiter at 60–66,000 feet. Israel is looking at possible use of its Hermes UAV or some form of the Teledyne Ryan Global Hawk UAV, which can loiter for 42 hours at 40,000 feet or beyond. Conceptual pictures of the UAV show some stealth characteristics. The UAVs would be flown in launch zone constellations, nominally of four UAVs. They would be controlled by a mobile command center which would use a data link with a low data rate of less than 1 kilobit per second and which would control flight and operations. The system would be integrated into the overall IAF C⁴I/BM theater air defense network.[862]

Cost and technical feasibility present major problems. The system is being designed by Rafael, and two cost-driven design characteristics include the use of engagement speeds below the aeroheating threshold of the missile to avoid cooling the infrared seeker, dome cooling, and a protective cap. The missile also locks on at launch to avoid an expensive data link. This design places considerable stress on the ability to design a missile with the required performance and the associated search/track systems and command and control capabilities. Much also depends on the threat being suitably close to Israel or an Israeli area of operations, the ability of Israeli intelligence to predict a narrow launch area for enemy missiles and the probable time of launch, since Israel may not be able to react to previous missile launches without risking the successful penetration of a first round or volley of enemy missiles.

Warning and Command and Control

Israel receives spaced-based warning, tracking, and point of impact data from the US as part of an agreement signed in April 1996. It also receives warning data, and substantial information on Iranian, Iraqi, Libyan, and Syrian programs. Much of these same data are also, in fact, provided to Egypt, Jordan, and the Southern Gulf states.

Israel is, however, studying the possibility of creating its own space-based system and a space-based queuing system for intercept purposes. Such a system hardly seems cost-effective, given Israel's financial constraints, but the Technion Space Research Institute in Haifa has carried out studies of such options.[863] Israel began to acquire the capability to launch satellites with electro-optical sensors and digital down-links. The Shavit I launched Israel's satellite payload on September 19, 1989. It used a three-stage booster system capable of launching a 4,000-pound payload over 1,200 miles or a 2,000-pound payload over 1,800 miles. It is doubtful that it had a payload capable of intelligence missions and seems to have been launched, in part, to offset the psychological impact of Iraq's missile launches.

This seems to be equally true of the Ofeq 2 launched in April 1990, one day after Saddam Hussein threatened to destroy Israel with chemical weapons if it should attack Baghdad. Israel used its three-stage Shavit launch vehicle to launch the Ofeq 3 from a secret launch site at the Palmachim test range near the coast south of Tel Aviv on April 5, 1995. Israeli radio almost certainly exaggerated in claiming that the satellite could transmit imagery "that allows identification of license numbers in downtown Baghdad." In fact some reports indicate that only about 36 kilograms of its 225-kilogram weight was payload and the rest was structure. Nevertheless, the Ofeq 3 had a much larger payload than the Ofeq 2, and the IDF spokesman confirmed that the 495-pound satellite was in a low orbit that circled the earth every 90 minutes and covered Syria, Iran, and Iraq. It is scarcely coincidental that the Ofeq 3's orbit takes it almost directly over the Golan and Damascus, about 90 miles north of Teheran and 240 miles north of Baghdad.[864]

Since that time, other launches of Israel's Ofeq and Amos series of satellites have demonstrated Israel's technical capability to launch sophisticated satellites. The Ofeq 3 launch in April 1995 seems to have been of a more capable photo reconnaissance satellite, although it evidently did not include advanced all-weather coverage and real-time data processing and transmission capability.[865] Nevertheless, there have been important technical failures like the failure to launch the Ofeq 4 intelligence satellite on February 4, 1998.[866] The Ofeq 4 was intended to be an all-weather photo reconnaissance satellite with real-time capability. It is unclear whether it was intended to replace the Ofeq 3 or work together with it. Changes in the orbit of the Ofeq 3 after the Ofeq 4 failed to reach orbit might suggest the latter.[867]

The IDF has concluded that its own warning system would require three or four satellites flying in a low earth orbit to provide continuous coverage of the most likely 1,000-by-1,000-kilometer launch area.[868] Israel's current space budget is only about $50 million a year and an effective program would cost hundreds of millions of dollars and provide less coverage and information than the US system. As a result, Israel may choose to rely on US capabilities. However, Israel may soon have another option. West Indian Space Ltd., a joint venture between US and Israeli companies, is trying to become the first commercial provider of high-resolution satellite images. It plans to operate eight small satellites based on the Ofeq design. Israel is believed to be the company's first customer.[869]

The Interoperable Defense Effort: Israeli and US Cooperation

Israel does not act alone in planning and developing such defenses. The US may oppose Israel's status as a nuclear power, but it works closely with Israel on theater missile defense. The US and Israel have formed a Binational Interoperability Working Group (BIWG) to implement full interoperability between US tactical and theater missile defense systems and Israeli developments like the Arrow. A ministerial level Policy Advisory Group (PAG) was established in April 1996 to facilitate such cooperation at the highest levels within the Israeli Ministry of Defense and the US. The end result is that Israel is developing both a national missile defense and a high degree of interoperable capability with the US.

The current goal the US has is to make the Arrow fully interoperable with US systems by 2001, using the US Link-16 and Joint Tactical Information Distribution System (JTIDS).[870] This would allow US ship-based systems like the Aegis and land-based US Army systems like the THAAD to be linked in a common, secure digital sensor and battle management system, greatly improving their synergy and ability to restrike a penetrating warhead and handle multiple targets at the same time. Israel and the US are also developing combined standard operating procedures for theater missile defense interoperability and will conduct joint simulations and exercises. The US is also providing technical support to Israel in its development of improved versions of the Arrow, related sensors and C^{4}I/BM, its use of US satellite-based warning and point-of-impact data, and its development of a UAV for boost-phase intercept purposes.

This US planning for missile defense cooperation with Israel does affect the Arab-Israeli balance. At the same time, Israel is examining cooperation with Jordan and Turkey and the US plans cooperation with key friendly Arab states like Egypt, Jordan, and the nations of the Southern Gulf. While US assistance to Arab states would not be based on the integration of interoperable indigenous defenses with US defenses, virtually all US theater defense planning examines scenarios for the deployment of Patriot PAC three and US mid-range (lower-tier) and theater-wide (upper-tier) missile defenses to Egypt and the Southern Gulf states.[871]

These points are often lost in the region's focus on the Arrow, but it is critical to understand that a major US program supports Israel's missile defenses and that missile defense is not simply relevant to Israeli defense scenarios but to the defense of friendly Arab states. This US policy has been briefed to every Arab country that is friendly to the US in the Southern Gulf at the ministerial level, as well as to Egypt and Jordan. The US began to hold detailed high-level conversations with members of the Gulf Cooperation Council in Abu Dhabi in April 1998. It has since organized a continuing series of conferences and planning sessions at the senior officer/expert level.

The Complex Structure of the Full Israeli Missile Defense Program

The following list, compiled by combining various media reports, shows recent trends in Israeli missile and anti-missile developments, including projects under way and recently acquired military hardware, and related developments in US capabilities to provide additional missile defenses:[872]

- Israel deploys three batteries of the US Patriot missile with improved anti-tactical ballistic missile capabilities, and will acquire the PAC-3 in the future. It has full access to US ATBM technology, including the improved missile, AN/MPQ-53 radar, and AN/MSQ-104 engagement ground stations. The US has also shown that it can rapidly reinforce Israel with three or more additional batteries.[873]

- The upgrading of the Patriot systems to the PAC-3 will provide improved coverage and lower "leakage" rates against short to medium-range ballistic missiles. It will also provide excellent air and cruise missile defenses. The PAC-3 is now scheduled to complete development around 2000. No deployment date for possible support of Israel is yet fixed. Even the PAC-3, however, will have a notably smaller defensive area coverage, or "footprint" against missiles closing with the kind of velocities produced by launch ranges in excess of 1,000 miles.

- Israel designed the Nautilus laser system, initially for rocket defense in a joint project with the US. The Nautilus was supposed to eventually be deployed in the north to counter Hizbollah rocket attacks. In February 1996 it destroyed a 122-mm Katyusha rocket in-flight during a test at White Sands. Because of the success of the prototype, it has developed into the Theater High Energy Laser (THEL). The project has recently been expanded to include interception of not only short-range rockets and artillery, but also medium-range Scuds and longer-range missiles such as Iran's Shahab series.[874] The US allocated $15 million for the THEL in FY1999.[875]

- The Arrow anti-tactical ballistic missile project, two-thirds of which is supported with US funding, continues into its fourth development phase. Intercept testing for the Arrow 2 missile has begun. The first Arrow units began to deploy in 1998.

- The Rafael Moab UAV forms part of the Israeli Boost-phase Intercept System. This is intended to engage TBMs soon after launch, using weapons fired from a UAV. Moab would launch an improved Rafael Python 4 air-to-air missile. Range is stated as 80–100 km depending on altitude of release.

- A ministerial level Policy Advisory Group (PAG) was established in April 1996 within the Israeli Ministry of Defense and US Department of Defense to facilitate US-Israeli cooperation at the highest levels. The end result is that Israel is developing both a national missile defense and a high degree of interoperable capability with the US. The US and Israel are seeking to make the Arrow fully interoperable with US TMD systems by sometime in 2001. This effort will use the Link-16 secure data exchange system and the US Joint Tactical Information Distribution System (JTIDS). At the same time, Israel and the US are developing combined standard operating procedures for theater missile defense interoperability and will conduct joint simulations and exercises. The US is also providing technical support to Israel in its development of improved versions of the Arrow, related sensors and C⁴I/BM, its use of US satellite-based warning and point of impact data, and its development of a UAV for boost-phase intercept purposes.

- The coverage provided by the Patriots and Arrows could be supplemented in the near to mid-term with US Navy Aegis ship-borne defenses which will be interoperable with US and Israeli-operated Patriots. The PAC-3 is now scheduled to complete development around 2003. No deployment date for possible support of Israel is yet fixed.

- Israel will benefit from US development of the land-based THAAD (Theater High Altitude Area Defense) and sea-based AEGIS upper-tier, wide area theater ballistic missile defense systems. These will provide wider area coverage than the Arrow, and high endo- and exo-atmospheric engagement capability. The US sea-based system will be capable of ascent, midcourse, and exo-descent phase intercepts. These systems are currently scheduled to complete development around FY2007. Any deployment would probably take place after 2008. Israel might also benefit from the USAF airborne laser development program, which might provide an additional layer of boost phase intercept capability.

- Israeli early warning and defenses would benefit from US national missile defense activities, particularly from improved battle management and C³ systems, and from the deployment of improved satellite detection systems on the space-based infrared system which will have both high and low orbit components. These systems will significantly improve plume detection, impact point estimates, and course to intercept detection and prediction. It might benefit from successful development and deployment of the ground-based interceptor endo-atmospheric kill vehicle.

Israeli Civil Defense

Israel is one of the few regional states to try to develop a serious civil defense program. This is partly a result of the Iraqi missile attacks on Israel in 1991, but Israel has been concerned with such options since the early 1960s. At present, the Israeli program is confined largely to issuing gas masks, basic passive defense measures for residences, and emergency services. Israel has looked at much more ambitious programs, including some defense against biological weapons.

These have been partially funded, often in reaction to a perceived crisis. For example, when a crisis between Iraq and UNSCOM threatened a new round of fighting, Israel budgeted $68 million on February 3, 1998, to buy vaccines and antidotes for anthrax, and rushed to buy 50,000 modern gas masks. It has provided enough gas masks for every citizen, modern gas detection devices that include the ability to detect VX, and AP2C vehicles from France to detect and characterize biological weapons.[876]

Some of these steps, however, are more political than military. An IDF study in 1996 found that a massive gas mask distribution program would only save a few dozen lives, and could not protect most of those exposed to nerve gas.[877] In spite of propaganda claims, IDF studies raise serious questions about whether available immunization programs really work, and Israeli medical services can survive a major attack and help the resulting flood of casualties. Other studies show that such programs can be extremely expensive, can require extensive training of the population, and have limited effectiveness against biological and nuclear attacks.[878]

At some point, Israel may have to make much harder choices about the need for a more comprehensive and adequate civil defense program. Its current program may help keep up morale and provide some limited protection, but it is far from adequate to deal with serious biological attacks and would have little or no effectiveness against a nuclear strike.

SYRIAN WEAPONS OF MASS DESTRUCTION

Israel does not have a monopoly on weapons of mass destruction. Egypt, Iran, Iraq, Libya, and Syria have significant capabilities that could threaten Israel, and Syria's capabilities could be critical in a future conflict.[879] Syria has made considerable progress in acquiring weapons of mass destruction since the mid-1970s. Syria has never shown a serious interest in nuclear weapons, although it did seek to buy two small research reactors from the PRC in 1992, including a 24-megawatt reactor, and purchased a small 30-kilowatt research reactor from the PRC in 1991. It allowed inspection by the International Atomic Energy Agency for the first time in February 1992.[880] It does, however, deploy sheltered missiles, armed with chemical warheads, as a means of both countering Israel's nuclear forces and maintaining its rivalry with Iraq.

Syrian Missile Programs

Syria obtained the FROG 7 in 1972, and the Scud B missile as early as 1974, but Syria did not seem to have given these missile forces a major role until Israel's invasion of Lebanon in 1982. In the ensuing fighting, Syria lost much of its air force in two brief clashes with Israeli fighters, and saw Israel suppress its land-based air defenses in Lebanon in a matter of hours. This experience persuaded Syria that surface-to-surface missiles were a potential means of overcoming Israel's advantage in the air, and furnished a means of attacking Israel's air bases and mobilization centers, and a deterrent to Israeli conventional air attacks. Syria does not seem to have felt that any missile force it could develop would allow it to risk engaging Israel in a war that could escalate to Israeli nuclear retaliation, but it seems to have concluded that missiles are its only option.[881]

Syria reorganized its surface-to-surface missile brigades. It obtained the SS-21, or Scarab, in 1983, and steadily improved the readiness and effectiveness of its missile units. In 1999, Syria had a force of 18 SS-21, 18 FROG-7, and 26 Scud B and Scud C surface-to-surface missile fire units, plus additional Sepal SS-1B and SSC-3 coastal defense missile fire units.[882]

Syria also improved its missile production facilities. It can currently produce its own Scud B missiles with ranges of approximately 260–300 kilometers, and a theoretical maximum accuracy or CEP of around 300 meters. The warhead weighs 985 kilograms and is large enough to carry a chemical, biological, or nuclear warhead. Syria is believed to have an inventory of around 200 Scud B missiles.[883]

The Scud B does, however, have important limitations. It has a maximum range of about 290 kilometers, and can only cover Israeli targets deep in the south of Israel (as far south as Halserim air base and Dimona) from vulnerable forward positions. This seems to have led to its deployment in sheltered locations near Damascus and this may have aided Israel's ability to track and target Scud B unit movements, although firing the Scud B at such short ranges might complicate Israel's detection and tracking problems in using theater ballistic missiles for defense.

The SS-21s in Syrian hands do not have chemical warheads and Syria would find it difficult to develop such a capability without Russian support. The problems of developing and testing an advanced missile warhead are beyond current Syrian capabilities. Given the accuracy of the SS-21, there is at least some long-term risk that Syria could eventually fire nerve agents successfully at Israeli air bases, C^{4}I sites, and mobilization centers—and seriously degrade Israeli conventional capabilities.[884] The SS-21s do not have the range to hit Dimona and most suspected Israeli nuclear weapons and missile storage sites.

These problems may help explain why Syria has put so much effort into obtaining longer-range missiles. They would give it the range to attack any target in Israel from sites as far away from Israel as possible, as well as a potential threat to Turkey. Such targets include the reserve assembly areas for Israel's ground forces, Israel's air bases in the south, and its nuclear facility at Dimona—although parts of the Dimona complex may be too well sheltered for such an attack. It would probably require missiles with nuclear warheads or with advanced penetrating conventional warheads and terminal guidance. These are weapons of a kind that Syria is unlikely to acquire in the near- to mid-term.[885]

From 1984–1989, Syria tried unsuccessfully to buy more SS-21s, and the SS-12 or SS-23 missile, from the USSR. It was particularly interested in the SS-23, which has a 500-kilometer range, and which could have hit targets throughout Israel and Jordan, and much of Iraq. It is clear that both President Hafez Assad and the Syrian Defense Minister actively sought such missiles, and they may even have asked for SS-25 ICBMs once it was clear that the USSR would agree to the INF treaty. The USSR, however, refused to provide any of these systems.[886]

Syria then sought M-9 missiles from the PRC. Reports surfaced in August 1989 that Syria ordered the new M-9 IRBM from the People's Republic of China.[887] While the PRC denied this, and the M-9 missile was still in development, it would meet many Syrian needs. It has a range in excess of 370 miles (600 kilometers), a projected CEP of around 600 meters, and a payload of 500 kilograms. There have also been reports that the PRC sold Syria the M-1B missile, with ranges of 50 to 60 miles, in March 1990.[888] The PRC is developing two other long-range mobile surface-to-surface missiles—the M-11 and the M-12—and Syria may have an interest in these systems as well. Syria purchased 30–90 tons of solid rocket fuel from the PRC in 1991.[889] There were unconfirmed reports in March 1999 that Syria had created a production facility to build both the M-11 (CSS-7/DF-11) and M-9 missiles with ranges of 280 and 600–800 kilometers respectively. It reports that production of the booster stage of the M-11 began in 1996, and that missile production is expected to start "soon."[890]

Syria finally succeeded in obtaining substantial deliveries of North Korean "Scud-C" missiles. These deliveries began on March 13, 1991, when a freighter called the Al-Yarmouk docked in Syria. Two more deliveries took place in 1991. When the US protested such shipments in February 1992, North Korea shifted freighter movements to route them through Iran. The first such shipment took place when the North Korean freighter Dae Hung Ho reached Iran in March 1992, and missile parts and manufacturing equipment were then airlifted to Syria.

Up to 50–80 missiles and 15–20 launchers have been delivered and manufactured since 1992, and several Syrian tests of the missile have taken place.[891] These missiles give Syria a weapon with an estimated range of 500–600 kilometers, a CEP of around 650–850 meters, and a payload of 450–600 kilograms. Syria has cooperated with Iran in importing these systems, and both countries seem to be interested in manufacturing the missile as well as importing it. According to some reports, Syria has built two missile plants near Hama, about 110 miles north of Damascus, one is for solid fueled rockets and the other is for liquid fueled systems. North Korea may have provided the equipment for the liquid fuel plant, and Syria may now be able to produce the missile.[892]

The "Scud C" offers Syria significant advantages in addition to longer range. While the North Korean missile is generally referred to as a "Scud C," the name may be highly misleading. The original Scud A was first seen in 1953 when it entered service. The improved Scud B, with a range of 300 kilometers entered service in 1965, and the "Scud C," with a range of 450 kilometers, was deployed in 1968. It is likely that the North Koreans have redesigned the now obsolete Soviet missile, and have either extended the single stage liquid propelled motor or have added strap-on boosters. It is nearly certain that they have improved the fusing options, and strap down inertial guidance system, and the reliability of the Scud's jet vane course correction system. These improvements are likely to produce a system not only superior to the Soviet Scud—which was being replaced by the SS-23 before the INF Treaty—but one that has a higher payload, more accuracy, and more reliability than any Iraqi Scud variant.[893]

It is also likely that Syria has improved versions of the Soviet MAZ-583 eight-wheeled transporter-erector-launcher, the refueling process and ZIL-157 propellant tanker, and the command vehicle, and improved position establishing and meteorological gear. If so, the set-up time for a Scud B or C unit being moved to a new position could be cut from a minimum of 45–60 minutes to as few as 15–20 minutes. This would not only greatly reduce the probability of detection and vulnerability to attack, but greatly improve operational accuracy as well. Commercially available Global Positioning Gear could further improve Syria's capabilities, particularly if reports of European GPS gear with military accuracy of 10 meters are true.

The new North Korean missile gives Syria the capability to strike at any part of Israel as well as its other neighbors, and Syria has long-range drones that can assist in targeting such missiles. It can cover all 11 of Israel's air bases, all of the 15-odd main armories for Israel's armored forces, and all major reserve force assembly areas.[894] The new missiles have better range-payload, reliability, and accuracy than the extended range Scuds that Saddam Hussein used in the Gulf War. Most experts believe that these missiles are armed with VX nerve gas warheads— joining the large number of sheltered Scud missiles with nerve gas warheads that Syria already deploys. They may well use bomblets to deliver such gas over a wider area. The possibility of biological warheads cannot be dismissed, although Syria is more likely to use the latter weapons in bombs or covert delivery systems.

Syria is also involved in a project to develop a long-range solid fueled missile, possibly with Iranian and North Korean assistance. The CIA reported in 1999 that Syria "continued work on establishing a solid-propellant rocket motor development and production capability. Foreign equipment and assistance have been and will continue to be essential for this effort."[895]

Syrian and Other Regional Use of Commercial Satellite Imagery

Syria has also improved its targeting capability in recent years by making extensive direct and indirect use of commercial satellite imagery, much of which is now highly detailed and comes with coordinate data with near GPS-like levels of accuracy. This is equally true of Egypt, Iran, Iraq, Israel, Jordan, Libya, and even Lebanon, and it represents a fundamental shift in regional intelligence and targeting capability.

It is impossible to determine the amount of photo coverage a given country has obtained from given commercial services, the quality of their photo interpretation, the links between data gathering and targeting, and national doctrine and procedures. A review of recent regional coverage does show, however, that photos are available of air bases, production facilities, and potential missile sites that offer considerable intelligence benefits. One thing is clear, the quality of coverage is improving steadily down to levels of resolution approaching a few meters, and 1-meter resolution should be broadly available by the early 2000s. No clear or enforceable policies exist regarding the sale of imagery that is crisis or war fighting relevant, and coverage can be used for both targeting weapons of mass destruction and conventional war fighting.[896]

In addition to commercial satellite imagery, several countries also have indigenous programs. Israel has the capability to launch military intelligence satellites for a wide range of missions. Egypt has launched its own commercial communications satellite and also has the potential to launch military satellites.[897] These satellites can only have a small fraction of the technical sophistication of US systems, but can still extend reconnaissance, surveillance, targeting, and SIGINT/COMINT capabilities far beyond the range of airborne sensors.

Syrian Missile Conversions and Cruise Missiles

Syria may also have tried to convert some of its SA-2 surface-to-air, SSC-1B, and SS-C-3 coastal defense missiles to deliver chemical agents.[898] This illustrates major potential problems in controlling missile technology. While the SA-2 Guideline is now an obsolete surface-to-air missile, it weighs 2,360 kilograms and is a fairly large system. The Soviet versions had nuclear warheads, and a 130-kilogram high explosive warhead. The slant range of the missile in the air intercept mode is about 50 kilometers, although the system would probably be accurate to over 100 kilometers in the surface-to-surface mode. It is not an ideal system for use against surface targets by any means, and would require substantial modification. It has been deployed in large numbers, however, and nations like Iraq have already developed major conversion programs to turn it into a surface-to-surface missile.

The SSC-1B Sepal is a relatively modern cruise missile in Third World terms. It entered Soviet service in 1970. It has a range of 450 kilometers and a warhead of up to 1,000 kilograms. While it receives little attention, it is a large 5,400-kilogram missile with radio command midcourse guidance, a radio altimeter to control altitude, command guidance at long ranges, and terminal active radar guidance. It can fly at preset altitudes from surface skimming to 3,000–5,000 meters. It is designed for attack against ships and the Soviet version has a 100–200 kiloton nuclear warhead. Its guidance system and accuracy make it difficult to modify for attacks on land targets that are much smaller than a large military base or small town, but its large warhead lends itself to chemical use against such area targets. Syria has several SSC-1B units, which normally have 16–18 missiles per battalion.

The SS-C-3 is another coastal defense missile based on the Styx. It is a modern system that was first deployed in Soviet forces in 1985. It has a much shorter range than the SS-C-1B. Its maximum range is only 80–90 kilometers and its warhead is unlikely to exceed 500 kilograms, although Soviet versions with yields of 1 to 200 kilotons have been reported. It uses inertial midcourse guidance (a programmed auto-pilot with precision accelerometers), and uses a mobile launcher based on the Soviet MAZ-543 8X8 all-terrain vehicle. It is specifically designed for export and has not been deployed with Soviet forces. It is normally used as a sea skimmer against naval targets, but can evidently be set for a high altitude cruise phase with accuracy sufficient to hit a small town or large air base. While converting such a system to chemical warheads would not normally be cost effective, the resulting system would be relatively mobile and easy to deploy. The possibility cannot be totally dismissed.

Syrian Aircraft Delivery Systems

Syria is slowly acquiring a significant long-range air strike capability. It already has at least 20 Su-24 strike attack aircraft. The exact performance of its export version of the Su-24 is unclear, and its avionics seem to be far less advanced than the Soviet version. Nevertheless, it is probably still a precision all-weather or night attack capable aircraft with some similarities to the F-111 or Tornado. It has a powerful pulse Doppler radar and is capable of very low altitude penetrations. It is a two-seat aircraft with a weapons/navigation officer sitting next to the pilot, and may be fitted with FLIR and electro-optical aids, and has good inertial navigation capabilities.

The Russian version has a moderate to good ECM/ECCM suite and radar homing/warning. It has the range/payload to attack Israel by flying around or through Jordan, or over the Mediterranean and from the south. It is a heavy aircraft that weighs 64,000 to 87,000 pounds loaded. It is a swing-wing aircraft with speeds of Mach 2.4 when clean of external munitions. Its LO-LO-LO combat radius with an eight-ton bomb load is 322 kilometers (200 miles). Its range with a 2.5-ton bomb load is 1,800 kilometers (1,115 miles). Its ferry range is about 6,400 kilometers (4,000 miles).[899]

The CIA reported in 1999 that Syria Damascus continued work on establishing a solid-propellant rocket motor development and production capability. Foreign equipment and assistance have been and will continue to be essential for this effort. In addition, Russia continued to deliver advanced antitank guided missiles to Syria. The vast majority of Syria's arsenal consists of weapons from the former Soviet Union. Russia wants to keep its predominant position as the key supplier of arms to Syria.[900]

While it is tempting to focus on missile systems, a well designed Syrian air raid on a city like Tel Aviv that saturated Israel's air defenses with other aircraft, and then raided with Syria's total inventory of Su-24s, might be able to deliver a considerable payload. Such an attack could be particularly lethal if that payload was toxins or biological weapons, rather than nerve gas. At the same time, it should be noted that a ship that took advantage of favorable winds, while sailing off the coast of Israel, could cover an area of up to several hundred square miles simply by releasing anthrax spores or some similar biological agent in a covert delivery mode.

Syrian Chemical Weapons

Syria probably acquired limited stocks of mustard gas shortly before or after the October War in 1973. It was only after Syria's clashes with Israel in 1982, however, that Syria seems to have started a major effort in chemical and biological warfare. As is the case with missiles, Syria saw weapons of mass destruction as a way of countering Israel's advantages and as a means of maintaining its status relative to its other regional military rivals.

Syrian troops steadily increased their NBC training after 1982, and Syria began to give chemical warfare training a serious priority. More significantly, Syria started a crash effort to produce nerve gas—setting up at least two major chemical weapons plants. US experts indicated in 1984 that Syria had begun manufacturing and deploying non-persistent nerve and other gases in 1982 or 1983. By the late 1980s, Syria seems to have been operating two, and possibly three, facilities for the production of chemical weapons. One seems to be the CERS Institute, which may also play a role in biological warfare research, another is near Homs, and a third is near Saffirah (a village near Allepo).

Both US and Israeli experts believe that Syria is stockpiling nerve gas, mustard gas, and other chemical agents, including non-persistent nerve gases like Sarin (GB) and persistent nerve gas agents like VX.[901] It is believed that VX is being produced at a plant near Damascus.[902] A full list of the kinds of chemical weapons Syria may have developed is shown in Table 15.3. The CIA reported in 1999 that, "Syria continued to seek CW-related precursors from various sources during the reporting period. Damascus already has a stockpile of the nerve agent Sarin and may be trying to develop more toxic and persistent nerve agents. Syria remains dependent on foreign sources for key elements of its CW program, including precursor chemicals and key production equipment."[903]

Syria was caught smuggling feedstocks from Russia in 1993 and 1994. It obtained 1,800 pounds of feedstocks for nerve gas in 1993, and attempted to smuggle out another 11,000 pounds in 1994. Ironically, the Russian responsible for the smuggling was General Anatoly Kuntsevich, once President Yeltsin's chief military liaison officer for chemical disarmament.[904] While most people do not need to be reminded of the severe consequences, Table 15.4 provides a general profile of some of the missions that can be carried out using chemical weapons and the possible amount of an agent necessary for that mission.

As for delivery systems and weapons, Syria may have modified a variant of the Soviet ZAB series incendiary bomb to deliver chemical agents, and may have modified the PTAB-500 cluster bomb to carry chemical bomblets. Syria has probably developed chemical artillery shells, and may be working on chemical rounds for its multiple rocket launchers. Syrian FROG missiles also seem to have been given chemical warheads, although there is no precise way to date when they acquired them.

The primary emphasis of the Syrian program, however, seems to have been strategic. Syria modified its Scud missiles to deliver chemical weapons no later than 1987.[905] In fact, a number of experts believe some Syrian surface-to-surface missiles armed with chemical weapons began to be stored in concrete shelters in the mountains near Damascus and in the Palmyra region no later than 1986, and that plans have long existed to deploy them forward in an emergency since that date.[906]

Putting chemical warheads on the Scud missile gives Syria a relatively effective weapons system, although such a weapon would have nothing like the lethality of Israel's nuclear weapons. For example, if Syria copied the Soviet designs for chemical warheads for the Scud, designs which the USSR seems to have made available to a number of Third World states in the late 1970s, and successfully produced an agent as lethal as the VX chemical warhead used on the Soviet version of the Scud missile, it would then have an 884-mm warhead weighing 2,170 pounds, of which 1,200 pounds would consist of chemical agent. The warhead would be fitted with a variable time fuse, and the agent would be dispersed by a bursting charge located along the center axis of the warhead.

Assuming a burst altitude of 1,100 meters, and a ground wind speed of 3 feet per second, and worst case conditions, the warhead could produce a contaminated area that would cover a band about 0.53 kilometers wide and 3.5 kilometers long—beginning about one kilometer from the burst. Assuming a flat plain and no protection, up to 50% of the exposed personnel would be casualties. This is a very impressive lethal area, and a VX nerve agent might remain lethal for several days. It is important to note, however, that this lethal area calculation does assume exposed personnel, a flat plain, and optimal delivery conditions. Real world lethality might be only 5% to 20% as high, although this would still halt military activity in many targets.[907]

Syrian warheads would be even more effective if—as US and Israeli intelligence experts believe—they now use bomblets in cluster munitions to disperse VX. The US Department of Defense has given briefings indicating that an underground production line to manufacture VX-loaded bomblets was set up near Damascus in early 1997, which is collocated with the Syrian Centre d'Etudes et de Recherche Scientifique (CERS). This facility seems to manufacture bomblets that can be loaded into either Scud B or Scud C warheads and bombs, and which could be modified to disseminate biological weapons. The missile warhead design is believed to be matched to the Syrian production of the Scud C booster. The fusing, dissemination mechanism, and effectiveness of the bomblets is unknown.[908]

Syrian Biological Weapons

Syria has also developed biological weapons, although it does not seem to have attempted to produce or stockpile them. It established at least one major biological warfare facility, and possibly two. One facility seems to exist near the Syrian coast and another facility may have been built underground. According to Israeli sources, Syria was able to produce Botulin or Ricin toxins in 1991 and probably anthrax as well.[909] US intelligence sources also believe that Syria has biological weapons.[910] A list of the kinds of biological weapons Syria may have developed is shown in Table 15.5.

While Syrian biological warfare capabilities receive only limited attention, it is important to note that Syrian sources indicate that the program dates back to at least the early 1980s. The world was never able to detect the true nature of Iraq's massive program until the defection of a leading Iraqi official in 1995—roughly half a decade after UNSCOM inspections had begun—and similar uncertainties may apply to Syria.

This raises major questions about Syria's strike capabilities. Older types of biological weapons using wet agents, and placed in older bomb and warhead designs with limited dissemination capability, can achieve only a small fraction of the potential effectiveness of dry agents in weapons with excellent dissemination capability. Dry micropowders using advanced agents—such as the most lethal forms of anthrax—can have the effectiveness of small theater nuclear weapons. It is difficult to design adequate missile warheads to disseminate such agents, but this is not beyond Syrian capabilities—particularly since much of the technology needed to make effective cluster munitions and bomblets for VX gas can be adapted to the delivery of biological weapons.[911]

The design of effective biological bombs and missile warheads may now be well within Syrian capabilities, as is the design of UAV, helicopter, cruise missile, or aircraft-borne systems to deliver the agent slowly over a long line of flight and taking maximum advantage of wind and weather conditions. US and Soviet tests proved that this kind of "line source" delivery could achieve lethalities as high as 50–100-kiloton weapons by the late 1950s, and the technology is well within Syria's grasp. So is the use of proxy or covert delivery.

This creates serious problems in understanding the balance, deterrence, and possible forms of war fighting. Both Israel and Syria may possess highly lethal capabilities, but nuclear weapons are largely a prompt and highly visible kill mechanism with few ambiguities. Biological weapons can be tailored to produce prompt or delayed kills, and different agents can be mixed to produce highly complicated effects that are very difficult to detect, characterize, and treat. The covert nature of both nations' programs makes it difficult for the other to fully understand either the enemy threat or exactly how it may be used. At the same time, Israeli nuclear capability is currently much more credible than a *potential* Syrian biological capability. Discussions with IDF and other Israeli experts indicate that they give comparatively little attention to the possibility that Syria could conduct a strike that would be massively more effective than a Syrian use of chemical weapons.

Neither Syria nor Israel seems likely to deliberately take existential risks, but several forms of escalation are at least possible:

- Syria or Israel invokes the direct or indirect threat of using its deterrent in a crisis or conventional war. While the original intent is to limit escalation or terminate conflict, the result is that the other side responds—the crisis slowly climbs the escalation ladder.

- Syria arms its missile and other forces with chemical weapons. Israel attempts to preemptively destroy Syrian delivery capabilities. Syria responds by launching under attack and using cruise missile/UAV platforms unknown to Israel.

- Iran or Iraq uses missiles with chemical and/or biological warheads successfully against Israeli population centers. Israel retaliates and strikes preemptively against Syria to limit damage.
- Syria faces a major Israeli advance on Damascus. It escalates demonstratively. Israel responds. Neither side can halt the resultant process of escalation before serious use.
- Syria or Israel misreads the other state and preempts or massively escalates while under attack.
- A nuclear or biological weapon designed for tactical use against enemy forces actually strikes against a population center by mistake. The resulting process of escalation is driven by the resulting misperceptions of the original intent and inability to effectively communicate and find some mutually agreeable point at which to halt escalation.

The key point is not the risk posed by any given scenario, but rather the inability to predict escalatory patterns, the lack of mutual understanding of the other side's intentions and capabilities, and the severe problems in trying to deal with fundamental asymmetric strike forces. Third party or terrorist strikes add a further complication, as do the asymmetries in vulnerability and different incentives for a first strike or launch under attack. At some point, escalation will also tend to become existential for either state. At this point, all restraint may cease. The 20th century also provides ample examples of the fact that the ability of leaders to act as rational bargainers in peacetime does not necessarily dictate crisis or war-time behavior.

Syrian Strategy, Doctrine, and Plans

While any use of long-range missiles would risk Israeli nuclear retaliation, some Israeli experts have suggested that Syria might risk limited strikes against Israeli air bases and mobilization assembly sites as part of a surprise attack on the Golan. Such an attack would not be designed to threaten Israel's existence or to capture the Galilee, but would rather attempt to establish new facts on the ground so rapidly that outside powers would force a cease-fire before Israel could counterattack and under conditions where it could not risk massive retaliation.

Other Israeli experts believe that Syria will try to use its chemically armed missiles as a deterrent to Israeli strategic strikes and to allow it to attack the Golan using its armored forces without fear of massive Israeli retaliation. Such scenarios would certainly involve massive risks for Syria, but cannot be dismissed. In fact, some Israelis argue that Syria's efforts to double its T-72 force with new purchases from the Russian Republic and the Czech Republic could support this contingency.[912]

Experts on Syrian forces do, however, raise questions about the extent to which Syria's missiles will be survivable even after Syria fully deploys its North Korean missiles. Some experts feel that Syria has a first strike or preemptive force, and must use its missiles the moment that it feels they are under attack. Others feel it would use some of its FROGs and Scuds on Israeli air bases, command centers, and mobilization staging areas, while holding others in reserve. Either tactic could be extremely destabilizing in a Syrian-Israeli conflict.

EGYPTIAN WEAPONS OF MASS DESTRUCTION

Egypt has kept a low profile compared to the other major military powers in the Middle East, and its efforts to proliferate now seem more a contingency program than a serious effort to proliferate. Egypt does have some long-range missile capability, although it is unclear if its weapons have chemical warheads. Egypt has had FROG-7 and Scud B missiles since the 1960s, and these remain operational in spite of the fact that former President Sadat severed military relations with the USSR in 1974. Egypt retains two active surface-to-surface missile regiments with 12 FROG-7 free rocket launchers and has a regiment with at least nine Scud B guided missile launchers.[913]

Egypt has developed an improved and domestically produced version of the FROG called the Saqr 80. This rocket is 6.5 meters long and 210 mm in diameter, and weighs 660 kilograms. It has a maximum range of 50 miles (80 kilometers) and a 440-pound (200-kilogram) warhead. It is a TEL mounted system, and can be mounted on both wheeled and tracked vehicles. Egypt uses a UAV with the system for long-range targeting. A variant is being studied that would hold four rockets per vehicle instead of the usual one. Egypt reports two types of conventional warheads for the Saqr 80, one with 950 AP/AT bomblets and one with 65 anti-tank mines, and it is developing an automatic survey and fire control system for the rocket. The Saqr 80 could, however, easily be used to deliver chemical weapons.[914]

Egyptian Missile Programs

Although the Scud Bs Egypt received in 1973 would normally have become inoperable due to age and lack of service, Egypt seems to have carried out a successful reverse engineering program and is attempting to mass produce its own version of the extended range Scud C missile. Egypt does seem to be building an improved version of the Scud B, using technology obtained with North Korean assistance.[915] Egypt has long had ties to North Korea in missile development and transferred some of the technology it got from the Soviet Union to North Korea in 1981.[916]

While the Scud B missile is normally credited with having a range of 190 miles (300 kilometers), and a 2,200-pound (1,000-kilogram) warhead, some sources claim that the range and warhead size of the improved Egyptian version of the Scud may be closer to that of the Iraqi Al Hussein, and the range may be 30% to 50% greater than that of a normal Scud.[917] Three Egyptian companies were sanctioned by the US State Department on March 23, 1999 for sending dual-use US technology to Pyongyang—Arab-British Dynamics, Helwan Machinery and Equipment Company, and the Kader Factory for Developed Industries.[918]

Egypt's most ambitious missile program has been the Condor. During the mid-1980s, Egypt began a covert program with Argentina and Iraq, in which Egypt and Iraq paid Argentina to develop the "Badar 2000" long-range missile and provide suitable production equipment. The Badar 2000 was based on the Argentine Condor II or Alacran missile, and was a solid fuel system with ranges from 480 to 1,000 kilometers, and warheads of 500 to 1,000 kilograms.[919] There is little doubt that the Badar 2000 was intended to use chemical warheads or other weapons of mass destruction.

Quiet US pressure on Argentina and Egypt, and key supplier countries, helped kill the Argentine and Egyptian efforts, although Iraq kept up work on the program. At the same time, it is unclear how well the program would have progressed without such US pressure. Argentina never operationally tested the Condor II, and there is some question as to Argentina's ability to provide the proper technical skills to develop such a system. According to some reports, a major program evaluation in 1988 revealed major technical problems in the original design, and Argentina may have decided to shift its efforts to a missile with a range of only 200 kilometers.

Other reports indicate, however, that the basic design was successful and that the US only succeeded in persuading Argentina to halt the program once its military government fell after a disastrous defeat in the Falklands. These sources also indicate that the US only succeeded in persuading Egypt to give up the program after President Mubarak was embarrassed by the arrest of the Egyptian officers attempting to smuggle missile technology out of the US.[920]

There are unconfirmed reports that Egypt has renewed its effort to develop and produce improved versions of the Scud since Israel's testing of the "Jericho II" missiles.[921] Many of these reports focus on the possible construction of a plant to produce an improved version of the Scud B, and possibly Scud C, with North Korean cooperation. The Scud C has a range of roughly 480 kilometers.

These reports indicate that North Korean transfers of technology include the equipment for building Scud body, special gyroscope measuring equipment and pulse-code modulation equipment for missile assembly and testing. Unconfirmed reports surfaced in June 1996 that Egypt had made a major missile purchase from North Korea, and would soon be able to assemble such missiles in Egypt. Seven shipments from North Korea were reported in March and April. The CIA did confirm in June 1997 that Egypt had acquired Scud B parts from Russia and North Korea during 1996. The were also new press reports that US satellites detected shipments of Scud C missile parts to Egypt in February-May 1996—including rocket motors and guidance. A number of US experts believe that Egypt does have a Scud C-like liquid-fueled missile under development known as "Project T" that has an estimated range of over 450 kilometers. They believe it has been designed with North Korean assistance.[922]

The CIA reported in 1999 that Egypt continued its effort to develop and produce the Scud B and Scud C and to develop the two-stage Vector short-range ballistic missiles (SRBM). Cairo also is interested in developing a medium-range ballistic missile (MRBM). During the first half of 1998, Egypt continued to obtain ballistic missile components and associated equipment from North Korea. This activity was part of a long-running program of ballistic missile cooperation between these two countries.[923]

In June, 1990, there were reports that Egypt had reached an agreement with the People's Republic of China to update Egypt's Saqr rocket factory to produce newer anti-aircraft missiles, the DF-4 Silkworm anti-ship missile, an improved version of the Scud, and three types of long-range Saqr surface-to-surface rockets.[924] The deal was reported to include an improved version of the DF-4, with its range extended from 50 to 90 nautical miles, and a DF-5 missile with a range of 170 miles. The regular DF-4 has a 1,000-pound warhead and can be used in a surface-to-surface as well as an anti-ship mode.[925] US experts have seen no evidence of such a program.

Egyptian Chemical Weapons

Egypt has been capable of delivering chemical weapons since the late 1950s, and may have acquired British stocks of mustard gas that Britain failed to remove from inventories it deployed in the northern desert in World War II. Egypt began low-level research efforts to develop long-range guided missiles and nuclear weapons in the 1950s. Egypt has had the capability to produce its own mustard gas and other chemical weapons since the early 1960s, and it used poison gas in its battles against the royalist faction in North Yemen in the period before its 1967 conflict with Israel.

Egypt has had large stockpiles of chemical defense equipment since the late 1960s—and substantial amounts of this equipment were captured during the fighting in October 1973. Egypt almost certainly had stockpiles of mustard gas at the time, and was probably producing limited amounts of non-persistent nerve gas. Egypt has also been less reticent about its possession of chemical weapons in the past. The former Egyptian Minister of War, General Abdel Ranny Gamassay, stated in 1975 that, "if Israel should decide to use a nuclear weapon in the battlefield, we shall use the weapons of mass destruction that are at our disposal."[926] In spite of the dramatic changes in its relations with Israel, and careful observance of its peace treaty, Egypt seems to have continued some production of chemical agents after the Camp David accords as well as maintained small stockpiles of chemical bombs and other chemical weapons.

While Egypt does not appear to have developed the significant chemical weapons production and delivery capabilities of states like Iraq, Syria, and Libya, it does seem to have stepped up its research effort since gas began to be used extensively in the Iran-Iraq War. Egypt probably retains the capability to produce mustard gas, non-persistent nerve gas, and perhaps to produce persistent nerve gas as well. Egypt was caught attempting to import the feedstock for nerve gas from Canada during 1988. Egypt has also placed highly specialized orders of fumigants, pesticides, arsenic, and strychnine for what seems to be used in a major poison gas production facility near or in the Beni Suef Air Base south of Cairo.[927]

Egypt also seems to have expanded its chemical weapons plant at Abu Zabaal, north of Cairo, and improved chemical weapons production equipment from firms like Krebs A. G. of Zurich, Switzerland. Egypt is believed to have approached Krebs in 1985, shortly after Iraq began to make large-scale use of chemical weapons in the Iran-Iraq War. Krebs built a plant for the El Nasr Pharmaceutical Plant at Abu Zabaal to make phosphorous trichloride, a basic chemical that can be used for both insecticides and chemical weapons. Krebs also was active in designing a phosphorous pentasulfide plant for Iran that seemed to be linked to Iran's chemical weapons efforts.[928]

Although President Mubarak has categorically denied that Egypt has chemical weapons, and a new long-range missile development effort, there are reasons to question such denials. Israeli sources believe that Egypt may be building new chemical weapons feedstock plants north of Cairo, and developing the capability to produce nerve and mustard gases without dependence on imports of precursor chemicals.

Egyptian Biological and Nuclear Weapons

Egypt also seems to have carried out extensive research on biological weapons, and has the capability to manufacture modern, effective biological weapons.[929] At the same time, there are few indications it has attempted to manufacture biological agents or load weapons with such agents. There have been rumors that Egypt is seeking to develop advanced chemical and biological warheads for its missiles systems and modern binary chemical bombs, and may be reviving its nuclear weapons research effort. If such Egyptian efforts exist, however, they are sufficiently covert so that few experts believe Egypt has gone beyond the research phase.

President Nasser did start an Egyptian nuclear program in the 1950s, but its main success was to help push Israel into building nuclear weapons. The Egyptian program was a failure, and there is no significant evidence of any serious Egyptian effort to acquire fissile material and build a bomb since the late 1970s. The only major recent development in Egyptian nuclear capability is that Egypt built a 22-megawatt reactor with Argentine help that went on-line in February 1998 at the Inshas research center north of Cairo. This reactor is under IAEA safeguards and can only produce a limited amount of weapons-grade Plutonium at best. Egypt certainly has the ability to design a nuclear weapon, manufacture all of the components other than fissile material, and carry out all aspects of testing except actual detonation. Most US experts believe, however, that Egypt has made no effort to invest in the required production technology and that it fully complies with the IAEA.

President Mubarak did say in October 1998 that Egypt could acquire nuclear weapons to match Israel's capability if this proves necessary.[930] "If the time comes when we need nuclear weapons, we will not hesitate. I say 'if' we have to because this is the last thing we think about. We do not think of joining the nuclear club." This speech was more an effort to push Israel towards disarmament talks, however, than any kind of threat.

Mubarak also said that Israel, "enhances its military expenditure and develops its missile systems that are used for military purposes. It knows very well that this will not benefit it or spare it from harm. Its efforts to use the help of foreign countries will plunge the region ban into a new arms race which serves nobody's interests."[931] Egypt has supported the indefinite extension of the NNPT, has long been officially committed to creating a nuclear weapons–free zone in the Middle East, and has advocated an agreement that would ban all weapons of mass destruction from the region.

ALGERIAN, LIBYAN, IRANIAN, AND IRAQI WEAPONS OF MASS DESTRUCTION

Other nations are also developing significant capabilities to produce weapons of mass destruction in ways that could affect the Arab-Israeli balance. These threats are currently limited, and are likely to remain so in the case of Libya. Iran, however, is beginning to develop significant missile capabilities and is moving towards the production of biological and nuclear weapons. Iraq seems to be a determined proliferator and is one of the few nations to have actually fired missiles and chemical weapons at other countries.[932]

Algeria

Algeria is only a potential proliferator and it poses the smallest potential threat to Israel or any of the Arab states on its borders. Algeria has conducted research into chemical and biological weapons, and seems to have stepped up its chemical weapons research effort significantly since 1988. Reports of significant surface-to-surface missile procurement efforts have never been confirmed, and Algeria does not have such weapons now.

The most threatening action that Algeria has taken is its creation of a secure nuclear research compound with a PRC-supplied reactor at Ain Ouserra, about 150 kilometers south of Algiers. Aside from this new reactor, Algeria had only a one-megawatt working reactor that it had acquired from Argentina in April 1989. The new reactor—which Algeria named Es Salam—was started in 1986 and was finished in 1992. It was located far from population centers in a defended military compound, with an SA-5 surface-to-air missile unit nearby, and was rated at 15 megawatts.[933]

The size of the reactor indicates that it was intended only as the first step in a contingency program and not as part of a major production effort. A 15-megawatt reactor would take about three years of full-time operation to produce enough material for one weapon, and is too small to produce significant amounts of

Plutonium. The 15-megawatt rating, however, is uncertain. A few experts feel that the oversized cooling towers of the facility indicated that the reactor might be capable of producing 45–60 megawatts. The facility's size, its defenses, and the fact that it was built in secret all produce concern that it might be used for a nuclear weapons program. Unconfirmed reports also indicated that a reprocessing facility, capable of separating weapons-usable plutonium from spent fuel or irradiated uranium targets, was under construction next to the reactor.

Some senior Western experts felt during the early 1990s that the reactor project was a reaction to tensions with Libya, Israel's 1985 raid on Tunis, and the US raids on Libya in 1981 and 1986. Algeria, however, has consistently denied any intention of building nuclear weapons. In May 1991, following the public exposure of the reactor by US intelligence, Algeria agreed to place the reactor under IAEA safeguards. As early as December 1993, Algerian officials pledged adherence to the NPT, and on January 12, 1995, Algeria formally acceded to the treaty. On March 30, 1996, Algeria signed a comprehensive IAEA safeguards agreement providing for IAEA inspections of all of Algeria's nuclear facilities and IAEA technical assistance to Algeria. The agreement entered into force on January 7, 1997.

Algeria, however, has not given up on its nuclear program. In spite of an ongoing civil war and severe economic problems, Algeria signed a "second stage" agreement for nuclear cooperation with China on June 1, 1996. According to an October 1996 "letter of intent," China was to assist Algeria with the construction of facilities for the research and production of radioactive isotopes for use in the medical, industrial, and agricultural sectors. China and Algeria intend to move into a third phase of cooperation under which China will share the know-how to enable Algeria to operate hot cells in the facility (mentioned previously) at the Es Salam compound. These hot cells would give Algeria the capability to separate plutonium from spent fuel. Algeria claims that the hot cells are intended for the purpose of producing medical isotopes, and the US is reportedly "satisfied" that the hot cells will be operated under IAEA safeguards.

A Spanish paper, *El Pais*, claimed on August 23, 1998 that Spain's military secret service, the CESID, had issued a report that said that Algeria will be able in two years to produce military-grade plutonium, a key ingredient for making atomic weapons. The report is said to have concluded that Algeria had forged ahead with a nuclear program with Chinese and Argentine technical support that far exceeded its civilian needs, despite having signed the international Nuclear Non-Proliferation Treaty.

The report is said to have been submitted to the Spanish government in July and to have sounded a warning of the danger involved if Algeria decided to divert its nuclear program to military purposes. The report indicated that the nuclear complex at Birine, 250 km (155 miles) south of Algiers, already had a heavy-water reactor in operation capable of producing weapons-grade plutonium. The CESID report stated that Algeria "has all the installations needed to carry out activities linked to the complete cycle for the creation of military plutonium" by the end of the century, the newspaper said. CESID concluded that if the Algerian government decided to change its current policy of not acquiring atomic weapons, "the knowledge gathered by a significant team of technicians and scientists, in addition to the availability of facilities . . . will place this country in the position of initiating a program of military purposes."

While it appears that the Zeroual government was only expanding Algeria's nuclear research program in compliance with the NPT, there are still serious uncertainties regarding Algeria's real long-term goals. The risk that Algeria may eventually seek the bomb is still a potential threat—although scarcely an urgent one.[934]

Libya

Libya has long sought to acquire long-range missiles and weapons of mass destruction, although Qadhafi's efforts have had more publicity than success. Its missile programs and nuclear programs have so far resulted in expensive failures. Its chemical weapons program has had only faltering success, and there is little evidence of any major Libyan successes in developing biological weapons.

Libyan Delivery Systems

Libya does have enough operational aircraft and pilots to deliver chemical or other weapons of mass destruction against other African states using its Tu-22s or Su-24s. Libya's missile capabilities are more limited. The USSR transferred 25 Scud B missiles to Libya by 1976. It now has at least 40 FROG launchers and 80 Scud missile launchers. Its total holdings of FROG rockets and Scud missiles are unknown. Libya has, however, obtained enough Scud missiles to sell or transfer some to Iran during the Iran-Iraq War.[935]

Libya has sought longer-range missiles for at least the past two decades, and Libya has sponsored missile development projects with a number of Warsaw Pact, European and Third World states. While sources differ, it seems likely that a West German firm called OTRAG helped Libya begin research on satellite launcher testing in the Libyan desert in the late 1970s and early 1980s. When OTRAG was forced to leave Libya by the West German government because of fears that it might be involved in ballistic missile development efforts, elements of the original OTRAG group stayed behind until the mid 1980s. These reports have never been confirmed, but indicate that the German team was working at a desert camp about 60 miles from Sebha on a missile with a 500–700-kilometer range called Ittisalt, and that there may have been a test in 1987.[936]

Another West German company called Technical Oil Productions may then have been set up to work on a missile project. This missile may have been called the Al-Fatih. Various sources report the missile had a range of at least 300 miles (490 kilometers), a range approximately 110 miles further than the range of the Scud B, and might have had a range of up to 640 miles (1,000 kilometers). The

Munich prosecutor later fined Globesat, another West German firm, for shipping rocket valves to Libya.[937]

Other reports cover a number of other potential suppliers. Some sources indicate that Libya was interested in the Chinese M-9 missile with a range of 600 kilometers, or the CSS-2.[938] There were reports of Libyan cooperation with Brazil in developing long-range missiles, and in the Brazilian MB/EE, Sonda V, and SS-300 missile programs. The MB/EE seems to be the most likely of the latter two candidates, and has a range of up to 620 miles (1,000 kilometers). There are also reports that Libya is interested in the North Korean No Dong family of missiles and has discussed possible purchase of, or cooperation on, the Shahab-3 missile with Iran.[939]

Still other reports indicate that Libya obtained French missile technology, and was trying to develop a short-range missile. These missiles are said to include the Ittisallat, with a range of 50 miles, and the Al-Fatah, with a range of over two hundred miles. British reporters indicate that Libya has a missile range or facility at al-Qarait and in Tauwlwa, and possible missile production facilities.[940]

The CIA reported in 1999 that Libya continued to obtain ballistic missile–related equipment, materials, and technology and that such outside assistance was critical to keeping its fledgling ballistic missile development programs from becoming moribund. Nevertheless, it also reported that the UN embargo had restricted the flow of ballistic missile goods and technology reaching Libya.[941]

No details have emerged to confirm any serious progress in any of Libya's missile efforts, however. There is little physical evidence of such developments, and there are no reports that Libya has tested a missile with ranges or performance better than that of the Scud.[942] The readiness of Libya's Scud, cruise missile, and other missile units is also believed to be low. Libya also sought to obtain spare parts and other support for its military aircraft and naval vessels from sources in the FSU and Eastern Europe. Once again, the UN embargo has greatly affected Tripoli, restricting its ability to keep Libya's Air Force operational.[943]

Libyan Chemical Warfare Programs

Libyan efforts to obtain chemical weapons have had some successes. The exact point at which Libya first began to acquire chemical weapons is unclear. While the evidence leading to the source is unclear—it could have been Egypt, the USSR, a third nation, or limited laboratory scale production—Libya seems to have had a small stock of mustard gas and possibly nerve gas by the late 1970s.[944]

Libya intensified its efforts to acquire chemical weapons in 1983–1984, as a reaction to Iraq's use of chemical weapons in the Iran-Iraq War and Israel's invasion of Lebanon. It is possible that it obtained East German and Cuban assistance in such efforts, and there are reports that it used an Iraqi citizen, Ihsan Barbouti, to purchase equipment and technology for the production of chemical weapons in early 1984.[945]

Libya established a chemical and biological research center in the Sabha area during 1984–1985, and conducted field tests of gas weapons in the Libyan desert. Qadhafi seems to have made a decision during this period to purchase a pilot plant for mustard and nerve gas production, and purchased a large, full-scale production plant during mid-1985. Some sources indicate that this pilot plant is located near Tripoli and began production in late-1987, and one report indicates that North Koreans operate it with some support by Iranian technicians.[946]

Some US government experts believe that Libya made limited, if ineffective, use of poison gas in Chad on several different occasions during 1986–1987. While some sources indicate that Libya used sarin nerve gas, most experts seem to believe that it used mustard gas. On at least one occasion, this gas seems to have blown back over Libyan troops.[947]

Libya then began construction of a massive chemical warfare complex that included weapons assembly and loading plants, as well as plants to produce chemical weapons. This plant was located at Rabta, 40 miles south of Tripoli, called "Pharma 150." This effort moved forward on a cash basis, and with the aid of a wide range of European, Japanese and other suppliers, Libya created a chemical warfare complex at Rabta, which now has around 30 buildings.

These buildings include a "Technical Center for Basic Research," equipped with a large entrance, reinforced steel floor, and mobile cranes, and a "Production Building," stocked with advanced machine tools. The assembly line bears no relation to pharmaceutical facilities in other countries. There are sheltered underground storage facilities near the main production centers at Rabta, and surface-to-air missiles and Libyan troops defend the plant. Its research staff and personnel operate under tight security controls, and all of its activities are classified. The dimensions of the support roads and certain nearby facilities seem to be linked with Libya's efforts to acquire surface-to-surface missiles.[948]

While protests from the outside world forced Libya to alter Rabta to look more like a civilian pharmaceutical plant, US experts feel it still has the potential to become the largest integrated single chemical weapons plant in the Third World, and the largest chemical warfare plant outside the CIS. Some experts feel it can eventually produce up to 40–45 metric tons a day of mustard gas, tabun and sarin. The plant is also designed to manufacture chemical warheads and munitions, as well as chemical agents, and seems capable of producing binary weapons. There also are some indications that it will produce napalm.[949] Libya acquired extensive key feed stocks like Thiodiglycol, and the equipment and technology to produce poison gas from firms like Imhausen-Chemie GmbH in Germany, and seemed capable of large-scale production of mustard gas without additional foreign supply. It has equally large stocks of the precursor chemicals to produce nerve gases like sarin.[950]

Libya has also had problems in making Rabta work ever since initial production testing began between the summer of 1988 and late 1989. It experienced further problems in operating its plant in early 1990. Then, in March 1990, a devastating fire of unknown origin swept the plant. This left Libya with small stocks of chemical weapons, but without any way to produce the massive numbers it once planned upon.[951] Libya's main source of poison gas still seems to be the 9,000 pounds a day of poison gas that it is producing at its prototype facility. It only seems to have produced a maximum of 30–50 tons of mustard gas by March 1990, and US experts have that it has only produced about 100 tons to date.[952]

Since 1990, Libya has carried out major new construction efforts that may be associated with its efforts to acquire missiles and aircraft that can use weapons of mass destruction. These projects include a major underground command site, and a new site near the ancient ruins at Sabha, some 460 miles south of Tripoli. Other sources indicate these reports are exaggerated or untrue, or that the plant at Sabha actually produces napalm.[953] Once again, reports differ sharply as to exactly what is happening, and Libya has denied such construction is under way.[954]

Other reports indicate that Libya has a second chemical weapons plant under construction in underground or sheltered facilities near Libya's OTRAG missile plant, whose primary purpose is the production of nerve gas, and that air defenses are being set up in the area.[955] The most likely location for any second chemical weapons plant is at Tarhunah, southeast of Tripoli. Libya has created a major underground facility, although it claims it has done this for its Great Man-made River Project. Much of the construction on this facility has been virtually halted since late 1996. There have been reports, however, that Libya has obtained support from some of the South African scientists who once worked on that country's chemical and biological programs.[956]

The CIA reported in 1999 that Libya remained heavily dependent on foreign suppliers for precursor chemicals and other key CW-related equipment. UN sanctions continued to severely limit that support during the first half of 1998. It also reported, however, that Tripoli had not given up its goal of establishing its own offensive CW capability and continued to pursue an independent production capability for the weapons.[957]

Libyan Biological Programs

Libya ratified the biological weapons convention in 1982, but has long had an interest in biological warfare. During the late 1980s, Libya funded some research into biological weapons and may acquire the capacity to produce limited amounts of such agents using the batch mode at some point during the next few years.[958] It is doubtful that Libya will make rapid progress in the mass production of such agents or the production of effective warheads and bombs, but Libyan chemical weapons production may eventually be joined by the production of biological weapons. There are some reports that it has sought technical support from Russian scientists.[959]

Libyan Nuclear Programs

Libya has made sporadic attempts to fund a nuclear weapon or "Islamic bomb" ever since the mid-1970s. Most of these efforts have done little more than enrich a few foreign advisors, suppliers, and outright con men. In spite of more than fifteen years of effort, there is no evidence that points to any serious Libyan nuclear weapons program.[960]

There are reports that Libya provided the financing for a substantial part of Pakistan's nuclear weapons effort in return for help in acquiring nuclear weapons materiel or weapons. These reports seem to be exaggerated, but Libya did sign some form of nuclear accord with Pakistan in 1973, and seems to have sought help in obtaining hot cell technology and training in order to acquire a capability to extract plutonium from uranium that was irradiated in a reactor. Libya also may have supplied Pakistan with substantial quantities of Yellow Cake between 1976 and 1980, some of which seems to have come from Niger. Further, while Libya reached a formal safeguard arrangement with the IAEA in 1980, it may not have declared all of its stocks to the IAEA. Even so, there are no convincing reports that Pakistan has given Libya serious assistance in its nuclear weapons effort.[961]

Libyan nuclear cooperation with the USSR is better documented, although it seems to have been no more productive. Libya and the USSR signed an agreement in 1975 that called for the USSR to build a small research reactor in Libya, and help set up some form of research center. This agreement resulted in the USSR building a small 10-megawatt reactor at Tajoura, which began operating in 1981 or 1982.[962] Two years later, the USSR agreed to build two 440-megawatt reactors. The USSR has never, however, provided any follow-up to the agreement. The same is true of a French agreement in 1976 to build a 660-megawatt reactor: construction has yet to start.[963]

Libya does seem to have begun to develop its own uranium deposits and sought to acquire the capability to produce uranium tetraflouride. As of 1992, however, both most private experts and US government experts felt that Libya was almost as far away from a nuclear weapons capability as it was in the early 1970s. Further, Libya allowed the IAEA to conduct a limited inspection of its nuclear research center at Tajura, near Tripoli. While Qadhafi is scarcely the most reliable witness on his own intentions, he has also declared that he was not interested in nuclear weapons, and there were no indications confirming reports that he had hired Russian scientists to work on a nuclear weapons effort as of early 1992.[964]

Since that time, UN sanctions have virtually precluded any serious effort.[965] Libya did grudgingly accept the indefinite extension of the NNPT in 1995, but largely because other Arab states convinced Qadhafi that the NNPT was useful as a political lever against Israel. Qadhafi repeated his view that the Arab world should develop nuclear weapons to counter Israel in an interview on January 26, 1997, and has taken the position that Arab states should also develop chemical and biological weapons.[966]

Libyan War Fighting Capability

Libya might be able to supply missiles and chemical weapons to Syria or another Arab power, or carry out token one-way air strikes on Israel or Egypt. However, it is as difficult to take this aspect of Libya's war fighting capabilities seriously as it is to take its conventional war fighting capabilities seriously.

Iran

Iran now has a relatively limited ability to strike Israel with weapons of mass destruction, but this capability will improve steadily in the future. It is acquiring relatively advanced long-range missiles, and is making considerable progress in developing biological and nuclear weapons.[967]

Iranian Delivery Systems

Iran retains some 50 F-4D/Es, has acquired roughly 30 Su-24s, and could easily adapt its 60 F-14s for lob delivery of weapons of mass destruction. It has significant numbers of F-5s and F-7s that could easily be sacrificed in one-way missions or even converted to drone attacks.[968] Iran would have trouble in massing large numbers of aircraft and sustaining high sortie rates, but it could probably mass 20–30 aircraft every few days to deliver significant numbers of chemical weapons against a force that did not have excellent air cover and ground-based air defense. Iran would have no sustainability and command and control problems in using limited numbers of aircraft more selectively to deliver nuclear or biological weapons against rear area, interdiction, or strategic targets. It is at least possible that Iran might adapt some of its tactical strike fighters to act as dedicated delivery systems to deliver a line-source attack with a biological agent.

Iran might commit such aircraft in one-way low-altitude strike profiles with a reasonable probability they could penetrate all but the best prepared air defenses— particularly if Iran is successful in developing an effective refueling capability. Pop-up attacks across the Gulf against coastal targets provide less than 10 minutes' radar warning in many cases, and only countries with an AWACS or aerostat warning system could hope to react unless they had advanced fighters patrolling their coast. Iraq had an extremely poor record of detecting and defending against isolated Iranian attacks on Baghdad during the Iran-Iraq War. The Iranian air force also had considerable success in US-Iranian military exercises during the time of the Shah when it flew extremely low-altitude attack profiles near its Gulf coast, and then suddenly broke out of terrain masking to surprise US Navy and Marine Corps forces. These exercises predate the deployment of the AWACS and Aegis, but indicate Iran might employ such tactics to reduce radar visibility and warning in the future.[969]

It is possible that Iran might use helicopters to deliver chemical and biological weapons, although this would require the forward deployment of the helicopters and weapons to Lebanon, Syria, or possibly Egypt and Jordan. The forward deployment of such systems seems doubtful and it would be difficult for Iran to support. Much of its helicopter force is now incapable of high-intensity combat operations but might well be employed in limited numbers of chemical and biological attacks using the helicopter as a sprayer or in line-source attacks using dry, storable biological agents.

There are, however, some potential advantages. While helicopters are vulnerable and shorter-ranged than strike aircraft, they are almost ideal platforms for medium-range biological attacks—particularly if flown in one-way dedicated attacks. Helicopters provide a high degree of mobility and dispersal and can fly map-of-the-earth profiles at low speeds that make them very difficult to defend against. They can deliver line-source attacks using biological agents, toxins, or persistent nerve gases against enemy rear areas sufficiently upwind to be outside the detection range of SHORAD radars and anti-aircraft weapons. The Iranian air force has about 50 helicopters that could be used in such missions, and the Iranian army could draw on a pool of roughly 100 AH-1s, 40 CH-47s, 130 Bell 214As, and nearly 200 other helicopters. At least some of these helicopters might be modified for drone delivery on one-way missions. None, however, could normally reach Israel.

Iran has used ballistic missiles like the Scud against Iraq. Iran acquired its Scuds in response to Iraq's invasion. Iran fired as many as 14 Scuds in 1985, 8 in 1986, 18 in 1987, and 77 in 1988. Iran fired 77 Scud missiles during a 52-day period in 1988, during what came to be known as the "war of the cities." Sixty-one were fired at Baghdad, nine at Mosul, five at Kirkuk, one at Tikrit, and one at Kuwait. Iran fired as many as five missiles on a single day, and once fired three missiles within 30 minutes. Iran's missile attacks were initially more effective than Iraq's attacks. This was largely a matter of geography. Many of Iraq's major cities were comparatively close to its border with Iran, but Tehran and most of Iran's major cities that had not already been targets in the war were outside the range of Iraqi Scud attacks. Iran's missiles, in contrast, could hit key Iraqi cities like Baghdad. This advantage ended when Iraq deployed extended range Scuds.

Most estimates indicate that Iran now has 6–12 Scud launchers and up to 200 Scud B (R-17E) missiles with 230–310 km range. Some estimates give higher figures. They estimate Iran bought 200–300 Scud Bs from North Korea between 1987 and 1992, and may have continued to buy such missiles after that time. Israeli experts estimate that Iran had at least 250–300 Scud B missiles, and at least 8–15 launchers on hand in 1997. Iran would have to deploy such systems to Syria to use them against Israel, and Syria already has Scud Bs of its own. The real threat Iran would pose in a future Arab-Israeli conflict would come from Iran's longer-range systems.

Iran now has the North Korean missile system, which is often referred to as a "Scud C." Typically, Iran formally denied the fact it had such systems long after the transfer of these missiles became a reality. Hassan Taherian, an Iranian foreign ministry official, stated in February 1995, "There is no missile cooperation between Iran and North Korea whatsoever. We deny this." In fact, a senior North Korean delegation traveled to Tehran to close the deal on November 29, 1990, and met with Mohsen Rezaei, the former commander of the IRGC. Iran either bought the missile then, or placed its order shortly thereafter. North Korea then exported the missile through its Lyongaksan Import Corporation. Iran imported some of these North Korean missile assemblies using its B-747s, and seems to have used ships to import others. In 1999, Iran probably had more than 60 of the same longer-range Scud missiles held by Syria, although some sources report 100 and one source reports 170.[970]

Iran has at least 5–10 Scud C launchers, each with several missiles. This total seems likely to include four new North Korean TELs received in 1995.[971] Iran seems to have set a goal of acquiring several hundred Scud C missiles by the late 1990s, and seems to want a large enough number of launchers to make its missile force highly dispersible.[972] The Scud B, however, lacks the range to reach a target in Israel from any point in Iran. The Scud C might reach some targets from the far western areas of Iran, but it would be marginal in terms of range-payload, particularly with a heavy warhead.

It has begun to test its new North Korean missiles. There are reports it has fired them from mobile launchers at a test site near Qom about 310 miles (500 kilometers) to a target area south of Shahroud. There are also reports that units equipped with such missiles have been deployed as part of Iranian exercises like the Saeqer-3 (Thunderbolt 3) exercise in late October 1993.

The Scud C missile is more advanced than the Scud B, although many aspects of its performance are unclear. North Korea seems to have completed development of the missile in 1987, after obtaining technical support from the People's Republic of China. While it is often called a "Scud C," it seems to differ substantially in detail from the original Soviet Scud B. It seems to be based more on the Chinese-made DF-61 than on a direct copy of the Soviet weapon.

The Scud C has a range of around 500 kilometers (310 miles) with a warhead with a high explosive payload of 700 kilograms, and has relatively good accuracy and reliability. While this payload is limited for a warhead designed for the effective delivery of chemical agents, Iran might modify the warhead to increase payload at the expense of range and restrict the using of chemical munitions to the most lethal agents such as persistent nerve gas. It might also concentrate its development efforts on arming its Scud C forces with more lethal biological agents.

In any case, such missiles have enough range-payload to give Iran the ability to strike at a much wider range of targets, although it still could not reach Israel without deploying forward to another country. The Scud Cs deployed in Iran can cover all targets on the southern coast of the Gulf and all of the populated areas in Iraq, although not all of western Iran. Iran could also reach targets in part of eastern Syria and the eastern third of Turkey, and cover targets in the border area of the former Soviet Union, western Afghanistan, and western Pakistan.

The accuracy and reliability of the Scud C involve major uncertainties, as does its operational CEP. Much would also depend on the precise level of technology Iran deployed in the warhead. Neither Russia nor the People's Republic of China seem to have transferred the warhead technology for biological and chemical weapons to Iran or Iraq when they sold them the Scud B missile and CSS-8. However, North Korea may have sold Iran such technology as part of the Scud C sale. If it did so, such a technology transfer would save Iran years of development and testing in obtaining highly lethal biological and chemical warheads. In fact, Iran would probably be able to deploy far more effective biological and chemical warheads than Iraq had at the time of the Gulf War.

Iran may be working with Syria in some of its development efforts, although Middle Eastern nations rarely cooperate in such sensitive areas. Iran served as a transshipment point for North Korean missile deliveries during 1992 and 1993. Some of this transshipment took place using the same Iranian B-747s that brought missile parts to Iran. Others moved by sea. For example, a North Korean vessel called the *Des Hung Ho*, bringing missile parts for Syria, docked at Bandar Abbas in May 1992. Iran then flew these parts to Syria. An Iranian ship coming from North Korea and a second North Korean ship followed, carrying missiles and machine tools for both Syria and Iran. At least 20 of the North Korean missiles have gone to Syria from Iran, and production equipment seems to have been transferred to Iran and to Syrian plants near Hama and Aleppo.

It is Iran's new missile developments which are most threatening in the case of an Arab-Israeli conflict. Iran is developing its own longer-range variants of the Scud C and No-Dong for indigenous production. It is using the technology developed for the North Korean Tapeo Dong as a technical base for a missile called the Shahab-3, and is using substantial Russian and some Chinese aid to develop even longer-range systems.

Iran can now assemble Scud B and Scud C missiles using foreign-made components. It may soon be able to make entire missile systems and warhead packages in Iran. Iran is developing an indigenous missile production capability with both solid and liquid fueled missiles, and seems to be seeking capability to produce MRBMs. The present scale of Iran's production and assembly efforts is unclear. Iran seems to have a design center, at least two rocket and missile assembly plants, a missile test range and monitoring complex, and a wide range of smaller design and refit facilities. The design center is said to be located at the Defense Technology and Science Research Center, which is a branch of Iran's Defense Industry Organization located outside Karaj, near Tehran. This center directs a number of other research efforts. Some experts believe it has support from Russian and Chinese scientists.

Iran's largest missile assembly and production plant is said to be a North Korean–built facility near Isfahan, although this plant may use Chinese equipment and technology. There are no confirmations of these reports, but this region is the center of much of Iran's advanced defense industry, including plants for munitions, tank overhaul, and helicopter and fixed wing aircraft maintenance. Some reports say the local industrial complex can produce liquid fuels and missile parts from a local steel mill. A second missile plant is said to be located 175 kilometers east of Tehran, near Semnan. Some sources indicate this plant is Chinese-built and began rocket production as early as 1987. It is supposed to be able to build 600–1,000 Oghab rockets per year, if Iran can import key ingredients for solid fuel motors like ammonium perchlorate. The plant is also supposed to produce the Iran-130.

Another facility may exist near Bandar Abbas for the assembly of the Seer-sucker. China is said to have built this facility in 1987, and is believed to be helping the naval branch of the Guards to modify the Seersucker to extend its range to 400 kilometers. It is possible that China is also helping Iran develop solid fuel rocket motors and produce or assemble missiles like the C-801 and C-802. There have, however, been reports that Iran is developing extended range Scuds with the support of Russian experts, as well as a missile called the Tondar 68, with a range of 700 kilometers. Still other reports claim that Iran has split its manufacturing facilities into plants near Pairzan, Seman, Shiraz, Maghdad, and Islaker. These reports indicate that the companies involved in building the Scuds are also involved in Iran's production of poison gas and include Defense Industries, Shahid, Bagheri Industrial Group, and Shahid Hemat Industrial Group. Iran's main missile test range is said to be further east, near Shahroud, along the Tehran-Mashhad railway. A telemetry station is supposed to be 350 kilometers to the south at Taba, along the Mashhad-Isfahan road. All of these facilities are reportedly under the control of the Islamic Revolutionary Guards Corps.

Iran has already begun advanced development testing of the Shahab-3, which is reported to have a range of 1,300–1,500 kilometers (800–930 miles) and a 1,650-pound warhead. Reports differ sharply on its size. *Jane's* estimates a launch weight up to 16,000 kilograms, based on the assumption that the Shahab system is derived from the No Dong. It could have a launch weight of 15,000 kilograms, a payload of 600 kilograms, and a range of 1,700–1,800 kilometers if it is based on a system similar to the Chinese CSS-5 (DF-21) and CSS-N3 ((JL-1). These systems entered service in 1983 and 1987.

Later reports and tests have provided more details on the Shahab system. Some US experts believe that Iran tested booster engines in 1997 capable of driving a missile in the range of 1,500 kilometers. Virtually all US experts believe that Iran is rapidly approaching the point where it will be able to manufacture missiles with much longer ranges than the Scud B. It is less clear when Iran will be able to bring such programs to the final development stage, carry out suitable test firings, develop effective warheads, and deploy actual units. Much still depends on the level of foreign assistance.

Eitan Ben Eliyahu, the commander of the Israeli Air Force, reported on April 14, 1997 that Iran had tested a missile capable of reaching Israel. The background briefings to his statement implied that Russia was assisting Iran in developing two missiles, with ranges of 620 and 780 miles. Follow-up intelligence briefings that Israel provided in September 1997 indicated that Russia was helping Iran develop four missiles. US intelligence reports indicate that China has also been helping Iran with some aspects of these missile efforts. These missiles included the Shahab ("meteor") missiles, with performance similar to those previously identified with Iranian missiles adapted from North Korean designs. Israel claimed the Shahab might be ready for deployment as early as 1999.

Iran openly tested the Shahab-3 on July 21, 1998, claiming that it was a defensive action to deal with potential threats from Israel. The missile flew for a distance of up to 620 miles before it exploded about 100 seconds after launch. US intelligence sources could not confirm whether the explosion was deliberate, but indicated that the final system might have a range of 800–940 miles (a maximum of 1,240 kilometers), depending on its payload. The test confirmed the fact the missile was a liquid fueled system.

Gen. Mohammad Bagher Qalibaf, head of the Islamic Revolutionary Guards Corps' air wing publicly reported on August 2, 1998 that the Shahab-3 is a 53-foot-long ballistic missile that can travel at 4,300 mph and carry a one-ton warhead at an altitude of nearly 82,000 feet. He claimed that the weapon was guided by an Iranian-made system that gives it great accuracy: "The final test of every weapon is in a real war situation but, given its warhead and size, the Shahab-3 is a very accurate weapon." Other Iranian sources reported that the missile had a range of 800 miles.

President Mohammad Khatami stated on August 1, 1998 that Iran was determined to continue to strengthen its armed forces, regardless of international concerns: "Iran will not seek permission from anyone for strengthening its defense capability." Martin Indyck, the US Assistant Secretary for Near East Affairs testified on July 28, 1998 that the US estimated that the system needed further refinement but might be deployed in its initial operational form between September 1998 and March 1999.

Iran publicly displayed the Shahab-3 on its launcher during a parade on September 25, 1998. The missile carrier bore signs saying, "The US can do nothing" and "Israel would be wiped from the map." There are some reports of a Shahab-3B missile with extended range and a larger booster. The resulting system seems to be close to both the No-Dong and Pakistani Ghauri or Haff-5 missile, first tested in April 1998, raising questions about Iranian-North Korean-Pakistani cooperation.

The CIA reported in 1999 that Russia and China continued to supply missile-related goods and technology to Iran. It reported that Iran used these goods and technologies to achieve its goal of becoming self-sufficient in the production of MRBMs, and that the July 1998 flight test of the Shahab-3 MRBM demonstrated the success Iran had achieved in realizing that goal. Iran already is producing Scud SRBMs with North Korean help and has begun production of the Shahab-3. In addition, the CIA stated that Iran's Defense Minister had publicly acknowledged the development of the Shahab-4 ballistic missile, with a "longer range and heavier payload than the 1,300-km Shahab-3."[973]

Iran announced on July 15, 2000 that it had successfully test-fired an upgraded version of its medium-range Shahab missile. An Iranian defence ministry source was quoted by state media as saying that the missile was test-fired to ensure it conforms to the latest technological standards. It was first tested in 1998. "This missile is part of our program for the defence industry and it would in no way threaten other countries." The Iranian announcement stated that the Shahab-3 was a ballistic missile, with a range of 800 miles, and could travel at a speed of 4,320 mph with a 1-ton warhead.

US experts indicated that they estimated the missile had a range of 1,300 km (800 miles), making it capable of hitting Israel, and that the Shahab-3 was modeled mainly on North Korea's No dong-1, but has been improved with Russian technology. Iran's Defence Minister, Admiral Ali Shamkhani, has said a larger missile, Shahab-4, was in production as a vehicle for launching satellites into space.[974] US officials agree that Iran is considering developing a rocket that can put satellites in orbit, but note that the development of such a booster would give Iran significantly enhanced capabilities to develop an intercontinental ballistic missile.[975] US Defense Department spokesman Ken Bacon stated that, "From everything we can tell, it was a successful firing. It is another sign they are determined to build longer-range weapons of mass destruction."[976]

Israel expressed its own concerns. Amos Yaron, director-general of the Defense Ministry, told Israeli Radio that, "We are looking at this matter for the moment with some concern because in any event they have the ability. We don't believe they have any intention whatsoever to attack the state of Israel for the moment . . . . It must be remembered that Iran developed these capabilities as a result of the lessons they had from the wars of the past, which is to say from its big war against Iraq. Iran didn't develop this missile against the state of Israel . . . . Now the Iranians have this ability. Between the ability and the intention, there is a great distance." A senior Israeli military source did predict, however, that by 2005, Iran would, with Russian help, achieve a military nuclear capability. Israel's army chief, Lieutenant-General Shaul Mofaz, told Israeli Radio that the combined development of the missile and a non-conventional capacity posed a threat not only to Israel, but also to any country within range of the missile.[977]

Iran's foreign minister Kamal Kharraz responded by stating that, "as it was announced before, the test was done to boost the country's defensive capability and as a deterring force. It looks like America and Israel are using Iran's efforts to boost its defensive capability, which are its natural and legitimate right, as a scapegoat to secure the budget to race for arms . . . Who says Israel has the right to be equipped with all kinds of offensive arms, including weapons of mass destruction, but other countries in the region should not even have defensive weapons? The propaganda against Iran is aimed at deflecting world concerns over the US missile shield."[978]

There are convincing reports that Iran is using Russian technology to develop a long-range missile with ranges from 2,000 to 6,250 kilometers. One of these is the Shahab-4, which is said to have improved guidance components, a range of up to 2,000 kilometers (1,240 miles), a warhead of up to 2,200 pounds, and a CEP of around 2,400 meters. Some estimates indicate that this system could be operational in 2–5 years. US Assistant Secretary for Near East Affairs testified on July 28, 1998, that the US estimated that the system still needed added foreign assistance to improve its motors and guidance system. These programs have had support from Russian, North Korean, and Chinese firms and technicians.[979] Shahab-3s based in launch sites near Iran's western border could reach any target in Israel. Shahab-4s could reach any target in Israel and most targets in Egypt from anywhere in Iran.[980]

Some reports indicate that the Shahab-4 is based on the Soviet SS-4 missile. Others say that there is a longer-range Shahab-5, based on the SS-4 or Taepo Dong missile. Reports saying the Shahab-4 is based on the SS-4 say it has a range of up to 4,000 kilometers and a payload in excess of one ton. Iran may have two other missile programs which include longer-range systems, variously reported as having maximum ranges of 3,650, 4,500–5,000, 6,250, or 10,000 kilometers.

It seems clear that Iran has obtained some of the technology and design details of the Russian SS-4. The SS-4 (also known as the R-12 or "Sandal") is an aging Russian liquid fuel design that first went into service in 1959 and which was supposedly destroyed as part of the IRBM Treaty. It is a very large missile, with technology dating back to the early 1950s, although it was evidently updated at least twice during the period between 1959 and 1980. It has a CEP of 2–4 kilometers and a maximum range of 2,000 kilometers, which means it can only be lethal with a nuclear warhead or a biological weapon with near-nuclear lethality.

At the same time, the SS-4's overall technology is relatively simple and it has a throw weight of nearly 1,400 kilograms (3,000 pounds). It is one of the few missile designs that a nation with a limited technology base could hope to manufacture or adapt, and its throw weight and range would allow Iran to use a relatively unsophisticated nuclear device or biological warhead. As a result, an updated version of the SS-4 might be a suitable design for a developing country.

Russia has been a key supplier of missile technology even though it agreed in 1994 that it would adhere to the terms of the Missile Technology Control Regime and would place suitable limits on the sale or transfer of rocket engines and technology. Nevertheless, the CIA has identified Russia as a leading source of Iranian missile technology, and the State Department has indicated that President Clinton expressed US concerns over this cooperation to President Yeltsin. This transfer is one reason the President appointed former Ambassador Frank Wisner, and then Robert Galluci, as his special representatives to try to persuade Russia to put a firm halt to aid support of Iran.

Iran's missile programs are reported to have continuing support from North Korea, and from Russian and Chinese firms and technicians. One such Chinese firm is Great Wall Industries. The Russian firms include the Russian Central Aerohydrodynamic Institute, which has provided Iran's Shahid Hemmat Industrial Group (SHIG) with wind tunnels for missile design, equipment for manufacturing missile models, and the software for testing launch and reentry performance. They may also include Rosvoorouzhenie, a major Russian arms-export agency; NPO Trud, a rocket motor manufacturer; a leading research center called the Bauman Institute; and Polyus (Northstar), a major laser test and manufacturing equipment firm.

Some sources have indicated that Russian military industries have signed contracts with Iran to help produce liquid fueled missiles and provide specialized wind tunnels, manufacture model missiles, and develop specialized computer software. For example, these reports indicate that the Russian Central Aerohydrodynamic Institute is cooperating with Iran's Defense Industries Organization (DIO) and the DIO's Shahid Hemmat Industrial Group (SHIG). The

Russian State Corporation for Export and Import or Armament and Military Equipment (Rosvoorouzhenie) and Infor are also reportedly involved in deals with the SHIG. These deals are also said to include specialized laser equipment, mirrors, tungsten-coat graphite material, and miraging steel for missile development and production. They could play a major role in helping Iran develop long-range versions of the Scud B and C, and more accurate variations of a missile similar to the No Dong.

The Israeli press reported in August 1997 that Israel had evidence that Iran was receiving Russian support. In September 1997, Israel urged the US to step up its pressure on Iran, and leaked reports indicating that private and state-owned Russian firms had provided gyroscopes, electronic components, wind tunnels, guidance and propulsion systems, and the components needed to build such systems to Iran. President Yeltsin and the Russian Foreign Ministry initially categorically denied that such charges were true. Following a meeting with Vice President Gore, President Yeltsin stated on September 26, 1997 that, "We are being accused of supplying Iran with nuclear or ballistic missile technologies. There is nothing further from the truth. I again and again categorically deny such rumors."

Russia agreed, however, that Ambassador Wisner and Yuri Koptyev, the head of the Russian space program, should jointly examine the US intelligence and draft a report on Russian transfers to Iran. This report reached a very different conclusion from President Yeltsin saying that Russia had provided such aid to Iran. Further, on October 1, 1997—roughly a week after Yeltsin issued his denial—the Russian security service issued a statement that it had "thwarted" an Iranian attempt to have parts for liquid fuel rocket motors manufactured in Russia, disguised as gas compressors and pumps.

Russian firms said to be helping Iran included the Russian Central Aerohydrodynamic Institute which developed a special wind tunnel, Rosvoorouzhenie, Kutznetzov (formerly NPO Trud), the Bauman National Technical University in Moscow, the Tsagi Research Institute for rocket propulsion development, and the Polyus (Northstar) Research Institute in Moscow. Iranians were also found to be studying rocket engineering at the Baltic State University in St. Petersburg and the Bauman State University.

The result was a new and often tense set of conversations between the US and Russia in January 1998. The US again sent Ambassador Frank Wisner to Moscow, Vice President Gore called Prime Minister Viktor Chernomyrdin, and Secretary of State Madeleine Albright made an indirect threat that the Congress might apply sanctions. Sergi Yastrzhembsky, a Kremlin spokesman, initially responded by denying that any transfer of technology had taken place.

This Russian denial was too categorical to have much credibility. Russia had previously announced the arrest of an Iranian diplomat on November 14, 1997 that it caught attempting to buy missile technology. The Iranian was seeking to buy blueprints and recruit Russian scientists to go to Iran. Yuri Koptev, the head of the Russian Space Agency, explained this, however, by stating that, "There have been several cases where some Russian organizations, desperately struggling to make ends meet and lacking responsibility, have embarked on some ambiguous projects...they were stopped long before they got to the point where any technology got out."

The end result of these talks was an agreement by Gore and Chernomyrdin to strengthen controls over technology transfer, but it was scarcely clear that it put an end to the problem. Conditions in Russia are getting worse, not better, and the desperation that drives sales has scarcely diminished. Prime Minister Chernomyrdin again promised to strengthen his efforts to restrict technology transfer to Iran in a meeting with Gore on March 12, 1998. The US informed Russia of 13 cases of possible Russian aid to Iran at the meeting and offered to increase the number of Russian commercial satellite launches it would license for US firms as an incentive.

Even so, new arrests of smugglers took place on April 9, 1998. The smugglers had attempted to ship 22 tons of specialized steel to Iran via Azerbaijan, using several Russian shell corporations as a cover. On April 16, 1998, the State Department declared 20 Russian agencies and research facilities were ineligible to receive US aid because of their role in transferring missile technology to Iran.

This level of technology transfer has led some US intelligence analysts to estimate that Iran may acquire missiles with ICBM-like ranges in the mid term.[981] The estimate stated that Iran is a hostile country most able to test an ICBM capable of delivering a weapon to the United States during the next 15 years. It summarized the US intelligence analysis as follows:

- Iran *could test* an ICBM that could deliver a several-hundred kilogram payload to many parts of the United States in the latter half of the next decade, using Russian technology and assistance.

- Iran *could pursue* a Taepo Dong-type ICBM. Most analysts believe it could test a three-stage ICBM patterned after the Taepo Dong-1 SLV or a three-stage Taepo Dong-2-type ICBM, possibly with North Korean assistance, in the next few years.

- Iran is *likely to test* an SLV by 2010 that—once developed—could be converted into an ICBM capable of delivering a several-hundred kilogram payload to the United States.

- Analysts differ on the likely timing of Iran's first flight test of an ICBM that could threaten the United States. Assessments include:

  - likely before 2010 and very likely before 2015 (noting that an SLV with ICBM capabilities will probably be tested within the next few years);
  - no more than an even chance by 2010 and a better than even chance by 2015;
  - and less than an even chance by 2015.

Iran has also acquired much of the technology necessary to build long-range cruise missile systems from China. The CIA reported in June 1997 that Iran obtained major new transfers of new long-range missile technology from Russian and Chinese firms during 1996. Since that time, there have been many additional reports of technology transfers from Russia. There have been past reports that Iran placed orders for PRC-made M-9 (CSS-6/DF-15) missile (280–620 kilometers range, launch weight of 6,000 kilograms). It is more likely, however, that PRC firms are giving assistance in developing indigenous missile R&D and production facilities for the production of an Iranian solid fueled missile. The US offered to provide China with added missile technology if it would agree to fully implement an end of technology transfer to Iran and Pakistan during meetings in Beijing on March 25–26, 1998.

Iran also has shorter missile range systems. In 1990, Iran bought CSS-8 surface-to-surface missiles (converted SA-2s) from China with ranges of 130–150 kilometers. It also has Chinese sea- and land-based anti-ship cruise missiles. Iran fired 10 such missiles at Kuwait during the Iran-Iraq war, hitting one US-flagged tanker. Such missiles would cost only 10% to 25% as much as ballistic missiles of similar range, and both the HY-2 Seersucker and CS-802 could be modified relatively quickly for land attacks against area targets.

Iran reported in December 1995 that it had already fired a domestically built anti-ship missile called the Saeqe-4 (Thunderbolt) during exercises in the Strait of Hormuz and Gulf of Oman. Other reports indicate that China is helping Iran build copies of the Chinese CS-801/CS-802 and the Chinese FL-2 or F-7 anti-ship cruise missiles. These missiles have relatively limited range. The range of the C-801 is 8–40 kilometers, the range of the CS-802 is 15–120 kilometers, the maximum range of the F-7 is 30 kilometers, and the maximum range of the FL-10 is 50 kilometers. Even a range of 120 kilometers would barely cover targets in the Southern Gulf from launch points on Iran's Gulf coast. These missiles also have relatively small high explosive warheads. As a result, Iran may well be seeking anti-ship capabilities, rather than platforms for delivering weapons of mass destruction.

A platform like the C-802 might, however, provide enough design data to develop a scaled-up, longer-range cruise missile for other purposes, and the Gulf is a relatively small area where most urban areas and critical facilities are near the coast. Aircraft or ships could launch cruise missiles with chemical or biological warheads from outside the normal defense perimeter of the Southern Gulf states, and it is at least possible that Iran might modify anti-ship missiles with chemical weapons to attack tankers—ships which are too large for most regular anti-ship missiles to be highly lethal.

Building an entire cruise missile would be more difficult. The technology for fusing CBW and cluster warheads would be within Iran's grasp. Navigation systems and jet engines, however, would still be a major potential problem. Current inertial navigation systems (INS) would introduce errors of at least several kilometers at ranges of 1,000 kilometers and would carry a severe risk of total guidance failure—probably exceeding two-thirds of the missiles fired. A differential global positioning system (GPS) integrated with the inertial navigation system (INS) and a radar altimeter, however, might produce an accuracy of 15 meters.

Some existing remotely piloted vehicles (UAVs), such as the South African Skua, claim such performance. Commercial technology is becoming available for differential global positioning system (GPS) guidance with accuracies of 2 to 5 meters.

There are commercially available reciprocating and gas turbine engines that Iran could adapt for use in a cruise missile, although finding a reliable and efficient turbofan engine for a specific design application might be difficult. An extremely efficient engine would have to be matched to a specific airframe. It is doubtful that Iran could design and build such an engine, but there are over 20 other countries with the necessary design and manufacturing skills. While airframe-engine-warhead integration and testing would present a challenge and might be beyond Iran's manufacturing skills, it is inherently easier to integrate and test a cruise missile than a long-range ballistic missile. Further, such developments would be far less detectable than developing a ballistic system if the program used coded or low-altitude directional telemetry.

Iran could bypass much of the problems inherent in developing its own cruise missile by modifying the HY-2 Seersucker for use as a land attack weapon and extending its range beyond 80 kilometers, or by modifying and improving the CS-801 (Ying Jai-1) anti-ship missile. There are reports that the Revolutionary Guards are working on such developments at a facility near Bandar Abbas.

Iran has made several indigenous long-range rockets that could carry CBW warheads and that might be transferred to the Hizbollah or brought into the Arab-Israeli theater. These include:

- The Iran-130, or Nazeat, since the end of the Iran-Iraq War. The full details of this system remain unclear, but it seems to use commercially available components, a solid fuel rocket, and a simple inertial guidance system to reach ranges of about 90–120 kilometers. It is 355 mm in diameter, 5.9 meters long, weighs 950 kilograms, and has a 150-kilogram warhead. It seems to have poor reliability and accuracy, and its payload only seems to be several hundred kilograms.

- The Shahin 2 has a 355-mm diameter, but is only 3.87 meters long, and weighs only 580 kilograms. It evidently can be equipped with three types of warheads: A 180-kilogram high explosive warhead, another warhead using high explosive submunitions, and a warhead that uses chemical weapons.

- Iranian Oghab (Eagle) rocket with 40+ kilometers range.

- New SSM with 125-mile range may be in production, but could be modified FROG.

A US examination of Iran's dispersal, sheltering, and hardening programs for its anti-ship missiles and other missile systems indicate that Iran has developed effective programs to ensure that they would survive a limited number of air strikes and that Iran had reason to believe that the limited number of preemptive strikes Israel could conduct against targets in the lower Gulf could not be effective in denying Iran the capability to deploy its missiles.

Iranian Chemical Warfare Capabilities

A CIA report in August 2000 summarized the state of proliferation in Iran as follows:[982]

Iran remains one of the most active countries seeking to acquire WMD and ACW technology from abroad. In doing so, Tehran is attempting to develop an indigenous capability to produce various types of weapons—nuclear, chemical, and biological—and their delivery systems. During the reporting period, the evidence indicates increased reflections of Iranian efforts to acquire WMD- and ACW-related equipment, materials, and technology primarily on entities in Russia, China, North Korea and Western Europe.

For the second half of 1999, entities in Russia, North Korea, and China continued to supply the largest amount of ballistic missile–related goods, technology, and expertise to Iran. Tehran is using this assistance to support current production programs and to achieve its goal of becoming self-sufficient in the production of ballistic missiles. Iran already is producing Scud short-range ballistic missiles (SRBMs) and has built and publicly displayed prototypes for the Shahab-3 medium-range ballistic missile (MRBM), which had its initial flight test in July 1998. In addition, Iran's Defense Minister last year publicly acknowledged the development of the Shahab-4, originally calling it a more capable ballistic missile than the Shahab-3, but later categorizing it as solely a space launch vehicle with no military applications. Iran's Defense Minister also has publicly mentioned plans for a "Shahab-5." Such statements, made against the backdrop of sustained cooperation with Russian, North Korean, and Chinese entities, strongly suggest that Tehran intends to develop a longer-range ballistic missile capability in the near future.

For the reporting period, Tehran expanded its efforts to seek considerable dual-use biotechnical materials, equipment, and expertise from abroad—primarily from entities in Russia and Western Europe—ostensibly for civilian uses. Iran began a biological warfare (BW) program during the Iran-Iraq war, and it may have some limited capability for BW deployment. Outside assistance is both important and difficult to prevent, given the dual-use nature of the materials, the equipment being sought, and the many legitimate end uses for these items.

Iran, a Chemical Weapons Convention (CWC) party, already has manufactured and stockpiled chemical weapons, including blister, blood, and choking agents and the bombs and artillery shells for delivering them. During the second half of 1999, Tehran continued to seek production technology, training, expertise, and chemicals that could be used as precursor agents in its chemical warfare (CW) program from entities in Russia and China. It also acquired or attempted to acquire indirectly through intermediaries in other countries equipment and material that could be used to create a more advanced and self-sufficient CW infrastructure.

Iran sought nuclear-related equipment, material, and technical expertise from a variety of sources, especially in Russia, during the second half of 1999. Work continues on the construction of a 1,000-megawatt nuclear power reactor in Bushehr, Iran, that will be subject to International Atomic Energy Agency (IAEA) safeguards. In addition, Russian entities continued to interact with Iranian research centers on various activities. These projects will help Iran augment its nuclear technology infrastructure, which in turn would be useful in supporting nuclear weapons research and development. The expertise and technology gained, along with the commercial channels and contacts established—even from cooperation that appears strictly civilian in nature—could be used to advance Iran's nuclear weapons research and developmental program.

Beginning in January 1998, the Russian Government took a number of steps to increase its oversight of entities involved in dealings with Iran and other states of proliferation concern. In 1999, it pushed a new export control law through the Duma. Russian firms, however, faced economic pressures to circumvent these controls and did so in some cases. The Russian Government, moreover, failed in some cases regarding Iran to enforce its export controls. Following repeated warnings, the US Government in January 1998 and January 1999 imposed administrative measures against Russian entities that had engaged in nuclear- and missile-related cooperation with Iran. The measures imposed on these and other Russian entities (which were penalized in 1998) remain in effect, although sanctions against two entities—Polyus and Inor—are being lifted.

China pledged in October 1997 not to engage in any new nuclear cooperation with Iran but said it would complete cooperation on two ongoing nuclear projects, a small research reactor and a zirconium production facility at Esfahan that Iran will use to produce cladding for reactor fuel. The pledge appears to be holding. As a party to the Nuclear Nonproliferation Treaty (NPT), Iran is required to apply IAEA safeguards to nuclear fuel, but safeguards are not required for the zirconium plant or its products.

Iran claims that it is attempting to establish a complete nuclear fuel cycle for its civilian energy program. In that guise, it seeks to obtain whole facilities, such as a uranium conversion facility, that, in fact, could be used in any number of ways in support of efforts to produce fissile material needed for a nuclear weapon. Despite international efforts to curtail the flow of critical technologies and equipment, Tehran continues to seek fissile material and technology for weapons development and has set up an elaborate system of military and civilian organizations to support its effort.

On the ACW side, Iran (which has acknowledged a need for Western military equipment and spare parts) continues to acquire Western equipment, such as attack helicopters, but also is developing indigenous production capabilities with assistance from countries such as Russia, China, and North Korea. Indigenous efforts involve such systems as tanks, TOW missiles, fighter aircraft, Chinese-designed SAMs and anti-ship missiles, and attack helicopters.

. . . Russian entities (have) continued to supply a variety of ballistic missile–related goods and technical know-how to countries such as Iran, India, and Libya. Iran's earlier success in gaining technology and materials from Russian entities accelerated Iranian development of the Shahab-3 MRBM, which was first flight-tested in July 1998. Russian entities during the second six months of 1999 have provided substantial missile-related technology, training, and expertise to Iran that almost certainly will continue to accelerate Iranian efforts to develop new ballistic missile systems.

During the second half of 1999, Russia also remained a key supplier for civilian nuclear programs in Iran, primarily focused on the Bushehr Nuclear Power Plant project. With respect to Iran's nuclear infrastructure, Russian assistance enhances Iran's ability to support a nuclear weapons development effort. By its very nature, even the transfer of civilian technology may be of use in Iran's nuclear weapons program. We remain concerned that Tehran is seeking more than a buildup of its civilian infrastructure, and the IC will be closely monitoring the relationship with Moscow for any direct assistance in support of a military program. In addition, Russia supplied India with material for its civilian nuclear program during this reporting period.

Russian entities remain a significant source of biotechnology and chemicals for Iran. Russia's world-leading expertise in biological and chemical weapons would make it an attractive target for Iranians seeking technical information and training on BW and CW agent production processes. Russia (along with its sister republics in the FSU) also remains an important source of conventional weapons and spare parts for Iran, which is seeking to upgrade and replace its existing conventional weapons inventories.

Following intense and continuing engagement with the US, Russian officials took some positive steps to strengthen the legal basis of export controls. President Yeltsin in July 1999 signed a federal export control law, which formally makes WMD-related transfers a violation of law and codifies several existing decrees—including catch-all controls—yet may lessen punishment for violators. Russian export enforcement and prosecution still remains weak, however. The export law is still awaiting completion of implementing decrees and its legal status is unclear. Public comments by the head of Russia's security council indicate that Russia obtained only three convictions for export control violations involving WMD and missile technology during 1998–99.

Nonetheless, the Russian government's commitment, willingness, and ability to curb proliferation-related transfers remain uncertain. Moreover, economic conditions in Russia continued to deteriorate, putting more pressure on Russian entities to circumvent export controls. Despite some examples of restraint, Russian businesses continue to be major suppliers of WMD equipment, materials, and technology to Iran. Specifically, Russia continues to provide Iran with nuclear technology that could be applied to Iran's weapons program. Monitoring Russian proliferation behavior, therefore, will remain a very high priority.

Throughout the second half of 1999, North Korea continued to export significant ballistic missile–related equipment and missile components, materials, and technical expertise to countries in the Middle East, South Asia, and North Africa. P'yongyang attaches a high priority to the development and sale of ballistic missiles, equipment, and related technology. Exports of ballistic missiles and related technology are one of the North's major sources of hard currency, which fuel continued missile development and production.

. . . Chinese missile-related technical assistance to Pakistan increased during this reporting period. In addition, firms in China provided missile-related items, raw materials, and/or assistance to several countries of proliferation concern—such as Iran, North Korea, and Libya. . . . China's 1997 pledge not to engage in any new nuclear cooperation with Iran has apparently held, but work associated with two remaining nuclear projects—a small research reactor and a zirconium production facility—continues. The Intelligence Community will continue to monitor carefully Chinese nuclear cooperation with Iran.

Prior to the reporting period, Chinese firms had supplied CW-related production equipment and technology to Iran. The US sanctions imposed in May 1997 on seven Chinese entities for knowingly and materially contributing to Iran's CW program remain in effect. Evidence during the current reporting period suggests Iran continues to seek such assistance from Chinese entities, but it is unclear to what extent these efforts have succeeded. In June 1998, China announced that it had expanded its chemical export controls to include 10 of the 20 Australia Group chemicals not listed on the CWC schedules.

Similarly, an analysis by the US National Intelligence Council of the missile threat during the period from 2000–2015 stated that:[983]

Iran sees its short- and medium-range missiles as deterrents, as force-multiplying weapons of war, primarily with conventional warheads, and as options for delivering biological, chemical, and eventually nuclear weapons. Iran could test an IRBM or land-attack cruise missile by 2004 and perhaps even an ICBM or space launch vehicle as early as 2001.

British, German, and US experts believe that Iran now has stockpiles of between several hundred and 2,000 tons of various lethal chemical agents. They believe that Iran has chemical warheads for its 155-mm artillery shells, 122-mm rockets, bombs, and mines, and may have chemical warheads for some of its longer-range rockets and guided missiles. It also may have a chemical package for its 2006 UAV, although this report is doubtful. There are reports that Iran has deployed chemical weapons on some of its ships. Israeli experts have claimed that Iran is already stockpiling nerve gas weapons.[984]

Iran purchased large amounts of chemical defense gear from the mid-1980s onwards. It also obtained stocks of non-lethal CS gas, although it quickly found such agents had very limited military impact since they could only be used effectively in closed areas or very small open areas. Acquiring poisonous chemical agents was more difficult. Iran did not have any internal capacity to manufacture poisonous chemical agents when Iraq first launched its attacks with such weapons. While Iran seems to have made limited use of chemical mortar and artillery rounds as early as 1985, and possibly as early as 1984, these rounds were almost certainly captured from Iraq.

Iran had to covertly import the necessary equipment and supplies, and it took several years to get substantial amounts of production equipment and the necessary feedstocks. Iran sought aid from European firms like Lurgi to produce large "pesticide" plants, and began to try to obtain the needed feedstock from a wide range of sources, relying heavily on its embassy in Bonn to manage the necessary deals. While Lurgi did not provide the pesticide plant Iran sought, Iran did obtain substantial support from other European firms and feedstocks from many other Western sources.

By 1986–1987, Iran developed the capability to produce enough lethal agents to load its own weapons. The Director of the CIA, and informed observers in the Gulf, made it clear that Iran could produce blood agents like hydrogen cyanide, phosgene gas, and/or chlorine gas. Iran was also able to weaponize limited quantities of blister (sulfur mustard) and blood (cyanide) agents beginning in 1987, and had some capability to weaponize phosgene gas, and/or chlorine gas. These chemical agents were produced in small batches, and evidently under laboratory scale conditions, which enabled Iran to load small numbers of weapons before any of its new major production plants went into full operation. These gas agents were loaded into bombs and artillery shells, and were used sporadically against Iraq in 1987 and 1988.

Reports regarding Iran's production and research facilities are highly uncertain. Iran seems to have completed a major poison gas plant at Qazvin, about 150 kilometers west of Tehran. This plant was reportedly completed between November 1987 and January 1988. While supposedly a pesticide plant, the facility's true purpose seems to have been poison gas production using organophosphorous compounds. It is impossible to trace all the sources of the major components and technology Iran used in its chemical weapons program during this period. Mujahideen sources claim Iran also set up a chemical bomb and warhead plant operated by the Zakaria Al-Razi chemical company near Mahshar in southern Iran, but it is unclear whether these reports are true.

Reports that Iran had chemical weapons plants at Damghan and Parchin that began operation as early as March 1988, and may have begun to test fire Scuds with chemical warheads as early as 1988–1989, are equally uncertain. Iran established at least one large research and development center under the control of the Engineering Research Centre of the Construction Crusade (Jhad e-Sazandegi), and had established a significant chemical weapons production capability by mid-1989.

Debates took place in the Iranian parliament or Majlis in late 1988 over the safety of Pasdaran gas plants located near Iranian towns, and that Rafsanjani described chemical weapons as follows: "Chemical and biological weapons are poor man's atomic bombs and can easily be produced. We should at least consider them for our defense. Although the use of such weapons is inhuman, the war taught us that international laws are only scraps of paper."

Post Iran-Iraq War estimates of Iran chemical weapons production are extremely uncertain. US experts believe Iran was beginning to produce significant mustard gas and nerve gas by the time of the August 1988 cease-fire in the Iran-Iraq War, although its use of chemical weapons remained limited and had little impact on the fighting. Iran's efforts to equip plants to produce V-agent nerve gases seem to have been delayed by US, British, and German efforts to limit technology transfers to Iran, but Iran may have acquired the capability to produce persistent nerve gas during the mid-1990s. Production of nerve gas weapons started no later than 1994. Iran began to stockpile cyanide (cyanogen chloride), phosgene, and mustard gas weapons after 1985. Recent CIA testimony indicates that production capacity may approach 1,000 tons annually.

Iran is seeking to buy more advanced chemical defense equipment, and has sought to buy specialized equipment on the world market to develop indigenous capability to produce advanced feedstocks for nerve weapons. CIA sources indicated in late 1996, that China might have supplied Iran with up to 400 tons of chemicals for the production of nerve gas. One report indicated in 1996, that Iran obtained 400 metric tons of chemicals for use in nerve gas weapons from China—including carbon sulfide.

Another report indicated that China supplied Iran with roughly two tons of calcium-hypochlorate in 1996, and loaded another 40,000 barrels in January or February of 1997. Calcium-hypochlorate is used for decontamination in chemical warfare. Iran placed several significant orders from China that were not delivered. Razak Industries in Tehran, and Chemical and Pharmaceutical Industries in Tabriz ordered 49 metric tons of alkyl dimethylamine, a chemical used in making detergents, and 17 tons of sodium sulfide, a chemical used in making mustard gas. The orders were never delivered, but they were brokered by Iran's International Movalled Industries Corporation (Imaco) and China's North Chemical Industries Co. (Nocinco). Both brokers have been linked to other transactions affecting Iran's chemical weapons program since early 1995, and Nocinco has supplied Iran with several hundred tons of carbon disulfide, a chemical used in nerve gas. Another Chinese firm, only publicly identified as Q. Chen, seems to have supplied glass vessels for chemical weapons.

The US imposed sanctions on seven Chinese firms in May 1997 for selling precursors for nerve gas and equipment for making nerve gas—although the US made it clear that it had, "no evidence that the Chinese government was involved." The Chinese firms were the Nanjing Chemical Industries Group and Jiangsu Yongli Chemical Engineering and Import/Export Corporation. Cheong Yee Ltd., a Hong Kong firm, was also involved. The precursors included tionyl chloride, dimethylamine, and ethylene chlorohydril. The equipment included special glass-lined vessels, and Nanjing Chemical and Industrial Group completed construction of a production plant to manufacture such vessels in Iran in June 1997.

Iran sought to obtain impregnated alumina, which is used to make phosphorous-oxychloride, a major component of VX and GB, from the US. It has obtained some additional equipment from Israel. Nahum Manbar, an Israeli national living in France, was convicted in an Israeli court in May 1997 for providing Iran with $16 million worth of production equipment for mustard and nerve gas during the period from 1990 to 1995.

The CIA reported in June 1997 that Iran had obtained new chemical weapons equipment technology from China and India in 1996. India is assisting in the construction of a major new plant at Qazvin, near Tehran, to manufacture phosphorous pentasulfide, a major precursor for nerve gas. The plant is fronted by Meli Agrochemicals, and Dr. Mejid Tehrani Abbaspour, a chief security advisor to Rafsanjani, negotiated the program.

A recent report by German intelligence indicates that Iran has made major efforts to acquire the equipment necessary to produce sarin and tabun, using the same cover of purchasing equipment for pesticide plants that Iraq used for its Sa'ad 16 plant in the 1980s. German sources note that three Indian companies (Tata Consulting Engineering, Transpek, and Rallis India) have approached German pharmaceutical and engineering concerns for such equipment and technology under conditions where German intelligence was able to trace the end user to Iran.

The lethality of these weapons is impossible to determine because so much depends on the technical details of the design of the weapon carrying chemical agents and the efficiency with which a chemical agent is dispersed. The chemical warheads for Iran's missiles are probably still of limited sophistication, but Iran has had ample time to develop effective artillery, rocket warheads, and bombs. Iran probably either has storable binary weapons, or can soon introduce them into its inventory, and there are recent indications Iran is seeking to buy equipment to support its forces in conducting nerve gas warfare.[985]

Iran ratified the Chemical Weapons Convention in June 1997, and has completed some of the necessary declaration, but it has not provided the CWC with all of the required data on its chemical weapons program. The CIA reported in 1999 that Iran continued to obtain material related to chemical warfare (CW) from various sources. It already has manufactured and stockpiled chemical weapons, including blister, blood, and choking agents and the bombs and artillery shells for delivering them. However, Tehran is seeking foreign equipment and expertise to create a more advanced and self-sufficient CW infrastructure.[986]

Iranian Biological Warfare Capabilities

The Iranian government conducted covert procurement operations linked to biological weapons research and production throughout much of the 1980s and 1990s. As early as 1982, reports surfaced that Iran had imported suitable type cultures from Europe and was working on the production of Mycotoxins, a relatively simple family of biological agents that require only limited laboratory facilities for small-scale production. US intelligence sources reported in August 1989 that Iran was trying to buy two new strains of fungus from Canada and the Netherlands that can be used to produce Mycotoxins. German sources indicated that Iran had successfully purchased such cultures several years earlier.

The Imam Reza Medical Center at Mashhad Medical Sciences University and the Iranian Research Organization for Science and Technology were identified as the end users for this purchasing effort, but it is likely that the true end user was an Iranian government agency specializing in biological warfare. Many experts believe that the Iranian biological weapons effort was placed under the control of the Islamic Revolutionary Guards Corps, which is known to have tried to purchase suitable production equipment for such weapons. It has conducted extensive research on more lethal active agents like anthrax, hoof and mouth disease, and biotoxins. In addition, Iranian groups have repeatedly approached various European firms for the equipment and technology necessary to work with these diseases and toxins.

Unclassified sources of uncertain reliability have identified a facility at Damghan as working on both biological and chemical weapons research and production, and believe that Iran may be producing biological weapons at a pesticide facility near Tehran.[987] Reports also surfaced in the spring of 1993 that Iran had succeeded in obtaining advanced biological weapons technology in Switzerland and containment equipment and technology from Germany. According to these reports, this led to serious damage to computer facilities in a Swiss biological research facility by unidentified agents. Similar reports indicated that agents had destroyed German bio-containment equipment destined for Iran.

More credible reports by US experts indicate that Iran has begun to stockpile anthrax and Botulinum in a facility near Tabriz, can now mass manufacture such agents, and has them in an aerosol form.[988] None of these reports, however, can be verified. The CIA has reported that Iran has, "sought dual-use biotech equipment from Europe and Asia, ostensibly for civilian use." It also reported in 1996 that Iran might be ready to deploy biological weapons.[989] Beyond this point, little unclassified information exists regarding the details of Iran's effort to "weaponize" and produce biological weapons.

There are reports that Iran has developed effective aerosol weapons and weapons designs with ceramic containers. This would allow it to develop suitable missile warheads and bombs and covert devices. Iran may have begun active weapons production in 1996, but probably only at limited scale suitable for advanced testing and development.

CIA testimony indicates that Iran is believed to have weaponized both live agents and toxins for artillery and bombs and may be pursuing biological warheads for its missiles. The CIA reported in 1996 that, "We believe that Iran holds some stocks of biological agents and weapons. Tehran probably has investigated both toxins and live organisms as biological warfare agents. Iran has the technical infrastructure to support a significant biological weapons program with little foreign assistance."

The CIA reported in June 1997 that Iran had obtained new dual use technology from China and India during 1996. Such uncertainties make it harder to determine the actual nature of Iran's current and probable future biological war fighting capabilities than is the case with chemical and nuclear weapons. The CIA reported in 1999 that Iran continued to pursue purchasing dual-use biotechnical equipment from Russia and other countries, ostensibly for civilian uses. Its biological warfare (BW) program began during the Iran-Iraq war, and Iran may have some limited capability for BW deployment. The CIA estimated that outside assistance was both important and difficult to prevent, given the dual-use nature of the materials and equipment being sought and the many legitimate end uses for these items.[990]

Iran may encounter continuing difficulties in developing effective ballistic missile warheads using biological agents, but it should be able to meet the technical challenges both in improving its targeting and in finding effective ways to disperse agents from cruise missile warheads and bombs. Iran may already have the technology to disperse agents like anthrax over a wide area by spreading them from a ship moving along a coast or out of a large container smuggled into a city or industrial complex. It also seems likely that Iran will be able to create a significant production capability for storable encapsulated biological agents by the year 2000,[991] even though it announced in June 1997 that it would not produce or employ chemical weapons, including toxins.

Iranian Nuclear Warfare Capabilities

There is no way to estimate when Iran will get nuclear weapons or to be certain that Iran will push its nuclear programs forward to the point where it has actual weapons. Iran has provided many indications over the years that it is going beyond a peaceful nuclear power program. In 1974, the Shah established the Atomic Energy Organization of Iran and rapidly began to negotiate for nuclear power plants. By the time the Shah fell in January 1979, he had six reactors under contract, and was attempting to purchase a total of 12 nuclear power plants from Germany, France, and the US. Two 1,300-megawatt German nuclear power plants at Bushehr were already 60% and 75% completed, and site preparation work had begun on the first of two 935-megawatt French plants at Darkhouin that were to be supplied by Framatome.

The Shah also started a nuclear weapons program in the early to mid-1970s, building upon his major reactor projects, investment in URENCO, and smuggling of nuclear enrichment and weapons related technology from US and Europe. He attempted to covertly import controlled technology from the US. US experts believe that the Shah began a low-level nuclear weapons research program centered at the Amirabad Nuclear Research Center. This research effort included studies of weapons designs and plutonium recovery from spent reactor fuel. It also involved a laser enrichment program, which began in 1975, and led to a complex and highly illegal effort to obtain laser separation technology from the US. This latter effort, which does not seem to have had any success, continued from 1976 until the Shah's fall, and four lasers operating in the critical 16-micron band were shipped to Iran in October 1978.

Iran worked on other ways to obtain plutonium, created a secret reprocessing research effort to use enriched uranium, and set up a small nuclear weapons design team. In 1976, Iran signed a secret contract to buy $700 million worth of yellow cake from South Africa, and appears to have reached an agreement to buy up to 1,000 metric tons a year. It is unclear how much of this ore South Africa shipped before it agreed to adopt IAEA export restrictions in 1984, and whether South Africa really honored such export restrictions. Some sources indicate that South Africa still made major deliveries as late as 1988–1989. Iran also tried to purchase 26.2 kilograms of highly enriched uranium; the application to the US for this purchase was pending when the Shah fell. The Shah did eventually accept full IAEA safeguards but their value is uncertain.

In 1984, Khomeini revived nuclear weapons programs begun under the Shah. He received significant West German and Argentine corporate support in some aspects of nuclear technology during the Iran-Iraq War. Iran also received limited transfers of centrifuge and other weapons-related technology from PRC, and possibly Pakistan. Bushehr I & II, on the Gulf Coast just southwest of Isfahan, were partially completed at the time of the Shah's fall. Khomeini attempted to revive the program and sought German and Argentine support, but the reactors were damaged by Iraqi air strikes in 1987 and 1988.

Iran has a Chinese-supplied heavy-water, zero-power research reactor at Isfahan Nuclear Research Center, and two Chinese-supplied sub-critical assemblies, of light water and graphite design. It has stockpiles of uranium and mines in Yazd area and it may have had a uranium-ore concentration facility at the University of Tehran.

Some experts feel that the IRGC moved experts and equipment from the Amirabad Nuclear Research Center to a new nuclear weapons research facility near Isfahan in the mid-1980s, and formed a new nuclear research center at the University of Isfahan in 1984, with French assistance. Unlike many Iranian facilities, the center at Isfahan was not declared to the IAEA until February 1992, when the IAEA was allowed to make a cursory inspection of six sites that various reports had claimed were the location of Iran's nuclear weapons efforts.

Iran began to show a renewed interest in laser isotope separation (LIS) in the mid-1980s, and held a conference on LIS in September 1987. It opened a new nuclear research center in Isfahan in 1984, located about four kilometers outside the city and between the villages of Shahrida and Fulashans. This facility was built at a scale far beyond the needs of peaceful research, and Iran sought French and Pakistani help for a new research reactor for this center.

Iran may have opened a new uranium ore processing plant close to its Shagand uranium mine in March 1990, and it seems to have extended its search for uranium ore into three additional areas. Iran may have also begun to exploit stocks of yellow cake that the Shah had obtained from South Africa in the late 1970s while obtaining uranium dioxide from Argentina by purchasing it through Algeria. The Khomeini government may also have obtained several thousand pounds of uranium dioxide from Argentina by purchasing it through Algeria. Uranium dioxide is considerably more refined than yellow cake, and is easier to use in irradiating material in a reactor to produce plutonium.

The status of Iran's nuclear program since the Iran-Iraq War is highly controversial, and Iran has denied the existence of such a program. On February 7, 1990, the speaker of the Majlis publicly toured the Atomic Energy Organization of Iran and opened the new Jabir Ibn al Hayyan laboratory to train Iranian nuclear technicians. Reports then surfaced that Iran had at least 200 scientists and a workforce of about 2,000 devoted to nuclear research. Iran's Deputy President Ayatollah Mohajerani stated in October 1991, that Iran should work with other Islamic states to create an "Islamic bomb."

The Iranian government has repeatedly made proposals to create a nuclear-free zone in the Middle East. For example, former President Rafsanjani was asked if Iran had a nuclear weapons program in an interview on the CBS program *60 Minutes* in February 1997. He replied, "Definitely not. I hate this weapon."

Other senior Iranian leaders, including President Khatami, have made similar categorical denials. Iran's new Foreign Minister, Kamal Kharrazi, stated on October 5, 1997, that, "We are certainly not developing an atomic bomb, because we do not believe in nuclear weapons. . . We believe in and promote the idea of the Middle East as a region free of nuclear weapons and other weapons of mass destruction. But why are we interested to develop nuclear technology? We need to diversify our energy sources. In a matter of a few decades, our oil and gas reserves would be finished and therefore, we need access to other sources of energy. . . Furthermore, nuclear technology has many other utilities in medicine and agriculture. The case of the United States in terms of oil reserve is not different from

Iran's. The United States also has large oil resources, but at the same time they have nuclear power plants. So there is nothing wrong with having access to nuclear technology if it is for peaceful purposes. . . . "

The IAEA reports that Iran has fully complied with its present requirements, and that it has found no indications of nuclear weapons effort, but IAEA only inspects Iran's small research reactors. The IAEA visits to other Iranian sites are not inspections, and do not use instruments, cameras, seals, etc. They are informal walk-throughs. It visited five suspect Iranian facilities in 1992 and 1993 in this manner, but did not conduct full inspections. Iran has not had any 93+2 inspections and its position on improved inspections is that it will not be either the first or the last to have them.

Iranian officials have repeatedly complained that the West tolerated Iraqi use of chemical weapons and its nuclear and biological buildup during the Iran-Iraq War, and has a dual standard where it does not demand inspections of Israel or that Israel sign the NPT.

There are many reasons to assume that Iran still has a nuclear weapons program. For one, Iran attempted to buy low enriched fissile material from Khazakstan. The US paid between $20 million and $30 million to buy 1,300 pounds of low enriched uranium from the Ust-Kamenogorsk facility in Khazakstan that Iran might have sought to acquire in 1992. A total of 120 pounds of the material, enough for two bombs, cannot be fully accounted for. Also, Iran has imported maraging steel, sometimes used for centrifuges, by smuggling it in through dummy fronts. Britain intercepted a 110-pound (50-kilo) shipment in August 1996. There are reports of a centrifuge research program at Sharif University of Technology in Tehran, although an IAEA "visit" did not confirm this.

Iran negotiated with Kraftwerke Union and CENA of Germany in the late 1980s and early 1990s. Iran attempted to import reactor parts from Siemens in Germany and Skoda in Czechoslovakia. None of these efforts solved Iran's problems in rebuilding its reactor program, but all demonstrate the depth of its interest. Iran took other measures to strengthen its nuclear program during the early 1990s. It installed a cyclotron from Ion Beam Applications in Belgium at a facility in Karzaj in 1991.

Iran conducted experiments in uranium enrichment and centrifuge technology at its Sharif University of Technology in Tehran. Sharif University was also linked to efforts to import cylinders of fluorine suitable for processing enriched material, and attempts to import specialized magnets that can be used for centrifuges, from Thyssen in Germany in 1991. It is clear from Iran's imports that it has sought centrifuge technology ever since. Although many of Iran's efforts have never been made public, British customs officials seized 110 pounds of maraging steel being shipped to Iran in July 1996.

Iran seems to have conducted research into plutonium separation and Iranians published research on uses of tritium that had applications to nuclear weapons boosting. Iran also obtained a wide range of US and other nuclear literature with applications for weapons designs. Italian inspectors seized eight steam condensers bound for Iran that could be used in a covert reactor program in 1993, and high technology ultrasound equipment suitable for reactor testing at the port of Bari in January 1994.

Other aspects of Iran's nuclear research effort had potential weapons applications. Iran continued to operate an Argentine-fueled 5-megawatt light water highly enriched uranium reactor at the University of Tehran. It is operated by a Chinese-supplied neutron source research reactor, and subcritical assemblies with 900 grams of highly enriched uranium, at its Isfahan Nuclear Research Center. This center has experimented with a heavy water zero-power reactor, a light water sub-critical reactor, and a graphite sub-critical reactor. In addition, it may have experimented with some aspects of nuclear weapons design.

The German Ministry of Economics has circulated a wide list of such Iranian fronts that are known to have imported or attempted to import controlled items. These fronts include the:

- Bonyad e-Mostazafan;
- Defense Industries Organization (Sazemane Sanaye Defa);
- Pars Garma Company, the Sadadja Industrial Group (Sadadja Sanaye Daryaee);
- Iran Telecommunications Industry (Sanaye Mokhaberet Iran);
- Shahid Hemat Industrial Group, the State Purchasing Organization, Education Research Institute (ERI);
- Iran Aircraft Manufacturing Industries (IAI);
- Iran Fair Deal Company, Iran Group of Surveyors;
- Iran Helicopter Support and Renewal Industries (IHI);
- Iran Navy Technical Supply Center;
- Iran Tehran Kohakd Daftar Nezarat, Industrial Development Group;
- Ministry of Defense (Vezerate Defa).

Iran claims it eventually needs to build enough nuclear reactors to provide 20% of its electric power. This Iranian nuclear power program presents serious problems in terms of proliferation. Although the reactors are scarcely ideal for irradiating material to produce plutonium or cannibalizing the core, they do provide Iran with the technology base to make its own reactors, have involved other technology transfer helpful to Iran in proliferating and can be used to produce weapons if Iran rejects IAEA safeguards.

Russia has agreed to build up to four reactors, beginning with a complex at Bushehr—with two 1,000–1,200-megawatt reactors and two 465-megawatt reactors, and provide significant nuclear technology. Russia has consistently claimed the light water reactor designs for Bushehr cannot be used to produce weapons grade Plutonium and are similar to the reactors the US is providing to North Korea.

The US has claimed, however, that Victor Mikhaliov, the head of Russia's Atomic Energy Ministry, proposed the sale of a centrifuge plant in April 1995. The

US also indicated that it had persuaded Russia not to sell Iran centrifuge technology as part of the reactor deal during the summit meeting between Presidents Clinton and Yeltsin in May 1995.

It was only after US pressure that Russia publicly stated that it never planned to sell centrifuge and advanced enrichment technology to Iran, and Iran denied that it had ever been interested in such technology. For example, the statement of Mohammed Sadegh Ayatollahi, Iran's representative to the IAEA, stated that, "We've had contracts before for the Bushehr plant in which we agreed that the spent fuel would go back to the supplier. For our contract with the Russians and Chinese, it is the same." According to some reports, Russia was to reprocess the fuel at its Mayak plant near Chelyabinsk in the Urals, and could store it at an existing facility, at Krasnoyarsk-26 in southern Siberia.

The CIA reported in June 1997 that Iran had obtained new nuclear technology from Russia during 1996. Furthermore, a nuclear accident at a plant at Rasht, six miles north of Gilan, exposed about 50 people to radiation in July 1996. Russian Nuclear Energy Minister Yevgeny Adamov and Russian Deputy Prime Minister Vladimir Bulgak visited Iran in March 1998 and dismissed US complaints about the risk that the reactors would be used to proliferate. Russia indicated that it would go ahead with selling two more reactors for construction at Bushehr within the next five years.

The first 1,000-megawatt reactor at Bushehr has experienced serious construction delays. In March 1998, Russia and Iran agreed to turn the construction project into a turnkey plant because the Iranian firms working on infrastructure had fallen well behind schedule. In February, Iran had agreed to fund improved safety systems. The reactor is reported to be on a 30-month completion cycle. The US persuaded the Ukraine not to sell Iran $45 million worth of turbines for its nuclear plant in early March 1998, and to strengthen its controls on Ukrainian missile technology under the MTCR.

China is reported to have agreed to provide significant nuclear technology transfer and possible sale of two 300-megawatt pressurized water reactors in the early 1990s, but then to agree to halt nuclear assistance to Iran after pressure from the US. Iran signed an agreement with China's Commission on Science, Technology, and Industry for National Defense on January 21, 1991, to build a small 27-kilowatt research reactor at Iran's nuclear weapons research facility at Isfahan. On November 4, 1991, China stated that it had signed commercial cooperation agreements with Iran in 1989 and 1991, and that it would transfer an electromagnetic isotope separator (Calutron) and a smaller nuclear reactor for "peaceful and commercial" purposes.

The Chinese reactor and Calutron were small research-scale systems and had no direct value in producing fissile material. They did, however, give Iran more knowledge of reactor and enrichment technology, and US experts believe that China provided Iran with additional data on chemical separation, other enrichment technology, the design for facilities to convert uranium to uranium hexaflouride to make reactor fuel, and help in processing yellow cake.

The US put intense pressure on China to halt such transfers. President Clinton and Chinese President Jiang Zemin reached an agreement at an October 1997 summit. China strengthened this pledge in negotiations with the US in February 1998. In March 1998, the US found that the China Nuclear Energy Corporation was negotiating to sell Iran several hundred tons of anhydrous hydrogen fluoride (AHF) to Isfahan Nuclear Research Corporation in central Iran, a site where some experts believe Iran is working on the development of nuclear weapons. AHF can be used to separate plutonium, help refine yellow cake into uranium hexaflouride to produce U-235, and as a feedstock for sarin. It is on two nuclear control lists. China agreed to halt the sale.

Iran denied that China had halted nuclear cooperation on March 15, 1998. Even so, the US acting Under Secretary of State for Arms Control and International Security Affairs stated that China was keeping its pledge not to aid Iran on March 26, 1998.

The CIA reported in 1999 that Russian entities continued to market and support a variety of nuclear-related projects in Iran during the first half of 1998, ranging from the sale of laboratory equipment for nuclear research institutes to the construction of a 1,000-megawatt nuclear power reactor in Bushehr, Iran, that will be subject to International Atomic Energy Agency (IAEA) safeguards. It estimated that these projects, along with other nuclear-related purchases, will help Iran augment its nuclear technology infrastructure, which in turn would be useful in supporting nuclear weapons research and development.[992]

The CIA also reported, however, that Russia has committed to observe certain limits on its nuclear cooperation with Iran. For example, President Yeltsin has stated publicly that Russia will not provide militarily useful nuclear technology to Iran. Beginning in January this year, the Russian Government has taken a number of steps. For example, in May 1998, Russia announced a decree intended to strengthen compliance of Russian businesses with existing export controls on proliferation-related items.

The CIA reported that China continued to work on one of its two remaining projects—to supply Iran's civil nuclear program with a zirconium production facility. This facility will be used by Iran to produce cladding for reactor fuel. As a party to the Nuclear Nonproliferation Treaty, Iran is required to apply IAEA safeguards to nuclear fuel, but safeguards are not required for the zirconium plant or its products. During the US-China October 1997 Summit, however, China had pledged not to engage in any new nuclear cooperation with Iran and to complete cooperation on two ongoing nuclear projects in a relatively short time. The CIA concluded that this pledge appeared to be holding. In addition, China promulgated new export regulations in June 1998 that cover the sale of dual-use nuclear equipment. The regulations took effect immediately and were intended to strengthen control over equipment and material that would contribute to proliferation. Promulgation of these regulations fulfills Jiang Zemin's commitment to the United States last fall to implement such controls by the middle of 1998.

The CIA summarized these efforts as follows, "Iran claims to desire the establishment of a complete nuclear fuel cycle for its civilian energy program. In that guise, it seeks to obtain whole facilities, such as a uranium conversion facility, that, in fact, could be used in any number of ways in support of efforts to produce fissile material needed for a nuclear weapon. Despite outside efforts to curtail the flow of critical technologies and equipment, Tehran continues to seek fissile material and technology for weapons development and has set up an elaborate system of military and civilian organizations to support its effort."[993]

If Iran does push forward with nuclear weapons, it seems unlikely that it will acquire them much before 2005, unless it can somehow buy fissile material from an outside source. The CIA has warned that such transfers may not be detected and that Iran could acquire a bomb under these conditions with little or no warning.[994] As Lt. General Binford Peay, then commander of USCENTCOM, stated in June 1997, "I would predict to you that it would be some time at the turn of the next century. . . . I wouldn't want to put a date on it. I don't know if it's 2010, 2007, 2003. I am just saying its coming closer. Your instincts tell you that that's the kind of speed they are moving at."[995]

Some sources have indicated that Iran may be able to build a weapon relatively quickly, but they have generally proved pessimistic. Robert Gates, then Director of Central Intelligence, testified to Congress in February 1992, that Iran was "building up its special weapons capability as part of a massive. . .effort to develop its military and defense capability."[996] In 1992 press reports by the US Central Intelligence Agency (CIA), National Intelligence Estimates (NIE) on this subject, indicated that the CIA estimated Iran could have a nuclear weapon by the year 2000. Reports coming out of Israel in January 1995, also claimed that the US and Israel estimated Iran could have a nuclear weapon in five years.[997]

As has been mentioned earlier, John Holum testified to Congress in 1995 that Iran could have the bomb by 2003. In 1997, he testified that Iran could have the bomb by 2005–2007.[998] Although two years had passed in which Iran might have made substantial progress, the US estimate of the earliest date at which Iran could make its own bomb slipped by two to four years. Other sources believe it may take Iran substantially longer to obtain nuclear weapons. US intelligence sources denied the reports coming out of Israel and estimated that it might take seven to fifteen years for Iran to acquire a nuclear weapon.[999]

Such estimates are inherently uncertain. US Secretary of Defense William Perry stated on January 9, 1995, "We believe that Iran is trying to develop a nuclear program. We believe it will be many, many years until they achieve such a capability. There are some things they might be able to do to short-cut that time."[1000] In referring to "short cuts," Secretary Perry was concerned with the risk that Iran could obtain fissile material and weapons technology from the former Soviet Union or some other nation capable of producing fissile material. This risk creates another serious uncertainty affecting Iran's future nuclear capabilities. Reports during 1992 and 1993 that Iran had hired large numbers of Soviet nuclear scientists have proven to be unreliable.[1001] Similarly, far more dramatic reports that Iran had succeeded in buying weapons-grade material from the former Soviet Union, or nuclear armed missiles from Kazakhstan are unsubstantiated.

At present, most experts feel that Iran has all the basic technology to build a bomb, but lacks any rapid route to getting fissile uranium and plutonium. They also believe that Iran is increasingly worried about preemptive strikes by Israel or the US. As a result, Iran deliberately has lowered the profile of its activities and only conducts a low-to-moderate level weapons design and development effort.[1002] No serious expert has claimed that a major weapons grade production effort has yet been detected. As a result, many feel that Iran is at least five to seven years away from acquiring a nuclear device using its own enriched material, and six to nine years away from acquiring the ability to design a nuclear weapon that can be fitted in the warhead of a long-range missile system.

The "wild card" in all these estimates is that the deadlines would change so radically if Iran could buy fissile material from another nation or source—such as the 500 kilograms of fissile material the US airlifted out of Kazakhstan in 1994. This was enough material to make up to 25 nuclear weapons, and the US acted primarily because Iran was actively seeking to buy such material.[1003] If Iran could obtain weapons grade material, a number of experts believe that it could probably develop a gun or simple implosion nuclear weapon in nine to 36 months.

The risk of such a transfer of fissile material is significant. US experts believe that all of the weapons and fissile material remaining in the former Soviet Union are now stored in Russian facilities. The security of these facilities is still erratic, however, and there is a black market in nuclear material. US estimates indicate the FSU left a legacy of some 1,485 tons of nuclear material. This includes 770 tons in some 27,000 weapons, including 816 strategic bombs, 5,434 missile warheads, and about 20,000 theater and tactical weapons. In addition, there was 715 tons of fissile or near-fissile material in eight countries of the FSU in over 50 sites: enough to make 35,000–40,000 bombs. Also, there are large numbers of experienced FSU technicians, including those at the Russian weapons design center at Arzamas, and at nuclear production complexes at Chelyabinsk, Krasnoyarsk, and Tomsk.

These factors led the US to conduct Operation Sapphire in 1994, where the US removed 600 kilograms of enriched uranium from the Ulba Metallurgy Plant in Kazakhstan at a time Iran was negotiating for the material. They also led to Britain and the US cooperating in Auburn Endeavor, and airlifting fissile material out of a nuclear research facility in Tiblisi, Georgia. There were 10 pounds of material at the institute, and 8.8 pounds were HEU. (It takes about 35 pounds to make a bomb.) This operation was reported in the *New York Times* on April 21, 1998. The British government confirmed it took place, but would not give the date.

In the spring of 1998, Pakistan successfully tested five nuclear devices of its own in response to India's four nuclear tests. With this development, Pakistan became the first Islamic country with proven nuclear capabilities. This opens up the possibility of eventual sales to nations like Saudi Arabia or Iran, although it is far from clear that such sales will take place.

Iranian War Fighting Options

Iran is developing capabilities that will allow it to strike at targets virtually anywhere in the greater Middle East. In time, it is likely to have missiles with nuclear and biological warheads that can strike at targets anywhere in Israel, Jordan, Lebanon, and Syria, and most of Egypt. If it can bring the Shahab-3 or -4 to full deployment with a nuclear weapon, it will have the equivalent of an existential strike capability—the ability to destroy the present political and social structure of any Middle Eastern state, and perhaps the very existence of Israel.

There is a danger, however, in over-reacting to Iran. Its actions are at least partly defensive, and they are focused on the Gulf. They are a reaction to Iraq's strikes and use of chemical weapons during the Iran-Iraq War and to the world's near-indifference. They are a reaction to the continuing threat from Iraq, and a political and strategic confrontation with the US and Israel. Iran has never been a risk-taking power in the sense that Iraq has. It also has to understand that its concentrated population and ethnic structure make it highly vulnerable to existential retaliation. A small number of nuclear strikes on Iranian population centers would destroy its present political and social structure and much of its Persian heritage and character. Furthermore, there are signs that Barak's government will try to improve relations with Iran.[1004]

Deterring Iran also goes far beyond the issue of Israel. If anything, the US faces the more direct challenge in terms of both deterrence and counterproliferation. Iran must seriously consider the US response as well as the Israeli response, and what would happen to Iran if it became the target of any such retaliation and Iraq was left unscathed.

In many ways, proliferation simply raises the cost to Iran if deterrence and containment fail, it does not give it a meaningful strategic edge and it at least partially legitimizes the use of weapons of mass destruction against its population centers. The game is not chess, but poker. Raising the ante only strengthens a losing hand if you can bluff your opponent. Betting the family ranch is still reckless and stupid. Once again, however, the image of the rational bargainer provides no guarantees regarding Iranian behavior. An Iranian hard-liner might launch the kind of covert or proxy attack using weapons of mass destruction that could trigger a sequence of events that would be extremely difficult to control. Threats and demonstrative strikes can lead to preemption and escalation. Different perceptions can lead Iran or any opponent to move up the escalation ladder in unpredictable ways.

Iraq

Iraq is a regime that has recently put proliferation into war fighting practice.[1005] It has used chemical weapons against Iran and its own Kurds. In 1991, Iraq used mobile launch units in both the western and southern parts of Iraq to hit targets in Israel and Saudi Arabia during the Gulf War.[1006] Iraq launched its first two Scuds against Israel late on the afternoon of January 17, 1991. The first strike on Saudi Arabia took place on January 18, and Iraq eventually launched a total of 93 missiles.[1007]

The Iraqi Scud strikes caused relatively limited direct damage to Israel. There are different estimates of the damage from the Scud attacks on Israel, but direct damage from the Iraqi Scud strikes killed a maximum of two people. Only 10 of the 232 people directly hurt by Scuds in Israel suffered more than superficial injuries, and only one was severely hurt, which indicates that the main damage was done by fear, shock, and misuse of civil defense equipment. In contrast, each V-1 falling on London directly killed 2.2 persons, and seriously injured 6.3, and each V-2 falling on London during World War II killed an average of 4.8 persons and seriously injured 11.7.[1008]

The physical impact of Iraq's Scud strikes was also limited. While some Israeli newspapers have talked about damage to 2,797 apartments before the deployment of the Patriot, and 9,029 after deployment of the Patriot, this damage generally consisted of broken windows. Only 74 apartments suffered significant damage, 40 before the deployment of Patriot and 34 afterwards.[1009] As was the case during the Iran-Iraq War, this experience is almost certainly an important "lesson" to Iraq's leadership that Iraq must have missiles armed with weapons of mass destruction and the option of using warheads lethal enough to pose major or existential threats—which require biological or nuclear warheads.

At the same time, the survivability of Iraq's missile launchers allowed Iraq to achieve its only real military "success" of the war. This success was political and psychological, rather than physical and military, and its continuing impact on Israel is still very real. The continuing Scud attacks gave Saddam Hussein immense prestige in some parts of the Arab world, and helped offset the impression of total defeat that surrounded most aspects of Iraq's performance during the war. The Scuds disrupted some aspects of the Coalition offensive air plan, and created the only real risk that the Coalition might be divided by Israel's entrance into the war.[1010]

Iraq's Current Delivery Capabilities

Iraq has lost most of its missile delivery capabilities as a result of the Gulf War and nearly nine years' worth of activity by UNSCOM. At the same time, it has made every possible effort to retain whatever capabilities it can. There is no way to know precisely what aspects of its missile program Iraq is concealing, or how far it has gotten in its post–Gulf War efforts to create new missile research, development, and production capabilities.

Prior to the Gulf War, Iraq had extensive delivery systems incorporating long-range strike aircraft with refueling capabilities and several hundred regular and improved, longer-range Scud missiles, some with chemical warheads. These systems included: Tu-16 and Tu-22 bombers, MiG-29 fighters, Mirage F-1, MiG-23BM, and Su-22 fighter attack aircraft, a Scud force with a minimum of 819 missiles, extended range Al Husayn Scud variants (600-kilometer range) extensively deployed throughout Iraq, and at three fixed sites in northern, western, and southern Iraq, developing Al-Abbas missiles (900-kilometer range), which could reach targets in Iran, the Persian Gulf, Israel, Turkey, and Cyprus, and long-range super guns with ranges of up to 600 kilometers. Iraq also engaged in efforts aimed at developing the Tamuz liquid fueled missile with a range of over 2,000 kilometers, and a solid fueled missile with a similar range. Clear evidence indicates that at least one design was to have a nuclear warhead.

Since the end of the war, the UN inspection regime has also destroyed many of Iraq's long-range missiles. UNSCOM has directly supervised the destruction of 48 Scud-type missiles. It has verified the Iraqi unilateral destruction of 83 more missiles and 9 mobile launchers. A State Department summary issued on November 16, 1998, indicates that UNSCOM has supervised the destruction of:

- 48 operational missiles;
- 14 conventional missile warheads;
- six operational mobile launchers; 28 operational fixed launch pads;
- 32 fixed launch pads;
- 30 missile chemical warheads;
- other missile support equipment and materials, and a variety of assembled and non-assembled supergun components;
- 38,537 filled and empty chemical munitions;
- 90 metric tons of chemical weapons agent;
- more than 3,000 metric tons of precursor chemicals;
- 426 pieces of chemical weapons production equipment; and
- 91 pieces of related analytical instruments.

UNSCOM and Western experts remain convinced, however, that Iraq continues to lie in its accounting of missile engines, missile launchers, and missile warheads. Iraq attempted to conceal a plant making missile engines from the UN inspectors. It only admitted this plant existed in 1995, raising new questions about how many of its missiles have been destroyed. Many also feel that Iraq retains the capability to rapidly deploy long-range missiles and some estimates go as high as 15–24 combat-capable long-range missiles.[1011]

More conservative estimates indicate that Iraq is concealing a number of mobile missile transporter-erector-launchers (TELs), and that it can rapidly build more—perhaps covertly. They indicate that Iraq probably has enough active propellant to fuel several dozen missiles, and possibly far more. Although Iraq has accounted for 817 of the known 819 Scud assemblies it imported before the cease-fire, it has never convincingly accounted for its indigenous production efforts. Accordingly, Iraq may have 5–12 operational Al Husayn missiles that it has disassembled and hidden in various places in Iraq. It could have major components for up to 25 more.

Former UNSCOM inspector Scott Ritter has testified that Iraq has lied about its missile production equipment. For example, it has described complex four-axis machine tools designed for missile production as much simpler three-axis machines.[1012] Iraq claims to have manufactured only 80 missile assemblies, 53 of which were unusable. UNSCOM has claimed that 10 are unaccounted for. The UN estimated in 1988 that it was able to account for 817 of the 819 long-range missiles that Iraq imported:

- Pre-1980 expenditures, such as training   8
- Expenditures during the Iran-Iraq War (1980–1981),
  including the war of the cities in February-April 1988   516
- Testing activities for the development of Iraq's modifications of
  imported missiles and other experimental activities (1985–1990)   69
- Expenditures during the Gulf War (January-March 1991)   93
- Destruction under the supervision of UNSCOM   48
- Unilateral destruction by Iraq (mid-July and October 1991)   83

Iraq also has a number of missile development programs under way that it can scale up into longer-range systems once UN sanctions cease to be effective, and which might be deployed forward to other Arab countries to use them against Israel. Such deployment seems unlikely. They present serious support problems, and Iraqi would risk the loss of the control of such systems to the host government. The deployment of such missiles would probably be detected and lead to Israeli interdictive strikes. If they were used they could provoke Israel into conventional or nuclear strikes against Iraq.

The Iraqi facilities involved took some damage during the US and British strikes against Iraq as part of Desert Fox in December 1998. However, they still include:[1013]

- *Luna/Frog-7*: A Russian unguided rocket with a 70-kilometer range currently in service and in limited production.
- *Astros II*: A Brazilian unguided rocket with a 60-kilometer range currently in service and in limited production.
- *SA-2*: A Russian surface-to-air missile that China has demonstrated can be converted into a 300-kilometer range surface-to-surface missile. Iraq has designed a surface-to-surface version.
- *SA-3*: A Russian surface-to-air missile that has some potential for conversion to a surface-to-surface missile.
- *Ababil-50*: A Yugoslav-designed, Iraqi-produced 50-kilometer range artillery rocket with very limited growth potential.
- *Ababil-100*: An Iraqi 100–150-kilometer range system with parallel solid-fuel and liquid fuel development programs. It seems to be a "legal" test bed and foundation for longer-range missile programs once sanctions are lifted.

- *"Al Samoud" (Defiance)*: Another Iraqi 100–150-kilometer range system with parallel liquid fuel development programs which reverse engineers certain features of the Scud, and which UNSCOM inspectors describe as a scaled-down Scud. It too seems to be a "legal" test bed and foundation for longer-range missile programs once sanctions are lifted. Many of the liquid fueled sub-programs are compatible with Scud production.

The CIA reported in 1999 that Iraq was developing two ballistic missiles that fall within the UN-allowed 150-km range restriction. The Al Samoud liquid-propellant missile—described as a scaled-down Scud—began flight-testing in 1997. Technicians for Iraq's pre-war Scud missiles were working on the Al Samoud program while UNSCOM still exercised supervision, and were developing technological improvements that could be applied to future longer-range missile programs. The CIA reported that the Ababil-100 solid-propellant missile was also under development, although progress on this system lagged the Al Samoud. It estimated Iraq could utilize expertise from these programs in the development of longer-range missile systems. Economic sanctions were lifted and UN-inspections ceased.[1014]

At various times during its long struggle with the UN over the implementation of the Security Council Resolutions that accompanied the cease-fire in the Gulf War and created UNSCOM, Iraq has admitted to:

- Hiding its capability to manufacture its own Scuds.
- Developing an extended range variant of the FROG-7 called the Laith. The UN claims to have tagged all existing FROG-7s to prevent any extension of their range beyond the UN-imposed limit of 150 kilometers for Iraqi missiles.
- Experimenting with cruise missile technology and ballistic missile designs with ranges up to 3,000 kilometers.
- Flight testing Al Husayn missiles with chemical warheads in April 1990.
- Developing biological warheads for the Al Husayn missile as part of Project 144 at Taji.
- Initiating a research and development program for a nuclear warhead missile delivery system.
- Successfully developing and testing a warhead separation system.
- Indigenously developing, testing, and manufacturing advanced rocket engines to include liquid-propellant designs.
- Conducting research into the development of Remotely Piloted Vehicles (UAVs) for the dissemination of biological agents.
- Attempting to expand its Ababil-100 program designed to build surface-to-surface missiles with ranges beyond the permitted 100–150 kilometers.
- Importing parts from Britain, Switzerland, and other countries for a 350-mm "super gun," as well as starting an indigenous 600-mm supergun design effort.

Iraq has other delivery systems. It can use covert or proxy delivery. Like Syria, it has the potential to develop cruise missiles. Despite its wartime losses, the Iraqi Air

Force's total surviving inventory of combat aircraft still seems to include 6 Tu-22s, 1–2 Tu-16s, 30 Mirage F-1s, 15 MiG-29s, 60 MiG-23s, 15 MiG-25s, 150 MiG-21s, 30 Su-25s, and 60 Su-17s, Su-20s, and Su-22s.[1015] Iraq has recently been able to fly peaks of 100 sorties per day, although many of these aircraft have been low-grade fighters and trainers, and it is not clear that the bombers are still operational.

US and UNSCOM officials have concluded that Iraq is trying to rebuild its ballistic missile program using a clandestine network of front companies to obtain the necessary materials and technology from European and Russian firms. This equipment is then concealed and stockpiled for assembly concomitant with the end of the UN inspection regime. The equipment clandestinely sought by Iraq includes advanced missile guidance components, such as accelerometers and gyroscopes, specialty metals, special machine tools, and a high-tech, French-made, million-dollar furnace designed to fabricate engine parts for missiles.

There have been several recent major violations and smuggling efforts. In November 1995, Iraq was found to have concealed an SS-21 missile it had smuggled in from Yemen. Also, Jordan found that Iraq was smuggling missile components through Jordan in early December 1995. These included 115 gyroscopes in 10 crates, and material for making chemical weapons. The shipment was worth an estimated $25 million. Iraq claimed the gyroscopes were for oil exploration but they are similar to those used in the Soviet SS-N-18 SLBM. UNSCOM also found some gyroscopes dumped in the Tigris.

Iraq has continued with its missile programs in spite of the US strikes on its production facilities as part of Desert Fox in December 1988.[1016] Iraq has rebuilt many of the facilities the US hit during these strikes, and retains the technology it acquired before the war.[1017] US and British experts indicate that they have evidence that clearly indicates an ongoing research and development effort, in spite of the UN sanctions regime. The fact that the agreement allows Iraq to continue producing and testing short-range missiles (less than 150-kilometer range) means it can retain significant missile development effort. The SA-2 is a possible test bed, but UNSCOM has tagged all missiles and monitors all high apogee tests. Iraq's Al Samoud and Ababil-100 programs are similar test beds. The Al Samoud is a scaled-down Scud, which Iraq seems to have tested. Iraq continues to expand its missile production facility at Ibn Al Haytham, which has two new buildings large enough to make much longer-range missiles. US satellite photographs reveal that Iraq has rebuilt its Al Kindi missile research facility.

Iraq could dedicate almost any part of its air forces to medium-to-long-range missions using weapons of mass destruction against area targets. It may also be able to modify otherwise unusable aircraft for single missions or as unguided drones. While Iraq could not mass large numbers of aircraft and sustain high sortie rates against Israel, it might be able to use limited numbers of aircraft selectively to deliver chemical or biological weapons against rear area, interdiction, or strategic targets in surprise strikes, and its aircraft could forward deploy to Syria or Jordan.

Iraq also probably has the technology to adapt some of its tactical strike fighters as dedicated delivery systems designed to deliver a line-source attack with a biological agent. These attacks would probably not be effective in penetrating a US-controlled fighter screen backed by systems like the Patriot, the AWACS/E-2C and the Aegis, but Iraq might commit aircraft to long-range, low altitude strike profiles with a reasonable probability that some could penetrate Iranian and all but the best prepared Southern Gulf air defenses.[1018]

It is possible that Iraq might use helicopters to deliver chemical and biological weapons, although these would involve the same problems in forward deployment as Iran's use of such systems. Iraq used helicopters from the early 1980s onwards to deliver chemical weapons against Iranian and Kurdish forces, with growing success in mountainous areas. The Iraqi Army seems to possess about 120 armed helicopters, including 20 PAH-1 (Bo-105) attack helicopters. No reliable estimate exists of its surviving heavy, medium, and light transports and utility helicopters, but it seems likely that Iraq retains as many as 200–300.[1019] The very fact that much of its helicopter force is now incapable of high-intensity combat operations may lead Iraq to consider employing selected aircraft in limited numbers of chemical and biological attacks using the helicopter as a sprayer or in line-source attacks using dry, storable biological agents. While helicopters are vulnerable and shorter-ranged than strike aircraft, they are almost ideal platforms for medium-range biological attacks, particularly if flown in one-way dedicated attacks.

More broadly, at least some US intelligence analysts estimate that Iraq might be able to strike at much longer distances in the mid term. A US National Intelligence Estimate of Iraq's missile program stated that although the Gulf War and subsequent United Nations activities destroyed much of Iraq's missile infrastructure, Iraq could test an ICBM capable of reaching the United States during the next 15 years. The assessment was summarized as follows:[1020]

- After observing North Korean activities, Iraq *most likely would pursue* a three-stage Taepo Dong-2 approach to an ICBM (or SLV), which could deliver a several-hundred-kilogram payload to parts of the United States. If Iraq could buy a Taepo·Dong-2 from North Korea, it *could have a launch capability* within months of the purchase; if it bought Taepo Dong engines, it *could test* an ICBM by the middle of the next decade. Iraq probably would take until the end of the next decade to develop the system domestically.

- Although much less likely, most analysts believe that if Iraq were to begin development today, it *could test* a much less capable ICBM in a few years using Scud components and based on its prior SLV experience or on the Taepo Dong-1.

- If it could acquire No Dongs from North Korea, Iraq *could test* a more capable ICBM along the same lines within a few years of the No Dong acquisition.

- Analysts differ on the likely timing of Iraq's first flight test of an ICBM that could threaten the United States. Assessments include *unlikely* before 2015; and *likely* before 2015, possibly before 2010—foreign assistance would affect the capability and timing.

Iraqi Chemical Weapons

Iraq retains significant chemical warfare capabilities and has not been under effective UN inspection since late 1997. In revelations to the UN, Iraq admitted that, prior to the Gulf War, it:

- Procured more than 1,000 key pieces of specialized production and support equipment for its chemical warfare program.
- Maintained large stockpiles of mustard gas, and the nerve agents sarin and tabun.
- Produced binary sarin filled artillery shells, 122-mm rockets, and aerial bombs.
- Manufactured enough precursors to produce 70 tons (70,000 kilograms) of the nerve agent VX. These precursors included 65 tons of choline and 200 tons of phosphorous pentasulfide and di-isopropylamine
- Tested ricin, a deadly nerve agent, for use in artillery shells.
- Had three flight tests of long-range Scuds with chemical warheads.
- Had a large VX production effort under way at the time of the Gulf War. The destruction of the related weapons and feedstocks has been claimed by Iraq, but not verified by UNSCOM. Iraq seems to have had at least 3,800 kilograms of V-agents by the time of the Gulf War, and 12–16 missile warheads.

During 1991–1994, UNSCOM supervised the destruction of 38,537 filled and unfilled chemical munitions, 690 tons of chemical warfare agents, more than 3,000 tons of precursor chemicals, and over 100 pieces of remaining production equipment at the Muthan State Establishment, Iraq's primary CW research, production, filling and storage site. Since that time, UNSCOM has forced new disclosures from Iraq that have led to the destruction of 325 newly identified pieces of production equipment, 120 of which were only disclosed in August, 1997. UNSCOM has also forced the destruction of 275 tons of additional precursors and 125 analytic instruments, as well as the return of 91 analytic pieces of equipment to Kuwait. As of February 1998, UNSCOM had supervised the destruction of a total of 40,000 munitions, 28,000 filled and 12,000 empty; 480,000 liters of chemical munitions; 1,800,000 liters of chemical precursors; and eight types of delivery systems including missile warheads.

In 1992, Iraq claimed that it had 45 missile warheads filled with chemical weapons. It stated in 1995 that it had 20 chemical and 25 biological warheads. UNSCOM established that it had a minimum of 75 operational warheads and 5 used for trials, and has evidence of the existence of additional warheads. However, it can only verify that 16 warheads were filled with sarin and 34 with chemical warfare binary components and that 30 were destroyed under its supervision—16 with sarin and 14 with binary components. UNSCOM reported in April 1998 that major uncertainties existed regarding 107,500 empty casings for chemical weapons, whether several thousand additional chemical weapons were filled with agents, the unilateral destruction of 15,620 weapons, and the fate of 16,038 additional weapons Iraq claimed it had discarded. "The margin of error" in the accounting presented by Iraq is in the neighborhood of 200 munitions.[1021]

Since this UNSCOM report, the US discovered that Iraq may have deployed stable VX nerve gas as a weapon and armed Scud missiles with VX gas. This discovery was particularly important because Iraq had initially denied that it was doing any work on VX gas. Iraq then admitted to have made 3.9 tons of the gas as part of a research project which it claimed it then destroyed in secret—although Tariq Aziz claimed in another letter to the Security Council that Iraq had only produced 1.7 tons of VX and that it was not of weapons grade. Iraq systematically lied about the existence of its production facilities for VX gas until 1995, and made "significant efforts" to conceal its production capabilities after that date. Uncertainties affecting the destruction of its VX gas still affect some 750 tons of imported precursor chemicals, and 55 tons of domestically produced precursors. Iraq has made unverifiable claims that 460 tons were destroyed by Coalition air attacks, and that it unilaterally destroyed 212 tons. UNSCOM has only been able to verify the destruction of 155 tons and destroy a further 36 tons on its own.

There have been other new discoveries. UNSCOM had the opportunity to briefly examine a document at any Iraqi Air Force headquarters on July 18, 1998 that indicated Iraq might have retained far more chemical weapons than had previously been suspected. The document showed that Iraq had used far fewer chemical weapons during the Iran-Iraq War than it had previously claimed. UNSCOM has good records of how many agents have been manufactured, and the discrepancies between what has been manufactured and what Iraq seems to have used are so great that they could account for as many as 6,300 air dropped bombs and 730 tons of agents.[1022] While US experts feel that the total is more likely to be several thousand bombs and several hundred tons, even the lower estimate is scarcely reassuring.

British and US intelligence experts warned in late 1998 that Iraq might be concealing significant war fighting capabilities during the military buildup to the crisis in October 1998. State Department spokesman James Rubin gave a briefing on the US estimate of Iraq's holdings on November 16, 1998, in which he stated that:

As for Chemical Weapons, Iraq has reported making 8,800 pounds (four tons) of VX nerve gas, 220,000 pounds (100 tons) to 330,000 pounds (150 tons) of nerve agents such as Sarin and 1.1 million pounds (500 tons) to 1.32 million pounds (600 tons) of mustard gas. Data from UN weapons inspectors indicates that Iraq may have produced an additional 1.32 million pounds (600 tons) of these agents, divided evenly among the three. In other words, these are the differences between what they say they have and what we have reason to believe they have.

It is scarcely surprising, therefore, that UNSCOM's October 6, 1998 report to the Security Council left many uncertainties regarding chemical weapons:[1023]

The Special Commission has sought to resolve the most important outstanding issues. These include the verification of the material balance of special munitions, including the accounting for 550 artillery shells filled with mustard chemical warfare agent, verification of the unilateral destruction of R-400 chemical and biological aerial bombs, and the provision by Iraq of the document sighted during the inspection at the headquarters of the Iraqi Air Force; accounting for the production of the chemical warfare agent VX; and verification of the completeness of declarations provided by Iraq on the material balance of chemical weapons production equipment.

Iraq declared that 550 shells filled with mustard had been lost shortly after the Gulf War. To date, no evidence of the missing munitions has been found. A dozen mustard-filled shells were recovered at a former chemical weapons storage facility in the period 1997–1998. The chemical sampling of these munitions in April 1998 revealed that the mustard was still of the highest quality. After seven years, the purity of mustard ranged between 94 per cent and 97 per cent. Iraq still has to account for the missing shells and to provide verifiable evidence of their disposition. In July 1998, Iraq promised to provide clarifications on this matter. To date, only preliminary information has been provided by Iraq on its continuing internal investigation;

R-400 aerial bombs. Among 1,550 R-400 bombs produced by Iraq, more than 1,000 bombs were declared as destroyed unilaterally by Iraq, including 157 bombs stated as filled with biological warfare agents. The accounting for about 500 bombs unilaterally destroyed was not possible owing to the state and extent of destruction. In order to bridge the gap, the Commission requested Iraq to provide the documentation on the disposition of the tail parachute sections of R-400 bombs. The accounting for these components would enable the Commission to verify the maximum number of R-400 bombs, which Iraq could have produced. Though this would not resolve the specific issue of the quantity and composition of biological weapons bombs, including allocation of biological weapons agents, it may facilitate the final accounting for the chemical R-400 bombs. Iraq presented the information sought on the disposition of tail sections but field inspection activities are still required;

According to Iraq, 3.9 tons of VX were produced in total: some 2.4 tons in 1988, the remainder in 1990. Iraq provided documents on the 1988 production but did not provide sufficient verifiable evidence on the status of its 1990 production. Iraq has claimed, however, that its VX production program failed owing to the low purity and instability of the agent produced. The Commission's view is that Iraq was certainly able to produce VX, and probably produced it in quantity. However, the achieved level of verification of precisely how much VX was produced by Iraq is not satisfactory. In addition, Iraq denies that it weaponized VX. Sampling by the Commission of special warheads has thrown significant doubt upon this claim;

In April 1998, the Commission decided to remove some remnants of special missile warheads destroyed unilaterally by Iraq and sample them in a laboratory outside Iraq. The purpose was to verify Iraq's declarations on the filling of the special warheads. Forty-four metal fragments of different types of warheads were selected for sampling. Initially Iraq did not permit the removal of samples for analysis. In May 1998, the samples were sent for analysis to a laboratory in the United States of America. This analysis was completed by mid-June. Degradation products of the chemical warfare agent VX were found in some samples. As Iraq had hitherto denied weaponization of VX, it was asked to provide its clarifications. To date no clarifications have been provided;

In July 1998, at Iraq's request, the Commission held an international expert meeting in Baghdad to present and to discuss with Iraq's authorities the results of analysis carried out earlier in the United States laboratory. Iraq did not challenge the analytical results presented, but continues to insist that VX had never been weaponized;

In June and July 1998, the Commission took different wipe samples from other special missile warhead remnants remaining in Iraq in order to collect more data on the types of their chemical fill. Forty-three samples were sent to the same laboratory in the United States, 40 samples sent to a laboratory in France and 40 samples to a laboratory in Switzerland. The analysis of all these samples is not yet complete.

US experts estimate that Iraq has rebuilt key portions of its chemical production infrastructure for industrial and commercial use. The facilities are currently subject to UN scrutiny, but they could be converted fairly quickly, allowing Iraq to restart limited agent production. Even though some foreign assistance for equipment and material would be required for all but a minimum effort, Iraq would only need several months to produce a usable stockpile of agents and several years to return to pre–Gulf War stockpile levels.

The CIA estimated in 1999 that, "Since the Gulf war, Baghdad has rebuilt key portions of its chemical production infrastructure for industrial and commercial use. Some of these facilities could be converted fairly quickly for production of CW agents. The recent discovery that Iraq had weaponized the advanced nerve agent VX and the convincing evidence that fewer CW munitions were consumed during the Iran-Iraq war than Iraq had declared provide strong indications that Iraq retains a CW capability and intends to reconstitute its pre-Gulf war capability as rapidly as possible once sanctions are lifted."[1024] Other sources indicate that Iraq was continuing with its chemical weapons development program in early 2000.[1025]

In spite of these uncertainties, some experts feel that it might take several years and several hundred million dollars worth of imported equipment to develop a major war fighting capability. They note that Iraq lost much of its feedstock production capacity during the bombing of Samara, which was very heavily damaged during the war. As a result, it will probably take Iraq three to five years to recover a significant capability to employ enough chemical shells, rockets, bombs and warheads to fight a major land war.[1026]

However, Iraq does not need the large amounts of chemical agents needed to support a major land offensive to arm several hundred missile warheads and aircraft bombs, and potentially play a serious role in an Arab-Israeli conflict Even limited numbers of chemical weapons can be highly effective in a number of war fighting contingencies. It is clear from UNSCOM's reports that Iraq may already have covertly produced enough chemical agents to arm several hundred weapons, including warheads, at small laboratory facilities. It is also clear from UNSCOM statements that it is virtually impossible for any inspection and control regime to prevent this.

Iraq has also had half a decade since the Gulf War in which to develop ways of producing purer chemical agents, and more effective bombs and warheads. Iraq, therefore, will almost certainly retain significant capabilities in spite of the "war of sanctions," and will be able to recover a significant capability to threaten enemy population centers and area targets with missile and air strikes shortly after it is freed from UN controls.[1027] This potential threat is serious enough to be an important factor behind US efforts to improve its chemical warfare defense capabilities, and US support of the efforts of the United Nations to create an Organization for the Prohibition of Chemical Weapons to enforce the Chemical Weapons Convention if sanctions on Iraq are lifted.[1028]

Iraq's Biological Warfare Capabilities

A senior UNSCOM inspector has described biological weapons as the "black hole" of the UN inspection effort. Iraq has continued to lie about virtually all of its biological weapons until 1995. UNSCOM uncovered substantial evidence that Iraq was concealing a major biological weapons effort by the spring of 1995. However, it was the defection of Lieutenant General Husayn Kamel Majid, formerly in charge of Iraq's weapons of mass destruction, in August 1995 that revealed the extent of this biological weapons program. Kamel's defection forced Iraq to admit that it:

- Imported 39 tons of growth media (31,000 kilograms or 68,200 pounds) for biological agents obtained from three European firms. According to UNSCOM, 3,500 kilograms or 7,700 pounds) remains unaccounted for. Some estimates go as high as 17 tons. Each ton can be used to produce 10 tons of bacteriological weapons.

- Imported type cultures from the US, which can be modified to develop biological weapons.

- Had a laboratory- and industrial-scale capability to manufacture various biological agents including the bacteria which cause anthrax and botulism; aflatoxin, a naturally occurring carcinogen; clostridium perfringens, a gangrene-causing agent; the protein toxin ricin; tricothecene mycotoxins, such as T-2 and DAS; and an anti-wheat fungus known as wheat cover smut. Iraq also conducted research into the rotavirus, the camel pox virus and the virus which causes haemorrhagic conjunctivitis.

- Created at least seven primary production facilities including the Sepp Institute at Muthanna, the Ghazi Research Institute at Amaria, the Daura Foot and Mouth Disease Institute, and facilities at Al Hakim, Salman Pak Taji, and Fudaliyah. According to UNSCOM, weaponization occurred primarily at Muthanna through May 1987 (largely Botulinum), and then moved to Al Salman. (anthrax). In March 1988 a plant was open at Al Hakim, and in 1989 an aflatoxin plant was set up at Fudaliyah.

- Had test site about 200 kilometers west of Baghdad, used animals in cages and tested artillery and rocket rounds against live targets at ranges up to 16 kilometers.

- Took fermenters and other equipment from Kuwait to improve effort during the Gulf War.

- Iraq had at least 79 civilian facilities capable of playing some role in biological weapons production still in existence in 1997.

UN inspectors found that Iraq weaponized at least three biological agents by the time of the Gulf War. The weaponization consisted of at least 100 bombs and 16 missile warheads loaded with botulinum, 50 R-400 air-delivered bombs and 5 missile warheads loaded with anthrax, and 4 missile warheads and 7 R-400 bombs loaded with aflatoxin, a natural carcinogen. The warheads were designed for operability with the Al Husayn Scud variant.

Iraq had other weaponization activities:

- Armed 155-mm artillery shells and 122-mm rockets with biological agents.
- Conducted field trials, weaponization tests, and live firings of 122-mm rockets armed with anthrax and botulinum toxin from March 1988 to May 1990.
- Tested ricin, a deadly protein toxin, for use in artillery shells.
- Produced at least 191 bombs and 25 missile warheads with biological agents.
- Developed and deployed 250-pound aluminum bombs covered in fiberglass. Bombs were designed so they could be mounted on both Soviet and French-made aircraft. They were rigged with parachutes for low altitude drops to allow efficient slow delivery and aircraft to fly under radar coverage. Some debate over whether bombs had cluster munitions or simply dispersed agents like LD-400 chemical bomb.
- Deployed at least 166 R-400 bombs with 85 liters of biological agents each during the Gulf War. Deployed them at two sites. One was near an abandoned runway where it could fly in aircraft, arm them quickly, and disperse with no prior indication of activity and no reason for the UN to target the runway.
- Filled at least 25 Scud missile warheads, and 157 bombs and aerial dispensers, with biological agents during the Gulf War.
- Developed and stored drop tanks ready for use for three aircraft or UAVs with the capability of dispersing 2,000 liters of anthrax. Development took place in December 1990. Claimed later that tests showed the systems were ineffective.

The UN found that Iraq equipped crop-spraying helicopters for biological warfare and held exercises and tests simulating the spraying of anthrax spores. Iraqi Mirages were given spray tanks to disperse biological agents and trials were held as late as January 13, 1991. The Mirages were chosen because they have large 2,200-liter belly tanks and could be refueled by air, giving them a longer endurance and greater strike range. The tanks had electric valves to allow the agent to be released and the system was tested by releasing simulated agent into desert areas with scattered petri dishes to detect the biological agent. UNSCOM has videotapes of the aircraft.

Project 144 at Taji produced at least 25 operational Al Husayn warheads. Ten of these were hidden deep in a railway tunnel, and 15 in holes dug in an unmanned hidden site along the Tigris. The biological weapons were only distinguished from regular weapons by a black stripe. The UN claims that Iraq has offered no evidence to corroborate its claims that it destroyed its stockpile of biological agents after the Gulf War. Further, Iraq retains the technology it acquired before the war and evidence clearly indicates an ongoing research and development effort, in spite of the UN sanctions regime.

There are still serious uncertainties about Iraq's exact motives in developing and producing aflatoxin. Iraqi research on aflatoxin began in May 1988 at Al Salman, where the toxin was produced by the growth of fungus aspergilus in 5.3-quart flasks. The motives behind Iraq's research on aflatoxin remain one of the most speculative aspects of its program. Aflatoxin is associated with fungal-contaminated food grains, and is considered nonlethal. It normally can produce liver cancer, but only after a period of months to years and in intense concentrations. There is speculation, however, that a weaponized form might cause death within days and some speculation that it can be used as an incapacitating agent.

Furthermore, Iraq has still not provided a convincing accounting of how many missile warheads it filled with anthrax and how many it filled with botulinum. Iraq has conducted experiments with water processing that indicate it may have examined ways to attack water supplies in ways that are not fully documented. It may have made considerably more progress in developing dry storable agents such as anthrax, and highly lethal encapsulated micro-powders than it has yet admitted. It may have mobile biological weapons production capabilities including fermenters, drying equipment, and grinding equipment. UNSCOM also has been unable to determine whether Iraq experimented on live subjects in 1991.

Total Iraqi production of more orthodox biological weapons reached at least 19,000 liters of concentrated botulinum (10,000 liters filled into munitions); 8,500 liters of concentrated anthrax (6,500 liters filled into munitions); and 2,500 liters of concentrated aflatoxin (1,850 liters filled into munitions). It manufactured 6,000 liters of concentrated botulinum toxin and 8,425 liters of anthrax at Al Hakim during 1990; 5,400 liters of concentrated botulinum toxin at the Daura Foot and Mouth Disease Institute from November 1990 to January 15, 1991; 400 liters of concentrated botulinum toxin at Taji; and 150 liters of concentrated anthrax at Salman Pak. Iraq is also known to have produced at least 1,850 liters of aflatoxin in solution at Fudaliyah; 340 liters of concentrated clostridium perfringens, a gangrene-causing biological agent, beginning in August 1990; and10 liters of concentrated ricin at Al Salam. Iraq claimed it abandoned work after tests failed.

At least one Iraqi defector—General Wafic al-Sammaral, a former senior officer in Iraqi military intelligence has claimed that Iraq, "retains 255 containers of biological warfare materials—230 with powder, which has no expiry date, and 25 with liquid, which will deteriorate over time."[1029] British, French, German, Swiss, US, and UNSCOM experts are aware of ongoing Iraqi import efforts that seemed to be designed to produce biological weapons. Most experts believe that Iraq has created the same highly secret and compartmentalized program to carry on with its biological weapons program after the Gulf War that it created for its missile, chemical warfare, and nuclear programs.

Such an Iraqi program is particularly difficult to trace since all key components are dual-use items that can be used for peaceful medical purposes and food processing. Dual-use items include everything from biomedical equipment and microencapsulation equipment for cold tablets to brewery fermenters and dry food storage equipment for infant formula. Both Iraq's research and production efforts can be widely dispersed and can be concealed in relatively small buildings—particularly if a government is willing to take moderate risks of contamination of the kind widely taken by the Soviet Union during the Cold War.

These factors led British and US intelligence experts to warn that Iraq might be concealing significant war fighting capabilities during the military buildup to the crisis in October 1998. More openly, State Department spokesman James Rubin gave a briefing on November 16, 1998, in which he stated that:

> There is a large discrepancy between the amount of biological growth media—that's the culture in which you grow biological weapons—procured and the amount of agents that were or could have been produced. Baghdad has not adequately explained where some 8,000 pounds (3,500 kg) of the material went out of some 68,000 pounds (31,000 kg) of biological growth media it imported. Iraq's accounting of the amount of the agent it produced and the number of failed batches is seriously flawed and cannot be reconciled on the basis of this full disclosure Iraq has made.

Much depends on whether Iraq did or did not have the capability to make dry, storable weapons at any point before or after the Gulf War. As has been touched upon earlier, some of Iraq's holdings and use of suitable equipment cannot be accounted for. Iraq also initially said that it had tried such production as early as 1989, and then denied this. Similarly, Iraq claims it did not succeed in weaponizing ricin and that its trials failed. This, however, is uncertain and therefore is a major potential risk. Iraq still produces tons of castor oil as a commercial lubricant, and 5% of the residual mash is ricin. UNSCOM experts indicate that the monitoring of this production effort is inadequate to control how the ricin is disposed or used.

UNSCOM reported in October 1997 that:

- Iraq has never provided a clear picture of the role of its military in its biological warfare program, and has claimed it only played a token role.
- It has never accounted for its disposal of growth media. The unaccounted for media is sufficient, in quantity, for the production of over three times more of the biological agent, anthrax, than Iraq claims to have been produced.
- Bulk warfare agent production appears to be vastly understated by Iraq. Expert calculations of possible agent production quantities, either by equipment capacity or growth media amounts, far exceed Iraq's stated results.
- Significant periods when Iraq claims its fermenters were not utilized are unexplained.
- Biological warfare field trials are underreported and inadequately described.
- Claims regarding field trials of chemical and biological weapons using R400 bombs are contradictory and indicate that, "more munitions were destroyed than were produced."
- The Commission is unable to verify that the unilateral destruction of the BW-filled Al Hussein warheads has taken place.
- There is no way to confirm whether Iraq destroyed 157 bombs of the R400 type, some of which were filled with botulin or anthrax spores.

- "The September 1997 FFCD fails to give a remotely credible account of Iraq's biological program. This opinion has been endorsed by an international panel of experts."

The US strikes on Iraq in December 1998 failed to target and destroy any known significant aspects of Iraq's biological weapons program. At this point, only another series of major defections is likely to reveal the full details of Iraq's accomplishments before 1991, or what it has done covertly since that time. At least one of the principal UNSCOM investigators of the Iraqi biological weapons program feels that no effort by UNSCOM can prevent Iraq from retaining a major biological weapons effort and resuming production and deployment within months of the end of the UNSCOM effort.

The CIA stated in 1999 that, "Iraq continues to refuse to disclose fully the extent of its BW program. After four years of denials, Iraq admitted to an offensive program resulting in the destruction of Al Hakam—a large BW production facility Iraq was trying to hide as a legitimate biological plant. Iraq still has not accounted for over a hundred BW bombs and over 80 percent of imported growth media-directly related to past and future Iraqi production of thousands of gallons of biological agent. This lack of cooperation is an indication that Baghdad intends to reconstitute its BW capability when possible."[1030] Other sources indicate that Iraq continues with its biological weapons program.[1031]

Further, any analysis of Iraq's intentions regarding biological weapons must take into account Iraq's probable reaction if it cannot revive its nuclear program. Biological weapons are sometimes described as the "poor man's nuclear weapons." They are also the "nuclear weapons" of the covert proliferator. As long as Saddam Hussein is in power, Iraq is virtually certain to seek highly lethal biological weapons as a means of compensating for the suppression of its nuclear program. Even when he is gone, successor regimes may feel compelled to follow a similar course because of the risks posed by Iran's nuclear and biological programs, Israel's nuclear forces, and US nuclear capabilities. Ironically, UNSCOM and the IAEA's success in dealing with the most visible aspects of Iraq's nuclear efforts may ultimately end in stimulating Iraq to develop the kind of biological option that is as close to a nuclear option as time, technology, delivery systems, and the ability to carry out a cover biological program permit.

Iraq's Nuclear Warfare Capabilities

Iraq has lost virtually all of the facilities and equipment it possessed for making fissile material at the time of the Gulf War. It did, however, have the technology to make fissile material, and had successfully designed at least two workable nuclear weapons. After the 1995 defection of Lt. Gen. Hussein Kamel, Iraq also provided the IAEA with technical drawings on the use of precision-shaped charges known as "explosive lenses." These consist of spherical shaped assemblies made of interlocking hexagonal blocks of explosives that are designed to detonate inward and crush enriched uranium to a critically dense mass.[1032]

The IAEA could not assess Iraq's final progress in completing such weapons designs because "the chart clearly illustrates several drawings are missing." It also reported major gaps in Iraq's disclosures. Iraq at first denied it had built molds for manufacture of explosive lenses. Later, it admitted it had such molds, but said that it "can't find" the molds. Iraq initially denied ever casting an explosive lens, and then admitted that Iraqi scientists "had cast one 120mm cylindrical charge and it was tested for 'velocity and pressure.'"[1033] This left the IAEA without the data needed to know either the level of sophistication Iraq reached in weapons design or how far it had gotten in manufacturing actual weapons components.

US experts feel that one of these nuclear weapons designs could have produced a weapon weighing about 1,000 kilograms (one metric ton).[1034] This mass, and the basic weapons design, was consistent with deployment in the warhead of a Scud missile, although the design of the warhead of the operational Al Husayn missile was 70–80 centimeters in diameter and the Iraqi weapon would have required a warhead 100–120 centimeters in diameter. The developmental Al-Abid could have carried a one-ton warhead with a diameter of 125 centimeters and a distance of up to 1,200 kilometers, and it would probably have been operational by 1993.[1035]

The basic design was similar in some ways to the US Trinity weapon that the US set off in New Mexico on July 16, 1945. It consisted of a soccer ball–shaped set of explosive lenses surrounding a pit of fissile material enclosed in a reflector made out of depleted uranium or beryllium. The pit was a solid sphere of uranium, with sufficient highly enriched uranium to approach one critical mass. Using such a large mass of uranium greatly increases the probability that a nuclear device will produce a significant yield even if the high explosive is relatively unsophisticated, and reduces the amount of explosive needed to compress the enriched material to supercriticality.

At the same time, Iraqi experts calculated that minor shifts in design could produce a yield as low as one kiloton, and lacked predetermined values for several critical calculations. As a result, they were using one-dimensional integrated codes for much of their design work. Iraq had not finalized its designs for high explosive lenses or neutron initiators, or its plans for converting HEU into the components that could be compressed into a fissile sphere. Completing these aspects of weapons design and manufacture could have taken Iraq until anytime from mid-1991 to as late as 1993.

The UN found that Iraq seemed to have carried out enough computation to support weaponization studies, hydrodynamic calculations, exploding wire studies, neutron initiator studies, energy source studies, neptunium and U-233 experiments, and lithium-6 experiments. The bulk of this calculation work seems to have been done at Tuwaitha, using an IBM 370 mainframe and smaller IBM PS/2 computers, although the hydrostatic calculations were performed on an NEC mainframe computer.[1036]

The UN also found that Iraq planned to use a hardened iron tamper and a polonium-210 metal/beryllium neutron initiator. The neutron initiator is the device needed to supply a burst of high energy neutrons at the correct instant necessary to start the chain reaction and keep it from damping out. Iraq obtained its polonium 210 from bismuth, and completed 20 tests of a polonium-beryllium neutron initiator.[1037] Iraq had designed and successfully tested its own neutron initiator using explosive lenses and dummy core material just before the Gulf War began. Iraq had also developed and tested high-energy pulse junction switches, which can act as a somewhat inferior substitute for krytron.[1038]

The current state of Iraq's nuclear efforts is unknown. Mohammed El Baradei, the Director General of the IAEA, made it quite clear in an editorial in the *Washington Post* on June 1, 1998 that the IAEA was in no position to state that it had found all of Iraq's nuclear weapons efforts and technology:[1039]

News stories have been circulating that the IAEA is about to issue Iraq a clean bill of health and to close the nuclear file. Nothing could be further from the truth . . . Does Iraq still possess nuclear weapons or weapon-usable material? Does Iraq retain the practical capability –i.e., the scientific and engineering hardware to produce dangerous amounts of weapon-usable fissile material? . . . My agency's answer is that there are "no indications" . . . but it must be understood that 'no indications' is not the same as "no existence." . . . no matter how comprehensive the inspection, any country-wide verification process, in Iraq or anywhere else, has a degree of uncertainty.

Because we need continuing reaffirmation that we have in fact neutralized the past program . . . we have introduced . . . a comprehensive and vigorous monitoring regime that . . . has the twin objectives of checking that Iraq's known technical and industrial assets are not used for prohibited purposes, and, perhaps more important, searching country-wide for indications of any prohibited activities. Monitoring inspections are intrusive and involve access to any and all facilities, including industrial sites, scientific establishments and universities, and the use of sensitive environmental sampling and analysis techniques anywhere in Iraq.

The IAEA warned in its October 1998 report to the Security Council that every point in El Baradei's statement remained just as valid if the Security Council decided to shift IAEA activity from the inspection phase to the monitoring phase. Further, UNSCOM provided an additional warning about the difficulties in controlling Iraq's efforts in its October 6, 1998 report to the Security Council on efforts to control Iraq's imports.[1040]

There are Western experts who feel that Iraq's nuclear programs remain active. Former UNSCOM Inspector Scott Ritter testified to Senate and House committees on September 4 and September 15 that Iraq might retain the components for three nuclear weapons. It later became clear that Ritter based his testimony on information compiled from three Iraqi defectors who came to UNSCOM by way of a "northern European" country.

While US and European policy makers initially indicated that they had no evidence to support Ritter's charges, reports surfaced on September 29, 1998, that UNSCOM inspectors had reported in both 1996 and 1997 that they had credible intelligence evidence that Iraq might have built and retained three to four nuclear implosion devices that only needed fissile-grade uranium cores to make kiloton nuclear weapons in the 10–25 kiloton range. US intelligence officials privately indicated that these UNSCOM reports might well be credible.[1041]

The defectors involved provided detailed and accurate descriptions of the methods used by Iraq's Special Security Services to hide weapons components that were known only to a handful of Western inspectors and intelligence experts at the time. These details include the Special Security Services' use of Mercedes trucks to shuttle the weapons between hiding places. These trucks had distinctive markings that included white cabins with red stripes, a red diesel tank and wheel rims, and Ministry of Trade license plates numbered between 30,000 and 87,000. Ritter stated that one defector sketched a map by hand depicting seven depots for those trucks. U-2 surveillance flights later found five of these sites. Ritter also disclosed that one of the defectors identified a secret concealment operations center in the Al Fao Building on Palestine Street in Baghdad. An UNSCOM no-notice inspection found in March 1996 that Iraq used this center to control several locations for concealing materials, although it seems to have been evacuated in January 1998.[1042]

Even the experts who feel that Iraq has nuclear weapons assemblies indicate that there is no evidence that Iraq has acquired fissile-grade uranium or plutonium, and obtaining fissile material has long been a more serious technical and supply problem than fabricating the rest of a working nuclear weapon. They also feel that any Iraqi devices are likely to be too large and too heavy to fit inside the 88-centimeter (roughly 34-inch) warhead of one of Iraq's Al Husayn missiles. At the same time, these uncertainties reinforce the warning of the Director General of the International Atomic Energy Agency that the IAEA cannot find every aspect of Iraq's nuclear program and that Iraq retains the technology base to make nuclear weapons.

Iraq does, however, continue to attempt to buy nuclear technology on the gray and black markets, and authorized its Iraqi Atomic Energy Organization to resume purchases of "peaceful" nuclear technology in 1998. It is also clear that Iraqi scientists are cooperating with other countries.

Khidhir Hamza, a former director of Iraq's program to devise a nuclear weapon who defected in 1994, has said in an interview in the *New York Times* that Iraq planned to produce nuclear components abroad, including devices to trigger nuclear reactions in warheads, or to import crucial parts to make arms in Iraq. He stated that there was "general planning for removal outside Iraq of some sensitive work or possibly work that requires some imports. The idea is to do it outside and bring the thing back home." Hamza said that at the time he left Iraq in 1995, a friend of his was importing electronic parts for the military from a front company in Jordan that bought the equipment in Malaysia and Singapore. "There are hundreds of these companies in Jordan. They have a whole system of runners in ordinary cars." He said that Iraq repaired its radar after the Gulf War by smuggling in parts. Hamza said there were other front companies in Southeast Asia and overseas bank accounts in areas ranging from the Persian Gulf region to Latin America to draw on to pay for purchases. He said that smugglers brought in parts in their personal luggage, that circuit boards were backed in foam-padded bags and brought into Jordan for a small bribe, and that plastic bags stuffed with goods were stored in the empty tanks of oil trucks returning from Turkey.

Other sources report that Abdulkadir Abdulrahman Ahmed, the director general of Iraq's nuclear research center, is regularly visiting India's leading nuclear research laboratory. This was only discovered when a computer hacker got into the Indian center's files. Hamza stated that Iraq had long worked to build up a "deep and multilayered cooperation" with India that "seems to be back now."[1043]

The CIA estimated in 1999 that, "Iraq continues to hide documentation, and probably some equipment, relating to key aspects of past nuclear activities. After years of Iraqi denials, the IAEA was able to get Iraq to admit to a far more advanced nuclear weapons program and a project based on advanced uranium enrichment technology. However, Baghdad continues to withhold significant information about enrichment techniques, foreign procurement, and weapons design."[1044]

Iraq's War Fighting Capabilities

Iraq is still devoting resources to biological, chemical, and nuclear research efforts. It retains significant technology, and much of the chemical and biological weapons equipment it dispersed before and during Desert Storm. It also retains a long-range air strike capability and probably retains some Scud and improved Scud missile assemblies. Table 15.7 and Figures 15.1 to 15.3 show that even relatively low performance chemical and biological weapons could still have a substantial killing effect.

A CIA report in August 2000 summarized the state of proliferation in Iraq as follows:[1045]

Since Operation Desert Fox in December 1998, Baghdad has refused to allow United Nations inspectors into Iraq as required by Security Council Resolution 687. Although UN Security Council Resolution (UNSCR) 1284, adopted in December 1999, established a follow-on inspection regime to the United Nations Special Commission on Iraq (UNSCOM) in the form of the United Nations Monitoring, Verification, and Inspection Committee (UNMOVIC), there have been no UN inspections during this reporting period. Moreover, the automated video monitoring system installed by the UN at known and suspect WMD facilities in Iraq has been dismantled by the Iraqis. Having lost this on-the-ground access, it is difficult for the UN or the US to accurately assess the current state of Iraq's WMD programs.

Since the Gulf war, Iraq has rebuilt key portions of its chemical production infrastructure for industrial and commercial use, as well as its missile production facilities. It has attempted to purchase numerous dual-use items for, or under the guise of, legitimate civilian use. This equipment—in principle subject to UN scrutiny—also could be diverted for WMD purposes. Since the suspension of UN inspections in December 1998, the risk of diversion has increased.

Following Desert Fox, Baghdad again instituted a reconstruction effort on those facilities destroyed by the US bombing, to include several critical missile production complexes and former dual-use CW production facilities. In addition, it appears to be installing or repairing dual-use equipment at CW-related facilities. Some of these facilities could be converted fairly quickly for production of CW agents.

UNSCOM reported to the Security Council in December 1998 that Iraq continued to withhold information related to its CW and BW programs. For example, Baghdad seized from UNSCOM inspectors an air force document discovered by UNSCOM that indicated that Iraq had not consumed as many CW munitions during the Iran-Iraq War in the 1980s as had been declared by Baghdad. This discrepancy indicates that Iraq may have an additional 6,000 CW munitions hidden.

We do not have any direct evidence that Iraq has used the period since Desert Fox to reconstitute its WMD programs, although given its past behavior, this type of activity must be regarded as likely. We assess that since the suspension of UN inspections in December of 1998, Baghdad has had the capability to reinitiate both its CW and BW programs within a few weeks to months, but without an inspection monitoring program, it is difficult to determine if Iraq has done so. We know, however, that Iraq has continued to work on its unmanned aerial vehicle (UAV) program, which involves converting L-29 jet trainer aircraft originally acquired from Eastern Europe. These modified and refurbished L-29s are believed to be intended for delivery of chemical or biological agents.

Iraq continues to pursue development of two SRBM systems which are not prohibited by the United Nations: the liquid-propellant Al-Samoud, and the solid-propellant Ababil-100. The Al-Samoud is essentially a scaled-down Scud, and the program allows Baghdad to develop technological improvements that could be applied to a longer range missile program. We believe that the Al-Samoud missile, as designed, is capable of exceeding the UN-permitted 150-km-range restriction with a potential operational range of about 180 kilometers. Personnel previously involved with the Condor II/Badr-2000 missile—which was largely destroyed during the Gulf War and eliminated by UNSCOM—are working on the Ababil-100 program. If economic sanctions against Iraq were lifted, Baghdad probably would attempt to convert these efforts into longer range missile systems, regardless of continuing UN monitoring and continuing restrictions on WMD and long-range missile programs.

An analysis by the US National Intelligence Council of the missile threat during the period from 2000–2015 stated that:[1046]

Iraq's ability to obtain WMD will be influenced, in part, by the degree to which the UN Security Council can impede development or procurement over the next 15 years. Under some scenarios, Iraq could test an ICBM capable of delivering nuclear-sized payloads to the United States before 2015; foreign assistance would affect the capabilities of the missile and the time it became available. Iraq could also develop a nuclear weapon during this period.

As is the case with Iran, the question arises as to how many risks Iraq would really take against a nuclear-armed Israel, particularly as long as it faces major potential threats from Iran and the US. Logically, Iraq's capability will remain more theoretical than real and far more of a limited possibility than a probability. Given Saddam Hussein's history, however, logic may not dictate action. Further-more, Iraq might join in an ongoing exchange by Israel and other powers if it thought it was to its advantage to do so or begin with threats and escalate into action. There are no rules to this game.

Proliferation and the Greater Middle East

The threat posed by the conventional capabilities of nations like Libya, Iran, and Iraq does not immediately alter the regional military balance, but the steady process of proliferation will. Iran will acquire significant new missile capabilities in the early 2000s, and Iraq is likely to develop significant covert biological and chemical capabilities in the near term and to resume its missile and nuclear weapons programs the moment UN sanctions cease to be effective. Libya is more bark than bite, but it does have chemical weapons.

Israel can neither plan on the basis that such nations will radically change their behavior in the near term, nor ignore the risks they pose to its arms control planning. Further, Egypt, Jordan, and Syria face the problem that the regional balance of power will shift, and that Libya, Iran, and Iraq presently have regimes which will attempt to exploit any shift in their favor in ways which may threaten Egyptian, Jordanian, and Syrian interests. Proliferation is not simply a matter of Israel versus the rest. Iranian and Iraqi efforts to proliferate are driven by Gulf security issues, not Israel. Jordan could easily be the victim of unintended strikes in any Iranian or Iraqi missile exchange with Israel, and Egypt faces difficult decisions in terms of both security and status if every other major regional power proliferates and Egypt does not.

THE WAR FIGHTING IMPLICATIONS OF WEAPONS OF MASS DESTRUCTION

The previous analysis of weapons programs shows that Israeli, Egyptian, and Syrian holdings of weapons of mass destruction, along with those of Iran, Iraq, and Libya, have important implications for regional war fighting arms control and the peace process. They are making fundamental changes in the potential scale and intensity of a future conflict, and are extending the zone of Arab-Israeli conflict to include radical states armed with weapons of mass destruction like Iran, Iraq, and Libya.

Weapons of mass destruction are creating the capability to conduct a fundamen-tally different level of warfare. Destructive as conventional wars may be, the process of creeping proliferation summarized in Table 15.1 is occurring in states that are relatively fragile when several of the most lethal types of weapon of mass destruction can destroy their major cities and kill a significant portion of their total population.

Arab and Iranian Forces and Capabilities

There is no easy way to translate this potential destructiveness into the analysis of specific contingencies for war fighting. Israel has never announced any specific doctrine of strategy for using its weapons of mass destruction, Egypt continues to deny it has such weapons, and Iran, Iraq, and Libya have either denied capability or made generalized threats to use such weapons in ways that tell little about their doctrine. Syria has never officially discussed its war fighting doctrine.

It is doubtful that Egypt, Iran, Iraq, and Libya as yet have any detailed war fighting doctrine for using weapons of mass destruction against Israel. Egypt almost certainly sees its limited contingency capabilities largely as a deterrent against a type of war with Israel that is already so unlikely that it would take a major change in the political situation, and months or years of Egyptian effort to produce chemical and biological weapons and train for their use, before it would be a serious risk.

Iran and Iraq will become more significant threats in the future, but currently lack the ability to deliver significant numbers of weapons against Israel. Iran and Iraq could conduct small one-way air strikes with chemical or biological weapons or use a civilian ship, civil aircraft, or proxy force to attempt the covert delivery of such weapons. However, the probable lethality of such strikes would currently be so limited that Iran and Iraq would have to risk national destruction for what would probably prove to be little more than mass terrorism and the provocation of an Israeli nuclear strike.

Libya has only a token capability to deliver chemical and possibly crude biological weapons. It could conduct very small one-way air strikes with chemical or biological weapons or it could again use a civilian ship, civil aircraft, or proxy force to attempt the covert delivery of such weapons, but Libya's capabilities are far weaker than those of Iran and Iraq. The current Libyan threat is much more likely to be that Qadhafi might take extreme risks for ideological reasons that would provoke Israel into a massive response and destabilize the regional political situation, than a military threat to Israel in serious war fighting terms.

Syria is the only Arab state that actively deploys weapons of mass destruction that are targeted exclusively against Israel. It does not, however, conduct large-scale land warfare or combined arms training to simulate the tactical use of chemical weapons, provide intensive small unit and squad training in chemical or biological warfare, or deploy the equivalent of a chemical corps in peacetime. Syria could almost certainly use its artillery and aircraft to deliver chemical weapons against tactical targets, but it is very poorly prepared to actually fight such a conflict, and it is unlikely that it could use such weapons with great effectiveness.

Syria seems most likely to use its chemical weapons, and any biological weapons, principally as a deterrent to Israel's exploitation of its conventional superiority—although they have some value as a deterrent to Israel's use of nuclear weapons and as a threat to fixed Israeli military installations and populated areas in order to deny Israel a potential nuclear monopoly. It places a heavy emphasis on having sheltered mobile missiles and the ability to survive conventional Israeli attacks, but there is no reliable unclassified description of Syrian C^4I/BM, deployment plans, doctrine, tactics or strategy. Some Syrians have privately discussed using "volleys" of biologically or chemically armed missiles to deter or retaliate against any Israeli use of nuclear weapons, but it is unclear whether Syria could rapidly deploy enough missiles to fire "volleys," or that they could survive deployment.

Some experts also question the quality of Syrian warhead and bomb design, Syria's ability to get anything approaching maximum lethality from missile weapons or bombs under operational circumstances, and its ability to conduct a large-scale attack in which it achieves high overall lethality. They feel that Syria has not yet demonstrated such sophistication, or even its possession of advanced fusing, in its conventional air weapons. Other experts believe that Syria has had access to Russian and Iranian designs, and significant technical assistance from China and North Korea. They feel Syria is now well armed with modern VX warheads and may have biological weapons.

Israeli Forces and Capabilities

Israel seems to have sophisticated attack capabilities ranging from the ability to employ tactical weapons to the ability to target and destroy any long-range enemy area target or population center. It does not conduct extensive offensive chemical warfare training or seem to conduct more than limited training for purely defensive biological warfare. If it has stocks of tactical chemical and biological weapons, it keeps them totally covert and reserves them for deterrent or demonstrative use against enemy forces and possibly to avoid leaving a "gap" between the use of conventional and nuclear weapons. Israel is also capable of retaliating against the use of limited chemical or biological attacks with strategic conventional bombing that could rapidly do major damage to enemy C^4I/BM capabilities, leadership facilities, utilities and water, and critical economic targets. It can almost certainly do more damage to any Arab neighbor using conventional weapons than that neighbor can currently do using chemical weapons.

Israel has the capability to use nuclear weapons to destroy the key population centers of any combination of enemies and effectively destroy them as modern states. If Israel used its full capabilities, it could probably do enough damage to delay the recovery of such states by a decade or more and to destroy their present political, ethnic, and economic structure beyond the capability to recover in anything approaching its current form. At the same time, Israel almost certainly brings the same sophistication in its C^4I/BM capabilities, targeting, and doctrine for nuclear warfare that it does to conventional air warfare. Further, Israel's large number of survivable weapons gives it the option of attacking a wide range of area targets like air bases and enemy rear areas without sacrificing its capability to destroy urban areas.

This aspect of Israeli capabilities is not fully understood by many Arab analysts, although senior Arab commanders probably understand it. Some Arabs discount Israeli nuclear capabilities on the grounds that Israel would not use nuclear weapons because it is too small and Arab targets are too close. In fact, Israel has had full access to the unclassified US literature on employing large numbers of theater nuclear weapons near friendly forces in Europe, and Israeli officers have participated in tactical nuclear exercises with US officers.

Israel is almost certainly able to fully target Syrian, Jordanian, and Egyptian air bases, and rear assembly areas, and to avoid any significant risk of fallout through a combination of varying weapons yield, varying the height of burst, and timing attacks according to accurate weather models. Israel could easily target 20–30 theater nuclear weapons on Syria, Jordan, or both; deliver them over a relatively short period; and do so safely, barring unusual weather conditions. Alternatively, Israel has the sophistication to vastly increase the killing effect of its nuclear weapons by using ground bursts to maximize fallout and by taking advantage of prevailing weather conditions to expand the lethal "footprint" of that fallout.

The only meaningful uncertainty affecting Israel's technical ability to use nuclear weapons relatively close to Israel is whether it would use tactical nuclear weapons near actual Israeli military operations. Some analysts feel that the IDF has tactical nuclear artillery shells for this purpose. It seems doubtful, however, that the IDF has more than remote contingency plans to use nuclear weapons in this way. It simply does not face sufficient risk to rely on nuclear weapons for minor tactical purposes and it can achieve far more damage far more safely by targeting further to the rear.

It is important to note that Israel's political and military leaders almost certainly see weapons of mass destruction primarily as a deterrent, and would only employ them in the event of an existential threat to Israel's security or to destroy an enemy that used weapons of mass destruction against it. Every aspect of Israel's current doctrine, force structure, and training indicates that it places primary reliance on conventional weapons. There is no evidence of any major IDF effort to organize or train personnel to use weapons of mass destruction and large-scale training and organization would be essential if Israel was planning to use such weapons at lower levels of conflict.

There is, however, one significant uncertainty affecting Israeli use of nuclear weapons on at least a demonstrative basis. It is unlikely that Israel would tolerate any major use of weapons of mass destruction on its civilian population or which led to high casualties, and it is uncertain that it would tolerate such attacks on the IDF. While Israel's reaction would almost certainly be highly contingency specific, and depend on the leadership of Israel at the time, Israel seems unlikely to "ride out" more than very limited uses of weapons of mass destruction against Israeli targets. Further, the retaliatory capabilities of present threats are so limited that it could escalate with relative military impunity, and would have relatively little to fear in terms of lasting reactions from world opinion if it did so as long as its attacker was clearly perceived to have used weapons of mass destruction first and to have done so aggressively.

THE EVOLVING WAR FIGHTING AND ARMS CONTROL IMPLICATIONS OF WEAPONS OF MASS DESTRUCTION

The uncertainties and risks created by the acquisition of long-range missiles; and chemical, biological, and nuclear weapons will grow steadily worse as proliferation proceeds and as the civil technology base of the region grows more sophisticated. There is no way to translate such mid- to long-term shifts into detailed changes in the war fighting capabilities that have just been discussed. Tables 15.1 to 15.6 do, however, show that weapons of mass destruction are likely to increase steadily in lethality.

War fighting and arms control planning must take these differences into consideration, as well as the potential interactions between using one or more different types of weapons of mass destruction. These tables show that chemical weapons may be weapons of mass destruction, but they do not have anything approaching the destructive power of biological and nuclear weapons. However, this might change if an attacking state should use aircraft or cruise missiles to deliver such weapons in bulk in aerosol form, rather than in the far less lethal form resulting from a few ballistic missile attacks. Chemical weapons could radically alter the nature of the escalation and targeting in a future Arab-Israeli conflict.

In contrast, the potential threat from biological weapons makes them a true weapon of mass destruction. These same figures show that biological weapons can be as destructive as small nuclear weapons, and all of the countries that have been discussed have biological weapons efforts. Further, covert delivery of such weapons is one of the most lethal ways of using them. One of the ironies of biological warfare is that it takes an extraordinarily advanced ballistic missile warhead and internal weapons system to disseminate at the right height a survivable and fully lethal biological agent over a wide area. However, Table 15.7 shows that states can use unconventional delivery systems and methods of attack that can be very effective in delivering highly lethal biological weapons strikes.

The US, for example, experimented during the Cold War with particulate matter the same size and weight as anthrax spores. It delivered such spores from commercial vessels moving along the coast of New Jersey and in "terrorist" attacks sprinkling the spores over commuters rushing home through Grand Central Station in New York. Both dissemination systems were highly effective and would have produced very high death rates. Both would have required human intelligence to prevent or identify the attackers. Metal detectors and other technological means would not have been effective, and most conventional anti-terrorist protective measures would have failed.

It is also important to note that many of the lethality estimates shown in Tables 15.1 to 15.6 understate the potential risks from biological and nuclear weapons.

They assume that the biological agent will be no more lethal than anthrax, but most Middle Eastern states are nearing the capability to produce and weaponize more lethal agents, and will probably acquire them at some point between 2000 and 2010 as part of the advances they are making in light manufacturing, food processing, pharmaceutical production, and civil biological research and biotechnology.

For example, the nuclear lethality estimates only consider prompt casualties from nuclear weapons (death within 24–48 hours). The longer-term deaths which would result from fallout after a ground burst, particularly if weather data were used to ensure the prevailing wind patterns carried fallout over additional urban areas, could more than double the casualties shown for a small fission weapon. Nations that can develop 12.5-kiloton weapons may well be able to get yields at least twice as high, and Israel may have boosted weapons with yields approaching 100 kilotons. Equally important, many Arab cities have large areas with population densities some 5 to 10 times higher than those assumed in these estimates—which are based on Western cities rather than Arab cities. The same lethality in weapons of mass destruction might easily kill three to five more times as many people in a city like Cairo than in a city like Tel Aviv.

If these lethality data are combined with the information on national military efforts, they show that the Middle East is already committed to a pattern of proliferation that will allow Israel and its neighbors to engage in a spectrum of conflicts ranging from the most advanced weapons available to crude unconventional weapons, and from localized attacks to weapons delivered over an area from Iran to Libya. Table 15.1 also shows that the process of regional proliferation also is very complex in character. It involves nations in producing both weapons of mass destruction requiring massive production facilities, and weapons which are remarkably easy to produce in small facilities and conceal. It involves developing weapons which lend themselves to models of deterrence, defense, and retaliation close to those that shaped the US-Russian balance during the Cold War, and weapons which lend themselves to covert use—which might make it impossible to conclusively identify a given attacker.

The most basic reasons for such proliferation are obvious, and center around a search for weapons of mass destruction that Israel, Egypt, and Syria embarked upon as long ago as the 1960s. At the same time, Iran, Iraq, and Libya have joined this race and other nations in the Middle East have reasons to proliferate, which include:

- Prestige
- Deterrence
- Intimidation
- War fighting
- Lessons of Iran-Iraq War and Gulf War: Missiles and weapons of mass destruction have been used against military and civilian targets.

- Arms race with neighbors: Algeria-Libya-Morocco, Egypt-Israel-Syria, Iran-Iraq-Southern Gulf.
- The "greater Middle East"—growing overlap of arms races listed above, plus impact of North Korea and India-Pakistan arms race.
- Deterrence and safeguards: No way to know the scale of the efforts of key threats and other major regional actors.
- Limit or attack US and other outside power projection options.
- Compensate for conventional weakness.
- Alternative to expensive conventional investments.
- "Glitter Factor"
- Create existential threat
- Force arms control; react to absence of meaningful arms control regimes.
- Momentum of arms race/respond to proliferation elsewhere.
- State, proxy, or private terrorism.

Table 15.8 outlines some of the war fighting options that affect the Arab-Israeli balance, but there is no way to know how each nation will develop its war fighting doctrine, war plans, safety procedures, leadership control procedures, release doctrine and procedures, targeting doctrine and capabilities, civil defense capabilities, and damage estimation and assessment capabilities. It seems unlikely that most leadership elites outside Israel will consider major existential risks or behave recklessly except under extreme crisis conditions. However, risk taking and miscalculation are long-standing historical realities and war fighting analysis that is based on scenarios and actions that seem prudent in peacetime can be terribly misleading.

The region is filled with leaders who believe in personal rule, are impatient with technical details, and may be poorly prepared for crises when they do occur. The region's military experts also tend to be far more interested in acquiring new weapons than the details of employing them, and it may be very difficult for many countries to estimate weapons reliability and effects—particularly when weapons development is covert. Restraint and rational deterrence in peacetime could quickly turn into uncontrolled escalation in a major crisis—particularly if leaders were confronted with the perceived need to preempt or a "use or lose" contingency. It is important to note that while some states may be proliferating, they may not yet have decided exactly how these weapons that they are producing are to be used. The uncertainties affecting their tactics and strategy may be summarized as follows:

- Israel is likely to be the only state to develop detailed war plans and tactical employment concepts, and its grand strategy precludes communicating any detailed doctrine of employment and deterrence before a war. Weapons of mass destruction are likely to be used only to prevent the military conquest of Israel after a conventional defeat or in response to major attacks on Israeli population centers.

- Many countries may not articulate detailed war plans and employment doctrine beyond the prestige of acquiring such weapons, broad threats, and efforts to intimidate their neighbors and the West.

- Even where nations appear to articulate a strategy of deterrence or employment, this may often consist more of words than detailed war fighting capabilities

- Most (all?) nations will engage in concealment, denial, and compartmentation—focusing more on the acquisition and development effort than employment. Targeting plans, test and evaluation, and understanding of lethality will be limited. Joint warfare concepts will rarely be articulated, and doctrine will not be practiced.

- WMD forces will often be covert or compartmented from other forces, and under the direct control of ruling elites with little real military experience. Separate lines of C^4I/BM reporting directly to the leadership will be common. Actual weapons may be held separately from delivery systems and by special units chosen more for loyalty than capability.

- Any actual employment will be crisis-driven, and utilization and escalation will be more a product of the attitudes and decisions of a narrow ruling political elite than any part of the military command chain. Risk taking will often be leader-specific and based on perceptions of a crisis shaped more by internal political attitudes than an objective understanding of the military situation.

- Employment is unlikely to be irrational or reckless, but restraint in attacking civilian targets or mass employment against armed forces may be limited. Regimes may also take existential risks in escalating if they feel they are likely to lose power.

- The use of proxies and unconventional delivery means may well be improvised without warning.

- Proliferating nations will pay highly detailed attention to US counterproliferation and ATBM efforts at the technical level, and the lessons of previous wars. They will seek to steadily improve concealment, denial, and countermeasures.

- Arms control will be seen as an extension of conflict and rivalry by other means; not as a valid security option.

The effects of any use of biological and nuclear weapons must be kept in perspective. Egypt, Iran, Iraq, Israel, Libya, and Syria are not "one bomb" states. A single nuclear device could not destroy a majority of the population except under the worst possible conditions, and where increases in the long-term death rate were included in the estimate of casualties along with short-term deaths within a 48-hour to seven-day period.

At the same time, Egypt, Iran, Iraq, Israel, Libya, and Syria are "few bomb" states. A nuclear or highly lethal biological attack on the capital and major population of any of the states just listed could destroy its current political leadership, much of its economy, and a great deal of the state's cohesion and national identity. Recovery would be questionable, and the social and economic impact of any such strike would last a decade or more.

Table 15.8
War Fighting Options

- Covert-indirect, unconventional warfare, "terrorism"

- Surprise attack to support conventional war fighting

- Avoid conventional defeat

- Pose political threat—intimidation

- Regional Deterrence—threatened or illustrative use

- Attack power projection facilities

- Counterproliferation

- Extended deterrence

- Controlled escalation ladder

- Asymmetric escalation/escalation dominance

- "Firebreaks"

- Launch on warning/launch under attack

- Seek to force conflict termination

- Destroy enemy as state

- Martyrdom

- Alter strategic nature of ongoing conflict

THE ARMS CONTROL IMPLICATIONS OF WEAPONS OF MASS DESTRUCTION

Advances in technology present growing problems for arms control at every level. While there have been no breakthroughs in the production of fissile material, there is a vast amount of fissile material in the former Soviet Union, and more and more countries could produce an aircraft-deliverable nuclear device in a matter of a few months or years if they could buy weapons-grade material.

The very nature of biotechnology means all of the countries in the Middle East are steadily acquiring the capability to make extremely lethal dry storable biological weapons, and can do so with fewer and fewer indicators in terms of imports of specialized technology, with more use of dual-use or civilian production facilities, and in smaller spaces. In most cases, their civil infrastructure will provide the capability to create such weapons without dedicated major military imports.

Long-range ballistic missile systems are being deployed in Iran and Syria as well as Israel; better strike fighters with performance capabilities superior to yesterday's bombers are becoming commonplace. The kind of cruise missile technology suited to long-range delivery of both nuclear and biological weapons against area targets like cities is becoming available to nations like Egypt, Iran, Iraq, Israel, and Syria. While improved air defenses and theater ballistic missile defenses—such as Patriot, Arrow, and THAAD—offer a potential countermeasure to such delivery systems, the peace process also will create more open borders and more civilian commercial traffic of a kind that makes it easier to use unconventional delivery means.

All of these developments create new uncertainties for war fighting and arms control. Nations that are just beginning to acquire a few nuclear weapons or serious biological weapons tend to see wars involving such weapons in terms of threats to enemy population centers and have little option other than to strike or concede if intimidation fails. They also tend to try to keep their capabilities covert, and remove them from their normal political decision making process. This can lead to rapid massive escalation or surprise attacks—particularly if a given side fears preemption, structures its forces to launch under attack, and/or seeks to strike before its opponent can bring its retaliatory forces and air and missile defenses to full readiness. Fewer weapons do not mean greater stability and security, and they almost inevitably mean counter-value targeting.

On the other hand, more weapons are hardly the solution. As the East-West arms race has shown, there is no logical stopping point. Broadening the number and type of weapons to allow strikes against military targets creates an incentive to be able to strike as many targets as possible. Obtaining the option to strike at tactical military targets lowers the threshold of escalation and may lead a given side to be more willing to attack. Reducing the vulnerability of steadily larger inventories of weapons and delivery systems may lead to a loss of control, or more lethal plans to preempt or launch under attack. Larger forces potentially increase the risk that weapons directed against military targets will hit population centers, and while the Middle East may not be filled with "one bomb" states, it is definitely filled with "few bomb" states. Further, a state under existential attack by one neighbor may lash out against other states—a pattern Iraq has already exhibited by launching missile attacks against Israel during the Gulf War.

Once again, it is important not to exaggerate the impact of these "worst case" risks or their probability. Such possibilities do not alter the basic rules of rational behavior. Weapons of mass destruction do not lead rational and moderate leaders to take existential risks or escalate to genocidal conflicts. At the same time, it is difficult to say that they lead to predictable crisis behavior or escalation ladders. Further, they create problems in terms of establishing any clear arms control or war fighting doctrine that determines how the potential possession and use of given types of weapons of mass destruction—like chemical weapons—relates to the use of biological weapons and nuclear weapons. Even if regional leadership elites had large cadres of experts and took them seriously, there would still be no "rules" for dealing with different mixes of different types of weapons of mass destruction— particularly since it is remarkably difficult to predict the exact damage any given use of such weapons will have against a given target.

One cannot, for example, talk about Israeli nuclear strategy, and then ignore the potential response in terms of Arab use of biological weapons. One cannot talk of potential uses of nuclear and biological weapons against military targets and be certain they will not produce massive collateral damage. One cannot talk about careful and rational decision-makers who may use a weapon with unintended effects, or whose perceptions of risk may be totally asymmetric.

It is also difficult to talk about plans and doctrine when most Middle Eastern states have only begun to think about the war fighting capabilities of the systems they or their neighbors are acquiring, and when perceptions and risk taking may change rapidly if a nation comes under actual attack or is faced with a decision to preempt or launch under attack that must be taken within hours, minutes, or seconds. Few chess players voluntarily engage in simultaneous games of Russian roulette.

Keeping these issues in mind, it is important for all countries in the region to start counterproliferation efforts. The following factors affect such efforts:

- No one area of focus can possibly be effective.
- There is no present prospect that any combination of arms control and active/passive counterproliferation can fully secure the region, any state in the region, or Western power projection forces.
- However, a synergistic effort blending arms control, containment, preemptive options, deterrence, retaliation, and civil defense should offer significant stability.
- There is no present prospect that such stability can be offered without at least tacit US threats to retaliate with nuclear weapons.
- Such policies cannot work by enforcing restraint on friends without enforcing them on enemies. There is no near to mid-term prospect that Israel can give up nuclear weapons.
- Creeping proliferation will follow the line of least resistance.
- There is no present prospect that any combination of measures can defend against biological warfare, and many proposed forms of counterproliferation act as incentive to develop biological weapons and use unconventional means of delivery.
- Theater missile defense will be meaningless without radical improvements in defense against air attacks, cruise missiles, and unconventional means of delivery.

Table 15.9 gives some examples of possible counterproliferation policies that states in the Middle East would need in order to achieve some form of arms control in the region. In addition, there will need to be force improvements to regulate any possible agreements and weapons development. These are listed in Table 15.10 and could possibly result in major budgetary problems for each of the countries participating in such efforts.

Weapons of mass destruction are the ultimate "wild card" in the trends in the Arab-Israeli military balance, and if such a card should ever be played, there is no way to predict its short- and long-term effects. The growth of existential risks involving unpredictable patterns of escalation and using different weapons of mass

Table 15.9
Possible Counterproliferation Policy

- Dissuasion to convince non-weapons of mass destruction states that their security interests are best served through not acquiring weapons of mass destruction.

- Denial to curtail access to technology and materials for weapons of mass destruction through export controls and other tools.

- Arms control efforts to reinforce the Nuclear Non-Proliferation Treaty, Biological and Chemical Weapons Conventions, nuclear free zones, conventional arms treaties that stabilize arms races, confidence and security building measures, and Anti-Ballistic Missile Treaty clarification efforts to allow US deployment of advanced theater ballistic missile defenses.

- Region-wide arms control agreements backed by intelligence sharing and ruthless, intrusive challenge inspection without regard for the niceties of sovereignty.

- International pressure to punish violators with trade sanctions to publicize and expose companies and countries that assist proliferators, and to share intelligence to heighten awareness of the proliferation problem.

- Defusing potentially dangerous situations by undertaking actions to reduce the threat from weapons of mass destruction already in the hands of selected countries – such as agreements to destroy, inspect, convert, monitor, or even reverse their capabilities.

- Military capabilities to be prepared to seize, disable, or destroy weapons of mass destruction in time of conflict.

- Improve tracking and detection of sales, technology transfer, research efforts, extremist groups.

- Defensive capabilities, both active (theater missile defenses) and passive (protective gear and vaccines) that will mitigate or neutralize the effects of weapons of mass destruction and enable US forces to fight effectively even on a contaminated battlefield.

- Declared and convincing counterstrike options ranging from conventional strikes devastating a user nation's economy, political structure and military forces to the use of nuclear weapons against the population centers of user nations and groups.

Table 15.10
Key Force Improvements Affecting Counterproliferation Policy

- *Detection and characterization of biological and chemical agents.* This initiative is intended to accelerate the fielding of stand-off and point detection and characterization systems by up to six years. It also addresses the integration of sensors into existing and planned carrier platforms, emphasizing manportability and compatibility with UAVs.

- *Detection, characterization, and defeat of hard, underground targets.* The US is seeking new sensors, enhanced lethality, and penetrating weapons to increase the probability of defeating the target while minimizing the risk of collateral damage.

- *Detection, localization and neutralization of weapons of mass destruction inside and outside the US.* The US is seeking to identify and evaluate systems, force structures, and operational plans to protect key military facilities and logistic nodes, and conduct joint exercises to improve the capability to respond to potential biological and chemical threats.

- *Development and deployment of additional passive defense capabilities for US forces, including development and production of biological agent vaccines.* This program will develop and field improved protective suits, shelters, filter systems, and equipment two to five years faster than previously planned. It also restores funding to the development of improved decontamination methods.

- *Support for weapons of mass destruction related armed control measures including strengthening the NNPT, CTB, and BWC.* They include establishing a COCOM successor regime, and improving controls on exports and technology by strengthening the MTCR, Nuclear Suppliers Group and Australia Group.

- *Missile defense capabilities, with primary emphasis on theater ballistic missile defenses.* This activity involves improvements in active and passive defenses, attack operations, and improvements in C^4I/BM as well as the deployment of theater missile defenses. The primary focus, however, is on antiballistic missile defenses, and in the near term, this involves the development of the Patriot Advanced Capability Level-3 (PAC-3/ERINT), Navy area theater missile defense (Aegis), and theater high altitude area defense (THAAD).

- *Publicized counterstrike options.* Options ranging from a convincing declared capability to conduct precision mass air and missile strikes with conventional weapons that can devastate user states to use of nuclear weapons escalating to the destruction of population centers.

- *New force tailored to dealing with terrorist and unconventional threats.* New intelligence and tracking systems dedicated to the prevention of mass terrorism, and tailored special forces to detect and attack terrorist groups and deal with unconventional uses of weapons of mass destruction.

destruction also presents steadily more serious problems for arms control. Limited numbers of weapons almost inevitably mean counter-value targeting against population centers and this scarcely means that fewer weapons are safer. If the number of weapons is more than zero, it is generally better to have a significant number of survivable weapons. In addition, the uncertainties pertaining to weapon design and performance pose great risks as well. The uncertainties which leaders in the countries need to consider, whether or not they have weapons of mass destruction, may be summarized as follows:

- Uncertain weapons accuracy, reliability, and effectiveness: The CEP problem, the weapons effect problem.
- Probable lack of full operational testing of all weapons used: The "Heisenberg factor."
- Acquisition does not mean war planning.
- C^4I/BM breakdowns/lack of accurate battle damage assessment by both attacker and attacks.
- Uncertainties coming from use of different types of WMDs and delivery systems.
- Unattributable attacks/proxy attacks.
- Unconventional warfare, mass terrorism, covert delivery, delayed effects.
- Impact of "Cocktails": mixes of different agents or types of weapons of mass destruction.
- Reliance on authoritarian leaders or elites who will never take the time to fully understand the technology and effects of weapons of mass destruction for sudden crisis decisions.
- Coupling effects—US linkages to allies.
- Different perceptions of values/escalation ladder.
- Risk of escalation "total war": willingness to risk use of infectious agents.
- Instability of preemption, launch on warning, launch under attack options.
- The risk of martyrdom and nothing to lose: Unplanned "doomsday machines."
- Unexpected collateral damage.
- Uncertain impact on conventional conflict.
- Uncertain capabilities for NBC defense/counterproliferation.
- Impact on peripheral states.
- Long-term damage effects.
- Next generation arms race.

The covert nature of proliferation makes it almost impossible for any nation to be sure its opponent has actually reduced its weapons to zero, and the very nature of biotechnology means that no presently conceivable arms control regime can deny states in the region a steadily growing "break out" capability to build and use bioweapons capable of decimating an opponent's capital city, potentially disrupting its government and threatening its existence as a state. Another such possibility which the countries in the region need to consider is the threat of terrorist use of weapons of mass destruction described in Table 15.8.

The common thread between all of these scenarios is the widespread use of chemical and biological weapons in areas of dense population. The easily accessible agents as well as the multitude of dense population centers in the Middle East make these scenarios increasingly probable. While many of the examples provided in this table include scenarios regarding states, it is important to note that many possibilities of a terrorist attack using these weapons:

- Unconventional and terrorist delivery of weapons of mass destruction can offer major advantages.
- Powers like Iran and Syria have used terrorists and extremists as proxies in attacking neighbors.
- Biological warfare—the easiest way to achieve extremely high lethalities—is best conducted in this manner.
- Past terrorist attacks have shown it can take months to years to firmly characterize the enemy, and this is particularly true when terrorism has indirect or direct support from a state like Libya, Syria, or Iran.
- "Plausible deniability" may exist indefinitely and a state subject to an existential attack has no meaningful way to retaliate.

These risks pose a critical—if not fatal—problem with global arms control regimes like the Nuclear Non-Proliferation Treaty and Biological Weapons Convention, and are a serious problem with the Chemical Weapons Convention. Such arms control regimes are inherently incapable of solving the "Nth Weapon" problem, and while they may be politically comforting, they cannot offer military security. If there is any hope for effective arms control, it must involve regional arms control measures that affect all forms of weapons of mass destruction, and which either rely on some level of possession to stabilize deterrence or on extremely intrusive technical means and unimpeded, sudden challenge inspection. Even then, it is far from clear that any regional arms control agreement can offer absolute assurance, no matter how many countries may be included or how demanding the proposed inspection system may be.

While many countries in the Middle East seek arms control as a method of defense, others see it as hindering their potential power and influence in the region. Further difficulties exist in the political arena, where signing a treaty might be seen as "giving in" to other nations or as a weakness in the leader signing it. The following factors affect the pursuit of arms control and counterproliferation:

- Egyptian-Israeli dispute has paralyzed ACRS and all near-term progress.
- NPT aids in early to mid-phases of proliferation. Transfer of technology for fuel cycle.
- IAEA inspection and "visits" to declared facilities help, but can also be manipulated to disguise proliferation.
- Dual use technology now allows states to carry out virtually all aspects of weapons design and manufacture—including simulated tests.

- In spite of Iraq's grandiose effort, the ability to carry out all aspects of nuclear proliferation except acquiring fissile materials is becoming steadily cheaper, smaller in scale, and easier to conceal.

- The CWC only affects signer countries and large efforts or those disclosed through SIGINT; it cannot prevent development and assembly of up to several hundred weapons and warheads.

- The steady expansion of petrochemical, industrial process plants, and insecticide plants will make it progressively easier to produce chemical weapons without extensive imports of telltale feedstocks.

- The technology to purify and stabilize mustard and nerve agents is now well known, as is the need for more lethal warhead technology. All major proliferators have nerve gas technology.

- The BWC has no enforcement provisions and no near to mid-term prospects of acquiring them.

- Advances in biotechnology, food processing systems, and pharmaceuticals mean all regional states will soon be able to covertly mass produce dry storage biological weapons in optimal aerosol form.

- The MTCR slows things down and is very valuable, but it has not prevented any determined regional actor from getting missiles.

- All credible regional proliferators already have long-range strike aircraft and a wide range of unconventional delivery options.

- Only a broadly based UNSCOM/IAEA effort of the kind going on in Iraq—supported by even more intrusive inspection and higher levels of technology—can really enforce arms control, and it might not work for biological weapons.

16

Deterrence, Arms Control, and Regional Stability

Two major policy conclusions are obvious. The first is that the military risks in the Arab-Israeli peace process remain extraordinarily high, and that only a comprehensive and stable peace process can address them. The second conclusion is that the cost of arms and military forces imposes a serious strain on Israel and all of its Arab neighbors, and that it is becoming progressively harder to maintain modern conventional forces with the resources available.

It is considerably harder to draw other general conclusions about the Arab-Israeli military balance. There are no simple punch lines and policy recommendations that can deal with the details and risks in this balance if the region does not move towards a broad and stable peace process. This analysis has shown that there are many possible "balances," each tied to different problems and potential sources of conflict that can suddenly escalate into crises or conflicts. The previous chapters have made it obvious that focusing on one possible contingency, or balance, at the expense of the others ignores real-world uncertainties affecting the region. The cumulative probability that one of many less probable events will actually happen is almost certainly higher than the probability that one of the few "most likely" contingencies will actually occur. As is often the case, the "devil is in the details."

At the same time, the analysis has revealed a number of broad trends in the balance. It has shown that the conventional military balance remains more stable than it has been in the past, in spite of the uncertainties in the peace process, and has strong elements of self-stabilizing deterrence. It has also shown, however, that a number of other trends are considerably more threatening—particularly the risks of low-intensity combat between Israeli and Palestinian and the use of weapons of mass destruction. These trends have a number of important implications for policy and arms control.

SELF-STABILIZING DETERRENCE

The current conventional military balance between Israel and its immediate neighbors is relatively stable largely because of Israel's peace with Egypt and Jordan and Israel's present "edge" in conventional war fighting capability. While it is possible to postulate a Syrian surprise attack that might achieve limited initial gains, or a breakdown in the peace process, Israel retains a major defensive "edge" in tactics, technology, and training. This Israeli conventional superiority translates into a strong deterrent against war, gives Israel the defensive strength to risk trading territory for peace, and acts as a strong incentive for the Arab states to pursue the peace process.

At the same time, Israel's conventional edge does not make it secure enough to provide enough offensive superiority that would allow it to threaten or intimidate its Arab neighbors. Israel badly needs peace with Egypt, Jordan, and the Palestinians. Any form of arrogance or aggressiveness undermines a security structure that is too fragile for Israel to exploit. The cost of offensive operations would be far greater to Israel than they could be worth, since Egypt has strong defensive capabilities, and Israel has nowhere to go and nothing it can usefully occupy.

The Nations Inside the Peace Process

The previous analysis has shown that a very different mix of trends has affected Egypt, Israel, and Jordan, the nations already participating in the peace process. The net effect of these trends has been to create further momentum behind self-stabilizing deterrence.

Egypt has benefited from loan forgiveness and massive amounts of US grant aid. The end result is that part of Egypt's force structure consists of modern, US-equipped units with improved tactics, training, and sustainability. Egypt's F-16s, E-2Cs, M-60s, and M-1s give it great defensive strength. This defensive strength is reinforced by its possession of the Improved Hawk, the Sinai accords and MFO, and strategic depth.

At the same time, Egypt has cut its real, domestically funded military spending by about 40% since the mid-1980s.[1047] These cuts have saved Egypt money, but they have made it even more difficult for Egypt to sustain its inflated military force structure than in the past and have reduced its offensive capabilities. About 35 to 40% of Egypt's force structure still consists of low-grade Soviet and European-equipped forces with obsolete equipment. Money and manpower that could have been allocated to high quality units and economic development have been wasted on these units, which have negligible value in offensive operations.

Egypt has also emphasized modernization over improvements in its infrastructure and sustainment capabilities. It is not organized to project forces across the Sinai and provide its armored maneuver forces with effective air defenses. At the same time, the Sinai accords and MFO do as much to prevent Egypt from being able to achieve strategic surprise in an attack on Israel as they do to limit Israeli offensive capabilities against Egypt.

Jordan is now a full partner in the peace process, and its military capabilities have been crippled by a lack of modernization since the early 1980s, and by the near cutoff in military and economic assistance that followed the Gulf War. Jordan has been forced to make major cuts in both its military expenditures and arms imports. Jordan's military expenditures in 1995 were only 66% of its expenditures in 1987, as measured in constant 1995 dollars.[1048] Jordan's arms imports totaled only about $100 million during 1990–1993, and $200 million during 1994–1997, versus a total of $2.4 billion during 1986–1989.

Arms deliveries to Jordan totaled around $400 million during 1990–1997, versus at least $5.6 billion for Israel and $9.9 billion for Egypt.[1049] New Jordanian arms agreements totaled around $800 million during 1991–1998, versus well over $6.8 billion for Israel and $9.5 billion for Egypt.[1050] As a result, Jordan has not been able to maintain its past force levels and its rates of modernization and recapitalization are so low that they are beginning to seriously undermine Jordan's military forces and strategic credibility.

Israel has cut real defense spending by about 40% since the early 1980s. Israel, however, has had the benefit of massive amounts of US grant aid. It has received well over $9.0 billion in US FMF aid in the last five years, and it has had billions of dollars' worth of additional ESF aid and $2 billion annually in loan guarantees. It also compares with a total of $6.5 billion in FMF aid for Egypt.

Israel has received about 40% more FMF aid than Egypt and it can use such aid far more efficiently. Egypt has had to buy fully assembled arms and support packages under the US FMS aid program, or has had to pay for facilities to assemble US weapons in Egypt. This has meant that much of the money Egypt spends under FMS goes to spares, special equipment, and overhead, and its weapons facilities have raised the unit cost of the arms that Egypt assembles above the unit cost of fully assembled US weapons.

In contrast, Israel can buy US weapons on a commercial basis and provide its own support packages, and its industries are so efficient that they can provide about 40% value added to the weapons components and technology Israel buys from the US. Israel has also benefited from free or low cost technology transfers, specially pricing arrangements, and Israeli military sales to the US. As a result, the net value of a given dollar's worth of FMF aid to Israel is about 50% higher than to any other Middle Eastern country.

Equally important, the preceding analysis has shown that Egypt and Israel are the only nations affecting the Arab-Israeli conventional balance that have been able to buy the kind of advanced technology and weapons necessary to react to the lessons of the Gulf War and take advantage of the "revolution in military affairs." While weapons numbers are still important, they are no longer the key measure of military strength. It is the ability to exploit technology in a fully integrated "system

of systems"—and to support this technology with new C⁴I/BM, training, munitions, joint operations, and sustainment capability—that will shape conventional
war fighting capability in the early 2000s. The only alternative for powers like
Syria—and for Iran and Iraq—has been to seek asymmetric approaches like
proliferation, proxy wars, and the use of terrorism.

Israel has had further advantages that have improved its defensive capabilities.
It has been able to exploit technology with its own industrial base. Unlike Egypt, it
has not had to convert from a Soviet bloc–supplied force structure. It has focused
on the tactics, training, infrastructure and sustainment capabilities necessary to
fully exploit modern technology while Egypt has concentrated on procurement. As
a result, Israel's defensive "edge" has steadily improved, while US arms and
technology transfers to Egypt have ensured that Egypt has no reason to feel
threatened or discriminated against.

In contrast, Syria has had to rely largely on aging Soviet bloc–designed
weapons, has lacked the money and access to technology to modernize and
restructure its forces, and has often chosen force quantity over force quality. Iraq
and Libya have been largely frozen in military technology for half a decade. Jordan
has lacked the money to compete.

The end result of these trends is a remarkable level of conventional military
deterrence that supports the peace process, with little chance of sudden destabilizing
changes that do not take the form of proliferation and asymmetric warfare. The
nations in the region also are already taking a "peace dividend"—although one that
events have forced on Iraq, Jordan, Lebanon, and Libya, and one that has been
financed by the US in the cases of Egypt and Israel. Only regional arms control can
ensure that this situation will not be reversed in the mid to long term, but the
destabilizing arms race and delicate conventional balance that have shaped
security developments in the region from the end of World War II to the early
1990s no longer exist.

The Nations Outside the Peace Process

This conventional stability is the product of broader forces that cannot be easily
reversed. The military capabilities of the nations outside the peace process have
been sharply reduced by the end of the Cold War, the outcome of the Gulf War, UN
sanctions, and their own political, strategic, and military incompetence. While
military expenditures and arms transfers are only one set of measures of military
capability, the previous analysis has shown that they can provide a good picture of
the overall trends in military effort. Syrian military expenditures in constant
dollars have dropped by more than 40% in constant dollar equivalents since the
mid-1980s. This drop in the dollar value of Syrian military spending has occurred
in spite of significant Syrian economic growth, and Syrian military expenditures
have dropped from a peak of 23% of GDP in the mid-1980s to less than 7.2% in
1995.[1051] Even if Syria could obtain massive new orders of arms, it would now

take close to half a decade for Syria to build back to the level of relative military capability it had in the mid-1980s.[1052]

The Gulf War has shown the continuing depth of the political divisions between Iraq and Syria, and the Coalition victory resulted in the destruction of about 40% of Iraq's major ground force weapons and the loss of many of its best combat aircraft. Since 1990, an import-dependent and inefficient Iraqi military machine has been without arms imports. In fact, deliveries of new conventional arms have dropped in value from $16.6 billion during 1987–1990 to nearly zero after that time. It has placed no significant new orders since mid-1990. Iraq has lost the imports it needs to sustain military operations and make up for its lack of effective organization and support capability. Iraq has lacked the ability to import the technology it needs to react to the lessons of the Gulf War, and will need years to "recapitalize" its conventional forces once the UN lifts its sanctions.[1053]

Libya never made effective use of its massive arms imports during the 1970s and 1980s, and its forces have been little more than a large military "parking lot." In recent years, however, Libya has failed to spend the money necessary to maintain and modernize its past imports. Deliveries of arms imports to Libya declined from $3.2 billion annually in current dollars in the early 1980s to around $700 million in the late 1980s. They dropped to less than $400 million in 1990, and averaged around $150 million annually during 1991–1994, and totaled far less than $50 billion a year during 1995–1998. Libya placed only about $75 million dollars a year worth of new arms orders during 1991–1994, and placed virtually no new orders during 1995–1998. Although the UN eased some sanctions on Libya in 1999, after it turned over two terrorists suspected of the Lockerbie bombing for trial in the Hague, the EC, and US maintained an embargo on arms exports. As a result, Libya has made no significant improvements in conventional military technology and its conventional military capabilities are declining from "parking lot" to "junkyard."[1054]

Lebanon remains a military cipher which has received an average of less than $50 million worth of arms a year since 1989, and only about $25 million a year since the Lebanese forces began to recover after 1993. Lebanon is beginning to receive more significant military aid from the US and France—its new arms orders averaged $50 million a year during 1994–1997—but for nation building and not for external conflict. It is a nation where the key military issue is the future of Syrian occupation and their proxies like the Hizbollah. Lebanon can be the scene of conflict, but the only military threat it poses is to itself.

Iran has never rebuilt the air strength it had at the time of the fall of the Shah. It has a total of around 307 aircraft, but less than 60 are modern Russian combat types. It has no real power projection capability, and its US-made aircraft are too old and too worn to play more than a token role against Israel. Like a number of Arab states on the periphery of the Arab-Israel balance, it can deploy token ground troops and large numbers of infantry "volunteers," but not effective armored and artillery forces in any strength. It lacks the training, sustainment, and mobility support systems for this kind of power projection.

The Stabilizing Role of the US

It is also important to note that the end of the Cold War, and the emergence of the US as the one state capable of massive global power projection, has tilted the balance towards stability in other ways. The US is Israel's closest ally. It cannot project power in time to be decisive in many Arab-Israeli contingencies, but its arms and technology export policies are shaped to ensure Israel's "edge." The US can provide Israel with massive resupply of weapons and munitions in a crisis and do so far more quickly than in 1973. It can support Israel by securing the seas and with sea- and bomber-launched cruise missiles. If the IAF should suffer a catastrophic defeat, it can also suddenly project massive amounts of air power into an environment that would otherwise be saturated by IAF aircraft. It can rapidly reinforce Israel's theater missile defenses.

It is important to note that the US will not assist in every conflict, but it is equally important to note that the US will not tolerate any Israeli defeat that threatens its existence as a nation or the safety of large numbers of its civilian population. The last quarter century has shown that it is irrelevant that this is not a formal treaty commitment.

At the same time, US ties to Israel are anything but a one-way alliance. The US would do everything possible to halt any Arab-Israeli conflict as soon as possible, and to enforce a rapid return to pre-conflict borders. It will provide Egypt with immediate military support against any threat other than Israel, and would immediately seek to reestablish an Egyptian-Israeli peace in the case of any clash or conflict. Both Egyptian and Israeli planners understand that the US would do everything in its power to prevent either state from making any territorial or strategic gains against the other in the event of a conflict. They also understand that any untoward escalation or incident involving the other nation's population could have a devastating impact on US political perceptions and the media, and US aid once a peace was reestablished.

The US commitment to Jordan is not as well structured, but the US has a clear commitment to Jordan's territorial integrity. It would do everything possible to prevent or terminate a conflict between Jordan and Israel, and would demand an Israeli withdrawal from Jordanian territory if Israel was foolish enough to try to occupy it. The US would immediately respond to any Jordanian request for aid in the event of Syrian and/or Iraqi military pressure and attacks.

The US places strategic pressure on both Israel and the Palestinians. It cannot force a peace, only encourage one. It cannot prevent some form of Second Intifada. The US can and will, however, press for peace and Israeli leaders of all parties know that US policy encourages the emergence of a Palestinian state once a final settlement is reached, and opposes any Israeli reoccupation of Palestinian territory. No nation in the Arab-Israeli struggle is immune to world opinion and the world media, but any Israeli action against the Palestinians must be taken in the context that Israel's leaders must be acutely sensitive to US public opinion and media.

There are no guarantees here. US attitudes and actions will be dependent on the nature of a particular crisis and contingency. As 1982 demonstrated, US support for Israel is dependent on Israeli moderation, restraint, and common sense. US support for Egypt and Jordan is dependent on their status as allies and the existence of friendly regimes. US support for the Palestinians is dependent on the existence of a Palestinian Authority that is willing to live with Israel and which has a commitment to at least an eventual peace. US interest in ensuring that Syria does not take serious losses is dependent on what Syria does and Syria's interest in resolving a given conflict. Nevertheless, the Arab-Israeli military balance does not exist in a strategic vacuum and the role of the US has unique importance.

Any major new successes in the peace process will also create military issues. A truly successful peace process will increase Israel's reliance on its strategic relationship with the US while it simultaneously increases the impact of the limitations of US military power projection capabilities. Israel's sacrifice of territory for peace means it needs every security guarantee the US can provide in securing the peace and helping Israel defend itself, but makes it progressively harder for the US to deploy decisive amounts of force in time to affect the balance in a sudden or surprise conflict.

US Intervention in an Arab-Israeli Conflict

Unlikely as such a contingency may be in political terms, a Syrian or broader Arab attack on Israel could be prepared and executed in a matter of a few days. US naval and air deployments could react in such a time frame, but they would face important limits. The US could provide Israel with important aid in the first days of such an attack. It could secure the seas around Israel. Depending on US deployments at the time, the US could probably provide one or two carriers' worth of air reinforcements, limited numbers of land-based fighter and fighter-attack aircraft, support from long-range bombers, and support with cruise missiles.

Much, however, would depend on US carrier and naval deployments at the time of such an attack, and on whether the US was involved in other contingencies. Israeli basing and C^4I/BM capabilities already are nearly saturated by the IAF, and Israel would find it difficult to base and protect land-based US air reinforcements.

The US could deploy units like the 82nd and 101st Airborne Divisions relatively rapidly, and possibly tailored reinforcement forces to meet critical needs—like the AH-64 and MLRS forces sent to Kosovo. Such forces could provide a significant punch and would have a major political and psychological impact.

There is little prospect the US could deploy heavy armored land forces until such a conflict was over. It would take a minimum of a month to deploy even one heavy division in sustainable combat-ready form. Even if the US provided prepositioned land force equipment, it would take US forces at least 7–10 days to marry up the required manpower with the prepositioned equipment and longer to deploy in a coherent combat-capable form—and this would depend on their movement and equipment being secure from attack.

These problems are not arguments against US reinforcement of Israel, or an Arab ally, in an ultimate crisis. Control of the seas, air space to the west of Israel, the threat of US strategic retaliation with conventional air power and cruise missiles, limited US air reinforcements, tailored, high-value US land reinforcements, and US re-supply of Israel or an Arab ally could be critical in some contingencies. At the same time, they indicate that Israel's security must ultimately rest on strong IDF forces, and not on US security guarantees.

These problems also indicate that any US presence on the Golan may have to be limited to an observer or peace-keeping mission, rather than a peace enforcement mission. Given the massive forces available to Israel and Syria, a US flag is not a secure deterrent unless it is backed by US forces in place. If Israel is to emerge from the peace process with the same level of deterrence and defense capabilities it has today, the IDF must be strong and effective enough to be largely self-reliant. Israel, its Arab neighbors, and future arms control efforts must accept this reality.

The Impact of US Military Assistance

The US needs to accept the fact that continued US aid to Israel and Egypt, and increased US aid to Jordan and the Palestinians are essential aspects of regional stability and the peace process. Both regional stability and peace require that Israel have enough US military aid to be able to sustain its defensive "edge."

Maintaining this "edge" is necessary to ensure Israeli public support for the peace process, encourage Arab states to fully accept the peace process, ensure that Israel does not revert to a reliance on preemption or strategic conventional attacks, and ensure Israel does not increase its reliance on deterrence using weapons of mass destruction. Having such an "edge" is also likely to be an essential precursor to Israeli willingness to negotiate conventional arms reductions and make any serious efforts towards creating a Weapons of Mass Destruction Free Zone or placing limits on its nuclear capabilities.

At the same time, US aid is equally important to ensuring Egyptian support for the peace process and Egyptian confidence that Israel's defensive "edge" has not become a destabilizing offensive superiority. The US must demonstrate that Israel's security does not come at the expense of its Arab allies, or the sacrifice of Arab strength and dignity. It must support Jordan and the Palestinian Authority through the difficult transitions still to come.

This hardly means the US should be the only source of aid to this region, and the US should do everything possible to encourage conventional arms reductions as an alternative to military assistance. At the same time, there is no short-term substitute for US aid, and US military assistance to Israel, Egypt, and Jordan will continue to play a critical role in ensuring regional stability and supporting the peace process.

BEYOND CONVENTIONAL DETERRENCE

Conventional deterrence, however, is only part of the story. The Arab-Israeli military balance and the peace process are being affected by other military trends and some of these trends are far less reassuring than those that shape the conventional balance. These trends include issues like the future of the Palestinians and Jordan, the need for a full Israeli-Syrian peace agreement, the problem of weapons of mass destruction, the role of US security guarantees and the need for US aid.

The Impact of the Peace Process, Low-intensity Combat, and the Palestinian Problem

The kind of delays in the peace process that took place under the Netanyahu government do threaten the stability of conventional deterrence. It is one thing to have a slow or cold peace, it is another to have the kind of peace process that falters so badly that a given side loses hope and belief in peace or concludes it simply cannot deal with the other. So far, this risk is limited to the Israeli-Palestinian negotiations. Egypt has lived with a cold peace even through such provocations as Israel's invasion of Lebanon in 1982. Jordan has not sought war in the past, but has had it thrust upon it by its Arab neighbors. It seems likely to firmly maintain its peace agreement as long as it remains under a Hashemite regime, and to seek a warm one. Ironically, Syria's very decoupling from the peace process makes it difficult for Syria to become permanently disenchanted or give up hope, and its proxy war with Israel in Lebanon gives it a lever that offers Syria some hope.

The tensions between Israel and the Palestinians, however, could sow the seeds of a much broader conflict. If the Palestinians abandon hope, and/or turn to some second form of Intifada, the impact will soon be felt outside Gaza, the West Bank, and Jerusalem. Any serious Israeli miscalculation in the way it conducts military action against the Palestinians could prove to be the one thing that would remobilize the Arab street and Arab nations against Israel. Similarly, continued Israeli near-indifference to the need to create some kind of viable economic structure that links Israel, the Palestinians and Jordan, and which provides tangible benefits from peace, represents the most probable way in which Israel could alienate Jordan.

Any analysis of the military balance that focuses solely on conventional war fighting ignores the risk that a breakdown of the peace process could transform the kind of conflict that took place during the Intifada into a far more serious level of low-intensity or unconventional war. Israel is not Ulster, Vietnam, or Afghanistan, but the issue of Israel's security may still be determined as much by its internal security, and the security of any Palestinian entity, as by the balance of military forces.

Efforts to find the proper balance between the security efforts of Israel and the Palestinian Authority Security, and efforts to enhance Palestinian dignity and provide the Palestinians with economic aid, is absolutely critical. Palestinian political development, jobs, and living conditions may be unfamiliar measures of the military balance, but they are critical measures in securing a peace. They may ultimately prove to be far more important than numbers of tanks and aircraft or arms control reductions, and they already have a higher immediate priority for policy planning. The human dimension of Israel and Palestinian security is the most important single factor threatening Arab-Israeli strategic stability in the near and mid-term.

The Impact of Jordan

Conventional deterrence, regional stability, and the peace process are equally dependent on giving Jordan added military self-reliance and self-stability, and on a consistent effort to help Jordan develop its economy and to broaden regional economic cooperation between Jordan, the Palestinian Authority, and Israel.

Jordan does not require massive amounts of new arms or military aid, but it does require continued US and other Western aid. It also needs US support in encouraging Jordanian-Israeli cooperation in areas like their F-16 programs. Unthinkable as it may have been a few years ago, Jordan and Israel need to cooperate in ways that go beyond mere confidence-building measures and which are beginning to shape their military planning in ways that deliberately secure their peace agreement.

At the same time, the US and the West need to show the Jordanian military and the Jordanian people need to be shown that peace does not come at the expense of self-reliance or dignity, and more is involved than arms transfers and military aid. As is the case with the Palestinians, Jordan's role in the military balance is dependent on internal security, and internal security is dependent on economic development.

These broader aspects of "human factors" are just as important in dealing with Jordanian security as they are in dealing with the Palestinian Authority, and it will be as important to ensure that the living standards of Jordanian Palestinians are improved as it will be to improve the living standards of Palestinians in Gaza and the West Bank.

The Impact of Syria, the Golan, and Lebanon

The military balance may achieve a high level of deterrence and stability even if Syria and Lebanon do not reach a peace agreement with Israel. At the same time, there can be little progress in conventional arms reductions, and Israel and Syria will continue to compete in acquiring weapons of mass destruction. Equally important, there will always be a risk of war, Syria and Iran will continue to use proxies to attack Israel, Syrian-backed Arab extremists will continue to challenge Israel's right to exist, and there will be little hope that Lebanon can regain its independence.

Reaching a full peace settlement does, therefore, have the same high priority it has had in the past and its urgency may be accelerating because of Hafez Assad's death and the risk of a succession crisis. At a minimum, such a peace would include an Israeli-Syrian peace treaty, an agreement that transfers the Golan to Syria in return for normalization, and an effective arms limitation agreement. Ideally, it will mean Syrian and Iranian withdrawal from Lebanon, and at least the beginning of a broad regional dialogue on the problem of weapons of mass destruction.

The Impact of Weapons of Mass Destruction

The demon lurking at the edges of the present military balance is the spread of weapons of mass destruction. The trends in the regional acquisition of weapons of mass destruction are almost directly opposed to the trends in the conventional balance. Israel's nuclear monopoly acts as both a destabilizing factor in its relations with Egypt, and as an essential deterrent for Israel in dealing with threats from Iran, Iraq, and Syria. Egypt continues to make covert efforts to acquire long-range missiles and chemical and biological weapons—partly for reasons of status and partly to create its own deterrent. Opponents of the peace process like Iran, Iraq, Libya, and Syria continue to make significant efforts to acquire or maintain their capability to manufacture and deliver such weapons.

Technology transfer is increasing the risks involved. New long-range missiles and strike aircraft are being transferred to Iran and Syria. There is little prospect that UNSCOM can deny Iraq the ability to produce biological and nerve gas weapons. Iran and Syria have biological and chemical weapons' development and production efforts that are not subject to control, and Libya continues to expand its chemical weapons' production efforts. Iran is seeking nuclear weapons. New biological technologies continue to increase the lethality of such weapons while making arms control more difficult. Regional powers are steadily improving their ability to manufacture the precursors for chemical weapons, and cruise missile technologies are becoming more widely available.

Uncertainty and ambiguity can deter, but they can also slaughter. There is no stable pattern of Arab-Israeli deterrence based on long practical political and military experience. Strategy, doctrine, war planning, and targeting are secret national concerns—to the extent they yet exist or exist in a carefully structured form. Conflicts outside Israel and the Arab "ring states" can suddenly involve Israel and/or its neighbors with little warning and in highly unstable and confusing contingencies. A crisis between Israel and Syria involving such weapons would give both sides significant potential incentives to preempt, launch under attack, or massively escalate.

There are significant incentives for cheating on arms control treaties and uncertain capabilities to verify such cheating. Further, as long as weapons of mass destruction are not constrained, it will be tempting for nations like Syria to try to compensate for conventional weakness by increasing their holdings of such weapons, or for nations like Egypt to covertly try to compensate for Israel's nuclear monopoly by acquiring weapons of mass destruction.

It is also important to understand that technology tends to favor the proliferator. Successful controls on nuclear weapons tend to drive proliferating states towards the development of equally lethal biological weapons, and biotechnology makes the development of such weapons progressively easier and at the same time makes them progressively harder to control. Large ballistic missiles still require a very complex and visible technology and manufacturing base and test process. They are also extremely expensive. Advances in cruise missile technology, however, are making cruise missiles much cheaper, extending ranges and payloads, and creating new commercially available dual-use components. Weapons development and manufacturing technologies are also making it progressively easier to suddenly produce several hundred highly effective biological and chemical weapons in covert ways and with little or no warning, bypassing most current proposals for inspection and control regimes. Advances in GPS, global commercial communications, and cyberwarfare are also making it progressively easier to use weapons of mass destruction through covert means of delivery and in asymmetric warfare.

IMPLICATIONS FOR ARMS CONTROL

These conflicting trends have important implications for arms control. On the one hand, there is less urgency in seeking near-term reductions in conventional forces. In fact, ongoing military aid and weapons transfers will be needed if Israel is to have the security to give up the Golan, if Egypt is to complete its ongoing conversions to US-supplied equipment, and if Jordan is to correct its major military weaknesses. The priority is to preserve and enhance the deterrence and defensive capabilities that underpin the peace process.

On the other hand, there is a clear priority for other forms of conventional arms control:

- Israel and Syria must reach an agreement on force limitations and confidence-building measures in the Golan—probably one that involves some form of multinational peacekeeping force. The details of such an agreement involves such vital national interests that they can only be shaped by Israel and Syria, and their mutual acceptance of an agreement they have both negotiated is more important than its precise form. At the same time, such an agreement will almost certainly require strong international support and some degree of US aid in terms of intelligence, warning, and verification.

- There is an equal need to reinforce the stabilizing trends in the conventional balance with confidence-building measures, added transparency, and expert dialogue. This is necessary to reduce exaggerated Israeli concerns with the Arab threat, and Egyptian and other Arab perceptions that Israel's defensive "edge" can somehow be translated into offensive dominance. More broadly, the region may not be able to simultaneously implement a peace process and reduce its conventional arms, but it does eventually need to reduce military spending and focus on economic development. Reaching an agreement on major conventional arms reductions may well take a decade, but it is scarcely too early for Israel and its neighbors to begin the process of planning and analysis that is an essential precondition to structuring arms reduction agreements.

- There is a need for outside suppliers to carefully consider the implications of any transfers to nations outside the Arab-Israeli peace process. There are a number of critical technologies and weapons systems that can affect the present trends in the conventional balance. These weapons and technologies include (a) advanced electronic warfare capability, (b) advanced AWACS or AEW aircraft, (c) advanced surface-to-air missiles like the S-3000 and S-400, (d) improved combat aircraft and air munitions for precision strike and beyond-visual-range combat, (e) advanced tanks and other armor with thermal sights, improved fire control, more lethal rounds, and spaced armor, (f) third or fourth generation anti-tank weapons, (g) large numbers of advanced infrared SHORADs, and (h) MLRS-like artillery weapons and advanced artillery fire control and targeting systems. Unless some qualitative limits are placed on such transfers to nations like Syria, Iran, Iraq, and Libya, the Middle East arms race is certain to continue and even accelerate in certain key areas.

- There is a need to find regional approaches to the problem of dealing with extremism and terrorism that can further limit the ability of outside powers and individuals to support Palestinian and Israeli extremists, and to improve cooperation between Israel, Jordan, and the Palestinian Authority. Security operations will inevitably be dominated by local security forces and human intelligence, but it may be possible to provide outside assistance in technology and in controlling technology transfer that will both improve security and reduce the need for intrusive security measures. Improved cooperation and dialogue may also find ways to improve security operations while simultaneously improving the treatment of Palestinians and reducing the barriers to Israeli-Palestinian economic cooperation.

Finally, arms control must begin to deal with the problem of proliferation. This requires all of the nations involved in the peace process to look beyond the issue of Nuclear Non-Proliferation Treaty and focus on the regional problem of all forms of weapons of mass destruction.

Egypt and the other Arab nations involved in the peace process need to recognize the difficulties Israel faces in dealing with any arms control effort that focuses solely on Israel's nuclear capabilities. Any negotiation that focuses on Israel's nuclear weapons without including Egyptian, Iranian, Iraqi, Libyan, and Syrian weapons of mass destruction singles out Israel's nuclear forces at a time when the capabilities of hostile neighboring states are growing, and are subject to temporary and uncertain controls, or no controls at all.

The threat posed by Syrian, Iranian, and Iraqi biological and chemical warfare capabilities, coupled with the threat posed by Iranian and Iraqi long-range missiles and aircraft, is not one Israel can ignore. They will soon approach the lethality of small nuclear forces, if they do not have this lethality already. If Israel brings its nuclear advantage to the conference table, Israeli nuclear capabilities may be constrained or reduced, while rogue states in the region can steadily increase the risk of nuclear-biological-chemical attacks on Israel.

Further, moderate Arab states need to take a more realistic view of exactly who threatens whom. Israeli nuclear capabilities are presently only a game-theoretic threat to Egypt, Jordan, and the moderate Gulf states. In contrast, Syrian, Iranian, and Iraqi weapons of mass destruction provide these nations with political status and leverage against their Arab neighbors, and create a considerably higher risk that moderate Arab states will become involved in actual war fighting contingencies.

If there is a way out of these problems, it seems to lie in a much broader approach to controlling weapons of mass destruction that clearly links region-wide progress in controlling nuclear weapons to region-wide progress in controlling chemical and biological weapons and long-range delivery systems. President Mubarak has advanced similar ideas in talking about a zone free of weapons of mass destruction, and such broader efforts could be made part of the existing Arms Control and Regional Security (ACRS) process if they defined the region to consider Iran, Iraq, and Libya as well as the states now in the ACRS process, and the risk of the transfer of related weapons and technology from outside the region. Attempting to focus on some particular agreement—such as the NPT—may suit the political passions of the moment, but it is scarcely a realistic solution for enhancing regional security.

This, however, means that Israel must recognize that such negotiations are necessary and that only a solid framework of arms control measures, coupled with a solid peace, can begin to provide security for both Israel and its Arab neighbors against weapons of mass destruction. At some point, Israel must emerge from the nuclear closet, and begin to provide its Arab neighbors with data on its forces and capabilities, just as they must begin to be frank about their biological, chemical, and missile programs.

Unfortunately Egypt, Israel, Jordan, and other moderate Arab states will need to consider the very real possibility that no amount of arms control negotiations may be able to stuff the genie of proliferation back into the bottle. In an ideal world, the Middle East should be free of weapons of mass destruction. In the real world, some mix of arms control and active counterproliferation measures may be the best that the nations in the peace process and ACRS can achieve.

There are obvious dangers in the Middle East where only extremist regimes have weapons of mass destruction, or where the only barrier to such a monopoly by extremists are arms control agreements where extremist regimes will find it far easier to cheat than moderate states. At least in the mid term, the nations in the peace process may find it equally necessary to cooperate in active counterproliferation efforts like air and missile defense. Egypt and Israel, in particular, may also find they have more to gain from a mix of such cooperation and efforts to structure region-wide arms control agreements that can be verified and secured, than from squabbling over issues like the NPT.

Sources and Methods

This text has stressed the fact that many of the statements and statistics mentioned here are highly uncertain. Middle Eastern governments go to great effort to conceal the nature of virtually every aspect of their national security activity, and the various unclassified sources available differ in many details.

SOURCES

It was possible to visit Egypt, Israel, Jordan, and Syria at various times during the preparation of this book and to talk to Egyptian, Israeli, Jordanian, and a few Syrian experts. Some provided detailed comments on the text. Interviews also took place with regional experts in the United States, United Kingdom, France, Switzerland, and Germany. Portions of the manuscript were circulated for informal review by officials and diplomats in several of the countries covered in the book, and some chapters were modified extensively in response. No such interviews or comments are referenced, however, unless those concerned specifically gave their permission and none of these sources is quoted by name. As a result, many of the sources shown in footnotes are supplemented by interviews and comments that cannot be referenced or attributed.

Data are drawn from a wide range of sources, but involve many detailed judgments by the author in reconciling different reports and data. In some cases, there was no "right" source, but one source was chosen for the sake of comparability and consistency. The CIA *World Factbook* was often chosen over other international data sources simply because it offered the most consistent basis for obtaining directly comparable data.

The sources for data on arms control are explained in depth in Chapter 2, along with the reasons for choosing given sources. The military manpower, force strength, and equipment estimated used throughout the book were made by the author using a wide range of sources, including computerized databases, interviews, and press clipping services.

Many key force strength statistics are taken from the latest edition of the International Institute for Strategic Studies *Military Balance* (IISS, London). Use has also been made of the annual editions of publications from *Jane's*, as well as the Jaffee Center for Strategic Studies, *The Military Balance in the Middle East* (JCSS, Tel Aviv). Other sources include the latest annual editions of various *Jane's* reference books. There were, however, many cases in which US government experts sharply differ from the figures available in these sources, and seem to have convincing reason to do so. Their estimates were used where unclassified data were available.

Extensive use has also been made of media sources, including Internet material, translations of broadcasts, newspapers, magazine articles, and similar materials. These are referenced in most cases, but some transcribed broadcasts and much of the Internet material did not permit detailed attribution. The Internet and several on-line services were used to retrieve data on US and Israeli government reporting and policy, descriptions of the details of the peace agreements, and examinations of Arab and Palestinian positions. Since most of the databases involved are dynamic, and either change or are deleted over time, there is no clear way to footnote much of this material. Recent press sources are generally cited, but are often only part of the material consulted.

Virtually all of the sources drawn upon in writing this analysis reveal data that are in partial conflict. They do not provide any consensus over demographic data, budget data, military expenditures and arms transfers, force numbers, unit designations, or weapons types. While the use of computer databases allowed some cross-correlation and checking of such sources, the reporting on factors like force strengths, unit types and identities, and tactics often could not be reconciled and citing multiple sources for each case is not possible.

Mapping and location names also presented a major problem. The author used US Army and US Air Force detailed maps, commercial maps, and in some cases commercial satellite photos. In many cases, however, the place names and terrain descriptions used in the combat reporting by both sides, and by independent observers, presented major contradictions that could not be resolved from available maps. No standardization emerged as to the spelling of place names. Sharp differences emerged in the data published by the US and Israeli governments, and private reporting reflects a complete lack of progress in reconciling the conflicting methods of transliterating Arabic and Hebrew names into English.

The same problem with transliterating names applied in reconciling the names of organizations and individuals—particularly those being transliterated from Arabic. A limited effort has been made to standardize the spellings used in this text, but many names are tied to relational databases where the preservation of the original spelling is necessary to identify the source and tie it to the transcript of related interviews.

METHODS

This book deliberately focuses on military capabilities, security issues, and the military aspects of arms control. It is only indirectly concerned with politics and economics. It also deliberately focuses on the details of security issues. It is intended primarily to help provide technical background for those who must assess the military balance, and its implications for peace negotiations and arms control, rather than provide policy recommendations.

In most cases, the author adjusted figures and data on a "best guess" basis, drawing on some thirty years of experience in the field. In some other cases, the original data provided by a given source were used without adjustment to ensure comparability, even though this leads to some conflicts in dates, place names, force strengths, and so on within the material presented—particularly between summary tables surveying a number of countries and the best estimates for a specific country in the text. In such cases, it seemed best to provide contradictory estimates to give the reader some idea of the range of uncertainty involved.

Most of the value judgments regarding military effectiveness are made on the basis of American military experience and standards. Although the author has lived in the Middle East, and worked as a US advisor to several Middle Eastern governments, he feels that any attempt to create some Middle Eastern standard of reference is likely to be far more arbitrary than basing such judgments on his own military background.

One final point: the emphasis on developments in Israel and Israeli literature is not deliberate. It is the result of a lack of substantive unclassified military literature in the Arab countries. Repeated efforts were made to obtain attributable sources with some degree of detail and reliability. Several countries did provide literature on a non-attributable basis, but the open literature is generally very vague and Arab news media proved to be difficult to search. Some good detailed reporting did emerge, but in general it proved better to rely on interviews and direct official inputs.

Notes

1. These estimates are extrapolated from the population growth data on the Arab-Israeli ring states in the CIA, *World Factbook, 1995, 1998, 1999, and 2000*, and from the military expenditure and arms import data over the preceding decade in ACDA, *World Military Expenditures and Arms Transfers,* Washington, GPO, various editions.

2. For a modern and well structured Israeli assessment of the balance, see Shlomo Bron and Yiftah Shapir, *The Middle East Military Balance, 1999–2000*, Tel Aviv University, Jaffee Center for Strategic Studies, 2000.

3. CIA, *World Factbook, 1995, 1998, 1999, and 2000;* World Bank, *Claiming the Future: Choosing Prosperity in the Middle East and North Africa*, Washington, World Bank, 1995, pp. 114–115.

4. CIA, *World Factbook, 1995, 1998, 1999, and 2000;* World Bank, *Claiming the Future: Choosing Prosperity in the Middle East and North Africa*, Washington, World Bank, 1995, pp. 114–115.

5. *Middle East Economic Digest*, August 13, 1999, p. 35.

6. CIA, *World Factbook, 1995, 1998, 1999, and 2000;* World Bank, *Claiming the Future: Choosing Prosperity in the Middle East and North Africa*, Washington, World Bank, 1995, pp. 114–115.

7. The Jaffee Center for Strategic Studies provides useful data on foreign advisors and sources of military aid, but does not estimate arms transfers.

8. The author has estimated the data for Lebanon for 1985–1989. ACDA did not report any figures.

9. Most of these statements are based on data taken from compilations of national reporting made by the US State Department. Some were provided informally by the embassies of the countries involved.

10. *Defense News*, September 4, 1995, p. 14; "Israeli defense budget in crisis," *Jane's International Defense Review*, September 1997, p. 10.

11. "Stiff opposition as Israeli MoD seeks 5% cash boost," *Jane's Defense Weekly*, July 1, 1998, p. 20.

12. *Jane's Defense Weekly*, September 22, 1999, p. 21.

13. Interviews in Jordan and Britain, *Defense News*, December 9, 1996, p. 10.

14. IISS, *The Military Balance, 1999–2000 and 2000–2001*.

15. CIA, *World Factbook, 1999 and 2000 editions*.

16. CIA, *World Factbook, 1999 and 2000 editions*.

17. World Bank, *Claiming the Future: Choosing Prosperity in the Middle East and North Africa*, Washington, World Bank, 1995, pp. 114–115.

18. Jehl, Douglas, "Jordan Now Succeeding in Mending Gulf Ties Frayed by Iraq," *New York Times*, February 8, 1996, p. A15

19. IISS, *The Military Balance, 1999–2000 and 2000–2001*.

20. *Jane's Defense Weekly*, July 12, 1995, p. 19.

21. Faraj, Caroline, "Funding, Politics Slow Jordanian Defense Plan," *Defense News*, December 9–15, 1996, p. 10.

22. Finnegan, Philip. Israel, Egypt Retain Huge Piece of IMF Pie, *Defense News*. February 15, 1999, p. 12.

23. Faraj, Caroline and Philip Finnegan, "Jordanian Border Defenses Boosted By US, British Aid," *Defense News*, April 12, 1999, p. 1.

24. CIA, *World Factbook, 1999 and 2000 editions*.

25. The defense budget is closely held and has not been provided to any international organizations. Portions of the military budget are reviewed in closed sessions by designated committees of the People's Assembly. Egypt has never submitted a standardized military expenditure report to the UN. In 1998, Egypt did not participate in the UN Register of Conventional Arms. In the past, Egypt has participated. Egypt provided information to the conventional arms register its first year but has declined to provide information since then in protest of what it considers deficiencies in the register which have not been addressed.

26. Ibid.

27. Ho, David, "US-Mideast," Associated Press, July 1, 1999.

28. US Department of State, *Congressional Presentation, Foreign Operations, Fiscal Years 1988, 1990, 1994, 1995, 1996, 1997, 1998, and 1999*, Department of State, Washington, DC; Source: Adapted from US Defense Security Assistance Agency (DSAA), "Foreign Military Sales, Foreign Military Construction Sales and Military Assistance Facts as of September 30, 1994," Department of Defense, Washington, 1995, and "Foreign Military Sales, Foreign Military Construction Sales and Military Assistance Facts as of September 30, 1997," Department of Defense, Washington, 1998.

29. CIA, *World Factbook, 1999 and 2000 editions*.

30. CIA, *World Factbook, 1999 and 2000 editions*.

31. Department of State, *Annual Report on Military Expenditures, 1999*, submitted to the Committee on Appropriations of the U.S. Senate and the Committee on Appropriations of the U.S. House of Representatives by the Department of State July 27, 2000, in accordance with section 511(b) of the Foreign Operations, Export Financing, and Related Programs Appropriations Act, 1993.

32. Scheer, Steven, "Israel economy in slump but pickup seen," Reuters, June 15, 1998.

33. "The Economy," *Israeli Office of Economic Affairs*, May 1998.

34. For a good discussion, see Alvin Rabushka, *A Scorecard on the Israeli Economy, a Review of 1998*, and Institute for Advanced Political and Strategic Studies, Jerusalem, February 1999.

35. CIA, *World Factbook, 1999 and 2000 editions.*

36. Neubach, Amnon. "Budget Deficits, Monetary Policies and the Peace Process," *Economic Slowdown and Peace Slowdown.* Israel Policy Papers No.3, January 15, 1997, p. 3.

37. Blanche, Ed. "Israeli Cabinet Votes to Cut Spending by $114m," *Jane's Defense Weekly*, September 17, 1997, p. 20.

38. Neubach, Amnon. "Budget Deficits, Monetary Policies and the Peace Process." *Economic Slowdown and Peace Slowdown.* Israel Policy Papers No.3, January 15, 1997, p. 3.

39. *Jane's Defense Weekly*, May 21, 1997, p. 13; *Jane's International Defense Review*, 9/1997, p. 10.

40. *Defense News*, September 13, 1999, pp. 1, 20; *Jane's Defense Weekly*, September 22, 1999, p. 21.

41. *Defense News*, September 13, 1999, p. 1, 20; *Jane's Defense Weekly*, September 22, 1999, p. 21.

42. *Jane's Defense Weekly*, August 30, 2000, p. 17.

43. *Jane's Defense Weekly*, November 29, 2000, p. 19.

44. *The Estimate*, September 8, 2000, p. 4.

45. *Jane's Defense Weekly*, August 30, 2000, p. 16, November 29, 2000, p. 19.

46. "Clinton Plans to Ask Syria to Resume Israel Talks," *The New York Times*, July 20, 1999, p. A8.

47. Ibid.

48. Ho, David, US-Mideast, Associated Press, July 1, 1999.

49. US Department of State, *Congressional Presentation, Foreign Operations, Fiscal Years 1988, 1990, 1994, 1995*, Department of State, Washington, DC; Source: Adapted from US Defense Security Assistance Agency (DSAA), "Foreign Military Sales, Foreign Military Construction Sales and Military Assistance Facts as of September 30, 1994," Department of Defense, Washington, 1995.

50. Richard Engel, "Reaping the Peace Dividend," *Jane's Defense Weekly*, January 12, 2000, pp. 23–29.

51. Faraj, Caroline; Finnegan, Philip, "Funding, Politics Slow Jordanian Defense Plan," Defense News, December 9–15, 1996, p. 10.

52. The reader should examine Tables IV and V in ACDA, *World Military Expenditures and Arms Transfers, 1993–1994*, Washington, GPO, 1995. To take only one example out of many, ACDA reports in Table IV that the US delivered $11.7 billion worth of weapons during 1991–1993 versus $3.6 billion for Russia/Soviet Union. These figures indicate that the US provided 3.25 times more weapons than Russia/Soviet Union. If one looks at the data on actual arms transfers to the Middle East in Table V, however, Russia provided slightly more tanks, 2.7 times more artillery weapons, 2.4 times more supersonic combat aircraft, and 2.1 times more helicopters. The only categories where the US led in weapons transfers were in APCs and light surface-to-air missiles.

53. Richard F. Grimmett, *Conventional Arms Transfers to the Middle East, 1986–1993*, Washington, Congressional Research Service, 94–612F, July 29, 1994; Richard F. Grimmett, "Conventional Arms Transfers to Developing Nations, 1987–1994," CRS 85–862F, Washington, Congressional Research Service, August 4, 1995, pp. 57 and 68.

54. Richard F. Grimmett, *Conventional Arms Transfers to the Middle East, 1991–1998*, Washington, Congressional Research Service, RL30275, August 4, 1999.

55. Richard F. Grimmett, *Conventional Arms Transfers to the Middle East, 1991–1998*, Washington, Congressional Research Service, RL30275, August 4, 1999.

56. United Press International, November 5, 1992, BC Cycle.

57. Blanch, Ed, "Syria discusses buying advanced Russian systems," *Jane's Defense Weekly*, May 19, 1999, p. 17; La Francere, Sharon, "Russia, Syria Hint at Weapons Deal," *The Washington Post*, July 7, 1999, p. A16; Kemp, Damian, "Russia pushes defense sales as exports hit highest for years," *Jane's Defense Weekly*, July 14, 1999, p. 17; Saradzhyan, Simon, "Bombing Spurs Interest in Russia Craft, Defenses," *Defense News*, July 19, 1999, p. 11.

58. La Francere, Sharon, "Russia, Syria Hint at Weapons Deal," *The Washington Post*, July 7, 1999, p. A16

59. Saradzhyan, Simon, "Bombing Spurs Interest in Russia Craft, Defenses," *Defense News*, July 19, 1999, p. 11.

60. Conversations with World Bank experts, *Middle East Economic Digest*, September 20, 1995, pp. 10–11.

61. Reuters, September 23, 1999, 0913.

62. "Syria: Gathering Clouds," *The Economist*, April 24, 1999, p. 4.

63. *Jane's Defense Weekly*, July 12, 1995, p. 19.

64. *Jane's Defense Weekly*, July 12, 1995, p. 19.

65. Richard F. Grimmett, *Conventional Arms Transfers to the Middle East, 1991–1998*, Washington, Congressional Research Service, RL30275, August 4, 1999.

66. Richard F. Grimmett, *Conventional Arms Transfers to the Middle East, 1991–1998*, Washington, Congressional Research Service, RL30275, August 4, 1999.

67. *Jane's Defense Weekly*, March 3, 1999, p. 18.

68. News Release, Office of the Secretary of Defense (Public Affairs), Defenselink, September 30, 1999.

69. Clyde R. Mark, "Israel: US Foreign Assistance," Congressional Research Service, CRS-IB85066, May 18, 1995; Clyde R. Mark, "Middle East and North Africa: US Aid FY1993, 1994, and 1995," CRS 94–274F, March 28, 1994; "Congressional Presentation for Foreign Operations," FY1996, US Department of State, 1995.

70. Opall-Rome, Barbara, "U.S., Israel Agree on Wye Accord Aid Package," *Defense News*, February 1, 1999, pp. 4, 19.

71. Opall-Rome, Barbara, "Barak Win Spurs US to Reopen Stalled Projects," *Defense News*, May 31, 1999, p. 4.

72. Twing, Shawn L., "Retired Israeli General Investigated for Embezzling $10 Million in U.S. Aid Funds," *The Washington Report on Middle East Affairs*, January/February 1997, p. 27.

73. Twing, Shawn L., "New US Foreign Aid Agreement Provides Israel a Net Increase in US Foreign Aid," *The Washington Report on Middle East Affairs*, July/Aug. 1998, p. 15.

74. Reuters, March 11, 1999, 0615.

75. *Jane's Defense Weekly*, August 11, 1999, p. 14.

76. Reuters, March 11, 1999, 0615.

77. Clyde R. Mark, "Middle East and North Africa: US Aid FY1993, 1994, and 1995," CRS 94–274F, March 28, 1994; "Congressional Presentation for Foreign Operations," FY1996, US Department of State, 1995.

78. Prados, Alfred B., "Jordan: U.S. Military Assistance and Cooperation," CRS 96–309F, April 5, 1996.

79. US Department of State, *Congressional Presentation, Foreign Operations, Fiscal Years 1988, 1990, 1994, 1995*, Department of State, Washington, DC; Prados, Alfred B., "Jordan: U.S. Military Assistance and Cooperation," CRS 96–309F, p. 3.

80. Faraj, Caroline, "Jordan Anticipates Boost From U.S. Cut in Israel, Egypt Aid," *Defense News*, April 13–19, 1998.

81. Based on interviews in Jordan and with US government experts; Prados, Alfred B., "Jordan: U.S. Military Assistance and Cooperation," CRS 96–309F, p. 5.

82. Faraj, Caroline, "Jordan Anticipates Boost From U.S. Cut in Israel, Egypt Aid," *Defense News*, April 13–19, 1998.

83. Redden, Jack, "Jordan hopes for air exercises with Israel, Turkey," Reuters Ltd., June 25, 1996.

84. *Jane's Defense Weekly*, March 3, 1999, p. 18.

85. Discussions with US officials, *Defense News*, October 2, 1995, p. 4; *Jane's Defense Weekly*, July 1, 1995, pp. 20–21; Schweid, Barry, "US-Jordan," The Associated Press, June 17, 1997.

86. *Jane's Defense Weekly*, September 30, 1995, p. 19.

87. Balman, Sid, "Lebanese PM seeks military aid," *United Press International*, Oct. 17, 1996; Finnegan, Philip, "Lebanon Seeks More US Aid," *Defense News*, Nov. 24–30, 1997.

88. Finnegan, Philip and Barbara Opall-Rome, "US to Expand Military Sales to Lebanon," *Defense News*, June 21, 1999, p. 4.

89. Additional data are estimated using Schlomo Gazit, ed., *The Middle East Military Balance, 1993–1994*, Jaffee Center for Strategic Studies, Tel Aviv, 1994; and Military Technology, *World Defense Almanac, 1994–1995*, Bonn, Monch Publishing Group, Issue 1, 1995. Material has also been drawn from computer printouts from NEXIS, the United States Naval Institute database, and from the DMS/FI Market Intelligence Reports database. Weapons data are taken from many sources, including computerized material available in NEXIS, and various editions of *Jane's Fighting Ships* (Jane's Publishing); *Jane's Naval Weapons Systems* (Jane's Publishing); *Jane's Armor and Artillery* (Jane's Publishing); *Jane's Infantry Weapons* (Jane's Publishing); *Jane's Military Vehicles and Logistics* (Jane's Publishing); *Jane's Land-Base Air Defense* (Jane's Publishing); *Jane's All the World's Aircraft* (Jane's Publishing); *Jane's Battlefield Surveillance Systems,* (Jane's Publishing); *Jane's Radar and Electronic Warfare Systems* (Jane's Publishing), *Jane's C⁴I Systems* (Jane's Publishing); *Jane's Air-Launched Weapons Systems* (Jane's Publishing); *Jane's Defense Appointments & Procurement Handbook (Middle East Edition)* (Jane's Publishing); *Tanks of the World* (Bernard and Grafe); *Weyer's Warships* (Bernard and Grafe); and *Warplanes of the World* (Bernard and Grafe). Other military background, effectiveness, strength, organizational, and history data are taken from Anthony H. Cordesman, *After the Storm: The Changing Military Balance in the Middle East*, Boulder, Westview, 1993; and *Weapons of Mass Destruction in the Middle East, London*, Brassey's/ RUSI, 1991; Anthony H. Cordesman and Abraham Wagner, *The Lessons of Modern War, Volume I*, Boulder, Westview, 1989; the relevant country or war sections of Herbert K. Tillema, *International Conflict Since 1945*, Boulder, Westview, 1991; Department of Defense and Department of State, *Congressional Presentation for Security Assistance Programs, Fiscal Year 1996*, Washington, Department of State, 1992; various annual editions of John Laffin's *The World in Conflict* or *War Annual*, London, Brassey's, and John Keegan, *World Armies*, London, Macmillan, 1983; "The IDF's Security Principles," Office of the IDF Spokesman, April, 1995, and Scotty Fisher, "Country Briefing Israel," *Jane's Defense Weekly*," February 18, 1995, pp. 29–38.

90. This analysis is based on interviews, the IISS, *Military Balance*, and *Jane's World Armies*, Issue 2, "Israel."

91. This analysis is based on interviews, the IISS, *Military Balance, Jane's World Armies*, Issue 2, "Syria," and *The Estimate*, August 13, 1999, p. 10.

92. Interviews and IISS, *Military Balance, 1998–1999, 1999–2000 and 2000–2001*.

93. Interviews, *Jane's Sentinel*, "Syria," *The Estimate*, August 13, 1999, p. 10.

94. *Jane's International Defense Review*, June 2000, pp. 3 and 17.

95. Interviews with Jordanian and US officials. *Jane's Defense Weekly*, July 12, 1995, p. 19.

96. This analysis is based on interviews, the IISS, *Military Balance*, and *Jane's World Armies*, Issue 2, "Lebanon."

97. Interviews and IISS, *Military Balance, 1998–1999, 1999–2000 and 2000–2001*.

98. This analysis is based on interviews, the IISS, *Military Balance*, and *Jane's World Armies*, Issue 1, "Egypt."

99. Richard Engel, "Reaping the Peace Dividend," *Jane's Defense Weekly*, January 12, 2000, pp. 23–29.

100. Interviews and IISS, *Military Balance, 1998–1999, 1999–2000* and *2000–2001*.

101. For an interesting argument that currently planned cuts mean a shift towards a more full time professional, or "peacetime," Israeli Army, see Stuart A. Cohen, "Studying the Israel Defense Forces: A Changing Contract With Israeli Society," BESA Center for Strategic Studies No. 20, Ramat Gan, Israel, Bar-Ilan University, 1995.

102. "The IDF's Security Principles," Office of the IDF Spokesman, April, 1995, and Scotty Fisher, "Country Briefing Israel," *Jane's Defense Weekly*," February 18, 1995, pp. 29–38.

103. *Jane's Defense Weekly*, April 17, 1996, p. 37, October 29, 1997, p. 17; *Washington Times*, October 22, 1997, p. A-13; *Armed Forces Journal*, May 1997, p. 42.

104. *Jane's Defense Weekly*, July 5, 2000, p. 16.

105. *Armed Forces Journal*, May 1997, p. 42; *Jane's Defense Weekly*, April 17, 1996, p. 37; *International Defense Review*, 8/1999, p. 3.

106. *Armed Forces Journal*, May 1997, p. 42; *Jane's Defense Weekly*, April 17, 1996, p. 37; *International Defense Review*, 8/1999, p. 3; R.M. Ogorkiewicz, "Israel advances with fourth-generation MBT armor and heavily protected fighting vehicles," *Jane's International Defense Review*, May 2000, pp. 55–59.

107. *Jane's Defense Weekly*, August 20 ,1997, p. 3.

108. Foss, Christopher F., "Jordan receives 120mm-armed M60A1 MBT," *Jane's Defense Weekly*, March 31, 1999, p. 16; "Jordan to trial upgunned M60," *Jane's International Defense Review*, May 1999, p. 61.

109. *Jane's International Defense Review*, July 2000, p. 19; *Jane's Defense Weekly*, April 5, 2000, p. 14.

110. *Jane's International Defense Review*, June 2000, p. 14.

111. "Looking to an arms industry of their own," *Jane's Defense Weekly*, January 15, 1997, p. 19.

112. *Jane's Defense Weekly*, September 22, 1999, p. 21; April 5, 2000, p. 14.

113. *Jane's Defense Weekly*, September 2000, p. 21; *Jane's International Defense Review*, July 2000, p. 8.

114. *Jane's Defense Weekly*, March 24, 1999, p. 20, September 22, 1999, p. 21; Reuters, March 15, 1999, 1403.

115. Reuters, March 11, 1999, 0615; *Jane's Defense Weekly*, March 17, 1999, p. 3.

116. *Jane's Defense Weekly*, December 15, 1999, p. 19.

117. Foss, Christopher F., "Egypt to be launch buyer for US-built 120mm round," *Jane's Defense Weekly*, April 28, 1999, p. 17.

118. *Defense News*, April 3, 1995, p. 3, October 30, 1995, p. 4; *Chicago Tribune*, January 4, 1993; *Jane's Defense Weekly*, February 21, 1996, p. 16.

119. *Jane's Defense Weekly*, November 19, 1997, p. 8; Richard Engel, "Reaping the Peace Dividend," *Jane's Defense Weekly*, January 12, 2000, pp. 23–29.

120. *Jane's Defense Weekly*, September 20, 2000, pp. 36–38.

121. R.M. Ogorkiewicz, "Israel advances with fourth-generation MBT armor and heavily protected fighting vehicles," *Jane's International Defense Review*, May 2000, pp. 55–59, and *International Defense Review*, September 1995, pp. 73–74.

122. *Jane's Defense Weekly*, September 20, 2000, pp. 36–38.

123. "The IDF's Security Principles," Office of the IDF Spokesman, April, 1995, and Scotty Fisher, "Country Briefing Israel," *Jane's Defense Weekly*," February 18, 1995, pp. 29–38.

124. *Jane's Intelligence Review*, Volume 7, Number 6, pp. 261–264, and Volume 7, Number 7, pp. 299–304.

125. *Jane's International Defense Review*, July 2000, p. 3.

126. Foss, Christopher F., "Jordan starts to test upgraded Scorpion vehicle," *Jane's Defense Weekly*, April 7, 1999, p. 20.

127. *Jane's Defense Weekly*, May 10, 2000, p. 16.

128. *Jane's Defense Weekly*, April 15, 1995, p. 20; March 6, 1996, p. 23; Richard Engel, "Reaping the Peace Dividend," *Jane's Defense Weekly*, January 12, 2000, pp. 23–29.

129. Richard Engel, "Reaping the Peace Dividend," *Jane's Defense Weekly*, January 12, 2000, pp. 23–29.

130. *Jane's Defense Weekly*, April 9, 1997, p. 27.

131. *Jane's Defense Weekly*, April 9, 1997, p. 27.

132. *Jane's Defense Weekly*, July 2, 1997, p. 16; *Jane's Defense Weekly*, Oct. 23, 1996, p. 3.

133. Foss, Christopher F., "Gill MR missile details released," *Jane's Defense Weekly*, April 28, 1999, p. 18.

134. *Jane's Defense Weekly*, October 11, 1999, p. 22.

135. *Jane's Defense Weekly*, July 2, 1997, p. 16; *Jane's Defense Weekly*, Oct. 23, 1996, p. 3.

136. *Jane's Defense Weekly*, November 3, 1999, p. 16; September 13, 2000, p. 4.

137. Foss, Christopher F., "LAHAT tested in Israel," *Jane's Defense Weekly*, August 4, 1999, p. 15.

138. Faraj, Caroline and Philip Finnegan, "Jordanian Border Defenses Boosted by US, British Aid," *Defense News*, April 12, 1999, p. 1.

139. *Defense News*, April 10, 1995, p. 24; January 20, 1997, p. 11; Richard Engel, "Reaping the Peace Dividend," *Jane's Defense Weekly*, January 12, 2000, pp. 23–29.

140. Both sides have long had some artillery weapons with such ranges. The difference is improvements in targeting, extended range projectiles, and projective lethality that give such weapons significant effectiveness.

141. *Jane's Defense Weekly*, September 20, 2000, p. 20.

142. Richard Engel, "Reaping the Peace Dividend," *Jane's Defense Weekly*, January 12, 2000, pp. 23–29, June 30, 1999, June 7, 2000, p. 15.

143. *Jane's Defense Weekly, August 25, 1999*, p. 18.

144. Richard Engel, "Reaping the Peace Dividend," *Jane's Defense Weekly*, January 12, 2000, pp. 23–29.

145. Richard Engel, "Reaping the Peace Dividend," *Jane's Defense Weekly*, January 12, 2000, pp. 23–29.

146. *Jane's International Defense Review*, 5/1998, p. 23.

147. "The IDF's Security Principles," Office of the IDF Spokesman, April 1995, and Scotty Fisher, "Country Briefing Israel," *Jane's Defense Weekly*," February 18, 1995, pp. 29–38; *Jane's Defense Weekly*, November 4, 1995, p. 8.

148. *Jane's Defense Weekly*, February 18, 1995, p. 38.

149. *Defense News*, October 18, 1999, p. 44; *Jane's Defense Weekly*, November 17, 1999, p. 19.

150. *Jane's Defense Weekly*, August 16, 2000, p. 23

151. *Jane's All the World's Aircraft*, Issue 5, March 1998.

152. *Wall Street Journal*, September 23, 1998, p. B-2.

153. Ed Blanche, "Changing the Face of Middle East Airpower," *Jane's Defense Weekly*, November 10, 1999, pp. 38–41.

154. *Jane's Defense Weekly*, December 1, 1999, p. 15.

155. *Jane's Defense Weekly*, November 18, 1998, p. 30.

156. *Jane's Defense Weekly*, November 18, 1998, p. 30.

157. *Jane's World Air Forces,* various editions, *Defense Weekly*, February 18, 1995, p. 38, October 12, 1998, p. 50; *Jane's Defense Weekly*, July 16, 1997, p. 17, September 30, 1998, p. 4, November 18, 1998, p. 30; Reuters, September 14, 1998, 0910 United Press, July 30, 1996, 1001; *Washington Times*, July 31, 1996, p. A-15.

158. *Jane's Defense Weekly*, April 30, 1997, p. 6.

159. *Jane's Defense Weekly*, April 30, 1997, p. 6, March 3, 1999, p. 3; "The IDF's Security Principles," Office of the IDF Spokesman, April, 1995; Scotty Fisher, "Country Briefing Israel," *Jane's Defense Weekly*," February 18, 1995, pp. 29–38; *Defense News*, February 21, 1993, p. 3, January 10, 1994, p. 6; *International Defense Review*, 10/1994, p. 6; *Wall Street Journal*, January 28, 1994, p. A-3.

160. Associated Press, March 27, 1999, 0150.

161. *Jane's Defense Weekly*, September 30, 1998, p. 4, February 3, 1999, pp. 31–32; *Jane's International Defense Review*, 12/1998, pp. 39–40; *Defense News*, June 3, 1996, p. 3, July 22, 1996, p. 3, May 12, 1997, p. 24, November 5, 1997, p. 17, April 20, 1998, p. 46, June 1, 1998, p. 3, June 7, 1998, p. 31; *Wall Street Journal*, September 23, 1998, p. B2.

162. "Barak Delays Decision on Israeli Aircraft Buy," *The Estimate*, June 4, 1999, p. 4.

163. "Israel Chooses Lockheed Martin," Associated Press, July 16, 1999; "Israel to buy 50 Lockheed Martin F-16 jets," Reuters, July 17, 1999; "Israel Will Buy 50 F-16's In Its Biggest Arms Deal Ever," *The New York Times*, July 19, 1999, p. A6; *Jane's Defense Weekly*, January 6, 2000, p. 6.

164. Ed Blanche, "Changing the Face of Middle East Airpower," *Jane's Defense Weekly*, November 10, 1999, pp. 38–41; Joris Janssen Lok, "New AGE F-16 Spans the Fighter Generations," *Jane's International Defense Review*, 2/2000. pp. 27–35.

165. Reuters, October 19, 1999, 2015.

166. *Jane's International Defense Review*, 8/1999, p. 11.

167. *Jane's Defense Weekly*, September 6, 2000.

168. *Jane's Defense Weekly*, October 13, 1999, p. 6.

169. *Defense News*, October 25, 1999, p. 14.

170. *Jane's Defense Weekly*, September 9, 1998, p. 79.

171. *Jane's Defense Weekly*, November 28, 1987, p. 1239; Rafael briefing sheet; manufacturer offprint of "Rafael: Lessons of Combat" from *Military Technology*, May 1991.

172. *Jane's Defense Weekly*, November 1, 2000, p. 13.

173. Reuters, April 21, 1998, 1753.

174. "Israel seeks to buy 42 U.S. missiles-Pentagon," Reuters, July 20, 1999, 1845.

175. *Jane's International Defense Review*, 5/1998, p. 18.

176. *Jane's International Defense Review*, May 1998.

177. *Jane's Defense Weekly*, August 16, 2000, p. 22.

178. *Defense News*, July 27, 1998, pp. 1 & 19; Tamir Eshel, "Israel's Defense Electronics," *Defense Electronics*, October 1991, pp. 87–90.

179. Tamir Eshel, "Israel's Defense Electronics," *Defense Electronics*, October 1991, pp. 87–90.

180. *Jane's Defense Weekly*, "USA, Israel sign LITENING team agreement," December 9, 1995, p. 21.

181. *Jane's Defense Weekly*, April 5, 2000, p. 3.

182. Dick Pawloski, *Changes in Threat Air Combat Doctrine and Force Structure, 24th Edition*, Fort Worth, General Dynamics DWIC-91, February 1992, pp. II-199 to II-211.

183. *Jane's Defense Weekly*, February 2, 1990, pp. 200–203, May 7, 1997, pp. 22–24.

184. *Jane's Defense Weekly*, February 2, 1990, pp. 200–203; *Air Force*, November, 1991, p. 50; *Jane's Defense Weekly*, June 24, 1989, p. 1324; *Aviation Week*, June 28, 1993, pp. 46–47; *International Defense Review*, 10/1992, p. 1015; *Jane's Defense Weekly*, February 18, 1995, pp. 29–37.

185. Ed Blanche, "Changing the Face of Middle East Airpower," *Jane's Defense Weekly*, November 10, 1999, pp. 38–41.

186. *Jane's Defense Weekly*, February 2, 1990, pp. 200–203; *Air Force*, November, 1991, p. 50; *Jane's Defense Weekly*, June 24, 1989, p. 1324; *Aviation Week*, June 28, 1993, pp. 46–47; *International Defense Review*, 10/1992, p. 1015; *Jane's Defense Weekly*, February 18, 1995, pp. 29–37.

187. *Jane's Defense Weekly*, February 2, 1990, pp. 200–203, May 7, 1997, pp. 22–24.

188. Reuters, July 12, 2000, 1109 and 1125; *The Estimate*, April 7, 2000, p. 4.

189. *Inside Defense Electronics*, April 10, 1992, p. 14; IAI Elta Brochure; *Air Force*, November 1991, p. 50; JINSA, *Security Affairs*, March 1992, p. 3; *Aviation Week*, June 28, 1993, pp. 46–47; *International Defense Review*, 10/1992, p. 1015; *Jane's Defense Weekly*, February 18, 1995, pp. 29–37.

190. *Jane's Defense Weekly*, February 2, 1990, pp. 200–203; *Air Force*, November 1991, p. 50; *Jane's Defense Weekly*, June 24, 1989, p. 1324; *Aviation Week*, June 28, 1993, pp. 46–47; *International Defense Review*, 10/1992, p. 1015; *Jane's Defense Weekly*, February 18, 1995, pp. 29–37; Reuters, November 12, 1999, 0749.

191. *Jane's Defense Weekly*, October 15, 1988, p. 959.

192. *Defense News*, July 13, 1998, p. 10; *Jane's Defense Weekly*, June 3, 1998, pp. 91–92; *Jane's International Defense Review*, 4/1998, p. 19.

193. *International Defense Review*, 9/1987, p. 1204.

194. *Defense News*, April 4, 1988, p. 1; *International Defense Review*, 9/1989, pp. 1237–1238; *Jane's Defense Weekly*, December 2, 1998, p. 19..

195. *International Defense Review*, 9/1989, pp. 1237–1238; *Defense News*, July 3, 1995, p. 8.

196. *International Defense Review*, 4/1998, p. 19

197. The Harpee and Star-1 may be different systems. *Defense News*, April 4, 1988, p. 1, May 11, 1992, p. 1, July 3, 1995, p. 8.

198. *Defense News*, November 28, 1988, p. 17; Israeli Military Industries (IMI) manufacturer brochures.

199. "The IDF's Security Principles," Office of the IDF Spokesman, April 1995; Scotty Fisher, "Country Briefing Israel," *Jane's Defense Weekly*," February 18, 1995, pp. 29–38; *Defense News*, February 21, 1993, p. 3; January 10, 1994, p. 6; *International Defense Review*, 10/1994, p. 6; *Wall Street Journal*, January 28, 1994, p. A-3.

200. *Jane's Defense Weekly*, August 30, 2000, p. 6.

201. Based on interviews, Jane's *Sentinel*, "Syria," and *Jane's World Air Forces*, Issue 4, November 1997.

202. Ed Blanche, "Changing the Face of Middle East Airpower," *Jane's Defense Weekly*, November 10, 1999, pp. 38–41.

203. Dick Pawloski, *Changes in Threat Air Combat Doctrine and Force Structure, 24th Edition*, General Dynamics DWIC-91, Fort Worth Division, February 1992, pp. I-85 to I-117.

204. Rostislav Belyakov and Nikolai Buntin, "The MiG 29M Light Multirole Fighter," Military Technology, 8/94, pp. 41–44; Dick Pawloski, *Changes in Threat Air Combat Doctrine and Force Structure, 24th Edition*, General Dynamics DWIC-91, Fort Worth Division, February 1992, pp. I-85 to I-117.

205. Dick Pawloski, *Changes in Threat Air Combat Doctrine and Force Structure, 24th Edition*, General Dynamics DWIC-91, Fort Worth Division, February 1992, pp. I-85 to I-117.

206. *Aviation Week and Space Technology*, April 10, 1989, pp. 19–20; *New York Times*, April 5, 1989, September 7, 1989; *Washington Times*, January 16, 1989; *FBIS/NES*, April 10, 1989.

207. The Su-24 has a wing area of 575 square feet, an empty weight of 41,845 pounds, carries 3,385 gallons or 22,000 pounds of fuel, has a take-off weight of 871,570 pounds with bombs and two external fuel tanks, carries 2,800 gallons or 18,200 pounds of external fuel, has a combat thrust to weight ratio of 1.02, a combat wing loading of 96 pounds per square foot, and a maximum load factor of 7.5G. *Jane's Intelligence Review*, July 1990, pp. 298–300; *Jane's Defense Weekly*, June 25, 1985, pp. 1226–1227; and Dick Pawloski, *Changes in Threat Air Combat Doctrine and Force Structure, 24th Edition*, General Dynamics DWIC-91, Fort Worth Division, February 1992, pp. I-65 and I-110 to I-117.

208. "Jordan to hire two Turkish transports," *Jane's Defense Weekly*, April 28, 1999, p. 17.

209. Faraj, Caroline and Philip Finnegan, "F-16s Top Jordanian Air Force Modernization Effort," *Defense News*, April 10, 1999, p. 12.

210. *Jane's Defense Weekly*, August 20, 1994, p. 6, July 12, 1995, p. 19; *Defense News*, June 26, 1995, p. 12; *Washington Times*, September 28, 1995, p. A-10.

211. Interviews, *Jane's Defense Weekly*, January 17, 1996, p.13, February 21, 1996, p. 16, March 20, 1996, August 7, 1996, p. 13; *New York Times*, February 28, 1996, p. A-9; *Washington Post*, February 14, 1996, p. A-12, June 12, 1996, p. A-17.

212. *Defense News*, August 11, 1997, p. 18.

213. *Jane's Defense Weekly*, August 20, 1994, p. 6, July 12, 1995, p. 19; *Defense News*, June 26, 1995, p. 12; *Washington Times*, September 28, 1995, p. A-10; Aldinger, Charles, "U.S. defense chief says Jordan seeks A-10 jets," *Reuters*, April 22, 1998.

214. Richard Engel, "Reaping the Peace Dividend," *Jane's Defense Weekly*, January 12, 2000, pp. 23–29.

215. Richard Engel, "Reaping the Peace Dividend," *Jane's Defense Weekly*, January 12, 2000, pp. 23–29.

216. *Jane's Defense Weekly*, May 7, 1997, pp. 22–25.

217. *Jane's Defense Weekly*, March 17, 1999, p. 3.

218. Joris Janssen Lok, "New Age F-16 Spans the Fighter Generations," *Jane's International Defense Review*, 2/2000. pp. 27–35.

219. Ed Blanche, "Changing the Face of Middle East Airpower," *Jane's Defense Weekly*, November 10, 1999, pp. 38–41.

220. IISS, *Military Balance, 1998–1999 and 1999–2000*; Reuters, April 2, 1996, 1141, April 4, 1996, 1351.

221. Richard Engel, "Reaping the Peace Dividend," *Jane's Defense Weekly*, January 12, 2000, pp. 23–29.

222. *Jane's Intelligence Review*, October, 1994, p. 456.

223. Reuters, April 2, 1997, 1851.

224. *Jane's Defense Weekly*, October 4, 2000, p. 4.

225. For a more detailed description of the Israeli AH-64 program, see *Jane's Defense Weekly*, October 10, 1992, p. 7.

226. *Jane's Defense Weekly*, November 10, 1999, p. 26.

227. *Jane's Defense Weekly*, October 4, 2000, p. 4.

228. *Defense Weekly*, October 4, 1999, p. 1; *Jane's Defense Weekly*, March 17, 1999, p. 17, December 22, 1999, p. 4.

229. *Defense News*, October 11, 1999, p. 1.

230. Jane's Defense Weekly, February 2, 2000, p. 21.

231. *Jane's Defense Weekly*, March 17, 1999, p. 17, December 22, 1999, p. 4.

232. *Jane's Defense Weekly*, June 5, 1996, p. 29, September 30, 1998, p. 4, February 3, 1999, pp. 31–32; *Defense News*, July 22, 1996, p. 3, October 7, 1996, p. 38.

233. *Jane's Defense Weekly*, January 20, 1999, p. 23.

234. "The IDF's Security Principles," Office of the IDF Spokesman, April 1995, and Scotty Fisher, "Country Briefing Israel," *Jane's Defense Weekly*," February 18, 1995, pp. 29–38.

235. Faraj, Caroline and Philip Finnegan, "Jordanian Border Defense Boosted by US, British Aid," *Defense News*, April 12, 1999, p. 1.

236. *Jane's Defense Weekly*, August 16, 2000, p. 22.

237. *Defense News*, June 30, 1997, p. 4.

238. *Flight International*, August 24, 1993, p. 12.

239. Saradzhyan, Simon, "Bombing Spurs Interest in Russian Craft, Defenses," *Defense News*, July 19, 1999, p. 11.

240. Based on interviews with British, US, and Israeli experts. *Washington Times*, January 16, 1992, p. G-4; *Washington Post*, February 1, 1992, p. A1, February 2, 1992, pp. A1 and A25, February 5, p. A-19; *Financial Times*, February 6, 1992, p. 4; *Christian Science Monitor*, February 6, 1992, p. 19; *Defense News*, February 17, 1992, p. 1.

241. Faraj, Caroline and Philip Finnegan, "Jordanian Border Defenses Boosted by US, British Aid," *Defense News*, April 12, 1999, p.1.

242. *Jane's Intelligence Review*, October 1994, p. 456.

243. *Washington Times*, May 30, 1997, p. A-10.

244. Goertz, Bill, "Egypt wants to buy high-tech Russian SAMs," *Washington Times*, May 30, 1997, p. A10.

245. "Russia to upgrade Egyptian missiles," *Jane's Defense Weekly,* March 31, 1999, p. 16.

246. Reuters, March 11, 1999, 0615; *Jane's Defense Weekly*, March 17, 1999, p. 3.

247. Jane's Defense Weekly, February 2, 2000, p. 21.

248. *Defense News*, January 20 ,1997, p. 11; Reuters, March 25, 1998, 2016; Richard Engel, "Reaping the Peace Dividend," *Jane's Defense Weekly*, January 12, 2000, pp. 23–29.

249. IISS, *Military Balance*, "Israel," various editions, *Jane's Fighting Ships (primarily the 1999–2000 and 2000–2001 editions)*; "Israel," various editions; *Jane's Sentinel, Eastern Mediterranean*; "Israel," various editions; Reuters, January 1, 1999, 0507; December 4, 1997, 1220; *Jane's International Defense Review*, 4/1998, pp. 29–30; *Washington Times*, July 1, 1998, p. A-1.

250. "Israel's newest sub sets out for Haifa," *Jane's Defense Weekly*, July 14, 1999, p. 14; *The Estimate*, July 30, 1999, p. 4.

251. *Jane's Defense Weekly*, November 10, 1999, p. 27, November 8, 2000, p. 16.

252. *Jane's Defense Weekly*, February 1999, p. 18, November 10, 1999, p. 27, November 8, 2000, p. 16.

253. *Jane's Defense Weekly*, November 8, 2000, p. 16.

254. *Jane's Defense Weekly*, November 8, 2000, p. 16.

255. *Jane's Defense Weekly*, November 29, 2000, p. 32.

256. Sieff, Martin, "Israel buying 3 submarines to carry nuclear missiles," *Washington Times*, July 1, 1998, p. A1; *Jane's Defense Weekly*, February 3, 1999, pp. 28–30.

257. *Jane's Defense Weekly*, February 24, 1999, p.19.

258. "Israel's newest sub sets out for Haifa," *Jane's Defense Weekly*, July 14, 1999, p. 14.

259. *Jane's Fighting Ships, 1998–1999 and 1999–2000 and 2000–2001*; IISS, *Military Balance, 1998–1999, 1999–2000, and 1999–2001*.

260. *Jane's International Defense Review*, April 1998, p. 29; "The IDF's Security Principles," Office of the IDF Spokesman, April 1995, and Scotty Fisher, "Country Briefing Israel," *Jane's Defense Weekly*," February 18, 1995, pp. 29–38.

261. *Jane's International Defense Review*, April 1998, p. 29.

262. *Jane's Defense Weekly*, February 3, 1999, pp. 28–30.

263. *Jane's Fighting Ships, 1998–1999, 1999–2000 and 2000–2001*; IISS, *Military Balance, 1998–1999, 1999–2000, and 2000–2001*; *Jane's Defense Weekly*, February 3, 1999, pp. 28–31.

264. *Jane's Fighting Ships, 1998–1999, 1999–2000 and 2000–2001*; IISS, *Military Balance, 1998–1999, 1999–2000, and 2000–2001*.

265. IISS, *Military Balance*, "Syria," various editions, *Jane's Fighting Ships*; "Syria," various editions; *Jane's Sentinel, Eastern Mediterranean*; "Syria," various editions.

266. *Jane's Fighting Ships, 1998–1999, 1999–2000 and 2000–2001*; IISS, *Military Balance, 1998–1999, 1999–2000, and 2000–2001*.

267. Interviews, *Jane's Sentinel*, "Syria."

268. Interviews, *Jane's Sentinel*, "Syria."

269. *Jane's Fighting Ships, 1998–1999, 1999–2000 and 2000–2001*; IISS, *Military Balance, 1998–1999, 1999–2000, and 2000–2001*.

270. *Jane's Fighting Ships, 1998–1999, 1999–2000 and 2000–2001*; IISS, *Military Balance, 1998–1999, 1999–2000, and 2000–2001*.

271. IISS, *Military Balance*, "Jordan," various editions, *Jane's Fighting Ships*; "Jordan," various editions; *Jane's Sentinel, Eastern Mediterranean*; "Jordan," various editions.

272. IISS, *Military Balance*, "Lebanon," various editions, *Jane's Fighting Ships*; "Lebanon," various editions; *Jane's Sentinel, Eastern Mediterranean*; "Lebanon," various editions.

273. *Jane's Fighting Ships, 1998–1999, 1999–2000 and 2000–2001*; IISS, *Military Balance, 1998–1999, 1999–2000, and 2000–2001*.

274. IISS, *Military Balance*, "Egypt," various editions, *Jane's Fighting Ships*; "Egypt," various editions; *Jane's Sentinel, Eastern Mediterranean*; "Egypt," various editions; *Defense News*, June 10, 1996, "Defense in Middle East;" *Jane's Defense Weekly*, July 23, 1997, p. 17.

275. *Jane's Defense Weekly*, October 18, 2000, p. 24.

276. *Defense News*, October 23, 1995, pp. 3, 45; *Jane's Defense Weekly*, July 23, 1997, p. 17; Reuters, July 13, 1997, 1240.

277. *Jane's International Defense Review*, July 2000, p. 18.

278. *Jane's Fighting Ships, 1998–1999, 1999–2000 and 2000–2001*; IISS, *Military Balance, 1998–1999, 1999–2000, and 2000–2001*.

279. *Jane's Defense Weekly*, May 6, 1995, p. 12.

280. For an interesting discussion of changes in Israel's manpower system that might affect these vulnerabilities, see Stuart A. Cohen, "Studying the Israel Defense Forces: A Changing Contract With Israeli Society," BESA Center for Strategic Studies No. 20, Ramat Gan, Israel, Bar-Ilan University, 1995.

281. Herbert J. Tillema, *International Armed Conflict since 1945*, Boulder, Westview, 1991.

282. Herbert J. Tillema, *International Armed Conflict since 1945*, Boulder, Westview, 1991.

283. "Security chief sees Israeli social rifts as threat," Reuters, July 21, 1999, 0517.

284. *Jane's Defense Weekly*, December 1, 1999, p. 15.

285. For example, see Reuters, November 12, 1999, 0749.

286. Elliot A. Cohen, Michael J. Eisenstadt, and Andre J. Bacevich, *Knives, Tanks, and Missiles*, Washington, Washington Institute, 1998; David, Eshel, "Crossroads 2000," *Jane's Defense Weekly*. February 3, 1999, pp. 23–32; Gerald M. Steinberg, "Israeli Security in a Changing Environment: Challenges and Responses," Ramat Gan, BESA/Bar Ilan University, October 26, 1998; *The Estimate*, July 3, 1998, pp. 4–5; Efraim Inbar, "Israeli National Security 1973–1996," Ramat Gan, BESA/Bar Ilan University, February 1998; Asher Arian, "Israeli Public Opinion on National Security, 1997," Tel Aviv, JCSS, Memo 47, April 1997.

287. Cohen, Eliot A., et al. *Knives, Tanks and Missiles: Israel's Security Revolution.* Washington, DC: Washington Institute for Near East Policy, 1998.

288. These issues take on added political sensitivity because Israeli field grade officers are very well paid by Israeli standards and receive generous payments when they leave active service. *Jane's Pointer*, May 1997, p. 5; Ed Blanche, "Is the myth fading for the Israeli Army? Part I & II," *Jane's Intelligence Review*, December 1996 and January 1997.

289. Stuart A. Cohen, "Towards a New Portrait of the (New) Israeli Soldier," Ramat Gan, BESA/Bar Ilan University, September 1997; Elliot A. Cohen, Michael J. Eisenstadt, and Andre J. Bacevich, *Knives, Tanks, and Missiles*, Washington, Washington Institute, 1998; David, Eshel, "Crossroads 2000," *Jane's Defense Weekly*. February 3, 1999, pp. 23–32; Gerald M. Steinberg, "Israeli Security in a Changing Environment: Challenges and Responses," Ramat Gan, BESA/Bar Ilan University, October 26, 1998; *The Estimate*, July 3, 1998, pp. 4–5; Efraim Inbar, "Israeli National Security 1973–1996," Ramat Gan, BESA/

Bar Ilan University, February 1998; Asher Arian, "Israeli Public Opinion on National Security, 1997, Tel Aviv, JCSS, Memo 47, April 1997.

290. *New York Times*, May 31, 1995, p. A-10; Elliot A. Cohen, Michael J. Eisenstadt, and Andre J. Bacevich, *Knives, Tanks, and Missiles*, Washington, Washington Institute, 1998, pp. 110–114.

291. *New York Times*, May 31, 1995, p. A-10; Elliot A. Cohen, Michael J. Eisenstadt, and Andre J. Bacevich, *Knives, Tanks, and Missiles*, Washington, Washington Institute, 1998, pp. 110–114.

292. "The IDF's Security Principles," Office of the IDF Spokesman, April 1995, and Scotty Fisher, "Country Briefing Israel," *Jane's Defense Weekly*," February 18, 1995, pp. 29–38.

293. Hockstader, Lee, "Israeli Platoon Brings Faith In Step With Military Duty," *The Washington Post*, July 30, 1999, p. A23.

294. Asher Arian, "Israeli Public Opinion on National Security, 1997, Tel Aviv, JCSS, Memo 47, April 1997; Stuart A. Cohen, "Towards a New Portrait of the (New) Israeli Soldier," Ramat Gan, BESA/Bar Ilan University, September 1997; Elliot A. Cohen, Michael J. Eisenstadt, and Andre J. Bacevich, *Knives, Tanks, and Missiles*, Washington, Washington Institute, 1998; Gerald M. Steinberg, "Israeli Security in a Changing Environment: Challenges and Responses," Ramat Gan, BESA/Bar Ilan University, October 26, 1998.

295. Ibid.

296. Ibid.

297. "The IDF's Security Principles," Office of the IDF Spokesman, April 1995, and Scotty Fisher, "Country Briefing Israel," *Jane's Defense Weekly*," February 18, 1995, pp. 29–38.

298. *The Estimate*, January 28, 2000, p. 4.

299. Stuart A. Cohen, "Towards a New Portrait of the (New) Israeli Soldier," Ramat Gan, BESA/Bar Ilan University, September, 1997; *Washington Post*, August 5, 1996, p. A-1; Reuters, June 22, 1998, 2107; Ed Blanche, "Is the myth fading for the Israeli Army? Part I & II," *Jane's Intelligence Review*, December 1996 and January 1997.

300. Cohen, Stuart A. "Towards a Portrait of the (New) Israeli Soldier." Security and Policy Studies No.35. Bar-Ilan University, Israel, 1997.

301. *Jane's Defense Weekly*," August 25, 1999, p. 18.

302. *Jerusalem Post*, May 7, 1996, p. 2, September 11, 1996; *Jane's Defense Weekly*, May 8, 1996, p. 19.

303. "The IDF's Security Principles," Office of the IDF Spokesman, April 1995, and Scotty Fisher, "Country Briefing Israel," *Jane's Defense Weekly*," February 18, 1995, pp. 29–38.

304. Asher Arian, "Israeli Public Opinion on National Security, 1997," Tel Aviv, JCSS, Memo 47, April 1997; Stuart A. Cohen, "Towards a New Portrait of the (New) Israeli Soldier," Ramat Gan, BESA/Bar Ilan University, September, 1997; *Washington Post*, August 5, 1996, p. A-1.

305. Ed Blanche, "Is the myth fading for the Israeli Army? Part I & II," *Jane's Intelligence Review*, December 1996 and January 1997; Stuart A. Cohen, "Towards a New Portrait of the (New) Israeli Soldier," Ramat Gan, BESA/Bar Ilan University, September, 1997; Reuters, June 22, 1998, 2107; *Jane's Defense Weekly*, November 26, 1997, p. 25.

306. Ibid.

307. *International Defense Review*, 1/1994, p. 20; *Jerusalem Report*, September 5, 1996, p. 20; Elliot A. Cohen, Michael J. Eisenstadt, and Andre J. Bacevich, *Knives, Tanks, and Missiles*, Washington, Washington Institute, 1998, pp. 115–116.

308. *Jane's International Defense Review*, April 1999, p. 22, December 6, 2000, p. 17.

309. "Israel Army Computer Corps Builds Success in Business," *The New York Times*, July 24, 1999, p. B2.

310. "International Defense Digest," working paper (no page number or date); Elliot A. Cohen, Michael J. Eisenstadt, and Andre J. Bacevich, *Knives, Tanks, and Missiles*, Washington, Washington Institute, 1998.

311. Based on data in the relevant country section of the IISS, *Military Balance, 1998–1999 and 1999–2000*. Estimates in other sources differ.

312. *New York Times*, June 24, 2000, pp. A-1, A-5, Reuters, August 24, 2000, 1017.

313. *Middle East Economic Digest (MEED)*, December 9, 1994, NEXIS edition; *Jane's Defense Weekly*, October 10, 1992, p. 7, February 3, 1999, pp. 27–31; *Defense Electronics and Computing*, 10/1992, p. 1035; *International Defense Review*, 10/1994, p. 6.

314. "Israel Will Buy 50 F-a6s In Its Biggest Arms Deal Ever," *The New York Times*, July 19, 1999, p. A6.

315. Dick Pawloski, *Changes in Threat Air Combat Doctrine and Force Structure, 24th Edition*, Fort Worth, General Dynamics DWIC-91, February , 1992, pp. II-199 to II-227.

316. *Jane's International Defense Review*, 5/1998, p. 18.

317. The defecting pilot was on maneuver near the Golan, and suddenly turned towards Israel and flew very fast and low over the Golan and the central Galilee. He landed in a remote civil strip near Megido. This led to a great deal of media comment in Israel, but such incidents are almost unavoidable. Although he flew for seven minutes without being intercepted, he flew at a time when IAF E-2Cs were not in the air and nearby aircraft were scrambled, when the IAF was in a state of low alert, and flew without using any radar or communications emissions. He also stated later that he did receive warning and was being tracked by Israeli radar. Israel later used the MiG-23ML (G) for training and test and evaluation purposes. *Washington Post*, October 13, 1989, p. A-35, October 14, 1989, p. A-18; *New York Times*, October 12, 1989, p. A-10, October 14, 1989, p. A-2; *Philadelphia Inquirer*, October 12, 1989, p. 18A, October 13, 1989, p. 17A; *Washington Times*, October 12, 1989, p. A-8; *Jane's Defense Weekly*, February 10, 1990, p. 221.

318. Samuel M. Katz, "Israeli Airpower on the Rise," *Air Force*, November 1991, pp. 44–51.

319. *Jane's Defense Weekly*, February 3, 1999, pp. 31–32.

320. *Jane's Defense Weekly*, February 3, 1999, pp. 31–32.

321. *Jane's Defense Weekly*, March 17, 1999, p. 17.

322. IISS, *Military Balance*, "Israel," various editions, *Jane's Fighting Ships*; "Israel," various editions; *Jane's Sentinel, Eastern Mediterranean*; "Israel," various editions; Reuters, January 1, 1999, 0507; December 4, 1997, 1220; *Jane's International Defense Review*, 4/1998, pp. 29–30; *Washington Times*, July 1, 1998, p. A-1.

323. *Defense News*, January 11, 1993; Agence France Presse, June 1, 1993; *International Defense Review*, March 1994, pp. 27–28.

324. *Jane's Fighting Ships, 1998–1999, 1999–2000 and 2000–2001*; IISS, *Military Balance, 1998–1999, 1999–2000, and 2000–2001*.

325. *Washington Times*, July 1, 1998, p. A-1.

326. Elliot A. Cohen, Michael J. Eisenstadt, and Andre J. Bacevich, *Knives, Tanks, and Missiles*, Washington, Washington Institute, 1998, pp. 81–143; David, Eshel, "Crossroads

2000," *Jane's Defense Weekly*. February 3, 1999, pp. 23–32; Gerald M. Steinberg, "Israeli Security in a Changing Environment: Challenges and Responses," Ramat Gan, BESA/Bar Ilan University, October 26, 1998; The Estimate, July 3, 1998, pp. 4–5; Efraim Inbar, "Israeli National Security 1973–1996," Ramat Gan, BESA/Bar Ilan University, February 1998; Asher Arian, "Israeli Public Opinion on National Security, 1997, Tel Aviv, JCSS, Memo 47, April 1997.

327. See Emanuel Wald, *The Wald Report: The Decline of Israeli National Security Since 1967*, Boulder, Westview Press, 1991.

328. *Jane's Defense Weekly*, July 27, 1991, p. 135; Eric Silver, "A Warrior for the Nineties," *The Jerusalem Report*, June 20, 1991, pp. 12–20.

329. Eshel, David, IDF Prepares for Radical Restructuring Programme. *Jane's Defense Weekly*, January 20, 1999, p. 23.

330. *The Estimate*, June 5, 1998.

331. Office of IDF spokesman; *Los Angeles Times*, November 1, 1995, p. A-1.

332. *Jane's Defense Weekly*, May 21, 1997, p. 13; *Jane's International Defense Review*, 9/1997, p. 10.

333. *Jane's Defense Weekly*, May 21, 1997, p. 13; *Jane's International Defense Review*, 9/1997, p. 10; *Jane's World Armies*, "Israel," Issue 2, November, 1997.

334. Gerald M. Steinberg, "Israeli Security in a Changing Environment: Challenges and Responses," Ramat Gan, BESA/Bar Ilan University, October 26, 1998; *The Estimate,* July 3, 1998, pp. 4–5; Efraim Inbar, "Israeli National Security 1973–1996," Ramat Gan, BESA/Bar Ilan University, February 1998; Asher Arian, "Israeli Public Opinion on National Security," 1997, Tel Aviv, JCSS, Memo 47, April 1997; Elliot A. Cohen, Michael J. Eisenstadt, and Andre J. Bacevich, *Knives, Tanks, and Missiles*, Washington, Washington Institute, 1998, pp. 6–81.

335. Sieff, Martin, "Is the Israeli army ready to fight a modern war?" *Washington Times*, July 15, 1998, A13; David, Eshel, "Crossroads 2000," *Jane's Defense Weekly*. February 3, 1999, pp. 23–32; Gerald M. Steinberg, "Israeli Security in a Changing Environment: Challenges and Responses," Ramat Gan, BESA/Bar Ilan University, October 26, 1998; The Estimate, July 3, 1998, pp. 4–5; Efraim Inbar, "Israeli National Security 1973–1996," Ramat Gan, BESA/Bar Ilan University, February 1998; Elliot A. Cohen, Michael J. Eisenstadt, and Andre J. Bacevich, *Knives, Tanks, and Missiles*, Washington, Washington Institute, 1998, pp. 125–129; *Jerusalem Post*, December 5, 1996, Ze'ev Schiff, "Facing Up to Reality," *Ha'aretz*, January 9, 1998.

336. For good reporting on the early phases of this effort, see Ed Blanche, "Israel Addresses the Threats of the New Millennium," *Jane's Intelligence Review*, February 1, 1999, p. 24 and March 1, 1999, p. 27.

337. *Jane's Defense Weekly*, February 10, 1999, p. 16; Gal Luft, "Israel's Impending Revolution in Security Affairs," March 17, 1999, p. 17; Peacewatch, No. 199, March 4, 1999; *Defense News*, March 22, 1999, p. 8

338. "Israeli cabinet approves National Security Council," Reuters, March 7, 1999.

339. "Country Survey: Israel," *Jane's Defense Weekly*, June 19, 1996, p. 30, January 20, 1999, p. 23, February 3, 1999, pp. 23–32, February 10, 1999, p. 16; *Jane's International Defense Review*, 9/1996, p. 10; Reuters, August 23, 1996, 1045, January 23, 1999, 1344, 1603, January 24, 1999, 0848; Associated Press, January 31, 1999, 0602; *Philadelphia Inquirer*, June 20, 1996, p. A-2; *Washington Times*, June 20, 1996, p. A-13.

340. David, Eshel, "Crossroads 2000," *Jane's Defense Weekly*. February 3, 1999, pp. 23–32; Gerald M. Steinberg, "Israeli Security in a Changing Environment: Challenges and

Responses," Ramat Gan, BESA/Bar Ilan University, October 26, 1998; The Estimate, July 3, 1998, pp. 4–5; Efraim Inbar, "Israeli National Security 1973–1996," Ramat Gan, BESA/ Bar Ilan University, February 1998; Elliot A. Cohen, Michael J. Eisenstadt, and Andre J. Bacevich, *Knives, Tanks, and Missiles*, Washington, Washington Institute, 1998, pp. 81–143.

341. "Israel's defense reforms will streamline manpower," *Jane's Defense Weekly*, June 30, 1999, p. 19.

342. Eshel, David, "Analysis: Israel's Future Forces," *Jane's Defense Weekly*, August 25, 1999, p. 21.

343. "Defense Briefs: Israel's New Ground Forces Service," *The Estimate*, July 2, 1999, p. 4.

344. David, Eshel, "Crossroads 2000," *Jane's Defense Weekly*, February 3, 1999, pp. 23–32; Gerald M. Steinberg, "Israeli Security in a Changing Environment: Challenges and Responses," Ramat Gan, BESA/Bar Ilan University, October 26, 1998; *The Estimate*, July 3, 1998, pp. 4–5; Efraim Inbar, "Israeli National Security 1973–1996," Ramat Gan, BESA/ Bar Ilan University, February 1998; Elliot A. Cohen, Michael J. Eisenstadt, and Andre J. Bacevich, *Knives, Tanks, and Missiles*, Washington, Washington Institute, 1998, pp. 81–143.

345. David, Eshel, "Crossroads 2000," *Jane's Defense Weekly*, February 3, 1999, pp. 23–32; Gerald M. Steinberg, "Israeli Security in a Changing Environment: Challenges and Responses," Ramat Gan, BESA/Bar Ilan University, October 26, 1998; The Estimate, July 3, 1998, pp. 4–5; Efraim Inbar, "Israeli National Security 1973–1996," Ramat Gan, BESA/ Bar Ilan University, February 1998; Elliot A. Cohen, Michael J. Eisenstadt, and Andre J. Bacevich, *Knives, Tanks, and Missiles*, Washington, Washington Institute, 1998, pp. 81–143.

346. *Jane's Defense Weekly*, August 16, 2000, p. 22.

347. David, Eshel, "Crossroads 2000," *Jane's Defense Weekly*, February 3, 1999, pp. 23–32; Gal Luft, "Israel's Impending Revolution in Security Affairs," *Peacewatch*, No. 199, March 4, 1999.

348. *Jane's Defense Weekly*, August 16, 2000, p. 22.

349. *Jane's Defense Weekly*, August 16, 2000, p. 22.

350. Opall-Rome, Barbara, "Barak Assembles Security Team," *Defense News*, July 19, 1999, p. 3.

351. Eshel, David, "New teams to manage Israel's security issues," *Jane's Defense Weekly*, June 23, 1999, p. 19.

352. Eshel, David, "Analysis: Barak's burden," *Jane's Defense Weekly*, July 21, 1999, p. 15.

353. Eshel, David, "Analysis: Israel's Future Forces," *Jane's Defense Weekly*, August 25, 1999, p. 21.

354. Eshel, David, "Analysis: Israel's Future Forces," *Jane's Defense Weekly*, August 25, 1999, p. 21.

355. Jaffee Center for Strategic Studies, *Bulletin*, Nos. 23–24, January 2000, pp. 4–5.

356. *Jane's Defense Weekly*, October 13, 1999, p. 21.

357. *Jane's Defense Weekly*, November 3, 1999, p. 16.

358. *Jane's Defense Weekly*, February 23, 2000, p. 4.

359. *The Estimate*, January 28, 2000, p. 4; *Jane's Defense Weekly*, January 12, 2000, p. 15, February 23, 2000, p. 4.

360. *Jane's Defense Weekly*, August 16, 2000, p. 22.

361. Reuters, September 19, 1999, 1002.

362. For example, see the maps in *The Economist*, February 19, 2000, p. 47, and the hostile Palestinian reaction in "Israel's Matrix of Control," *For the Record*, The Center for Policy Analysis of Palestine, No. 26, January 21, 2000 and No. 30, February 14, 2000.

363. *Jane's Defense Weekly*, October 11, 2000, p. 30.

364. Cody, Edward, "Israel Takes Another Tack," *Washington Post*, November 1, 2000.

365. Reuters "Israelis Kill Palestinian in New 'Assassination'," December 14, 2000; Arieh O'Sullivan, "IDF soldiers killing of a Hamas Activist spurs charges of assassination," *Jerusalem Post*, December 15, 2000; Sontong, Deborah "Israel Acknowledges Hunting Down Arab Militants," *New York Times*, December 21, 2000.

366. Deutsche Press Agentur, "Israel Destroys Six Homes in Gaza" January 4, 2001.

367. Sontag, Deborah. "Gun Lessons Are Suddenly All the Rage in Israel," *New York Times*, October 25, 2000.

368. *Washington Post*, November 30, 2000, pp. A-32 and A-33.

369. "Report of the United Nations High Commissioner for Human Rights and Follow-Up to the World Conference on Human Rights," New York United Nations, E/CN.42001/114, November 29, 2000.

370. "Report of the United Nations High Commissioner for Human Rights and Follow-Up to the World Conference on Human Rights," New York United Nations, E/CN.42001/114, November 29, 2000, pp. 8 and 16.

371. "Report of the United Nations High Commissioner for Human Rights and Follow-Up to the World Conference on Human Rights," New York United Nations, E/CN.42001/114, November 29, 2000, p. 15.

372. "Report of the United Nations High Commissioner for Human Rights and Follow-Up to the World Conference on Human Rights," New York United Nations, E/CN.42001/114, November 29, 2000, pp. 8 and 14.

373. Sontag, Deborah. "Gun Lessons Are Suddenly All the Rage in Israel," *New York Times,* October 25, 2000.

374. Morris, Nomi and Barbara Demick. "Financial Toll Now Begins in Mideast," *Philadelphia Inquirer*, October 30, 2000.

375. *New York Times*, June 24, 2000, pp. A-1, A-5; Reuters, August 24, 2000, 1017.

376. The original peace agreement authorized 9,000 PLO police officers. IDF reports indicate that 14,000–17,000 have been hired. Prime Minister Rabin also authorized 2,000 more police for Gaza in February 1995. *Los Angeles Times*, February 10, 1995, p. A-2; *Washington Times*, February 8, 1995, p. A-1; *Christian Science Monitor*, May 17, 1995, p. 7.

377. US Department of State, "Patterns of Global Terrorism, 1994," Washington, GPO, April 1995, pp. 15–20.

378. Israeli Ministry of Foreign Affairs, "Terrorism and the Peace Process, Background Paper," September 14, 1998, www.mfa.gov.il/mfa/go.asp?MFAH02lm0.

379. Reuters, June 16, 1998.

380. See "The Charter of the Hamas" Articles One to Thirty-Six," *www.womeningreen.org/hama.htm.*

381. See the summary in Alisa Mandrel and Joshua Obstfeld, "Trends in Israeli-Palestinian Political Fatalities, 1987–1999," *Research Notes*, The Washington Institute, No. 8, October 1999.

382. Alisa Mandel and Joshua Obstfeld, "Trends in Israeli-Palestinian Political Fatalities, 1987–1999," Research Notes, No. 8, Washington, The Washington Institute for Near East Policy, October 1999.

383. Alisa Mandel and Joshua Obstfeld, "Trends in Israeli-Palestinian Political Fatalities, 1987–1999," Research Notes, No. 8, Washington, The Washington Institute for Near East Policy, October 1999.

384. See "The Charter of the Hamas" Articles One to Thirty-Six, *www.womeningreen.org/hama.htm*, and US Department of State, "Patterns of Global Terrorism, 1998," Washington, GPO, April 1999, Appendix B, "Syria," and "Iran."

385. US Department of State, "Patterns of Global Terrorism, 1994," Washington, GPO, April 1995, pp. 15–19; *Washington Post*, November 5, 1995, p. A-33.

386. "HAMAS—The Islamic Terrorist Movement," Background Paper, September 1998, Israeli Foreign Ministry, *www.mfa.gov.il/mfa/go.asp?MFAH02mj0*.

387. Alisa Mandel and Joshua Obstfeld, "Trends in Israeli-Palestinian Political Fatalities, 1987–1999," Research Notes, No. 8, Washington, The Washington Institute for Near East Policy, October 1999.

388. *Washington Post*, October 17, 1995, p. A-1; *Washington Times*, September 4, 1995, p. A-9.

389. See Reuven Paz, "Sleeping with the Enemy: A Reconciliation Process as Part of Counter Terrorism—Is Hamas Capable of Hudna," The International Policy Institute for Counter-Terrorism, Herzliya, June 1998.

390. *New York Times*, October 13, 1995, p. A-5; Executive News Service, October 12, 1995, p. 1330.

391. *Peacewatch*, October 30, 1995, pp. 1–3; *Philadelphia Inquirer*, November 1, 1995, p. A-3; Executive News, October 11, 1995, 0611.

392. Associated Press, February 11, 1999, 0139 February 12, 1999, 0352; Reuters, February 12, 1999, 0234.

393. Executive News Service, November 6, 1996, 1643.

394. "The HAMAS—Background, August, 1997, Israeli Foreign Ministry, *www.mfa.gov.il/mfa/go.asp?MFAH0cbq0*.

395. Dr. Reuven Ehrlich (Avi-Ran), "Terrorism as a Preferred Instrument of Syrian Policy," ICT Research Fellow, *www.ict.org.il/*, accessed October 16, 1999.

396. al-Mughrabi, Nidal. Palestinian Police Link Hamas Men to Iran. Reuters, February 4, 1999.

397. For a detailed discussion of this issue, see Elie Rekhess, "The Terrorist Connection—Iran, the Islamic Jihad, and Hamas," *Justice*, Volume 5, May 1995.

398. See US Department of State, "Patterns of Global Terrorism, 1998," Washington, GPO, April 1999, "Overview of State-Sponsored Terrorism."

399. The bombings failed because the bombs exploded prematurely, killing some of the Hamas agents involved. United Press, September 9, 1999, 1902.

400. International Policy Institute for Counter-Terrorism, "Iran and Terrorism," Herzliya, Israel, *www.ict.org.il/*, accessed October 16, 1999.

401. Associated Press, September 19, 1999, 0801; Reuters, October 6, 1999, 1132.

402. *Washington Post*, September 22, 1999, p. A-22, September 23, 1999, p. A-21.

403. Reuters, September 22, 1999, 0842.

404. *Los Angeles Times*, June 19, 1998.

405. Reuters, June 25, 1998.

406. *Washington Post*, November 2, 1998, p. A-1.

407. See US Department of State, "Patterns of Global Terrorism, 1998," Washington, GPO, April 1999, Appendix B, "Syria," and "Iran."

408. For a detailed discussion of this issue, see Elie Rekhess, "The Terrorist Connection—Iran, the Islamic Jihad, and Hamas," *Justice*, Volume 5, May 1995.

409. Elie Rekhess, "The Terrorist Connection—Iran, the Islamic Jihad, and Hamas," *Justice*, Volume 5, May 1995.

410. *Al-Hayat*, December 12, 1994; *Al-Wassat*, December 12, 1994.

411. Radio Nur, December 11, 1994; Iranian TV, November 23, 1994; Associated Press, November 11, 1994.

412. Reuters, September 27, 1999, 1223.

413. See US Department of State, "Patterns of Global Terrorism, 1998," Washington, GPO, April 1999, "Overview of State-Sponsored Terrorism."

414. Dr. Reuven Ehrlich (Avi-Ran), "Terrorism as a Preferred Instrument of Syrian Policy," ICT Research Fellow, *www.ict.org.il/*, accessed October 16, 1999.

415. Dr. Reuven Ehrlich (Avi-Ran), "Terrorism as a Preferred Instrument of Syrian Policy," ICT Research Fellow, *www.ict.org.il/*, accessed October 16, 1999.

416. *New York Times*, October 15, 2000, p. A-11.

417. *New York Times*, October 15, 2000, p. A-11.

418. Al-Issawi, Tarek "Lebanese On Israeli Border Prepare" Associated Press October 16, 2000.

419. *New York Times*, October 15, 2000, p. A-11.

420. New York Times, October 14, 2000, p. A-7.

421. US Department of State, "Patterns of Global Terrorism, 1994," Washington, GPO, April 1995, pp. 17–21, and 20–69 and "Patterns of Global Terrorism, 1998," Washington, GPO, April 1999; *Washington Post*, November 5, 1995, p. A-33.

422. Dr. Reuven Ehrlich (Avi-Ran), "Terrorism as a Preferred Instrument of Syrian Policy," ICT Research Fellow, *www.ict.org.il/*, accessed October 16, 1999.

423. US Department of State, "Patterns of Global Terrorism, 1994," Washington, GPO, April 1995, pp. 15–18,19.

424. See US Department of State, "Patterns of Global Terrorism, 1998," Washington, GPO, April 1999, Appendix B, "Syria," and "Iran."

425. International Policy Institute for Counter-Terrorism, "Iran and Terrorism," Herzliya, Israel, *www.ict.org.il/*, accessed October 16, 1999.

426. *Washington Post*, September 26, 1995, p. A-1; ; *Washington Post*, November 5, 1995, p. A-33; US Department of State, "Patterns of Global Terrorism, 1994," Washington, GPO, April 1995, pp. 17–21 and 20–69.

427. This analysis is based on US State Department reporting on the Palestinian Authority's compliance with the peace accords in dealing with terrorism.

428. US Department of State, "Patterns of Global Terrorism, 1994," Washington, GPO, April 1995, pp. 15–19 and "Patterns of Global Terrorism, 1998," Washington, GPO, April 1999; Executive News, July 13, 1995, 1544.

429. Executive News Service, October 2, 1995, 1147.

430. *Washington Post*, October 17, 1995, p. A-1; *Washington Times*, September 4, 1995, p. A-9.

431. For a summary of criticism and charges by major Israeli officials, see *Near East Report*, April 24, 1995, p. 54. These criticisms do, however, predate many of the measures taken to strengthen the Palestinian Authority Security forces after April 1995.

432. "Israeli-Palestinian Security Cooperation Contributes to Terror Decline." Israeli Policy Forum, *Washington Bulletin*, June 22, 1999.

433. See Reuters, November 16, 1999, 0837.

434. *Mideast Mirror*, October 1, 1999, Israeli Section.

435. Summary text of peace accords, US State Department; Israeli government Internet database, accessed October 1995; information sheets provided by the Palestinian Authority; *Washington Post*, September 27, 1995, p. A-27. Also see *The Estimate*, October 13–26, 1995, pp. 5–8.

436. Text of the Wye River Memorandum, US Information Agency Web pages, accessed March 1, 1999.

437. Lahoud, Lamia. "Tanzime Leader: The Intifada must go on," *Jerusalem Post* November 6, 2000.

438. *New York Times*, August 3, 2000, pp. A-1 and A-12.

439. Luft, Gal. "The Palestinian Security Services: Between Police and Army." *Washington Institute Research Memorandum No. 36*. November 1998.

440. Discussions with US and Israeli experts; *Philadelphia Inquirer*, July 28, 1995, p. A-23.

441. Summary text of peace accords, US State Department; Israeli government Internet database, accessed October 1995; information sheets provided by the Palestinian Authority; *Washington Post*, September 27, 1995, p. A-27; *Jane's Intelligence Review*, February 1994, pp. 69–70; *Washington Times*, September 28, 1995, p. A-13.

442. *Calgary Herald*, September 27, 1996, p. D1; *The Boston Globe*, September 29, 1996, p. A1; *New York Times*, September 29, 1996, p. A-12.

443. CIA, *Atlas of the Middle East*, Washington, GPO, January 1993, pp. 52–53, 62–63.

444. CIA, *World Factbook 2000*, "Gaza."

445. CIA, *World Factbook 2000*, "Gaza."

446. CIA, *World Factbook 2000*, "Gaza."

447. CIA, *World Factbook 2000*, "Gaza."

448. CIA, *World Factbook 2000*, "West Bank."

449. Many of these comments in this section are based on interviews in Gaza, Israel, and Cairo in 1994 and 1995; on detailed security maps of Gaza, and IDF Spokesman, "Gaza-Jericho Agreement: Security Aspects," Tel Aviv, IDF, May 1994.

450. Based on the data in the CIA, *World Factbook, 1995, 1998, and 1999*, "Gaza." Other sources report an Israeli per capita income of $14,000 and a Gazan per capita income of $1,400. (*New York Times*, November 8, 1995, p. A-19.)

451. *New York Times*, February 8, 1995, p. A-19; *Wall Street Journal*, September 26, 1995, p. A-18.

452. *New York Times*, February 8, 1995, p. A-19; *Wall Street Journal*, September 26, 1995, p. A-18.

453. Based on data released by the International Labor Organization on December 3, 1995, and the data in the CIA, *World Factbook, 1995* and *1999*, "Gaza." Other sources report an Israeli per capita income of $14,000 and a Gazan per capita income of $1,400. (*New York Times*, November 8, 1995, p. A-19.) Also see *Middle East Economic Digest*, August 27, 1999, p. 20 and BBC, July 6, 1999, "Excerpts from Al-Ayyam." Unemployment for Palestinians has already dropped from 20.3% in 1997 to 14.4% in 1998. Israel had a decline in its border closures in 1998, which led to the decrease in unemployment of Palestinians.

454. *MEED*, July 17, 1998, pp. 9–16; Palestinian Unemployment Falls Sharply in 1998," Reuters, June 22, 1999.

455. Based on data released by the International Labor Organization on December 3, 1995, and the data in the CIA, *World Factbook, 1995, 1998, and 1999*, "Gaza." Other

sources report an Israeli per capita income of $14,000 and a Gazan per capita income of $1,400. (*New York Times*, November 8, 1995, p. A-19.)

456. "Palestinian Unemployment Falls Sharply in 1998," Reuters, June 22, 1999 and CIA, *World Factbook, 1998 and 1999*, "Gaza."

457. *Washington Post*, October 16, 2000, p. A-23.

458. O'Sullivan, Arieh, "Navy has contingency plan to evacuate Gaza settlers by sea" *Jerusalem Post*, November 6, 2000.

459. Foundation for Middle East Peace, "Report on the Israeli Settlement in the Occupied Territories," November-December 2000.

460. Greenberg, Joel. "Five Palestinians Are Killed In Gaza and the West Bank," *New York Times*, December 13, 2000.

461. *Ha'aretz*, August 23, 1995 and September 13, 1995; *Yediot Ahronont*, August 25, 1995.

462. For detailed complaints about arms smuggling in Gaza and other security problems, see "Peace Watch Report: Weapons Control and the Palestinian Authority," Tel Aviv, Jaffee Center for Strategic Studies, June 1995.

463. *Washington Post*, October 22, 2000, p. A-28.

464. CIA, *Atlas of the Middle East*, Washington, GPO, January 1993, pp. 52–53, 62–63.

465. Gold, Dore, "Fundamental Factors in a Stabilized Middle East: Security, Territory, and Peace," Washington, JINSA, 1993.

466. CIA, *World Factbook, 1998 1999, and 2000*.

467. CIA, *World Factbook, 2000*.

468. CIA *World Factbook 2000*, "West Bank."

469. *Washington Post*, October 16, 2000, p. A-23.

470. CIA *World Factbook 2000*, "West Bank."

471. "Israeli Settlements and US Policy." The Center for Policy Analysis on Palestine, June 22, 1999.

472. "US, Israel Clash over Settlements in the West Bank." *The Baltimore Sun*, April 22, 1999.

473. "Freeze, Please." *The Economist*, June 5, 1999, p. 4. Bashi, Sari. "Barak Promises to Curtail Building." *The Associated Press*, June 7, 1999.

474. Greenberg, Joel, "Israel Shows Sign of Curbing Settlement Spending," *New York Times*, July 13, 1999, p. A3.

475. "Barak's Election Portends Modifications in Israel's Foreign Policy," *Report on Israeli Settlement in the Occupied Territories*, Foundation for Middle East Peace, July-August 1999.

476. Deborah Sontag, "Israel Weighs Border Pal to Proclaim if Talks Fail," *New York Times*, October 22, 2000, p. A-8

477. Deborah Sontag, "Israel Weighs Border Pal to Proclaim if Talks Fail," *New York Times*, October 22, 2000, p. A-8

478. Deborah Sontag, "Israel Weighs Border Pal to Proclaim if Talks Fail," *New York Times*, October 22, 2000, p. A-8

479. Summary text of peace accords, US State Department; Israeli government Internet database, accessed October 1995; information sheets provided by the Palestinian Authority; *Washington Post*, September 27, 1995, p. A-27.

480. Summary text of peace accords, US State Department; Israeli government Internet database, accessed October 1995; information sheets provided by the Palestinian Authority;

Washington Post, September 27, 1995, p. A-27; *Christian Science Monitor*, January 18, 1995, p. 19.

481. Assad, Samar. "PLO Statehood Meeting Delayed," *Associated Press*, June 21, 1999.

482. Stamas, Vicky, "Barak sets 15-month goal for peace breakthrough," Reuters, July 18, 1999, 1142.

483. Gazit, Shlomo, *The Palestinian Refugee Problem, Final Status Issues: Israel-Palestinians*, Study No. 2, Tel Aviv, Jaffee Center for Strategic Studies, 1995, p. 36.

484. World Bank, *World Development Indicators, 1998*, Washington, World Bank, p. 44.

485. *The Palestinian Refugee Crisis*, Information Brief No. 1, Washington, Center for Policy Analysis on Palestine, July 14, 1999. Also, some statistics based on UNRWA data obtained by telephone. For a discussion of the compensation issue, see Center for Policy Analysis on Palestine, *Palestinian Refugee Compensation*, Information Paper No. 3, Washington, Center for Policy Analysis on Palestine, April 1995. Also see Center for Policy Analysis on Palestine, *Palestinian Refugees: Their Problem and Future*, Information Paper No. 3, Washington, Center for Policy Analysis on Palestine, October 1994.

486. Gazit, Shlomo, *The Palestinian Refugee Problem, Final Status Issues: Israel-Palestinians*, Study No. 2, Tel Aviv, Jaffee Center for Strategic Studies, 1995, p. 36; Judy Dempsy, "Palestinian's Right of Return Turns on Israel's Moral Responsibility," *Financial Times*, October 13, 1999, p. 10 .

487. CIA, *World Factbook, 1995, 1998, and 1999*; Clyde Mark, "Palestinians and the Middle East Peace: Issues for the United States," Congressional Research Service, IB92052, December 5, 1994; *Wall Street Journal*, September 25, 1995, p. A-18; *Washington Times*, August 7, 1995, p. A-11.

488. See World Bank, *Integrated Development of the Jordan Rift Valley*, Washington, World Bank, October 1994; World Bank, *Emergency Assistance Program for the Occupied Territories*, Washington, World Bank, October 1994; World Bank, *Developing the Occupied Territories: An Investment for Peace*, Washington, World Bank, October 1994; World Bank, *Peace and the Jordanian Economy*, Washington, World Bank, October 1994.

489. Statistics based on UNRWA data obtained by telephone. For a discussion of the options from an Israeli perspective, see Gazit, Shlomo, *The Palestinian Refugee Problem, Final Status Issues: Israel-Palestinians*, Study No. 2, Tel Aviv, Jaffee Center for Strategic Studies, 1995.

490. Reuters, October 6, 1998.

491. Institute for Public Affairs In These Times, "Will the Peace Process Lead to Apartheid?," Oct. 17, 1999, p. 3.

492. Reuters, "Jerusalem Mayor Urges Boost to Jewish Population," September 14, 1999.

493. *Middle East Insight*, "Defining Jerusalem," Jan-Feb. 1999, pp. 27–52.

494. *The Jerusalem Monitor*, "Poll Reveals Palestinian Opinion on Jerusalem," Sept/Oct. 1999, p. 7.

495. White House Statement on Jerusalem Embassy Act Waiver, June 18, 1999.

496. *Washington Times*, October 26, 1995, p. A-17; *Washington Post*, October 25, 1995, p. A-22; *New York Times*, July 6, 1995, p. A-3; Executive News Service, December 3, 1995, 1433.

497. White House Statement on Jerusalem Embassy Act Waiver, June 18, 1999.

498. CIA, *Atlas of the Middle East*, Washington, GPO, January 1993, pp. 52–53, 62–63.

499. Dore Gold , *Jerusalem*, Tel Aviv, Jaffee Center for Strategic Studies, 1995, p. 7.

500. There are many demographic and historical studies of Jerusalem, and a number of studies of options for peace that are referenced in the bibliography. A number of Palestinian

studies have been done on this issue, including draft work by Walid Khalidi, a report by Hisham Sharabi, ed. "Settlements and Peace: The Problem of Jewish Colonization in Palestine," Washington, Center for Policy Analysis on Palestine, July 1995, and Center for Policy Analysis on Palestine, *Jerusalem*, Center for Policy Analysis on Palestine, Washington, February 1994. There are a number of excellent Israeli studies as well. Two of the best recent studies are Dore Gold, *Jerusalem*, Tel Aviv, Jaffee Center for Strategic Studies, 1995, and Hirsch, Moshe, Deborah Housen-Couriel, and Ruth Lapidoth, *Whither Jerusalem?*, London, Martinus Nijhoff, 1995.

501. Stamas, Vicky, "Barak sets 15-month goal for peace breakthrough," Reuters, July 18, 1999, 1142.

502. Executive News Service, October 18, 1995, 1430; *Report on Israeli Settlements in the Occupied Territories*, Volume 5, Number 6, November 1995, p. 3. There are a number of Israeli studies of "adjustments" to the 1967 borders, but they rarely are supported by exact borders and significant demographic details. Discussions with Israeli officials indicate that negotiations are not likely to be based on the assumptions in most such studies, particularly the Allon Plan, and that most such studies will need to be revised as a result of the September 1995 peace accords. For an excellent Israeli study of the options involved, see Joseph Alpher, *Settlements and Borders*, Tel Aviv, Jaffee Center for Strategic Studies, 1994. There are also a number of good Palestinian studies, including Hisham Sharabi, "Settlements and Peace: The Problem of Jewish Colonization in Palestine" Washington, The Center for Policy Analysis on Palestine, July 1995. Even the most recent of these studies, however, are now dated because of the September 1995 peace accords.

503. Prime Minister Rabin made these points several times before his assassination. They were repeated afterwards by Shimon Peres, and his new Foreign Minister Ehud Barak and Yossi Belin, a normally "dovish" minister in Peres's office. See Executive News Service, November 28, 1995, 0419.

504. Associated Press, March 4, 1999.

505. Executive News, July 17, 1995, 0705; *Christian Science Monitor*, August 3, 1995, p. 6; *Baltimore Sun*, August 25, 1995, p., 6A; *Washington Post*, July 24, 1995, p. A-14, September 10, 1995, p. C-2; *Washington Times*, August 8, 1995, p. A-12. For a discussion of the water issue from a Palestinian perspective, see Center for Policy Analysis on Palestine, *The Water Issue and the Palestinian-Israeli Conflict*, Information Paper No. 2, Washington, Center for Policy Analysis on Palestine, September 1993.

506. Summary text of peace accords, US State Department; Israeli government Internet database, accessed October 1995; information sheets provided by the Palestinian Authority; *Washington Post*, September 27, 1995, p. A-27.

507. Executive News Service, December 4, 1995, 0755.

508. Aronson, Geoffrey, "The Wye River Memorandum and Israeli Settlements," Information Brief, no. 3, Center for Policy Analysis on Palestine, August 4, 1999.

509. *Report on Israeli Settlement in the Occupied Territories*, Vol. 8, No. 6, November-December 1998.

510. "Wye, or not?" *The Economist*, July 17, 1999.

511. Hockstader, Lee, "Israel Will Resume West Bank Pullback," *The Washington Post*, August 2, 1999, p. A1.

512. Reuters, October 5, 1999, 1042.

513. Reuters, March 19, 2000, 0812; Associated Press, March 19, 2000, 0749.

514. *Jane's Defense Weekly*, July 2, 1997, p. 15; *Mariv*, July 19,1997; Reuters, July 20, 1997, 0910; *Washington Times*, July 21, 1997, p. A-11.

515. *Jane's Defense Weekly*, July 15, 1998, pp. 25–26.

516. *Report on Israeli Settlement*, January-February 1999, p.3

517. *Christian Science Monitor*, September 20, 1995, p. 6.

518. *Washington Post*, October 22, 2000, p. A-28.

519. Army Spokesperson quoted in Orme, William, "Israeli Army Removes Angry Settlers Blocking Gaza Road," *New York Times*, December 5, 2000.

520. Camiel, Deborah. "Israeli Copters Attack Palestinian Gunmen," *Washington Post*, December 5, 2000.

521. Reuters, October 4, 1999, 1116.

522. Hockstader, Lee "Pings and E-Arrows Fly in the Middle East Cyber-War" *Washington Post,* October 27, 2000.

523. BBC "Israel Lobby Group Hacked," November 3, 2000.

524. *Ha'aretz*, August 23, 1995 and September 13, 1995; *Yediot Ahronont*, August 25, 1995.

525. Foundation for Middle East Peace "Report on Israeli Settlement in the Occupied Territories," November-December; MSNBC "Fatah official, Israeli militant shot dead," December 31, 2000.

526. *Ha'aretz*, August 23, 1995 and September 12, 1995.

527. *Yedit Ahronot*, August 25, 1995.

528. Estimates vary from 68% to 73%. *Christian Science Monitor*, October 17, 1995, p. A-20; *Peacewatch*, October 5, 1995, p. 1.

529. Washington Institute, *Supporting Peace*, Washington, Washington Institute, 1994, p. 83; *Economist*, September 12, 1998, p. 48; "Arafat's Palestine—Closure, Corruption, and Poverty," *Swiss Review of World Affairs*, September 1, 1997; *Business Week*, November 9, 1998, p. 504; *Israel Business Today*, July 31, 1997, p. 6.

530. *Economist*, September 12, 1998, p. 48; "Arafat's Palestine—Closure, Corruption, and Poverty," *Swiss Review of World Affairs*, September 1, 1997; *Business Week*, November 9, 1998, p. 504; *Israel Business Today*, July 31, 1997, p. 6.

531. William A. Orme, "Palestinian Economy in Ruins," *New York Times*, December 6, 2000, Internet edition; Reuters, Jerusalem, December 6, 2000; Lee Hackstander, "Gaza's Fragile Economy Suffocated by Sanctions," *Washington Post*, December 6, 2000, p. A-1.

532. Office of the United Nations Special Coordinator, "The Impact on the Palestinian Economy of Confrontations, Mobility Restrictions and Border Closures September 28-November 26, 2000," United Nations.

533. William A. Orme, "Palestinian Economy in Ruins," *New York Times*, December 6, 2000, Internet edition; Reuters, Jerusalem, December 6, 2000; Lee Hackstander, "Gaza's Fragile Economy Suffocated by Sanctions," *Washington Post*, December 6, 2000, p. A-1.

534. William A. Orme, "Palestinian Economy in Ruins," *New York Times*, December 6, 2000, Internet edition; Reuters, Jerusalem, December 6, 2000; Lee Hackstander, "Gaza's Fragile Economy Suffocated by Sanctions," *Washington Post*, December 6, 2000, p. A-1.

535. William A. Orme, "Palestinian Economy in Ruins," *New York Times*, December 6, 2000, Internet edition; Reuters, Jerusalem, December 6, 2000; Lee Hackstander, "Gaza's Fragile Economy Suffocated by Sanctions," *Washington Post*, December 6, 2000, p. A-1.

536. Reuters, Jerusalem, December 6, 2000; William A. Orme, "Palestinian Economy in Ruins," *New York Times*, December 6, 2000, Internet edition; Lee Hackstander, "Gaza's Fragile Economy Suffocated by Sanctions," *Washington Post*, December 6, 2000, p. A-1.

537. These points are drawn from conversations with Israeli civilian experts, and not with active Israeli officers or officials.

538. "Report on Israeli Settlement in the Occupied Territories," *Foundation for Middle East Peace*, November-December 2000.

539. Kiley, Sam, "Cairo Pulls Out Israel Envoy After Bombing," *The Times*, November 22, 2000.

540. Kiley, Sam, "Cairo Pulls Out Israel Envoy After Bombing," *The Times*, November 22, 2000.

541. Khalaf, Roula, "It's Tough Going for the Monarch," *Financial Times* November 8, 2000.

542. *Washington Post*, April 28, 1995.

543. Luft, Gal. The Palestinian Security Services: Between Police and Army. The Washington Institute Policy Focus Research Memorandum, No. 36, November 1998.

544. *Washington Post*, October 17, 1995, p. A-1, October 26, 1995, p. A-20.

545. "Israeli-Palestinian Security Cooperation Contribute to Terror Decline." Israel Policy Forum, *Washington Bulletin*, June 22, 1999.

546. Executive News Service, October 19, 1995, 1507, November 11, 1995, 1632.

547. Heath Minister Ephraiam Sneh admitted Israel's role in killing a leader of Islamic Jihad in an interview on November 2, 1995, but retracted his remarks. Executive News Service, October 29, 1995, 1431, November 2, 1995, 0704.

548. US State Department, *Country Reports on Human Rights, 1998*, Internet version, accessed March 25, 1999.

549. *New York Times*, September 7, 1999, p. A-1; *Washington Post*, September 7, 1999, p. A-1.

550. For Palestinian criticism of Israeli security operations, see Center for Policy Analysis on Palestine, *Targeting to Kill: Israel's Undercover Units*, Center for Policy Analysis on Palestine, Washington, May 1992, and Center for Policy Analysis on Palestine, *Palestinian Human Rights Under Israeli Rule*, Center for Policy Analysis on Palestine, Washington, May 1993.

551. Executive News Service, June 28, 1995, 1240, *Philadelphia Inquirer*, June 28, 1995, 1240, September 13, 1995, p. A-1; *Baltimore Sun*, September 9, 1995, p. 4A; *Washington Post*, September 9, 1995, p. A-19.

552. For typical quotes and exchanges see Reuters, September 9, 1999, 0343, September 16, 1999, 1211, September 19, 1999, 1002.

553. *The Estimate*, June 16, 2000, pp. 5–8.

554. *The Estimate*, February 13, 1998, July 17, 1998, and August 13, 1999.

555. *Washington Post,* June 11, 2000, p. A-27, June 13, 2000, p. A-28, June 18, 2000, pp. A-21 and B-2; *The Estimate,* Volume XII, Number 10, May 19, 2000; Eyal Zisser, "Can Bashar al-Assad Hold on in Syria?" Policywatch, 470, June 12, 2000; Middle East Economic Digest, June 16, 2000; "Bashar's World, *Economist,* June 17, 2000, pp. 24–26; *New York Times*, June 11, 2000, pp. A-1 and A-14, June 13, 2000, p. A-10.

556. *Washington Post*, June 18, 2000, p. B-2.

557. Based on interviews and the relevant country sections of the IISS, *Military Balance, 1998–1999, 1999–2000 and 2000–2001,* and *Jane's World Air Forces,* various editions, *Jane's World Armies*, various editions, *Jane's Fighting Ships*, various editions, the Jane's *Sentinel* series; the CSIS, Military East Military Balance (On-Line editions), and Anthony H. Cordesman, *After The Storm: The Changing Military Balance in the Middle East*, Boulder, Westview, 1993.

558. *Jane's Defense Weekly*, July 1, 1995, p. 13; Syrian *Official Gazette*, June 6, 1995.

559. *Jane's Defense Weekly*, November 2, 1999, p. 20.

560. UPI, November 5, 1992, BC cycle.

561. *New York Times*, April 29, 1994, p. A-7; *Middle East Economic Digest MEED*, December 9, 1994, NEXIS edition. *Defense News*, July 4, 1994, p. 15.

562. *Jane's Defense Weekly*, November 2, 1999, p. 20.

563. Syria Plans Russian Arms Purchase, United Press International, February 17, 1999.

564. Blanche, Ed. "Syria Discusses Buying Advanced Russian Systems." *JDW*, May 19, 1999, p. 17.

565. Saradzhyan, Simon, "Bombing Spurs Interest in Russian Craft, Defenses," *Defense News*, July 19, 1999, p. 11.

566. LaFraniere, Sharon, "Russia, Syria Hint at Weapons Deal," *The Washington Post*, July 7, 1999, p. A6.

567. Kemp, Damian, "Russia pushes defense sales as exports hit highest for years," *Jane's Defense Weekly*, July 14, 1999, p. 17.

568. *Jane's Defense Weekly*, November 2, 1999, p. 20.

569. Jaffee Center for Strategic Studies, The *Middle East Military Balance, 1999–2000*, Tel Aviv, JCSS, Tel Aviv University, 2000; *Haaretz,* English edition, December 22, 1999.

570. *Jane's Defense Weekly*, January 26, 2000, p. 20; *Near East Report*, October 4, 1999, pp. 77–80; Reuters, December 23, 1999, 0952.

571. The strength estimates here are based on interviews, various editions of the IISS, *Military Balance*, and *Jane's World Armies*, Issue 2, "Syria."

572. Based on data in the relevant country section of the IISS, *Military Balance, 1998–1999 and 1999–2000*. Estimates in other sources differ.

573. Based on the data in the CIA, *World Factbook, 1999 and 2000 editions*; "Syria." For a good summary analysis of the location and population of Israeli settlements, and related security issues, see "Report on Israeli Settlements in the Occupied Territories: A Golan Heights Primer," Washington, Foundation for Middle East Peace, February 1995. Extensive additional data are available from the Israel government and Golani web servers on the Internet.

574. For a good discussion of the geography of the peace issue, see Alon Ben-Meir, "Peace with Syria First," Middle East Insight, July-August, 1999, pp. 17–23.

575. For more detail on this contingency, see the author's *After the Storm*, Boulder, Westview, 1993, and Edward B. Atkeson, "The Syrian-Israeli Military Balance: A Pot That Bears Watching," Arlington, Institute of Land Warfare, Paper No. 10, January 1992.

576. Some estimates go as low as 900 square kilometers. See David Eshel, "Compromise on the Golan," *Jane's Defense Weekly*, November 10, 1999, pp. 36–41.

577. CIA, *Atlas of the Middle East*, Washington, GPO, January, 1993, pp. 52–53, 62–63; Shlomo Bron, "The Negotiations With Syria: Quo Vadis? *Strategic Assessment*, Vol. 2, No. 3, December 1999; Frederic C. Hof, *Line of Battle, Border of Peace?* Washington, Middle East Insight, 1999; Bashar Tarabieh, "The Reality of Israeli Occupation: A Syrian Golani Perspective, *Information Brief*, No. 17, Center for Policy Analysis on Palestine, January 3, 2000.

578. David Eshel, "Compromise on the Golan," *Jane's Defense Weekly*, November 10, 1999, pp. 36–41.

579. David Eshel, "Compromise on the Golan," *Jane's Defense Weekly*, November 10, 1999, pp. 36–41.

580. Washington Institute, *Supporting Peace*, Washington, Washington Institute, 1994, pp. 9–12, 79–82; Aryeh Shalev, *Israel and Syria, Peace and Security on the Golan*, Boulder, Westview, 1994.

581. *Jane's Defense Weekly*, April 22, 1995, p. 24; W. Seth Carus and Hirsh Goodman, *The Future Battlefield and the Arab-Israeli Conflict*, London, Transaction Press, 1990, pp. 64–176.

582. This discussion is adapted from a US State Department working paper, the Golan Heights Information Server (*www.golan.org,* and www.golan-syria.org).

583. This discussion is adapted from a US State Department working paper and the Golan Heights Information Server (*www.golan.org*).

584. Reuters, January 19, 2000, 0933; *Mideast Mirror*, January 13, 1999, Israel section; Frederick C. Hof, Center for Policy Analysis on Palestine, "The Ongoing Dispute over the Line of 4 June, 1967," *Information Brief*, Number 31, March 31, 2000; Frederic C. Hof and Patrick Clawson, "Who Will Control the Share and Waters of the Galilee," Peacewatch, Number 254, April 13, 2000; and Frederic C. Hof, "Why the Geneva Talks Failed: Redrawing the Syrian-Israeli Border," *Information Brief*, Number 30, March 29, 2000.

585. This analysis is based largely on the work of Frederick C. Hof.

586. David Eshel, "Compromise on the Golan," *Jane's Defense Weekly*, November 10, 1999, pp. 36–41.

587. Washington Institute, *Supporting Peace*, Washington, Washington Institute, pp. 1994, p. 83.

588. UPI, August 3, 1993.

589. United Nations Peacekeeping Operations, "Current Peacekeeping Operations, Syrian Golan Heights, United Nations Disengagement Observer Force," UNDOF Mission Profile, July 14, 1999. The budget for the force is roughly $$33.66 million per year.

590. Kenneth S. Brower, "The Middle East Military Balance: Israel versus the Rest," *International Defense Review*, 7/1986, pp. 910–911.

591. "The IDF's Security Principles," Office of the IDF Spokesman, April 1995, and Scotty Fisher, "Country Briefing Israel," *Jane's Defense Weekly*," February 18, 1995, pp. 29–38.

592. For more detail on this contingency, see the author's *After the Storm*, Boulder, Westview, 1993, *Perilous Prospects*, Boulder, Westview, 1996, and Edward B. Atkeson, "The Syrian-Israeli Military Balance: A Pot That Bears Watching," Arlington, Institute of Land Warfare, Paper No. 10, January 1992 and *The Powder Keg*, Falls Church, Nova, 1996.

593. Reuters, December 23, 1999, 0952; *Jane's Defense Weekly*, February 2, 2000, p. 5.

594. Some systems can fire rounds longer range, but not accurately. Syria's S-23 guns are its only long-range weapons with effective ranges beyond 28 kilometers and they have been in storage for several years.

595. Reuters, January 19, 2000, 0933; *Mideast Mirror*, January 13, 1999, Israel section; Frederick C. Hof, Center for Policy Analysis on Palestine, "The Ongoing Dispute over the Line of 4 June, 1967," *Information Brief*, Number 30, March 31, 2000.

596. Reuters, March 5, 1999, 0441.

597. Sontag, Deborah. "Sadly, Golan Settlers Concede Peace Could Mean Eviction." *New York Times*, June 14, 1999, p. A1.

598. David Eshel, "Compromise on the Golan," *Jane's Defense Weekly*, November 10, 1999, pp. 36–41.

599. Wines, Michael, "Syria Signals Its Willingness To Reopen Talks With Israel," *The New York Times*, July 7, 1999, p. A6; Schneider, Howard, "Syria, Israel Seem Eager to Reopen Peace Talks," *The Washington Post*, June 24, 1999, p. A19.

600. "Syria's nods and winks," *The Economist*, July 24, 1999; "Syria tells Palestinian Groups to Cease Fire," Reuters, July 19, 1999, p. 41.

601. *Mideast Mirror*, January 13, 1999, Israel section.

602. Interviews, *Boston Globe*, June 23, 1995, p. 14; *Los Angeles Times*, May 2, 1994, p. A-4; *Washington Post*, May 3, 1995, p. A-15, May 16 ,1995, p. A-7, May 25, 1995, p. A-23; *New York Times,* May 16, 1995, p. A-6, May 25, 1995, p. A-1, May 26, 1995, p. A-2; Reuters, January 19, 2000, 0933; *Mideast Mirror*, January 13, 1999, Israel section. The bulk of this discussion is based on the draft US terms of peace and reporting by Akiva Eldar in *Haaretz* in January 2000. Also see Reuters, March 5, 1999, 0441; David Eshel, "Compromise on the Golan," *Jane's Defense Weekly*, November 10, 1999, pp. 36–41; *The Estimate*, January 14, 2000, p. 4.

603. "Syrian army chief asks troops to remain vigilant," Reuters, May 10, 1999.

604. The bulk of this discussion is based on the draft US terms of peace and reporting by Akiva Eldar in *Haaretz* in January 2000. Also see Reuters, March 5, 1999, 0441; David Eshel, "Compromise on the Golan," *Jane's Defense Weekly*, November 10, 1999, pp. 36–41; *The Estimate*, January 14, 2000, p. 4. For historical background see The Washington Institute, *Policywatch*, Number 117, October 27, 1995; *Christian Science Monitor*, September 28 ,1995, p. 6; Executive News, October 11, 1995, 0604, October 15, 1995, 0629; *Armed Forces Journal*, October, 1995, p. 15.

605. CIA, *Atlas of the Middle East*, Washington, GPO, January, 1993, pp. 52–53, 62–63; Shlomo Bron, "The Negotiations With Syria: Quo Vadis?" *Strategic Assessment*, Vol. 2, No. 3, December 1999; Frederick C. Hof, *Line of Battle, Border of Peace?* Washington, Middle East Insight, 1999; Bashar Tarabieh, "The Reality of Israeli Occupation: A Syrian Golani Perspective," *Information Brief*, No. 17, Center for Policy Analysis on Palestine, January 3, 2000,

606. Reuters, March 4, 1999.

607. Executive News Service, November 28, 1995, 0859, 1614.

608. "Syria's nods and winks," *The Economist*, July 24, 1999, p. 41.

609. *New York Times*, May 16, 1995, p. A-6, May 25, 1995, p. A-1; *Washington Post*, May 25, 1995, p. A-23.

610. A comprehensive discussion of the technical issues involved require a detailed knowledge of Israeli intelligence sources and methods that is not available to the author. For another view, see Aryeh Shalev, *Israel and Syria, Peace and Security on the Golan*, Boulder, Westview, 1994, pp. 128–139.

611. Hamza, Issam, "UN force marks 25 years of presence in Golan," Reuters, June 3, 1999, 0828.

612. "Syria asks Canada to keep soldiers on after peace."

613. Brent Scowcroft, "A US Role in the Golan Heights," *New York Times,* January 6, 2000.

614. *Jane's Defense Weekly*, November 3, 1999, p. 16.

615. *Jane's Defense Weekly*, February 23, 2000, p. 4.

616. *Jane's Defense Weekly*, December 22, 1999, p. 2; *The Estimate*, January 14, 2000, p. 4.

617. *The Estimate*, January 28, 2000, p. 4; *Jane's Defense Weekly*, February 23, 2000, p. 4.

618. *The Estimate*, January 28, 2000, p. 4; *Jane's Defense Weekly*, February 23, 2000, p. 4.

619. CIA, *World Factbook, 1999 and 2000 editions*.

620. For a discussion of the Syrian military operation that took control of Lebanon, see John Laffin, *The World in Conflict, War Annual 6*, London, Brassey's, 1995, pp. 133–144.

621. *Christian Science Monitor*, September 28, 1995, p. 7; *Middle East Economic Digest*, October 27, 1995, pp. 2–3; IISS. *Military Balance, 1998–1999 and 1999–2000*.

622. CIA, *World Factbook, 1999 and 2000 editions*; Reuters, May 21, 2000, 2002.

623. Interviews with US experts in February 2000; Reuters, May 21, 2000, 2002.

624. Reuters, March 5, 2000, 1144; *New York Times International*, February 12, 2000, p. A-4, February 14, 2000, p. A-10, March 8, 2000, p. A-8; Jehl, Douglas, "Killing Highlights Lebanon's Palestinian Problem," *The New York Times*, June 11, 1999, p. A3; *Washington Post*, February 13, 2000, p. A-23; Shlomo Bron, *Israel and South Lebanon*, Tel Aviv, The Jaffee Center for Strategic Studies, November 1999.

625. *Economist*, December 18, 1999, p. 40; *Jane's Defense Weekly*, February 16, 2000, p. 32; Nichole Brackman, "Israeli-Lebanese Negotiations: The Palestinian Refugee Issue," *Peacewatch*, No. 288, December 28, 1999.

626. Interviews with US experts in February 2000; Reuters, May 21, 2000, 2002.

627. Based on interviews and the relevant country sections of the *Military Balance, 1998–1999, 1999–2000, and 2000–2001*, and *Jane's World Air Forces*, various editions, *Jane's World Armies*, various editions, Jane's Fighting Ships, various editions, the *Jane's Sentinel* Series; the CSIS, Military East Military Balance (On-Line editions), Anthony H. Cordesman, *After The Storm: The Changing Military Balance in the Middle East*, Boulder, Westview, 1993, A.J. Venter, "Lebanon: A Pawn in the Power Struggle," *Jane's Intelligence Review*, June 1998, pp. 18–23; Shmuel Gordan, *The Vulture and the Snake*, Ramat Gan, BESA, Security and Policy Studies No. 39, Bar Ilan University, June 1998; David Eshel, "The Vietnam Syndrome," *Jane's Defense Weekly*, January 6, 1999, pp. 19–25; Edward Blanche, "A Bizarre yet Bloody Conflict Drags on in South Lebanon Part I & II," *Jane's Intelligence Review*, September and October 1997.

628. Reuters, June 15, 2000.

629. The strength estimates here are based on interviews, various editions of the IISS, *Military Balance*, and *Jane's World Armies*, Issue 2, "Lebanon" and "Israel," and Issue 1, "Syria."

630. *The Washington Post*, December 5, 1998, p. A-18.

631. Finnegan, Philip and Barbara Opall-Rome. "U.S. to Expand Military Sales to Lebanon." *Defense News*, June 21, 1999, p. 4.

632. *Defense News*, November 24–30, 1997, p. 30.

633. *Jane's Sentinel*, "Syria," 1996.

634. *Christian Science Monitor*, October 16, 1995, p. 7; *Baltimore Sun*, October 12, 1995, p. 4; *Middle East Economic Digest*, September 29, 1995, p. 21, October 27, 1995, pp. 2–3; *Washington Post*, October 16, 1995, p. A-1; *New York Times*, October 16, 1995, p. A-1; A.J. Venter, "Lebanon: A Pawn in the Power Struggle," *Jane's Intelligence Review*, June 1998, pp. 18–23; Shmuel Gordan, *The Vulture and the Snake*, Ramat Gan, BESA, Security and Policy Studies No. 39, Bar Ilan University, June 1998; David Eshel, "The Vietnam Syndrome," *Jane's Defense Weekly*, January 6, 1999, pp. 19–25; Edward Blanche, "A Bizarre yet Bloody Conflict Drags on in South Lebanon Part I & II," *Jane's Intelligence Review*, September and October 1997.

635. *Middle East Economic Digest*, September 29, 1995, p. 21.

636. *Washington Post*, December 20, 1994, p. A-30; Reuters, May 21, 2000, 0449; Interviews in November 1999 with US experts.

637. IISS, *Military Balance, 1999–2000*; interviews with US experts, November 1999.

638. Washington Institute, *Supporting Peace*, Washington, Washington Institute, pp. 1994, p. 83; interviews in November 1999 with US experts.

639. The strength estimates here are based on interviews, various editions of the IISS, *Military Balance*, and *Jane's World Armies*, Issue 2, "Lebanon" and "Israel," and Issue 1, "Syria."

640. See A.J. Venter, "Lebanon: A Pawn in the Power Struggle," *Jane's Intelligence Review*, June 1998, pp. 18–23; Shmuel Gordan, *The Vulture and the Snake*, Ramat Gan, BESA, Security and Policy Studies No. 39, Bar Ilan University, June 1998; David Eshel, "The Vietnam Syndrome," *Jane's Defense Weekly*, January 6, 1999, pp. 19–25; Edward Blanche, "A Bizarre yet Bloody Conflict Drags on in South Lebanon Part I & II," *Jane's Intelligence Review*, September and October 1997.

641. Interviews with US experts, November 1999 and February 2000.

642. Lebanese sources claim that this is a "kill ratio" of 1,889 Lebanese killed for every Israeli killed.

643. These estimates are based on the work of Nicholas Blandford, and Jerusalem Fund. See Nicholas Blandford, "Israeli Occupation of South Lebanon," *Information Brief*, Number 8, Jerusalem Fund, September 29, 1999, and "Hizbullah: Lebanon's Heir Apparent," *Jane's Intelligence Review*, November 1999.

644. Associated Press, November 30, 1998.

645. Patrick Clawson and Michael Eisenstadt, *The Last Arab-Israeli Battlefield*, Washington, Washington Institute, 2000, pp. 7–8; Nicholas Blandford, "Hizbullah: Lebanon's Heir Apparent," *Jane's Intelligence Review*, November 1999; A. J. Venter, "Hezbollah Defies Onslaught," *International Defense Review*, p. 81.

646. Reuters, March 5, 2000, 1144; *New York Times International*, February 12, 2000, p. A-4, February 14, 2000, p. A-10, March 8, 2000, p. A-8; Jehl, Douglas, "Killing Highlights Lebanon's Palestinian Problem," *The New York Times*, June 11, 1999, p. A3; *Washington Post*, February 13, 2000, p. A-23; Shlomo Bron, *Israel and South Lebanon*, Tel Aviv, The Jaffee Center for Strategic Studies, November 1999.

647. *Jane's Intelligence Review*, June 1998, p. 21; National Public Radio, March 9, 1999, 1609.

648. See *Jane's World Armies*, Issue 2, "Lebanon" and "Israel," and Issue 1, "Syria."

649. A full description of the Hizbollah's goals and political views can be found at www.hezbollah.org. Also see Patrick Clawson and Michael Eisenstadt, *The Last Arab-Israeli Battlefield*, Washington, Washington Institute, 2000, pp. 17–19; Sadi al-Husayni, "Lebanon: Interview with Hizballah Secretary General Hassanm Nasrallah on Iran and Arab Regimes," al-Sharq al-Awsat, FBIS-NES-97-289, October 16, 1997; Nasri Hajjaj, "Interview with Hizballah Secretary General Hassanm Nasrallah," al-Ayyam, FBIS-NES-2000-0105, January 1, 2000, *Los Angeles Times*, November 28, 1997, p. A-5; *Atlanta Constitution*, March 4, 1999, p. B-1

650. Dr. Reuven Ehrlich (Avi-Ran), "Terrorism as a Preferred Instrument of Syrian Policy," ICT Research Fellow, *www.ict.org.il/*, accessed October 16, 1999.

651. Reuters, February 14, 2000, 0809; *New York Times International*, February 12, 2000, p. A-4, February 14, 2000, p. A-10.

652. *al-Was*t , March 11, 1996.

653. International Policy Institute for Counter-Terrorism, "Iran and Terrorism," Herzliya, Israel, *www.ict.org.il/*, accessed October 16, 1999; US Department of State, "Patterns of Global Terrorism, 1998," Washington, GPO, April 1999, Appendix B, "Syria," and "Iran."

654. International Policy Institute for Counter-Terrorism, "Iran and Terrorism," Herzliya, Israel, *www.ict.org.il/*, accessed October 16, 1999.

655. Associated Press, September 27, 1999, 1546.

656. "Hizbollah Applies Israel, U.S. Military Strategies to Guerrilla War in Lebanon." Defense News, June 21, 1999, p. 4.

657. *Washington Post*, October 16, 1995, p. A-1; *New York Times*, October 16, 1995, p. A-1.

658. *Jane's Defense Weekly*, June 1998, pp. 18–23.

659. See *Jane's World Armies*, Issue 2, "Lebanon" and "Israel," and Issue 1, "Syria."

660. Patrick Clawson and Michael Eisenstadt, *The Last Arab-Israeli Battlefield*, Washington, Washington Institute, 2000, pp. 8–9; Kenneth Katzman, "Terrorism: Middle Eastern Groups and State Sponsors," Washington, Congressional Research Service, CRS Report 98–722F, August 27, 1998, pp. 5–6; "Islamic Jihad to Expand in Lebanon," al-Quds, FBIS-NES-1999–117, November 16, 1999.

661. US Department of State, "Patterns of Global Terrorism, 1994," Washington, GPO, April 1995, pp. 15–18,19; "Patterns of Global Terrorism, 1998," Washington, GPO, April 1999, and ; "Patterns of Global Terrorism, 1999," Washington, GPO, April 2000.

662. Patrick Clawson and Michael Eisenstadt, *The Last Arab-Israeli Battlefield*, Washington, Washington Institute, 2000, p. 12.

663. *Jane's Intelligence Review*, September 1997, p. 413; *Christian Science Monitor*, October 9, 1997, p. 6.

664. The strength estimates here are based on interviews, various editions of the IISS, *Military Balance*, and *Jane's World Armies*, Issue 2, "Lebanon" and "Israel," and Issue 1, "Syria."

665. See Patrick Clawson and Michael Eisenstadt, *The Last Arab-Israeli Battlefield*, Washington, Washington Institute, 2000, pp. 86–88.

666. See Ed Blanche, "Israel's Human Sandbags Set to Collapse in Lebanon," *Jane's Intelligence Review*, August 1, 1999; Nicholas Blandford, "Hizbollah Attacks Force Israel to Take a Hard Look at Lebanon," *Jane's Intelligence Review*, April 1999, pp. 32–37.

667. See the detailed chronology in Associated Press, May 23, 2000, 2259.

668. Associated Press, May 24, 2000.

669. Reuters, May 24, 2000, 064.

670. Associated Press, May 24, 2000.

671. *New York Times*, May 24, 2000, p. A-1.

672. Associated Press, May 24, 2000.

673. Reuters, May 24, 2000, 0210.

674. Reuters, May 24, 2000, 0549.

675. Reuters, May 24, 2000, 0549.

676. Eshel, David. The Vietnam Syndrome. *Jane's Defense Weekly*, January 6, 1999, pp. 19–26.

677. See A. J. Venter, "Lebanon: A Pawn in the Power Struggle," *Jane's Intelligence Review*, June 1998, pp. 18–23; Shmuel Gordan, *The Vulture and the Snake*, Ramat Gan, BESA, Security and Policy Studies No. 39, Bar Ilan University, June 1998; David Eshel, "The Vietnam Syndrome," *Jane's Defense Weekly*, January 6, 1999, pp. 19–25; Edward Blanche, "A Bizarre yet Bloody Conflict Drags on in South Lebanon Part I & II," *Jane's Intelligence Review*, September and October 1997.

678. This analysis draws heavily on the work of Shmuel Gordan, *The Vulture and the Snake*, Ramat Gan, BESA, Security and Policy Studies No. 39, Bar Ilan University, June 1998; and David Eshel, "The Vietnam Syndrome," *Jane's Defense Weekly*, January 6, 1999, pp. 19–25; Edward Blanche, "A Bizarre yet Bloody Conflict Drags on in South Lebanon Part I & II," *Jane's Intelligence Review*, September and October 1997.

679. *Washington Post*, October 16, 1995, p. A-1; *New York Times*, October 16, 1995, p. A-1.

680. For example, an ambush that killed six Israeli soldiers on October 15, 1995. *Washington Times*, October 16, 1995, p. A-1; Executive News Service, October 14, 1995, 0556; October 16, 1995, 1654; *Washington Post*, October 16, 1995, p. A-1; *New York Times*, October 16, 1995, p. A-1.

681. *Washington Post*, April 12, 1996, p. A-27; *Jane's Defense Weekly*, April 24, 1996, p. 14; *Armed Forces Journal*, June 1996, p. 22.

682. *Jane's Defense Weekly*, April 24, 1996, p. 14; *Armed Forces Journal*, June 1996, p. 22.

683. Eshel, David. The Vietnam Syndrome," *Jane's Defense Weekly*, October 20, 1999, pp. 19–26.

684. Gordan, Shmuel. "The Vulture and the Snake: Counter-Guerilla Air Warfare: The War in Southern Lebanon." Bar-Ilan University, Israel, 1998.

685. "IDF Training to Prevent Friendly Fire," *Jane's Defense Weekly*, July 14, 1999, p. 14.

686. *Christian Science Monitor*, October 9, 1997, p. 6.

687. *Washington Times*, March 3, 1999, p. A-14.

688. *Pharaohs*, June 2000, p. 47.

689. John Kifner, "In Long Fight With Israel, Hezbollah Tactics Evolved," *New York Times*, July 19, 2000.

690. John Kifner, "In Long Fight With Israel, Hezbollah Tactics Evolved," *New York Times*, July 19, 2000.

691. John Kifner, "In Long Fight With Israel, Hezbollah Tactics Evolved," *New York Times*, July 19, 2000.

692. Edward Blanche, "Pressure Mounts on Israel to Quit Lebanon's Security Zone." *Jane's Defense Weekly*, March 5, 1997, p. 17.

693. Blanche, Ed. "Israel Signals Conditions for Lebanon Withdrawal." *Jane's Defense Weekly*, March 18, 1998, p. 21.

694. Redden, Jack, "Analysis- SLA flight shows need for Syria-Israel deal," Reuters, June 3, 1999; Blandford, Nicholas, "South Lebanon Army in Retreat," *Jane's Defense Weekly*, June 9, 1999.

695. Lee Hockstader, "Stopping Trouble at the Border," *The Washington Post*, December 4, 1998, p. A37.

696. *Jane's Defense Weekly*, March 5, 1997, p. 17.

697. Eshel, David. IDF Pulls Back from Lebanon Withdrawal. *Jane's Defense Weekly*. December 9, 1998, p. 19.

698. Blanford, Nicholas. Israeli Cabinet Endorses Strikes on Lebanon. *Jane's Defense Weekly*, January 13, 1999, p. 20.

699. *Washington Times*, February 24, 1999, p. A-11, March 3, 1999, p. A-14.

700. *Washington Times*, February 24, 1999, p. A-11, March 1, 1999, p. A-1, March 3, 1999, p. A-14; *Los Angeles Times*, March 2, 1999, p. A-3; *Philadelphia Inquirer*, March 4, 1999, p. A-2.

701. Reuters, July, 17, 1997; *Washington Times*, March 3, 1999, p. A-14.

702. *Christian Science Monitor*, October 9, 1997, p. 6.

703. *Christian Science Monitor*, October 9, 1997, p. 6.

704. "Hezbollah: No Truce In S. Lebanon," AP, March 8, 1999.

705. Blanford, Nicholas, "Hezbollah hit 22 outposts in Lebanon," *Jane's Defense Weekly*, May 5, 1999, p. 19.

706. *Los Angeles Times*, March 2, 1999, p. A-3; *Philadelphia Inquirer*, March 4, 1999, p. A-2; *Washington Times*, March 3, 1999, p. A-14.

707. Reuters, February 24, 1999, 1816, March 2, 1999, 0453, March 4, 1999, March 5, 1999, 0441.

708. Associated Press, March 2, 1999, 2231.

709. Blanford, Nicholas, "South Lebanon Army in Retreat," *Jane's Defense Weekly*, June 9, 1999, p. 50.

710. "IDF Reduces Lebanon Security Forces, "*JDW*, April 21, 1999, p. 17.

711. "Time to Leave the Insecurity Zone." *The Economist*, May 29, 1999, p. 42.

712. "Exit in Disorder," *The Economist*, June 5, 1999, p. 45; Sleiman, Sultan, "Israel's Lebanon Allies Retreat from Jezzine," Reuters, June 3, 1999; Blanford, Nicholas, "South Lebanon Army in Retreat," *JDW,* June 9, 1999, p. 50.

713. Blanford, Nicholas, "Latest clashes are worst since 'Grapes of Wrath,'" *Jane's Defense Weekly*, July 7, 1999, p. 16.

714. Ghattas, Sam F., "Lebanon-Israel," AP, June 25, 1999, 0846.

715. Blanford, Nicholas, "Latest clashes are worst since 'Grapes of Wrath,'" *Jane's Defense Weekly*, July 7, 1999, p. 16.

716. Ghattas, Sam F., "Lebanon-Israel," AP, June 25, 1999, 0846; Sontag, Deborah, "Lebanon and Israel Still Tense After Clash," *The New York Times*, June 25, 1999, p. A5.

717. Associated Press, September 30, 1999, 0810.

718. Much of this discussion is based on interviews with senior Israeli officers.

719. Reuters, February 14, 2000, 0809; *Washington Post*, February 13, 2000, p. A-23.

720. *Washington Post*, March 12, 2000, p. A-26.

721. For a good summary of the issues at this time, see Michael Young, "Impending Lebanese-Israeli Talks," *Information Brief*, Center for Policy Analysis on Palestine, No. 20, January 19, 2000.

722. Associated Press, March 8, 2000, 1142.

723. Reuters, May 22, 2000, 0615.

724. Eshel, David, "The leaving of Lebanon . . ." *Jane's Defense Weekly,* June 7, 2000, p. 20.

725. Eshel, David. The Vietnam Syndrome. *Jane's Defense Weekly,* January 6, 1999, pp. 19–26.

726. Patrick Clawson and Michael Eisenstadt, *The Last Arab-Israeli Battlefield*, Washington, Washington Institute, 2000, pp. 97–100.

727. These cost figures were presented to the Knesset on October 12, 1999. Associated Press, October 18, 1999, 1049; *Jane's Defense Weekly*, January 6, 1999, p. 17.

728. Associated Press, October 18, 1999, 1049; *Jane's Defense Weekly*, January 6, 1999, p. 17.

729. *Jane's Defense Weekly*, January 6, 1999, p. 17.

730. *Jane's Defense Weekly*, July 10, 1996, p. 3

731. Lennox, Duncan and David Eshel, "Israeli high-energy laser project may face more delays," *Jane's Defense Weekly*, April 7, 1999, p. 21.

732. Bender, Bryan, "Future of US-Israeli laser project in doubt," *Jane's Defense Weekly,* June 2, 1999, p. 6.

733. Bender, Bryan, "US and Israeli governments to bail out THEL," *Jane's Defense Weekly*, June 16, 1999, p. 6.

734. *Jane's International Defense Review*, 2/2000, p. 4.

735. Reuters, June 7, 2000, 2127.

736. Associated Press, April 30, 2000, 1628.

737. *Washington Post*, March 12, 2000, p. A-26.

738. See Reuters, March 5, 2000, 1144; *New York Times International*, February 12, 2000, p. A-4, February 14, 2000, p. A-10, March 8, 2000, p. A-8; Jehl, Douglas, "Killing Highlights Lebanon's Palestinian Problem," *The New York Times*, June 11, 1999, p. A3; *Washington Post*, February 13, 2000, p. A-23; Shlomo Bron, *Israel and South Lebanon*, Tel Aviv, The Jaffee Center for Strategic Studies, November 1999.

739. *Economist,* June 17, 2000.

740. "Lebanon—UNIFIL Background," Information Technology Section/Department of Public Information. *www.un.org/depts/DPKO/Missions/unifil/unifilB.htm*, accessed June 19, 2000.

741. For further details, see Clyde R. Mark, "Lebanon," IB89118, Washington, Congressional Research Service, November 14, 1995.

742. *Jane's Defense Weekly*, February 24, 1999, p. 19.

743. Reuters, May 24, 2000, 0543.

744. This history is modified in large part from the UNIFIL history provided in the UNIFIL Web site at *www.un.org/Depts/DPKO/Missions/unifil/unifilB.htm*, as of October 2000.

745. Hof, Frederick, *Peacewatch,* "The Israeli-Lebanon Border: A Primer," The Washington Institute for Near East Policy, April 25, 2000.

746. BBC News, "Lebanon Border 'Close'," June 2, 2000, 2145, accessed June 19, 2000.

747. *Los Angeles Times*, December 3, 1997, p. A3, *Washington Times*, March 3, 1999, p. A-14.

748. MEMRI, *Special Dispatch*, "The Future of the Armed Struggle, An Arab Debate," No. 25, May 23, 2000; Reuters, May 18, 2000, 0923.

749. Reuters, May 19, 2000, 1211, May 21, 2000, 1508.

750. *New York Times*, October 15, 2000, p. A-11.

751. *Jane's Defense Weekly*, July 19, 2000, p. 8.

752. *New York Times*, October 15, 2000, p. A-11.

753. For example, Hizbollah rocket attacks on Qiryat Shemona and other settlements on November 28, 1995, after clashes that killed three members of the Hizbollah. *New York Times*, November 29, 1995, p. A-6; *Washington Post*, November 29, 1995, p. A-1.

754. Reuters, June 26, 2000, 0833.

755. *Jane's Defense Weekly*, August 16, 2000, p. 5.

756. *The Economist*, August 26, 2000, p. 33; Reuters, August 1, 2000, 1252; *New York Times*, August 13, 2000, p. 7.

757. Reuters, June 26, 2000, 2157; *The Economist*, June 24, 2000, p. 50.

758. *New York Times*, September 5, 2000, p. A-4.

759. Based on interviews and the relevant country sections of the *Military Balance, 1998–1999, 1999–2000 and 2000–2001,* and *Jane's World Air Forces,* various editions, *Jane's World Armies*, various editions, *Jane's Fighting Ships*, various editions, the Jane's *Sentinel* series; the CSIS, Military East Military Balance (On-Line editions), and Anthony H. Cordesman, *After The Storm: The Changing Military Balance in the Middle East*, Boulder, Westview, 1993.

760. *Jane's Defense Weekly*, March 24, 1999, p. 20; Reuters, March 15, 1999, 1403.

761. Based largely on data in the relevant country section of the IISS, *Military Balance, 1998–1999, 1999–2000 and 2000–2001;* and *Jane's World Armies*, Issue 2, "Jordan," November 1997. Estimates in other sources differ.

762. Based largely on data in the relevant country section of the IISS, *Military Balance, 1998–1999, 1999–2000 and 2000–2001*. Estimates in other sources differ.

763. Based largely on data in the relevant country section of the IISS, *Military Balance, 1998–1999, 1999–2000 and 2000–2001*. Estimates in other sources differ.

764. *Defense News*, December 12, 1994, p. 3; March 8, 1993, p. 1.

765. *Jane's Defense Weekly*, January 6, 1999, p.15; *Defense News*, January 1, 1999, p. 18.

766. Faraj, Caroline and Philip Finnegan, "Jordan Pursues Closer Gulf Ties in Hopes of Joint Training," *Defense News*, April 19, 1999.

767. Faraj, Caroline and Philip Finnegan, "Egyptian Military Explores Industrial Teaming With Jordan," *Defense News*, April 19, 1999, p. 22.

768. *Defense News*, December 12, 1994, p. 3, March 8, 1993, p. 1, November 7, 1994, p. 1, November 29, 1993, p. 1

769. Press Association Newsfile, July 7, 1993; *The Independent*, June 23, 1993; *Washington Times*, June 17, 1993.

770. Associated Press, February 21, 1999, 1248; *Washington Post*, February 22, 1999, p. A-10.

771. *Washington Post*, August 16, 1995, p. A-26.

772. For an excellent detailed discussion of the military details, see Ed Blanche, "The Phantom Alliance," *Jane's Defense Weekly*, March 10, 1999, pp. 53–57. Also see Alan Makovsky, Cengiz Candar, and Efriam Inbar, "The Turkish-Israeli-Syrian Triangle," *Peacewatch*, No. 249, March 15, 2000.

773. *Jane's Defense Weekly*, August 25, 1999, p. 5; Alan Makovsky, "Syrian-Israeli Negotiations and Turkey, *Peacewatch*, No. 236, December 17, 1999; General Cevik Bir, "Reflections on Turkish-Israeli Relations and Turkish Security, *Policywatch*, 422, November 5, 1999.

774. Ed Blanche, "The Phantom Alliance," *Jane's Defense Weekly*, March 10, 1999, pp. 53–57.

775. Opall-Rome, Barbara, "Israel, GDLS Join Forces For Turkish Tank Contest," *Defense News*, June 21, 1999, p. 8.

776. Bekdil, Ege and Barbara Opall-Rome, "Turkey Fears New Israeli Government May Dilute Ties," *Defense News*, June 14, 1999, p. 56.

777. See the quotes in *Defense News*, March 15, 1999, p. 4.

778. Reuters, March 11, 1999, 0615.

779. *Jane's Defense Weekly,* May 24, 2000, p. 3.

780. Based on interviews and the relevant country sections of the IISS *Military Balance, 1998–1999, 1999–2000 and 2000–2001,* and *Jane's World Air Forces,* various editions, *Jane's World Armies*, various editions, Jane's Fighting Ships, various editions, the Jane's *Sentinel* series; the CSIS, Military East Military Balance (On-Line editions), and Anthony H. Cordesman, *After The Storm: The Changing Military Balance in the Middle East*, Boulder, Westview, 1993.

781. Based largely on data in the relevant country section of the IISS, *Military Balance, 1998–1999, 1999–2000 and 2000–2001;* and *Jane's World Armies*, Issue 1, "Egypt," June, 1997. Estimates in other sources differ.

782. Based largely on data in the relevant country section of the IISS, *Military Balance, 1998–1999, 1999–2000 and 2000–2001*. Estimates in other sources differ.

783. Reuters, March 11, 1999, 0615; *Jane's Defense Weekly*, March 17, 1999, p. 3.

784. Based largely on data in the relevant country section of the IISS, *Military Balance, 1998–1999, 1999–2000 and 2000–2001*, and Reuters, March 11, 1999, 0615. Estimates in other sources differ.

785. Based largely on data in the relevant country section of the IISS, *Military Balance, 1998–1999, 1999–2000 and 2000–2001*. Estimates in other sources differ.

786. "Russia to upgrade Egyptian missiles," *Jane's Defense Weekly*, March 31, 1999, p. 16.

787. *Jane's Defense Weekly*, March 17, 1999, p. 3.

788. Based largely on data in the relevant country section of the IISS, *Military Balance, 1998–1999, 1999–2000 and 2000–2001*. Estimates in other sources differ.

789. This summary is adapted from work by Aryeh Shalev in *Israel and Syria: Peace and Security on the Golan*, JCSS Study Number 24, Tel Aviv, 1994, pp. 173–177.

790. The technical history of the MFO can be traced through the annual reports of the US State Department and through the annual reports to Congress by the General Accounting Office (*Assessment of US Participation in the Multinational Force and Observers*).

791. The author examined both Egyptian and Israeli complaints about such violations in some in-depth discussions with Egyptian and Israeli officials. These violations are not normally reported publicly in detail, but they are largely technical in character and have had little—if any—strategic significance.

792. Associated Press, March 12, 1999, 1313.

793. Associated Press, March 12, 1999, 1313.

794. Based on interviews and the relevant country sections of the *Military Balance, 1998–1999, 1999–2000 and 2000–2001,* and *Jane's World Air Forces,* various editions, *Jane's World Armies,* various editions, Jane's Fighting Ships, various editions, the Jane's *Sentinel Series*; the CSIS, Military East Military Balance (On-Line editions), and Anthony H. Cordesman, *After The Storm: The Changing Military Balance in the Middle East*, Boulder, Westview, 1993.

795. Based on interviews and the relevant country sections of the *Military Balance, 1998–1999, 1999–2000 and 2000–2001,* and *Jane's World Air Forces,* various editions, *Jane's World Armies*, various editions, *Jane's Fighting Ships*, various editions, the Jane's *Sentinel Series*; the CSIS, Military East Military Balance (On-Line editions), and Anthony H. Cordesman, *After The Storm: The Changing Military Balance in the Middle East*, Boulder, Westview, 1993.

796. IISS, *The Military Balance, 1998–1999, 1999–2000 and 2000–2001*. Some estimates show totals for the Gendarmerie alone. This is incorrect. They have been merged with the national police and some elements of the internal security forces.

797. *New York Times*, May 17, 1995, p. A-3.

798. "Report: Barak Rejected Iranian Offer," Associated Press, July 21, 1999, 1017.

799. Based on interviews and the relevant country sections of the *Military Balance, 1998–1999, 1999–2000 and 2000–2001,* and *Jane's World Air Forces,* various editions, *Jane's World Armies*, various editions, *Jane's Fighting Ships*, various editions, the *Jane's Sentinel Series*; the CSIS, Military East Military Balance (On-Line editions), and Anthony H. Cordesman, *After The Storm: The Changing Military Balance in the Middle East*, Boulder, Westview, 1993.

800. For a detailed discussion, see Anthony H. Cordesman, *The Threat from the Northern Gulf*, Boulder, Westview, 1994; and Dr. Andrew Rathmell, "Iraq—The Endgame?" *Jane's Intelligence Review*, Volume 7, Number 5, pp. 224–228.

801. Avner Cohen, *Israel and the Bomb*, New York, Columbia University Press, 1998; Reuters, October 4, 1998, 2202; Associated Press, September 16, 1998, 0122; *Defense News*, October 12, 1998, p. 46.

802. A detailed description of Israel's nuclear and missile effort, accompanied by satellite photos is provided in Harold Hough,"Israel's Nuclear Infrastructure," *Jane's Intelligence Weekly*, November 1994, pp. 505–511. Also see *Chicago Sun-Times*, July 7, 1993, p. 29; *Washington Times*, June 27, 1994, p. A-15; *Sunday Times*, October 5, 1986, pp. 1–3 and October 12, 1986, pp. 1 and 12; Frank Barnaby, *The Invisible Bomb*, London, I. B. Taurus, 1989, Avner Cohen, *Israel and the Bomb*, New York, Columbia University Press, 1998; Jones, Rodney W., March C. McDonough, Toby F. Dalton and Gregory D. Koblentz, *Tracking Nuclear Proliferation*, Washington, Carnegie Endowment, 1998; Office of the Secretary of Defense, *Proliferation: Threat and Response*, Washington, Department of Defense, November 1997; Office of the Secretary of Defense, *Proliferation: Threat and Response*, Washington, Department of Defense, November 1998; *Science*, March 22, 1974, p. 15; *Washington Times*, October 6, 1986; *Boston Globe*, October 14, 1986; *New York Times*, October 27, 1986; *Washington Post*, October 31, 1986. Recent BBC and ITV reporting efforts seem to give more credibility to the idea that Israel has some form of relatively short-range nuclear-armed missile. Ranges of anywhere from 75–930 NM have been reported for the Jericho, with accuracies of anywhere from 0.1 km to radar correlator guidance packages capable of CEPs of 100 meters.

803. Some US experts like Theodore Taylor speculate that Israel has the technology to build plutonium weapons using only 8.8 pounds (4 kilograms) of material versus the 16–18 pounds normally used to calculate the amount required per weapon. Other work by Frank Barnaby indicates that Israel may have at least 35 weapons with yields boosted up to 100 kilotons or more. Such high-yield weapons would largely remove the need for thermonuclear weapons—since Israeli missiles almost certainly have CEPs good enough to high any regional target close enough to destroy it with such yields, and there are no targets hardened enough to survive such blasts. Based on work by Leonard Spector; *Sunday Times*, October 5, 1986, pp. 1–3 and October 12, 1986, pp. 1 and 12; *Washington Times*, October 6, 1986; *Boston Globe*, October 14, 1986; *New York Times*, October 27, 1986; and *Washington Post*, October 31, 1986; Avner Cohen, *Israel and the Bomb*, New York, Columbia University Press, 1998.

804. *Washington Times*, November 3, 1989, p. A-6; *Defense News*, October 12, 1998, p. 46.

805. Adapted from Matthew Meselson and Julian Perry Robinson, "Chemical Warfare and Chemical Disarmament," Scientific American, Vol. 242, No. 4, April 1980, pp. 38–47; "Chemical Warfare: Extending the Range of Destruction," *Jane's Defense Weekly*, August 25, 1990, p. 267; Dick Palowski, *Changes in Threat Air Combat Doctrine and Force Structure, 24th Edition*, Fort Worth, General Dynamics DWIC-01, February 1992, pp. II-335 to II-339; US Marine Corps, *Individual Guide For NBC Defense*, Field Manual OH-11–1A, August 1990; and unpublished testimony to the Special Investigations Subcommittee of the Government Operations Committee, US Senate, by Mr. David Goldberg, Foreign Science and Technology Center, US Army Intelligence Center on February 9, 1989.

806. Israeli weapons designers seem to have had remarkable access to French design work in the late 1950s and early 1960s. There are even unconfirmed rumors that France permitted Israel to conduct a test in Algeria in the early 1960s.

807. Avner Cohen, *Israel and the Bomb*, New York, Columbia University Press, 1998; Leonard S. Spector, Mark G. McDonough, and Evan S. Medeiros, *Tracking Nuclear*

Proliferation, Washington, Carnegie Endowment; Jones, Rodney W., March C. McDonough, Toby F. Dalton and Gregory D. Koblentz, *Tracking Nuclear Proliferation*, Washington, Carnegie Endowment, 1998; Office of the Secretary of Defense, *Proliferation: Threat and Response*, Washington, Department of Defense, November 1997; Office of the Secretary of Defense, *Proliferation: Threat and Response*, Washington, Department of Defense, November 1998; *The Estimate*, June 5, 1998, pp. 5–8. Israel also acquired Meiko Scientific Supercomputers in December 1992. These supercomputers are sometimes associated with thermonuclear weapons and missile trajectory analysis. While such systems might be an aid to creating such weapons, Israel's existing mini-computers have long been adequate. There is also little incentive to use thermonuclear weapons with accurate IRBMs or in bombs because they consume added material, are more complex, and boosted weapons are adequate to destroy virtually any regional target. *New York Times*, January 9, 1992, p. D-1, June 1, 1998, p. A-7; Associated Press, April 20, 1997, 2152, September 16, 1998, 0122; *Washington Times*, April 23, 1997, p. A-12; Reuters, October 4, 1998, 2202; *Defense News*, October 12, 1998, p. 46.

808. Enhanced radiation or neutron weapons maximize radiation at the expense of blast, and do less physical damage, although they still produce large amounts of blast and thermal technology. Enhanced yield weapons boost a nuclear explosion to yields in excess of 100 kilotons and largely eliminate the need for thermonuclear weapons with highly accurate systems. Thermonuclear weapons allow explosions in excess of 25 megatons.

809. Anthony H. Cordesman and Abraham R. Wagner, *The Lessons of Modern War*, Volume 1, Boulder, Westview, 1990, pp. 244–246; *Jane's Defense Weekly*, August 8, 1987, p. 21.

810. For recent reporting on the Israeli nuclear effort, see the *Sunday Times*, October 5, 1986; *Washington Times*, October 6, 1986; *Boston Globe*, October 14, 1986; *New York Times*, October 27, 1986; and *Washington Post*, October 31, 1986.

811. Other reports indicate that the Jericho surface-to-surface missile had a range of up to 300 miles and a 1,000–1,500-pound warhead. Other reports indicate that it could reach a 400-mile range with a 226-pound (100-kilogram) nuclear warhead. Data published by Iran after the seizure of the US Embassy in Tehran claimed to have found evidence that Israel was giving Iran missile technology in return for oil, and had tested new guidance systems in flights in Iran. *Aerospace Daily*, May 1, 1985, May 7, 1985; Shuey et al., *Missile Proliferation: Survey of Emerging Missile Forces*, p. 56; *International Defense Review*, July 1987, p. 857; *Defense and Foreign Affairs Daily*, May 9, 1985, pp. 1–2; CIA, "Prospects for Further Proliferation of Nuclear Weapons," DCI NIO 1945/74, September 4, 1974; NBC Nightly News, July 30, 1985; *New York Times*, April 1, 1986; US Arms Control and Disarmament Agency, *World Military Expenditures and Arms Transfers*, Washington, GPO, 1989, p. 18; *Jane's Defense Weekly*, November 25, 1989, p. 1143; Avner Cohen, *Israel and the Bomb*, New York, Columbia University Press, 1998; *The Estimate*, June 5, 1998, pp. 5–8.

812. *Jane's Defense Weekly*, March 10, 1999, pp. 50–64.

813. Some reports give the range as 500 kilometers; *Jane's Defense Weekly*, March 10, 1999, pp. 50–64.

814. *Jane's Defense Weekly*, June 10, 1989, p. 1135.

815. *Baltimore Sun*, November 23, 1988; *Washington Post*, September 16, 1989.

816. Tass International, 1216 GMT, September 15, 1989; *Washington Post*, September 16, 1989; *Jane's Defense Weekly*, November 19, 1988, September 23, 1989, p. 549; *Washington Times*, July 22, 1987, p. D-4; *International Defense Review*, 7/1987, p. 857, and

New York Times, July 22, 1987, p. A-6, July 29, 1987; *Mideast Markets*, November 23, 1987, p. 11; in Harold Hough,"Israel's Nuclear Infrastructure," *Jane's Intelligence Weekly*, November 1994, pp. 505–511.

817. BBC and ITV reporting efforts seem to give more credibility to the idea that Israel has some form of relatively short-range nuclear-armed missile. Ranges of anywhere from 750–930 NM have been reported, with accuracies of anywhere from 0.1 km to radar correlator guidance packages capable of CEPs of 100 meters. *Bulletin of Atomic Scientists*, Vol. 46, Jan/Feb. 1998, p. 48; *Washington Post*, September 16, 1989, p. A-17, November 15, 1989, p. A-14; *Economist*, August 1, 1987, p. 41; *Washington Times*, July 22, 1987, p. D-4; July 24, 1987, p. A-9 and April 4, 1988, p. 17; *International Defense Review*, 7/1987, p. 857, and *New York Times*, July 29, 1987, p. A-10.

818. Tass International, 1216 GMT, September 15, 1989; *Washington Post*, September 16, 1989; *Jane's Defense Weekly*, November 19, 1988, September 23, 1989, p. 549; *Washington Times*, July 22, 1987, p. D-4; *International Defense Review*, 7/1987, p. 857, and *New York Times*, July 22, 1987, p. A-6, July 29, 1987; *Mideast Markets*, November 23, 1987, p. 11; in Harold Hough, "Israel's Nuclear Infrastructure, *Jane's Intelligence Weekly*, November 1994, pp. 505–511.

819. *International Defense Review, Extra*, 2/1997, p. 2; Associated Press, April 20, 1997, 2152.

820. Tass International, 1216 GMT, September 15, 1989; *Washington Post*, September 16, 1989; *Jane's Defense Weekly*, November 19, 1988, September 23, 1989, p. 549; *Washington Times*, July 22, 1987, p. D-4; *International Defense Review*, 7/1987, p. 857, and *New York Times*, July 22, 1987, p. A-6, July 29, 1987; *Mideast Markets*, November 23, 1987, p. 11; in Harold Hough, "Israel's Nuclear Infrastructure," *Jane's Intelligence Weekly*, November, 1994, pp. 505–511.

821. *Washington Post*, October 26, 1989, p. A-36; *Boston Globe*, October 30, 1989, p. 2; *Newsweek*, November 6, 1989, p. 52.

822. *Jane's Intelligence Review*, September 1997, pp. 407–410; *Jane's Defense Weekly*, March 10, 1999, pp. 50–64; *International Defense Review, Extra*, 2/1997, p. 2.

823. It is also possible that Israel may have deployed nuclear warheads for its MGM-55C Lance missiles. Israel has 12 Lance transporter-erector-launchers, and at least 36 missiles. The Lance is a stored liquid fueled missile with inertial guidance and a range of 5–125 kilometers. It has a warhead weight of 251 kilograms, and a CEP of 375 meters. It was deployed in US forces with the W-70 nuclear warhead. *International Defense Review*, 7/1987, p. 857; *Economist*, May 4, 1968, pp. 67–68; *New York Times*, July 22, 1987, p. A-6; *Washington Times*, July 22, 1987, p. D-4; *Defense and Foreign Affairs*, June 1985, p. 1; *Aerospace Daily*, May 1, 1985, p. 5 and May 17, 1985, p. 100; *Aerospace Daily*, May 1, 1985, May 7, 1985; Shuey et al., Missile Proliferation: Survey of Emerging Missile Forces, p. 56; CIA, "Prospects for Further Proliferation of Nuclear Weapons, "DCI NIO 1945/74, September 4, 1974; NBC Nightly News, July 30, 1985; *New York Times*, April 1, 1986; US Arms Control and Disarmament Agency, *World Military Expenditures and Arms Transfers*, Washington, GPO, 1989, p. 18; Michael A. Ottenberg, "Israel and the Atom," *American Sentinel*, August 16, 1992, p. 1.

824. Harold Hough, "Could Israel's Nuclear Assets Survive a First Strike?" *Jane's Intelligence Review*, September 1997, pp. 407–410.

825. Harold Hough, "Could Israel's Nuclear Assets Survive a First Strike?" *Jane's Intelligence Review*, September 1997, pp. 407–410.

826. Harold Hough, "Could Israel's Nuclear Assets Survive a First Strike?" *Jane's Intelligence Review*, September 1997, pp. 407–410.

827. Some experts also feel that Israel deployed large numbers of nuclear artillery rounds after the 1973 war, including rounds for its 175-mm and 203-mm weapons. A few experts feel such rounds include enhanced radiation variants. Such capabilities are very controversial, but they would give Israel the ability to use low-yield weapons against Syrian and other Arab armor and artillery formations at ranges of 18–29 kilometers, and could stop massed army formations as long as they remained as much as 12 kilometers from Israeli Army formations or civilians. *Jane's Defense Weekly*, July 15, 1989, p. 59 and December 23, 1989, p. 1385; Johannesburg Domestic Service, 1600 GMT, July 5, 1989; *Boston Globe*, October 27, 1989; Fred Francis, NBC Nightly News, October 25 and 26, 1989; *New York Times*, October 27, 1989, p. A-1, November 15, 1989; *Newsweek*, November 6, 1989, p. 52; *Washington Times*, June 20, 1989, p. A-1; *Washington Post*, October 27, 1989, p. A-1, October 29, 1989; Michael A. Ottenberg, "Israel and the Atom," *American Sentinel*, August 16, 1992, p. 1.

828. This information is unconfirmed, and based on only one source. Israel does, however, have excellent research facilities, laboratory production of poison gas is essential to test protection devices as is the production of biological weapons to test countermeasures and antidotes.

829. *Philadelphia Inquirer*, November 1, 1998, p. A-7; Associated Press, October 8, 1998, 1350.

830. Associated Press, October 5, 1998, 0316, October 8, 1998, 1350; *Philadelphia Inquirer*, November 1, 1998, p. A-7; *Washington Post*, March 15, 1999, p. A-11.

831. *Washington Times*, October 7, 1998, p. A-14.

832. *Defense News*, June 29, 1998, p. 3; *New York Times*, June 21, 1998, p. A-6.

833. *Defense News*, July 29, 1996, p. 3.

834. *Washington Times*, May 2, 1998, p. A-6.

835. *Washington Times*, May 2, 1998, p. A-6.

836. *Ma'ariv*, August 10, 1990.

837. *Davar*, August 10, 1990, *Ha'aretz*, August 10, 1990.

838. *Strategic Assessment*, Vol. 1, No. 1, p. 3, April 1998; *Ma'ariv*, January 30, 1998, February 2, 1998, February 6, 1998.

839. *Defense News*, June 29, 1998, p. 3; *New York Times*, June 21, 1998, p. A-6.

840. January 21, 2000, 0645.

841. Associated Press, February 2, 2000, 0834.

842. *Strategic Assessment*, Vol. 1, No. 1, p. 3, April 1998.

843. *Ha'aretz*, May 22, 1997, Reuters, May 23, 1997, 0821, *Washington Times*, May 24, 1997, p. A-8

844. Much of this analysis is based on interviews with US and Israeli officials. It includes data drawn from *Jane's Defense Weekly*, April 29, 1998, p. 3, June 3, 1998, p. 3, October 21, 1998, p. 4, December 9, 1998, p. 18; *Defense News*, June 8., 1998, p. 8, July 6, 1998, p. 3; *Wall Street Journal*, September 28, 1998, p. A-23.

845. *Jane's Defense Weekly*, July 10, 1996, p. 3

846. David Martin, "Ballistic Missile Defense Overview," Washington, Ballistic Missile Defense Office, Department of Defense, March 3, 1999; *Defense News*, July 8, 1996, p. 4, July 6, 1998, p. 6.

847. Lennox, Duncan and David Eshel, "Israeli high-energy laser project may face more delays," *Jane's Defense Weekly*, April 7, 1999, p. 21.

848. Bender, Bryan, "Future of US-Israeli laser project in doubt," *Jane's Defense Weekly*, June 2, 1999, p. 6.

849. Bender, Bryan, "US and Israeli governments to bail out THEL," *Jane's Defense Weekly*, June 16, 1999, p. 6.

850. *Jane's International Defense Review*, 2/2000, p. 4, *Jane's Defense Weekly*, June 14, 2000, p. 4, May 31, 2000, p. 4, May 26, 2000, p. 26; Reuters, June 7, 2000, 1748.

851. "US approves extra patriot sales to bolster Israeli defenses," *Jane's Defense Weekly*, June 24, 1998, p. 17, March 24, 1999, p. 3; Associated Press, December 10, 1998, 1704.

852. *Jane's Defense Weekly*, November 17, 1999, p. 3.

853. *Jane's Defense Weekly*, May 6, 1995, p. 15, March 19, 1997, p. 19, August 27, 1997, p. 4, November 12, 1997, p. 29, January 14, 1998, p. 4, July 8, 1998, p. 17, September 23, 1998, p. 3, December 2, 1998, p. 22, December 9, 1998, p. 18; *Defense News*, May 20, 1996, p. 33, July 22, 1996, p. 6; *Washington Times*, March 9, 1996, p., A-1 *Aviation Week*, June 21, 1993, p. 39; Reuters, March 27, 1998, 1733, September 15, 1998, 0528, November 29, 1998, 1044; Associated Press, August 3, 1998, 1125; *Washington Post*, September 16, 1998, p. A-37.

854. *Jane's Defense Weekly*, May 6, 1995, p. 15, March 11, 1998, June 24, 1998, p. 17, p. 18, December 2, 1998, p. 22, December 9, 1998, p. 18; *Aviation Week*, June 21, 1993, p. 39; Reuters, November 29, 1998, 1044; *Jane's International Defense Review*, 8/1999, p. 10.

855. Opall-Rome, Barbara, "Israel Promotes Regional Arrow," *Defense News*, May 10, 1999, p. 3.

856. *Jane's Defense Weekly*, January 14, 1998, February 4, 1998, p. 18, March 11, 1998, p. 18, November 10, 1999, p. 5; Reuters, February 26, 1998, 1409, November 1, 1999, 0914.

857. The program manager referred to a 100% leak-proof system. Then Israeli Defense Minister Yitzhak Mordecai referred to it as, "an almost complete shield against the present and future threat," on November 29, 1998. Reuters, November 29, 1998, 1044; *Jane's Defense Weekly*, January 5, 2000, p. 15.

858. *Jane's Defense Weekly*, "Arrow missile intercepts," September 20, 2000.

859. Ibid.

860. *Jane's Defense Weekly*, March 10, 1999, pp. 71–73, January 5, 2000, p. 15; Angelo M. Codevilla, "Missiles, Defense, and Israel," Washington, IASP Papers in Strategy, No. 5, November 1997.

861. David Martin, "Ballistic Missile Defense Overview," Washington, Ballistic Missile Defense Office, Department of Defense, March 3, 1999; *Jane's International Defense Review*, 7/1996, p. 5, 9/1997, p. 9; *Jane's Defense Weekly*, March 10, 1999, pp. 71–73; *Defense News*, March 29, 1999, pp. 1 & 28.

862. David Martin, "Ballistic Missile Defense Overview," Washington, Ballistic Missile Defense Office, Department of Defense, March 3, 1999; *Jane's International Defense Review*, 7/1996, p. 5, 9/1997, p. 9; *Jane's Defense Weekly*, March 10, 1999, pp. 71–73.

863. *Defense News*, June 8, 1998, p. 8; May 6, 1996, p. 24; *Jane's Defense Weekly*, March 10, 1999, pp. 71–73.

864. Israel launched the Ofeq 1 prototype on September 19, 1988. It has a satellite mass of 156 kilograms. It sent up the Ofeq 2 on April 3, 1990, one day after Saddam Hussein threatened to destroy half of Israel with chemical weapons if Israel attacked Baghdad. The Ofeq satellite has a mass of 160 kilograms. *Washington Post*, April 6, 1995, p. 1; *Jane's*

Intelligence Review, Volume 7, Number 6, June, 1995, pp. 265–268; *Washington Post*, April 6, 1995, p. 1.

865. Jane's *Pointer*, August 1998, p. 7.

866. *Jane's Defense Weekly*, February 4 ,1996, p. 18; *Jane's Pointer*, August 1998, p. 7.

867. Clarke, Philip, "Another Israeli satellite fails," *Jane's Intelligence Review*, August 1998, p. 7; *Jane's Pointer*, August 1998, p. 7.

868. *Jane's Defense Weekly*, March 6 ,1996, p. 23.

869. "US-Israeli venture aims to capture high-res satellite image market," *Jane's Defense Weekly*, March 31, 1999, p. 17.

870. David Martin, "Ballistic Missile Defense Overview," Washington, Ballistic Missile Defense Office, Department of Defense, March 3, 1999; *Jane's Defense Weekly*, October 21, 1998, p. 4.

871. *Jane's Defense Weekly*, April 29, 1998, p. 3.

872. Much of this assessment is based on work provided by the Ballistic Missile Defense Office of the US Department of Defense in February 1999.

873. *Jane's Defense Weekly*, June 24, 1998, p. 17; Associated Press, June 12, 1998, 1719; December 10, 1998, 1704; IISS, *Military Balance, 1998–1999 and 1999–2000*, "Israel"; David Martin, "Ballistic Missile Defense Overview," Washington, Ballistic Missile Defense Office, Department of Defense, March 3, 1999.

874. Opall-Rome, Barbara. Israelis Broaden Missile Defense Role for Laser: THEL is Among Counterforce Options. *Defense News*, July 6–12, 1998, p. 3.

875. Opall-Rome, Barbara. Senate May Add $37 Million for Arrow, Other Israel Defense Programs, *Defense News*. June 8–14, 1998, p. 4.

876. *Jane's Defense Weekly*, February 18, 1998, p. 19.

877. *Defense News*, February 9, 1998, p. 30.

878. For summary background, see David Klein, "Defending the Rear: When is Enough?" *Strategic Assessment*, Vol. 2, No. 2, October 1999.

879. This section draws extensively on interviews in the US, Britain, France, Switzerland and Israel, and Anthony H. Cordesman "Weapons of Mass Destruction in the Middle East," Washington, CSIS, March 7, 1999, Internet edition; Anthony H. Cordesman, *Perilous Prospects*, Boulder, Westview, 1996, pp. 230–267; the "Syria" sections of the 1996, 1997, and 1998 editions of Office of the Secretary of Defense, *Proliferation: Threat and Response*, Washington, Department of Defense, and the "Syria" sections of Rodney W. Jones, Mark G. McDonough, Toby F. Dalton, and Gregory D. Koblenz, *Tracking Nuclear Proliferation*, Washington, Carnegie Endowment, 1998.

880. Michael Eisenstadt, "Syria's Strategic Weapons," *Jane's Intelligence Review*, April 1993, pp. 168–171; Agence French Presse, computer printout, February 10, 1992; *Christian Science Monitor*, March 10, 1992, p. 1; *Washington Post*, December 7, 1991, p. A-26, February 11, 1992, p. A-16; *Daily Telegraph*, November 23, 1991, p. 10; *London Financial Times*, March 27, 1992, p. 4; *Washington Times*, November 24, 1991, p. A-17.

881. Office of the Secretary of Defense, *Proliferation: Threat and Response*, Washington, Department of Defense, 1997, pp. 37–40.

882. J. M. Moreaux, "The Syrian Army," *Defense Update*, No. 69, p. 31.

883. *Jane's Defense Weekly*, September 3, 1997, p. 3.

884. *New York Times*, June 6, 1986, p. 11; *Washington Post*, June 11, 1986, p. 36, and *Defense Week*, April 14, 1986, p. 5; Michael Eisenstadt, "Syria's Strategic Weapons," *Jane's Intelligence Review*, April 1993, pp. 168–171.

885. *Jane's Defense Weekly*, July 26, 1982, p. 92.

886. Although various other press reports have appeared at different times that Syria has established an SS-23 site, had a brigade of SS-23s, and even had deployed the SS-25, none of these reports are true. See J. M. Moreaux, "The Syrian Army," *Defense Update*, No. 69, p. 31.

887. The *Sunday Correspondent*, October 15, 1989, p. 3; *Al-Ittihad*, July 31, 1989, p. 1; Hong Kong AFP, 0629 GMT, August 7, 1989.

888. *Washington Post*, March 30, 1990, p. 1; *Washington Times*, November 22, 1989; *Defense and Foreign Affairs*, August 14–20, 1989, p. 2.

889. *Jane's Defense Weekly*, December 23, 1989, pp. 1384–1385, September 3, 1997. p. 3; *Washington Post*, June 23, 1988, p. A-2, March 29, 1990, pp. A-1 and A-34; *New York Times International*, March 30, 1990, p. A-7; *New York Times*, June 22, 1988, p. 1, January 31, 1992, p. A-1.

890. *Jane's Defense Weekly*, March 10, 1999, pp. 50–69.

891. *Jane's Defense Weekly*, January 15, 1997, p. 3.

892. *Wall Street Journal*, July 10, 1991, p. 12; *Washington Times*, March 10, 1992, p. A-3, March 11, 1992, p. A-3, July 16, 1992, p. A-3; *Time*, March 23, 1992, p. 34; *Washington Post*, February 22, 1992, p. A-15, March 11, 1992, p. A-11, March 13, 1992, p. A-18; July 14, 1992, p. A-1, August 14, 1992, p. A-25; *New York Times*, January 31, 1992, p. A-1, February 21, 1992, p. A-9; *Sunday Times*, December 21, 1991, p. 1.

893. *Defense News*, October 16, 1989, p. 60; *Washington Times*, June 18, 1990, p. A1; Lora Lumpe, Lisbeth Gronlund, and David C. Wright, "Third World Missiles Fall Short," *The Bulletin of the Atomic Scientists*, March, 1992, pp. 30–36.

894. Michael Eisenstadt, "Syria's Strategic Weapons," *Jane's Intelligence Review*, April 1993, pp. 168–171.

895. CIA, *Unclassified Report to Congress on the Acquisition of Technology Relating to Weapons of Mass Destruction and Advanced Conventional Munitions 1 January Through 30 June 1998*, January 1999, Internet edition.

896. The author examined actual imagery of the region from a number of commercial sources. For a regional discussion of this issue see Gerald M. Steinberg, "Dual Use Aspects of Commercial High-Resolution Imaging Satellites," BESA Security and Policy Study No. 37, Ramat Gan, Bar-Ilan University, February 1998.

897. *Middle East Economic Digest*, June 19, 1998, p. 3.

898. The following analysis involves considerable technical speculation by the author. It is based on various *Jane's* publications, and General Dynamics, *The World's Missile Systems*, Pomona, General Dynamics, 8th Edition, 1988.

899. Adapted by the author from various editions of *Jane's* and Ray Bonds, *Modern Soviet Weapons*, New York, ARCO, 1986, pp. 432–435.

900. CIA, *Unclassified Report to Congress on the Acquisition of Technology Relating to Weapons of Mass Destruction and Advanced Conventional Munitions 1 January Through 30 June 1998*, January 1999, Internet edition.

901. *Jane's Defense Weekly*, August 21, 1996, p. 15.

902. Office of the Secretary of Defense, *Proliferation: Threat and Response*, Washington, Department of Defense, 1997, pp. 37–40 and 1998 edition; *Washington Times*, March 4, 1997, p. A-19; United Press, November 18, 1996, 1227; Reuters, April 29, 1997, 0651, September 24, 1999, 0644.

903. CIA, *Unclassified Report to Congress on the Acquisition of Technology Relating to Weapons of Mass Destruction and Advanced Conventional Munitions 1 January Through 30 June 1998*, January 1999, Internet edition.

904. *Baltimore Sun*, October 24, 1995, p. 1A.

905. *London Sunday Times*, January 10, 1988, p. 1; *Washington Times*, April 8, 1988, p. 9, January 11, 1988, p. 1; *Los Angeles Times*, January 14, 1988, p. 13.

906. Syrian units deploy as close as 10 kilometers from the front line versus 20–25 kilometers for Soviet units.

907. The FROG with a VX chemical warhead carried much less agent. The Soviet version is 540 mm in diameter, and weighs about 960 pounds, of which 475 is VX agent. The FROG with a chemical warhead has a maximum range of 40 miles versus 190 miles for the Scud. Michael Eisenstadt, "Syria's Strategic Weapons," *Jane's Intelligence Review*, April 1993, pp. 168–171; Shuey, Lenhart, Snyder, Donnelly, Mielke, and Moteff, *Missile Proliferation: Survey of Emerging Missile Forces*, Washington, DC, Congressional Research Service, Report 88–642F, February 9, 1989, pp. 34–35; *Jane's Defense Weekly*, February 27, 1988, pp. 370–371; Defense Intelligence Agency, Soviet Chemical Weapons Threat, DST-1620F-051–85, 1985, p. 8.

908. Interviews, *Jane's Defense Weekly*, September 3, 1997, p. 3.

909. The analysis in this section is based largely on various interviews. Also see *Jane's Defense Weekly*, July 26, 1986, p. 92, April 2, 1988, p. 613; April 30, 1988, p. 853; *Washington Post*, June 23, 1988, p.33; September 7, 1988, p. A-25; *Los Angeles Times*, July 14, 1988, p. I-1; *Washington Times*, September 18, 1987, p. 2; *New York Times*, June 22, 1988, p. A-6.

910. *Jane's Defense Weekly*, August 21, 1996, p. 15; Office of the Secretary of Defense, *Proliferation: Threat and Response*, Washington, Department of Defense, 1997, pp. 37–40.

911. *Jane's Defense Weekly*, September 3, 1997, p. 3

912. Interviews in Israel, January 1992 and 1994.

913. This section draws extensively on interviews in the US, Britain, France, Switzerland, Israel and Egypt: and Anthony H. Cordesman, "Weapons of Mass Destruction in the Middle East," Washington, CSIS, March 7, 1999, Internet edition; Anthony H. Cordesman, *Perilous Prospects*, Boulder, Westview, 1996, pp. 230–271.

914. *Jane's Defense Weekly*, March 12, 1988, pp. 462–463; *Washington Times*, October 7, 1996, p. A-14; United Press, June 21, 1999, 1509.

915. *Atlanta Constitution*, October 5, 1988, p. 17A463; *Washington Times*, October 7, 1996, p. A-14; United Press, June 21, 1999, 1509.

916. *Jane's Defense Weekly*, February 23, 2000, p. 18.

917. *London Financial Times*, December 21, 1987, p. 1; June 8, 1988, pp. 20, 38.

918. *Jane's Defense Weekly*, February 23, 2000, p. 18.

919. *Jane's Defense Weekly*, December 16, 1989; *Defense Electronics*, August 1988, pp. 17 & 20; *La Nacion*, July 4, 1988; *Economist*, May 4, 1988, pp. 67–68; *Defense and Foreign Affairs*, June 1985, p. 1, *Defense and Foreign Affairs Daily*, May 9, 1985, pp. 1–2; International Defense Review, July 1987, p. 857; *New York Times*, July 22, 1987, p. A-6; *Washington Times*, July 22, 197, p. D-4.

920. For a good summary report, see *Jane's Defense Weekly*, February 17, 1990, p. 295. Also see *Financial Times*, November 21, 1989, p. 1; *Washington Post*, September 20, 1989.

921. *London Financial Times*, December 21, 1987, p. 1; June 8, 1988, pp. 20, 38.

922. *Jane's Defense Weekly*, March 10, 1999, pp. 50–69.

923. CIA, *Unclassified Report to Congress on the Acquisition of Technology Relating to Weapons of Mass Destruction and Advanced Conventional Munitions 1 January Through 30 June 1998*, January 1999, Internet edition.

924. The US also detected Egyptian efforts to build additional types of missiles. In 1987 and 1988, Egypt became involved in an attempt to smuggle missile equipment out of the US in a complex operation involving front organizations like the IFAT Corporation of Zug, Switzerland. As a result, the US arrested two Egyptian military officers based at the Egyptian embassy in Washington on June 23, 1988. They were arrested for conspiring with an Egyptian-born rocket scientist called Abdelkadr Helmy, and other Egyptian agents, to export 32 tons of rocket fuel chemicals, 432 pounds of carbon fiber materials for nose cones and rocket motor nozzles, propulsion hardware, telemetry tracking equipment, equipment and materials for making rocket motor casings, and missile assembly plans for the Pershing II missile. These missile plans had been obtained from Messerschmidt in Germany and an Italian firm. The material was carbon-phenolic fabric that is used to make rocket nozzles and rocket heat shields. Helmy received at least one million dollars from Egyptian sources to purchase the carbon fabric and other missile components. *Washington Post*, August 20, 1988, p. A-1, April 1, 1989, p. A-15, April 16, 1989, p. A-29; *New York Times*, March 10, 1989, p. A-1, June 11, 1989, p. 6, June 25, 1988, p. 1; *Los Angeles Times*, June 10, 1989, p. 10; *Washington Times*, April 17, 1989, p. A-8; *London Financial Times*, April 18, 1989, p. 5; *Wall Street Journal*, April 4, 1989, p. A-1; *Philadelphia Inquirer*, March 11, 1989, p. 9-A.

925. Abdel Darwish, "China to Update Egypt's Missiles," *The Independent*, (UK), June 14, 1990, p. 2.

926. *Al-Ahram*, July 25, 1975; *Al-Akhbar*, July 25, 1975.

927. The results of these orders are uncertain, and there are no confirmed reports of actual production. *Washington Post*, August 20, 1988, p. A-1; *New York Times*, June 25, 1988, p. 1.

928. *Washington Post*, April 1, 1989, p. A-15, April 16, 1989, p. A-29; *Washington Times*, April 17, 1989, p. A-8; *London Financial Times*, April 18, 1989, p. 5.; *Wall Street Journal*, April 4, 1989, p. A-1; *Philadelphia Inquirer*, March 11, 1989, p. 9-A; *New York Times*, March 10, 1989, p. A-1.

929. Interviews with US experts, informal testimony to the US Congress, *Jane's Defense Weekly*, August 21, 1996, p. 15.

930. *Jane's Defense Weekly*, October 14, 1998.

931. *Jane's Defense Weekly*, October 14, 1998.

932. This section draws extensively on interviews in the US, Britain, France, Switzerland and Israel, and Anthony H. Cordesman "Weapons of Mass Destruction in the Middle East," Washington, CSIS, March 7, 1999, Internet edition; Anthony H. Cordesman, *Perilous Prospects*, Boulder, Westview, 1996, pp. 230–267; the "Libya" sections of the 1996, 1997, and 1998 editions of Office of the Secretary of Defense, *Proliferation: Threat and Response*, Washington, Department of Defense, and the "Libya" sections of Rodney W. Jones, Mark G. McDonough, Toby F. Dalton, and Gregory D. Koblenz, *Tracking Nuclear Proliferation*, Washington, Carnegie Endowment, 1998.

933. Statement of the Director of Central Intelligence before the Senate Armed Services Committee, January 27, 1991 and testimony before Senator Glenn's Governmental Affairs Committee, January 15, 1992; *Economist*, January 11, 1992, p. 38; *Washington Times*, April 11, 1991, p. 3.

934. Jones, Rodney W. and Mark G. McDonough. *Tracking Nuclear Proliferation.* Washington, Carnegie Endowment for International Peace, 1998.

935. Estimates based on the IISS *Military Balance, 1998–1999 and 1999–2000*; ACDA, *World Military Expenditures and Arms Transfers, 1988*, Washington, GPO, March 1988, p. 22.

936. Lora Lumpe, Lisbeth Gronlund, and David C. Wright, "Third World Missiles Fall Short," *Bulletin of the Atomic Scientists*, March 1992, pp. 30–36.

937. ACDA, *World Military Expenditures and Arms Transfers*, 1988, Washington, GPO, March 1988, p. 18; *Washington Times*, October 9, 1989, p. A-2; ABC Network News, April 28, 1988; *Stern*, No. 1/1987; *Bulletin of Atomic Scientists*, June 1988, p. 15; Shuey, Lenhart, Snyder, Donnelly, Mielke, and Moteff, Missile Proliferation: Survey of Emerging Missile Forces, Washington, D.C., Congressional Research Service, Report 88–642F, February 9, 1989, pp. 61–63; Fred Donovan, Mideast Missile Flexing, Arms Control Today, May 1990, p. 31; Duncan Lennox, "The Global Proliferation of Ballistic Missiles," *Jane's Defense Weekly*, December 25, 1989, pp. 1384–1385; Lora Lumpe, Lisbeth Gronlund, and David C. Wright, "Third World Missiles Fall Short," *Bulletin of the Atomic Scientists*, March, 1992, pp. 30–36.

938. *Flight International*, May 23–29, 1990, p. 18.

939. *Jane's Defense Weekly*, March 10, 1999, pp. 50–69.

940. Sources include working material provided by Leonard Specter of the Carnegie Endowment; discussions with reporter from an independent British television network; *Jane's Defense Weekly*, December 23, 1989, pp. 1384-1385; *Washington Post*, January 28, 1988; *New York Times*, March 13, 1981; *Aviation Week and Space Technology*, April 10, 1989, pp. 19–20; *Christian Science Monitor*, July 3, 1990, p. 19; *Washington Times*, July 18, 1989, p. A-1.

941. CIA, *Unclassified Report to Congress on the Acquisition of Technology Relating to Weapons of Mass Destruction and Advanced Conventional Munitions 1 January Through 30 June 1998*, January 1999, Internet edition.

942. Office of the Secretary of Defense, *Proliferation: Threat and Response*, Washington, Department of Defense, 1997, pp. 33–37; Rodney W. Jones, Mark G. McDonough, Toby F. Dalton, and Gregory D. Koblenz, *Tracking Nuclear Proliferation*, Washington, Carnegie Endowment, 1998, pp. 215–217; Reuters, May 17, 1995, January 27, 1996; *Jane's Defense Weekly*, September 9, 1996, p. 24.

943. CIA, *Unclassified Report to Congress on the Acquisition of Technology Relating to Weapons of Mass Destruction and Advanced Conventional Munitions 1 January Through 30 June 1998*, January 1999, Internet edition.

944. Yoseff Bodansky and Vaughn Forrest,"Chemical Weapons in the Third World," 4. Libya's Chemical-Biological Warfare Capabilities, Task Force on Terrorism and Unconventional Warfare, House Republican Research Committee, U.S. House of Representatives, Washington, D.C., June 12, 1990, p. 3; El-Hussini Mohrez, Soviet Egyptian Relations, New York, St. Martin's Press, 1987, p. 187.

945. *Time*, February 27, 1989; Yoseff Bodansky and Vaughn Forrest,"Chemical Weapons in the Third World," 4. Libya's Chemical-Biological Warfare Capabilities, Task Force on Terrorism and Unconventional Warfare, House Republican Research Committee, U.S. House of Representatives, Washington, D.C. , June 12, 1990, pp. 4 and 8.

946. *Washington Times*, January 20, 1989; Al-Dustur, December 25, 1988, Ha'aretz, December 27, 1988.

947. Yoseff Bodansky and Vaughn Forrest, "Chemical Weapons in the Third World, 4. Libya's Chemical-Biological Warfare Capabilities", Task Force on Terrorism and Unconventional Warfare, House Republican Research Committee, U.S. House of Representatives, Washington, D.C., June 12, 1990, pp. 2–4; *Moscow News*, July 6; 1986; Ha'aretz, August 14, 1986, December 23, 1989, December 25, 1988.

948. Focus on Libya, DoD Current News, "Special Edition: Chemical Weapons," February 1990, pp. 36–37; *London Sunday Times*, April 5, 1992, pp. 1 and 26.

949. Yoseff Bodansky and Vaughn Forrest, "Chemical Weapons in the Third World, 4. Libya's Chemical-Biological Warfare Capabilities, Task Force on Terrorism and Unconventional Warfare, House Republican Research Committee, U.S. House of Representatives, Washington, D.C., June 12, 1990, pp. 4 and 5; Ha'aretz, December 27, 1988; *New York Times*, January 1, 1989, *Washington Times*, May 21, 1990.

950. *Wall Street Journal*, March 23, 1990, p. A-12.

951. *Washington Post*, December 19, 1988, p. A-1; January 4, 1989, p. 12; January 8, 1989, p. C-4; January 23, 1989, p. 12; January 19, 1989, p. A-1; January 24, 1989, p. 18, March 15, 1990, p. A-1, March 31, 1990, p. A-28, April 7, 1990, p. A-11; *New York Times*, January 4, 1989, p. 1; January 14, 1989, pp. 1 and 5; January 18, 1989, p. 7, March 31, 1990, p. A-3; *Wall Street Journal*, January 16, 1989, p. 5; January 17, 1989, p. 17, March 23, 1990, p. A-12; *Newsweek*, March 19, 1990, p. 33, March 26, 1990, p. 27.

952. Statement of the Director of Central Intelligence before the Senate Armed Services Committee, January 27, 1991 and testimony before Senator Glenn's Governmental Affairs Committee, January 15, 1992, p. 10. *Washington Post*, December 19, 1988, p. A-1; January 4, 1989, p. 12; January 8, 1989, p. C-4; January 23, 1989, p. 12; January 19, 1989, p. A-1; January 24, 1989, p. 18, March 8, 1990, p. A-26; *New York Times*, January 4, 1989, p. 1; January 14, 1989, pp. 1 and 5; January 18, 1989, p. 7, March 7, 1990, pp. A-1 and A-5, June 7, 1990, p. A-14, June 19, 1990, p. A-8; *Wall Street Journal*, January 16, 1989, p. 5; January 17, 1989, p. 17; *Washington Times*, May 21, 1990, p. A-3.

953. *Washington Post*, March 16, 1990, pp. A-1 & A-38, March 31, 1990, p. A-28, April 7, 1990, p. A-11, May 3, 1990, pp. A-33 and A-36, June 19, 1990; *Christian Science Monitor*, March 16, 1990, p. 3; March 22, 1990, p. 20; *Washington Times*, May 21, 1990, p. A-3, June 18, 1990, p. 1, June 19, 1990, p. 3, July 12, 1990, p. 6; *Newsweek*, March 19, 1990, p. 33, March 26, 1990, p. 27, April 9, 1990, p. A-3; *Wall Street Journal*, March 8, 1990, p. A16; *New York Times*, March 31, 1990, p. 3. Ha'aretz, May 6, 1990; *Der Spiegel*, May 7, 1990, *Insight*, June 11, 1990; *Washington Post*, June 28, 1990, p. A-33.

954. *Washington Times*, May 7, 1990, p. A-2; *New York Times*, January 22, 1992, p. A-1.

955. Statement of the Director of Central Intelligence before the Senate Armed Services Committee, January 27, 1991 and testimony before Senator Glenn's Governmental Affairs Committee, January 15, 1992.

956. *Washington Times*, June 24, 1996; *Defense News*, December 16, 1996, p. 1; Office of the Secretary of Defense, *Proliferation: Threat and Response*, Washington, Department of Defense, 1997, pp. 33–37; Rodney W. Jones, Mark G. McDonough, Toby F. Dalton, and Gregory D. Koblenz, *Tracking Nuclear Proliferation*, Washington, Carnegie Endowment, 1998, pp. 215–217.

957. CIA, *Unclassified Report to Congress on the Acquisition of Technology Relating to Weapons of Mass Destruction and Advanced Conventional Munitions 1 January Through 30 June 1998*, January 1999, Internet edition.

958. There are reports that Libya used biological agents like the Mycotoxins in Chad and even tested them against political prisoners. There are also claims that Libya received the necessary technology from the USSR, Cuba, and East Germany. These reports seem dubious, and many of the symptoms described are characteristic of poor medical discipline in the field and poor medical treatment of prisoners. *Washington Times*, January 20, 1989; R. Harris and J. Paxman, A Higher Form of Killing, New York, Hill and Wang, 1982, p. 220; Yoseff Bodansky and Vaughn Forrest, "Chemical Weapons in the Third World, 4. Libya's

Chemical-Biological Warfare Capabilities, Task Force on Terrorism and Unconventional Warfare, House Republican Research Committee, U.S. House of Representatives, Washington, D.C., June 12, 1990, pp. 4 and 5.

959. Office of the Secretary of Defense, *Proliferation: Threat and Response*, Washington, Department of Defense, 1997, pp. 33–37; Statement of the Director of Central Intelligence before the Senate Armed Services Committee, January 27, 1991 and testimony before Senator Glenn's Governmental Affairs Committee, January 15, 1992. *Washington Post*, December 19, 1988, p. A-1; January 4, 1989, p. 12; January 8, 1989, p. C-4; January 23, 1989, p. 12; January 19, 1989, p. A-1; January 24, 1989, p. 18, March 8, 1990, p. A-26; *New York Times*, January 4, 1989, p. 1; January 14, 1989, pp. 1 and 5; January 18, 1989, p. 7, March 7, 1990, pp. A-1 and A-5, June 7, 1990, p. A-14; *Wall Street Journal*, January 16, 1989, p. 5; January 17, 1989, p. 17; *Washington Times*, May 21, 1990, p. A-3.

960. Many of the conclusions and facts in this section are based on working papers made available by Leonard Specter of the Carnegie Endowment.

961. Steve Weissman and Herbert Krosney, The Islamic Bomb, New York, Times Books, 1981, pp. 60 and 211–212; *Washington Star*, April 14, 1981.

962. The reactor is subject to IAEA inspection. Libya ratified the NPT in 1975.

963. *Bulletin of Atomic Scientists*, August-September 1981, p. 14; The Middle East, February 1982, p. 47; *New York Times*, March 23, 1976; *Washington Post*, December 12, 1977; *Nuclear Engineering International*, April 1986, p. 6; *Nucleonics Week*, March 31, 1983, p. 11, September 27, 1984, p. 1.

964. Agence France Presse, February 10, 1992; BBC, February 4, 1992, ME 1295A1; *Washington Post*, February 4, 1992, p. A-11; AP AM cycle, January 25, 1992; Reuters, January 25, 1992, BC cycle.

965. Office of the Secretary of Defense, *Proliferation: Threat and Response*, Washington, Department of Defense, 1997, pp. 33–37, and Rodney W. Jones, Mark G. McDonough, Toby F. Dalton, and Gregory D. Koblentz, *Tracking Nuclear Proliferation*, Washington, Carnegie Endowment, 1998, pp. 215–217.

966. Reuters, May 17, 1995, January 27, 1996; *Jane's Defense Weekly*, September 9, 1996, p. 24.

967. The primary source used in this section is Anthony H. Cordesman, *Iran in Transition*, Westport, Greenwood, 1999; the "Iran" sections of the 1996, 1997, and 1998 editions of Office of the Secretary of Defense, *Proliferation: Threat and Response*, Washington, Department of Defense, and the "Iran" sections of Rodney W. Jones, Mark G. McDonough, Toby F. Dalton, and Gregory D. Koblenz, *Tracking Nuclear Proliferation*, Washington, Carnegie Endowment, 1998.

968. Force estimates are based on the IISS, *Military Balance, 1998–1999 and 1999–2000*, and Office of the Secretary of Defense, *Proliferation: Threat and Response*, Washington, Department of Defense, April 1996.

969. The author participated in one such exercise during the time he was stationed at the US Embassy in Tehran.

970. Defense Intelligence Agency, *The Scud Missile: An Unclassified Overview for Policy Makers*, forwarded under U-3,148/SVI-FOIA, October 22, 1997; Associated Press, July 11, 1996, 0720; *Jane's Defense Weekly*, July 17, 1996, p. 3.

971. Some US experts believe Iran has less than 100 missiles. *Jane's Defense Weekly*, May 13, 1995, p. 5; July 17, 1996, p. 3.

972. Dr. Robert A. Nagler, *Ballistic Missile Proliferation: An Emerging Threat*; Systems Planning Corporation, Arlington, 1992.

973. CIA, *Unclassified Report to Congress on the Acquisition of Technology Relating to Weapons of Mass Destruction and Advanced Conventional Munitions 1 January Through 30 June 1998*, January 1999, Internet edition.

974. Associated Press, July 15, 2000, 0935; Reuters, July 15, 2000, 0714.

975. Elaine Sciolino and Steven Lee Myers, "U.S. Study Reopens Division Over Nuclear Missile Threat," *New York Times*, July 4, 2000.

976. July 16, 2000, 0826.

977. Reuters, July 15, 2000, 2158.

978. Reuters, July 18, 2000, 0634.

979. *Washington Times*, September 10, 1997, p. A-1; Associated Press, September 10, 1997, 1620; *Jane's Defense Weekly*, February 17, 1999, p. 5.

980. The nominal range for full coverage from Western Iran is around 1,300 kilometers; the nominal range for coverage of all of Israel from anywhere in Iran is around 1,800–2,000 kilometers. Much depends, however, on the special warhead configuration and the resulting range-payload.

981. US National Intelligence Council, "Foreign Missile Developments and the Ballistic Missile Threat to the United States Through 2015," Washington, NIC, September 1999.

982. CIA, August 10, 2000, Unclassified Report to Congress on the Acquisition of Technology Relating to Weapons of Mass Destruction and Advanced Conventional Munitions, 1 July through 31 December 1999. Internet edition.

983. National Intelligence Council, "Global Trends 2015: A Dialogue About the Future With Nongovernment Experts," Washington, CIA, December 2000, *http://www.odci.gov/cia/publications/globaltrends2015/index.html.*

984. *Jane's Intelligence Review*, Special Report, No. 6, May, 1995, pp. 16–18; *Jane's Defense Weekly*, March 10, 1999, pp. 50–69; *Insight*, February 27, 1995, p. 13; Agence France Presse, January 4, 1995, 0522; *Christian Science Monitor*, April 28, 1997, p. 3.

985. Based on discussions with various experts, the sources listed earlier, , and working papers by Leonard Spector; *Observer*, June 12, 1988; *US News and World Report*, February 12, 1990; *FBIS-NES*, March 23, 1990, p. 57; *Defense and Foreign Affairs*, November 20, 1989, p. 2; *New York Times*, July 1, 1989, May 9, 1989, June 27, 1989; *Financial Times*, February 6, 1992, p. 3, *Washington Times*, January 8, 1995, p. A-9; Kenneth Katzman, "Iran: Arms and Technology Acquisitions," Library of Congress, CRS-97–474F, October 1, 1997; Kenneth Katzman, "Iran: Military Relations With China," Library of Congress, CRS-967–572F, June 26, 1996; Shirley A. Kan, "Chinese Proliferation of Weapons of Mass Destruction, Background and Analysis," Library of Congress, CRS-96–767F, September 13, 1996.

986. CIA, *Unclassified Report to Congress on the Acquisition of Technology Relating to Weapons of Mass Destruction and Advanced Conventional Munitions 1 January Through 30 June 1998*, January 1999, Internet edition.

987. James Smith, "Biological Weapons Developments," *Jane's Intelligence Review*, November, 1991, pp. 483–487; *New York Times*, August 13, 1989, p. 11; Kenneth R. Timmerman, *Weapons of Mass Destruction: The Cases of Iran, Syria, and Libya*, Simon Wiesenthal Center, Los Angeles, August, 1992, pp. 28–45.

988. *Sunday Telegraph*, August 10, 1996, on-line edition; *Sunday Times*, August 10, 1996, fax edition; United Press, August 11, 1996, 0530.

989. Director of Central Intelligence, "The Acquisition of Technology Relating to Weapons of Mass Destruction and Advanced Conventional Munitions," Washington, CIA, June 1997.

990. CIA, *Unclassified Report to Congress on the Acquisition of Technology Relating to Weapons of Mass Destruction and Advanced Conventional Munitions 1 January Through 30 June 1998*, January 1999, Internet edition.

991. The technical content of this discussion is adapted in part from the author's discussion of the technical aspects of such weapons in *After the Storm: The Changing Military Balance in the Middle East*, Boulder, Westview, 1993 and *Iran and Iraq: The Threat from the Northern Gulf*, Boulder, Westview, 1994; working material on biological weapons prepared for the United Nations, and from Office of the Secretary of Defense, *Proliferation: Threat and Response*, Washington, Department of Defense, April 1996, pp. 12–16; Office of Technology Assessment, *Proliferation of Weapons of Mass Destruction: Assessing the Risks*, United States Congress OTA-ISC-559, Washington, DC, August, 1993; Kenneth R. Timmerman, *Weapons of Mass Destruction: The Cases of Iran, Syria, and Libya*, Simon Wiesenthal Center, Los Angeles, August 1992; Dr. Robert A. Nagler, *Ballistic Missile Proliferation: An Emerging Threat*; Systems Planning Corporation, Arlington, 1992; and translations of unclassified documents on proliferation by the Russian Foreign Intelligence Bureau provided to the author by the staff of the Government Operations Committee of the US Senate.

992. CIA, *Unclassified Report to Congress on the Acquisition of Technology Relating to Weapons of Mass Destruction and Advanced Conventional Munitions 1 January Through 30 June 1998*, January 1999, Internet edition.

993. CIA, *Unclassified Report to Congress on the Acquisition of Technology Relating to Weapons of Mass Destruction and Advanced Conventional Munitions 1 January Through 30 June 1998*, January 1999, Internet edition.

994. Reuters, January 26, 2000, 1121; *New York Times*, January 16, 2000, p. A-1; Associated Press, January 18, 2000, 1831.

995. Speech at the annual USCENTCOM conference, June 26, 1997.

996. *Los Angeles Times*, March 17, 1992, p. 1.

997. *New York Times*, November 30, 1992, pp. A-1 and A-6, January 5, 1995, p. A-10; *Washington Times*, January 6, 1995, p. A-15.

998. Associated Press, May 5, 1997, 0126.

999. *New York Times*, January 10, 1995, p. A-3; *Jane's Intelligence Review*, "Iran's Weapons of Mass Destruction," Special Report Number 6, May 1995, pp., 4–14; Gerald White, *The Risk Report*, Volume 1, Number 7, September, 1995; *Jane's Intelligence Review*, October, 1995, p. 452.

1000. *Chalk Times*, January 10, 1995, p. 31; *Washington Times*, January 19, 1995, p. A-18.

1001. Although the possibility is a real one. *Financial Times*, January 30, 1992, p. 4; Agence France Presse, January 26, 1992; *Sunday Times*, January 26, 1992; *Der Spiegel*, July 20, 1992, p. 117; Patrick Clawson, *Iran's Challenge to the West, How, When, and Why*, Washington, The Washington Institute Policy Papers, Number Thirty Three, 1993, pp. 63–65; *United States News and World Report*, November 14, 1994, p. 88; *Jane's Intelligence Review*, "Iran's Weapons of Mass Destruction," Special Report Number 6, May 1995, pp. 4–14; Gerald White, *The Risk Report*, Volume 1, Number 7, September 1995; *Jane's Intelligence Review*, October 1995, p. 452.

1002. *Washington Times*, May 17, 1995, p. A-15; Office of the Secretary of Defense, *Proliferation: Threat and Response*, Washington, Department of Defense, April 1996, pp. 12–16.

1003. *New York Times*, May 14, 1995; *Washington Post*, November 5, 1997, p. A-1.

1004. "Report: Barak Rejected Iran Offer," Associated Press, July 21, 1999, 1017.

1005. The primary source used in this section is Anthony H. Cordesman, *Iraq and the War of Sanctions*, Westport, Greenwood, 1999; the "Iraq" sections of the 1996, 1997, and 1998 editions of Office of the Secretary of Defense, *Proliferation: Threat and Response*, Washington, Department of Defense, and the "Iraq" sections of Rodney W. Jones, Mark G. McDonough, Toby F. Dalton, and Gregory D. Koblenz, *Tracking Nuclear Proliferation*, Washington, Carnegie Endowment, 1998.

1006. See the deliberate furor Saddam Hussein created over the fixed sites in March 1990. *New York Times*, March 30, 1990. p. 6.

1007. Note by the Secretary General, "Report by the Secretary-General on the Activities of the Special Commission established by the Secretary-General," UN Security Council, S/;1997/774, October 6, 1997, paragraph 23.

1008. Widely different figures on the level of physical damage done in Israel have been published in various sources. See Theodore A. Postal, "Lessons of the Gulf War Experience with Patriot," *International Security*, Winter 1991–1992, pp. 139–151 for high damage estimates and a useful chronology of damage effects in Israel. For a very different examination of the damage effects from the Scud attacks, see Steve Fedtter, George N. Lewis, and Lisbeth Gronlund, "Why were Scud Casualties so low?" *Nature*, Vol. 361, January 28, 1993, pp. 293–296.

1009. Iran has claimed that each Scud that fell on Tehran killed 10–15 and injured at least 30, but these claims are dubious. Steve Fedtter, George N. Lewis, and Lisbeth Gronlund, "Why were Scud Casualties so low?" *Nature*, Vol. 361, January 28, 1993, pp. 293–296.

1010. For good accounts of these impacts, see General H. Norman Schwarzkopf, *It Doesn't Take a Hero*, pp. 409, 415–421, 430, 452, 460–461, 470–472, and 475; also see Rick Atkinson, *Crusade*, pp. 18, 33, 38–50, 66, 81–85, 90–94, 96–103, 124–126, 144–148, 173–175, 181–182, 217–218, 222, 232, 277–278, 417, 496.

1011. Note by the Secretary-General, S/1998/920(1998), October 6, 1998.

1012. Speech by Scott Ritter, Washington Institute, September 4, 1998.

1013. Data from UNSCOM and *Jane's Defense Weekly*, March 10, 1999, pp. 50–69.

1014. CIA, *Unclassified Report to Congress on the Acquisition of Technology Relating to Weapons of Mass Destruction and Advanced Conventional Munitions 1 January Through 30 June 1998*, January 1999, Internet edition.

1015. The IISS estimates are similar.

1016. *Sunday Times*, February 6, 2000; February 20, 2000.

1017. *New York Times*, February 1, 2000, p. A-1, February 8, 2000; *Sunday Times*, February 6, 2000 and February 20, 2000; *Washington Post*, February 10, 2000, p. A-23.

1018. The author participated in one such exercise during the time he was stationed at the US Embassy in Teheran.

1019. The IISS estimates 500. It is doubtful that this many are operational.

1020. US National Intelligence Council, "Foreign Missile Developments and the Ballistic Missile Threat to the United States Through 2015," Washington, NIC, September 1999.

1021. Note by the Secretary-General, "Report of the Secretary-General on the Activities of the Special Commission," S/1997/774, October 6, 1997, paragraph 48.

1022. *Washington Post*, August 17, 1998, p. A-1.

1023. Note by the Secretary-General, S/1998/920(1998), October 6, 1998.

1024. CIA, *Unclassified Report to Congress on the Acquisition of Technology Relating to Weapons of Mass Destruction and Advanced Conventional Munitions 1 January Through 30 June 1998*, January 1999, Internet edition.

1025. *New York Times*, February 1, 2000, p. A-1, February 8, 2000; *Sunday Times*, February 6, 2000 and February 20, 2000; *Washington Post*, February 10, 2000, p. A-23.

1026. The technical content of this discussion is adapted in part from the author's discussion of the technical aspects of such weapons in *After the Storm: The Changing Military Balance in the Middle East*, Boulder, Westview, 1993; working material on biological weapons prepared for the United Nations, and from the Office of Technology Assessment, *Proliferation of Weapons of Mass Destruction: Assessing the Risks*, United States Congress OTA-ISC-559, Washington, DC, August 1993; Kenneth R. Timmerman, *Weapons of Mass Destruction: The Cases of Iran, Syria, and Libya*, Simon Wiesenthal Center, Los Angeles, August 1992; Dr. Robert A. Nagler, *Ballistic Missile Proliferation: An Emerging Threat*; Systems Planning Corporation, Arlington, 1992; and translations of unclassified documents on proliferation by the Russian Foreign Intelligence Bureau provided to the author by the staff of the Government Operations Committee of the US Senate.

1027. *After the Storm: The Changing Military Balance in the Middle East*, Boulder, Westview, 1993; working material on biological weapons prepared for the United Nations, Office of Technology Assessment, *Proliferation of Weapons of Mass Destruction: Assessing the Risks*, United States Congress OTA-ISC-559, Washington, DC, August 1993; Kenneth R. Timmerman, *Weapons of Mass Destruction: The Cases of Iran, Syria, and Libya*, Simon Wiesenthal Center, Los Angeles, August 1992; Dr. Robert A. Nagler, *Ballistic Missile Proliferation: An Emerging Threat*; Systems Planning Corporation, Arlington, 1992; and translations of unclassified documents on proliferation by the Russian Foreign Intelligence Bureau.

1028. *Jane's Defense Weekly*, May 14, 1997, p. 4, June 4, 1997, pp. 19–27.

1029. Jane's *Pointer*, September 1996, p. 6.

1030. CIA, *Unclassified Report to Congress on the Acquisition of Technology Relating to Weapons of Mass Destruction and Advanced Conventional Munitions 1 January Through 30 June 1998*, January 1999, Internet edition.

1031. *New York Times*, February 1, 2000, p. A-1, February 8, 2000; *Sunday Times*, February 6, 2000 and February 20, 2000; *Washington Post*, February 10, 2000, p. A-23.

1032. *Washington Post*, September 29, 1998, p. A-1.

1033. *Washington Post*, September 29, 1998, p. A-1.

1034. Many of these details are taken from Peter D. Zimmerman, *Iraq's Nuclear Achievements: Components, Sources, and Stature*, Washington, Congressional Research Service, 93–323F, February 18, 1993. Also see J. Carson Mark, "Some Remarks on Iraq's Possible Nuclear Weapons Capability in Light of Some of the Known Facts Concerning Nuclear Weapons," Nuclear Control Institute, Washington, May 16, 1991.

1035. David Albright, Frans Berkhout and William Walker, *Plutonium and Highly Enriched Uranium, 1996—World Inventories, Capabilities, and Policies*, Oxford, SIPRI-Oxford Press, 1997, p. 311.

1036. United Nations Security Council, *Report on the Eighth IAEA Inspection in Iraq Under Security Council Resolution 687*, 11–18 November, 1991, New York, United Nations, S/23283 (English), pp. 14–15, 29; Gary Milhollin, "Building Saddam Hussein's Bomb," *New York Times*, March 8, 1992, pp. 30–31; *Report on the Seventh IAEA Inspection in Iraq Under Security Council Resolution 687*, November 14, 1991, New York, United Nations, S/232215 (English), p. 30.

1037. *US News and World Report*, November 25, 1991, p. 36; United Nations Security Council, *Report on the Eighth IAEA Inspection in Iraq Under Security Council Resolution 687*, November 11–18, 1991, New York, United Nations, S/23283 (English), p. 29.

1038. Peter D. Zimmerman, *Iraq's Nuclear Achievements: Components, Sources, and Stature*, Washington, Congressional Research Service, 93–323F, February 18, 1993; J. Carson Mark, "Some Remarks on Iraq's Possible Nuclear Weapons Capability in Light of Some of the Known Facts Concerning Nuclear Weapons," Nuclear Control Institute, Washington, May 16, 1991; and A. J. Venter, "How Saddam Almost Built His Bomb," *Jane's Intelligence Review*, December 1997, fax from *Jane's*.

1039. *Washington Post*, June 1, 1998, p. A-17.

1040. Note by the Secretary-General, S/1998/920(1998), October 6, 1998.

1041. *Washington Post*, September 29, 1998, p. A-1.

1042. *Washington Post*, September 29, 1998, p. A-1.

1043. *New York Times*, November 20, 1998, p. A-1.

1044. CIA, *Unclassified Report to Congress on the Acquisition of Technology Relating to Weapons of Mass Destruction and Advanced Conventional Munitions 1 January Through 30 June 1998*, January 1999, Internet edition.

1045. CIA, August 10, 2000, Unclassified Report to Congress on the Acquisition of Technology Relating to Weapons of Mass Destruction and Advanced Conventional Munitions, 1 July Through 31 December 1999, Internet edition.

1046. National Intelligence Council, "Global Trends 2015: A Dialogue About the Future With Nongovernment Experts, Washington, CIA, December 2000, *http://www.odci.gov/cia/publications/globaltrends2015/index.html.*

1047. The figures cited are based on work published by ACDA and Richard F. Grimmett, updated on the basis of discussion with US government experts.

1048. ACDA, *World Military Expenditures and Arms Transfers, 1993–1994*, Table I.

1049. The figures cited are based on work published by ACDA and Richard F. Grimmett, updated on the basis of discussion with US government experts.

1050. The figures cited are based on work published by ACDA and Richard F. Grimmett, updated on the basis of discussion with US government experts.

1051. The figures cited are based on work published by ACDA and Richard F. Grimmett, updated on the basis of discussion with US government experts.

1052. Richard F. Grimmett, *Conventional Arms Transfers to the Middle East, 1991–1998*, Washington, Congressional Research Service, RL30275, August 4, 1999.

1053. The figures cited are based on work published by ACDA and Richard F. Grimmett, updated on the basis of discussion with US government experts.

1054. The figures cited are based on work published by ACDA and Richard F. Grimmett, updated on the basis of discussion with US government experts.

Bibliography

Abdelnour, Ziad K., "Lebanon: Israel's True Partner?" *Middle East Quarterly*, Vol. II, No. 2, June 1995, pp. 39–44.

Adan, Avrahham (Bren), *On the Banks of the Suez*, San Francisco, Presidio, 1980.

Aerospace Daily, various editions.

Air Force, various editions.

Ajami, Fouad, "The Sorrows of Egypt," *Foreign Affairs*, September-October 1995, pp. 72–88.

Albright, David, Frans Berkhout and William Walker, *Plutonium and Highly Enriched Uranium, 1996—World Inventories, Capabilities, and Policies*, Oxford, SIPRI-Oxford Press, 1997, p. 311.

al-Mughrabi, Nidal. Palestinian Police Link Hamas Men to Iran. Reuters, February 4, 1999.

Alpher, Joseph, "Israel: Security After Oslo," *International Affairs*, Vol. 70, No. 2, April 1994, pp. 229–242.

Alpher, Joseph, Settlements and Borders, Final Status-Israel—Palestinians, Study No. 3, Tel Aviv, JCSS, 1994.

Arian, Asher "Israeli Public Opinion on National Security, 1997," Tel Aviv, JCSS, Memo 47, April 1997.

Arian, Asher, "Israeli Public Opinion on National Security," 1997, Tel Aviv, JCSS, Memo 47, April 1997.

Armed Forces Journal International, various editions.

Asher, Jerry, and Eric Hammel, *Duel for the Golan*, New York, Morrow, 1987.

Assad, Hafiz al-, "Interview with Syrian President Hafiz al-Assad," *Journal of Palestine Studies*, Summer 1993, pp. 111–121.

Atkeson, Edward B, "The Syrian-Israeli Military Balance: A Pot That Bears Watching," Arlington, Institute of Land Warfare, Paper No. 10, January 1992.

Aviation Week and Space Technology, various editions.

Badri, Magdoub, and Zohdy, *The Ramadan War, 1973*, New York, Hippocrene, 1974.

Bailey, Clinton, *Jordan's Palestinian Challenge, 1948–1983,* Westview, Boulder, 1984.

Barker, A. J., *Arab-Israeli Wars,* New York, Hippocrene, 1980.

Barnaby, Frank, *The Invisible Bomb,* London, I. B. Taurus, 1989

Bass, Gail, and Bonnie Jean Cordes, *Actions Against Non-Nuclear Energy Facilities: September 1981-September 1982,* Santa Monica, Calif., Rand Corporation, April 1983.

Beit-Hallahmi, Benjamin, *The Israeli Connection: Who Arms Israel and Why,* New York, Pantheon, 1987.

Belyakov, Rostislav and Nikolai Buntin, "The MiG 29M Light Multirole Fighter," *Military Technology,* 8/94, pp. 41–44.

Ben Horin, Yoav, and Barry Posen, *Israel's Strategic Doctrine,* Santa Monica, Calif., Rand Corporation, September 1981.

Ben Porat et al., *Kippur, Special Edition,* Tel Aviv, 1973.

Ben-Meir, Alon, "The Israeli-Syrian Battle for Equitable Peace," *Middle East Policy,* Vol. III, No. 1, 1994, pp. 70–83.

Beres, Louis, Rene, *Security or Armageddon,* Lexington, Lexington Books, 1986.

Beres, Rene, "After the Gulf War: Israel, Palestine, and the Risk of Nuclear War in the Middle East," *Strategic Review,* Fall 1991, pp. 48–55.

Berger, Marshall, "The New Battle for Jerusalem," *Middle East Quarterly,* Vol. I, No. 4, December 1994, pp. 23–34.

Bitzinger, Richard, "The Globalization of the Arms Industry," *Foreign Policy,* Summer 1995, pp. 170–182.

Blanche, Edward, "Is the Myth Fading for the Israeli Army? Part I & II," *Jane's Intelligence Review,* December 1996 and January 1997.

Blanche, Edward, "A Bizarre yet Bloody Conflict Drags on in South Lebanon Part I & II," *Jane's Intelligence Review,* September and October 1997.

Blanford, Nicholas, "Hizbullah Attacks Force Israel to Take a Hard Look at Lebanon," *Jane's Intelligence Review,* April 1999, pp. 32–37.

Blechman, Barry M., Stephan S. Kaplan, *Force Without War,* Washington, Brookings Institution, 1978.

Bonds, Ray, *Modern Soviet Weapons,* New York, ARCO, 1986, pp. 432–435.

Bowen, David, and Laura Drake, "The Syrian-Israeli Border Conflict, 1949–1967," *The Middle East,* Vol. 1, No. 4, 1992, pp. 17–28.

Braizat, Musa S., *The Jordanian-Palestinian Relationship,* New York, St. Martin's Press, 1998.

Bulletin of Atomic Scientists, various editions.

Carus, W. Seth, "The Genie Unleashed: Iraq's Chemical and Biological Weapons Production," *Policy Papers No. 14,* The Washington Institute for Near East Policy, Washington, 1989.

Carus, W. Seth, and Hirsh Goodman, *The Future Battlefield and the Arab-Israeli Conflict,* London, Transaction Press, 1990.

Carver, Michael, *War Since 1945,* London, Weidenfeld and Nicholson, 1980.

Casandra, "The Impending Crisis in Egypt," *Middle East Journal,* Volume 49, No. 1, Winter, 1995, pp. 9–27.

Center for Policy Analysis of Palestine, *Settlements and Peace: The Problem of Jewish Colonization in Palestine, A Special Report,* Washington, Center for Policy Analysis of Palestine, July 1995.

Center for Policy Analysis on Palestine, *Jerusalem,* Washington, Center for Policy Analysis on Palestine, February 1994.

Center for Policy Analysis on Palestine, *Palestinian Human Rights Under Israeli Rule*, Center for Policy Analysis on Palestine, Washington, May 1993.

Center for Policy Analysis on Palestine, *Palestinian Refugee Compensation*, Information Paper No. 3, Washington, Center for Policy Analysis on Palestine, April 1995.

Center for Policy Analysis on Palestine, *Palestinian Refugees: Their Problem and Future*, Information Paper No. 3, Washington, Center for Policy Analysis on Palestine, October 1994.

Center for Policy Analysis on Palestine, *Targeting to Kill: Israel's Undercover Units*, Center for Policy Analysis on Palestine, Washington, May 1992.

Center for Policy Analysis on Palestine, *The Water Issue and the Palestinian-Israeli Conflict*, Information Paper No. 2, Washington, Center for Policy Analysis on Palestine, September 1993.

Clarke, Duncan, "Israel's Unauthorized Arms Transfers," *Foreign Policy*, Summer 1995, pp. 89–111.

Clawson, Patrick, *Iran's Challenge to the West, How, When, and Why*, Washington, The Washington Institute Policy Papers, Number 33, 1993.

Clawson, Patrick, and Howard Rosen, *Economic Consequences of Peace of Israel, The Palestinians, and Jordan*, Washington Institute Policy Papers, No. 25, 1991.

Codevilla, Angelo M., "Missiles, Defense, and Israel," Washington, IASP Papers in Strategy, No. 5, November 1997.

Cohen, Avner, *Israel and the Bomb*, New York, Columbia University Press, 1998.

Cohen, Elliot A., Michael J. Eisenstadt, and Andre J. Bacevich, *Knives, Tanks, and Missiles*, Washington, Washington Institute, 1998.

Cohen, Howard A., and Steven Plant, "Quenching the Levant's Thirst," *Middle East Quarterly*, Vol. II, No. 1, March 1995, pp. 37–46.

Cohen, Michael J., *Fighting World War Three from the Middle East*, Portland, Frank Cass Publishers, 1997.

Cohen, Saul, *The Geopolitics of Israel's Border Question*, Tel Aviv, Jaffee Center for Strategic Studies, 1986.

Cohen, Stuart A., "How Did the Intifada Affect the IDF?" *Conflict Quarterly*, Vol. 14, No. 3 (Summer 1994).

Cohen, Stuart A., "Israel's Changing Military Commitments, 1981–1991," *Journal of Strategic Studies*, Vol. 15, No. 31, September 1993, pp. 330–351.

Cohen, Stuart A., "Towards a New Portrait of the (New) Israeli Soldier," Ramat Gan, BESA/Bar Ilan University, September 1997.

Cohen, Stuart A., "Studying the Israel Defense Forces: A Changing Contract With Israeli Society," BESA Center for Strategic Studies No. 20, Ramat Gan, Israel, Bar-Ilan University, 1995.

Collins, John N., *Military Geography*, Washington, National Defense University, 1998.

Combat Fleets of The World, Their Ships, Aircraft, and Armament, A. D. Baker III ed., Annapolis Md., Naval Institute Press.

Congressional Budget Office, *Limiting Conventional Arms Transfers to the Middle East*, Washington, A CBO Study, September 1992.

Cordesman, Anthony H., *After The Storm: The Changing Military Balance in the Middle East*, Boulder, Westview, 1993.

Cordesman, Anthony H., *Iran and Iraq: The Threat from the Northern Gulf*, Boulder, Westview, 1994.

Cordesman, Anthony H., "The Military Balance in the Maghreb: The Next Decade," in *Brassey's Military Annual, 1986*, London, Brassey's, pp. 227–254.

Cordesman, Anthony H., *Iraq and the War of Sanctions*, Westport, Greenwood, 1999.

Cordesman, Anthony H., *Iran in Transition*, Westport, Greenwood, 1999.

Cordesman, Anthony H., *Jordan and the Middle East Balance*, Washington, Middle East Institute, 1978 and 1985.

Cordesman, Anthony H., *Perilous Prospects*, Boulder, Westview, 1996.

Cordesman, Anthony H., *The Lessons of Modern War: Volume I—The Arab-Israeli Conflicts*, with Abraham R. Wagner, Westview, Boulder, 1990.

Cordesman, Anthony H., *The Lessons of Modern War: Volume II—The Iran-Iraq Conflict*, with Abraham R. Wagner, Westview, Boulder, 1990.

Cordesman, Anthony H., *Weapons of Mass Destruction in the Middle East*, London, Brassey's/RUSI, 1991.

Cordesman, Anthony H., *The Arab-Israeli Military Balance and the Art of Operations*, Washington, University Press of America-AEI, 1987.

Cordesman, Anthony H., and Abraham R. Wagner, *The Lessons of Modern War, Volume IV*, Boulder, Westview, 1995.

Darwish, Abdel, "China to Update Egypt's Missiles," *The Independent*, (UK), June 14, 1990, p. 2.

Defense and Foreign Affairs Daily, various editions.

Defense Intelligence Agency, *The Scud Missile: An Unclassified Overview for Policy Makers*, forwarded under U-3,148/SVI-FOIA, October 22, 1997.

Defense News, various editions.

Diab, M. Zuhair, "Have Syria and Israel Opted for Peace?," *Middle East Policy*, Vol. III, No. 2, 1994, pp. 77–90.

Director of Central Intelligence, "The Acquisition of Technology Relating to Weapons of Mass Destruction and Advanced Conventional Munitions, July-December, 1996," Washington, CIA, June 1997.

DMS/FI Market Intelligence Reports database.

Drake, C.J.M., *Terrorist's Target Selection*, New York, St. Martin's Press, 1998.

Dunn, Michael C., "Fundamentalism in Egypt, *Middle East Policy*, Vol. II, No. 3, 1993, pp. 49–61.

Dunn, Michael C., Islamist Parties in Jordan and Yemen," *Middle East Policy*, Vol. II, No. 2, 1993, pp. 16–28.

Dupuy, Trevor N., and Paul Martell, *Flawed Victory*, Washington, Hero Books, 1985.

Dupuy, Trevor N., *Elusive Victory: The Arab-Israeli Wars, 1947–1974*, New York, Harper & Row, 1978.

Economist, various editions.

Economist Intelligence Unit, various country reports.

Ehrlich, Dr. Reuven (Avi-Ran), "Terrorism as a Preferred Instrument of Syrian Policy," ICT Research Fellow, *www.ict.org.il/*, accessed October 16, 1999.

Eisenberg, Laur Zittrain, "Passive Belligerence, Israel and the 1991 Gulf War," *Journal of Strategic Studies*, Vol. 15, No. 31, September 1993, pp. 304–330.

Eisenstadt, Michael, "Syria's Strategic Weapons," *Jane's Intelligence Review*, April 1993, pp. 168–171.

Eisenstadt, Michael, *Like A Phoenix from the Ashes? The Future of Iraqi Military Power*, Washington, The Washington Institute, 1993.

Elazar, Daniel J., *Judea, Samaria, and Gaza: Views on the Present and the Future*, Washington, AEI, 1982.

El-Edroos, Brigadier S. A., *The Hashemite Arab Army, 1908–1979*, Amman, Publishing Committee, 1980.

Elmusa, Sharif, "Dividing the Common Palestinian-Israeli Waters: An International Water Law Approach," *Journal of Palestine Studies*, Spring 1993, pp. 57–77.

Elmusa, Sharif, "The Jordan-Israel Water Agreement," *Journal of Palestine Studies*, Spring 1995, pp. 63–73.

El-Shazly, Lt. General Saad, *The Crossing of Suez*, San Francisco, American Mideast Research, 1980.

Eshel, David, *War of Desperation*, London, Osprey, 1985. Strongly pro-Israeli books on the impact of the 1973 and 1982 fighting on the balance with a great deal of useful data on the war.

Eshel, David, *Peace for Galilee, Special edition of the Born in Battle Series*, Tel Aviv, Eshel-Dramit, 1982.

Eshel, David, *The Yom Kippur War*, Tel Aviv, Eshel Dramit, 1978.

Eshel, David, "IDF 2000," *Jane's Defense Weekly*, February 3, 1999, pp. 23–32.

Eshel, David, "The Vietnam Syndrome," *Jane's Defense Weekly*, pp. 19–25.

Eshel, Tamir, "Israel's Defense Electronics," *Defense Electronics*, October 1991, pp. 87–90.

Estimate, various editions.

Executive News Service, on-line database.

Fandy, Mamoun, "The Tensions Behind the Violence in Egypt," *Middle East Policy*, Vol. II, No. 1, 1993, pp. 1–14.

Feiler, Gil, "Palestinian Employment Prospects," *The Middle East Journal*, Vol. 47, No. 4, Autumn, 1993, pp. 633–651.

Feldman, Shai, *Israeli Nuclear Deterrence, A Strategy for the 1980s*, New York, Columbia University Press, 1982.

Feldman, Shai, ed., *Confidence Building and Verification: Prospects in the Middle East*, Tel Aviv, Jaffee Center For Strategic Studies, 1994.

Feldman, Shai, Nuclear Weapons and Arms Control in the Middle East, Cambridge, MIT Press, 1997.

Feldman, Shai, and Ariel Levite, *Arms Control and the New Middle East Security Environment*, Boulder, Westview, 1994.

Fisher, Scotty, "Country Briefing Israel," *Jane's Defense Weekly*, February 18, 1995, pp. 29–38.

Fisher, Stanley, Dani Rodrik, and Elia Turner, *The Economics of a Middle East Peace*, Cambridge, MIT Press, 1993.

Flight International, various editions.

Foreign Intelligence Service of the Russian Federation, *A New Challenge After the Cold War: The Proliferation of Weapons of Mass Destruction*, Moscow, 1993. Available in a FBIS translation of February 1993 from the Government Operations Committee of the US Senate.

Foundation for Middle East Peace, "Report on Israeli Settlements in the Occupied Territories: A Golan Heights Primer," Washington, Foundation for Middle East Peace, February 1995.

Fromkin, David, *A Peace to End All Peace: The Fall of the Ottoman Empire and the Creation of the Modern Middle East*, New York, Avon Books, 1989.

Gabriel, Richard A., *Fighting Armies: Antagonists in the Middle East, A Combat Assessment*, Westport, Greenwood Press, 1983.

Gabriel, Richard A., *Operation Peace for Galilee*, New York, Hill and Norton, 1983.

Gazit, Shlomo, *The Palestinian Refugee Problem, Final Status Issues: Israel-Palestinians*, Study No. 2, Tel Aviv, Jaffee Center for Strategic Studies, 1995.

General Dynamics, *The World's Missile Systems*, Pomona, General Dynamics, 8th Edition, 1988.

Gilbert, Martin, *Jerusalem: Illustrated History Atlas*, London, Martin Gilbert, 1977.

Golan, Galia, " A Palestinian State from an Israeli Point of View," *Middle East Policy*, Vol. III, No. 1, 1994, pp. 56–70.

Golan, Galia, *The Soviet Union and the Israeli War in Lebanon*, Research Paper 46, Jerusalem, Soviet and East European Research Center, 1982.

Golan Heights Information Server (www.golan.org, and www.golan-syria.org).

Gold, Dore, "Fundamental Factors in a Stabilized Middle East: Security, Territory, and Peace," Washington, JINSA, 1993.

Goodman, Hirsch, and W. Seth Carus, *The Future Battlefield and the Arab-Israeli Conflict*, Transaction Publishers, Rutgers, New Brunswick, New Jersey, 1989 (Washington Institute for Middle East Policy).

Gordan, Shmuel, *The Vulture and the Snake*, Ramat Gan, BESA, Security and Policy Studies No. 39, Bar Ilan University, June 1998.

Grossman, David, *Yellow Wind*, New York, Farrar, Straus, and Giroux, 1988.

Guyatt, Nicholas, *The Absence of Peace*, New York, St. Martin's Press, 1998.

Harkabi, Yehoshafat, "Reflections on National Defense Policy," *Jerusalem Quarterly*, no. 18, Winter 1981, pp. 121–140.

Harris, R., and J. Paxman, *A Higher Form of Killing*, New York, Hill and Wang, 1982.

Heikel, Mohammed, *The Road to Ramadan*, New York, Quadrangle, 1975.

Held, Colbert, *Middle East Patterns*, Westview, Boulder, 1989.

Heller, Mark, and Sari Nuseibeh, *No Trumpets, No Drums: A Two-State Settlement of the Israeli-Palestinian Conflict*, New York, Hill and Wang, 1991.

Hersh, Seymour M., *The Samson Option, Israel's Nuclear Arsenal and American Foreign Policy*, New York, Random House, 1991.

Herzog, Chaim, *The Arab-Israeli Wars*, New York, Random House, 1982.

Hirsch, Moshe, Deborah Housen-Couriel, and Ruth Lapidoth, *Whither Jerusalem?* London, Martinus Nijhoff, 1995.

Hof, Frederick C., "The Yarmouk and Jordan Rivers in the Israel-Jordan Peace Treaty," *Middle East Policy*, Vol. III, No. 3, 1, pp. 47–56.

Hough, Harold, "Israel's Nuclear Infrastructure," *Jane's Intelligence Weekly*, November 1994, pp. 505–511.

Hough, Harold, "Could Israel's Nuclear Assets Survive a First Strike?" *Jane's Intelligence Review*, September 1997, pp. 407–410.

Hoveyda, Fereydoun, *The Broken Crescent*, Westport, Praeger, 1998.

Inbar, Efraim, and Shmuel Sandler, *Middle Eastern Security, Prospects for an Arms Control Regime,* Portland, Frank Cass Publishers, 1995.

Inbar, Efraim, "Israeli National Security 1973–1996," Ramat Gan, BESA/Bar Ilan University, February 1998.

Inside Defense Electronics, various editions.

International Defense Review, various editions.

International Policy Institute for Counter-Terrorism, "Iran and Terrorism," Herzliya, Israel, *www.ict.org.il/,* accessed October 16, 1999.

Isby, David C., Weapons and Tactics of the Soviet Army, Fully Revised Edition, London, *Jane's,* 1987.

Israeli government Internet database.

Israeli Military Industries (IMI) manufacturer brochures.

Jaffee Center for Strategic Studies, *Israel's Options for Peace,* Report of a JCSS Study Group, Tel Aviv, Jaffee Center, 1989.

Jaffee Center for Strategic Studies, *The Middle East Military Balance,* Boulder, Westview.

Jaffee Center for Strategic Studies, *The Middle East Military Balance,* Tel Aviv, Jaffee Center for Strategic Studies, various editions.

Jane's All the World's Aircraft, London, Jane's Publishing, various editions.

Jane's Air-Launched Weapons Systems, London, Jane's Publishing, various editions.

Jane's Armor and Artillery, London, Jane's Publishing, various editions.

Jane's Battlefield Surveillance Systems, London, Jane's Publishing, various editions.

Jane's C⁴I Systems, London, Jane's Publishing, various editions.

Jane's Defense Appointments & Procurement Handbook (Middle East Edition), London, Jane's Publishing, various editions.

Jane's Defense Weekly, various editions.

Jane's Fighting Ships, London, Jane's Publishing, various editions.

Jane's Infantry Weapons, London, Jane's Publishing, various editions.

Jane's Intelligence Review, various editions.

Jane's International Defense Review, various editions.

Jane's Land-Base Air Defense, London, Jane's Publishing, various editions.

Jane's Military Vehicles and Logistics, London, Jane's Publishing, various editions.

Jane's Naval Weapons Systems, London, Jane's Publishing, various editions.

Jane's Radar and Electronic Warfare Systems, London, Jane's Publishing, various editions.

Jane's Sentinel Series—Eastern Mediterranean, Gulf States, and North Africa.

Jane's Strategic Weapons Systems, London, Jane's Publishing, various editions.

Jane's World Air Forces, London, Jane's Publishing, various editions.

Jane's World Armies, London, Jane's Publishing, various editions.

JINSA, *Security Affairs,* various editions.

Johnson, Major Maxwell Orme, USMC, The Military as an Instrument of US Policy in Southwest Asia: The Rapid Deployment Joint Task Force, 1979–1982, Boulder, Westview, 1983.

Jones, Rodney W., ed., *Small Nuclear Forces and US Security Policy,* Lexington, Mass., Lexington Books, 1984.

Jones, Rodney W., March C. McDonough, Toby F. Dalton and Gregory D. Koblentz, *Tracking Nuclear Proliferation,* Washington, Carnegie Endowment, 1998.

Kan, Shirley A., "Chinese Proliferation of Weapons of Mass Destruction, Background and Analysis," Library of Congress, CRS-96–767F, September 13, 1996.

Kanovsky, Eliyahu, "Will Arab-Israeli Peace Bring Prosperity?" *Middle East Quarterly,* Vol. II, No. 2, June 1994, pp. 3–12.

Kaplan, Stephen S., *Diplomacy of Power,* Washington, Brookings Institution, 1981.

Karam, Simon, "Lebanon, Collapse and Revival," *Middle East Policy,* Vol. III, No. 1, 1994, pp. 15–24.

Katz, Samuel M., "Israeli Airpower on the Rise," *Air Force,* November 1991, pp. 44–51.

Katzman, Kenneth, "Iran: Military Relations With China," Library of Congress, CRS-967–572F, June 26, 1996.

Katzman, Kenneth, "Iran: Arms and Technology Acquisitions," Library of Congress, CRS-97–474F, October 1, 1997.

Kechichian, Joseph, and Jeanne Nazimek, "Challenges to the Military in Egypt," *Middle East Policy*, Vol. V, No. 3, September 1997, pp. 125–139.

Keegan, John, *World Armies*, London, Macmillan, 1983.

Kemp, Geoffrey, *The Control of the Middle East Arms Race,* Washington, Carnegie Endowment, 1991.

Kemp, Geoffrey, and Robert E. Harkavy, *Strategic Geography and the Changing Middle East*, Washington, Carnegie Endowment/Brookings, 1997.

Khalidi, Rashid, *Under Siege*, New York, Columbia, 1986.

Khalidi Walid, *Conflict and Violence in Lebanon*, Cambridge, Harvard Center for International Affairs, 1984.

Khashan, Hillel, "The Levant: Treaties Without Normalization," *Middle East Quarterly*, June 1995, pp. 3–14.

Khazen, Farid el, "Lebanon's First Postwar Parliamentary Election," *Middle East Policy*, Vol. II, No. 1, 1993, pp. 102–119.

Kienle, Eberhard, *Contemporary Syria*, New York, St. Martin's Press, 1997.

Klieman, Aaron S., *Israel's Global Reach*, London, Pergamon-Brassey's, 1985.

Kollek, Teddy, *Jerusalem*, Washington, The Washington Institute for Near East Policy, Policy Papers No. 22, 1990.

Kramer, Martin, *The Islamism Debate*, Tel Aviv University, Dayan Center Papers 120, 1997.

Kramer, Martin, "Hizbollah's Vision of the West," *Policy Papers No. 16*, The Washington Institute for Near East Policy, Washington, 1989.

Kronsky, Herbert, and Stephen Weissman, *The Islamic Bomb*, New York, Times Books, 1981.

Laffin, John, *The World in Conflict* or *War Annual*, London, Brassey's, various editions.

Lambeth, Benjamin S., *Moscow's Lessons From the 1982 Lebanon Air War*, Santa Monica, Rand Corporation, 1984.

Lesch, Ann M., and Dan Tschirgi, *Origins and Development of the Arab-Israeli Conflict*, Westport, Greenwood, 1998.

Levite, Ariel, *Offense and Defense in Israeli Strategy*, Westview, Boulder, 1989.

Levran, Aharon, *Israeli Strategy After Desert Storm*, Portland, Frank Cass Publishers, 1997.

Lowi, Miriam R., "Bridging the Divide: Transboundary Resource Disputes & The Case of West Bank Water," *International Security*, Summer 1993, pp. 113–139.

Luft, Gal, "Israel's Impending Revolution in Security Affairs," *Peacewatch*, No. 199, March 4, 1999.

Luft, Gal, "The Palestinian Security Services: Between Police and Army," *Washington Institute Research Memorandum No. 36*. November 1998.

Luttwak, Edward, and Dan Horowitz, *The Israeli Army*, New York, Harper & Row, 1975.

Maoz, Zeev, *Regional Security in the Middle East*, Portland, Frank Cass Publishers, 1997.

Mark, Clyde R., "Israel: US Foreign Assistance," Congressional Research Service, CRS-IB85066, May 18, 1995.

Mark, Clyde R., "Middle East and North Africa: US Aid FY1993, 1994, and 1995," CRS 94–274F, March, *Jane's Defense Weekly*, July 12, 1995, p. 19.

Mark, Clyde, "Palestinians and the Middle East Peace: Issues for the United States," Congressional Research Service, IB92052, December 5, 1994.

Martin, David, "Ballistic Missile Defense Overview," Washington, Ballistic Missile Defense Office, Department of Defense, March 3, 1999.

Mauroni, Albert J., *Chemical-Biological Defense*, Westport, Praeger, 1998.

McLaurin, R. D., "Golan Security in a Middle East Settlement," *Oriente Moderno*, December 1981, pp. 43–58.

Meir, Alon Ben, "Jerusalem's Final Status," *Middle East Policy*, Vol. III, No. 3, 1994, pp. 93–110.

Merari, Ariel, and Shlomi Elad, *The International Dimension of Palestinian Terrorism*, Tel Aviv, Jaffee Center, 1986.

Middle East Economic Digest, various editions.

Middle East Policy (formerly Arab-American Affairs), various editions.

Military Technology, various editions.

Military Technology, *World Defense Almanac*, Bonn, Monch Publishing Group, various editions.

Moore, James H., "Parting the Waters: Israeli and Palestinian Entitlements to West Bank Aquifers and the Jordan River Basin," *Middle East Policy*, Vol. III, No. 2, 1994, pp. 91–108.

Moreaux , J. M., "The Syrian Army," *Defense Update*, No. 69, p. 31.

Mushih, Muhammed, "The Golan: Israel, Syria, and Strategic Calculations," *The Middle East Journal*, Vol. 47, No. 4, Autumn 1993, pp. 611–633.

Nakhleh, Emile A., "Palestinians and Israelis: Options for Coexistence," *Journal of Palestine Studies*, Winter 1993, pp. 5–16.

National Intelligence Council, "Foreign Missile Developments and the Ballistic Missile Threat to the United States Through 2015," Washington, NIC, September 1999.

Neff, Donald, *Warriors Against Israel*, Battleboro, Amana, 1988.

Neubach, Amnon, "Budget Deficits, Monetary Policies and the Peace Process." *Economic Slowdown and Peace Slowdown*. Israel Policy Papers No. 3, January 15, 1997.

Norton, Augustus Richard, and Robin Wright, "The Post-Peace Crisis in the Middle East," *Survival*, Winter 1994–1995, pp. 7–20.

Nuclear Engineering, various editions.

Nuclear Fuel, various editions.

Nucleonics Week, various editions.

O'Ballance, Edgar, *The Electronic War in the Middle East, 1968–1970*, Hamden, CT, Archon, 1974.

O'Ballance, Edgar, *The Palestinian Intifada*, New York, St. Martin's Press, 1998.

O'Ballance, Edgar, *The Civil War in Lebanon, 1975–1992*, New York, St. Martin's Press, 1998.

Office of Technology Assessment, *Global Arms Trade: Commerce in Advanced Military Technology and Weapons*, Washington, OTA, Congress of the United States, June 1991.

Office of the IDF Spokesman, "The IDF's Security Principles," Office of the IDF Spokesman, April 1995, Fisher, Scotty, "Country Briefing Israel," *Jane's Defense Weekly*, February 18, 1995, pp. 29–38.

Office of the Secretary of Defense, *Proliferation: Threat and Response*, Washington, Department of Defense, November 1997.

Office of the Secretary of Defense, *Proliferation: Threat and Response*, Washington, Department of Defense, November 1998.

Ottenbergy, Michael A. G., "Israel and the Atom," *American Sentinel*, August 16, 1992, p. 1.

Palestinian Authority, briefing papers.

Pawloski, Dick, *Changes in Threat Air Combat Doctrine and Force Structure, 24th Edition*, Fort Worth, General Dynamics DWIC-91, February 1992, pp. II-199 to II-227.

Peretz, Don, *Intifada: The Palestinian Uprising*, Boulder, Westview, 1993.

Perthes, Volker, *The Political Economy of Syria*, New York, St. Martin's Press, 1997.

Pipes, Daniel, *Damascus Courts the West: Syrian Politics, 1989–1991*, Washington Institute Policy Papers No. 26, Washington, Washington Institute for Near East Policy, 1992.

Policywatch, various editions.

Pry, Peter, *Israel's Nuclear Arsenal*, Boulder, Westview Press, 1984.

Quandt, William B., *The Middle East Ten Years After Camp David*, Brookings, Washington, September 1988.

Quandt, William B., *Camp David, Peacemaking and Politics*, Washington, Brookings, 1986.

Quandt, William B., *Peace Process: American Diplomacy and the Arab-Israeli Conflict*, Berkeley, University of California Press, 1993.

Quandt, William B., *The United States and Egypt*, Washington, Brookings, 1990.

Rabin, Yitzhak, "Deterrence in an Israeli Security Context," in Aharon Klieman and Ariel Levite, eds., *Deterrence in the Middle East: Where Theory and Practice Converge*, Boulder, Westview, 1993, pp. 6–16.

Rabinovich, Itamar, *The War for Lebanon, 1970–1983*, Ithaca, Cornell University, 1984.

Rabushka. Alvin, "Scorecard on the Israeli Economy," Washington, IASP Papers in Strategy, No. 5, March 1998.

Rafael briefing sheet; manufacturer offprint of "Rafael: Lessons of Combat" from *Military Technology*, May 1991.

Randall, Jonathan C., *Going All The Way*, New York, Viking Press, 1983.

Rathnell, Dr. Andrew, "Iraq—The Endgame?" *Jane's Intelligence Review*, Volume 7, Number 5, pp. 224–228.

Reich, Bernard, and Gershon R. Kieval, *Israeli National Security Policy: Political Actors and Perspectives*, New York, Macmillan, 1985.

Rekhess, Elie, "The Terrorist Connection—Iran, the Islamic Jihad, and Hamas," *Justice*, Volume 5, May 1995.

Reuters, on-line access.

Rubenstein, Alvin Z., *Red Star Over the Nile*, New Jersey, Princeton, 1977.

Safran, Nadav, *From War to War*, New York, Pegasus, 1969.

Safran, Nadav, *Israel: The Embattled Ally*, Cambridge, Belknap/Harvard,

Satloff, Robert B., *The Politics of Change in the Middle East*, Boulder, Westview, 1993.

Satloff, Robert, "The Jordan-Israel Peace Treaty," *Middle East Quarterly*, Vol. II, No. 1, March 1995, pp. 47–52.

Scarlott, Jennifer, "Nuclear Proliferation After the Gulf War," *World Policy Journal*, Fall 1991, pp. 687–695.

Schiff, Ze'ev, *Earthquake*, Jerusalem, 1973.

Schiff, Ze'ev, *A History of the Israeli Army*, New York, Macmillan, 1985.

Schiff, Ze'ev, and Ehud Ya'ari, *Intifada: The Palestinian Uprising—Israel's Third Front*, New York, Simon and Schuster, 1990.

Schiff, Ze'ev, and Ehud Ya'ari, *Israel's War in Lebanon*, New York, Simon and Schuster.

Schiff, Ze'ev, "Security for Peace: Israel's Minimal Security Requirements in Negotiations with the Palestinians," Policy Papers No. 15, The Washington Institute for Near East Policy, Washington, 1989.

Schmid, Alex P., *Soviet Military Interventions Since 1945*, New Brunswick, Transaction, Inc., 1985.

SDIO, Ballistic Missile Proliferation: An Emerging Threat, 1992, Washington, SDIO, October 1992.

Seale, Patrick, *Assad, The Struggle for the Middle East*, Berkeley, University of California Press, 1988.

Sela, Avraham, and Moshe Ma'oz, *The PLO and Israel*, New York, St. Martin's Press, 1997.

Sella, Amon, Soviet Political and Military Conduct in the Middle East, London, Macmillan, 1981.

Shalev, Aryeh, *Israel and Syria: Peace and Security on the Golan*, Tel Aviv, Jaffee Center for Strategic Studies, 1993.

Shalev, Aryeh, *The West Bank: Line of Defense*, New York, Praeger, 1985.

Shimshoni, Jonathan, *Israel and Conventional Deterrence*, Ithaca, Cornell University Press, 1988.

Shuey, Lenhart, Snyder, Donnelly, Mielke, and Moteff, *Missile Proliferation: Survey of Emerging Missile Forces*, Washington, Congressional Research Service, Report 88–642F, February 9, 1989.

Sicherman, Harvey, *Palestinian Self-Government (Autonomy): Its Past and Future*, Washington, Washington Institute, 1991.

Sicker, Martin, *Israel's Quest for Security*, New York, Praeger, 1989.

Sirriyeh, Hussein, *Lebanon: Dimensions of Conflict*, Adelphi Paper 243, IISS, London, 1989.

Skogmo, Bjorn, *UNIFIL: International Peacekeeping in Lebanon, 1978–1988*, Lynne Reiner, Boulder, 1988.

Spector, Leonard S., Mark G. McDonough, and Evan S. Medeiros, *Tracking Nuclear Proliferation*, Washington, Carnegie Endowment, 1995.

Spencer, Claire, *The Maghreb in the 1990s*, London, International Institute of Strategic Studies, Adelphi Paper 274, IISS-Brassey's, February 1993.

Steinberg, Gerald M., "Israeli Security in a Changing Environment: Challenges and Responses," Ramat Gan, BESA/Bar Ilan University, October 26, 1998.

Stockholm International Peace Research Institute, *World Armaments and Disarmament: SIPRI Yearbook*, Oxford Press, London, various editions.

Survival, various editions.

Susser, Asher, *In the Back Door: Jordan's Disengagement and the Middle East Peace Process*, Washington, The Washington Institute, Policy Papers 19, 1990.

Tal, David, *The 1956 War, Portland*, Frank Cass Publishers, 1999.

Tal, Lawrence, "Dealing with Radical Islam: The Case of Jordan," *Survival*, Autumn 1995, pp. 139–157.

Tal, Lawrence, "Is Jordan Doomed," *Foreign Affairs*, Vol. 72, No. 5, November/December 1993, pp. 110–126.

Talal, Hassan Bin, Palestinian Self-Determination, A Study of the West Bank and Gaza Strip, New York, Quartet, 1981.

Tanks of the World (Bernard and Grafe), various editions.

Tanter, Raymond, *Rogue Regimes*, New York, St. Martin's Press, 1998.

The Jerusalem Report, various editions.

Tillema, Herbert K., *International Conflict Since 1945*, Boulder, Westview, 1991.

United States Naval Institute database.

UN, Note by the Secretary-General, "Report of the Secretary-General on the Activities of the Special Commission," S/1997/774, October 6, 1997.

UN, Report on the Eighth IAEA Inspection in Iraq Under Security Council Resolution 687, 11–18 November, 1991, New York, United Nations, S/23283 (English).

UN, Report on the Seventh IAEA Inspection in Iraq Under Security Council Resolution 687, 14 November, 1991, New York, United Nations, S/232215 (English).

UPI, on-line access.

Urban, Mark, "Fire in Galilee," a three-part series in *Armed Forces*, March.

US Arms Control and Disarmament Agency (ACDA), *World Military Expenditures and Arms Transfers,* Washington, GPO, various editions.

US Central Intelligence Agency (CIA), *Handbook of Economic Statistics,* Washington, GPO, various editions.

US Central Intelligence Agency (CIA), "Prospects for Further Proliferation of Nuclear Weapons," DCI NIO, 2000.

US Central Intelligence Agency (CIA), *World Factbook*, Washington, CIA, various editions.

US Central Intelligence Agency (CIA), Unclassified Report to Congress on the Acquisition of Technology Relating to Weapons of Mass Destruction and Advanced Conventional Munitions 1 January Through 30 June 1998, January 1999, Internet edition.

US Defense Intelligence Agency (DIA), *Soviet Chemical Weapons Threat*, DST-1620F-051–85, 1985, p. 8.

US Defense Security Assistance Agency (DSAA), "Foreign Military Sales, Foreign Military Construction Sales and Military Assistance Facts as of September 30, 1994," Department of Defense, Washington, 1995.

US Department of Defense, *Conduct of the Persian Gulf War: Final Report to Congress*, Washington, Department of Defense, April 1992.

US Department of State, "Patterns of Global Terrorism," various years, Internet version.

US Department of State, *Congressional Presentation for Security Assistance Programs, Fiscal Year 1996*, Washington, Department of State, 1995.

US Department of State, *Country Reports on Human Rights, various editions*, Internet version.

van Creveld, Martin, *Military Lessons of the Yom Kippur War: Historical Perspectives*, Washington Paper no. 24, Beverly Hills, Sage Publications, 1975.

Vandewalle, Dirk, "The Middle East Peace Process and Economic Integration," *Survival*, Winter, 1994–95, pp. 21–34.

Vatikiotis, J. P., *Politics and the Military in Jordan*, New York, Praeger, 1967.

Venter, A. J., "Lebanon: A Pawn in the Power Struggle," *Jane's Intelligence Review*, June 1998, pp. 18–23.

von Pikva, Otto, *Armies of the Middle East*, New York, Mayflower, 1979.

Wald, Emanuel, *The Wald Report: The Decline of Israeli National Security Since 1967*, Boulder, Westview, 1991.

Warplanes of the World (Bernard and Grafe), various editions.

Weinberger, Naomi, "The Palestinian National Security Debate," *Journal of Palestine Studies*, Winter 1995, pp. 16–30.

Wendt, James C., and Richard Darilek, *Possible US Roles in Support of a Syrian-Israeli Peace Agreement*, Washington, Rand, 1994.

Weyer's Warships (Bernard and Grafe), various editions.

Whetten, Lawrence L., *The Canal War: Four Power Conflict in the Middle East*, Cambridge, MIT, 1974.

Woolsey, James, "Testimony by Director of Central Intelligence before the Senate Governmental Affairs Committee," February 24, 1993.

World Bank, *A Population Perspective on Development in the Middle East and North Africa*, World Bank, August 1994.

World Bank, *Claiming the Future: Choosing Prosperity in the Middle East and North Africa*, Washington, World Bank, 1995.

World Bank, *Developing the Occupied Territories: An Investment for Peace*, Washington, World Bank, October 1994.

World Bank, *Emergency Assistance Program for the Occupied Territories*, Washington, World Bank, October 1994.

World Bank, *Forging A Partnership for Environmental Action, Washington*, World Bank, December 1994.

World Bank, *Integrated Development of the Jordan Rift Valley*, Washington, World Bank, October 1994.

World Bank, *Peace and the Jordanian Economy*, Washington, World Bank, October 1994.

World Bank, *Will Arab Workers Prosper or Be Left Out in the Twenty-First Century*, World Bank, 1995.

Yaacov, Bar Siman Tov, *The Israeli-Egyptian War of Attrition, 1969–1970*, New York, Columbia, 1980.

Yaniv, Avner, *Deterrence Without the Bomb, The Politics of Israeli Strategy*, Lexington, Lexington Books, 1987.

Zak, Moshe, "The Jordan-Israel Peace Treaty," *Middle East Quarterly*, Vol. II, No. 1, March 1995, pp. 53–60.

Zunes, Stephen, "Israeli-Syrian Peace, The Long Road Ahead," *Middle East Policy*, Vol. II, No. 3, 1993, pp. 62–68.

Zunes, Stephen, "The Israeli-Jordanian Agreement: Peace or Pax Americana," *Middle East Policy*, Vol. III, No. 3, 1995, pp. 57–68.

About the Author

ANTHONY H. CORDESMAN holds the Arleigh A. Burke Chair in Strategy at the Center for Strategic and International Studies, and is a special consultant on military affairs for ABC News. The author of numerous books on international security issues, he has served in senior positions for the Secretary of Defense, NATO, State Department, Department of Energy, and the U.S. Senate.